IVOR HORTON'S
BEGINNING VISUAL C++® 2010

IVOR HORTON'S
BEGINNING

Visual C++® 2010

Ivor Horton

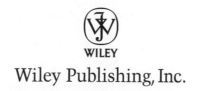

WILEY
Wiley Publishing, Inc.

Ivor Horton's Beginning Visual C++® 2010

Published by
Wiley Publishing, Inc.
10475 Crosspoint Boulevard
Indianapolis, IN 46256
www.wiley.com

Published by Wiley Publishing, Inc., Indianapolis, Indiana

Published simultaneously in Canada

ISBN: 978-0-470-50088-0

Manufactured in the United States of America

10 9 8 7 6 5 4 3 2 1

For general information on our other products and services please contact our Customer Care Department within the United States at (877) 762-2974, outside the United States at (317) 572-3993 or fax (317) 572-4002.

Wiley also publishes its books in a variety of electronic formats. Some content that appears in print may not be available in electronic books.

Library of Congress Control Number: 2010921242

This book is for Edward Gilbey, who arrived in September 2009 and has been a joy to have around ever since.

ABOUT THE AUTHOR

 IVOR HORTON graduated as a mathematician and was lured into information technology by promises of great rewards for very little work. In spite of the reality usually being a great deal of work for relatively modest rewards, he has continued to work with computers to the present day. He has been engaged at various times in programming, systems design, consultancy, and the management and implementation of projects of considerable complexity.

Horton has many years of experience in the design and implementation of computer systems applied to engineering design and manufacturing operations in a variety of industries. He has considerable experience in developing occasionally useful applications in a wide variety of programming languages, and in teaching scientists and engineers primarily to do likewise. He has been writing books on programming for more than 15 years now, and his currently published works include tutorials on C, C++, and Java. At the present time, when he is not writing programming books or providing advice to others, he spends his time fishing, traveling, and enjoying life in general.

ABOUT THE TECHNICAL EDITOR

MARC GREGOIRE is a software engineer from Belgium. He graduated from the Catholic University Leuven, Belgium, with a degree in "Burgerlijk ingenieur in de computer wetenschappen" (equivalent to Master of Science in Engineering in Computer Science). After that, he received the cum laude degree of Master in Artificial Intelligence at the same university, started working for a big software consultancy company (Ordina: `http://www.ordina.be`). His main expertise is C/C++, specifically Microsoft VC++ and the MFC framework. Next to C/C++, Marc also likes C# and uses PHP for creating web pages. In addition to his main interest for Windows development, he also has experience in developing C++ programs running 24x7 on Linux platforms, and in developing critical 2G and 3G software running on Solaris for big telecom operators.

In April of the years 2007, 2008, and 2009 he received the Microsoft MVP (Most Valuable Professional) award for his Visual C++ expertise.

Marc is an active member on the CodeGuru forum (as Marc G) and also wrote some articles and FAQ entries for CodeGuru. He creates freeware and shareware programs that are distributed through his website at `www.nuonsoft.com` and maintains a blog on `www.nuonsoft.com/blog/`.

CREDITS

EXECUTIVE EDITOR
Robert Elliott

PROJECT EDITOR
John Sleeva

TECHNICAL EDITOR
Marc Gregoire

PRODUCTION EDITOR
Eric Charbonneau

COPY EDITOR
Sadie Kleinman

EDITORIAL DIRECTOR
Robyn B. Siesky

EDITORIAL MANAGER
Mary Beth Wakefield

MARKETING MANAGER
Ashley Zurcher

PRODUCTION MANAGER
Tim Tate

VICE PRESIDENT AND EXECUTIVE GROUP PUBLISHER
Richard Swadley

VICE PRESIDENT AND EXECUTIVE PUBLISHER
Barry Pruett

ASSOCIATE PUBLISHER
Jim Minatel

PROJECT COORDINATOR, COVER
Lynsey Stanford

PROOFREADERS
Maraya Cornell and Paul Sagan, Word One

INDEXER
Johnna VanHoose Dinse

COVER DESIGNER
Michael E. Trent

COVER IMAGE
©istockphoto

ACKNOWLEDGMENTS

THE AUTHOR IS ONLY ONE MEMBER of the large team of people necessary to get a book into print. I'd like to thank the John Wiley & Sons and Wrox Press editorial and production teams for their help and support throughout.

I would particularly like to thank my technical editor, Marc Gregoire, for doing such an outstanding job of reviewing the text and checking out all the code fragments and examples in the book. His many constructive comments and suggestions for better ways of presenting the material has undoubtedly made the book a much better tutorial.

As always, the love and support of my wife, Eve, has been fundamental to making it possible for me to write this book alongside my other activities. She provides for my every need and remains patient and cheerful in spite of the effect that my self-imposed workload has on family life.

CONTENTS

INTRODUCTION

WELCOME TO *IVOR HORTON'S BEGINNING VISUAL C++ 2010*. With this book, you can become an effective C++ programmer using Microsoft's latest application-development system. I aim to teach you the C++ programming language, and then how to apply C++ in the development of your own Windows applications. Along the way, you will also learn about many of the exciting new capabilities introduced by this latest version of Visual C++, including how you can make full use of multi-core processors in your programs.

PROGRAMMING IN C++

Visual C++ 2010 supports two distinct, but closely related flavors of the C++ language, ISO/IEC standard C++ (which I will refer to as native C++) and C++/CLI. Although native C++ is the language of choice for many professional developers, especially when performance is the primary consideration, the speed and ease of development that C++/CLI and the Windows Forms capability bring to the table make that essential, too. This is why I cover both flavors of C++ in depth in this book.

Visual C++ 2010 fully supports the original ISO/IEC standard C++ language, with the added advantage of some powerful new native C++ language features from the upcoming ISO/IEC standard for C++. This is comprehensively covered in this book, including the new language features.

Visual C++ 2010 also supports C++/CLI, which is a dialect of C++ that was developed by Microsoft as an extension to native C++. The idea behind C++/CLI is to add features to native C++ that allow you to develop applications that target the virtual machine environment supported by .NET. This adds C++ to the other languages such as BASIC and C# that can use the .NET Framework. The C++/CLI language is now an ECMA standard alongside the CLI standard that defines the virtual machine environment for .NET.

The two versions of C++ available with Visual C++ 2010 are complementary and fulfill different roles. ISO/IEC C++ is there for the development of high-performance applications that run natively on your computer, whereas C++/CLI has been developed specifically for writing applications that target the .NET Framework. Once you have learned the essentials of how you write applications in both versions of C++, you will be able to make full use of the versatility and scope of Visual C++ 2010.

DEVELOPING WINDOWS APPLICATIONS

With a good understanding of C++, you are well placed to launch into Windows application development. The Microsoft Foundation Classes (MFC) encapsulate the Windows API to provide comprehensive, easy-to-use capabilities for developing high-performance Windows applications in native C++.

You get quite a lot of assistance from automatically generated code when writing native C++ programs, but you still need to write a lot of C++ yourself. You need a solid understanding of object-oriented programming (OOP) techniques, as well as a good appreciation of what's involved in programming for Windows. You will learn all that you need using this book.

C++/CLI targets the .NET Framework and is the vehicle for the development of Windows Forms applications. With Windows Forms, you can create much, if not all of the user interface required for an application interactively, without writing a single line of code. Of course, you still must customize a Windows Forms application to make it do what you want, but the time required for development is a fraction of what you would need to create the application using native C++. Even though the amount of customizing code you have to add may be a relatively small proportion of the total, you still need an in-depth knowledge of the C++/CLI language to do it successfully. This book aims to provide you with that.

ADVANCED LIBRARY CAPABILITIES

The Parallel Patterns Library (PPL) is an exciting new capability introduced in Visual C++ 2010 that makes it easy to program for using multiple processors. Programming for multiple processors has been difficult in the past, but the PPL really does make it easy. I'll show you the various ways in which you can use the PPL to speed up your compute-intensive applications.

WHO THIS BOOK IS FOR

This book is for anyone who wants to learn how to write C++ applications for the Microsoft Windows operating system using Visual C++ 2010. I make no assumptions about prior knowledge of any particular programming language, so there are no prerequisites other than some aptitude for programming and sufficient enthusiasm and commitment for learning to program in C++ to make it through this book. This tutorial is for you if:

➤ You are a newcomer to programming and sufficiently keen to jump into the deep end with C++. To be successful, you need to have at least a rough idea of how your computer works, including the way in which the memory is organized and how data and instructions are stored.

➤ You have a little experience of programming in some other language, such as BASIC, and you are keen to learn C++ and develop practical Microsoft Windows programming skills.

➤ You have some experience in C or C++, but not in a Microsoft Windows context and want to extend your skills to program for the Windows environment using the latest tools and technologies.

➤ You have some knowledge of C++ and you want to extend your C++ skills to include C++/CLI.

WHAT THIS BOOK COVERS

Essentially, this book covers two broad topics: the C++ programming language, and Windows application programming using either MFC or the .NET Framework. Before you can develop fully-fledged Windows applications, you need to have a good level of knowledge of C++, so the C++ tutorial comes first.

The first part of the book teaches you the essentials of C++ programming using both of the C++ language technologies supported by Visual C++ 2010, through a detailed, step-by-step tutorial on both flavors of the C++ language. You'll learn the syntax and use of the native ISO/IEC C++ language and gain experience and confidence in applying it in a practical context through an extensive range of working examples. There are also exercises that you can use to test your knowledge, with solutions available for download if you get stuck. You'll learn C++/CLI as an extension to native C++, again through working examples that illustrate how each language feature works.

Of course, the language tutorial also introduces and demonstrates the use of the C++ standard library facilities you are most likely to need. You'll add to your knowledge of the standard libraries incrementally as you progress through the C++ language. Additionally, you will learn about the powerful tools provided by the Standard Template Library (STL) in both its forms: the native C++ version and the C++/CLI version. There is also a chapter dedicated to the new Parallel Patterns Library that enables you to harness the power of the multi-core processing capabilities of your PC for computationally intensive applications.

Once you are confident in applying C++, you move on to Windows programming. You will learn how to develop native Windows applications using the MFC by creating a substantial working application of more than 2000 lines of code. You develop the application over several chapters, utilizing a broad range of user interface capabilities provided by the MFC. To learn Windows programming with C++/CLI, you develop a Windows Forms application with similar functionality user interface features to the native C++ application.

HOW THIS BOOK IS STRUCTURED

The book is structured as follows:

➤ **Chapter 1** introduces you to the basic concepts you need to understand for programming in C++, for native applications and for .NET Framework applications, together with the main ideas embodied in the Visual C++ 2010 development environment. It describes how you use the capabilities of Visual C++ 2010 for creating the various kinds of C++ applications you learn about in the rest of the book.

➤ **Chapters 2 through 9** teach you both versions of the C++ language. The content of each of Chapters 2 through 9 is structured in a similar way; the first part of each chapter deals with native C++ language elements, and the second part deals with how the same capabilities are provided in C++/CLI.

➤ **Chapter 10** teaches you how you use the STL, which is a powerful and extensive set of tools for organizing and manipulating data in your native C++ programs. The STL is application-neutral, so you will be able to apply it in a wide range of contexts. Chapter 10 also teaches you the STL/CLR, which is new in Visual C++ 2010. This is a version of the STL for use in C++/CLI applications.

➤ **Chapter 11** introduces you to techniques for finding errors in your C++ programs. It covers the general principles of debugging your programs and the basic features that Visual C++ 2010 provides to help you find errors in your code.

➤ **Chapter 12** discusses how Microsoft Windows applications are structured and describes and demonstrates the essential elements that are present in every application written for the Windows operating system. The chapter explains elementary examples of how Windows applications work, with programs that use native C++ and the Windows API, native C++ and the MFC, as well as an example of a basic Windows Forms application using C++/CLI.

➤ **Chapter 13** introduces how you can program to use multiple processors if your PC has a multi-core processor. You learn about the basic techniques for parallel processing through complete working examples of Windows API applications that are very computationally intensive.

➤ **Chapters 14 through 19** teach you Windows programming. You learn to write native C++ Windows applications using the MFC for building a GUI. You will also learn how you use the .NET Framework in a C++/CLI Windows application. You learn how you create and use common controls to build the graphical user interface for your application, and how you handle the events that result from user interaction with your program. In addition to the techniques you learn for building a GUI, the application that you develop also shows you how you handle printing and how you can save your application data on disk.

➤ **Chapter 20** teaches you the essentials you need to know for creating your own libraries using MFC. You learn about the different kinds of libraries you can create, and you develop working examples of these that work with the application that you have evolved over the preceding six chapters.

All chapters in the book include numerous working examples that demonstrate the programming techniques discussed. Every chapter concludes with a summary of the key points that were covered, and most chapters include a set of exercises at the end that you can attempt, to apply what you have learned. Solutions to the exercises, together with all the code from the book, are available for download from the publisher's Web site (see the "Source Code" section later in this Introduction for more details). The tutorial on the C++ language uses examples that are console programs, with simple command-line input and output. This approach enables you to learn the various capabilities of C++ without getting bogged down in the complexities of Windows GUI programming. Programming for Windows is really practicable only after you have a thorough understanding of the programming language.

If you want to keep things as simple as possible, or if you are new to programming, you can just learn the native C++ programming language in the first instance. Each of the chapters that cover the C++ language (Chapters 2 through 9) first discuss particular aspects of the capabilities of native C++, and then the new features introduced by C++/CLI in the same context. The reason for organizing things this way is that C++/CLI is defined as an extension to the ISO/IEC standard language, so an understanding of C++/CLI is predicated on knowledge of ISO/IEC C++. Thus, you can just work through the native topics in each of the chapters and ignore the C++/CLI sections that follow. You then can to progress to Windows application development using native C++ without having to keep the two versions of the language in mind. You can return to C++/CLI when you are comfortable with ISO/IEC C++. Of course, if you already have some programming expertise, you can also work straight through and add to your knowledge of both versions of the C++ language incrementally.

WHAT YOU NEED TO USE THIS BOOK

To fully use this book, you need a version of Visual C++ 2010 (or Visual Studio 2010) that supports the Microsoft Foundation Classes (MFC). Note that the free Visual C++ 2010 Express Edition is *not* sufficient. The Express Edition provides only the C++ compiler and access to the basic Windows API; it does not provide the MFC library. Thus, any fee edition of either Visual C++ 2010 or Visual Studio 2010 will enable you to compile and execute all the examples in the book.

CONVENTIONS

To help you get the most from the text and keep track of what's happening, we've used a number of conventions throughout the book.

TRY IT OUT

The *Try It Out* is an exercise you should work through, following the text in the book.

1. They usually consist of a set of steps.
2. Each step has a number.
3. Follow the steps through with your copy of the database.

How It Works

After each *Try It Out*, the code you've typed will be explained in detail.

 WARNING *Boxes like this one hold important, not-to-be forgotten information that is directly relevant to the surrounding text.*

 NOTE *Notes, tips, hints, tricks, and asides to the current discussion are offset and placed in italics like this.*

As for styles in the text:

➤ We *highlight* new terms and important words when we introduce them.

➤ We show keyboard strokes like this: Ctrl+A.

➤ We show file names, URLs, and code within the text like so: `persistence.properties`.

➤ We present code in two different ways:

```
We use a monofont type with no highlighting for most code examples.
We use bold highlighting to emphasize code that is of particular importance in the
present context.
```

SOURCE CODE

As you work through the examples in this book, you may choose either to type in all the code manually, or to use the source code files that accompany the book. All the source code used in this book is available for download at `http://www.wrox.com`. When at the site, simply locate the book's title (use the Search box or one of the title lists) and click the Download Code link on the book's detail page to obtain all the source code for the book. Code that is included on the Web site is highlighted by the following icon:

Available for
download on
Wrox.com

Listings include the filename in the title. If it is just a code snippet, you'll find the filename in a code note such as this:

code snippet filename

 NOTE *Because many books have similar titles, you may find it easiest to search by ISBN; this book's ISBN is 978-0-470-50088-0.*

Once you download the code, just decompress it with your favorite compression tool. Alternately, you can go to the main Wrox code download page at `http://www.wrox.com/dynamic/books/download.aspx` to see the code available for this book and all other Wrox books.

ERRATA

We make every effort to ensure that there are no errors in the text or in the code. However, no one is perfect, and mistakes do occur. If you find an error in one of our books, like a spelling mistake or faulty piece of code, we would be very grateful for your feedback. By sending in errata, you may save another reader hours of frustration, and at the same time, you will be helping us provide even higher quality information.

To find the errata page for this book, go to `http://www.wrox.com` and locate the title using the Search box or one of the title lists. Then, on the book's detail page, click the Book Errata link. On this page, you can view all errata that has been submitted for this book and posted by Wrox editors. A complete book list, including links to each book's errata, is also available at `www.wrox.com/misc-pages/booklist.shtml`.

If you don't spot "your" error on the Book Errata page, go to `www.wrox.com/contact/techsupport.shtml` and complete the form there to send us the error you have found. We'll check the information and, if appropriate, post a message to the book's errata page and fix the problem in subsequent editions of the book.

P2P.WROX.COM

For author and peer discussion, join the P2P forums at `p2p.wrox.com`. The forums are a Web-based system for you to post messages relating to Wrox books and related technologies and interact with other readers and technology users. The forums offer a subscription feature to e-mail you topics of interest of your choosing when new posts are made to the forums. Wrox authors, editors, other industry experts, and your fellow readers are present on these forums.

At `http://p2p.wrox.com`, you will find a number of different forums that will help you, not only as you read this book, but also as you develop your own applications. To join the forums, just follow these steps:

1. Go to `p2p.wrox.com` and click the Register link.
2. Read the terms of use and click Agree.
3. Complete the required information to join, as well as any optional information you wish to provide, and click Submit.
4. You will receive an e-mail with information describing how to verify your account and complete the joining process.

 NOTE *You can read messages in the forums without joining P2P, but in order to post your own messages, you must join.*

Once you join, you can post new messages and respond to messages other users post. You can read messages at any time on the Web. If you would like to have new messages from a particular forum e-mailed to you, click the Subscribe to this Forum icon by the forum name in the forum listing.

For more information about how to use the Wrox P2P, be sure to read the P2P FAQs for answers to questions about how the forum software works, as well as many common questions specific to P2P and Wrox books. To read the FAQs, click the FAQ link on any P2P page.

Programming with Visual C++ 2010

WHAT YOU WILL LEARN IN THIS CHAPTER:

➤ What the principal components of Visual C++ 2010 are

➤ What the .NET Framework consists of and the advantages it offers

➤ What solutions and projects are and how you create them

➤ About console programs

➤ How to create and edit a program

➤ How to compile, link, and execute C++ console programs

➤ How to create and execute basic Windows programs

Windows programming isn't difficult. Microsoft Visual C++ 2010 makes it remarkably easy, as you'll see throughout the course of this book. There's just one obstacle in your path: Before you get to the specifics of Windows programming, you have to be thoroughly familiar with the capabilities of the C++ programming language, particularly the object-oriented aspects of the language. Object-oriented techniques are central to the effectiveness of all the tools provided by Visual C++ 2010 for Windows programming, so it's essential that you gain a good understanding of them. That's exactly what this book provides.

This chapter gives you an overview of the essential concepts involved in programming applications in C++. You'll take a rapid tour of the integrated development environment (IDE) that comes with Visual C++ 2010. The IDE is straightforward and generally intuitive in its operation, so you'll be able to pick up most of it as you go along. The best way to get familiar with it is to work through the process of creating, compiling, and executing a simple program.

So power up your PC, start Windows, load the mighty Visual C++ 2010, and begin your journey.

THE .NET FRAMEWORK

The **.NET Framework** is a central concept in Visual C++ 2010 as well as in all the other .NET development products from Microsoft. The .NET Framework consists of two elements: the **Common Language Runtime (CLR)** in which your application executes, and a set of libraries called the .NET Framework class libraries. The .NET Framework class libraries provide the functional support your code will need when executing with the CLR, regardless of the programming language used, so .NET programs written in C++, C#, or any of the other languages that support the .NET Framework all use the same .NET libraries.

There are two fundamentally different kinds of C++ applications you can develop with Visual C++ 2010. You can write applications that natively execute on your computer. These applications will be referred to as **native C++ programs**; you write native C++ programs in the version of C++ defined by the ISO/IEC (International Standards Organization/International Electrotechnical Commision) language standard. You can also write applications to run under the control of the CLR in an extended version of C++ called **C++/CLI**. These programs will be referred to as **CLR programs**, or **C++/CLI programs**.

The .NET Framework is not strictly part of Visual C++ 2010 but rather a component of the Windows operating system that makes it easier to build software applications and Web services. The .NET Framework offers substantial advantages in code reliability and security, as well as the ability to integrate your C++ code with code written in over 20 other programming languages that target the .NET Framework. A slight disadvantage of targeting the .NET Framework is that there is a small performance penalty compared to native code, but you won't notice this in the majority of circumstances.

THE COMMON LANGUAGE RUNTIME

The **Common Language Runtime (CLR)** is a standardized environment for the execution of programs written in a wide range of high-level languages including Visual Basic, C#, and of course C++. The specification of the CLR is now embodied in the European Computer Manufacturers Association (ECMA) standard for the **Common Language Infrastructure (CLI)**, the ECMA-335, and also in the equivalent ISO standard, ISO/IEC 23271, so the CLR is an implementation of this standard. You can see why C++ for the CLR is referred to as C++/CLI — it's C++ for the Common Language Infrastructure, so you are likely to see C++/CLI compilers on other operating systems that implement the CLI.

 NOTE *Information about all ECMA standards is available from* `www.ecma-international.org`, *and ECMA-335 is currently available as a free download.*

The CLI is essentially a specification for a **virtual machine** environment that enables applications written in diverse high-level programming languages to be executed in different system environments without the original source code's being changed or replicated. The CLI specifies a standard intermediate language for the virtual machine to which the high-level language source code is compiled. With the .NET Framework, this intermediate language is referred to as **Microsoft Intermediate Language (MSIL)**. Code in the intermediate language is ultimately mapped to machine code by a **just-in-time (JIT)** compiler when you execute a program. Of course, code in the CLI intermediate language can be executed within any other environment that has a CLI implementation.

The CLI also defines a common set of data types called the **Common Type System (CTS)** that should be used for programs written in any programming language targeting a CLI implementation. The CTS specifies how data types are used within the CLR and includes a set of predefined types. You may also define your own data types, and these must be defined in a particular way to be consistent with the CLR, as you'll see. Having a standardized type system for representing data allows components written in different programming languages to handle data in a uniform way and makes it possible to integrate components written in different languages into a single application.

Data security and program reliability is greatly enhanced by the CLR, in part because dynamic memory allocation and release for data is fully automatic, but also because the MSIL code for a program is comprehensively checked and validated before the program executes. The CLR is just one implementation of the CLI specification that executes under Microsoft Windows on a PC; there will undoubtedly be other implementations of the CLI for other operating system environments and hardware platforms. You'll sometimes find that the terms CLI and CLR are used interchangeably, although it should be evident that they are not the same thing. The CLI is a standard specification; the CLR is Microsoft's implementation of the CLI.

WRITING C++ APPLICATIONS

You have tremendous flexibility in the types of applications and program components that you can develop with Visual C++ 2010. As noted earlier in this chapter, you have two basic options for Windows applications: You can write code that executes with the CLR, and you can also write code that compiles directly to machine code and thus executes natively. For window-based applications targeting the CLR, you use Windows Forms as the base for the GUI provided by the .NET Framework libraries. Using Windows Forms enables rapid GUI development because you assemble the GUI graphically from standard components and have the code generated completely automatically. You then just need to customize the code that has been generated to provide the functionality that you require.

For natively executing code, you have several ways to go. One possibility is to use the Microsoft Foundation Classes (MFC) for programming the graphical user interface for your Windows application. The MFC encapsulates the Windows operating system Application Programming Interface (API) for GUI creation and control and greatly eases the process of program development. The Windows API originated long before the C++ language arrived on the scene, so it has none of the object-oriented characteristics that would be expected if it were written today; however, you are not obliged to use the MFC. If you want the ultimate in performance, you can write your C++ code to access the Windows API directly.

C++ code that executes with the CLR is described as **managed C++** because data and code are managed by the CLR. In CLR programs, the release of memory that you have allocated dynamically for storing data is taken care of automatically, thus eliminating a common source of error in native C++ applications. C++ code that executes outside the CLR is sometimes described by Microsoft as **unmanaged C++** because the CLR is not involved in its execution. With unmanaged C++ you must take care of all aspects of allocating and releasing memory during execution of your program yourself, and also forego the enhanced security provided by the CLR. You'll also see unmanaged C++ referred to as **native C++** because it compiles directly to native machine code.

Figure 1-1 shows the basic options you have for developing C++ applications.

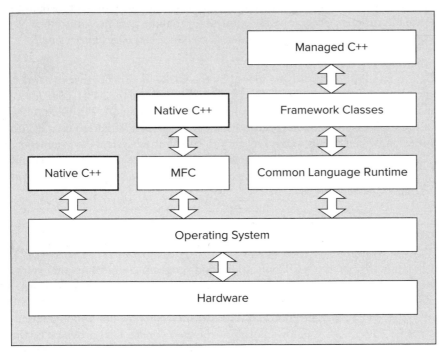

FIGURE 1-1

Figure 1-1 is not the whole story. An application can consist partly of managed C++ and partly of native C++, so you are not obliged to stick to one environment or the other. Of course, you do lose out somewhat by mixing code, so you would choose to follow this approach only when necessary, such as when you want to convert an existing native C++ application to run with the CLR. You obviously won't get the benefits inherent in managed C++ in the native C++ code, and there can also be appreciable overhead involved in communications between the managed and unmanaged code components. The ability to mix managed and unmanaged code can be invaluable, however, when you need to develop or extend existing unmanaged code but also want to obtain the advantages of using the CLR. Of course, for new applications you should decide at the outset whether you want to create a managed C++ application or a native C++ application.

LEARNING WINDOWS PROGRAMMING

There are always two basic aspects to interactive applications executing under Windows: You need code to create the **graphical user interface (GUI)** with which the user interacts, and you need code to process these interactions to provide the functionality of the application. Visual C++ 2010 provides you with a great deal of assistance in both aspects of Windows application development. As you'll see later in this chapter, you can create a working Windows program with a GUI without writing any code yourself at all. All the basic code to create the GUI can be generated automatically by Visual C++ 2010; however, it's essential to understand how this automatically generated code works because you need to extend and modify it to make it do what you want, and to do that you need a comprehensive understanding of C++.

For this reason you'll first learn C++ — both the native C++ and C++/CLI versions of the language — without getting involved in Windows programming considerations. After you're comfortable with C++ you'll learn how to develop fully-fledged Windows applications using native C++ and C++/CLI. This means that while you are learning C++, you'll be working with programs that involve only command line input and output. By sticking to this rather limited input and output capability, you'll be able to concentrate on the specifics of how the C++ language works and avoid the inevitable complications involved in GUI building and control. After you become comfortable with C++ you'll find that it's an easy and natural progression to applying C++ to the development of Windows application programs.

Learning C++

Visual C++ 2010 fully supports two versions of C++, defined by two separate standards:

> ➤ The **ISO/IEC C++** standard is for implementing native applications — unmanaged C++. This version of C++ is supported on the majority of computer platforms.

> ➤ The **C++/CLI** standard is designed specifically for writing programs that target the CLR and is an extension of the ISO/IEC C++.

Chapters 2 through 9 of this book teach you the C++ language. Because C++/CLI is an extension of ISO/IEC C++, the first part of each chapter introduces elements of the ISO/IEC C++ language; the second part explains the additional features that C++/CLI introduces.

Writing programs in C++/CLI enables you to take full advantage of the capabilities of the .NET Framework, something that is not possible with programs written in ISO/IEC C++. Although C++/CLI is an extension of ISO/IEC C++, to be able to execute your program fully with the CLR means that it must conform to the requirements of the CLR. This implies that there are some features of ISO/IEC C++ that you cannot use in your CLR programs. One example of this that you might deduce from what I have said up to now is that the dynamic memory allocation and release facilities offered by ISO/IEC C++ are not compatible with the CLR; you must use the CLR mechanism for memory management, and this implies that you must use C++/CLI classes, not native C++ classes.

The C++ Standards

At the time of writing, the currently approved C++ language standard is defined by the document ISO/IEC 14882:1998, published by the International Organization for Standardization (ISO). This is the well-established version of C++ that has been around since 1998 and is supported by compilers on the majority of computer hardware platforms and operating systems. There is a new standard for C++ in draft form that is expected to be approved in the near future. Visual C++ 2010 already supports several of the new language capabilities offered by this new standard, and these are described in this book.

Programs that you write in standard C++ can be ported from one system environment to another reasonably easily, although the library functions that a program uses — particularly those related to building a graphical user interface — are a major determinant of how easy or difficult it will be. ISO/IEC standard C++ is the first choice of many professional program developers because it is so widely supported, and because it is one of the most powerful programming languages available today.

C++/CLI is a version of C++ that extends the ISO/IEC standard for C++ to better support the **Common Language Infrastructure (CLI)** defined by the standard ECMA-355. The C++/CLI language specification is defined by the standard ECMA-372 and is available for download from the ECMA web site. This standard was developed from an initial technical specification that was produced by Microsoft to support the execution of C++ programs with the .NET Framework. Thus, both the CLI and C++/CLI were originated by Microsoft in support of the .NET Framework. Of course, standardizing the CLI and C++/CLI greatly increases the likelihood of implementation in environments other than Windows. It's important to appreciate that although C++/CLI is an extension of ISO/IEC C++, there are features of ISO/IEC C++ that you must not use when you want your program to execute fully under the control of the CLR. You'll learn what these are as you progress through the book.

The CLR offers substantial advantages over the native environment. If you target your C++ programs at the CLR, they will be more secure and not prone to the potential errors you can make when using the full power of ISO/IEC C++. The CLR also removes the incompatibilities introduced by various high-level languages by standardizing the target environment to which they are compiled, and thus permits modules written in C++ to be combined with modules written in other languages, such as C# or Visual Basic.

Attributes

Attributes are an advanced feature of programming with C++/CLI that enable you to add descriptive declarations to your code. At the simplest level, you can use attributes to annotate particular programming elements in your program, but there's more to attributes than just additional descriptive data. Attributes can affect how your code behaves at run time by modifying the way the code is compiled or by causing extra code to be generated that supports additional capabilities. A range of standard attributes is available for C++/CLI, and it is also possible to create your own.

A detailed discussion of attributes is beyond the scope of this book, but I mention them here because you will make use of attributes in one or two places in the book, particularly in Chapter 19, where you learn how to write objects to a file.

Console Applications

As well as developing Windows applications, Visual C++ 2010 also enables you to write, compile, and test C++ programs that have none of the baggage required for Windows programs — that is, applications that are essentially character-based, command-line programs. These programs are called **console applications** in Visual C++ 2010 because you communicate with them through the keyboard and the screen in character mode.

When you write console applications it might seem as if you are being sidetracked from the main objective of Windows programming, but when it comes to learning C++ (which you do need to do before embarking on Windows-specific programming) it's the best way to proceed. There's a lot of code in even a simple Windows program, and it's very important not to be distracted by the complexities of Windows when learning the ins and outs of C++. Therefore, in the early chapters of the book, which are concerned with how C++ works, you'll spend time walking with a few lightweight console applications before you get to run with the heavyweight sacks of code in the world of Windows.

While you're learning C++, you'll be able to concentrate on the language features without worrying about the environment in which you're operating. With the console applications that you'll write, you have only a text interface, but this will be quite sufficient for understanding all of C++ because there's no graphical capability within the definition of the language. Naturally, I will provide extensive coverage of graphical user interface programming when you come to write programs specifically for Windows using Microsoft Foundation Classes (MFC) in native C++ applications, and Windows Forms with the CLR.

There are two distinct kinds of console applications, and you'll be using both.

➤ **Win32 console applications** compile to native code. You'll be using these to try out the capabilities of ISO/IEC C++.

➤ **CLR console applications** target the CLR. You'll be using these when you are working with the features of C++/CLI.

Windows Programming Concepts

The project creation facilities provided with Visual C++ 2010 can generate skeleton code for a wide variety of native C++ application programs automatically, including basic Windows programs. For Windows applications that you develop for the CLR you get even more automatic code generation. You can create complete applications using Windows Forms that require only a small amount of customized code to be written by you, and some that require no additional code at all. Creating a project is the starting point for all applications and components that you develop with Visual C++ 2010, and to get a flavor of how this works you'll look at the mechanics of creating some examples, including an outline Windows program, later in this chapter.

A Windows program, whether a native C++ program or a program written for the CLR, has a different structure from that of the typical console program you execute from the command line, and it's more complicated. In a console program you can get input from the keyboard and write output back to the command line directly, whereas a Windows program can access the input and output facilities of the computer only by way of functions supplied by the host environment; no direct access to the hardware resources is permitted. Because several programs can be active at one time under Windows, Windows has to determine which application a given raw input, such as a mouse click or the pressing of a key on the keyboard, is destined for, and signal the program concerned accordingly. Thus, the Windows operating system has primary control of all communications with the user.

The nature of the interface between a user and a Windows application is such that a wide range of different inputs is usually possible at any given time. A user may select any of a number of menu options, click a toolbar button, or click the mouse somewhere in the application window. A well-designed Windows application has to be prepared to deal with any of the possible types of input at any time because there is no way of knowing in advance which type of input is going to occur. These user actions are received by the operating system in the first instance, and are all regarded by Windows as **events**. An event that originates with the user interface for your application will typically result in a particular piece of your program code being executed. How program execution proceeds is therefore determined by the sequence of user actions. Programs that operate in this way are referred to as **event-driven programs,** and are different from traditional procedural programs that have a single order of execution. Input to a procedural program is controlled by the program code and can occur only when the program permits it; therefore, a Windows program consists primarily of pieces of code that respond to events caused by the action of the user, or by Windows itself. This sort of program structure is illustrated in Figure 1-2.

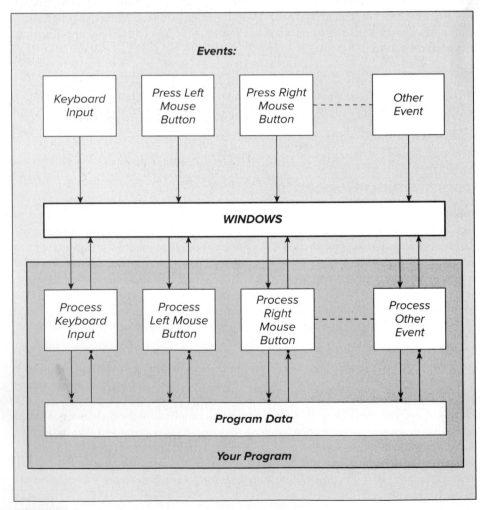

FIGURE 1-2

Each square block in Figure 1-2 represents a piece of code written specifically to deal with a particular event. The program may appear to be somewhat fragmented because of the number of disjointed blocks of code, but the primary factor welding the program into a whole is the Windows operating system itself. You can think of your program as customizing Windows to provide a particular set of capabilities.

Of course, the modules servicing various external events, such as the selection of a menu or a mouse click, all typically have access to a common set of application-specific data in a particular program. This application data contains information that relates to what the program is about — for example, blocks of text recording scoring records for a player in a program aimed at tracking how your baseball team is doing — as well as information about some of the events that have occurred during execution of the program. This shared collection of data allows various parts of the program that look independent to communicate and operate in a coordinated and integrated fashion. I will go into this in much more detail later in the book.

Even an elementary Windows program involves several lines of code, and with Windows programs generated by the application wizards that come with Visual C++ 2010, "several" turns out to be "many." To simplify the process of understanding how C++ works, you need a context that is as uncomplicated as possible. Fortunately, Visual C++ 2010 comes with an environment that is ready-made for the purpose.

WHAT IS THE INTEGRATED DEVELOPMENT ENVIRONMENT?

The integrated development environment (IDE) that comes with Visual C++ 2010 is a completely self-contained environment for creating, compiling, linking, and testing your C++ programs. It also happens to be a great environment in which to learn C++ (particularly when combined with a great book).

Visual C++ 2010 incorporates a range of fully integrated tools designed to make the whole process of writing C++ programs easy. You will see something of these in this chapter, but rather than grind through a boring litany of features and options in the abstract, you can first take a look at the basics to get a view of how the IDE works, and then pick up the rest in context as you go along.

The fundamental parts of Visual C++ 2010, provided as part of the IDE, are the editor, the compiler, the linker, and the libraries. These are the basic tools that are essential to writing and executing a C++ program. Their functions are as follows.

The Editor

The editor provides an interactive environment in which to create and edit C++ source code. As well as the usual facilities, such as cut and paste, which you are certainly already familiar with, the editor also provides color cues to differentiate between various language elements. The editor automatically recognizes fundamental words in the C++ language and assigns a color to them according to what they are. This not only helps to make your code more readable, but also provides a clear indicator of when you make errors in keying such words.

The Compiler

The compiler converts your source code into **object code,** and detects and reports errors in the compilation process. The compiler can detect a wide range of errors caused by invalid or unrecognized program code, as well as structural errors, such as parts of a program that can never be executed. The object code output from the compiler is stored in files called **object files** that have names with the extension .obj.

The Linker

The linker combines the various modules generated by the compiler from source code files, adds required code modules from program libraries supplied as part of C++, and welds everything into an executable whole. The linker can also detect and report errors — for example, if part of your program is missing, or a nonexistent library component is referenced.

The Libraries

A **library** is simply a collection of prewritten routines that supports and extends the C++ language by providing standard professionally-produced code units that you can incorporate into your programs to carry out common operations. The operations implemented by routines in the various libraries provided by Visual C++ 2010 greatly enhance productivity by saving you the effort of writing and testing the code for such operations yourself. I have already mentioned the .NET Framework library, and there are a number of others — too many to enumerate here — but I'll identify the most important ones.

The **Standard C++ Library** defines a basic set of routines common to all ISO/IEC C++ compilers. It contains a wide range of routines, including numerical functions, such as the calculation of square roots and the evaluation of trigonometrical functions; character- and string-processing routines, such as the classification of characters and the comparison of character strings; and many others. You'll get to know quite a number of these as you develop your knowledge of ISO/IEC C++. There are also libraries that support the C++/CLI extensions to ISO/IEC C++.

Native window-based applications are supported by a library called the **Microsoft Foundation Classes** (MFC). The MFC greatly reduces the effort needed to build the graphical user interface for an application. (You'll see a lot more of the MFC when you finish exploring the nuances of the C++ language.) Another library contains a set of facilities called **Windows Forms,** which are roughly the equivalent of the MFC for Windows-based applications executed with the .NET Framework. You'll be seeing how you make use of Windows Forms to develop applications, too.

USING THE IDE

All program development and execution in this book is performed from within the IDE. When you start Visual C++ 2010 you'll notice an application window similar to that shown in Figure 1-3.

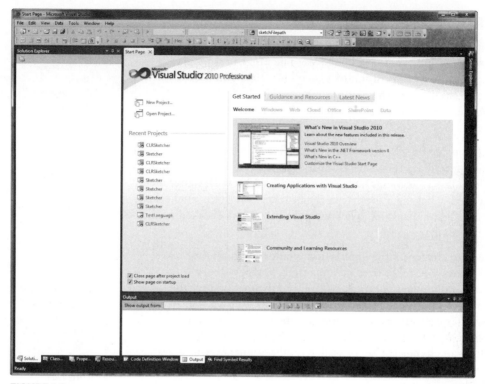

FIGURE 1-3

The pane to the left in Figure 1-3 is the **Solution Explorer window,** the top right pane presently showing the Start page is the **Editor window,** and the tab visible in the pane at the bottom is the **Output window.** The Solution Explorer window enables you to navigate through your program files and display their contents in the Editor window, and to add new files to your program. The Solution Explorer window has an additional tab (only three are shown in Figure 1-3) that displays the **Resource View** for your application, and you can select which tabs are to be displayed from the View menu. The Editor window is where you enter and modify source code and other components of your application. The Output window displays the output from build operations in which a project is compiled and linked. You can choose to display other windows by selecting from the View menu.

Note that a window can generally be undocked from its position in the Visual C++ application window. Just right-click the title bar of the window you want to undock and select Float from the pop-up menu. In general, I will show windows in their undocked state in the book. You can restore a window to its docked state by right-clicking its title bar and selecting Dock from the pop-up.

Toolbar Options

You can choose which toolbars are displayed in your Visual C++ window by right-clicking in the toolbar area. The range of toolbars in the list depends on which edition of Visual C++ 2010 you have installed. A pop-up menu with a list of toolbars (Figure 1-4) appears, and the toolbars currently displayed have checkmarks alongside them.

This is where you decide which toolbars are visible at any one time. You can make your set of toolbars the same as those shown in Figure 1-3 by making sure the Build, Class Designer, Debug, Standard, and View Designer menu items are checked. Clicking a toolbar in the list checks it if it is unchecked, and results in its being displayed; clicking a toolbar that is checked unchecks it and hides the toolbar.

You don't need to clutter up the application window with all the toolbars you think you might need at some time. Some toolbars appear automatically when required, so you'll probably find that the default toolbar selections are perfectly adequate most of the time. As you develop your applications, from time to time you might think it would be more convenient to have access to toolbars that aren't displayed. You can change the set of visible toolbars whenever it suits you by right-clicking in the toolbar area and choosing from the context menu.

FIGURE 1-4

 NOTE *As in many other Windows applications, the toolbars that make up Visual C++ 2010 come complete with tooltips. Just let the mouse pointer linger over a toolbar button for a second or two, and a white label will display the function of that button.*

Dockable Toolbars

A **dockable toolbar** is one that you can move around to position it at a convenient place in the window. You can arrange for any of the toolbars to be docked at any of the four sides of the application window. If you right-click in the toolbar area and select Customize from the pop-up, the Customize dialog will be displayed. You can choose where a particular toolbar is docked by selecting it and clicking the Modify Selection button. You can then choose from the drop-down list to dock the toolbar where you want. Figure 1-5 shows how the dialog looks after the user selects the Build toolbar on the left and clicks the Modify Selection button.

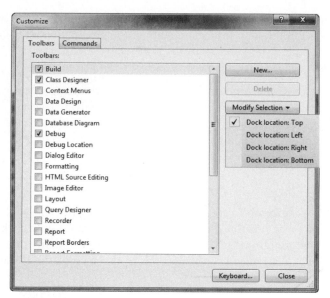

FIGURE 1-5

You'll recognize many of the toolbar icons that Visual C++ 2010 uses from other Windows applications, but you may not appreciate exactly what these icons do in the context of Visual C++, so I'll describe them as we use them.

Because you'll use a new project for every program you develop, looking at what exactly a project is and understanding how the mechanism for defining a project works is a good place to start finding out about Visual C++ 2010.

Documentation

There will be plenty of occasions when you'll want to find out more information about Visual C++ 2010 and its features and options. Press Ctrl+Alt+F1 to access the product documentation. The Help menu also provides various routes into the documentation, as well as access to program samples and technical support.

Projects and Solutions

A **project** is a container for all the things that make up a program of some kind — it might be a console program, a window-based program, or some other kind of program — and it usually consists of one or more source files containing your code, plus possibly other files containing auxiliary data. All the files for a project are stored in the **project folder**; detailed information about the project is stored in an XML file with the extension .vcxproj, also in the project folder. The project folder also contains other folders that are used to store the output from compiling and linking your project.

The idea of a **solution** is expressed by its name, in that it is a mechanism for bringing together all the programs and other resources that represent a solution to a particular data-processing problem. For example, a distributed order-entry system for a business operation might be composed of several different programs that could each be developed as a project within a single solution; therefore, a solution is a folder in which all the information relating to one or more projects is stored, and one or more project folders are subfolders of the solution folder. Information about the projects in a solution is stored in two files with the extensions .sln and .suo, respectively. When you create a project a new solution is created automatically unless you elect to add the project to an existing solution.

When you create a project along with a solution, you can add further projects to the same solution. You can add any kind of project to an existing solution, but you will usually add only a project related in some way to the existing project, or projects, in the solution. Generally, unless you have a good reason to do otherwise, each of your projects should have its own solution. Each example you create with this book will be a single project within its own solution.

Defining a Project

The first step in writing a Visual C++ 2010 program is to create a project for it using the File ⇨ New ⇨ Project menu option from the main menu or by pressing Ctrl+Shift+N; you can also simply click New Project . . . on the Start page. As well as containing files that define all the code and any other data that makes up your program, the project XML file in the project folder also records the Visual C++ 2010 options you're using.

That's enough introductory stuff for the moment. It's time to get your hands dirty.

TRY IT OUT   Creating a Project for a Win32 Console Application

You'll now take a look at creating a project for a console application. First, select File ⇨ New ⇨ Project or use one of the other possibilities mentioned earlier to bring up the New Project dialog box, as shown in Figure 1-6.

FIGURE 1-6

The left pane in the New Project dialog box displays the types of projects you can create; in this case, click Win32. This also identifies an application wizard that creates the initial contents for the project. The right pane displays a list of templates available for the project type you have selected in the left pane. The template you select is used by the application wizard in creating the files that make up the project. In the next dialog box you have an opportunity to customize the files that are created when you click the OK button in this dialog box. For most of the type/template options, a basic set of program source modules is created automatically.

You can now enter a suitable name for your project by typing into the "Name:" edit box — for example, you could call this one Ex1_01, or you can choose your own project name. Visual C++ 2010 supports long file names, so you have a lot of flexibility. The name of the solution folder appears in the bottom edit box and, by default, the solution folder has the same name as the project. You can change this if you want. The dialog box also enables you to modify the location for the solution that contains your project — this appears in the "Location:" edit box. If you simply enter a name for your project, the solution folder is automatically set to a folder with that name, with the path shown in the "Location:" edit box. By default the solution folder is created for you, if it doesn't already exist. If you want to specify a different path for the solution folder, just enter it in the "Location:" edit box. Alternatively, you can use the Browse button to select another path for your solution. Clicking OK displays the Win32 Application Wizard dialog box shown in Figure 1-7.

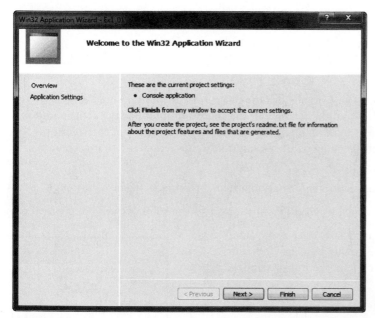

FIGURE 1-7

This dialog box explains the settings currently in effect. If you click the Finish button the wizard creates all the project files based on the settings in this box. In this case, you can click Application Settings on the left to display the Application Settings page of the wizard, shown in Figure 1-8.

FIGURE 1-8

The Application Settings page enables you to choose options that you want to apply to the project. Here, you can leave things as they are and click Finish. The application wizard then creates the project with all the default files.

The project folder will have the name that you supplied as the project name and will hold all the files making up the project definition. If you didn't change it, the solution folder has the same name as the project folder and contains the project folder plus the files defining the contents of the solution. If you use Windows Explorer to inspect the contents of the solution folder, you'll see that it contains four files:

➤   A file with the extension .sln that records information about the projects in the solution.

➤   A file with the extension .suo in which user options that apply to the solution will be recorded.

➤   A file with the extension .sdf that records data about Intellisense for the solution. Intellisense is the facility that provides auto-completion and prompts you for code in the Editor window as you enter it.

➤   A file with the extension .opensdf that records information about the state of the project. This file exists only while the project is open.

If you use Windows Explorer to look in the project folder, you will see that there are eight files initially, including a file with the name ReadMe.txt that contains a summary of the contents of the files that have been created for the project. The project you have created will automatically open in Visual C++ 2010 with the Solution Explorer pane, as in Figure 1-9.

FIGURE 1-9

The **Solution Explorer** pane presents a view of all the projects in the current solution and the files they contain — here, of course, there is just one project. You can display the contents of any file as an additional tab in the Editor pane just by double-clicking the name in the Solution Explorer tab. In the Editor pane, you can switch instantly to any of the files that have been displayed just by clicking on the appropriate tab.

The **Class View** tab displays the classes defined in your project and also shows the contents of each class. You don't have any classes in this application, so the view is empty. When I discuss classes you will see that you can use the Class View tab to move around the code relating to the definition and implementation of all your application classes quickly and easily.

The **Property Manager** tab shows the properties that have been set for the Debug and Release versions of your project. I'll explain these versions a little later in this chapter. You can change any of the properties shown by right-clicking a property and selecting Properties from the context menu; this displays a dialog box where you can set the project property. You can also press Alt+F7 to display the properties dialog box at any time. I'll discuss this in more detail when we go into the Debug and Release versions of a program.

You can display the **Resource View** tab by selecting from the View menu or by pressing Ctrl+Shift+E. The Resource View shows the dialog boxes, icons, menus, toolbars, and other resources used by the program. Because this is a console program, no resources are used; however, when you start writing Windows applications, you'll see a lot of things here. Through this tab you can edit or add to the resources available to the project.

As with most elements of the Visual C++ 2010 IDE, the Solution Explorer and other tabs provide context-sensitive pop-up menus when you right-click items displayed in the tab, and in some cases when you right-click in the empty space in the tab, too. If you find that the Solution Explorer pane gets in your way when you're writing code, you can hide it by clicking the Autohide icon. To redisplay it, click the Name tab on the left of the IDE window.

Modifying the Source Code

The application wizard generates a complete Win32 console program that you can compile and execute. Unfortunately, the program doesn't do anything as it stands, so to make it a little more interesting you need to change it. If it is not already visible in the Editor pane, double-click Ex1_01.cpp in the Solution Explorer pane. This is the main source file for the program that the application wizard generated, and it looks like what is shown in Figure 1-10.

```
Ex1_01.cpp                                                    ▾ ☐ ✕
(Global Scope)                          ▾                            ▾
    1  // Ex1_01.cpp : Defines the entry point for the console application.
    2  //
    3
    4  #include "stdafx.h"
    5
    6
    7  int _tmain(int argc, _TCHAR* argv[])
    8  {
    9      return 0;
   10  }
   11
   12  |

100 %  ▾
```

FIGURE 1-10

If the line numbers are not displayed on your system, select Tools ➪ Options from the main menu to display the Options dialog box. If you extend the C/C++ option in the Text Editor subtree in the left pane and select General from the extended tree, you can select Line Numbers in the right pane of the dialog box. I'll first give you a rough guide to what this code in Figure 1-10 does, and you'll see more on all of this later.

The first two lines are just comments. Anything following "//" in a line is ignored by the compiler. When you want to add descriptive comments in a line, precede your text with "//".

Line 4 is an `#include` directive that adds the contents of the file `stdafx.h` to this file in place of this `#include` directive. This is the standard way to add the contents of `.h` source files to a `.cpp` source file in a C++ program.

Line 7 is the first line of the executable code in this file and the beginning of the function `_tmain()`. A function is simply a named unit of executable code in a C++ program; every C++ program consists of at least one — and usually many more — functions.

Lines 8 and 10 contain left and right braces, respectively, that enclose all the executable code in the function `_tmain()`. The executable code is, therefore, just the single line 9, and all this does is end the program.

Now you can add the following two lines of code in the Editor window:

```
// Ex1_01.cpp : Defines the entry point for the console application.
//

#include "stdafx.h"
#include <iostream>

int _tmain(int argc, _TCHAR* argv[])
{
  std::cout << "Hello world!\n";
  return 0;
}
```

code snippet Ex1_01.cpp

The new lines you should add are shown in bold; the others are generated for you. To introduce each new line, place the cursor at the end of the text on the preceding line and press Enter to create an empty line in which you can type the new code. Make sure it is exactly as shown in the preceding example; otherwise the program may not compile.

The first new line is an `#include` directive that adds the contents of one of the standard libraries for ISO/IEC C++ to the source file. The `iostream` library defines facilities for basic I/O operations, and the one you are using in the second line that you added writes output to the command line. `std::cout` is the name of the standard output stream, and you write the string "`Hello world!\n`" to `std::cout` in the second addition statement. Whatever appears between the pair of double-quote characters is written to the command line.

Building the Solution

To build the solution, press F7 or select the Build ➪ Build Solution menu item. Alternatively, you can click the toolbar button corresponding to this menu item. The toolbar buttons for the Build menu may not be displayed, but you can easily fix this by right-clicking in the toolbar area and selecting the Build toolbar from those in the list. The program should then compile successfully. If there are errors, it may be that you created them while entering the new code, so check the two new lines very carefully.

Files Created by Building a Console Application

After the example has been built without error, take a look in the project folder by using Windows Explorer to see a new subfolder to the solution folder Ex1_01 called Debug. This is the folder Ex1_01\Debug, not the folder Ex1_01\Ex1_01\Debug. This folder contains the output of the build you just performed on the project. Notice that this folder contains three files.

Other than the .exe file, which is your program in executable form, you don't need to know much about what's in these files. In case you're curious, however, the .ilk file is used by the linker when you rebuild your project. It enables the linker to incrementally link the object files produced from the modified source code into the existing .exe file. This avoids the need to relink everything each time you change your program. The .pdb file contains debugging information that is used when you execute the program in debug mode. In this mode, you can dynamically inspect information generated during program execution.

There's a Debug subdirectory in the Ex1_01 project folder too. This contains a large number of files that were created during the build process, and you can see what kind of information they contain from the Type description in Windows Explorer.

Debug and Release Versions of Your Program

You can set a range of options for a project through the Project ➪ Ex1_01 Properties menu item. These options determine how your source code is processed during the compile and link stages. The set of options that produces a particular executable version of your program is called a **configuration**. When you create a new project workspace, Visual C++ 2010 automatically creates configurations for producing two versions of your application. One version, called the Debug version, includes additional information that helps you debug the program. With the Debug version of your program, you can step through the code when things go wrong, checking on the data values in the program. The other, called the Release version, has no debug information included and has the code-optimization options for the compiler turned on to provide you with the most efficient executable module. These two configurations are sufficient for your needs throughout this book, but when you need to add other configurations for an application you can do so through the Build ➪ Configuration Manager menu. (Note that this menu item won't appear if you haven't got a project loaded. This is obviously not a problem, but might be confusing if you're just browsing through the menus to see what's there.)

You can choose which configuration of your program to work with by selecting from the dropdown list in the toolbar. If you select Configuration Manager . . . from the dropdown list, the Configuration Manager dialog box will be displayed, as shown in Figure 1-11.

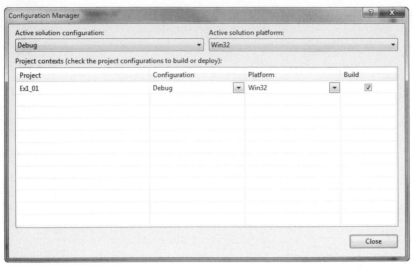

FIGURE 1-11

You use this dialog when your solution contains multiple projects. Here you can choose configurations for each of the projects and choose which ones you want to build.

After your application has been tested using the debug configuration and appears to be working correctly, you typically rebuild the program as a release version; this produces optimized code without the debug and trace capability, so the program runs faster and occupies less memory.

Executing the Program

After you have successfully compiled the solution, you can execute your program by pressing Ctrl+F5. You should see the window shown in Figure 1-12.

As you can see, you get the text between the double quotes written to the command line. The "\n" that

FIGURE 1-12

appeared at the end of the text string is a special sequence called an **escape sequence** that denotes a newline character. Escape sequences are used to represent characters in a text string that you cannot enter directly from the keyboard.

TRY IT OUT **Creating an Empty Console Project**

The previous project contained a certain amount of excess baggage that you don't need when working with simple C++ language examples. The precompiled headers option chosen by default resulted in the stdafx.h file being created in the project. This is a mechanism for making the compilation process more efficient when there are a lot of files in a program, but it won't be necessary for many of our examples. In these instances, you start with an empty project to which you can add your own source files. You can see how this works by creating a new project in a new solution for a Win32 console program with the name Ex1_02. After you have entered the project name and clicked OK, click Application Settings on the left side of the dialog box that follows. You can then select "Empty project" from the additional options, as Figure 1-13 shows.

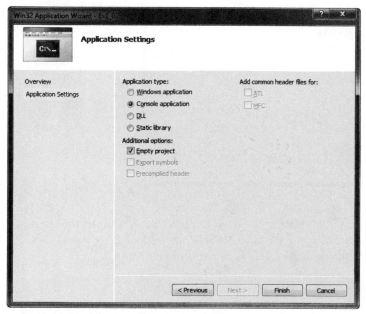

FIGURE 1-13

When you click Finish, the project is created as before, but this time without any source files.

By default, the project options will be set to use Unicode libraries. This makes use of a non-standard name for the main function in the program. In order to use standard native C++ in your console programs, you need to switch off the use of Unicode libraries.

Select the Project ➪ Properties menu item, or press Alt+F7, to display the Property Pages dialog for the project. Select the General option under Configuration Properties in the left pane and select the Character Set property in the right pane. You will then be able to set the value of this property to Not Set from the drop-down list to the right of the property name, as shown in Figure 1-14. Click OK to close the dialog. You should do this for all the native C++ console program examples in the book. If you forget to do so, they won't build. You will be using Unicode libraries in the Windows examples, though.

FIGURE 1-14

Next, add a new source file to the project. Right-click the Solution Explorer pane, and then select Add ⇨ New Item . . . from the context menu. A dialog box displays: click Code in the left pane and C++ File(.cpp) in the right pane. Enter the file name as **Ex1_02**, as shown in Figure 1-15.

FIGURE 1-15

When you click Add, the new file is added to the project and is displayed in the Editor window. The file is empty, of course, so nothing will be displayed. Enter the following code in the Editor window:

```cpp
// Ex1_02.cpp A simple console program
#include <iostream>                         // Basic input and output library

int main()
{
    std::cout << "This is a simple program that outputs some text." << std::endl;
    std::cout << "You can output more lines of text" << std::endl;
    std::cout << "just by repeating the output statement like this." << std::endl;
    return 0;                               // Return to the operating system
}
```

code snippet Ex1_02.cpp

Note the automatic indenting that occurs as you type the code. C++ uses indenting to make programs more readable, and the editor automatically indents each line of code that you enter based on what was in the previous line. You can change the indenting by selecting the Tools ⇨ Options . . . menu item to display the Options dialog. Selecting Text Editor ⇨ C/C++ ⇨ Tabs in the left pane of the dialog displays the indenting options in the right pane. The editor inserts tabs by default, but you can change it to insert spaces if you want.

You can also see the syntax color highlighting in action as you type. Some elements of the program are shown in different colors, as the editor automatically assigns colors to language elements depending on what they are.

The preceding code is the complete program. You probably noticed a couple of differences compared to the code generated by the application wizard in the previous example. There's no #include directive for the stdafx.h file. You don't have this file as part of the project here because you are not using the precompiled headers facility. The name of the function here is main; before it was _tmain. In fact all ISO/IEC C++ programs start execution in a function called main(). Microsoft also provides for this function to be called wmain when Unicode characters are used, and the name _tmain is defined to be either main or wmain (in the tchar.h header file), depending on whether or not the program is going to use Unicode characters. In the previous example the name _tmain is defined behind the scenes to be main. I'll use the standard name main in all the native C++ examples, which is why you need to change the Character Set property value for these projects to Not Set.

The output statements are a little different. The first statement in main() is the following:

```cpp
std::cout << "This is a simple program that outputs some text." << std::endl;
```

You have two occurrences of the << operator, and each one sends whatever follows to std::cout, which is the standard output stream. First, the string between double quotes is sent to the stream, and then std::endl, where std::endl is defined in the standard library as a newline character. Earlier, you used the escape sequence \n for a newline character within a string between double quotes. You could have written the preceding statement as follows:

```cpp
std::cout << "This is a simple program that outputs some text.\n";
```

You can now build this project in the same way as the previous example. Note that any open source files in the Editor pane are saved automatically if you have not already saved them. When you have compiled the program successfully, press Ctrl+F5 to execute it. If everything works as it should, the output will be as follows:

```
This is a simple program that outputs some text.
You can output more lines of text
just by repeating the output statement like this.
```

Dealing with Errors

Of course, if you didn't type the program correctly, you get errors reported. To see how this works you could deliberately introduce an error into the program. If you already have errors of your own, you can use those to perform this exercise. Go back to the Editor pane and delete the semicolon at the end of the second-to-last line between the braces (line 8); then rebuild the source file. The Output pane at the bottom of the application window will include the following error message:

```
C2143: syntax error : missing ';' before 'return'
```

Every error message during compilation has an error number that you can look up in the documentation. Here the problem is obvious; however, in more obscure cases, the documentation may help you figure out what is causing the error. To get the documentation on an error, click the line in the Output pane that contains the error number and then press F1. A new window displays containing further information about the error. You can try it with this simple error, if you like.

When you have corrected the error, you can then rebuild the project. The build operation works efficiently because the project definition keeps track of the status of the files making up the project. During a normal build, Visual C++ 2010 recompiles only the files that have changed since the program was last compiled or built. This means that if your project has several source files, and you've edited only one of the files since the project was last built, only that file is recompiled before linking to create a new .exe file.

You'll also use CLR console programs, so the next section shows you what a CLR console project looks like.

TRY IT OUT Creating a CLR Console Project

Press Ctrl+Shift+N to display the New Project dialog box; then select the project type as CLR and the template as CLR Console Application, as shown in Figure 1-16.

FIGURE 1-16

Enter the name as **Ex1_03**. When you click OK, the files for the project are created. There are no options for a CLR console project, so you always start with the same set of files in a project with this template. If you want an empty project — something you won't need with this book — there's a separate template for this.

If you look at the Solution Explorer pane, you'll see that there are some extra files, compared to a Win32 console project.

There are a couple of files in the virtual `Resource Files` folder. The `.ico` file stores an icon for the application that is displayed when the program is minimized; the `.rc` file records the resources for the application — just the icon in this case.

There is also a file with the name `AssemblyInfo.cpp`. Every CLR program consists of one or more **assemblies**, an assembly being a collection of code and resources that forms a functional unit. An assembly also contains extensive data for the CLR; there are specifications of the data types being used, versioning information about the code, and information that determines if the contents of the assembly can be accessed from another assembly. In short, an assembly is a fundamental building block in all CLR programs.

If the source code in the `Ex1_03.cpp` file is not displayed in the Editor window, double-click the file name in the Solution Explorer pane. The source code has the same `#include` directive as the default native C++ console program because CLR programs use precompiled headers for efficiency. The next line is new:

```
using namespace System;
```

The .NET library facilities are all defined within a **namespace**, and all the standard sort of stuff you are likely to use is in a namespace with the name `System`. This statement indicates the program code that follows uses the `System` namespace, but what exactly is a namespace?

A namespace is a very simple concept. Within your program code and within the code that forms the .NET libraries, names have to be given to lots of things — data types, variables, and blocks of code called functions all have to have names. The problem is that if you happen to invent a name that is already used in the library, there's potential for confusion. A namespace provides a way of getting around this problem. All the names in the library code defined within the `System` namespace are implicitly prefixed with the namespace name. So a name such as `String` in the library is really `System::String`. This means that if you have inadvertently used the name `String` for something in your code, you can use `System::String` to refer to `String` from the .NET library without confusing it with the name `String` in your code.

The two colons (`::`) are an operator called the **scope resolution operator**. Here the scope resolution operator separates the namespace name `System` from the type name `String`. You have seen this operator in the native C++ examples earlier in this chapter with `std::cout` and `std::endl`. This is the same story — `std` is the namespace name for native C++ libraries, and `cout` and `endl` are the names that have been defined within the `std` namespace to represent the standard output stream and the newline character, respectively.

In fact, the `using namespace` statement in this example enables you to use any name from the `System` namespace without having to use the namespace name as a prefix. If you did end up with a name conflict between a name you defined and a name in the library, you could resolve the problem by removing the `using namespace` statement and explicitly qualifying the name from the library with the namespace name. You learn more about namespaces in Chapter 2.

You can compile and execute the program by pressing Ctrl+F5. The output window should contain the following:

```
Hello World
```

NOTE *At the time of writing, the console window for a C++/CLI program does not remain on the screen when you press Ctrl+F5. It is displayed briefly, and then immediately disappears. If you find this is still the case with your installation, put the following line immediately before any return statement in the* main() *function:*

```
Console::ReadLine();
```

The program will pause with the console window displayed when this statement executes. Just press the Enter key to continue and allow the program to end. You may need to do this for all C++/CLI console program examples to see the output.

The other possibility is to open a command prompt window for the folder that contains the .exe *file for the program. With Windows Vista or Windows 7, you can do this by holding down the Shift key while you right-click the folder in Windows Explorer and then selecting Open Command Window Here from the context menu. You can then execute the program from the command prompt by entering the name of the* .exe *file.*

The output is similar to that from the first example. This output is produced by the following line:

```
Console::WriteLine(L"Hello World");
```

This uses a .NET library function to write the information between the double quotes to the command line, so this is the CLR equivalent of the native C++ statement that you added to Ex1_01:

```
std::cout << "Hello world!\n";
```

What the CLR statement does is more immediately apparent than what the native C++ statement does.

Setting Options in Visual C++ 2010

Two sets of options are available. You can set options that apply to the tools provided by Visual C++ 2010, which apply in every project context. You also can set options that are specific to a project, and that determine how the project code is to be processed when it is compiled and linked. Options that apply to every project are set through the Options dialog box that's displayed when you select Tools ➪ Options from the main menu. You used this dialog earlier to change the code indenting used by the editor. The Options dialog box is shown in Figure 1-17.

FIGURE 1-17

Clicking the [unfilled] symbol for any of the items in the left pane displays a list of subtopics. Figure 1-17 shows the options for the General subtopic under Projects and Solutions. The right pane displays the options you can set for the topic you have selected in the left pane. You should concern yourself with only a few of these at this time, but you'll find it useful to spend a little time browsing the range of options available to you. Clicking the Help button (the one with the question mark) at the top right of the dialog box displays an explanation of the current options.

You probably want to choose a path to use as a default when you create a new project, and you can do this through the first option shown in Figure 1-17. Just set the path to the location where you want your projects and solutions stored.

You can set options that apply to every C++ project by selecting the Projects and Solutions ➪ VC++ Project Settings topic in the left pane. You can also set options specific to the current project through the Project ➪ Properties menu item in the main menu, or by pressing Alt+F7. This menu item label is tailored to reflect the name of the current project. You used this to change the value of the Character Set property for the Ex1_02 console program.

Creating and Executing Windows Applications

Just to show how easy it's going to be, you can now create two working Windows applications. You'll create a native C++ application using MFC, and then you'll create a Windows Forms application that runs with the CLR. I'll defer discussion of the programs that you'll generate until I've covered the necessary ground for you to understand it in detail. You will see, though, that the processes are straightforward.

Creating an MFC Application

To start with, if an existing project is active — as indicated by the project name's appearing in the title bar of the Visual C++ 2010 main window — you can select Close Solution from the File menu. Alternatively, you can create a new project and have the current solution closed automatically.

To create the Windows program, select New ➪ Project from the File menu or press Ctrl+Shift+N; then set the project type as MFC, and select MFC Application as the project template. You can then enter the project name as **Ex1_04**. When you click OK the MFC Application Wizard dialog box is displayed. The dialog box has a range of options that let you choose which features you'd like to have included in your application. These are identified by the items in the list on the left of the dialog box.

Click Application Type to display these options. Click the Tabbed documents option to deselect it and select Windows Native/Default from the drop-down list to the right. The dialog should then look as shown in Figure 1-18.

FIGURE 1-18

Click Advanced Features next, and uncheck Explorer docking pane, Output docking pane, Properties docking pane, ActiveX controls, and Common Control Manifest so that the dialog looks as shown in Figure 1-19.

FIGURE 1-19

Finally, click Finish to create the project. The undocked Solution Explorer pane in the IDE window will look as shown in Figure 1-20.

The list shows the large number of source files that have been created, and several resource files. You need plenty of space on your hard drive when writing Windows programs! The files with the extension .cpp contain executable C++ source code, and the .h files contain C++ code consisting of definitions that are used by the executable code. The .ico files contain icons. The files are grouped into subfolders you can see for ease of access. These aren't real folders, though, and they won't appear in the project folder on your disk.

If you now take a look at the Ex1_04 solution folder and subfolders using Windows Explorer or whatever else you may have handy for looking at the files on your hard disk, you'll notice that you have generated a total of 29 files. Four of these are in the solution folder that includes the transient .opensdf file, a further 20 are in the project folder, and the rest are in a subfolder, res, of the project folder. The files in the res subfolder contain the resources used by the program, such as the menus and icons. You get all this as a result of just entering the name you want to assign to the project. You can see why, with so many files and file names being created automatically, a separate directory for each project becomes more than just a good idea.

FIGURE 1-20

One of the files in the Ex1_04 project directory is ReadMe.txt, and it provides an explanation of the purpose of each of the files that the MFC Application Wizard has generated. You can take a look at it if you want, using Notepad, WordPad, or even the Visual C++ 2010 editor. To view it in the Editor window, double-click it in the Solution Explorer pane.

Building and Executing the MFC Application

Before you can execute the program, you have to build the project — that is, compile the source code and link the program modules. You do this in exactly the same way as with the console application example. To save time, press Ctrl+F5 to get the project built and then executed in a single operation.

After the project has been built, the Output window indicates that there are no errors, and the executable starts running. The window for the program you've generated is shown in Figure 1-21.

FIGURE 1-21

As you see, the window is complete with menus and a toolbar. Although there is no specific functionality in the program — that's what you need to add to make it *your* program — all the menus work. You can try them out. You can even create further windows by selecting New from the File menu.

I think you'll agree that creating a Windows program with the MFC Application Wizard hasn't stressed too many brain cells. You'll need to get a few more ticking away when it comes to developing the basic program you have here into a program that does something more interesting, but it won't be that hard. Certainly, for many people, writing a serious Windows program the old-fashioned way, without the aid of Visual C++ 2010, required at least a couple of months on a brain-enhancing fish diet before making the attempt. That's why so many programmers used to eat sushi. That's all gone now with Visual C++ 2010. You never know, however, what's around the corner in programming technology. If you like sushi, it's best to continue eating it to be on the safe side.

Creating a Windows Forms Application

This is a job for another application wizard. So, create yet another new project, but this time select the type as CLR in the left pane of the New Project dialog box, and the template as Windows Forms Application. You can then enter the project name as **Ex1_05**. There are no options to choose from in this case, so click OK to create the project.

FIGURE 1-22

The Solution Explorer pane in Figure 1-22 shows the files that have been generated for this project.

There are considerably fewer files in this project — if you look in the directories, you'll see that there are a total of 15, including the solution files. One reason is that the initial GUI is much simpler than the native C++ application using MFC. The Windows Forms application has no menus or toolbars, and there is only one window. Of course you can add all these things quite easily, but the wizard for a Windows Forms application does not assume you want them from the start.

The Editor window looks rather different for this project, as Figure 1-23 shows.

The Editor window shows an image of the application window rather than code. The reason for this is that developing the GUI for a Windows Forms application is oriented toward a graphical design approach rather than a coding approach. You add GUI components to the application window by dragging or placing them there graphically, and Visual C++ 2010 automatically generates the code to display them. If you press Ctrl+Alt+X or select View ⇨ Toolbox you'll see an additional window showing a list of GUI components, as in Figure 1-24.

FIGURE 1-23

FIGURE 1-24

The Toolbox window presents a list of standard components that you can add to a Windows Forms application. If you scroll down you will see there are many more groups of controls available. You can try adding some buttons to the window for Ex1_05. Click Button in the Toolbox window list and then click in the client area of the Ex1_05 application window, displayed in the Editor window, where you want the button to be placed. You can adjust the size of the button by dragging its borders, and you can reposition the button by dragging it around. You can also change the caption. Right-click the button, select Properties from the pop-up, and then select the button1 value for the Text property in the Appearance group of properties. You can then enter **Start** on the keyboard and then press Enter to change the button label. The Properties window shows many other properties for the button as well. I won't go into these now, but essentially they are the specifications that affect the appearance of the button, and you can change them to suit your application.

Try adding another button with the label Stop, for example. The Editor window will look as shown in Figure 1-25.

You can graphically edit any of the GUI components at any time, and the code adjusts automatically. Try adding a few other components in the same way and then compile and execute the example by pressing Ctrl+F5. The application window displays in all its glory. Couldn't be easier, could it?

SUMMARY

FIGURE 1-25

In this chapter you have run through the basic mechanics of using Visual C++ 2010 to create applications of various kinds. You created and executed native and CLR console programs, and with the help of the application wizards you created an MFC-based Windows program and a Windows Forms program that executes with the CLR.

Starting with the next chapter, you'll use console applications extensively throughout the first half of the book. All the examples illustrating how C++ language elements are used are executed using either Win32 or CLR console applications. You will return to the application wizard for MFC-based programs and Windows Forms applications as soon as you have finished delving into the secrets of C++.

▶ **WHAT YOU LEARNED IN THIS CHAPTER**

TOPIC	CONCEPT
The Common Language Runtime	The Common Language Runtime (CLR) is the Microsoft implementation of the Common Language Infrastructure (CLI) standard.
The .NET Framework	The .NET Framework comprises the CLR plus the .NET libraries that support applications targeting the CLR.
Native C++	Native C++ applications are written in the ISO/IEC C++ language.
C++/CLI	Programs written in the C++/CLI language execute with the CLR.
Attributes	Attributes can provide additional information to the compiler to instruct it to modify or extend particular programming elements in a program.
Solutions	A solution is a container for one or more projects that form a solution to an information-processing problem of some kind.
Projects	A project is a container for the code and resource elements that make up a functional unit in a program.
Assemblies	An assembly is a fundamental unit in a CLR program. All CLR programs are made up of one or more assemblies.

2

Data, Variables, and Calculations

WHAT YOU WILL LEARN IN THIS CHAPTER:

➤ C++ program structure

➤ Namespaces

➤ Variables in C++

➤ Defining variables and constants

➤ Basic input from the keyboard and output to the screen

➤ Performing arithmetic calculations

➤ Casting operands

➤ Variable scope

➤ What the auto keyword does

➤ How to discover the type of an expression

In this chapter, you'll get down to the essentials of programming in C++. By the end of the chapter, you will be able to write a simple C++ program of the traditional form: input-process-output. I'll first discuss the ISO/IEC standard C++ language features, and then cover any additional or different aspects of the C++/CLI language.

As you explore aspects of the language using working examples, you'll have an opportunity to get some additional practice with the Visual C++ Development Environment. You should create a project for each of the examples before you build and execute them. Remember that when you are defining projects in this chapter and the following chapters through to Chapter 11, they are all console applications.

THE STRUCTURE OF A C++ PROGRAM

Programs that will run as console applications under Visual C++ 2010 are programs that read data from the command line and output the results to the command line. To avoid having to dig into the complexities of creating and managing application windows before you have enough knowledge to understand how they work, all the examples that you'll write to understand how the C++ language works will be console programs, either Win32 console programs or .NET console programs. This will enable you to focus entirely on the C++ language in the first instance; once you have mastered that, you'll be ready to deal with creating and managing application windows. You'll first look at how console programs are structured.

A program in C++ consists of one or more **functions**. In Chapter 1, you saw an example that was a Win32 console program consisting simply of the function main(), where main is the name of the function. Every ISO/IEC standard C++ program contains the function main(), and all C++ programs of any size consist of several functions — the main() function where execution of the program starts, plus a number of other functions. A function is simply a self-contained block of code with a unique name that you invoke for execution by using the name of the function. As you saw in Chapter 1, a Win32 console program that is generated by the Application Wizard has a main function with the name _tmain. This is a programming device to allow the name to be main or wmain, depending on whether or not the program is using Unicode characters. The names wmain and _tmain are Microsoft-specific. The name for the main function conforming to the ISO/IEC standard for C++ is main. I'll use the name main for all our ISO/IEC C++ examples because this is the most portable option. If you intend to compile your code only with Microsoft Visual C++, then it is advantageous to use the Microsoft-specific names for main, in which case you can use the Application Wizard to generate your console applications. To use the Application Wizard with the console program examples in this book, just copy the code shown in the body of the main function in the book to _tmain.

Figure 2-1 shows how a typical console program might be structured. The execution of the program shown starts at the beginning of the function main(). From main(), execution transfers to a function input_names(), which returns execution to the position immediately following the point where it was called in main(). The sort_names() function is then called from main(), and, once control returns to main(), the final function output_names() is called. Eventually, once output has been completed, execution returns once again to main() and the program ends.

Of course, different programs may have radically different functional structures, but they all start execution at the beginning of main(). If you structure your programs as a number of functions, you can write and test each function separately. Segmenting your programs in this way gives you a further advantage in that functions you write to perform a particular task can be re-used in other programs. The libraries that come with C++ provide a lot of standard functions that you can use in your programs. They can save you a great deal of work.

FIGURE 2-1

 NOTE *You'll see more about creating and using functions in Chapter 5.*

TRY IT OUT A Simple Program

A simple example can help you to understand the elements of a program a little better. Start by creating a new project — you can use the Ctrl+Shift+N key combination as a shortcut for this. When the dialog shown in Figure 2-2 appears, select Win32 as the project type and Win32 Console Application as the template. You can name the project Ex2_01.

FIGURE 2-2

If you click the OK button, you'll see a new dialog in the form shown in Figure 2-3 that shows an overview of what the Application Wizard will generate.

If you now click Application Settings on the left of this dialog, you'll see further options for a Win32 application displayed, as shown in Figure 2-4.

FIGURE 2-3

FIGURE 2-4

The default setting is a Console application that will include a file containing a default version of `main()`, but you'll start from the most basic project structure, so choose Empty project from the set of additional options and click the Finish button. Now you have a project created, but it contains no files at all. You can see what the project contains from the Solution Explorer pane on the left of the

Visual C++ 2010 main window, as shown in Figure 2-5. Because you are starting with an empty project, you need to check that the project properties are set appropriately. You can display the project properties dialog by selecting Properties from the Project menu or just pressing Alt+F7. Select Configuration in the left pane, and then General in the left pane if it is not already highlighted. In the right pane, you'll see a list of properties, so select Character Set in the Project Defaults set. To the right of the property name, you'll see a drop-down list, from which you should select Not Set. The default value for this property for a Win32 console implies you are going to use the Unicode character set in the application. This will cause the compiler to look for _wmain, which won't be present. If you fail to reset this project property, then you will get an error message during the build operation because _wmain cannot be found. Having set the Character Set property, you are ready to create the program code.

FIGURE 2-5

You'll start by adding a new source file to the project, so right-click Source Files in the Solution Explorer pane and select the Add ➪ New Item. . . menu option. The Add New Item dialog, similar to that shown in Figure 2-6, displays.

FIGURE 2-6

Make sure the C++ File(.cpp) template is highlighted by clicking on it, and enter the file name, as shown in Figure 2-6. The file will automatically be given the extension .cpp, so you don't have to enter the extension. There is no problem having the name of the file the same as the name of the project. The project file will have the extension .vcxproj, so that will differentiate it from the source file.

Click the Add button to create the file. You can then type the following code in the Editor pane of the IDE window:

```
// Ex2_01.cpp
// A Simple Example of a Program
#include <iostream>

using std::cout;
using std::endl;

int main()
{
    int apples, oranges;                  // Declare two integer variables
    int fruit;                            // ...then another one

    apples = 5; oranges = 6;              // Set initial values
    fruit = apples + oranges;             // Get the total fruit

    cout << endl;                         // Start output on a new line
    cout << "Oranges are not the only fruit... " << endl
        << "- and we have " << fruit << " fruits in all.";
    cout << endl;                         // Output a new line character

    return 0;                             // Exit the program
}
```

code snippet Ex2_01.cpp

The preceding example is intended to illustrate some of the ways in which you can write C++ statements and is not a model of good programming style.

The editor will check the code as you type. Anything it thinks is not correct will be underlined with a red squiggle, so look out for these. If you see one, it usually means that you have mistyped something somewhere.

Since the file is identified by its extension as a file containing C++ code, the keywords in the code that the editor recognizes will be colored to identify them. You will be able to see if you have entered `Int` where you should have entered `int`, because `Int` will not have the color used to highlight keywords in your source code.

If you look at the Solution Explorer pane (press Ctrl+Alt+L to display it) for your new project, you'll see the newly created source file. Solution Explorer will always show all the files in a project. You can display the Class View pane by selecting from the View menu or by pressing Ctrl+Shift+C. This consists of two panes, the upper pane showing global functions and macros within the project (and classes when you get to create a project involving classes), and the lower pane presently empty. The `main()` function will appear in the lower pane if you select Global Functions and Variables in the upper Class View pane; this is shown in Figure 2-7. I'll consider what this means

FIGURE 2-7

in more detail later, but essentially, **globals** are functions and/or variables that are accessible from anywhere in the program.

You can display the Property Manager pane by selecting from the View menu. If you extend the items in the tree that is displayed by clicking the [unfilled] symbols, it will look like Figure 2-8.

This shows the two possible versions you can build, the Debug version for testing and the Release version when your program has been tested. The properties for each version of the project are shown, and double-clicking on any of them will display a dialog showing the Property Pages, where you can change properties, if necessary.

FIGURE 2-8

You have three ways to compile and link the program; you can select the Build Ex2_01 menu item from the Build menu, you can press the F7 function key, or you can select the appropriate toolbar button — you can identify what a toolbar button does by hovering the mouse cursor over it. If there is no toolbar button that shows the tooltip Build Ex2_01 when the cursor is over it, then the Build toolbar is not currently displayed. You can remedy this by right-clicking on an empty part of the toolbar area and selecting Build from the list of toolbars that is displayed. It's a very long list and you will probably want to choose different sets of toolbars to be displayed, depending on what you are doing.

Assuming the build operation was successful, you can execute the program by pressing the Ctrl+F5 keys or by selecting Start Without Debugging from the Debug menu. You should get the following output in a command line window:

```
Oranges are not the only fruit...
- and we have 11 fruits in all.
Press any key to continue ...
```

The first two lines were produced by the program, and the last line indicates how you can end the execution and close the command-line window. I won't show this last line of output from other console examples, but it's always there.

Program Comments

The first two lines in the program are **comments**. Comments are an important part of any program, but they're not executable code — they are there simply to help the human reader. All comments are ignored by the compiler. On any line of code, two successive slashes // that are not contained within a text string (you'll see what text strings are later) indicate that the rest of the line is a comment.

You can see that several lines of the program contain comments as well as program statements. You can also use an alternative form of comment bounded by /* and */. For example, the first line of the program could have been written:

```
/*    Ex2_01.cpp    */
```

The comment using // covers only the portion of the line following the two successive slashes, whereas the /*...*/ form defines whatever is enclosed between the /* and the */ as a comment, and this can span several lines. For example, you could write:

```
/*
   Ex2_01.cpp
   A Simple Program Example
*/
```

All four lines are comments and are ignored by the compiler. If you want to highlight some particular comment lines, you can always embellish them with a frame of some description:

```
/****************************
 *  Ex2-01.cpp               *
 *  A Simple Program Example *
 ****************************/
```

As a rule, you should always comment your programs comprehensively. The comments should be sufficient for another programmer or you at a later date to understand the purpose of any particular piece of code and how it works. I will often use comments in examples to explain in more detail than you would in a production program.

The #include Directive — Header Files

Following the comments, you have a #include directive:

```
#include <iostream>
```

This is called a **directive** because it directs the compiler to do something — in this case, to insert the contents of the file, iostream, that is identified between the angled brackets, <>, into the program source file before compilation. The iostream file is called a **header file** because it's invariably inserted at the beginning of a program file. The iostream header file is part of the standard C++ library, and it contains definitions that are necessary for you to be able to use C++ input and output statements. If you didn't include the contents of iostream into the program, it wouldn't compile, because you use output statements in the program that depend on some of the definitions in this file. There are many different header files provided by Visual C++ that cover a wide range of capabilities. You'll be seeing more of them as you progress through the language facilities.

The name of the file to be inserted by a #include directive does not have to be written between angled brackets. The name of the header file can also be written between double quotes, thus:

```
#include "iostream"
```

The only difference between this and the version above between angled brackets is the places where the compiler is going to look for the file.

If you write the header file name between double quotes, the compiler searches for the header file first in the directory that contains the source file in which the directive appears. If the header file is not there, the compiler then searches the directories where the standard header files are stored.

If the file name is enclosed between angled brackets, the compiler only searches the directories it expects to find the standard header files. Thus, when you want to include a standard header in a source, you should place the name between angled brackets because they will be found more quickly. When you are including other header files, typically ones that you create yourself, you should place the name between double quotes; otherwise, they will not be found at all.

A #include statement is one of several available **preprocessor directives**, and I'll be introducing more of these as you need them throughout the book. The Visual C++ editor recognizes preprocessor directives and highlights them in blue in your edit window. Preprocessor directives are commands executed by the preprocessor phase of the compiler that executes before your code is compiled into object code, and preprocessor directives generally act on your source code in some way before it is compiled. They all start with the # character.

Namespaces and the Using Declaration

As you saw in Chapter 1, the **standard library** is an extensive set of routines that have been written to carry many common tasks: for example, dealing with input and output, and performing basic mathematical calculations. Since there are a very large number of these routines, as well as other kinds of things that have names, it is quite possible that you might accidentally use the same name as one of the names defined in the standard library for your own purposes. A **namespace** is a mechanism in C++ for avoiding problems that can arise when duplicate names are used in a program for different things, and it does this by associating a given set of names, such as those from the standard library, with a sort of family name, which is the namespace name.

Every name that is defined in code that appears within a namespace also has the namespace name associated with it. All the standard library facilities for ISO/IEC C++ are defined within a namespace with the name std, so every item from this standard library that you can access in your program has its own name, plus the namespace name, std, as a qualifier. The names cout and endl are defined within the standard library so their full names are std::cout and std::endl, and you saw these in action in Chapter 1. The two colons that separate the namespace name from the name of an entity form an operator called the **scope resolution operator,** and I'll discuss other uses for this operator later on in the book. Using the full names in the program will tend to make the code look a bit cluttered, so it would be nice to be able to use their simple names, unqualified by the namespace name, std. The two lines in our program that follow the #include directive for iostream make this possible:

```
using std::cout;
using std::endl;
```

These are **using declarations** that tell the compiler that you intend to use the names cout and endl from the namespace std without specifying the namespace name. The compiler will now assume that wherever you use the name cout in the source file subsequent to the first using declaration, you mean the cout that is defined in the standard library. The name cout represents the standard output stream that, by default, corresponds to the command line, and the name endl represents the newline character.

You'll learn more about namespaces, including how you define your own namespaces, a little later this chapter.

The main() Function

The function `main()` in the example consists of the function header defining it as `main()` plus everything from the first opening curly brace ({) to the corresponding closing curly brace (}). The braces enclose the executable statements in the function, which are referred to collectively as the **body** of the function.

As you'll see, all functions consist of a header that defines (among other things) the function name, followed by the function body that consists of a number of program statements enclosed between a pair of braces. The body of a function may contain no statements at all, in which case, it doesn't do anything.

A function that doesn't do anything may seem somewhat superfluous, but when you're writing a large program, you may map out the complete program structure in functions initially, but omit the code for many of the functions, leaving them with empty or minimal bodies. Doing this means that you can compile and execute the whole program with all its functions at any time and add detailed coding for the functions incrementally.

Program Statements

The program statements making up the function body of `main()` are each terminated with a *semicolon*. It's the semicolon that marks the end of a statement, not the end of the line. Consequently, a statement can be spread over several lines when this makes the code easier to follow, and several statements can appear in a single line. The program statement is the basic unit in defining what a program does. This is a bit like a sentence in a paragraph of text, where each sentence stands by itself in expressing an action or an idea, but relates to and combines with the other sentences in the paragraph in expressing a more general idea. A statement is a self-contained definition of an action that the computer is to carry out, but that can be combined with other statements to define a more complex action or calculation.

The action of a function is always expressed by a number of statements, each ending with a semicolon. Take a quick look at each of the statements in the example just written, just to get a general feel for how it works. I will discuss each type of statement more fully later in this chapter.

The first statement in the body of the `main()` function is:

```
int apples, oranges;            // Declare two integer variables
```

This statement declares two variables, `apples` and `oranges`. A **variable** is just a named bit of computer memory that you can use to store data, and a statement that introduces the names of one or more variables is called a **variable declaration**. The keyword `int` in the preceding statement indicates that the variables with the names `apples` and `oranges` are to store values that are whole numbers, or integers. Whenever you introduce the name of a variable into a program, you always specify what kind of data it will store, and this is called the `type` of the variable.

The next statement declares another integer variable, `fruit`:

```
int fruit;                              // ...then another one
```

While you can declare several variables in the same statement, as you did in the preceding statement for apples and oranges, it is generally a good idea to declare each variable in a separate statement on its own line, as this enables you to comment them individually to explain how you intend to use them.

The next line in the example is:

```
apples = 5; oranges = 6;        // Set initial values
```

This line contains two statements, each terminated by a semicolon. I put this here just to demonstrate that you can put more than one statement in a line. While it isn't obligatory, it's generally good programming practice to write only one statement on a line, as it makes the code easier to understand. Good programming practice is about adopting approaches to coding that make your code easy to follow, and minimize the likelihood of errors.

The two statements in the preceding line store the values 5 and 6 in the variables apples and oranges, respectively. These statements are called **assignment statements**, because they assign a new value to a variable, and the = is the assignment operator.

The next statement is:

```
fruit = apples + oranges;       // Get the total fruit
```

This is also an assignment statement, but is a little different because you have an **arithmetic expression** to the right of the assignment operator. This statement adds together the values stored in the variables apples and oranges and stores the result in the variable fruit.

The next three statements are:

```
cout << endl;                   // Start output on a new line
cout << "Oranges are not the only fruit... " << endl
     << "- and we have " << fruit << " fruits in all.";
cout << endl;                   // Start output on a new line
```

These are all **output statements**. The first statement is the first line here, and it sends a newline character, denoted by the word endl, to the command line on the screen. In C++, a source of input or a destination for output is referred to as a **stream**. The name cout specifies the "standard" output stream, and the operator << indicates that what appears to the right of the operator is to be sent to the output stream, cout. The << operator "points" in the direction that the data flows — from the variable or string that appears on the right of the operator to the output destination on the left. Thus, in the first statement, the value represented by the name endl — which represents a newline character — is sent to the stream identified by the name cout — and data transferred to cout is written to the command line.

The meaning of the name cout and the operator << are defined in the standard library header file iostream, which you added to the program code by means of the #include directive at the beginning of the program. cout is a name in the standard library and, therefore, is within the namespace std. Without the using directive, it would not be recognized unless you used its fully qualified name, which is std::cout, as I mentioned earlier. Because cout has been defined to represent the standard output stream, you shouldn't use the name cout for other purposes, so you can't use it as the name of a variable in your program, for example. Obviously, using the same name for different things is likely to cause confusion.

The second output statement of the three is spread over two lines:

```
cout << "Oranges are not the only fruit... " << endl
     << "- and we have " << fruit << " fruits in all.";
```

As I said earlier, you can spread each statement in a program over as many lines as you wish if it helps to make the code clearer. The end of a statement is always signaled by a semicolon, not the end of a line. Successive lines are read and combined into a single statement by the compiler until it finds the semicolon that defines the end of the statement. Of course, this means that if you forget to put a semicolon at the end of a statement, the compiler will assume the next line is part of the same statement and join them together. This usually results in something the compiler cannot understand, so you'll get an error message.

The statement sends the text string `"Oranges are not the only fruit..."` to the command line, followed by another newline character (`endl`), then another text string, `"- and we have "`, followed by the value stored in the variable `fruit`, then, finally, another text string, `" fruits in all."`. There is no problem stringing together a sequence of things that you want to output in this way. The statement executes from left to right, with each item being sent to `cout` in turn. Note that each item to be sent to `cout` is preceded by its own `<<` operator.

The third and last output statement just sends another newline character to the screen, and the three statements produce the output from the program that you see.

The last statement in the program is:

```
return 0;                    // Exit the program
```

This terminates execution of the `main()` function, which stops execution of the program. Control returns to the operating system, and the `0` is a return code that tells the operating system that the application terminated successfully after completing its task. I'll discuss all these statements in more detail later.

The statements in a program are executed in the sequence in which they are written, unless a statement specifically causes the natural sequence to be altered. In Chapter 3, you'll look at statements that alter the sequence of execution.

Whitespace

Whitespace is the term used in C++ to describe blanks, tabs, newline characters, form feed characters, and comments. Whitespace serves to separate one part of a statement from another and enables the compiler to identify where one element in a statement, such as `int`, ends and the next element begins. Otherwise, whitespace is ignored and has no effect.

For example, consider the following statement

```
int fruit;                   // ...then another one
```

There must be at least one whitespace character (usually a space) between `int` and `fruit` for the compiler to be able to distinguish them, but if you add more whitespace characters, they will be ignored. The content of the line following the semicolon is all whitespace and is therefore ignored.

On the other hand, look at this statement:

```
fruit = apples + oranges;        // Get the total fruit
```

No whitespace characters are necessary between `fruit` and `=`, or between `=` and `apples`, although you are free to include some if you wish. This is because the `=` is not alphabetic or numeric, so the compiler can separate it from its surroundings. Similarly, no whitespace characters are necessary on either side of the + sign, but you can include some if you want to aid the readability of your code.

As I said, apart from its use as a separator between elements in a statement that might otherwise be confused, whitespace is ignored by the compiler (except, of course, in a string of characters between quotes). Therefore, you can include as much whitespace as you like to make your program more readable, as you did when you spread an output statement in the last example over several lines. Remember that in C++, the end of a statement is wherever the semicolon occurs.

Statement Blocks

You can enclose several statements between a pair of braces, in which case, they become a **block**, or a **compound statement**. The body of a function is an example of a block. Such a compound statement can be thought of as a single statement (as you'll see when you look at the decision-making possibilities in C++ in Chapter 3). In fact, wherever you can put a single statement in C++, you could equally well put a block of statements between braces. As a consequence, blocks can be placed inside other blocks. In fact, blocks can be nested, one within another, to any depth.

 NOTE *A statement block also has important effects on variables, but I will defer discussion of this until later in this chapter when I discuss something called variable scope.*

Automatically Generated Console Programs

In the last example, you opted to produce the project as an empty project with no source files, and then you added the source file subsequently. If you just allow the Application Wizard to generate the project, as you did in Chapter 1, the project will contain several files, and you should explore their contents in a little more depth. Create a new Win32 console project with the name `Ex2_01A`, and this time, just allow the Application Wizard to finish without choosing to set any of the options in the Application Settings dialog. The project will have four files containing code: the `Ex2_01A.cpp` and `stdafx.cpp` source files, the `stdafx.h` header file, and the `targetver.h` file that specifies the earliest version of Windows that is capable of running your application. This is to provide for basic capability that you might need in a console program, and represents a working program as it stands, which does nothing. If you have a project open, you can close it by selecting the File ➪ Close Solution item on the main menu. You can create a new project with an existing project open, in which case, the old project will be closed automatically unless you elect to add it to the same solution.

First of all, the contents of `Ex2_01A.cpp` will be:

```
// Ex2_01A.cpp : Defines the entry point for the console application.
//

#include "stdafx.h"

int _tmain(int argc, _TCHAR* argv[])
{
  return 0;
}
```

code snippet Ex2_01A.cpp

This is decidedly different from the previous example. There is a `#include` directive for the `stdafx.h` header file that was not in the previous version, and the function where execution starts is called `_tmain()`, not `main()`.

The Application Wizard has generated the `stdafx.h` header file as part of the project, and if you take a look at the code in there, you'll see there are three further `#include` directives for the `targetver.h` header that I mentioned earlier, plus the standard library header files `stdio.h` and `tchar.h` The old-style header `stdio.h` is for standard I/O and was used before the current ISO/IEC standard for C++; this covers the same functionality as the `iostream` header. `tchar.h` is a Microsoft-specific header file defining text functions. The idea is that `stdafx.h` should define a set of standard system include files for your project — you would add `#include` directives for any other system headers that you need in this file. While you are learning ISO/IEC C++, you won't be using either of the headers that appear in `stdafx.h`, which is one reason for not using the default file generation capability provided by the Application Wizard.

As I already explained, Visual C++ 2010 supports `wmain()` as an alternative to `main()` when you are writing a program that's using Unicode characters — `wmain()` being a Microsoft-specific command that is not part of ISO/IEC standard C++. In support of that, the `tchar.h` header defines the name `_tmain` so that it will normally be replaced by `main`, but will be replaced by `wmain` if the symbol `_UNICODE` is defined. Thus, to identify a program as using Unicode, you would add the following statement to the beginning of the `stdafx.h` header file:

```
#define _UNICODE
```

Actually, you don't need to do this with the Ex2_01A project you have just created, because the `Character Set` project property will have been set to use the Unicode character set by default.

Now that I've explained all that, I'll stick to plain old `main()` for our ISO/IEC C++ examples that are console applications, because this option is standard C++ and, therefore, the most portable coding approach.

DEFINING VARIABLES

A fundamental objective in all computer programs is to manipulate some data and get some answers. An essential element in this process is having a piece of memory that you can call your own, that you can refer to using a meaningful name, and where you can store an item of data. Each individual piece of memory so specified is called a **variable**.

As you already know, each variable will store a particular kind of data, and the type of data that can be stored is fixed when you define the variable in your program. One variable might store whole numbers (that is, integers), in which case, you couldn't use it to store numbers with fractional values. The value that each variable contains at any point is determined by the statements in your program, and, of course, its value will usually change many times as the program calculation progresses.

The next section looks first at the rules for naming a variable when you introduce it into a program.

Naming Variables

The name you give to a variable is called an **identifier** or, more conveniently, a **variable name**. Variable names can include the letters A–z (upper- or lowercase), the digits 0–9, and the underscore character. No other characters are allowed, and if you happen to use some other character, you will typically get an error message when you try to compile the program. Variable names must also begin with either a letter or an underscore. Names are usually chosen to indicate the kind of information to be stored.

Because variable names in Visual C++ 2010 can be up to 2048 characters long, you have a reasonable amount of flexibility in what you call your variables. In fact, as well as variables, there are quite a few other things that have names in C++, and they, too, can have names of up to 2048 characters, with the same definition rules as a variable name. Using names of the maximum length allowed can make your programs a little difficult to read, and unless you have amazing keyboard skills, they are the very devil to type in. A more serious consideration is that not all compilers support such long names. If you anticipate compiling your code in other environments, it's a good idea to limit names to a maximum of 31 characters; this will usually be adequate for devising meaningful names and will avoid problems of compiler name length constraints in most instances.

Although you can use variable names that begin with an underscore (for example, _this and _that), this is best avoided because of potential clashes with standard system variables that have the same form. You should also avoid using names starting with a double underscore for the same reason.

Examples of good variable names include the following:

- ➤ `price`
- ➤ `discount`
- ➤ `pShape`
- ➤ `value_`
- ➤ `COUNT`

8_Ball, 7Up, and 6_pack are not legal. Neither is Hash! nor Mary-Ann. This last example is a common mistake, although Mary_Ann with an underscore in place of the hyphen would be quite acceptable. Of course, Mary Ann would not be, because blanks are not allowed in variable names. Note that the variable names republican and Republican are quite different, as names are case-sensitive, so upper- and lowercase letters are differentiated. Of course, whitespace characters in general cannot appear within a name, and if you inadvertently include whitespace characters, you will have two or more names instead of one, which will usually cause the compiler to complain.

A convention that is often adopted in C++ is to reserve names beginning with a capital letter for naming classes and use names beginning with a lowercase letter for variables. I'll discuss classes in Chapter 8.

Keywords in C++

There are reserved words in C++ called **keywords** that have special significance within the language. They will be highlighted with a particular color by the Visual C++ 2010 editor as you enter your program — in my system, the default color is blue. If a keyword you type does not appear highlighted, then you have entered the keyword incorrectly. Incidentally, if you don't like the default colors used by the text editor, you can change them by selecting Options from the Tools menu and making changes when you select Environment/Fonts and Colors in the dialog.

Remember that keywords, like the rest of the C++ language, are case-sensitive. For example, the program that you entered earlier in the chapter contained the keywords int and return; if you write Int or Return, these are not keywords and, therefore, will not be recognized as such. You will see many more as you progress through the book. You must ensure that the names you choose for entities in your program, such as variables, are not the same as any of the keywords in C++.

Declaring Variables

As you saw earlier, a variable **declaration** is a program statement that specifies the name of a variable of a given type. For example:

```
int value;
```

This declares a variable with the name value that can store integers. The type of data that can be stored in the variable value is specified by the keyword int, so you can only use value to store data of type int. Because int is a keyword, you can't use int as a name for one of your variables.

 NOTE *A variable declaration always ends with a semicolon.*

A single declaration can specify the names of several variables, but as I have said, it is generally better to declare variables in individual statements, one per line. I'll deviate from this from time to time in this book, but only in the interests of not spreading code over too many pages.

In order to store data (for example, the value of an integer), you not only need to have defined the name of the variable, you also need to have associated a piece of the computer's memory with the variable name. This process is called variable **definition**. In C++, a variable declaration is also a definition (except in a few special cases, which we shall come across during the book). In the course of a single statement, we introduce the variable name, and also tie it to an appropriately sized piece of memory.

So, the statement

```
int value;
```

is both a declaration and a definition. You use the variable *name* value that you have declared to access the piece of the computer's *memory* that you have defined, and that can store a single value of type int.

 NOTE *You use the term declaration when you introduce a name into your program, with information on what the name will be used for. The term definition refers to the allotment of computer memory to the name. In the case of variables, you can declare and define in a single statement, as in the preceding line. The reason for this apparently pedantic differentiation between a declaration and a definition is that you will meet statements that are declarations but not definitions.*

You must declare a variable at some point between the beginning of your program and when the variable is used for the first time. In C++, it is good practice to declare variables close to their first point of use.

Initial Values for Variables

When you declare a variable, you can also assign an initial value to it. A variable declaration that assigns an initial value to a variable is called an **initialization**. To initialize a variable when you declare it, you just need to write an equals sign followed by the initializing value after the variable name. You can write the following statements to give each of the variables an initial value:

```
int value = 0;
int count = 10;
int number = 5;
```

In this case, value will have the value 0, count will have the value 10, and number will have the value 5.

There is another way of writing the initial value for a variable in C++ called **functional notation**. Instead of an equals sign and the value, you can simply write the value in parentheses following the variable name. So, you could rewrite the previous declarations as:

```
int value(0);
int count(10);
int number(5);
```

Generally, it's a good idea to use either one notation or the other consistently when you are initializing variables. However, I'll use one notation in some examples and the other notation in others, so you get used to seeing both of them in working code.

If you don't supply an initial value for a variable, then it will usually contain whatever garbage was left in the memory location it occupies by the previous program you ran (there is an exception to this that you will meet later in this chapter). Wherever possible, you should initialize your variables when you declare them. If your variables start out with known values, it makes it easier to work out what is happening when things go wrong. And one thing you can be sure of — things *will* go wrong.

FUNDAMENTAL DATA TYPES

The sort of information that a variable can hold is determined by its **data type**. All data and variables in your program must be of some defined type. ISO/IEC standard C++ provides you with a range of **fundamental data types**, specified by particular keywords. Fundamental data types are so called because they store values of types that represent fundamental data in your computer, essentially numerical values, which also includes characters because a character is represented by a numerical character code. You have already seen the keyword int for defining integer variables. C++/CLI also defines fundamental data types that are not part of ISO/IEC C++, and I'll go into those a little later in this chapter.

The fundamental types fall into three categories: types that store integers, types that store non-integral values — which are called floating-point types — and the void type that specifies an empty set of values or no type.

Integer Variables

Integer variables are variables that can have only values that are whole numbers. The number of players in a football team is an integer, at least at the beginning of the game. You already know that you can declare integer variables using the keyword int. Variables of type int occupy 4 bytes in memory and can store both positive and negative integer values. The upper and lower limits for the values of a variable of type int correspond to the maximum and minimum signed binary numbers, which can be represented by 32 bits. The upper limit for a variable of type int is $2^{31}-1$, which is 2,147,483,647, and the lower limit is $-(2^{31})$, which is −2,147,483,648. Here's an example of defining a variable of type int:

```
int toeCount = 10;
```

In Visual C++ 2010, the keyword short also defines an integer variable, this time occupying 2 bytes. The keyword short is equivalent to short int, and you could define two variables of type short with the following statements:

```
short feetPerPerson = 2;
short int feetPerYard = 3;
```

Both variables are of the same type here because short means exactly the same as short int. I used both forms of the type name to show them in use, but it would be best to stick to one representation of the type in your programs, and of the two, short is used most often.

C++ also provides the integer type, long, which can also be written as long int. Here's how you declare variables of type long:

```
long bigNumber = 1000000L;
long largeValue = 0L;
```

Of course, you could also use functional notation when specifying the initial values:

```
long bigNumber(1000000L);
long largeValue(0L);
```

These statements declare the variables `bigNumber` and `largeValue` with initial values `1000000` and `0`, respectively. The letter `L` appended to the end of the literals specifies that they are integers of type `long`. You can also use the small letter `l` for the same purpose, but it has the disadvantage that it is easily confused with the digit `1`. Integer literals without an `L` appended are of type `int`.

NOTE *You must not include commas when writing large numeric values in a program. In text, you might write the number 12,345, but in your program code, you must write this as 12345.*

Integer variables declared as `long` in Visual C++ 2010 occupy 4 bytes and can have values from −2,147,483,648 to 2,147,483,647. This is the same range as for variables declared as type `int`.

NOTE *With other C++ compilers, variables of type `long` (which is the same as type `long int`) may not be the same as type `int`, so if you expect your programs to be compiled in other environments, don't assume that `long` and `int` are equivalent. For truly portable code, you should not even assume that an `int` is 4 bytes (for example, under older 16-bit versions of Visual C++, a variable of type `int` was 2 bytes).*

If you need to store integers of an even greater magnitude, you can use variables of type `long long`:

```
long long huge = 100000000LL;
```

Variables of type `long long` occupy 8 bytes and can store values from −9223372036854775808 to 9223372036854775807. The suffix to identify an integer constant as type `long long` is `LL` or `ll`, but the latter is best avoided.

Character Data Types

The `char` data type serves a dual purpose. It specifies a one-byte variable that you can use either to store integers within a given range, or to store the code for a single **ASCII** character, which is the American Standard Code for Information Interchange. You can declare a `char` variable with this statement:

```
char letter = 'A';
```

Or you could write this as:

```
char letter('A');
```

This declares the variable with the name `letter` and initializes it with the constant `'A'`. Note that you specify a value that is a single character between single quotes, rather than the double quotes used previously for defining a string of characters to be displayed. A string of characters is a series of values of type `char` that are grouped together into a single entity called an **array**. I'll discuss arrays and how strings are handled in C++ in Chapter 4.

Because the character `'A'` is represented in ASCII by the decimal value 65, you could have written the statement as:

```
char letter = 65;           // Equivalent to A
```

This produces the same result as the previous statement. The range of integers that can be stored in a variable of type `char` with Visual C++ is from −128 to 127.

NOTE *The ISO/IEC C++ standard does not require that type* char *should represent signed 1-byte integers. It is the compiler implementer's choice as to whether type* char *represents signed integers in the range −128 to 127 or unsigned integers in the range 0 to 255. You need to keep this in mind if you are porting your C++ code to a different environment.*

The type `wchar_t` is so called because it is a **wide char**acter type, and variables of this type store 2-byte character codes with values in the range from 0 to 65,535. Here's an example of defining a variable of type `wchar_t`:

```
wchar_t letter = L'Z';      // A variable storing a 16-bit character code
```

This defines a variable, `letter`, that is initialized with the 16-bit code for the letter Z. The `L` preceding the character constant, `'Z'`, tells the compiler that this is a 16-bit character code value. A `wchar_t` variable stores Unicode code values.

You could have used functional notation here, too:

```
wchar_t letter(L'Z');       // A variable storing a 16-bit character code
```

You can also use hexadecimal constants to initialize integer variables, including those of type `char`, and it is obviously going to be easier to use this notation when character codes are available as hexadecimal values. A hexadecimal number is written using the standard representation for hexadecimal digits: 0 to 9, and A to F (or a to f) for digits with values from 10 to 15. It's also prefixed by 0x (or 0X) to distinguish it from a decimal value. Thus, to get exactly the same result again, you could rewrite the last statement as follows:

```
wchar_t letter(0x5A);       // A variable storing a 16-bit character code
```

NOTE *Don't write decimal integer values with a leading zero. The compiler will interpret such values as octal (base 8), so a value written as 065 will be equivalent to 53 in normal decimal notation.*

Notice that Windows XP, Vista, and Windows 7 provide a Character Map utility that enables you to locate characters from any of the fonts available to Windows. It will show the character code in hexadecimal and tell you the keystroke to use for entering the character. You'll find the Character Map utility if you click on the Start button and look in the System Tools folder that is within the Accessories folder.

Integer Type Modifiers

Variables of the integral types `char`, `int`, `short`, or `long` store `signed` integer values by default, so you can use these types to store either positive or negative values. This is because these types are assumed to have the default **type modifier** `signed`. So, wherever you wrote `int` or `long`, you could have written `signed int` or `signed long`, respectively.

You can also use the `signed` keyword by itself to specify the type of a variable, in which case, it means `signed int`. For example:

```
signed value = -5;              // Equivalent to signed int
```

This usage is not particularly common, and I prefer to use `int`, which makes it more obvious what is meant.

The range of values that can be stored in a variable of type `char` is from −128 to 127, which is the same as the range of values you can store in a variable of type `signed char`. In spite of this, type `char` and type `signed char` are different types, so you should not make the mistake of assuming they are the same.

If you are sure that you don't need to store negative values in a variable (for example, if you were recording the number of miles you drive in a week), then you can specify a variable as `unsigned`:

```
unsigned long mileage = 0UL;
```

Here, the minimum value that can be stored in the variable `mileage` is zero, and the maximum value is 4,294,967,295 (that's $2^{32}-1$). Compare this to the range of −2,147,483,648 to 2,147,483,647 for a `signed long`. The bit that is used in a `signed` variable to determine the sign of the value is used in an `unsigned` variable as part of the numeric value instead. Consequently, an `unsigned` variable has a larger range of positive values, but it can't represent a negative value. Note how a `U` (or `u`) is appended to `unsigned` constants. In the preceding example, I also have `L` appended to indicate that the constant is `long`. You can use either upper- or lowercase for `U` and `L`, and the sequence is unimportant. However, it's a good idea to adopt a consistent way of specifying such values.

You can also use `unsigned` by itself as the type specification for a variable, in which case, you are specifying the variable to be of type `unsigned int`.

> **NOTE** *Remember, both* `signed` *and* `unsigned` *are keywords, so you can't use them as variable names.*

The Boolean Type

Boolean variables are variables that can have only two values: a value called `true` and a value called `false`. The type for a logical variable is `bool`, named after George Boole, who developed Boolean algebra, and type `bool` is regarded as an integer type. Boolean variables are also referred to as **logical variables**. Variables of type `bool` are used to store the results of tests that can be either `true` or `false`, such as whether one value is equal to another.

You could declare the name of a variable of type `bool` with the statement:

```
bool testResult;
```

Of course, you can also initialize variables of type `bool` when you declare them:

```
bool colorIsRed = true;
```

Or like this:

```
bool colorIsRed(true);
```

> **NOTE** *You will find that the values* TRUE *and* FALSE *are used quite extensively with variables of numeric type, and particularly of type* int. *This is a hangover from the time before variables of type* `bool` *were implemented in C++, when variables of type* int *were typically used to represent logical values. In this case, a zero value is treated as false and a non-zero value as true. The symbols* TRUE *and* FALSE *are still used within the MFC where they represent a non-zero integer value and 0, respectively. Note that* TRUE *and* FALSE — *written with capital letters* — *are not keywords in C++; they are just symbols defined within the MFC. Note also that* TRUE *and* FALSE *are not legal* `bool` *values, so don't confuse* true *with* TRUE.

Floating-Point Types

Values that aren't integral are stored as **floating-point** numbers. A floating-point number can be expressed as a decimal value such as 112.5, or with an exponent such as 1.125E2 where the decimal part is multiplied by the power of 10 specified after the E (for Exponent). Our example is, therefore, 1.125×10^2, which is 112.5.

> **NOTE** *A floating-point constant must contain a decimal point, or an exponent, or both. If you write a numerical value with neither, you have an integer.*

You can specify a floating-point variable using the keyword `double`, as in this statement:

```
double in_to_mm = 25.4;
```

A variable of type `double` occupies 8 bytes of memory and stores values accurate to approximately 15 decimal digits. The range of values stored is much wider than that indicated by the 15 digits accuracy, being from 1.7×10^{-308} to 1.7×10^{308}, positive and negative.

If you don't need 15 digits' precision, and you don't need the massive range of values provided by `double` variables, you can opt to use the keyword `float` to declare floating-point variables occupying 4 bytes. For example:

```
float pi = 3.14159f;
```

This statement defines a variable `pi` with the initial value 3.14159. The `f` at the end of the constant specifies that it is of type `float`. Without the `f`, the constant would have been of type `double`. Variables that you declare as `float` have approximately 7 decimal digits of precision and can have values from 3.4×10^{-38} to 3.4×10^{38}, positive and negative.

The ISO/IEC standard for C++ also defines the `long double` floating-point type, which in Visual C++ 2010, is implemented with the same range and precision as type `double`. With some compilers, `long double` corresponds to a 16-byte floating-point value with a much greater range and precision than type `double`.

Fundamental Types in ISO/IEC C++

The following table contains a summary of all the fundamental types in ISO/IEC C++ and the range of values that are supported for these in Visual C++ 2010.

TYPE	SIZE IN BYTES	RANGE OF VALUES
bool	1	true or false
char	1	By default, the same as type signed char: −128 to 127. Optionally, you can make char the same range as type unsigned char.
signed char	1	−128 to 127
unsigned char	1	0 to 255
wchar_t	2	0 to 65,535
short	2	−32,768 to 32,767
unsigned short	2	0 to 65,535
int	4	−2,147,483,648 to 2,147,483,647
unsigned int	4	0 to 4,294,967,295

continues

(continued)

TYPE	SIZE IN BYTES	RANGE OF VALUES
long	4	−2,147,483,648 to 2,147,483,647
unsigned long	4	0 to 4,294,967,295
long long	8	−9223372036854775808 to 9223372036854775807
unsigned long long	4	0 to 18446744073709551615
float	4	$\pm 3.4 \times 10^{\pm 38}$ with approximately 7 digits accuracy
double	8	$\pm 1.7 \times 10^{\pm 308}$ with approximately 15 digits accuracy
long double	8	$\pm 1.7 \times 10^{\pm 308}$ with approximately 15 digits accuracy

Literals

I have already used a lot of explicit constants to initialize variables, and in C++, constant values of any kind are referred to as **literals**. A literal is a value of a specific type, so values such as 23, 3.14159, 9.5f, and true are examples of literals of type int, type double, type float, and type bool, respectively. The literal "Samuel Beckett" is an example of a literal that is a string, but I'll defer discussion of exactly what type this is until Chapter 4. Here's a summary of how you write literals of various types.

TYPE	EXAMPLES OF LITERALS
char, signed char, or unsigned char	'A', 'Z', '8', '* '
wchar_t	L'A', L'Z', L'8', L'* '
Int	-77, 65, 12345, 0x9FE
unsigned int	10U, 64000u
long	-77L, 65L, 123451
unsigned long	5UL, 999999UL, 25ul, 35Ul
long long	-777LL, 66LL, 123456711
unsigned long long	55ULL, 999999999ULL, 885ull, 445Ull
float	3.14f, 34.506F
double	1.414, 2.71828
long double	1.414L, 2.718281
bool	true, false

You can't specify a literal to be of type short or unsigned short, but the compiler will accept initial values that are literals of type int for variables of these types, provided the value of the literal is within the range of the variable type.

You will often need to use literals in calculations within a program, for example, conversion values such as 12 for feet into inches or 25.4 for inches to millimeters, or a string to specify an error message. However, you should avoid using numeric literals within programs explicitly where their significance is not obvious. It is not necessarily apparent to everyone that when you use the value 2.54, it is the number of centimeters in an inch. It is better to declare a variable with a fixed value corresponding to your literal instead — you might name the variable inchesToCentimeters, for example. Then, wherever you use inchesToCentimeters in your code, it will be quite obvious what it is. You will see how to fix the value of a variable a little later on in this chapter.

Defining Synonyms for Data Types

The typedef keyword enables you to define your own type name for an existing type. Using typedef, you could define the type name BigOnes as equivalent to the standard long int type with the declaration:

```
typedef long int BigOnes;        // Defining BigOnes as a type name
```

This defines BigOnes as an alternative type specifier for long int, so you could declare a variable mynum as long int with the declaration:

```
BigOnes mynum = 0L;              // Define a long int variable
```

There's no difference between this declaration and the one using the built-in type name. You could equally well use

```
long int mynum = 0L;             // Define a long int variable
```

for exactly the same result. In fact, if you define your own type name such as BigOnes, you can use both type specifiers within the same program for declaring different variables that will end up as having the same type.

Because typedef only defines a synonym for an existing type, it may appear to be a bit superficial, but it is not at all. You'll see later that it fulfills a very useful role in enabling you to simplify more complex declarations by defining a single name that represents a somewhat convoluted type specification. This can make your code much more readable.

Variables with Specific Sets of Values

You will sometimes be faced with the need for variables that have a limited set of possible values that can be usefully referred to by labels — the days of the week, for example, or months of the year. There is a specific facility in C++ to handle this situation, called an **enumeration**. Take one of the examples I have just mentioned — a variable that can assume values corresponding to days of the week. You can define this as follows:

```
enum Week{Mon, Tues, Wed, Thurs, Fri, Sat, Sun} thisWeek;
```

This declares an enumeration type with the name Week and the variable thisWeek, which is an instance of the enumeration type Week that can assume only the constant values specified between the braces. If you try to assign to thisWeek anything other than one of the set of values specified, it will cause an error. The symbolic names listed between the braces are known as **enumerators**. In fact, each of the names of the days will be automatically defined as representing a fixed integer value. The first name in the list, Mon, will have the value 0, Tues will be 1, and so on.

You could assign one of the enumeration constants as the value of the variable thisWeek like this:

```
thisWeek = Thurs;
```

Note that you do not need to qualify the enumeration constant with the name of the enumeration. The value of thisWeek will be 3 because the symbolic constants that an enumeration defines are assigned values of type int by default in sequence, starting with 0.

By default, each successive enumerator is one larger than the value of the previous one, but if you would prefer the implicit numbering to start at a different value, you can just write:

```
enum Week {Mon = 1, Tues, Wed, Thurs, Fri, Sat, Sun} thisWeek;
```

Now, the enumeration constants will be equivalent to 1 through 7. The enumerators don't even need to have unique values. You could define Mon and Tues as both having the value 1, for example, with the statement:

```
enum Week {Mon = 1, Tues = 1, Wed, Thurs, Fri, Sat, Sun} thisWeek;
```

As the type of the variable thisWeek is type int, it will occupy 4 bytes, as will all variables that are of an enumeration type.

Note that you are *not* allowed to use functional notation for initializing enumerators. You must use the assignment operator as in the examples you have seen.

Having defined the form of an enumeration, you can define another variable as follows:

```
enum Week nextWeek;
```

This defines a variable nextWeek as an enumeration that can assume the values previously specified. You can also omit the enum keyword in declaring a variable, so, instead of the previous statement, you could write:

```
Week next_week;
```

If you wish, you can assign specific values to all the enumerators. For example, you could define this enumeration:

```
enum Punctuation {Comma = ',', Exclamation = '!', Question = '?'} things;
```

Here, you have defined the possible values for the variable things as the numerical equivalents of the appropriate symbols. The symbols are 44, 33, and 63, respectively, in decimal. As you can see, the values assigned don't have to be in ascending order. If you don't specify all the values explicitly, each enumerator will be assigned a value incrementing by 1 from the last specified value, as in our second Week example.

You can omit the enumeration type if you don't need to define other variables of this type later. For example:

```
enum {Mon, Tues, Wed, Thurs, Fri, Sat, Sun} thisWeek, nextWeek, lastWeek;
```

Here, you have three variables declared that can assume values from Mon to Sun. Because the enumeration type is not specified, you cannot refer to it. Note that you cannot define other variables for this enumeration *at all*, because you would not be permitted to repeat the definition. Doing so would imply that you were redefining values for Mon to Sun, and this isn't allowed.

BASIC INPUT/OUTPUT OPERATIONS

Here, you will only look at enough of native C++ input and output to get you through learning about C++. It's not that it's difficult — quite the opposite, in fact — but for Windows programming, you won't need it at all. C++ input/output revolves around the notion of a data stream, where you can insert data into an output stream or extract data from an input stream. You have already seen that the ISO/IEC C++ standard output stream to the command line on the screen is referred to as cout. The complementary input stream from the keyboard is referred to as cin. Of course, both stream names are defined within the std namespace.

Input from the Keyboard

You obtain input from the keyboard through the standard input stream, cin, using the extraction operator for a stream, >>. To read two integer values from the keyboard into integer variables num1 and num2, you can write this statement:

```
std::cin >> num1 >> num2;
```

The **extraction operator,** >>, "points" in the direction that data flows — in this case, from cin to each of the two variables in turn. Any leading whitespace is skipped, and the first integer value you key in is read into num1. This is because the input statement executes from left to right. Any whitespace following num1 is ignored, and the second integer value that you enter is read into num2. There has to be some whitespace between successive values, though, so that they can be differentiated. The stream input operation ends when you press the Enter key, and execution then continues with the next statement. Of course, errors can arise if you key in the wrong data, but I will assume that you always get it right!

Floating-point values are read from the keyboard in exactly the same way as integers, and of course, you can mix the two. The stream input and operations automatically deal with variables and data of any of the fundamental types. For example, in the statements,

```
int num1 = 0, num2 = 0;
double factor = 0.0;
std::cin >> num1 >> factor >> num2;
```

the last line will read an integer into num1, then a floating-point value into `factor`, and finally, an integer into num2.

Output to the Command Line

You have already seen output to the command line, but I want to revisit it anyway. Writing information to the display operates in a complementary fashion to input. As you have seen, the standard output stream is called `cout`, and you use the insertion operator, <<, to transfer data to the output stream. This operator also "points" in the direction of data movement. You have already used this operator to output a text string between quotes. I can demonstrate the process of outputting the value of a variable with a simple program.

TRY IT OUT   Output to the Command Line

I'll assume that you've got the hang of creating a new empty project by adding a new source file to the project and building it into an executable. Here's the code that you need to put in the source file once you have created the Ex2_02 project:

Available for download on Wrox.com

```cpp
// Ex2_02.cpp
// Exercising output
#include <iostream>

using std::cout;
using std::endl;

int main()
{
   int num1 = 1234, num2 = 5678;
   cout << endl;                      // Start on a new line
   cout << num1 << num2;              // Output two values
   cout << endl;                      // End on a new line
   return 0;                          // Exit program
}
```

code snippet Ex2_02.cpp

How It Works

Because you have `using` declarations for `std::cout` and `std::endl`, you can use the unqualified stream names in the code. The first statement in the body of `main()` declares and initializes two integer variables, num1 and num2. This is followed by two output statements, the first of which moves the screen cursor position to a new line. Because output statements execute from left to right, the second output statement displays the value of num1 followed by the value of num2.

When you compile and execute this, you will get the output:

```
12345678
```

The output is correct, but it's not exactly helpful. You really need the two output values to be separated by at least one space. The default for stream output is to just output the digits in the output value, which doesn't provide for spacing successive output values out nicely so they can be differentiated. As it is, you have no way to tell where the first number ends and the second number begins.

Formatting the Output

You can fix the problem of there being no spaces between items of data quite easily, though, just by outputting a space between the two values. You can do this by replacing the following line in your original program:

```
cout << num1 << num2;                    // Output two values
```

Just substitute the statement:

```
cout << num1 << ' ' << num2;             // Output two values
```

Of course, if you had several rows of output that you wanted to align in columns, you would need some extra capability because you do not know how many digits there will be in each value. You can take care of this situation by using what is called a **manipulator**. A manipulator modifies the way in which data output to (or input from) a stream is handled.

Manipulators are defined in the standard library header file iomanip, so you need to add a #include directive for it. The manipulator that you'll use is setw(n), which will output the value that follows right-justified in a field n spaces wide, so setw(6) causes the next output value to be presented in a field with a width of six spaces. Let's see it working.

TRY IT OUT   **Using Manipulators**

To get something more like the output you want, you can change the program to the following:

Available for download on Wrox.com

```
// Ex2_03.cpp
// Exercising output
#include <iostream>
#include <iomanip>

using std::cout;
using std::endl;
using std::setw;

int main()
{
   int num1 = 1234, num2 = 5678;
   cout << endl;                                // Start on a new line
   cout << setw(6) << num1 << setw(6) << num2;  // Output two values
   cout << endl;                                // Start on a new line
   return 0;                                    // Exit program
}
```

code snippet Ex2_03.cpp

How It Works

The changes from the last example are the addition of the `#include` directive for the `iomanip` header file, the addition of a `using` declaration for the `setw` name in the `std` namespace, and the insertion of the `setw()` manipulator in the output stream preceding each value so that the output values are presented in a field six characters wide. Now you get nice, neat output where you can actually separate the two values:

```
1234  5678
```

Note that the `setw()` manipulator works only for the single output value immediately following its insertion into the stream. You have to insert the manipulator into the stream immediately preceding each value that you want to output within a given field width. If you put only one `setw()`, it would apply to the first value to be output after it was inserted. Any following value would be output in the default manner. You could try this out by deleting the second `setw(6)` and its insertion operator in the example.

Another useful manipulator that is defined in the `iomanip` header is `std::setiosflags`. This enables you to have the output left-aligned in a given field width instead of right-aligned by default. Here's how you can do that:

```
cout << std::setiosflags(std::ios::left);
```

You can also use the `std::setiosflags` manipulator to control the appearance of numerical output, so it is worth exploring.

Escape Sequences

When you write a character string between double quotes, you can include special character sequences called **escape sequences** in the string. They are called escape sequences because they allow characters to be included in a string that otherwise could not be represented in the string, and they do this by escaping from the default interpretation of the characters. An escape sequence starts with a backslash character, \, and the backslash character cues the compiler to interpret the character that follows in a special way. For example, a tab character is written as \t, so the t is understood by the compiler to represent a tab in the string, and not the letter t. Look at these two output statements:

```
cout << endl << "This is output.";
cout << endl << "\tThis is output after a tab.";
```

They will produce these lines:

```
This is output.
        This is output after a tab.
```

The \t in the second output statement causes the output text to be indented to the first tab position.

In fact, instead of using `endl`, you could use the escape sequence for the newline character, `\n`, in each string, so you could rewrite the preceding statements as follows:

```
cout << "\nThis is output.";
cout << "\n\tThis is output after a tab.";
```

Here are some escape sequences that may be particularly useful:

ESCAPE SEQUENCE	WHAT IT DOES
\a	Sounds a beep
\n	Newline
\'	Single quote
\\	Backslash
\b	Backspace
\t	Tab
\"	Double quote
\?	Question mark

Obviously, if you want to be able to include a backslash or a double quote as a character to appear in a string, you must use the appropriate escape sequences to represent them. Otherwise, the backslash would be interpreted as the start of another escape sequence, and the double quote would indicate the end of the character string.

You can also use characters specified by escape sequences in the initialization of variables of type `char`. For example:

```
char Tab = '\t';                // Initialize with tab character
```

Because a character literal is delimited by single quote characters, you must use an escape sequence to specify a character literal that is a single quote, thus `'\''`.

TRY IT OUT   Using Escape Sequences

Here's a program that uses some of the escape sequences from the table in the previous section:

```
// Ex2_04.cpp
// Using escape sequences
#include <iostream>
#include <iomanip>

using std::cout;
```

```
int main()
{
   char newline = '\n';                      // Newline escape sequence
   cout << newline;                          // Start on a new line
   cout << "\"We\'ll make our escapes in sequence\", he said.";
   cout << "\n\tThe program\'s over, it\'s time to make a beep beep.\a\a";
   cout << newline;                          // Start on a new line
   return 0;                                 // Exit program
}
```

code snippet Ex2_04.cpp

If you compile and execute this example, it will produce the following output:

```
"We'll make our escapes in sequence", he said.
          The program's over, it's time to make a beep beep.
```

How It Works

The first line in `main()` defines the variable `newline` and initializes it with a character defined by the escape sequence for a new line. You can then use `newline` instead of `endl` from the standard library.

After writing `newline` to `cout`, you output a string that uses the escape sequences for a double quote (`\"`) and a single quote (`\'`). You don't have to use the escape sequence for a single quote here because the string is delimited by double quotes, and the compiler will recognize a single quote character as just that, and not a delimiter. You must use the escape sequences for the double quotes in the string, though. The string starts with a newline escape sequence followed by a tab escape sequence, so the output line is indented by the tab distance. The string also ends with two instances of the escape sequence for a beep, so you should hear a double beep from your PC's speaker.

CALCULATING IN C++

This is where you actually start doing something with the data that you enter. You know how to carry out simple input and output; now, you are beginning the bit in the middle, the "processing" part of a C++ program. Almost all of the computational aspects of C++ are fairly intuitive, so you should slice through this like a hot knife through butter.

The Assignment Statement

You have already seen examples of the assignment statement. A typical assignment statement looks like this:

```
whole = part1 + part2 + part3;
```

The assignment statement enables you to calculate the value of an expression that appears on the right-hand side of the equals sign, in this case, the sum of part1, part2, and part3, and store the result in the variable specified on the left-hand side, in this case, the variable with the name whole. In this statement, the whole is exactly the sum of its parts, and no more.

 NOTE *Note how the statement, as always, ends with a semicolon.*

You can also write repeated assignments, such as:

```
a = b = 2;
```

This is equivalent to assigning the value 2 to b and then assigning the value of b to a, so both variables will end up storing the value 2.

Arithmetic Operations

The basic arithmetic operators you have at your disposal are addition, subtraction, multiplication, and division, represented by the symbols +, -, *, and /, respectively. Generally, these operate as you would expect, with the exception of division, which has a slight aberration when working with integer variables or constants, as you'll see. You can write statements such as the following:

```
netPay = hours * rate - deductions;
```

Here, the product of hours and rate will be calculated and then deductions subtracted from the value produced. The multiply and divide operators are executed before addition and subtraction, as you would expect. I will discuss the order of execution of the various operators in expressions more fully later in this chapter. The overall result of evaluating the expression hours*rate-deductions will be stored in the variable netPay.

The minus sign used in the last statement has two operands — it subtracts the value of its right operand from the value of its left operand. This is called a **binary operation** because two values are involved. The minus sign can also be used with one operand to change the sign of the value to which it is applied, in which case it is called a **unary minus**. You could write this:

```
int a = 0;
int b = -5;
a = -b;                          // Changes the sign of the operand
```

Here, a will be assigned the value +5 because the unary minus changes the sign of the value of the operand b.

Note that an assignment is not the equivalent of the equations you saw in high-school algebra. It specifies an action to be carried out rather than a statement of fact. The expression to the right of the assignment operator is evaluated and the result is stored in the location specified on the left.

> **NOTE** *Typically, the expression on the left of an assignment is a single variable name, but it doesn't have to be. It can be an expression of some kind, but if it is an expression, then the result of evaluating it must be an **lvalue**. An lvalue, as you will see later, is a persistent location in memory where the result of the expression to the right of the assignment operator can be stored.*

Look at this statement:

```
number = number + 1;
```

This means "add 1 to the current value stored in number and then store the result back in number." As a normal algebraic statement, it wouldn't make sense, but as a programming action, it obviously does.

TRY IT OUT Exercising Basic Arithmetic

You can exercise basic arithmetic in C++ by calculating how many standard rolls of wallpaper are needed to paper a room. The following example does this:

```cpp
// Ex2_05.cpp
// Calculating how many rolls of wallpaper are required for a room
#include <iostream>

using std::cout;
using std::cin;
using std::endl;

int main()
{
   double height = 0.0, width = 0.0, length = 0.0;  // Room dimensions
   double perimeter = 0.0;                          // Room perimeter

   const double rollWidth = 21.0;                   // Standard roll width
   const double rollLength = 12.0*33.0;             // Standard roll length(33ft.)

   int strips_per_roll = 0;                         // Number of strips in a roll
   int strips_reqd = 0;                             // Number of strips needed
   int nrolls = 0;                                  // Total number of rolls

   cout << endl                                     // Start a new line
        << "Enter the height of the room in inches: ";
   cin >> height;

   cout  << endl                                    // Start a new line
        << "Now enter the length and width in inches: ";
   cin >> length >> width;

   strips_per_roll = rollLength / height;           // Get number of strips per roll
   perimeter = 2.0*(length + width);                // Calculate room perimeter
   strips_reqd = perimeter / rollWidth;             // Get total strips required
   nrolls = strips_reqd / strips_per_roll;          // Calculate number of rolls
```

```
        cout << endl
            << "For your room you need " << nrolls << " rolls of wallpaper."
            << endl;

        return 0;
    }
```

code snippet Ex2_05.cpp

Unless you are more adept than I am at typing, chances are, there will be a few errors when you compile this for the first time. Once you have fixed the typos, it will compile and run just fine. You'll get a couple of warning messages from the compiler. Don't worry about them — the compiler is just making sure you understand what's going on. I'll explain the reason for the warning messages in a moment.

How It Works

One thing needs to be clear at the outset — I assume no responsibility for you running out of wallpaper as a result of using this program! As you'll see, all errors in the estimate of the number of rolls required are due to the way C++ works and to the wastage that inevitably occurs when you hang your own wallpaper — usually 50 percent plus!

I'll work through the statements in this example in sequence, picking out the interesting, novel, or even exciting features. The statements down to the start of the body of main() are familiar territory by now, so I will take those for granted.

A couple of general points about the layout of the program are worth noting. First, the statements in the body of main() are indented to make the extent of the body easier to see, and second, various groups of statements are separated by a blank line to indicate that they are functional groups. Indenting statements is a fundamental technique in laying out program code in C++. You will see that this is applied universally to provide visual cues to help you identify the various logical blocks in a program.

The const Modifier

You have a block of declarations for the variables used in the program right at the beginning of the body of main(). These statements are also fairly familiar, but there are two that contain some new features:

```
    const double rollWidth = 21.0;              // Standard roll width
    const double rollLength = 12.0*33.0;        // Standard roll length(33ft.)
```

They both start out with a new keyword: const. This is a **type modifier** that indicates that the variables are not just of type double, but are also constants. Because you effectively tell the compiler that these are constants, the compiler will check for any statements that attempt to change the values of these variables, and if it finds any, it will generate an error message. You could check this out by adding, anywhere after the declaration of rollWidth, a statement such as:

```
    rollWidth = 0;
```

You will find the program no longer compiles, returning `'error C3892: 'rollWidth' : you cannot assign to a variable that is const'`.

It can be very useful to define constants that you use in a program by means of `const` variable types, particularly when you use the same constant several times in a program. For one thing, it is much better than sprinkling literals throughout your program that may not have blindingly obvious meanings; with the value 42 in a program, you could be referring to the meaning of life, the universe, and everything, but if you use a `const` variable with the name `myAge` that has a value of 42, it becomes obvious that you are not. For another thing, if you need to change the value of a `const` variable that you are using, you will need to change its definition only in a source file to ensure that the change automatically appears throughout. You'll see this technique used quite often.

Constant Expressions

The `const` variable `rollLength` is also initialized with an arithmetic expression (`12.0*33.0`). Being able to use constant expressions to initialize variables saves having to work out the value yourself. It can also be more meaningful, as it is in this case, because 33 feet times 12 inches is a much clearer expression of what the value represents than simply writing 396. The compiler will generally evaluate constant expressions accurately, whereas if you do it yourself, depending on the complexity of the expression and your ability to number-crunch, there is a finite probability that it may be wrong.

You can use any expression that can be calculated as a constant at compile time, including `const` objects that you have already defined. So, for instance, if it were useful in the program to do so, you could declare the area of a standard roll of wallpaper as:

```
const double rollArea = rollWidth*rollLength;
```

This statement would need to be placed after the declarations for the two `const` variables used in the initialization of `rollArea`, because all the variables that appear in a constant expression must be known to the compiler at the point in the source file where the constant expression appears.

Program Input

After declaring some integer variables, the next four statements in the program handle input from the keyboard:

```
cout << endl                                    // Start a new line
     << "Enter the height of the room in inches: ";
cin >> height;

cout << endl                                    // Start a new line
     << "Now enter the length and width in inches: ";
cin >> length >> width;
```

Here, you have written text to `cout` to prompt for the input required, and then read the input from the keyboard using `cin`, which is the standard input stream. You first obtain the value for the room `height` and then read the `length` and `width`, successively. In a practical program, you would need to check for errors and possibly make sure that the values that are read are sensible, but you don't have enough knowledge to do that yet!

Calculating the Result

You have four statements involved in calculating the number of standard rolls of wallpaper required for the size of room given:

```
strips_per_roll = rollLength / height;      // Get number of strips in a roll
perimeter = 2.0*(length + width);           // Calculate room perimeter
strips_reqd = perimeter / rollWidth;        // Get total strips required
nrolls = strips_reqd / strips_per_roll;     // Calculate number of rolls
```

The first statement calculates the number of strips of paper with a length corresponding to the height of the room that you can get from a standard roll, by dividing one into the other. So, if the room is 8 feet high, you divide 96 into 396, which would produce the floating-point result 4.125. There is a subtlety here, however. The variable where you store the result, `strips_per_roll`, was declared as `int`, so it can store only integer values. Consequently, any floating-point value to be stored as an integer is rounded down to the nearest integer, 4 in this case, and this value is stored. This is actually the result that you want here because, although they may fit under a window or over a door, fractions of a strip are best ignored when estimating.

The conversion of a value from one type to another is called **type conversion**. This particular example is called an **implicit type conversion**, because the code doesn't explicitly state that a conversions is needed, and the compiler has to work it out for itself. The two warnings you got during compilation were issued because information could be lost as a result of the implicit conversion that were inserted due to the process of changing a value from one type to another.

You should beware when your code necessitates implicit conversions. Compilers do not always supply a warning that an implicit conversion is being made, and if you are assigning a value of one type to a variable of a type with a lesser range of values, then there is always a danger that you will lose information. If there are implicit conversions in your program that you have included accidentally, then they may represent bugs that may be difficult to locate.

Where such a conversion that may result in the loss of information is unavoidable, you can specify the conversion explicitly to demonstrate that it is no accident and that you really meant to do it. You do this by making an **explicit type conversion** or **cast** of the value on the right of the assignment to `int`, so the statement would become:

```
strips_per_roll = static_cast<int>(rollLength / height);   // Get number
                                                           // of strips in
                                                           // a roll
```

The addition of `static_cast<int>` with the parentheses around the expression on the right tells the compiler explicitly that you want to convert the value of the expression between the parentheses to type `int`. Although this means that you still lose the fractional part of the value, the compiler assumes that you know what you are doing and will not issue a warning. You'll see more about `static_cast<>()` and other types of explicit type conversion later in this chapter.

Note how you calculate the perimeter of the room in the next statement. To multiply the sum of the `length` and the `width` by 2.0, you enclose the expression summing the two variables between parentheses. This ensures that the addition is performed first and the result is multiplied by 2.0 to produce the correct value for the perimeter. You can use parentheses to make sure that a calculation is carried out in the order you require because expressions in parentheses are always evaluated first. Where there are nested parentheses, the expressions within the parentheses are evaluated in sequence, from the innermost to the outermost.

The third statement, calculating how many strips of paper are required to cover the room, uses the same effect that you observed in the first statement: the result is rounded down to the nearest integer because it is to be stored in the integer variable, `strips_reqd`. This is not what you need in practice. It would be best to round up for estimating, but you don't have enough knowledge of C++ to do this yet. Once you have read the next chapter, you can come back and fix it!

The last arithmetic statement calculates the number of rolls required by dividing the number of strips required (an integer) by the number of strips in a roll (also an integer). Because you are dividing one integer by another, the result has to be an integer, and any remainder is ignored. This would still be the case if the variable `nrolls` were floating-point. The integer value resulting from the expression would be converted to floating-point form before it was stored in `nrolls`. The result that you obtain is essentially the same as if you had produced a floating-point result and rounded down to the nearest integer. Again, this is not what you want, so if you want to use this, you will need to fix it.

Displaying the Result

The following statement displays the result of the calculation:

```
cout << endl
     << "For your room you need " << nrolls << " rolls of wallpaper."
     << endl;
```

This is a single output statement spread over three lines. It first outputs a newline character and then the text string `"For your room you need"`. This is followed by the value of the variable `nrolls` and, finally, the text string `" rolls of wallpaper."`. As you can see, output statements are very easy in C++.

Finally, the program ends when this statement is executed:

```
return 0;
```

The value zero here is a return value that, in this case, will be returned to the operating system. You will see more about return values in Chapter 5.

Calculating a Remainder

You saw in the last example that dividing one integer value by another produces an integer result that ignores any remainder, so that 11 divided by 4 gives the result 2. Because the remainder after division can be of great interest, particularly when you are dividing cookies amongst children, for example, C++ provides a special operator, `%`, for this. So you can write the following statements to handle the cookie-sharing problem:

```
int residue = 0, cookies = 19, children = 5;
residue = cookies % children;
```

The variable `residue` will end up with the value 4, the number left after dividing 19 by 5. To calculate how many cookies each child receives, you just need to use division, as in the statement:

```
each = cookies / children;
```

Modifying a Variable

It's often necessary to modify the existing value of a variable, such as by incrementing it or doubling it. You could increment a variable called `count` using the statement:

```
count = count + 5;
```

This simply adds 5 to the current value stored in `count` and stores the result back in `count`, so if `count` started out as 10, it would end up as 15.

You also have an alternative, shorthand way of writing the same thing in C++:

```
count += 5;
```

This says, "Take the value in `count`, add 5 to it, and store the result back in `count`." We can also use other operators with this notation. For example,

```
count *= 5;
```

has the effect of multiplying the current value of `count` by 5 and storing the result back in `count`. In general, you can write statements of the form,

```
lhs op=  rhs;
```

lhs stands for any legal expression for the left-hand side of the statement and is usually (but not necessarily) a variable name. *rhs* stands for any legal expression on the right-hand side of the statement. *op* is any of the following operators:

You have already met the first five of these operators, and you'll see the others, which are the shift and logical operators, later in this chapter.

The general form of the statement is equivalent to this:

```
lhs = lhs op (rhs);
```

The parentheses around rhs imply that this expression is evaluated first, and the result becomes the right operand for op.

This means that you can write statements such as:

```
a /= b + c;
```

This will be identical in effect to this statement:

```
a = a/(b + c);
```

Thus, the value of a will be divided by the sum of b and c, and the result will be stored back in a.

The Increment and Decrement Operators

This section introduces some unusual arithmetic operators called the **increment** and **decrement operators**. You will find them to be quite an asset once you get further into applying C++ in earnest. These are unary operators that you use to increment or decrement the value stored in a variable that holds an integral value. For example, assuming the variable count is of type int, the following three statements all have exactly the same effect:

```
count = count + 1;      count += 1;       ++count;
```

They each increment the variable count by 1. The last form, using the increment operator, is clearly the most concise.

The increment operator not only changes the value of the variable to which you apply it, but also results in a value. Thus, using the increment operator to increase the value of a variable by 1 can also appear as part of a more complex expression. If incrementing a variable using the ++ operator, as in ++count, is contained within another expression, then the action of the operator is to *first* increment the value of the variable and *then* use the incremented value in the expression. For example, suppose count has the value 5, and you have defined a variable total of type int. Suppose you write the following statement:

```
total = ++count + 6;
```

This results in count being incremented to 6, and this result is added to 6, so total is assigned the value 12.

So far, you have written the increment operator, ++, in front of the variable to which it applies. This is called the **prefix** form of the increment operator. The increment operator also has a **postfix** form, where the operator is written *after* the variable to which it applies; the effect of this is slightly different. The variable to which the operator applies is incremented only *after* its value has been used in context. For example, reset count to the value 5 and rewrite the previous statement as:

```
total = count++ + 6;
```

Then `total` is assigned the value 11, because the initial value of `count` is used to evaluate the expression before the increment by 1 is applied. The preceding statement is equivalent to the two statements:

```
total = count + 6;
++count;
```

The clustering of `"+"` signs in the preceding example of the postfix form is likely to lead to confusion. Generally, it isn't a good idea to write the increment operator in the way that I have written it here. It would be clearer to write:

```
total = 6 + count++;
```

Where you have an expression such as `a++ + b`, or even `a+++b`, it becomes less obvious what is meant or what the compiler will do. They are actually the same, but in the second case, you might really have meant `a + ++b`, which is different. It evaluates to one more than the other two expressions.

Exactly the same rules that I have discussed in relation to the increment operator apply to the decrement operator, `--`. For example, if `count` has the initial value 5, then the statement

```
total = --count + 6;
```

results in `total` having the value 10 assigned, whereas,

```
total = 6 + count--;
```

sets the value of `total` to 11. Both operators are usually applied to integers, particularly in the context of **loops**, as you will see in Chapter 3. You will see in later chapters that they can also be applied to other data types in C++, notably variables that store addresses.

TRY IT OUT   The Comma Operator

The comma operator allows you to specify several expressions where normally only one might occur. This is best understood by looking at an example that demonstrates how it works:

```
// Ex2_06.cpp
// Exercising the comma operator
#include <iostream>

using std::cout;
using std::endl;

int main()
{
    long num1(0L), num2(0L), num3(0L), num4(0L);

    num4 = (num1 = 10L, num2 = 20L, num3 = 30L);
    cout << endl
        << "The value of a series of expressions "
```

```
           << "is the value of the rightmost: "
           << num4;
    cout << endl;

    return 0;
}
```

code snippet Ex2_06.cpp

How It Works

If you compile and run this program you will get this output:

```
The value of a series of expressions is the value of the rightmost: 30
```

This is fairly self-explanatory. The first statement in `main()` creates four variables, `num1` through `num4`, and initializes them to zero using functional notation. The variable `num4` receives the value of the last of the series of three assignments, the value of an assignment being the value assigned to the left-hand side. The parentheses in the assignment for `num4` are essential. You could try executing this without them to see the effect. Without the parentheses, the first expression separated by commas in the series will become:

```
num4 = num1 = 10L
```

So, `num4` will have the value `10L`.

Of course, the expressions separated by the comma operator don't have to be assignments. You could equally well write the following statements:

```
long num1(1L), num2(10L), num3(100L), num4(0L);
num4 = (++num1, ++num2, ++num3);
```

The effect of the assignment statement will be to increment the variables `num1`, `num2`, and `num3` by 1, and to set `num4` to the value of the last expression, which will be 101L. This example is aimed at illustrating the effect of the comma operator and is not an example of how to write good code.

The Sequence of Calculation

So far, I haven't talked about how you arrive at the sequence of calculations involved in evaluating an expression. It generally corresponds to what you will have learned at school when dealing with basic arithmetic operators, but there are many other operators in C++. To understand what happens with these, you need to look at the mechanism used in C++ to determine this sequence. It's referred to as **operator precedence**.

Operator Precedence

Operator precedence orders the operators in a priority sequence. In any expression, operators with the highest precedence are always executed first, followed by operators with the next highest precedence, and so on, down to those with the lowest precedence of all. The precedence of the operators in C++ is shown in the following table.

OPERATORS	ASSOCIATIVITY
`::`	Left
`()`　`[]`　`->`　`.`	Left

`!`　`~`　`+(unary)` `-(unary)` `++`　`--`　`&(unary)` `*(unary)` `(typecast)`
`static_cast`　`const_cast`　`dynamic_cast`　`reinterpret_cast`
`sizeof`　`new`　`delete typeid decltype`
	Right

`.*(unary)` `->*`	Left
`*`　`/`　`%`	Left
`+`　`-`	Left
`<<` `>>`	Left
`< <=`　`> >=`	Left
`==`　`!=`	Left
`&`	Left
`^`	Left
`|`	Left
`&&`	Left
`||`	Left
`?:`(conditional operator)	Right
`=`　`*=`　`/=`　`%=`　`+=`　`-=`　`&=`　`^=`　`|=`　`<<=`　`>>=`	Right
`,`	Left

There are a lot of operators here that you haven't seen yet, but you will know them all by the end of the book. Rather than spreading them around, I have put all the C++ operators in the precedence table so that you can always refer back to it if you are uncertain about the precedence of one operator relative to another.

Operators with the highest precedence appear at the top of the table. All the operators that appear in the same cell in the table have equal precedence. If there are no parentheses in an expression, operators with equal precedence are executed in a sequence determined by their **associativity**. Thus, if the associativity is "left," the left-most operator in an expression is executed first, progressing through the expression to the right-most. This means that an expression such as a + b + c + d is executed as though it was written (((a + b) + c) + d) because binary + is left-associative.

Note that where an operator has a unary (working with one operand) and a binary (working with two operands) form, the unary form is always of a higher precedence and is, therefore, executed first.

 NOTE *You can always override the precedence of operators by using parentheses. Because there are so many operators in C++, it's sometimes hard to be sure what takes precedence over what. It is a good idea to insert parentheses to make sure. A further plus is that parentheses often make the code much easier to read.*

TYPE CONVERSION AND CASTING

Calculations in C++ can be carried out only between values of the same type. When you write an expression involving variables or constants of different types, for each operation to be performed, the compiler has to arrange to convert the type of one of the operands to match that of the other. This process is called **implicit type conversion**. For example, if you want to add a double value to a value of an integer type, the integer value is first converted to double, after which the addition is carried out. Of course, the variable that contains the value to be converted is, itself, not changed. The compiler will store the converted value in a temporary memory location, which will be discarded when the calculation is finished.

There are rules that govern the selection of the operand to be converted in any operation. Any expression to be calculated breaks down into a series of operations between two operands. For example, the expression 2*3-4+5 amounts to the series 2*3 resulting in 6, 6-4 resulting in 2, and finally 2+5 resulting in 7. Thus, the rules for converting the type of operands where necessary need to be defined only in terms of decisions about pairs of operands. So, for any pair of operands of different types, the compiler decides which operand to convert to the other considering types to be in the following rank from high to low:

1. `long double`	2. `double`	3. `float`
4. `unsigned long long`	5. `long long`	
6. `unsigned long`	7. `long`	
8. `unsigned int`	9. `int`	

Thus, if you have an operation where the operands are of type `long long` and type `unsigned int`, the latter will be converted to type `long long`. Any operand of type `char`, `signed char`, `unsigned char`, `short`, or `unsigned short` is at least converted to type `int` before an operation.

Implicit type conversions can produce some unexpected results. For example, consider the following statements:

```
unsigned int a(10u);
signed int b(20);
std::cout << a - b << std::endl;
```

You might expect this code fragment to output the value −10, but it doesn't. It outputs the value 4294967286. This is because the value of b is converted to unsigned int to match the type of a, and the subtraction operation results in an unsigned integer value. This implies that if you have to write integer operations that apply to operands of different types, you should not rely on implicit type conversion to produce the result you want unless you are quite certain it will do so.

Type Conversion in Assignments

As you saw in example Ex2_05.cpp earlier in this chapter, you can cause an implicit type conversion by writing an expression on the right-hand side of an assignment that is of a different type from the variable on the left-hand side. This can cause values to be changed and information to be lost. For instance, if you assign an expression that results in a float or double value to a variable of type int or a long, the fractional part of the float or double result will be lost, and just the integer part will be stored. (You may lose even more information if the value of your floating-point result exceeds the range of values available for the integer type concerned.)

For example, after executing the following code fragment,

```
int number = 0;
float decimal = 2.5f;
number = decimal;
```

the value of number will be 2. Note the f at the end of the constant 2.5f. This indicates to the compiler that this constant is single-precision floating-point. Without the f, the default would have been type double. Any constant containing a decimal point is floating-point. If you don't want it to be double-precision, you need to append the f. A capital letter F would do the job just as well.

Explicit Type Conversion

With mixed expressions involving the basic types, your compiler automatically arranges casting where necessary, but you can also force a conversion from one type to another by using an explicit type conversion, which is also referred to as a **cast**. To cast the value of an expression to a given type, you write the cast in the form:

```
static_cast<the_type_to_convert_to>(expression)
```

The keyword static_cast reflects the fact that the cast is checked statically — that is, when your program is compiled. No further checks are made when you execute the program to see if this cast is safe to apply. Later, when you get to deal with classes, you will meet dynamic_cast, where the conversion is checked dynamically — that is, when the program is executing. There are also two other kinds of cast — const_cast for removing the const-ness of an expression, and reinterpret_cast, which is an unconditional cast — but I'll say no more about these here.

The effect of the static_cast operation is to convert the value that results from evaluating *expression* to the type that you specify between the angled brackets. The *expression* can be anything from a single variable to a complex expression involving lots of nested parentheses.

Here's a specific example of the use of `static_cast<>()`:

```
double value1 = 10.5;
double value2 = 15.5;
int whole_number = static_cast<int>(value1) + static_cast<int>(value2);
```

The initializing value for the variable `whole_number` is the sum of the integral parts of `value1` and `value2`, so they are each explicitly cast to type `int`. The variable `whole_number` will therefore have the initial value 25. The casts do *not* affect the values stored in `value1` and `value2`, which will remain as 10.5 and 15.5, respectively. The values 10 and 15 produced by the casts are just stored temporarily for use in the calculation and then discarded. Although both casts cause a loss of information in the calculation, the compiler will always assume that you know what you are doing when you specify a cast explicitly.

Also, as I described in `Ex2_05.cpp` relating to assignments involving different types, you can always make it clear that you know the cast is necessary by making it explicit:

```
strips_per_roll = static_cast<int>(rollLength / height);      //Get number of strips
                                                              // in a roll
```

You can write an explicit cast for a numerical value to any numeric type, but you should be conscious of the possibility of losing information. If you cast a value of type `float` or `double` to type `long`, for example, you will lose the fractional part of the value when it is converted, so if the value started out as less than 1.0, the result will be 0. If you cast a value of type `double` to type `float`, you will lose accuracy because a `float` variable has only 7 digits precision, whereas `double` variables maintain 15. Even casting between integer types provides the potential for losing data, depending on the values involved. For example, the value of an integer of type `long long` can exceed the maximum that you can store in a variable of type `int`, so casting from a `long long` value to an `int` may lose information.

In general, you should avoid casting as far as possible. If you find that you need a lot of casts in your program, the overall design of your program may well be at fault. You need to look at the structure of the program and the ways in which you have chosen data types to see whether you can eliminate, or at least reduce, the number of casts in your program.

Old-Style Casts

Prior to the introduction of `static_cast<>()` (and the other casts: `const_cast<>()`, `dynamic_cast<>()`, and `reinterpret_cast<>()`, which I'll discuss later in the book) into C++, an explicit cast of the result of an expression to another type was written as:

```
(the_type_to_convert_to)expression
```

The result of *expression* is cast to the type between the parentheses. For example, the statement to calculate `strips_per_roll` in the previous example could be written:

```
strips_per_roll = (int)(rollLength / height);      //Get number of strips in a roll
```

Essentially, there are four different kinds of casts, and the old-style casting syntax covers them all. Because of this, code using the old-style casts is more error-prone — it is not always clear what you intended, and you may not get the result you expected. Although you will still see the old style of casting used extensively (it's still part of the language and you will see it in MFC code for historical reasons), I strongly recommend that you stick to using only the new casts in your code.

THE AUTO KEYWORD

You can use the auto keyword as the type of a variable in a definition statement and have its type deduced from the initial value you supply. Here are some examples:

```
auto n = 16;                    // Type is int
auto pi = 3.14159;              // Type is double
auto x = 3.5f;                  // Type is float
auto found = false;             // Type is bool
```

In each case, the type assigned to the variable you are defining is the same as that of the literal used as the initializer. Of course, when you use the auto keyword in this way, you must supply an initial value for the variable.

Variables defined using the auto keyword can also be specified as constants:

```
const auto e = 2.71828L;        // Type is const long double
```

Of course, you can also use functional notation:

```
const auto dozen(12);                 // Type is const int
```

The initial value for a variable you define using the auto keyword can also be an expression:

```
auto factor(n*pi*pi);           // Type is double
```

In this case, the definitions for the variables n and pi that are used in the initializing expression must precede this statement.

The auto keyword may seem at this point to be a somewhat trivial feature of C++, but you'll see later in the book, especially in Chapter 10, that it can save a lot of effort in determining complicated variable types and make your code more elegant.

DISCOVERING TYPES

The typeid operator enables you to discover the type of an expression. To obtain the type of an expression, you simply write typeid(expression), and this results in an object of type type_info that encapsulates the type of the expression. Suppose that you have defined variables x and y that are of type int and type double, respectively. The expression typeid(x*y) results in a type_info object representing the type of x*y, which by now you know to be double. Because the result of the typeid operator is an object, you can't write it to the standard output stream just as it is. However, you can output the type of the expression x*y like this:

```
cout << "The type of x*y is " << typeid(x*y).name() << endl;
```

This will result in the output:

```
The type of x*y is double
```

You will understand better how this works when you have learned more about classes and functions in Chapter 7. When you use the `typeid` operator, you must add a `#include` directive for the `typeinfo` header file to your program:

```
#include <typeinfo>
```

This provides the definition for the `type_info` type that the `typeid` operator returns. You won't need to use the `typeid` operator very often, but when you do need it, it is invaluable.

THE BITWISE OPERATORS

The bitwise operators treat their operands as a series of individual bits rather than a numerical value. They work only with integer variables or integer constants as operands, so only data types `short`, `int`, `long`, `long long`, `signed char`, and `char`, as well as the unsigned variants of these, can be used. The bitwise operators are useful in programming hardware devices, where the status of a device is often represented as a series of individual flags (that is, each bit of a byte may signify the status of a different aspect of the device), or for any situation where you might want to pack a set of on-off flags into a single variable. You will see them in action when you look at input/output in detail, where single bits are used to control various options in the way data is handled.

There are six bitwise operators:

& bitwise AND	| bitwise OR	^ bitwise exclusive OR
~ bitwise NOT	>> shift right	<< shift left

The following sections take a look at how each of them works.

The Bitwise AND

The bitwise AND, `&`, is a binary operator that combines corresponding bits in its operands in a particular way. If both corresponding bits are 1, the result is a 1 bit, and if either or both bits are 0, the result is a 0 bit.

The effect of a particular binary operator is often shown using what is called a **truth table**. This shows, for various possible combinations of operands, what the result is. The truth table for `&` is as follows:

Bitwise AND	0	1
0	0	0
1	0	1

For each row and column combination, the result of & combining the two is the entry at the intersection of the row and column. You can see how this works in an example:

```
char letter1 = 'A', letter2 = 'Z', result = 0;
result = letter1 & letter2;
```

You need to look at the bit patterns to see what happens. The letters 'A' and 'Z' correspond to hexadecimal values 0x41 and 0x5A, respectively. The way in which the bitwise AND operates on these two values is shown in Figure 2-9.

You can confirm this by looking at how corresponding bits combine with & in the truth table. After the assignment, result will have the value 0x40, which corresponds to the character "@".

FIGURE 2-9

Because the & produces zero if *either* bit is zero, you can use this operator to make sure that unwanted bits are set to 0 in a variable. You achieve this by creating what is called a "mask" and combining with the original variable using &. You create the mask by specifying a value that has 1 where you want to keep a bit, and 0 where you want to set a bit to zero. The result of AND-ing the mask with another integer will be 0 bits where the mask bit is 0, and the same value as the original bit in the variable where the mask bit is 1. Suppose you have a variable letter of type char where, for the purposes of illustration, you want to eliminate the high-order 4 bits, but keep the low-order 4 bits. This is easily done by setting up a mask as 0x0F and combining it with the value of letter using & like this:

```
letter = letter & 0x0F;
```

or, more concisely:

```
letter &= 0x0F;
```

If letter started out as 0x41, it would end up as 0x01 as a result of either of these statements. This operation is shown in Figure 2-10.

The 0 bits in the mask cause corresponding bits in letter to be set to 0, and the 1 bits in the mask cause corresponding bits in letter to be kept as they are.

Similarly, you can use a mask of 0xF0 to keep the 4 high-order bits, and zero the 4 low-order bits. Therefore, this statement,

FIGURE 2-10

```
letter &= 0xF0;
```

will result in the value of letter being changed from 0x41 to 0x40.

The Bitwise OR

The bitwise OR, |, sometimes called the **inclusive OR**, combines corresponding bits such that the result is a 1 if either operand bit is a 1, and 0 if both operand bits are 0. The truth table for the bitwise OR is:

Bitwise OR	0	1
0	0	1
1	1	1

You can exercise this with an example of how you could set individual flags packed into a variable of type int. Suppose that you have a variable called `style` of type `short` that contains 16 individual 1-bit flags. Suppose further that you are interested in setting individual flags in the variable `style`. One way of doing this is by defining values that you can combine with the OR operator to set particular bits on. To use in setting the rightmost bit, you can define:

```
short vredraw = 0x01;
```

For use in setting the second-to-rightmost bit, you could define the variable `hredraw` as:

```
short hredraw = 0x02;
```

So, you could set the rightmost two bits in the variable `style` to 1 with the statement:

```
style = hredraw | vredraw;
```

The effect of this statement is illustrated in Figure 2-11. Of course, to set the third bit of `style` to 1, you would use the constant `0x04`.

Because the OR operation results in 1 if either of two bits is a 1, OR-ing the two variables together produces a result with both bits set on.

FIGURE 2-11

A common requirement is to be able to set flags in a variable without altering any of the others that may have been set elsewhere. You can do this quite easily with a statement such as:

```
style |= hredraw | vredraw;
```

This statement will set the two rightmost bits of the variable `style` to 1, leaving the others at whatever they were before the execution of this statement.

The Bitwise Exclusive OR

The **exclusive OR**, ^, is so called because it operates similarly to the inclusive OR but produces 0 when both operand bits are 1. Therefore, its truth table is as follows:

Bitwise EOR	0	1
0	0	1
1	1	0

Using the same variable values that we used with the AND, you can look at the result of the following statement:

```
result = letter1 ^ letter2;
```

This operation can be represented as:

```
letter1  0100 0001
letter2  0101 1010
```

EOR-ed together produce:

```
result  0001 1011
```

The variable `result` is set to `0x1B`, or 27 in decimal notation.

The ^ operator has a rather surprising property. Suppose that you have two `char` variables, `first` with the value `'A'`, and `last` with the value `'Z'`, corresponding to binary values 0100 0001 and 0101 1010. If you write the statements,

```
first ^= last;          // Result first is 0001 1011
last ^= first;          // Result last is 0100 0001
first ^= last;          // Result first is 0101 1010
```

the result of these is that `first` and `last` have exchanged values without using any intermediate memory location. This works with any integer values.

The Bitwise NOT

The bitwise NOT, ~, takes a single operand, for which it inverts the bits: 1 becomes 0, and 0 becomes 1. Thus, if you execute the statement,

```
result = ~letter1;
```

if `letter1` is 0100 0001, the variable `result` will have the value 1011 1110, which is 0xBE, or 190 as a decimal value.

The Bitwise Shift Operators

These operators shift the value of an integer variable a specified number of bits to the left or right. The operator >> is for shifts to the right, while << is the operator for shifts to the left. Bits that "fall off" either end of the variable are lost. Figure 2-12 shows the effect of shifting the 2-byte variable left and right, with the initial value shown.

FIGURE 2-12

You declare and initialize a variable called `number` with the statement:

```
unsigned short number = 16387U;
```

As you saw earlier in this chapter, you write unsigned integer literals with a letter `U` or `u` appended to the number. You can shift the contents of this variable to the left with the statement:

```
number <<= 2;               // Shift left two bit positions
```

The left operand of the shift operator is the value to be shifted, and the number of bit positions that the value is to be shifted is specified by the right operand. The illustration shows the effect of the operation. As you can see, shifting the value 16,387 two positions to the left produces the value 12. The rather drastic change in the value is the result of losing the high-order bit when it is shifted out.

You can also shift the value to the right. Let's reset the value of number to its initial value of 16,387. Then you can write:

```
number >>= 2;            // Shift right two bit positions
```

This shifts the value 16,387 two positions to the right, storing the value 4,096. Shifting right 2 bits is effectively dividing the value by 4 (without remainder). This is also shown in the illustration.

As long as bits are not lost, shifting n bits to the left is equivalent to multiplying the value by 2, n times. In other words, it is equivalent to multiplying by 2^n. Similarly, shifting right n bits is equivalent to dividing by 2^n. But beware: as you saw with the left shift of the variable number, if significant bits are lost, the result is nothing like what you would expect. However, this is no different from the multiply operation. If you multiplied the 2-byte number by 4, you would get the same result, so shifting left and multiply are still equivalent. The problem of accuracy arises because the value of the result of the multiplication is outside the range of a 2-byte integer.

You might imagine that confusion could arise between the operators that you have been using for input and output and the shift operators. As far as the compiler is concerned, the meaning will always be clear from the context. If it isn't, the compiler will generate a message, but you need to be careful. For example, if you want to output the result of shifting a variable number left by 2 bits, you could write the following statement:

```
cout << (number << 2);
```

Here, the parentheses are essential. Without them, the shift operator will be interpreted by the compiler as a stream operator, so you won't get the result that you intended; the output will be the value of number followed by the value 2.

The right-shift operation is similar to the left-shift. For example, suppose the variable number has the value 24, and you execute the following statement:

```
number >>= 2;
```

This will result in number having the value 6, effectively dividing the original value by 4. However, the right shift operates in a special way with signed integer types that are negative (that is, the sign bit, which is the leftmost bit, is 1). In this case, the sign bit is propagated to the right. For example, declare and initialize a variable number of type char with the value −104 in decimal:

```
char number = -104;      // Binary representation is 1001 1000
```

Now you can shift it right 2 bits with the operation:

```
number >>= 2;            // Result 1110 0110
```

The decimal value of the result is −26, as the sign bit is repeated. With operations on `unsigned` integer types, of course, the sign bit is not repeated and zeros appear.

> **NOTE** *You may be wondering how the shift operators, << and >>, can be the same as the operators used with the standard streams for input and output. These operators can have different meanings in the two contexts because* `cin` *and* `cout` *are stream objects, and because they are objects, it is possible to redefine the meaning of operators in context by a process called* operator overloading. *Thus, the* >> *operator has been redefined for input stream objects such as* `cin`, *so you can use it in the way you have seen. The* << *operator has also been redefined for use with output stream objects such as* `cout`. *You will learn about operator overloading in Chapter 8.*

INTRODUCING LVALUES AND RVALUES

Every expression in C++ results in either an **lvalue** or an **rvalue** (sometimes written **l-value** and **r-value** and pronounced like that). An lvalue refers to an address in memory in which something is stored on an ongoing basis. An rvalue, on the other hand, is the result of an expression that is stored transiently. An lvalue is so called because any expression that results in an lvalue can appear on the left of the equals sign in an assignment statement. If the result of an expression is not an lvalue, it is an rvalue.

Consider the following statements:

```
int a(0), b(1), c(2);
a = b + c;
b = ++a;
c = a++;
```

The first statement declares the variables a, b, and c to be of type `int` and initializes them to 0, 1, and 2, respectively. In the second statement, the expression b+c is evaluated and the result is stored in the variable a. The result of evaluating the expression b+c is stored temporarily in a memory location and the value is copied from this location to a. Once execution of the statement is complete, the memory location holding the result of evaluating b+c is discarded. Thus, the result of evaluating the expression b+c is an rvalue.

In the third statement, the expression ++a is an lvalue because its result is a after its value is incremented. The expression a++ in the third statement is an rvalue because it stores the value of a temporarily as the result of the expression and then increments a.

An expression that consists of a single named variable is always an lvalue.

NOTE *This is by no means all there is to know about lvalues and rvalues. Most of the time, you don't need to worry very much about whether an expression is an lvalue or an rvalue, but sometimes, you do. Lvalues and rvalues will pop up at various times throughout the book, so keep the idea in mind.*

UNDERSTANDING STORAGE DURATION AND SCOPE

All variables have a finite lifetime when your program executes. They come into existence from the point at which you declare them and then, at some point, they disappear — at the latest, when your program terminates. How long a particular variable lasts is determined by a property called its **storage duration**. There are three different kinds of storage duration that a variable can have:

➤ Automatic storage duration

➤ Static storage duration

➤ Dynamic storage duration

Which of these a variable will have depends on how you create it. I will defer discussion of variables with dynamic storage duration until Chapter 4, but you will be exploring the characteristics of the other two in this chapter.

Another property that variables have is **scope**. The scope of a variable is simply that part of your program over which the variable name is valid. Within a variable's scope, you can legally refer to it, either to set its value or to use it in an expression. Outside of the scope of a variable, you cannot refer to its name — any attempt to do so will cause a compiler error. Note that a variable may still *exist* outside of its scope, even though you cannot refer to it by name. You will see examples of this situation a little later in this discussion.

All the variables that you have declared up to now have had **automatic storage duration**, and are therefore called **automatic variables**. Let's take a closer look at these first.

Automatic Variables

The variables that you have declared so far have been declared within a block — that is, within the extent of a pair of braces. These are called **automatic** variables and are said to have **local scope** or **block scope**. An automatic variable is "in scope" from the point at which it is declared until the end of the block containing its declaration. The space that an automatic variable occupies is allocated automatically in a memory area called the **stack** that is set aside specifically for this purpose. The default size for the stack is 1MB, which is adequate for most purposes, but if it should turn out to be insufficient, you can increase the size of the stack by setting the /STACK option for the project to a value of your choosing.

An automatic variable is "born" when it is defined and space for it is allocated on the stack, and it automatically ceases to exist at the end of the block containing the definition of the variable. This will be at the closing brace matching the first opening brace that precedes the declaration of the variable. Every time the block of statements containing a declaration for an automatic variable is executed, the variable is created anew, and if you specified an initial value for the automatic variable, it will be reinitialized each time it is created. When an automatic variable dies, its memory on the stack will be freed for use by other automatic variables. Let's look at an example demonstrating some of what I've discussed so far about scope.

TRY IT OUT   **Automatic Variables**

The following example shows the effect of scope on automatic variables:

Available for download on Wrox.com

```cpp
// Ex2_07.cpp
// Demonstrating variable scope
#include <iostream>

using std::cout;
using std::endl;

int main()
{                                       // Function scope starts here
   int count1 = 10;
   int count3 = 50;
   cout << endl
        << "Value of outer count1 = " << count1
        << endl;

   {                                    // New scope starts here...
      int count1 = 20;                  // This hides the outer count1
      int count2 = 30;
      cout << "Value of inner count1 = " << count1
           << endl;
      count1 += 3;                      // This affects the inner count1
      count3 += count2;
   }                                    // ...and ends here

   cout << "Value of outer count1 = " << count1
        << endl
        << "Value of outer count3 = " << count3
        << endl;

   // cout << count2 << endl;          // uncomment to get an error

   return 0;
}                                       // Function scope ends here
```

code snippet Ex2_07.cpp

The output from this example will be:

```
Value of outer count1 = 10
Value of inner count1 = 20
```

```
Value of outer count1 = 10
Value of outer count3 = 80
```

How It Works

The first two statements declare and define two integer variables, `count1` and `count3`, with initial values of 10 and 50, respectively. Both these variables exist from this point to the closing brace at the end of the program. The scope of these variables also extends to the closing brace at the end of `main()`.

Remember that the lifetime and scope of a variable are two different things. It's important not to get these two ideas confused. The lifetime is the period during execution from when the variable is first created to when it is destroyed and the memory it occupies is freed for other uses. The scope of a variable is the region of program code over which the variable may be accessed.

Following the variable definitions, the value of `count1` is output to produce the first of the lines shown above. There is then a second brace, which starts a new block. Two variables, `count1` and `count2`, are defined within this block, with values 20 and 30, respectively. The `count1` declared here is *different* from the first `count1`. The first `count1` still exists, but its name is masked by the second `count1`. Any use of the name `count1` following the declaration within the inner block refers to the `count1` declared within that block.

I used a duplicate of the variable name `count1` here only to illustrate what happens. Although this code is legal, it isn't a good approach to programming in general. In a real-world programming environment, it would be confusing, and if you use duplicate names, it makes it very easy to hide variables defined in an outer scope accidentally.

The value shown in the second output line shows that within the inner block, you are using the `count1` in the inner scope — that is, inside the innermost braces:

```
cout << "Value of inner count1 = " << count1
     << endl;
```

Had you still been using the outer `count1`, then this would display the value 10. The variable `count1` is then incremented by the statement:

```
count1 += 3;              // This affects the inner count1
```

The increment applies to the variable in the inner scope, since the outer one is still hidden. However, `count3`, which was defined in the outer scope, is incremented in the next statement without any problem:

```
count3 += count2;
```

This shows that the variables that were declared at the beginning of the outer scope are accessible from within the inner scope. (Note that if `count3` had been declared *after* the second of the inner pair of braces, then it would still be within the outer scope, but in that case, `count3` would not exist when the above statement was executed.)

After the brace ending the inner scope, `count2` and the inner `count1` cease to exist. The variables `count1` and `count3` are still there in the outer scope, and the values displayed show that `count3` was indeed incremented in the inner scope.

If you uncomment the line,

```
// cout << count2 << endl;          // uncomment to get an error
```

the program will no longer compile correctly because it attempts to output a nonexistent variable. You will get an error message something like,

```
c:\microsoft visual studio\myprojects\Ex2_07\Ex2_07.cpp(29) : error
    C2065: 'count2' : undeclared identifier
```

This is because `count2` is out of scope at this point.

Positioning Variable Declarations

You have great flexibility as to where you can place the declarations for your variables. The most important aspect to consider is what scope the variables need to have. Beyond that, you should generally place a declaration close to where the variable is to be first used in a program. You should write your programs with a view to making them as easy as possible for another programmer to understand, and declaring a variable at its first point of use can be helpful in achieving that.

It is possible to place declarations for variables outside of all of the functions that make up a program. The next section looks what effect that has on the variables concerned.

Global Variables

Variables that are declared outside of all blocks and classes (I will discuss classes later in the book) are called **globals** and have **global scope** (which is also called **global namespace scope** or **file scope**). This means that they are accessible throughout all the functions in the file, following the point at which they are declared. If you declare them at the very top of your program, they will be accessible from anywhere in the file.

Globals also have **static storage duration** by default. Global variables with static storage duration will exist from the start of execution of the program until execution of the program ends. If you do not specify an initial value for a global variable, it will be initialized with 0 by default. Initialization of global variables takes place before the execution of `main()` begins, so they are always ready to be used within any code that is within the variable's scope.

Figure 2-13 shows the contents of a source file, `Example.cpp`, and the arrows indicate the scope of each of the variables.

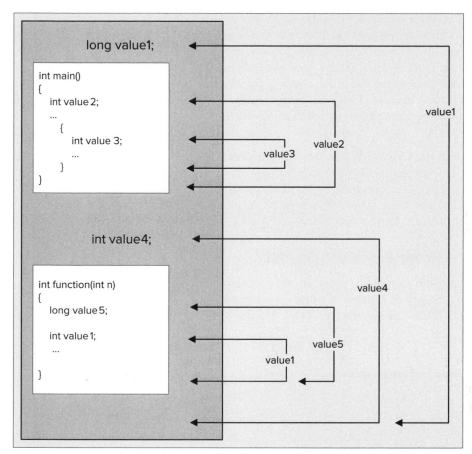

FIGURE 2-13

The variable value1, which appears at the beginning of the file, is declared at global scope, as is value4, which appears after the function main(). The scope of each global variable extends from the point at which it is defined to the end of the file. Even though value4 exists when execution starts, it cannot be referred to in main() because main() is not within the variable's scope. For main() to use value4, you would need to move its declaration to the beginning of the file. Both value1 and value4 will be initialized with 0 by default, which is not the case for the automatic variables. Note that the local variable called value1 in function() hides the global variable of the same name.

Since global variables continue to exist for as long as the program is running, this might raise the question in your mind, "Why not make all variables global and avoid this messing about with local variables that disappear?" This sounds very attractive at first, but as with the Sirens of mythology, there are serious side effects that completely outweigh any advantages you may gain.

Real programs are generally composed of a large number of statements, a significant number of functions, and a great many variables. Declaring all variables at the global scope greatly magnifies the possibility of accidental erroneous modification of a variable, as well as making the job of naming them sensibly quite intractable. They will also occupy memory for the duration of program execution. By keeping variables local to a function or a block, you can be sure they have almost complete protection from external effects, they will only exist and occupy memory from the point at which they are defined to the end of the enclosing block, and the whole development process becomes much easier to manage. That's not to say you should never define variables at global scope. Sometimes, it can be very convenient to define constants that are used throughout the program code at global scope.

If you take a look at the Class View pane for any of the examples that you have created so far and extend the class tree for the project by clicking on the [unfilled] symbol, you will see an entry called Global Functions and Variables. If you click on this, you will see a list of everything in your program that has global scope. This will include all the global functions, as well as any global variables that you have declared.

TRY IT OUT   **The Scope Resolution Operator**

As you have seen, a global variable can be hidden by a local variable with the same name. However, it's still possible to get at the global variable by using the **scope resolution operator** (::), which you saw in Chapter 1 when I was discussing namespaces. I can demonstrate how this works with a revised version of the last example:

```cpp
// Ex2_08.cpp
// Demonstrating variable scope
#include <iostream>

using std::cout;
using std::endl;

int count1 = 100;                          // Global version of count1

int main()
{                                          // Function scope starts here
   int count1 = 10;
   int count3 = 50;
   cout << endl
        << "Value of outer count1 = " << count1
        << endl;
   cout << "Value of global count1 = " << ::count1        // From outer block
        << endl;

   {                                   // New scope starts here...
      int count1 = 20;                 // This hides the outer count1
      int count2 = 30;
      cout << "Value of inner count1 = " << count1
           << endl;
      cout << "Value of global count1 = " << ::count1        // From inner block
           << endl;

      count1 += 3;                     // This affects the inner count1
      count3 += count2;
```

```
    }                                   // ...and ends here.

    cout << "Value of outer count1 = " << count1
        << endl
        << "Value of outer count3 = " << count3
        << endl;

    //cout << count2 << endl;          // uncomment to get an error
    return 0;
}                                       // Function scope ends here
```

code snippet Ex2_08.cpp

If you compile and run this example, you'll get the following output:

```
Value of outer count1 = 10
Value of global count1 = 100
Value of inner count1 = 20
Value of global count1 = 100
Value of outer count1 = 10
Value of outer count3 = 80
```

How It Works

The shaded lines of code indicate the changes I have made to the previous example; I just need to discuss the effects of those. The declaration of count1 prior to the definition of the function main() is global, so in principle, it is available anywhere through the function main(). This global variable is initialized with the value of 100:

```
int count1 = 100;                       // Global version of count1
```

However, you have two other variables called count1, which are defined within main(), so, throughout the program, the global count1 is hidden by the local count1 variables. The first new output statement is:

```
cout << "Value of global count1 = " << ::count1            // From outer block
    << endl;
```

This uses the scope resolution operator (::) to make it clear to the compiler that you want to reference the global variable count1, *not* the local one. You can see that this works from the value displayed in the output.

In the inner block, the global count1 is hidden behind *two* variables called count1: the inner count1 and the outer count1. We can see the global scope resolution operator doing its stuff within the inner block, as you can see from the output generated by the statement we have added there:

```
cout << "Value of global count1 = " << ::count1            // From inner block
    << endl;
```

This outputs the value 100, as before — the long arm of the scope resolution operator used in this fashion always reaches a global variable.

You have seen earlier that you can refer to a name in the std namespace by qualifying the name with the namespace name, such as with std::cout or std::endl. The compiler searches the namespace that has the name specified by the left operand of the scope resolution operator for the name that you specify as the right operand. In the preceding example, you are using the scope resolution operator to search the global namespace for the variable count1. By not specifying a namespace name in front of the operator, you are telling the compiler to search the global namespace for the name that follows it.

You'll see a lot more of this operator when you get to explore object-oriented programming in Chapter 9, where it is used extensively.

Static Variables

It's conceivable that you might want to have a variable that's defined and accessible locally, but which also continues to exist after exiting the block in which it is declared. In other words, you need to declare a variable within a block scope, but to give it **static storage duration**. The static specifier provides you with the means of doing this, and the need for this will become more apparent when we come to deal with functions in Chapter 5.

In fact, a static variable will continue to exist for the life of a program even though it is declared within a block and available only from within that block (or its sub-blocks). It still has block scope, but it has static storage duration. To declare a static integer variable called count, you would write:

```
static int count;
```

If you don't provide an initial value for a static variable when you declare it, then it will be initialized for you. The variable count declared here will be initialized with 0. The default initial value for a static variable is always 0, converted to the type applicable to the variable. Remember that this is *not* the case with automatic variables.

 NOTE *If you don't initialize your automatic variables, they will contain junk values left over from the program that last used the memory they occupy.*

NAMESPACES

I have mentioned namespaces several times, so it's time you got a better idea of what they are about. They are not used in the libraries supporting MFC, but the libraries that support the CLR and Windows forms use namespaces extensively, and of course, the C++ standard library does, too.

You know already that all the names used in the ISO/IEC C++ standard library are defined in a namespace with the name std. This means that all the names used in the standard library have an additional qualifying name, std; for example, cout is really std::cout. You have already seen how you can add a using declaration to import a name from the std namespace into your source file. For example:

```
using std::cout;
```

This allows you to use the name `cout` in your source file and have it interpreted as `std::cout`.

Namespaces provide a way to separate the names used in one part of a program from those used in another. This is invaluable with large projects involving several teams of programmers working on different parts of the program. Each team can have its own namespace name, and worries about two teams accidentally using the same name for different functions disappear.

Look at this line of code:

```
using namespace std;
```

This statement is a **using directive** and is different from a `using` declaration. The effect of this is to import *all* the names from the `std` namespace into the source file so you can refer to anything that is defined in this namespace without qualifying the name in your program. Thus, you can write the name `cout` instead of `std::cout` and `endl` instead of `std::endl`. This sounds like a big advantage, but the downside of this blanket `using` directive is that it effectively negates the primary reason for using a namespace — that is, preventing accidental name clashes. There are two ways to access names from a namespace without negating its intended effect. One way is to qualify each name explicitly with the namespace name; unfortunately, this tends to make the code very verbose and reduce its readability. The other possibility that I mentioned early on in this chapter is to introduce just the names that you use in your code with `using` declarations as you have seen in earlier examples, like this, for example:

```
using std::cout;            // Allows cout usage without qualification
using std::endl;            // Allows endl usage without qualification
```

Each `using` declaration introduces a single name from the specified namespace and allows it to be used unqualified within the program code that follows. This provides a much better way of importing names from a namespace, as you only import the names that you actually use in your program. Because Microsoft has set the precedent of importing all names from the `System` namespace with C++/CLI code, I will continue with that in the C++/CLI examples. In general, I recommend that you use `using` declarations in your own code rather than `using` directives when you are writing programs of any significant size.

Of course, you can define your own namespace that has a name that you choose. The following section shows how that's done.

Declaring a Namespace

You use the keyword `namespace` to declare a namespace — like this:

```
namespace myStuff
{
   // Code that I want to have in the namespace myStuff...
}
```

This defines a namespace with the name `myStuff`. All name declarations in the code between the braces will be defined within the `myStuff` namespace, so to access any such name from a point outside this namespace, the name must be qualified by the namespace name, myStuff, or have a using declaration that identifies that the name is from the myStuff namespace.

You can't declare a namespace inside a function. It's intended to be used the other way around; you use a namespace to contain functions, global variables, and other named entities such as classes in your program. You must not put the definition of main() in a namespace, though. The function main() is where execution starts, and it must always be at global namespace scope; otherwise, the compiler won't recognize it.

You could put the variable value in the previous example in a namespace:

```cpp
// Ex2_09.cpp
// Declaring a namespace
#include <iostream>

namespace myStuff
{
  int value = 0;
}

int main()
{
  std::cout << "enter an integer: ";
  std::cin  >> myStuff::value;
  std::cout << "\nYou entered " << myStuff::value
            << std::endl;
  return 0;
}
```

code snippet Ex2_09.cpp

The myStuff namespace defines a scope, and everything within the namespace scope is qualified with the namespace name. To refer to a name declared within a namespace from outside, you must qualify it with the namespace name. Inside the namespace scope, any of the names declared within it can be referred to without qualification — they are all part of the same family. Now, you must qualify the name value with myStuff, the name of our namespace. If not, the program will not compile. The function main() now refers to names in two different namespaces, and in general, you can have as many namespaces in your program as you need. You could remove the need to qualify value by adding a using directive:

```cpp
// Ex2_10.cpp
// Using a using directive
#include <iostream>

namespace myStuff
{
  int value = 0;
}

using namespace myStuff;          // Make all the names in myStuff available

int main()
{
```

```
        std::cout << "enter an integer: ";
        std::cin  >> value;
        std::cout << "\nYou entered " << value
              << std::endl;
        return 0;
    }
```

code snippet Ex2_10.cpp

You could also have a `using` directive for `std` as well, so you wouldn't need to qualify standard library names either, but as I said, this defeats the whole purpose of namespaces. Generally, if you use namespaces in your program, you should not add `using` directives all over your program; otherwise, you might as well not bother with namespaces in the first place. Having said that, I will add a `using` directive for `std` in some of our examples to keep the code less cluttered and easier for you to read. When you are starting out with a new programming language, you can do without clutter, no matter how useful it is in practice.

Multiple Namespaces

A real-world program is likely to involve multiple namespaces. You can have multiple declarations of a namespace with a given name, and the contents of all namespace blocks with a given name are within the same namespace. For example, you might have a program file with two namespaces:

```
    namespace sortStuff
    {
       // Everything in here is within sortStuff namespace
    }

    namespace calculateStuff
    {
       // Everything in here is within calculateStuff namespace
       // To refer to names from sortStuff they must be qualified
    }

    namespace sortStuff
    {
       // This is a continuation of the namespace sortStuff
       // so from here you can refer to names in the first sortStuff namespace
       // without qualifying the names
    }
```

A second declaration of a namespace with a given name is just a continuation of the first, so you can reference names in the first namespace block from the second without having to qualify them. They are all in the same namespace. Of course, you would not usually organize a source file in this way deliberately, but it can arise quite naturally with header files that you include into a program. For example, you might have something like this:

```
    #include <iostream>       // Contents are in namespace std
    #include "myheader.h"     // Contents are in namespace myStuff
```

```
#include <string>          // Contents are in namespace std

// and so on...
```

Here, `iostream` and `string` are ISO/IEC C++ standard library headers, and `myheader.h` represents a header file that contains our program code. You have a situation with the namespaces that is an exact parallel of the previous illustration.

This has given you a basic idea of how namespaces work. There is a lot more to namespaces than I have discussed here, but if you grasp this bit, you should be able to find out more about it without difficulty, if the need arises.

NOTE The two forms of `#include` directive in the previous code fragment cause the compiler to search for the file in different ways. When you specify the file to be included between angled brackets, you are indicating to the compiler that it should search for the file along the path specified by the `/I` compiler option, and failing that, along the path specified by the `INCLUDE` environment variable. These paths locate the C++ library files, which is why this form is reserved for library headers. The `INCLUDE` environment variable points to the folder holding the library header, and the `/I` option allows an additional directory containing library headers to be specified. When the file name is between double quotes, the compiler will search the folder that contains the file in which the `#include` directive appears. If the file is not found, it will search in any directories that `#include` the current file. If that fails to find the file, it will search the library directories.

C++/CLI PROGRAMMING

C++/CLI provides a number of extensions and additional capabilities to what I have discussed in this chapter up to now. I'll first summarize these additional capabilities before going into details. The additional C++/CLI capabilities are:

➤ All the ISO/IEC fundamental data types can be used as I have described in a C++/CLI program, but they have some extra properties in certain contexts that I'll come to.

➤ C++/CLI provides its own mechanism for keyboard input and output to the command line in a console program.

➤ C++/CLI introduces the `safe_cast` operator that ensures that a cast operation results in verifiable code being generated.

➤ C++/CLI provides an alternative enumeration capability that is class-based and offers more flexibility than the ISO/IEC C++ `enum` declaration you have seen.

You'll learn more about CLR reference class types beginning in Chapter 4, but because I have introduced global variables for native C++, I'll mention now that variables of CLR reference class types cannot be global variables.

Let's begin by looking at fundamental data types in C++/CLI.

C++/CLI Specific: Fundamental Data Types

You can and should use the ISO/IEC C++ fundamental data type names in your C++/CLI programs, and with arithmetic operations, they work exactly as you have seen in native C++. Although all the operations with fundamental types you have seen work in the same way in C++/CLI, the fundamental type names in a C++/CLI program have a different meaning and introduce additional capabilities in certain situations. A fundamental type in a C++/CLI program is a value class type and can behave either as an ordinary value or as an object if the circumstances require it.

Within the C++/CLI language, each ISO/IEC fundamental type name maps to a **value class type** that is defined in the System namespace. Thus, in a C++/CLI program, the ISO/IEC fundamental type names are shorthand for the associated value class type. This enables the value of a fundamental type to be treated simply as a value or be automatically converted to an object of its associated value class type when necessary. The fundamental types, the memory they occupy, and the corresponding value class types are shown in the following table:

FUNDAMENTAL TYPE	SIZE (BYTES)	CLI VALUE CLASS
bool	1	System::Boolean
char	1	System::SByte
signed char	1	System::SByte
unsigned char	1	System::Byte
short	2	System::Int16
unsigned short	2	System::UInt16
int	4	System::Int32
unsigned int	4	System::UInt32
long	4	System::Int32
unsigned long	4	System::UInt32
long long	8	System::Int64
unsigned long long	8	System::UInt64
float	4	System::Single
double	8	System::Double
long double	8	System::Double
wchar_t	2	System::Char

By default, type char is equivalent to signed char, so the associated value class type is System::SByte. Note that you can change the default for char to unsigned char by setting the compiler option /J, in which case, the associated value class type will be System::Byte. System is the root namespace name in which the C++/CLI value class types are defined. There are many other types defined within the System namespace, such as the type String for representing strings that you'll meet in Chapter 4. C++/CLI also defines the System::Decimal value class type within the System namespace, and variables of type Decimal store exact decimal values with 28 decimal digits precision.

As I said, the value class type associated with each fundamental type name adds important additional capabilities for such variables in C++/CLI. When necessary, the compiler will arrange for automatic conversions from the original value to an object of a value class type, and vice versa; these processes are referred to as **boxing** and **unboxing**, respectively. This allows a variable of any of these types to behave as a simple value or as an object, depending on the circumstances. You'll learn more about how and when this happens in Chapter 9.

Because the ISO/IEC C++ fundamental type names are aliases for the value class type names in a C++/CLI program, in principle, you can use either in your C++/CLI code. For example, you already know you can write statements creating integer and floating-point variables like this:

```
int count = 10;
double value = 2.5;
```

You could use the value class names that correspond with the fundamental type names and have the program compile without any problem, like this:

```
System::Int32 count = 10;
System::Double value = 2.5;
```

Note that this is not exactly the same as using the fundamental type names such as int and double in your code, rather than the value class names System::Int32 and System::Double. The reason is that the mapping between fundamental type names and value class types I have described applies to the Visual C++ 2010 compiler; other compilers are not obliged to implement the same mapping. Type long in Visual C++ 2010 maps to type Int32, but it is quite possible that it could map to type Int64 on some other implementation. On the other hand, the representations of the value class type that are equivalents to the fundamental native C++ types are fixed; for example, type System::Int32 will always be a 32-bit signed integer on any C++/CLI implementation.

Having data of the fundamental types being represented by objects of a value class type is an important feature of C++/CLI. In ISO/IEC C++, fundamental types and class types are quite different, whereas in C++/CLI, all data is stored as objects of a class type, either as a value class type or as a reference class type. You'll learn how you define reference class types in Chapter 7.

Next, you'll try a CLR console program.

TRY IT OUT **A Fruity CLR Console Program**

Create a new project and select the project type as CLR and the template as CLR Console Application. You can then enter the project name as Ex2_11, as shown in Figure 2-14.

FIGURE 2-14

When you click on the OK button, the Application Wizard will generate the project containing the following code:

```
// Ex2_11.cpp : main project file.

#include "stdafx.h"

using namespace System;

int main(array<System::String ^> ^args)
{
    Console::WriteLine(L"Hello World");
    return 0;
}
```

I'm sure you noticed the extra stuff between the parentheses following main. This is concerned with passing values to the function main() when you initiate execution of the program from the command line, and you'll learn more about this when you explore functions in detail. If you compile and execute the default project, it will write "Hello World" to the command line. Now, you'll convert this program to a CLR version of `Ex2_02` so you can see how similar it is. To do this, you can modify the code in `Ex2_11.cpp` as follows:

```
// Ex2_11.cpp : main project file.
#include "stdafx.h"

using namespace System;

int main(array<System::String ^> ^args)
{
    int apples, oranges;               // Declare two integer variables
    int fruit;                         // ...then another one

    apples = 5; oranges = 6;           // Set initial values
    fruit = apples + oranges;          // Get the total fruit

    Console::WriteLine(L"\nOranges are not the only fruit...");
    Console::Write(L"- and we have ");
    Console::Write(fruit);
    Console::Write(L" fruits in all.\n");
    return 0;
}
```

code snippet Ex2_11.cpp

The new lines are shown shaded and those in the lower block replace the two lines in the automatically generated version of `main()`. You can now compile and execute the project. The program should produce the following output:

```
Oranges are not the only fruit...
- and we have 11 fruits in all.
```

Remember, if the command window showing the output disappears before you can see it, you can add the following statement immediately before the return statement in the preceding code:

```
Console::ReadLine();
```

The program will pause when this statement is reached, waiting for you to press the Enter key.

How It Works

The only significant difference is in how the output is produced. The definitions for the variables and the computation are the same. Although you are using the same type names as in the ISO/IEC C++ version of the example, the effect is not the same. The variables `apples`, `oranges`, and `fruit` will be of the C++/CLI type, `System::Int32`, that is specified by type `int`, and they have some additional capabilities compared with the ISO/IEC type. The variables here can act as objects in some circumstances or as simple values as they do here. If you want to confirm that `Int32` is the same as `int` in this case, you could replace the `int` type name with `Int32` and recompile the example. It should work in exactly the same way.

Evidently, the following line of code produces the first line of output:

```
Console::WriteLine(L"\nOranges are not the only fruit...");
```

The `WriteLine()` function is a C++/CLI function that is defined in the `Console` class in the `System` namespace. You'll learn about classes in detail in Chapter 7, but for now, the `Console` class represents the standard input and output streams that correspond to the keyboard and the command line in a command-line window. Thus, the `WriteLine()` function writes whatever is between the parentheses following the function name to the command line and then writes a newline character to move the cursor to the next line ready for the next output operation. Thus, the preceding statement writes the text `"\nOranges are not the only fruit..."` between the double quotes to the command line. The `L` that precedes the string indicates that it is a wide-character string where each character occupies two bytes.

The `Write()` function in the `Console` class is essentially the same as the `WriteLine()` function, the only difference being that it does not automatically write a newline character following the output that you specify. You can therefore use the `Write()` function when you want to write two or more items of data to the same line in individual output statements.

Values that you place between the parentheses that follow the name of a function are called **arguments**. Depending on how a function was written, it will accept zero, one, or more arguments when it is called. When you need to supply more than one argument, they must be separated by commas. There's more to the output functions in the `Console` class, so I want to explore `Write()` and `WriteLine()` in a little more depth.

C++/CLI Output to the Command Line

You saw in the previous example how you can use the `Console::Write()` and `Console::WriteLine()` methods to write a string or other items of data to the command line. You can put a variable of any of the types you have seen between the parentheses following the function name, and the value will be written to the command line. For example, you could write the following statements to output information about a number of packages:

```
int packageCount = 25;                   // Number of packages
Console::Write(L"There are ");           // Write string - no newline
Console::Write(packageCount);            // Write value - no newline
Console::WriteLine(L" packages.");       // Write string followed by newline
```

Executing these statements will produce the output:

```
There are 25 packages.
```

The output is all on the same line because the first two output statements use the `Write()` function, which does not output a newline character after writing the data. The last statement uses the `WriteLine()` function, which does write a newline after the output, so any subsequent output will be on the next line.

It looks a bit of a laborious process having to use three statements to write one line of output, and it will be no surprise to you that there is a better way. That capability is bound up with formatting the output to the command line in a .NET Framework program, so you'll explore that a little next.

C++/CLI Specific — Formatting the Output

Both the `Console::Write()` and `Console::WriteLine()` functions have a facility for you to control the format of the output, and the mechanism works in exactly the same way with both. The easiest way to understand it is through some examples. First, look at how you can get the output that was produced by the three output statements in the previous section with a single statement:

```
int packageCount = 25;
Console::WriteLine(L"There are {0} packages.", packageCount);
```

The second statement here will output the same output as you saw in the previous section. The first argument to the `Console::WriteLine()` function here is the string `L"There are {0}` `packages."`, and the bit that determines that the value of the second argument should be placed in the string is "`{0}`." The braces enclose a format string that applies to the second argument to the function, although in this instance, the format string is about as simple as it could get, being just a zero. The arguments that follow the first argument to the `Console::WriteLine()` function are numbered in sequence starting with zero, like this:

```
referenced by:                       0    1    2    etc.
Console::WriteLine("Format string", arg2, arg3, arg4,... );
```

Thus, the zero between the braces in the previous code fragment indicates that the value of the `packageCount` argument should replace the `{0}` in the string that is to be written to the command line.

If you want to output the weight as well as the number of packages, you could write this:

```
int packageCount = 25;
double packageWeight = 7.5;
Console::WriteLine(L"There are {0} packages weighing {1} pounds.",
                                            packageCount, packageWeight);
```

The output statement now has three arguments, and the second and third arguments are referenced by 0 and 1, respectively, between the braces. So, this will produce the output:

```
There are 25 packages weighing 7.5 pounds.
```

You could also write the statement with the last two arguments in reverse sequence, like this:

```
Console::WriteLine(L"There are {1} packages weighing {0} pounds.",
                                            packageWeight, packageCount);
```

The `packageWeight` variable is now referenced by 0 and `packageCount` by 1 in the format string, and the output will be the same as previously.

You also have the possibility to specify how the data is to be presented on the command line. Suppose that you wanted the floating-point value `packageWeight` to be output with two places of decimals. You could do that with the following statement:

```
Console::WriteLine(L"There are {0} packages weighing {1:F2} pounds.",
                                            packageCount, packageWeight);
```

In the substring {1:F2}, the colon separates the index value, 1, that identifies the argument to be selected from the format specification that follows, F2. The F in the format specification indicates that the output should be in the form "±ddd.dd. . ." (where *d* represents a digit) and the 2 indicates that you want to have two decimal places after the point. The output produced by the statement will be:

```
There are 25 packages weighing 7.50 pounds.
```

In general, you can write the format specification in the form {n,w : Axx} where the *n* is an index value selecting the argument following the format string, *w* is an optional field width specification, the *A* is a single letter specifying how the value should be formatted, and the *xx* is an optional one or two digits specifying the precision for the value. The field-width specification is a signed integer. The value will be right-justified in the field if w is positive and left-justified when it is negative. If the value occupies less than the number of positions specified by w, the output is padded with spaces; if the value requires more positions than that specified by w, the width specification is ignored. Here's another example:

```
Console::WriteLine(L"Packages:{0,3} Weight: {1,5:F2} pounds.",
                                            packageCount, packageWeight);
```

The package count is output with a field width of 3 and the weight with a field width of 5, so the output will be:

```
Packages:  25 Weight:  7.50 pounds.
```

There are other format specifiers that enable you to present various types of data in different ways. Here are some of the most useful format specifications:

FORMAT SPECIFIER	DESCRIPTION
C or c	Outputs the value as a currency amount.
D or d	Outputs an integer as a decimal value. If you specify the precision to be more than the number of digits, the number will be padded with zeroes to the left.
E or e	Outputs a floating-point value in scientific notation, that is, with an exponent. The precision value will indicate the number of digits to be output following the decimal point.
F or f	Outputs a floating-point value as a fixed-point number of the form ±dddd.dd. . . .
G or g	Outputs the value in the most compact form, depending on the type of the value and whether you have specified the precision. If you don't specify the precision, a default precision value will be used.
N or n	Outputs the value as a fixed-point decimal value using comma separators between each group of three digits when necessary.
X or x	Outputs an integer as a hexadecimal value. Upper or lowercase hexadecimal digits will be output depending on whether you specify X or x.

That gives you enough of a toehold in output to continue with more C++/CLI examples. Now, you'll take a quick look at some of this in action.

Here's an example that calculates the price of a carpet in order to demonstrate output in a CLR console program:

```cpp
// Ex2_12.cpp : main project file.
// Calculating the price of a carpet
#include "stdafx.h"

using namespace System;

int main(array<System::String ^> ^args)
{
  double carpetPriceSqYd = 27.95;
  double roomWidth = 13.5;              // In feet
  double roomLength = 24.75;            // In feet
  const int feetPerYard = 3;
  double roomWidthYds = roomWidth/feetPerYard;
  double roomLengthYds = roomLength/feetPerYard;
  double carpetPrice = roomWidthYds*roomLengthYds*carpetPriceSqYd;

  Console::WriteLine(L"Room size is {0:F2} yards by {1:F2} yards",
                                 roomLengthYds, roomWidthYds);
  Console::WriteLine(L"Room area is {0:F2} square yards",
                                 roomLengthYds*roomWidthYds);
  Console::WriteLine(L"Carpet price is ${0:F2}", carpetPrice);
  return 0;
}
```

code snippet Ex2_12.cpp

The output should be:

```
Room size is 8.25 yards by 4.50 yards
Room area is 37.13 square yards
Carpet price is $1037.64
```

How It Works

The dimensions of the room are specified in feet whereas the carpet is priced per square yard, so you have defined a constant, `feetPerYard`, to use in the conversion from feet to yards. In the expression to convert each dimension, you are dividing a value of type `double` by a value of type `int`. The compiler will insert code to convert the value of type `int` to type `double` before carrying out the multiplication. After converting the room dimensions to yards, you calculate the price of the carpet by multiplying the dimensions in yards to obtain the area in square yards and multiplying that by the price per square yard.

The output statements use the F2 format specification to limit the output values to two decimal places. Without this, there would be more decimal places in the output that would be inappropriate, especially for the price. You could try removing the format specification to see the difference.

Note that the statement to output the area has an arithmetic expression as the second argument to the `WriteLine()` function. The compiler will arrange to first evaluate the expression, and then, the result will be passed as the actual argument to the function. In general, you can always use an expression as an argument to a function, as long as the result of evaluating the expression is of a type that is consistent with the function parameter type.

C++/CLI Input from the Keyboard

The keyboard input capabilities that you have with a .NET Framework console program are somewhat limited. You can read a complete line of input as a string using the `Console::ReadLine()` function, or you can read a single character using the `Console::Read()` function. You can also read which key was pressed using the `Console::ReadKey()` function.

You would use the `Console::ReadLine()` function like this:

```
String^ line = Console::ReadLine();
```

This reads a complete line of input text that is terminated when you press the Enter key. The variable `line` is of type `String^` and stores a reference to the string that results from executing the `Console::ReadLine()` function; the little hat character, ^, following the type name, `String`, indicates that this is a **handle** that references an object of type `String`. You'll learn more about type `String` and handles for `String` objects in Chapter 4.

A statement that reads a single character from the keyboard looks like this:

```
char ch = Console::Read();
```

With the `Read()` function, you could read input data character by character, and then, analyze the characters read and convert the input to a corresponding numeric value.

The `Console::ReadKey()` function returns the key that was pressed as an object of type `ConsoleKeyInfo`, which is a value class type defined in the `System` namespace. Here's a statement to read a key press:

```
ConsoleKeyInfo keyPress = Console::ReadKey(true);
```

The argument `true` to the `ReadKey()` function results in the key press not being displayed on the command line. An argument value of `false` (or omitting the argument) will cause the character corresponding to the key pressed being displayed. The result of executing the function will be stored in `keyPress`. To identify the character corresponding to the key (or keys) pressed, you use the expression `keyPress.KeyChar`. Thus, you could output a message relating to a key press with the following statement:

```
Console::WriteLine(L"The key press corresponds to the character: {0}",
                                        keyPress.KeyChar);
```

The key that was pressed is identified by the expression keyPress.Key. This expression refers to a value of a C++/CLI enumeration (which you'll learn about very soon) that identifies the key that was pressed. There's more to the ConsoleKeyInfo objects than I have described. You'll meet them again later in the book.

While not having formatted input in a C++/CLI console program is a slight inconvenience while you are learning, in practice, this is a minor limitation. Virtually all the real-world programs you are likely to write will receive input through components of a window, so you won't typically have the need to read data from the command line. However, if you do, the value classes that are the equivalents of the fundamental types can help.

Reading numerical values from the command line will involve using some facilities that I have not yet discussed. You'll learn about these later in the book, so I'll gloss over some of the details at this point.

If you read a string containing an integer value using the Console::ReadLine() function, the Parse() function in the Int32 class will convert it to a 32-bit integer for you. Here's how you might read an integer using that:

```
Console::Write(L"Enter an integer: ");
int value = Int32::Parse(Console::ReadLine());
Console::WriteLine(L"You entered {0}", value);
```

The first statement just prompts for the input that is required, and the second statement reads the input. The string that the Console::ReadLine() function returns is passed as the argument to the Parse() function that belongs to the Int32 class. This will convert the string to a 32-bit integer and store it in value. The last statement outputs the value to show that all is well. Of course, if you enter something that is not an integer, disaster will surely follow.

The other value classes that correspond to native C++ fundamental types also define a Parse() function, so, for example, when you want to read a floating-point value from the keyboard, you can pass the string that Console::ReadLine() returns to the Double::Parse() function. The result will be a value of type double.

Using safe_cast

The safe_cast operation is for explicit casts in the CLR environment. In most instances, you can use static_cast to cast from one type to another in a C++/CLI program without problems, but because there are exceptions that will result in an error message, it is better to use safe_cast. You use safe_cast in exactly the same way as static_cast. For example:

```
double value1 = 10.5;
double value2 = 15.5;
int whole_number = safe_cast<int>(value1) + safe_cast<int>(value2);
```

The last statement casts each of the values of type double to type int before adding them together and storing the result in whole_number.

C++/CLI Enumerations

Enumerations in a C++/CLI program are significantly different from those in an ISO/IEC C++ program. For a start, you define an enumeration in C++/CLI like this:

```
enum class Suit{Clubs, Diamonds, Hearts, Spades};
```

This defines an enumeration type, `Suit`, and variables of type `Suit` can be assigned only one of the values defined by the enumeration — `Hearts`, `Clubs`, `Diamonds`, or `Spades`. When you refer to the constants in a C++/CLI enumeration, you must always qualify the constant you are using with the enumeration type name. For example:

```
Suit suit = Suit::Clubs;
```

This statement assigns the value `Clubs` from the `Suit` enumeration to the variable with the name `suit`. The `::` operator that separates the type name, `Suit`, from the name of the enumeration constant, `Clubs`, is the scope resolution operator that you have seen before, and it indicates that `Clubs` exists within the scope of the `Suit` enumeration.

Note the use of the word `class` in the definition of the enumeration, following the `enum` keyword. This does not appear in the definition of an ISO/IEC C++ enumeration as you saw earlier, and it identifies the enumeration as C++/CLI. In fact, the two words combined, `enum class`, are a keyword in C++/CLI that is different from the two keywords, `enum` and `class`. The use of the `enum class` keyword gives a clue to another difference from an ISO/IEC C++ enumeration; the constants here that are defined within the enumeration — `Hearts`, `Clubs`, and so on — are *objects*, not simply values of a fundamental type as in the ISO/IEC C++ version. In fact, by default, they are objects of type `Int32`, so they each encapsulate a 32-bit integer value; however, you must cast a constant to the fundamental type `int` before attempting to use it as such.

> **NOTE** *You can use* `enum struct` *instead of* `enum class` *when you define an enumeration. These are equivalent so it comes down to personal choice as to which you use. I will use* `enum class` *throughout.*

Because a C++/CLI enumeration is a class type, you cannot define it locally, within a function, for example, so if you want to define such an enumeration for use in `main()`, for example, you would define it at global scope.

This is easy to see with an example.

TRY IT OUT   Defining a C++/CLI Enumeration

Here's a very simple example using an enumeration:

Available for download on Wrox.com

```
// Ex2_13.cpp : main project file.
// Defining and using a C++/CLI enumeration.
#include "stdafx.h"
```

```
using namespace System;

// Define the enumeration at global scope
enum class Suit{Clubs, Diamonds, Hearts, Spades};

int main(array<System::String ^> ^args)
{
    Suit suit = Suit::Clubs;
    int value = safe_cast<int>(suit);
    Console::WriteLine(L"Suit is {0} and the value is {1} ", suit, value);
    suit = Suit::Diamonds;
    value = safe_cast<int>(suit);
    Console::WriteLine(L"Suit is {0} and the value is {1} ", suit, value);
    suit = Suit::Hearts;
    value = safe_cast<int>(suit);
    Console::WriteLine(L"Suit is {0} and the value is {1} ", suit, value);
    suit = Suit::Spades;
    value = safe_cast<int>(suit);
    Console::WriteLine(L"Suit is {0} and the value is {1} ", suit, value);
    return 0;
}
```

code snippet Ex2_13.cpp

This example will produce the following output:

```
Suit is Clubs and the value is 0
Suit is Diamonds and the value is 1
Suit is Hearts and the value is 2
Suit is Spades and the value is 3
```

How It Works

Because it is a class type, the Suit enumeration cannot be defined within the function main(), so its definition appears before the definition of main() and is therefore defined at global scope. The example defines a variable, suit, of type Suit and allocates the value Suit::Clubs to it initially with the statement:

```
Suit suit = Suit::Clubs;
```

The qualification of the constant name Clubs with the type name Suit is essential; without it, Clubs would not be recognized by the compiler.

If you look at the output, the value of suit is displayed as the name of the corresponding constant — "Clubs" in the first instance. This is quite different from what happens with native enums. To obtain the constant value that corresponds to the object in a C++/CLI enum, you must explicitly cast the value to the underlying type, type int in this instance:

```
value = safe_cast<int>(suit);
```

You can see from the output that the enumeration constants have been assigned values starting from 0. In fact, you can change the type that is used for the enumeration constants. The next section looks at how that's done.

Specifying a Type for Enumeration Constants

The constants in a C++/CLI enumeration can be any of the following types:

```
short       int        long       long long    signed char   char
unsigned    unsigned   unsigned   unsigned     unsigned      bool
short       int        long       long long    char
```

To specify the type for the constants in an enumeration, you write the type after the enumeration type name, but separated from it by a colon, just as with the native C++ enum. For example, to specify the enumeration constant type as char, you could write:

```
enum class Face : char {Ace, Two, Three, Four, Five, Six, Seven,
                        Eight, Nine, Ten, Jack, Queen, King};
```

The constants in this enumeration will be of type System::Sbyte and the underlying fundamental type will be type char. The first constant will correspond to code value 0 by default, and the subsequent values will be assigned in sequence. To get at the underlying value, you must explicitly cast the value to the type.

Specifying Values for Enumeration Constants

You don't have to accept the default for the underlying values. You can explicitly assign values to any or all of the constants defined by an enumeration. For example:

```
enum class Face : char {Ace = 1, Two, Three, Four, Five, Six, Seven,
                        Eight, Nine, Ten, Jack, Queen, King};
```

This will result in Ace having the value 1, Two having the value 2, and so on, with King having the value 13. If you wanted the values to reflect the relative face card values with Ace high, you could write the enumeration as:

```
enum class Face : char {Ace = 14, Two = 2, Three, Four, Five, Six, Seven,
                        Eight, Nine, Ten, Jack, Queen, King};
```

In this case, Two will have the value 2, and successive constants will have values in sequence, so King will still be 13. Ace will be 14, the value you have explicitly assigned.

The values you assign to enumeration constants do not have to be unique. This provides the possibility of using the values of the constants to convey some additional property. For example:

```
enum class WeekDays : bool { Mon = true, Tues = true, Wed = true,
                             Thurs = true, Fri = true, Sat = false, Sun = false };
```

This defines the enumeration WeekDays where the enumeration constants are of type bool. The underlying values have been assigned to identify which represent workdays as opposed to rest days. In the particular case of enumerators of type bool, you must supply all enumerators with explicit values.

Operations on Enumeration Constants

You can increment or decrement variables of an enum type using ++ or --, providing the enumeration constants are of an integral type other than bool. For example, consider this fragment using the Face type from the previous section:

```
Face card = Face::Ten;
++card;
Console::WriteLine(L"Card is {0}", card);
```

Here, you initialize the card variable to Face::Ten and then increment it. The output from the last statement will be:

```
Card is Jack
```

Incrementing or decrementing an enum variable does not involve any validation of the result, so it is up to you to ensure that the result corresponds to one of the enumerators so that it makes sense.

You can also use the + or - operators with enum values:

```
card = card - Face::Two;
```

This is not a very likely statement in practice, but the effect is to reduce the value of card by 2 because that is the value of Face::Two. Note that you cannot write:

```
card = card - 2;                      // Wrong! Will not compile.
```

This will not compile because the operands for the subtraction operator are of different types and there is no automatic conversion here. To make this work, you must use a cast:

```
card = card - safe_cast<Face>(2);      //OK!
```

Casting the integer to type Face allows card to be decremented by 2.

You can also use the bitwise operators ^, |, &, and ~ with enum values but, these are typically used with enums that represent flags, which I'll discuss in the next section. As with the arithmetic operations, the enum type must have enumeration constants of an integral type other than bool.

Finally, you can compare enum values using the relational operators:

```
==    !=    <    <=    >    >=
```

I'll be discussing the relational operators in the next chapter. For now, these operators compare two operands and result in a value of type `bool`. This allows you to use expressions such as `card == Face::Eight`, which will result in the value `true` if `card` is equal to `Face::Eight`.

Using Enumerators as Flags

It is possible to use an enumeration in quite a different way from what you have seen up to now. You can define an enumeration such that the enumeration constants represent **flags** or **status bits** for something. Most hardware storage devices use status bits to indicate the status of the device before or after an I/O operation, for example, and you can also use status bits or flags in your programs to record events of one kind or another.

Defining an enumeration to represent flags involves using an attribute. Attributes are additional information that you add to program statements to instruct the compiler to modify the code in some way or to insert code. This is rather an advanced topic for this book so I won't discuss attributes in general, but I'll make an exception in this case. Here's an example of an `enum` defining flags:

```
[Flags] enum class FlagBits{ Ready = 1, ReadMode = 2, WriteMode = 4,
                                          EOF = 8, Disabled = 16};
```

The `[Flags]` part of this statement is the attribute and it tells the compiler that the enumeration constants are single bit values; note the choice of explicit values for the constants. It also tells the compiler to treat a variable of type `FlagBits` as a collection of flag bits rather than a single value, for example:

```
FlagBits status = FlagBits::Ready | FlagBits::ReadMode | FlagBits::EOF;
```

The `status` variable will have the value,

```
0000 0000 0000 0000 0000 0000 0000 1011
```

with bits set to 1 corresponding to the enumeration constants that have been OR-ed together. This corresponds to the decimal value 11. If you now output the value of `status` with the following statement:

```
Console::WriteLine(L"Current status: {0}", status);
```

the output will be:

```
Current status: Ready, ReadMode, EOF
```

The conversion of the value of `status` to a string is not considering status as an integer value, but as a collection of bits, and the output is the names of the flags that have been set in the variable separated by commas.

To reset one of the bits in a `FlagBits` variable, you use the bitwise operators. Here's how you could switch off the `Ready` bit in status:

```
status = status & ~FlagBits::Ready;
```

The expression ~`FlagBits::Ready` results in a value with all bits set to 1 except the bit corresponding to `FlagBits::Ready`. When you AND this with `status`, only the `FlagBits::Ready` bit in status will be set to 0; all other bits in status will be left at their original setting.

Note that the `op=` operators are not defined for enum values so you cannot write:

```
status &= ~FlagBits::Ready;          // Wrong! Will not compile.
```

Native Enumerations in a C++/CLI Program

You can use the same syntax as native C++ enumerations in a C++/CLI program, and they will behave the same as they do in a native C++ program. The syntax for native C++ enums is extended in a C++/CLI program to allow you to specify the type for the enumeration constants explicitly. I recommend that you stick to C++/CLI enums in your CLR programs, unless you have a good reason to do otherwise.

DISCOVERING C++/CLI TYPES

The native `typeid` operator does not work with CLR reference types. However, C++/CLI has its own mechanism for discovering the type of an expression. For variables x and y, the expression `(x*y).GetType()` will produce an object of type `System::Type` that encapsulates the type of an expression. This will automatically be converted to a `System::String` object when you output it. For example:

```
int x = 0;
double y = 2.0;
Console::WriteLine(L"Type of x*y is {0}", (x*y).GetType());
```

Executing this fragment will result in the following output:

```
Type of x*y is System.Double
```

Of course, you could use the native `typeid` operator with the variables x and y and get a `type_info` object, but because C++/CLI represents a type as a `System::Type` object, I recommend that you stick to using `GetType()`.

C++/CLI also has its own version of `typeid` that you can only apply to a single variable or a type name. You can write `x::typeid` to get the `System::Type` object encapsulating the type of x. You can also write `String::typeid` to get the `System::Type` object for `System::String`.

SUMMARY

This chapter covered the basics of computation in C++. You have learned about all the elementary types of data provided for in the language, and all the operators that manipulate these types directly.

Although I have discussed all the fundamental types, don't be misled into thinking that's all there is. There are more complex types based on the basic set, as you'll see, and eventually, you will be creating original types of your own.

You can adopt the following coding strategies when writing a C++/CLI program:

➤ You should use the fundamental type names for variables, but keep in mind that they are really synonyms for the value class type names in a C++/CLI program. The significance of this will be more apparent when you learn more about classes.

➤ You should use `safe_cast` and not `static_cast` in your C++/CLI code. The difference will be much more important in the context of casting class objects, but if you get into the habit of using `safe_cast`, you generally can be sure you will avoid problems.

➤ You should use `enum class` to declare enumeration types in C++/CLI.

➤ To get the `System::Type` object for the type of an expression or variable, use `GetType()`.

EXERCISES

1. Write an ISO/IEC C++ program that asks the user to enter a number and then prints it out, using an integer as a local variable.

2. Write a program that reads an integer value from the keyboard into a variable of type `int`, and uses one of the bitwise operators (i.e. not the `%` operator!) to determine the positive remainder when divided by 8. For example, 29 = (3x8)+5 and −14 = (−2x8)+2 have positive remainder 5 and 2, respectively, when divided by 8.

3. Fully parenthesize the following expressions, in order to show the precedence and associativity:

```
1 + 2 + 3 + 4

16 * 4 / 2 * 3

a > b? a: c > d? e: f

a & b && c & d
```

4. Create a program that will calculate the aspect ratio of your computer screen, given the width and height in pixels, using the following statements:

```
int width = 1280;
int height = 1024;

double aspect = width / height;
```

When you output the result, what answer will you get? Is it satisfactory — and if not, how could you modify the code, without adding any more variables?

5.   (Advanced) Without running it, can you work out what value the following code is going to output, and why?

```
unsigned s = 555;

int i = (s >> 4) & ~(~0 << 3);
cout << i;
```

6.   Write a C++/CLI console program that uses an enumeration to identify months in the year, with the values associated with the months running from 1 to 12. The program should output each enumeration constant and its underlying value.

7.   Write a C++/CLI program that will calculate the areas of three rooms to the nearest number of whole square feet that have the following dimensions in feet:

Room1: 10.5 by 17.6   Room2: 12.7 by 18.9   Room3: 16.3 by 15.4

The program should also calculate and output the average area of the three rooms and the total area; in each case, the result should be to the nearest whole number of square feet.

▶ WHAT YOU LEARNED IN THIS CHAPTER

TOPIC	CONCEPT
The `main()` function	A program in C++ consists of at least one function called `main()`.
The function body	The executable part of a function is made up of statements contained between braces.
Statements	A statement in C++ is terminated by a semicolon.
Names	Named objects in C++, such as variables or functions, can have names that consist of a sequence of letters and digits, the first of which is a letter, and where an underscore is considered to be a letter. Uppercase and lowercase letters are distinguished.
Reserved words	All the objects, such as variables, that you name in your program must not have a name that coincides with any of the reserved words in C++.
Fundamental types	All constants and variables in C++ are of a given type. The fundamental types in ISO/IEC C++ are `char`, `signed char`, `unsigned char`, `wchar_t`, `short`, `unsigned short`, `int`, `unsigned int`, `long`, `unsigned long`, `long long`, `unsigned long long`, `bool`, `float`, `double`, and `long double`.
Declarations	The name and type of a variable is defined in a declaration statement ending with a semicolon. Variables may also be given initial values in a declaration.
The `const` modifier	You can protect the value of a variable of a basic type by using the modifier `const`. This will prevent direct modification of the variable within the program and give you compiler errors everywhere that a constant's value is altered.
Automatic variables	By default, a variable is automatic, which means that it exists only from the point at which it is declared to the end of the scope in which it is defined, indicated by the corresponding closing brace after its declaration.
`static` variables	A variable may be declared as `static`, in which case, it continues to exist for the life of the program. It can be accessed only within the scope in which it was defined.
Global variables	Variables can be declared outside of all blocks within a program, in which case, they have global namespace scope. Variables with global namespace scope are accessible throughout a program, except where a local variable exists with the same name as the global variable. Even then, they can still be reached by using the scope resolution operator.
Namespaces	A namespace defines a scope where each of the names declared within it is qualified by the namespace name. Referring to names from outside a namespace requires the names to be qualified.

continues

(continued)

The native C++ standard library	The ISO/IEC C++ Standard Library contains functions and operators that you can use in your program. They are contained in the namespace std. The root namespace for C++/CLI libraries has the name System. You can access individual objects in a namespace by using the namespace name to qualify the object name by using the scope resolution operator, or you can supply a using declaration for a name from the namespace.
lvalues	An lvalue is an object that can appear on the left-hand side of an assignment. Non-const variables are examples of lvalues.
Mixed expressions	You can mix different types of variables and constants in an expression, but they will be automatically converted to a common type where necessary. Conversion of the type of the right-hand side of an assignment to that of the left-hand side will also be made where necessary. This can cause loss of information when the left-hand side type can't contain the same information as the right-hand side: double converted to int, or long converted to short, for example.
Explicit casts	You can explicitly cast the value of an expression to another type. You should always make an explicit cast to convert a value when the conversion may lose information. There are also situations where you need to specify an explicit cast in order to produce the result that you want.
Using typedef	The typedef keyword allows you to define synonyms for other types.
The auto keyword	You can use the auto keyword instead of a type name when defining a variable and have the type deduced from the initial value.
The typeid operator	The typeid operator is used to obtain the type of an expression.

3

Decisions and Loops

WHAT YOU WILL LEARN IN THIS CHAPTER:

➤ How to compare data values

➤ How to alter the sequence of program execution based on the result

➤ How to apply logical operators and expressions

➤ How to deal with multiple choice situations

➤ How to write and use loops in your programs

In this chapter, you will look at how to add decision-making capabilities to your C++ programs. You'll also learn how to make your programs repeat a set of actions until a specific condition is met. This will enable you to handle variable amounts of input, as well as make validity checks on the data that you read in. You will also be able to write programs that can adapt their actions depending on the input data, and that can deal with problems where logic is fundamental to the solution.

I'll start with one of the most powerful and fundamental tools in programming: the ability to compare variables and expressions with other variables and expressions and, based on the outcome, execute one set of statements or another.

COMPARING VALUES

Unless you want to make decisions on a whim, you need a mechanism for comparing things. This involves some new operators called **relational operators**. Because all information in your computer is ultimately represented by numerical values (in the last chapter you saw how character information is represented by numeric codes), comparing numerical values is the essence of practically all decision making. You have six fundamental operators for comparing two values available:

<	less than	<=	less than or equal to
>	greater than	>=	greater than or equal to
==	equal to	!=	not equal to

NOTE *The "equal to" comparison operator has two successive = signs. This is not the same as the assignment operator, which consists only of a single = sign. It's a common mistake to use the assignment operator instead of the comparison operator, so watch out for this potential cause of confusion.*

Each of these operators compares the values of two operands and returns one of the two possible values of type `bool`: `true` if the comparison is true, or `false` if it is not. You can see how this works by having a look at a few simple examples of comparisons. Suppose you have created integer variables i and j with the values 10 and −5, respectively. The expressions,

```
i > j     i != j     j > -8     i <= j + 15
```

all return the value `true`.

Assume that you have defined the following variables:

```
char first = 'A', last = 'Z';
```

Here are some examples of comparisons using these character variables:

```
first == 65   first < last 'E' <= first   first != last
```

All four expressions involve comparing ASCII code values. The first expression returns `true` because `first` was initialized with `'A'`, which is the equivalent of decimal 65. The second expression checks whether the value of `first`, which is `'A'`, is less than the value of `last`, which is `'Z'`. If you check the ASCII codes for these characters in Appendix B, notice that the capital letters are represented by an ascending sequence of numerical values from 65 to 90, 65 representing `'A'` and 90 representing `'Z'`, so this comparison also returns the value `true`. The third expression returns the value `false` because `'E'` is greater than the value of `first`. The last expression returns `true` because `'A'` is definitely not equal to `'Z'`.

Consider some slightly more complicated numerical comparisons. With variables defined by the statements

```
int i = -10, j = 20;
double x = 1.5, y = -0.25E-10;
```

take a look at the following expressions:

```
-1 < y     j < (10 - i)     2.0*x >= (3 + y)
```

As you can see, you can use expressions that result in numerical values as operands in comparisons. The precedence table for operators that you saw in Chapter 2 shows that none of the parentheses are strictly necessary, but they do help to make the expressions clearer. The first comparison is true, and so returns the bool value true. The variable y has a very small negative value, -0.000000000025, and so is greater than -1. The second comparison returns the value false. The expression 10 - i has the value 20, which is the same as j. The third expression returns true because the expression 3 + y is slightly less than 3.

You can use relational operators to compare values of any of the fundamental types, or of the enumeration types as I mentioned in Chapter 2, so all you need now is a practical way of using the results of a comparison to modify the behavior of a program.

The if Statement

The basic if statement allows your program to execute a single statement — or a block of statements enclosed within braces — if a given condition expression evaluates to true, or to skip the statement or block of statements if the condition evaluates to false. This is illustrated in Figure 3-1.

A simple example of an if statement is:

if(condition)

condition
evaluates to true

condition
evaluates to false

```
{

    // Statements

}
```

// More statements

FIGURE 3-1

```
if('A' == letter)
    cout << "The first capital, alphabetically speaking.";
```

The condition to be tested appears in parentheses immediately following the keyword, if, and this is followed by the statement to be executed when the condition is true. Note the position of the semicolon here. It goes after the statement *following* the if and the condition between parentheses; there shouldn't be a semicolon after the condition in parentheses because the two lines essentially make up a single statement. You also can see how the statement following the if is indented, to indicate that it is only executed when the if condition returns the value true. The indentation is not necessary for the program to execute, but it helps you to recognize the relationship between the if condition and the statement that depends on it. The output statement in the code fragment is executed only if the variable letter has the value 'A'.

NOTE *When you are comparing a variable to a constant of some kind using the == operator, it is a good idea to write the constant on the left of the == operator, as in* 'A' == letter. *That way, if you accidentally write* 'A' = letter, *you will get an error message from the compiler. If you write* letter = 'A', *this is perfectly legal, though not what you intended, so no error message will be produced.*

You could extend this example to change the value of `letter` if it contains the value `'A'`:

```
if('A' == letter)
{
   cout << "The first capital, alphabetically speaking.";
   letter = 'a';
}
```

The block of statements that is controlled by the `if` statement is delimited by the curly braces. Here you execute the statements in the block only if the condition (`'A' == letter`) evaluates to `true`. Without the braces, only the first statement would be the subject of the `if`, and the statement assigning the value `'a'` to `letter` would always be executed. Note that there is a semicolon after each of the statements in the block, but not after the closing brace at the end of the block. There can be as many statements as you like within the block. Now, as a result of `letter` having the value `'A'`, you change its value to `'a'` after outputting the same message as before. If the condition returns `false`, neither of these statements is executed.

Nested if Statements

The statement to be executed when the condition in an `if` statement is true can also be an `if`. This arrangement is called a **nested** `if`. The condition for the inner `if` is only tested if the condition for the outer `if` is true. An `if` that is nested inside another can also contain a nested `if`. You can generally continue nesting `if`s one inside the other like this for as long as you know what you are doing.

TRY IT OUT   **Using Nested Ifs**

The following is a working example of the nested `if`.

```
// Ex3_01.cpp
// A nested if demonstration
#include <iostream>

using std::cin;
using std::cout;
using std::endl;

int main()
{
   char letter(0);                     // Store input in here

   cout << endl
        << "Enter a letter: ";         // Prompt for the input
   cin >> letter;                      // then read a character

   if(letter >= 'A')                   // Test for 'A' or larger
   {
      if(letter <= 'Z')                // Test for 'Z' or smaller
      {
         cout << endl
              << "You entered a capital letter."
              << endl;
```

```
            return 0;
        }
    }

    if(letter >= 'a')                  // Test for 'a' or larger
    {
        if(letter <= 'z')              // Test for 'z' or smaller
        {
            cout << endl
                << "You entered a small letter."
                << endl;
            return 0;
        }
    }

    cout << endl << "You did not enter a letter." << endl;
    return 0;
}
```

code snippet Ex3_01.cpp

How It Works

This program starts with the usual comment lines, then the #include statement for the header file supporting input/output, followed by the using declarations for cin, cout, and endl that are in the std namespace. The first action in the body of main() is to prompt for a letter to be entered. This is stored in the char variable with the name letter.

The if statement that follows the input checks whether the character entered is 'A' or larger. Because the ASCII codes for lowercase letters (97 to 122) are greater than those for uppercase letters (65 to 90), entering a lowercase letter causes the program to execute the first if block, since (letter >= 'A') returns true for all letters. In this case, the nested if, which checks for an input of 'Z' or less, is executed. If it is 'Z' or less, you know that you have a capital letter, the message is displayed, and you are done, so you execute a return statement to end the program. Both statements are enclosed between braces, so they are both executed when the nested if condition returns true.

The next if checks whether the character entered is lowercase, using essentially the same mechanism as the first if, displays a message and returns.

If the character entered is not a letter, the output statement following the last if block is executed. This displays a message to the effect that the character entered was not a letter. The return is then executed.

You can see that the relationship between the nested ifs and the output statement is much easier to follow because of the indentation applied to each.

A typical output from this example is:

```
Enter a letter: T
You entered a capital letter.
```

You could easily arrange to change uppercase to lowercase by adding just one extra statement to the `if`, checking for uppercase:

```
if(letter >= 'A')                  // Test for 'A' or larger
    if(letter <= 'Z')              // Test for 'Z' or smaller
    {
        cout << endl
            << "You entered a capital letter.";
            << endl;
        letter += 'a' - 'A';       // Convert to lowercase
        return 0;
    }
```

This involves adding one additional statement. This statement for converting from uppercase to lowercase increments the `letter` variable by the value `'a'` - `'A'`. It works because the ASCII codes for `'A'` to `'Z'` and `'a'` to `'z'` are two groups of consecutive numerical codes, decimal 65 to 90 and 97 to 122 respectively, so the expression `'a'` - `'A'` represents the value to be added to an uppercase letter to get the equivalent lowercase letter and corresponds to 97 - 65, which is 32. Thus , if you add 32 to the code value for `'K'`, which is 75, you get 107, which is the code value for `'k'`.

You could equally well use the equivalent ASCII values for the letters here, but by using the letters you've ensured that this code would work on computers where the characters were not ASCII, as long as both the upper- and lowercase sets are represented by a contiguous sequence of numeric values.

There is a standard library function to convert letters to uppercase, so you don't normally need to program this yourself. It has the name `toupper()` and appears in the standard header file `ctype`. You will see more about standard library facilities when you get to look specifically at how functions are written.

The Extended if Statement

The `if` statement that you have been using so far executes a statement if the condition specified returns `true`. Program execution then continues with the next statement in sequence. You also have a version of the `if` that allows one statement to be executed if the condition returns `true`, and a different statement to be executed if the condition returns `false`. Execution then continues with the next statement in sequence. As you saw in Chapter 2, a block of statements can always replace a single statement, so this also applies to these `if`s.

TRY IT OUT   **Extending the If**

Here's an extended `if` example.

```
// Ex3_02.cpp
// Using the extended if
#include <iostream>

using std::cin;
using std::cout;
```

```
using std::endl;

int main()
{
    long number(0L);              // Store input here
    cout << endl
        << "Enter an integer number less than 2 billion: ";
    cin >> number;

    if(number % 2L)               // Test remainder after division by 2
        cout << endl              // Here if remainder 1
            << "Your number is odd." << endl;
    else
        cout << endl              // Here if remainder 0
            << "Your number is even." << endl;

    return 0;
}
```

code snippet Ex3_02.cpp

Typical output from this program is:

```
Enter an integer less than 2 billion: 123456
Your number is even.
```

How It Works

After reading the input value into `number`, the value is tested by taking the remainder after division by two (using the remainder operator `%` that you saw in the last chapter) and using that as the condition for the `if`. In this case, the condition of the `if` statement returns an integer, not a boolean. The `if` statement interprets a non-zero value returned by the condition as `true`, and interprets zero as `false`. In other words, the condition expression for the `if` statement

```
(number % 2L)
```

is equivalent to

```
(number % 2L != 0)
```

If the remainder is 1, the condition is `true`, and the statement immediately following the `if` is executed. If the remainder is 0, the condition is `false`, and the statement following the `else` keyword is executed. It's obvious here what the `if` expression is doing, but with more complicated expressions it's better to add the extra few characters needed for the comparison with zero to ensure that the code is easily understood.

NOTE *In an* `if` *statement, the condition can be an expression that results in a value of any of the fundamental data types that you saw in Chapter 2. When the condition expression evaluates to a numerical value rather than the* `bool` *value required by the* `if` *statement, the compiler inserts an automatic conversion of the result of the expression to type* `bool`. *A non-zero value that is cast to type* `bool` *results in* `true`, *and a zero value results in* `false`.

The remainder from the division of an integer by two can only be one or zero. After either outcome, the `return` statement is executed to end the program.

 NOTE *The* `else` *keyword is written without a semicolon, similar to the if part of the statement. Again, indentation is used as a visible indicator of the relationship between various statements. You can clearly see which statement is executed for a true or non-zero result, and which for a false or zero result. You should always indent the statements in your programs to show their logical structure.*

The `if-else` combination provides a choice between two options. The general logic of the `if-else` is shown in Figure 3-2.

The arrows in the diagram indicate the sequence in which statements are executed, depending on whether the `if` condition returns `true` or `false`.

Nested if-else Statements

As you have seen, you can nest `if` statements within `if` statements. You can also nest `if-else` statements within `if`s, `if`s within `if-else` statements, and `if-else` statements within `if-else` statements. This provides considerable room for confusion, so take a look at a few examples. The following is an example of an `if-else` nested within an `if`.

```
if('y' == coffee)
    if('y' == donuts)
        cout << "We have coffee and donuts.";
    else
        cout << "We have coffee, but not donuts";
```

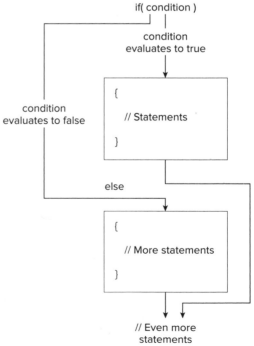

FIGURE 3-2

The test for `donuts` is executed only if the result of the test for `coffee` returns `true`, so the messages reflect the correct situation in each case; however, it is easy to get this confused. If you write much the same thing with incorrect indentation, you can be trapped into the wrong conclusion:

```
if('y' == coffee)
    if('y' == donuts)
        cout << "We have coffee and donuts.";
else                                      // This else is indented incorrectly
    cout << "We have no coffee...";       // Wrong!
```

The mistake is easy to see here, but with more complicated `if` structures you need to keep in mind the rule about which `if` owns which `else`.

 NOTE An `else` *always belongs to the nearest preceding* `if` *that is not already spoken for by another* `else`.

Whenever things look a bit complicated, you can apply this rule to sort things out. When you are writing your own programs you can always use braces to make the situation clearer. It isn't really necessary in such a simple case, but you could write the last example as follows:

```
if('y' == coffee)
{
    if('y' == donuts)
        cout << "We have coffee and donuts.";
    else
        cout << "We have coffee, but not donuts";
}
```

and it should be absolutely clear. Now that you know the rules, understanding the case of an `if` nested within an `if-else` becomes easy.

```
if('y' == coffee)
{
    if('y' == donuts)
        cout << "We have coffee and donuts.";
}
else
    if('y' == tea)
        cout << "We have tea, but not coffee";
```

Here the braces are essential. If you leave them out, the `else` would belong to the second `if`, which is looking out for `donuts`. In this kind of situation, it is easy to forget to include the braces and create an error that may be hard to find. A program with this kind of error compiles fine and even produces the right results some of the time.

If you removed the braces in this example, you get the correct results only as long as `coffee` and `donuts` are both equal to `'y'` so that the `if('y' == tea)` check wouldn't be executed.

Here you'll look at `if-else` statements nested in `if-else` statements. This can get very messy, even with just one level of nesting.

```
if('y' == coffee)
   if('y' == donuts)
      cout << "We have coffee and donuts.";
   else
      cout << "We have coffee, but not donuts";
else
   if('y' == tea)
      cout << "We have no coffee, but we have tea, and maybe donuts...";
   else
      cout << "No tea or coffee, but maybe donuts...";
```

The logic here doesn't look quite so obvious, even with the correct indentation. No braces are necessary, as the rule you saw earlier verifies that each `else` belongs to the correct `if`, but it would look a bit clearer if you included them.

```
if('y' == coffee)
{
   if('y' == donuts)
      cout << "We have coffee and donuts.";
   else
      cout << "We have coffee, but not donuts";
}
else
{
   if('y' == tea)
      cout << "We have no coffee, but we have tea, and maybe donuts...";
   else
      cout << "No tea or coffee, but maybe donuts...";
}
```

There are much better ways of dealing with this kind of logic in a program. If you put enough nested `if`s together, you can almost guarantee a mistake somewhere. The following section will help to simplify things.

Logical Operators and Expressions

As you have just seen, using `if`s where you have two or more related conditions can be a bit cumbersome. We have tried our `if`fy talents on looking for coffee and donuts, but in practice you may want to test much more complex conditions.

Logical operators provide a neat and simple solution. Using logical operators, you can combine a series of comparisons into a single logical expression, so you end up needing just one `if`, virtually regardless of the complexity of the set of conditions, as long as the decision ultimately boils down to a choice between two possibilities — true or false.

You have just three logical operators:

&&	Logical AND
||	Logical OR
!	Logical negation (NOT)

Logical AND

You would use the AND operator, `&&`, where you have two conditions that must both be `true` for a true result. You want to be rich *and* healthy. Thus the `&&` operator produces the result `true` when both operands have the value `true`, and `false` otherwise.

You could use the `&&` operator when you are testing a character to determine whether it's an uppercase letter; the value being tested must be both greater than or equal to `'A'` AND less than or equal to `'Z'`. Both conditions must return `true` for the value to be a capital letter.

 NOTE *As before, the conditions you combine using logical operators may return numerical values. Remember that in this case a non-zero value converts to the value* `true`; *zero converts to* `false`.

Taking the example of a value stored in a `char` variable `letter`, you could replace the test that uses two `if`s with one that uses only a single `if` and the `&&` operator:

```
if((letter >= 'A') && (letter <= 'Z'))
   cout << "This is a capital letter.";
```

The parentheses inside the expression that is the `if` condition ensure that there is no doubt that the comparison operations are executed first, which makes the statement clearer. Here, the output statement is executed only if *both* of the conditions that are combined by the `&&` operator are `true`.

 NOTE *If the left operand for the* `&&` *operator is* `false`, *the right operand will not be evaluated. This becomes significant if the right operand is an expression that can change something, such as an expression involving the* `++` *or* `--` *operator. For example, in the expression* x>=5 && ++n<10, n *will not be incremented if x is less than* 5.

Logical OR

The OR operator, `||`, applies when you have two conditions and you want a `true` result if either or both of them are true. For example, you might be considered creditworthy for a loan from the bank if your income was at least $100,000 a year, or if you had $1,000,000 in cash. This could be tested using the following `if`.

```
if((income >= 100000.00) || (capital >= 1000000.00))
   cout << "How much would you like to borrow, Sir (grovel, grovel)?";
```

The ingratiating response emerges when either or both of the conditions are `true`. (A better response might be, "Why do you *want* to borrow?" It's strange how banks lend you money only if you don't need it.)

You only get a `false` result with the `||` operator when both operands are `false`.

> **NOTE** If the left operand for the || operator is `true`, the right operand will not be evaluated. For example, in the expression x>=5 || ++n<10, the variable n will not be incremented if x is greater than or equal to 5.

Logical NOT

The third logical operator, `!`, takes one operand of type `bool` and inverts its value. So, if the value of a variable `test` is `true`, `!test` is `false`; and if `test` is `false`, `!test` is `true`. To take the example of a simple expression, if x has the value 10, consider the expression

```
!(x > 5)
```

The result is `false`, because `x > 5` is `true`.

You could also apply the `!` operator in an expression that was a favorite of Charles Dickens':

```
!(income > expenditure)
```

If this expression is `true`, the result is misery, at least as soon as the bank starts bouncing your checks.

Finally, you can apply the `!` operator to other basic data types. Suppose you have a variable, `rate`, that is of type `float` and has the value 3.2. For some reason, you might want to verify that the value of `rate` is non-zero, in which case you could use the expression:

```
!(rate)
```

The value 3.2 is non-zero and thus converts to the `bool` value `true`, so the result of this expression is `false`.

TRY IT OUT   Combining Logical Operators

You can combine conditional expressions and logical operators to any degree that you feel comfortable with. For example, using just a single if, you could construct a test for whether a variable contained a letter. Let's write it as a working example:

Available for download on Wrox.com

```cpp
// Ex3_03.cpp
// Testing for a letter using logical operators
#include <iostream>

using std::cin;
using std::cout;
using std::endl;

int main()
{
   char letter(0);                              // Store input in here
```

```
    cout << endl
        << "Enter a character: ";
    cin >> letter;

    if(((letter >= 'A') && (letter <= 'Z')) ||
       ((letter >= 'a') && (letter <= 'z')))          // Test for alphabetic
        cout << endl
            << "You entered a letter." << endl;
    else
        cout << endl
            << "You didn't enter a letter." << endl;

    return 0;
}
```

code snippet Ex3_03.cpp

How It Works

This example starts out in the same way as Ex3_01.cpp, by reading a character after a prompt for input. The interesting part of the program is in the if statement condition. This consists of two logical expressions combined with the || (OR) operator, so that if either is true, the condition returns true and the message

```
    You entered a letter.
```

is displayed. If both logical expressions are false, the else statement is executed, which displays the message

```
    You didn't enter a letter.
```

Each of the logical expressions combines a pair of comparisons with the operator && (AND), so both comparisons must return true if the logical expression is to be true. The first logical expression returns true if the input is an uppercase letter, and the second returns true if the input is a lowercase letter.

The Conditional Operator

The conditional operator is sometimes called the **ternary operator** because it involves three operands. It is best understood by looking at an example. Suppose you have two variables, a and b, and you want to assign the maximum of a and b to a third variable, c. You can do this with the following statement:

```
    c = a > b ? a : b;          // Set c to the maximum of a or b
```

The first operand for the conditional operator must be an expression that results in a bool value, true or false, and in this case it is a > b. If this expression returns true, the second operand — in this case a — is selected as the value resulting from the operation. If the first argument returns false, the third operand — in this case b — is selected as the value that results from the operation. Thus, the result of the conditional expression a > b ? a : b is a if a is greater than b, and b otherwise. This value is stored in `c` as a result of the assignment operation. The use of the conditional operator in this assignment statement is equivalent to the `if` statement:

```
if(a > b)
   c = a;
else
   c = b;
```

The conditional operator can be written generally as:

```
condition ? expression1 : expression2
```

If the *condition* evaluates as `true`, the result is the value of *expression1*, and if it evaluates to `false`, the result is the value of *expression2*.

TRY IT OUT   Using the Conditional Operator with Output

A common use of the conditional operator is to control output based on the result of an expression or the value of a variable. You can vary a message by selecting one text string or another, depending on the condition specified.

```cpp
// Ex3_04.cpp
// The conditional operator selecting output
#include <iostream>

using std::cout;
using std::endl;

int main()
{
    int nCakes(1);            // Count of number of cakes

    cout << endl
         << "We have " << nCakes << " cake" << ((nCakes > 1) ? "s." : ".")
         << endl;

    ++nCakes;

    cout << endl
         << "We have " << nCakes << " cake" << ((nCakes > 1) ? "s." : ".")
         << endl;
    return 0;
}
```

code snippet Ex3_04.cpp

The output from this program is:

```
We have 1 cake.
We have 2 cakes.
```

How It Works

You first create the `nCakes` variable with the initial value 1; then you have an output statement that shows the number of cakes. The part that uses the conditional operator simply tests the variable to determine whether you have a singular cake or several cakes:

```
((nCakes>1) ? "s." : ".")
```

This expression evaluates to `"s."` if `nCakes` is greater than 1, or `"."` otherwise. This enables you to use the same output statement for any number of cakes and get grammatically correct output. You make use of this in the example by incrementing the `nCakes` variable and repeating the output statement.

There are many other situations where you can apply this sort of mechanism; selecting between `"is"` and `"are"`, for example.

The switch Statement

The `switch` statement enables you to select from multiple choices based on a set of fixed values for a given expression. It operates like a physical rotary switch in that you can select one of a fixed number of choices. Some makes of washing machine provide a means of choosing an operation for processing your laundry in this way. There are a given number of possible positions for the switch, such as cotton, wool, synthetic fiber, and so on, and you can select any one of them by turning the knob to point to the option you want.

In the `switch` statement, the selection is determined by the value of an expression that you specify. You define the possible `switch` positions by one or more **case values,** a particular one being selected if the value of the `switch` expression is the same as the particular case value. There is one case value for each possible choice in the `switch`, and all the case values must be distinct.

If the value of the `switch` expression does not match any of the case values, the `switch` automatically selects the `default` case. You can, if you want, specify the code for the default case, as you will do below; otherwise, the default is to do nothing.

TRY IT OUT   **The switch Statement**

You can examine how the `switch` statement works with the following example.

```cpp
// Ex3_05.cpp
// Using the switch statement
#include <iostream>

using std::cin;
using std::cout;
using std::endl;

int main()
{
   int choice(0);                     // Store selection value here

   cout << endl
```

```
                << "Your electronic recipe book is at your service." << endl
                << "You can choose from the following delicious dishes: "
                << endl
                << endl << "1 Boiled eggs"
                << endl << "2 Fried eggs"
                << endl << "3 Scrambled eggs"
                << endl << "4 Coddled eggs"
                << endl << endl << "Enter your selection number: ";
        cin >> choice;

        switch(choice)
        {
            case 1: cout << endl << "Boil some eggs." << endl;
                    break;
            case 2: cout << endl << "Fry some eggs." << endl;
                    break;
            case 3: cout << endl << "Scramble some eggs." << endl;
                    break;
            case 4: cout << endl << "Coddle some eggs." << endl;
                    break;
            default: cout << endl <<"You entered a wrong number, try raw eggs."
                            << endl;
        }

        return 0;
    }
```

code snippet Ex3_05.cpp

How It Works

The stream output statement displays the input options, and then a selection number is read into the variable `choice`. The `switch` statement has the condition specified as simply `choice`, in parentheses, immediately following the keyword `switch`. The possible options in the `switch` are enclosed between braces and are each identified by a **case label**. A case label is the keyword `case`, followed by the value of `choice` that corresponds to this option, and terminated by a colon.

As you can see, the statements to be executed for a particular `case` follow the colon at the end of the case label, and are terminated by a `break` statement. The `break` transfers execution to the statement after the `switch`. The `break` isn't mandatory, but if you don't include it, execution continues with the statements for the case that follows, which isn't usually what you want. You can demonstrate this by removing the `break` statements from this example and seeing what happens.

The statements to be executed for a particular case can also be between braces, and sometimes this is necessary. For example, if you create a variable within a case statement, you must include braces. The following statement will result in an error message:

```
switch(choice)
{
case 1:
  int count = 2;
  cout << "Boil " << count
```

```
          << " eggs." << endl;
    // Code to do something with count...
    break;

default:
    cout << endl <<"You entered a wrong number, try raw eggs." << endl;
    break;
}
```

Because it is possible that the `count` variable may not get initialized within the block for the `switch`, you get the following error:

```
error C2360: initialization of 'count' is skipped by 'case' label
```

You can fix this by writing it as:

```
switch(choice)
{
case 1:
  {
    int count = 2;
    cout << "Boil " << count
        << " eggs." << endl;
    // Code to do something with count...
    break;
  }

default:
    cout << endl <<"You entered a wrong number, try raw eggs." << endl;
    break;
}
```

If the value of `choice` doesn't correspond with any of the case values specified, the statements preceded by the `default` label are executed. A `default` case isn't essential. In its absence, if the value of the test expression doesn't correspond to any of the cases, the `switch` is exited, and the program continues with the next statement after the `switch`.

TRY IT OUT   **Sharing a Case**

Each of the expressions that you specify to identify the cases in a switch statement must be constant expressions that can be evaluated at compile time and must evaluate to a unique integer value. The reason that no two case values can be the same is that the compiler would have no way of knowing which case statement should be executed for that particular value; however, different cases don't need to have a unique action. Several cases can share the same action, as shown here.

Available for
download on
Wrox.com

```
// Ex3_06.cpp
// Multiple case actions
#include <iostream>
```

```cpp
using std::cin;
using std::cout;
using std::endl;

int main()
{
   char letter(0);
   cout << endl
        << "Enter a small letter: ";
   cin >> letter;

   switch(letter*(letter >= 'a' && letter <= 'z'))
   {
      case 'a':  case 'e': case 'i': case 'o': case 'u':
        cout << endl << "You entered a vowel.";
        break;

      case 0:
        cout << endl << "That is not a small letter.";
        break;

      default: cout << endl << "You entered a consonant.";
   }

   cout << endl;
   return 0;
}
```

code snippet Ex3_06.cpp

How It Works

In this example, you have a more complex expression in the switch. If the character entered isn't a lowercase letter, the expression

```cpp
(letter >= 'a' && letter <= 'z')
```

results in the value false; otherwise it evaluates to true. Because letter is multiplied by this expression, the value of the logical expression is converted to an integer — 0 if the logical expression is false and 1 if it is true. Thus, the switch expression evaluates to 0 if a lowercase letter was not entered, and to the value of letter if it was. The statements following the case label case 0 are executed whenever the character code stored in letter does not represent a lowercase letter.

If a lowercase letter was entered, the switch expression evaluates to the same value as letter; so, for all values corresponding to vowels, the output statement following the sequence of case labels that have vowels as values is executed. The same statement executes for any vowel because when any of these case labels is chosen, successive statements are executed until the break statement is reached. You can see that a single action can be taken for a number of different cases by writing each of the case labels, one after the other, before the statements to be executed. If a lowercase letter that is a consonant is entered as program input, the default case label statement is executed.

Unconditional Branching

The `if` statement provides you with the flexibility to choose to execute one set of statements or another, depending on a specified condition, so the statement execution sequence is varied, depending on the values of the data in the program. The `goto` statement, in contrast, is a blunt instrument. It enables you to branch to a specified program statement unconditionally. The statement to be branched to must be identified by a statement label, which is an identifier defined according to the same rules as a variable name. This is followed by a colon and placed before the statement requiring labeling. Here is an example of a labeled statement:

```
myLabel: cout << "myLabel branch has been activated" << endl;
```

This statement has the label `myLabel`, and an unconditional branch to this statement would be written as follows:

```
goto myLabel;
```

Whenever possible, you should avoid using `goto`s in your program. They tend to encourage convoluted code that can be extremely difficult to follow.

 NOTE *Because the `goto` is theoretically unnecessary in a program — there's always an alternative approach to using `goto` — a significant cadre of programmers say you should never use it. I don't subscribe to such an extreme view. It is a legal statement, after all, and there are occasions when it can be convenient, such as when you must exit from a deeply nested set of loops (you learn about loops in the next section). I do, however, recommend that you only use it where you can see an obvious advantage over other options that are available; otherwise, you may end up with convoluted, error-prone code that is hard to understand and even harder to maintain.*

REPEATING A BLOCK OF STATEMENTS

The capability to repeat a group of statements is fundamental to most applications. Without this capability, an organization would need to modify the payroll program every time an extra employee was hired, and you would need to reload your favorite game every time you wanted to play. So, let's first understand how a loop works.

What Is a Loop?

A loop executes a sequence of statements until a particular condition is `true` (or `false`). You can actually write a loop with the C++ statements that you have met so far. You just need an `if` and the dreaded `goto`. Look at the following example.

Available for download on Wrox.com

```
// Ex3_07.cpp
// Creating a loop with an if and a goto
#include <iostream>

using std::cin;
```

```
    using std::cout;
    using std::endl;

    int main()
    {
        int i(1), sum(0);
        const int max(10);

loop:
        sum += i;               // Add current value of i to sum
        if(++i <= max)
            goto loop;          // Go back to loop until i = 11

        cout << endl
            << "sum = " << sum << endl
            << "i = "   << i    << endl;
        return 0;
    }
```

code snippet Ex3_07.cpp

This example accumulates the sum of integers from 1 to 10. The first time through the sequence of statements, i has the initial value 1 and is added to sum, which starts out as zero. In the if, i is incremented to 2 and, as long as it is less than or equal to max, the unconditional branch to loop occurs, and the value of i, now 2, is added to sum. This continues with i being incremented and added to sum each time, until finally, when i is incremented to 11 in the if, the branch back is not executed. If you run this example, you get the following output:

```
    sum = 55
    i = 11
```

This shows quite clearly how the loop works; however, it uses a goto and introduces a label into the program, both of which you should avoid, if possible. You can achieve the same thing, and more, with the for statement, which is specifically for writing a loop.

TRY IT OUT   Using the for Loop

You can rewrite the last example using what is known as a for loop.

```
// Ex3_08.cpp
// Summing integers with a for loop
#include <iostream>

using std::cin;
using std::cout;
using std::endl;

int main()
```

```
{
    int i(1), sum(0);
    const int max(10);

    for(i = 1; i <= max; i++)          // Loop specification
        sum += i;                      // Loop statement

    cout << endl
         << "sum = " << sum << endl
         << "i = "   << i    << endl;
    return 0;
}
```

code snippet Ex3_08.cpp

How It Works

If you compile and run this, you get exactly the same output as the previous example, but the code is much simpler here. The conditions determining the operation of the loop appear in parentheses after the keyword for. There are three expressions that appear within the parentheses, separated by semicolons:

➤ The first expression executes once at the outset and sets the initial conditions for the loop. In this case, it sets i to 1.

➤ The second expression is a logical expression that determines whether the loop statement (or block of statements) should continue to be executed. If the second expression is true, the loop continues to execute; when it is false, the loop ends, and execution continues with the statement that follows the loop. In this case, the loop statement on the following line is executed as long as i is less than or equal to max.

➤ The third expression is evaluated after the loop statement (or block of statements) executes, and in this case increments i at each iteration. After this expression has been evaluated, the second expression is evaluated once more to see whether the loop should continue.

Actually, this loop is not *exactly* the same as the version in Ex3_07.cpp. You can demonstrate this if you set the value of max to 0 in both programs and run them again; then, you will find that the value of sum is 1 in Ex3_07.cpp and 0 in Ex3_08.cpp, and the value of i differs too. The reason for this is that the if version of the program always executes the loop at least once because you don't check the condition until the end. The for loop doesn't do this, because the condition is actually checked at the beginning.

The general form of the for loop is:

```
for (initializing_expression ; test_expression ; increment_expression)
    loop_statement;
```

Of course, *loop_statement* can be a single statement, or a block of statements between braces. The sequence of events in executing the for loop is shown in Figure 3-3.

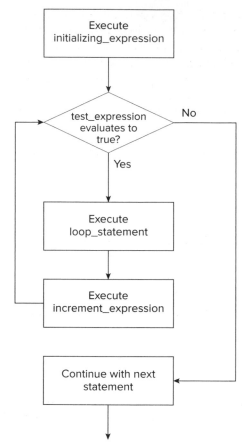

FIGURE 3-3

As I have said, the loop statement shown in Figure 3-3 can also be a block of statements. The expressions controlling the `for` loop are very flexible. You can even write two or more expressions, separated by the comma operator, for each control expression. This gives you a lot of scope in what you can do with a `for` loop.

Variations on the for Loop

Most of the time, the expressions in a `for` loop are used in a fairly standard way: the first to initialize one or more loop counters, the second to test if the loop should continue, and the third to increment or decrement one or more loop counters. You are not obliged to use these expressions in this way, however, and quite a few variations are possible.

The initialization expression in a `for` loop can also include a declaration for a loop variable. In the previous example, you could have written the loop to include the declaration for the loop counter `i` in the first control expression.

```
for(int i = 1; i <= max; i++)      // Loop specification
    sum += i;                      // Loop statement
```

Naturally, the original declaration for i would need to be omitted in the program. If you make this change to the last example, you will find that it does not compile because the loop variable, i, ceases to exist after the loop, so you cannot refer to it in the output statement. A loop has a scope which extends from the for expression to the end of the body of the loop, which of course can be a block of code between braces, as well as just a single statement. The counter i is now declared within the loop scope, so you cannot refer to it in the output statement, which is outside the scope of the loop. If you need to use the value in the counter after the loop has executed, you must declare the counter variable *outside the scope of the loop.*

You can omit the initialization expression altogether from the loop. Because i has the initial value 1, you can write the loop as:

```
for(; i <= max; i++)              // Loop specification
    sum += i;                     // Loop statement
```

You still need the semicolon that separates the initialization expression from the test condition for the loop. In fact, both semicolons must always be present, regardless of whether any or all of the control expressions are omitted. If you omit the first semicolon, the compiler is unable to decide which expression has been omitted, or even which semicolon is missing.

The loop statement can be empty. For example, you could place the loop statement in the for loop from the previous example inside the increment expression; in this case the loop becomes

```
for(; i <= max; sum += i++);      // The whole loop
```

You still need the semicolon after the closing parentheses, to indicate that the loop statement is now empty. If you omit this, the statement immediately following this line is interpreted as the loop statement. Sometimes you'll see the empty loop statement written on a separate line, like the following:

```
for(; i <= max; sum += i++)       // The whole loop
    ;
```

TRY IT OUT   Using Multiple Counters

You can use the comma operator to include multiple counters in a for loop. You can see this in operation in the following program.

```
// Ex3_09.cpp
// Using multiple counters to show powers of 2
#include <iostream>
#include <iomanip>

using std::cin;
using std::cout;
using std::endl;
using std::setw;

int main()
{
    const int max(10);

    for(long i = 0L, power = 1L; i <= max; i++, power += power)
```

```
        cout << endl
              << setw(10) << i << setw(10) << power;      // Loop statement

    cout << endl;
    return 0;
}
```

How It Works

You create and initialize two variables in the initialization section of the `for` loop and increment each of them in the increment section. You can create as many variables as you want here, as long as they are of the same type.

You can also specify multiple conditions, separated by commas, in the second expression that represents the test part of the `for` loop that determines whether it should continue, but this is not generally useful because only the right-most condition affects when the loop ends.

For each increment of `i`, the value of the variable `power` is doubled by adding it to itself. This produces the powers of two that we are looking for, and so the program produces the following output.

```
        0           1
        1           2
        2           4
        3           8
        4          16
        5          32
        6          64
        7         128
        8         256
        9         512
       10        1024
```

You use the `setw()` manipulator that you saw in the previous chapter to align the output nicely. You have included the `iomanip` header file and added a using declaration for the name in the `std` namespace, so you can use `setw()` without qualifying the name.

TRY IT OUT   The Indefinite for Loop

If you omit the second control expression that specifies the test condition for a `for` loop, the value is assumed to be `true`, so the loop continues indefinitely unless you provide some other means of exiting from it. In fact, if you like, you can omit all the expressions in the parentheses after `for`. This may not seem to be useful, but the reverse is true. You will often come across situations where you want to execute a loop a number of times, but you do not know in advance how many iterations you will need. Have a look at the following:

```
// Ex3_10.cpp
// Using an infinite for loop to compute an average
#include <iostream>
```

```cpp
using std::cin;
using std::cout;
using std::endl;

int main()
{
   double value(0.0);                 // Value entered stored here
   double sum(0.0);                   // Total of values accumulated here
   int i(0);                          // Count of number of values
   char indicator('n');               // Continue or not?

   for(;;)                            // Indefinite loop
   {
      cout << endl
           << "Enter a value: ";
      cin >> value;                   // Read a value
      ++i;                            // Increment count
      sum += value;                   // Add current input to total

      cout << endl
           << "Do you want to enter another value (enter y or n)? ";
      cin >> indicator;               // Read indicator
      if (('n' == indicator) || ('N' == indicator))
         break;                       // Exit from loop
   }

   cout << endl
        << "The average of the " << i
        << " values you entered is " << sum/i << "."
        << endl;
   return 0;
}
```

code snippet Ex3_10.cpp

How It Works

This program computes the average of an arbitrary number of values. After each value is entered, you
need to indicate whether you want to enter another value, by entering a single character, y or n. Typical
output from executing this example is:

```
Enter a value: 10

Do you want to enter another value (enter y or n)? y

Enter a value: 20

Do you want to enter another value (enter y or n)? y

Enter a value: 30

Do you want to enter another value (enter y or n)? n

The average of the 3 values you entered is 20.
```

After declaring and initializing the variables that you're going to use, you start a `for` loop with no expressions specified, so there is no provision for ending it here. The block immediately following is the subject of the loop that is to be repeated.

The loop block performs three basic actions:

➤ It reads a value.

➤ It adds the value read from `cin` to `sum`.

➤ It checks whether you want to continue to enter values.

The first action within the block is to prompt you for input and then read a value into the variable `value`. The value that you enter is added to `sum`, and the count of the number of values, `i`, is incremented. After accumulating the value in `sum`, you are asked if you want to enter another value, and prompted to enter `'y'` — or `'n'` if you have finished. The character that you enter is stored in the variable `indicator`, for testing against `'n'` or `'N'` in the `if` statement. If neither is found, the loop continues; otherwise, a `break` is executed. The effect of `break` in a loop is similar to its effect in the context of the `switch` statement. In this instance, it exits the loop immediately by transferring control to the statement following the closing brace of the loop block.

Finally, you output the count of the number of values entered and their average, which is calculated by dividing `sum` by `i`. Of course, `i` is promoted to type `double` before the calculation, as you remember from the casting discussion in Chapter 2.

Using the continue Statement

There is another statement, besides `break`, that you can use to affect the operation of a loop: the `continue` statement. This is written simply as:

```
continue;
```

Executing `continue` within a loop starts the next loop iteration immediately, skipping over any statements remaining in the body of the loop. I can show how this works with the following code:

```
#include <iostream>

using std::cin;
using std::cout;
using std::endl;

int main()
{
  int value(0), product(1);

  for(int i = 1; i <= 10; i++)
  {
    cout << "Enter an integer: ";
    cin >> value;

    if(0 == value)           // If value is zero
      continue;              // skip to next iteration

    product *= value;
```

```
    }

    cout << "Product (ignoring zeros): " << product
         << endl;

    return 0;                              // Exit from loop
}
```

This loop reads 10 values with the intention of producing the product of the values entered. The `if` checks each value entered, and if it is zero, the `continue` statement skips to the next iteration. This is so that you don't end up with a zero product if one of the values is zero. Obviously, if a zero value occurred on the last iteration, the loop would end. There are clearly other ways of achieving the same result, but `continue` provides a very useful capability, particularly with complex loops where you may need to skip to the end of the current iteration from various points in the loop.

The effect of the `break` and `continue` statements on the logic of a `for` loop is illustrated in Figure 3-4.

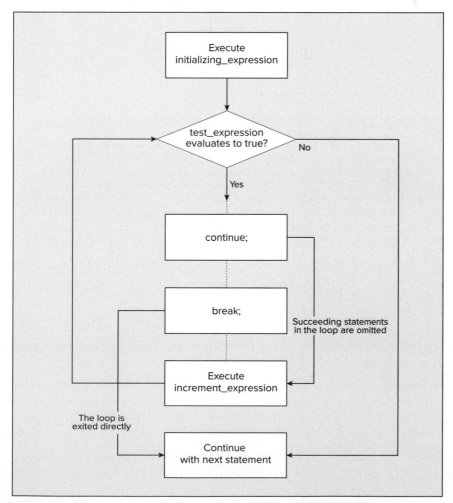

FIGURE 3-4

Obviously, in a real situation, you would use the break and continue statements with some condition-testing logic to determine when the loop should be exited, or when an iteration of the loop should be skipped. You can also use the break and continue statements with the other kinds of loop, which I'll discuss later on in this chapter, where they work in exactly the same way.

TRY IT OUT   Using Other Types in Loops

So far, you have only used integers to count loop iterations. You are in no way restricted as to what type of variable you use to count iterations. Look at the following example:

```cpp
// Ex3_11.cpp
// Display ASCII codes for alphabetic characters
#include <iostream>
#include <iomanip>

using std::cout;
using std::endl;
using std::hex;
using std::dec;
using std::setw;

int main()
{
   for(char capital = 'A', small = 'a'; capital <= 'Z'; capital++, small++)
      cout << endl
            << "\t" << capital                          // Output capital as a character
            << hex << setw(10) << static_cast<int>(capital)   // and as hexadecimal
            << dec << setw(10) << static_cast<int>(capital)   // and as decimal
            << " " << small                    // Output small as a character
            << hex << setw(10) << static_cast<int>(small)     // and as hexadecimal
            << dec << setw(10) << static_cast<int>(small);    // and as decimal

   cout << endl;
   return 0;
}
```

code snippet Ex3_11.cpp

How It Works

Here we have using declarations for the names of some new manipulators that are used in the program to affect how the output is presented.

The loop in this example is controlled by the char variable capital, which you declare along with the variable small in the initializing expression. You also increment both variables in the third control expression for the loop, so that the value of capital varies from 'A' to 'Z', and the value of small correspondingly varies from 'a' to 'z'.

The loop contains just one output statement spread over seven lines. The first line is:

```cpp
cout << endl
```

This starts a new line on the screen.

The next three lines are:

```
<< "\t" << capital                            // Output capital as a character
<< hex << setw(10) << static_cast<int>(capital)   // and as hexadecimal
<< dec << setw(10) << static_cast<int>(capital)   // and as decimal
```

After outputting a tab character on each iteration, the value of capital is displayed three times: as a character, as a hexadecimal value, and as a decimal value.

When you insert the manipulator hex into the cout stream, this causes subsequent integer data values to be displayed as hexadecimal values, rather than the default decimal representation, so the second output of capital is as a hexadecimal representation of the character code.

You then insert the dec manipulator into the stream to cause succeeding values to be output as decimals once more. By default, a variable of type char is interpreted by the stream as a character, not a numerical value. You get the char variable capital to output as a numerical value by casting its value to type int, using the static_cast<>() operator that you saw in the previous chapter, in the discussion following the Try It Out – Exercising Basic Arithmetic exercise.

The value of small is output in a similar way by the next three lines of the output statement:

```
<< " " << small                               // Output small as a character
<< hex << setw(10) << static_cast<int>(small)     // and as hexadecimal
<< dec << setw(10) << static_cast<int>(small);    // and as decimal
```

As a result, the program generates the following output:

```
A        41        65     a        61        97
B        42        66     b        62        98
C        43        67     c        63        99
D        44        68     d        64       100
E        45        69     e        65       101
F        46        70     f        66       102
G        47        71     g        67       103
H        48        72     h        68       104
I        49        73     i        69       105
J        4a        74     j        6a       106
K        4b        75     k        6b       107
L        4c        76     l        6c       108
M        4d        77     m        6d       109
N        4e        78     n        6e       110
O        4f        79     o        6f       111
P        50        80     p        70       112
Q        51        81     q        71       113
R        52        82     r        72       114
S        53        83     s        73       115
T        54        84     t        74       116
U        55        85     u        75       117
```

V	56	86	v	76	118
W	57	87	w	77	119
X	58	88	x	78	120
Y	59	89	y	79	121
Z	5a	90	z	7a	122

Floating-Point Loop Counters

You can also use a floating-point value as a loop counter. Here's an example of a for loop with this kind of counter:

```
double a(0.3), b(2.5);
for(double x = 0.0; x <= 2.0; x += 0.25)
    cout << "\n\tx = " << x
         << "\ta*x + b = " << a*x + b;
```

This code fragment calculates the value of a*x+b for values of x from 0.0 to 2.0, in steps of 0.25; however, you need to take care when using a floating-point counter in a loop. Many decimal values cannot be represented exactly in binary floating-point form, so discrepancies can build up with cumulative values. This means that you should not code a for loop such that ending the loop depends on a floating-point loop counter reaching a precise value. For example, the following poorly-designed loop never ends.

```
for(double x = 0.0 ; x != 1.0 ; x += 0.2)
    cout << x;
```

The intention with this loop is to output the value of x as it varies from 0.0 to 1.0; however, 0.2 has no exact representation as a binary floating-point value, so the value of x is never exactly 1. Thus, the second loop control expression is always false, and the loop continues indefinitely.

The while Loop

A second kind of loop in C++ is the while loop. Where the for loop is primarily used to repeat a statement or a block for a prescribed number of iterations, the while loop is used to execute a statement or block of statements as long as a specified condition is true. The general form of the while loop is:

```
while(condition)
    loop_statement;
```

Here *loop_statement* is executed repeatedly, as long as the *condition* expression has the value true. After the condition becomes false, the program continues with the statement following the loop. As always, a block of statements between braces could replace the single *loop_statement*.

The logic of the while loop can be represented as shown in Figure 3-5.

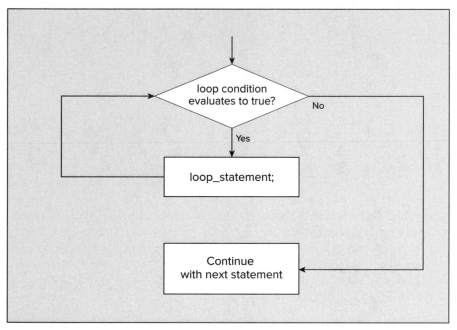

FIGURE 3-5

Using the while Loop

You could rewrite the earlier example that computes averages (Ex3_10.cpp) to use the while loop.

Available for
download on
Wrox.com

```cpp
// Ex3_12.cpp
// Using a while loop to compute an average
#include <iostream>

using std::cin;
using std::cout;
using std::endl;

int main()
{
   double value(0.0);            // Value entered stored here
   double sum(0.0);              // Total of values accumulated here
   int i(0);                     // Count of number of values
   char indicator('y');          // Continue or not?

   while('y' == indicator )      // Loop as long as y is entered
   {
      cout << endl
           << "Enter a value: ";
      cin >> value;              // Read a value
      ++i;                       // Increment count
      sum += value;              // Add current input to total

      cout << endl
           << "Do you want to enter another value (enter y or n)? ";
```

```
        cin >> indicator;              // Read indicator
    }

    cout << endl
        << "The average of the " << i
        << " values you entered is " << sum/i << "."
        << endl;
    return 0;
}
```

How It Works

For the same input, this version of the program produces the same output as before. One statement has been updated, and another has been added — they are highlighted in the code. The `for` loop statement has been replaced by the `while` statement, and the test for `indicator` in the `if` has been deleted, as this function is performed by the `while` condition. You have to initialize `indicator` with `'y'`, in place of the `'n'` which appeared previously — otherwise the `while` loop terminates immediately. As long as the condition in the `while` returns `true`, the loop continues.

You can use any expression resulting in `true` or `false` as a `while` loop condition. The example would be a better program if the loop condition were extended to allow `'Y'` to be entered to continue the loop, as well as `'y'`. You could modify the `while` as follows to do the trick.

```
while(('y' == indicator) || ('Y' == indicator))
```

You can also create a `while` loop that potentially executes indefinitely, by using a condition that is always `true`. This can be written as follows:

```
while(true)
{
...
}
```

You could also write the loop control expression as the integer value 1, which would be converted to the `bool` value `true`. Naturally, the same requirement applies here as in the case of the indefinite `for` loop: namely, that you must provide some way of exiting the loop within the loop block. You'll see other ways to use the `while` loop in Chapter 4.

The do-while Loop

The `do-while` loop is similar to the `while` loop in that the loop continues as long as the specified loop condition remains `true`. The main difference is that the condition is checked at the end of the loop — which contrasts with the `while` loop and the `for` loop, where the condition is checked at the beginning of the loop. Consequently, the `do-while` loop statement is *always* executed at least once. The general form of the `do-while` loop is:

```
do
{
    loop_statements;
}while(condition);
```

The logic of this form of loop is shown in Figure 3-6.

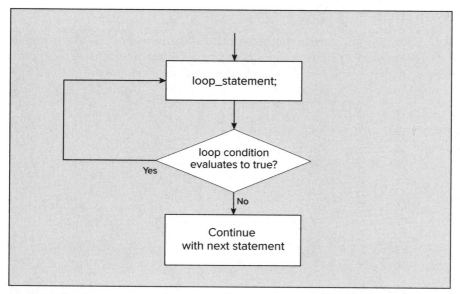

FIGURE 3-6

You could replace the `while` loop in the last version of the program to calculate an average with a do-while loop:

```
do
{
    cout << endl
         << "Enter a value: ";
    cin >> value;                   // Read a value
    ++i;                            // Increment count
    sum += value;                   // Add current input to total

    cout << "Do you want to enter another value (enter y or n)?";
    cin >> indicator;               // Read indicator
} while(('y' == indicator) || ('Y' == indicator));
```

There's little difference between the two versions of the loop, except that this version doesn't depend on the initial value set in `indicator` for correct operation. As long as you want to enter at least one value, which is not unreasonable for the calculation in question, this version of the loop is preferable.

Nested Loops

You can nest one loop inside another. The usual application for this will become more apparent in Chapter 4 — it's typically applied to repeating actions at different levels of classification. An example might be calculating the total marks for each student in a class, and then repeating the process for each class in a school.

TRY IT OUT   **Nested Loops**

You can see the effects of nesting one loop inside another by calculating the values of a simple formula. A factorial of an integer is the product of all the integers from 1 to the integer in question; the factorial of 3, for example, is 1 times 2 times 3, which is 6. The following program computes the factorial of integers that you enter (until you've had enough):

Available for
download on
Wrox.com

```cpp
// Ex3_13.cpp
// Demonstrating nested loops to compute factorials
#include <iostream>

using std::cin;
using std::cout;
using std::endl;

int main()
{
   char indicator('n');
   long value(0L), factorial(0L);

   do
   {
      cout << endl << "Enter an integer value: ";
      cin >> value;

      factorial = 1L;
      for(long i = 2L; i <= value; i++)
         factorial *= i;

      cout << "Factorial " << value << " is " << factorial;
      cout << endl << "Do you want to enter another value (y or n)? ";
      cin >> indicator;
   } while(('y' == indicator) || ('Y' == indicator));

   return 0;
}
```

code snippet Ex3_13.cpp

If you compile and execute this example, the typical output produced is:

```
Enter an integer value: 5
Factorial 5 is 120
```

```
Do you want to enter another value (y or n)? y

Enter an integer value: 10
Factorial 10 is 3628800
Do you want to enter another value (y or n)? y

Enter an integer value: 13
Factorial 13 is 1932053504
Do you want to enter another value (y or n)? y

Enter an integer value: 22
Factorial 22 is -522715136
Do you want to enter another value (y or n)? n
```

How It Works

Factorial values grow very fast. In fact, 12 is the largest input value for which this example produces a correct result. The factorial of 13 is actually 6,227,020,800, not 1,932,053,504, as the program tells you. If you run it with even larger input values, leading digits are lost in the result stored in the variable `factorial`, and you may well get negative values for the factorial, as you do when you ask for the factorial of 22.

This situation doesn't cause any error messages, so it is of paramount importance that you are sure that the values you're dealing with in a program can be contained in the permitted range of the type of variable you're using. You also need to consider the effects of incorrect input values. Errors of this kind, which occur silently, can be very hard to find.

The outer of the two nested loops is the `do-while` loop, which controls when the program ends. As long as you keep entering y or Y at the prompt, the program continues to calculate factorial values. The factorial for the integer entered is calculated in the inner `for` loop. This is executed `value` times, to multiply the variable `factorial` (with an initial value of 1) with successive integers from 2 to `value`.

TRY IT OUT   **Another Nested Loop**

Nested loops can be a little confusing, so let's try another example. This program generates a multiplication table of a given size.

```cpp
// Ex3_14.cpp
// Using nested loops to generate a multiplication table
#include <iostream>
#include <iomanip>

using std::cout;
using std::endl;
using std::setw;

int main()
{
  const int size(12);                   // Size of table
```

```
    int i(0), j(0);                      // Loop counters

    cout << endl                         // Output table title
        << size << " by " << size << " Multiplication Table" << endl << endl;

    cout << endl << "    |";

    for(i = 1; i <= size; i++)           // Loop to output column headings
       cout << setw(3) << i << " ";

    cout << endl;                        // Newline for underlines

    for(i = 0; i <= size; i++)
       cout << "_____";                  // Underline each heading

    for(i = 1; i <= size; i++)           // Outer loop for rows
    {
       cout << endl
           << setw(3) << i << " |";      // Output row label
       for(j = 1; j <= size; j++)            // Inner loop for the rest of the row
          cout << setw(3) << i*j << " ";    // End of inner loop
    }                                         // End of outer loop
    cout << endl;

    return 0;
}
```

code snippet Ex3_14.cpp

The output from this example is:

```
12 by 12 Multiplication Table
```

	1	2	3	4	5	6	7	8	9	10	11	12
1	1	2	3	4	5	6	7	8	9	10	11	12
2	2	4	6	8	10	12	14	16	18	20	22	24
3	3	6	9	12	15	18	21	24	27	30	33	36
4	4	8	12	16	20	24	28	32	36	40	44	48
5	5	10	15	20	25	30	35	40	45	50	55	60
6	6	12	18	24	30	36	42	48	54	60	66	72
7	7	14	21	28	35	42	49	56	63	70	77	84
8	8	16	24	32	40	48	56	64	72	80	88	96
9	9	18	27	36	45	54	63	72	81	90	99	108
10	10	20	30	40	50	60	70	80	90	100	110	120
11	11	22	33	44	55	66	77	88	99	110	121	132
12	12	24	36	48	60	72	84	96	108	120	132	144

How It Works

The table title is produced by the first output statement in the program. The next output statement, combined with the loop following it, generates the column headings. Each column is five characters wide, so the heading value is displayed in a field width of three, specified by the setw(3) manipulator, followed by two spaces. The output statement preceding the loop outputs four spaces and a vertical bar above the first column, which contains the row headings. A series of underline characters is then displayed beneath the column headings.

The nested loop generates the main table contents. The outer loop repeats once for each row, so i is the row number. The output statement

```
cout << endl
     << setw(3) << i << " |";    // Output row label
```

goes to a new line for the start of a row, and then outputs the row heading given by the value of i in a field width of three, followed by a space and a vertical bar.

A row of values is generated by the inner loop:

```
for(j = 1; j <= size; j++)              // Inner loop for the rest of the row
    cout << setw(3) << i*j << " ";    // End of inner loop
```

This loop outputs values i*j, corresponding to the product of the current row value i, and each of the column values in turn by varying j from 1 to size. So, for each iteration of the outer loop, the inner loop executes size iterations. The values are positioned in the same way as the column headings. When the outer loop is completed, the return is executed to end the program.

C++/CLI PROGRAMMING

Everything I have discussed in this chapter applies equally well in a C++/CLI program. Just to illustrate the point, we can look at some examples of CLR console programs that demonstrate some of what you have learned so far in this chapter. The following is a CLR program that's a slight variation on Ex3_01.

TRY IT OUT **A CLR Program Using Nested if Statements**

Create a CLR console program with the default code and modify the main() function like this:

```
// Ex3_15.cpp : main project file.

#include "stdafx.h"

using namespace System;

int main(array<System::String ^> ^args)
{
  wchar_t letter;                        // Corresponds to the C++/CLI Char type
  Console::Write(L"Enter a letter: ");
```

```
    letter = Console::Read();

    if(letter >= 'A')                    // Test for 'A' or larger
     if(letter <= 'Z')                   // Test for 'Z' or smaller
     {
       Console::WriteLine(L"You entered a capital letter.");
       return 0;
     }

    if(letter >= 'a')                    // Test for 'a' or larger
     if(letter <= 'z')                   // Test for 'z' or smaller
     {
        Console::WriteLine(L"You entered a small letter.");
        return 0;
     }

    Console::WriteLine(L"You did not enter a letter.");
     return 0;
   }
```

code snippet Ex3_15.cpp

As always, the **shaded** lines are the new code you should add.

How It Works

The logic is the same as in the Ex3_01 example — in fact, all the statements are the same except for those producing the output and the declaration of letter. I changed the type to wchar_t because type System::Char has some extra facilities that I'll mention. The Console::Read() function reads a single character from the keyboard. Because you use the Console::Write() function to output the initial prompt, there is no newline character issued; so, you can enter the letter on the same line as the prompt.

The .NET Framework provides its own functions for converting character codes to upper- or lowercase within the Char class. These are the functions Char::ToUpper() and Char::ToLower(); you put the character to be converted between the parentheses as the argument to the function. For example:

```
wchar_t uppcaseLetter = Char::ToUpper(letter);
```

Of course, you could store the result of the conversion back in the original variable, as in the following:

```
letter = Char::ToUpper(letter);
```

The Char class also provides IsUpper() and IsLower() functions that test whether a letter is upper- or lowercase. You pass the letter to be tested as the argument to the function, and the function returns a bool value as a result. You could use these functions to code the main() function quite differently.

```
wchar_t letter;                          // Corresponds to the C++/CLI Char type
Console::Write(L"Enter a letter: ");
letter = Console::Read();
wchar_t upper = Char::ToUpper(letter);
if(upper >= 'A' && upper <= 'Z')         // Test for between 'A' and 'Z'
```

```
                Console::WriteLine(L"You entered a {0} letter.",
                              Char::IsUpper(letter) ? "capital" : "small");
          else
              Console::WriteLine(L"You did not enter a letter.");
          return 0;
```

This simplifies the code considerably. After converting a letter to uppercase, you test the uppercase value to check whether it's between `'A'` and `'Z'`. If it is, you output a message that depends on the result of the conditional operator expression that forms the second argument to the `WriteLine()` function. The conditional operator expression evaluates to `"capital"` if `letter` is uppercase, and `"small"` if it is not, and this result is inserted in the output as determined by the position of the format string `{0}`.

Try another CLR example that uses the `Console::ReadKey()` function in a loop and explores the `ConsoleKeyInfo` class a little more.

TRY IT OUT   Reading Key Presses

Create a CLR console program and add the following code to `main()`:

Available for download on Wrox.com

```cpp
// Ex3_16.cpp : main project file.
// Testing key presses in a loop.

#include "stdafx.h"
using namespace System;

int main(array<System::String ^> ^args)
{
  Console::WriteLine(L"Press a key combination - press Escape to quit.");

  ConsoleKeyInfo keyPress;

  do
  {
    keyPress = Console::ReadKey(true);
    Console::Write(L"You pressed");
    if(safe_cast<int>(keyPress.Modifiers)>0)
        Console::Write(L" {0},", keyPress.Modifiers);
      Console::WriteLine(L" {0} which is the {1} character",
                                      keyPress.Key, keyPress.KeyChar);
  }while(keyPress.Key != ConsoleKey::Escape);
  return 0;
}
```

code snippet Ex3_16.cpp

The following is some sample output from this program:

```
    Press a key combination - press Escape to quit.
    You pressed Shift, B which is the B character
    You pressed Shift, Control, N which is the ? character
```

```
You pressed Oem1 which is the ; character
You pressed Oem3 which is the ' character
You pressed Shift, Oem3 which is the @ character
You pressed Shift, Oem7 which is the ~ character
You pressed D3 which is the 3 character
You pressed Shift, D3 which is the ? character
You pressed Shift, D5 which is the % character
You pressed Oem8 which is the ` character
You pressed Escape which is the ? character
```

Of course, there are key combinations that do not represent a displayable character, and in these cases there is no character in the output. The program also ends if you press Ctrl+C because the operating system recognizes this as the command to end the program.

How It Works

Key presses are tested in the do-while loop, and this loop continues until the Escape key is pressed. The Console::ReadKey() function is called within the loop, and the result is stored in the variable keyPress, which is of type ConsoleKeyInfo. The ConsoleKeyInfo class has three properties that you can access to help identify the key or keys that were pressed — the Key property identifies the key that was pressed, the KeyChar property represents the Unicode character code for the key, and the Modifiers property is a bitwise combination of ConsoleModifiers constants that represent the Shift, Alt, and Ctrl keys. ConsoleModifiers is an enumeration that is defined in the System library; the constants defined in the enumeration have the names Alt, Shift, and Control.

As you can see from the arguments to the WriteLine() function in the last output statement, to access a property for an object you place the property name following the object name, separated by a period; the period is referred to as the **member access** operator. To access the KeyChar property for the object keyPress, you write keyPress.KeyChar.

The operation of the program is very simple. Within the loop, you call the ReadKey() function to read a key press, and the result is stored in the variable keyPress. Next you write the initial part of the output to the command line using the Write() function; because no newline is written in this case, the next output statement writes to the same line. You then test whether the Modifiers property is greater than zero. If it is, modifier keys were pressed and you output them; otherwise, you skip the output for modifier keys. You will probably remember that a C++/CLI enumeration constant is an object that you must explicitly convert to an integer type before you can use it as a numerical value — hence the cast to type int in the if expression.

The output of the Modifiers value is interesting. As you can see from the output, when more than one modifier key is pressed, you get all the modifier keys from the single output statement. This is because the Modifiers enumeration is defined with bit flags. As you saw in Chapter 2, this allows a variable of the enumeration type to consist of several flags OR-ed together, and the individual flags recognized and output by the Write() or WriteLine() functions.

The loop continues as long as the condition keyPress.Key != ConsoleKey::Escape is true. It is false when the keyPress.Key property is equal to ConsoleKey::Escape, which is when the Escape key is pressed.

The for each Loop

All the loop statements I have discussed apply equally well to C++/CLI programs, and the C++/CLI language provides you with the luxury of an additional kind of loop called the `for each` loop. This loop also works with native C++ code in Visual C++ 2010, although formally the `for each` loop is not part of the ISO/IEC standard C++ language. The `for each` loop is specifically for iterating through all the objects in a particular kind of set of objects, and because you haven't learned about these yet, I'll just introduce the `for each` loop briefly here, and elaborate on it some more a bit later in the book.

Since you do know a little about the `String` object, which represents a set of characters, you can use a `for each` loop to iterate through all the characters in a string. Let's try an example of that.

TRY IT OUT   Using a for each Loop to Access the Characters in a String

Create a new CLR console program project with the name Ex3_17 and modify the code to the following:

```cpp
// Ex3_17.cpp : main project file.
// Analyzing a string using a for each loop

#include "stdafx.h"
using namespace System;

int main(array<System::String ^> ^args)
{
  int vowels(0), consonants(0);
  String^ proverb(L"A nod is as good as a wink to a blind horse.");

  for each(wchar_t ch in proverb)
  {
   if(Char::IsLetter(ch))
   {
    ch = Char::ToLower(ch);        // Convert to lowercase
    switch(ch)
    {
    case 'a': case 'e': case 'i': case 'o': case 'u':
      ++vowels;
      break;
    default:
      ++consonants;
      break;
    }
   }
  }

  Console::WriteLine(proverb);
  Console::WriteLine(L"The proverb contains {0} vowels and {1} consonants.",
                                          vowels, consonants);

   return 0;
}
```

code snippet Ex3_17.cpp

This example produces the following output:

```
A nod is as good as a wink to a blind horse.
The proverb contains 14 vowels and 18 consonants.
```

How It Works

The program counts the number of vowels and consonants in the string referenced by the `proverb` variable. The program does this by iterating through each character in the string using a `for each` loop. You first define the two variables used to accumulate the total number of vowels and the total number of consonants.

```
int vowels(0), consonants(0);
```

Under the covers, both are of the C++/CLI `Int32` type, which stores a 32-bit integer.

Next, you define the string to analyze.

```
String^ proverb(L"A nod is as good as a wink to a blind horse.");
```

The `proverb` variable is of type `String^`, which is described as type "handle to `String`"; a handle is used to store the location of an object on the garbage-collected heap that is managed by the CLR. You'll learn more about handles and type `String^` when we get into C++/CLI class types; for now, just take it that this is the type you use for C++/CLI variables that store strings.

The `for each` loop that iterates over the characters in the string referenced by `proverb` is of this form:

```
for each(wchar_t ch in proverb)
{
    // Process the current character stored in ch...
}
```

The characters in the `proverb` string are Unicode characters, so you use a variable of type `wchar_t` (equivalent to type `Char`) to store them. The loop successively stores characters from the `proverb` string in the loop variable `ch`, which is of the C++/CLI type `Char`. This variable is local to the loop — in other words, it exists only within the loop block. On the first iteration `ch` contains the first character from the string, on the second iteration it contains the second character, on the third iteration the third character, and so on until all the characters have been processed and the loop ends.

Within the loop you determine whether the character is a letter in the `if` expression:

```
if(Char::IsLetter(ch))
```

The `Char::IsLetter()` function returns the value `true` if the argument — `ch` in this case — is a letter, and `false` otherwise. Thus, the block following the `if` only executes if `ch` contains a letter. This is necessary because you don't want punctuation characters to be processed as though they were letters.

Having established that `ch` is indeed a letter, you convert it to lowercase with the following statement:

```
ch = Char::ToLower(ch);      // Convert to lowercase
```

This uses the `Char::ToLower()` function from the .NET Framework library, which returns the lowercase equivalent of the argument — ch in this case. If the argument is already lowercase, the function just returns the same character code. By converting the character to lowercase, you avoid having to test subsequently for both upper- and lowercase vowels.

You determine whether ch contains a vowel or a consonant within the `switch` statement.

```
switch(ch)
{
case 'a': case 'e': case 'i': case 'o': case 'u':
  ++vowels;
  break;
default:
  ++consonants;
  break;
}
```

For any of the five cases where ch is a vowel, you increment the value stored in `vowels`; otherwise, you increment the value stored in `consonants`. This `switch` is executed for each character in `proverb`, so when the loop finishes, `vowels` contains the number of vowels in the string and `consonants` contains the number of consonants. You then output the result with the following statements:

```
Console::WriteLine(proverb);
Console::WriteLine(L"The proverb contains {0} vowels and {1} consonants.",
                                          vowels, consonants);
```

In the last statement, the value of `vowels` replaces the `"{0}"` in the string and the value of `consonants` replaces the `"{1}"`. This is because the arguments that follow the first format string argument are referenced by index values starting from 0.

SUMMARY

In this chapter, you learned all the essential mechanisms for making decisions in C++ programs. The ability to compare values and change the course of program execution is what differentiates a computer from a simple calculator. You need to be comfortable with all of the decision-making statements I have discussed because they are all used very frequently. You have also gone through all the facilities for repeating a group of statements. Loops are a fundamental programming technique that you will need to use in every program of consequence that you write. You will find you use the `for` loop most often in native C++, closely followed by the `while` loop. The `for each` loop in C++/CLI is typically more efficient than other loop forms, so be sure to use that where you can.

You can download the source code for the examples in the book and the solutions to the following exercises from www.wrox.com.

1.   Write a program that reads numbers from `cin` and then sums them, stopping when 0 has been entered. Construct three versions of this program, using the `while`, `do-while`, and `for` loops.

2.   Write an ISO/IEC C++ program to read characters from the keyboard and count the vowels. Stop counting when a Q (or a q) is encountered. Use a combination of an indefinite loop to get the characters, and a `switch` statement to count them.

3.   Write a program to print out the multiplication table from 2 to 12, in columns.

4.   Imagine that in a program you want to set a 'file open mode' variable based on two attributes: the file type, which can be text or binary, and the way in which you want to open the file to read or write it, or append data to it. Using the bitwise operators (`&` and `|`) and a set of flags, devise a method to allow a single integer variable to be set to any combination of the two attributes. Write a program that sets such a variable and then decodes it, printing out its setting, for all possible combinations of the attributes.

5.   Repeat `Ex3_2` as a C++/CLI program — you can use `Console::ReadKey()` to read characters from the keyboard.

6.   Write a CLR console program that defines a string (as type `String^`) and then analyzes the characters in the string to discover the number of uppercase letters, the number of lowercase letters, the number of non-alphabetic characters, and the total number of characters in the string.

▶ WHAT YOU LEARNED IN THIS CHAPTER

TOPIC	CONCEPT
Relational operators	The decision-making capability in C++ is based on the set of relational operators, which allow expressions to be tested and compared, and yield a `bool` value – `true` or `false` – as the result.
Decisions based on numerical values	You can also make decisions based on conditions that return non-`bool` values. Any non-zero value is cast to `true` when a condition is tested; zero casts to `false`.
Statements for decision-making	The primary decision-making capability in C++ is provided by the `if` statement. Further flexibility is provided by the `switch` statement, and by the conditional operator.
Loop statements	There are three basic methods provided in ISO/IEC C++ for repeating a block of statements: the `for` loop, the `while` loop, and the `do-while` loop. The `for` loop allows the loop to repeat a given number of times. The `while` loop allows a loop to continue as long as a specified condition returns `true`. Finally, `do-while` executes the loop at least once and allows continuation of the loop as long as a specified condition returns `true`.
The `for each` statement	C++/CLI provides the `for each` loop statement in addition to the three loop statements defined in ISO/IEC C++.
Nested loops	Any kind of loop may be nested within any other kind of loop.
The `continue` keyword	The keyword `continue` allows you to skip the remainder of the current iteration in a loop and go straight to the next iteration.
The `break` keyword	The keyword `break` provides an immediate exit from a loop. It also provides an exit from a `switch` at the end of statements in a `case`.

Arrays, Strings, and Pointers

WHAT YOU WILL LEARN IN THIS CHAPTER:

➤   How to use arrays

➤   How to declare and initialize arrays of different types

➤   How to declare and use multidimensional arrays

➤   How to use pointers

➤   How to declare and initialize pointers of different types

➤   The relationship between arrays and pointers

➤   How to declare references and some initial ideas on their uses

➤   How to allocate memory for variables dynamically in a native C++ program

➤   How dynamic memory allocation works in a Common Language Runtime (CLR) program

➤   Tracking handles and tracking references and why you need them in a CLR program

➤   How to work with strings and arrays in C++/CLI programs

➤   How to create and use interior pointers

So far, we have covered all the fundamental data types of consequence, and you have a basic knowledge of how to perform calculations and make decisions in a program. This chapter is about broadening the application of the basic programming techniques that you have learned so far, from using single items of data to working with whole collections of data items.

In this chapter, you'll be using objects more extensively. Although you have not yet explored the details of how they are created, don't worry if everything is not completely clear. You'll learn about classes and objects in detail starting in Chapter 7.

HANDLING MULTIPLE DATA VALUES OF THE SAME TYPE

You already know how to declare and initialize variables of various types that each holds a single item of information; I'll refer to single items of data as **data elements**. The most obvious extension to the idea of a variable is to be able to reference several data elements of a particular type with a single variable name. This would enable you to handle applications of a much broader scope.

Let's consider an example of where you might need this. Suppose that you needed to write a payroll program. Using a separately named variable for each individual's pay, their tax liability, and so on, would be an uphill task to say the least. A much more convenient way to handle such a problem would be to reference an employee by some kind of generic name — `employeeName` to take an imaginative example — and to have other generic names for the kinds of data related to each employee, such as `pay`, `tax`, and so on. Of course, you would also need some means of picking out a particular employee from the whole bunch, together with the data from the generic variables associated with them. This kind of requirement arises with any collection of like entities that you want to handle in your program, whether they're baseball players or battleships. Naturally, C++ provides you with a way to deal with this.

Arrays

The basis for the solution to all of these problems is provided by the **array** in ISO/IEC C++. An array is simply a number of memory locations called **array elements** or simply **elements**, each of which can store an item of data of the same given data type, and which are all referenced through the same variable name. The employee names in a payroll program could be stored in one array, the pay for each employee in another, and the tax due for each employee could be stored in a third array.

Individual items in an array are specified by an index value which is simply an integer representing the sequence number of the elements in the array, the first having the sequence number 0, the second 1, and so on. You can also envisage the index value of an array element as being an offset from the first element in an array. The first element has an offset of 0 and therefore an index of 0, and an index value of 3 will refer to the fourth element of an array. For the payroll, you could arrange the arrays so that if an employee's name was stored in the `employeeName` array at a given index value, then the arrays `pay` and `tax` would store the associated data on pay and tax for the same employee in the array positions referenced by the same index value.

The basic structure of an array is illustrated in Figure 4-1.

The height array has 6 elements.

FIGURE 4-1

Figure 4-1 shows an array with the name `height` that has six elements, each storing a different value. These might be the heights of the members of a family, for instance, recorded to the nearest inch. Because there are six elements, the index values run from 0 through 5. To refer to a particular element, you write the array name, followed by the index value of the particular element between square brackets. The third element is referred to as `height[2]`, for example. If you think of the index as being the offset from the first element, it's easy to see that the index value for the fourth element will be 3.

The amount of memory required to store each element is determined by its type, and all the elements of an array are stored in a contiguous block of memory.

Declaring Arrays

You declare an array in essentially the same way as you declared the variables that you have seen up to now, the only difference being that the number of elements in the array is specified between square brackets immediately following the array name. For example, you could declare the integer array `height`, shown in the previous figure, with the following declaration statement:

```
long height[6];
```

Because each `long` value occupies 4 bytes in memory, the whole array requires 24 bytes. Arrays can be of any size, subject to the constraints imposed by the amount of memory in the computer on which your program is running.

You can declare arrays to be of any type. For example, to declare arrays intended to store the capacity and power output of a series of engines, you could write the following:

```
double cubic_inches[10];    // Engine size
double horsepower[10];      // Engine power output
```

If auto mechanics is your thing, this would enable you to store the cubic capacity and power output of up to 10 engines, referenced by index values from 0 to 9. As you have seen before with other variables, you can declare multiple arrays of a given type in a single statement, but in practice it is almost always better to declare variables in separate statements.

TRY IT OUT   Using Arrays

As a basis for an exercise in using arrays, imagine that you have kept a record of both the amount of gasoline you have bought for the car and the odometer reading on each occasion. You can write a program to analyze this data to see how the gas consumption looks on each occasion that you bought gas:

```
// Ex4_01.cpp
// Calculating gas mileage
#include <iostream>
#include <iomanip>

using std::cin;
using std::cout;
using std::endl;
```

```cpp
using std::setw;

int main()
{
   const int MAX(20);                     // Maximum number of values
   double gas[ MAX ];                     // Gas quantity in gallons
   long miles[ MAX ];                     // Odometer readings
   int count(0);                          // Loop counter
   char indicator('y');                   // Input indicator

   while( ('y' == indicator || 'Y' == indicator) && count < MAX )
   {
      cout << endl << "Enter gas quantity: ";
      cin >> gas[count];                  // Read gas quantity
      cout << "Enter odometer reading: ";
      cin >> miles[count];                // Read odometer value

      ++count;
      cout << "Do you want to enter another(y or n)? ";
      cin >> indicator;
   }

   if(count <= 1)                         // count = 1 after 1 entry completed
   {                                      // ... we need at least 2
      cout << endl << "Sorry - at least two readings are necessary.";
      return 0;
   }

   // Output results from 2nd entry to last entry
   for(int i = 1; i < count; i++)
   {
      cout << endl
           << setw(2) << i << "."           // Output sequence number
           << "Gas purchased = " << gas[i] << " gallons" // Output gas
           << " resulted in "               // Output miles per gallon
           << (miles[i] - miles[i - 1])/gas[i] << " miles per gallon.";
   }
   cout << endl;
   return 0;
}
```

code snippet Ex4_01.cpp

The program assumes that you fill the tank each time so the gas bought was the amount consumed by
driving the distance recorded. Here's an example of the output produced by this example:

```
Enter gas quantity: 12.8
Enter odometer reading: 25832
Do you want to enter another(y or n)? y

Enter gas quantity: 14.9
Enter odometer reading: 26337
Do you want to enter another(y or n)? y

Enter gas quantity: 11.8
```

```
Enter odometer reading: 26598
Do you want to enter another(y or n)? n

 1.Gas purchased = 14.9 gallons resulted in 33.8926 miles per gallon.
 2.Gas purchased = 11.8 gallons resulted in 22.1186 miles per gallon.
```

How It Works

Because you need to take the difference between two odometer readings to calculate the miles covered for the gas used, you use only the odometer reading from the first pair of input values — you ignore the gas bought in the first instance as that would have been consumed during miles driven earlier.

During the second period shown in the output, the traffic must have been really bad — or maybe the parking brake was left on.

The dimensions of the two arrays gas and miles used to store the input data are determined by the value of the constant with the name MAX. By changing the value of MAX, you can change the program to accommodate a different maximum number of input values. This technique is commonly used to make a program flexible in the amount of information that it can handle. Of course, all the program code must be written to take account of the array dimensions, or of any other parameters being specified by const variables. This presents little difficulty in practice, however, so there's no reason why you should not adopt this approach. You'll also see later how to allocate memory for storing data as the program executes, so that you don't need to fix the amount of memory allocated for data storage in advance.

Entering the Data

The data values are read in the while loop. Because the loop variable count can run from 0 to MAX - 1, we haven't allowed the user of our program to enter more values than the array can handle. You initialize the variables count and indicator to 0 and 'y' respectively, so that the while loop is entered at least once. There's a prompt for each input value required and the value is read into the appropriate array element. The element used to store a particular value is determined by the variable count, which is 0 for the first input. The array element is specified in the cin statement by using count as an index, and count is then incremented, ready for the next value.

After you enter each value, the program prompts for confirmation that another value is to be entered. The character entered is read into the variable indicator and then tested in the loop condition. The loop will terminate unless 'y' or 'Y' is entered and the variable count is less than the specified maximum value, MAX.

After the input loop ends (by whatever means), the value of count contains one more than the index value of the last element entered in each array. (Remember, you increment it after you enter each new element). This is checked in order to verify that at least two pairs of values were entered. If this wasn't the case, the program ends with a suitable message because two odometer values are necessary to calculate a mileage value.

Producing the Results

The output is generated in the for loop. The control variable i runs from 1 to count-1, allowing mileage to be calculated as the difference between the current element, miles[i] and the previous element, miles[i - 1]. Note that an index value can be any expression evaluating to an integer that represents a legal index for the array in question, which is an index value from 0 to one less than the number of elements in the array.

If the value of an index expression lies outside of the range corresponding to legitimate array elements, you will reference a spurious data location that may contain other data, garbage, or even program code. If the reference to such an element appears in an expression, you will use some arbitrary data value in the calculation, which certainly produces a result that you did not intend. If you are storing a result in an array element using an illegal index value, you will overwrite whatever happens to be in that location. When this is part of your program code, the results are catastrophic. If you use illegal index values, there are no warnings produced either by the compiler or at runtime. The only way to guard against this is to code your program to prevent it happening.

The output is generated by a single `cout` statement for all values entered, except for the first. A line number is also generated for each line of output using the loop control variable `i`. Miles per gallon is calculated directly in the output statement. You can use array elements in exactly the same way as any other variables in an expression.

Initializing Arrays

To initialize an array in its declaration, you put the initializing values, separated by commas, between braces, and you place the set of initial values following an equals sign after the array name. Here's an example of how you can declare and initialize an array:

```
int cubic_inches[5] = { 200, 250, 300, 350, 400 };
```

The array has the name `cubic_inches` and has five elements that each store a value of type `int`. The values in the initializing list between the braces correspond to successive index values of the array, so in this case `cubic_inches[0]` has the value 200, `cubic_inches[1]` the value 250, `cubic_inches[2]` the value 300, and so on.

You must not specify more initializing values than there are elements in the array, but you can include fewer. If there *are* fewer, the values are assigned to successive elements, starting with the first element — which is the one corresponding to the index value 0. The array elements for which you didn't provide an initial value are initialized with zero. This isn't the same as supplying no initializing list. Without an initializing list, the array elements contain junk values. Also, if you include an initializing list, there must be at least one initializing value in it; otherwise the compiler generates an error message. I can illustrate this with the following rather limited example.

TRY IT OUT Initializing an Array

```cpp
// Ex4_02.cpp
// Demonstrating array initialization
#include <iostream>
#include <iomanip>

using std::cout;
using std::endl;
```

```
using std::setw;

int main()
{
    int value[5] = { 1, 2, 3 };
    int junk [5];

    cout << endl;
    for(int i = 0; i < 5; i++)
        cout << setw(12) << value[i];

    cout << cndl;
    for(int i = 0; i < 5; i++)
        cout << setw(12) << junk[i];

    cout << endl;
    return 0;
}
```

code snippet Ex4_02.cpp

In this example, you declare two arrays, the first of which, value, you initialize in part, and the second, junk, you don't initialize at all. The program generates two lines of output, which on my computer look like this:

```
          1           2           3           0           0
 -858993460  -858993460  -858993460  -858993460  -858993460
```

The second line (corresponding to values of junk[0] to junk[4]) may well be different on your computer.

How It Works

The first three values of the array value are the initializing values, and the last two have the default value of 0. In the case of junk, all the values are spurious because you didn't provide any initial values at all. The array elements contain whatever values were left there by the program that last used these memory locations.

A convenient way to initialize a whole array to zero is simply to specify a single initializing value as 0. For example:

```
long data[100] = {0};          // Initialize all elements to zero
```

This statement declares the array data, with all one hundred elements initialized with 0. The first element is initialized by the value you have between the braces, and the remaining elements are initialized to zero because you omitted values for these.

You can also omit the dimension of an array of numeric type, provided you supply initializing values. The number of elements in the array is determined by the number of initializing values you specify. For example, the array declaration

```
int value[] = { 2, 3, 4 };
```

defines an array with three elements that have the initial values 2, 3, and 4.

Character Arrays and String Handling

An array of type `char` is called a **character array** and is generally used to store a character string. A character string is a sequence of characters with a special character appended to indicate the end of the string. The string-terminating character indicates the end of the string; this character is defined by the escape sequence '\0', and is sometimes referred to as a **null character,** since it's a byte with all bits as zero. A string of this form is often referred to as a C-style string because defining a string in this way was introduced in the C language from which C++ was developed by Bjarne Stroustrup (you can find his home page at `http://www.research.att.com/~bs/`).

This is not the only representation of a string that you can use — you'll meet others later in the book. In particular, C++/CLI programs use a different representation of a string, and the MFC defines a `CString` class to represent strings.

The representation of a C-style string in memory is shown in Figure 4-2.

FIGURE 4-2

Figure 4-2 illustrates how a string looks in memory and shows a form of declaration for a string that I'll get to in a moment.

> **NOTE** *Each character in the string occupies one byte, so together with the terminating null character, a string requires a number of bytes that is one greater than the number of characters contained in the string.*

You can declare a character array and initialize it with a string literal. For example:

```
char movie_star[15] = "Marilyn Monroe";
```

Note that the terminating '\0' is supplied automatically by the compiler. If you include one explicitly in the string literal, you end up with two of them. You must, however, allow for the terminating null in the number of elements that you allot to the array.

You can let the compiler work out the length of an initialized array for you, as you saw in Figure 4-1. Here's another example:

```
char president[] = "Ulysses Grant";
```

Because the dimension is unspecified, the compiler allocates space for enough elements to hold the initializing string, plus the terminating null character. In this case it allocates 14 elements for the array `president`. Of course, if you want to use this array later for storing a different string, its length (including the terminating null character) must not exceed 14 bytes. In general, it is your responsibility to ensure that the array is large enough for any string you might subsequently want to store.

You can also create strings that comprise Unicode characters, the characters in the string being of type `wchar_t`. Here's a statement that creates a Unicode string:

```
wchar_t president[] = L"Ulysses Grant";
```

The `L` prefix indicates that the string literal is a wide character string, so each character in the string, including the terminating null character, will occupy two bytes. Of course, indexing the string references characters, not bytes, so `president[2]` corresponds to the character `L'y'`.

String Input

The `iostream` header file contains definitions of a number of functions for reading characters from the keyboard. The one that you'll look at here is the function `getline()`, which reads a sequence of characters entered through the keyboard and stores it in a character array as a string terminated by `'\0'`. You typically use the `getline()` function statements like this:

```
const int MAX(80);                // Maximum string length including \0
char name[MAX];                   // Array to store a string
cin.getline(name, MAX, '\n');     // Read input line as a string
```

These statements first declare a `char` array name with `MAX` elements and then read characters from `cin` using the function `getline()`. The source of the data, `cin`, is written as shown, with a period separating it from the function name. The period indicates that the `getline()` function you are calling is the one belonging to the `cin` object. The significance of the arguments to the `getline()` function is shown in Figure 4-3.

The maximum number of characters to be read. When the specified maximum has been read, input stops.

The character that is to stop the input process. You can specify any character here, and the first occurance of that character will stop the input process.

The name of the array of type char[] in which the characters read from cin are to be stored.

cin.getline(name , MAX, '\n');

FIGURE 4-3

Because the last argument to the `getline()` function is `'\n'` (newline or end line character) and the second argument is `MAX`, characters are read from `cin` until the '\n' character is read, or when `MAX` - 1 characters have been read, whichever occurs first. The maximum number of characters read is `MAX` - 1 rather than `MAX` to allow for the '\0' character to be appended to the sequence of characters stored in the array. The '\n' character is generated when you press the *Return* key on your keyboard and is therefore usually the most convenient character to end input. You can, however, specify something else by changing the last argument. The '\n' isn't stored in the input array name, but as I said, a '\0' is added at the end of the input string in the array.

You will learn more about this form of syntax when classes are discussed later on. Meanwhile, just take it for granted as you use it in an example.

TRY IT OUT **Programming with Strings**

You now have enough knowledge to write a simple program to read a string and then count how many characters it contains.

```cpp
// Ex4_03.cpp
// Counting string characters
#include <iostream>
using std::cin;
using std::cout;
using std::endl;

int main()
{
   const int MAX(80);                 // Maximum array dimension
   char buffer[MAX];                  // Input buffer
   int count(0);                      // Character count

   cout << "Enter a string of less than "
        << MAX << " characters:\n";
   cin.getline(buffer, MAX, '\n');    // Read a string until \n

   while(buffer[count] != '\0')       // Increment count as long as
      count++;                        // the current character is not null

   cout << endl
        << "The string \"" << buffer
        << "\" has " << count << " characters.";
   cout << endl;
   return 0;
}
```

code snippet Ex4_03.cpp

Typical output from this program is as follows:

```
Enter a string of less than 80 characters:
Radiation fades your genes
The string "Radiation fades your genes" has 26 characters.
```

How It Works

This program declares a character array `buffer` and reads a character string into the array from the keyboard after displaying a prompt for the input. Reading from the keyboard ends when the user presses *Return*, or when MAX-1 characters have been read.

A `while` loop is used to count the number of characters read. The loop continues as long as the current character referenced with `buffer[count]` is not '\0'. This sort of checking on the current character while stepping through an array is a common technique in native C++. The only action in the loop is to increment `count` for each non-null character.

There is a library function, `strlen()`, that will do what this loop does; you'll learn about it later in this chapter.

Finally, in the example, the string and the character count is displayed with a single output statement. Note the use of the escape sequence '\"' to output a double quote.

Multidimensional Arrays

The arrays that you have defined so far with one index are referred to as **one-dimensional** arrays. An array can also have more than one index value, in which case it is called a **multidimensional** array. Suppose you have a field in which you are growing bean plants in rows of 10, and the field contains 12 such rows (so there are 120 plants in all). You could declare an array to record the weight of beans produced by each plant using the following statement:

```
double beans[12][10];
```

This declares the two-dimensional array `beans`, the first index being the row number, and the second index the number within the row. To refer to any particular element requires two index values. For example, you could set the value of the element reflecting the fifth plant in the third row with the following statement:

```
beans[2][4] = 10.7;
```

Remember that the index values start from zero, so the row index value is 2 and the index for the fifth plant within the row is 4.

Being a successful bean farmer, you might have several identical fields planted with beans in the same pattern. Assuming that you have eight fields, you could use a three-dimensional array to record data about these, declared thus:

```
double beans[8][12][10];
```

This records production for all of the plants in each of the fields, the leftmost index referencing a particular field. If you ever get to bean farming on an international scale, you are able to use a four-dimensional array, with the extra dimension designating the country. Assuming that you're as good a salesman as you are a farmer, growing this quantity of beans to keep up with the demand may well start to affect the ozone layer.

Arrays are stored in memory such that the rightmost index value varies most rapidly. Thus, the array `data[3][4]` is three one-dimensional arrays of four elements each. The arrangement of this array is illustrated in Figure 4-4.

The elements of the array are stored in a contiguous block of memory, as indicated by the arrows in Figure 4-4. The first index selects a particular row within the array, and the second index selects an element within the row.

Note that a two-dimensional array in native C++ is really a one-dimensional array of one-dimensional arrays. A native C++ array with three dimensions is actually a one-dimensional array of elements where each element is a one-dimensional array of one-dimensional arrays. This is not something you need to worry about most of the time, but as you will see later, C++/CLI arrays are not the same as this. It also implies that for the array in Figure 4-4, the expressions data[0], data[1], and data[2], represent one-dimensional arrays.

data[0][0]	data[0][1]	data[0][2]	data[0][3]

data[1][0]	data[1][1]	data[1][2]	data[1][3]

data[2][0]	data[2][1]	data[2][2]	data[2][3]

The array elements are stored in contiguous locations in memory.

FIGURE 4-4

Initializing Multidimensional Arrays

To initialize a multidimensional array, you use an extension of the method used for a one-dimensional array. For example, you can initialize a two-dimensional array, data, with the following declaration:

```
long data[2][4] = {
                     { 1,  2,  3,  5 },
                     { 7, 11, 13, 17 }
                   };
```

Thus, the initializing values for each row of the array are contained within their own pair of braces. Because there are four elements in each row, there are four initializing values in each group, and because there are two rows, there are two groups between braces, each group of initializing values being separated from the next by a comma.

You can omit initializing values in any row, in which case the remaining array elements in the row are zero. For example:

```
long data[2][4] = {
                      { 1,  2,  3        },
                      { 7, 11            }
                  };
```

I have spaced out the initializing values to show where values have been omitted. The elements `data[0][3]`, `data[1][2]`, and `data[1][3]` have no initializing values and are therefore zero.

If you wanted to initialize the whole array with zeros you could simply write:

```
long data[2][4] = {0};
```

If you are initializing arrays with even more dimensions, remember that you need as many nested braces for groups of initializing values as there are dimensions in the array — unless you're initializing the array with zeros

TRY IT OUT | **Storing Multiple Strings**

You can use a single two-dimensional array to store several C-style strings. You can see how this works with an example:

```cpp
// Ex4_04.cpp
// Storing strings in an array
#include <iostream>
using std::cout;
using std::cin;
using std::endl;

int main()
{
    char stars[6][80] = { "Robert Redford",
                          "Hopalong Cassidy",
                          "Lassie",
                          "Slim Pickens",
                          "Boris Karloff",
                          "Oliver Hardy"
                        };
    int dice(0);

    cout << endl
         << "Pick a lucky star!"
         << "Enter a number between 1 and 6: ";
    cin >> dice;

    if(dice >= 1 && dice <= 6)          // Check input validity
       cout << endl                     // Output star name
            << "Your lucky star is " << stars[dice - 1];
    else
       cout << endl                     // Invalid input
            << "Sorry, you haven't got a lucky star.";

    cout << endl;
    return 0;
}
```

code snippet Ex4_04.cpp

How It Works

Apart from its incredible inherent entertainment value, the main point of interest in this example is the declaration of the array `stars`. It is a two-dimensional array of elements of type `char` that can hold up to six strings, each of which can be up to 80 characters long (including the terminating null character that is automatically added by the compiler). The initializing strings for the array are enclosed between braces and separated by commas.

One disadvantage of using arrays in this way is the memory that is almost invariably left unused. All of the strings are fewer than 80 characters, and the surplus elements in each row of the array are wasted.

You can also let the compiler work out how many strings you have by omitting the first array dimension and declaring it as follows:

```
char stars[][80] = {  "Robert Redford",
                      "Hopalong Cassidy",
                      "Lassie",
                      "Slim Pickens",
                      "Boris Karloff",
                      "Oliver Hardy"
                   };
```

This causes the compiler to define the first dimension to accommodate the number of initializing strings that you have specified. Because you have six, the result is exactly the same, but it avoids the possibility of an error. Here, you can't omit both array dimensions. With an array of two or more dimensions, the rightmost dimension must always be defined.

 NOTE *Note the semicolon at the end of the declaration. It's easy to forget it when there are initializing values for an array.*

Where you need to reference a string for output in the following statement, you need only specify the first index value:

```
cout << endl                            // Output star name
     << "Your lucky star is " << stars[dice - 1];
```

A single index value selects a particular 80-element sub-array, and the output operation displays the contents up to the terminating null character. The index is specified as `dice - 1` as the `dice` values are from 1 to 6, whereas the index values clearly need to be from 0 to 5.

INDIRECT DATA ACCESS

The variables that you have dealt with so far provide you with the ability to name a memory location in which you can store data of a particular type. The contents of a variable are either entered from an external source, such as the keyboard, or calculated from other values that are entered. There is another kind of variable in C++ that does not store data that you normally enter or calculate, but greatly extends the power and flexibility of your programs. This kind of variable is called a **pointer**.

What Is a Pointer?

Each memory location that you use to store a data value has an address. The address provides the means for your PC hardware to reference a particular data item. A pointer is a variable that stores the address of another variable of a particular type. A pointer has a variable name just like any other variable and also has a type that designates what kind of variables its contents refer to. Note that the type of a pointer variable includes the fact that it's a pointer. A variable that is a pointer, that can hold addresses of locations in memory containing values of type int, is of type 'pointer to int'.

Declaring Pointers

The declaration for a pointer is similar to that of an ordinary variable, except that the pointer name has an asterisk in front of it to indicate that it's a variable that is a pointer. For example, to declare a pointer pnumber of type long, you could use the following statement:

```
long* pnumber;
```

This declaration has been written with the asterisk close to the type name. If you want, you can also write it as:

```
long *pnumber;
```

The compiler won't mind at all; however, the type of the variable pnumber is 'pointer to long', which is often indicated by placing the asterisk close to the type name. Whichever way you choose to write a pointer type, be consistent.

You can mix declarations of ordinary variables and pointers in the same statement. For example:

```
long* pnumber, number (99);
```

This declares the pointer pnumber of type 'pointer to long' as before, and also declares the variable number, of type long. On balance, it's probably better to declare pointers separately from other variables; otherwise, the statement can appear misleading as to the type of the variables declared, particularly if you prefer to place the * adjacent to the type name. The following statements certainly look clearer, and putting declarations on separate lines enables you to add comments for them individually, making for a program that is easier to read.

```
long number(99);     // Declaration and initialization of long variable
long* pnumber;       // Declaration of variable of type pointer to long
```

It's a common convention in C++ to use variable names beginning with p to denote pointers. This makes it easier to see which variables in a program are pointers, which in turn can make a program easier to follow.

Let's take an example to see how this works, without worrying about what it's for. I will get to how you use pointers very shortly. Suppose you have the long integer variable number containing the value 99 because you declared it above. You also have the pointer pnumber of type pointer to long, which you could use to store the address of the variable number. But how do you obtain the address of a variable?

The Address-Of Operator

What you need is the **address-of operator,** &. This is a unary operator that obtains the address of a variable. It's also called the reference operator, for reasons I will discuss later in this chapter. To set up the pointer that I have just discussed, you could write this assignment statement:

```
pnumber = &number;            // Store address of number in pnumber
```

The result of this operation is illustrated in Figure 4-5.

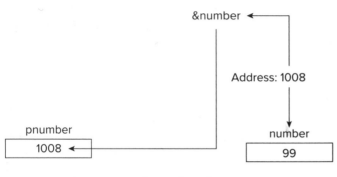

pnumber = &number;

FIGURE 4-5

You can use the operator & to obtain the address of any variable, but you need a pointer of the appropriate type to store it. If you want to store the address of a double variable, for example, the pointer must have been declared as type double*, which is type 'pointer to double'.

Using Pointers

Taking the address of a variable and storing it in a pointer is all very well, but the really interesting aspect is how you can use it. Fundamental to using a pointer is accessing the data value in the variable to which a pointer points. This is done using the **indirection operator** *.

The Indirection Operator

You use the **indirection operator,** *, with a pointer to access the contents of the variable that it points to. The name 'indirection operator' stems from the fact that the data is accessed indirectly. It is also called the **dereference operator,** and the process of accessing the data in the variable pointed to by a pointer is termed **de-referencing the pointer.**

One aspect of this operator that can seem confusing is the fact that you now have several different uses for the same symbol, *. It is the multiply operator, it serves as the indirection operator, and it is used in the declaration of a pointer. Each time you use *, the compiler is able to distinguish its meaning by the context. When you multiply two variables, A*B for instance, there's no meaningful interpretation of this expression for anything other than a multiply operation.

Why Use Pointers?

A question that usually springs to mind at this point is, "Why use pointers at all?" After all, taking the address of a variable you already know and sticking it in a pointer so that you can dereference it seems like overhead you can do without. There are several reasons why pointers are important.

As you will see shortly, you can use pointer notation to operate on data stored in an array, which often executes faster than if you use array notation. Also, when you get to define your own functions later in the book, you will see that pointers are used extensively for enabling access within a function to large blocks of data, such as arrays, that are defined outside the function. Most importantly, however, you will also see that you can allocate space for variables dynamically — that is, during program execution. This sort of capability allows your program to adjust its use of memory depending on the input to the program. Because you don't know in advance how many variables you are going to create dynamically, a primary way you have for doing this is using pointers — so make sure you get the hang of this bit.

Initializing Pointers

Using pointers that aren't initialized is extremely hazardous. You can easily overwrite random areas of memory through an uninitialized pointer. The resulting damage depends on how unlucky you are, so it's more than just a good idea to initialize your pointers. It's very easy to initialize a pointer to the address of a variable that has already been defined. Here you can see that I have initialized the pointer pnumber with the address of the variable number just by using the operator & with the variable name:

```
int number(0);                  // Initialized integer variable
int* pnumber(&number);          // Initialized pointer
```

When initializing a pointer with the address of another variable, remember that the variable must already have been declared prior to the pointer declaration.

Of course, you may not want to initialize a pointer with the address of a specific variable when you declare it. In this case, you can initialize it with the pointer equivalent of zero. For this, Visual C++ provides the literal nullptr — a pointer literal that does not point to anything — so you can declare and initialize a pointer using the following statement:

```
int* pnumber(nullptr);          // Pointer not pointing to anything
```

This ensures that the pointer doesn't contain an address that will be accepted as valid, and provides the pointer with a value that you can check in an if statement, such as:

```
if(pnumber == nullptr)
   cout << endl << "pnumber does not point to anything.";
```

nullptr is a feature introduced by the new standard for C++ that is supported by the Visual C++ 2010 compiler. In the past, 0 or NULL (which is a macro for which the compiler will substitute 0) have been used to initialize a pointer, and of course, these still work. However, it is much better to use nullptr to initialize your pointers.

> **NOTE** *The reason for introducing* `nullptr` *into the C++ language is to remove potential confusion between the literal 0 as an integral value and 0 as a pointer. Having a dual meaning for the literal 0 can cause problems in some circumstances.* `nullptr` *is of type* `std::nullptr_t` *and cannot be confused with a value of any other type.* `nullptr` *can be implicitly converted to any pointer type but cannot be implicitly converted to any integral type except type* `bool`.

Because the literal `nullptr` can be implicitly converted to type `bool`, you can check the status of the pointer `pnumber` like this:

```
if(!pnumber)
    cout << endl << "pnumber does not point to anything.";
```

`nullptr` converts to the `bool` value `false`, and any other pointer value converts to `true`. Thus, if `pnumber` contains `nullptr`, the `if` expression will be `true` and will cause the message to be written to the output stream.

TRY IT OUT   Using Pointers

You can try out various aspects of pointer operations with an example:

Available for
download on
Wrox.com

```
// Ex4_05.cpp
// Exercising pointers
#include <iostream>
using std::cout;
using std::endl;
using std::hex;
using std::dec;

int main()
{
    long* pnumber(nullptr);          // Pointer declaration & initialization
    long number1(55), number2(99);

    pnumber = &number1;              // Store address in pointer
    *pnumber += 11;                  // Increment number1 by 11
    cout << endl
        << "number1 = " << number1
        << "   &number1 = " << hex << pnumber;

    pnumber = &number2;              // Change pointer to address of number2
    number1 = *pnumber*10;           // 10 times number2

    cout << endl
        << "number1 = " << dec << number1
        << "    pnumber = " << hex << pnumber
```

```
                    << "    *pnumber = " << dec << *pnumber;

          cout << endl;
          return 0;
        }
```

You should compile and execute the release version of this example. The debug version will add extra bytes, used for debugging purposes, that will cause the variables to be separated by 12 bytes instead of 4. On my computer, this example generates the following output:

```
number1 = 66    &number1 = 0012FEC8
number1 = 990    pnumber = 0012FEBC    *pnumber = 99
```

How It Works

There is no input to this example. All operations are carried out with the initializing values for the variables. After storing the address of number1 in the pointer pnumber, the value of number1 is incremented indirectly through the pointer in this statement:

```
        *pnumber += 11;                     // Increment number1 by 11
```

The indirection operator determines that you are adding 11 to the contents of the variable pointed to by pnumber, which is number1. If you forgot the * in this statement, you would be attempting to add 11 to the address stored in the pointer.

The values of number1, and the address of number1 that is stored in pnumber, are displayed. You use the hex manipulator to generate the address output in hexadecimal notation.

You can obtain the value of ordinary integer variables as hexadecimal output by using the manipulator hex. You send it to the output stream in the same way that you have applied endl, with the result that all following output is in hexadecimal notation. If you want the following output to be decimal, you need to use the manipulator dec in the next output statement to switch the output back to decimal mode again.

After the first line of output, the contents of pnumber is set to the address of number2. The variable number1 is then changed to the value of 10 times number2:

```
        number1 = *pnumber*10;               // 10 times number2
```

This is calculated by accessing the contents of number2 indirectly through the pointer. The second line of output shows the results of these calculations.

The address values you see in your output may well be different from those shown in the output here since they reflect where the program is loaded in memory, which depends on how your operating system is configured. The 0x prefixing the address values indicates that they are hexadecimal numbers.

Note that the addresses &number1 and pnumber (when it contains &number2) differ by four bytes. This shows that number1 and number2 occupy adjacent memory locations, as each variable of type long occupies four bytes. The output demonstrates that everything is working as you would expect.

Pointers to char

A pointer of type char* has the interesting property that it can be initialized with a string literal. For example, you can declare and initialize such a pointer with the statement:

```
char* proverb ("A miss is as good as a mile.");
```

This looks similar to initializing a char array, but it's slightly different. This creates a string literal (actually an array of type const char) with the character string appearing between the quotes and terminating with '\0', and stores the address of the literal in the pointer proverb. The address of the literal will be the address of its first character. This is shown in Figure 4-6.

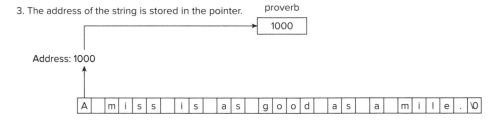

1. The pointer proverb is created.

3. The address of the string is stored in the pointer.

proverb

1000

Address: 1000

| A | m | i | s | s | | i | s | | a | s | | g | o | o | d | | a | s | | a | | m | i | l | e | . | \0 |

2. The constant string is created, terminated with \0.

FIGURE 4-6

TRY IT OUT   Lucky Stars With Pointers

You could rewrite the lucky stars example using pointers instead of an array to see how that would work:

```cpp
// Ex4_06.cpp
// Initializing pointers with strings
#include <iostream>
using std::cin;
using std::cout;
using std::endl;

int main()
{
```

```cpp
   char* pstr1("Robert Redford");
   char* pstr2("Hopalong Cassidy");
   char* pstr3("Lassie");
   char* pstr4("Slim Pickens");
   char* pstr5 ("Boris Karloff");
   char* pstr6("Oliver Hardy");
   char* pstr("Your lucky star is ");

   int dice(0);

   cout << endl
        << "Pick a lucky star!"
        << "Enter a number between 1 and 6: ";
   cin >> dice;

   cout << endl;
   switch(dice)
   {
      case 1: cout << pstr << pstr1;
              break;
      case 2: cout << pstr << pstr2;
              break;
      case 3: cout << pstr << pstr3;
              break;
      case 4: cout << pstr << pstr4;
              break;
      case 5: cout << pstr << pstr5;
              break;
      case 6: cout << pstr << pstr6;
              break;

      default: cout << "Sorry, you haven't got a lucky star.";
   }

   cout << endl;
   return 0;
}
```

code snippet Ex4_06.cpp

How It Works

The array in Ex4_04.cpp has been replaced by the six pointers, pstr1 to pstr6, each initialized with a name. You have also declared an additional pointer, pstr, initialized with the phrase that you want to use at the start of a normal output line. Because you have discrete pointers, it is easier to use a switch statement to select the appropriate output message than to use an if, as you did in the original version. Any incorrect values entered are all taken care of by the default option of the switch.

Outputting the string pointed to by a pointer couldn't be easier. As you can see, you simply write the pointer name. It may cross your mind at this point that in Ex4_05.cpp you wrote a pointer name in the output statement, and the address that it contained was displayed. Why is it different here? The answer is in the way the output operation views a pointer of type 'pointer to char.' It treats a pointer of this type in a special way, in that it regards it as a string (which is an array of char), and so outputs the string itself, rather than its address.

Using pointers in the example has eliminated the waste of memory that occurred with the array version of this program, but the program seems a little long-winded now. There must be a better way. Indeed there is — using an array of pointers.

TRY IT OUT **Arrays of Pointers**

With an array of pointers of type char, each element can point to an independent string, and the lengths of each of the strings can be different. You can declare an array of pointers in the same way that you declare a normal array. Let's go straight to rewriting the previous example using a pointer array:

```cpp
// Ex4_07.cpp
// Initializing pointers with strings
#include <iostream>
using std::cin;
using std::cout;
using std::endl;

int main()
{
    char* pstr[] =  { "Robert Redford",      // Initializing a pointer array
                      "Hopalong Cassidy",
                      "Lassie",
                      "Slim Pickens",
                      "Boris Karloff",
                      "Oliver Hardy"
                    };
    char* pstart("Your lucky star is ");

    int dice(0);

    cout << endl
         << "Pick a lucky star!"
         << "Enter a number between 1 and 6: ";
    cin >> dice;

    cout << endl;
    if(dice >= 1 && dice <= 6)              // Check input validity
        cout << pstart << pstr[dice - 1];   // Output star name

    else
        cout << "Sorry, you haven't got a lucky star."; // Invalid input

    cout << endl;
    return 0;
}
```

code snippet Ex4_07.cpp

How It Works

In this case, you are nearly getting the best of all possible worlds. You have a one-dimensional array of pointers to type char declared, such that the compiler works out what the dimension should be from the number of initializing strings. The memory usage that results from this is illustrated in Figure 4-7.

Compared to using a 'normal' array, the pointer array generally carries less overhead in terms of space. With an array, you would need to make each row the length of the longest string, and six rows of seventeen bytes each is 102 bytes, so by using a pointer array you have saved a whole -1 bytes! What's gone wrong? The simple truth is that for this small number of relatively short strings, the size of the extra array of pointers is significant. You *would* make savings if you were dealing with more strings that were longer and had more variable lengths.

Space saving isn't the only advantage that you get by using pointers. In a lot of circumstances you save time, too. Think of what happens if you want to move "Oliver Hardy" to the first position and "Robert Redford" to the end. With the pointer array as above, you just need to swap the pointers — the strings themselves stay where they are. If you had stored these simply as strings, as you did in Ex4_04.cpp, a great deal of copying would be necessary — you'd need to copy the whole string "Robert Redford" to a temporary location while you copied "Oliver Hardy" in its place, and then you'd need to copy "Robert Redford" to the end position. This requires significantly more computer time to execute.

Because you are using pstr as the name of the array, the variable holding the start of the output message needs to be different; it is called pstart. You select the string that you want to output by means of a very simple if statement, similar to that of the original version of the example. You either display a star selection or a suitable message if the user enters an invalid value.

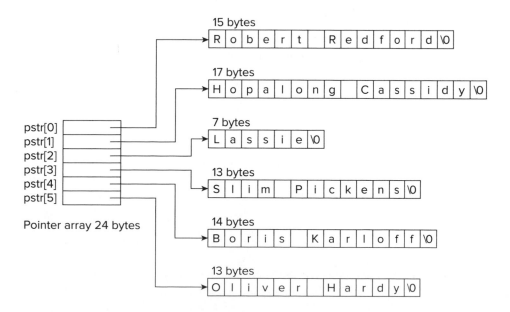

Total Memory is 103 bytes

FIGURE 4-7

One weakness of the way the program is written is that the code assumes there are six options, even though the compiler is allocating the space for the pointer array from the number of initializing strings that you supply. So if you add a string to the list, you have to alter other parts of the program to take account of this. It would be nice to be able to add strings and have the program automatically adapt to however many strings there are.

The sizeof Operator

A new operator can help us here. The `sizeof` operator produces an integer value of type `size_t` that gives the number of bytes occupied by its operand, where `size_t` is a type defined by the standard library. Many standard library functions return a value of type `size_t`, and the `size_t` type is defined within the standard library using a `typedef` statement to be equivalent to one of the fundamental types, usually `unsigned int`. The reason for using `size_t` rather than a fundamental type directly is that it allows flexibility in what the actual type is in different C++ implementations. The C++ standard permits the range of values accommodated by a fundamental type to vary, to make the best of a given hardware architecture, and `size_t` can be defined to be the equivalent of the most suitable fundamental type in the current machine environment.

Look at this statement that refers to the variable `dice` from the previous example:

```
cout << sizeof dice;
```

The value of the expression `sizeof dice` is 4 because `dice` was declared as type `int` and therefore occupies 4 bytes. Thus this statement outputs the value 4.

The `sizeof` operator can be applied to an element in an array or to the whole array. When the operator is applied to an array name by itself, it produces the number of bytes occupied by the whole array, whereas when it is applied to a single element with the appropriate index value or values, it results in the number of bytes occupied by that element. Thus, in the last example, you could output the number of elements in the `pstr` array with the expression:

```
cout << (sizeof pstr)/(sizeof pstr[0]);
```

The expression `(sizeof pstr)/(sizeof pstr[0])` divides the number of bytes occupied by the whole pointer array, by the number of bytes occupied by the first element of the array. Because each element in the array occupies the same amount of memory, the result is the number of elements in the array.

 NOTE *Remember that* `pstr` *is an array of pointers — using the* `sizeof` *operator on the array or on individual elements will not tell us anything about the memory occupied by the text strings.* `pstr[0]` *is a pointer to a character array and thus occupies just 4 bytes.*

You can also apply the `sizeof` operator to a type name rather than a variable, in which case the result is the number of bytes occupied by a variable of that type. In this case, the type name should be enclosed in parentheses. For example, after executing the statement,

```
size_t long_size(sizeof(long));
```

the variable `long_size` will be initialized with the value 4. The variable `long_size` is declared to be of type `size_t` to match the type of the value produced by the `sizeof` operator. Using a different integer type for `long_size` may result in a warning message from the compiler.

TRY IT OUT   Using the sizeof Operator

You can amend the last example to use the `sizeof` operator so that the code automatically adapts to an arbitrary number of string values from which to select:

```cpp
// Ex4_08.cpp
// Flexible array management using sizeof
#include <iostream>
using std::cin;
using std::cout;
using std::endl;

int main()
{
    char* pstr[] = { "Robert Redford",        // Initializing a pointer array
                     "Hopalong Cassidy",
                     "Lassie",
                     "Slim Pickens",
                     "Boris Karloff",
                     "Oliver Hardy"
                   };
    char* pstart("Your lucky star is ");

    int count((sizeof pstr)/(sizeof pstr[0]));  // Number of array elements

    int dice(0);

    cout << endl
         << " Pick a lucky star!"
         << " Enter a number between 1 and " << count << ": ";
    cin >> dice;

    cout << endl;
    if(dice >= 1 && dice <= count)                 // Check input validity
        cout << pstart << pstr[dice - 1];          // Output star name
    else
        cout << "Sorry, you haven't got a lucky star."; // Invalid input

    cout << endl;
    return 0;
}
```

code snippet Ex4_08.cpp

How It Works

As you can see, the changes required in the example are very simple. You just calculate the number of elements in the pointer array `pstr` and store the result in `count`. Then, wherever the total number of elements in the array was referenced as 6, you just use the variable `count`. You could now just add a few more names to the list of lucky stars, and everything affected in the program is adjusted automatically.

Constant Pointers and Pointers to Constants

The array `pstr` in the last example is clearly not intended to be modified in the program, and nor are the strings being pointed to, nor is the variable `count`. It would be a good idea to ensure that these didn't get modified by mistake in the program. You could very easily protect the variable `count` from accidental modification by writing this:

```
const int count = (sizeof pstr)/(sizeof pstr[0]);
```

However, the array of pointers deserves closer examination. You declared the array like this:

```
char* pstr[] = { "Robert Redford",    // Initializing a pointer array
                 "Hopalong Cassidy",
                 "Lassie",
                 "Slim Pickens",
                 "Boris Karloff",
                 "Oliver Hardy"
               };
```

Each pointer in the array is initialized with the address of a string literal, "Robert Redford", "Hopalong Cassidy", and so on. The type of a string literal is 'array of const char,' so you are storing the address of a const array in a non-const pointer. The compiler allows us to use a string literal to initialize an element of an array of char* for reasons of backward compatibility with existing code.

If you try to alter the character array with a statement like this:

```
*pstr[0] = "Stan Laurel";
```

the program does not compile.

If you were to reset one of the elements of the array to point to a character using a statement like this:

```
*pstr[0] = 'X';
```

the program compiles, but crashes when this statement is executed.

You don't really want to have unexpected behavior, like the program crashing at run time, and you can prevent it. A far better way of writing the declaration is as follows:

```
const char* pstr[] = { "Robert Redford",      // Array of pointers
                       "Hopalong Cassidy",    // to constants
                       "Lassie",
                       "Slim Pickens",
                       "Boris Karloff",
                       "Oliver Hardy"
                     };
```

In this case, there is no ambiguity about the const-ness of the strings pointed to by the elements of the pointer array. If you now attempt to change these strings, the compiler flags this as an error at compile time.

However, you could still legally write this statement:

```
pstr[0] = pstr[1];
```

Those lucky individuals due to be awarded Mr. Redford would get Mr. Cassidy instead because both pointers now point to the same name. Note that this isn't changing the values of the objects pointed to by the pointer array element — it is changing the value of the pointer stored in pstr[0]. You should therefore inhibit this kind of change as well, because some people may reckon that good old Hoppy may not have the same sex appeal as Robert. You can do this with the following statement:

```
// Array of constant pointers to constants
const char* const pstr[] = { "Robert Redford",
                             "Hopalong Cassidy",
                             "Lassie",
                             "Slim Pickens",
                             "Boris Karloff",
                             "Oliver Hardy"
                           };
```

To summarize, you can distinguish three situations relating to const, pointers, and the objects to which they point:

➤   A pointer to a constant object

➤   A constant pointer to an object

➤   A constant pointer to a constant object

In the first situation, the object pointed to cannot be modified, but you can set the pointer to point to something else:

```
const char* pstring("Some text");
```

In the second, the address stored in the pointer can't be changed, but the object pointed to can be:

```
char* const pstring("Some text");
```

Finally, in the third situation, both the pointer and the object pointed to have been defined as constant and, therefore, neither can be changed:

```
const char* const pstring("Some text");
```

> **NOTE** *Of course, all this applies to pointers that point to any type. A pointer to type* char *is used here purely for illustrative purposes. In general, to interpret more complex types correctly, you just read them from right to left. The type* const char* *is a pointer to characters that are* const *and the type* char* const *is a* const *pointer to characters.*

Pointers and Arrays

Array names can behave like pointers under some circumstances. In most situations, if you use the name of a one-dimensional array by itself, it is automatically converted to a pointer to the first element of the array. Note that this is not the case when the array name is used as the operand of the sizeof operator.

If you have these declarations,

```
double* pdata(nullptr);
double data[5];
```

you can write this assignment:

```
pdata = data;        // Initialize pointer with the array address
```

This is assigning the address of the first element of the array data to the pointer pdata. Using the array name by itself refers to the address of the array. If you use the array name data with an index value, it refers to the contents of the element corresponding to that index value. So, if you want to store the address of that element in the pointer, you have to use the address-of operator:

```
pdata = &data[1];
```

Here, the pointer pdata contains the address of the second element of the array.

Pointer Arithmetic

You can perform arithmetic operations with pointers. You are limited to addition and subtraction in terms of arithmetic, but you can also perform comparisons of pointer values to produce a logical result. Arithmetic with a pointer implicitly assumes that the pointer points to an array, and that the arithmetic operation is on the address contained in the pointer. For the pointer pdata, for example, you could assign the address of the third element of the array data to a pointer with this statement:

```
pdata = &data[2];
```

In this case, the expression pdata+1 would refer to the address of data[3], the fourth element of the data array, so you could make the pointer point to this element by writing this statement:

```
pdata += 1;              // Increment pdata to the next element
```

This statement increments the address contained in pdata by the number of bytes occupied by one element of the array data. In general, the expression pdata+n, where n can be any expression resulting in an integer, adds n*sizeof(double) to the address contained in the pointer pdata, because it was declared to be of type pointer to double. This is illustrated in Figure 4-8.

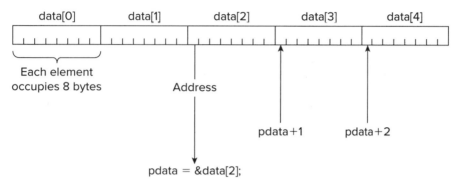

double data[5];

data[0]   data[1]   data[2]   data[3]   data[4]

Each element occupies 8 bytes

Address

pdata+1   pdata+2

pdata = &data[2];

FIGURE 4-8

In other words, incrementing or decrementing a pointer works in terms of the type of the object pointed to. Increasing a pointer to long by one changes its contents to the next long address, and so increments the address by four. Similarly, incrementing a pointer to short by one increments the address by two. The more common notation for incrementing a pointer is using the increment operator. For example:

```
pdata++;                // Increment pdata to the next element
```

This is equivalent to (and more common than) the += form. However, I used the preceding += form to make it clear that although the increment value is actually specified as one, the effect is usually an address increment greater than one, except in the case of a pointer to type char.

> **NOTE** *The address resulting from an arithmetic operation on a pointer can be a value ranging from the address of the first element of the array to the address that is one beyond the last element. Accessing an address that does not refer to an element within the array results in undefined behavior.*

You can, of course, dereference a pointer on which you have performed arithmetic (there wouldn't be much point to it otherwise). For example, assuming that pdata is still pointing to data[2], this statement,

```
*(pdata + 1) = *(pdata + 2);
```

is equivalent to this:

```
data[3] = data[4];
```

When you want to dereference a pointer after incrementing the address it contains, the parentheses are necessary because the precedence of the indirection operator is higher than that of the arithmetic operators, + and -. If you write the expression *pdata+1, instead of *(pdata+1), this adds one to the value stored at the address contained in pdata, which is equivalent to executing data[2]+1. Because this isn't an lvalue, its use in the previous assignment statement causes the compiler to generate an error message.

You can use an array name as though it were a pointer for addressing elements of an array. If you have the same one-dimensional array as before, declared as

```
long data[5];
```

using pointer notation, you can refer to the element data[3], for example, as *(data+3). This kind of notation can be applied generally so that, corresponding to the elements data[0], data[1], data[2], you can write *data, *(data+1), *(data+2), and so on.

TRY IT OUT   Array Names as Pointers

You could practice this aspect of array addressing with a program to calculate prime numbers (a prime number is divisible only by itself and one).

```cpp
// Ex4_09.cpp
// Calculating primes
#include <iostream>
#include <iomanip>
using std::cout;
using std::endl;
using std::setw;

int main()
{
    const int MAX(100);             // Number of primes required
    long primes[MAX] = { 2,3,5 };   // First three primes defined
    long trial(5);                  // Candidate prime
    int count(3);                   // Count of primes found
    bool found(false);              // Indicates when a prime is found

    do
    {
        trial += 2;                 // Next value for checking
        found = false;              // Set found indicator

        for(int i = 0; i < count; i++)   // Try division by existing primes
        {
            found = (trial % *(primes + i)) == 0;// True for exact division
              if(found)                            // If division is exact
                break;                             // it's not a prime
        }
```

```
        if (!found)                          // We got one...
            *(primes + count++) = trial;  // ...so save it in primes array
    }while(count < MAX);

    // Output primes 5 to a line
    for(int i = 0; i < MAX; i++)
    {
        if(i % 5 == 0)                      // New line on 1st, and every 5th line
            cout << endl;
        cout << setw(10) << *(primes + i);
    }
    cout << endl;

    return 0;
}
```

code snippet Ex4_09.cpp

If you compile and execute this example, you should get the following output:

2	3	5	7	11
13	17	19	23	29
31	37	41	43	47
53	59	61	67	71
73	79	83	89	97
101	103	107	109	113
127	131	137	139	149
151	157	163	167	173
179	181	191	193	197
199	211	223	227	229
233	239	241	251	257
263	269	271	277	281
283	293	307	311	313
317	331	337	347	349
353	359	367	373	379
383	389	397	401	409
419	421	431	433	439
443	449	457	461	463
467	479	487	491	499
503	509	521	523	541

How It Works

You have the usual `#include` statements for the `iostream` header file for input and output, and for `iomanip`, because you will use a stream manipulator to set the field width for output.

You use the constant MAX to define the number of primes that you want the program to produce. The `primes` array, which stores the results, has the first three primes already defined to start the process off. All the work is done in two loops: the outer `do-while` loop, which picks the next value to be checked and adds the value to the `primes` array if it is prime, and the inner `for` loop that actually checks the value to see whether it's prime or not.

The algorithm in the `for` loop is very simple and is based on the fact that if a number is not a prime, it must be divisible by one of the primes found so far — all of which are less than the number in question because all numbers are either prime or a product of primes. In fact, only division by primes less than or equal to the square root of the number in question need to be checked, so this example isn't as efficient as it might be.

```
found = (trial % *(primes + i)) == 0;   // True for exact division
```

This statement sets the variable `found` to `true` if there's no remainder from dividing the value in `trial` by the current prime `*(primes+i)` (remember that this is equivalent to `primes[i]`), and to `0` otherwise. The `if` statement causes the `for` loop to be terminated if `found` has the value `true` because the candidate in `trial` can't be a prime in that case.

After the `for` loop ends (for whatever reason), it's necessary to decide whether or not the value in `trial` was prime. This is indicated by the value in the indicator variable `found`.

```
*(primes + count++) = trial;   // ...so save it in primes array
```

If `trial` *does* contain a prime, this statement stores the value in `primes[count]` and then increments `count` through the postfix increment operator.

After `MAX` number of primes have been found, they are output with a field width of 10 characters, 5 to a line, as a result of this statement:

```
if(i % 5 == 0)                  // New line on 1st, and every 5th line
    cout << endl;
```

This starts a new line when `i` has the values `0, 5, 10,` and so on.

TRY IT OUT   Counting Characters Revisited

To see how handling strings works in pointer notation, you could produce a version of the program you looked at earlier for counting the characters in a string:

```
// Ex4_10.cpp
// Counting string characters using a pointer
#include <iostream>
using std::cin;
using std::cout;
using std::endl;

int main()
{
    const int MAX(80);                 // Maximum array dimension
    char buffer[MAX];                  // Input buffer
    char* pbuffer(buffer);             // Pointer to array buffer

    cout << endl                       // Prompt for input
         << "Enter a string of less than "
```

```
                << MAX << " characters:"
                << endl;

    cin.getline(buffer, MAX, '\n');      // Read a string until \n

    while(*pbuffer)                      // Continue until \0
        pbuffer++;

    cout << endl
         << "The string \"" << buffer
         << "\" has " << pbuffer - buffer << " characters.";
    cout << endl;

    return 0;
}
```

code snippet Ex4_10.cpp

Here's an example of typical output from this example:

```
Enter a string of less than 80 characters:
The tigers of wrath are wiser than the horses of instruction.
The string "The tigers of wrath are wiser than the horses of
instruction." has 61 characters.
```

How It Works

Here the program operates using the pointer pbuffer rather than the array name buffer. You don't need the count variable because the pointer is incremented in the while loop until '\0' is found. When the '\0' character is found, pbuffer will contain the address of that position in the string. The count of the number of characters in the string entered is therefore the difference between the address stored in the pointer pbuffer, and the address of the beginning of the array denoted by buffer.

You could also have incremented the pointer in the loop by writing the loop like this:

```
    while(*pbuffer++);                      // Continue until \0
```

Now the loop contains no statements, only the test condition. This would work adequately, except for the fact that the pointer would be incremented after '\0' was encountered, so the address would be one more than the last position in the string. You would therefore need to express the count of the number of characters in the string as pbuffer-buffer-1.

Note that you can't use the array name here in the same way that you have used the pointer. The expression buffer++ is strictly illegal because you can't modify the address value that an array name represents. Even though you can use an array name in an expression as though it is a pointer, it isn't a pointer, because the address value that it represents is fixed.

Using Pointers with Multidimensional Arrays

Using a pointer to store the address of a one-dimensional array is relatively straightforward, but with multidimensional arrays, things can get a little complicated. If you don't intend to use pointers with multidimensional arrays, you can skip this section, as it's a little obscure; however, if you have previous experience with C, this section is worth a glance.

If you have to use a pointer with multidimensional arrays, you need to keep clear in your mind what is happening. By way of illustration, you can use an array beans, declared as follows:

```
double beans[3][4];
```

You can declare and assign a value to the pointer pbeans, as follows:

```
double* pbeans;
pbeans = &beans[0][0];
```

Here you are setting the pointer to the address of the first element of the array, which is of type double. You could also set the pointer to the address of the first row in the array with the statement:

```
pbeans = beans[0];
```

This is equivalent to using the name of a one-dimensional array, which is replaced by its address. You used this in the earlier discussion; however, because beans is a two-dimensional array, you cannot set an address in the pointer with the following statement:

```
pbeans = beans;                // Will cause an error!!
```

The problem is one of type. The type of the pointer you have defined is double*, but the array is of type double[3][4]. A pointer to store the address of this array must be of type double*[4]. C++ associates the dimensions of the array with its type, and the statement above is only legal if the pointer has been declared with the dimension required. This is done with a slightly more complicated notation than you have seen so far:

```
double (*pbeans)[4];
```

The parentheses here are essential; otherwise, you would be declaring an array of pointers. Now the previous statement is legal, but this pointer can only be used to store addresses of an array with the dimensions shown.

Pointer Notation with Multidimensional Arrays

You can use pointer notation with an array name to reference elements of the array. You can reference each element of the array beans that you declared earlier, which had three rows of four elements, in two ways:

➤ Using the array name with two index values

➤ Using the array name in pointer notation

Therefore, the following two statements are equivalent:

```
beans[i][j]
*(*(beans + i) + j)
```

Let's look at how these work. The first line uses normal array indexing to refer to the element with offset j in row i of the array.

You can determine the meaning of the second line by working from the inside outwards. beans refers to the address of the first row of the array, so beans+i refers to row i of the array. The expression *(beans+i) is the address of the first element of row i, so *(beans+i)+j is the address of the element in row i with offset j. The whole expression therefore refers to the value of that element.

If you really want to be obscure — and it isn't recommended that you should be — the following two statements, where you have mixed array and pointer notation, are also legal references to the same element of the array:

```
*(beans[i] + j)
(*(beans + i))[j]
```

There is yet another aspect to the use of pointers that is really the most important of all: the ability to allocate memory for variables dynamically. You'll look into that next.

DYNAMIC MEMORY ALLOCATION

Working with a fixed set of variables in a program can be very restrictive. You will often want to decide the amount of space to be allocated for storing different types of variables at execution time, depending on the input data for the program. Any program that involves reading and processing a number of data items that is not known in advance can take advantage of the ability to allocate memory to store the data at run time. For example, if you need to implement a program to store information about the students in a class, the number of students is not fixed, and their names will vary in length, so to deal with the data most efficiently, you'll want to allocate space dynamically at execution time.

Obviously, because dynamically allocated variables can't have been defined at compile time, they can't be named in your source program. When they are created, they are identified by their address in memory, which is contained within a pointer. With the power of pointers, and the dynamic memory management tools in Visual C++ 2010, writing your programs to have this kind of flexibility is quick and easy.

The Free Store, Alias the Heap

In most instances, when your program is executed, there is unused memory in your computer. This unused memory is called the **heap** in C++, or sometimes the **free store**. You can allocate space within the free store for a new variable of a given type using a special operator in C++ that returns the address of the space allocated. This operator is new, and it's complemented by the operator delete, which de-allocates memory previously allocated by new.

You can allocate space in the free store for some variables in one part of a program, and then release the allocated space and return it to the free store after you have finished with it. This makes the memory available for reuse by other dynamically allocated variables, later in the same program. This can be a powerful technique; it enables you to use memory very efficiently, and in many cases, it results in programs that can handle much larger problems, involving considerably more data than otherwise might be possible.

The new and delete Operators

Suppose that you need space for a `double` variable. You can define a pointer to type `double` and then request that the memory be allocated at execution time. You can do this using the operator `new` with the following statements:

```
double* pvalue(nullptr);
pvalue = new double;        // Request memory for a double variable
```

This is a good moment to recall that *all pointers should be initialized*. Using memory dynamically typically involves a number of pointers floating around, so it's important that they should not contain spurious values. You should try to arrange for a pointer not containing a legal address value to be set to `nullptr`.

The `new` operator in the second line of code above should return the address of the memory in the free store allocated to a `double` variable, and this address is stored in the pointer `pvalue`. You can then use this pointer to reference the variable using the indirection operator, as you have seen. For example:

```
*pvalue = 9999.0;
```

Of course, the memory may not have been allocated because the free store had been used up, or because the free store is fragmented by previous usage — meaning that there isn't a sufficient number of contiguous bytes to accommodate the variable for which you want to obtain space. You don't have to worry too much about this, however. The `new` operator will *throw an exception* if the memory cannot be allocated for any reason, which terminates your program. Exceptions are a mechanism for signaling errors in C++; you learn about these in Chapter 6.

You can also initialize a variable created by `new`. Taking the example of the `double` variable that was allocated by `new` and the address stored in `pvalue`, you could have set the value to 999.0, as it was created with this statement:

```
pvalue = new double(999.0);    // Allocate a double and initialize it
```

Of course, you could create the pointer and initialize it in a single statement, like this:

```
double* pvalue(new double(999.0));
```

When you no longer need a variable that has been dynamically allocated, you can free up the memory that it occupies in the free store with the `delete` operator:

```
delete pvalue;                  // Release memory pointed to by pvalue
```

This ensures that the memory can be used subsequently by another variable. If you don't use `delete`, and subsequently store a different address value in the pointer `pvalue`, it will be impossible to free up the memory, or to use the variable that it contains, because access to the address is lost. In this situation, you have what is referred to as a memory leak, especially when it recurs in your program.

Allocating Memory Dynamically for Arrays

Allocating memory for an array dynamically is very straightforward. If you wanted to allocate an array of type `char`, assuming `pstr` is a pointer to `char`, you could write the following statement:

```
pstr = new char[20];     // Allocate a string of twenty characters
```

This allocates space for a `char` array of 20 characters and stores its address in `pstr`.

To remove the array that you have just created in the free store, you must use the `delete` operator. The statement would look like this:

```
delete [] pstr;          // Delete array pointed to by pstr
```

Note the use of square brackets to indicate that what you are deleting is an array. When removing arrays from the free store, you should always include the square brackets, or the results will be unpredictable. Note also that you do not specify any dimensions here, simply `[]`.

Of course, the `pstr` pointer now contains the address of memory that may already have been allocated for some other purpose, so it certainly should not be used. When you use the `delete` operator to discard some memory that you previously allocated, you should always reset the pointer, like this:

```
pstr = nullptr;
```

This ensures that you do not attempt to access the memory that has been deleted.

TRY IT OUT   Using Free Store

You can see how dynamic memory allocation works in practice by rewriting the program that calculates an arbitrary number of primes, this time using memory in the free store to store the primes.

```
// Ex4_11.cpp
// Calculating primes using dynamic memory allocation
#include <iostream>
#include <iomanip>
using std::cin;
using std::cout;
using std::endl;
using std::setw;

int main()
{
    long* pprime(nullptr);              // Pointer to prime array
```

```
long trial(5);                    // Candidate prime
int count(3);                     // Count of primes found
int found(0);                     // Indicates when a prime is found
int max(0);                       // Number of primes required

cout << endl
     << "Enter the number of primes you would like (at least 4): ";
cin >> max;                       // Number of primes required

if(max < 4)                       // Test the user input, if less than 4
   max = 4;                       // ensure it is at least 4

pprime = new long[max];

*pprime = 2;                      // Insert three
*(pprime + 1) = 3;                // seed primes
*(pprime + 2) = 5;

do
{
   trial += 2;                              // Next value for checking
   found = 0;                               // Set found indicator

   for(int i = 0; i < count; i++)           // Division by existing primes
   {
      found =(trial % *(pprime + i)) == 0;// True for exact division
      if(found)                             // If division is exact
         break;                             // it's not a prime
   }

   if (found == 0)                  // We got one...
      *(pprime + count++) = trial;  // ...so save it in primes array
} while(count < max);

// Output primes 5 to a line
for(int i = 0; i < max; i++)
{
   if(i % 5 == 0)                   // New line on 1st, and every 5th line
      cout << endl;
   cout << setw(10) << *(pprime + i);
}

delete [] pprime;                            // Free up memory
pprime = nullptr;                            // and reset the pointer
cout << endl;
return 0;
}
```

code snippet Ex4_11.cpp

Here's an example of the output from this program:

```
Enter the number of primes you would like (at least 4): 20
      2          3          5          7         11
     13         17         19         23         29
     31         37         41         43         47
     53         59         61         67         71
```

How It Works

In fact, the program is similar to the previous version. After receiving the number of primes required in the int variable max, you allocate an array of that size in the free store using the operator new. Note that you have made sure that max can be no less than 4. This is because the program requires space to be allocated in the free store for at least the three seed primes, plus one new one. You specify the size of the array that is required by putting the variable max between the square brackets following the array type specification:

```
pprime = new long[max];
```

You store the address of the memory area that is allocated by new in the pointer pprime. The program would terminate at this point if the memory could not be allocated.

After the memory that stores the prime values has been successfully allocated, the first three array elements are set to the values of the first three primes:

```
*pprime = 2;                    // Insert three
*(pprime + 1) = 3;              // seed primes
*(pprime + 2) = 5;
```

You are using the dereference operator to access the first three elements of the array. As you saw earlier, the parentheses in the second and third statements are there because the precedence of the * operators is higher than that of the + operator.

You can't specify initial values for elements of an array that you allocate dynamically. You have to use explicit assignment statements if you want to set initial values for elements of the array.

The calculation of the prime numbers is exactly as before; the only change is that the name of the pointer you have here, pprime, is substituted for the array name, primes, that you used in the previous version. Equally, the output process is the same. Acquiring space dynamically is really not a problem at all. After it has been allocated, it in no way affects how the computation is written.

After you finish with the array, you remove it from the free store using the delete operator, remembering to include the square brackets to indicate that it is an array you are deleting.

```
delete [] pprime;               // Free up memory
```

Although it's not essential here, you also reset the pointer:

```
pprime = nullptr;               // and reset the pointer
```

All memory allocated in the free store is released when your program ends, but it is good to get into the habit of resetting pointers to nullptr when they no longer point to valid memory areas.

Dynamic Allocation of Multidimensional Arrays

Allocating memory in the free store for a multidimensional array involves using the new operator in a slightly more complicated form than is used for a one-dimensional array. Assuming that you have already declared the pointer pbeans appropriately, to obtain the space for the array beans[3][4] that you used earlier in this chapter, you could write this:

```
pbeans = new double [3][4];            // Allocate memory for a 3x4 array
```

You just specify both array dimensions between square brackets after the type name for the array elements.

Allocating space for a three-dimensional array simply requires that you specify the extra dimension with new, as in this example:

```
pBigArray = new double [5][10][10]; // Allocate memory for a 5x10x10 array
```

However many dimensions there are in the array that has been created, to destroy it and release the memory back to the free store, you write the following:

```
delete [] pBigArray;                   // Release memory for array
pBigArray = nullptr;
```

You always use just one pair of square brackets following the delete operator, regardless of the dimensionality of the array with which you are working.

You have already seen that you can use a variable as the specification of the dimension of a one-dimensional array to be allocated by new. This extends to two or more dimensions, but with the restriction that only the leftmost dimension may be specified by a variable. All the other dimensions must be constants or constant expressions. So, you could write this:

```
pBigArray = new double[max][10][10];
```

where max is a variable; however, specifying a variable for any dimension other than the left-most causes an error message to be generated by the compiler.

USING REFERENCES

A *reference* appears to be similar to a pointer in many respects, which is why I'm introducing it here, but it really isn't the same thing at all. The real importance of references becomes apparent only when you get to explore their use with functions, particularly in the context of object-oriented programming. Don't be misled by their simplicity and what might seem to be a trivial concept. As you will see later, references provide some extraordinarily powerful facilities, and in some contexts enable you to achieve results that would be impossible without them.

What Is a Reference?

There are two kinds of references: **lvalue references** and **rvalue references**. Essentially, a reference is a name that can be used as an alias for something else.

An lvalue reference is an alias for another variable; it is called an lvalue reference because it refers to a persistent storage location that can appear on the left of an assignment operation. Because an lvalue reference is an alias and not a pointer, the variable for which it is an alias has to be specified when the reference is declared; unlike a pointer, a reference cannot be altered to represent another variable.

An rvalue reference can be used as an alias for a variable, just like an lvalue reference, but it differs from an lvalue reference in that it can also reference an rvalue, which is a temporary value that is essentially transient.

Declaring and Initializing Lvalue References

Suppose that you have declared a variable as follows:

```
long number(0L);
```

You can declare an lvalue reference for this variable using the following declaration statement:

```
long& rnumber(number);      // Declare a reference to variable number
```

The ampersand following the type name `long` and preceding the variable name `rnumber`, indicates that an lvalue reference is being declared, and that the variable name it represents, `number`, is specified as the initializing value following the equals sign; therefore, the variable `rnumber` is of type 'reference to `long`'. You can now use the reference in place of the original variable name. For example, this statement,

```
rnumber += 10L;
```

has the effect of incrementing the variable `number` by 10.

Note that you cannot write:

```
int& refData = 5;          // Will not compile!
```

The literal 5 is constant and cannot be changed. To protect the integrity of constant values, you must use a `const` reference:

```
const int & refData = 5;    // OK
```

Now you can access the literal 5 through the `refData` reference. Because you declare `refData` as `const`, it cannot be used to change the value it references.

Let's contrast the lvalue reference `rnumber` defined above with the pointer `pnumber`, declared in this statement:

```
long* pnumber(&number);       // Initialize a pointer with an address
```

This declares the pointer pnumber, and initializes it with the address of the variable number. This then allows the variable number to be incremented with a statement such as:

```
*pnumber += 10L;                    // Increment number through a pointer
```

There is a significant distinction between using a pointer and using a reference. The pointer needs to be dereferenced, and whatever address it contains is used to access the variable to participate in the expression. With a reference, there is no need for de-referencing. In some ways, a reference is like a pointer that has already been dereferenced, although it can't be changed to reference something else. An lvalue reference is the complete equivalent of the variable for which it is a reference.

Defining and Initializing Rvalue References

You specify an rvalue reference type using two ampersands following the type name. Here's an example:

```
int x(5);
int&& rx = x;
```

The first statement defines the variable x with the initial value 5, and the second statement defines an rvalue reference, rx, that references x. This shows that you can initialize an rvalue reference with an lvalue so it that can work just like an lvalue reference. You can also write this as:

```
int&& rExpr = 2*x + 3;
```

Here, the rvalue reference is initialized to reference the result of evaluating the expression 2*x+3, which is a temporary value — an rvalue. You cannot do this with an lvalue reference. Is this useful? In this case, no; but in a different context, it is very useful.

While the code fragments relating to references illustrate how lvalue and rvalue reference variables *can* be defined and initialized, this is not how they are typically used. The primary application for both types of references is in defining functions where they can be of immense value; you'll learn more about this later in the book, starting in Chapter 5.

NATIVE C++ LIBRARY FUNCTIONS FOR STRINGS

The standard library provides the cstring header that contains functions that operate on null-terminated strings. These are a set of functions that are specified to the C++ standard. There are also alternatives to some of these functions that are not standard, but which provide a more secure implementation of the function than the original versions. In general, I'll mention both where they exist in the cstring header, but I'll use the more secure versions in examples. Let's explore some of the most useful functions provided by the cstring header.

NOTE *The* `string` *standard header for native C++ defines the* `string` *and* `wstring` *classes that represent character strings. The* `string` *class represents strings of characters of type* `char` *and the* `wstring` *class represents strings of characters of type* `wchar_t`. *Both are defined in the* `string` *header as template classes that are instances of the* `basic_string<T>` *class template. A class template is a parameterized class (with parameter* `T` *in this case) that you can use to create new classes to handle different types of data. I won't be discussing templates and the* `string` *and* `wstring` *classes until Chapter 8, but I thought I'd mention them here because they have some features in common with the functions provided by the* `String` *type that you'll be using in C++/CLI programs later in this chapter. If you are really interested to see how they compare, you could always have a quick look at the section in Chapter 8 that has the same title as this section. It should be reasonably easy to follow at this point, even without knowledge of templates and classes.*

Finding the Length of a Null-Terminated String

The `strlen()` function returns the length of the argument string of type `char*` as a value of type `size_t`. The type `size_t` is an implementation-defined type that corresponds to an unsigned integer type that is used generally to represent the lengths of sequences of various kinds. The `wcslen()` function does the same thing for strings of type `wchar_t*`.

Here's how you use the `strlen()` function:

```
char * str("A miss is as good as a mile.");
cout << "The string contains " <<  strlen(str) << " characters." << endl;
```

The output produced when this fragment executes is:

```
The string contains 28 characters.
```

As you can see from the output, the length value that is returned does not include the terminating null. It is important to keep this in mind, especially when you are using the length of one string to create another string of the same length.

Both `strlen()` and `wcslen()` find the length by looking for the null at the end. If there isn't one, the functions will happily continue beyond the end of the string, checking throughout memory in the hope of finding a null. For this reason, these functions represent a security risk when you are working with data from an untrusted external source. In this situation you can use the `strnlen()` and `wcsnlen()` functions, both of which require a second argument that specifies the length of the buffer in which the string specified by the first argument is stored.

Joining Null-Terminated Strings

The `strcat()` function concatenates two null-terminated strings. The string specified by the second argument is appended to the string specified by the first argument. Here's an example of how you might use it:

```
char str1[30]= "Many hands";
char* str2(" make light work.");
strcat(str1, str2);
cout << str1 << endl;
```

Note that the first string is stored in the array `str1` of 30 characters, which is far more than the length of the initializing string, "Many hands". The string specified by the first argument must have sufficient space to accommodate the two strings when they are joined. If it doesn't, disaster will surely result because the function will then try to overwrite the area beyond the end of the first string.

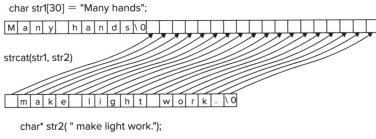

FIGURE 4-9

As Figure 4-9 shows, the first character of the string specified by the second argument overwrites the terminating null of the first argument, and all the remaining characters of the second string are copied across, including the terminating null. Thus, the output from the fragment will be:

```
Many hands make light work.
```

The `strcat()` function returns the pointer that is the first argument, so you could combine the last two statements in the fragment above into one:

```
cout << strcat(str1, str2) << endl;
```

The `wcscat()` function concatenates wide-character strings, but otherwise works exactly the same as the `strcat()` function.

With the `strncat()` function you can append part of one null-terminated string to another. The first two arguments are the destination and source strings respectively, and the third argument is a count of the number of characters from the source string that are to be appended. With the strings as defined in Figure 4-9, here's an example of using `strncat()`:

```
cout << strncat(str1, str2, 11) << endl;
```

After executing this statement, str1 contains the string "Many hands make light". The operation appends 11 characters from str2 to str1, overwriting the terminating '\0' in str1, and then appends a final '\0' character. The wcsncat() provides the same capability as strncat() but for wide-character strings.

All the functions for concatenating strings that I have introduced up to now rely on finding the terminating nulls in the strings to work properly, so they are also insecure when it comes to dealing with untrusted data. The strcat_s(), wcscat_s(), strncat_s(), and wcsncat_s() functions in <cstring> provide secure alternatives. Just to take one example, here's how you could use strcat_s() to carry out the operation shown in Figure 4-9:

```
const size_t count = 30;
char str1[count]= "Many hands";
char* str2(" make light work.");

errno_t error = strcat_s(str1, count, str2);

if(error == 0)
  cout << " Strings joined successfully." << endl;

else if(error == EINVAL)
  cout << "Error! Source or destination string is NULL." << endl;

else if(error == ERANGE)
  cout << " Error! Destination string too small." << endl;
```

For convenience, I defined the array size as the constant count. The first argument to strcat_s() is the destination string to which the source string specified by the third argument is to be appended. The second argument is the total number of bytes available at the destination. The function returns an integer value of type errno_t to indicate how things went. The error return value will be zero if the operation is successful, EINVAL if the source or destination is NULLPTR, or ERANGE if the destination length is too small. In the event of an error occurring, the destination will be left unchanged. The error code values EINVAL and ERANGE are defined in the cerrno header, so you need an #include directive for this, as well as for cstring, to compile the fragment above correctly. Of course, you are not obliged to test for the error codes that the function might return, and if you don't, you won't need the #include directive for cerrno.

Copying Null-Terminated Strings

The standard library function strcpy() copies a string from a source location to a destination. The first argument is a pointer to the destination location, and the second argument is a pointer to the source string; both arguments are of type char*. The function returns a pointer to the destination string. Here's an example of how you use it:

```
const size_t LENGTH = 22;
const char source[LENGTH] ="The more the merrier!";
char destination[LENGTH];
cout << "The destination string is: " << strcpy(destination, source)
     << endl;
```

The source string and the destination buffer can each accommodate a string containing 21 characters plus the terminating null. You copy the source string to destination in the last statement. The output statement makes use of the fact that the strcpy() function returns a pointer to the destination string, so the output is:

```
The destination string is: The more the merrier!
```

You must ensure that the destination string has sufficient space to accommodate the source string. If you don't, something will get overwritten in memory, and disaster is the likely result.

The strcpy_s() function is a more secure version of strcpy(). It requires an extra argument between the destination and source arguments that specifies the size of the destination string buffer. The strcpy_s() function returns an integer value of type errno_t that indicates whether an error occurred. Here's how you might use this function:

```
const size_t LENGTH(22);
const char source[LENGTH] ="The more the merrier!";
char destination[LENGTH];

errno_t error = strcpy_s(destination, LENGTH, source);

if(error == EINVAL)
cout << "Error. The source or the destination is NULLPTR." << endl;
else if(error == ERANGE)
  cout << "Error. The destination is too small." << endl;
else
  cout << "The destination string is: " << destination << endl;
```

You need to include the cstring and cerrno headers for this to compile. The strcpy_s() function verifies that the source and destination are not NULLPTR and that the destination buffer has sufficient space to accommodate the source string. When either or both the source and destination are NULLPTR, the function returns the value EINVAL. If the destination buffer is too small, the function returns ERANGE. If the copy is successful, the return value is 0.

You have analogous wide-character versions of these copy functions; these are wcscpy() and wcscpy_s().

Comparing Null-Terminated Strings

The strcmp() function compares two null-terminated strings that you specify by arguments that are pointers of type char*. The function returns a value of type int that is less than zero, zero, or greater than 0, depending on whether the string pointed to by the first argument is less than, equal to, or greater than the string pointed to by the second argument. Here's an example:

```
char* str1("Jill");
char* str2("Jacko");
int result = strcmp(str1, str2);
if(result < 0)
  cout << str1 << " is less than " << str2 << '.' << endl;
else if(0 == result)
```

```
    cout << str1 << " is equal to " << str2 << '.' << endl;
  else
    cout << str1 << " is greater than " << str2 << '.' << endl;
```

This fragment compares the strings str1 and str2, and uses the value returned by strcmp() to execute one of three possible output statements.

Comparing the strings works by comparing the character codes of successive pairs of corresponding characters. The first pair of characters that are different determines whether the first string is less than or greater than the second string. Two strings are equal if they contain the same number of characters, and the corresponding characters are identical. Of course, the output is:

```
Jill is greater than Jacko.
```

The wcscmp() function is the wide-character string equivalent of strcmp().

Searching Null-Terminated Strings

The strspn() function searches a string for the first character that is *not* contained in a given set and returns the index of the character found. The first argument is a pointer to the string to be searched, and the second argument is a pointer to a string containing the set of characters. You could search for the first character that is not a vowel like this:

```
char* str = "I agree with everything.";
char* vowels = "aeiouAEIOU ";
size_t index = strspn(str, vowels);
cout << "The first character that is not a vowel is '" << str[index]
     << "' at position " << index << endl;
```

This searches str for the first character that is not contained in vowels. Note that I included a space in the vowels set, so a space will be ignored so far as the search is concerned. The output from this fragment is:

```
The first character that is not a vowel is 'g' at position 3
```

Another way of looking at the value the strspn() function returns is that it represents the length of the substring, starting from the first character in the first argument string that consists entirely of characters in the second argument string. In the example it is the first three characters "I a".

The wcsspn() function is the wide-character string equivalent of strspn().

The strstr() function returns a pointer to the position in the first argument of a substring specified by the second argument. Here's a fragment that shows this in action:

```
char* str = "I agree with everything.";
char* substring = "ever";
char* psubstr = strstr(str, substring);

if(!psubstr)
  cout << "\"" << substring << "\" not found in \"" << str << "\"" << endl;
else
  cout << "The first occurrence of \"" << substring
       << "\" in \"" << str << "\" is at position "
       << psubstr-str << endl;
```

The third statement calls the `strstr()` function to search `str` for the first occurrence of the substring. The function returns a pointer to the position of the substring if it is found, or NULL when it is not found. The `if` statement outputs a message, depending on whether or not `substring` was found in `str`. The expression `psubstr-str` gives the index position of the first character in the substring. The output produced by this fragment is:

```
The first occurrence of "ever" in "I agree with everything." is at position 13
```

TRY IT OUT   **Searching Null-Terminated Strings**

This example searches a given string to determine the number of occurrences of a given substring.

Available for download on Wrox.com

```cpp
// Ex4_12.cpp
// Searching a string
#include <iostream>
#include <cstring>
using std::cout;
using std::endl;
using std::strlen;
using std::strstr;

int main()
{
  char* str("Smith, where Jones had had \"had had\" had had \"had\"."
                        "\n\"Had had\" had had the examiners' approval.");
  char* word("had");
  cout << "The string to be searched is: "
       << endl << str << endl;

  int count(0);                   // Number of occurrences of word in str
  char* pstr(str);                // Pointer to search start position
  char* found(nullptr);           // Pointer to occurrence of word in str

  while(true)
  {
    found = strstr(pstr, word);
    if(!found)
      break;
    ++count;
    pstr = found+strlen(word);    // Set next search start as 1 past the word found
  }

  cout << "\"" << word << "\" was found "
       << count << " times in the string." << endl;
  return 0;
}
```

code snippet Ex4_12.cpp

The output from this example is:

```
The string to be searched is: Smith, where Jones had had "had had" had had "had".
"Had had" had had the examiners' approval.
"had" was found 10 times in the string.
```

How It Works

All the action takes place in the indefinite `while` loop:

```
while(true)
{
  found = strstr(pstr, word);
  if(!found)
    break;
  ++count;
  pstr = found+strlen(word);      // Set next search start as 1 past the word found
}
```

The first step is to search the string for `word` starting at position `pstr`, which initially is the beginning of the string. You store the address that `strstr()` returns in `found`; this will be `nullptr` if `word` was not found in `pstr`, so the `if` statement ends the loop in that case.

If `found` is not `nullptr`, you increment the count of the number of occurrences of `word`, and update the `pstr` pointer so that it points to one character past the `word` instance that was found in `pstr`. This will be the starting point for the search on the next loop iteration.

From the output, you can see that `word` was found ten times in `str`. Of course, "Had" doesn't count because it starts with an uppercase letter.

C++/CLI PROGRAMMING

Dynamic memory allocation works differently with the CLR, and the CLR maintains its own memory heap that is independent of the native C++ heap. The CLR automatically deletes memory that you allocate on the CLR heap when it is no longer required, so you do not need to use the `delete` operator in a program written for the CLR. The CLR may also compact heap memory to avoid fragmentation from time to time. Thus, at a stroke, the CLR greatly reduces the possibility of memory leaks and memory fragmentation. The management and clean-up of the heap that the CLR provides is described as **garbage collection** — the garbage being your discarded variables and objects. The heap that is managed by the CLR is called the **garbage-collected heap**. You use the `gcnew` operator instead of `new` to allocate memory in a C++/CLI, program; the 'gc' prefix is a cue to the fact that you are allocating memory on the garbage-collected heap, and not the native C++ heap, where all the housekeeping is down to you.

The CLR garbage collector is able to delete objects and release the memory that they occupy when they are no longer required. An obvious question arises: How does the garbage collector know when an object on the heap is no longer required? The answer is quite simple. The CLR keeps track of every variable that references each object in the heap; when there are no variables containing the address of a given object, the object can no longer be referred to in a program, and therefore can be deleted.

Because the garbage collection process can involve compacting the heap memory area to remove fragmented unused blocks of memory, the addresses of data items that you have stored in the heap can change. Consequently, you cannot use ordinary native C++ pointers with the garbage-collected heap, because if the location of the data that is pointed to changes, the pointer will no longer be valid. You need a way to access objects on the heap that enables the address to be updated when the garbage collector relocates the data item in the heap. This capability is provided in two ways: by a **tracking handle** (also referred to simply as a **handle**) that is analogous to a pointer in native C++, and by a tracking reference that provides the equivalent of a native C++ reference in a CLR program.

Tracking Handles

A tracking handle has similarities to a native C++ pointer, but there are significant differences, too. A tracking handle does store an address, which is automatically updated by the garbage collector if the object it references is moved during compaction of the heap. However, you cannot perform address arithmetic with a tracking handle as you can with a native pointer, and casting a tracking handle is not permitted.

You use tracking handles to reference objects created in the CLR heap. All objects that are reference class types are stored in the heap; therefore, the variables you create to refer to such objects must be tracking handles. For instance, the String class type is a reference class type, so variables that reference String objects must be tracking handles. The memory for value class types is allocated on the stack by default, but you can choose to store values in the heap by using the gcnew operator. This is also a good time to remind you of a point I mentioned in Chapter 2 — that variables allocated on the CLR heap, which includes all CLR reference types, cannot be declared at global scope.

Creating Tracking Handles

You specify a handle for a type by placing the ^ symbol (commonly referred to as a 'hat') following the type name. For example, here's how you could declare a tracking handle with the name proverb that can store the address of a String object:

```
String^ proverb;
```

This defines the variable proverb to be a tracking handle of type String^. When you declare a handle it is automatically initialized with null, so it will not refer to anything. To explicitly set a handle to null you use the keyword nullptr like this:

```
proverb = nullptr;                    // Set handle to null
```

Note that you cannot use 0 to represent null here, as you can with native pointers (even though it is now not recommended). If you initialize a tracking handle with 0, the value 0 is converted to the type of object that the handle references, and the address of this new object is stored in the handle.

 WARNING *The* nullptr *keyword in C++/CLI has a different meaning from the* nullptr *keyword in native C++. This doesn't matter, as long as you are not mixing native C++ code that uses native pointers with C++/CLI code. If you are, you must use* __nullptr *as the null pointer value for your native C++ pointers and* nullptr *for the value of handles in the C++/CLI code. Although you can mix native C++ and C++/CLI code, it is best avoided as far as possible.*

Of course, you can initialize a handle explicitly when you declare it. Here's another statement that defines a handle to a `String` object:

```
String^ saying(L"I used to think I was indecisive but now I'm not so sure");
```

This statement creates a `String` object on the heap that contains the string between the parentheses; the address of the new object is stored in `saying`. Note that the type of the string literal is `const wchar_t*`, not type `String`. The way the `String` class has been defined makes it possible for such a literal to be used to create an object of type `String`.

Here's how you could create a handle for a value type:

```
int^ value(99);
```

This statement creates the handle `value` of type `int^`; the value it points to on the heap is initialized to 99. Remember that you have created a kind of pointer, so `value` cannot participate in arithmetic operations without dereferencing it. To dereference a tracking handle, you use the `*` operator in the same way as you do for native pointers. For example, here is a statement that uses the value pointed to by a tracking handle in an arithmetic operation:

```
int result(2*(*value)+15);
```

The expression `*value` between the parentheses accesses the integer stored at the address held in the tracking handle, so the variable `result` is set to 213.

Note that when you use a handle on the left of an assignment, there's no need to explicitly dereference it to store a result; the compiler takes care of it for you. For example:

```
int^ result(nullptr);
result = 2*(*value)+15;
```

Here you first create the handle `result`, initialized to null. Because `result` appears on the left of an assignment in the next statement, and the right-hand side produces a value, the compiler is able to determine that `result` must be dereferenced to store the value. Of course, you could write it explicitly like this:

```
*result = 2*(*value)+15;
```

Here you explicitly dereference the handle on the left of the assignment.

CLR Arrays

CLR arrays are different from the native C++ arrays. Memory for a CLR array is allocated on the garbage-collected heap, but there's more to it than that. CLR arrays have built-in functionality that you don't get with native C++ arrays, as you'll see shortly. You specify an array variable type using the keyword `array`. You must also specify the type for the array elements between angled brackets following the `array` keyword. The general form for specifying the type of variable to reference a one-dimensional array is `array<element_type>^`. Because a CLR array is created on the heap, an array variable is always a tracking handle. Here's an example of a declaration for an array variable:

```
array<int>^ data;
```

The array variable, `data`, that you create here can store a reference to any one-dimensional array of elements of type `int`.

You can create a CLR array using the `gcnew` operator at the same time that you declare the array variable:

```
array<int>^ data = gcnew array<int>(100);   // Create an array to store 100 integers
```

This statement creates a one-dimensional array with the name `data`. Note that an array variable is a tracking handle, so you must not forget the hat following the element type specification between the angled brackets. The number of elements appears between parentheses following the array type specification, so this array contains 100 elements, each of which can store a value of type `int`. Of course, you can also use functional notation to initialize the variable `data`:

```
array<int>^ data(gcnew array<int>(100));    // Create an array to store 100 integers
```

Just like native C++ arrays, CLR array elements are indexed from zero, so you could set values for the elements in the `data` array like this:

```
for(int i = 0 ; i<100 ; i++)
  data[i] = 2*(i+1);
```

This loop sets the values of the elements to 2, 4, 6, and so on up to 200. Elements in a CLR array are objects; here you are storing objects of type `Int32` in the array. Of course, these behave like ordinary integers in arithmetic expressions, so the fact that they are objects is transparent in such situations.

The number of elements appears in the loop control expression as a literal value. It would be better to use the `Length` property of the array that records the number of elements, like this:

```
for(int i = 0 ; i < data->Length ; i++)
  data[i] = 2*(i+1);
```

To access the `Length` property, you use the `->` operator, because `data` is a tracking handle and works like a pointer. The `Length` property records the number of elements in the array as a 32-bit integer value. If you need it, you can get the array length as a 64-bit value through the `LongLength` property.

You can also use the `for each` loop to iterate over all the elements in an array:

```
array<int>^ values = { 3, 5, 6, 8, 6};
for each(int item in values)
{
  item = 2*item + 1;
  Console::Write("{0,5}",item);
}
```

The first statement demonstrates that you can initialize an array handle with an array defined by a set of values. The size of the array is determined by the number of initial values between the braces, in this case five, and the values are assigned to the elements in sequence. Thus the handle `values` will reference an array of 5 integers where the elements have the values 3, 5, 6, 8 and 6. Within the loop, `item` references each of the elements in the `values` array in turn. The first statement in the body of the loop stores twice the current element's value plus 1 in `item`. The second statement in the loop outputs the new value, right-justified in a field width of five characters; the output produced by this code fragment is:

```
    7   11   13   17   13
```

It is easy to get the wrong idea about what is going on here. The `for each` loop above does not change the elements in the `values` array. `item` is a variable that accesses the value of each array element in turn; it does not reference the array elements themselves.

An array variable can store the address of any array of the same rank (the rank being the number of dimensions, which in the case of the `data` array is 1) and element type. For example:

```
data = gcnew array<int>(45);
```

This statement creates a new one-dimensional array of 45 elements of type `int` and stores its address in `data`. The original array referenced by the handle, `data`, is discarded.

Of course, the elements in an array can be of any type, so you can easily create an array of strings:

```
array<String^>^ names = { "Jack", "Jane", "Joe", "Jessica", "Jim", "Joanna"};
```

The elements of this array are initialized with the strings that appear between the braces, and the number of strings between the braces determines the number of elements in the array. `String` objects are created on the CLR heap, so each element in the array is a tracking handle of type `String^`.

If you declare the array variable without initializing it and then want it to reference an array you create subsequently, you must explicitly create the array in order to use a list of initial values. Here's an example:

```
array<String^>^ names;                  // Declare the array variable
names = gcnew array<String^>{ "Jack", "Jane", "Joe", "Jessica", "Jim", "Joanna"};
```

The first statement creates the array variable `names`, which will be initialized with `nullptr` by default. The second statement creates an array of elements of type `String^` and initializes it with handles to the strings between the braces. Without the explicit `gcnew` definition the statement will not compile.

You can use the static `Clear()` function that is defined in the `Array` class to set any sequence of numeric elements in an array to zero. You call a static function using the class name. You'll learn more about such functions when you explore classes in detail. Here's an example of how you could use the `Clear()` function to clear an array of elements of type `double`:

```
Array::Clear(samples, 0, samples->Length);          // Set all elements to zero
```

The first argument to `Clear()` is the array that is to be cleared, the second argument is the index for the first element to be cleared, and the third argument is the number of elements to be cleared. Thus, this example sets all the elements of the `samples` array to 0.0. If you apply the `Clear()` function to an array of tracking handles such as `String^`, the elements are set to `nullptr` and if you apply it to an array of `bool` elements they are set to `false`.

It's time to let a CLR array loose in an example.

TRY IT OUT   Using a CLR Array

In this example, you generate an array containing random values and then find the maximum value. Here's the code:

```cpp
// Ex4_13.cpp : main project file.
// Using a CLR array
#include "stdafx.h"

using namespace System;

int main(array<System::String ^> ^args)
{
  array<double>^ samples = gcnew array<double>(50);

  // Generate random element values
  Random^ generator = gcnew Random;
  for(int i = 0 ; i< samples->Length ; i++)
    samples[i] = 100.0*generator->NextDouble();

  // Output the samples
  Console::WriteLine(L"The array contains the following values:");
  for(int i = 0 ; i< samples->Length ; i++)
  {
    Console::Write(L"{0,10:F2}", samples[i]);
    if((i+1)%5 == 0)
      Console::WriteLine();
  }

  // Find the maximum value
  double max(0);
  for each(double sample in samples)
    if(max < sample)
      max = sample;

  Console::WriteLine(L"The maximum value in the array is {0:F2}", max);
  return 0;
}
```

code snippet Ex4_13.cpp

Typical output from this example looks like this:

```
The array contains the following values:
    30.38     73.93     29.82     93.00     78.14
    89.53     75.87      5.98     45.29     89.83
```

```
     5.25      53.86      11.40       3.34      83.39
    69.94      82.43      43.05      32.87      59.50
    58.89      96.69      34.67      18.81      72.99
    89.60      25.53      34.00      97.35      55.26
    52.64      90.85      10.35      46.14      82.03
    55.46      93.26      92.96      85.11      10.55
    50.50       8.10      29.32      82.98      76.48
    83.94      56.95      15.04      21.94      24.81
The maximum value in the array is 97.35
```

How It Works

You first create an array that stores 50 values of type `double`:

```
array<double>^ samples = gcnew array<double>(50);
```

The array variable, `samples`, must be a tracking handle, because CLR arrays are created on the garbage-collected heap.

You populate the array with pseudo-random values of type `double` with the following statements:

```
Random^ generator = gcnew Random;
for(int i = 0 ; i< samples->Length ; i++)
   samples[i] = 100.0*generator->NextDouble();
```

The first statement creates an object of type `Random` on the CLR heap. A `Random` object has functions that will generate pseudo-random values. Here you use the `NextDouble()` function in the loop, which returns a random value of type `double` that lies between 0.0 and 1.0. By multiplying this by 100.0 you get a value between 0.0 and 100.0. The `for` loop stores a random value in each element of the samples array.

A `Random` object also has a `Next()` function that returns a random non-negative value of type `int`. If you supply an integer argument when you call the `Next()` function, it will return a random non-negative integer which is less than the argument value. You can also supply two integer arguments that represent the minimum and maximum values for the random integer to be returned.

The next loop outputs the contents of the array, five elements to a line:

```
Console::WriteLine(L"The array contains the following values:");
for(int i = 0 ; i< samples->Length ; i++)
{
  Console::Write(L"{0,10:F2}", samples[i]);
  if((i+1)%5 == 0)
    Console::WriteLine();
}
```

Within the loop, you write the value of each element with a field width of 10 and 2 decimal places. Specifying the field width ensures the values align in columns. You also write a newline character to the output whenever the expression `(i+1)%5` is zero, which is after every fifth element value, so you get five to a line in the output.

Finally, you figure out what the maximum element value is:

```
double max = 0;
for each(double sample in samples)
  if(max < sample)
    max = sample;
```

This uses a `for each` loop just to show that you can. The loop compares `max` with each element value in turn, and whenever the element is greater than the current value in `max`, `max` is set to that value. You end up with the maximum element value in `max`.

You could use a `for` loop here if you also wanted to record the index position of the maximum element as well as its value — for example:

```
double max = 0;
int index = 0;
for (int i = 0 ; i < samples->Length ; i++)
  if(max < samples[i])
  {
    max = samples[i];
    index = i;
  }
```

Sorting One-Dimensional Arrays

The `Array` class in the `System` namespace defines a `Sort()` function that sorts the elements of a one-dimensional array so that they are in ascending order. To sort an array, you just pass the array handle to the `Sort()` function. Here's an example:

```
array<int>^ samples = { 27, 3, 54, 11, 18, 2, 16};
Array::Sort(samples);                           // Sort the array elements

for each(int value in samples)                  // Output the array elements
  Console::Write(L"{0, 8}", value);
Console::WriteLine();
```

The call to the `Sort()` function rearranges the values of the elements in the samples array into ascending sequence. The result of executing this code fragment is:

```
     2    3    11    16    18    27    54
```

You can also sort a range of elements in an array by supplying two more arguments to the `Sort()` function, specifying the index for the first element of those to be sorted, and the number of elements to be sorted. For example:

```
array<int>^ samples = { 27, 3, 54, 11, 18, 2, 16};
Array::Sort(samples, 2, 3);                      // Sort elements 2 to 4
```

This statement sorts the three elements in the samples array that begin at index position 2. After executing these statements, the elements in the array will have the values:

```
27   3   11   18   54   2   16
```

There are several other versions of the Sort() function that you can find if you consult the documentation, but I'll introduce one other that is particularly useful. This version presumes you have two arrays that are associated such that the elements in the first array represent keys to the corresponding elements in the second array. For example, you might store names of people in one array and the weights of the individuals in a second array. The Sort() function sorts the array of names in ascending sequence and also rearranges the elements of the weights array so that the weights still match the appropriate person. Let's try it in an example.

TRY IT OUT   Sorting Two Associated Arrays

This example creates an array of names, and stores the weights of each person in the corresponding element of a second array. It then sorts both arrays in a single operation.

Available for download on Wrox.com

```cpp
// Ex4_14.cpp : main project file.
// Sorting an array of keys(the names) and an array of objects(the weights)

#include "stdafx.h"

using namespace System;

int main(array<System::String ^> ^args)
{
  array<String^>^ names = { "Jill", "Ted", "Mary", "Eve", "Bill", "Al"};
  array<int>^ weights = { 103, 168, 128, 115, 180, 176};

  Array::Sort( names,weights);                    // Sort the arrays
  for each(String^ name in names)                 // Output the names
    Console::Write(L"{0, 10}", name);
  Console::WriteLine();

  for each(int weight in weights)                 // Output the weights
    Console::Write(L"{0, 10}", weight);
  Console::WriteLine();
    return 0;
}
```

code snippet Ex4_14.cpp

The output from this program is:

```
        Al      Bill       Eve      Jill      Mary       Ted
       176       180       115       103       128       168
```

How It Works

The values in the `weights` array correspond to the weight of the person at the same index position in the `names` array. The `Sort()` function you call here sorts both arrays using the first array argument — names, in this instance — to determine the order of both arrays. You can see from the output that after sorting, everyone still has his or her correct weight recorded in the corresponding element of the weights array.

Searching One-Dimensional Arrays

The `Array` class provides functions that search the elements of a one-dimensional array. Versions of the `BinarySearch()` function use a binary search algorithm to find the index position of a given element in the entire array, or in a given range of elements. The binary search algorithm requires that the elements are ordered, if it is to work, so you need to sort the elements before you search an array.

Here's how you could search an entire array:

```
array<int>^ values = { 23, 45, 68, 94, 123, 127, 150, 203, 299};
int toBeFound(127);
int position = Array::BinarySearch(values, toBeFound);
if(position<0)
  Console::WriteLine(L"{0} was not found.", toBeFound);
else
  Console::WriteLine(L"{0} was found at index position {1}.", toBeFound, position);
```

The value to be found is stored in the `toBeFound` variable. The first argument to the `BinarySearch()` function is the handle of the array to be searched, and the second argument specifies what you are looking for. The result of the search is returned by the `BinarySearch()` function as a value of type `int`. If the second argument to the function is found in the array specified by the first argument, its index position is returned; otherwise a negative integer is returned. Thus, you must test the value returned to determine whether or not the search target was found. Because the values in the `values` array are already in ascending sequence, there is no need to sort the array before searching it. This code fragment would produce the output:

```
127 was found at index position 5.
```

To search a given range of elements in an array you use a version of the `BinarySearch()` function that accepts four arguments. The first argument is the handle of the array to be searched, the second argument is the index position of the element where the search should start, the third argument is the number of elements to be searched, and the fourth argument is what you are looking for. Here's how you might use that:

```
array<int>^ values = { 23, 45, 68, 94, 123, 127, 150, 203, 299};
int toBeFound(127);
int position = Array::BinarySearch(values, 3, 6, toBeFound);
```

This searches the values array from the fourth array element through to the last. As with the previous version of `BinarySearch()`, the function returns the index position found, or a negative integer if the search fails.

Let's try a searching example.

TRY IT OUT Searching Arrays

This is a variation on the previous example with a search operation added:

```cpp
// Ex4_15.cpp : main project file.
// Searching an array

#include "stdafx.h"

using namespace System;

int main(array<System::String ^> ^args)
{
  array<String^>^ names = { "Jill", "Ted", "Mary", "Eve", "Bill",
                            "Al", "Ned", "Zoe", "Dan", "Jean"};
  array<int>^ weights = { 103, 168, 128, 115, 180,
                          176, 209, 98,  190, 130 };
  array<String^>^ toBeFound = {"Bill", "Eve", "Al", "Fred"};

  Array::Sort( names, weights);                    // Sort the arrays

  int result(0);                                   // Stores search result
  for each(String^ name in toBeFound)              // Search to find weights
  {
    result = Array::BinarySearch(names, name);     // Search names array

    if(result<0)                                   // Check the result
      Console::WriteLine(L"{0} was not found.", name);
    else
      Console::WriteLine(L"{0} weighs {1} lbs.", name, weights[result]);
  }
  return 0;
}
```

code snippet Ex4_15.cpp

This program produces the output:

```
Bill weighs 180 lbs.
Eve weighs 115 lbs.
Al weighs 176 lbs.
Fred was not found.
```

How It Works

You create two associated arrays — an array of names and an array of corresponding weights in pounds. You also create the toBeFound array that contains the names of the people whose weights you'd like to know.

You sort the names and weights arrays, using the names array to determine the order. You then search the names array for each name in the toBeFound array using a for each loop. The loop variable, name, is assigned each of the names in the `toBeFound` array in turn. Within the loop, you search for the current name with the statement:

```
result = Array::BinarySearch(names, name);    // Search names array
```

This returns the index of the element from `names` that contains `name`, or a negative integer if the name is not found. You then test the result and produce the output in the `if` statement:

```
if(result<0)                                  // Check the result
  Console::WriteLine(L"{0} was not found.", name);
else
  Console::WriteLine(L"{0} weighs {1} lbs.", name, weights[result]);
```

Because the ordering of the `weights` array was determined by the ordering of the `names` array, you are able to index the `weights` array with `result`, the index position in the `names` array where `name` was found. You can see from the output that "Fred" was not found in the `names` array.

When the binary search operation fails, the value returned is not just any old negative value. It is, in fact, the bitwise complement of the index position of the first element that is greater than the object you are searching for, or the bitwise complement of the `Length` property of the array if no element is greater than the object sought. Knowing this, you can use the `BinarySearch()` function to work out where you should insert a new object in an array, and still maintain the order of the elements. Suppose you wanted to insert "Fred" in the `names` array. You can find the index position where it should be inserted with these statements:

```
array<String^>^ names = { "Jill", "Ted", "Mary", "Eve", "Bill",
                          "Al", "Ned", "Zoe", "Dan", "Jean"};
Array::Sort(names);                   // Sort the array
String^ name = L"Fred";
int position(Array::BinarySearch(names, name));
if(position<0)                        // If it is negative
 position = ~position;                // flip the bits to get the insert index
```

If the result of the search is negative, flipping all the bits gives you the index position of where the new name should be inserted. If the result is positive, the new name is identical to the name at this position, and you can use the result as the new position directly.

You can now copy the `names` array into a new array that has one more element, and use the position value to insert `name` at the appropriate place:

```
array<String^>^ newNames = gcnew array<String^>(names->Length+1);

// Copy elements from names to newNames
for(int i = 0 ; i<position ; i++)
  newNames[i] = names[i];

newNames[position] = name;                    // Copy the new element

if(position<names->Length)                    // If any elements remain in
                                              // names
  for(int i = position ; i<names->Length ; i++)
    newNames[i+1] = names[i];                 // copy them to newNames
```

This creates a new array with a length that is one greater than the length of the old array. You then copy all the elements from the old to the new, up to index position `position-1`. You then copy the new name followed by the remaining elements from the old array. To discard the old array, you would just write:

```
names = nullptr;
```

Multidimensional Arrays

You can create arrays that have two or more dimensions; the maximum number of dimensions an array can have is 32, which should accommodate most situations. You specify the number of dimensions that your array has between the angled brackets immediately following the element type, and separated from it by a comma. The dimension of an array is 1 by default, which is why you did not need to specify it up to now. Here's how you can create a two-dimensional array of integer elements:

```
array<int, 2>^ values = gcnew array<int, 2>(4, 5);
```

This statement creates a two-dimensional array with four rows and five columns for a total of 20 elements. To access an element of a multidimensional array, you specify a set of index values, one for each dimension; these are placed, between square brackets, separated by commas, following the array name. Here's how you could set values for the elements of a two-dimensional array of integers:

```
int nrows(4);
int ncols(5);
array<int, 2>^ values(gcnew array<int, 2>(nrows, ncols));
for(int i = 0 ; i<nrows ; i++)
  for(int j = 0 ; j<ncols ; j++)
    values[i,j] = (i+1)*(j+1);
```

The nested loop iterates over all the elements of the array. The outer loop iterates over the rows, and the inner loop iterates over every element in the current row. As you can see, each element is set to a value that is given by the expression `(i+1)*(j+1)`, so elements in the first row will be set to 1,2,3,4,5; elements in the second row will be 2,4,6,8,10; and so on, through to the last row, which will be 4,6,12,16,20.

I'm sure you will have noticed that the notation for accessing an element of a two-dimensional array here is different from the notation used for native C++ arrays. This is no accident. A C++/CLI array is not an array of arrays like a native C++ array; it is a true two-dimensional array. You cannot use a single index with a two-dimensional C++/CLI array, because this has no meaning; the array is a two-dimensional array of elements. As I said earlier, the dimensionality of an array is referred to as its *rank*, so the rank of the `values` array in the previous fragment is 2. Of course, you can also define C++/CLI arrays of rank 3 or more, up to an array of rank 32. In contrast, native C++ arrays are actually always of rank 1, because native C++ arrays of two or more dimensions are really arrays of arrays. As you'll see later, you can also define arrays of arrays in C++/CLI.

Let's put a multidimensional array to use in an example.

TRY IT OUT   Using a Multidimensional Array

This CLR console example creates a 12x12 multiplication table in a two-dimensional array:

```cpp
// Ex4_16.cpp : main project file.
// Using a two-dimensional array

#include "stdafx.h"

using namespace System;

int main(array<System::String ^> ^args)
{
  const int SIZE(12);
  array<int, 2>^ products(gcnew array<int, 2>(SIZE,SIZE));

  for (int i = 0 ; i < SIZE ; i++)
    for(int j = 0 ; j < SIZE ; j++)
      products[i,j] = (i+1)*(j+1);

  Console::WriteLine(L"Here is the {0} times table:",  SIZE);

  // Write horizontal divider line
  for(int i = 0 ; i <= SIZE ; i++)
    Console::Write(L"_____");
  Console::WriteLine();                  // Write newline

  // Write top line of table
  Console::Write(L" |");
  for(int i = 1 ; i <= SIZE ; i++)
    Console::Write(L"{0,3} |", i);
  Console::WriteLine();                  // Write newline

  // Write horizontal divider line with verticals
  for(int i = 0 ; i <= SIZE ; i++)
    Console::Write(L"____|");
  Console::WriteLine();                  // Write newline

  // Write remaining lines
  for(int i = 0 ; i<SIZE ; i++)
  {
    Console::Write(L"{0,3} |", i+1);
    for(int j = 0 ; j<SIZE ; j++)
      Console::Write(L"{0,3} |", products[i,j]);

    Console::WriteLine();                // Write newline
  }

  // Write horizontal divider line
  for(int i = 0 ; i <= SIZE ; i++)
```

```
        Console::Write(L"_____");
      Console::WriteLine();                    // Write newline

        return 0;
    }
```

code snippet Ex4_16.cpp

This example should produce the following output:

```
Here is the 12 times table:
```

	1	2	3	4	5	6	7	8	9	10	11	12
1	1	2	3	4	5	6	7	8	9	10	11	12
2	2	4	6	8	10	12	14	16	18	20	22	24
3	3	6	9	12	15	18	21	24	27	30	33	36
4	4	8	12	16	20	24	28	32	36	40	44	48
5	5	10	15	20	25	30	35	40	45	50	55	60
6	6	12	18	24	30	36	42	48	54	60	66	72
7	7	14	21	28	35	42	49	56	63	70	77	84
8	8	16	24	32	40	48	56	64	72	80	88	96
9	9	18	27	36	45	54	63	72	81	90	99	108
10	10	20	30	40	50	60	70	80	90	100	110	120
11	11	22	33	44	55	66	77	88	99	110	121	132
12	12	24	36	48	60	72	84	96	108	120	132	144

How It Works

It looks like a lot of code, but most of it is concerned with making the output pretty. You create the two-dimensional array with the following statements:

```
const int SIZE(12);
array<int, 2>^ products(gcnew array<int, 2>(SIZE,SIZE));
```

The first line defines a constant integer value that specifies the number of elements in each array dimension. The second line defines an array of rank 2 that has 12 rows of 12 elements. This array stores the products in the 12 × 12 table.

You set the values of the elements in the products array in a nested loop:

```
for (int i = 0 ; i < SIZE ; i++)
  for(int j = 0 ; j < SIZE ; j++)
    products[i,j] = (i+1)*(j+1);
```

The outer loop iterates over the rows, and the inner loop iterates over the columns. The value of each element is the product of the row and column index values after they are incremented by 1. The rest of the code in `main()` is concerned solely with generating output.

After writing the initial table heading, you create a row of bars to mark the top of the table, like this:

```
for(int i = 0 ; i <= SIZE ; i++)
  Console::Write(L"_____");
Console::WriteLine();                // Write newline
```

Each iteration of the loop writes five horizontal bar characters. Note that the upper limit for the loop is inclusive, so you write 13 sets of five bars to allow for the row labels in the table plus the 12 columns.

Next you write the row of column labels for the table with another loop:

```
// Write top line of table
Console::Write(L"  |");
for(int i = 1 ; i <= SIZE ; i++)
  Console::Write(L"{0,3} |", i);
Console::WriteLine();                // Write newline
```

You have to write the space over the row label position separately because that is a special case with no output value. Each of the column labels is written in the loop. You then write a newline character, ready for the row outputs that follow.

The row outputs are written in a nested loop:

```
for(int i = 0 ; i<SIZE ; i++)
{
  Console::Write(L"{0,3} |", i+1);
  for(int j = 0 ; j<SIZE ; j++)
    Console::Write(L"{0,3} |", products[i,j]);

  Console::WriteLine();              // Write newline
}
```

The outer loop iterates over the rows, and the code inside the outer loop writes a complete row, including the row label on the left. The inner loop writes the values from the `products` array that correspond to the `ith` row, with the values separated by vertical bars.

The remaining code writes more horizontal bars to finish off the bottom of the table.

Arrays of Arrays

Array elements can be of any type, so you can create arrays where the elements are tracking handles that reference arrays. This gives you the possibility of creating so-called *jagged arrays*, because each handle referencing an array can have a different number of elements. This is most easily understood by looking at an example. Suppose you want to store the names of children in a class grouped by the grade they scored, where there are five classifications corresponding to grades A, B, C, D, and E. You could first create an array of five elements where each element stores an array of names. Here's the statement that will do that:

```
array< array< String^ >^ >^ grades(gcnew array< array< String^ >^ >(5));
```

Don't let all the hats confuse you — it's simpler than it looks. The array variable, grades, is a handle of type `array<type>^`. Each element in the array is also a handle to an array, so the type of the array elements is of the same form — `array<type>^`; this has to go between the angled brackets in the original array type specification, which results in `array< array<type>^ >^`. The elements stored in the array are also handles to String objects, so you must replace type in the last expression with `String^`; thus you end up with the array type being `array< array< String^ >^ >^`.

With the array of arrays worked out, you can now create the arrays of names. Here's an example of what that might look like:

```
grades[0] = gcnew array<String^>{"Louise", "Jack"};                  // Grade A
grades[1] = gcnew array<String^>{"Bill", "Mary", "Ben", "Joan"};     // Grade B
grades[2] = gcnew array<String^>{"Jill", "Will", "Phil"};            // Grade C
grades[3] = gcnew array<String^>{"Ned", "Fred", "Ted", "Jed", "Ed"}; // Grade D
grades[4] = gcnew array<String^>{"Dan", "Ann"};                      // Grade E
```

The expression grades[n] accesses the nth element of the grades array, and, of course, this is a handle to an array of String^ handles in each case. Thus, each of the five statements creates an array of String object handles and stores the address in one of the elements of the grades array. As you see, the arrays of strings vary in length, so clearly you can manage a set of arrays with arbitrary lengths in this way.

You could create and initialize the whole array of arrays in a single statement:

```
array< array< String^ >^ >^ grades = gcnew array< array< String^ >^ >
        {
            gcnew array<String^>{"Louise", "Jack"},                  // Grade A
            gcnew array<String^>{"Bill", "Mary", "Ben", "Joan"},     // Grade B
            gcnew array<String^>{"Jill", "Will", "Phil"},            // Grade C
            gcnew array<String^>{"Ned", "Fred", "Ted", "Jed", "Ed"}, // Grade D
            gcnew array<String^>{"Dan", "Ann"}                       // Grade E
        };
```

The initial values for the elements are between the braces.

Let's put this in a working example that demonstrates how you can process arrays of arrays.

TRY IT OUT   Using an Array of Arrays

Create a CLR console program project and modify it as follows:

```
// Ex4_17.cpp : main project file.
// Using an array of arrays

#include "stdafx.h"

using namespace System;

int main(array<System::String ^> ^args)
{
    array< array< String^ >^ >^ grades = gcnew array< array< String^ >^ >
        {
```

```
            gcnew array<String^>{"Louise", "Jack"},                   // Grade A
            gcnew array<String^>{"Bill", "Mary", "Ben", "Joan"},      // Grade B
            gcnew array<String^>{"Jill", "Will", "Phil"},             // Grade C
            gcnew array<String^>{"Ned", "Fred", "Ted", "Jed", "Ed"},  // Grade D
            gcnew array<String^>{"Dan", "Ann"}                        // Grade E
          };

  wchar_t gradeLetter('A');

  for each(array< String^ >^ grade in grades)
  {
    Console::WriteLine(L"Students with Grade {0}:", gradeLetter++);

    for each( String^ student in grade)
      Console::Write(L"{0,12}",student);          // Output the current name

    Console::WriteLine();                         // Write a newline
  }
  return 0;
}
```

code snippet Ex4_17.cpp

This example produces the following output:

```
Students with Grade A:
      Louise        Jack
Students with Grade B:
        Bill        Mary        Ben         Joan
Students with Grade C:
        Jill        Will        Phil
Students with Grade D:
         Ned        Fred        Ted         Jed          Ed
Students with Grade E:
         Dan         Ann
```

How It Works

The array definition is exactly as you saw in the previous section. Next, you define the gradeLetter variable as type wchar_t with the initial value 'A'. This is to be used to present the grade classification in the output.

The students and their grades are listed by the nested loops. The outer for each loop iterates over the elements in the grades array:

```
for each(array< String^ >^ grade in grades)
{
  // Process students in the current grade...
}
```

The loop variable grade is of type array< String^ >^ because that's the element type in the grades array. The variable grade references each of the arrays of String^ handles in turn: the first time around the loop references the array of grade A student names, the second time around it references grade B student names, and so on until the last loop iteration when it references the grade E student names.

On each iteration of the outer loop, you execute the following code:

```
Console::WriteLine(L"Students with Grade {0}:", gradeLetter++);

for each( String^ student in grade)
    Console::Write(L"{0,12}",student);          // Output the current name

Console::WriteLine();                           // Write a newline
```

The first statement writes a line that includes the current value of `gradeLetter`, which starts out as `'A'`. The statement also increments `gradeLetter` to be, `'B'`, `'C'`, `'D'`, and `'E'` successively on subsequent iterations of the outer loop.

Next, you have the inner `for each` loop that iterates over each of the names in the current grade array in turn. The output statement uses the `Console::Write()` function so all the names appear on the same line. The names are presented right-justified in the output in a field width of 12, so the names in the lines of output are aligned. After the loop, the `WriteLine()` just writes a newline to the output, so the next grade output starts on a new line.

You could have used a `for` loop for the inner loop:

```
for (int i  = 0 ; i < grade->Length ; i++)
    Console::Write(L"{0,12}",grade[i]);         // Output the current name
```

Here the loop is constrained by the `Length` property of the current array of names that is referenced by the `grade` variable.

You could have used a `for` loop for the outer loop as well, in which case the inner loop needs to be changed further, and the nested loop looks like this:

```
for (int j = 0 ; j < grades->Length ; j++)
{
  Console::WriteLine(L"Students with Grade {0}:", gradeLetter+j);
  for (int i  = 0 ; i < grades[j]->Length ; i++)
    Console::Write(L"{0,12}",grades[j][i]);        // Output the current name
  Console::WriteLine();
}
```

Now `grades[j]` references the jth array of names; the expression `grades[j][i]` references the ith name in the jth array of names.

Strings

You have already seen that the `String` class type that is defined in the `System` namespace represents a string in C++/CLI — in fact, a string consists of Unicode characters. To be more precise, it represents a string consisting of a sequence of characters of type `System::Char`. You get a huge amount of powerful functionality with `String` class objects, making string processing very easy. Let's start at the beginning with string creation.

You can create a `String` object like this:

```
System::String^ saying(L"Many hands make light work.");
```

The variable `saying` is a tracking handle that references the `String` object initialized with the string that appears between the parentheses. You must always use a tracking handle to store a reference to a `String` object. The string literal here is a wide character string because it has the prefix `L`. If you omit the `L` prefix, you have a string literal containing 8-bit characters, but the compiler ensures it is converted to a wide-character string.

You can access individual characters in a string by using a subscript, just like an array; the first character in the string has an index value of 0. Here's how you could output the third character in the string `saying`:

```
Console::WriteLine(L"The third character in the string is {0}", saying[2]);
```

Note that you can only retrieve a character from a string using an index value; you cannot update the string in this way. String objects are immutable and therefore cannot be modified.

You can obtain the number of characters in a string by accessing its `Length` property. You could output the length of `saying` with this statement:

```
Console::WriteLine(L"The string has {0} characters.", saying->Length);
```

Because `saying` is a tracking handle — which, as you know, is a kind of pointer — you must use the `->` operator to access the `Length` property (or any other member of the object). You'll learn more about properties when you get to investigate C++/CLI classes in detail.

Joining Strings

You can use the `+` operator to join strings to form a new `String` object. Here's an example:

```
String^ name1(L"Beth");
String^ name2(L"Betty");
String^ name3(name1 + L" and " + name2);
```

After executing these statements, `name3` contains the string "Beth and Betty". Note how you can use the `+` operator to join `String` objects with string literals. You can also join `String` objects with numerical values or `bool` values, and have the values converted automatically to a string before the join operation. The following statements illustrate this:

```
String^ str(L"Value: ");
String^ str1(str + 2.5);        // Result is new string L"Value: 2.5"
String^ str2(str + 25);         // Result is new string L"Value: 25"
String^ str3(str + true);       // Result is new string L"Value: True"
```

You can also join a string and a character, but the result depends on the type of character:

```
char ch('Z');
wchar_t wch(L'Z');
String^ str4(str + ch);            // Result is new string L"Value: 90"
String^ str5(str + wch);           // Result is new string L"Value: Z"
```

The comments show the results of the operations. A character of type `char` is treated as a numerical value, so you get the character code value joined to the string. The `wchar_t` character is of the same type as the characters in the `String` object (type `Char`), so the character is appended to the string.

Don't forget that `String` objects are immutable; once created, they cannot be changed. This means that *all* operations that apparently modify `String` objects always result in new `String` objects being created.

The `String` class also defines a `Join()` function that you use when you want to join a series of strings stored in an array into a single string with separators between the original strings. Here's how you could join names together in a single string with the names separated by commas:

```
array<String^>^ names = { L"Jill", L"Ted", L"Mary", L"Eve", L"Bill"};
String^ separator(L", ");
String^ joined = String::Join(separator, names);
```

After executing these statements, `joined` references the string `L"Jill, Ted, Mary, Eve, Bill"`. The `separator` string has been inserted between each of the original strings in the `names` array. Of course, the separator string can be anything you like — it could be `L" and "`, for example, which results in the string `L"Jill and Ted and Mary and Eve and Bill"`.

Let's try a full example of working with `String` objects.

TRY IT OUT   Working with Strings

Suppose you have an array of integer values that you want to output aligned in columns. You want the values aligned, but you want the columns to be just sufficiently wide to accommodate the largest value in the array with a space between columns. This program does that.

```
// Ex4_18.cpp : main project file.
// Creating a custom format string

#include "stdafx.h"

using namespace System;

int main(array<System::String ^> ^args)
{

  array<int>^ values = { 2, 456, 23, -46, 34211, 456, 5609, 112098,
    234, -76504, 341, 6788, -909121, 99, 10};
  String^ formatStr1(L"{0,");               // 1st half of format string
  String^ formatStr2(L"}");                 // 2nd half of format string
```

```
String^ number;                       // Stores a number as a string

// Find the length of the maximum length value string
int maxLength(0);                     // Holds the maximum length found
for each(int value in values)
{
  number = L"" + value;               // Create string from value
  if(maxLength<number->Length)
    maxLength = number->Length;
}

// Create the format string to be used for output
String^ format(formatStr1 + (maxLength+1) + formatStr2);

// Output the values
int numberPerLine(3);
for(int i = 0 ; i< values->Length ; i++)
{
  Console::Write(format, values[i]);
  if((i+1)%numberPerLine == 0)
    Console::WriteLine();
}
return 0;
}
```

code snippet Ex4_18.cpp

The output from this program is:

```
      2     456      23
    -46   34211     456
   5609  112098     234
 -76504     341    6788
-909121      99      10
```

How It Works

The objective of this program is to create a format string to align the output of integers from the values array in columns, with a width sufficient to accommodate the maximum length string representation of the integers. You create the format string initially in two parts:

```
String^ formatStr1(L"{0,");           // 1st half of format string
String^ formatStr2(L"}");             // 2nd half of format string
```

These two strings are the beginning and end of the format string you ultimately require. You need to work out the length of the maximum-length number string, and sandwich that value between formatStr1 and formatStr2, to form the complete format string.

You find the length you require with the following code:

```
int maxLength(0);                     // Holds the maximum length found
for each(int value in values)
```

```
    {
      number = L"" + value;                 // Create string from value
      if(maxLength<number->Length)
        maxLength = number->Length;
    }
```

Within the loop you convert each number from the array to its `String` representation by joining it to an empty string. You compare the `Length` property of each string to `maxLength`, and if it's greater than the current value of `maxLength`, it becomes the new maximum length.

The statement that creates a string from `value` shows how an integer is automatically converted to a string when you combine it with a string using the addition operator. You could also obtain `value` as a string with the following statement:

```
        number = value.ToString();
```

This uses the `ToString()` function that is defined in the `System::Int32` value class that converts an integer value to a string.

Creating the format string is simple:

```
        String^ format(formatStr1 + (maxLength+1) + formatStr2);
```

You need to add 1 to `maxLength` to allow one additional space in the field when the maximum length string is displayed. Placing the expression `maxLength+1` between parentheses ensures that it is evaluated as an arithmetic operation before the string-joining operations are executed.

Finally, you use the `format` string in the code to output values from the array:

```
        int numberPerLine(3);
        for(int i = 0 ; i< values->Length ; i++)
        {
          Console::Write(format, values[i]);
          if((i+1)%numberPerLine == 0)
            Console::WriteLine();
        }
```

The output statement in the loop uses `format` as the string for output. With the `maxLength` plugged into the `format` string, the output is in columns that are one greater than the maximum length output value. The `numberPerLine` variable determines how many values appear on a line, so the loop is quite general in that you can vary the number of columns by changing the value of `numberPerLine`.

Modifying Strings

The most common requirement for trimming a string is to trim spaces from both the beginning and the end. The `Trim()` function for a string object does that:

```
        String^ str = {L" Handsome is as handsome does... "};
        String^ newStr(str->Trim());
```

The `Trim()` function in the second statement removes any spaces from the beginning and end of `str` and returns the result as a new `String` object stored in `newStr`. Of course, if you did not want to retain the original string, you could store the result back in `str`.

There's another version of the `Trim()` function that allows you to specify the characters that are to be removed from the start and end of the string. This function is very flexible because you have more than one way of specifying the characters to be removed. You can specify the characters in an array and pass the array handle as the argument to the function:

```
String^ toBeTrimmed(L"wool wool sheep sheep wool wool wool");
array<wchar_t>^ notWanted = {L'w',L'o',L'l',L' '};
Console::WriteLine(toBeTrimmed->Trim(notWanted));
```

Here you have a string, `toBeTrimmed`, that consists of sheep covered in wool. The array of characters to be trimmed from the string is defined by the `notWanted` array; passing that to the `Trim()` function for the string removes any of the characters in the array from both ends of the string. Remember, `String` objects are immutable, so the original string is not being changed in any way — a new string is created and returned by the `Trim()` operation. Executing this code fragment produces the output:

```
sheep sheep
```

If you happen to specify the character literals without the `L` prefix, they will be of type `char` (which corresponds to the `SByte` value class type); however, the compiler arranges that they are converted to type `wchar_t`.

You can also specify the characters that the `Trim()` function is to remove explicitly as arguments, so you could write the last line of the previous fragment as:

```
Console::WriteLine(toBeTrimmed->Trim(L'w', L'o', L'l', L' '));
```

This produces the same output as the previous version of the statement. You can have as many arguments of type `wchar_t` as you like, but if there are a lot of characters to be specified, an array is the best approach.

If you want to trim only one end of a string, you can use the `TrimEnd()` or `TrimStart()` functions. These come in the same variety of versions as the `Trim()` function. So: without arguments you trim spaces, with an array argument you trim the characters in the array, and with explicit `wchar_t` arguments those characters are removed.

The inverse of trimming a string is padding it at either end with spaces or other characters. You have `PadLeft()` and `PadRight()` functions that pad a string at the left or right end, respectively. The primary use for these functions is in formatting output where you want to place strings either left- or right-justified in a fixed width field. The simpler versions of the `PadLeft()` and `PadRight()` functions accept a single argument specifying the length of the string that is to result from the operation. For example:

```
String^ value(L"3.142");
String^ leftPadded(value->PadLeft(10));      // Result is L"     3.142"
String^ rightPadded(value->PadRight(10));    // Result is L"3.142     "
```

If the length you specify as the argument is less than or equal to the length of the original string, either function returns a new String object that is identical to the original.

To pad a string with a character other than a space, you specify the padding character as the second argument to the PadLeft() or PadRight() functions. Here are a couple of examples of this:

```
String^ value(L"3.142");
String^ leftPadded(value->PadLeft(10, L'*'));     // Result is L"*****3.142"
String^ rightPadded(value->PadRight(10, L'#'));   // Result is L"3.142#####"
```

Of course, with all these examples, you could store the result back in the handle referencing the original string, which would discard the original string.

The String class also has the ToUpper() and ToLower() functions to convert an entire string to upper- or lowercase. Here's how that works:

```
String^ proverb(L"Many hands make light work.");
String^ upper(proverb->ToUpper());     // Result L"MANY HANDS MAKE LIGHT WORK."
```

The ToUpper() function returns a new string that is the original string converted to uppercase.

You use the Insert() function to insert a string at a given position in an existing string. Here's an example of doing that:

```
String^ proverb(L"Many hands make light work.");
String^ newProverb(proverb->Insert(5, L"deck "));
```

The function inserts the string specified by the second argument, starting at the index position in the old string, which is specified by the first argument. The result of this operation is a new string containing:

```
Many deck hands make light work.
```

You can also replace all occurrences of a given character in a string with another character, or all occurrences of a given substring with another substring. Here's a fragment that shows both possibilities:

```
String^ proverb(L"Many hands make light work.");
Console::WriteLine(proverb->Replace(L' ', L'*'));
Console::WriteLine(proverb->Replace(L"Many hands", L"Pressing switch"));
```

Executing this code fragment produces the output:

```
Many*hands*make*light*work.
Pressing switch make light work.
```

The first argument to the Replace() function specifies the character or substring to be replaced, and the second argument specifies the replacement.

Comparing Strings

You can compare two String objects using the Compare() function in the String class. The function returns an integer that is less than zero, equal to zero, or greater than zero, depending on whether the first argument is less than, equal to, or greater than the second argument. Here's an example:

```
String^ him(L"Jacko");
String^ her(L"Jillo");
int result(String::Compare(him, her));
if(result < 0)
  Console::WriteLine(L"{0} is less than {1}.", him, her);
else if(result > 0)
  Console::WriteLine(L"{0} is greater than {1}.", him, her);
else
  Console::WriteLine(L"{0} is equal to {1}.", him, her);
```

You store the integer that the `Compare()` function returns in `result`, and use that in the `if` statement to decide the appropriate output. Executing this fragment produces the output:

```
Jacko is less than Jillo.
```

There's another version of `Compare()` that requires a third argument of type `bool`. If the third argument is `true`, then the strings referenced by the first two arguments are compared, ignoring case; if the third argument is `false`, then the behavior is the same as the previous version of `Compare()`.

Searching Strings

Perhaps the simplest search operation is to test whether a string starts or ends with a given substring. The `StartsWith()` and `EndsWith()` functions do that. You supply a handle to the substring you are looking for as the argument to either function, and the function returns a `bool` value that indicates whether or not the substring is present. Here's a fragment showing how you might use the `StartsWith()` function:

```
String^ sentence(L"Hide, the cow's outside.");
if(sentence->StartsWith(L"Hide"))
  Console::WriteLine(L"The sentence starts with 'Hide'.");
```

Executing this fragment results in the output:

```
The sentence starts with 'Hide'.
```

Of course, you could also apply the `EndsWith()` function to the `sentence` string:

```
Console::WriteLine(L"The sentence does{0} end with 'outside'.",
                        sentence->EndsWith(L"outside") ? L"" : L" not");
```

The result of the conditional operator expression is inserted into the output string. This is an empty string if `EndsWith()` returns `true`, and `L"not"` if it returns `false`. In this instance the function returns `false` (because of the period at the end of the `sentence` string).

The `IndexOf()` function searches a string for the first occurrence of a specified character or substring, and returns the index if it is present, or -1 if it is not found. You specify the character or the substring you are looking for as the argument to the function. For example:

```
String^ sentence(L"Hide, the cow's outside.");
int ePosition(sentence->IndexOf(L'e'));          // Returns 3
int thePosition(sentence->IndexOf(L"the"));      // Returns 6
```

The first search is for the letter 'e' and the second is for the word "the". The values returned by the IndexOf() function are indicated in the comments.

More typically, you will want to find all occurrences of a given character or substring. Another version of the IndexOf() function is designed to be used repeatedly, to enable you to do that. In this case, you supply a second argument specifying the index position where the search is to start. Here's an example of how you might use the function in this way:

```
String^ words(L"wool wool sheep sheep wool wool wool");
String^ word(L"wool");
int index(0);
int count(0);
while((index = words->IndexOf(word,index)) >= 0)
{
  index += word->Length;
  ++count;
}
Console::WriteLine(L"'{0}' was found {1} times in:\n{2}", word, count, words);
```

This fragment counts the number of occurrences of "wool" in the words string. The search operation appears in the while loop condition, and the result is stored in index. The loop continues as long as index is non-negative; when IndexOf() returns -1 the loop ends. Within the loop body, the value of index is incremented by the length of word, which moves the index position to the character following the instance of word that was found, ready for the search on the next iteration. The count variable is incremented within the loop, so when the loop ends it has accumulated the total number of occurrences of word in words. Executing the fragment results in the following output:

```
'wool' was found 5 times in:
wool wool sheep sheep wool wool wool
```

The LastIndexOf() function is similar to the IndexOf() function except that it searches backwards through the string from the end or from a specified index position. Here's how the operation performed by the previous fragment could be performed using the LastIndexOf() function:

```
int index(words->Length - 1);
int count(0);
while(index >= 0 && (index = words->LastIndexOf(word,index)) >= 0)
{
  --index;
  ++count;
}
```

With the word and words strings the same as before, this fragment produces the same output. Because LastIndexOf() searches backwards, the starting index is the last character in the string, which is words->Length-1. When an occurrence of word is found, you must now decrement index by 1, so that the next backward search starts at the character preceding the current occurrence of word. If word occurs right at the beginning of words — at index position 0 — decrementing index results in –1, which is not a legal argument to the LastIndexOf() function because the search starting position must always be within the string. The additional check for a negative value of index in the loop condition prevents this from happening; if the left operand of the && operator is false, the right operand is not evaluated.

The last search function I want to mention is IndexOfAny(), which searches a string for the first occurrence of any character in the array of type array<wchar_t> that you supply as the argument. Similar to the IndexOf() function, the IndexOfAny() function comes in versions that search from the beginning of a string or from a specified index position. Let's try a full working example of using the IndexOfAny() function.

TRY IT OUT   Searching for Any of a Set of Characters

This example searches a string for punctuation characters:

```cpp
// Ex4_19.cpp : main project file.
// Searching for punctuation

#include "stdafx.h"

using namespace System;

int main(array<System::String ^> ^args)
{
  array<wchar_t>^ punctuation = {L'"', L'\'', L'.', L',', L':', L';', L'!', L'?'};
  String^ sentence(L"\"It's chilly in here\", the boy's mother said coldly.");

  // Create array of space characters same length as sentence
  array<wchar_t>^ indicators(gcnew array<wchar_t>(sentence->Length){L' '});

  int index(0);                    // Index of character found
  int count(0);                    // Count of punctuation characters
  while((index = sentence->IndexOfAny(punctuation, index)) >= 0)
  {
    indicators[index] = L'^';      // Set marker
    ++index;                       // Increment to next character
    ++count;                       // Increase the count
  }
  Console::WriteLine(L"There are {0} punctuation characters in the string:",
                                                              count);
  Console::WriteLine(L"\n{0}\n{1}", sentence, gcnew String(indicators));
  return 0;
  }
```

code snippet Ex4_19.cpp

This example should produce the following output:

```
There are 6 punctuation characters in the string:

"It's chilly in here", the boy's mother said coldly.
 ^  ^                  ^^        ^                 ^
```

How It Works

You first create an array containing the characters to be found and the string to be searched:

```
array<wchar_t>^ punctuation = {L'"', L'\'', L'.', L',', L':', L';', L'!', L'?'};
String^ sentence(L"\"It's chilly in here\", the boy's mother said coldly.");
```

Note that you must specify a single quote character using an escape sequence because a single quote is a delimiter in a character literal. You can use a double quote explicitly in a character literal, as there's no risk of it being interpreted as a delimiter in this context.

Next you define an array of characters with the elements initialized to a space character:

```
array<wchar_t>^ indicators(gcnew array<wchar_t>(sentence->Length){L' '});
```

This array has as many elements as the sentence string has characters. You'll be using this array in the output to mark where punctuation characters occur in the sentence string. You'll just change the appropriate array element to '^' whenever a punctuation character is found. Note how a single initializer between the braces following the array specification can be used to initialize all the elements in the array.

The search takes place in the while loop:

```
while((index = sentence->IndexOfAny(punctuation, index)) >= 0)
{
  indicators[index] = L'^';        // Set marker
  ++index;                         // Increment to next character
  ++count;                         // Increase the count
}
```

The loop condition is essentially the same as you have seen in earlier code fragments. Within the loop body, you update the indicators array element at position index to be a '^' character, before incrementing index, ready for the next iteration. When the loop ends, count will contain the number of punctuation characters that were found, and indicators will contain '^' characters at the positions in the sentence where such characters were found.

The output is produced by the following statements:

```
Console::WriteLine(L"There are {0} punctuation characters in the string:",
                                                              count);
Console::WriteLine(L"\n{0}\n{1}" sentence, gcnew String(indicators));
```

The second statement creates a new String object on the heap from the indicators array by passing the array to the String class **constructor**. A class constructor is a function that will create a class object when it is called. You'll learn more about constructors when you get into defining your own classes.

Tracking References

A tracking reference provides a similar capability to a native C++ reference in that it represents an alias for something on the CLR heap. You can create tracking references to value types on the stack and to handles in the garbage-collected heap; the tracking references themselves are always created on the stack. A tracking reference is automatically updated if the object referenced is moved by the garbage collector.

You define a tracking reference using the % operator. For example, here's how you could create a tracking reference to a value type:

```
int value(10);
int% trackValue(value);
```

The second statement defines `trackValue` to be a tracking reference to the variable `value`, which has been created on the stack. You can now modify `value` using `trackValue`:

```
trackValue *= 5;
Console::WriteLine(value);
```

Because `trackValue` is an alias for `value`, the second statement outputs 50.

Interior Pointers

Although you cannot perform arithmetic on the address in a tracking handle, C++/CLI does provide a form of pointer with which it is possible to apply arithmetic operations; it's called an **interior pointer,** and it is defined using the keyword `interior_ptr`. The address stored in an interior pointer can be updated automatically by the CLR garbage collection when necessary. An interior pointer is always an automatic variable that is local to a function.

Here's how you could define an interior point containing the address of the first element in an array:

```
array<double>^ data = {1.5, 3.5, 6.7, 4.2, 2.1};
interior_ptr<double> pstart(&data[0]);
```

You specify the type of object pointed to by the interior pointer between angled brackets following the `interior_ptr` keyword. In the second statement here you initialize the pointer with the address of the first element in the array using the `&` operator, just as you would with a native C++ pointer. If you do not provide an initial value for an interior pointer, it is initialized with `nullptr` by default. An array is always allocated on the CLR heap, so here's a situation where the garbage collector may adjust the address contained in an interior pointer.

There are constraints on the type specification for an interior pointer. An interior pointer can contain the address of a value class object on the stack, or the address of a handle to an object on the CLR heap; it cannot contain the address of a whole object on the CLR heap. An interior pointer can also point to a native class object or a native pointer.

You can also use an interior pointer to hold the address of a value class object that is part of an object on the heap, such as an element of a CLR array. This way, you can create an interior pointer that can store the address of a tracking handle to a `System::String` object, but you cannot create an interior pointer to store the address of the `String` object itself. For example:

```
interior_ptr<String^> pstr1;      // OK - pointer to a handle
interior_ptr<String> pstr2;       // Will not compile - pointer to a String object
```

All the arithmetic operations that you can apply to a native C++ pointer you can also apply to an interior pointer. You can increment and decrement an interior pointer to change the address it contains, to refer to the following or preceding data item. You can also add or subtract integer values and compare interior pointers. Let's put together an example that does some of that.

TRY IT OUT   Creating and Using Interior Pointers

This example exercises interior pointers with numerical values and strings:

```
// Ex4_20.cpp : main project file.
// Creating and using interior pointers

#include "stdafx.h"

using namespace System;

int main(array<System::String ^> ^args)
{
  // Access array elements through a pointer
  array<double>^ data = {1.5, 3.5, 6.7, 4.2, 2.1};
  interior_ptr<double> pstart(&data[0]);
  interior_ptr<double> pend(&data[data->Length - 1]);
  double sum(0.0);
  while(pstart <= pend)
    sum += *pstart++;

  Console::WriteLine(L"Total of data array elements = {0}\n", sum);

  // Just to show we can - access strings through an interior pointer
  array<String^>^ strings = { L"Land ahoy!",
                              L"Splice the mainbrace!",
                              L"Shiver me timbers!",
                              L"Never throw into the wind!"
                            };

  for(interior_ptr<String^> pstrings = &strings[0] ;
            pstrings-&strings[0] < strings->Length ; ++pstrings)
   Console::WriteLine(*pstrings);
  return 0;
}
```

code snippet Ex4_20.cpp

The output from this example is:

```
Total of data array elements = 18
Land ahoy!
Splice the mainbrace!
Shiver me timbers!
Never throw into the wind!
```

How It Works

After creating the `data` array of elements of type `double`, you define two interior pointers:

```
interior_ptr<double> pstart(&data[0]);
interior_ptr<double> pend(&data[data->Length - 1]);
```

The first statement creates `pstart` as a pointer to type `double` and initializes it with the address of the first element in the array, `data[0]`. The interior pointer, `pend`, is initialized with the address of the last element in the array, `data[data->Length - 1]`. Because `data->Length` is the number of elements in the array, subtracting 1 from this value produces the index for the last element.

The `while` loop accumulates the sum of the elements in the array:

```
while(pstart <= pend)
  sum += *pstart++;
```

The loop continues as long as the interior pointer, `pstart`, contains an address that is not greater than the address in `pend`. You could equally well have expressed the loop condition as `!(pstart > pend)`.

Within the loop, `pstart` starts out containing the address of the first array element. The value of the first element is obtained by dereferencing the pointer with the expression `*pstart`; the result of this is added to `sum`. The address in the pointer is then incremented using the `++` operator. On the last loop iteration, `pstart` contains the address of the last element, which is the same as the address value that `pend` contains So, incrementing `pstart` makes the loop condition `false` because `pstart` is then greater than `pend`. After the loop ends the value of `sum` is written out, so you can confirm that the `while` loop is working as it should.

Next you create an array of four strings:

```
array<String^>^ strings = { L"Land ahoy!",
                            L"Splice the mainbrace!",
                            L"Shiver me timbers!",
                            L"Never throw into the wind!"
                          };
```

The `for` loop then outputs each string to the command line:

```
for(interior_ptr<String^> pstrings = &strings[0] ;
        pstrings-&strings[0] < strings->Length ; ++pstrings)
  Console::WriteLine(*pstrings);
```

The first expression in the `for` loop condition declares the interior pointer, `pstrings`, and initializes it with the address of the first element in the `strings` array. The second expression determines whether the `for` loop continues:

```
pstrings-&strings[0] < strings->Length
```

As long as `pstrings` contains the address of a valid array element, the difference between the address in `pstrings` and the address of the first element in the array is less than the number of elements in the array, given by the expression `strings->Length`. Thus, when this difference equals the length of the array, the loop ends. You can see from the output that everything works as expected.

The most frequent use of an interior pointer is referencing objects that are part of a CLR heap object, and you'll see more about this later in the book.

SUMMARY

You are now familiar with all of the basic types of values in C++, how to create and use arrays of those types, and how to create and use pointers. You have also been introduced to the idea of a reference. However, we have not exhausted all of these topics. I'll come back to the topics of arrays, pointers, and references later in the book.

The pointer mechanism is sometimes a bit confusing because it can operate at different levels within the same program. Sometimes it is operating as an address, and at other times it can be operating with the value stored at an address. It's very important that you feel at ease with the way pointers are used, so if you find that they are in any way unclear, try them out with a few examples of your own until you feel confident about applying them.

EXERCISES

You can download the source code for the examples in the book and the solutions to the following exercises from www.wrox.com.

1. Write a native C++ program that allows an unlimited number of values to be entered and stored in an array allocated in the free store. The program should then output the values, five to a line, followed by the average of the values entered. The initial array size should be five elements. The program should create a new array with five additional elements, when necessary, and copy values from the old array to the new.

2. Repeat the previous exercise but use pointer notation throughout instead of arrays.

3. Declare a character array, and initialize it to a suitable string. Use a loop to change every other character to uppercase.

Hint: In the ASCII character set, values for uppercase characters are 32 less than their lowercase counterparts.

4.   Write a C++/CLI program that creates an array with a random number of elements of type `int`. The array should have from 10 to 20 elements. Set the array elements to random values between 100 and 1000. Output the elements, five to a line, in ascending sequence without sorting the array; for example, find the smallest element and output that, then the next smallest, and so on.

5.   Write a C++/CLI program that will generate a random integer greater than 10,000. Output the integer and then output the digits in the integer in words. For example, if the integer generated were 345678, then the output should be:

```
The value is 345678
three four five six seven eight
```

6.   Write a C++/CLI program that creates an array containing the following strings:

```
"Madam I'm Adam."
"Don't cry for me, Marge and Tina."
"Lid off a daffodil."
"Red lost soldier."
"Cigar? Toss it in a can. It is so tragic."
```

The program should examine each string in turn, output the string, and indicate whether it is or is not a palindrome (that is, whether it is the same sequence of letters reading backward or forward, ignoring spaces and punctuation).

▶ WHAT YOU LEARNED IN THIS CHAPTER

TOPIC	CONCEPT
Native C++ arrays	An array allows you to manage a number of variables of the same type using a single name. Each dimension of an array is defined between square brackets, following the array name in the declaration of the array.
Array dimensions	Each dimension of an array is indexed starting from zero. Thus, the fifth element of a one-dimensional array has the index value 4.
Initializing arrays	Arrays can be initialized by placing the initializing values between curly braces in the declaration.
Pointers	A pointer is a variable that contains the address of another variable. A pointer is declared as a 'pointer to *type*' and may only be assigned addresses of variables of the given type.
Pointers to `const` and `const` pointers	A pointer can point to a constant object. Such a pointer can be reassigned to another object. A pointer may also be defined as `const`, in which case it can't be reassigned.
References	A reference is an alias for another variable, and can be used in the same places as the variable it references. A reference must be initialized in its declaration. A reference can't be reassigned to another variable.
The `sizeof` operator	The operator `sizeof` returns the number of bytes occupied by the object specified as its argument. Its argument may be a variable or a type name between parentheses.
The `new` operator	The operator `new` allocates memory dynamically in the free store in a native C++ application. When memory has been assigned as requested, it returns a pointer to the beginning of the memory area provided. If memory cannot be assigned for any reason, an exception is thrown that by default causes the program to terminate.
The `gcnew` operator	In a CLR program, you allocate memory in the garbage-collected heap using the `gcnew` operator.
Reference class objects	Reference class objects in general, and `String` objects in particular, are always allocated on the CLR heap.
`String` class objects	You use `String` objects when working with strings in a CLR program.
CLR arrays	The CLR has its own array types with more functionality that native array types. CLR arrays are created on the CLR heap.
Tracking handles	A tracking handle is a form of pointer used to reference variables defined on the CLR heap. A tracking handle is automatically updated if what it refers to is relocated in the heap by the garbage collector. Variables that reference objects and arrays on the heap are always tracking handles.

TOPIC	CONCEPT
Tracking references	A tracking reference is similar to a native reference, except that the address it contains is automatically updated if the object referenced is moved by the garbage collector.
Interior pointers	An interior pointer is a C++/CLI pointer type to which you can apply the same operation as a native pointer.
Modifying interior pointers	The address contained in an interior pointer can be modified using arithmetic operations and still maintain an address correctly, even when referring to something stored in the CLR heap.

5

Introducing Structure into Your Programs

WHAT YOU WILL LEARN IN THIS CHAPTER:

➤ How to declare and write your own C++ functions

➤ How function arguments are defined and used

➤ How to pass arrays to and from a function

➤ What pass-by-value means

➤ How to pass pointers to functions

➤ How to use references as function arguments, and what pass-by-reference means

➤ How the `const` modifier affects function arguments

➤ How to return values from a function

➤ How to use recursion

Up to now, you haven't really been able to structure your program code in a modular fashion, because you have only been able to construct a program as a single function, `main()`; but you *have* been using library functions of various kinds as well as functions belonging to objects. Whenever you write a C++ program, you should have a modular structure in mind from the outset, and as you'll see, a good understanding of how to implement functions is essential to object-oriented programming in C++.

There's quite a lot to structuring your C++ programs, so to avoid indigestion, you won't try to swallow the whole thing in one gulp. After you have chewed over and gotten the full flavor of these morsels, you'll move on to the next chapter, where you will get further into the meat of the topic.

UNDERSTANDING FUNCTIONS

First, let us take a look at the broad principles of how a function works. A function is a self-contained block of code with a specific purpose. A function has a name that both identifies it and is used to call it for execution in a program. The name of a function is global but is not necessarily unique in C++, as you'll see in the next chapter; however, functions that perform different actions should generally have different names.

The name of a function is governed by the same rules as those for a variable. A function name is, therefore, a sequence of letters and digits, the first of which is a letter, where an underscore (_) counts as a letter. The name of a function should generally reflect what it does, so, for example, you might call a function that counts beans count_beans().

You pass information to a function by means of **arguments** specified when you invoke it. These arguments need to correspond with **parameters** that appear in the definition of the function. The arguments that you specify replace the parameters used in the definition of the function when the function executes. The code in the function then executes as though it were written using your argument values. Figure 5-1 illustrates the relationship between arguments in the function call and the parameters specified in the definition of the function.

FIGURE 5-1

In this example, the function returns the sum of the two arguments passed to it. In general, a function returns either a single value to the point in the program where it was called, or nothing at all, depending on how the function is defined. You might think that returning a single value from a function is a constraint, but the single value returned can be a pointer that might contain the address of an array, for example. You will see more about how data is returned from a function a little later in this chapter.

Why Do You Need Functions?

One major advantage that a function offers is that it can be executed as many times as necessary from different points in a program. Without the ability to package a block of code into a function, programs would end up being much larger because you would typically need to replicate the same code at various points in them. But the real reason that you need functions is to break up a program into easily manageable chunks for development and testing; small blocks of code are easier to understand than large blocks of code.

Imagine a really big program — let's say a million lines of code. A program of this size would be virtually impossible to write and debug without functions. Functions enable you to segment a program so that you can write the code piecemeal, and test each piece independently before bringing it together with the other pieces. It also allows the work to be divided among members of a programming team, with each team member taking responsibility for a tightly specified piece of the program, with a well-defined functional interface to the rest of the code.

Structure of a Function

As you have seen when writing the function `main()`, a function consists of a **function header** that identifies the function, followed by the **body** of the function between curly braces containing the executable code for the function. Let's look at an example. You could write a function to raise a value to a given power; that is, to compute the result of multiplying the value x by itself n times, which is x^n:

```
// Function to calculate x to the power n, with n greater than or
// equal to 0
double power(double x, int n)          // Function header
{                                      // Function body starts here...
   double result(1.0);                 // Result stored here
   for(int i = 1; i <= n; i++)
     result *= x;

   return result;
}                                      // ...and ends here
```

The Function Header

Let's first examine the function header in this example. The following is the first line of the function.

```
double power(double x, int n)          // Function header
```

It consists of three parts:

➤ The type of the **return value** (`double`, in this case)

➤ The name of the function (`power`, in this case)

➤ The parameters of the function enclosed between parentheses (`x` and `n`, in this case, of types `double` and `int`, respectively)

The return value is returned to the calling function when the function is executed, so when the function is called, it results in a value of type `double` in the expression in which it appears.

Our function has two parameters: `x`, the value to be raised to a given power, which is of type `double`, and the value of the power, `n`, which is of type `int`. The computation that the function performs is written using these parameter variables together with another variable, `result`, declared in the body of the function. The parameter names and any variables defined in the body of the function are local to the function.

 NOTE *No semicolon is required at the end of the function header or after the closing brace for the function body.*

The General Form of a Function Header

The general form of a function header can be written as follows:

```
return_type function_name(parameter_list)
```

The `return_type` can be any legal type. If the function does not return a value, the return type is specified by the keyword `void`. The keyword `void` is also used to indicate the absence of parameters, so a function that has no parameters and doesn't return a value would have the following function header.

```
void my_function(void)
```

An empty parameter list also indicates that a function takes no arguments, so you could omit the keyword `void` between the parentheses like:

```
void my_function()
```

 NOTE *A function with a return type specified as void should not be used in an expression in the calling program. Because it doesn't return a value, it can't sensibly be part of an expression, so using it in this way causes the compiler to generate an error message.*

The Function Body

The desired computation in a function is performed by the statements in the function body following the function header. The first of these in our example declares a variable `result` that is initialized with the value 1.0. The variable `result` is local to the function, as are all automatic variables declared within the function body. This means that the variable `result` ceases to exist after the function has completed execution. What might immediately strike you is that if `result` ceases to exist on completing execution of the function, how is it returned? The answer is that a copy of the value being returned is made automatically, and this copy is available to the return point in the program.

The calculation is performed in the `for` loop. A loop control variable `i` is declared in the `for` loop, which assumes successive values from 1 to n. The variable `result` is multiplied by x once for each loop iteration, so this occurs n times to generate the required value. If n is 0, the statement in the loop won't be executed at all because the loop continuation condition immediately fails, and so `result` is left as 1.0.

As I've said, the parameters and all the variables declared within the body of a function are local to the function. There is nothing to prevent you from using the same names for variables in other functions for quite different purposes. Indeed, it's just as well this is so because it would be extremely difficult to ensure variables' names were always unique within a program containing a large number of functions, particularly if the functions were not all written by the same person.

The scope of variables declared within a function is determined in the same way that I have already discussed. A variable is created at the point at which it is defined and ceases to exist at the end of the block containing it. There is one type of variable that is an exception to this — variables declared as `static`. I'll discuss static variables a little later in this chapter.

 NOTE *Take care not to mask global variables with local variables of the same name. You first met this situation back in Chapter 2, where you saw how you could use the scope resolution operator* `::` *to access global variables.*

The return Statement

The `return` statement returns the value of `result` to the point where the function was called. The general form of the `return` statement is

```
return expression;
```

where `expression` must evaluate to a value of the type specified in the function header for the return value. The expression can be any expression you want, as long as you end up with a value of the required type. It can include function calls — even a call of the same function in which it appears, as you'll see later in this chapter.

If the type of return value has been specified as `void`, there must be no expression appearing in the `return` statement. It must be written simply as:

```
return;
```

You can also omit the `return` statement when there is no return value and it otherwise would be placed as the last statement in the function body.

Using a Function

At the point at which you use a function in a program, the compiler must know something about it to compile the function call. It needs enough information to be able to identify the function, and to verify that you are using it correctly. Unless the definition of the function that you intend to use appears earlier in the same source file, you must declare the function using a statement called a **function prototype**.

Function Prototypes

The prototype of a function provides the basic information that the compiler needs to check that you are using a function correctly. It specifies the parameters to be passed to the function, the function name, and the type of the return value — basically, it contains the same information as appears in the function header, with the addition of a semicolon. Clearly, the number of parameters and their types must be the same in the function prototype as they are in the function header in the definition of the function.

The prototypes for the functions that you call from within another function must appear before the statements doing the calling, and are usually placed at the beginning of the program source file. The header files that you've been including for standard library functions contain the prototypes of the functions provided by the library, amongst other things.

For the `power()` function example, you could write the prototype as:

```
double power(double value, int index);
```

 NOTE *Don't forget that a semicolon is required at the end of a function prototype. Without it, you get error messages from the compiler.*

Note that I have specified names for the parameters in the function prototype that are different from those I used in the function header when I defined the function. This is just to indicate that it's possible. Most often, the same names are used in the prototype and in the function header in the definition of the function, but this doesn't *have* to be so. You can use longer, more expressive parameter names in the function prototype to aid understanding of the significance of the parameters, and then use shorter parameter names in the function definition where the longer names would make the code in the body of the function less readable.

If you like, you can even omit the names altogether in the prototype, and just write:

```
double power(double, int);
```

This provides enough information for the compiler to do its job; however, it's better practice to use some meaningful name in a prototype because it aids readability and, in some cases, makes all the difference between clear code and confusing code. If you have a function with two parameters of the same type (suppose our index was also of type `double` in the function `power()`, for example), the use of suitable names indicates which parameter appears first and which second.

TRY IT OUT   Using a Function

You can see how all this goes together in an example exercising the `power()` function.

```cpp
// Ex5_01.cpp
// Declaring, defining, and using a function
#include <iostream>
using std::cout;
using std::endl;

double power(double x, int n);     // Function prototype

int main(void)
{
   int index(3);                  // Raise to this power
   double x(3.0);                 // Different x from that in function power
   double y(0.0);

   y = power(5.0, 3);             // Passing constants as arguments
   cout << endl << "5.0 cubed = " << y;

   cout << endl << "3.0 cubed = "
        << power(3.0, index);     // Outputting return value

   x = power(x, power(2.0, 2.0)); // Using a function as an argument
   cout << endl                   // with auto conversion of 2nd parameter
        << "x = " << x;

   cout << endl;
   return 0;
}

// Function to compute positive integral powers of a double value
// First argument is value, second argument is power index
double power(double x, int n)
{                                 // Function body starts here...
   double result(1.0);            // Result stored here
   for(int i = 1; i <= n; i++)
      result *= x;
   return result;
}                                 // ...and ends here
```

code snippet Ex5_01.cpp

This program shows some of the ways in which you can use the function `power()`, specifying the arguments to the function in a variety of ways. If you run this example, you get the following output:

```
5.0 cubed = 125
3.0 cubed = 27
x = 81
```

How It Works

After the usual `#include` statement for input/output and the `using` declarations, you have the prototype for the function `power()`. If you were to delete this and try recompiling the program, the compiler wouldn't be able to process the calls to the function in `main()` and would instead generate a whole series of error messages:

```
error C3861: 'power': identifier not found
```

In a change from previous examples, I've used the new keyword `void` in the function `main()` where the parameter list would usually appear to indicate that no parameters are to be supplied. Previously, I left the parentheses enclosing the parameter list empty, which is also interpreted in C++ as indicating that there are no parameters; but it's better to specify the fact by using the keyword `void`. As you saw, the keyword `void` can also be used as the return type for a function to indicate that no value is returned. If you specify the return type of a function as `void`, you must not place a value in any `return` statement within the function; otherwise, you get an error message from the compiler.

You gathered from some of the previous examples that using a function is very simple. To use the function `power()` to calculate 5.0^3 and store the result in a variable `y` in our example, you have the following statement:

```
y = power(5.0, 3);
```

The values 5.0 and 3 here are the arguments to the function. They happen to be constants, but you can use any expression as an argument, as long as a value of the correct type is ultimately produced. The arguments to the `power()` function substitute for the parameters x and n, which were used in the definition of the function. The computation is performed using these values, and then, a copy of the result, 125, is returned to the calling function, `main()`, which is then stored in `y`. You can think of the function as having this value in the statement or expression in which it appears. You then output the value of `y`:

```
cout << endl << "5.0 cubed = " << y;
```

The next call of the function is used within the output statement:

```
cout << endl << "3.0 cubed = "
     << power(3.0, index);        // Outputting return value
```

Here, the value returned by the function is transferred directly to the output stream. Because you haven't stored the returned value anywhere, it is otherwise unavailable to you. The first argument in the call of the function here is a constant; the second argument is a variable.

The function `power()` is used next in this statement:

```
x = power(x, power(2.0, 2.0));    // Using a function as an argument
```

Here, the `power()` function is called twice. The first call to the function is the rightmost in the expression, and the result supplies the value for the second argument to the leftmost call. Although the arguments in the sub-expression `power(2.0, 2.0)` are both specified as the `double` literal 2.0, the function is actually called with the first argument as 2.0 and the second argument as the integer literal, 2. The compiler converts the `double` value specified for the second argument to type `int`, because it knows from the function prototype (shown again below) that the type of the second parameter has been specified as `int`.

```
double power(double x, int n);        // Function prototype
```

The `double` result 4.0 is returned by the first call to the `power()` function, and after conversion to type `int`, the value 4 is passed as the second argument in the next call of the function, with `x` as the first argument. Because `x` has the value 3.0, the value of 3.0^4 is computed and the result, 81.0, stored in `x`. This sequence of events is illustrated in Figure 5-2.

This statement involves two implicit conversions from type `double` to type `int` that were inserted by the compiler. There's a possible loss of data when converting from type `double` to type `int`, so the compiler issues warning message when this occurs, even though the compiler itself has inserted this conversion. Generally, relying on automatic conversions where there is potential for data loss is a dangerous programming practice, and it is not at all obvious from the code that this conversion is intended. It is far better to be explicit in your code by using the `static_cast` operator when necessary. The statement in the example is much better written as:

```
x = power(x, static_cast<int>(power(2.0, 2)));
```

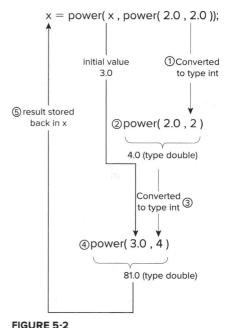

FIGURE 5-2

Coding the statement like this avoids both the compiler warning messages that the original version caused. Using a static cast does not remove the possibility of losing data in the conversion of data from one type to another. Because you specified it, though, it is clear that this is what you intended, recognizing that data loss might occur.

PASSING ARGUMENTS TO A FUNCTION

It's very important to understand how arguments are passed to a function, as it affects how you write functions and how they ultimately operate. There are also a number of pitfalls to be avoided, so we'll look at the mechanism for this quite closely.

The arguments you specify when a function is called should usually correspond in type and sequence to the parameters appearing in the definition of the function. As you saw in the last example, if the type of an argument you specify in a function call doesn't correspond with the type of the parameter in the function definition, the compiler arranges for the argument to be converted to the required type, obeying the same rules as those for converting operands that I discussed in Chapter 2. If the conversion is not to be possible, you get an error message from the compiler. However, even if the conversion is possible and the code compiles, it could well result in the loss of data (for example, from type `long` to type `short`) and should therefore be avoided.

There are two mechanisms used generally in C++ to pass arguments to functions. The first mechanism applies when you specify the parameters in the function definition as ordinary variables (*not* references). This is called the **pass-by-value** method of transferring data to a function, so let's look into that first of all.

The Pass-by-value Mechanism

With this mechanism, the variables, constants, or expression values that you specify as arguments are not passed to a function at all. Instead, copies of the argument values are created, and these copies are used as the values to be transferred to the function. Figure 5-3 shows this in a diagram using the example of our `power()` function.

```
int index = 2;
double value = 10.0;
double result = power(value, index);
```

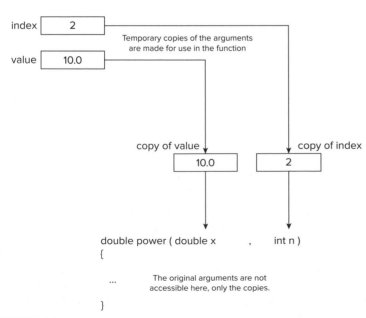

FIGURE 5-3

Each time you call the function power(), the compiler arranges for copies of the arguments that you specify to be stored in a temporary location in memory. During execution of the functions, all references to the function parameters are mapped to these temporary copies of the arguments.

TRY IT OUT   Passing-by-value

One consequence of the pass-by-value mechanism is that a function can't directly modify the arguments passed. You can demonstrate this by deliberately trying to do so in an example:

```cpp
// Ex5_02.cpp
// A futile attempt to modify caller arguments
#include <iostream>
using std::cout;
using std::endl;

int incr10(int num);            // Function prototype

int main(void)
{
   int num(3);

   cout << endl << "incr10(num) = " << incr10(num) << endl
        << "num = " << num << endl;
   return 0;
}

// Function to increment a variable by 10
int incr10(int num)            // Using the same name might help...
{
   num += 10;                  // Increment the caller argument - hopefully
   return num;                 // Return the incremented value
}
```

code snippet Ex5_02.cpp

Of course, this program is doomed to failure. If you run it, you get this output:

```
incr10(num) = 13
num = 3
```

How It Works

The output confirms that the original value of num remains untouched. The copy of num that was generated and passed as the argument to the incr10() function was incremented and was eventually discarded on exiting from the function.

Clearly, the pass-by-value mechanism provides you with a high degree of protection from having your caller arguments mauled by a rogue function, but it is conceivable that you might actually want to arrange to modify caller arguments. Of course, there is a way to do this. Didn't you just know that pointers would turn out to be incredibly useful?

Pointers as Arguments to a Function

When you use a pointer as an argument, the pass-by-value mechanism still operates as before; however, a pointer is an address of another variable, and if you take a copy of this address, the copy still points to the same variable. This is how specifying a pointer as a parameter enables your function to get at a caller argument.

TRY IT OUT   Pass-by-pointer

You can change the last example to use a pointer to demonstrate the effect:

Available for download on Wrox.com

```cpp
// Ex5_03.cpp
// A successful attempt to modify caller arguments
#include <iostream>
using std::cout;
using std::endl;

int incr10(int* num);                  // Function prototype

int main(void)
{
   int num(3);

   int* pnum(&num);                    // Pointer to num

   cout << endl << "Address passed = " << pnum;

   int result = incr10(pnum);
   cout << endl << "incr10(pnum) = " << result;

   cout << endl << "num = " << num << endl;
   return 0;
}

// Function to increment a variable by 10
int incr10(int* num)                   // Function with pointer argument
{
   cout << endl << "Address received = " << num;

   *num += 10;                         // Increment the caller argument
                                       //  - confidently
   return *num;                        // Return the incremented value
}
```

code snippet Ex5_03.cpp

The output from this example is:

```
Address passed = 0012FF6C
Address received = 0012FF6C
incr10(pnum) = 13
num = 13
```

The address values produced by your computer may be different from those shown above, but the two values should be identical to each other.

How It Works

In this example, the principal alterations from the previous version relate to passing a pointer, pnum, in place of the original variable, num. The prototype for the function now has the parameter type specified as a pointer to int, and the main() function has the pointer pnum declared and initialized with the address of num. The function main(), and the function incr10(), output the address sent and the address received, respectively, to verify that the same address is indeed being used in both places. Because the incr10() function is writing to cout, you now call it before the output statement and store the return value in result:

```
int result = incr10(pnum);
cout << endl << "incr10(pnum) = " << result;
```

This ensures proper sequencing of the output. The output shows that this time, the variable num has been incremented and has a value that's now identical to that returned by the function.

In the rewritten version of the function incr10(), both the statement incrementing the value passed to the function and the return statement now de-reference the pointer to use the value stored.

Passing Arrays to a Function

You can also pass an array to a function, but in this case, the array is not copied, even though a pass-by-value method of passing arguments still applies. The array name is converted to a pointer, and a copy of the pointer to the beginning of the array is passed by value to the function. This is quite advantageous because copying large arrays is very time-consuming. As you may have worked out, however, elements of the array may be changed within a function, and thus, an array is the only type that cannot be passed by value.

TRY IT OUT   Passing Arrays

You can illustrate the ins and outs of this by writing a function to compute the average of a number of values passed to a function in an array.

```
// Ex5_04.cpp
// Passing an array to a function
#include <iostream>
using std::cout;
using std::endl;

double average(double array[], int count);       //Function prototype

int main(void)
{
    double values[] = { 1.0, 2.0, 3.0, 4.0, 5.0, 6.0, 7.0, 8.0, 9.0, 10.0 };

    cout << endl << "Average = "
```

```
               << average(values, (sizeof values)/(sizeof values[0])) << endl;
      return 0;
   }

   // Function to compute an average
   double average(double array[], int count)
   {
      double sum(0.0);                    // Accumulate total in here
      for(int i = 0; i < count; i++)
         sum += array[i];                 // Sum array elements

      return sum/count;                   // Return average
   }
```

code snippet Ex5_04.cpp

The program produces the following output:

```
Average = 5.5
```

How It Works

The average() function is designed to work with an array of any length. As you can see from the prototype, it accepts two arguments: the array and a count of the number of elements. The function is called in main() in this statement,

```
cout << endl << "Average = "
     << average(values, (sizeof values)/(sizeof values[0])) << endl;
```

The function is called with the first argument as the array name, values, and the second argument as an expression that evaluates to the number of elements in the array.

You'll recall this expression, using the operator sizeof, from when you looked at arrays in Chapter 4.

Within the body of the function, the computation is expressed in the way you would expect. There's no significant difference between this and the way you would write the same computation if you implemented it directly in main().

The output confirms that everything works as we anticipated.

TRY IT OUT   **Using Pointer Notation When Passing Arrays**

You haven't exhausted all the possibilities here. As you determined at the outset, the array name is passed as a pointer — to be precise, as a copy of a pointer — so within the function, you are not obliged to work with the data as an array at all. You could modify the function in the example to work with pointer notation throughout, in spite of the fact that you are using an array.

Available for download on Wrox.com

```
// Ex5_05.cpp
// Handling an array in a function as a pointer

#include <iostream>
using std::cout;
using std::endl;

double average(double* array, int count);        //Function prototype

int main(void)
{
    double values[] = { 1.0, 2.0, 3.0, 4.0, 5.0, 6.0, 7.0, 8.0, 9.0, 10.0 };

    cout << endl << "Average = "
         << average(values, (sizeof values)/(sizeof values[0])) << endl;
    return 0;
}

// Function to compute an average
double average(double* array, int count)
{
    double sum(0.0);                      // Accumulate total in here
    for(int i = 0; i < count; i++)
        sum += *array++;                  // Sum array elements

    return sum/count;                     // Return average
}
```

code snippet Ex5_05.cpp

The output is exactly the same as in the previous example.

How It Works

As you can see, the program needed very few changes to make it work with the array as a pointer. The prototype and the function header have been changed, although neither change is absolutely necessary. If you change both back to the original version, with the first parameter specified as a double array, and leave the function body written in terms of a pointer, it works just as well. The most interesting aspect of this version is the body of the for loop statement:

```
        sum += *array++;                    // Sum array elements
```

Here, you apparently break the rule about not being able to modify an address specified as an array name because you are incrementing the address stored in array. In fact, you aren't breaking the rule at all. Remember that the pass-by-value mechanism makes a copy of the original array address and passes that to the function, so you are just modifying the copy here — the original array address is quite unaffected. As a result, whenever you pass a one-dimensional array to a function, you are free to treat the value passed as a pointer in every sense, and change the address in any way that you want.

Passing Multidimensional Arrays to a Function

Passing a multidimensional array to a function is quite straightforward. The following statement declares a two-dimensional array, `beans`:

```
double beans[2][4];
```

You could then write the prototype of a hypothetical function, `yield()`, like this:

```
double yield(double beans[2][4]);
```

> **NOTE** *You may be wondering how the compiler can know that this is defining an array of the dimensions shown as an argument, and not a single array element. The answer is simple — you can't write a single array element as a parameter in a function definition or prototype, although you can pass one as an argument when you call a function. For a parameter accepting a single element of an array as an argument, the parameter would have just a variable name and its type. The array context doesn't apply.*

When you are defining a multi-dimensional array as a parameter, you can also omit the first dimension value. Of course, the function needs some way of knowing the extent of the first dimension. For example, you could write this:

```
double yield(double beans[][4], int index);
```

Here, the second parameter provides the necessary information about the first dimension. The function can operate with a two-dimensional array, with the value for the first dimension specified by the second argument to the function and with the second dimension fixed at 4.

TRY IT OUT   **Passing Multidimensional Arrays**

You define such a function in the following example:

Available for download on Wrox.com

```
// Ex5_06.cpp
// Passing a two-dimensional array to a function
#include <iostream>
using std::cout;
using std::endl;

double yield(double array[][4], int n);

int main(void)
{
    double beans[3][4] = {   { 1.0,  2.0,  3.0,  4.0 },
                             { 5.0,  6.0,  7.0,  8.0 },
                             { 9.0, 10.0, 11.0, 12.0 }   };

    cout << endl << "Yield = " << yield(beans, sizeof beans/sizeof beans[0])
```

```
                   << endl;
        return 0;
    }

    // Function to compute total yield
    double yield(double beans[][4], int count)
    {
        double sum(0.0);
        for(int i = 0; i < count; i++)        // Loop through number of rows
            for(int j = 0; j < 4; j++)        // Loop through elements in a row
                sum += beans[i][j];
        return sum;
    }
```

code snippet Ex5_06.cpp

The output from this example is:

```
Yield = 78
```

How It Works

I have used different names for the parameters in the function header from those in the prototype, just to remind you that this is possible — but in this case, it doesn't really improve the program at all. The first parameter is defined as an array of an arbitrary number of rows, each row having four elements. You actually call the function using the array beans with three rows. The second argument is specified by dividing the total size of the array in bytes by the size of the first row. This evaluates to the number of rows in the array.

The computation in the function is simply a nested for loop with the inner loop summing elements of a single row and the outer loop repeating this for each row.

Using a pointer in a function rather than a multidimensional array as an argument doesn't really apply particularly well in this example. When the array is passed, it passes an address value that points to an array of four elements (a row). This doesn't lend itself to an easy pointer operation within the function. You would need to modify the statement in the nested for loop to the following:

```
    sum += *(*(beans + i) + j);
```

So the computation is probably clearer in array notation.

References as Arguments to a Function

We now come to the second of the two mechanisms for passing arguments to a function. Specifying a parameter to a function as a reference changes the method of passing data for that parameter. The method used is not pass-by-value, where an argument is copied before being transferred to the function, but **pass-by-reference**, where the parameter acts as an alias for the argument passed. This eliminates any copying of the argument supplied and allows the function to access the caller argument directly. It also means that the de-referencing, which is required when passing and using a pointer to a value, is also unnecessary.

Using reference parameters to a function has particular significance when you are working with objects of a class type. Objects can be large and complex, in which case, the copying process can be very time-consuming. Using reference parameters in these situations can make your code execute considerably faster.

TRY IT OUT Pass-by-reference

Let's go back to a revised version of a very simple example, `Ex5_03.cpp`, to see how it would work using reference parameters:

```
// Ex5_07.cpp
// Using an lvalue reference to modify caller arguments
#include <iostream>
using std::cout;
using std::endl;

int incr10(int& num);                   // Function prototype

int main(void)
{
   int num(3);
   int value(6);

   int result = incr10(num);
   cout << endl  << "incr10(num) = " << result
        << endl << "num = " << num;

   result = incr10(value);
   cout << endl << "incr10(value) = " << result
        << endl << "value = " << value << endl;
   return 0;
}

// Function to increment a variable by 10
int incr10(int& num)                     // Function with reference argument
{
   cout << endl << "Value received = " << num;
   num += 10;                            // Increment the caller argument
                                         //  - confidently
   return num;                           // Return the incremented value
}
```

code snippet Ex5_07.cpp

This program produces the output:

```
Value received = 3
incr10(num) = 13
num = 13
Value received = 6
incr10(value) = 16
value = 16
```

How It Works

You should find the way this works quite remarkable. This is essentially the same as Ex5_03.cpp, except that the function uses an lvalue reference as a parameter. The prototype has been changed to reflect this. When the function is called, the argument is specified just as though it were a pass-by-value operation, so it's used in the same way as the earlier version. The argument value isn't passed to the function. The function parameter is *initialized* with the address of the argument, so whenever the parameter num is used in the function, it accesses the caller argument directly.

Just to reassure you that there's nothing fishy about the use of the identifier num in main() as well as in the function, the function is called a second time with the variable value as the argument. At first sight, this may give you the impression that it contradicts what I said was a basic property of a reference — that after being declared and initialized, it couldn't be reassigned to another variable. The reason it isn't contradictory is that a reference as a function parameter is created and initialized each time the function is called, and is destroyed when the function ends, so you get a completely new reference created each time you use the function.

Within the function, the value received from the calling program is displayed onscreen. Although the statement is essentially the same as the one used to output the address stored in a pointer, because num is now a reference, you obtain the data value rather than the address.

This clearly demonstrates the difference between a reference and a pointer. A reference is an alias for another variable, and therefore can be used as an alternative way of referring to it. It is equivalent to using the original variable name.

The output shows that the function incr10() is directly modifying the variable passed as a caller argument.

You will find that if you try to use a numeric value, such as 20, as an argument to incr10(), the compiler outputs an error message. This is because the compiler recognizes that a reference parameter can be modified within a function, and the last thing you want is to have your constants changing value now and again. This would introduce a kind of excitement into your programs that you could probably do without. You also cannot use an expression for an argument corresponding to an lvalue reference parameter unless the expression is an lvalue. Essentially, the argument for an lvalue reference parameter must result in a persistent memory location in which something can be stored.

NOTE *I'm sure that you remember that there is another type of reference called an* **rvalue reference** *that I mentioned in Chapter 4. A parameter of an rvalue reference type allows an expression that is an rvalue to be passed to a function.*

The security you get by using an lvalue reference parameter is all very well, but if the function didn't modify the value, you wouldn't want the compiler to create all these error messages every time you passed a reference argument that was a constant. Surely, there ought to be some way to accommodate this? As Ollie would have said, "There most certainly is, Stanley!"

Use of the const Modifier

You can apply the const modifier to a parameter to a function to tell the compiler that you don't intend to modify it in any way. This causes the compiler to check that your code indeed does not modify the argument, and there are no error messages when you use a constant argument.

TRY IT OUT Passing a const

You can modify the previous program to show how the const modifier changes the situation.

Available for download on Wrox.com

```cpp
// Ex5_08.cpp
// Using a reference to modify caller arguments
#include <iostream>
using std::cout;
using std::endl;

int incr10(const int& num);                 // Function prototype

int main(void)
{
   const int num(3);         // Declared const to test for temporary creation
   int value(6);

   int result = incr10(num);
   cout << endl << "incr10(num) = " << result
        << endl << "num = " << num;

   result = incr10(value);
   cout << endl << "incr10(value) = " << result;
   cout << endl << "value = " << value;

   cout << endl;
   return 0;
}

// Function to increment a variable by 10
int incr10(const int& num)        // Function with const reference argument
{
   cout << endl << "Value received = " << num;
//    num += 10;                    // this statement would now be illegal
   return num+10;                 // Return the incremented value
}
```

code snippet Ex5_08.cpp

The output when you execute this is:

```
Value received = 3
incr10(num) = 13
num = 3
Value received = 6
incr10(value) = 16
value = 6
```

How It Works

You declare the variable num in main() as const to show that when the parameter to the function incr10() is declared as const, you no longer get a compiler message when passing a const object.

It has also been necessary to comment out the statement that increments num in the function incr10(). If you uncomment this line, you'll find the program no longer compiles, because the compiler won't allow num to appear on the left side of an assignment. When you specified num as const in the function header and prototype, you promised not to modify it, so the compiler checks that you kept your word.

Everything works as before, except that the variables in main() are no longer changed in the function.

By using lvalue reference parameters, you now have the best of both worlds. On one hand, you can write a function that can access caller arguments directly and avoid the copying that is implicit in the pass-by-value mechanism. On the other hand, where you don't intend to modify an argument, you can get all the protection against accidental modification you need by using a const modifier with an lvalue reference type.

Rvalue Reference Parameters

I'll now illustrate briefly how parameters that are rvalue reference types differ from parameters that are lvalue reference types. Keep in mind that this won't be how rvalue references are intended to be used. You'll learn about that later in the book. Let's look at an example that is similar to Ex5_07.cpp.

TRY IT OUT   Using rvalue Reference Parameters

Here's the code for this example:

Available for
download on
Wrox.com

```
// Ex5_09.cpp
// Using an rvalue reference parameter

#include <iostream>
using std::cout;
using std::endl;

int incr10(int&& num);               // Function prototype

int main(void)
{
   int num(3);
   int value(6);
   int result(0);
\*
   result = incr10(num);                       // Increment num
   cout << endl << "incr10(num) = " << result
        << endl << "num = " << num;

   result = incr10(value);                     // Increment value
   cout << endl << "incr10(value) = " << result
        << endl << "value = " << value;
*\
```

```
       result = incr10(value+num);                        // Increment an expression
       cout << endl << "incr10(value+num) = " << result
            << endl << "value = " << value;

       result = incr10(5);                                 // Increment a literal
       cout << endl << "incr10(5) = " << result
            << endl << "5 = " << 5;

       cout << endl;
       return 0;
}

// Function to increment a variable by 10
int incr10(int&& num)        // Function with rvalue reference argument
{
    cout << endl << "Value received = " << num;
    num += 10;
    return num;              // Return the incremented value
}
```

code snippet Ex5_09.cpp

Compiling and executing this produces the output:

```
Value received = 9
incr10(value+num) = 19
value = 6
Value received = 5
incr10(5) = 15
5 = 5
```

How It Works

The `Incr10()` function now has an rvalue reference parameter type. In `main()`, you call the function with the expression `value+num` as the argument. The output shows that the function returns the value of the expression incremented by 10. Of course, you saw earlier that if you try to pass an expression as the argument for an lvalue reference parameter, the compiler will not allow it.

Next, you pass the literal, 5, as the argument, and again, the value returned shows the incrementing works. The output also shows that the literal 5 has not been changed, but why not? The argument in this case is an expression consisting of just the literal 5. The expression has the value 5 when it is evaluated, and this is stored in a temporary location that is referenced by the function parameter.

If you uncomment the statements at the beginning of `main()`, the code will not compile. A function that has an rvalue reference parameter can only be called with an argument that is an rvalue. Because `sum` and `value` are lvalues, the compiler flags the statements that pass these as arguments to `incr10()` as errors.

While this example shows that you can pass an expression as the argument corresponding to an rvalue reference, and that within the function, the temporary location holding the value of the expression can be accessed and changed, this serves no purpose in this context. You will see when we get to look into defining classes that in some circumstances, rvalue reference parameters offer significant advantages.

NOTE *An important point to keep in mind is that even though an rvalue reference parameter may refer to an rvalue — the result of an expression that is temporary — the rvalue reference parameter itself is not an rvalue, it is an lvalue. There are circumstances where you will want to convert the rvalue reference parameter from an lvalue to an rvalue. You will see in Chapter 8 how this can arise and how you can use the* `std::move()` *library function to convert an lvalue to an rvalue.*

Arguments to main()

You can define `main()` with no parameters (or better, with the parameter list as `void`), or you can specify a parameter list that allows the `main()` function to obtain values from the command line from the execute command for the program. Values passed from the command line as arguments to `main()` are always interpreted as strings. If you want to get data into `main()` from the command line, you must define it like this:

```cpp
int main(int argc, char* argv[])
{
    // Code for main()…
}
```

The first parameter is the count of the number of strings found on the command line, including the program name, and the second parameter is an array that contains pointers to these strings plus an additional element that is null. Thus, `argc` is always at least 1, because you at least must enter the name of the program. The number of arguments received depends on what you enter on the command line to execute the program. For example, suppose that you execute the `DoThat` program with the command:

```
DoThat.exe
```

There is just the name of the .exe file for the program, so `argc` is 1 and the `argv` array contains two elements — `argv[0]` pointing to the string `"DoThat.exe"`, and `argv[1]` that contains null.

Suppose you enter this on the command line:

```
DoThat or else "my friend" 999.9
```

Now `argc` is 5 and `argv` contains six elements, the last element being 0 and the first five pointing to the strings:

```
"DoThat" "or" "else" "my friend" "999.9"
```

You can see from this that if you want to have a string that includes spaces received as a single string, you must enclose it between double quotes. You can also see that numerical values are read as strings, so if you want conversion to the numerical value, that is up to you.

Let's see it working.

TRY IT OUT **Receiving Command-Line Arguments**

This program just lists the arguments it receives from the command line.

```cpp
// Ex5_10.cpp
// Reading command line arguments
#include <iostream>
using std::cout;
using std::endl;

int main(int argc, char* argv[])
{
  cout << endl << "argc = " << argc << endl;
  cout << "Command line arguments received are:" << endl;
  for(int i = 0 ; i <argc ; i++)
    cout << "argument " << (i+1) << ": " << argv[i] << endl;
  return 0;
}
```

code snippet Ex5_10.cpp

You have two choices when entering the command-line arguments. After you build the example in the IDE, you can open a command window at the folder containing the .exe file, and then enter the program name followed by the command-line arguments. Alternatively, you can specify the command-line arguments in the IDE before you execute the program. Just open the project properties window by selecting Project ⇨ Properties from the main menu and then extend the Configuration Properties tree in the left pane by clicking the plus sign (+). Click the Debugging folder and enter the items to be passed to the application as values for the Command Arguments property.

I enter the following in the command window with the current directory containing the .exe file for the program:

```
Ex5_10 trying multiple "argument values" 4.5 0.0
```

Here is the output from resulting from my input:

```
argc = 6
Command line arguments received are:
argument 1: Ex5_10
argument 2: trying
argument 3: multiple
argument 4: argument values
argument 5: 4.5
argument 6: 0.0
```

How It Works

The program first outputs the value of `argc` and then the values of each argument from the `argv` array in the `for` loop. You can see from the output that the first argument value is the program name. `"argument values"` is treated as a single argument because of the enclosing double quotes.

You could make use of the fact that the last element in `argv` is null and code the output of the command-line argument values like this:

```
int i(0);
while(argv[i] != nullptr)
  cout << "argument " << (i+1) << ": " << argv[i++] << endl;
```

The `while` loop ends when `argv[argc]` is reached because that element is a null pointer.

Accepting a Variable Number of Function Arguments

You can define a function so that it allows any number of arguments to be passed to it. You indicate that a variable number of arguments can be supplied when a function is called by placing an ellipsis (which is three periods, . . .) at the end of the parameter list in the function definition. For example:

```
int sumValues(int first,...)
{
  //Code for the function
}
```

There must be at least one ordinary parameter, but you can have more. The ellipsis must always be placed at the end of the parameter list.

Obviously, there is no information about the type or number of arguments in the variable list, so your code must figure out what is passed to the function when it is called. The native C++ library defines `va_start`, `va_arg`, and `va_end` macros in the `cstdarg` header to help you do this. It's easiest to show how these are used with an example.

TRY IT OUT   Receiving a Variable Number of Arguments

This program uses a function that just sums the values of a variable number of arguments passed to it.

```
// Ex5_11.cpp
// Handling a variable number of arguments
#include <iostream>
#include <cstdarg>
using std::cout;
using std::endl;

int sum(int count, ...)
{
  if(count <= 0)
```

```
      return 0;

    va_list arg_ptr;                          // Declare argument list pointer
    va_start(arg_ptr, count);                 // Set arg_ptr to 1st optional argument

    int sum(0);
    for(int i = 0 ; i<count ; i++)
      sum += va_arg(arg_ptr, int);            // Add int value from arg_ptr and increment

    va_end(arg_ptr);                          // Reset the pointer to null
    return sum;
  }

  int main(int argc, char* argv[])
  {
    cout << sum(6, 2, 4, 6, 8, 10, 12) << endl;
    cout << sum(9, 11, 22, 33, 44, 55, 66, 77, 66, 99) << endl;
    return 0;
  }
```

code snippet Ex5_11.cpp

This example produces the following output:

```
42
473
```

How It Works

The main() function calls the sum() function in the two output statements, in the first instance with seven arguments and in the second with ten arguments. The first argument in each case specifies the number of arguments that follow. It's important not to forget this, because if you omit the first count argument, the result will be rubbish.

The sum() function has a single normal parameter of type int that represents the count of the number of arguments that follow. The ellipsis in the parameter list indicates that an arbitrary number of arguments can be passed. Basically, you have two ways of determining how many arguments there are when the function is called — you can require that the number of arguments is specified by a fixed parameter, as in the case of sum(), or you can require that the last argument has a special marker value that you can check for and recognize.

To start processing the variable argument list, you declare a pointer of type va_list:

```
    va_list arg_ptr;                          // Declare argument list pointer
```

The va_list type is defined in the cstdarg header file, and the pointer is used to point to each argument in turn.

The va_start macro is used to initialize arg_ptr so that it points to the first argument in the list:

```
    va_start(arg_ptr, count);                 // Set arg_ptr to 1st optional argument
```

The second argument to the macro is the name of the fixed parameter that precedes the ellipsis in the parameter, and this is used by the macro to determine where the first variable argument is.

You retrieve the values of the arguments in the list in the `for` loop:

```
int sum(0);
for(int i = 0 ; i<count ; i++)
   sum += va_arg(arg_ptr, int);       // Add int value from arg_ptr and increment
```

The `va_arg` macro returns the value of the argument at the location specified by `arg_ptr` and increments `arg_ptr` to point to the next argument value. The second argument to the `va_arg` macro is the argument type, and this determines the value that you get as well as how `arg_ptr` increments, so if this is not correct, you get chaos; the program probably executes, but the values you retrieve are rubbish, and `arg_ptr` is incremented incorrectly to access more rubbish.

When you are finished retrieving argument values, you reset `arg_ptr` with the statement:

```
va_end(arg_ptr);                    // Reset the pointer to null
```

The `va_end` macro resets the pointer of type `va_list` that you pass as the argument to it to null. It's a good idea to always do this because after processing the arguments, `arg_ptr` points to a location that does not contain valid data.

RETURNING VALUES FROM A FUNCTION

All the example functions that you have created have returned a single value. Is it possible to return anything other than a single value? Well, not directly, but as I said earlier, the single value returned need not be a numeric value; it could also be an address, which provides the key to returning any amount of data. You simply use a pointer. Unfortunately, this also is where the pitfalls start, so you need to keep your wits about you for the adventure ahead.

Returning a Pointer

Returning a pointer value is easy. A pointer value is just an address, so if you want to return the address of some variable `value`, you can just write the following:

```
return &value;                     // Returning an address
```

As long as the function header and function prototype indicate the return type appropriately, you have no problem — or at least, no apparent problem. Assuming that the variable `value` is of type `double`, the prototype of a function called `treble`, which might contain the above `return` statement, could be as follows:

```
double* treble(double data);
```

I have defined the parameter list arbitrarily here.

So let's look at a function that returns a pointer. It's only fair that I warn you in advance — this function doesn't work, but it is educational. Let's assume that you need a function that returns a pointer to a memory location containing three times its argument value. Our first attempt to implement such a function might look like this:

```cpp
// Function to treble a value - mark 1
double* treble(double data)
{
   double result(0.0);

   result = 3.0*data;
   return &result;
}
```

TRY IT OUT Returning a Bad Pointer

You could create a little test program to see what happens (remember that the `treble` function won't work as expected):

```cpp
// Ex5_12.cpp
#include <iostream>
using std::cout;
using std::endl;

double* treble(double);                  // Function prototype

int main(void)
{
   double num(5.0);                      // Test value
   double* ptr(nullptr);                 // Pointer to returned value

   ptr = treble(num);

   cout << endl << "Three times num = " << 3.0*num;

   cout << endl << "Result = " << *ptr;   // Display 3*num

   cout << endl;
   return 0;
}

// Function to treble a value - mark 1
double* treble(double data)
{
   double result(0.0);
   result = 3.0*data;
   return &result;
}
```

code snippet Ex5_12.cpp

There's a hint that everything is not as it should be, because compiling this program results in a warning from the compiler:

```
warning C4172: returning address of local variable or temporary
```

The output that I got from executing the program was:

```
Three times num = 15
Result = 4.10416e-230
```

How It Works (or Why It Doesn't)

The function `main()` calls the function `treble()` and stores the address returned in the pointer `ptr`, which should point to a value that is three times the argument, `num`. You then display the result of computing three times `num`, followed by the value at the address returned from the function.

Clearly, the second line of output doesn't reflect the correct value of 15, but where's the error? Well, it's not exactly a secret because the compiler gives fair warning of the problem. The error arises because the variable `result` in the function `treble()` is created when the function begins execution, and is destroyed on exiting from the function — so the memory that the pointer is pointing to no longer contains the original variable value. The memory previously allocated to `result` becomes available for other purposes, and here, it has evidently been used for something else.

A Cast-Iron Rule for Returning Addresses

There is an absolutely cast-iron rule for returning addresses:

Never, ever, return the address of a local automatic variable from a function.

You obviously can't use a function that doesn't work, so what can you do to rectify that? You could use a reference parameter and modify the original variable, but that's not what you set out to do. You are trying to return a pointer to some useful data so that, ultimately, you can return more than a single item of data. One answer lies in dynamic memory allocation (you saw this in action in the previous chapter). With the operator `new`, you can create a new variable in the free store that continues to exist until it is eventually destroyed by `delete` — or until the program ends. With this approach, the function looks like this:

```
// Function to treble a value - mark 2
double* treble(double data)
{
    double* result(new double(0.0));
    *result = 3.0*data;
    return result;
}
```

Rather than declaring `result` to be type `double`, you now declare it to be of type `double*` and store in it the address returned by the operator `new`. Because the result is a pointer, the rest of the function is changed to reflect this, and the address contained in the result is finally returned to the calling program. You could exercise this version by replacing the function in the last working example with this version.

You need to remember that with dynamic memory allocation from within a native C++ function such as this, more memory is allocated each time the function is called. The onus is on the calling program to delete the memory when it's no longer required. It's easy to forget to do this in practice, with the result that the free store is gradually eaten up until, at some point, it is exhausted and the program fails. As mentioned before, this sort of problem is referred to as a **memory leak**.

Here you can see how the function would be used. The only necessary change to the original code is to use `delete` to free the memory as soon as you have finished with the pointer returned by the `treble()` function.

```
#include <iostream>

using std::cout;
using std::endl;

double* treble(double);                  // Function prototype

int main(void)
{
   double num(5.0);                      // Test value
   double* ptr(nullptr);                 // Pointer to returned value

   ptr = treble(num);

   cout << endl << "Three times num = " << 3.0*num;

   cout << endl << "Result = " << *ptr;          // Display 3*num
   delete ptr;                           // Don't forget to free the memory
   ptr = 0;
   cout << endl;
   return 0;
}

// Function to treble a value - mark 2
double* treble(double data)
{
   double* result(new double(0.0));
   *result = 3.0*data;
   return result;
}
```

Returning a Reference

You can also return an lvalue reference from a function. This is just as fraught with potential errors as returning a pointer, so you need to take care with this, too. Because an lvalue reference has no existence in its own right (it's always an alias for something else), you must be sure that the object that it refers to still exists after the function completes execution. It's very easy to forget this when you use references in a function because they appear to be just like ordinary variables.

References as return types are of primary significance in the context of object-oriented programming. As you will see later in the book, they enable you to do things that would be impossible without them. (This particularly applies to "operator overloading," which I'll come to in

Chapter 8). Returning an lvalue reference from a function means that you can use the result of the function on the left side of an assignment statement.

TRY IT OUT Returning a Reference

Let's look at an example that illustrates the use of reference return types, and also demonstrates how a function can be used on the left of an assignment operation when it returns an lvalue. This example assumes that you have an array containing a mixed set of values. Whenever you want to insert a new value into the array, you want to replace the element with the lowest value.

```cpp
// Ex5_13.cpp
// Returning a reference
#include <iostream>
#include <iomanip>
using std::cout;
using std::endl;
using std::setw;

double& lowest(double values[], int length);  // Function prototype

int main(void)
{
    double array[] = { 3.0, 10.0, 1.5, 15.0, 2.7, 23.0,
                       4.5, 12.0, 6.8, 13.5, 2.1, 14.0 };
    int len(sizeof array/sizeof array[0]);    // Initialize to number
                                              // of elements

    cout << endl;
    for(int i = 0; i < len; i++)
        cout << setw(6) << array[i];

    lowest(array, len) = 6.9;                 // Change lowest to 6.9
    lowest(array, len) = 7.9;                 // Change lowest to 7.9

    cout << endl;
    for(int i = 0; i < len; i++)
        cout << setw(6) << array[i];

    cout << endl;
    return 0;
}

// Function returning a reference
double& lowest(double a[], int len)
{
    int j(0);                                 // Index of lowest element
    for(int i = 1; i < len; i++)
        if(a[j] > a[i])                       // Test for a lower value...
            j = i;                            // ...if so update j
    return a[j];                              // Return reference to lowest
                                              // element
}
```

code snippet Ex5_13.cpp

The output from this example is:

```
3    10   1.5    15   2.7   23   4.5   12   6.8  13.5   2.1   14
3    10   6.9    15   2.7   23   4.5   12   6.8  13.5   7.9   14
```

How It Works

Let's first take a look at how the function is implemented. The prototype for the function `lowest()` uses `double&` as the specificaition of the return type, which is therefore of type "reference to `doubl`." You write a reference type return value in exactly the same way as you have already seen for variable declarations, appending the `&` to the data type. The function has two parameters specified — a one-dimensional array of type `double` and a parameter of type `int` that specifies the length of the array.

The body of the function has a straightforward `for` loop to determine which element of the array passed contains the lowest value. The index, `j`, of the array element with the lowest value is arbitrarily set to 0 at the outset, and then modified within the loop if the current element, `a[i]`, is less than `a[j]`. Thus, on exit from the loop, `j` contains the index value corresponding to the array element with the lowest value. The `return` statement is as follows:

```
return a[j];                    // Return reference to lowest element
```

In spite of the fact that this looks identical to the statement that would return a value, because the return type was declared as a reference, this returns a reference to the array element `a[j]` rather than the value that the element contains. The address of `a[j]` is used to initialize the reference to be returned. This reference is created by the compiler because the return type was declared as a reference.

Don't confuse returning `&a[j]` with returning a reference. If you write `&a[j]` as the return value, you are specifying the address of `a[j]`, which is a *pointer*. If you do this after having specified the return type as a *reference*, you get an error message from the compiler. Specifically, you get this:

```
error C2440: 'return' : cannot convert from 'double * ' to 'double &'
```

The function `main()`, which exercises the `lowest()` function, is very simple. An array of type `double` is declared and initialized with 12 arbitrary values, and an `int` variable `len` is initialized to the length of the array. The initial values in the array are output for comparison purposes.

Again, the program uses the stream manipulator `setw()` to space the values uniformly, requiring the `#include` directive for `iomanip`.

The function `main()` then calls the function `lowest()` on the left side of an assignment to change the lowest value in the array. This is done twice to show that it does actually work and is not an accident. The contents of the array are then output to the display again, with the same field width as before, so corresponding values line up.

As you can see from the output with the first call to `lowest()`, the third element of the array, `array[2]`, contained the lowest value, so the function returned a reference to it and its value was changed to 6.9. Similarly, on the second call, `array[10]` was changed to 7.9. This demonstrates quite clearly that returning a reference allows the use of the function on the left side of an assignment statement. The effect is as if the variable specified in the `return` statement appeared on the left of the assignment.

Of course, if you want to, you can also use it on the right side of an assignment, or in any other suitable expression. If you had two arrays, x and y, with the number of array elements specified by `lenx` and `leny`, respectively, you could set the lowest element in the array x to twice the lowest element in the array y with this statement:

```
lowest(x, lenx) = 2.0*lowest(y, leny);
```

This statement would call your `lowest()` function twice — once with arguments y and `leny` in the expression on the right side of the assignment, and once with arguments x and `lenx` to obtain the address where the result of the right-hand expression is to be stored.

A Teflon-Coated Rule: Returning References

A similar rule to the one concerning the return of a pointer from a function also applies to returning references:

Never, ever, return a reference to a local variable from a function.

I'll leave the topic of returning a reference from a function for now, but I haven't finished with it yet. I will come back to it again in the context of user-defined types and object-oriented programming, when you will unearth a few more magical things that you can do with references.

Static Variables in a Function

There are some things you can't do with automatic variables within a function. You can't count how many times a function is called, for example, because you can't accumulate a value from one call to the next. There's more than one way to get around this if you need to. For instance, you could use a reference parameter to update a count in the calling program, but this wouldn't help if the function was called from lots of different places within a program. You could use a global variable that you incremented from within the function, but globals are risky things to use. Because globals can be accessed from anywhere in a program, it is very easy to change them accidentally.

Global variables are also risky in applications that have multiple threads of execution that access them, and you must take special care to manage how globals are accessed from different threads. The basic problem that has to be addressed when more than one thread can access a global variable is that one thread can change the value of a global variable while another thread is working with it. The best solution in such circumstances is to avoid the use of global variables altogether.

To create a variable whose value persists from one call of a function to the next, you can declare a variable within a function as `static`. You use exactly the same form of declaration for a `static` variable that you saw in Chapter 2. For example, to declare a variable `count` as `static`, you could use this statement:

```
static int count(0);
```

This also initializes the variable to zero.

> **NOTE** *Initialization of a static variable within a function only occurs the first time that the function is called. In fact, on the first call of a function, the static variable is created and initialized. It then continues to exist for the duration of program execution, and whatever value it contains when the function is exited is available when the function is next called.*

TRY IT OUT   Using Static Variables in Functions

You can demonstrate how a static variable behaves in a function with the following simple example:

```cpp
// Ex5_14.cpp
// Using a static variable within a function
#include <iostream>
using std::cout;
using std::endl;

void record(void);        // Function prototype, no arguments or return value

int main(void)
{
   record();

   for(int i = 0; i <= 3; i++)
      record();

   cout << endl;
   return 0;
}

// A function that records how often it is called
void record(void)
{
   static int count(0);
   cout << endl << "This is the " << ++count;
   if((count > 3) && (count < 21))        // All this....
      cout <<"th";
   else
      switch(count%10)                     // is just to get...
      {
         case 1: cout << "st";
                 break;
         case 2: cout << "nd";
                 break;
         case 3: cout << "rd";
                 break;
```

```
        default: cout << "th";      // the right ending for...
    }                               // 1st, 2nd, 3rd, 4th, etc.
    cout << " time I have been called";
    return;
}
```

code snippet Ex5_14.cpp

Our function here serves only to record the fact that it was called. If you build and execute it, you get this output:

```
This is the 1st time I have been called
This is the 2nd time I have been called
This is the 3rd time I have been called
This is the 4th time I have been called
This is the 5th time I have been called
```

How It Works

You initialize the static variable count with 0 and increment it in the first output statement in the function. Because the increment operation is prefixed, the incremented value is displayed by the output statement. It will be 1 on the first call, 2 on the second, and so on. Because the variable count is static, it continues to exist and retain its value from one call of the function to the next.

The remainder of the function is concerned with working out when "**st**", "**nd**", "**rd**", or "**th**" should be appended to the value of count that is displayed. It's surprisingly irregular.

Note the return statement. Because the return type of the function is void, to include a value would cause a compiler error. You don't actually need to put a return statement in this particular case, as running off the closing brace for the body of the function is equivalent to the return statement without a value. The program would compile and run without error even if you didn't include the return.

RECURSIVE FUNCTION CALLS

When a function contains a call to itself, it's referred to as a **recursive function**. A recursive function call can also be indirect, where a function fun1 calls a function fun2, which, in turn, calls fun1.

Recursion may seem to be a recipe for an indefinite loop, and if you aren't careful, it certainly can be. An indefinite loop will lock up your machine and require *Ctrl+Alt+Del* to end the program, which is always a nuisance. A prerequisite for avoiding an indefinite loop is that the function contains some means of stopping the process.

Unless you have come across the technique before, the sort of things to which recursion may be applied may not be obvious. In physics and mathematics, there are many things that can be thought of as involving recursion. A simple example is the factorial of an integer, which, for a given integer N, is the product 1x2x3...xN. This is very often the example given to show recursion in operation. Recursion can also be applied to the analysis of programs during the compilation process; however, you will look at something even simpler.

TRY IT OUT **A Recursive Function**

At the start of this chapter (see Ex5_01.cpp), you produced a function to compute the integral power of a value; that is, to compute x^n. This is equivalent to x multiplied by itself n times. You can implement this as a recursive function as an elementary illustration of recursion in action. You can also improve the implementation of the function to deal with negative index values, where x^{-n} is equivalent to $1/x^n$.

Available for download on Wrox.com

```cpp
// Ex5_15.cpp (based on Ex5_01.cpp)
// A recursive version of x to the power n
#include <iostream>
using std::cout;
using std::endl;

double power(double x, int n);     // Function prototype

int main(void)
{
  double x(2.0);                    // Different x from that in function power
  double result(0.0);

  // Calculate x raised to powers -3 to +3 inclusive
  for(int index = -3 ; index<=3 ; index++)
    cout << x << " to the power " << index << " is " << power(x, index)<< endl;

  return 0;
}

// Recursive function to compute integral powers of a double value
// First argument is value, second argument is power index
double power(double x, int n)
{
  if(n < 0)
  {
    x = 1.0/x;
    n = -n;
  }
  if(n > 0)
    return x*power(x, n-1);
  else
    return 1.0;
}
```

code snippet Ex5_15.cpp

The output from this program is:

```
2 to the power -3 is 0.125
2 to the power -2 is 0.25
2 to the power -1 is 0.5
2 to the power 0 is 1
2 to the power 1 is 2
2 to the power 2 is 4
2 to the power 3 is 8
```

How It Works

The function now supports positive and negative powers of x, so the first action is to check whether the value for the power that x is to be raised to, n, is negative:

```
if(n < 0)
{
    x = 1.0/x;
    n = -n;
}
```

Supporting negative powers is easy; it just uses the fact that x^{-n} can be evaluated as $(1/x)^n$. Thus, if n is negative, you set x to be 1.0/x and change the sign of n so it's positive.

The next `if` statement decides whether or not the power() function should call itself once more:

```
if(n > 0)
    return x*power(x, n-1);
else
    return 1.0;
```

The `if` statement provides for the value 1.0 being returned if n is zero, and in all other cases, it returns the result of the expression, x*power(x, n-1). This causes a further call to the function power() with the index value reduced by 1. Thus, the `else` clause in the `if` statement provides the essential mechanism necessary to avoid an indefinite sequence of recursive function calls.

Clearly, within the function power(), if the value of n is other than zero, a further call to the function power() occurs. In fact, for any given value of n other than 0, the function calls itself n times, ignoring the sign of n. The mechanism is illustrated in Figure 5-4, where the value 3 for the index argument is assumed.

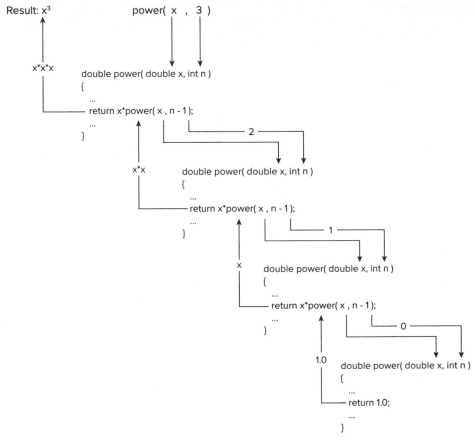

FIGURE 5-4

As you see, the power() function is called a total of four times to generate x^3, three of the calls being recursive where the function is calling itself.

Using Recursion

Unless you have a problem that particularly lends itself to using recursive functions, or if you have no obvious alternative, it's generally better to use a different approach, such as a loop. This is much more efficient than using recursive function calls. Think about what happens with our last example to evaluate a simple product, x*x*...x, n times. On each call, the compiler generates copies of the two arguments to the function, and also has to keep track of the location to return to when each return is executed. It's also necessary to arrange to save the contents of various registers in your computer so that they can be used within the function power(), and, of course, these need to be restored to their original state at each return from the function. With a quite modest depth of recursive call, the overhead can be considerably greater than if you use a loop.

This is not to say you should never use recursion. Where the problem suggests the use of recursive function calls as a solution, it can be an immensely powerful technique, greatly simplifying the code. You'll see an example where this is the case in the next chapter.

C++/CLI PROGRAMMING

For the most part, functions in a C++/CLI program work in exactly the same way as in a native program. Of course, you deal in handles and tracking references when programming for the CLR, not native pointers and references, and that introduces some differences. There are a few other things that are a little different, so let's itemize them.

➤ Function parameters and return values in a CLR program can be value class types, tracking handles, tracking references, and interior pointers.

➤ When a parameter is an array, there is no need to have a separate parameter for the size of the array because C++/CLI arrays have the size built into the Length property.

➤ You cannot do address arithmetic with array parameters in a C++/CLI program as you can in a native C++ program, so you must always use array indexing.

➤ Returning a handle to memory you have allocated on the CLR heap is not a problem because the garbage collector takes care of releasing the memory when it is no longer in use.

➤ The mechanism for accepting a variable number of arguments in C++/CLI is different from the native C++ mechanism.

➤ Accessing command-line arguments in main() in a C++/CLI program is also different from the native C++ mechanism.

Let's look at the last two differences in more detail.

Functions Accepting a Variable Number of Arguments

The C++/CLI language provides for a variable number of arguments by allowing you to specify the parameter list as an array with the array specification preceded by an ellipsis. Here's an example of a function with this parameter list:

```
int sum(... array<int>^ args)
{
  // Code for sum
}
```

The sum() function here accepts any number of arguments of type int. To process the arguments, you just access the elements of the array args. Because it is a CLR array, the number of elements is recorded as its Length property, so you have no problem determining the number of arguments in the body of the function. This mechanism is also an improvement over the native C++ mechanism you saw earlier because it is type-safe. The arguments clearly have to be of type int to be accepted by this function. Let's try a variation on Ex5_11 to see the CLR mechanism working.

TRY IT OUT A Variable Number of Function Arguments

Here's the code for this CLR project.

```
// Ex5_16.cpp : main project file.
// Passing a variable number of arguments to a function

#include "stdafx.h"

using namespace System;

double sum(... array<double>^ args)
{
  double sum(0.0);
  for each(double arg in args)
    sum += arg;
  return sum;
}

int main(array<System::String ^> ^args)
{
  Console::WriteLine(sum(2.0, 4.0, 6.0, 8.0, 10.0, 12.0));
  Console::WriteLine(sum(1.1, 2.2, 3.3, 4.4, 5.5, 6.6, 7.7, 8.8, 9.9));
  return 0;
}
```

code snippet Ex5_16.cpp

This example produces the following output:

```
42
49.5
```

How It Works

The sum() function here has been implemented to accept arguments of type double. The ellipsis preceding the array parameter tells the compiler to expect an arbitrary number of arguments, and the argument values should be stored in an array of elements of type double. Of course, without the ellipsis, the function would expect just one argument when it was called that was a tracking handle for an array.

Compared with the native version in Ex5_11, the definition of the sum() function is remarkably simple. All the problems associated with the type and the number of arguments have disappeared in the C++/CLI version. The sum is accumulated in a simple for each loop that iterates over all the elements in the array.

Arguments to main()

You can see from the previous example that there is only one parameter to the main() function in a C++/CLI program, and it is an array of elements of type String^. Accessing and processing command-line arguments in a C++/CLI program boils down to just accessing the elements in the array parameter. You can try it out.

TRY IT OUT   Accessing Command-Line Arguments

Here's a C++/CLI version of `Ex5_10`.

```
// Ex5_17.cpp : main project file.
// Receiving multiple command line arguments.

#include "stdafx.h"

using namespace System;

int main(array<System::String ^> ^args)
{
  Console::WriteLine(L"There were {0} command line arguments.", args->Length);
  Console::WriteLine(L"Command line arguments received are:");
    int i(1);
  for each(String^ str in args)
    Console::WriteLine(L"Argument {0}: {1}", i++, str);

    return 0;
}
```

code snippet Ex5_17.cpp

You can enter the command-line arguments in the command window or through the project properties window, as described earlier in the chapter. I entered the following on the command line:

```
Ex5_17 trying multiple "argument values" 4.5 0.0
```

I got the following output:

```
There were 5 command line arguments.
Command line arguments received are:
Argument 1: trying
Argument 2: multiple
Argument 3: argument values
Argument 4: 4.5
Argument 5: 0.0
```

How It Works

From the output, you can see that one difference between this and the native C++ version is that you don't get the program name passed to `main()` as an argument — not really a great disadvantage, really a positive feature in most circumstances. Accessing the command-line arguments is now a trivial exercise involving just iterating through the elements in the `args` array.

SUMMARY

In this chapter, you learned about the basics of program structure. You should have a good grasp of how functions are defined, how data can be passed to a function, and how results are returned to a calling program. Functions are fundamental to programming in C++, so everything you do from here on will involve using multiple functions in a program.

The use of references as arguments is a very important concept, so make sure you are confident about using them. You'll see a lot more about references as arguments to functions when you look into object-oriented programming.

EXERCISES

You can download the source code for the examples in the book and the solutions to the following exercises from www.wrox.com.

1. The **factorial** of 4 (written as 4!) is 4*3*2*1 = 24, and 3! is 3*2*1 = 6, so it follows that 4! = 4*3!, or more generally:

    ```
    fact(n) = n*fact(n - 1)
    ```

    The limiting case is when n is 1, in which case, 1! = 1. Write a recursive function that calculates factorials, and test it.

2. Write a function that swaps two integers, using pointers as arguments. Write a program that uses this function and test that it works correctly.

3. The trigonometry functions (sin(), cos(), and tan()) in the standard cmath library take arguments in radians. Write three equivalent functions, called sind(), cosd(), and tand(), which take arguments in degrees. All arguments and return values should be type double.

4. Write a native C++ program that reads a number (an integer) and a name (less than 15 characters) from the keyboard. Design the program so that the data entry is done in one function, and the output in another. Keep the data in the main program. The program should end when zero is entered for the number. Think about how you are going to pass the data between functions — by value, by pointer, or by reference?

5. (Advanced) Write a function that, when passed a string consisting of words separated by single spaces, returns the first word; calling it again with an argument of NULL returns the second word, and so on, until the string has been processed completely, when NULL is returned. This is a simplified version of the way the native C++ run-time library routine strtok() works. So, when passed the string **'one two three'**, the function returns you **'one'**, then **'two'**, and finally **'three'**. Passing it a new string results in the current string being discarded before the function starts on the new string.

▶ **WHAT YOU LEARNED IN THIS CHAPTER**

TOPIC	CONCEPT
Functions	Functions should be compact units of code with a well-defined purpose. A typical program will consist of a large number of small functions, rather than a small number of large functions.
Function prototypes	Always provide a function prototype for each function defined in your program, positioned before you call that function.
Reference parameters	Passing values to a function using a reference can avoid the copying implicit in the pass-by-value transfer of arguments. Parameters that are not modified in a function should be specified as `const`.
Returning references or pointers	When returning a reference or a pointer from a native C++ function, ensure that the object being returned has the correct scope. Never return a pointer or a reference to an object that is local to a native C++ function.
Returning handles in C++/CLI	In a C++/CLI program, there is no problem with returning a handle to memory that has been allocated dynamically, because the garbage collector takes care of deleting it when it is no longer required.
Passing C++/CLI arrays to a function	When you pass a C++/CLI array to a function, there is no need for another parameter for the length of the array, as the number of elements is available in the function body as the `Length` property for the array.

More about Program Structure

In the previous chapter, you learned about the basics of defining functions and the various ways in which data can be passed to a function. You also saw how results are returned to a calling program. In this chapter, you will explore the further aspects of how functions can be put to good use.

POINTERS TO FUNCTIONS

A pointer stores an address value that, up to now, has been the address of another variable with the same basic type as the pointer. This has provided considerable flexibility in allowing you to use different variables at different times through a single pointer. A pointer can also point to the address of a function. This enables you to call a function through a pointer, which will be the function at the address that was last assigned to the pointer.

Obviously, a pointer to a function must contain the memory address of the function that you want to call. To work properly, however, the pointer must also maintain information about the parameter list for the function it points to, as well as the return type. Therefore, when you declare a pointer to a function, you have to specify the parameter types and the return type of the functions that it can point to, in addition to the name of the pointer. Clearly, this is going to restrict what you can store in a particular pointer to a function. If you have declared a pointer to functions that accept one argument of type int and return a value of type double, you can only store the address of a function that has exactly the same form. If you want to store the address of a function that accepts two arguments of type int and returns type char, you must define another pointer with these characteristics.

Declaring Pointers to Functions

You can declare a pointer pfun that you can use to point to functions that take two arguments, of type char* and int, and return a value of type double. The declaration would be as follows:

```
double (*pfun)(char*, int);          // Pointer to function declaration
```

At first, you may find that the parentheses make this look a little weird. This statement declares a pointer with the name pfun that can point to functions that accept two arguments of type pointer to char and of type int, and return a value of type double. The parentheses around the pointer name, pfun, and the asterisk are necessary; without them, the statement would be a function declaration rather than a pointer declaration. In this case, it would look like this:

```
double *pfun(char*, int);            // Prototype for a function
                                     // returning type double*
```

This statement is a prototype for a function pfun() that has two parameters, and returns a pointer to a double value. Because you intended to declare a pointer, this is clearly not what you want at the moment.

The general form of a declaration of a pointer to a function looks like this:

```
return_type (*pointer_name)(list_of_parameter_types);
```

 NOTE *The pointer can only point to functions with the same* return_type *and* list_of_parameter_types *specified in the declaration.*

This shows that the declaration of a pointer to a function consists of three components:

➤ The return type of the functions that can be pointed to

➤ The pointer name preceded by an asterisk to indicate it is a pointer

➤ The parameter types of the functions that can be pointed to

NOTE *If you attempt to assign a function to a pointer that does not conform to the types in the pointer declaration, the compiler generates an error message.*

You can initialize a pointer to a function with the name of a function within the declaration of the pointer. The following is an example of this:

```
long sum(long num1, long num2);      // Function prototype
long (*pfun)(long, long) = sum;      // Pointer to function points to sum()
```

In general, you can set the `pfun` pointer that you declared here to point to any function that accepts two arguments of type `long` and returns a value of type `long`. In the first instance, you initialized it with the address of the `sum()` function that has the prototype given by the first statement.

Of course, you can also initialize a pointer to a function by using an assignment statement. Assuming the pointer `pfun` has been declared as above, you could set the value of the pointer to a different function with these statements:

```
long product(long, long);            // Function prototype
...
pfun = product;                      // Set pointer to function product()
```

As with pointers to variables, you must ensure that a pointer to a function is initialized before you use it to call a function. Without initialization, catastrophic failure of your program is guaranteed.

TRY IT OUT   Pointers to Functions

To get a proper feeling for these newfangled pointers and how they perform in action, try one out in a program.

```
// Ex6_01.cpp
// Exercising pointers to functions
#include <iostream>
using std::cout;
using std::endl;

long sum(long a, long b);            // Function prototype
long product(long a, long b);        // Function prototype

int main(void)
{
  long (*pdo_it)(long, long);        // Pointer to function declaration

  pdo_it = product;
  cout << endl
       << "3*5 = " << pdo_it(3, 5);  // Call product thru a pointer

  pdo_it = sum;                      // Reassign pointer to sum()
  cout << endl
       << "3*(4 + 5) + 6 = "
```

```
             << pdo_it(product(3, pdo_it(4, 5)), 6);   // Call thru a pointer,
                                                        // twice
  cout << endl;
  return 0;
}

// Function to multiply two values
long product(long a, long b)
{
  return a*b;
}

// Function to add two values
long sum(long a, long b)
{
  return a + b;
}
```

code snippet Ex6_01.cpp

This example produces the output:

```
3*5 = 15
3*(4 + 5) + 6 = 33
```

How It Works

This is hardly a useful program, but it does show very simply how a pointer to a function is declared, assigned a value, and subsequently used to call a function.

After the usual preamble, you declare a pointer to a function, pdo_it, which can point to either of the other two functions that you have defined, sum() or product(). The pointer is given the address of the function product() in this assignment statement:

```
pdo_it = product;
```

You just supply the name of the function as the initial value for the pointer, and no parentheses or other adornments are required. The function name is automatically converted to an address, which is stored in the pointer.

The function product() is called indirectly through the pointer pdo_it in the output statement.

```
      cout << endl
           << "3*5 = " << pdo_it(3, 5);          // Call product thru a pointer
```

You use the name of the pointer just as if it was a function name, followed by the arguments between parentheses exactly as they would appear if you were using the original function name directly.

Just to show that you can do it, you change the pointer to point to the function sum().

```
  pdo_it = sum;                                  // Reassign pointer to sum()
```

You then use it again in a ludicrously convoluted expression to do some simple arithmetic:

```
        cout << endl
            << "3*(4 + 5) + 6 = "
            << pdo_it(product(3, pdo_it(4, 5)), 6);    // Call thru a pointer,
                                                        // twice
```

This shows that a pointer to a function can be used in exactly the same way as the function that it points to. The sequence of actions in the expression is shown in Figure 6-1.

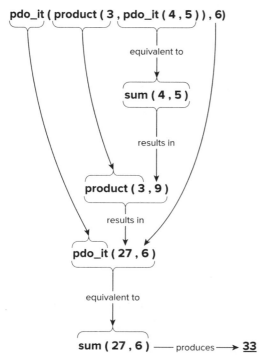

FIGURE 6-1

A Pointer to a Function as an Argument

Because "pointer to a function" is a perfectly reasonable type, a function can also have a parameter that is a pointer to a function. The function can then call the function pointed to by the argument. Because the pointer can be made to point at different functions in different circumstances, this allows the particular function that is to be called from inside a function to be determined in the calling program. In this case, you can pass a function explicitly as an argument.

TRY IT OUT   Passing a Function Pointer

You can look at this with an example. Suppose you need a function that processes an array of numbers by producing the sum of the squares of each of the numbers on some occasions, and the sum of the cubes on other occasions. One way of achieving this is by using a pointer to a function as an argument.

```cpp
// Ex6_02.cpp
// A pointer to a function as an argument
#include <iostream>
using std::cout;
using std::endl;

// Function prototypes
double squared(double);
double cubed(double);
double sumarray(double array[], int len, double (*pfun)(double));

int main(void)
{
  double array[] = { 1.5, 2.5, 3.5, 4.5, 5.5, 6.5, 7.5 };
  int len(sizeof array/sizeof array[0]);

  cout << endl << "Sum of squares = " << sumarray(array, len, squared);
  cout << endl << "Sum of cubes = " << sumarray(array, len, cubed);
  cout << endl;
  return 0;
}

// Function for a square of a value
double squared(double x)
{
  return x*x;
}

// Function for a cube of a value
double cubed(double x)
{
  return x*x*x;
}

// Function to sum functions of array elements
double sumarray(double array[], int len, double (*pfun)(double))
{
  double total(0.0);                       // Accumulate total in here

  for(int i = 0; i < len; i++)
    total += pfun(array[i]);

  return total;
}
```

code snippet Ex6_02.cpp

If you compile and run this code, you should see the following output:

```
Sum of squares = 169.75
Sum of cubes = 1015.88
```

How It Works

The first statement of interest is the prototype for the function `sumarray()`. Its third parameter is a pointer to a function that has a parameter of type `double`, and returns a value of type `double`.

```
double sumarray(double array[], int len, double (*pfun)(double));
```

The function `sumarray()` processes each element of the array passed as its first argument with whatever function is pointed to by its third argument. The function then returns the sum of the processed array elements.

You call the function `sumarray()` twice in `main()`, the first time with the function name `squared` as the third argument, and the second time using `cubed`. In each case, the address corresponding to the function name that you use as the argument is substituted for the function pointer in the body of the function `sumarray()`, so the appropriate function is called within the `for` loop.

There are obviously easier ways of achieving what this example does, but using a pointer to a function provides you with a lot of generality. You could pass any function to `sumarray()` that you care to define as long as it takes one `double` argument and returns a value of type `double`.

Arrays of Pointers to Functions

In the same way as with regular pointers, you can declare an array of pointers to functions. You can also initialize them in the declaration. Here is an example of declaring an array of pointers.

```
double sum(double, double);                           // Function prototype
double product(double, double);                       // Function prototype
double difference(double, double);                    // Function prototype
double (*pfun[3])(double,double) =
                   { sum, product, difference };      // Array of function pointers
```

Each of the elements in the array is initialized by the corresponding function address appearing in the initializing list between braces. To call the function `product()` using the second element of the pointer array, you would write:

```
pfun[1](2.5, 3.5);
```

The square brackets that select the function pointer array element appear immediately after the array name and before the arguments to the function being called. Of course, you can place a function call through an element of a function pointer array in any appropriate expression that the original function might legitimately appear in, and the index value selecting the pointer can be any expression producing a valid index value.

INITIALIZING FUNCTION PARAMETERS

With all the functions you have used up to now, you have had to take care to provide an argument corresponding to each parameter in a function call. It can be quite handy to be able to omit one or more arguments in a function call and have some default values for the arguments that you leave out supplied automatically. You can arrange this by initializing the parameters to a function in its prototype.

For example, suppose that you write a function to display a message, where the message to be displayed is passed as an argument. Here is the definition of such a function:

```
void showit(const char message[])
{
  cout << endl
       << message;
  return;
}
```

You can initialize the parameter to this function by specifying the initializing string value in the function prototype, as follows:

```
void showit(const char message[] = "Something is wrong.");
```

Here, the parameter `message` is initialized with the string literal shown. Once you initialize a parameter to a function in the prototype, if you leave out that argument when you call the function, the initializing value is used in the call.

TRY IT OUT   **Omitting Function Arguments**

Leaving out the function argument when you call the function executes it with the default value. If you supply the argument, it replaces the default value. You can use the `showit()` function to output a variety of messages.

Available for
download on
Wrox.com

```
// Ex6_03.cpp
// Omitting function arguments
#include <iostream>
using std::cout;
using std::endl;

void showit(const char message[] = "Something is wrong.");

int main(void)
{
  const char mymess[] = "The end of the world is nigh.";

  showit();                                  // Display the basic message
  showit("Something is terribly wrong!");    // Display an alternative
  showit();                                  // Display the default again
  showit(mymess);                            // Display a predefined message

  cout << endl;
```

```
    return 0;
}

void showit(const char message[])
{
  cout << endl
       << message;
  return;
}
```

If you execute this example, it produces the following apocalyptic output:

```
Something is wrong.
Something is terribly wrong!
Something is wrong.
The end of the world is nigh.
```

How It Works

As you can see, you get the default message specified in the function prototype whenever the argument is left out; otherwise, the function behaves normally.

If you have a function with several arguments, you can provide initial values for as many of them as you like. If you want to omit more than one argument to take advantage of a default value, all arguments to the right of the leftmost argument that you omit must also be left out. For example, suppose you have this function:

```
int do_it(long arg1 = 10, long arg2 = 20, long arg3 = 30, long arg4 = 40);
```

and you want to omit one argument in a call to it. You can omit only the last one, arg4. If you want to omit arg3, you must also omit arg4. If you omit arg2, arg3 and arg4 must also be omitted, and if you want to use the default value for arg1, you have to omit all of the arguments in the function call.

You can conclude from this that you need to put the arguments which have default values in the function prototype together in sequence at the end of the parameter list, with the argument most likely to be omitted appearing last.

EXCEPTIONS

If you've had a go at the exercises that appear at the end of the previous chapters, you've more than likely come across compiler errors and warnings, as well as errors that occur while the program is running. **Exceptions** are a way of flagging errors or unexpected conditions that occur in your C++ programs, and you already know that the new operator throws an exception if the memory you request cannot be allocated.

So far, you have typically handled error conditions in your programs by using an if statement to test some expression, and then executing some specific code to deal with the error. C++ also provides another, more general mechanism for handling errors that allows you to separate the code that deals with these conditions from the code that executes when such conditions do not arise. It is important to realize that exceptions are not intended to be used as an alternative to the normal data checking and validating that you might do in a program. The code that is generated when you use exceptions carries quite a bit of overhead with it, so exceptions are really intended to be applied in the context of exceptional, near-catastrophic conditions that might arise, but are not normally expected to occur in the normal course of events. An error reading from a disk might be something that you use exceptions for. An invalid data item being entered is not a good candidate for using exceptions.

The exception mechanism uses three new keywords:

➤ **try** — identifies a code block in which an exception can occur

➤ **throw** — causes an exception condition to be originated

➤ **catch** — identifies a block of code in which the exception is handled

In the following Try It Out, you can see how they work in practice.

TRY IT OUT   **Throwing and Catching Exceptions**

You can easily see how exception handling operates by working through an example. Let's use a very simple context for this. Suppose that you are required to write a program that calculates the time it takes in minutes to make a part on a machine. The number of parts made in each hour is recorded, but you must keep in mind that the machine breaks down regularly and may not make any parts.

You could code this using exception handling as follows:

```cpp
// Ex6_04.cpp  Using exception handling
#include <iostream>
using std::cout;
using std::endl;

int main(void)
{
  int counts[] = {34, 54, 0, 27, 0, 10, 0};
  int time(60);                         // One hour in minutes

  for(int i = 0 ; i < sizeof counts/sizeof counts[0] ; i++)
    try
    {
      cout << endl << "Hour " << i+1;

      if(0 == counts[i])
        throw "Zero count - calculation not possible.";

      cout << " minutes per item: " << static_cast<double>(time)/counts[i];
    }
```

```
      catch(const char aMessage[])
      {
        cout << endl << aMessage << endl;
      }
    return 0;
  }
```

code snippet Ex6_04.cpp

If you run this example, the output is:

```
Hour 1 minutes per item: 1.76471
Hour 2 minutes per item: 1.11111
Hour 3
Zero count - calculation not possible.

Hour 4 minutes per item: 2.22222
Hour 5
Zero count - calculation not possible.

Hour 6 minutes per item: 6
Hour 7
Zero count - calculation not possible.
```

How It Works

The code in the `try` block is executed in the normal sequence. The `try` block serves to define where an exception can be raised. You can see from the output that when an exception is thrown, the sequence of execution continues with the `catch` block and, after the code in the catch block has been executed, execution continues with the next loop iteration. Of course, when no exception is thrown, the `catch` block is not executed. Both the `try` block and the `catch` block are regarded as a single unit by the compiler, so they both form the `for` loop block and the loop continues after an exception is thrown.

The division is carried out in the output statement that follows the `if` statement checking the divisor. When a `throw` statement is executed, control passes immediately to the first statement in the `catch` block, so the statement that performs the division is bypassed when an exception is thrown. After the statement in the `catch` block executes, the loop continues with the next iteration, if there is one.

Throwing Exceptions

Exceptions can be thrown anywhere within a `try` block, and the operand of the `throw` statements determines a type for the exception — the exception thrown in the example is a string literal and, therefore, of type `const char[]`. The operand following the `throw` keyword can be any expression, and the type of the result of the expression determines the type of exception thrown.

Exceptions can also be thrown in functions called from within a try block and caught by a catch block following the try block. You could add a function to the previous example to demonstrate this, with the definition:

```
void testThrow(void)
{
  throw " Zero count - calculation not possible.";
}
```

You place a call to this function in the previous example in place of the throw statement:

```
if(0 == counts[i])
  testThrow();              // Call a function that throws an exception
```

The exception is thrown by the testThrow() function and caught by the catch block whenever the array element is zero, so the output is the same as before. Don't forget the function prototype if you add the definition of testThrow() to the end of the source code.

Catching Exceptions

The catch block following the try block in our example catches any exception of type const char[]. This is determined by the parameter specification that appears in parentheses following the keyword catch. You must supply at least one catch block for a try block, and the catch blocks must immediately follow the try block. A catch block catches all exceptions (of the correct type) that occur anywhere in the code in the immediately preceding try block, including those thrown in any functions called directly or indirectly within the try block.

If you want to specify that a catch block is to handle any exception thrown in a try block, you must put an ellipsis (...) between the parentheses enclosing the exception declaration:

```
catch (...)
{
  // code to handle any exception
}
```

This catch block must appear last if you have other catch blocks defined for the try block.

TRY IT OUT   Nested try Blocks

You can nest try blocks one within another. With this situation, if an exception is thrown from within an inner try block that is not followed by a catch block corresponding to the type of exception thrown, the catch handlers for the outer try block are searched. You can demonstrate this with the following example:

```
// Ex6_05.cpp
// Nested try blocks
#include <iostream>
using std::cin;
using std::cout;
using std::endl;

int main(void)
```

```
{
  int height(0);
  const double inchesToMeters(0.0254);
  char ch('y');

  try                                           // Outer try block
  {
    while('y' == ch || 'Y' == ch)
    {
      cout << "Enter a height in inches: ";
      cin >> height;                            // Read the height to be
                                                // converted

      try                                       // Defines try block in which
      {                                         // exceptions may be thrown
        if(height > 100)
          throw "Height exceeds maximum";       // Exception thrown
        if(height < 9)
          throw height;                         // Exception thrown

          cout << static_cast<double>(height)*inchesToMeters
               << " meters" << endl;
      }
      catch(const char aMessage[])              // start of catch block which
      {                                         // catches exceptions of type
        cout << aMessage << endl;               // const char[]
      }
      cout << "Do you want to continue(y or n)?";
      cin >> ch;
    }
  }
  catch(int badHeight)
  {
    cout << badHeight << " inches is below minimum" << endl;
  }
  return 0;
}
```

code snippet Ex6_05.cpp

How It Works

Here, there is a `try` block enclosing the `while` loop and an inner try block in which two different types of exception may be thrown. The exception of type `const char[]` is caught by the `catch` block for the inner `try` block, but the exception of type `int` has no catch handler associated with the inner `try` block; therefore, the `catch` handler in the outer try block is executed. In this case, the program ends immediately because the statement following the `catch` block is a `return`.

Exception Handling in the MFC

This is a good point to raise the question of MFC and exceptions because they are used to some extent. If you browse the documentation that came with Visual C++ 2010, you may come across

TRY, THROW, and CATCH in the index. These are macros defined within MFC that were created before the exception handling was implemented in the C++ language. They mimic the operation of try, throw, and catch in the C++ language, but the language facilities for exception handling really render these obsolete, so you should not use them. They are, however, still there for two reasons. There are large numbers of programs still around that use these macros, and it is important to ensure that, as far as possible, old code still compiles. Also, most of the MFC that throws exceptions was implemented in terms of these macros. In any event, any new programs should use the try, throw, and catch keywords in C++ because they work with the MFC.

There is one slight anomaly you need to keep in mind when you use MFC functions that throw exceptions. The MFC functions that throw exceptions generally throw exceptions of class types — you will find out about class types before you get to use the MFC. Even though the exception that an MFC function throws is of a given class type — CDBException, say — you need to catch the exception as a pointer, not as the type of the exception. So, with the exception thrown being of type CDBException, the type that appears as the catch block parameter is CBDException*.

HANDLING MEMORY ALLOCATION ERRORS

When you used the operator new to allocate memory for our variables (as you saw in Chapters 4 and 5), you ignored the possibility that the memory might not be allocated. If the memory isn't allocated, an exception is thrown that results in the termination of the program. Ignoring this exception is quite acceptable in most situations because having no memory left is usually a terminal condition for a program that you can usually do nothing about. However, there can be circumstances where you might be able to do something about it if you had the chance, or you might want to report the problem in your own way. In this situation, you can catch the exception that the new operator throws. Let's contrive an example to show this happening.

TRY IT OUT Catching an Exception Thrown by the new Operator

The exception that the new operator throws when memory cannot be allocated is of type bad_alloc. bad_alloc is a class type defined in the new standard header file, so you'll need a #include directive for that. Here's the code:

```cpp
// Ex6_06.cpp
// Catching an exception thrown by new
#include<new>                        // For bad_alloc type
#include<iostream>
using std::bad_alloc;
using std::cout;
using std::endl;

int main( )
{
  char* pdata(nullptr);
  size_t count(~static_cast<size_t>(0)/2);
  try
  {
```

```
      pdata = new char[count];
      cout << "Memory allocated." << endl;
    }
    catch(bad_alloc &ex)
    {
      cout << "Memory allocation failed." << endl
           << "The information from the exception object is: "
           << ex.what() << endl;
    }
    delete[] pdata;
    return 0;
  }
```

code snippet Ex6_06.cpp

On my machine, this example produces the following output:

```
Memory allocation failed.
The information from the exception object is: bad allocation
```

If you are in the fortunate position of having many gigabytes of memory in your computer, you may not get the exception thrown.

How It Works

The example allocates memory dynamically for an array of type `char[]` where the length is specified by the `count` variable that you define as:

```
size_t count(~static_cast<size_t>(0)/2);
```

The size of an array is an integer of type `size_t`, so you declare `count` to be of this type. The value for `count` is generated by a somewhat complicated expression. The value 0 is type `int`, so the value produced by the expression `static_cast<size_t>(0)` is a zero of type `size_t`. Applying the `~` operator to this flips all the bits so you then have a `size_t` value with all the bits as 1, which corresponds to the maximum value you can represent as `size_t`, because `size_t` is an unsigned type. This value exceeds the maximum amount of memory that the `new` operator can allocate in one go, so you divide by 2 to bring it within the bounds of what is possible. This is still a very large value, so, unless your machine is exceptionally well endowed with memory, the allocation request will fail.

The allocation of the memory takes place in the `try` block. If the allocation succeeds, you'll see a message to that effect, but if, as you expect, it fails, an exception of type `bad_alloc` will be thrown by the new operator. This causes the code in the `catch` block to be executed. Calling the `what()` function for the `bad_alloc` object reference ex returns a string describing the problem that caused the exception, and you see the result of this call in the output. Most exception classes implement the `what()` function to provide a string describing why the exception was thrown.

To handle out-of-memory situations with some positive effect, clearly, you must have some means of returning memory to the free store. In most practical cases, this involves some serious work on the program to manage memory, so it is not often undertaken.

FUNCTION OVERLOADING

Suppose you have written a function that determines the maximum value in an array of values of type `double`:

```
// Function to generate the maximum value in an array of type double
double maxdouble(double array[], int len)
{
   double maximum(array[0]);

   for(int i = 1; i < len; i++)
      if(maximum < array[i])
         maximum = array[i];

   return maximum;
}
```

You now want to create a function that produces the maximum value from an array of type `long`, so you write another function similar to the first, with this prototype:

```
long maxlong(long array[], int len);
```

You have chosen the function name to reflect the particular task in hand, which is OK for two functions, but you may also need the same function for several other types of argument. It seems a pity that you have to keep inventing names. Ideally, you would use the same function name `max()` regardless of the argument type, and have the appropriate version executed. It probably won't be any surprise to you that you can, indeed, do this, and the C++ mechanism that makes it possible is called **function overloading**.

What Is Function Overloading?

Function overloading allows you to use the same function name for defining several functions as long as they each have different parameter lists. When the function is called, the compiler chooses the correct version for the job based on the list of arguments you supply. Obviously, the compiler must always be able to decide unequivocally which function should be selected in any particular instance of a function call, so the parameter list for each function in a set of overloaded functions must be unique. Following on from the `max()` function example, you could create overloaded functions with the following prototypes:

```
int max(int array[], int len);          // Prototypes for
long max(long array[], int len);        // a set of overloaded
double max(double array[], int len);    // functions
```

These functions share a common name, but have a different parameter list. In general, overloaded functions can be differentiated by having corresponding parameters of different types, or by having a different number of parameters.

Note that a different return type does not distinguish a function adequately. You can't add the following function to the previous set:

```
double max(long array[], int len);         // Not valid overloading
```

The reason is that this function would be indistinguishable from the function that has this prototype:

```
long max(long array[], int len);
```

If you define functions like this, it causes the compiler to complain with the following error:

```
error C2556: 'double max(long [],int)' : overloaded function differs only by
    return type from 'long max(long [],int)'
```

and the program does not compile. This may seem slightly unreasonable, until you remember that you can write statements such as these:

```
long numbers[] = {1, 2, 3, 3, 6, 7, 11, 50, 40};
int len(sizeof numbers/sizeof numbers[0]);
max(numbers, len);
```

The fact that the call for the max() function doesn't make much sense here because you discard the result does not make it illegal. If the return type were permitted as a distinguishing feature, the compiler would be unable to decide whether to choose the version with a long return type or a double return type in the instance of the preceding code. For this reason, the return type is not considered to be a differentiating feature of overloaded functions.

In fact, every function — not just overloaded functions — is said to have a **signature**, where the signature of a function is determined by its name and its parameter list. All functions in a program must have unique signatures; otherwise, the program does not compile.

TRY IT OUT   Using Overloaded Functions

You can exercise the overloading capability with the function max() that you have already defined. Try an example that includes the three versions for int, long, and double arrays.

```
// Ex6_07.cpp
// Using overloaded functions
#include <iostream>
using std::cout;
using std::endl;

int max(int array[], int len);              // Prototypes for
long max(long array[], int len);            // a set of overloaded
double max(double array[], int len);        // functions

int main(void)
{
    int small[] = {1, 24, 34, 22};
    long medium[] = {23, 245, 123, 1, 234, 2345};
    double large[] = {23.0, 1.4, 2.456, 345.5, 12.0, 21.0};

    int lensmall(sizeof small/sizeof small[0]);
    int lenmedium(sizeof medium/sizeof medium[0]);
    int lenlarge(sizeof large/sizeof large[0]);

    cout << endl << max(small, lensmall);
```

```
      cout << endl << max(medium, lenmedium);
      cout << endl << max(large, lenlarge);

      cout << endl;
      return 0;
   }

   // Maximum of ints
   int max(int x[], int len)
   {
      int maximum(x[0]);
      for(int i = 1; i < len; i++)
         if(maximum < x[i])
            maximum = x[i];
      return maximum;
   }

   // Maximum of longs
   long max(long x[], int len)
   {
      long maximum (x[0]);
      for(int i = 1; i < len; i++)
         if(maximum < x[i])
            maximum = x[i];
      return maximum;
   }

   // Maximum of doubles
   double max(double x[], int len)
   {
      double maximum(x[0]);
      for(int i = 1; i < len; i++)
         if(maximum < x[i])
            maximum = x[i];
      return maximum;
   }
```

code snippet Ex6_07.cpp

The example works as you would expect and produces this output:

```
34
2345
345.5
```

How It Works

You have three prototypes for the three overloaded versions of the function max(). In each of the three output statements, the appropriate version of the function max() is selected by the compiler based on the argument list types. This works because each of the versions of the max() function has a unique signature, because its parameter list is different from that of the other max() functions.

Reference Types and Overload Selection

Of course, you can use reference types for parameters in overloaded functions, but you must take care to ensure the compiler can select an appropriate overload. Suppose you define functions with the following prototype:

```
void f(int n);
void f(int& rn);
```

These functions are differentiated by the type of the single parameter, but code using these will not compile. When you call `f()` with an argument of type `int`, the compiler has no means of determining which function should be selected because either function is equally applicable. In general, you cannot overload on a given type, `type`, and an lvalue reference to that type, `type&`.

However, the compiler can distinguish the overloaded functions with the following prototypes:

```
void f(int& arg);          // Lvalue reference parameter
void f(int&& arg);         // Rvalue reference parameter
```

Even though for some argument types, either function could apply, the compiler adopts a preferred choice. The `f(int&)` function will always be selected when the argument is an lvalue. The `f(int&&)` version will be selected only when the argument is an rvalue. For example:

```
int num(5);
f(num);                    // Calls f(int&)
f(2*num);                  // Calls f(int&&)
f(25);                     // Calls f(int&&)
f(num++);                  // Calls f(int&&)
f(++num);                  // Calls f(int&)
```

Only the first and last statements call the overload with the lvalue reference parameter, because the other statements call the function with arguments that are rvalues.

> **NOTE** The rvalue reference type parameter is intended primarily for addressing specific problems that you'll learn about when we look into defining classes.

When to Overload Functions

Function overloading provides you with the means of ensuring that a function name describes the function being performed and is not confused by extraneous information such as the type of data being processed. This is akin to what happens with basic operations in C++. To add two numbers, you use the same operator, regardless of the types of the operands. Our overloaded function `max()` has the same name, regardless of the type of data being processed. This helps to make the code more readable and makes these functions easier to use.

NOTE *The intent of function overloading is clear: to enable the same operation to be performed with different operands using a single function name. So, whenever you have a series of functions that do essentially the same thing, but with different types of arguments, you should overload them and use a common function name.*

FUNCTION TEMPLATES

The last example was somewhat tedious in that you had to repeat essentially the same code for each function, but with different variable and parameter types. However, there is a way of avoiding this. You have the possibility of creating a recipe that will enable the compiler to automatically generate functions with various parameter types. The code defining the recipe for generating a particular group of functions is called a **function template**.

A function template has one or more **type parameters**, and you generate a particular function by supplying a concrete type argument for each of the template's parameters. Thus, the functions generated by a function template all have the same basic code, but customized by the type arguments that you supply. You can see how this works in practice by defining a function template for the function max() in the previous example.

Using a Function Template

You can define a template for the function max() as follows:

```
template<class T> T max(T x[], int len)
{
   T maximum(x[0]);
   for(int i = 1; i < len; i++)
      if(maximum < x[i])
          maximum = x[i];
   return maximum;
}
```

The template keyword identifies this as a template definition. The angled brackets following the template keyword enclose the type parameters that are used to create a particular instance of the function separated by commas; in this instance, you have just one type parameter, T. The keyword class before the T indicates that the T is the type parameter for this template, class being the generic term for type. Later in the book, you will see that defining a class is essentially defining your own data type. Consequently, you have fundamental types in C++, such as type int and type char, and you also have the types that you define yourself. Note that you can use the keyword typename instead of class to identify the parameters in a function template, in which case, the template definition would look like this:

```
template<typename T> T max(T x[], int len)
{
   T maximum(x[0]);
```

```
        for(int i = 1; i < len; i++)
            if(maximum < x[i])
                maximum = x[i];
        return maximum;
    }
```

Some programmers prefer to use the typename keyword as the class keyword tends to connote a user-defined type, whereas typename is more neutral and, therefore, is more readily understood to imply fundamental types as well as user-defined types. In practice, you'll see both keywords used widely.

Wherever T appears in the definition of a function template, it is replaced by the specific type argument, such as long, that you supply when you create an instance of the template. If you try this out manually by plugging in long in place of T in the template, you'll see that this generates a perfectly satisfactory function for calculating the maximum value from an array of type long:

```
long max(long x[], int len)
{
    long maximum(x[0]);
    for(int i = 1; i < len; i++)
        if(maximum < x[i])
            maximum = x[i];
    return maximum;
}
```

The creation of a particular function instance is referred to as **instantiation**.

Each time you use the function max() in your program, the compiler checks to see if a function corresponding to the type of arguments that you have used in the function call already exists. If the function required does not exist, the compiler creates one by substituting the argument type that you have used in your function call in place of the parameter T throughout the source code in the corresponding template definition. You could exercise the template for max() function with the same main() function that you used in the previous example.

TRY IT OUT   Using a Function Template

Here's a version of the previous example modified to use a template for the max() function:

```
// Ex6_08.cpp
// Using function templates

#include <iostream>
using std::cout;
using std::endl;

// Template for function to compute the maximum element of an array
template<typename T> T max(T x[], int len)
{
    T maximum(x[0]);
    for(int i = 1; i < len; i++)
        if(maximum < x[i])
```

```
            maximum = x[i];
    return maximum;
}

int main(void)
{
   int small[] = { 1, 24, 34, 22};
   long medium[] = { 23, 245, 123, 1, 234, 2345};
   double large[] = { 23.0, 1.4, 2.456, 345.5, 12.0, 21.0};

   int lensmall(sizeof small/sizeof small[0]);
   int lenmedium(sizeof medium/sizeof medium[0]);
   int lenlarge(sizeof large/sizeof large[0]);

   cout << endl << max(small, lensmall);
   cout << endl << max(medium, lenmedium);
   cout << endl << max(large, lenlarge);

   cout << endl;
   return 0;
}
```

code snippet Ex6_08.cpp

If you run this program, it produces exactly the same output as the previous example.

How It Works

For each of the statements outputting the maximum value in an array, a new version of max() is instantiated using the template. Of course, if you add another statement calling the function max() with one of the types used previously, no new version of the code is generated.

Note that using a template doesn't reduce the size of your compiled program in any way. The compiler generates a version of the source code for each function that you require. In fact, using templates can generally *increase* the size of your program, as functions can be created automatically even though an existing version might satisfactorily be used by casting the argument accordingly. You can force the creation of particular instances of a template by explicitly including a declaration for it. For example, if you wanted to ensure that an instance of the template for the function max() was created corresponding to the type float, you could place the following declaration after the definition of the template:

```
float max(float, int);
```

This forces the creation of this version of the function template. It does not have much value in the case of our program example, but it can be useful when you know that several versions of a template function might be generated, but you want to force the generation of a subset that you plan to use with arguments cast to the appropriate type, where necessary.

USING THE DECLTYPE OPERATOR

You use the decltype operator to obtain the type of an expression, so decltype(exp) is the type of value that results from evaluating the expression exp. For example, you could write the following statements:

```
double x(100.0);
int n(5);
decltype(x*n) result(x*n);
```

The last statement specifies the type of result to be the type of the expression x*n, which is type double. While this shows the mechanics of what the decltype operator does, the primary use for the decltype operator is in defining function templates. Occasionally, the return type of a template function with multiple type parameters may depend on the types used to instantiate the template. Suppose you want to write a template function to multiply corresponding elements of two arrays, possibly of different types, and return the sum of these products. Because the types of the two arrays may be different, the type of the result will depend on the actual types of the array arguments, so you cannot specify a particular return type. Here's how you can use the decltype operator to take care of it:

```
template<class T1, class T2>
auto f(T1 v1[], T2 v2[], size_t count) ->decltype(v1[0]*v2[0])
{
  decltype(v1[0]*v2[0]) sum(0);
  for(size_t i = 0; i<count ; i++) sum += v1[i]*v2[i];
  return sum;
}
```

This is a slightly different syntax for a function template from what you have seen earlier. The return type is specified using the auto keyword that I introduced in Chapter 2. The actual return type is determined by the compiler when an instance of the template is created because, at that point, the type arguments corresponding to T1 and T2 are known. The decltype expression following the -> will determine the return type for any instance of the template. Let's see if it works.

> **TRY IT OUT**   Using the decltype Operator

Here's a simple example to exercise the template you have just seen:

Available for download on Wrox.com

```
// Ex6_09.cpp Using the decltype operator
#include <iostream>
#include <typeinfo>
using std::cout;
using std::endl;

template<class T1, class T2>
auto product(T1 v1[], T2 v2[], size_t count) ->decltype(v1[0]*v2[0])
{
  decltype(v1[0]*v2[0]) sum(0);
  for(size_t i = 0; i<count ; i++) sum += v1[i]*v2[i];
```

```
      return sum;
    }

    int main()
    {
      double x[] = {100.5, 99.5, 88.7, 77.8};
      short y[] = {3, 4, 5, 6};
      long z[] = {11L, 12L, 13L, 14L};
      size_t n = 4;
      cout << "Result type is "<< typeid(product(x, y, n)).name() << endl;
      cout << "Result is " << product(x, y, n) << endl;
      cout << "Result type is "<< typeid(product(z, y, n)).name() << endl;
      cout << "Result is " << product(z, y, n) << endl;
      return 0;
    }
```

code snippet Ex6_09.cpp

This produces the following output:

```
Result type is double
Result is 1609.8
Result type is long
Result is 230
```

How It Works

You have a `#include` directive for the `typeinfo` header because this is required to use the `typeid` operator that you first saw back in Chapter 2. The return types for functions generated from the `product()` function template are determined by the expression `decltype(v1[0]*v2[0])`. The first instantiations of the template in `main()` are due to the statements:

```
    cout << "Result type is "<< typeid(product(x, y, n)).name() << endl;
    cout << "Result is " << product(x, y, n) << endl;
```

You can see from the output that the type of the value returned by the `product()` function instance is type `double` when the first two arguments are arrays of type `double` and type `short`, respectively, which is as it should be. Executing the next two statements shows that the type for the value returned is type `long` when the arguments are arrays of type `short` and `long`. Clearly, the `decltype` operator is working exactly as advertized.

AN EXAMPLE USING FUNCTIONS

You have covered a lot of ground in C++ up to now and a lot on functions in this chapter alone. After wading through a varied menu of language capabilities, it's not always easy to see how they relate to one another. Now would be a good point to see how some of this goes together to produce something with more meat than a simple demonstration program.

Let's work through a more realistic example to see how a problem can be broken down into functions. The process involves defining the problem to be solved, analyzing the problem to see how it can be implemented in C++, and, finally, writing the code. The approach here is aimed at illustrating how various functions go together to make up the final result, rather than providing a tutorial on how to develop a program.

Implementing a Calculator

Suppose you need a program that acts as a calculator; not one of these fancy devices with lots of buttons and gizmos designed for those who are easily pleased, but one for people who know where they are going, arithmetically speaking. You can really go for it and enter a calculation from the keyboard as a single arithmetic expression, and have the answer displayed immediately. An example of the sort of thing that you might enter is:

```
2*3.14159*12.6*12.6 / 2 + 25.2*25.2
```

To avoid unnecessary complications for the moment, you won't allow parentheses in the expression and the whole computation must be entered in a single line; however, to allow the user to make the input look attractive, you *will* allow spaces to be placed anywhere. The expression entered may contain the operators multiply, divide, add, and subtract represented by *, /, +, and –, respectively, and the expression entered will be evaluated with normal arithmetic rules, so that multiplication and division take precedence over addition and subtraction.

The program should allow as many successive calculations to be performed as required, and should terminate if an empty line is entered. It should also have helpful and friendly error messages.

Analyzing the Problem

A good place to start is with the input. The program reads in an arithmetic expression of any length on a single line, which can be any construction within the terms given. Because nothing is fixed about the elements making up the expression, you have to read it as a string of characters and then work out within the program how it's made up. You can decide arbitrarily that you will handle a string of up to 80 characters, so you could store it in an array declared within these statements:

```
const int MAX(80);          // Maximum expression length including '\0'
char buffer[MAX];           // Input area for expression to be evaluated
```

To change the maximum length of the string processed by the program, you will only need to alter the initial value of MAX.

> **NOTE** Chapter 8 discusses the `string` class, which enables you to handle strings of any length without having to decide the length in advance.

You need to understand the basic structure of the information that appears in the input string, so let's break it down step by step.

You will want to make sure that the input is as uncluttered as possible when you are processing it, so before you start analyzing the input string, you will get rid of any spaces in it. You can call the function that will do this `eatspaces()`. This function can work by stepping through the input buffer — which is the array `buffer[]` — and shuffling characters up to overwrite any spaces. This process uses two indexes to the buffer array, `i` and `j`, which start out at the beginning of the buffer; in general, you'll store element `j` at position `i`. As you progress through the array elements, each time you find a space, you increment `j` but not `i`, so the space at position `i` gets overwritten by the next character you find at index position `j` that is not a space. Figure 6-2 illustrates the logic of this.

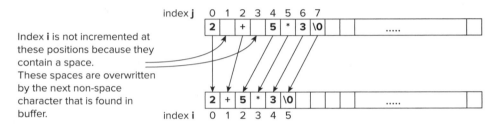

The buffer array before copying its contents to itself

Index **i** is not incremented at
these positions because they
contain a space.
These spaces are overwritten
by the next non-space
character that is found in
buffer.

The buffer array after copying its contents to itself

FIGURE 6-2

This process is one of copying the contents of the array `buffer[]` to itself, excluding any spaces. Figure 6-2 shows the **buffer** array before and after the copying process, and the arrows indicate which characters are copied and the position to which each character is copied.

When you have removed spaces from the input, you are ready to evaluate the expression. You define the function `expr()`, which returns the value that results from evaluating the whole expression in the input buffer. To decide what goes on inside the `expr()` function, you need to look into the structure of the input in more detail. The add and subtract operators have the lowest precedence and so are evaluated last. You can think of the input string as comprising one or more **terms** connected by operators, which can be either the operator + or the operator -. You can refer to either operator as an `addop`. With this terminology, you can represent the general form of the input expression like this:

```
expression: term addop term ... addop term
```

The expression contains at least one `term` and can have an arbitrary number of following `addop` `term` combinations. In fact, assuming that you have removed all the blanks, there are only three legal possibilities for the character that follows each `term`:

➤   The next character is `'\0'`, so you are at the end of the string.

➤   The next character is `'-'`, in which case you should subtract the next `term` from the value accrued for the expression up to this point.

➤   The next character is `'+'`, in which case you should add the value of the next `term` to the value of the expression accumulated so far.

If anything else follows a term, the string is not what you expect, so you'll display an error message and exit from the program. Figure 6-3 illustrates the structure of a sample expression.

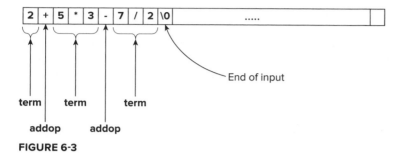

FIGURE 6-3

Next, you need a more detailed and precise definition of a term. A term is simply a series of numbers connected by either the operator * or the operator /. Therefore, a term (in general) looks like this:

```
term: number multop number ... multop number
```

multop represents either a multiply or a divide operator. You could define a function term() to return the value of a term. This needs to scan the string to a number first and then to look for a multop followed by another number. If a character is found that isn't a multop, the term() function assumes that it is an addop and returns the value that has been found up to that point.

The last thing you need to figure out before writing the program is how you recognize a number. To minimize the complexity of the code, you'll only recognize unsigned numbers; therefore, a number consists of a series of digits that optionally may be followed by a decimal point and some more digits. To determine the value of a number, you step through the buffer looking for digits. If you find anything that isn't a digit, you check whether it's a decimal point. If it's not a decimal point, it has nothing to do with a number, so you return what you have got. If you find a decimal point, you look for more digits. As soon as you find anything that's not a digit, you have the complete number and you return that. Imaginatively, you'll call the function to recognize a number and return its value number(). Figure 6-4 shows an example of how an expression breaks down into terms and numbers.

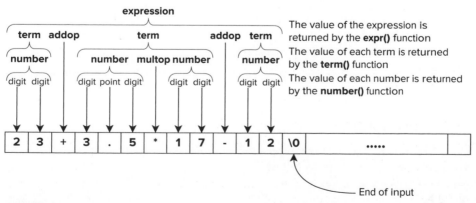

FIGURE 6-4

You now have enough understanding of the problem to write some code. You can work through the functions you need and then write a main() function to tie them all together. The first and, perhaps, easiest function to write is eatspaces(), which is going to eliminate the blanks from the input string.

Eliminating Blanks from a String

You can write the prototype for the eatspaces() function as follows:

```
void eatspaces(char* str);          // Function to eliminate blanks
```

The function doesn't need to return any value because the blanks can be eliminated from the string *in situ*, modifying the original string directly through the pointer that is passed as the argument. The process for eliminating blanks is a very simple one. You copy the string to itself, overwriting any spaces as you saw earlier in this chapter.

You can define the function to do this as follows:

Available for download on Wrox.com

```
// Function to eliminate spaces from a string
void eatspaces(char* str)
{
  int i(0);                                 // 'Copy to' index to string
  int j(0);                                 // 'Copy from' index to string

  while((*(str + i) = *(str + j++)) != '\0')  // Loop while character is not \0
    if(*(str + i) != ' ')                   // Increment i as long as
      i++;                                  // character is not a space
  return;
}
```

code snippet Ex6_10.cpp

How the Function Functions

All the action is in the while loop. The loop condition copies the string by moving the character at position j to the character at position i, and then increments j to the next character. If the character copied was '\0', you have reached the end of the string and you're done.

The only action in the loop statement is to increment i to the next character if the last character copied was not a blank. If it *is* a blank, i is not to be incremented and the blank can therefore be overwritten by the character copied on the next iteration.

That wasn't hard, was it? Next, you can try writing the function that returns the result of evaluating the expression.

Evaluating an Expression

The expr() function returns the value of the expression specified in the string that is supplied as an argument, so you can write its prototype as follows:

```
double expr(char* str);               // Function evaluating an expression
```

The function declared here accepts a string as an argument and returns the result as type `double`. Based on the structure for an expression that you worked out earlier, you can draw a logic diagram for the process of evaluating an expression, as shown in Figure 6-5.

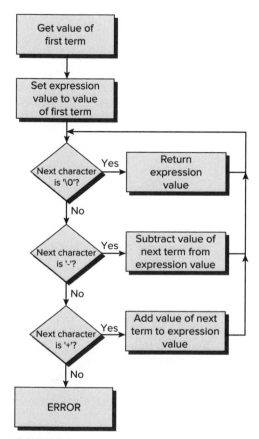

FIGURE 6-5

Using this basic definition of the logic, you can now write the function:

Available for download on Wrox.com

```cpp
// Function to evaluate an arithmetic expression
double expr(char* str)
{
  double value(0.0);                  // Store result here
  int index(0);                       // Keeps track of current character position

  value = term(str, index);           // Get first term

  for(;;)                             // Indefinite loop, all exits inside
  {
    switch(*(str + index++))          // Choose action based on current character
```

```
    {
      case '\0':                        // We're at the end of the string
         return value;                  // so return what we have got

      case '+':                         // + found so add in the
         value += term(str, index);     // next term
         break;

      case '-':                         // - found so subtract
         value -= term(str, index);     // the next term
         break;

      default:                          // If we reach here the string
         cout << endl                   // is junk
              << "Arrrgh!*#!! There's an error"
              << endl;
         exit(1);
    }
  }
}
```

code snippet Ex6_10.cpp

How the Function Functions

Considering this function is analyzing any arithmetic expression that you care to throw at it (as long as it uses our operator subset), it's not a lot of code. You define a variable `index` of type `int`, which keeps track of the current position in the string where you are working, and you initialize it to 0, which corresponds to the index position of the first character in the string. You also define a variable `value` of type `double` in which you'll accumulate the value of the expression that is passed to the function in the `char` array `str`.

Because an expression must have at least one term, the first action in the function is to get the value of the first term by calling the function `term()`, which you have yet to write. This actually places three requirements on the function `term()`:

1. It should accept a `char*` pointer and an `int` variable as parameters, the second parameter being an index to the first character of the term in the string supplied.

2. It should update the index value passed to reference the character following the last character of the term found.

3. It should return the value of the term as type `double`.

The rest of the program is an indefinite `for` loop. Within the loop, the action is determined by a `switch` statement, which is controlled by the current character in the string. If it is a `'+'`, you call the `term()` function to get the value of the next term in the expression and add it to the variable `value`. If it is a `'-'`, you subtract the value returned by `term()` from the variable `value`. If it is a `'\0'`, you are at the end of the string, so you return the current contents of the variable `value` to the calling program. If it is any other character, it shouldn't be there, so after remonstrating with the user, you end the program!

As long as either a '+' or a '-' is found, the loop continues. Each call to `term()` moves the value of the `index` variable to the character following the term that was evaluated, and this should be either another '+' or '-', or the end-of-string character '\0'. Thus, the function either terminates normally when '\0' is reached, or abnormally by calling `exit()`. You need to remember the `#include` directive for `cstdlib` header file that provides the definition of the function `exit()` when you come to put the whole program together.

You could also analyze an arithmetic expression using a recursive function. If you think about the definition of an expression slightly differently, you could specify it as being either a term, or a term followed by an expression. The definition here is recursive (i.e. the definition involves the item being defined), and this approach is very common in defining programming language structures. This definition provides just as much flexibility as the first, but using it as the base concept, you could arrive at a recursive version of `expr()` instead of using a loop as you did in the implementation above. You might want to try this alternative approach as an exercise after you have completed the first version.

Getting the Value of a Term

The `term()` function returns a value for a term as type `double` and receives two arguments: the string being analyzed and an index to the current position in the string. There are other ways of doing this, but this arrangement is quite straightforward. You can, therefore, write the prototype of the function `term()` as follows:

```
double term(char* str, int& index);        // Function analyzing a term
```

You have specified the second parameter as a reference. This is because you want the function to be able to modify the value of the variable `index` in the calling program to position it at the character following the last character of the term found in the input string. You could return `index` as a value, but then you would need to return the value of the term in some other way, so this arrangement seems quite natural.

The logic for analyzing a term is going to be similar in structure to that for an expression. A term is a number, potentially followed by one or more combinations of a multiply or a divide operator and another number. You can write the definition of the `term()` function as follows:

```
// Function to get the value of a term
double term(char* str, int& index)
{
  double value(0.0);                    // Somewhere to accumulate
                                        // the result

  value = number(str, index);           // Get the first number in the term

  // Loop as long as we have a good operator
  while(true)
  {
    if(*(str + index) == '*')           // If it's multiply,
```

```
      value *= number(str, ++index);    // multiply by next number

    else if(*(str + index) == '/')     // If it's divide,
      value /= number(str, ++index);   // divide by next number
    else
      break;
  }
  return value;                        // We've finished, so return what
                                       // we've got
}
```

code snippet Ex6_10.cpp

How the Function Functions

You first declare a local `double` variable, `value`, in which you'll accumulate the value of the current term. Because a term must contain at least one number, the first action in the function is to obtain the value of the first number by calling the `number()` function and storing the result in `value`. You implicitly assume that the function `number()` accepts the string and an index to a position in the string as arguments, and returns the value of the number found. Because the `number()` function must also update the index to the string to the position after the number that was found, you'll again specify the second parameter as a reference when you come to define that function.

The rest of the `term()` function is a `while` loop that continues as long as the next character is `'*'` or `'/'`. Within the loop, if the character found at the current position is `'*'`, you increment the variable `index` to position it at the beginning of the next number, call the function `number()` to get the value of the next number, and then multiply the contents of `value` by the value returned. In a similar manner, if the current character is `'/'`, you increment the `index` variable and divide the contents of `value` by the value returned from `number()`. Because the function `number()` automatically alters the value of the variable index to the character following the number found, `index` is already set to select the next available character in the string on the next iteration.

The loop terminates when a character other than a multiply or divide operator is found, whereupon the current value of the term accumulated in the variable `value` is returned to the calling program.

The last analytical function that you require is `number()`, which determines the numerical value of any number appearing in the string.

Analyzing a Number

Based on the way you have used the `number()` function within the `term()` function, you need to declare it with this prototype:

```
double number(char* str, int& index);    // Function to recognize a number
```

The specification of the second parameter as a reference allows the function to update the argument in the calling program directly, which is what you require.

You can make use of a function provided in a standard C++ library here. The cctype header file provides definitions for a range of functions for testing single characters. These functions return values of type int where nonzero values correspond to true and zero corresponds to false. Four of these functions are shown in the following table:

FUNCTIONS	DESCRIPTION
int isalpha(int c)	Returns nonzero if the argument is alphabetic; otherwise, returns 0.
int isupper(int c)	Returns nonzero if the argument is an uppercase letter; otherwise, returns 0.
int islower(int c)	Returns nonzero if the argument is a lowercase letter; otherwise, returns 0.
int isdigit(int c)	Returns nonzero if the argument is a digit; otherwise, returns 0.

 NOTE *A number of other functions are provided by* <cctype>, *but I won't grind through all the details. If you're interested, you can look them up in the Visual C++ 2010 Help. A search on "is routines" should find them.*

You only need the last of the functions shown above in the program. Remember that isdigit() is testing a character, such as the character '9' (ASCII character 57 in decimal notation) for instance, not a numeric 9, because the input is a string.

You can define the function number() as follows:

```
// Function to recognize a number in a string
double number(char* str, int& index)
{
  double value(0.0);                    // Store the resulting value

  // There must be at least one digit...
  if(!isdigit(*(str + index)))
  { // There's no digits so input is junk...
    cout << endl
         << "Arrrgh!*#!! There's an error"
         << endl;
    exit(1);
  }

  while(isdigit(*(str + index)))        // Loop accumulating leading digits
    value = 10*value + (*(str + index++) - '0');

                                        // Not a digit when we get to here
  if(*(str + index) != '.')             // so check for decimal point
```

```
      return value;                        // and if not, return value

   double factor(1.0);                     // Factor for decimal places
   while(isdigit(*(str + (++index))))      // Loop as long as we have digits
   {
      factor *= 0.1;                       // Decrease factor by factor of 10
      value = value + (*(str + index) - '0')*factor;   // Add decimal place
   }

   return value;                          // On loop exit we are done
}
```

code snippet Ex6_10.cpp

How the Function Functions

You declare the local variable `value` as type `double` that holds the value of the number that is found. You initialize it with 0.0 because you add in the digit values as you go along. There must always be at least one digit present for the number to be valid, so the first step is to verify that this is the case. If there is no initial digit, the input is badly formed, so you terminate the program after issuing a message.

As the number in the string is a series of digits as ASCII characters, the function steps through the string accumulating the value of the number digit by digit. This occurs in two phases — the first phase accumulates digits before the decimal point; then, if you find a decimal point, the second phase accumulates the digits after it.

The first step is in the `while` loop that continues as long as the current character selected by the variable `index` is a digit. The value of the digit is extracted and added to the variable `value` in the loop statement:

```
value = 10*value + (*(str + index++) - '0');
```

The way this is constructed bears a closer examination. A digit character has an ASCII value between 48, corresponding to the digit 0, and 57, corresponding to the digit 9. Thus, if you subtract the ASCII code for `'0'` from the code for a digit, you convert it to its equivalent numeric digit value from 0 to 9. You have parentheses around the subexpression `*(str + index++) - '0'`; these are not essential, but they do make what's going on a little clearer. The contents of the variable `value` are multiplied by 10 to shift the value one decimal place to the left before adding in the digit value, because you'll find digits from left to right — that is, the most significant digit first. This process is illustrated in Figure 6-6.

As soon as you come across something other than a digit, it is either a decimal point or something else. If it's not a decimal point, you've finished, so you return the current contents of the variable `value` to the calling program. If it is a decimal point, you accumulate the digits corresponding to the fractional part of the number in the second loop. In this loop, you use the `factor` variable, which has the initial value 1.0, to set the decimal place for the current digit, and, consequently, `factor` is multiplied by 0.1 for each digit found. Thus, the first digit after the decimal point is multiplied by 0.1, the second by 0.01, the third by 0.001, and so on. This process is illustrated in Figure 6-7.

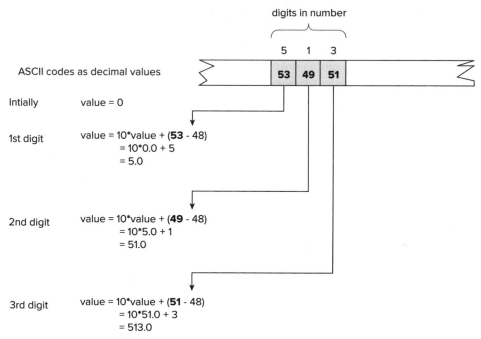

digits in number

5 1 3

ASCII codes as decimal values   53 49 51

Intially   value = 0

1st digit   value = 10*value + (**53** - 48)
                      = 10*0.0 + 5
                      = 5.0

2nd digit   value = 10*value + (**49** - 48)
                      = 10*5.0 + 1
                      = 51.0

3rd digit   value = 10*value + (**51** - 48)
                      = 10*51.0 + 3
                      = 513.0

FIGURE 6-6

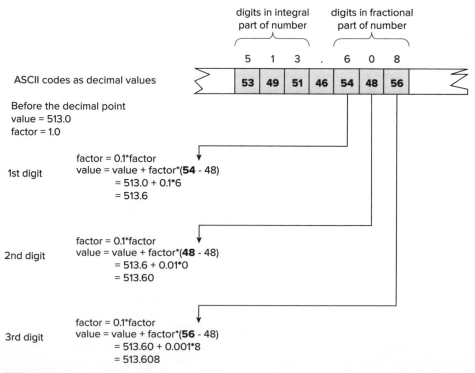

digits in integral   digits in fractional
part of number   part of number

5 1 3 . 6 0 8

ASCII codes as decimal values   53 49 51 46 54 48 56

Before the decimal point
value = 513.0
factor = 1.0

1st digit   factor = 0.1*factor
                 value = value + factor*(**54** - 48)
                      = 513.0 + 0.1*6
                      = 513.6

2nd digit   factor = 0.1*factor
                 value = value + factor*(**48** - 48)
                      = 513.6 + 0.01*0
                      = 513.60

3rd digit   factor = 0.1*factor
                 value = value + factor*(**56** - 48)
                      = 513.60 + 0.001*8
                      = 513.608

FIGURE 6-7

As soon as you find a non-digit character, you are done, so, after the second loop, you return the value of the variable `value`. You almost have the whole thing now. You just need a `main()` function to read the input and drive the process.

Putting the Program Together

You can collect the `#include` statements together and assemble the function prototypes at the beginning of the program for all the functions used in this program:

Available for download on Wrox.com

```
// Ex6_10.cpp
// A program to implement a calculator

#include <iostream>                    // For stream input/output
#include <cstdlib>                     // For the exit() function
#include <cctype>                      // For the isdigit() function
using std::cin;
using std::cout;
using std::endl;

void eatspaces(char* str);            // Function to eliminate blanks
double expr(char* str);               // Function evaluating an expression
double term(char* str, int& index);  // Function analyzing a term
double number(char* str, int& index);// Function to recognize a number

const int MAX(80);                    // Maximum expression length,
                                      // including '\0'
```

code snippet Ex6_10.cpp

You have also defined a global variable MAX, which is the maximum number of characters in the expression processed by the program (including the terminating `'\0'` character).

Now, you can add the definition of the `main()` function, and your program is complete. The `main()` function should read a string and exit if it is empty; otherwise, call the function `expr()` to evaluate the input and display the result. This process should repeat indefinitely. That doesn't sound too difficult, so let's give it a try.

Available for download on Wrox.com

```
int main()
{
  char buffer[MAX] = {0};    // Input area for expression to be evaluated

  cout << endl
       << "Welcome to your friendly calculator."
       << endl
       << "Enter an expression, or an empty line to quit."
       << endl;

  for(;;)
```

```
    {
      cin.getline(buffer, sizeof buffer);          // Read an input line
      eatspaces(buffer);                           // Remove blanks from input

      if(!buffer[0])                               // Empty line ends calculator
        return 0;

      cout << "\t= " << expr(buffer)               // Output value of expression
           << endl << endl;
    }
  }
```

code snippet Ex6_10.cpp

How the Function Functions

In main(), you set up the char array buffer to accept an expression up to 80 characters long (including the string termination character). The expression is read within the indefinite for loop using the getline() input function, and, after obtaining the input, spaces are removed from the string by calling the function eatspaces().

All the other things that the function main() provides for are within the loop. They are to check for an empty string, which consists of just the null character, '\0', in which case the program ends, and to output the value of the string produced by the function expr().

After you type all the functions, you should get output similar to the following:

```
2 * 35
       = 70
2/3 + 3/4 + 4/5 + 5/6 + 6/7
       = 3.90714
1 + 2.5 + 2.5*2.5 + 2.5*2.5*2.5
       = 25.375
```

You can enter as many calculations as you like, and when you are fed up with it, just press Enter to end the program.

Extending the Program

Now that you have got a working calculator, you can start to think about extending it. Wouldn't it be nice to be able to handle parentheses in an expression? It can't be that difficult, can it? Let's give it a try.

Think about the relationship between something in parentheses that might appear in an expression and the kind of expression analysis that you have made so far. Look at an example of the kind of expression you want to handle:

```
2*(3 + 4) / 6 - (5 + 6) / (7 + 8)
```

Notice that the expressions in parentheses always form part of a `term` in your original parlance. Whatever sort of computation you come up with, this is always true. In fact, if you could substitute the value of the expressions within parentheses back into the original string, you would have something that you can already deal with. This indicates a possible approach to handling parentheses. You might be able to treat an expression in parentheses as just another number, and modify the function `number()` to sort out the value of whatever appears between the parentheses.

That sounds like a good idea, but "sorting out" the expression in parentheses requires a bit of thought: the clue to success is in the terminology used here. An expression that appears within parentheses is a perfectly good example of a full-blown expression, and you already have the `expr()` function that will return the value of an expression. If you can get the `number()` function to work out what the contents of the parentheses are and extract those from the string, you could pass the substring that results to the `expr()` function, so recursion would really simplify the problem. What's more, you don't need to worry about nested parentheses. Because any set of parentheses contains what you have defined as an expression, they are taken care of automatically. Recursion wins again.

Take a stab at rewriting the `number()` function to recognize an expression between parentheses.

```cpp
// Function to recognize an expression in parentheses
// or a number in a string
double number(char* str, int& index)
{
  double value(0.0);                    // Store the resulting value

  if(*(str + index) == '(')             // Start of parentheses
  {
    char* psubstr(nullptr);             // Pointer for substring
    psubstr = extract(str, ++index);    // Extract substring in brackets
    value = expr(psubstr);              // Get the value of the substring
    delete[]psubstr;                    // Clean up the free store
    return value;                       // Return substring value
  }

  // There must be at least one digit...
  if(!isdigit(*(str + index)))
  { // There's no digits so input is junk...
    cout << endl
         << "Arrrgh!*#!! There's an error"
         << endl;
    exit(1);
  }

  while(isdigit(*(str + index)))        // Loop accumulating leading digits
    value = 10*value + (*(str + index++) - '0');
                                        // Not a digit when we get to here
  if(*(str + index)!= '.')              // so check for decimal point
```

```
    return value;                           // and if not, return value

  double factor(1.0);                       // Factor for decimal places
  while(isdigit(*(str + (++index))))        // Loop as long as we have digits
  {
    factor *= 0.1;                          // Decrease factor by factor of 10
    value = value + (*(str + index) - '0')*factor;  // Add decimal place
  }
  return value;                             // On loop exit we are done
}
```

code snippet Ex6_10Extended.cpp

This is not yet complete, because you still need the `extract()` function, but you'll fix that in a moment.

How the Function Functions

Look how little has changed to support parentheses. I suppose it is a bit of a cheat, because you use a function (`extract()`) that you haven't written yet, but for one extra function, you get as many levels of nested parentheses as you want. This really is icing on the cake, and it's all down to the magic of recursion!

The first thing that the function `number()` does now is to test for a left parenthesis. If it finds one, it calls another function, `extract()` to extract the substring between the parentheses from the original string. The address of this new substring is stored in the pointer `psubstr`, so you then apply the `expr()` function to the substring by passing this pointer as an argument. The result is stored in `value`, and after releasing the memory allocated on the free store in the function `extract()` (as you will eventually implement it), you return the value obtained for the substring as though it were a regular number. Of course, if there is no left parenthesis to start with, the function `number()` continues exactly as before.

Extracting a Substring

You now need to write the function `extract()`. It's not difficult, but it's also not trivial. The main complication comes from the fact that the expression within parentheses may also contain other sets of parentheses, so you can't just go looking for the first right parenthesis you can find. You must watch out for more left parentheses as well, and for every one you find, ignore the corresponding right parenthesis. You can do this by maintaining a count of left parentheses as you go along, adding one to the count for each left parenthesis you find. If the left parenthesis count is not zero, you subtract one for each right parenthesis. Of course, if the left parenthesis count is zero and you find a right parenthesis, you're at the end of the substring. The mechanism for extracting a parenthesized substring is illustrated in Figure 6-8.

FIGURE 6-8

Because the string you extract here contains subexpressions enclosed within parentheses, eventually extract() is called again to deal with those.

The function extract() also needs to allocate memory for the substring and return a pointer to it. Of course, the index to the current position in the original string must end up selecting the character following the substring, so the parameter for that should be specified as a reference. The prototype of extract(), therefore, is as follows:

```
char* extract(char* str, int& index); //Function to extract a substring
```

You can now have a shot at the definition of the function.

Available for
download on
Wrox.com

```
// Function to extract a substring between parentheses
// (requires <cstring> header file)
char* extract(char* str, int& index)
{
  char buffer[MAX];                     // Temporary space for substring
  char* pstr(nullptr);                  // Pointer to new string for return
  int numL(0);                          // Count of left parentheses found
  int bufindex(index);                  // Save starting value for index

  do
  {
    buffer[index - bufindex] = *(str + index);
    switch(buffer[index - bufindex])
    {
      case ')':
        if(0 == numL)
        {
          buffer[index - bufindex] = '\0';  // Replace ')' with '\0'
          ++index;
          pstr = new char[index - bufindex];
          if(!pstr)
          {
```

```
                cout << "Memory allocation failed,"
                    << " program terminated.";
                exit(1);
            }
            strcpy_s(pstr, index-bufindex, buffer); // Copy substring to new memory
            return pstr;                  // Return substring in new memory
        }
        else
            numL--;                       // Reduce count of '(' to be matched
            break;

        case '(':
          numL++;                         // Increase count of '(' to be
                                          // matched

          break;
        }
    } while(*(str + index++) != '\0');    // Loop - don't overrun end of string

    cout << "Ran off the end of the expression, must be bad input."
        << endl;
    exit(1);
}
```

code snippet Ex6_10Extended.cpp

How the Function Functions

You declare a char array to temporarily hold the substring. You don't know how long the substring will be, but it can't be more than MAX characters. You can't return the address of buffer to the calling function, because it is local and will be destroyed on exit from the function; therefore, you need to allocate some memory on the free store when you know how long the string is. You do this by declaring a variable pstr of type "pointer to char," which you return by value when you have the substring safe and sound in the free store memory.

You declare a counter numL to keep track of left parentheses in the substring (as I discussed earlier). The initial value of index (when the function begins execution) is stored in the variable bufindex. You use this in combination with incremented values of index to index the array buffer.

The executable part of the function is basically one big do-while loop. The substring is copied from str to buffer one character on each loop iteration, with a check for left or right parentheses during each cycle. If a left parenthesis is found, numL is incremented, and if a right parenthesis is found and numL is non-zero, it is decremented. When you find a right parenthesis and numL is zero, you have found the end of the substring. The ')' in the substring in buffer is then replaced by '\0', and sufficient memory is obtained on the free store to hold the substring. The substring in buffer is then copied to the memory you obtained through the operator new by using the strcpy_s() function that is declared in the cstring header file; this is a safe version of the old strcpy() function that is declared in the same header. This function copies the string specified by the third argument, buffer, to the address specified by the first argument, pstr. The second argument is the length of the destination string, pstr.

If you fall through the bottom of the loop, it means that you hit the `'\0'` at the end of the expression in `str` without finding the complementary right bracket, so you display a message and terminate the program.

Running the Modified Program

After replacing the `number()` function in the old version of the program, adding the `#include` statement for `<cstring>`, and incorporating the prototype and the definition for the new `extract()` function you have just written, you're ready to roll with an all-singing, all-dancing calculator. If you have assembled all that without error, you can get output something like this:

```
Welcome to your friendly calculator.
Enter an expression, or an empty line to quit.
1/(1+1/(1+1/(1+1)))
        = 0.6
(1/2-1/3)*(1/3-1/4)*(1/4-1/5)
        = 0.000694444
3.5*(1.25-3/(1.333-2.1*1.6))-1
        = 8.55507
2,4-3.4
Arrrgh!*#!! There's an error
```

The friendly and informative error message in the last output line is due to the use of the comma instead of the decimal point in the expression above it, in what should be 2.4. As you can see, you get nested parentheses to any depth with a relatively simple extension of the program, all due to the amazing power of recursion.

C++/CLI PROGRAMMING

Just about everything discussed so far in relation to functions for native C++ applies equally well to C++/CLI language code with the proviso that parameter types and return types will be fundamental types, which, as you know, are equivalent to value class types in a CLR program, tracking handle types, or tracking reference types. Because you cannot perform arithmetic on the address stored in a tracking handle, the coding techniques that I demonstrated for treating parameters that are native C++ arrays as pointers on which you can perform arithmetic operations do not apply to C++/CLI arrays. Many of the complications that can arise with arguments to native C++ functions disappear, but there is still the odd trap in C++/CLI for the unwary. A CLR version of the calculator can help you understand how functions look written in C++/CLI.

The `throw` and `catch` mechanism for exceptions works much the same in CLR programs as it does in native C++ programs, but there are some differences. The exceptions that you throw in a C++/CLI program must always be thrown using tracking handles. Consequently, you should always be throwing exception objects and, as far as possible, you should avoid throwing literals, especially string literals. For example, consider this try-catch code:

```
try
{
  throw L"Catch me if you  can.";
}
```

```
catch(String^ ex)                      // The exception will not be caught by this
{
  Console::WriteLine(L"String^: {0}",ex);
}
```

The `catch` block cannot catch the object thrown here, because the `throw` statement throws an exception of type `const wchar_t*`, not of type `String^`. To catch the exception as thrown, the `catch` block needs to be:

```
try
{
  throw L"Catch me if you  can.";
}
catch(const wchar_t* ex)               // OK. The exception thrown is of this type
{
  String^ exc = gcnew String(ex);
  Console::WriteLine(L"wchar_t:{0}", exc);
}
```

This `catch` block catches the exception because it now has the correct type.

To throw the exception so that it can be caught by the original `catch` block, you must change the code in the `try` block:

```
try
{
  throw gcnew String(L"Catch me if you  can.");
}
catch(String^ ex)                      // OK. Exception thrown is of this type
{
  Console::WriteLine(L"String^: {0}",ex);
}
```

Now, the exception is a `String` object and is thrown as type `String^`, a handle that references the string.

You can use function templates in your C++/CLI programs, but you have an additional capability called **generic functions** that looks remarkably similar; however, there are significant differences.

Understanding Generic Functions

Although generic functions appear to do the same thing as function templates and, therefore, at first sight, seem superfluous, generic functions work rather differently from template functions, and the differences make them a valuable additional capability in CLR programs. When you use a function template, the compiler generates the source code for each function that you require from the template; this generated code is then compiled along with the rest of your program code. In some cases, this can result in many functions being generated, and the size of the execution module may be increased substantially. On the other hand, a generic function specification is itself compiled, and when you call a function that matches the generic function specification, actual types are substituted for the type parameters at execution time. No extra code is generated at compile time, and the code-bloat that can arise with template functions does not occur.

Some aspects of defining a generic function depend on knowledge of stuff that comes in later chapters, but it will all be clear eventually. I'll provide minimal explanations here of the things that are new, and you'll learn the details later in the book.

Defining Generic Functions

You define a generic function using type parameters that are replaced by actual types when the function is called. Here's an example of a generic function definition:

```
generic<typename T> where T:IComparable
T MaxElement(array<T>^ x)
{
  T max(x[0]);
  for(int i = 1; i < x->Length; i++)
    if(max->CompareTo(x[i]) < 0)
        max = x[i];
  return max;
}
```

This generic function does the same job as the native C++ function template you saw earlier in this chapter. The `generic` keyword in the first line identifies what follows as a generic specification, and the first line defines the type parameter for the function as `T`; the `typename` keyword between the angled brackets indicates that the `T` that follows is the name of a type parameter in the generic function, and that this type parameter is replaced by an actual type when the generic function is used. For a generic function with multiple type parameters, the parameter names go between the angled brackets, each preceded by the `typename` keyword and separated by commas.

The `where` keyword that follows the closing angled bracket introduces a `constraint` on the actual type that may be substituted for `T` when you use the generic function. This particular constraint says that any type that is to replace `T` in the generic function must implement the `IComparable` interface. You'll learn about interfaces later in the book, but for now, I'll say that it implies that the type must define the `CompareTo()` function that allows two objects of the type to be compared. Without this constraint, the compiler has no knowledge of what operations are possible for the type that is to replace `T` because, until the generic function is used, this is completely unknown. With the constraint, you can use the `CompareTo()` function to compare `max` with an element of the array. The `CompareTo()` function returns an integer value that is less than zero when the object for which it is called (`max`, in this case) is less than the argument, zero if it equals the argument, and greater than zero if it is greater than the argument.

The second line specifies the generic function name `MaxElement`, its return type `T`, and its parameter list. This looks rather like an ordinary function header, except that it involves the generic type parameter `T`. The return type for the generic function and the array element type that is part of the parameter type specification are both of type `T`, so both these types are determined when the generic function is used.

Using Generic Functions

The simplest way of calling a generic function is just to use it like any ordinary function. For example, you could use the generic `MaxElement()` from the previous section like this:

```
array<double>^ data = {1.5, 3.5, 6.7, 4.2, 2.1};
double maxData = MaxElement(data);
```

The compiler is able to deduce that the type argument to the generic function is `double` in this instance, and generates the code to call the function accordingly. The function executes with instances of T in the function being replaced by `double`. As I said earlier, this is not like a template function; there is no creation of function instances at compile time. The compiled generic function is able to handle type argument substitutions when it is called.

Note that if you pass a string literal as an argument to a generic function, the compiler deduces that the type argument is `String^`, regardless of whether the string literal is a narrow string constant such as `"Hello!"` or a wide string constant such as `L"Hello!"`.

It is possible that the compiler may not be able to deduce the type argument from a call of a generic function. In these instances, you can specify the type argument(s) explicitly between angled brackets following the function name in the call. For example, you could write the call in the previous fragment as:

```
double maxData = MaxElement<double>(data);
```

With an explicit type argument specified, there is no possibility of ambiguity.

There are limitations on what types you can supply as a type argument to a generic function. A type argument cannot be a native C++ class type, nor a native pointer or reference, nor a handle to a value class type such as `int^`. Thus, only value class types such as `int` or `double` and tracking handles such as `String^` are allowed (but not a handle to a value class type).

Let's try a working example.

TRY IT OUT   Using a Generic Function

Here's an example that defines and uses three generic functions:

```
// Ex6_11.cpp : main project file.
// Defining and using generic functions

#include "stdafx.h"

using namespace System;

// Generic function to find the maximum element in an array
generic<typename T> where T:IComparable
T MaxElement(array<T>^ x)
{
  T max(x[0]);
  for(int i = 1; i < x->Length; i++)
    if(max->CompareTo(x[i]) < 0)
      max = x[i];
  return max;
}


// Generic function to remove an element from an array
generic<typename T> where T:IComparable
```

```cpp
array<T>^ RemoveElement(T element, array<T>^ data)
{
  array<T>^ newData = gcnew array<T>(data->Length - 1);
  int index(0);                       // Index to elements in newData array
  bool found(false);                  // Indicates that the element to remove was found
  for each(T item in data)
  {
    // Check for invalid index or element found
    if((!found) && item->CompareTo(element) == 0)
    {
      found = true;
       continue;
    }
    else
    {
      if(newData->Length == index)
      {
        Console::WriteLine(L"Element to remove not found");
        return data;
      }
      newData[index++] = item;
    }
  }
    return newData;
}

// Generic function to list an array
generic<typename T>
void ListElements(array<T>^ data)
{
  for each(T item in data)
    Console::Write(L"{0,10}", item);
  Console::WriteLine();
}

int main(array<System::String ^> ^args)
{
  array<double>^ data = {1.5, 3.5, 6.7, 4.2, 2.1};
  Console::WriteLine(L"Array contains:");
  ListElements(data);
  Console::WriteLine(L"\nMaximum element = {0}\n", MaxElement(data));
  array<double>^ result = RemoveElement(MaxElement(data), data);
  Console::WriteLine(L" After removing maximum, array contains:");
  ListElements(result);

  array<int>^ numbers = {3, 12, 7, 0, 10, 11};
  Console::WriteLine(L"\nArray contains:");
  ListElements(numbers);
  Console::WriteLine(L"\nMaximum element = {0}\n", MaxElement(numbers));
  Console::WriteLine(L"\nAfter removing maximum, array contains:");
  ListElements(RemoveElement(MaxElement(numbers), numbers));

  array<String^>^ strings = {L"Many", L"hands", L"make", L"light", L"work"};
  Console::WriteLine(L"\nArray contains:");
  ListElements(strings);
```

```
    Console::WriteLine(L"\nMaximum element = {0}\n", MaxElement(strings));
    Console::WriteLine(L"\nAfter removing maximum, array contains:");
    ListElements(RemoveElement(MaxElement(strings), strings));
    return 0;
}
```

code snippet Ex6_11.cpp

The output from this example is:

```
Array contains:
      1.5        3.5        6.7        4.2        2.1

Maximum element = 6.7

  After removing maximum, array contains:
      1.5        3.5        4.2        2.1

Array contains:
      3         12          7          0         10         11

Maximum element = 12

After removing maximum, array contains:
      3          7          0         10         11

Array contains:
    Many       hands       make      light       work

Maximum element = work


After removing maximum, array contains:
    Many       hands       make      light
```

How It Works

The first generic function that this example defines is MaxElement(), which is identical to the one you saw in the preceding section that finds the maximum element in an array, so I won't discuss it again.

The next generic function, RemoveElement(), removes the element passed as the first argument from the array specified by the second argument, and the function returns a handle to the new array that results from the operation. You can see from the first two lines of the function definition that both parameter types and the return type involve the type parameter, T.

```
generic<typename T> where T:IComparable
array<T>^ RemoveElement(T element, array<T>^ data)
```

The constraint on T is the same as for the first generic function and implies that whatever type is used as the type argument must implement the CompareTo() function to allow objects of the type to be compared. The second parameter and the return type are both handles to an array of elements of type T. The first parameter is simply type T.

The function first creates an array to hold the result:

```
array<T>^ newData = gcnew array<T>(data->Length - 1);
```

The `newData` array is of the same type as the second argument — an array of elements of type `T` — but has one fewer element because one element is to be removed from the original.

The elements are copied from the `data` array to the `newData` array in the `for each` loop:

```
int index(0);                     // Index to elements in newData array
bool found(false);                // Indicates that element to remove was found
for each(T item in data)
{
  // Check for invalid index or element found
  if((!found) && item->CompareTo(element) == 0)
  {
    found = true;
    continue;
  }
  else
  {
    if(newData->Length == index)
    {
      Console::WriteLine(L"Element to remove not found");
      return data;
    }
    newData[index++] = item;
  }
}
```

All elements are copied except the one identified by the first argument to the function. You use the `index` variable to select the next `newData` array element that is to receive the next element from the `data` array. Each element from `data` is copied unless it is equal to `element`, in which case, `found` is set to `true` and the `continue` statement skips to the next iteration. It is quite possible that an array could have more than one element equal to the first argument, and the `found` variable prevents subsequent elements that are the same as `element` from being skipped in the loop.

You also have a check for the index variable exceeding the legal limit for indexing elements in `newData`. This could arise if there is no element in the data array equal to the first argument to the function. In this eventuality, you just return the handle to the original array.

The third generic function just lists the elements from an array of type `array<T>`:

```
generic<typename T>
void ListElements(array<T>^ data)
{
  for each(T item in data)
    Console::Write(L"{0,10}", item);
  Console::WriteLine();
}
```

This is one of the few occasions when no constraint on the type parameter is needed. There is very little you can do with objects that are of a completely unknown type, so, typically, generic function type parameters will have constraints. The operation of the function is very simple — each element from the array is written to the command line in an output field with a width of 10 in the `for each` loop. If you want, you could add a little sophistication by adding a parameter for the field width and creating the format string to be used as the first argument to the `Write()` function in the `Console` class. You could also add logic to the loop to write a specific number of elements per line based on the field width.

The `main()` function exercises these generic functions with type parameters of types `double`, `int`, and `String^`. Thus, you can see that all three generic functions work with value types and handles. In the second and third examples, the generic functions are used in combination in a single statement. For example, look at this statement in the third sample use of the functions:

```
ListElements(RemoveElement(MaxElement(strings), strings));
```

The first argument to the `RemoveElement()` generic function is produced by the `MaxElement()` generic function call, so these generic functions can be used in the same way as equivalent ordinary functions.

The compiler is able to deduce the type argument in all instances where the generic functions are used but you could specify them explicitly if you wanted to. For example, you could write the previous statement like this:

```
ListElements(RemoveElement<String^>(MaxElement<String^>(strings), strings));
```

A Calculator Program for the CLR

Let's re-implement the calculator as a C++/CLI example. We'll assume the same program structure and hierarchy of functions as you saw for the native C++ program, but the functions will be declared and defined as C++/CLI functions. A good starting point is the set of function prototypes at the beginning of the source file — I have used `Ex6_12` as the CLR project name:

```
// Ex6_12.cpp : main project file.
// A CLR calculator supporting parentheses

#include "stdafx.h"
#include <cstdlib>                              // For exit()

using namespace System;
String^ eatspaces(String^ str);                // Function to eliminate blanks
double expr(String^ str);                       // Function evaluating an expression
double term(String^ str, int^ index);           // Function analyzing a term
double number(String^ str, int^ index);         // Function to recognize a number
String^ extract(String^ str, int^ index);       // Function to extract a substring
```

code snippet Ex6_12.cpp

All the parameters are now handles; the string parameters are type String^ and the index parameter that records the current position in the string is also a handle of type int^. Of course, a string is returned as a handle of type String^.

The main() function implementation looks like this:

```cpp
int main(array<System::String ^> ^args)
{
  String^ buffer;     // Input area for expression to be evaluated

  Console::WriteLine(L"Welcome to your friendly calculator.");
  Console::WriteLine(L"Enter an expression, or an empty line to quit.");

  for(;;)
  {
    buffer = eatspaces(Console::ReadLine());        // Read an input line

    if(String::IsNullOrEmpty(buffer))               // Empty line ends calculator
      return 0;

    Console::WriteLine(L" = {0}\n\n",expr(buffer)); // Output value of expression
  }
  return 0;
}
```

code snippet Ex6_12.cpp

The function is a lot shorter and easier to read. Within the indefinite for loop, you call the String class function, IsNullOrEmpty(). This function returns true if the string passed as the argument is null or of zero length, so it does exactly what you want here.

Removing Spaces from the Input String

The function to remove spaces is much simpler and shorter:

```cpp
// Function to eliminate spaces from a string
String^ eatspaces(String^ str)
{
  return str->Replace(L" ", L"");
}
```

code snippet Ex6_12.cpp

You use the Replace() function that the System::String class defines to replace any space in str by an empty string, thus removing all spaces from str. The Replace() function returns the new string with the spaces removed.

Evaluating an Arithmetic Expression

You can implement the function to evaluate an expression like this:

```cpp
// Function to evaluate an arithmetic expression
double expr(String^ str)
{
  int^ index(0);                       // Keeps track of current character position

  double value(term(str, index));      // Get first term

  while(*index < str->Length)
  {
    switch(str[*index])                // Choose action based on current character
    {
      case '+':                        // + found so
          ++(*index);                  // increment index and add
          value += term(str, index);   // the next term
          break;

      case '-':                        // - found so
          ++(*index);                  // increment index and subtract
        value -= term(str, index);     // the next term
        break;

      default:                         // If we reach here the string is junk
        Console::WriteLine(L"Arrrgh!*#!! There's an error.\n");
        exit(1);
    }
  }
  return value;
}
```

code snippet Ex6_12.cpp

The index variable is declared as a handle because you want to pass it to the `term()` function and allow the `term()` function to modify the original variable. If you declared index simply as type `int`, the `term()` function would receive a copy of the value and could not refer to the original variable to change it.

The declaration of `index` results in a warning message from the compiler, because the statement relies on autoboxing of the value 0 to produce the `Int32` value class object that the handle references, and the warning is because people often write the statement like this but intend to initialize the handle to null. Of course, to do this, you must use `nullptr` as the initial value in place of 0. If you want to eliminate the warning, you could rewrite the statement as:

```cpp
int^ index(gcnew int(0));
```

This statement uses a constructor explicitly to create the object and initialize it with 0, so there's no warning from the compiler.

After processing the initial term by calling the `term()` function, the `while` loop steps through the string looking for + or – operators followed by another term. The `switch` statement identifies and processes the operators. If you have been using native C++ for a while, you might be tempted to write the case statements in the `switch` a little differently — for example:

```
// Incorrect code!! Does not work!!
case '+':                                    // + found so
   value += term(str, ++(*index));       // increment index & add the next term
   break;
```

Of course, this would typically be written without the first comment. This code is wrong, but why is it wrong? The `term()` function expects a handle in type `int^` as the second argument, and that is what is supplied here, although maybe not as you expect. The compiler arranges for the expression `++(*index)` to be evaluated and the result stored in a temporary location. The expression indeed updates the value referenced by `index`, but the handle that is passed to the `term()` function is a handle to the temporary location holding the result of evaluating the expression, not the handle `index`. This handle is produced by autoboxing the value stored in the temporary location. When the `term()` function updates the value referenced by the handle that is passed to it, the temporary location is updated, not the location referenced by `index`; thus, all the updates to the index position of the string made in the `term()` function are lost. If you expect a function to update a variable in the calling program, you must not use an expression as the function argument — you must always use the handle variable name.

Obtaining the Value of a Term

As in the native C++ version, the `term()` function steps through the string that is passed as the first argument, starting at the character position referenced by the second argument:

```
// Function to get the value of a term
double term(String^ str, int^ index)
{
   double value(number(str, index));           // Get the first number in the term

   // Loop as long as we have characters and a good operator
   while(*index < str->Length)
   {
     if(L'*' == str[*index])                    // If it's multiply,
     {
       ++(*index);                              // increment index and
       value *= number(str, index);            // multiply by next number
     }
     else if(L'/' == str[*index])              // If it's divide
     {
       ++(*index);                              // increment index and
       value /= number(str, index);            // divide by next number
     }
     else
       break;                                   // Exit the loop
   }
```

```
    // We've finished, so return what we've got
    return value;
}
```

code snippet Ex6_12.cpp

After calling the `number()` function to get the value of the first number or parenthesized expression in a term, the function steps through the string in the `while` loop. The loop continues while there are still characters in the input string, as long as a `*` or `/` operator followed by another number or parenthesized expression is found.

Evaluating a Number

The `number()` function extracts and evaluates a parenthesized expression if there is one; otherwise, it determines the value of the next number in the input.

```
// Function to recognize a number
double number(String^ str, int^ index)
{
  double value(0.0);                            // Store for the resulting value

  // Check for expression between parentheses
  if(L'(' == str[*index])                       // Start of parentheses
  {
    ++(*index);
    String^ substr = extract(str, index);       // Extract substring in brackets
    return expr(substr);                        // Return substring value
  }

  // There must be at least one digit...
  if(!Char::IsDigit(str, *index))
  {
    Console::WriteLine(L"Arrrgh!*#!! There's an error.\n");
    exit(1);
  }

  // Loop accumulating leading digits
  while((*index < str->Length) && Char::IsDigit(str, *index))
  {
    value = 10.0*value + Char::GetNumericValue(str[(*index)]);
    ++(*index);
  }

  // Not a digit when we get to here
  if((*index == str->Length) || str[*index] != '.')   // so check for decimal point
    return value;                                      // and if not, return value

  double factor(1.0);                     // Factor for decimal places
  ++(*index);                             // Move to digit

  // Loop as long as we have digits
  while((*index < str->Length) && Char::IsDigit(str, *index))
```

```
  {
    factor *= 0.1;                        // Decrease factor by factor of 10
    value = value + Char::GetNumericValue(str[*index])*factor; // Add decimal place
    ++(*index);
  }

  return value;                           // On loop exit we are done
}
```

code snippet Ex6_12.cpp

As in the native C++ version, the `extract()` function is used to extract a parenthesized expression, and the substring that results is passed to the `expr()` function to be evaluated. If there's no parenthesized expression — indicated by the absence of an opening parenthesis — and there is at least one digit, the input is scanned for a number, which is a sequence of zero or more digits followed by an optional decimal point plus fractional digits. The `IsDigit()` function in the `Char` class returns `true` if a character is a digit and `false` otherwise. The character here is in the string passed as the first argument to the function at the index position specified by the second argument. There's another version of the `IsDigit()` function that accepts a single argument of type `wchar_t`, so you could use this with the argument `str[*index]`. The `GetNumericValue()` function in the `Char` class returns the value of a Unicode digit character that you pass as the argument as a value of type `double`. There's another version of this function to which you can pass a string handle and an index position to specify the character.

Extracting a Parenthesized Substring

You can implement the `extract()` function that returns a parenthesized substring from the input like this:

```
// Function to extract a substring between parentheses
String^ extract(String^ str, int^ index)
{
  int numL(0);                            // Count of left parentheses found
  int bufindex(*index);                   // Save starting value for index

  while(*index < str->Length)
  {
    switch(str[*index])
    {
      case ')':
        if(0 == numL)
          return str->Substring(bufindex, (*index)++ - bufindex);
        else
          numL--;                         // Reduce count of '(' to be matched
        break;

      case '(':
        numL++;                           // Increase count of '(' to be
                                          // matched

        break;
    }
```

```
    ++(*index);
  }

  Console::WriteLine(L"Ran off the end of the expression, must be bad input.");
  exit(1);
}
```

code snippet Ex6_12.cpp

The strategy is similar to the native C++ version, but the code is a lot simpler. To find the complementary right parenthesis, the function keeps track of how many new left parentheses are found using the variable numL. When a right parenthesis is found and the left parenthesis count in numL is zero, the Substring() member of the System::String class is used to extract the substring that was between the parentheses. The substring is then returned.

If you assemble all the functions in a CLR console project, you'll have a C++/CLI implementation of the calculator running with the CLR. The output should be much the same as the native C++ version.

SUMMARY

You now have a reasonably comprehensive knowledge of writing and using functions, and you have used overloading to implement a set of functions providing the same operation with different types of parameters. You'll see more about overloading functions in the following chapters.

You also got some experience of using several functions in a program by working through the calculator example. But remember that all the uses of functions up to now have been in the context of a traditional procedural approach to programming. When you come to look at object-oriented programming, you will still use functions extensively, but with a very different approach to program structure and to the design of a solution to a problem.

EXERCISES

You can download the source code for the examples in the book and the solutions to the following exercises from www.wrox.com.

1. Consider the following function:

```
int ascVal(size_t i, const char* p)
{
  // print the ASCII value of the char
  if (!p || i > strlen(p))
    return -1;
  else
    return p[i];
}
```

Write a program that will call this function through a pointer and verify that it works. You'll need a #include directive for the cstring header in your program to use the strlen() function.

2. Write a family of overloaded functions called `equal()`, which take two arguments of the same type, returning 1 if the arguments are equal, and 0 otherwise. Provide versions having `char`, `int`, `double`, and `char*` arguments. (Use the `strcmp()` function from the runtime library to test for equality of strings. If you don't know how to use `strcmp()`, search for it in the online help. You'll need a `#include` directive for the `cstring` header file in your program.) Write test code to verify that the correct versions are called.

3. At present, when the calculator hits an invalid input character, it prints an error message, but doesn't show you where the error was in the line. Write an error routine that prints out the input string, putting a caret (^) below the offending character, like this:

```
12 + 4,2*3
        ^
```

4. Add an exponentiation operator, ^, to the calculator, fitting it in alongside * and /. What are the limitations of implementing it in this way, and how can you overcome them?

5. (Advanced) Extend the calculator so it can handle trig and other math functions, allowing you to input expressions such as:

```
2 * sin(0.6)
```

The math library functions all work in radians; provide versions of the trigonometric functions so that the user can use degrees, for example:

```
2 * sind(30)
```

▶ WHAT YOU LEARNED IN THIS CHAPTER

TOPIC	CONCEPT
Pointers to functions	A pointer to a function stores the address of a function, plus information about the number and types of parameters and return type for a function.
Pointers to functions	You can use a pointer to a function to store the address of any function with the appropriate return type, and number and types of parameters.
Pointers to functions	You can use a pointer to a function to call the function at the address it contains. You can also pass a pointer to a function as a function argument.
Exceptions	An exception is a way of signaling an error in a program so that the error handling code can be separated from the code for normal operations.
Throwing exceptions	You throw an exception with a statement that uses the keyword `throw`.
`try` blocks	Code that may throw exceptions should be placed in a `try` block, and the code to handle a particular type of exception is placed in a `catch` block immediately following the try block. There can be several `catch` blocks following a `try` block, each catching a different type of exception.
Overloaded functions	Overloaded functions are functions with the same name, but with different parameter lists.
Calling an overloaded function	When you call an overloaded function, the function to be called is selected by the compiler based on the number and types of the arguments that you specify.
Function templates	A function template is a recipe for generating overloaded functions automatically.
Function template parameters	A function template has one or more parameters that are type variables. An instance of the function template — that is, a function definition — is created by the compiler for each function call that corresponds to a unique set of type arguments for the template.
Function template instances	You can force the compiler to create a particular instance from a function template by specifying the function you want in a prototype declaration.
The `decltype` operator	The `decltype` operator produces the type that results from evaluating an expression. You can use the `decltype` operator to determine the return type of a template function when the return type depends on the particular template parameters.

7

Defining Your Own Data Types

WHAT YOU WILL LEARN IN THIS CHAPTER:

➤   How structures are used

➤   How classes are used

➤   The basic components of a class and how you define class types

➤   How to create, and use, objects of a class

➤   How to control access to members of a class

➤   How to create constructors

➤   The default constructor

➤   References in the context of classes

➤   How to implement the copy constructor

➤   How C++/CLI classes differ from native C++ classes

➤   How to define and use properties in a C++/CLI class

➤   How to define and use literal fields

➤   How to define and use `initonly` fields

➤   What a static constructor is

This chapter is about creating your own data types to suit your particular problem. It's also about creating objects, the building blocks of object-oriented programming. An object can seem a bit mysterious to the uninitiated, but as you will see in this chapter, an object can be just an instance of one of your own data types.

THE STRUCT IN C++

A structure is a user-defined type that you define using the keyword `struct`, so it is often referred to as a struct. The `struct` originated back in the C language, and C++ incorporates and expands on the C `struct`. A struct in C++ is functionally replaceable by a class insofar as anything you can do with a `struct`, you can also achieve by using a class; however, because Windows was written in C before C++ became widely used, the `struct` appears pervasively in Windows programming. It is also widely used today, so you really need to know something about structs. We'll first take a look at (C-style) structs in this chapter before exploring the more extensive capabilities offered by classes.

What Is a struct?

Almost all the variables that you have seen up to now have been able to store a single type of entity — a number of some kind, a character, or an array of elements of the same type. The real world is a bit more complicated than that, and just about any physical object you can think of needs several items of data to describe it even minimally. Think about the information that might be needed to describe something as simple as a book. You might consider title, author, publisher, date of publication, number of pages, price, topic or classification, and ISBN number, just for starters, and you can probably come up with a few more without too much difficulty. You could specify separate variables to contain each of the parameters that you need to describe a book, but ideally, you would want to have a single data type, BOOK, say, which embodied all of these parameters. I'm sure you won't be surprised to hear that this is exactly what a `struct` can do for you.

Defining a struct

Let's stick with the notion of a book, and suppose that you just want to include the title, author, publisher, and year of publication within your definition of a book. You could declare a structure to accommodate this as follows:

```
struct BOOK
{
  char Title[80];
  char Author[80];
  char Publisher[80];
  int Year;
};
```

This doesn't define any variables, but it does create a new type for variables, and the name of the type is BOOK. The keyword `struct` defines BOOK as such, and the elements making up an object of this type are defined within the braces. Note that each line defining an element in the `struct` is terminated by a semicolon, and that a semicolon also appears after the closing brace. The elements of a `struct` can be of any type, except the same type as the `struct` being defined. You couldn't have an element of type BOOK included in the structure definition for BOOK, for example. You may think this is a limitation, but note that you could include a pointer to a variable of type BOOK, as you'll see a little later on.

The elements `Title`, `Author`, `Publisher`, and `Year` enclosed between the braces in the definition above may also be referred to as **members** or **fields** of the `BOOK` structure. Each object of type `BOOK` contains the members `Title`, `Author`, `Publisher`, and `Year`. You can now create variables of type `BOOK` in exactly the same way that you create variables of any other type:

```
BOOK Novel;                          // Declare variable Novel of type BOOK
```

This declares a variable with the name `Novel` that you can now use to store information about a book. All you need now is to understand how you get data into the various members that make up a variable of type `BOOK`.

Initializing a struct

The first way to get data into the members of a `struct` is to define initial values in the declaration. Suppose you wanted to initialize the variable `Novel` to contain the data for one of your favorite books, *Paneless Programming*, published in 1981 by the Gutter Press. This is a story of a guy performing heroic code development while living in an igloo, and, as you probably know, inspired the famous Hollywood box office success, *Gone with the Window*. It was written by I.C. Fingers, who is also the author of that seminal three-volume work, *The Connoisseur's Guide to the Paper Clip*. With this wealth of information, you can write the declaration for the variable `Novel` as:

```
BOOK Novel =
{
 "Paneless Programming",           // Initial value for Title
 "I.C. Fingers",                   // Initial value for Author
 "Gutter Press",                   // Initial value for Publisher
  1981                             // Initial value for Year
};
```

The initializing values appear between braces, separated by commas, in much the same way that you defined initial values for members of an array. As with arrays, the sequence of initial values obviously needs to be the same as the sequence of the members of the `struct` in its definition. Each member of the structure `Novel` has the corresponding value assigned to it, as indicated in the comments.

Accessing the Members of a struct

To access individual members of a `struct`, you can use the **member selection operator**, which is a period; this is sometimes referred to as the **member access operator**. To refer to a particular member, you write the `struct` variable name, followed by a period, followed by the name of the member that you want to access. To change the `Year` member of the `Novel` structure, you could write:

```
Novel.Year = 1988;
```

This would set the value of the `Year` member to 1988. You can use a member of a structure in exactly the same way as any other variable of the same type as the member. To increment the member `Year` by two, for example, you can write:

```
Novel.Year += 2;
```

This increments the value of the `Year` member of the `struct`, just like any other variable.

TRY IT OUT   **Using structs**

You can use another console application example to exercise a little further how referencing the members of a `struct` works. Suppose you want to write a program to deal with some of the things you might find in a yard, such as those illustrated in the professionally landscaped yard in Figure 7-1.

FIGURE 7-1

I have arbitrarily assigned the coordinates 0,0 to the top-left corner of the yard. The bottom-right corner has the coordinates 100,120. Thus, the first coordinate value is a measure of the horizontal position relative to the top-left corner, with values increasing from left to right, and the second coordinate is a measure of the vertical position from the same reference point, with values increasing from top to bottom. Figure 7-1 also shows the position of the pool and those of the two huts relative to the top-left corner of the yard. Because the yard, huts, and pool are all rectangular, you could define a `struct` type to represent any of these objects:

```
struct RECTANGLE
{
    int Left;                          // Top-left point
```

```
    int Top;                            // coordinate pair

    int Right;                          // Bottom-right point
    int Bottom;                         // coordinate pair
};
```

The first two members of the RECTANGLE structure type correspond to the coordinates of the top-left point of a rectangle, and the next two to the coordinates of the bottom-right point. You can use this in an elementary example dealing with the objects in the yard as follows:

```
// Ex7_01.cpp
// Exercising structures in the yard
#include <iostream>
using std::cout;
using std::endl;


// Definition of a struct to represent rectangles
struct RECTANGLE
{
  int Left;                          // Top-left point
  int Top;                           // coordinate pair

  int Right;                         // Bottom-right point
  int Bottom;                        // coordinate pair
};

// Prototype of function to calculate the area of a rectangle
long Area(const RECTANGLE& aRect);

// Prototype of a function to move a rectangle
void MoveRect(RECTANGLE& aRect, int x, int y);

int main(void)
{
  RECTANGLE Yard = { 0, 0, 100, 120 };
  RECTANGLE Pool = { 30, 40, 70, 80 };
  RECTANGLE Hut1, Hut2;

  Hut1.Left = 70;
  Hut1.Top = 10;
  Hut1.Right = Hut1.Left + 25;
  Hut1.Bottom = 30;

  Hut2 = Hut1;                        // Define Hut2 the same as Hut1
  MoveRect(Hut2, 10, 90);            // Now move it to the right position

  cout << endl
       << "Coordinates of Hut2 are "
       << Hut2.Left << "," << Hut2.Top << " and "
       << Hut2.Right << "," << Hut2.Bottom;

  cout << endl
       << "The area of the yard is "
```

```
            << Area(Yard);

     cout << endl
          << "The area of the pool is "
          << Area(Pool)
          << endl;

     return 0;
   }

   // Function to calculate the area of a rectangle
   long Area(const RECTANGLE& aRect)
   {
     return (aRect.Right - aRect.Left)*(aRect.Bottom - aRect.Top);
   }

   // Function to Move a Rectangle
   void MoveRect(RECTANGLE& aRect, int x, int y)
   {
     int length(aRect.Right - aRect.Left);     // Get length of rectangle
     int width(aRect.Bottom - aRect.Top);      // Get width of rectangle

     aRect.Left = x;                           // Set top-left point
     aRect.Top = y;                            // to new position
     aRect.Right = x + length;                 // Get bottom-right point as
     aRect.Bottom = y + width;                 // increment from new position
     return;
   }
```

code snippet Ex7_01.cpp

The output from this example is:

```
Coordinates of Hut2 are 10,90 and 35,110
The area of the yard is 12000
The area of the pool is 1600
```

How It Works

Note that the struct definition appears at global scope in this example. You'll be able to see it in the Class View tab for the project. Putting the definition of the struct at global scope allows you to declare a variable of type RECTANGLE anywhere in the .cpp file. In a program with a more significant amount of code, such definitions would normally be stored in a .h file and then added to each .cpp file where necessary by using a #include directive.

You have defined two functions to process RECTANGLE objects. The function Area() calculates the area of the RECTANGLE object that you pass as a reference argument as the product of the length and the width, where the length is the difference between the horizontal positions of the defining points, and the width is the difference between the vertical positions of the defining points. The parameter is const because the function does not change the argument that is passed to it. By passing a reference, the code runs a little faster because the argument is not copied. The MoveRect() function modifies the defining points of a RECTANGLE object to position it at the coordinates x, y, which are passed as arguments.

The position of a RECTANGLE object is assumed to be the position of the Left, Top point. Because the RECTANGLE object is passed as a reference, the function is able to modify the members of the RECTANGLE object directly. After calculating the length and width of the RECTANGLE object passed, the Left and Top members are set to x and y, respectively, and the new Right and Bottom members are calculated by incrementing x and y by the length and width of the original RECTANGLE object.

In the main() function, you initialize the Yard and Pool RECTANGLE variables with their coordinate positions, as shown in Figure 7-1. The variable Hut1 represents the hut at the top-right in the illustration, and its members are set to the appropriate values using assignment statements. The variable Hut2, corresponding to the hut at the bottom-left of the yard, is first set to be the same as Hut1 in the assignment statement:

```
Hut2 = Hut1;                           // Define Hut2 the same as Hut1
```

This statement results in the values of the members of Hut1 being copied to the corresponding members of Hut2. You can only assign a struct of a given type to another of the same type. You can't increment a struct directly or use a struct in an arithmetic expression.

To alter the position of Hut2 to its place at the bottom-left of the yard, you call the MoveRect() function with the coordinates of the required position as arguments. This roundabout way of getting the coordinates of Hut2 is totally unnecessary, and serves only to show how you can use a struct as an argument to a function.

IntelliSense Assistance with Structures

You've probably noticed that the editor in Visual C++ 2010 is quite intelligent — it knows the types of variables, for instance. This is because of the IntelliSense feature. If you hover the mouse cursor over a variable name in the editor window, it pops up a little box showing its type. It also can help a lot with structures (and classes, as you will see) because not only does it know the types of ordinary variables, it also knows the members that belong to a variable of a particular structure type. As long as your computer is reasonably fast, as you type the member selection operator following a structure variable name, the editor pops a window showing the list of members. If you click one of the members, it shows the comment that appeared in the original definition of the structure, so you know what it is. This is shown in Figure 7-2, using a fragment of the previous example.

```
58   }
59
60   // Function to Move a Rectangle
61   void MoveRect(RECTANGLE& aRect, int x, int y)
62   {
63       int length = aRect.Right - aRect.Left;    // Get length of rectangle
64       int width = aRect.Bottom - aRect.Top;     // Get width of rectangle
65
66       aRect.Left = x;                           // Set top left point
67       aRect.Top = y;                            // to new position
68       aRect.Right = x + length;                 // Get bottom right point as
69       aRect.
70           ● Botto          coordinate pair
71           ● Left           File: ex7_01.cpp
72           ● Right
73           ● Top
74
75
```

FIGURE 7-2

Now, there's a real incentive to add comments, and to keep them short and to the point. If you double-click on a member in the list or press the Enter key when the item is highlighted, it is automatically inserted after the member selection operator, thus eliminating one source of typos in your code. Great, isn't it?

You can turn any or all of the IntelliSense features off if you want to, but I guess the only reason you would want to is if your machine is too slow to make them useful. To turn the various IntelliSense features on or off, first select Options from the Tools menu. Expand the Text Editor tree in the left pane of the dialog that displays by clicking the [unfilled] symbol, then click the [unfilled] symbol alongside C/C++. Click on the Advanced option and you will see the IntelliSense options displayed in the right pane.

The editor also shows the parameter list for a function when you are typing the code to call it — it pops up as soon as you enter the left parenthesis for the argument list. This is particularly helpful with library functions, as it's tough to remember the parameter list for all of them. Of course, the `#include` directive for the header file must already be there in the source code for this to work. Without it, the editor has no idea what the library function is. Also beware of omitting the `std` namespace prefix when you have also failed to include a using statement for a library function; the editor won't recognize the function. You will see more things that the editor can help with as you learn more about classes.

After that interesting little diversion, let's get back to structures.

The struct RECT

Rectangles are used a great deal in Windows programs. For this reason, there is a `RECT` structure predefined in the header file `windows.h`. Its definition is essentially the same as the structure that you defined in the last example:

```
struct RECT
{
  LONG left;                          // Top-left point
  LONG top;                           // coordinate pair

  LONG right;                         // Bottom-right point
  LONG bottom;                        // coordinate pair
};
```

Type `LONG` is a Windows type that is equivalent to the fundamental type `long`. This `struct` is usually used to define rectangular areas on your display for a variety of purposes. Because `RECT` is used so extensively, `windows.h` also contains prototypes for a number of functions to manipulate and modify rectangles. For example, `windows.h` provides the function `InflateRect()` to increase the size of a rectangle, and the function `EqualRect()` to compare two rectangles.

MFC also defines a class called `CRect`, which is the equivalent of a `RECT` structure. After you understand classes, you will be using this in preference to the `RECT` structure. The `CRect` class provides a very extensive range of functions for manipulating rectangles, and you will be using a number of these when you are writing Windows programs using MFC.

Using Pointers with a struct

As you might expect, you can create a pointer to a variable of a structure type. In fact, many of the functions declared in windows.h that work with RECT objects require pointers to a RECT as arguments, because this avoids the copying of the whole structure when a RECT argument is passed to a function. To define a pointer to a RECT object, for example, this declaration is what you might expect:

```
RECT* pRect(nullptr);                  // Define a pointer to RECT
```

Assuming that you have defined a RECT object, aRect, you can set the pointer to the address of this variable in the normal way, using the address-of operator:

```
pRect = &aRect;                        // Set pointer to the address of aRect
```

As you saw when the idea of a struct was introduced, a struct can't contain a member of the same type as the struct being defined, but it can contain a pointer to a struct, including a pointer to a struct of the same type. For example, you could define a structure like this:

```
struct ListElement
{
  RECT aRect;                          // RECT member of structure
  ListElement* pNext;                  // Pointer to a list element
};
```

The first element of the ListElement structure is of type RECT, and the second element is a pointer to a structure of type ListElement — the same type as that being defined. (Remember that this element isn't of type ListElement, it's of type "pointer to ListElement.") This allows objects of type ListElement to be daisy-chained together, where each ListElement can contain the address of the next ListElement object in a chain, the last in the chain having the pointer as nullptr. This is illustrated in Figure 7-3.

FIGURE 7-3

Each box in the diagram represents an object of type ListElement, and the pNext member of each object stores the address of the next object in the chain, except for the last object, where pNext is nullptr. This kind of arrangement is usually referred to as a **linked list**. It has the advantage that as long as you know the first element in the list, you can find all the others. This is particularly important when variables are created dynamically, since a linked list can be used to keep track of them all. Every time a new one is created, it's simply added to the end of the list by storing its address in the pNext member of the last object in the chain.

Accessing Structure Members through a Pointer

Consider the following statements:

```
RECT aRect = {0, 0, 100, 100};
RECT* pRect(&aRect);
```

The first declares and defines the aRect object to be of type RECT with the first pair of members initialized to (0, 0) and the second pair to (100, 100). The second statement declares pRect as a pointer to type RECT and initializes it with the address of aRect. You can now access the members of aRect through the pointer with a statement such as this:

```
(*pRect).Top += 10;                    // Increment the Top member by 10
```

The parentheses to dereference the pointer here are essential, because the member access operator takes precedence over the dereferencing operator. Without the parentheses, you would be attempting to treat the pointer as a struct and to dereference the member, so the statement would not compile. After executing this statement, the Top member will have the value 10 and, of course, the remaining members will be unchanged.

The method that you used here to access the member of a struct through a pointer looks rather clumsy. Because this kind of operation crops up very frequently in C++, the language includes a special operator to enable you to express the same thing in a much more readable and intuitive form, so let's look at that next.

The Indirect Member Selection Operator

The **indirect member selection operator**, ->, is specifically for accessing members of a struct (or a class) through a pointer; this operator is also referred to as the **indirect member access operator**. The operator looks like a little arrow (->) and is formed from a minus sign (-) followed by the symbol for greater than (>). You could use it to rewrite the statement to access the Top member of aRect through the pointer pRect, as follows:

```
pRect->Top += 10;                      // Increment the Top member by 10
```

This is much more expressive of what is going on, isn't it? The indirect member selection operator is also used with classes, and you'll see a lot more of it throughout the rest of the book.

DATA TYPES, OBJECTS, CLASSES, AND INSTANCES

Before I get into the language, syntax, and programming techniques of classes, I'll start by considering how your existing knowledge relates to the concept of classes.

So far, you've learned that native C++ lets you create variables that can be any of a range of fundamental data types: int, long, double, and so on. You have also seen how you can use the struct keyword to define a structure that you could then use as the type for a variable representing a composite of several other variables.

The variables of the fundamental types don't allow you to model real-world objects (or even imaginary objects) adequately. It's hard to model a box in terms of an int, for example; however, you can use the members of a struct to define a set of attributes for such an object. You could define variables length, width, and height to represent the dimensions of the box and bind them together as members of a Box structure, as follows:

```
struct Box
{
  double length;
  double width;
  double height;
};
```

With this definition of a new data type called Box, you define variables of this type just as you did with variables of the basic types. You can then create, manipulate, and destroy as many Box objects as you need to in your program. This means that you can model objects using structs and write your programs around them. So — that's object-oriented programming all wrapped up, then?

Well, not quite. You see, object-oriented programming (OOP) is based on three basic concepts relating to object types (*encapsulation*, *polymorphism*, and *inheritance*), and what you have seen so far doesn't quite fit the bill. Don't worry about what these terms mean for the moment — you'll explore that in the rest of this chapter and throughout the book.

The notion of a struct in C++ goes far beyond the original concept of struct in C — it incorporates the object-oriented notion of a **class**. This idea of classes, from which you can create your own data types and use them just like the native types, is fundamental to C++, and the new keyword class was introduced into the language to describe this concept. The keywords struct and class are almost identical in C++, except for the access control to the members, which you will find out more about later in this chapter. The keyword struct is maintained for backwards compatibility with C, but everything that you can do with a struct, and more, you can achieve with a class.

Take a look at how you might define a class representing boxes:

```
class CBox
{
  public:
    double m_Length;
    double m_Width;
    double m_Height;
};
```

When you define CBox as a class, you are essentially defining a new data type, similar to when you defined the Box structure. The only differences here are the use of the keyword class instead of struct, and the use of the keyword public followed by a colon that precedes the definition of the members of the class. The variables that you define as part of the class are called **data members** of the class, because they are variables that store data.

You have also called the class CBox instead of Box. You could have called the class Box, but the MFC adopts the convention of using the prefix C for all class names, so you might as well get used to it. MFC also prefixes data members of classes with m_ to distinguish them from other variables, so I'll use this convention, too. Remember, though, that in other contexts where you might use C++ and in C++/CLI in particular, this will not be the case; in some instances, the convention for naming classes and their members may be different, and in others, there may be no particular convention adopted for naming entities.

The public keyword is a clue as to the difference between a structure and a class. It just specifies that the members of the class that follow the keyword are generally accessible, in the same way as the members of a structure are. By default, the members of a class are not generally accessible and are said to be **private**, and to make members accessible, you must precede their definitions with the keyword public. The members of a struct, on the other hand, are public by default. The reason that class members are private by default is because, in general, an object of a class should be a self-contained entity such that the data that make the object what it is should be *encapsulated* and only changed under controlled circumstances. As you'll see a little later in the chapter, though, it's also possible to place other restrictions on the accessibility of members of a class.

You can declare a variable, bigBox, say, which represents an instance of the CBox class type like this:

```
CBox bigBox;
```

This is exactly the same as declaring a variable for a struct, or, indeed, for any other variable type. After you have defined the class CBox, declarations for variables of this type are quite standard.

First Class

The notion of class was invented by an Englishman to keep the general population happy. It derives from the theory that people who knew their place and function in society would be much more secure and comfortable in life than those who did not. The famous Dane, Bjarne Stroustrup, who invented C++, undoubtedly acquired a deep knowledge of class concepts while at Cambridge University in England and appropriated the idea very successfully for use in his new language.

Class in C++ is similar to the English concept, in that each class usually has a very precise role and a permitted set of actions. However, it differs from the English idea because class in C++ has largely socialist overtones, concentrating on the importance of working classes. Indeed, in some ways, it is the reverse of the English ideal, because, as you will see, working classes in C++ often live on the backs of classes that do nothing at all.

Operations on Classes

In C++, you can create new data types as classes to represent whatever kinds of objects you like. As you'll come to see, classes (and structures) aren't limited to just holding data; you can also define member functions or even operations that act on objects of your classes using the standard C++ operators. You can define the class CBox, for example, so that the following statements work and have the meanings you want them to have:

```
CBox box1;
CBox box2;

if(box1 > box2)              // Fill the larger box
  box1.fill();
else
  box2.fill();
```

You could also implement operations as part of the CBox class for adding, subtracting or even multiplying boxes — in fact, almost any operation to which you could ascribe a sensible meaning in the context of boxes.

I'm talking about incredibly powerful medicine here, and it constitutes a major change in the approach that you can take to programming. Instead of breaking down a problem in terms of what are essentially computer-related data types (integer numbers, floating-point numbers, and so on) and then writing a program, you're going to be programming in terms of problem-related data types, in other words, classes. These classes might be named CEmployee, or CCowboy, or CCheese, or CChutney, each defined specifically for the kind of problem that you want to solve, complete with the functions and operators that are necessary to manipulate instances of your new types.

Program design now starts with deciding what new application-specific data types you need to solve the problem in hand and writing the program in terms of operations on the specifics that the problem is concerned with, be it CCoffins or CCowpokes.

Terminology

I'll first summarize some of the terminology that I will be using when discussing classes in C++:

➤ A **class** is a user-defined data type.

➤ **Object-oriented programming** (OOP) is the programming style based on the idea of defining your own data types as classes, where the data types are specific to the domain of the problem you intend to solve.

➤ Declaring an object of a class type is sometimes referred to as **instantiation** because you are creating an **instance** of a class.

➤ Instances of a class are referred to as **objects**.

➤ The idea of an object containing the data implicit in its definition, together with the functions that operate on that data, is referred to as **encapsulation**.

When I get into the details of object-oriented programming, it may seem a little complicated in places, but getting back to the basics of what you're doing can often help to make things clearer, so always keep in mind what objects are really about. They are about writing programs in terms of the objects that are specific to the domain of your problem. All the facilities around classes in C++ are there to make this as comprehensive and flexible as possible. Let's get down to the business of understanding classes.

UNDERSTANDING CLASSES

A class is a specification of a data type that you define. It can contain data elements that can either be variables of the basic types in C++, or of other user-defined types. The data elements of a class may be single data elements, arrays, pointers, arrays of pointers of almost any kind, or objects of other classes, so you have a lot of flexibility in what you can include in your data type. A class also can contain functions that operate on objects of the class by accessing the data elements that they include. So, a class combines both the definition of the elementary data that makes up an object and the means of manipulating the data that belongs to individual objects of the class.

The data and functions within a class are called **members** of the class. Oddly enough, the members of a class that are data items are called **data members** and the members that are functions are called **function members** or **member functions**. The member functions of a class are also sometimes referred to as **methods**; I will not use this term in this book, but keep it in mind, as you may see it used elsewhere. The data members are also referred to as **fields**, and this terminology is used with C++/CLI, so I will be using this terminology from time to time.

When you define a class, you define a blueprint for a data type. This doesn't actually define any data, but it does define what the class name means, that is, what an object of the class will consist of and what operations can be performed on such an object. It's much the same as if you wrote a description of the basic type `double`. This wouldn't be an actual variable of type `double`, but a definition of how it's made up and how it operates. To create a variable of a basic data type, you need to use a declaration statement. It's exactly the same with classes, as you will see.

Defining a Class

Take a look again at the class example mentioned earlier — a class of boxes. You defined the `CBox` data type using the keyword `class` as follows:

```
class CBox
{
  public:
    double m_Length;                // Length of a box in inches
    double m_Width;                 // Width of a box in inches
    double m_Height;                // Height of a box in inches
};
```

The name of the class appears following the `class` keyword, and the three data members are defined between the curly braces. The data members are defined for the class using the declaration statements that you already know and love, and the whole class definition is terminated with a semicolon. The names of all the members of a class are local to the class. You can therefore use the same names elsewhere in a program without causing any problems.

Access Control in a Class

The `public` keyword determines the access attributes of the members of the class that follow it. Specifying the data members as `public` means that these members of an object of the class can be accessed anywhere within the scope of the class object to which they belong. You can also specify the members of a class as `private` or `protected`. If you omit the access specification altogether, the members have the default attribute, `private`. (This is the only difference between a class and a struct in C++ — the default access specifier for a struct is `public`.) You will look into the effects of all these keywords in a bit later.

Remember that all you have defined so far is a class, which is a data type. You haven't declared any objects of the class type. When I talk about accessing a class member, say `m_Height`, I'm talking about accessing the data member of a particular object, and that object needs to be defined somewhere.

Declaring Objects of a Class

You declare objects of a class with exactly the same sort of declaration that you use to declare objects of basic types, so you could declare objects of the `CBox` class type with these statements:

```
CBox box1;                          // Declare box1 of type CBox
CBox box2;                          // Declare box2 of type CBox
```

Both of the objects `box1` and `box2` will, of course, have their own data members. This is illustrated in Figure 7-4.

FIGURE 7-4

The object name `box1` embodies the whole object, including its three data members. They are not initialized to anything, however — the data members of each object will simply contain junk values, so you need to look at how you can access them for the purpose of setting them to some specific values.

Accessing the Data Members of a Class

You can refer to the data members of objects of a class using the **direct member selection operator** that you used to access members of a struct. So, to set the value of the data member `m_Height` of the object `box2` to, say, 18.0, you could write this assignment statement:

```
box2.m_Height = 18.0;                 // Setting the value of a data member
```

You can only access the data member in this way in a function that is outside the class, because the `m_Height` member was specified as having `public` access. If it wasn't defined as `public`, this statement would not compile. You'll see more about this shortly.

TRY IT OUT Your First Use of Classes

Verify that you can use your class in the same way as the structure. Try it out in the following console application:

```cpp
// Ex7_02.cpp
// Creating and using boxes
#include <iostream>
using std::cout;
using std::endl;

class CBox                              // Class definition at global scope
{
  public:
    double m_Length;                    // Length of a box in inches
    double m_Width;                     // Width of a box in inches
    double m_Height;                    // Height of a box in inches
};

int main()
{
  CBox box1;                            // Declare box1 of type CBox
  CBox box2;                            // Declare box2 of type CBox

  double boxVolume(0.0);                // Stores the volume of a box

  box1.m_Height = 18.0;                 // Define the values
  box1.m_Length = 78.0;                 // of the members of
  box1.m_Width = 24.0;                  // the object box1

  box2.m_Height = box1.m_Height - 10;   // Define box2
  box2.m_Length = box1.m_Length/2.0;    // members in
  box2.m_Width = 0.25*box1.m_Length;    // terms of box1

  // Calculate volume of box1
  boxVolume = box1.m_Height*box1.m_Length*box1.m_Width;

  cout << endl
       << "Volume of box1 = " << boxVolume;

  cout << endl
       << "box2 has sides which total "
       << box2.m_Height+ box2.m_Length+ box2.m_Width
       << " inches.";

  cout << endl                          // Display the size of a box in memory
       << "A CBox object occupies "
       << sizeof box1 << " bytes.";

  cout << endl;
  return 0;
}
```

code snippet Ex7_02.cpp

As you type in the code for main(), you should see the editor prompting you with a list of member names whenever you enter a member selection operator following the name of a class object. You can then select the member you want from the list by double-clicking it. Hovering the mouse cursor for a moment over any of the variables in your code will result in the type being displayed.

How It Works

Back to console application examples again for the moment, so you should define the project accordingly. Everything here works, as you would have expected from your experience with structures. The definition of the class appears outside of the function main() and, therefore, has global scope. This enables you to declare objects in any function in the program and causes the class to show up in the Class View tab.

You have declared two objects of type CBox within the function main(), box1 and box2. Of course, as with variables of the basic types, the objects box1 and box2 are local to main(). Objects of a class type obey the same rules with respect to scope as variables declared as one of the basic types (such as the variable boxVolume used in this example).

The first three assignment statements set the values of the data members of box1. You define the values of the data members of box2 in terms of the data members of box1 in the next three assignment statements.

You then have a statement that calculates the volume of box1 as the product of its three data members, and this value is output to the screen. Next, you output the sum of the data members of box2 by writing the expression for the sum of the data members directly in the output statement. The final action in the program is to output the number of bytes occupied by box1, which is produced by the operator sizeof.

If you run this program, you should get this output:

```
Volume of box1 = 33696
box2 has sides which total 66.5 inches.
A CBox object occupies 24 bytes.
```

The last line shows that the object box1 occupies 24 bytes of memory, which is a result of having three data members of 8 bytes each. The statement that produced the last line of output could equally well have been written like this:

```
cout << endl                        // Display the size of a box in memory
    << "A CBox object occupies "
    << sizeof (CBox) << " bytes.";
```

Here, I have used the type name between parentheses, rather than a specific object name as the operand for the sizeof operator. You'll remember that this is standard syntax for the sizeof operator, as you saw in Chapter 4.

This example has demonstrated the mechanism for accessing the public data members of a class. It also shows that they can be used in exactly the same way as ordinary variables. You are now ready to break new ground by taking a look at member *functions* of a class.

Member Functions of a Class

A member function of a class is a function that has its definition or its prototype within the class definition. It operates on any object of the class of which it is a member, and has access to all the members of a class for that object.

TRY IT OUT   Adding a Member Function to CBox

To see how you access the members of the class from within a function member, create an example extending the CBox class to include a member function that calculates the volume of the CBox object.

```cpp
// Ex7_03.cpp
// Calculating the volume of a box with a member function
#include <iostream>
using std::cout;
using std::endl;

class CBox                              // Class definition at global scope
{
  public:
    double m_Length;                    // Length of a box in inches
    double m_Width;                     // Width of a box in inches
    double m_Height;                    // Height of a box in inches

  // Function to calculate the volume of a box
  double Volume()
  {
    return m_Length*m_Width*m_Height;
  }
};

int main()
{
  CBox box1;                            // Declare box1 of type CBox
  CBox box2;                            // Declare box2 of type CBox

  double boxVolume(0.0);               // Stores the volume of a box

  box1.m_Height = 18.0;                // Define the values
  box1.m_Length = 78.0;                // of the members of
  box1.m_Width = 24.0;                 // the object box1

  box2.m_Height = box1.m_Height - 10;  // Define box2
  box2.m_Length = box1.m_Length/2.0;   // members in
  box2.m_Width = 0.25*box1.m_Length;   // terms of box1

  boxVolume = box1.Volume();           // Calculate volume of box1
  cout << endl
       << "Volume of box1 = " << boxVolume;

  cout << endl
       << "Volume of box2 = "
       << box2.Volume();

  cout << endl
       << "A CBox object occupies "
```

```
            << sizeof box1 << " bytes.";

    cout << endl;
    return 0;
}
```

code snippet Ex7_03.cpp

How It Works

The new code that you add to the CBox class definition is shaded. It's just the definition of the Volume()
function, which is a member function of the class. It also has the same access attribute as the data
members: public. This is because every class member that you declare following an access attribute
will have that access attribute, until another access attribute is specified within the class definition. The
Volume() function returns the volume of a CBox object as a value of type double. The expression in the
return statement is just the product of the three data members of the class.

There's no need to qualify the names of the class members in any way when you access them in member
functions. The unqualified member names automatically refer to the members of the object that is
current when the member function is executed.

The member function Volume() is used in the highlighted statements in main(), after initializing
the data members (as in the first example). You can call a member function of a particular object by
writing the name of the object to be processed, followed by a period, followed by the member function
name. As noted previously, the function automatically accesses the data members of the object for
which it was called, so the first use of Volume() calculates the volume of box1. Using only the name of
a member will always refer to the member of the object for which the member function has been called.

The member function is used a second time directly in the output statement to produce the volume of
box2. If you execute this example, it produces this output:

```
Volume of box1 = 33696
Volume of box2 = 6084
A CBox object occupies 24 bytes.
```

Note that the CBox object is still the same number of bytes. Adding a function member to a class doesn't
affect the size of the objects. Obviously, a member function has to be stored in memory somewhere, but
there's only one copy regardless of how many class objects you create, and the memory occupied by member
functions isn't counted when the sizeof operator produces the number of bytes that an object occupies.

NOTE *Adding a* virtual *function to a class, which you will learn about in
Chapter 9, will increase the size of a class object.*

*The names of the class data members in the member function automatically
refer to the data members of the specific object used to call the function, and the
function can only be called for a particular object of the class. In this case, this is
done by using the direct member access operator with the name of an object.*

NOTE *If you try to call a member function without specifying an object name, your program will not compile.*

Positioning a Member Function Definition

A member function definition need not be placed inside the class definition. If you want to put it outside the class definition, you need to put the prototype for the function inside the class. If you rewrite the previous class with the function definition outside, the class definition looks like this:

```
class CBox                          // Class definition at global scope
{
  public:
    double m_Length;                // Length of a box in inches
    double m_Width;                 // Width of a box in inches
    double m_Height;                // Height of a box in inches
    double Volume(void);            // Member function prototype
};
```

Now, you need to write the function definition, but because it appears outside the definition of the class, there has to be some way of telling the compiler that the function belongs to the class CBox. This is done by prefixing the function name with the name of the class and separating the two with the **scope resolution operator,** ::, which is formed from two successive colons. The function definition would now look like this:

```
// Function to calculate the volume of a box
double CBox::Volume()
{
  return m_Length*m_Width*m_Height;
}
```

It produces the same output as the last example; however, it isn't exactly the same program. In the second case, all calls to the function are treated in the way that you're already familiar with. However, when you define a function within the definition of the class, as in Ex7_03.cpp, the compiler implicitly treats the function as an **inline function**.

Inline Functions

With an inline function, the compiler tries to expand the code in the body of the function in place of a call to the function. This avoids much of the overhead of calling the function and, therefore, speeds up your code. This is illustrated in Figure 7-5.

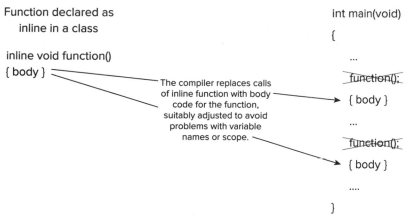

Function declared as inline in a class

inline void function()
{ body }

The compiler replaces calls of inline function with body code for the function, suitably adjusted to avoid problems with variable names or scope.

int main(void)
{
...
function();
{ body }
...
function();
{ body }
....
}

FIGURE 7-5

NOTE *Of course, the compiler ensures that expanding a function inline doesn't cause any problems with variable names or scope.*

The compiler may not always be able to insert the code for a function inline (such as with recursive functions or functions for which you have obtained an address), but generally, it will work. It's best used for very short, simple functions, such as our function Volume() in the CBox class, because such functions execute faster and inserting the body code does not significantly increase the size of the executable module.

With the function definition outside of the class definition, the compiler treats the function as a normal function, and a call of the function will work in the usual way; however, it's also possible to tell the compiler that, if possible, you would like the function to be considered as inline. This is done by simply placing the keyword inline at the beginning of the function header. So, for this function, the definition would be as follows:

```
// Function to calculate the volume of a box
inline double CBox::Volume()
{
  return m_Length*m_Width*m_Height;
}
```

With this definition for the function, the program would be exactly the same as the original. This enables you to put the member function definitions outside of the class definition, if you so choose, and still retain the execution performance benefits of inlining.

You can apply the keyword inline to ordinary functions in your program that have nothing to do with classes and get the same effect. Remember, however, that it's best used for short, simple functions.

You now need to understand a little more about what happens when you declare an object of a class.

CLASS CONSTRUCTORS

In the previous program example, you declared the CBox objects, box1 and box2, and then laboriously worked through each of the data members for each object in order to assign an initial value to it. This is unsatisfactory from several points of view. First of all, it would be easy to overlook initializing a data member, particularly with a class that had many more data members than our CBox class. Initializing the data members of several objects of a complex class could involve pages of assignment statements. The final constraint on this approach arises when you get to defining data members of a class that don't have the attribute public — you won't be able to access them from outside the class, anyway. There has to be a better way and, of course, there is — it's known as the class **constructor**.

What Is a Constructor?

A class constructor is a special function in a class that is responsible for creating new objects when required. A constructor, therefore, provides the opportunity to initialize objects as they are created and to ensure that data members only contain valid values. A class may have several constructors, enabling you to create objects in various ways.

You have no leeway in naming the constructors in a class — they always have the same name as the class in which they are defined. The function CBox(), for example, is a constructor for our class CBox. It also has no return type. It's wrong to specify a return type for a constructor; you must not even write it as void. The primary purpose of a class constructor is to assign initial values to the data elements of the class, and no return type for a constructor is necessary or permitted. If you inadvertently specify a return type for a constructor, the compiler will report it as an error with error number C2380.

TRY IT OUT   Adding a Constructor to the CBox class

Let's extend our CBox class to incorporate a constructor.

```cpp
// Ex7_04.cpp
// Using a constructor
#include <iostream>
using std::cout;
using std::endl;

class CBox                              // Class definition at global scope
{
  public:
    double m_Length;                    // Length of a box in inches
    double m_Width;                     // Width of a box in inches
    double m_Height;                    // Height of a box in inches

    // Constructor definition
    CBox(double lv, double bv, double hv)
    {
      cout << endl << "Constructor called.";
      m_Length = lv;                    // Set values of
```

```
      m_Width = bv;                      // data members
      m_Height = hv;
    }

    // Function to calculate the volume of a box
    double Volume()
    {
      return m_Length* m_Width* m_Height;
    }
};

int main()
{
  CBox box1(78.0,24.0,18.0);           // Declare and initialize box1
  CBox cigarBox(8.0,5.0,1.0);          // Declare and initialize cigarBox

  double boxVolume(0.0);               // Stores the volume of a box

  boxVolume = box1.Volume();           // Calculate volume of box1
  cout << endl
       << "Volume of box1 = " << boxVolume;

  cout << endl
       << "Volume of cigarBox = "
       << cigarBox.Volume();

  cout << endl;
  return 0;
}
```

code snippet Ex7_04.cpp

How It Works

The CBox() constructor has been written with three parameters of type double, corresponding to the initial values for the m_Length, m_Width, and m_Height members of a CBox object. The first statement in the constructor outputs a message so that you can tell when it's been called. You wouldn't do this in production programs, but because it's very helpful in showing when a constructor is called, it's often used when testing a program. I'll use it regularly for the purposes of illustration. The code in the body of the constructor is very simple. It just assigns the arguments that you pass to the constructor when you call it to the corresponding data members. If necessary, you could also include checks that valid, non-negative arguments are supplied and, in a real context, you probably would want to do this, but our primary interest here is in seeing how the mechanism works.

Within main(), you declare the object box1 with initializing values for the data members m_Length, m_Width, and m_Height, in sequence. These are in parentheses following the object name. This uses the functional notation for initialization that, as you saw in Chapter 2, can also be applied to initializing ordinary variables of basic types. You also declare a second object of type CBox, called cigarBox, which also has initializing values.

The volume of `box1` is calculated using the member function `Volume()` as in the previous example, and is then displayed on the screen. You also display the value of the volume of `cigarBox`. The output from the example is:

```
Constructor called.
Constructor called.
Volume of box1 = 33696
Volume of cigarBox = 40
```

The first two lines are output from the two calls of the constructor `CBox()`, once for each object declared. The constructor that you have supplied in the class definition is automatically called when a `CBox` object is declared, so both `CBox` objects are initialized with the initializing values appearing in the declaration. These are passed to the constructor as arguments, in the sequence that they are written in the declaration. As you can see, the volume of `box1` is the same as before and `cigarBox` has a volume looking suspiciously like the product of its dimensions, which is quite a relief.

The Default Constructor

Try modifying the last example by adding the declaration for `box2` that you had previously in `Ex7_03.cpp`:

```
CBox box2;                              // Declare box2 of type CBox
```

Here, you've left `box2` without initializing values. When you rebuild this version of the program, you get the error message:

```
error C2512: 'CBox': no appropriate default constructor available
```

This means that the compiler is looking for a **default constructor** for `box2` (also referred to as the **noarg** constructor because it doesn't require arguments when it is called) because you haven't supplied any initializing values for the data members. A default constructor is one that does not require any arguments to be supplied, which can be either a constructor that has no parameters specified in the constructor definition, or one whose arguments are all optional. Well, this statement was perfectly satisfactory in `Ex7_02.cpp`, so why doesn't it work now?

The answer is that the previous example used a default no-argument constructor that was supplied by the compiler, and the compiler provided this constructor because you didn't supply one. Because in this example, you *did* supply a constructor, the compiler assumed that you were taking care of everything and didn't supply the default. So, if you still want to use declarations for `CBox` objects that aren't initialized, you have to include a definition for the default constructor yourself. What exactly does the default constructor look like? In the simplest case, it's just a constructor that accepts no arguments; it doesn't even need to do anything:

```
CBox()                        // Default constructor
{}                            // Totally devoid of statements
```

You can see such a constructor in action.

TRY IT OUT Supplying a Default Constructor

Let's add our version of the default constructor to the last example, along with the declaration for box2, plus the original assignments for the data members of box2. You must enlarge the default constructor just enough to show that it is called. Here is the next version of the program:

```cpp
// Ex7_05.cpp
// Supplying and using a default constructor
#include <iostream>
using std::cout;
using std::endl;

class CBox                              // Class definition at global scope
{
  public:
    double m_Length;                    // Length of a box in inches
    double m_Width;                     // Width of a box in inches
    double m_Height;                    // Height of a box in inches

    // Constructor definition
    CBox(double lv, double bv, double hv)
    {
      cout << endl << "Constructor called.";
      m_Length = lv;                    // Set values of
      m_Width = bv;                     // data members
      m_Height = hv;
    }

    // Default constructor definition
    CBox()
    {
      cout << endl << "Default constructor called.";
    }

    // Function to calculate the volume of a box
    double Volume()
    {
      return m_Length*m_Width*m_Height;
    }
};

int main()
{
  CBox box1(78.0,24.0,18.0);            // Declare and initialize box1
  CBox box2;                            // Declare box2 - no initial values
  CBox cigarBox(8.0, 5.0, 1.0);        // Declare and initialize cigarBox

  double boxVolume(0.0);                // Stores the volume of a box

  boxVolume = box1.Volume();            // Calculate volume of box1
  cout << endl
       << "Volume of box1 = " << boxVolume;

  box2.m_Height = box1.m_Height - 10;  // Define box2
  box2.m_Length = box1.m_Length / 2.0; // members in
```

```
    box2.m_Width = 0.25*box1.m_Length;    // terms of box1

  cout << endl
      << "Volume of box2 = "
      << box2.Volume();

  cout << endl
        << "Volume of cigarBox = "
        << cigarBox.Volume();

  cout << endl;
  return 0;
}
```

code snippet Ex7_05.cpp

How It Works

Now that you have included your own version of the default constructor, there are no error messages from the compiler and everything works. The program produces this output:

```
Constructor called.
Default constructor called.
Constructor called.
Volume of box1 = 33696
Volume of box2 = 6084
Volume of cigarBox = 40
```

All that the default constructor does is display a message. Evidently, it was called when you declared the object box2. You also get the correct value for the volumes of all three CBox objects, so the rest of the program is working as it should.

One aspect of this example that you may have noticed is that you now know you can overload constructors just as you overloaded functions in Chapter 6. You have just executed an example with two constructors that differ only in their parameter list. One has three parameters of type `double` and the other has no parameters at all.

Assigning Default Parameter Values in a Class

You have seen how you can specify default values for the parameters to a function in the function prototype. You can also do this for class member functions, including constructors. If you put the definition of the member function inside the class definition, you can put the default values for the parameters in the function header. If you include only the prototype of a function in the class definition, the default parameter values should go in the prototype.

If you decided that the default size for a CBox object was a unit box with all sides of length 1, you could alter the class definition in the last example to this:

```
class CBox                         // Class definition at global scope
{
  public:
```

```
    double m_Length;                    // Length of a box in inches
    double m_Width;                     // Width of a box in inches
    double m_Height;                    // Height of a box in inches

    // Constructor definition
    CBox(double lv = 1.0, double bv = 1.0, double hv = 1.0)
    {
      cout << endl << "Constructor called.";
      m_Length = lv;                    // Set values of
      m_Width = bv;                     // data members
      m_Height = hv;
    }

    // Default constructor definition
    CBox()
    {
      cout << endl << "Default constructor called.";
    }

    // Function to calculate the volume of a box
    double Volume()
    {
      return m_Length*m_Width*m_Height;
    }
};
```

If you make this change to the last example, what happens? You get another error message from the compiler, of course. Amongst a lot of other stuff, you get these useful comments from the compiler:

```
warning C4520: 'CBox': multiple default constructors specified
error C2668: 'CBox::CBox': ambiguous call to overloaded function
```

This means that the compiler can't work out which of the two constructors to call — the one for which you have set default values for the parameters or the constructor that doesn't accept any parameters. This is because the declaration of box2 requires a constructor without parameters and either constructor can now be called without parameters. The obvious solution to this is to get rid of the constructor that accepts no parameters. This is actually beneficial. Without this constructor, any CBox object declared without being explicitly initialized will automatically have its members initialized to 1.

TRY IT OUT   Supplying Default Values for Constructor Arguments

You can demonstrate this with the following simplified example:

```
// Ex7_06.cpp
// Supplying default values for constructor arguments
#include <iostream>
using std::cout;
using std::endl;

class CBox                             // Class definition at global scope
```

```cpp
{
  public:
    double m_Length;                    // Length of a box in inches
    double m_Width;                     // Width of a box in inches
    double m_Height;                    // Height of a box in inches

    // Constructor definition
    CBox(double lv = 1.0, double bv = 1.0, double hv = 1.0)
    {
      cout << endl << "Constructor called.";
      m_Length = lv;                    // Set values of
      m_Width = bv;                     // data members
      m_Height = hv;
    }

    // Function to calculate the volume of a box
    double Volume()
    {
      return m_Length*m_Width*m_Height;
    }
};

int main()
{
  CBox box2;                            // Declare box2 - no initial values

  cout << endl
       << "Volume of box2 = "
       << box2.Volume();

  cout << endl;
  return 0;
}
```

code snippet Ex7_06.cpp

How It Works

You only declare a single uninitialized CBox variable — box2 — because that's all you need for demonstration purposes. This version of the program produces the following output:

```
Constructor called.
Volume of box2 = 1
```

This shows that the constructor with default parameter values is doing its job of setting the values of objects that have no initializing values specified.

You should not assume from this that this is the only, or even the recommended, way of implementing the default constructor. There will be many occasions where you won't want to assign default values in this way, in which case, you'll need to write a separate default constructor. There will even be times when you don't want to have a default constructor operating at all, even though you have defined another constructor. This would ensure that all declared objects of a class must have initializing values explicitly specified in their declaration.

Using an Initialization List in a Constructor

Previously, you initialized the members of an object in the class constructor using explicit assignment. You could also have used a different technique, which is called an **initialization list**. I can demonstrate this with an alternative version of the constructor for the class CBox:

```
// Constructor definition using an initialization list
CBox(double lv = 1.0, double bv = 1.0, double hv = 1.0):
                          m_Length(lv), m_Width(bv), m_Height(hv)
{
  cout << endl << "Constructor called.";
}
```

The way this constructor definition is written assumes that it appears within the body of the class definition. Now, the values of the data members are not set in assignment statements in the body of the constructor. As in a declaration, they are specified as initializing values using functional notation and appear in the initializing list as part of the function header. The member m_Length is initialized by the value of lv, for example. This can be more efficient than using assignments as you did in the previous version. If you substitute this version of the constructor in the previous example, you will see that it works just as well.

Note that the initializing list for the constructor is separated from the parameter list by a colon, and each of the initializers is separated by a comma. This technique for initializing parameters in a constructor is important, because, as you will see later, it's the only way of setting values for certain types of data members of an object. The MFC also relies heavily on the initialization list technique.

Making a Constructor Explicit

If you define a constructor with a single parameter, the compiler will use this constructor for implicit conversions, which may not be what you want. For example, suppose you define a constructor for the CBox class like this:

```
CBox(double side): m_Length(side), m_Width(side), m_Height(side) {}
```

This is a handy constructor to have when you want to define a CBox object that is a cube, where all the dimensions are the same. Because this constructor has a single parameter, the compiler will use it for implicit conversions when necessary. For example, consider the following code fragment:

```
CBox box;
box = 99.0;
```

The first statement calls the default constructor to create box, so this must be present in the class. The second statement will call the constructor CBox(double) with the argument as 99.0, so you are getting an implicit conversion from a value of type double to type CBox. This may be what you want, but there will be many classes with single argument constructors where you don't want this to happen. In these situations, you can use the `explicit` keyword in the definition of the constructor to prevent it:

```
explicit CBox(double side): m_Length(side), m_Width(side), m_Height(side) {}
```

With the constructor declared as `explicit`, it will only be called when it is explicitly invoked, and it will not be used for implicit conversions. With the constructor declared as `explicit`, the statement assigning the value 99.0 to the `box` object will not compile. In general, unless you want your single-parameter constructors to be used as implicit-type conversions, it is best to declare all such constructors as `explicit`.

There's another way you can get implicit conversions that you may not intend. In the previous version of the `CBox` class, the constructor has default values for all three parameters. This is how it looks using an initialization list:

```
CBox(double lv = 1.0, double bv = 1.0, double hv = 1.0):
                         m_Length(lv), m_Width(bv), m_Height(hv)
{
  cout << endl << "Constructor called.";
}
```

Because there are default values for the second and third parameters, the following statements will compile:

```
CBox box;
box = 99.0;
```

This time, you will get an implicit call to the constructor above with the first argument value as 99.0 and the other two arguments with default values. This is unlikely to be what you want. To prevent this, make the constructor explicit:

```
explicit CBox(double lv = 1.0, double bv = 1.0, double hv = 1.0):
                         m_Length(lv), m_Width(bv), m_Height(hv)
{
  cout << endl << "Constructor called.";
}
```

PRIVATE MEMBERS OF A CLASS

Having a constructor that sets the values of the data members of a class object, but still admits the possibility of any part of a program being able to mess with what are essentially the guts of an object, is almost a contradiction in terms. To draw an analogy, after you have arranged for a brilliant surgeon such as Dr. Kildare, whose skills were honed over years of training, to do things to your insides, letting the local plumber or bricklayer have a go hardly seems appropriate. You need some protection for your class data members.

You can get the security you need by using the keyword `private` when you define the class members. Class members that are `private` can, in general, be accessed only by member functions of a class. There's one exception, but we'll worry about that later. A normal function has no direct means of accessing the `private` members of a class. This is shown in Figure 7-6.

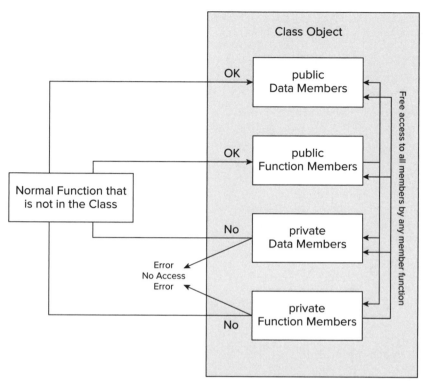

FIGURE 7-6

Having the possibility of specifying class members as `private` also enables you to separate the interface to the class from its internal implementation. The interface to a class is composed of the `public` members and the `public` member functions, in particular, because they can provide indirect access to all the members of a class, including the `private` members. By keeping the internals of a class `private`, you can later modify them to improve performance, for example, without necessitating modifications to the code that uses the class through its public interface. To keep data and function members of a class safe from unnecessary meddling, it's good practice to declare those that don't need to be exposed as `private`. Only make `public` what is essential to the use of your class.

TRY IT OUT   **Private Data Members**

You can rewrite the `CBox` class to make its data members `private`.

```cpp
// Ex7_07.cpp
// A class with private members
#include <iostream>
using std::cout;
```

```cpp
using std::endl;

class CBox                              // Class definition at global scope
{
  public:
    // Constructor definition using an initialization list
    explicit CBox(double lv = 1.0, double bv = 1.0, double hv = 1.0):
                          m_Length(lv), m_Width(bv), m_Height(hv)
    {
      cout << endl << "Constructor called.";
    }

    // Function to calculate the volume of a box
    double Volume()
    {
      return m_Length*m_Width*m_Height;
    }

  private:
    double m_Length;                    // Length of a box in inches
    double m_Width;                     // Width of a box in inches
    double m_Height;                    // Height of a box in inches
};

int main()
{
  CBox match(2.2, 1.1, 0.5);           // Declare match box
  CBox box2;                           // Declare box2 - no initial values

  cout << endl
       << "Volume of match = "
       << match.Volume();

// Uncomment the following line to get an error
// box2.m_Length = 4.0;

  cout << endl
       << "Volume of box2 = "
       << box2.Volume();
  cout << endl;

  return 0;
}
```

code snippet Ex7_07.cpp

How It Works

The CBox constructor is now explicit to prevent unwanted implicit conversions. The definition of the CBox class now has two sections. The first is the public section containing the constructor and the member function Volume(). The second section is specified as private and contains the data members. Now, the data members can only be accessed by the member functions of the class. You don't have to modify any of the member functions — they can access all the data members of the class, anyway. If you uncomment the statement in the function main() that assigns a value to the m_Length member of the object box2, however, you'll get a compiler error message confirming that the data member is inaccessible. If you haven't already done so, take a look at the members of the CBox class in Class View; you'll see that the icon alongside each member indicates its accessibility; a small padlock in the icon shows when a member is private.

A point to remember is that using a constructor or a member function is now the only way to get a value into a private data member of an object. You have to make sure that all the ways in which you might want to set or modify private data members of a class are provided for through member functions.

You can also put functions into the private section of a class. In this case, they can only be called by other function members of the same class. If you put the function Volume() in the private section, you will get a compiler error from the statements that attempt to use it in the function main(). If you put the constructor in the private section, you won't be able to declare any objects of the class type.

The preceding example generates this output:

```
Constructor called.
Constructor called.
Volume of match = 1.21
Volume of box2 = 1
```

The output demonstrates that the class is still working satisfactorily, with its data members defined as having the access attribute private. The major difference is that they are now completely protected from unauthorized access and modification.

If you don't specify otherwise, the default access attribute that applies to members of a class is private. You could, therefore, put all your private members at the beginning of the class definition and let them default to private by omitting the keyword. It's better, however, to take the trouble to explicitly state the access attribute in every case, so there can be no doubt about what you intend.

Of course, you don't have to make all your data members private. If the application for your class requires it, you can have some data members defined as private and some as public. It all depends on what you're trying to do. If there's no reason to make members of a class public, it is better to make them private, as it makes the class more secure. Ordinary functions won't be able to access any of the private members of your class.

Accessing private Class Members

On reflection, declaring the data members of a class as private is rather extreme. It's all very well protecting them from unauthorized modification, but that's no reason to keep their values a secret. What you need is a Freedom of Information Act for private members.

You don't have to start writing to your state senator to get it — it's already available to you. All that's necessary is to write a member function to return the value of a data member. Look at this member function for the class CBox:

```
inline double CBox::GetLength()
{
  return m_Length;
}
```

Just to show how it looks, this has been written as a member function definition, which is external to the class. I've specified it as `inline`, since we'll benefit from the speed increase without increasing the size of the code too much. Assuming that you have the declaration of the function in the `public` section of the class, you can use it by writing statements such as this:

```
double len = box2.GetLength();              // Obtain data member length
```

All you need to do is to write a similar function for each data member that you want to make available to the outside world, and their values can be accessed without prejudicing the security of the class. Of course, if you put the definitions for these functions within the class definition, they will be `inline` by default.

The friend Functions of a Class

There may be circumstances when, for one reason or another, you want certain selected functions that are not members of a class to, nonetheless, be able to access all the members of a class — a sort of elite group with special privileges. Such functions are called **friend functions** of a class and are defined using the keyword `friend`. You can either include the prototype of a friend function in the class definition, or you can include the whole function definition. Functions that are friends of a class and are defined within the class definition are also, by default, `inline`.

> **NOTE** *Friend functions are not members of the class, and therefore, the access attributes do not apply to them. They are just ordinary global functions with special privileges.*

Imagine that you want to implement a friend function in the CBox class to compute the surface area of a CBox object.

You can see how a friend function works in the following example:

```
// Ex7_08.cpp
// Creating a friend function of a class
#include <iostream>
using std::cout;
using std::endl;

class CBox                             // Class definition at global scope
{
  public:

    // Constructor definition
    explicit CBox(double lv = 1.0, double bv = 1.0, double hv = 1.0)
    {
      cout << endl << "Constructor called.";
      m_Length = lv;                   // Set values of
```

```
      m_Width = bv;                    // data members
      m_Height = hv;
    }

    // Function to calculate the volume of a box
    double Volume()
    {
      return m_Length*m_Width*m_Height;
    }

  private:
    double m_Length;                   // Length of a box in inches
    double m_Width;                    // Width of a box in inches
    double m_Height;                   // Height of a box in inches

  // Friend function
  friend double BoxSurface(CBox aBox);
};

// friend function to calculate the surface area of a Box object
double BoxSurface(CBox aBox)
{
  return 2.0*(aBox.m_Length*aBox.m_Width +
              aBox.m_Length*aBox.m_Height +
              aBox.m_Height*aBox.m_Width);
}

int main()
{
  CBox match(2.2, 1.1, 0.5);          // Declare match box
  CBox box2;                          // Declare box2 - no initial values

  cout << endl
       << "Volume of match = "
       << match.Volume();

  cout << endl
       << "Surface area of match = "
       << BoxSurface(match);

  cout << endl
       << "Volume of box2 = "
       << box2.Volume();

  cout << endl
       << "Surface area of box2 = "
       << BoxSurface(box2);

  cout << endl;
  return 0;
}
```

code snippet Ex7_08.cpp

How It Works

You declare the function `BoxSurface()` as a friend of the `CBox` class by writing the function prototype with the keyword `friend` at the front. Since the `BoxSurface()` function itself is a global function, it makes no difference where you put the `friend` declaration within the definition of the class, but it's a good idea to be consistent when you position this sort of declaration. You can see that I have chosen to position ours after all the `public` and `private` members of the class. Remember that a `friend` function isn't a member of the class, so access attributes don't apply.

The definition of the function follows that of the class. Note that you specify access to the data members of the object within the definition of `BoxSurface()`, using the `CBox` object passed to the function as a parameter. Because a `friend` function isn't a class member, the data members can't be referenced just by their names. They each have to be qualified by the object name in exactly the same way as they might in an ordinary function, except, of course, that an ordinary function can't access the `private` members of a class. A `friend` function is the same as an ordinary function, except that it can access all the members of the class or classes for which it is a friend, without restriction.

The example produces the following output:

```
Constructor called.
Constructor called.
Volume of match = 1.21
Surface area of match = 8.14
Volume of box2 = 1
Surface area of box2 = 6
```

This is exactly what you would expect. The `friend` function is computing the surface area of the `CBox` objects from the values of the `private` members.

Placing friend Function Definitions Inside the Class

You could have combined the definition of the function with its declaration as a friend of the `CBox` class within the class definition, and the code would run as before. The function definition in the class would be:

```
friend double BoxSurface(CBox aBox)
{
  return 2.0*(aBox.m_Length*aBox.m_Width +
              aBox.m_Length*aBox.m_Height +
              aBox.m_Height*aBox.m_Width);
}
```

However, this has a number of disadvantages relating to the readability of the code. Although the function would still have global scope, this might not be obvious to readers of the code, because the function would be hidden in the body of the class definition.

The Default Copy Constructor

Suppose that you declare and initialize a `CBox` object `box1` with this statement:

```
CBox box1(78.0, 24.0, 18.0);
```

You now want to create another CBox object, identical to the first. You would like to initialize the second CBox object with box1. Let's try it.

TRY IT OUT   Copying Information Between Instances

The following example shows this in action:

```cpp
// Ex7_09.cpp
// Initializing an object with an object of the same class
#include <iostream>
using std::cout;
using std::endl;

class CBox                              // Class definition at global scope
{
  public:
    // Constructor definition
    explicit CBox(double lv = 1.0, double bv = 1.0, double hv = 1.0)
    {
      cout << endl << "Constructor called.";
      m_Length = lv;                    // Set values of
      m_Width = bv;                     // data members
      m_Height = hv;
    }

    // Function to calculate the volume of a box
    double Volume()
    {
      return m_Length*m_Width*m_Height;
    }

  private:
    double m_Length;                    // Length of a box in inches
    double m_Width;                     // Width of a box in inches
    double m_Height;                    // Height of a box in inches
};

int main()
{
  CBox box1(78.0, 24.0, 18.0);
  CBox box2 = box1;                     // Initialize box2 with box1

  cout << endl
       << "box1 volume = " << box1.Volume()
       << endl
       << "box2 volume = " << box2.Volume();

  cout << endl;
  return 0;
}
```

code snippet Ex7_09.cpp

This example produces the following output:

```
Constructor called.
box1 volume = 33696
box2 volume = 33696
```

How It Works

Clearly, the program is working as you would want, with both boxes having the same volume. However, as you can see from the output, our constructor was called only once for the creation of box1. The question is, how was box2 created? The mechanism is similar to the one that you experienced when you had no constructor defined and the compiler supplied a default constructor to allow an object to be created. In this case, the compiler generates a default version of what is referred to as a **copy constructor**.

A copy constructor does exactly what we're doing here — it creates an object of a class by initializing it with an existing object of the same class. The default version of the copy constructor creates the new object by copying the existing object, member by member.

This is fine for simple classes such as CBox, but for many classes — classes that have pointers or arrays as members, for example — it won't work properly. Indeed, with such classes the default copy constructor can create serious errors in your program. In these cases, you must create your own class copy constructor. This requires a special approach that you'll look into more fully toward the end of this chapter and again in the next chapter.

THE POINTER this

In the CBox class, you wrote the Volume() function in terms of the class member names in the definition of the class. Of course, every object of type CBox that you create contains these members, so there has to be a mechanism for the function to refer to the members of the particular object for which the function is called.

When any member function executes, it automatically contains a hidden pointer with the name this, which points to the object used with the function call. Therefore, when the member m_Length is accessed in the Volume() function during execution, it's actually referring to this->m_Length, which is the fully specified reference to the object member that is being used. The compiler takes care of adding the necessary pointer name this to the member names in the function.

If you need to, you can use the pointer this explicitly within a member function. You might, for example, want to return a pointer to the current object.

Explicit Use of this

You could add a public function to the CBox class that compares the volume of two CBox objects.

```
// Ex7_10.cpp
// Using the pointer this
#include <iostream>
using std::cout;
using std::endl;
```

```
class CBox                                // Class definition at global scope
{
  public:
    // Constructor definition
    explicit CBox(double lv = 1.0, double bv = 1.0, double hv = 1.0)
    {
      cout << endl << "Constructor called.";
      m_Length = lv;                      // Set values of
      m_Width = bv;                       // data members
      m_Height = hv;
    }

    // Function to calculate the volume of a box
    double Volume()
    {
      return m_Length*m_Width*m_Height;
    }

    // Function to compare two boxes which returns true
    // if the first is greater than the second, and false otherwise
    bool Compare(CBox& xBox)
    {
      return this->Volume() > xBox.Volume();
    }

  private:
    double m_Length;                      // Length of a box in inches
    double m_Width;                       // Width of a box in inches
    double m_Height;                      // Height of a box in inches
};

int main()
{
  CBox match(2.2, 1.1, 0.5);             // Declare match box
  CBox cigar(8.0, 5.0,1.0);              // Declare cigar box

  if(cigar.Compare(match))
    cout << endl
         << "match is smaller than cigar";
  else
    cout << endl
         << "match is equal to or larger than cigar";

  cout << endl;
  return 0;
}
```

code snippet Ex7_10.cpp

How It Works

The member function `Compare()` returns `true` if the prefixed `CBox` object in the function call has a greater volume than the `CBox` object specified as an argument, and `false` if it doesn't. The parameter to the `Compare()` function is a reference to avoid unnecessary copying of the argument. In the `return` statements, the prefixed object is referred to through the pointer `this`, used with the indirect member access operator, `->`, that you saw earlier in this chapter.

Remember that you use the direct member access operator when accessing members through objects and the indirect member access operator when accessing members through pointers to objects. `this` is a pointer, so you use the `->` operator.

The `->` operator works the same for pointers to class objects as it did when you were dealing with a `struct`. Here, using the pointer `this` demonstrates that it exists and *does* work, but it's quite unnecessary to use it explicitly in this case. If you change the `return` statement in the `Compare()` function to be:

```
return Volume() > xBox.Volume();
```

you'll find that the program works just as well. Any references to unadorned member names are automatically assumed to be the members of the object pointed to by `this`.

You use the `Compare()` function in `main()` to check the relationship between the volumes of the objects `match` and `cigar`. The output from the program is:

```
Constructor called.
Constructor called.
match is smaller than cigar
```

This confirms that the `cigar` object is larger than the `match` object.

It also wasn't essential to define the `Compare()` function as a class member. You could just as well have written it as an ordinary function with the objects as arguments. Note that this isn't true of the function `Volume()`, because it needs to access the `private` data members of the class. Of course, if you implemented the `Compare()` function as an ordinary function, it wouldn't have access to the pointer `this`, but it would still be very simple:

```
// Comparing two CBox objects - ordinary function version
int Compare(CBox& B1, CBox& B2)
{
    return B1.Volume() > B2.Volume();
}
```

This has both objects as arguments and returns `true` if the volume of the first is greater than the last. You would use this function to perform the same function as in the last example, with this statement:

```
if(Compare(cigar, match))
    cout << endl
        << "match is smaller than cigar";
else
    cout << endl
        << "match is equal to or larger than cigar";
```

If anything, this looks slightly better and easier to read than the original version; however, there's a much better way to do this, which you will learn about in the next chapter.

CONST OBJECTS

The Volume() function that you defined for the CBox class does not alter the object for which it is called; neither does a function such as getHeight() that returns the value of the m_Height member. Likewise, the Compare() function in the previous example didn't change the class objects at all. This may seem at first sight to be a mildly interesting but largely irrelevant observation, but it isn't — it's quite important. Let's think about it.

You will undoubtedly want to create class objects that are fixed from time to time, just like values such as pi or inchesPerFoot that you might declare as const double. Suppose you wanted to define a CBox object as const — because it was a very important standard-sized box, for instance. You might define it with the following statement:

```
const CBox standard(3.0, 5.0, 8.0);
```

Now that you have defined your standard box having dimensions 3 × 5 × 8, you don't want it messed about with. In particular, you don't want to allow the values stored in its data members to be altered. How can you be sure they won't be?

Well, you already are. If you declare an object of a class as const, the compiler will not allow any member function to be called for it that might alter it. You can demonstrate this quite easily by modifying the declaration for the object, cigar, in the previous example to:

```
const CBox cigar(8.0, 5.0, 1.0);              // Declare cigar box
```

If you try recompiling the program with this change, it won't compile. You see the error message:

```
error C2662: 'cBox::Compare' : cannot convert 'this' pointer
from 'const CBox' to CBox &' Conversion loses qualifiers
```

This is produced for the if statement that calls the Compare() member of cigar. An object that you declare as const will always have a this pointer that is const, so the compiler will not allow any member function to be called that does not assume the this pointer that is passed to it is const. You need to find out how to make the this pointer in a member function const.

const Member Functions of a Class

To make the this pointer in a member function const, you must declare the function as const within the class definition. Take a look at how you do that with the Compare() member of CBox. The class definition needs to be modified to the following:

```
class CBox                              // Class definition at global scope
{
  public:
    // Constructor definition
    explicit CBox(double lv = 1.0, double bv = 1.0, double hv = 1.0)
```

```
  {
    cout << endl << "Constructor called.";
    m_Length = lv;                       // Set values of
    m_Width = bv;                        // data members
    m_Height = hv;
  }

  // Function to calculate the volume of a box
  double Volume() const
  {
    return m_Length*m_Width*m_Height;
  }

  // Function to compare two boxes which returns true (1)
  // if the first is greater than the second, and false (0) otherwise
  bool Compare(const CBox& xBox) const
  {
    return this->Volume() > xBox.Volume();
  }

private:
  double m_Length;                       // Length of a box in inches
  double m_Width;                        // Width of a box in inches
  double m_Height;                       // Height of a box in inches
};
```

To specify that a member function is const, you just append the const keyword to the function header. Note that you can only do this with class member functions, not with ordinary global functions. Declaring a function as const is only meaningful in the case of a function that is a member of a class. The effect is to make the this pointer in the function const, which, in turn, means that you cannot write a data member of the class on the left of an assignment within the function definition; it will be flagged as an error by the compiler. A const member function cannot call a non-const member function of the same class, since this would potentially modify the object. This means that because the Compare() function calls Volume(), the Volume() member must be declared as const, too. With the Volume() function declared as const, you can make the parameter to the Compare() function const. When Volume() was a non-const member of the class, making the Compare() function parameter const would result in a C2662 error message from the compiler. When you declare an object as const, the member functions that you call for it must be declared as const; otherwise, the program will not compile. The Compare() function now works with both const and non-const CBox objects.

Member Function Definitions Outside the Class

When the definition of a const member function appears outside the class, the header for the definition must have the keyword const added, just as the declaration within the class does. In fact, you should always declare all member functions that do not alter the class object for which they are called as const. With this in mind, the CBox class could be defined as:

```
class CBox                              // Class definition at global scope
{
  public:
    // Constructor
    explicit CBox(double lv = 1.0, double bv = 1.0, double hv = 1.0);

    double Volume() const;              // Calculate the volume of a box
    bool Compare(CBox xBox) const;      // Compare two boxes

  private:
    double m_Length;                    // Length of a box in inches
    double m_Width;                     // Width of a box in inches
    double m_Height;                    // Height of a box in inches
};
```

This assumes that all function members are defined separately, including the constructor. Both the Volume() and Compare() members have been declared as const. The Volume() function is now defined outside the class as:

```
double CBox::Volume() const
{
  return m_Length*m_Width*m_Height;
}
```

The Compare() function definition is:

```
int CBox::Compare(CBox xBox) const
{
  return this->Volume() > xBox.Volume();
}
```

As you can see, the const modifier appears in both definitions. If you leave it out, the code will not compile. A function with a const modifier is a different function from one without, even though the name and parameters are exactly the same. Indeed, you can have both const and non-const versions of a function in a class, and sometimes, this can be very useful.

With the class declared as shown, the constructor also needs to be defined separately, like this:

```
CBox::CBox(double lv, double bv, double hv):
                  m_Length(lv), m_Width(bv), m_Height(hv)
{
  cout << endl << "Constructor called.";
}
```

ARRAYS OF OBJECTS

You can create an array of objects in exactly the same way as you created an ordinary array where the elements were one of the built-in types. Each element of an array of class objects causes the default constructor to be called.

TRY IT OUT   Arrays of Class Objects

We can use the class definition of CBox from the last example, but modified to include a specific default constructor:

```cpp
// Ex7_11.cpp
// Using an array of class objects
#include <iostream>
using std::cout;
using std::endl;

class CBox                              // Class definition at global scope
{
  public:
    // Constructor definition
    CBox(double lv, double bv = 1.0, double hv = 1.0)
    {
      cout << endl << "Constructor called.";
      m_Length = lv;                    // Set values of
      m_Width = bv;                     // data members
      m_Height = hv;
    }

    CBox()                              // Default constructor
    {
      cout << endl
           << "Default constructor called.";
      m_Length = m_Width = m_Height = 1.0;
    }

    // Function to calculate the volume of a box
    double Volume() const
    {
      return m_Length*m_Width*m_Height;
    }

  private:
    double m_Length;                    // Length of a box in inches
    double m_Width;                     // Width of a box in inches
    double m_Height;                    // Height of a box in inches

};

int main()
{
  CBox boxes[5];                        // Array of CBox objects declared
  CBox cigar(8.0, 5.0, 1.0);            // Declare cigar box

  cout << endl
       << "Volume of boxes[3] = " << boxes[3].Volume()
       << endl
```

```
                  << "Volume of cigar = " << cigar.Volume();

     cout << endl;
     return 0;
   }
```

code snippet Ex7_11.cpp

The program produces this output:

```
Default constructor called.
Default constructor called.
Default constructor called.
Default constructor called.
Default constructor called.
Constructor called.
Volume of boxes[3] = 1
Volume of cigar = 40
```

How It Works

You have modified the constructor that accepts arguments so that only two default values are supplied, and you have added a default constructor that initializes the data members to 1 after displaying a message that it was called. You are now able to see *which* constructor was called *when*. The constructors now have quite distinct parameter lists, so there's no possibility of the compiler confusing them.

You can see from the output that the default constructor was called five times, once for each element of the boxes array. The other constructor was called to create the cigar object. It's clear from the output that the default constructor initialization is working satisfactorily, as the volume of the array element boxes[3] is 1.

STATIC MEMBERS OF A CLASS

Both data members and function members of a class can be declared as static. Because the context is a class definition, there's a little more to it than the effect of the static keyword outside of a class, so let's look at static data members.

Static Data Members

When you declare data members of a class to be static, the effect is that the static data members are defined only once and are shared between all objects of the class. Each object gets its own copies of each of the ordinary data members of a class, but only one instance of each static data member exists, regardless of how many class objects have been defined. Figure 7-7 illustrates this.

Class Definition

```
class CBox
{
    public:
        static int objectCount;


        ...
    private:
        double m_Length;
        double m_Width;
        double m_Height;
        ...
```

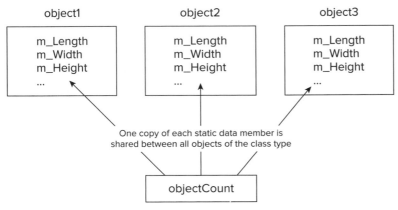

FIGURE 7-7

One use for a static data member is to count how many objects actually exist. You could add a static data member to the public section of the CBox class by adding the following statement to the previous class definition:

```
static int objectCount;              // Count of objects in existence
```

You now have a problem. How do you initialize the static data member?

You can't initialize the static data member in the class definition — that's simply a blueprint for an object, and initializing values are not allowed. You don't want to initialize it in a constructor, because you want to increment it every time the constructor is called so the count of the number of objects created is accumulated. You can't initialize it in another member function because a member function is associated with an object, and you want it initialized before any object is created. The answer is to write the initialization of the static data member outside of the class definition with this statement:

```
int CBox::objectCount(0);            // Initialize static member of class CBox
```

> **NOTE** Notice that the `static` keyword is not included here; however, you do need to qualify the member name by using the class name and the scope resolution operator so that the compiler understands that you are referring to a static member of the class. Otherwise, you would simply create a global variable that had nothing to do with the class.

TRY IT OUT   Counting Instances

Let's add the `static` data member and the object-counting capability to the last example.

Available for download on Wrox.com

```cpp
// Ex7_12.cpp
// Using a static data member in a class
#include <iostream>
using std::cout;
using std::endl;

class CBox                             // Class definition at global scope
{
  public:
    static int objectCount;            // Count of objects in existence

    // Constructor definition
    CBox(double lv, double bv = 1.0, double hv = 1.0)
    {
      cout << endl << "Constructor called.";
      m_Length = lv;                   // Set values of
      m_Width = bv;                    // data members
      m_Height = hv;
      objectCount++;
    }

    CBox()                             // Default constructor
    {
      cout << endl
           << "Default constructor called.";
      m_Length = m_Width = m_Height = 1.0;
      objectCount++;
    }

    // Function to calculate the volume of a box
    double Volume() const
    {
      return m_Length*m_Width*m_Height;
    }

  private:
    double m_Length;                   // Length of a box in inches
    double m_Width;                    // Width of a box in inches
    double m_Height;                   // Height of a box in inches
```

```
    };

    int CBox::objectCount(0);              // Initialize static member of CBox class

    int main()
    {
      CBox boxes[5];                       // Array of CBox objects declared
      CBox cigar(8.0, 5.0, 1.0);           // Declare cigar box

      cout << endl << endl
           << "Number of objects (through class) = "
           << CBox::objectCount;

      cout << endl
           << "Number of objects (through object) = "
           << boxes[2].objectCount;

      cout << endl;
      return 0;
    }
```

code snippet Ex7_12.cpp

This example produces the following output:

```
Default constructor called.
Default constructor called.
Default constructor called.
Default constructor called.
Default constructor called.
Constructor called.
Number of objects (through class) = 6
Number of objects (through object) = 6
```

How It Works

This code shows that it doesn't matter how you refer to the static member objectCount (whether through the class itself or any of the objects of that class). The value is the same and it is equal to the number of objects of that class that have been created. The six objects are obviously the five elements of the boxes array, plus the cigar object. It's interesting to note that static members of a class exist even though there may be no members of the class in existence. This is evidently the case, because you initialized the static member objectCount before any class objects were declared.

 NOTE *Static data members are automatically created when your program begins, and they will be initialized with 0 unless you initialize them with some other value. Thus, you need only to initialize static data members of a class if you want them to start out with a value other than 0.*

Static Function Members of a Class

By declaring a function member as `static`, you make it independent of any particular object of the class. Referencing members of the class from within a static function must be done using qualified names (as you would do with an ordinary global function accessing a public data member). The static member function has the advantage that it exists, and can be called, even if no objects of the class exist. In this case, only static data members can be used because they are the only ones that exist. Thus, you can call a static function member of a class to examine static data members, even when you do not know for certain that any objects of the class exist. You could, therefore, use a static member function to determine whether some objects of the class have been created or, indeed, how many have been created.

Of course, after the objects have been defined, a static member function can access `private` as well as `public` members of class objects. A static function might have this prototype:

```
static void Afunction(int n);
```

A static function can be called in relation to a particular object by a statement such as the following:

```
aBox.Afunction(10);
```

where `aBox` is an object of the class. The same function could also be called without reference to an object. In this case, the statement would take the following form,

```
CBox::Afunction(10);
```

where `CBox` is the class name. Using the class name and the scope resolution operator serves to tell the compiler to which class the function `Afunction()` belongs.

POINTERS AND REFERENCES TO CLASS OBJECTS

Using pointers, and particularly references to class objects, is very important in object-oriented programming and, in particular, in the specification of function parameters. Class objects can involve considerable amounts of data, so using the pass-by-value mechanism by specifying parameters to a function to be objects can be very time-consuming and inefficient because each argument object will be copied. There are also some techniques involving the use of references that are essential to some operations with classes. As you'll see, you can't write a copy constructor without using a reference parameter.

Pointers to Objects

You declare a pointer to a class object in the same way that you declare other pointers. For example, a pointer to objects of type `CBox` is declared in this statement:

```
CBox* pBox(nullptr);                  // Declare a pointer to CBox
```

You can now use this to store the address of a CBox object in an assignment in the usual way, using the address operator:

```
pBox = &cigar;                    // Store address of CBox object cigar in pBox
```

As you saw when you used the `this` pointer in the definition of the `Compare()` member function, you can call a function using a pointer to an object. You can call the function `Volume()` for the pointer `pBox` in a statement like this:

```
cout << pBox->Volume();           // Display volume of object pointed to by pBox
```

Again, this uses the indirect member selection operator. This is the typical notation used by most programmers for this kind of operation, *so from now on, I'll use it universally.*

TRY IT OUT   **Pointers to Classes**

Let's try exercising the indirect member access operator a little more. We will use the example `Ex7_10.cpp` as a base, but change it a little.

```
// Ex7_13.cpp
// Exercising the indirect member access operator
#include <iostream>
using std::cout;
using std::endl;

class CBox                                // Class definition at global scope
{
  public:
    // Constructor definition
    explicit CBox(double lv = 1.0, double bv = 1.0, double hv = 1.0)
    {
      cout << endl << "Constructor called.";
      m_Length = lv;                      // Set values of
      m_Width = bv;                       // data members
      m_Height = hv;
    }

    // Function to calculate the volume of a box
    double Volume() const
    {
      return m_Length*m_Width*m_Height;
    }

    // Function to compare two boxes which returns true
    // if the first is greater than the second, and false otherwise
    bool Compare(CBox* pBox) const
    {
      if(!pBox)
        return 0;
      return this->Volume() > pBox->Volume();
```

```cpp
    }

  private:
    double m_Length;              // Length of a box in inches
    double m_Width;               // Width of a box in inches
    double m_Height;              // Height of a box in inches
};

int main()
{
  CBox boxes[5];                  // Array of CBox objects declared
  CBox match(2.2, 1.1, 0.5);      // Declare match box
  CBox cigar(8.0, 5.0, 1.0);      // Declare cigar Box
  CBox* pB1(&cigar);              // Initialize pointer to cigar object address
  CBox* pB2(nullptr);             // Pointer to CBox initialized to null

  cout << endl
       << "Address of cigar is " << pB1      // Display address
       << endl
       << "Volume of cigar is "
       << pB1->Volume();          // Volume of object pointed to

  pB2 = &match;
  if(pB2->Compare(pB1))           // Compare via pointers
    cout << endl
         << "match is greater than cigar";
  else
    cout << endl
         << "match is less than or equal to cigar";

  pB1 = boxes;                    // Set to address of array
  boxes[2] = match;               // Set 3rd element to match
  cout << endl                    // Now access thru pointer
       << "Volume of boxes[2] is " << (pB1 + 2)->Volume();

  cout << endl;
  return 0;
}
```

code snippet Ex7_13.cpp

If you run the example, the output looks something like that shown here:

```
Constructor called.
Constructor called.
Constructor called.
Constructor called.
Constructor called.
Constructor called.
Constructor called.
Address of cigar is 0012FE20
Volume of cigar is 40
match is less than or equal to cigar
Volume of boxes[2] is 1.21
```

Of course, the value of the address for the object `cigar` may well be different on your PC.

How It Works

The only change to the class definition isn't one of great substance. You have modified the `Compare()` function to accept a pointer to a `CBox` object as an argument. You have an `if` statement added to the function that guards against the possibility for the argument to be null. Now that you know about `const` member functions, you declare the `Compare()` as `const` because it doesn't alter the object. The function `main()` merely exercises pointers to `CBox` type objects in various, rather arbitrary, ways.

Within the `main()` function, you declare two pointers to `CBox` objects after declaring an array, `boxes`, and the `CBox` objects `cigar` and `match`. The first, `pB1`, is initialized with the address of the object `cigar`, and the second, `pB2`, is initialized to `nullptr`. All of this uses the pointer in exactly the same way you would when you're applying a pointer to a basic type. The fact that you are using a pointer to a type that you have defined yourself makes no difference.

You use `pB1` with the indirect member access operator to generate the volume of the object pointed to, and the result is displayed. You then assign the address of `match` to `pB2` and use both pointers in calling the compare function. Because the argument of the function `Compare()` is a pointer to a `CBox` object, the function uses the indirect member selection operator in calling the `Volume()` function for the object.

To demonstrate that you can use address arithmetic on the pointer `pB1` when using it to select the member function, you set `pB1` to the address of the first element of the array of type `CBox`, `boxes`. In this case, you select the third element of the array and calculate its volume. This is the same as the volume of `match`.

You can see from the output that there were seven calls of the constructor for `CBox` objects: five because of the array `boxes`, plus one each for the objects `cigar` and `match`.

Overall, there's virtually no difference between using a pointer to a class object and using a pointer to a basic type, such as `double`.

References to Class Objects

References really come into their own when they are used with classes. As with pointers, there is virtually no difference between the way you declare and use references to class objects and the way in which we've already declared and used references to variables of basic types. To declare a reference to the object `cigar`, for instance, you would write this:

```
CBox& rcigar(cigar);                    // Define reference to object cigar
```

To use a reference to calculate the volume of the object `cigar`, you would just use the reference name where the object name would otherwise appear:

```
cout << rcigar.Volume();                // Output volume of cigar thru a reference
```

As you may remember, a reference acts as an alias for the object it refers to, so the usage is exactly the same as using the original object name.

Implementing a Copy Constructor

The importance of references is really in the context of parameters and return values in functions, particularly class member functions. Let's return to the question of the copy constructor as a first toe in the water. For the moment, I'll sidestep the question of *when* you need to write your own copy constructor and concentrate on the problem of *how* you can write one. I'll use the CBox class just to make the discussion more concrete.

The copy constructor is a constructor that creates an object by initializing it with an existing object of the same class. It therefore needs to accept an object of the class as an argument. You might consider writing the prototype like this:

```
CBox(CBox initB);
```

Now, consider what happens when this constructor is called. If you write this declaration,

```
CBox myBox(cigar);
```

this generates a call of the copy constructor, as follows:

```
CBox::CBox(cigar);
```

This seems to be no problem, until you realize that the argument is passed by value. So, before the object cigar can be passed, the compiler needs to arrange to make a copy of it. Therefore, it calls the copy constructor to make a copy of the argument for the call of the copy constructor. Unfortunately, since it is passed by value, this call also needs a copy of its argument to be made, so the copy constructor is called, and so on and so on. You end up with an infinite number of calls to the copy constructor.

The solution, as I'm sure you have guessed, is to use a const reference parameter. You can write the prototype of the copy constructor like this:

```
CBox(const CBox& initB);
```

Now, the argument to the copy constructor doesn't need to be copied. It is used to initialize the reference parameter, so no copying takes place. As you remember from the discussion on references, if a parameter to a function is a reference, no copying of the argument occurs when the function is called. The function accesses the argument variable in the caller function directly. The const qualifier ensures that the argument can't be modified in the function.

NOTE *This is another important use of the* const *qualifier. You should always declare a reference parameter of a function as* const *unless the function will modify it.*

You could implement the copy constructor as follows:

```
CBox::CBox(const CBox& initB)
{
  m_Length = initB.m_Length;
  m_Width = initB.m_Width;
  m_Height = initB.m_Height;
}
```

This definition of the copy constructor assumes that it appears outside of the class definition. The constructor name is therefore qualified with the class name using the scope resolution operator. Each data member of the object being created is initialized with the corresponding member of the object passed as an argument. Of course, you could equally well use the initialization list to set the values of the object.

This case is not an example of when you need to write a copy constructor. As you have seen, the default copy constructor works perfectly well with CBox objects. I will get to *why* and *when* you need to write your own copy constructor in the next chapter.

C++/CLI PROGRAMMING

The C++/CLI programming language has its own struct and class types. In fact, C++/CLI allows the definition of two different struct and class types that have different characteristics; value struct types and value class types, and ref struct types and ref class types. Each of the two-word combinations, value struct, ref struct, value class, and ref class, is a keyword and distinct from the keywords struct and class; value and ref are not, by themselves, keywords. As in native C++, the only difference between a struct and a class in C++/CLI is that members of a struct are public by default, whereas members of a class are private by default. One essential difference between value classes (or value structs) and reference classes (or ref structs) is that variables of value class types contain their own data, whereas variables to access reference class types must be handles, and therefore contain an address.

Note that member functions of C++/CLI classes cannot be declared as const. Another difference from native C++ is that the this pointer in a non-static function member of a value class type T is an interior pointer of type interior_ptr<T>, whereas the this pointer in a ref class type T is a handle of type T^. You need to keep this in mind when returning the this pointer from a C++/CLI function or storing it in a local variable. There are three other restrictions that apply to both value classes and reference classes:

➤ A value class or ref class cannot contain fields that are native C++ arrays or native C++ class types.

➤ Friend functions are not allowed.

➤ A value class or ref class cannot have members that are bit-fields.

You have already heard back in Chapter 2 that the fundamental type names such as type int and type double are shorthand for value class types in a CLR program. When you declare a data item of a value class type, memory for it will be allocated on the stack, but you can create value class objects on the heap using the `gcnew` operator, in which case, the variable that you use to access the value class object must be a handle. For example:

```
double pi(3.142);            // pi is stored on the stack
int^ lucky(gcnew int(7));    // lucky is a handle and 7 is stored on the heap
double^ two(2.0);            // two is a handle, and 2.0 is stored on the heap
```

You can use any of these variables in an arithmetic expression but you must use the * operator to dereference the handle to access the value. For example:

```
Console::WriteLine(L"2pi = {0}", *two*pi);
```

Note that you could write the product as `pi**two` and get the right result, but it is better to use parentheses in such instances and write `pi*(*two)`, as this makes the code clearer.

Defining Value Class Types

I won't discuss `value struct` types separately from `value class` types as the only difference is that the members of a `value struct` type are `public` by default, whereas `value class` members are private by default. A value class is intended to be a relatively simple class type that provides the possibility for you to define new primitive types that can be used in a similar way to the fundamental types; however, you won't be in a position to do this fully until you learn about a topic called **operator overloading** in the next chapter. A variable of a value class type is created on the stack and stores the value directly, but as you have already seen, you can also use a tracking handle to reference a value class type stored on the CLR heap.

Take an example of a simple value class definition:

```
// Class representing a height
value class Height
{
private:
  // Records the height in feet and inches
  int feet;
  int inches;

public:
  // Create a height from inches value
  Height(int ins)
  {
    feet = ins/12;
    inches = ins%12;
  }

  // Create a height from feet and inches
  Height(int ft, int ins) : feet(ft), inches(ins){}
};
```

This defines a value class type with the name `Height`. It has two private fields that are both of type `int` that record a height in feet and inches. The class has two constructors — one to create a `Height` object from a number of inches supplied as the argument, and the other to create a `Height` object from both a feet-and-inches specification. The latter should really check that the number of inches supplied as an argument is less than 12, but I'll leave you to add that as a fine point. To create a variable of type `Height`, you could write:

```
Height tall = Height(7, 8);                // Height is 7 feet 8 inches
```

This creates the variable, `tall`, containing a `Height` object representing 7 feet, 8 inches; this object is created by calling the constructor with two parameters.

```
Height baseHeight;
```

This statement creates a variable, `baseHeight`, that will be automatically initialized to a height of zero. The `Height` class does not have a no-arg constructor specified, and because it is a value class, you are not permitted to supply one in the class definition. There will be a no-arg constructor included automatically in a value class that will initialize all value type fields to the equivalent of zero and all fields that are handles to `nullptr`, and you cannot override the implicit constructor with your own version. It's this default constructor that will be used to create the value of `baseHeight`.

There are a couple of other restrictions on what a value class can contain:

➤ You must not include a copy constructor in a value class definition.

➤ You cannot overload the assignment operator in a value class. (I'll discuss how you overload operators in a class in Chapter 8.)

Value class objects are always copied by just copying fields, and the assignment of one value class object to another is done in the same way. Value classes are intended to be used to represent simple objects defined by a limited amount of data, so for objects that don't fit this specification or where the value class restrictions are problematical, you should use `ref class` types to represent them.

Let's take the `Height` class for a test drive.

TRY IT OUT Defining and Using a Value Class Type

Here's the code to exercise the `Height` value class:

Available for download on Wrox.com

```
// Ex7_14.cpp : main project file.
// Defining and using a value class type

#include "stdafx.h"

using namespace System;

// Class representing a height
value class Height
{
private:
  // Records the height in feet and inches
  int feet;
```

```
    int inches;

  public:
    // Create a height from inches value
    Height(int ins)
    {
      feet = ins/12;
      inches = ins%12;
    }

    // Create a height from feet and inches
    Height(int ft, int ins) : feet(ft), inches(ins){}
};

int main(array<System::String ^> ^args)
{
  Height myHeight(Height(6,3));
  Height^ yourHeight(Height(70));
  Height hisHeight(*yourHeight);

  Console::WriteLine(L"My height is {0}", myHeight);
  Console::WriteLine(L"Your height is {0}", yourHeight);
  Console::WriteLine(L"His height is {0}", hisHeight);
  return 0;
}
```

code snippet Ex7_14.cpp

Executing this program results in the following output:

```
My height is Height
Your height is Height
His height is Height
```

How It Works

Well, the output is a bit monotonous and perhaps less than we were hoping for, but let's come back to that a little later. In the `main()` function, you create three variables with the following statements:

```
Height myHeight(Height(6,3));
Height^ yourHeight(Height(70));
Height hisHeight(*yourHeight);
```

The first variable is of type `Height` so the object that represents a height of 6 feet, 3 inches is allocated on the stack. The second variable is a handle of type `Height^` so the object representing a height of 5 feet, 10 inches is created on the CLR heap. The third variable is another stack variable that is a copy of the object referenced by `yourHeight`. Because `yourHeight` is a handle, you have to dereference it to assign it to the `hisHeight` variable, and the result is that `hisHeight` contains a duplicate of the object referenced by `yourHeight`. Variables of a value class type always contain a unique object, so two such variables cannot reference the same object; assigning one variable of a value class type to another always involves copying. Of course, several handles can reference a single object, and assigning the value of one handle to another simply copies the address (or `nullptr`) from one to the other so that both objects reference the same object.

The output is produced by the three calls of the `Console::WriteLine()` function. Unfortunately, the output is not the values of the value class objects, but simply the class name. So how did this come about? It was optimistic to expect the values to be produced — after all, how is the compiler to know how they should be presented? `Height` objects contain two values — which one should be presented as the value? The class has to have a way to make the value available in this context.

The ToString() Function in a Class

Every C++/CLI class that you define has a `ToString()` function — I'll explain how this comes about in Chapter 9 when I discuss class inheritance — that returns a handle to a string that is supposed to represent the class object. The compiler arranges for the `ToString()` function for an object to be called whenever it recognizes that a string representation of an object is required, and you can call it explicitly, if necessary. For example, you could write this:

```
double pi(3.142);
Console::WriteLine(pi.ToString());
```

This outputs the value of `pi` as a string, and it is the `ToString()` function that is defined in the `System::Double` class that provides the string. Of course, you would get the same output without explicitly calling the `ToString()` function.

The default version of the `ToString()` function that you get in the `Height` class just outputs the class name, because there is no way to know ahead of time what value should be returned as a string for an object of your class type. To get an appropriate value output by the `Console::WriteLine()` function in the previous example, you must add a `ToString()` function to the `Height` class that presents the value of an object in the form that you want.

Here's how the class looks with a `ToString()` function:

```
// Class representing a height
value class Height
{
private:
  // Records the height in feet and inches
  int feet;
  int inches;

public:
  // Create a height from inches value
  Height(int ins)
  {
    feet = ins/12;
    inches = ins%12;
  }

  // Create a height from feet and inches
```

```
Height(int ft, int ins) : feet(ft), inches(ins){}

// Create a string representation of the object
virtual String^ ToString() override
{
  return feet + L" feet "+ inches + L" inches";
}
};
```

The combination of the `virtual` keyword before the return type for `ToString()` and the `override` keyword following the parameter list for the function indicates that this version of the `ToString()` function overrides the version of the function that is present in the class by default. You'll hear a lot more about this in Chapter 9. Our new version of the `ToString()` function now outputs a string expressing a height in feet and inches. If you add this function to the class definition in the previous example, you get the following output when you compile and execute the program:

```
My height is 6 feet 3 inches
Your height is 5 feet 10 inches
His height is 5 feet 10 inches
```

This is more like what you were expecting to get before. You can see from the output that the `WriteLine()` function quite happily deals with an object on the CLR heap that you reference through the `yourHeight` handle, as well as the `myHeight` and `hisHeight` objects that were created on the stack.

Literal Fields

The factor 12 that you use to convert from feet to inches and vice versa is a little troubling. It is an example of what is called a "magic number," where a person reading the code has to guess or deduce its significance and origin. In this case, it's fairly obvious what the 12 is, but there will be many instances where the origin of a numerical constant in a calculation is not so apparent. C++/CLI has a **literal field** facility for introducing named constants into a class that will solve the problem in this case. Here's how you can eliminate the magic number from the code in the single-argument constructor in the `Height` class:

```
value class Height
{
private:
  // Records the height in feet and inches
  int feet;
  int inches;
  literal int inchesPerFoot = 12;

public:
  // Create a height from inches value
  Height(int ins)
  {
    feet = ins/ inchesPerFoot;
    inches = ins% inchesPerFoot;
  }

  // Create a height from feet and inches
```

```
    Height(int ft, int ins) : feet(ft), inches(ins){}

    // Create a string representation of the object
    virtual  String^ ToString() override
    {
       return feet + L" feet "+ inches + L" inches";
    }
  };
```

Now, the constructor uses the name `inchesPerFoot` instead of 12, so there is no doubt as to what is going on.

You can define the value of a literal field in terms of other literal fields as long as the names of the fields you are using to specify the value are defined first. For example:

```
value class Height
{
  // Other code...
  literal int inchesPerFoot = 12;
  literal double millimetersPerInch = 25.4;
  literal double millimetersPerFoot = inchesPerFoot*millimetersPerInch;

  // Other code...
};
```

Here, you define the value for the literal field `millimetersPerFoot` as the product of the other two literal fields. If you were to move the definition of the `millimetersPerFoot` field so that it precedes either or both of the other two, the code would not compile.

A literal field can only be initialized with a value that is a constant integral value, an enum value, or a string; this obviously limits the possible types for a literal field to those you can initialize in this way. You should also note that you cannot use functional notation to initialize a literal field. If you do, the compiler will think you are specifying a function. Of course, literal fields cannot be changed. If you attempt to alter the value of `inchesPerFoot` in the `Height` class, you will get the following error message from the compiler:

```
"error C3891: 'Height::inchesPerFoot' : a literal data member cannot
be used as a l-value"
```

Defining Reference Class Types

A reference class is comparable to a native C++ class in capabilities and does not have the restrictions that a value class has. Unlike a native C++ class, however, a reference class does not have a default copy constructor or a default assignment operator. If your class needs to support either of these operators, you must explicitly add a function for the capability — you'll see how in the next chapter.

You define a reference class using the `ref class` keyword — both words together separated by one or more spaces represent a single keyword. Here's the CBox class from the Ex7_07 example redefined as a reference class.

```cpp
ref class Box
{
  public:
    // No-arg constructor supplying default field values
    Box(): Length(1.0), Width(1.0), Height(1.0)
    {
      Console::WriteLine(L"No-arg constructor called.");
    }

    // Constructor definition using an initialization list
    Box(double lv, double bv, double hv):
                            Length(lv), Width(bv), Height(hv)
    {
      Console::WriteLine(L"Constructor called.");
    }

    // Function to calculate the volume of a box
    double Volume()
    {
      return Length*Width*Height;
    }

  private:
    double Length;                        // Length of a box in inches
    double Width;                         // Width of a box in inches
    double Height;                        // Height of a box in inches
};
```

Note first that I have removed the C prefix for the class name and the m_ prefix for member names because this notation is not recommended for C++/CLI classes. You cannot specify default values for function and constructor parameters in C++/CLI classes, so you have to add a no-arg constructor to the Box class to fulfill this function. The no-arg constructor just initializes the three private fields with 1.0.

TRY IT OUT   Using a Reference Class Type

Here's an example that uses the Box class that you saw in the previous section.

```cpp
// Ex7_15.cpp : main project file.
// Using the Box reference class type
#include "stdafx.h"

using namespace System;

ref class Box
{
  public:
    // No-arg constructor supplying default field values
```

```
  Box(): Length(1.0), Width(1.0), Height(1.0)
  {
    Console::WriteLine(L"No-arg constructor called.");
  }

   // Constructor definition using an initialization list
   Box(double lv, double bv, double hv):
                           Length(lv), Width(bv), Height(hv)
   {
     Console::WriteLine(L"Constructor called.");
   }

   // Function to calculate the volume of a box
   double Volume()
   {
     return Length*Width*Height;
   }

 private:
   double Length;                   // Length of a box in inches
   double Width;                    // Width of a box in inches
   double Height;                   // Height of a box in inches
};

int main(array<System::String ^> ^args)
{
  Box^ aBox;                       // Handle of type Box^
  Box^ newBox = gcnew Box(10, 15, 20);
  aBox = gcnew Box;                // Initialize with default Box
  Console::WriteLine(L"Default box volume is {0}", aBox->Volume());
  Console::WriteLine(L"New box volume is {0}", newBox->Volume());
  return 0;
}
```

code snippet Ex7_15.cpp

The output from this example is:

```
Constructor called.
No-arg constructor called.
Default box volume is 1
New box volume is 3000
```

How It Works

The first statement in main() creates a handle to a Box object.

```
  Box^ aBox;                       // Handle of type Box^
```

No object is created by this statement, just the tracking handle, aBox. The aBox variable is initialized by default with nullptr so it does not point to anything yet. In contrast, a variable of a value class type always contains an object.

The next statement creates a handle to a new Box object.

```
Box^ newBox = gcnew Box(10, 15, 20);
```

The constructor accepting three arguments is called to create the Box object on the heap, and the address is stored in the handle, newBox. As you know, objects of ref class types are always created on the CLR heap and are referenced generally using a handle.

You create a Box object by calling the no-arg constructor, and store its address in aBox.

```
aBox = gcnew Box;                      // Initialize with default Box
```

This object has the Length, Width, and Height fields set to 1.0.

Finally, you output the volumes of the two Box objects you have created.

```
Console::WriteLine(L"Default box volume is {0}", aBox->Volume());
Console::WriteLine(L"New box volume is {0}", newBox->Volume());
```

Because aBox and newBox are handles, you use the -> operator to call the Volume() function for the objects to which they refer.

Defining a Copy Constructor for a Reference Class Type

You are unlikely to be doing it very often, but if you do pass objects of a reference class type to a function by value, you must implement a public copy constructor; this situation can arise with the Standard Template Library implementation for the CLR, which you will learn about in Chapter 10. The parameter to the copy constructor must be a const reference, so you would define the copy constructor for the Box class like this:

```
Box(const Box% box) : Length(box.Length), Width(box.Width), Height(box.Height)
{}
```

In general, the form of the copy constructor for a ref class T that allows a ref type object of type T to be passed by value to a function is:

```
T(const T% t)
{
  // Code to make the copy...
}
```

Occasionally, you may also need to implement a copy constructor that takes an argument that is a handle. Here's how you could do that for the Box class:

```
Box(const Box^ box) : Length(box->Length), Width(box->Width), Height(box->Height)
{}
```

As you can see, there is little difference between this and the previous version.

Class Properties

A **property** is a member of either a value class or a reference class that you access as though it were a field, but it really isn't a field. The primary difference between a property and a field is that the name of a field refers to a storage location, whereas the name of a property does not — it calls a function. A property has get() and set() accessor functions to retrieve and set its value, respectively, so when you use a property name to obtain its value, behind the scenes, you are calling the get() function for the property, and when you use the name of a property on the left of an assignment statement, you are calling its set() function. If a property only provides a definition for the get() function, it is called a **read-only property** because the set() function is not available to set the property value. A property may just have the set() function defined for it, in which case, it is described as a **write-only property**.

A class can contain two different kinds of properties: **scalar properties** and **indexed properties**. A scalar property is a single value accessed using the property name, whereas indexed properties are a set of values that you access using an index between square brackets following the property name. The String class has the scalar property, Length, that provides you with the number of characters in a string, and for a String object str, you access the Length property using the expression str->Length because str is a handle. Of course, to access a property with the name MyProp for a value class object stored in the variable val, you would use the expression val.MyProp, just like accessing a field. The Length property for a string is an example of a read-only property because no set() function is defined for it — you cannot set the length of a string because a String object is immutable. The String class also gives you access to individual characters in the string as indexed properties. For a string handle, str, you can access the third indexed property with the expression str[2], which corresponds to the third character in the string.

Properties can be associated with, and specific to, a particular object, in which case, the properties are described as instance properties. The Length property for a String object is an example of an instance property. You can also specify a property as static, in which case, the property is associated with the class, and the property value will be the same for all objects of the class type. Let's explore properties in a little more depth.

Defining Scalar Properties

A scalar property has a single value and you define a scalar property in a class using the property keyword. The get() function for a scalar property must have a return type that is the same as the property type, and the set() function must have a parameter of the same type as the property. Here's an example of a property in the Height value class that you saw earlier.

```
value class Height
{
private:
  // Records the height in feet and inches
  int feet;
  int inches;
  literal int inchesPerFoot = 12;
  literal double inchesToMeters = 2.54/100;

public:
```

```
    // Create a height from inches value
    Height(int ins)
    {
      feet = ins / inchesPerFoot;
      inches = ins % inchesPerFoot;
    }

    // Create a height from feet and inches
    Height(int ft, int ins) : feet(ft), inches(ins){}

    // The height in meters as a property
    property double meters
    {
      // Returns the property value
      double get()
      {
        return inchesToMeters*(feet*inchesPerFoot+inches);
      }

      // You would define the set() function for the property here...
    }

    // Create a string representation of the object
    virtual  String^ ToString() override
    {
      return feet + L" feet "+ inches + L" inches";
    }
  };
```

The `Height` class now contains a property with the name `meters`. The definition of the `get()` function for the property appears between the braces following the property name. You would put the `set()` function for the property here, too, if there were one. Note that there is no semicolon following the braces that enclose the `get()` and `set()` function definitions for a property. The `get()` function for the `meters` property makes use of a new literal class member, `inchesToMeters`, to convert the height in inches to meters. Accessing the `meters` property for an object of type `Height` makes the height available in meters. Here's how you could do that:

```
    Height ht(Height(6, 8));                    // Height of 6 feet 8 inches
    Console::WriteLine(L"The height is {0} meters", ht.meters);
```

The second statement outputs the value of `ht` in meters using the expression `ht.meters`.

You are not obliged to define the `get()` and `set()` functions for a property inline; you can define them outside the class definition in a `.cpp` file. For example, you could specify the `meters` property in the `Height` class like this:

```
    value class Height
    {
      // Code as before...
```

```
public:
  // Code as before...


  // The height in meters
  property double meters
  {
    double get();                         // Returns the property value

    // You would define the set() function for the property here...
  }

  // Code as before...
};
```

The `get()` function for the meters property is now declared but not defined in the `Height` class, so a definition must be supplied outside the class definition. In the `get()` function definition in the `Height.cpp` file, the function name must be qualified by the class name and the property name, so the definition looks like this:

```
double Height::meters::get()
{
  return inchesToMeters*(feet*inchesPerFoot+inches);
}
```

The `Height` qualifier indicates that this function definition belongs to the `Height` class, and the `meters` qualifier indicates the function is for the `meters` property in the class.

Of course, you can define properties for a reference class. Here's an example:

```
ref class Weight
{
private:
  int lbs;
  int oz;

public:
  property int pounds
  {
    int get() { return lbs;  }
    void set(int value) {  lbs = value;  }
  }

  property int ounces
  {
    int get() { return oz;  }
    void set(int value) {  oz = value;  }
  }
};
```

Here, the `pounds` and `ounces` properties are used to provide access to the values of the private fields, `lbs` and `oz`. You can set values for the properties of a `Weight` object and access them subsequently like this:

```
Weight^ wt(gcnew Weight);
wt->pounds = 162;
wt->ounces = 12;
Console::WriteLine(L"Weight is {0} lbs {1} oz.", wt->pounds, wt->ounces);
```

A variable accessing a `ref class` object is generally a handle, so you must use the `->` operator to access properties of an object of a reference class type.

Trivial Scalar Properties

You can define a scalar property for a class without providing definitions for the `get()` and `set()` functions, in which case, it is called a trivial scalar property. To specify a trivial scalar property, you just omit the braces containing the `get()` and `set()` function definitions and end the property declaration with a semicolon. Here's an example of a value class with trivial scalar properties:

```
value class Point
{
public:
  property int x;                          // Trivial property
  property int y;                          // Trivial property

  virtual String^ ToString() override
  {
    return L"(" + x + L"," + y + L")";     // Returns "(x,y)"
  }
};
```

Default `get()` and `set()` function definitions are supplied automatically for each trivial scalar property, and these return the property value and set the property value to the argument of the type specified for the property. Private space is allocated to accommodate the property value behind the scenes.

Let's see some scalar properties working.

TRY IT OUT   Using Scalar Properties

This example uses three classes, two value classes, and a ref class:

Available for download on Wrox.com

```
// Ex7_16.cpp : main project file.
// Using scalar properties

#include "stdafx.h"

using namespace System;

// Class defining a person's height
value class Height
{
private:
  // Records the height in feet and inches
  int feet;
```

```
    int inches;

    literal int inchesPerFoot = 12;
    literal double inchesToMeters = 2.54/100;

public:
    // Create a height from inches value
    Height(int ins)
    {
        feet = ins / inchesPerFoot;
        inches = ins % inchesPerFoot;
    }

    // Create a height from feet and inches
    Height(int ft, int ins) : feet(ft), inches(ins){}

    // The height in meters
    property double meters                              // Scalar property
    {
        // Returns the property value
        double get()
        {
            return inchesToMeters*(feet*inchesPerFoot+inches);
        }

        // You would define the set() function for the property here...
    }

    // Create a string representation of the object
    virtual  String^ ToString() override
    {
        return feet + L" feet "+ inches + L" inches";
    }
};

// Class defining a person's weight
value class Weight
{
private:
    int lbs;
    int oz;

    literal int ouncesPerPound = 16;
    literal double lbsToKg = 1.0/2.2;

public:
    Weight(int pounds, int ounces)
    {
        lbs = pounds;
        oz = ounces;
    }

    property int pounds                                 // Scalar property
    {
```

```
    int get() { return lbs;  }
    void set(int value) {  lbs = value;  }
  }

  property int ounces                          // Scalar property
  {
    int get() { return oz;  }
    void set(int value) {  oz = value;  }
  }

  property double kilograms                    // Scalar property
  {
    double get() { return lbsToKg*(lbs + oz/ouncesPerPound);  }
  }

  virtual String^ ToString() override
  { return lbs + L" pounds " + oz + L" ounces"; }
};

// Class defining a person
ref class Person
{
private:
  Height ht;
  Weight wt;

public:
  property String^ Name;                       // Trivial scalar property
  Person(String^ name, Height h, Weight w) : ht(h), wt(w)
  {
    Name = name;
  }

  property Height height
  {
    Height get(){ return ht;  }
  }

  property Weight weight
  {
    Weight get(){ return wt;  }
  }
};

int main(array<System::String ^> ^args)
{
  Weight hisWeight(185, 7);
  Height hisHeight(6, 3);
  Person^ him(gcnew Person(L"Fred", hisHeight, hisWeight));

  Weight herWeight(Weight(105, 3));
  Height herHeight(Height(5, 2));
  Person^ her(gcnew Person(L"Freda", herHeight, herWeight));

  Console::WriteLine(L"She is {0}", her->Name);
```

```
Console::WriteLine(L"Her weight is {0:F2} kilograms.",
                                       her->weight.kilograms);
Console::WriteLine(L"Her height is {0} which is {1:F2} meters.",
                                    her->height, her->height.meters);

Console::WriteLine(L"He is {0}", him->Name);
Console::WriteLine(L"His weight is {0}.", him->weight);
Console::WriteLine(L"His height is {0} which is {1:F2} meters.",
                                    him->height,him->height.meters);

  return 0;
}
```

code snippet Ex7_16.cpp

This example produces the following output:

```
She is Freda
Her weight is 47.73 kilograms.
Her height is 5 feet 2 inches which is 1.57 meters.
He is Fred
His weight is 185 pounds 7 ounces.
His height is 6 feet 3 inches which is 1.91 meters.
```

How It Works

The two value classes, Height and Weight, define the height and weight of a person. The Person class has fields of type Height and Weight to store the height and weight of a person, and the name of a person is stored in the Name property, which is a trivial property because no explicit get() and set() functions have been defined for it; it therefore has the default get() and set() functions. The values of the ht and wt fields are accessible through the read-only properties height and weight, respectively.

The first two statements in main() define Height and Weight objects, and these are then used to define him:

```
Weight hisWeight(185, 7);
Height hisHeight(6, 3);
Person^ him(gcnew Person(L"Fred", hisHeight, hisWeight));
```

Height and Weight are value classes so the variables of these types store the values directly. Person is a reference class so him is a handle. The first argument to the Person class constructor is a string literal so the compiler arranges for a String object to be created from this, and the handle to this object is passed as the argument. The second and third arguments are the value class objects that you create in the first two statements. Of course, copies of these are passed as arguments because of the pass-by-value mechanism for function arguments. Within the Person class constructor, the assignment statement sets the value of the Name parameter, and the values of the two fields, ht and wt, are set in the initialization list. The only way to set a property is through an implicit call of its set() function; a property cannot be initialized in the initializer list of a constructor.

There is a similar sequence of three statements to those for him that define her. With two Person objects created on the heap, you first output information about her with these statements:

```
Console::WriteLine(L"She is {0}", her->Name);
Console::WriteLine(L"Her weight is {0:F2} kilograms.",
                                        her->weight.kilograms);
Console::WriteLine(L"Her height is {0} which is {1:F2} meters.",
                              her->height,her->height.meters);
```

In the first statement, you access the Name property for the object referenced by the handle, her, with the expression her->Name; the result of executing this is a handle to the string that the property's get() value returns, so it is of type String^.

In the second statement, you access the kilograms property of the wt field for the object referenced by her with the expression her->weight.kilograms. The her->weight part of this expression returns a copy of the wt field, and this is used to access the kilograms property; thus, the value returned by the get() function for the kilograms property becomes the value of the second argument to the WriteLine() function.

In the third output statement, the second argument is the result of the expression, her->getHeight, which returns a copy of ht. To produce the value of this in a form suitable for output, the compiler arranges for the ToString() function for the object to be called, so the expression is equivalent to her->Height.ToString(), and, in fact, you could write it like this if you want. The third argument to the WriteLine() function is the meters property for the Height object that is returned by the height property for the Person object, her.

The last three output statements output information about the him object in a similar fashion to the her object. In this case, the weight is produced by an implicit call of the ToString() function for the wt field in the him object.

Defining Indexed Properties

Indexed properties are a set of property values in a class that you access using an index between square brackets, just like accessing an array element. You have already made use of indexed properties for strings because the String class makes characters from the string available as indexed properties. As you have seen, if str is the handle to a String object, then the expression str[4] accesses the fifth indexed property value, which corresponds to the fifth character in the string. A property that you access by placing an index in square brackets following the name of the variable referencing the object, this is an example of a **default indexed property**. An indexed property that has a property name is described as a **named indexed property**.

Here's a class containing a default indexed property:

```
ref class Name
{
  private:
  array<String^>^ Names;              // Stores names as array elements

public:
  Name(...array<String^>^ names) : Names(names) {}

  // Indexed property to return any name
```

```
  property String^ default[int]
  {
    // Retrieve indexed property value
    String^ get(int index)
    {
      if(index >= Names->Length)
        throw gcnew Exception(L"Index out of range");
      return Names[index];
    }
  }
};
```

The idea of the Name class is to store a person's name as an array of individual names. The constructor accepts an arbitrary number of arguments of type String^ that are then stored in the Names field, so a Name object can accommodate any number of names.

The indexed property here is a *default* indexed property because the name is specified by the default keyword. If you supplied a regular name in this position in the property specification, it would be a named indexed property. The square brackets following the default keyword indicate that it is, indeed, an indexed property, and the type they enclose — type int, in this case — is the type of the index values that is to be used when retrieving values for the property. The type of the index does not have to be a numeric type and you can have more than one index parameter for accessing indexed property values.

For an indexed property accessed by a single index, the get() function must have a parameter specifying the index that is of the same type as that which appears between the square brackets following the property name. The set() function for such an indexed property must have two parameters: the first parameter is the index, and the second is the new value to be set for the property corresponding to the first parameter.

Let's see how indexed properties behave in practice.

TRY IT OUT **Using a Default Indexed Property**

Here's an example that makes use of a slightly extended version of the Name class:

```
// Ex7_17.cpp : main project file.
// Defining and using default indexed properties

#include "stdafx.h"

using namespace System;

ref class Name
{
  private:
  array<String^>^ Names;

public:
  Name(...array<String^>^ names) : Names(names) {}

  // Scalar property specifying number of names
```

```
      property int NameCount
      {
        int get() {return Names->Length; }
      }

      // Indexed property to return names
      property String^ default[int]
      {
        String^ get(int index)
        {
          if(index >= Names->Length)
            throw gcnew Exception(L"Index out of range");
          return Names[index];
        }
      }
  };

  int main(array<System::String ^> ^args)
  {
    Name^ myName = gcnew Name(L"Ebenezer", L"Isaiah", L"Ezra", L"Inigo",
                                                    L"Whelkwhistle");

    // List the names
    for(int i = 0 ; i < myName->NameCount ; i++)
      Console::WriteLine(L"Name {0} is {1}", i+1, myName[i]);
    return 0;
  }
```

code snippet Ex7_17.cpp

This example produces the following output:

```
Name 1 is Ebenezer
Name 2 is Isaiah
Name 3 is Ezra
Name 4 is Inigo
Name 5 is Whelkwhistle
```

How It Works

The Name class in the example is basically the same as in the previous section, but with a scalar property with the name NameCount added that returns the number of names in the Name object. In main(), you first create a Name object with five names:

```
    Name^ myName = gcnew Name(L"Ebenezer", L"Isaiah", L"Ezra", L"Inigo",
                                                    L"Whelkwhistle");
```

The parameter list for the constructor in the Name class starts with an ellipsis, so it accepts any number of arguments. The arguments that are supplied when it is called will be stored in the elements of the names array, so initializing the Names field with names makes Names reference the names array. In the previous statement, you supply five arguments to the constructor, so the Names field in the object referenced by myName is an array with five elements.

You access the properties for myName in a for loop to list the names that the object contains:

```
for(int i = 0 ; i < myName->NameCount ; i++)
  Console::WriteLine(L"Name {0} is {1}", i+1, myName[i]);
```

You use the NameCount property value to control the for loop. Without this property, you would not know how many names there are to be listed. Within the loop, the last argument to the WriteLine() function accesses the ith indexed property. As you see, accessing the default indexed property just involves placing the index value in square brackets after the myName variable name. The output demonstrates that the indexed properties are working as expected.

The indexed property is read-only because the Name class only includes a get() function for the property. To allow properties to be changed, you could add a definition for the set() function for the default indexed property like this:

```
ref class Name
{
  // Code as before...

  // Indexed property to return names
  property String^ default[int]
  {
    String^ get(int index)
    {
      if(index >= Names->Length)
        throw gcnew Exception(L"Index out of range");
      return Names[index];
    }

    void set(int index, String^ name)
    {
      if(index >= Names->Length)
        throw gcnew Exception(L"Index out of range");
      Names[index] = name;
    }
  }
};
```

You can now use the ability to set indexed properties by adding a statement in main() to set the last indexed property value:

```
Name^ myName = gcnew Name(L"Ebenezer", L"Isaiah", L"Ezra",
                                      L"Inigo", L"Whelkwhistle");

myName[myName->NameCount - 1] = L"Oberwurst";  // Change last indexed property

// List the names
```

```
for(int i = 0 ; i < myName->NameCount ; i++)
  Console::WriteLine(L"Name {0} is {1}", i+1, myName[i]);
```

With this addition, you'll see from the output for the new version of the program that the last name has, indeed, been updated by the statement assigning a new value to the property at index position `myName->NameCount-1`.

You could also try adding a named indexed property to the class:

```
ref class Name
{
  // Code as before...

  // Indexed property to return initials
  property wchar_t Initials[int]
  {
    wchar_t get(int index)
    {
      if(index >= Names->Length)
        throw gcnew Exception(L"Index out of range");
      return Names[index][0];
    }
  }
};
```

The indexed property has the name `Initials` because its function is to return the initial of a name specified by an index. You define a named indexed property in essentially the same way as a default indexed property, but with the property name replacing the default keyword.

To use this indexed property, add the following statements at the end of `main()` before the `return` statement:

```
Console::Write(L"The initials are: ");
  for (int i = 0 ; i < myName->NameCount ; i++)
    Console::Write(myName->Initials[i] + ".");
  Console::WriteLine();
```

If you recompile the program and execute it once more, you see the following output.

```
Name 1 is Ebenezer
Name 2 is Isaiah
Name 3 is Ezra
Name 4 is Inigo
Name 5 is Oberwurst
The initials are: E.I.E.I.O.
```

The initials are produced by accessing the named indexed property in the `for` loop, and the output shows that they work as expected.

More Complex Indexed Properties

As mentioned, indexed properties can be defined so that more than one index is necessary to access a value, and the indexes need not be numeric. Here's an example of a class with such an indexed property:

```
enum class Day{Monday, Tuesday, Wednesday, Thursday, Friday, Saturday, Sunday};

// Class defining a shop
ref class Shop
{
public:
  property String^ Opening[Day, String^]            // Opening times
  {
    String^ get(Day day, String^ AmOrPm)
    {
      switch(day)
      {
        case Day::Saturday:                         // Saturday opening:
          if(L"am" == AmOrPm)
            return L"9:00";                          //          morning is 9 am
          else
            return L"14:30";                         //          afternoon is 2:30 pm
          break;

        case Day::Sunday:                           // Saturday opening:
          return L"closed";                         //          closed all day
          break;

        default:
          if(L"am" == AmOrPm)                        // Monday to Friday opening:
            return L"9:30";                          //          morning is 9:30 am
          else
            return L"14:00";                         //          afternoon is 2 pm
          break;
      }
    }
  }
};
```

The class representing a shop has an indexed property specifying opening times. The first index is an enumeration value of type Day that identifies the day of the week, and the second index is a handle to a string that determines whether it is morning or afternoon. You could output the Opening property value for a Shop object like this:

```
Shop^ shop(gcnew Shop);
Console::WriteLine(shop->Opening[Day::Saturday, L"pm"]);
```

The first statement creates the Shop object and the second displays the opening time for the shop for Saturday afternoon. As you see, you just place the two index values for the property between square brackets and separate them by a comma. The output from the second statement is the string "14:30". If you can dream up a reason why you need them, you could also define indexed properties with three or more indexes in a class.

Static Properties

Static properties are similar to static class members in that they are defined for the class and are the same for all objects of the class type. You define a static property by adding the `static` keyword in the definition of the property. Here's how you might define a static property in the `Height` class you saw earlier:

```
value class Height
{
  // Code as before...
public:
  static property String^ Units
  {
    String^ get() {  return L"feet and inches";  }
  }
};
```

This is a simple property that makes available the units that are assumed by the class as a string. You access a static property by qualifying the property name with the name of the class, just as you would any other static member of the class:

```
Console::WriteLine(L"Class units are {0}.", Height::Units);
```

Static class properties exist whether or not any objects of the class type have been created. This differs from instance properties, which are specific to each object of the class type. Of course, if you have defined a class object, you can access a static property using the variable name. If you have created a `Height` object with the name `myHt`, for example, you could output the value of the static `Units` property with the statement:

```
Console::WriteLine(L"Class units are {0}.", myHt.Units);
```

For accessing a static property in a reference class through a handle to an object of that type, you would use the `->` operator.

Reserved Property Names

Although properties are different from fields, the values for properties still have to be stored somewhere and the storage locations need to be identified somehow. Internally, properties have names created for the storage locations that are needed, and such names are reserved in a class that has properties, so you must not use these names for other purposes.

If you define a scalar or named indexed property with the name NAME in a class, the names `get_NAME` and `set_NAME` are reserved in the class so you must not use them for other purposes. Both names are reserved regardless of whether or not you define the `get()` and `set()` functions for the property. When you define a default indexed property in a class, the names `get_Item` and `set_Item` are reserved. The possibility of there being reserved names that use underscore characters is a good reason for avoiding the use of the underscore character in your own names in a C++/CLI program.

initonly Fields

Literal fields are a convenient way of introducing constants into a class, but they have the limitation that their values must be defined when you compile the program. C++/CLI also provides `initonly` fields in a class that are constants that you can initialize in a constructor. Here's an example of an initonly field in a skeleton version of the Height class:

```
value class Height
{
private:
  int feet;
  int inches;

public:
    initonly int inchesPerFoot;                    // initonly field

  // Constructor
  Height(int ft, int ins) :
            feet(ft), inches(ins),                 // Initialize fields
            inchesPerFoot(12)                      // Initialize initonly field
  {}
};
```

Here, the initonly field has the name inchesPerFoot and is initialized in the initializer list for the constructor. This is an example of a non-static initonly field and each object will have its own copy, just like the ordinary fields, feet and inches. Of course, the big difference between initonly fields and ordinary fields is that you cannot subsequently change the value of an initonly field — after it has been initialized, it is fixed for all time. Note that you must not specify an initial value for a non-static initonly field when you declare it; this implies that you *must* initialize all non-static initonly fields in a constructor.

You don't have to initialize non-static initonly fields in the constructor's initializer list — you could do it in the body of the constructor:

```
Height(int ft, int ins) :
            feet(ft), inches(ins),                 // Initialize fields
  {
    inchesPerFoot = 12;                            // Initialize initonly field
  }
```

Now, the field is initialized in the body of the constructor. You would typically pass the value for a non-static initonly field as an argument to the constructor rather than use an explicit literal, as we have done here, because the point of such fields is that their values are instance-specific. If the value is known when you write the code, you might as well use a literal field.

You can also define an initonly field in a class to be static, in which case, it is shared between all members of the class, and if it is a public initonly field, it's accessible by qualifying the field name with the class name. The inchesPerFoot field would make much more sense as a static initonly field — the value really isn't going to vary from one object to another. Here's a new version of the Height class with a static initonly field:

```
value class Length
{
private:
  int feet;
  int inches;
```

```
public:
  initonly static int inchesPerFoot = 12;          // Static initonly field

  // Constructor
  Height(int ft, int ins) :
            feet(ft), inches(ins)                  // Initialize fields
  {}
};
```

Now, the `inchesPerFoot` field is static, and it has its value specified in the declaration rather than in the constructor initializer list. Indeed, you are not permitted to set values for static fields of any kind in the constructor. If you think about it, this makes sense because static fields are shared among all objects of the class, and therefore, setting values for such fields each time a constructor is called would conflict with this notion.

You now seem to be back with `initonly` fields only being initialized at compile time, where literal fields could do the job anyway; however, you have another way to initialize static `initonly` fields at runtime — through a **static constructor**.

Static Constructors

A static constructor is a constructor that you declare using the `static` keyword and that you use to initialize static fields and static `initonly` fields. A static constructor has no parameters and cannot have an initializer list. A static constructor is always private, regardless of whether or not you put it in a public section of the class. You can define a static constructor for value classes and for reference classes. You cannot call a static constructor directly — it will be called automatically prior to the execution of a normal constructor. Any static fields that have initial values specified in their declarations will be initialized prior to the execution of the static constructor. Here's how you could initialize the `initonly` field in the `Length` class using a static constructor:

```
value class Height
{
private:
  int feet;
  int inches;

  // Static constructor
  static Height() { inchesPerFoot = 12; }

public:
  initonly static int inchesPerFoot;               // Static initonly field

  // Constructor
  Height(int ft, int ins) :
            feet(ft), inches(ins)                  // Initialize fields
  {}
};
```

This example of using a static constructor has no particular advantage over explicit initialization of `inchesPerFoot`, but bear in mind that the big difference is that the initialization is now occurring at runtime and the value could be acquired from an external source.

SUMMARY

You now understand the basic ideas behind classes in C++. You're going to see more and more about using classes throughout the rest of the book.

EXERCISES

You can download the source code for the examples in the book and the solutions to the following exercises from www.wrox.com.

1. Define a struct Sample that contains two integer data items. Write a program that declares two objects of type Sample, called a and b. Set values for the data items that belong to a and then check that you can copy the values into b by simple assignment.

2. Add a char* member to struct Sample in the previous exercise called sPtr. When you fill in the data for a, dynamically create a string buffer initialized with "Hello World!" and make a.sptr point to it. Copy a into b. What happens when you change the contents of the character buffer pointed to by a.sPtr and then output the contents of the string pointed to by b.sPtr? Explain what is happening. How would you get around this?

3. Create a function that takes a pointer to an object of type Sample as an argument, and that outputs the values of the members of any object Sample that is passed to it. Test this function by extending the program that you created for the previous exercise.

4. Define a class CRecord with two private data members that store a name up to 14 characters long and an integer item number. Define a getRecord() function member of the CRecord class that will set values for the data members by reading input from the keyboard, and a putRecord() function member that outputs the values of the data members. Implement the getRecord() function so that a calling program can detect when a zero item number is entered. Test your CRecord class with a main() function that reads and outputs CRecord objects until a zero item number is entered.

5. Define a class to represent a **push-down stack** of integers. A stack is a list of items that permits adding ("pushing") or removing ("popping") items only from one end and works on a last-in, first-out principle. For example, if the stack contained [10 4 16 20], pop() would return 10, and the stack would then contain [4 16 20]; a subsequent push(13) would leave the stack as [13 4 16 20]. You can't get at an item that is not at the top without first popping the ones above it. Your class should implement push() and pop() functions, plus a print() function so that you can check the stack contents. Store the list internally as an array, for now. Write a test program to verify the correct operation of your class.

6. What happens with your solution to the previous exercise if you try to pop() more items than you've pushed, or save more items than you have space for? Can you think of a robust way to trap this? Sometimes, you might want to look at the number at the top of the stack without removing it; implement a peek() function to do this.

7. Repeat Ex7-4 but as a CLR console program using ref classes.

► WHAT YOU LEARNED IN THIS CHAPTER

TOPIC	CONCEPT
Classes	A class provides a means of defining your own data types. They can reflect whatever types of objects your particular problem requires.
Class members	A class can contain data members and function members. The function members of a class always have free access to the data members of the same class. Data members of a C++/CLI class are referred to as fields.
Class constructors	Objects of a class are created and initialized using functions called constructors. These are automatically called when an object declaration is encountered. Constructors may be overloaded to provide different ways of initializing an object.
C++/CLI classes	Classes in a C++/CLI program can be value classes or ref classes.
C++/CLI class objects	Variables of a value class type store data directly whereas variables referencing ref class objects are always handles.
Static constructors	C++/CLI classes can have a static constructor defined that initializes the static members of a class.
Class member access	Members of a class can be specified as `public`, in which case, they are freely accessible by any function in a program. Alternatively, they may be specified as `private`, in which case, they may only be accessed by member functions or `friend` functions of the class.
Static class members	Members of a class can be defined as `static`. Only one instance of each static member of a class exists, which is shared amongst all instances of the class, no matter how many objects of the class are created.
The pointer this	Every non-static object of a class contains the pointer `this`, which points to the current object for which the function was called.
this in value classes and ref classes	In non-static function members of a value class type, the `this` pointer is an interior pointer, whereas in a ref class type, it is a handle.
const member functions	A member function that is declared as `const` has a `const this` pointer, and therefore cannot modify data members of the class object for which it is called. It also cannot call another member function that is not `const`.
Calling const member functions	You can only call `const` member functions for a class object declared as `const`.
Calling const member functions	Function members of value classes and ref classes cannot be declared as `const`.
Passing objects to a function by reference	Using references to class objects as arguments to function calls can avoid substantial overheads in passing complex objects to a function.
The copy constructor	A copy constructor, which is a constructor for an object initialized with an existing object of the same class, must have its parameter specified as a `const` reference.
Copying value class objects	You cannot define a copy constructor in a value class because copying value class objects is always done by member-by-member copying.

More on Classes

WHAT YOU WILL LEARN IN THIS CHAPTER:

➤ What a class destructor is and when and why it is necessary

➤ How to implement a class destructor

➤ How to allocate data members of a native C++ class in the free store and how to delete them when they are no longer required

➤ When you must write a copy constructor for a class

➤ What a union is and how it can be used

➤ How to make objects of your class work with C++ operators such as + or *

➤ How to use rvalue reference parameters to avoid unnecessary copying of class objects

➤ What class templates are and how to define and use them

➤ How to use the standard `string` class for string operations in native C++ programs

➤ How to overload operators in C++/CLI classes

In this chapter, you will extend your knowledge of classes by understanding how you can make your class objects work more like the basic types in C++.

CLASS DESTRUCTORS

Although this section heading refers to destructors, it's also about dynamic memory allocation. When you allocate memory in the free store for class members, you are invariably obliged to make use of a destructor, in addition to a constructor, of course, and, as you'll see later in this chapter, using dynamically allocated class members will also require you to write your own copy constructor.

What Is a Destructor?

A **destructor** is a function that destroys an object when it is no longer required or when it goes out of scope. The class destructor is called automatically when an object goes out of scope. Destroying an object involves freeing the memory occupied by the data members of the object (except for static members, which continue to exist even when there are no class objects in existence). The destructor for a class is a member function with the same name as the class, preceded by a tilde (~). The class destructor doesn't return a value and doesn't have parameters defined. For the CBox class, the prototype of the class destructor is:

```
~CBox();                    // Class destructor prototype
```

Because a destructor has no parameters, there can only ever be one destructor in a class.

 NOTE *It's an error to specify a return value or parameters for a destructor.*

The Default Destructor

All the objects that you have been using up to now have been destroyed automatically by the **default destructor** for the class. The default destructor is always generated automatically by the compiler if you do not define your own class destructor. The default destructor doesn't delete objects or object members that have been allocated in the free store by the operator new. If space for class members has been allocated dynamically in a contructor, then you must define your own destructor that will explicitly use the `delete` operator to release the memory that has been allocated by the constructor using the operator new, just as you would with ordinary variables. You need some practice in writing destructors, so let's try it out.

TRY IT OUT   **A Simple Destructor**

To get an appreciation of when the destructor for a class is called, you can include a destructor in the class CBox. Here's the definition of the example including the CBox class with a destructor:

```
// Ex8_01.cpp
// Class with an explicit destructor
#include <iostream>
using std::cout;
using std::endl;

class CBox                      // Class definition at global scope
{
  public:
    // Destructor definition
    ~CBox()
```

```cpp
    {
      cout << "Destructor called." << endl;
    }

    // Constructor definition
    explicit CBox(double lv = 1.0, double wv = 1.0, double hv = 1.0):
                            m_Length(lv), m_Width(wv), m_Height(hv)
    {
      cout << endl << "Constructor called.";
    }

    // Function to calculate the volume of a box
    double Volume() const
    {
      return m_Length*m_Width*m_Height;
    }

    // Function to compare two boxes which returns true
    // if the first is greater that the second, and false otherwise
    bool compare(CBox* pBox) const
    {
      return this->Volume() > pBox->Volume();
    }

  private:
    double m_Length;          // Length of a box in inches
    double m_Width;           // Width of a box in inches
    double m_Height;          // Height of a box in inches
};

// Function to demonstrate the CBox class destructor in action
int main()
{
  CBox boxes[5];             // Array of CBox objects declared
  CBox cigar(8.0, 5.0, 1.0); // Declare cigar box
  CBox match(2.2, 1.1, 0.5); // Declare match box
  CBox* pB1(&cigar);         // Initialize pointer to cigar object address
  CBox* pB2(0);              // Pointer to CBox initialized to null

  cout << endl
       << "Volume of cigar is "
       << pB1->Volume();     // Volume of obj. pointed to

  pB2 = boxes;               // Set to address of array
  boxes[2] = match;          // Set 3rd element to match
  cout << endl
       << "Volume of boxes[2] is "
       << (pB2 + 2)->Volume();  // Now access thru pointer

  cout << endl;
  return 0;
}
```

code snippet Ex8_01.cpp

How It Works

The only thing that the CBox class destructor does is to display a message showing that it was called. The output is:

```
Constructor called.
Constructor called.
Constructor called.
Constructor called.
Constructor called.
Constructor called.
Constructor called.
Volume of cigar is 40
Volume of boxes[2] is 1.21
Destructor called.
Destructor called.
Destructor called.
Destructor called.
Destructor called.
Destructor called.
Destructor called.
```

You get one call of the destructor at the end of the program for each of the objects that exist at that time. For each constructor call that occurred, there's a matching destructor call. You don't need to call the destructor explicitly here. When an object of a class goes out of scope, the compiler will arrange for the destructor for the class to be called automatically. In our example, the destructor calls occur after main() has finished executing, so it's quite possible for an error in a destructor to cause a program to crash after main() has safely terminated.

Destructors and Dynamic Memory Allocation

You will find that you often want to allocate memory for class data members dynamically. You can use the operator new in a constructor to allocate memory for an object member. In such a case, you must assume responsibility for releasing the memory when the object is no longer required by providing a suitable destructor. Let's first define a simple class where we can do this.

Suppose you want to define a class where each object is a message of some description — for example, a text string. The class should be as memory-efficient as possible, so, rather than defining a data member as a char array big enough to hold the maximum length string that you might require, you'll allocate memory in the free store for the message when an object is created. Here's the class definition:

Available for download on Wrox.com

```
//Listing 08_01
class CMessage
{
  private:
    char* pmessage;                    // Pointer to object text string

  public:

    // Function to display a message
```

```
    void ShowIt() const
    {
      cout << endl << pmessage;
    }

    // Constructor definition
    CMessage(const char* text = "Default message")
    {
      pmessage = new char[strlen(text) + 1];        // Allocate space for text
      strcpy_s(pmessage, strlen(text) + 1, text);   // Copy text to new memory
    }

    ~CMessage();                                     // Destructor prototype
};
```

code snippet Ex8_02.cpp

This class has only one data member defined, pmessage, which is a pointer to a text string. This is defined in the private section of the class, so that it can't be accessed from outside the class.

In the public section, you have the ShowIt() function that will output a CMessage object to the screen. You also have the definition of a constructor and you have the prototype for the class destructor, ~CMessage(), which I'll come to in a moment.

The constructor for the class requires a string as an argument, but if none is passed, it uses the default string that is specified for the parameter. The constructor obtains the length of the string supplied as the argument, excluding the terminating NULL, by using the library function strlen(). For the constructor to use this library function, there must be a #include statement for the cstring header file. The constructor determines the number of bytes of memory necessary to store the string in the free store by adding 1 to the value that the function strlen() returns.

 NOTE *Of course, if the memory allocation fails, an exception will be thrown that will terminate the program. If you wanted to manage such a failure to provide a more graceful end to the program, you would catch the exception within the constructor code. (See Chapter 6 for information on handling out-of-memory conditions.)*

Having obtained the memory for the string using the operator new, you use the strcpy_s() library function that is also declared in the cstring header file to copy the string supplied as the argument to the constructor into the memory allocated for it. The strcpy_s() function copies the string specified by the third argument to the address contained in the first argument. The second argument specifies the length of the destination location.

You now need to write a class destructor that will free up the memory allocated for a message. If you don't provide a destructor for the class, there's no way to delete the memory allocated for an object. If you use this class as it stands in a program where a large number of CMessage objects are created, the free store will be gradually eaten away until the program fails. It's easy for this to occur in circumstances where it may not be obvious that it is happening. For example, if you create a temporary CMessage object in a function that is called many times in a program, you might assume that the objects are being destroyed at the return from the function. You'd be right about that, of course, but the free store memory will not be released. Thus, for each call of the function, more of the free store will be occupied by memory for discarded CMessage objects.

The code for the CMessage class destructor is as follows:

```
// Listing 08_02
// Destructor to free memory allocated by new
CMessage::~CMessage()
{
   cout << "Destructor called."      // Just to track what happens
        << endl;
   delete[] pmessage;                // Free memory assigned to pointer
}
```

code snippet Ex8_02.cpp

Because you're defining the destructor outside of the class definition, you must qualify the name of the destructor with the class name, CMessage. All the destructor does is to first display a message so that you can see what's going on, and then use the delete operator to free the memory pointed to by the member pmessage. Note that you have to include the square brackets with delete because you're deleting an array (of type char).

TRY IT OUT   **Using the Message Class**

You can exercise the CMessage class with a little example:

```
// Ex8_02.cpp
// Using a destructor to free memory
#include <iostream>          // For stream I/O
#include <cstring>           // For strlen() and strcpy()
using std::cout;
using std::endl;

// Put the CMessage class definition here (Listing 08_01)

// Put the destructor definition here (Listing 08_02)

int main()
{
   // Declare object
   CMessage motto("A miss is as good as a mile.");

   // Dynamic object
   CMessage* pM(new CMessage("A cat can look at a queen."));

   motto.ShowIt();            // Display 1st message
   pM->ShowIt();              // Display 2nd message
```

```
        cout << endl;

    // delete pM;                    // Manually delete object created with new
        return 0;
    }
```

code snippet Ex8_02.cpp

Don't forget to replace the comments in the code with the CMessage class and destructor definitions from the previous section; it won't compile without this (the source code in the download contains all the code for the example).

How It Works

At the beginning of main(), you declare and define an initialized CMessage object, motto, in the usual manner. In the second declaration, you define a pointer to a CMessage object, pM, and allocate memory for the CMessage object that is pointed to by using the operator new. The call to new invokes the CMessage class constructor, which has the effect of calling new again to allocate space for the message text pointed to by the data member pmessage. If you build and execute this example, it will produce the following output:

```
A miss is as good as a mile.
A cat can look at a queen.
Destructor called.
```

You have only one destructor call recorded in the output, even though you created two CMessage objects. I said earlier that the compiler doesn't take responsibility for objects created in the free store. The compiler arranged to call your destructor for the object motto because this is a normal automatic object, even though the memory for the data member was allocated in the free store by the constructor. The object pointed to by pM is different. You allocated memory for the *object* in the free store, so you have to use delete to remove it. You need to uncomment the following statement that appears just before the return statement in main():

```
    // delete pM;                    // Manually delete object created with new
```

If you run the code now, it will produce this output:

```
A miss is as good as a mile.
A cat can look at a queen.
Destructor called.
Destructor called.
```

Now you get an extra call of your destructor. This is surprising in a way. Clearly, delete is only dealing with the memory allocated by the call to new in the function main(). It only freed the memory pointed to by pM. Because your pointer pM points to a CMessage object (for which a destructor has been defined), delete also calls your destructor to allow you to release the memory for the members of the object. So when you use delete for an object created dynamically with new, it will always call the destructor for the object before releasing the memory that the object occupies. This ensures that any memory allocated dynamically for members of the class will also be freed.

IMPLEMENTING A COPY CONSTRUCTOR

When you allocate space for class members dynamically, there are demons lurking in the free store. For the CMessage class, the default copy constructor is woefully inadequate. Suppose you write these statements:

```
CMessage motto1("Radiation fades your genes.");
CMessage motto2(motto1);     // Calls the default copy constructor
```

The effect of the default copy constructor will be to copy the address that is stored in the pointer member of the class from motto1 to motto2 because the copying process implemented by the default copy constructor involves simply copying the values stored in the data members of the original object to the new object. Consequently, there will be only one text string shared between the two objects, as Figure 8-1 illustrates.

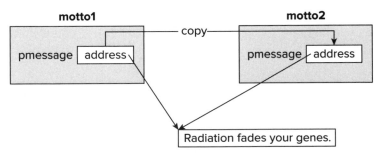

FIGURE 8-1

If the string is changed from either of the objects, it will be changed for the other object as well, because both objects share the same string. If motto1 is destroyed, the pointer in motto2 will be pointing at a memory area that has been released, and may now be used for something else, so chaos will surely ensue. Of course, the same problem arises if motto2 is deleted; motto1 would then contain a member pointing to a nonexistent string.

The solution is to supply a class copy constructor to replace the default version. You could implement this in the public section of the class as follows:

```
CMessage(const CMessage& aMess)
{
  size_t len = strlen(aMess.pmessage)+1;
  pmessage = new char[len];
  strcpy_s(pmessage, len, aMess.pmessage);
}
```

Remember from the previous chapter that, to avoid an infinite spiral of calls to the copy constructor, the parameter must be specified as a const reference. This copy constructor first allocates enough memory to hold the string in the object aMess, storing the address in the data member of the new object, and then copies the text string from the initializing object. Now, the new object will be identical to, but quite independent of, the old one.

Just because you don't initialize one CMessage class object with another, don't think that you're safe and need not bother with the copy constructor. Another monster lurks in the free store that can emerge to bite you when you least expect it. Consider the following statements:

```
CMessage thought("Eye awl weighs yews my spell checker.");
DisplayMessage(thought);      // Call a function to output a message
```

where the function DisplayMessage() is defined as:

```
void DisplayMessage(CMessage localMsg)
{
  cout << endl << "The message is: " << localMsg.ShowIt();
  return;
}
```

Looks simple enough, doesn't it? What could be wrong with that? A catastrophic error, that's what! What the function DisplayMessage() does is actually irrelevant. The problem lies with the parameter. The parameter is a CMessage object, so the argument in a call is passed by value. With the default copy constructor, the sequence of events is as follows:

1. The object thought is created with the space for the message "Eye awl weighs yews my spell checker" allocated in the free store.

2. The function DisplayMessage() is called and, because the argument is passed by value, a copy, localMsg, is made using the default copy constructor. Now, the pointer in the copy points to the same string in the free store as the original object.

3. At the end of the function, the local object goes out of scope, so the destructor for the CMessage class is called. This deletes the local object (the copy) by deleting the memory pointed to by the pointer pmessage.

4.   On return from the function `DisplayMessage()`, the pointer in the original object, `thought`, still points to the memory area that has just been deleted. Next time you try to use the original object (or even if you don't, since it will need to be deleted sooner or later), your program will behave in weird and mysterious ways.

Any call to a function that passes by value an object of a class that has a member defined dynamically will cause problems. So, out of this, you have an absolutely 100-percent, 24-carat golden rule:

> **NOTE** *If you allocate space for a member of a native C++ class dynamically, always implement a copy constructor.*

SHARING MEMORY BETWEEN VARIABLES

As a relic of the days when 64KB was quite a lot of memory, you have a facility in C++ that allows more than one variable to share the same memory (but, obviously, not at the same time). This is called a **union**, and there are four basic ways in which you can use one:

➤   You can use it so that a variable A occupies a block of memory at one point in a program, which is later occupied by another variable B of a different type, because A is no longer required. I recommend that you don't do this. It's not worth the risk of error that is implicit in such an arrangement. You can achieve the same effect by allocating memory dynamically.

➤   Alternatively, you could have a situation in a program where a large array of data is required, but you don't know in advance of execution what the data type will be — it will be determined by the input data. I also recommend that you don't use unions in this case, since you can achieve the same result using a couple of pointers of different types and, again, allocating the memory dynamically.

➤   A third possible use for a union is one that you may need now and again — when you want to interpret the same data in two or more different ways. This could happen when you have a variable that is of type `long`, and you want to treat it as two values of type `short`. Windows will sometimes package two `short` values in a single parameter of type `long` passed to a function. Another instance arises when you want to treat a block of memory containing numeric data as a string of bytes, just to move it around.

➤   You can use a union as a means of passing an object or a data value around where you don't know in advance what its type is going to be. The union can provide for storing any one of the possible range of types that you might have.

Defining Unions

You define a union using the keyword `union`. It is best understood by taking an example of a definition:

```
union shareLD                     // Sharing memory between long and double
{
  double dval;
  long lval;
};
```

This defines a union type `shareLD` that provides for the variables of type `long` and `double` to occupy the same memory. The union type name is usually referred to as a **tag name**. This statement is rather like a class definition, in that you haven't actually defined a union instance yet, so you don't have any variables at this point. Once the union type has been defined, you can define instances of a union in a declaration. For example:

```
shareLD myUnion;
```

This defines an instance of the union type, `shareLD`, that you defined previously. You could also have defined `myUnion` by including it in the union definition statement:

```
union shareLD                     // Sharing memory between long and double
{
  double dval;
  long lval;
} myUnion;
```

To refer to a member of the union, you use the direct member selection operator (the period) with the union instance name, just as you have done when accessing members of a class. So, you could set the `long` variable `lval` to 100 in the union instance `MyUnion` with this statement:

```
myUnion.lval = 100;               // Using a member of a union
```

Using a similar statement later in a program to initialize the double variable `dval` will overwrite `lval`. The basic problem with using a union to store different types of values in the same memory is that, because of the way a union works, you also need some means of determining which of the member values is current. This is usually achieved by maintaining another variable that acts as an indicator of the type of value stored.

A union is not limited to sharing between two variables. If you wish, you can share the same memory between several variables. The memory occupied by the union will be that which is required by its largest member. For example, suppose you define this union:

```
union shareDLF
{
  double dval;
  long lval;
  float fval;
} uinst = {1.5};
```

An instance of `shareDLF` will occupy 8 bytes, as illustrated in Figure 8-2.

FIGURE 8-2

In the example, you defined an instance of the union, `uinst`, as well as the tag name for the union. You also initialized the instance with the value 1.5.

 NOTE *You can only initialize the first member of the union when you declare an instance.*

Anonymous Unions

You can define a union without a union type name, in which case, an instance of the union is automatically declared. For example, suppose you define a union like this:

```
union
{
  char* pval;
  double dval;
  long lval;
};
```

This statement defines both a union with no name and an instance of the union with no name. Consequently, you can refer to the variables that it contains just by their names, as they appear in the union definition, `pval`, `dval`, and `lval`. This can be more convenient than a normal union with a type name, but you need to be careful that you don't confuse the union members with ordinary variables. The members of the union will still share the same memory. As an illustration of how the anonymous union above works, to use the `double` member, you could write this statement:

```
dval = 99.5;                   // Using a member of an anonymous union
```

As you can see, there's nothing to distinguish the variable `dval` as a union member. If you need to use anonymous unions, you could use a naming convention to make the members more obvious and thus make your code a little less obscure.

Unions in Classes and Structures

You can include an instance of a union in a class or in a structure. If you intend to store different types of value at different times, this usually necessitates maintaining a class data member to indicate what kind of value is stored in the union. There isn't usually a great deal to be gained by using unions as class or struct members.

OPERATOR OVERLOADING

Operator overloading is a very important capability because it enables you to make standard C++ operators, such as +, -, *, and so on, work with objects of your own data types. It allows you to write a function that redefines a particular operator so that it performs a particular action when it's used with objects of a class. For example, you could redefine the operator > so that, when it was used with objects of the class CBox that you saw earlier, it would return true if the first CBox argument had a greater volume than the second.

Operator overloading doesn't allow you to invent new operators, nor can you change the precedence of an operator, so your overloaded version of an operator will have the same priority in the sequence of evaluating an expression as the original base operator. The operator precedence table can be found in Chapter 2 of this book and in the MSDN Library.

Although you can't overload all the operators, the restrictions aren't particularly oppressive. These are the operators that you can't overload:

: :	The scope resolution operator
? :	The conditional operator
.	The direct member selection operator
sizeof	The size-of operator
. *	The de-reference pointer to class member operator

Anything else is fair game, which gives you quite a bit of scope. Obviously, it's a good idea to ensure that your versions of the standard operators are reasonably consistent with their normal usage, or at least reasonably intuitive in their operation. It wouldn't be a very sensible approach to produce an overloaded + operator for a class that performed the equivalent of a multiply on class objects. The best way to understand how operator overloading works is to work through an example, so let's implement what I just referred to, the greater-than operator, >, for the CBox class.

Implementing an Overloaded Operator

To implement an overloaded operator for a class, you have to write a special function. Assuming that it is a member of the class CBox, the declaration for the function to overload the > operator within the class definition will be as follows:

```
class CBox
{
  public:
    bool operator>(CBox& aBox) const;  // Overloaded 'greater than'

  // Rest of the class definition...
};
```

The word operator here is a keyword. Combined with an operator symbol or name, in this case, >, it defines an operator function. The function name in this case is operator>. You can write an operator function with or without a space between the keyword operator and the operator itself, as long as there's no ambiguity. The ambiguity arises with operators with names rather than symbols such as new or delete. If you were to write operatornew and operatordelete without a space, they are legal names for ordinary functions, so for operator functions with these operators, you must leave a space between the keyword operator and the operator name itself. The strangest-looking function name for an overloaded operator function is operator()(). This looks like a typing error, but it is, in fact, a function that overloads the function call operator, (). Note that you declare the `operator>()` function as `const` because it doesn't modify the data members of the class.

With the `operator>()` operator function, the right operand of the operator will be defined by the function parameter. The left operand will be defined implicitly by the pointer `this`. So, if you have the following `if` statement:

```
if(box1 > box2)
    cout << endl << "box1 is greater than box2";
```

then the expression between the parentheses in the `if` will call our operator function, and is equivalent to this function call:

```
box1.operator>(box2);
```

The correspondence between the CBox objects in the expression and the operator function parameters is illustrated in Figure 8-3.

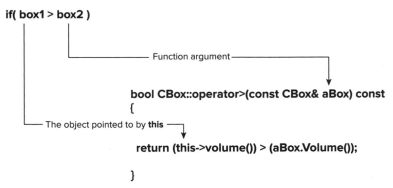

FIGURE 8-3

Let's look at how the code for the `operator>()` function works:

```
// Operator function for 'greater than' which
// compares volumes of CBox objects.
bool CBox::operator>(const CBox& aBox) const
{
    return this->Volume() > aBox.Volume();
}
```

You use a reference parameter to the function to avoid unnecessary copying when the function is called. Because the function does not alter the object for which it is called, you can declare it as `const`. If you don't do this, you cannot use the operator to compare `const` objects of type CBox at all.

The `return` expression uses the member function `Volume()` to calculate the volume of the CBox object pointed to by `this`, and compares the result with the volume of the object `aBox` using the basic operator `>`. The basic `>` operator returns a value of type `int` (not a type `bool`), and thus, 1 is returned if the CBox object pointed to by the pointer `this` has a larger volume than the object `aBox` passed as a reference argument, and 0 otherwise. The value that results from the comparison will be automatically converted to the return type of the operator function, type `bool`.

TRY IT OUT   Operator Overloading

You can exercise the `operator>()` function with an example:

```cpp
// Ex8_03.cpp
// Exercising the overloaded 'greater than' operator
#include <iostream>                           // For stream I/O
using std::cout;
using std::endl;

class CBox                                    // Class definition at global scope
{
  public:
    // Constructor definition
    explicit CBox(double lv = 1.0, double wv = 1.0, double hv = 1.0):
                            m_Length(lv), m_Width(wv), m_Height(hv)
    {
      cout << endl << "Constructor called.";
    }

    // Function to calculate the volume of a box
    double Volume() const
    {
      return m_Length*m_Width*m_Height;
    }

    bool operator>(const CBox& aBox) const;  // Overloaded 'greater than'

    // Destructor definition
    ~CBox()
    {
      cout << "Destructor called." << endl;
    }

  private:
    double m_Length;                          // Length of a box in inches
    double m_Width;                           // Width of a box in inches
    double m_Height;                          // Height of a box in inches
};

// Operator function for 'greater than' that
// compares volumes of CBox objects.
bool CBox::operator>(const CBox& aBox) const
{
  return this->Volume() > aBox.Volume();
}
int main()
{
  CBox smallBox(4.0, 2.0, 1.0);
  CBox mediumBox(10.0, 4.0, 2.0);
  CBox bigBox(30.0, 20.0, 40.0);

  if(mediumBox > smallBox)
```

```
       cout << endl << "mediumBox is bigger than smallBox";

   if(mediumBox > bigBox)
       cout << endl << "mediumBox is bigger than bigBox";
   elsecout << endl << "mediumBox is not bigger than bigBox";

   cout << endl;
   return 0;
}
```

code snippet Ex8_03.cpp

How It Works

The prototype of the `operator>()` operator function appears in the `public` section of the class. As the function definition is outside the class definition, it won't default to `inline`. This is quite arbitrary. You could just as well have put the definition in place of the prototype in the class definition. In this case, you wouldn't need to qualify the function name with `CBox::` in front of it. As you'll remember, this is necessary when you define a function member outside the class definition because this tells the compiler that the function is a member of the `CBox` class.

The function `main()` has two `if` statements using the operator > with class members. These automatically invoke the overloaded operator function. If you wanted to get confirmation of this, you could add an output statement to the operator function. The output from this example is:

```
Constructor called.
Constructor called.
Constructor called.
mediumBox is bigger than smallBox
mediumBox is not bigger than bigBox
Destructor called.
Destructor called.
Destructor called.
```

The output demonstrates that the `if` statements work fine with our operator function, so being able to express the solution to `CBox` problems directly in terms of `CBox` objects is beginning to be a realistic proposition.

Implementing Full Support for a Comparison Operator

With the current version of the operator function `operator>()`, there are still a lot of things that you can't do. Specifying a problem solution in terms of `CBox` objects might well involve statements such as the following:

```
if(aBox > 20.0)
   // Do something...
```

Our function won't deal with that. If you try to use an expression comparing a CBox object with a numerical value, you'll get an error message. To support this capability, you would need to write another version of the operator>() function as an overloaded function.

You can quite easily support the type of expression that you've just seen. The declaration of the member function within the class would be:

```
// Compare a CBox object with a constant
bool operator>(const double& value) const;
```

This would appear in the definition of the class, and the right operand for the > operator corresponds to the function parameter here. The CBox object that is the left operand will be passed as the implicit pointer this.

The implementation of this overloaded operator is also easy. It's just one statement in the body of the function:

```
// Function to compare a CBox object with a constant
bool CBox::operator>(const double& value) const
{
   return this->Volume() > value;
}
```

This couldn't be much simpler, could it? But you still have a problem using the > operator with CBox objects. You may well want to write statements such as this:

```
if(20.0 > aBox)
   // do something...
```

You might argue that this could be done by implementing the operator<() operator function that accepted a right argument of type double, and rewriting the statement above to use it, which is quite true. Indeed, implementing the < operator is likely to be a requirement for comparing CBox objects, anyway, but an implementation of support for an object type shouldn't artificially restrict the ways in which you can use the objects in an expression. The use of the objects should be as natural as possible. The problem is how to do it.

A member operator function always provides the left argument as the pointer this. Because the left argument, in this case, is of type double, you can't implement it as a member function. That leaves you with two choices: an ordinary function or a friend function. Because you don't need to access the private members of the class, it doesn't need to be a friend function, so you can implement the overloaded > operator with a left operand of type double as an ordinary function. The prototype would need to be:

```
bool operator>(const double& value, const CBox& aBox);
```

This is placed outside the class definition, of course, because the function isn't a member of the CBox class. The implementation would be this:

```
// Function comparing a constant with a CBox object
bool operator>(const double& value, const CBox& aBox)
```

```
  {
    return value > aBox.Volume();
  }
```

As you have seen already, an ordinary function (and a `friend` function, too, for that matter) accesses the members of an object by using the direct member selection operator and the object name. Of course, an ordinary function only has access to the public members. The member function `Volume()` is `public`, so there's no problem using it here.

If the class didn't have the `public` function `Volume()`, you could either declare the operator function a `friend` function that could access the `private` data members directly, or you could provide a set of member functions to return the values of the `private` data members and use those in an ordinary function to implement the comparison.

TRY IT OUT   Complete Overloading of the > Operator

We can put all this together in an example to show how it works:

```cpp
// Ex8_04.cpp
// Implementing a complete overloaded 'greater than' operator
#include <iostream>                     // For stream I/O
using std::cout;
using std::endl;

class CBox                              // Class definition at global scope
{
  public:
    // Constructor definition
    explicit CBox(double lv = 1.0, double wv = 1.0, double hv = 1.0):
                        m_Length(lv), m_Width(wv), m_Height(hv)
    {
      cout << endl << "Constructor called.";
    }

    // Function to calculate the volume of a box
    double Volume() const
    {
      return m_Length*m_Width*m_Height;
    }

    // Operator function for 'greater than' that
    // compares volumes of CBox objects.
    bool operator>(const CBox& aBox) const
    {
      return this->Volume() > aBox.Volume();
    }

    // Function to compare a CBox object with a constant
    bool operator>(const double& value) const
    {
      return this->Volume() > value;
    }
```

```
         // Destructor definition
         ~CBox()
         { cout << "Destructor called." << endl;}

     private:
       double m_Length;                // Length of a box in inches
       double m_Width;                 // Width of a box in inches
       double m_Height;                // Height of a box in inches
   };

   bool operator>(const double& value, const CBox& aBox); // Function prototype

   int main()
   {
     CBox smallBox(4.0, 2.0, 1.0);
     CBox mediumBox(10.0, 4.0, 2.0);

     if(mediumBox > smallBox)
       cout << endl << "mediumBox is bigger than smallBox";

     if(mediumBox > 50.0)
       cout << endl << "mediumBox capacity is more than 50";
     else
       cout << endl << "mediumBox capacity is not more than 50";
     if(10.0 > smallBox)
       cout << endl << "smallBox capacity is less than 10";
     else
       cout << endl << "smallBox capacity is not less than 10";

     cout << endl;
     return 0;
   }

   // Function comparing a constant with a CBox object
   bool operator>(const double& value, const CBox& aBox)
   {
     return value > aBox.Volume();
   }
```

code snippet Ex8_04.cpp

How It Works

Note the position of the prototype for the ordinary function version of `operator>()`. It needs to follow the class definition, because it refers to a CBox object in the parameter list. If you place it before the class definition, the example will not compile.

There is a way to place it at the beginning of the program file following the `#include` statement: use an **incomplete class declaration**. This would precede the prototype and would look like this:

```
   class CBox;                                  // Incomplete class declaration
   bool operator>(const double& value, const CBox& aBox);  // Function prototype
```

The incomplete class declaration identifies CBox to the compiler as a class and is sufficient to allow the compiler to process the prototype for the function properly, since the compiler now knows that CBox is a user-defined type to be specified later.

This mechanism is also essential in circumstances such as those where you have two classes, each of which has a pointer to an object of the other class as a member. They will each require the other to be declared first. It is only possible to resolve such an impasse through the use of an incomplete class declaration.

The output from the example is:

```
Constructor called.
Constructor called.
mediumBox is bigger than smallBox
mediumBox capacity is more than 50
smallBox capacity is less than 10
Destructor called.
Destructor called.
```

After the constructor messages due to the declarations of the objects smallBox and mediumBox, you have the output lines from the three if statements, each of which is working as you would expect. The first of these calls the operator function that is a class member and works with two CBox objects. The second calls the member function that has a parameter of type double. The expression in the third if statement calls the operator function that you have implemented as an ordinary function.

As it happens, you could have made both the operator functions that are class members ordinary functions, because they only need access to the member function Volume(), which is public.

 NOTE *Any comparison operator can be implemented in much the same way as you have implemented these. They would only differ in the minor details, and the general approach to implementing them would be exactly the same.*

Overloading the Assignment Operator

If you don't provide an overloaded assignment operator function for your class, the compiler will provide a default. The default version will simply provide a member-by-member copying process, similar to that of the default copy constructor. However, don't confuse the default copy constructor with the default assignment operator. The default copy constructor is called by a declaration of a class object that's initialized with an existing object of the same class, or by passing an object to a function by value. The default assignment operator, on the other hand, is called when the left side and the right side of an assignment statement are objects of the same class type.

For the CBox class, the default assignment operator works with no problem, but for any class which has space for members allocated dynamically, you need to look carefully at the requirements of the class in question. There may be considerable potential for chaos in your program if you leave the assignment operator out under these circumstances.

For a moment, let's return to the CMessage class that you used when I was talking about copy constructors. You'll remember it had a member, pmessage, that was a pointer to a string. Now, consider the effect that the default assignment operator could have. Suppose you had two instances of the class, motto1 and motto2. You could try setting the members of motto2 equal to the members of motto1 using the default assignment operator, as follows:

```
motto2 = motto1;                    // Use default assignment operator
```

The effect of using the default assignment operator for this class is essentially the same as using the default copy constructor: disaster will result! Since each object will have a pointer to the same string, if the string is changed for one object, it's changed for both. There is also the problem that when one of the instances of the class is destroyed, its destructor will free the memory used for the string, and the other object will be left with a pointer to memory that may now be used for something else.

What you need the assignment operator to do is to copy the text to a memory area owned by the destination object.

Fixing the Problem

You can fix this with your own assignment operator function, which we will assume is defined within the class definition:

```
// Overloaded assignment operator for CMessage objects
CMessage& operator=(const CMessage& aMess)
{
  // Release memory for 1st operand
  delete[] pmessage;
  pmessage = new char[strlen(aMess.pmessage) + 1];

  // Copy 2nd operand string to 1st
  strcpy_s(this->pmessage, strlen(aMess.pmessage) + 1, aMess.pmessage);

  // Return a reference to 1st operand
  return *this;
}
```

An assignment might seem very simple, but there's a couple of subtleties that need further investigation. First of all, note that you return a *reference* from the assignment operator function. It may not be immediately apparent why this is so — after all, the function does complete the assignment operation entirely, and the object on the right of the assignment will be copied to that on the left. Superficially, this would suggest that you don't need to return anything, but you need to consider in a little more depth how the operator might be used.

There's a possibility that you might need to use the result of an assignment operation on the right-hand side of an expression. Consider a statement such as this:

```
motto1 = motto2 = motto3;
```

Because the assignment operator is right-associative, the assignment of `motto3` to `motto2` will be carried out first, so this will translate into the following statement:

```
motto1 = (motto2.operator=(motto3));
```

The result of the operator function call here is on the right of the equals sign, so the statement will finally become this:

```
motto1.operator=(motto2.operator=(motto3));
```

If this is to work, you certainly have to return something. The call of the `operator=()` function between the parentheses must return an object that can be used as an argument to the other `operator=()` function call. In this case, a return type of either `CMessage` or `CMessage&` would do it, so a reference is not mandatory in this situation, but you must at least return a `CMessage` object.

However, consider the following example:

```
(motto1 = motto2) = motto3;
```

This is perfectly legitimate code — the parentheses serve to make sure the leftmost assignment is carried out first. This translates into the following statement:

```
(motto1.operator=(motto2)) = motto3;
```

When you express the remaining assignment operation as the explicit overloaded function call, this ultimately becomes:

```
(motto1.operator=(motto2)).operator=(motto3);
```

Now, you have a situation where the object returned from the `operator=()` function is used to call the `operator=()` function. If the return type is just `CMessage`, this will not be legal because a temporary copy of the original object is actually returned, and the compiler will not allow a member function call using a temporary object. In other words, the return value when the return type is `CMessage` is not an lvalue. The only way to ensure this sort of thing will compile and work correctly is to return a reference, which is an lvalue, so the only possible return type if you want to allow fully flexible use of the assignment operator with your class objects is `CMessage&`.

Note that the native C++ language does not enforce any restrictions on the accepted parameter or return types for the assignment operator, but it makes sense to declare the operator in the way I have just described if you want your assignment operator functions to support normal C++ usage of assignment.

The second subtlety you need to keep in mind is that each object already has memory for a string allocated, so the first thing that the operator function has to do is to delete the memory allocated to the first object and reallocate sufficient memory to accommodate the string belonging to the second object. Once this is done, the string from the second object can be copied to the new memory now owned by the first.

There's still a defect in this operator function. What if you were to write the following statement?

```
motto1 = motto1;
```

Obviously, you wouldn't do anything as stupid as this directly, but it could easily be hidden behind a pointer, for instance, as in the following statement,

```
Motto1 = *pMess;
```

If the pointer pMess points to motto1, you essentially have the preceding assignment statement. In this case, the operator function as it stands would delete the memory for motto1, allocate some more memory based on the length of the string that has already been deleted, and try to copy the old memory, which, by then, could well have been corrupted. You can fix this with a check for identical left and right operands at the beginning of the function, so now, the definition of the operator=() function would become this:

```
// Overloaded assignment operator for CMessage objects
CMessage& operator=(const CMessage& aMess)
{
  if(this == &aMess)                   // Check addresses, if equal
    return *this;                      // return the 1st operand

  // Release memory for 1st operand
  delete[] pmessage;
  pmessage = new char[strlen(aMess.pmessage) + 1];

  // Copy 2nd operand string to 1st
  strcpy_s(this->pmessage, strlen(aMess.pmessage)+1, aMess.pmessage);

  // Return a reference to 1st operand
  return *this;
}
```

This code assumes that the function definition appears within the class definition.

TRY IT OUT   **Overloading the Assignment Operator**

Let's put this together in a working example. We'll add a function, called Reset(), to the class at the same time. This just resets the message to a string of asterisks.

```
// Ex8_05.cpp
// Overloaded assignment operator working well
#include <iostream>
#include <cstring>
using std::cout;
using std::endl;

class CMessage
{
  private:
    char* pmessage;                    // Pointer to object text string

  public:
    // Function to display a message
    void ShowIt() const
    {
      cout << endl << pmessage;
```

```
    }

    //Function to reset a message to *
    void Reset()
    {
      char* temp = pmessage;
      while(*temp)
        *(temp++) = '*';
    }

    // Overloaded assignment operator for CMessage objects
    CMessage& operator=(const CMessage& aMess)
    {
      if(this == &aMess)                    // Check addresses, if equal
        return *this;                       // return the 1st operand

      // Release memory for 1st operand
      delete[] pmessage;
      pmessage = new char[strlen(aMess.pmessage) + 1];

      // Copy 2nd operand string to 1st
      strcpy_s(this->pmessage, strlen(aMess.pmessage) + 1, aMess.pmessage);

      // Return a reference to 1st operand
      return *this;
    }

    // Constructor definition
    CMessage(const char* text = "Default message")
    {
      pmessage = new char[strlen(text) + 1];      // Allocate space for text
      strcpy_s(pmessage, strlen(text)+1, text);   // Copy text to new memory
    }

    // Copy constructor definition
    CMessage(const CMessage& aMess)
    {
      size_t len = strlen(aMess.pmessage)+1;
      pmessage = new char[len];
      strcpy_s(pmessage, len, aMess.pmessage);
    }

    // Destructor to free memory allocated by new
    ~CMessage()
    {
      cout << "Destructor called."       // Just to track what happens
           << endl;
      delete[] pmessage;                 // Free memory assigned to pointer
    }
};

int main()
{
  CMessage motto1("The devil takes care of his own");
  CMessage motto2;

  cout << "motto2 contains - ";
```

```
            motto2.ShowIt();
            cout << endl;

            motto2 = motto1;                    // Use new assignment operator

            cout << "motto2 contains - ";
            motto2.ShowIt();
            cout << endl;

            motto1.Reset();                     // Setting motto1 to * doesn't
                                                // affect motto2
            cout << "motto1 now contains - ";
            motto1.ShowIt();
            cout << endl;

            cout << "motto2 still contains - ";
            motto2.ShowIt();
            cout << endl;

            return 0;
            }
```

code snippet Ex8_05.cpp

You can see from the output of this program that everything works exactly as required, with no linking between the messages of the two objects, except where you explicitly set them equal:

```
motto2 contains -
Default message
motto2 contains -
The devil takes care of his own
motto1 now contains -
******************************
motto2 still contains -
The devil takes care of his own
Destructor called.
Destructor called.
```

So let's have another golden rule out of all of this:

Always implement an assignment operator if you allocate space dynamically for a data member of a class.

Having implemented the assignment operator, what happens with operations such as +=? Well, they don't work unless you implement them. For each form of op= that you want to use with your class objects, you need to write another operator function.

Overloading the Addition Operator

Let's look at overloading the addition operator for our CBox class. This is interesting because it involves creating and returning a new object. The new object will be the sum (whatever you define that to mean) of the two CBox objects that are its operands.

So what do we want the sum of two boxes to mean? Well, there are quite a few legitimate possibilities, but we'll keep it simple here. Let's define the sum of two CBox objects as a CBox object that is large enough to contain the other two boxes stacked on top of each other. You can do this by making the new object have an m_Length member that is the larger of the m_Length members of the objects being added, and an m_Width member derived in a similar way. The m_Height member will be the sum of the m_Height members of the two operand objects, so that the resultant CBox object can contain the other two CBox objects. This isn't necessarily an optimal solution, but it will be sufficient for our purposes. By altering the constructor, we'll also arrange that the m_Length member of a CBox object is always greater than or equal to the m_Width member.

Our version of the addition operation for boxes is easier to explain graphically, so it's illustrated in Figure 8-4.

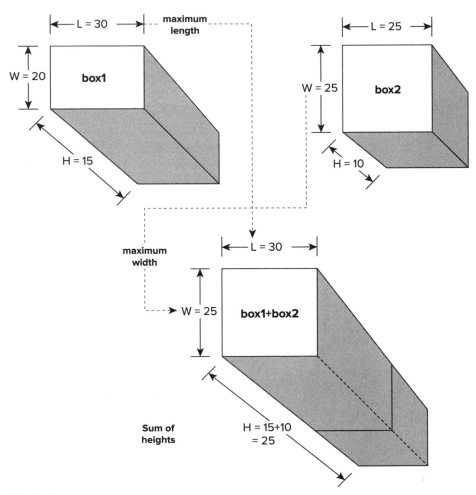

FIGURE 8-4

Because you need to get at the members of a CBox object directly, you will make the operator+() a member function. The declaration of the function member within the class definition will be this:

```
CBox operator+(const CBox& aBox) const;  // Function adding two CBox objects
```

You define the parameter as a reference to avoid unnecessary copying of the right argument when the function is called, and you make it a const reference because the function does not modify the argument. If you don't declare the parameter as a const reference, the compiler will not allow a const object to be passed to the function, so it would then not be possible for the right operand of + to be a const CBox object. You also declare the function as const as it doesn't change the object for which it is called. Without this, the left operand of + could not be a const CBox object.

The operator+() function definition would now be as follows:

```
// Function to add two CBox objects
CBox CBox::operator+(const CBox& aBox) const
{
  // New object has larger length and width, and sum of heights
  return CBox(m_Length > aBox.m_Length ? m_Length : aBox.m_Length,
              m_Width  > aBox.m_Width  ? m_Width  : aBox.m_Width,
              m_Height + aBox.m_Height);
}
```

You construct a local CBox object from the current object (*this) and the object that is passed as the argument, aBox. Remember that the return process will make a temporary copy of the local object and that is what is passed back to the calling function, not the local object, which is discarded on return from the function.

TRY IT OUT   **Exercising Our Addition Operator**

You'll be able to see how the overloaded addition operator in the CBox class works in this example:

```
// Ex8_06.cpp
// Adding CBox objects
#include <iostream>                          // For stream I/O
using std::cout;
using std::endl;

class CBox                                   // Class definition at global scope
{
  public:
    // Constructor definition
    explicit CBox(double lv = 1.0, double wv = 1.0, double hv = 1.0): m_Height(hv)
    {
      m_Length = lv > wv ? lv : wv;          // Ensure that
      m_Width  = wv < lv ? wv : lv;          // length >= width
    }

    // Function to calculate the volume of a box
    double Volume() const
    {
      return m_Length*m_Width*m_Height;
```

```
      }

      // Operator function for 'greater than' which
      // compares volumes of CBox objects.
      bool operator>(const CBox& aBox) const
      {
        return this->Volume() > aBox.Volume();
      }

      // Function to compare a CBox object with a constant
      bool operator>(const double& value) const
      {
        return Volume() > value;
      }

      // Function to add two CBox objects
      CBox operator+(const CBox& aBox) const
      {
        // New object has larger length & width, and sum of heights
        return CBox(m_Length > aBox.m_Length ? m_Length : aBox.m_Length,
                    m_Width > aBox.m_Width   ?  m_Width : aBox.m_Width,
                    m_Height + aBox.m_Height);
      }

      // Function to show the dimensions of a box
      void ShowBox() const
      {
        cout << m_Length << " " << m_Width  << " " << m_Height << endl;
      }

  private:
    double m_Length;                    // Length of a box in inches
    double m_Width;                     // Width of a box in inches
    double m_Height;                    // Height of a box in inches
};

bool operator>(const double& value, const CBox& aBox); // Function prototype

int main()
{
  CBox smallBox(4.0, 2.0, 1.0);
  CBox mediumBox(10.0, 4.0, 2.0);
  CBox aBox;
  CBox bBox;

  aBox = smallBox + mediumBox;
  cout << "aBox dimensions are ";
  aBox.ShowBox();

  bBox = aBox + smallBox + mediumBox;
  cout << "bBox dimensions are ";
  bBox.ShowBox();

  return 0;
```

```
    }

// Function comparing a constant with a CBox object
bool operator>(const double& value, const CBox& aBox)
{
  return value > aBox.Volume();
}
```

code snippet Ex8_06.cpp

You'll be using the CBox class definition again a few pages down the road in this chapter, so make a note that you'll want to return to this point in the book.

How It Works

In this example, I have changed the CBox class members a little. I have deleted the destructor because it isn't necessary for this class, and I have modified the constructor to ensure that the m_Length member isn't less than the m_Width member. Knowing that the length of a box is always at least as big as the width makes the add operation a bit easier. I've also added the ShowBox() function to output the dimensions of a CBox object. Using this, we'll be able to verify that our overloaded add operation is working as we expect.

The output from this program is:

```
aBox dimensions are 10 4 3
bBox dimensions are 10 4 6
```

This seems to be consistent with the notion of adding CBox objects that we have defined, and, as you can see, the function also works with multiple add operations in an expression. For the computation of bBox, the overloaded addition operator will be called twice.

You could equally well have implemented the add operation for the class as a friend function. Its prototype would then be this:

```
friend CBox operator+(const CBox& aBox, const CBox& bBox);
```

The process for producing the result would be much the same, except that you'd need to use the direct member selection operator to obtain the members for both the arguments to the function. It would work just as well as the first version of the operator function.

Overloading the Increment and Decrement Operators

I'll briefly introduce the mechanism for overloading the increment and decrement operators in a class because they have some special characteristics that make them different from other unary operators. You need a way to deal with the fact that the ++ and -- operators come in a prefix and postfix form, and the effect is different depending on whether the operator is applied in its prefix or postfix form. In native C++, the overloaded operator is different for the prefix and postfix forms of the increment and decrement operators. Here's how they would be defined in a class with the name `Length`, for example:

```
class Length
{
  private:
    double len;                         // Length value for the class

  public:
    Length& operator++();               // Prefix increment operator
    const Length operator++(int);       // Postfix increment operator

    Length& operator--();               // Prefix decrement operator
    const Length operator--(int);       // Postfix decrement operator

  // rest of the class...

}
```

This simple class assumes a length is stored just as a value of type `double`. You would probably, in reality, make a length class more sophisticated than this, but it will serve to illustrate how you overload the increment and decrement operators.

The primary way the prefix and postfix forms of the overloaded operators are differentiated is by the parameter list; for the prefix form, there are no parameters, and for the postfix form, there is a parameter of type `int`. The parameter in the postfix operator function is only to distinguish it from the prefix form and is otherwise unused in the function implementation.

The prefix increment and decrement operators increment or decrement the operand before its value is used in an expression, so you just return a reference to the current object after it has been incremented or decremented. Here's how an implementation of the prefix `operator++()` function would look for the `Length` class:

```
Length& Length::operator++()
{
  ++(this->len);
  return *this;
}
```

With the postfix forms, the operand is incremented after its current value is used in an expression. This is achieved by creating a new object that is a copy of the current object before incrementing the current object and returning the copy after the current object has been modified. Here's how you might implement the function to overload the postfix ++ operator for the `Length` class:

```
const Length Length::operator++(int)
{
  Length length = *this;              // Copy the current object
  ++*this;                            // Increment the current object
  return length;                      // Return the original copy
}
```

After copying the current object, you increment it using the prefix ++ operator for the class. You then return the original, unincremented copy of the current object; it is this value that will be used in the expression in which the operator appears. Specifying the return value as const prevents expressions such as data++++ from compiling.

Overloading the Function Call Operator

The function call operator is (), so the function overload for this is operator()(). An object of a class that overloads the function call operator is referred to as a **function object** or **functor** because you can use the object name as though it is the name of a function. Let's look at a simple example. Here's a class that overloads the function call operator:

```
class Area
{
  public:
    int operator()(int length, int width) { return length*width; }
};
```

The operator function in this class calculates an area as the product of its integer arguments. To use this operator function, you just need to create an object of type Area, for example:

```
Area area;                                // Create function object
int pitchLength(100), pitchWidth(50);
int pitchArea = area(pitchLength, pitchWidth);   // Execute function call overload
```

The first statement creates the area object that is used in the third statement to call the function call operator for the object. This returns the area of a football pitch, in this case.

Of course, you can pass a function object to another function, just as you would any other object. Look at this function:

```
void printArea(int length, int width, Area& area)
{
  cout << "Area is " << area(length, width);
}
```

Here is a statement that uses this function:

```
printArea(20, 35, Area());
```

This statement calls the printArea() function with the first two arguments specifying the length and width of a rectangle. The third argument calls the default constructor to create an Area object that is used in the function to calculate an area. Thus, a function object provides you with a way of passing a function as an argument to another function that is simpler and easier to work with than using pointers to functions.

Classes that define function objects typically do not need data members and do not have a constructor defined, so there is minimal overhead in creating and using function objects. Function object classes are also usually defined as templates because this makes them very flexible, as you'll see later in this chapter.

THE OBJECT COPYING PROBLEM

Copying is implicit in passing arguments by value to a function. This is not a problem when the argument is of a fundamental type, but for arguments that are objects of a class type, it can be. The overhead arising from the copy operation for an object can be considerable, especially when the object owns memory that was allocated dynamically. Copying an object is achieved by calling the class copy constructor, so the efficiency of this class function is critical to execution performance. As you have seen with the CMessage class, the assignment operator also involves copying an object. However, there can be circumstances where such copy operations are not really necessary, and if you can find a way to avoid them in such situations, execution time may be substantially reduced. Rvalue reference parameters are the key to making this possible.

Avoiding Unnecessary Copy Operations

A modified version of the CMessage class from Ex8_05.cpp will provide a basis for seeing how this works. Here's a version of the class that implements the addition operator:

```
class CMessage
{
  private:
    char* pmessage;                       // Pointer to object text string

  public:
    // Function to display a message
    void ShowIt() const
    {
      cout << endl << pmessage;
    }

    // Overloaded addition operator
    CMessage operator+(const CMessage& aMess) const
    {
      cout << "Add operator function called." << endl;
      size_t len = strlen(pmessage) + strlen(aMess.pmessage) + 1;
      CMessage message;
      message.pmessage = new char[len];
      strcpy_s(message.pmessage, len, pmessage);
      strcat_s(message.pmessage, len, aMess.pmessage);
      return message;
    }

    // Overloaded assignment operator for CMessage objects
    CMessage& operator=(const CMessage& aMess)
```

```
    {
      cout << "Assignment operator function called." << endl;
      if(this == &aMess)                // Check addresses, if equal
        return *this;                   // return the 1st operand

      // Release memory for 1st operand
      delete[] pmessage;
      pmessage = new char[strlen(aMess.pmessage) + 1];

      // Copy 2nd operand string to 1st
      strcpy_s(this->pmessage, strlen(aMess.pmessage)+1, aMess.pmessage);

      // Return a reference to 1st operand
      return *this;
    }

    // Constructor definition
    CMessage(const char* text = "Default message")
    {
      cout << "Constructor called." << endl;
      pmessage = new char[strlen(text) + 1];      // Allocate space for text
      strcpy_s(pmessage, strlen(text)+1, text);   // Copy text to new memory
    }

    // Copy constructor definition
    CMessage(const CMessage& aMess)
    {
      cout << "Copy constructor called." << endl;
      size_t len = strlen(aMess.pmessage)+1;
      pmessage = new char[len];
      strcpy_s(pmessage, len, aMess.pmessage);
    }

    // Destructor to free memory allocated by new
    ~CMessage()
    {
      cout << "Destructor called."      // Just to track what happens
           << endl;
      delete[] pmessage;                // Free memory assigned to pointer
    }
};
```

code snippet Ex8_07.cpp

The changes from the version in Ex8_05.cpp are highlighted. There is now output from the constructor and the assignment operator function to trace when they are called. There is also a copy constructor and the addition operator function in the class. The operator+() function is for adding two CMessage objects. You could add versions for concatenating a CMessage object with a string literal, but it's not necessary for our purposes here.

Let's see what copying occurs with some simple operations on CMessage objects.

TRY IT OUT Tracing Object Copy Operations

Here's the code to exercise the CMessage class:

```
// Ex8_07.cpp
// How many copy operations?
#include <iostream>
#include <cstring>
using std::cout;
using std::endl;

// Insert CMessage class definition here...

int main()
{
  CMessage motto1("The devil takes care of his own. ");
  CMessage motto2("If you sup with the devil use a long spoon.\n");
  CMessage motto3;
  cout << " Executing: motto3 = motto1 + motto2 " << endl;;
  motto3 = motto1 + motto2;
  cout << " Done!! " << endl << endl;

  cout << " Executing: motto3 = motto3 + motto1 + motto2 " << endl;
  motto3 = motto3 + motto1 + motto2;
  cout << " Done!! " << endl << endl;

  cout << "motto3 contains - ";
   motto3.ShowIt();
  cout << endl;
  return 0;
}
```

code snippet Ex8_07.cpp

This example produces the following output:

```
Constructor called.
Constructor called.
Constructor called.
   Executing: motto3 = motto1 + motto2
Add operator function called.
Constructor called.
Copy constructor called.
Destructor called.
Assignment operator function called.
Destructor called.
   Done!!

   Executing: motto3 = motto3 + motto1 + motto2
Add operator function called.
Constructor called.
Copy constructor called.
```

```
Destructor called.
Add operator function called.
Constructor called.
Copy constructor called.
Destructor called.
Assignment operator function called.
Destructor called.
Destructor called.
  Done!!

motto3 contains -
The devil takes care of his own. If you sup with the devil use a long spoon.
The devil takes care of his own. If you sup with the devil use a long spoon.


Destructor called.
Destructor called.
Destructor called.
```

How It Works

The first statement of interest is:

```
motto3 = motto1 + motto2;                // Use new addition operator
```

This calls operator+() to add motto1 and motto2, and the operator function calls the constructor to create the temporary object to be returned. The returned object is then copied by the copy constructor, and the returned object is destroyed, as you can see from the destructor call. The copy is then copied into motto3 by the operator=() function. Finally, the temporary object that is the right operand for the assignment operation is destroyed by calling the destructor. There are two operations that copy temporary objects (rvalues) as a result of this statement.

The second statement of interest is:

```
motto3 = motto3 + motto1 + motto2;
```

The operator+() function is called to concatenate motto3 and motto1, and the function calls the constructor to create the result that is returned. The object returned is then copied using the copy constructor, and after the original object created within the function is destroyed by the destructor, the copy is concatenated with motto2 by calling operator+() once more, and the sequence of calls is repeated. Finally, the operator=() function is called to store the result. Thus, for this simple statement, we have three copy operations from temporary objects, two from copy constructor calls, and one from the assignment operator.

All these copy operations could be very expensive in elapsed time if CMessage were a really complex object involving a lot of data on the heap. If these copy operations could be avoided, you could improve execution efficiency considerably. Let's look at how you can do this.

Applying Rvalue Reference Parameters

When the source object is a temporary object that is going to be destroyed immediately after the copy operation, the alternative to copying is to steal the heap memory belonging to the temporary object that is pointed to by its pmessage member and transfer it to the destination object. If you can do this, you avoid the need to allocate more heap memory for the destination object, and there will be no need to release the memory owned by the source object. The source object is going to be destroyed immediately after the operation, so there is no risk in doing this — just faster execution. The key to being able to perform this trick is to detect when the source object in a copy operation is an rvalue. This is exactly what an rvalue reference parameter enables you to do.

You can create an additional overload for the operator=() function like this:

```
CMessage& operator=(CMessage&& aMess)
{
    cout << "Move assignment operator function called." << endl;
    delete[] pmessage;          // Release memory for left operand
    pmessage = aMess.pmessage;  // Steal string from rhs object
    aMess.pmessage = nullptr;   // Null rhs pointer
    return *this;               // Return a reference to 1st operand
}
```

code snippet Ex8_08.cpp

This operator function will be called when the right operand is an rvalue — a temporary object. When the right operand is an lvalue, the original function with an lvalue reference parameter will be called. The rvalue reference version of the function deletes the string pointed to by the pmessage member of the destination object and copies the address stored in the pmessage member of the source object. The pmessage member of the source object is then set to nullptr. It is essential that you do this; otherwise, the message would be deleted by the destructor call for the source object. Note that you must not specify the parameter as const in this case, because you are modifying it.

You can apply exactly the same logic to copy constructor operations by adding an overloaded copy constructor with an rvalue reference parameter:

```
CMessage(CMessage&& aMess)
{
    cout << "Move copy constructor called." << endl;
    pmessage = aMess.pmessage;
    aMess.pmessage = nullptr;
}
```

code snippet Ex8_08.cpp

Instead of copying the message belonging to the source object to the object being constructed, you simply transfer the address of the message string from the source object to the new object, so, in this case, the copy is just a move operation. As before, you set pmessage for the source object to nullptr to prevent the message string from being deleted by the destructor.

TRY IT OUT Efficient Object Copy Operations

You can create a new console application, Ex8_08, and copy the code from Ex8_07. You can then add the overloaded operator=() and copy constructor functions that I just discussed to the CMessage class definition. This example will produce the following output:

```
Constructor called.
Constructor called.
Constructor called.
 Executing: motto3 = motto1 + motto2
Add operator function called.
Constructor called.
Move copy constructor called.
Destructor called.
Move assignment operator function called.
Destructor called.
 Done!!

Executing: motto3 = motto3 + motto1 + motto2
Add operator function called.
Constructor called.
Move copy constructor called.
Destructor called.
Add operator function called.
Constructor called.
Move copy constructor called.
Destructor called.
Move assignment operator function called.
Destructor called.
Destructor called.
 Done!!

motto3 contains -
The devil takes care of his own. If you sup with the devil use a long spoon.
The devil takes care of his own. If you sup with the devil use a long spoon.


Destructor called.
Destructor called.
Destructor called.
```

How It Works

You can see from the output that all of the operations in the previous example that involved copying an object now execute as move operations. The assignment operator function calls now use the version with the rvalue reference parameter, as do the copy constructor calls. The output also shows that motto3 ends up with the same string as before, so everything is working as it should.

For classes that define complex objects with data stored on the heap, overloading the assignment operator and copy constructor with versions that have an rvalue reference parameter can significantly improve performance.

>
>
> **NOTE** *If you define the* `operator=()` *function and copy constructor in a class with the parameters as non-const rvalue references, make sure you also define the standard versions with* `const` *lvalue reference parameters. If you don't, you will get the compiler-supplied default versions of these that perform member-by-member copying. This will certainly not be what you want.*

Named Objects are Lvalues

When the assignment operator function with the rvalue reference parameter in the CMessage class is called, we know for certain that the argument — the right operand — is an rvalue and is, therefore, a temporary object from which we can steal memory. However, within the body of this operator function, the parameter, aMess, is an lvalue. This is because any expression that is a named variable is an lvalue. This can result in inefficiencies creeping back in, as I can demonstrate through an example that uses a modified version of the CMessage class:

```cpp
class CMessage
{
  private:
    CText text;                      // Object text string

  public:
    // Function to display a message
    void ShowIt() const
    {
      text.ShowIt();
    }

    // Overloaded addition operator
    CMessage operator+(const CMessage& aMess) const
    {
      cout << "CMessage add operator function called." << endl;
      CMessage message;
      message.text = text + aMess.text;
      return message;
    }

    // Copy assignment operator for CMessage objects
    CMessage& operator=(const CMessage& aMess)
    {
      cout << "CMessage copy assignment operator function called." << endl;
      if(this == &aMess)               // Check addresses, if equal
        return *this;                  // return the 1st operand

      text = aMess.text;
      return *this;                    // Return a reference to 1st operand
    }

    // Move assignment operator for CMessage objects
    CMessage& operator=(CMessage&& aMess)
    {
      cout << "CMessage move assignment operator function called." << endl;
      text = aMess.text;
```

```
      return *this;                      // Return a reference to 1st operand
    }

    // Constructor definition
    CMessage(const char* str = "Default message")
    {
      cout << "CMessage constructor called." << endl;
      text = CText(str);
    }

    // Copy constructor definition
    CMessage(const CMessage& aMess)
    {
      cout << "CMessage copy constructor called." << endl;
      text = aMess.text;
    }

    // Move constructor definition
    CMessage(CMessage&& aMess)
    {
      cout << "CMessage move constructor called." << endl;
      text = aMess.text;
    }
};
```

code snippet Ex8_09.cpp

The text for the message is now stored as an object of type CText, and the member functions of the CMessage class have been changed accordingly. Note that the class is kitted out with rvalue reference versions of the copy constructor and the assignment operator, so it should move rather than create new objects when it is feasible to do so. Here's the definition of the CText class:

```
class CText
{
private:
    char* pText;

public:
    // Function to display text
    void ShowIt() const
    {
      cout << pText << endl;
    }

    // Constructor
    CText(const char* pStr="No text")
    {
      cout << "CText constructor called." << endl;
      size_t len(strlen(pStr)+1);
      pText = new char[len];                    // Allocate space for text
      strcpy_s(pText, len, pStr);               // Copy text to new memory
    }

    // Copy constructor definition
    CText(const CText& txt)
```

```
{
  cout << "CText copy constructor called." << endl;
  size_t len(strlen(txt.pText)+1);
  pText = new char[len];
  strcpy_s(pText, len, txt.pText);
}

// Move constructor definition
CText(CText&& txt)
{
  cout << "CText move constructor called." << endl;
  pText = txt.pText;
  txt.pText = nullptr;
}

// Destructor to free memory allocated by new
~CText()
{
  cout << "CText destructor called." << endl;      // Just to track what happens
  delete[] pText;                                   // Free memory
}

// Assignment operator for CText objects
CText& operator=(const CText& txt)
{
  cout << "CText assignment operator function called." << endl;
  if(this == &txt)                                  // Check addresses, if equal
    return *this;                                   // return the 1st operand

  delete[] pText;                                   // Release memory for 1st operand
  size_t len(strlen(txt.pText)+1);
  pText = new char[len];

  // Copy 2nd operand string to 1st
  strcpy_s(this->pText, len, txt.pText);
  return *this;                                     // Return a reference to 1st operand
}

// Move assignment operator for CText objects
CText& operator=(CText&& txt)
{
  cout << "CText move assignment operator function called." << endl;
  delete[] pText;                                   // Release memory for 1st operand
  pText = txt.pText;
  txt.pText = nullptr;
  return *this;                                     // Return a reference to 1st operand
}

// Overloaded addition operator
CText operator+(const CText& txt) const
{
  cout << "CText add operator function called." << endl;
  size_t len(strlen(pText) + strlen(txt.pText) + 1);
  CText aText;
  aText.pText = new char[len];
  strcpy_s(aText.pText, len, pText);
```

```
        strcat_s(aText.pText, len, txt.pText);
        return aText;
    }
};
```

code snippet Ex8_09.cpp

It looks like a lot of code, but this is because the class has overloaded versions of the copy constructor and the assignment operator, and it has the `operator+()` function defined. The `CMessage` class makes use of these in the implementation of its member functions. There are also output statements to trace when each function is called. Let's exercise these classes with an example.

TRY IT OUT Creeping Inefficiencies

Here's a simple `main()` function that uses the `CMessage` copy constructor and assignment operator:

```cpp
// Ex8_09.cpp Creeping inefficiencies
#include <iostream>
#include <cstring>
using std::cout;
using std::endl;

// Insert CText class definition here...
// Insert CMessage class definition here...

int main()
{
  CMessage motto1("The devil takes care of his own. ");
  CMessage motto2("If you sup with the devil use a long spoon.\n");

  cout << endl << " Executing: CMessage motto3(motto1+motto2); " << endl;
  CMessage motto3(motto1+motto2);
  cout << " Done!! " << endl << endl << "motto3 contains - ";
   motto3.ShowIt();
  CMessage motto4;
  cout << endl << " Executing: motto4 = motto3 + motto2; " << endl;
  motto4 = motto3 + motto2;
  cout << " Done!! " << endl << endl << "motto4 contains - ";
   motto4.ShowIt();
  cout << endl;
  return 0;
}
```

code snippet Ex8_09.cpp

How It Works

It's a lot of output from relatively few statements in `main()`. I'll just discuss the interesting bits. Let's first consider the output arising from executing the statement:

```
CMessage motto3(motto1+motto2);
```

The output looks like this:

```
CMessage add operator function called.
CText constructor called.
CMessage constructor called.
CText constructor called.
CText move assignment operator function called.
CText destructor called.
CText add operator function called.
CText constructor called.
CText move copy constructor called.
CText destructor called.
CText move assignment operator function called.
CText destructor called.
CText constructor called.
CMessage move constructor called.
CText assignment operator function called.
CText destructor called.
```

To see what is happening, you need to relate the output messages to the code in the functions that are called. First, the `operator+()` function for the `CMessage` class is called to concatenate `motto1` and `motto2`. In the body of this function, the `CMessage` constructor is called to create the message object, and within this process, the `CText` constructor is called. Everything is going swimmingly until we get to the second to last line of output, following the line indicating the `CMessage` move constructor is called. When this constructor executes, the argument must have been a temporary — an rvalue — so the assignment statement in the body of the function that stores the value of the `text` member should be a move assignment operation for `CText` objects, not a copy assignment. The problem arises because within the `CMessage` move constructor function, the `aMess` parameter is an lvalue because it has a name, in spite of the fact that we know for certain that the argument passed to the function was an rvalue. This means that `aMess.text` is also an lvalue. If it weren't, the `CMessage` copy constructor would have been called.

The same problem arises with the statement:

```
motto4 = motto3 + motto2;
```

If you look at the output from this, you'll see that exactly the same problem arises when the move assignment operator for `CMessage` objects is called. The `text` member of the argument is copied when, really, it could be moved.

We could fix these inefficiencies if we had a way to force `aMess.text` to be an `rvalue` in the move assignment and move constructor functions in the `CMessage` class. The C++ library thoughtfully provides you with the `std::move()` function that will do precisely what you want. This function returns whatever argument you pass to it as an rvalue. You can change the `CMessage` move constructor like this:

```
CMessage(CMessage&& aMess)
{
  cout << "CMessage move constructor called." << endl;
  text = std::move(aMess.text);
}
```

Now, the right-hand side of the assignment that sets up the text member of the new object is an rvalue.

You can modify the move assignment operator function in a similar way:

```
CMessage& operator=(CMessage&& aMess)
{
   cout << "CMessage move assignment operator function called." << endl;
   text = std::move(aMess.text);
   return *this;                        // Return a reference to 1st operand
}
```

The `std::move()` function is declared in the `utility` header, so you need to add a `#include` directive for this to the example. If you recompile the program and execute it once more, the output will show that you now get the `CText` move assignment operator function called from the two functions you have modified.

CLASS TEMPLATES

You saw back in Chapter 6 that you could define a function template that would automatically generate functions varying in the type of arguments accepted, or in the type of values returned. C++ has a similar mechanism for classes. A **class template** is not, in itself, a class, but a sort of "recipe" for a class that will be used by the compiler to generate the code for a class. As you can see from Figure 8-5, it's like the function template — you determine the class that you want generated by specifying your choice of type for the parameter (T, in this case) that appears between the angled brackets in the template. Doing this generates a particular class that is referred to as an **instance** of the class template. The process of creating a class from a template is described as **instantiating** the template.

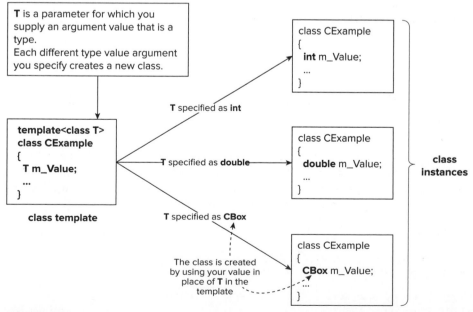

FIGURE 8-5

An appropriate class definition is generated when you instantiate an object of a template class for a particular type, so you can generate any number of different classes from one class template. You'll get a good idea of how this works in practice by looking at an example.

Defining a Class Template

I'll choose a simple example to illustrate how you define and use a class template, and I won't complicate things by worrying too much about possible errors that can arise if it's misused. Suppose you want to define classes that can store a number of data samples of some kind, and each class is to provide a Max() function to determine the maximum sample value of those stored. This function will be similar to the one you saw in the function template discussion in Chapter 6. You can define a class template, which will generate a class CSamples to store samples of whatever type you want:

```
template <class T>
class CSamples
{
  public:
    // Constructor definition to accept an array of samples
    CSamples(const T values[], int count)
    {
      m_Free = count < 100 ? Count : 100; // Don't exceed the array
      for(int i = 0; i < m_Free; i++)
        m_Values[i] = values[i];         // Store count number of samples
    }

    // Constructor to accept a single sample
    CSamples(const T& value)
    {
      m_Values[0] = value;            // Store the sample
      m_Free = 1;                     // Next is free
    }

    // Default constructor
    CSamples(){ m_Free = 0 }          // Nothing stored, so first is free

    // Function to add a sample
    bool Add(const T& value)
    {
      bool OK = m_Free < 100;         // Indicates there is a free place
      if(OK)
        m_Values[m_Free++] = value;   // OK true, so store the value
      return OK;
    }

    // Function to obtain maximum sample
    T Max() const
    {
      // Set first sample or 0 as maximum
      T theMax = m_Free ? m_Values[0] : 0;

      for(int i = 1; i < m_Free; i++)  // Check all the samples
        if(m_Values[i] > theMax)
          theMax = m_Values[i];        // Store any larger sample
```

```
        return theMax;
    }

  private:
    T m_Values[100];              // Array to store samples
    int m_Free;                   // Index of free location in m_Values
};
```

To indicate that you are defining a template, rather than a straightforward class, you insert the `template` keyword and the type parameter, `T`, between angled brackets, just before the `class` keyword and the class name, `CSamples`. This is essentially the same syntax that you used to define a function template back in Chapter 6. The parameter `T` is the type variable that will be replaced by a specific type when you declare a class object. Wherever the parameter `T` appears in the class definition, it will be replaced by the type that you specify in your object declaration; this creates a class definition corresponding to this type. You can specify any type (a basic data type or a class type), but it has to make sense in the context of the class template, of course. Any class type that you use to instantiate a class from a template must have all the operators defined that the member functions of the template will use with such objects. If your class hasn't implemented `operator>()`, for example, it will not work with the `CSamples` class template above. In general, you can specify multiple parameters in a class template if you need them. I'll come back to this possibility a little later in the chapter.

Getting back to the example, the type of the array in which the samples will be stored is specified as `T`. The array will, therefore, be an array of whatever type you specify for `T` when you declare a `CSamples` object. As you can see, you also use the type `T` in two of the constructors for the class, as well as in the `Add()` and `Max()` functions. Each of these occurrences will also be replaced when you instantiate a class object using the template.

The constructors support the creation of an empty object, an object with a single sample, and an object initialized with an array of samples. The `Add()` function allows samples to be added to an object one at a time. You could also overload this function to add an array of samples. The class template includes some elementary provision to prevent the capacity of the `m_Values` array being exceeded in the `Add()` function, and in the constructor that accepts an array of samples.

As I said earlier, in theory, you can create objects of `CSamples` classes that will handle any data type: type `int`, type `double`, or any class type that you've defined. In practice, this doesn't mean it will necessarily compile and work as you expect. It all depends on what the template definition does, and usually, a template will only work for a particular range of types. For example, the `Max()` function implicitly assumes that the > operator is available for whatever type is being processed. If it isn't, your program will not compile. Clearly, you'll usually be in the position of defining a template that works for some types but not others, but there's no way you can restrict what type is applied to a template.

Template Member Functions

You may want to place the definition of a class template member function outside of the template definition. The syntax for this isn't particularly obvious, so let's look at how you do it. You put the function declaration in the class template definition in the normal way. For instance:

```
template <class T>
class CSamples
{
```

```
  // Rest of the template definition...
  T Max() const;                   // Function to obtain maximum sample
  // Rest of the template definition...
}
```

This declares the `Max()` function as a member of the class template, but doesn't define it. You now need to create a separate function template for the definition of the member function. You must use the template class name plus the parameters in angled brackets to identify the class template to which the function template belongs:

```
template<class T>
T CSamples<T>::Max() const
{
  // Set first sample or 0 as maximum
  T theMax = m_Free ? m_Values[0] : 0;

  for(int i = 1; i < m_Free; i++)          // Check all the samples
    if(m_Values[i] > theMax)
      theMax = m_Values[i];                // Store any larger sample
  return theMax;
}
```

You saw the syntax for a function template back in Chapter 6. Since this function template is for a member of the class template with the parameter T, the function template definition here should have the same parameters as the class template definition. There's just one in this case — T — but in general, there can be several. If the class template had two or more parameters, then so would each template defining a member function.

Note how you only put the parameter name, T, along with the class name before the scope resolution operator. This is necessary — the parameters are fundamental to the identification of the class to which a function, produced from the template, belongs. The type will be `CSamples<T>` with whatever type you assign to T when you create an instance of the class template. Your type is plugged into the class template to generate the class definition, and into the function template to generate the definition for the `Max()` function for the class. Each class that's produced from the class template needs to have its own definition for the function `Max()`.

Defining a constructor or a destructor outside of the class template definition is very similar. You could write the definition of the constructor that accepts an array of samples as:

```
template<class T>
CSamples<T>::CSamples(const T values[], int count)
{
  m_Free = count < 100 ? count : 100;    // Don't exceed the array

  for(int i = 0; i < m_Free; i++)
    m_Values[i] = values[i];             // Store count number of samples
}
```

The class to which the constructor belongs is specified in the template in the same way as for an ordinary member function. Note that the constructor name doesn't require the parameter specification — it is just `CSamples`, but it needs to be qualified by the class template type `CSamples<T>`. You only use the parameter with the class template name *preceding* the scope resolution operator.

Creating Objects from a Class Template

When you use a function defined by a function template, the compiler is able to generate the function from the types of the arguments used. The type parameter for the function template is implicitly defined by the specific use of a particular function. Class templates are a little different. To create an object based on a class template, you must always specify the type parameter following the class name in the declaration.

For example, to declare a `CSamples<>` object to handle samples of type `double`, you could write the declaration as:

```
CSamples<double> myData(10.0);
```

This defines an object of type `CSamples<double>` that can store samples of type `double`, and the object is created with one sample stored with the value 10.0.

Class Templating

You could create an object from the `CSamples<>` template that stores `CBox` objects. This will work because the `CBox` class implements the `operator>()` function to overload the greater-than operator. You could exercise the class template with the `main()` function in the following listing:

```cpp
// Ex8_10.cpp
// Using a class template
#include <iostream>
using std::cout;
using std::endl;

// Put the CBox class definition from Ex8_06.cpp here...

// CSamples class template definition
template <class T> class CSamples
{
  public:
    // Constructors
    CSamples(const T values[], int count);
    CSamples(const T& value);
    CSamples(){ m_Free = 0; }

    bool Add(const T& value);        // Insert a value
    T Max() const;                   // Calculate maximum

  private:
    T m_Values[100];                 // Array to store samples
    int m_Free;                      // Index of free location in m_Values
};
```

```cpp
// Constructor template definition to accept an array of samples
template<class T> CSamples<T>::CSamples(const T values[], int count)
{
  m_Free = count < 100? count:100;      // Don't exceed the array
  for(int i = 0; i < m_Free; i++)
    m_Values[i] = values[i];            // Store count number of samples
}

// Constructor to accept a single sample
template<class T> CSamples<T>::CSamples(const T& value)
{
  m_Values[0] = value;                  // Store the sample
  m_Free = 1;                           // Next is free
}

// Function to add a sample
template<class T> bool CSamples<T>::Add(const T& value)
{
  bool OK = m_Free < 100;               // Indicates there is a free place
  if(OK)
    m_Values[m_Free++] = value;         // OK true, so store the value
  return OK;
}

// Function to obtain maximum sample
template<class T> T CSamples<T>::Max() const
{
  T theMax = m_Free ? m_Values[0] : 0; // Set first sample or 0 as maximum
  for(int i = 1; i < m_Free; i++)      // Check all the samples
    if(m_Values[i] > theMax)
      theMax = m_Values[i];             // Store any larger sample
  return theMax;
}

int main()
{
  CBox boxes[] = {                              // Create an array of boxes
               CBox(8.0, 5.0, 2.0),     // Initialize the boxes...
               CBox(5.0, 4.0, 6.0),
               CBox(4.0, 3.0, 3.0)
             };

  // Create the CSamples object to hold CBox objects
  CSamples<CBox> myBoxes(boxes, sizeof boxes / sizeof CBox);

  CBox maxBox = myBoxes.Max();                  // Get the biggest box
  cout << endl                                  // and output its volume
       << "The biggest box has a volume of "
       << maxBox.Volume() << endl;
  return 0;
}
```

code snippet Ex8_10.cpp

You should replace the comment with the CBox class definition from Ex8_06.cpp. You need not worry about the operator>() function that supports comparison of a CBox object with a value of type double, as this example does not need it. With the exception of the default constructor, all the member functions of the template are defined by separate function templates, just to show you a complete example of how it's done.

In main(), you create an array of three CBox objects and then use this array to initialize a CSamples object that can store CBox objects. The declaration of the CSamples object is basically the same as it would be for an ordinary class, but with the addition of the type parameter in angled brackets following the template class name.

The program will generate the following output:

```
The biggest box has a volume of 120
```

Note that when you create an instance of a class template, it does not follow that instances of the function templates for function members will also be created. The compiler will only create instances of templates for member functions that you actually call in your program. In fact, your function templates can even contain coding errors and, as long as you don't call the member function that the template generates, the compiler will not complain. You can test this out with the example. Try introducing a few errors into the template for the Add() member. The program will still compile and run because it doesn't call the Add() function.

You could try modifying the example and perhaps seeing what happens when you instantiate classes by using the template with various other types.

 NOTE *You might be surprised at what happens if you add some output state-ments to the class constructors. The constructor for the CBox is being called 103 times! Look at what is happening in the main() function. First, you create an array of three CBox objects, so that's three calls. You then create a CSamples object to hold them, but a CSamples object contains an array of 100 variables of type CBox, so you call the default constructor another 100 times, once for each element in the array. Of course, the maxBox object will be created by the default copy constructor that is supplied by the compiler.*

Class Templates with Multiple Parameters

Using multiple type parameters in a class template is a straightforward extension of the example using a single parameter that you have just seen. You can use each of the type parameters wherever you want in the template definition. For example, you could define a class template with two type parameters:

```
template<class T1, class T2>
class CExampleClass
{
```

```
      // Class data members

   private:
      T1 m_Value1;
      T2 m_Value2;

      // Rest of the template definition...
   };
```

The types of the two class data members shown will be determined by the types you supply for the parameters when you instantiate an object.

The parameters in a class template aren't limited to types. You can also use parameters that require constants or constant expressions to be substituted in the class definition. In our CSamples template, we arbitrarily defined the m_Values array with 100 elements. You could, however, let the user of the template choose the size of the array when the object is instantiated, by defining the template as:

```
template <class T, int Size> class CSamples
  {
    private:
      T m_Values[Size];                  // Array to store samples
      int m_Free;                        // Index of free location in m_Values

    public:
      // Constructor definition to accept an array of samples
      CSamples(const T values[], int count)
      {
        m_Free = count < Size ? count : Size; // Don't exceed the array

        for(int i = 0; i < m_Free; i++)
          m_Values[i] = values[i];            // Store count number of samples
      }

      // Constructor to accept a single sample
      CSamples(const T& value)
      {
        m_Values[0] = value;             // Store the sample
        m_Free = 1;                      // Next is free
      }

      // Default constructor
      CSamples()
      {
        m_Free = 0;                      // Nothing stored, so first is free
      }

      // Function to add a sample
      int Add(const T& value)
      {
        int OK = m_Free < Size;          // Indicates there is a free place
        if(OK)
```

```
      m_Values[m_Free++] = value;    // OK true, so store the value
    return OK;
  }

  // Function to obtain maximum sample
  T Max() const
  {
    // Set first sample or 0 as maximum
    T theMax = m_Free ? m_Values[0] : 0;

    for(int i = 1; i < m_Free; i++)    // Check all the samples
      if(m_Values[i] > theMax)
        theMax = m_Values[i];          // Store any larger sample
    return theMax;
  }
};
```

The value supplied for Size when you create an object will replace the appearance of the parameter throughout the template definition. Now, you can declare the CSamples object from the previous example as:

```
CSamples<CBox, 3> myBoxes(boxes, sizeof boxes/sizeof CBox);
```

Because you can supply *any* constant expression for the Size parameter, you could also have written this as:

```
CSamples<CBox, sizeof boxes/sizeof CBox>
                          myBoxes(boxes, sizeof boxes/sizeof CBox);
```

The example is a poor use of a template, though — the original version was much more usable. A consequence of making Size a template parameter is that instances of the template that store the same types of objects but have different size parameter values are totally different classes and cannot be mixed. For instance, an object of type CSamples<double, 10> cannot be used in an expression with an object of type CSamples<double, 20>.

You need to be careful with expressions that involve comparison operators when instantiating templates. Look at this statement:

```
CSamples<aType, x > y ? 10 : 20 > MyType();      // Wrong!
```

This will not compile correctly because the > preceding y in the expression will be interpreted as a right-angled bracket. Instead, you should write this statement as:

```
CSamples<aType, (x > y ? 10 : 20) > MyType();    // OK
```

The parentheses ensure that the expression for the second template argument doesn't get mixed up with the angled brackets.

Templates for Function Objects

A class that defines function objects is typically defined by a template, for the obvious reason that it allows function objects to be defined that will work with a variety of argument types. Here's a template for the Area class that you saw earlier:

```
template<class T> class Area
{
public:
  T operator()(T length, T width){ return length*width;  }
};
```

This template will allow you to define function objects to calculate areas with the dimensions of any numeric type. You could define the printArea() function that you saw earlier as a function template:

```
template<class T> void printArea(T length, T width, Area<T> area)
{  cout << "Area is " <<  area(length, width); }
```

Now, you can call to the printArea() function like this:

```
printArea(1.5, 2.5, Area<double>());
printArea(100, 50, Area<int>());
```

Function objects are applied extensively with the Standard Template Library that you will learn about in Chapter 10, so you will see practical examples of their use in that context.

USING CLASSES

I've touched on most of the basic aspects of defining a native C++ class, so maybe we should look at how a class might be used to solve a problem. The problem has to be simple in order to keep this book down to a reasonable number of pages, so we'll consider problems in which we can use an extended version of the CBox class.

The Idea of a Class Interface

The implementation of an extended CBox class should incorporate the notion of a **class interface**. You are going to provide a tool kit for anyone wanting to work with CBox objects, so you need to assemble a set of functions that represents the interface to the world of boxes. Because the interface will represent the only way to deal with CBox objects, it needs to be defined to cover adequately the likely things one would want to do with a CBox object, and be implemented, as far as possible, in a manner that protects against misuse or accidental errors.

The first question that you need to consider in designing a class is the nature of the problem you intend to solve, and, from that, determine the kind of functionality you need to provide in the class interface.

Defining the Problem

The principal function of a box is to contain objects of one kind or another, so, in a word, the problem is **packaging**. We'll attempt to provide a class that eases packaging problems in general and then see how it might be used. We will assume that we'll always be working on packing CBox objects into other CBox objects since, if you want to pack candy in a box, you can always represent each of the pieces of candy as an idealized CBox object. The basic operations that you might want to provide in the CBox class include:

➤ Calculate the volume of a CBox. This is a fundamental characteristic of a CBox object, and you have an implementation of this already.

➤ Compare the volumes of two CBox objects to determine which is the larger. You probably should support a complete set of comparison operators for CBox objects. You already have a version of the > operator.

➤ Compare the volume of a CBox object with a specified value, and vice versa. You also have an implementation of this for the > operator, but you will also need to implement functions supporting the other comparison operators.

➤ Add two CBox objects to produce a new CBox object that will contain both the original objects. Thus, the result will be at least the sum of the volumes, but may be larger. You have a version of this already that overloads the + operator.

➤ Multiply a CBox object by an integer (and vice versa) to provide a new CBox object that will contain a specified number of the original objects. This is effectively designing a carton.

➤ Determine how many CBox objects of a given size can be packed in another CBox object of a given size. This is effectively division, so you could implement this by overloading the / operator.

➤ Determine the volume of space remaining in a CBox object after packing it with the maximum number of CBox objects of a given size.

I had better stop right there! There are undoubtedly other functions that would be very useful but, in the interest of saving trees, we'll consider the set to be complete, apart from ancillaries such as accessing dimensions, for example.

Implementing the CBox Class

You really need to consider the degree of error protection that you want to build into the CBox class. The basic class that you defined to illustrate various aspects of classes is a starting point, but you should also consider some points a little more deeply. The constructor is a little weak in that it doesn't ensure that the dimensions for a CBox are valid, so, perhaps, the first thing you should do is to ensure that you always have valid objects. You could redefine the basic class as follows to do this:

```
class CBox                              // Class definition at global scope
{
  public:
    // Constructor definition
    explicit CBox(double lv = 1.0, double wv = 1.0, double hv = 1.0)
```

```
      {
        lv = lv <= 0 ? 1.0 : lv;      // Ensure positive
        wv = wv <= 0 ? 1.0 : wv;      // dimensions for
        hv = hv <= 0 ? 1.0 : hv;      // the object

        m_Length = lv > wv ? lv : wv;   // Ensure that
        m_Width = wv < lv ? wv : lv;    // length >= width
        m_Height = hv;
      }

      // Function to calculate the volume of a box
      double Volume() const
      {
        return m_Length*m_Width*m_Height;
      }

      // Function providing the length of a box
      double GetLength() const { return m_Length; }

      // Function providing the width of a box
      double GetWidth() const { return m_Width; }

      // Function providing the height of a box
      double GetHeight() const { return m_Height; }

    private:
      double m_Length;                // Length of a box in inches
      double m_Width;                 // Width of a box in inches
      double m_Height;                // Height of a box in inches
  };
```

The constructor is now secure because any dimension that the user of the class tries to set to a negative number or zero will be set to 1 in the constructor. You might also consider displaying a message for a negative or zero dimension because there is obviously an error when this occurs, and arbitrarily and silently setting a dimension to 1 might not be the best solution.

The default copy constructor is satisfactory for our class, because you have no dynamic memory allocation for data members, and the default assignment operator will also work as you would like. The default destructor also works perfectly well in this case, so you do not need to define it. Perhaps now, you should consider what is required to support comparisons of objects of our class.

Comparing CBox Objects

You should include support for the operators >, >=, ==, <, and <= so that they work with both operands as CBox objects, as well as between a CBox object and a value of type double. You can implement these as ordinary global functions because they don't need to be member functions. You can write the functions that compare the volumes of two CBox objects in terms of the functions that compare the volume of a CBox object with a double value, so let's start with the latter. You can start by repeating the operator>() function that you had before:

```
// Function for testing if a constant is > a CBox object
bool operator>(const double& value, const CBox& aBox)
{
```

```
    return value > aBox.Volume();
}
```

You can now write the `operator<()` function in a similar way:

```
// Function for testing if a constant is < CBox object
bool operator<(const double& value, const CBox& aBox)
{
  return value < aBox.Volume();
}
```

You can code the implementations of the same operators with the arguments reversed in terms of the two functions you have just defined:

```
// Function for testing if CBox object is > a constant
bool operator>(const CBox& aBox, const double& value)
{ return value < aBox; }

// Function for testing if CBox object is < a constant
int operator<(const CBox& aBox, const double& value)
{ return value > aBox; }
```

You just use the appropriate overloaded operator function that you wrote before, with the arguments from the call to the new function switched.

The functions implementing the >= and <= operators will be the same as the first two functions, but with the <= operator replacing each use of <, and >= instead of >; there's little point in reproducing them at this stage. The `operator==()` functions are also very similar:

```
// Function for testing if constant is == the volume of a CBox object
bool operator==(const double& value, const CBox& aBox)
{
    return value == aBox.Volume();
}

// Function for testing if CBox object is == a constant
bool operator==(const CBox& aBox, const double& value)
{
    return value == aBox;
}
```

You now have a complete set of comparison operators for CBox objects. Keep in mind that these will also work with expressions, as long as the expressions result in objects of the required type, so you will be able to combine them with the use of other overloaded operators.

Combining CBox Objects

Now, you come to the question of overloading the operators +, *, /, and %. I will take them in order. The add operation that you already have from Ex8_06.cpp has this prototype:

```
CBox operator+(const CBox& aBox) const;    // Function adding two CBox objects
```

Although the original implementation of this isn't an ideal solution, let's use it anyway to avoid overcomplicating the class. A better version would need to examine whether the operands had any faces with the same dimensions and, if so, join along those faces, but coding that could get a bit messy. Of course, if this were a practical application, a better add operation could be developed later and substituted for the existing version, and any programs written using the original would still run without change. The separation of the interface to a class from its implementation is crucial to good C++ programming.

Notice that I conveniently forgot the subtraction operator. This is a judicious oversight to avoid the complications inherent in implementing this. If you're really enthusiastic about it, and you think it's a sensible idea, you can give it a try — but you need to decide what to do when the result has a negative volume. If you allow the concept, you need to resolve which box dimension or dimensions are to be negative, and how such a box is to be handled in subsequent operations.

The multiply operation is very easy. It represents the process of creating a box to contain n boxes, where n is the multiplier. The simplest solution would be to take the m_Length and m_Width of the object to be packed and multiply the height by n to get the new CBox object. You can make it a little cleverer by checking whether or not the multiplier is even and, if it is, stack the boxes side by side by doubling the m_Width value and only multiplying the m_Height value by half of n. This mechanism is illustrated in Figure 8-6.

CBox Multiply: n odd
: 3*aBox

aBox

CBox Multiply: n even
: 6*aBox

Two stacks of three boxes
side by side

FIGURE 8-6

Of course, you don't need to check which is the larger of the length and width for the new object because the constructor will sort it out automatically. You can write the version of the `operator*()` function as a member function with the left operand as a `CBox` object:

```
// CBox multiply operator this*n
CBox operator*(int n) const
{
  if(n % 2)
    return CBox(m_Length, m_Width, n*m_Height);           // n odd
  else
    return CBox(m_Length, 2.0*m_Width, (n/2)*m_Height);   // n even
}
```

Here, you use the `%` operator to determine whether `n` is even or odd. If `n` is odd, the value of `n % 2` is 1 and the `if` statement is `true`. If it's even, `n % 2` is 0 and the statement is `false`.

You can now use the function you have just written in the implementation of the version with the left operand as an integer. You can write this as an ordinary non-member function:

```
// CBox multiply operator n*aBox
CBox operator*(int n, const CBox& aBox)
{
  return aBox*n;
}
```

This version of the multiply operation simply reverses the order of the operands so as to use the previous version of the function directly. That completes the set of arithmetic operators for `CBox` objects that you defined. You can finally look at the two analytical operator functions, `operator/()` and `operator%()`.

Analyzing CBox Objects

As I have said, the division operation will determine how many `CBox` objects identical to that specified by the right operand can be contained in the `CBox` object specified by the left operand. To keep it relatively simple, assume that all the `CBox` objects are packed the right way up, that is, with the height dimensions vertical. Also assume that they are all packed the same way round, so that their length dimensions are aligned. Without these assumptions, it can get rather complicated.

The problem will then amount to determining how many of the right-operand objects can be placed in a single layer, and then deciding how many layers you can get inside the left-operand `CBox`.

You can code this as a member function like this:

```
int operator/(const CBox& aBox) const
{
  int tc1 = 0;        // Temporary for number in horizontal plane this way
  int tc2 = 0;        // Temporary for number in a plane that way

  tc1 = static_cast<int>((m_Length / aBox.m_Length))*
        static_cast<int>((m_Width / aBox.m_Width));   // to fit this way
  tc2 = static_cast<int>((m_Length / aBox.m_Width))*
```

```
                 static_cast<int>((m_Width / aBox.m_Length)); // and that way

    //Return best fit
    return static_cast<int>((m_Height/aBox.m_Height)*(tc1>tc2 ? tc1 : tc2));
  }
```

This function first determines how many of the right-operand CBox objects can fit in a layer with their lengths aligned with the length dimension of the left-operand CBox. This is stored in tc1. You then calculate how many can fit in a layer with the lengths of the right-operand CBoxes lying in the width direction of the left-operand CBox. Finally, you multiply the larger of tc1 and tc2 by the number of layers you can pack in, and return that value. This process is illustrated in Figure 8-7.

How aBox/bBox is calculated

L = 8

L = 3

W = 2 | bBox

W = 6 | aBox

H = 1

H = 2

There are two rectangular arrangements possible for fitting a number of bBox objects within aBox, as shown below.

With this configuration
12 can be stored
8/3 = 2

With this configuration
16 can be stored
8/2 = 4

| bBox | bBox |
6/2 = 3 | bBox | bBox |
| bBox | bBox |

6/3 = 2 | bBox bBox bBox bBox |
| bBox bBox bBox bBox |

2/1 = 2

2/1 = 2

Result is 16

FIGURE 8-7

Consider two possibilities: fitting bBox into aBox with the length aligned with that of aBox, and then with the length of bBox aligned with the width of aBox. You can see from Figure 8-7 that the best packing results from rotating bBox so that the width divides into the length of aBox.

The other analytical operator function, `operator%()`, for obtaining the free volume in a packed `aBox` is easier, because you can use the operator you have just written to implement it. You can write it as an ordinary global function because you don't need access to the `private` members of the class.

```
// Operator to return the free volume in a packed box
double operator%(const CBox& aBox, const CBox& bBox)
{
   return aBox.Volume() - ((aBox/bBox)*bBox.Volume());
}
```

This computation falls out very easily using existing class functions. The result is the volume of the big box, `aBox`, minus the volume of the `bBox` boxes that can be stored in it. The number of `bBox` objects packed into `aBox` is given by the expression `aBox/bBox`, which uses the previous overloaded operator. You multiply this by the volume of `bBox` objects to get the volume to be subtracted from the volume of the large box, `aBox`.

That completes the class interface. Clearly, there are many more functions that might be required for a production problem solver but, as an interesting working model demonstrating how you can produce a class for solving a particular kind of problem, it will suffice. Now you can go ahead and try it out on a real problem.

TRY IT OUT   A Multifile Project Using the CBox Class

Before you can actually start writing the code to *use* the `CBox` class and its overloaded operators, first you need to assemble the definition for the class into a coherent whole. You're going to take a rather different approach from what you've seen previously, in that you're going to write multiple files for the project. You're also going to start using the facilities that Visual C++ 2010 provides for creating and maintaining code for our classes. This will mean that you do rather less of the work, but it will also mean that the code will be slightly different in places.

Start by creating a new WIN32 project for a console application called `Ex8_11` and check the `Empty project` application option. If you select the Class View tab, you'll see the window shown in Figure 8-8.

This shows a view of all the classes in a project but, of course, there are none here for the moment. Although there are no classes defined — or anything else, for that matter — Visual C++ 2010 has already made provision for including some. You can use Visual C++ 2010 to create a skeleton for our `CBox` class, and the files that relate to it, too. Right-click `Ex8_11` in Class View and select Add/Class . . . from the pop-up menu that appears. You can then select C++ from the class categories in the left pane of the Add Class dialog that is displayed and the C++ Class template in the right pane, and press

FIGURE 8-8

Enter. You will then be able to enter the name of the class that you want to create, `CBox`, in the Generic C++ Class Wizard dialog, as shown in Figure 8-9.

FIGURE 8-9

The name of the file that's indicated on the dialog, `Box.cpp`, will be used to contain the **class implementation**, which consists of the definitions for the function members of the class. This is the executable code for the class. You can change the name of this file, if you want, but `Box.cpp` looks like a good name for the file in this case. The class definition will be stored in a file called `Box.h`. This is the standard way of structuring a program. Code that consists of class definitions is stored in files with the extension `.h`, and code that defines functions is stored in files with the extension `.cpp`. Usually, each class definition goes in its own `.h` file, and each class implementation goes in its own `.cpp` file.

When you click the Finish button in the dialog, two things happen:

1.   A file `Box.h` is created, containing a skeleton definition for the class `CBox`. This includes a no-argument constructor and a destructor.

2.   A file `Box.cpp` is created, containing a skeleton implementation for the functions in the class with definitions for the constructor and the destructor — both bodies are empty, of course.

The editor pane displaying the code should be as shown in Figure 8-10. If it is not presently displayed, just double-click `CBox` in `Class View`, and it should appear.

As you can see, above the pane containing the code listing for the class, there are two controls. The left control displays the current class name, `CBox`, and clicking the button to the right of the class

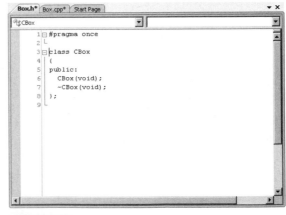

FIGURE 8-10

name will display the list of all the classes in the project. In general, you can use this control to switch to another class by selecting it from the list, but here, you have just one class defined. The control to the right relates to the members defined in the .cpp file for the current class, and clicking its button will display the members of the class. Selecting a member from the list will cause its code to be visible in the pane below.

Let's start developing the CBox class based on what Visual C++ has provided automatically for us.

DEFINING THE CBOX CLASS

If you click the ▲ to the left of Ex8_11 in the Class View, the tree will be expanded and you will see that CBox is now defined for the project. All the classes in a project are displayed in this tree. You can view the source code supplied for the definition of a class by double-clicking the class name in the tree, or by using the controls above the pane displaying the code, as I described in the previous section.

The CBox class definition that was generated starts with a preprocessor directive:

```
#pragma once
```

The effect of this is to prevent the file from being opened and included into the source code more than once by the compiler in a build. Typically, a class definition will be included into several files in a project because each file that references the name of a particular class will need access to its definition. In some instances, a header file may, itself, have #include directives for other header files. This can result in the possibility of the contents of a header file appearing more than once in the source code. Having more than one definition of a class in a build is not allowed and will be flagged as an error. Having the #pragma once directive at the start of every header file will ensure this cannot happen.

Note that #pragma once is a Microsoft-specific directive that may not be supported in other development environments. If you are developing code that you anticipate may need to be compiled in other environments, you can use the following form of directive in a header file to achieve the same effect:

```
// Box.h header file
#ifndef BOX_H
#define BOX_H
// Code that must not be included more than once
// such as the CBox class definition
#endif
```

The important lines are bolded and correspond to directives that are supported by any ISO/ANSI C++ compiler. The lines following the #ifndef directive down to the #endif directive will be included in a build as long as the symbol BOX_H is not defined. The line following #ifndef defines the symbol BOX_H, thus ensuring that the code in this header file will not be included a second time. Thus, this has the same effect as placing the #pragma once directive at the beginning of a header file. Clearly, the #pragma once directive is simpler and less cluttered, so it's better to use that when you only expect to be using your code in the Visual C++ 2010 development environment. You will sometimes see the #ifndef/#endif combination written as:

```
#if !defined BOX_H
#define BOX_H
```

```
// Code that must not be included more than once
// such as the CBox class definition
#endif
```

The `Box.cpp` file that was generated by Class Wizard contains the following code:

```
#include "Box.h"

CBox::CBox(void)
{
}

CBox::~CBox(void)
{
}
```

The first line is a `#include` preprocessor directive that has the effect of including the contents of the `Box.h` file — the class definition — into this file, `Box.cpp`. This is necessary because the code in `Box.cpp` refers to the `CBox` class name, and the class definition needs to be available to assign meaning to the name `CBox`.

ADDING DATA MEMBERS

First, you can add the private data members `m_Length`, `m_Width`, and `m_Height`. Right-click CBox in Class View and select Add/Add Variable . . . from the pop-up menu. You can then specify the name, type, and access for the first data member that you want to add to the class in the Add Member Variable Wizard dialog.

The way you specify a new data member in this dialog is quite self-explanatory. If you specify a lower limit for a data member, you must also specify an upper limit. When you specify limits, the constructor definition in the `.cpp` file will be modified to add a default value for the data member corresponding to the lower limit. You can add a comment in the lower input field, if you wish. When you click the OK button, the variable will be added to the class definition, along with the comment if you have supplied one. You should repeat the process for the other two class data members, `m_Width` and `m_Height`. The class definition in `Box.h` will then be modified to look like this:

```
#pragma once

class CBox
{
public:
  CBox(void);
  ~CBox(void);
private:
  // Length of a box in inches
  double m_Length;
  // Width of a box in inches
  double m_Width;
  // Height of a box in inches
  double m_Height;
};
```

Of course, you're quite free to enter the declarations for these members manually, directly into the code, if you want. You always have the choice of whether you use the automation provided by the IDE. You can also manually delete anything that was generated automatically, but don't forget that sometimes, both the .h and .cpp file will need to be changed. It's a good idea to save all the files whenever you make manual changes, as this will cause the information in Class View to be updated.

If you look in the Box.cpp file, you'll see that the Wizard has also added an initialization list to the constructor definition for the data members you have added, with each variable initialized to 0. You'll modify the constructor to do what you want next.

DEFINING THE CONSTRUCTOR

You need to change the declaration of the no-arg constructor in the class definition so that it has arguments with default values, so modify it to:

```
explicit CBox(double lv = 1.0, double wv = 1.0, double hv = 1.0);
```

Now, you're ready to implement it. Open the Box.cpp file, if it isn't open already, and modify the constructor definition to:

```
CBox::CBox(double lv, double wv, double hv)
{
  lv = lv <= 0.0 ? 1.0 : lv;          // Ensure positive
  wv = wv <= 0.0 ? 1.0 : wv;          // dimensions for
  hv = hv <= 0.0 ? 1.0 : hv;          // the object

  m_Length = lv > wv ? lv : wv;       // Ensure that
  m_Width = wv < lv ? wv : lv;        // length >= width
  m_Height = hv;
}
```

Remember that the initializers for the parameters to a member function should only appear in the member declaration in the class definition, not in the definition of the function. If you put them in the function definition, your code will not compile. You've seen this code already, so I won't discuss it again. It would be a good idea to save the file at this point by clicking on the Save toolbar button. Get into the habit of saving the file you're editing before you switch to something else. If you need to edit the constructor again, you can get to it easily by either double-clicking its entry in the lower pane on the Class View tab, or selecting it from the right drop-down menu above the pane displaying the code.

You can also get to a member function's definition in a .cpp file or to its declaration in a .h file directly by right-clicking its name in the Class View pane and selecting the appropriate item from the context menu that appears.

ADDING FUNCTION MEMBERS

You need to add all the functions you saw earlier to the CBox class. Previously, you defined several function members within the class definition, so that these functions were automatically inline. You can achieve the same result by entering the code in the class definition for these functions manually, or you can use the Add Member Function Wizard.

You might think that you can define each inline function in the .cpp file, and add the keyword inline to the function definitions, but the problem here is that inline functions end up not being "real" functions. Because the code from the body of each function has to be inserted directly at the position it is called, the definitions of the functions need to be available when the file containing calls to the functions is compiled. If they're not, you'll get linker errors and your program will not run. If you want member functions to be inline, you *must* include the function definitions in the .h file for the class. They can be defined either within the class definition, or immediately following it in the .h file. You should put any global inline functions you need into a .h file, and #include that file into any .cpp file that uses them.

To add the GetHeight() function as inline, right-click CBox on the Class View tab and select Add/Add Function. . . from the context menu. You then can enter the data defining the function in the dialog that is displayed, as Figure 8-11 shows.

FIGURE 8-11

You can specify the return type to be double by selecting from the drop-down list, but you could equally well type it in. For a type that does not appear in the list, you can just enter it from the keyboard. Selecting the inline checkbox ensures that GetHeight() will be created as an inline function. Note the other options to declare a function as static, virtual, or pure. As you know, a static member function exists independently of any objects of a class. You'll get to virtual and pure virtual functions in Chapter 9. The GetHeight() function has no parameters, so nothing further needs to be added. Clicking the OK button will add the function definition to the class definition in Box.h. If you repeat this process for the GetWidth(), GetLength(), and Volume() member functions, the CBox class definition in Box.h will look like this:

```
#pragma once

class CBox
{
public:
    explicit CBox(double lv = 1.0, double wv = 1.0, double hv = 1.0);
    ~CBox(void);
private:
    // Length of a box in inches
    double m_Length;
    // Width of a box in inches
    double m_Width;
    // Height of a box in inches
    double m_Height;
public:
    double GetHeight(void)
    {
      return 0;
    }

    double GetWidth(void)
    {
      return 0;
    }

    double CBox::GetLength(void)
    {
      return 0;
    }

    // Calculate the volume of a box
    double Volume(void)
    {
      return 0;
    }
};
```

An additional public section has been added to the class definition that contains the inline function definitions. You need to modify each of the definitions to provide the correct return value and to declare the functions to be const. For example, the code for the GetHeight() function should be changed to:

```
double GetHeight(void) const
{
  return m_Height;
}
```

You can change the definitions of the GetWidth() and GetLength() functions in a similar way. The Volume() function definition should be changed to:

```
double Volume(void) const
{
  return m_Length*m_Width*m_Height;
}
```

You could enter the other non-inline member functions directly in the editor pane that shows the code, but, of course, you can also use the Add Member Function Wizard to do it, and the practice will be useful. Right-click CBox in the Class View tab and select the Add/Add Function. . . menu item from the context menu, as before. You can then enter the details of the first function you want to add in the dialog that appears, as Figure 8-12 shows.

FIGURE 8-12

Here, I have defined the operator+() function as public with a return type of CBox. The parameter type and name have also been entered in the appropriate fields. You must click the Add button to register the parameter as being in the parameter list before clicking the Finish button. This will also update the function signature shown at the bottom of the Add Member Function Wizard dialog. You could then enter details of another parameter, if there were more than one, and click Add once again to add it. I have also entered a comment in the dialog, and the Wizard will insert this in both Box.h and Box.cpp. When you click Finish, the declaration for the function will be added to the class definition in the Box.h file, and a skeleton definition for the function will be added to the Box.cpp file. The function needs to be declared as const, so you must add this keyword to the declaration of the operator+() function within the class definition, and to the definition of the function on Box.cpp. You must also add the code in the body of the function, like this:

```
CBox CBox::operator +(const CBox& aBox) const
{
    // New object has larger length and width of the two,
    // and sum of the two heights
    return CBox(m_Length > aBox.m_Length ? m_Length : aBox.m_Length,
```

```
            m_Width > aBox.m_Width ? m_Width : aBox.m_Width,
            m_Height + aBox.m_Height);
}
```

You need to repeat this process for the `operator*()` and `operator/()` functions that you saw earlier. When you have completed this, the class definition in `Box.h` will look something like this:

```cpp
#pragma once

class CBox
{
public:
    explicit CBox(double lv = 1.0, double wv = 1.0, double hv = 1.0);
    ~CBox(void);
    double GetHeight(void) const   {  return m_Height;  }
    double GetWidth(void) const    {  return m_Width;   }
    double GetLength(void) const   {  return m_Length;  }
    double Volume(void) const      {  return m_Length*m_Width*m_Height;  }

    // Overloaded addition operator
    CBox operator+(const CBox& aBox) const;

    // Multiply a box by an integer
    CBox operator*(int n) const;

    // Divide one box into another
    int operator/(const CBox& aBox) const;

private:
    // Length of a box in inches
    double m_Length;

    // Width of a box in inches
    double m_Width;

    // Height of a box in inches
    double m_Height;
};
```

You can edit or rearrange the code in any way that you want — as long as it's still correct, of course. I have modified the code and removed the repeated `public` keyword occurrences so that the code occupies a bit less space on this page.

The contents of the `Box.cpp` file ultimately look something like this:

```cpp
#include ".\box.h"

CBox::CBox(double lv, double wv, double hv)
{
  lv = lv <= 0.0 ? 1.0 : lv;            // Ensure positive
  wv = wv <= 0.0 ? 1.0 : wv;            // dimensions for
```

```
  hv = hv <= 0.0 ? 1.0 : hv;              // the object

  m_Length = lv>wv ? lv : wv;             // Ensure that
  m_Width = wv<lv ? wv : lv;              // length >= width
  m_Height = hv;
}

CBox::~CBox(void)
{
}

// Overloaded addition operator
CBox CBox::operator+(const CBox& aBox) const
{
  // New object has larger length and width of the two,
  // and sum of the two heights
  return CBox(m_Length > aBox.m_Length ? m_Length : aBox.m_Length,
              m_Width > aBox.m_Width ? m_Width : aBox.m_Width,
              m_Height + aBox.m_Height);
}

// Multiply a box by an integer
CBox CBox::operator*(int n) const
{
  if(n%2)
    return CBox(m_Length, m_Width, n*m_Height);          // n odd
  else
    return CBox(m_Length, 2.0*m_Width, (n/2)*m_Height);  // n even
}

// Divide one box into another
int CBox::operator/(const CBox& aBox) const
{
  // Temporary for number in horizontal plane this way
  int tc1 = 0;
  // Temporary for number in a plane that way
  int tc2 = 0;

  tc1 = static_cast<int>((m_Length/aBox.m_Length))*
        static_cast<int>((m_Width/aBox.m_Width));   // to fit this way

  tc2 = static_cast<int>((m_Length/aBox.m_Width))*
        static_cast<int>((m_Width/aBox.m_Length)); // and that way

  //Return best fit
  return static_cast<int>((m_Height/aBox.m_Height))*(tc1>tc2 ? tc1 : tc2);
}
```

The bolded lines are those that you should have modified or added manually.

The very short functions, particularly those that just return the value of a data member, have their definitions within the class definition so that they are inline. If you take a look at ClassView by clicking on the tab, and then click the ▲ beside the CBox class name, you'll see that all the members of the class are shown in the lower pane.

This completes the CBox class, but you still need to define the global functions that implement operators to compare the volume of a CBox object with a numerical value.

ADDING GLOBAL FUNCTIONS

You need to create a .cpp file that will contain the definitions for the global functions supporting operations on CBox objects. The file also needs to be part of the project. Click the Solution Explorer tab to display it (you currently will have the Class View tab displayed) and right-click the Source Files folder. Select Add ⇨ New Item. . . from the context menu to display the dialog. Choose the category as Code and the template as C++ File (.cpp) in the right pane of the dialog, and enter the file name as **BoxOperators**.

You can now enter the following code in the editor pane:

```
// BoxOperators.cpp
// CBox object operations that don't need to access private members
#include "Box.h"

// Function for testing if a constant is > a CBox object
bool operator>(const double& value, const CBox& aBox)
{ return value > aBox.Volume(); }

// Function for testing if a constant is < CBox object
bool operator<(const double& value, const CBox& aBox)
{ return value < aBox.Volume(); }

// Function for testing if CBox object is > a constant
bool operator>(const CBox& aBox, const double& value)
{ return value < aBox; }

// Function for testing if CBox object is < a constant
bool operator<( const CBox& aBox, const double& value)
{ return value > aBox; }

// Function for testing if a constant is >= a CBox object
bool operator>=(const double& value, const CBox& aBox)
{ return value >= aBox.Volume(); }

// Function for testing if a constant is <= CBox object
bool operator<=(const double& value, const CBox& aBox)
{ return value <= aBox.Volume(); }

// Function for testing if CBox object is >= a constant
bool operator>=( const CBox& aBox, const double& value)
{ return value <= aBox; }

// Function for testing if CBox object is <= a constant
bool operator<=( const CBox& aBox, const double& value)
{ return value >= aBox; }

// Function for testing if a constant is == CBox object
bool operator==(const double& value, const CBox& aBox)
{ return value == aBox.Volume(); }
```

```
// Function for testing if CBox object is == a constant
bool operator==(const CBox& aBox, const double& value)
{ return value == aBox; }

// CBox multiply operator n*aBox
CBox operator*(int n, const CBox& aBox)
{ return aBox * n; }

// Operator to return the free volume in a packed CBox
double operator%( const CBox& aBox, const CBox& bBox)
{ return aBox.Volume() - (aBox / bBox) * bBox.Volume(); }
```

You have a #include directive for Box.h because the functions refer to the CBox class. Save the file. When you have completed this, you can select the Class View tab. The Class View tab now includes a Global Functions and Variables folder that will contain all the functions you have just added.

You have seen definitions for all these functions earlier in the chapter, so I won't discuss their implementations again. When you want to use any of these functions in another .cpp file, you'll need to be sure that you declare all the functions that you use so the compiler will recognize them. You can achieve this by putting a set of declarations in a header file. Switch back to the Solution Explorer pane once more and right-click the Header Files folder name. Select Add ⇨ New Item . . . from the context menu to display the dialog, but this time, select category as Code and the template to be Header File(.h), and enter the name as **BoxOperators**. After you click the Add button, an empty header file is added to the project, and you can add the following code in the editor window:

```
// BoxOperators.h - Declarations for global box operators
#pragma once
#include "box.h"

bool operator>(const double& value, const CBox& aBox);
bool operator<(const double& value, const CBox& aBox);
bool operator>(const CBox& aBox, const double& value);
bool operator<(const CBox& aBox, const double& value);
bool operator>=(const double& value, const CBox& aBox);
bool operator<=(const double& value, const CBox& aBox);
bool operator>=(const CBox& aBox, const double& value);
bool operator<=(const CBox& aBox, const double& value);
bool operator==(const double& value, const CBox& aBox);
bool operator==(const CBox& aBox, const double& value);
CBox operator*(int n, const CBox aBox);
double operator%(const CBox& aBox, const CBox& bBox);
```

The #pragma once directive ensures that the contents of the file will not be included more than once in a build. It's important to place this directive in all your own header files, as it is easy to inadvertently attempt to include a header more than once. If you do end up with a header file included more than once into a source file, then you will have multiple definitions for the same thing in the source file and your code will not compile. You just need to add a #include directive for BoxOperators.h to any source file that makes use of any of these functions.

You're now ready to start applying these functions, along with the CBox class, to a specific problem in the world of boxes.

USING THE CBOX CLASS

Suppose that you are packaging candies. The candies are on the big side, real jawbreakers, occupying an envelope 1.5 inches long by 1 inch wide by 1 inch high. You have access to a standard candy box that is 4.5 inches by 7 inches by 2 inches, and you want to know how many candies will fit in the box so that you can set the price. You also have a standard carton that is 2 feet, 6 inches long by 18 inches wide and 18 inches deep, and you want to know how many boxes of candy it can hold and how much space you're wasting when it has been filled.

In case the standard candy box isn't a good solution, you would also like to know what custom candy box would be suitable. You know that you can get a good price on boxes with a length from 3 inches to 7 inches, a width from 3 inches to 5 inches, and a height from 1 inch to 2.5 inches, where each dimension can vary in steps of half an inch. You also know that you need to have at least 30 candies in a box, because this is the minimum quantity consumed by your largest customers at a sitting. Also, the candy box should not have empty space, because the complaints from customers who think they are being cheated go up. Further, ideally, you want to pack the standard carton completely so the candies don't rattle around. You don't want to be too stringent about this; otherwise, packing could become difficult, so let's say you have no wasted space if the free space in the packed carton is less than the volume of a single candy box.

With the CBox class, the problem becomes almost trivial; the solution is represented by the following main() function. Add a new C++ source file, Ex8_11.cpp, to the project through the context menu you get when you right-click Source Files in the Solution Explorer pane, as you've done before. You can then type in the code shown here:

```cpp
// Ex8_11.cpp
// A sample packaging problem
#include <iostream>
#include "Box.h"
#include "BoxOperators.h"
using std::cout;
using std::endl;

int main()
{
    CBox candy(1.5, 1.0, 1.0);              // Candy definition
    CBox candyBox(7.0, 4.5, 2.0);           // Candy box definition
    CBox carton(30.0, 18.0, 18.0);          // Carton definition

    // Calculate candies per candy box
    int numCandies = candyBox/candy;

    // Calculate candy boxes per carton
    int numCboxes = carton/candyBox;

    // Calculate wasted carton space
    double space = carton%candyBox;

    cout << endl << "There are " << numCandies << " candies per candy box" << endl
         << "For the standard boxes there are " << numCboxes
         << " candy boxes per carton " << endl << "with "
```

```
                    << space << " cubic inches wasted.";

          cout << endl << endl << "CUSTOM CANDY BOX ANALYSIS (No Waste)";

          // Try the whole range of custom candy boxes
          for(double length = 3.0 ; length <= 7.5 ; length += 0.5)
          {
             for(double width = 3.0 ; width <= 5.0 ; width += 0.5)
             {
                for(double height = 1.0 ; height <= 2.5 ; height += 0.5)
                {
                   // Create new box each cycle
                   CBox tryBox(length, width, height);

                   if(carton%tryBox < tryBox.Volume() &&
                                 tryBox % candy == 0.0 && tryBox/candy >= 30)
                      cout << endl << endl
                           << "Trial Box L = " << tryBox.GetLength()
                           << " W = " << tryBox.GetWidth()
                           << " H = " << tryBox.GetHeight()
                           << endl
                           << "Trial Box contains " << tryBox / candy << " candies"
                           << " and a carton contains " << carton / tryBox
                           << " candy boxes.";
                }
             }
          }
          cout << endl;
          return 0;
       }
```

code snippet Ex8_11.cpp

Let's first look at how the program is structured. You have divided it into a number of files, which is common when writing in C++. You will be able to see them if you look at the Solution Explorer tab, which will look as shown in Figure 8-13.

The file `Ex8_11.cpp` contains the `main()` function and a `#include` directive for the file `BoxOperators.h` that contains the prototypes for the functions in `BoxOperators.cpp` (which aren't class members). It also has a `#include` directive for the definition of the class `CBox` in `Box.h`. A C++ console program is usually divided into a number of files that will each fall into one of three basic categories:

1.   `.h` files containing library `#include` commands, global constants and variables, class definitions, and function prototypes — in other words, everything except executable code. They also contain inline function definitions. Where a program has several class definitions, they are often placed in separate `.h` files.

FIGURE 8-13

2. .cpp files containing the executable code for the program, plus #include commands for all the definitions required by the executable code.

3. Another .cpp file containing the function main().

The code in our main() function really doesn't need a lot of explanation — it's almost a direct expression of the definition of the problem in words, because the operators in the class interface perform problem-oriented actions on CBox objects.

The solution to the question of the use of standard boxes is in the declaration statements, which also compute the answers we require as initializing values. You then output these values with some explanatory comments.

The second part of the problem is solved using the three nested for loops iterating over the possible ranges of m_Length, m_Width, and m_Height so that you evaluate all possible combinations. You could output them all as well, but because this would involve 200 combinations, of which you might only be interested in a few, you have an if statement which identifies the options that you're actually interested in. The if expression is only true if there's no space wasted in the carton *and* the current trial candy box has no wasted space *and* it contains at least 30 candies.

How It Works

Here's the output from this program:

```
There are 42 candies per candy box
For the standard boxes there are 144 candy boxes per carton
with 648 cubic inches wasted.

CUSTOM CANDY BOX ANALYSIS (No Waste)

Trial Box L = 5 W = 4.5 H = 2
Trial Box contains 30 candies and a carton contains 216 candy boxes.

Trial Box L = 5 W = 4.5 H = 2
Trial Box contains 30 candies and a carton contains 216 candy boxes.

Trial Box L = 6 W = 4.5 H = 2
Trial Box contains 36 candies and a carton contains 180 candy boxes.

Trial Box L = 6 W = 5 H = 2
Trial Box contains 40 candies and a carton contains 162 candy boxes.

Trial Box L = 7.5 W = 3 H = 2
Trial Box contains 30 candies and a carton contains 216 candy boxes.
```

You have a duplicate solution due to the fact that, in the nested loop, you evaluate boxes that have a length of 5 and a width of 4.5, as well as boxes that have a length of 4.5 and a width of 5. Because the CBox class constructor ensures that the length is not less than the width, these two are identical. You could include some additional logic to avoid presenting duplicates, but it hardly seems worth the effort. You could treat it as a small exercise if you like.

ORGANIZING YOUR PROGRAM CODE

In example Ex8_11, you distributed the code among several files for the first time. Not only is this common practice with C++ applications generally, but with Windows programming, it is essential. The sheer volume of code involved in even the simplest program necessitates dividing it into workable chunks.

As I discussed in the previous section, there are basically two kinds of source code files in a C++ program, .h files and .cpp files. This is illustrated in Figure 8-14.

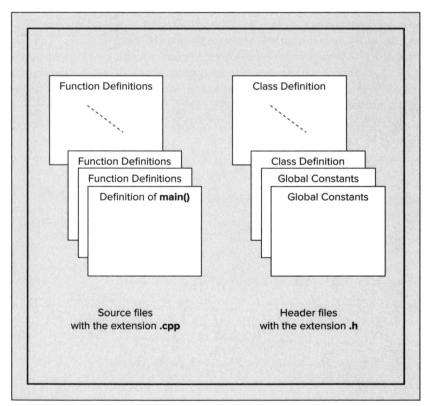

FIGURE 8-14

First, there's the executable code that corresponds to the definitions of the functions that make up the program. Second, there are definitions of various kinds that are necessary for the executable code to compile correctly. These are global constants and variables; data types that include classes, structures, and unions; and function prototypes. The executable source code is stored in files with the extension .cpp, and the definitions are stored in files with the extension .h.

From time to time, you might want to use code from existing files in a new project. In this case, you only have to add the .cpp files to the project, which you can do by using the Project ⇨ Add Existing Item. . . menu option, or by right-clicking either Source Files or Header Files in the Solution

Explorer tab and selecting Add ⇨ Existing Item. . . from the context menu to add the file to your project. You don't need to add .h files to your project, although you can if you want them to be shown in the Solution Explorer pane immediately. The code from .h files will be added at the beginning of the .cpp files that require them as a result of the #include directives that you specify. You need #include directives for header files containing standard library functions and other standard definitions, as well as for your own header files. Visual C++ 2010 automatically keeps track of all these files, and enables you to view them in the Solution Explorer tab. As you saw in the last example, you can also view the class definitions and global constants and variables in the Class View tab.

In a Windows program, there are other kinds of definitions for the specification of such things as menus and toolbar buttons. These are stored in files with extensions like .rc and .ico. Just like .h files, these do not need to be explicitly added to a project, as they are created and tracked automatically by Visual C++ 2010 when you need them.

Naming Program Files

As I have already said, for classes of any complexity, it's usual to store the class definition in a .h file with a file name based on the class name, and to store the implementation of the function members of the class that are defined outside the class definition in a .cpp file with the same name. On this basis, the definition of our CBox class appeared in a file with the name Box.h. Similarly, the class implementation was stored in the file Box.cpp. We didn't follow this convention in the earlier examples in the chapter because the examples were very short, and it was easier to reference the examples with names derived from the chapter number and the sequence number of the example within the chapter. With programs of any size, though, it becomes essential to structure the code in this way, so it would be a good idea to get into the habit of creating .h and .cpp files to hold your program code from now on.

Segmenting a C++ program into .h and .cpp files is a very convenient approach, as it makes it easy for you to find the definition or implementation of any class, particularly if you're working in a development environment that doesn't have all the tools that Visual C++ provides. As long as you know the class name, you can go directly to the file you want. This isn't a rigid rule, however. It's sometimes useful to group the definitions of a set of closely related classes together in a single file and assemble their implementations similarly. However you choose to structure your files, the Class View still displays all the individual classes, as well as all the members of each class, as you can see in Figure 8-15.

I adjusted the size of the Class View pane so all the elements in the project are visible. Here, you can see the details of the classes and globals for the last example. As I've mentioned, double-clicking any of the entries in the tree will take you directly to the relevant source code.

FIGURE 8-15

NATIVE C++ LIBRARY CLASSES FOR STRINGS

As I mentioned in Chapter 4, the `string` standard header defines the `string` and `wstring` classes that represent character strings. Both are defined in the `string` header as template classes that are instances of the `basic_string<T>` class template. The `string` class is defined as `basic_string<char>`, and `wstring` is defined as `basic_string<wchar_t>`, so the `string` class represents strings of characters of type `char`, and `wstring` represents strings of characters of type `wchar_t`.

These string types are much easier to use than null-terminated strings and bring with them a whole range of powerful functions. Because `string` and `wstring` are both instances of the same template, `basic_string<T>`, they provide the same functionality, so I'll only discuss the features and use in the context of the `string` type. The `wstring` type will work just the same, except that the strings contain Unicode character codes and you must use the `L` prefix for string literals in your code.

Creating String Objects

Creating `string` objects is very easy but you have a lot of choices as to how you do it. First, you can create and initialize a string object like this:

```
string sentence = "This sentence is false.";
```

The `sentence` object will be initialized with the string literal that appears to the right of the assignment operator. A string object has no terminating null character, so the string length is the number of characters in the string, 23 in this instance. You can discover the length of the string encapsulated by a string object at any time by calling its `length()` member function. For example:

```
cout << "The string is of length " << sentence.length() << endl;
```

Executing the statement produces the output:

```
The string is of length 23
```

Incidentally, you can output a `string` object to `stdout` in the same way as any other variable:

```
cout << sentence << endl;
```

This displays the `sentence` string on a line by itself. You can also read a character string into a string object like this:

```
cin >> sentence;
```

However, reading from `stdin` in this way ignores leading whitespace until a non-whitespace character is found, and also terminates input when you enter a space following one or more non-whitespace characters. You will often want to read text into a string object that includes spaces and may span several lines. In this case, the `getline()` function template that is defined in the `string` header is much more convenient. For example:

```
getline(cin, sentence, '*');
```

This function template is specifically for reading data from a stream into a string or wstring object. The first argument is the stream that is the source of input — it doesn't have to be cin; the second argument is the object that is to receive the input; and the third argument is the character that terminates reading. Here, I have specified the terminating character as '*', so this statement will read text from cin, including spaces, into sentence, until the end of input is indicated by an asterisk being read from the input stream.

Of course, you can also use functional notation to initialize a string object:

```
string sentence("This sentence is false.");
```

If you don't specify an initial string literal when you create a string object, the object will contain an empty string:

```
string astring;                         // Create an empty string
```

Calling the length() of the string astring will result in zero.

Another possibility is to initialize a string object with a single character repeated a specified number of times:

```
string bees(7, 'b');                    // String is "bbbbbbb"
```

The first argument to the constructor is the number of repetitions of the character specified by the second argument.

Finally, you can initialize a string object with all or part of another string object. Here's an example of using another string object as an initializer:

```
string letters(bees);
```

The letters object will be initialized with the string contained in bees.

To select part of a string object as initializer, you call the string constructor with three arguments, the first being the string object that is the source of the initializing string, the second being the index position of the first character to be selected, and the third argument being the number of characters to be selected. Here's an example:

```
string sentence("This sentence is false.");
string part(sentence, 5, 11);
```

The part object will be initialized with 11 characters from sentence beginning with the sixth character (the first character is at index position 0). Thus, part will contain the string "sentence is".

Of course, you can create arrays of string objects and initialize them using the usual notation. For example:

```
string animals[] = { "dog", "cat", "horse", "donkey", "lion"};
```

This creates an array of string objects that has five elements initialized with the string literals between the braces.

Concatenating Strings

Perhaps the most common operation with strings is joining two strings to form a single string. You can use the + operator to concatenate two string objects or a string object and a string literal. Here are some examples:

```
string sentence1("This sentence is false.");
string sentence2("Therefore the sentence above must be true!");
string combined;                   // Create an empty string
sentence1 = sentence1 + "\n";      // Append string containing newline
combined = sentence1 + sentence2;  // Join two strings
cout << combined << endl;          // Output the result
```

Executing these statements will result in the following output:

```
This sentence is false.
Therefore the sentence above must be true!
```

The first three statements create string objects. The next statement appends the string literal "\n" to sentence1 and stores the result in sentence1. The next statement joins sentence1 and sentence2 and stores the result in combined. The last statement outputs the string combined.

String concatenation using the + operator is possible because the string class implements operator+(). This implies that one of the operands must be a string object, so you can't use the + operator to join two string literals. Keep in mind that each time you use the + operator to join two strings, you are creating a new string object, which involves a certain amount of overhead. You'll see in the next section how you can modify and extend an existing string object, and this may be a more efficient alternative in some cases, because it does not involve creating new objects.

You can also use the + operator to join a character to a string object, so you could have written the fourth statement in the previous code fragment as:

```
sentence1 = sentence1 + '\n';          // Append newline character to string
```

The string class also implements operator+=() such that the right operand can be a string literal, a string object, or a single character. You could write the previous statement as:

```
sentence1 += '\n';
```

or

```
sentence1 += "\n";
```

There is a difference between using the += operator and using the + operator. As I said, the + operator creates a new string object containing the combined string. The += operator appends the string or character that is the right operand to the `string` object that is the left operand, so the `string` object is modified directly and no new object is created.

Let's exercise some of what I have described in an example.

TRY IT OUT   Creating and Joining Strings

This is a simple example that reads names and ages from the keyboard and then lists what you entered. Here's the code:

```cpp
// Ex8_12.cpp
// Creating and joining string objects
#include <iostream>
#include <string>
using std::cin;
using std::cout;
using std::endl;
using std::string;
using std::getline;

// List names and ages
void listnames(string names[], string ages[], size_t count)
{
  cout << endl << "The names you entered are: " << endl;
  for(size_t i = 0 ; i < count && !names[i].empty() ; ++i)
    cout << names[i] + " aged " + ages[i] + '.' << endl;
}

int main()
{
  const size_t count = 100;
  string names[count];
  string ages[count];
  string firstname;
  string secondname;

  for(size_t i = 0 ; i<count ; i++)
  {
    cout << endl << "Enter a first name or press Enter to end: ";
    getline(cin, firstname, '\n');
    if(firstname.empty())
    {
      listnames(names, ages, i);
      cout << "Done!!" << endl;
      return 0;
    }

    cout << "Enter a second name: ";
    getline(cin, secondname, '\n');

    names[i] = firstname + ' ' + secondname;
    cout << "Enter " + firstname + "'s age: ";
    getline(cin, ages[i], '\n');
```

```
      }
      cout << "No space for more names." << endl;
      listnames(names, ages, count);
      return 0;
   }
```

This example produces output similar to the following:

```
Enter a first name or press Enter to end: Marilyn
Enter a second name: Munroe
Enter Marilyn's age: 26

Enter a first name or press Enter to end: Tom
Enter a second name: Crews
Enter Tom's age: 45

Enter a first name or press Enter to end: Arnold
Enter a second name: Weisseneggar
Enter Arnold's age: 52

Enter a first name or press Enter to end:

The names you entered are:
Marilyn Munroe aged 26.
Tom Crews aged 45.
Arnold Weisseneggar aged 52.
Done!!
```

How It Works

The `listnames` function lists names and ages stored in arrays that are passed as the first two arguments. The third argument is a count of the number of elements in the array. Listing of the data occurs in a loop:

```
for(size_t i = 0 ; i < count && !names[i].empty() ; ++i)
  cout << names[i] + " aged " + ages[i] + '.' << endl;
```

The loop condition is a belt-and-braces control mechanism in that it not only checks that the index `i` is less than the value of `count` that is passed as the third argument, but it also calls the `empty()` function for the current element to verify that it is not an empty string. The single statement in the body of the loop concatenates the current string in `names[i]` with the literal `" aged "`, the `ages[i]` string, and the character `'.'` using the + operator, and writes the resultant string to `cout`. The expression concatenating the strings is equivalent to:

```
((names[i].operator+(" aged ")).operator+(ages[i])).operator+('.')
```

Each call of the `operator+()` function returns a new `string` object that results from the operation. Thus, the expression demonstrates combining a `string` object with a string literal, a `string` object with another `string` object, and a `string` object with a character literal.

Although the code above demonstrates the use of the `string::operator+()` function, for performance reasons, you would use the following:

```
cout << names[i] << " aged " << ages[i] << '.' << endl;
```

This avoids the calls to the operator function and the creation of all the string objects that result from that.

In `main()`, you first create two arrays of `string` objects of length `count` with the statements:

```
const size_t count = 100;
string names[count];
string ages[count];
```

The `names` and `ages` arrays will store names and corresponding age values that are entered from the keyboard.

Within the `for` loop in `main()`, you read the first and second names separately using the `getline()` function template that is defined in the `string` header:

```
cout << endl << "Enter a first name or press Enter to end: ";
getline(cin, firstname, '\n');
if(firstname.empty())
{
  listnames(names, ages, i);
  cout << "Done!!" << endl;
  return 0;
}

cout << "Enter a second name: ";
getline(cin, secondname, '\n');
```

The `getline()` function allows an empty string to be read, something you cannot do using the `>>` operator with `cin`. The first argument to `getline()` is the stream that is the source of the input, the second argument is the destination for the input, and the third argument is the character that signals the end on the input operation. If you omit the third argument, entering `'\n'` will terminate the input process, so you could have omitted it here. You use the ability to read an empty string here as you test for an empty string in `firstname` by calling its `empty()` function. An empty string signals the end of input, so you call `listnames()` to output the data and end program execution.

When `firstname` is not empty, you continue with reading the second name into `secondname`, again using the `getline()` template function. You concatenate `firstname` and `secondname` using the `+` operator and store the result in `names[i]`, the currently unused element in the `names` array.

Finally in the loop, you read a string for the age of the person and store the result in `ages[i]`. The `for` loop limits the number of entries to `count`, which corresponds to the number of elements in the arrays. If you fall through the end of the loop, the arrays are full, so after displaying a message, you output the data that was entered.

Accessing and Modifying Strings

You can access any character in a `string` object to read it or overwrite it by using the subscript operator, `[]`. Here's an example:

```
string sentence("Too many cooks spoil the broth.");
for(size_t i = 0; i < sentence.length(); i++)
{
  if(' ' == sentence[i])
    sentence[i] = '*';
}
```

This just inspects each character in the `sentence` string in turn to see if it is a space, and if it is, replaces the character with an asterisk.

You can use the `at()` member function to achieve the same result as the `[]` operator:

```
string sentence("Too many cooks spoil the broth.");
for(size_t i = 0; i < sentence.length(); i++)
{
  if(' ' == sentence.at(i))
    sentence.at(i) = '*';
}
```

This does exactly the same as the previous fragment, so what's the difference between using `[]` and using `at()`? Well, subscripting is faster than using the `at()` function, but the downside is the validity of the index is not checked. If the index is out of range, the result of using the subscript operator is undefined. The `at()` function, on the other hand, is a bit slower, but it does check the index, and if it is not valid, the function will throw an `out_of_range` exception. You would use the `at()` function when there is the possibility of the index value being out of range, and in this situation, you should put the code in a `try` block and handle the exception appropriately. If you are sure index out of range conditions cannot arise, then use the `[]` operator.

You can extract a part of an existing `string` object as a new `string` object. For example:

```
string sentence("Too many cooks spoil the broth.");
string substring = sentence.substr(4, 10);              // Extracts "many cooks"
```

The first argument to the `substr()` function is the first character of the substring to be extracted, and the second argument is the count of the number of characters in the substring.

By using the `append()` function for a string object, you can add one or more characters to the end of the string. This function comes in several versions; there are versions that append one or more of a given character, a string literal, or a `string` object to the object for which the function is called. For example:

```
string phrase("The higher");
string word("fewer");
phrase.append(1, ' ');              // Append one space
phrase.append("the ");              // Append a string literal
phrase.append(word);                // Append a string object
phrase.append(2, '!');              // Append two exclamation marks
```

After executing this sequence, `phrase` will have been modified to `"The higher the fewer!!"`. With the version of `append()` with two arguments, the first argument is the count of the number of times the character specified by the second argument is to be appended. When you call `append()`, the function returns a reference to the object for which it was called, so you could write the four `append()` calls above in a single statement:

```
phrase.append(1, ' ').append("the ").append(word).append(2, '!');
```

You can also use `append()` to append part of a string literal or part of a `string` object to an existing string:

```
string phrase("The more the merrier.");
string query("Any");
query.append(phrase, 3, 5).append(1, '?');
```

The result of executing these statements is that `query` will contain the string `"Any more?"`. In the last statement, the first call to the `append()` function has three arguments:

➤   The first argument, `phrase`, is the `string` object from which characters are to be extracted and appended to `query`.

➤   The second argument, 3, is the index position of the first character to be extracted.

➤   The third argument, 5, is the count of the total number of characters to be appended.

Thus, the substring `" more"` is appended to `query` by this call. The second call for the `append()` function appends a question mark to `query`.

When you want to append a single character to a string object, you could use the `push_back()` function as an alternative to `append()`. Here's how you would use that:

```
query.push_back('*');
```

This appends an asterisk character to the end of the `query` string.

Sometimes, adding characters to the end of a string just isn't enough. There will be occasions when you want to insert one or more characters at some position in the interior of a string. The various flavors of the `insert()` function will do that for you:

```
string saying("A horse");
string word("blind");
string sentence("He is as good as gold.");
string phrase("a wink too far");
saying.insert(1, " ");                  // Insert a space character
saying.insert(2, word);                 // Insert a string object
saying.insert(2, "nodding", 3);         // Insert 3 characters of a string literal
saying.insert(5, sentence, 2, 15);      // Insert part of a string at position 5
saying.insert(20, phrase, 0, 9);        // Insert part of a string at position 20
saying.insert(29, " ").insert(30, "a poor do", 0, 2);
```

I'm sure you'll be interested to know that after executing the statements above, saying will contain the string "A nod is as good as a wink to a blind horse". The parameters to the various versions of insert() are:

FUNCTION PROTOTYPE	DESCRIPTION
```string& insert(size_t index, const char* pstring)```	Inserts the null-terminated string pstring at position index.
```string& insert(size_t index, const string& astring)```	Inserts the string object astring at position index.
```string& insert(size_t index, const char* pstring, size_t count)```	Inserts the first count characters from the null-terminated string pstring at position index.
```string& insert(size_t index, size_t count, char ch)```	Inserts count copies of the character ch at position index.
```string& insert(size_t index, const string& astring, size_t start, size_t count)```	Inserts count characters from the string object astring, beginning with the character at position start; the substring is inserted at position index.

In each of these versions of insert(), a reference to the string object for which the function is called is returned; this allows you to chain calls together, as in the last statement in the code fragment.

This is not the complete set of insert() functions, but you can do everything you need with those in the table. The other versions use **iterators** as arguments, and you'll learn about iterators in Chapter 10.

You can interchange the strings encapsulated by two string objects by calling the swap() member function. For example:

```
string phrase("The more the merrier.");
string query("Any");
query.swap(phrase);
```

This results in query containing the string "The more the merrier." and phrase containing the string "Any". Of course, executing phrase.swap(query) would have the same effect.

If you need to convert a string object to a null-terminated string, the `c_str()` function will do this. For example:

```
string phrase("The higher the fewer");
const char *pstring = phrase.c_str();
```

The `c_str()` function returns a pointer to a null-terminated string with the same contents as the `string` object.

You can also obtain the contents of a string object as an array of elements of type `char` by calling the `data()` member function. Note that the array contains just the characters from the string object without a terminating null.

You can replace part of a string object by calling its `replace()` member function. This also comes in several versions, as the following table shows.

FUNCTION PROTOTYPE	DESCRIPTION

`string& replace(`
`  size_t index,`
`  size_t count,`
`  const char* pstring)`
	Replaces count characters, starting at position index, with the first count characters from `pstring`.

`string& replace(`
`  size_t index,`
`  size_t count,`
`  const string& astring)`
	Replaces count characters, starting at position index, with the first count characters from `astring`.

`string& replace(`
`  size_t index,`
`  size_t count1,`
`  const char* pstring,`
`  size_t count2)`
	Replaces count1 characters, starting at position index, with up to count2 characters from `pstring`. This allows the replacement substring to be longer or shorter than the substring that is replaced.

`string& replace(`
`  size_t index1,`
`  size_t count1,`
`  const string& astring,`
`  size_t index2,`
`  size_t count2)`
	Replaces count1 characters, starting at position index1, with count2 characters from `astring`, starting at position index2.

`string& replace(`
`  size_t index,`
`  size_t count1,`
`  size_t count2,`
`  char ch)`
	Replaces count1 characters, starting at index, with count2 occurrences of the character ch.

In each case, a reference to the `string` object for which the function is called is returned.

Here's an example:

```
string proverb("A nod is as good as a wink to a blind horse");
string sentence("It's bath time!");
proverb.replace(38, 5, sentence, 5, 3);
```

This fragment uses the fifth version of the `replace()` function from the preceding table to substitute "`bat`" in place of "`horse`" in the string `proverb`.

Comparing Strings

You have a full complement of operators for comparing two string objects or comparing a string object with a string literal. Operator overloading has been implemented in the `string` class for the following operators:

```
==    !=    <    <=    >    >=
```

Here's an example of the use of these operators:

```
string dog1("St Bernard");
string dog2("Tibetan Mastiff");
if(dog1 < dog2)
  cout << "dog2 comes first!" << endl;
else if(dog1 > dog2)
  cout << "dog1 comes first!" << endl;
```

When you compare two strings, corresponding characters are compared until a pair of characters is found that differ, or the end of one or both strings is reached. When two corresponding characters are found to be different, the values of the character codes determine which string is less than the other. If no character pairs are found to be different, the string with fewer characters is less than the other string. Two strings will be equal if they contain the same number of characters and corresponding characters are identical.

TRY IT OUT   **Comparing Strings**

This example illustrates the use of the comparison operators by implementing an extremely inefficient sorting method. Here's the code:

Available for download on Wrox.com

```
// Ex8_13.cpp
// Comparing and sorting words
#include <iostream>
#include <iomanip>
#include <string>
using std::cin;
using std::cout;
using std::endl;
using std::ios;
using std::setiosflags;
```

```cpp
using std::setw;
using std::string;

string* sort(string* strings, size_t count)
{
  bool swapped(false);
  while(true)
  {
    for(size_t i = 0 ; i < count-1 ; i++)
    {
      if(strings[i] > strings[i+1])
      {
        swapped = true;
        strings[i].swap(strings[i+1]);
      }
    }
    if(!swapped)
      break;
    swapped = false;
  }
  return strings;
}

int main()
{
  const size_t maxstrings(100);
  string strings[maxstrings];
  size_t nstrings(0);
  size_t maxwidth(0);

  // Read up to 100 words into the strings array
  while(nstrings < maxstrings)
  {
    cout << "Enter a word or press Enter to end: ";
    getline(cin, strings[nstrings]);
    if(maxwidth < strings[nstrings].length())
      maxwidth = strings[nstrings].length();
    if(strings[nstrings].empty())
      break;
    ++nstrings;
  }

  // Sort the input in ascending sequence
  sort(strings,nstrings);
  cout << endl
       << "In ascending sequence, the words you entered are:"
       << endl
       << setiosflags(ios::left);            // Left-justify the output
  for(size_t i = 0 ; i < nstrings ; i++)
  {
    if(i % 5 == 0)
      cout << endl;
    cout << setw(maxwidth+2) << strings[i];
  }
```

```
    cout << endl;
    return 0;
}
```

code snippet Ex8_13.cpp

Here's some typical output from this example:

```
Enter a word or press Enter to end: loquacious
Enter a word or press Enter to end: transmogrify
Enter a word or press Enter to end: abstemious
Enter a word or press Enter to end: facetious
Enter a word or press Enter to end: xylophone
Enter a word or press Enter to end: megaphone
Enter a word or press Enter to end: chauvinist
Enter a word or press Enter to end:

In ascending sequence, the words you entered are:

abstemious    chauvinist    facetious    loquacious    megaphone
transmogrify  xylophone
```

How It Works

The most interesting part is the `sort()` function that accepts two arguments, the address of a string array and the count of the number of array elements.

The function implements the bubble sort, which works by scanning through the elements in sequences and comparing successive elements. All the work is done in the `while` loop:

```
bool swapped(false);
while(true)
{
  for(size_t i = 0 ; i < count-1 ; i++)
  {
    if(strings[i] > strings[i+1])
    {
      swapped = true;
      strings[i].swap(strings[i+1]);
    }
  }
  if(!swapped)
    break;
  swapped = false;
}
```

Successive elements in the `strings` array are compared using the `>` operator. If the first element is greater than the second in a pair, the elements are swapped. In this case, the elements are interchanged by calling the `swap()` function for one `string` object with the second `string` object as argument. Comparing successive elements and swapping when necessary continues for the entire array of elements. This process is repeated until there is a pass through all the elements where no elements are swapped. The elements are then in ascending sequence. The `bool` variable `swapped` acts as an indicator for whether swapping occurs on any given pass. It is only set to `true` when two elements are swapped.

The `main()` function reads up to 100 words into the strings array in a loop:

```
while(nstrings < maxstrings)
{
  cout << "Enter a word or press Enter to end: ";
  getline(cin, strings[nstrings]);
  if(maxwidth < strings[nstrings].length())
    maxwidth = strings[nstrings].length();
  if(strings[nstrings].empty())
    break;
  ++nstrings;
}
```

The `getline()` function here reads characters from `cin` until `'\n'` is read. The input is stored in the `string` object specified by the second argument `strings[nstrings]`. Just pressing the Enter key will result in an `empty()` string, so the loop is terminated when the `empty()` function for the last `string` object read returns `true`. The `maxwidth` variable is used to record the length of the longest string entered. This will be used later in the output process after the input has been sorted.

Calling the `sort()` function sorts the contents of the `strings` array in ascending sequence. The result is output in a loop:

```
cout << endl
     << "In ascending sequence, the words you entered are:"
     << endl
     << setiosflags(ios::left);         // Left-justify the output
for(size_t i = 0 ; i < nstrings ; i++)
{
  if(i % 5 == 0)
    cout << endl;
  cout << setw(maxwidth+2) << strings[i];
}
```

This outputs each element in a field width of `maxwidth+2` characters. Each word is left-justified in the field because of the call to the `setiosflags()` manipulator with the argument `ios::left`. Unlike the `setw()` manipulator, the `setiosflags()` manipulator remains in effect until you reset it.

Searching Strings

You have four versions of the `find()` function that search a `string` object for a given character or substring, and they are described in the following table. All the `find()` functions are defined as being `const`.

FUNCTION	DESCRIPTION

`size_t find(`
   `char ch,`
   `size_t offset=0)`
	Searches a `string` object for the character `ch` starting at index position `offset`. You can omit the second argument, in which case, the default value is 0.

`size_t find(`
   `const char* pstr,`
   `size_t offset=0)`
	Searches a `string` object for the null-terminated string `pstr`, starting at index position `offset`. You can omit the second argument, in which case, the default value is 0.

`size_t find(`
   `const char* pstr,`
   `size_t offset,`
   `size_t count)`
	Searches a `string` object for the first `count` characters of the null-terminated string `pstr`, starting at index position `offset`.

`size_t find(`
   `const string& str,`
   `size_t offset=0)`
	Searches a `string` object for the string object `str`, starting at index position `offset`. You can omit the second argument, in which case, the default value is 0.

In each case, the `find()` function returns the index position where the character or first character of the substring was found. The function returns the value `string::npos` if the item was not found. This latter value is a constant defined in the `string` class that represents an illegal position in a `string` object; it is used generally to signal a search failure.

Here's a fragment showing some of the ways you might use the `find()` function:

```
string phrase("So near and yet so far");
string str("So near");
cout << phrase.find(str) << endl;          // Outputs 0
cout << phrase.find("so far") << endl;     // Outputs 16
cout << phrase.find("so near") << endl;    // Outputs string::npos = 4294967295
```

The value of `string::npos` can vary with different C++ compiler implementations, so to test for it, you should always use `string::npos` and not the explicit value.

Here's another example that scans the same string repeatedly, searching for occurrences of a particular substring:

```
string str( "Smith, where Jones had had \"had had\", \"had had\" had."
            " \"Had had\" had had the examiners' approval.");
string substr("had");

cout << "The string to be searched is:"
     << endl << str << endl;
size_t offset(0);
size_t count(0);
size_t increment(substr.length());

while(true)
```

```
  {
    offset = str.find(substr, offset);
    if(string::npos == offset)
      break;
    offset += increment;
    ++count;
  }
  cout << endl << " The string \"" << substr
      << "\" was found " << count << " times in the string above."
      << endl;
```

Here, you search the string `str` to see how many times "`had`" appears. The search is done in the `while` loop, where `offset` records the position found, and is also used as the start position for the search. The search starts at index position 0, the start of the string, and each time the substring is found, the new starting position for the next search is set to the found position plus the length of the substring. This ensures that the substring that was found is bypassed. Every time the substring is found, count is incremented. If `find()` returns `string::npos`, then the substring was not found and the search ends. Executing this fragment produces the output:

```
The string to be searched is:
Smith, where Jones had had "had had", "had had" had. "Had had" had had the
examiners' approval.

The string "had" was found 10 times in the string above.
```

Of course, `"Had"` is not a match for the substring "`had`," so 10 is the correct result.

The `find_first_of()` and `find_last_of()` member functions search a `string` object for an occurrence of any character from a given set. You could search a string to find spaces or punctuation characters, for example, which would allow you to break a string up into individual words. Both functions come in several flavors, as the following table shows. All functions in the table are defined as `const` and return a value of type `size_t`.

FUNCTION	DESCRIPTION

`find_first_of(`
  `char ch,`
  `size_t offset = 0)`
	Searches a `string` object for the first occurrence of the character, ch, starting at position `offset`, and returns the index position where the character is found as a value of type `size_t`. If you omit the second argument, the default value of `offset` is 0.

`find_first_of(`
  `const char* pstr,`
  `size_t offset = 0)`
	Searches a `string` object for the first occurrence of any character in the null-terminated string, `pstr`, starting at position `offset`, and returns the index position where the character is found as a value of type `size_t`. If you omit the second argument, the default value of `offset` is 0.

`find_first_of(`
  `const char* pstr,`
  `size_t offset,`
  `size_t count)`
	Searches a `string` object for the first occurrence of any character in the first count characters of the null-terminated string, `pstr`, starting at position `offset`, and returns the index position where the character is found as a value of type `size_t`.

continues

(continued)

FUNCTION	DESCRIPTION

find_first_of(
 	
  const string& str,
 	
  size_t offset = 0)
	Searches a string object for the first occurrence of any character in the string, str, starting at position offset, and returns the index position where the character is found as a value of type size_t. If you omit the second argument, the default value of offset is 0.

find_last_of(
 	
  char ch,
 	
  size_t offset=npos)
	Searches backward through a string object for the last occurrence of the character, ch, starting at position offset, and returns the index position where the character is found as a value of type size_t. If you omit the second argument, the default value of offset is npos, which is the end of the string.

find_last_of(
 	
  const char* pstr,
 	
  size_t offset=npos)
	Searches backward through a string object for the last occurrence of any character in the null-terminated string, pstr, starting at position offset, and returns the index position where the character is found as a value of type size_t. If you omit the second argument, the default value of offset is npos, which is the end of the string.

find_last_of(
 	
  const char* pstr,
 	
  size_t offset,
 	
  size_t count)
	Searches backward through a string object for the last occurrence of any of the first count characters in the null-terminated string, pstr, starting at position offset, and returns the index position where the character is found as a value of type size_t.

find_last_of(
 	
  const string& str,
 	
  size_t offset=npos)
	Searches backward through a string object for the last occurrence of any character in the string, str, starting at position offset, and returns the index position where the character is found as a value of type size_t. If you omit the second argument, the default value of offset is npos, which is the end of the string.

With all versions of the find_first_of() and find_last_of() functions, string::npos will be returned if no matching character is found.

With the same string as the last fragment, you could see what the find_last_of() function does with the same search string "had."

```
size_t count(0);
size_t offset(string::npos);
while(true)
{
  offset = str.find_last_of(substr, offset);
  if(string::npos == offset)
    break;
  --offset;
  ++count;
}
```

```
cout << endl << " Characters from the string \"" << substr
     << "\" were found " << count << " times in the string above."
     << endl;
```

This time, you are searching backward starting at index position `string::npos`, the end of the string, because this is the default starting position. The output from this fragment is:

```
The string to be searched is:
Smith, where Jones had had "had had", "had had" had. "Had had" had had
the examiners' approval.

Characters from the string "had" were found 38 times in the string above.
```

The result should not be a surprise. Remember, you are searching for occurrences of *any* of the characters in "had" in the string `str`. There are 32 in the "Had" and "had" words, and 6 in the remaining words. Because you are searching backward through the string, you decrement `offset` within the loop when you find a character.

The last set of search facilities are versions of the `find_first_not_of()` and `find_last_not_of()` functions. All of the functions in the following table are `const` and return a value of type `size_t`.

FUNCTION	DESCRIPTION
find_first_not_of(char ch, size_t offset = 0)	Searches a `string` object for the first occurrence of a character that is not the character, ch, starting at position `offset`. The function returns the index position where the character is found as a value of type `size_t`. If you omit the second argument, the default value of `offset` is 0.
find_first_not_of(const char* pstr, size_t offset = 0)	Searches a `string` object for the first occurrence of a character that is not in the null-terminated string, pstr, starting at position `offset`, and returns the index position where the character is found as a value of type `size_t`. If you omit the second argument, the default value of `offset` is 0.
find_first_ not_of(char* pstr, size_t offset, size_t count)	Searches a `string` object for the first occurrence of a character that is not in the first count characters of the null-terminated string, pstring, starting at position `offset`. The function returns the index position where the character is found as a value of type `size_t`.
find_first_not_of(const string& str, size_t offset = 0)	Searches a `string` object for the first occurrence of any character that is not in the string, pstr, starting at position `offset`. The function returns the index position where the character is found as a value of type `size_t`. If you omit the second argument, the default value of `offset` is 0.

continues

(continued)

FUNCTION	DESCRIPTION

find_last_not_of(
   char ch,
   size_t offset=npos)
	Searches backward through a string object for the last occurrence of a character that is not the character, ch, starting at position offset. The index position where the character is found is returned as a value of type size_t. If you omit the second argument, the default value of offset is npos, which is the end of the string.

find_last_not_of(
   const char* pstr,
   size_t offset=npos)
	Searches backward through a string object for the last occurrence of any character that is not in the null-terminated string, pstr, starting at position offset. The index position where the character is found is returned as a value of type size_t. If you omit the second argument, the default value of offset is npos, which is the end of the string.

find_last_not_of(
   const char* pstr,
   size_t offset,
   size_t count)
	Searches backward through a string object for the last occurrence of a character that is not among the first count characters in the null-terminated string, pstr, starting at position offset. The function returns the index position where the character is found as a value of type size_t.

find_last_not_of(
   const string& str,
   size_t offset=npos)
	Searches backward through a string object for the last occurrence of any character not in the string, str, starting at position offset. The function returns the index position where the character is found as a value of type size_t. If you omit the second argument, the default value of offset is npos, which is the end of the string.

As with previous search functions, string::npos will be returned if the search does not find a character. These functions have many uses, typically finding tokens in a string that may be separated by characters of various kinds. For example, text consists of words separated by spaces and punctuation characters, so you could use these functions to find the words in a block of text. Let's see that working in an example.

TRY IT OUT   **Sorting Words from Text**

This example will read a block of text, and then extract the words and output them in ascending sequence. I'll use the somewhat inefficient bubble sort function that you saw in Ex8_11 here. In Chapter 10, you will use a library function for sorting that would be much better, but you need to learn about some other stuff before you can use that. The program will also figure out how many times each word occurs and output the count for each word. Such an analysis is called a **collocation**. Here's the code:

```cpp
// Ex8_14.cpp
// Extracting words from text
#include <iostream>
#include <iomanip>
#include <string>
using std::cin;
```

```cpp
using std::cout;
using std::endl;
using std::ios;
using std::setiosflags;
using std::resetiosflags;
using std::setw;
using std::string;

// Sort an array of string objects
string* sort(string* strings, size_t count)
{
  bool swapped(false);
  while(true)
  {
    for(size_t i = 0 ; i < count-1 ; i++)
    {
      if(strings[i] > strings[i+1])
      {
        swapped = true;
        strings[i].swap(strings[i+1]);
      }
    }
    if(!swapped)
      break;
    swapped = false;
  }
  return strings;
}

int main()
{
  const size_t maxwords(100);
  string words[maxwords];
  string text;
  string separators(" \".,:;!?()\n");
  size_t nwords(0);
  size_t maxwidth(0);

  cout << "Enter some text on as many lines as you wish."
    << endl << "Terminate the input with an asterisk:" << endl;

  getline(cin, text, '*');

  size_t start(0), end(0), offset(0);   // Record start & end of word & offset
  while(true)
  {
    // Find first character of a word
    start = text.find_first_not_of(separators, offset);  // Find non-separator
    if(string::npos == start)              // If we did not find it, we are done
      break;
    offset = start + 1;                    // Move past character found


    // Find first separator past end of current word
```

```
      end = text.find_first_of(separators,offset);        // Find separator
      if(string::npos == end)            // If it's the end of the string
      {                                  // current word is last in string
        offset = end;                    // We use offset to end loop later
        end = text.length();             // Set end as 1 past last character
      }
      else
        offset = end + 1;                // Move past character found

      words[nwords] = text.substr(start, end-start);      // Extract the word

      // Keep track of longest word
      if(maxwidth < words[nwords].length())
        maxwidth = words[nwords].length();

      if(string::npos == offset)         // If we reached the end of the string
        break;                           // We are done

      if(++nwords == maxwords)           // Check for array full
      {
        cout << endl << "Maximum number of words reached."
             << endl << "Processing what we have." << endl;
        break;
      }
    }

  sort(words, nwords);

  cout << endl
       << "In ascending sequence, the words in the text are:"
       << endl;

  size_t count(0);                                    // Count of duplicate words
  // Output words and number of occurrences
  for(size_t i = 0 ; i<nwords ; i++)
  {
    if(0 == count)
      count = 1;
    if(i < nwords-2 && words[i] == words[i+1])
    {
      ++count;
      continue;
    }
    cout << setiosflags(ios::left)                    // Output word left-justified
         << setw(maxwidth+2) << words[i];
    cout << resetiosflags(ios::right)                 // and word count right-justified
         << setw(5) << count << endl;
    count = 0;
  }
  cout << endl;
  return 0;
}
```

code snippet Ex8_14.cpp

Here's an example of some output from this program:

```
Enter some text on as many lines as you wish.
Terminate the input with an asterisk:
I sometimes think I'd rather crow
And be a rooster than to roost
And be a crow. But I dunno.

A rooster he can roost also,
Which don't seem fair when crows can't crow
Which may help some. Still I dunno.*

In ascending sequence, the words in the text are:
A          1
And        2
But        1
I          3
I'd        1
Still      1
Which      2
a          2
also       1
be         2
can        1
can't      1
crow       3
crows      1
don't      1
dunno      2
fair       1
he         1
help       1
may        1
rather     1
roost      2
rooster    2
seem       1
some       1
sometimes  1
than       1
think      1
to         1
when       1
```

How It Works

The input is read from `cin` using the `getline()` with the termination character specified as an asterisk. This allows an arbitrary number of lines of input to be entered. Individual words are extracted from the input in the string object `text` and stored in the `words` array. This is done in the `while` loop.

The first step in extracting a word from text is to find the index position of the first character of the word:

```
start = text.find_first_not_of(separators, offset);   // Find non-separator
if(string::npos == start)            // If we did not find it, we are done
  break;
offset = start + 1;                  // Move past character found
```

The `find_first_not_of()` function call returns the index position of the first character from the position offset that is not one of the characters in separators. You could use the `find_first_of()` function here to search for any of A to Z, a to z to achieve the same result. When the last word has been extracted, the search will reach the end of the string without finding a character, so you test for this by comparing the value that was returned with `string::npos`. If it is the end of the string, all words have been extracted, so you exit the loop. In any other instance, you set offset at one past the character that was found.

The next search is for any separator character:

```
end = text.find_first_of(separators,offset);       // Find separator
if(string::npos == end)           // If it's the end of the string
{                                 // current word is last in string
  offset = end;                   // We use offset to end loop later
  end = text.length();            // Set end as 1 past last character
}
else
  offset = end + 1;               // Move past character found
```

The search for any separator is from index position offset, which is one past the first character of the word, so usually, you will find the separator that is one past the last character of the word. When the word is the last in the text and there is no separator following the last character of the word, the function will return `string::npos`, so you deal with this situation by setting end to one past the last character in the string and setting offset to `string::npos`. The offset variable will be tested later in the loop after the current word has been extracted to determine whether the loop should end.

Extracting a word is easy:

```
words[nwords] = text.substr(start, end-start);       // Extract the word
```

The `substr()` function extracts end-start characters from text, starting with the character at start. The length of the word is end-start because start is the first character and end is one past the last character in the word.

The rest of the while loop body keeps track of the maximum word length in the way you have seen before, checks for the end-of-string condition, and checks whether the words array is full.

The words are output in a for loop that iterates over all the elements in the words array. The if statements in the loop deal with counting duplicate words:

```
if(0 == count)
  count = 1;
if(i < nwords-2 && words[i] == words[i+1])
{
```

```
        ++count;
        continue;
    }
```

The `count` variable records the number of duplicate words, so it is always a minimum of 1. At the end of the loop, `count` is set to 0 when a word and its count are written out. This acts as an indicator that a new word count is starting, so when `count` is 0, the first `if` statement sets it to 1; otherwise, it is left at its current value.

The second `if` statement checks if the next word is the same as the current word, and if it is, `count` is incremented and the rest of the current loop iteration is skipped. This mechanism accumulates the number of times a word is duplicated in `count`. The loop condition also checks that the index, `i`, is less than `nwords-2`, because we don't want to check the next word when the current word is the last in the array. Thus, we only output a word and its count when the next word is different, or the current word is the last in the array.

The last step in the `for` loop is to output a word and its count:

```
    cout << setiosflags(ios::left)              // Output word left-justified
         << setw(maxwidth+2) << words[i];
    cout << resetiosflags(ios::right)           // and word count right-justified
         << setw(5) << count << endl;
    count = 0;
```

The output statement left-justifies the word in a field width that is two greater than the longest word. The count is output right-justified in a field width of five.

C++/CLI PROGRAMMING

While you can define a destructor in a reference class in the same way as you do for native C++ classes, most of the time it is not necessary. However, I'll return to the topic of destructors for reference classes in the next chapter. You can also call delete for a handle to a reference class, but again, this is not normally necessary as the garbage collector will delete unwanted objects automatically.

C++/CLI classes support overloading of operators, but there are some differences from operator overloading in native classes that you need to explore. A couple of differences you have already heard about. You'll probably recall that you must not overload the assignment operator in your value classes because the process for the assignment of one value class object to another of the same type is already defined to be member-by-member copying, and you cannot change this. I also mentioned that, unlike native classes, a ref class does not have a default assignment operator — if you want the assignment operator to work with your ref class objects, then you must implement the appropriate function. Another difference from native C++ classes is that functions that implement operator overloading in C++/CLI classes can be static members of a class as well as instance members. This means that you have the option of implementing binary operators in C++/CLI classes with static member functions with two parameters in addition to the possibilities you have seen in the context of native C++ for operator functions as instance functions with one parameter or non-member functions with two parameters. Similarly, in C++/CLI, you have the additional possibility to implement a prefix unary operator as a static member function with no parameters. Finally, although in native C++ you can overload the `new` operator, you cannot overload the `gcnew` operator in a C++/CLI class.

Let's look into some of the specifics, starting with value classes.

Overloading Operators in Value Classes

Let's define a class to represent a length in feet and inches and use that as a base for demonstrating how you can implement operator overloading for a value class. Addition seems like a good place to start, so here's the `Length` value class, complete with the addition operator function:

```
value class Length
{
private:
  int feet;                            // Feet component
  int inches;                          // Inches component

public:
  static initonly int inchesPerFoot = 12;

  // Constructor
  Length(int ft, int ins) : feet(ft), inches(ins){ }

  // A length as a string
  virtual String^ ToString() override
  {
    return feet.ToString() + (1 == feet ? L" foot " : L" feet ") +
           inches + (1 == inches ? L" inch" : L" inches");
  }

  // Addition operator
  Length operator+(Length len)
  {
    int inchTotal = inches+len.inches+inchesPerFoot*(feet+len.feet);
    return Length(inchTotal/inchesPerFoot, inchTotal%inchesPerFoot);
  }
};
```

The constant, `inchesPerFoot`, is `static`, so it will be directly available to static and non-static function members of the class. Declaring `inchesPerFoot` as `initonly` means that it cannot be modified, so it can be a public member of the class. There's a `ToString()` function override defined for the class, so you can write `Length` objects to the command line using the `Console::WriteLine()` function. The `operator+()` function implementation is very simple. The function returns a new `Length` object produced by combining the `feet` and `inches` component for the current object and the parameter, `len`. The calculation is done by combining the two lengths in inches and then computing the arguments to the `Length` class constructor for the new object from the value for the combined lengths in inches.

The following code fragment would exercise the new operator function for addition:

```
Length len1 = Length(6, 9);
Length len2 = Length(7, 8);
Console::WriteLine(L"{0} plus {1} is {2}", len1, len2, len1+len2);
```

The last argument to the WriteLine() function is the sum of two Length objects, so this will invoke the operator+() function. The result will be a new Length object for which the compiler will arrange to call the ToString() function, so the last statement is really the following:

```
Console::WriteLine(L"{0} plus {1} is {2}", len1, len2,
                                       len1.operator+(len2).ToString());
```

The execution of the code fragment will result in the following output:

```
6 feet 9 inches plus 7 feet 8 inches is 14 feet 5 inches
```

Of course, you could define the operator+() function as a static member of the Length class, like this:

```
static Length operator+(Length len1, Length len2)
{
  int inchTotal = len1.inches+len2.inches+inchesPerFoot*(len1.feet+len2.feet);
  return Length(inchTotal/inchesPerFoot, inchTotal%inchesPerFoot);
}
```

The parameters are the two Length objects to be added together to produce a new Length object. Because this is a static member of the class, the operator+() function is fully entitled to access the private members, feet and inches, of both the Length objects passed as arguments. Friend functions are not allowed in C++/CLI classes, and an external function would not have access to private members of the class, so you have no other possibilities for implementing the addition operator.

Because you are not working with areas resulting from the product of two Length objects, it really only makes sense to provide for multiplying a Length object by a numerical value. You can implement multiply operator overloading as a static member of the class, but let's define the function outside the class. The class would look like this:

```
value class Length
{
private:
  int feet;
  int inches;

public:
  static initonly int inchesPerFoot = 12;

  // Constructor
  Length(int ft, int ins) : feet(ft), inches(ins){ }

  // A length as a string
```

```
virtual String^ ToString() override
{
  return feet.ToString() + (1 == feet ? L" foot " : L" feet ") +
         inches + (1 == inches ? L" inch" : L" inches");
}

// Addition operator
Length operator+(Length len)
{
  int inchTotal = inches+len.inches+inchesPerFoot*(feet+len.feet);
  return Length(inchTotal/inchesPerFoot, inchTotal%inchesPerFoot);
}

static Length operator*(double x, Length len); // Pre-multiply by a double value
static Length operator*(Length len, double x); // Post-multiply by a double value
};
```

The new function declarations in the class provide for overloaded * operator functions to pre-
and post-multiply a Length object by a value of type double. The definition of the operator*()
function outside the class for pre-multiplication would be:

```
Length Length::operator *(double x, Length len)
{
  int ins = safe_cast<int>(x*len.inches +x*len.feet*inchesPerFoot);
  return Length(ins/12, ins %12);
}
```

The post-multiplication version can now be implemented in terms of this:

```
Length Length::operator *(Length len, double x)
{ return operator*(x, len);   }
```

This just calls the pre-multiply version with the arguments reversed. You could exercise these
functions with the following fragment:

```
double factor = 2.5;
Console::WriteLine(L"{0} times {1} is {2}", factor, len2, factor*len2);
Console::WriteLine(L"{1} times {0} is {2}", factor, len2, len2*factor);
```

Both lines of output from this code fragment should reflect the same result from
multiplication — 19 feet, 2 inches. The argument expression factor*len2 is equivalent to:

```
Length::operator*(factor, len2).ToString()
```

The result of calling the static operator*() function is a new Length object, and the ToString()
function for that is called to produce the argument to the WriteLine() function. The expression
len2*factor is similar but calls the operator*() function that has the parameters reversed.
Although the operator*() functions have been written to deal with a multiplier of type double,
they will also work with integers. The compiler will automatically promote an integer value to type
double when you use it in an expression such as 12*(len1+len2).

We could expand a little further on overloaded operators in the `Length` class with a working example.

TRY IT OUT   A Value Class with Overloaded Operators

This example implements operator overloading for addition, multiplication, and division for the `Length` class:

```cpp
// Ex8_15.cpp : main project file.
// Overloading operators in the value class, Length
#include "stdafx.h"
using namespace System;

value class Length
{
private:
  int feet;
  int inches;

public:
  static initonly int inchesPerFoot = 12;

  // Constructor
  Length(int ft, int ins) : feet(ft), inches(ins){ }

  // A length as a string
  virtual String^ ToString() override
  {
    return feet.ToString() + (1 == feet ? L" foot " : L" feet ") +
           inches + (1 == inches ? L" inch" : L" inches");
  }

  // Addition operator
  Length operator+(Length len)
  {
    int inchTotal = inches+len.inches+inchesPerFoot*(feet+len.feet);
    return Length(inchTotal/inchesPerFoot, inchTotal%inchesPerFoot);
  }

  // Division operator
  static Length operator/(Length len, double x)
  {
    int ins = safe_cast<int>((len.feet*inchesPerFoot + len.inches)/x);
    return Length(ins/inchesPerFoot, ins%inchesPerFoot);
  }

  static Length operator*(double x, Length len); // Pre-multiply by double value
  static Length operator*(Length len, double x); // Post-multiply by double value
};
Length Length::operator *(double x, Length len)
{
  int ins = safe_cast<int>(x*len.inches +x*len.feet*inchesPerFoot);
  return Length(ins/inchesPerFoot, ins%inchesPerFoot);
}
```

```
Length Length::operator *(Length len, double x)
{ return operator*(x, len);   }


int main(array<System::String ^> ^args)
{
  Length len1 = Length(6, 9);
  Length len2 = Length(7, 8);
  double factor(2.5);

  Console::WriteLine(L"{0} plus {1} is {2}", len1, len2, len1+len2);
  Console::WriteLine(L"{0} times {1} is {2}", factor, len2, factor*len2);
  Console::WriteLine(L"{1} times {0} is {2}", factor, len2, len2*factor);
  Console::WriteLine(L"The sum of {0} and {1} divided by {2} is {3}",
                                  len1, len2, factor, (len1+len2)/factor);


  return 0;
}
```

code snippet Ex8_15.cpp

The output from the example is:

```
6 feet 9 inches plus 7 feet 8 inches is 14 feet 5 inches
2.5 times 7 feet 8 inches is 19 feet 2 inches
7 feet 8 inches times 2.5 is 19 feet 2 inches
The sum of 6 feet 9 inches and 7 feet 8 inches divided by 2.5 is 5 feet 9 inches
```

How It Works

The new operator overloading function in the Length class is for division, and it allows division of a Length value by a value of type double. Dividing a double value by a Length object does not have an obvious meaning, so there's no need to implement this version. The operator/() function is implemented as another static member of the class, and the definition appears within the body of the class definition to contrast how that looks compared with the operator*() functions. You would normally define all these functions inside the class definition.

Of course, you could define the operator/() function as a non-static class member like this:

```
Length operator/(double x)
{
  int ins = safe_cast<int>((feet*inchesPerFoot + inches)/x);
  return Length(ins/inchesPerFoot, ins%inchesPerFoot);
}
```

It now has one argument, which will be the right operand for the / operator. The left operand is the current object that is referenced by the this pointer (implicitly in this case).

The operators are exercised in the four output statements. Only the last one is new to you, and this combines the use of the overloaded + operator for Length objects with the overloaded / operator. The last argument to the `Console::WriteLine()` function in the fourth output statement is `(len1+len2)/factor` which is equivalent to the expression:

```
Length::operator/(len1.operator+(len2), factor) .ToString()
```

The first argument to the static `operator/()` function is the `Length` object that is returned by the `operator+()` function, and the second argument is the `factor` variable, which is the divisor. The `ToString()` function for the `Length` object returned by `operator/()` is called to produce the argument string that is passed to the `Console::WriteLine()` function.

It is possible that you might want the capability to divide one `Length` object by another and have a value of type `int` as the result. This would allow you to figure out how many 17-inch lengths you can cut from a piece of timber 12 feet, 6 inches long, for instance. You can implement this quite easily like this:

```
static int operator/(Length len1, Length len2)
{
  return
  (len1.feet*inchesPerFoot + len1.inches)/( len2.feet*inchesPerFoot + len2.inches);
}
```

This just returns the result of dividing the first length in inches by the second in inches.

To complete the set, you could add a function to overload the `%` operator to tell you how much is left over. This could be implemented as:

```
static Length operator%(Length len1, Length len2)
{
  int ins = (len1.feet*inchesPerFoot + len1.inches)%
                              (len2.feet*inchesPerFoot + len2.inches);
  return Length(ins/inchesPerFoot, ins%inchesPerFoot);
}
```

You compute the residue in inches after dividing `len1` by `len2`, and return it as a new `Length` object.

With all these operators, you really can use your `Length` objects in arithmetic expressions. You can write statements such as:

```
Length len1 = Length(2,6);          // 2 feet 6 inches
Length len2 = Length(3,5);          // 3 feet 5 inches
Length len3 = Length(14,6);         // 14 feet 6 inches
Length total = 12*(len1 + len2 + len3) + (len3/Length(1,7))*len2;
```

The value of `total` will be 275 feet, 9 inches. The last statement makes use of the assignment operator that comes with every value class as well as the `operator*()`, `operator+()`, and `operator/()` functions in the `Length` class. This operator overloading is not only powerful stuff, it really is easy, isn't it?

Overloading the Increment and Decrement Operators

Overloading the increment and decrement operators is simpler in C++/CLI than in native C++. As long as you implement the operator function as a static class member, the same function will serve as both the prefix and postfix operator functions. Here's how you could implement the increment operator for the Length class:

```
value class Length
{
public:
  // Code as before...

  // Overloaded increment operator function - increment by 1 inch
  static Length operator++(Length len)
  {
    ++len.inches;
    len.feet += len.inches/len.inchesPerFoot;
    len.inches %= len.inchesPerFoot;
    return len;
  }
};
```

This implementation of the operator++() function increments a length by 1 inch. The following code would exercise the function:

```
Length len = Length(1, 11);              // 1 foot 11 inches
Console::WriteLine(len++);
Console::WriteLine(++len);
```

Executing this fragment will produce the output:

```
1 foot 11 inches
2 feet 1 inch
```

Thus, the prefix and postfix increment operations are working as they should using a single operator function in the Length class. This occurs because the compiler is able to determine whether to use the value of the operand in a surrounding expression before or after the operand has been incremented, and compile the code accordingly.

Overloading Operators in Reference Classes

Overloading operators in a reference class is essentially the same as overloading operators in a value class, the primary difference being that parameters and return values are typically handles. Let's see how the Length class looks implemented as a reference class, then you'll be able to compare the two versions.

TRY IT OUT   Overloaded Operators in a Reference Class

This example defines `Length` as a reference class with the same set of overloaded operators as the value class version:

```cpp
// Ex8_16.cpp : main project file.
// Defining and using overloaded operator

#include "stdafx.h"
using namespace System;

ref class Length
{
private:
  int feet;
  int inches;

public:
  static initonly int inchesPerFoot = 12;

  // Constructor
  Length(int ft, int ins) : feet(ft), inches(ins){ }

  // A length as a string
  virtual String^ ToString() override
  {
    return feet.ToString() + (1 == feet ? L" foot " : L" feet ") +
           inches + (1 == inches ? L" inch" : L" inches");
  }

  // Overloaded addition operator
  Length^ operator+(Length^ len)
  {
    int inchTotal = inches+len->inches+inchesPerFoot*(feet+len->feet);
    return gcnew Length(inchTotal/inchesPerFoot, inchTotal%inchesPerFoot);
  }

  // Overloaded divide operator - right operand type double
  static Length^ operator/(Length^ len, double x)
  {
    int ins = safe_cast<int>((len->feet*inchesPerFoot + len->inches)/x);
    return gcnew Length(ins/inchesPerFoot, ins%inchesPerFoot);
  }

  // Overloaded divide operator - both operands type Length
  static int operator/(Length^ len1, Length^ len2)
  {
    return (len1->feet*inchesPerFoot + len1->inches)/
                                 (len2->feet*inchesPerFoot + len2->inches);
  }

  // Overloaded remainder operator
  static Length^ operator%(Length^ len1, Length^ len2)
  {
```

```
      int ins = (len1->feet*inchesPerFoot + len1->inches)%
                              (len2->feet*inchesPerFoot + len2->inches);
      return gcnew Length(ins/inchesPerFoot, ins%inchesPerFoot);
  }

  static Length^ operator*(double x, Length^ len); // Multiply - L operand double
  static Length^ operator*(Length^ len, double x); // Multiply - R operand double

  // Pre- and postfix increment operator
  static Length^ operator++(Length^ len)
  {
    Length^ temp = gcnew Length(len->feet, len->inches);
    ++temp->inches;
    temp->feet += temp->inches/temp->inchesPerFoot;
    temp->inches %= temp->inchesPerFoot;
    return temp;
  }
};

// Multiply operator implementation - left operand double
Length^ Length::operator*(double x, Length^ len)
{
  int ins = safe_cast<int>(x*len->inches +x*len->feet*inchesPerFoot);
  return gcnew Length(ins/inchesPerFoot, ins%inchesPerFoot);
}

// Multiply operator implementation - right operand double
Length^ Length::operator*(Length^ len, double x)
{ return operator*(x, len);   }

int main(array<System::String ^> ^args)
{
  Length^ len1 = gcnew Length(2,6);            // 2 feet 6 inches
  Length^ len2 = gcnew Length(3,5);            // 3 feet 5 inches
  Length^ len3 = gcnew Length(14,6);           // 14 feet 6 inches

  // Use +, * and / operators
  Length^ total = 12*(len1+len2+len3) + (len3/gcnew Length(1,7))*len2;
  Console::WriteLine(total);

  // Use remainder operator
  Console::WriteLine(
            L"{0} can be cut into {1} pieces {2} long with {3} left over.",
                                    len3, len3/len1, len1, len3%len1);
  Length^ len4 = gcnew Length(1, 11);          // 1 foot 11 inches

  // Use pre- and postfix increment operator
  Console::WriteLine(len4++);                  // Use postfix increment operator
  Console::WriteLine(++len4);                  // Use prefix increment operator
  Console::WriteLine(len4);                    // Final value of len4
  return 0;
}
```

code snippet Ex8_16.cpp

This example will produce the following output:

```
275 feet 9 inches
14 feet 6 inches can be cut into 5 pieces 2 feet 6 inches long
with 2 feet 0 inches left over.
1 foot 11 inches
2 feet 1 inch
2 feet 1 inch
```

How It Works

Compared to a value class, there are differences in the parameter and return types for the overloaded operator functions, the use of the -> operator as a consequence of that, and objects of type Length are now created on the CLR heap using the gcnew keyword. In addition, the overloaded increment operator function returns a temporary object and does not modify the original object using the reference argument.

It is important that you do not modify the original object when you are overloading the increment or decrement operator in a reference class, because the code that the compiler generates relies on the object that is passed to the overload function being left unchanged. When the function is called for a postfix increment or decrement operation, the code that is generated uses the object in the expression in which it appears, and then stores the object that you return to replace the original. Apart from these changes, the code is basically the same and the operator functions work just as effectively as in the previous example.

Implementing the Assignment Operator for Reference Types

There are relatively few circumstances where you will need to implement the assignment operator for a reference type because you will typically use handles to refer to objects, and the need for a copy constructor does not arise. However, if you use the Standard Template Library for the CLR that you will meet in Chapter 10, in some situations, you will need to implement the assignment operator, and the compiler will never supply one by default. The form of the function to overload the assignment operator in a reference class is very simple, and is easily understood if you look at an example. Here's how the assignment operator would look for the Length class, for instance:

```
Length% operator=(const Length% len)
{
  if(this != %len)
  {
    feet = len.feet;
    inches = len.inches;
  }
  return *this;
}
```

The function parameter is const because it will not be changed, and if you don't declare it as const, the argument will be passed by value and will cause the copy constructor to be called.

The return type is also a reference because you always return the object pointed to by `this`. The `if` statement checks whether or not the argument and the current object are identical, and if they are, the function just returns `*this`, which will be the current object. If they are not, you copy each of the data members of `len` to the current object before returning it.

SUMMARY

In this chapter, you have learned the basics of how you can define classes and how you create and use class objects. You have also learned about how you can overload operators in a class to allow the operators to be applied to class objects.

EXERCISES

1. Define a native C++ class to represent an estimated integer, such as "about 40." These are integers whose value may be regarded as exact or estimated, so the class needs to have as data members a value and an "estimation" flag. The state of the estimation flag affects arithmetic operations, so that "2 * about 40" is "about 80." The state of variables should be switchable between "estimated" and "exact."

   Provide one or more constructors for such a class. Overload the + operator so that these integers can be used in arithmetic expressions. Do you want the + operator to be a global or a member function? Do you need an assignment operator? Provide a `Print()` member function so that they can be printed out, using a leading "E" to denote that the "estimation" flag is set. Write a program to test the operation of your class, checking especially that the operation of the estimation flag is correct.

2. Implement a simple string class in native C++ that holds a `char*` and an integer length as `private` data members. Provide a constructor that takes an argument of type `const char*`, and implement the copy constructor, assignment operator, and destructor functions. Verify that your class works. You will find it easiest to use the string functions from the `cstring` header file.

3. What other constructors might you want to supply for your string class? Make a list, and code them up.

4. (Advanced) Does your class correctly deal with cases such as this?

   ```
   string s1;
   ...
   s1 = s1;
   ```

   If not, how should it be modified?

5. (Advanced) Overload the + and += operators of your class for concatenating strings.

6. Modify the stack example from Exercise 7 in the previous chapter so that the size of the stack is specified in the constructor and dynamically allocated. What else will you need to add? Test the operation of your new class.

7. Define a `Box` ref class with the same functionality as the `CBox` class in Ex8_10.cpp, and reimplement the example as a program for the CLR.

8. This exercise might be of use to someone working with sensitive documents. Write a native C++ program that uses the `string` class that is declared in the `string` header to read a text string of arbitrary length from the keyboard. The program should then prompt for entry of one or more words that appear in the input text. All occurrences of the chosen words in the input text, regardless of case, should be replaced, with as many asterisks as there are letters in the word. Only whole words should be replaced, so if the string is `"Our friend Wendy is at the end of the road."` and the chosen word is `"end"`, the result should be `"Our friend Wendy is at the *** of the road."`, not `"Our fri*** W***y is at the *** of the road."`.

9. Write a class called `CTrace` that you can use to show at run time when code blocks have been entered and exited, by producing output like this:

```
function 'f1' entry
'if' block entry
'if' block exit
function 'f1' exit
```

10. Can you think of a way to automatically control the indentation in the last exercise so that the output looks like this?

```
function 'f1' entry
 'if' block entry
 'if' block exit
function 'f1' exit
```

▶ **WHAT YOU LEARNED IN THIS CHAPTER**

TOPIC	CONCEPT
Destructors	Objects are destroyed using functions called **destructors**. It is essential to define a destructor in native C++ classes to destroy objects which contain members that are allocated on the heap, because the default constructor will not do this.
The default copy constructor	The compiler will supply a default copy constructor for a native C++ class if you do not define one. The default copy constructor will not deal correctly with objects of classes that have data members allocated on the free store.
Defining a copy constructor	When you define your own copy constructor in a native C++ class, you must use a reference parameter.
The copy constructor in value classes	You must not define a copy constructor in value classes; copies of value class objects are always created by copying fields.
The copy constructor in reference classes	No default copy constructor is supplied for a reference class, although you can define your own when this is necessary.
The assignment operator in native C++ classes	If you do not define an assignment operator for your native C++ class, the compiler will supply a default version. As with the copy constructor, the default assignment operator will not work correctly with classes that have data members allocated on the free store.
The assignment operator in value classes	You must not define the assignment operator in a value class. Assignment of value class objects is always done by copying fields.
The assignment operator in reference classes	A default assignment operator is not provided for reference classes, but you can define your own assignment operator function when necessary.
Native C++ classes that allocate memory on the heap.	It is essential that you provide a destructor, a copy constructor, and an assignment operator for native C++ classes that have members allocated by `new`.
Unions	A union is a mechanism that allows two or more variables to occupy the same location in memory.
Fields in C++/CLI classes	C++/CLI classes can contain **literal fields** that define constants within a class. They can also contain **initonly fields** that cannot be modified once they have been initialized.
Operator overloading	Most basic operators can be overloaded to provide actions specific to objects of a class. You should only implement operator functions for your classes that are consistent with the normal interpretation of the basic operators.

TOPIC	CONCEPT
The `string` class	The `string` class in the standard library for native C++ provides a powerful and superior way to process strings in your programs.
Class templates	A class template is a pattern that you can use to create classes with the same structure, but which support different data types.
Class template parameters	You can define a class template that has multiple parameters, including parameters that can assume constant values rather than types.
Organizing your code	You should put definitions for your programs in `.h` files, and executable code — function definitions — in `.cpp` files. You can then incorporate `.h` files into your `.cpp` files by using `#include` directives.

Class Inheritance
and Virtual Functions

In this chapter, you're going to look into a topic that lies at the heart of object-oriented programming (OOP): **class inheritance**. Simply put, inheritance is the means by which you can define a new class in terms of one you already have. This is fundamental to programming in C++, so it's important that you understand how inheritance works.

OBJECT-ORIENTED PROGRAMMING BASICS

As you have seen, a class is a data type that you define to suit your own application requirements. Classes in OOP also define the objects to which your program relates. You program the solution to a problem in terms of the objects that are specific to the problem, using operations that work directly with those objects. You can define a class to represent something abstract, such as a complex number, which is a mathematical concept, or a truck, which is decidedly physical (especially if you run into one on the highway). So, as well as being a data type, a class can also be a definition of a set of real-world objects of a particular kind, at least to the degree necessary to solve a given problem.

You can think of a class as defining the characteristics of a particular group of things that are specified by a common set of parameters and share a common set of operations that may be performed on them. The operations that you can apply to objects of a given class type are defined by the class interface, which corresponds to the functions contained in the public section of the class definition. The CBox class that you used in the previous chapter is a good example — it defined a box in terms of its dimensions plus a set of public functions that you could apply to CBox objects to solve a problem.

Of course, there are many different kinds of boxes in the real world: there are cartons, coffins, candy boxes, and cereal boxes, to name but a few, and you will certainly be able to come up with many others. You can differentiate boxes by the kinds of things they hold, the materials from which they are made, and in a multitude of other ways, but even though there are many different kinds of boxes, they share some common characteristics — the essence of *boxiness*, perhaps. Therefore, you can still visualize all kinds of boxes as actually being related to one another, even though they have many differentiating features. You could define a particular kind of box as having the generic characteristics of all boxes — perhaps just a length, a width, and a height. You could then add some additional characteristics to the basic box type to differentiate a particular kind of box from the rest. You may also find that there are new things you can do with your specific kind of box that you can't do with other boxes.

It's also possible that some objects may be the result of combining a particular kind of box with some other type of object: a box of candy or a crate of beer, for example. To accommodate this, you could define one kind of box as a generic box with basic "boxiness" characteristics and then specify another sort of box as a further specialization of that. Figure 9-1 illustrates an example of the kinds of relationships you might define between different sorts of boxes.

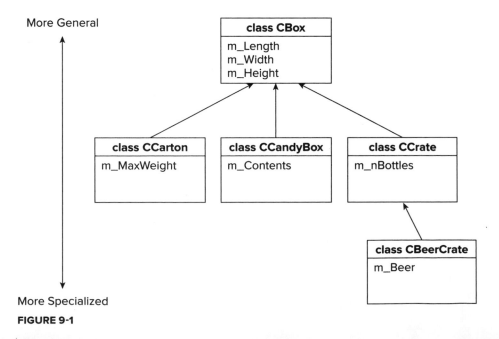

FIGURE 9-1

The boxes become more specialized as you move down the diagram, and the arrows run from a given box type to the one on which it is based. Figure 9-1 defines three different kinds of boxes based on the generic type, CBox. It also defines beer crates as a further refinement of crates designed to hold bottles.

Thus, a good way to approximate the real world relatively well using classes in C++ is through the ability to define classes that are interrelated. A candy box can be considered to be a box with all the characteristics of a basic box, plus a few characteristics of its own. This precisely illustrates the relationship between classes in C++ when one class is defined based on another. A more specialized class has all the characteristics of the class on which it is based, plus a few characteristics of its own that identify what makes it special. Let's look at how this works in practice.

INHERITANCE IN CLASSES

When you define one class based on an existing class, the new class is referred to as a **derived class**. A derived class automatically contains all the data members of the class that you used to define it and, with some restrictions, the function members as well. The class is said to **inherit** the data members and function members of the class on which it is based.

The only members of a base class that are not inherited by a derived class are the destructor, the constructors, and any member functions overloading the assignment operator. All other function members, together with all the data members of a base class, are inherited by a derived class. Of course, the reason for certain base members not being inherited is that a derived class always has its own constructors and destructor. If the base class has an assignment operator, the derived class provides its own version. When I say these functions are not inherited, I mean that they don't exist as members of a derived class object. However, they still exist for the base class part of an object, as you will see.

What Is a Base Class?

A **base class** is any class that you use as a basis for defining another class. For example, if you define a class, B, directly in terms of a class, A, A is said to be a **direct base class** of B. In Figure 9-1, the CCrate class is a direct base class of CBeerCrate. When a class such as CBeerCrate is defined in terms of another class, CCrate, CBeerCrate is said to be derived from CCrate. Because CCrate is itself defined in terms of the class CBox, CBox is said to be an **indirect base class** of CBeerCrate. You'll see how this is expressed in the class definition in a moment. Figure 9-2 illustrates the way in which base class members are inherited in a derived class.

FIGURE 9-2

Just because member functions are inherited doesn't mean that you won't want to replace them in the derived class with new versions, and, of course, you can do that when necessary.

Deriving Classes from a Base Class

Let's go back to the original CBox class with `public` data members that you saw at the beginning of the previous chapter:

```
// Header file Box.h in project Ex9_01
#pragma once

class CBox
{
  public:
    double m_Length;
    double m_Width;
    double m_Height;

    CBox(double lv = 1.0, double wv = 1.0, double hv = 1.0):
                          m_Length(lv), m_Width(wv), m_Height(hv){}
};
```

Create a new empty WIN32 console project with the name Ex9_01 and save this code in a new header file in the project with the name Box.h. The #pragma once directive ensures the definition of CBox appears only once in a build. There's a constructor in the class so that you can initialize objects when you declare them. Suppose you now need another class of objects, CCandyBox, that are the same as CBox objects but also have another data member — a pointer to a text string — that identifies the contents of the box.

You can define CCandyBox as a derived class with the CBox class as the base class, as follows:

```
// Header file CandyBox.h in project Ex9_01
#pragma once
#include "Box.h"
class CCandyBox: CBox
{
  public:
    char* m_Contents;

    CCandyBox(char* str = "Candy")                  // Constructor
    {
      m_Contents = new char[ strlen(str) + 1 ];
      strcpy_s(m_Contents, strlen(str) + 1, str);
    }

    ~CCandyBox()                                    // Destructor
    { delete[] m_Contents; };
};
```

Add this header file to the project Ex9_01. You need the #include directive for the Box.h header file because you refer to the CBox class in the code. If you were to leave this directive out, CBox would be unknown to the compiler, so the code would not compile. The base class name, CBox, appears after the name of the derived class, CCandyBox, and is separated from it by a colon. In all other respects, it looks like a normal class definition. You have added the new member, m_Contents, and, because it is a pointer to a string, you need a constructor to initialize it and a destructor to release the memory for the string. You have also put a default value for the string describing the contents of a CCandyBox object in the constructor. Objects of the CCandyBox class type contain all the members of the base class, CBox, plus the additional data member, m_Contents.

Note the use of the strcpy_s() function that you first saw in Chapter 6. Here, there are three arguments — the destination for the copy operation, the length of the destination buffer, and the source. If both arrays were static — that is, not allocated on the heap — you could omit the second argument and just supply the destination and source pointers. This is possible because the strcpy_s() function is also available as a template function that can infer the length of the destination string automatically. You can therefore call the function just with the destination and source strings as arguments when you are working with static strings.

TRY IT OUT   Using a Derived Class

Now, you'll see how the derived class works in an example. Add the following code to the Ex9_01 project as the source file Ex9_01.cpp:

```cpp
// Ex9_01.cpp
// Using a derived class
#include <iostream>                     // For stream I/O
#include <cstring>                      // For strlen() and strcpy()
#include "CandyBox.h"                   // For CBox and CCandyBox
using std::cout;
using std::endl;

int main()
{
  CBox myBox(4.0, 3.0, 2.0);                     // Create CBox object
  CCandyBox myCandyBox;
  CCandyBox myMintBox("Wafer Thin Mints");       // Create CCandyBox object

  cout << endl
       << "myBox occupies " << sizeof myBox      // Show how much memory
       << " bytes" << endl                       // the objects require
       << "myCandyBox occupies " << sizeof myCandyBox
       << " bytes" << endl
       << "myMintBox occupies " << sizeof myMintBox
       << " bytes";

  cout << endl
       << "myBox length is " << myBox.m_Length;

  myBox.m_Length = 10.0;

  // myCandyBox.m_Length = 10.0;         // uncomment this for an error
```

```
    cout << endl;
    return 0;
}
```

code snippet Ex9_01.cpp

How It Works

You have a `#include` directive for the `CandyBox.h` header here, and because you know that that contains a `#include` directive for `Box.h`, you don't need to add a directive to include `Box.h`. You could put a `#include` directive for `Box.h` in this file, in which case, the `#pragma once` directive in `Box.h` would prevent its inclusion more than once. This is important because each class can only be defined once; two definitions for a class in the code would be an error.

After declaring a `CBox` object and two `CCandyBox` objects, you output the number of bytes that each object occupies. Let's look at the output:

```
myBox occupies 24 bytes
myCandyBox occupies 32 bytes
myMintBox occupies 32 bytes
myBox length is 4
```

The first line is what you would expect from the discussion in the previous chapter. A `CBox` object has three data members of type `double`, each of which is 8 bytes, making 24 bytes in all. Both the `CCandyBox` objects are the same size — 32 bytes. The length of the string doesn't affect the size of an object, as the memory to hold the string is allocated in the free store. The 32 bytes are made up of 24 bytes for the three `double` members inherited from the base class `CBox`, plus 4 bytes for the pointer member `m_Contents`, which makes 28 bytes. So, where did the other 4 bytes come from? This is due to the compiler aligning members at addresses that are multiples of 8 bytes. You should be able to demonstrate this by adding an extra member of type `int`, say, to the class `CCandyBox`. You will find that the size of a class object is still 32 bytes.

You also output the value of the `m_Length` member of the `CBox` object, `myBox`. Even though you have no difficulty accessing this member of the `CBox` object, if you uncomment the following statement in the function `main()`,

```
// myCandyBox.m_Length = 10.0;      // uncomment this for an error
```

the program no longer compiles. The compiler generates the following message:

```
error C2247: 'CBox::m_Length' not accessible because 'CCandyBox'
uses 'private' to inherit from 'CBox'
```

It says quite clearly that the `m_Length` member from the base class is not accessible because `m_Length` has become `private` in the derived class. This is because there is a default access specifier of `private` for a base class when you define a derived class — it's as if the first line of the derived class definition had been:

```
class CCandyBox: private CBox
```

There always has to be an access specification for a base class that determines the status of the inherited members in the derived class. If you omit the access specification for a base class, the compiler assumes that it's `private`. If you change the definition of the CCandyBox class in CandyBox.h to the following,

```
class CCandyBox: public CBox
{
  public:
    char* m_Contents;

    CCandyBox(char* str = "Candy")                    // Constructor
    {
      m_Contents = new char[ strlen(str) + 1 ];
      strcpy_s(m_Contents, strlen(str) + 1, str);
    }

    ~CCandyBox()                                       // Destructor
    { delete[] m_Contents; };
};
```

the m_Length member is inherited in the derived class as `public`, and is accessible in the function main(). With the access specifier `public` for the base class, all the inherited members originally specified as `public` in the base class have the same access level in the derived class.

ACCESS CONTROL UNDER INHERITANCE

The access to inherited members in a derived class needs to be looked at more closely. Consider the status of the `private` members of a base class in a derived class.

There was a good reason to choose the version of the class CBox with `public` data members in the previous example, rather than the later, more secure version with `private` data members. The reason was that although `private` data members of a base class are also members of a derived class, they remain `private` to the base class in the derived class, so member functions added to the derived class cannot access them. They are only accessible in the derived class through function members of the base class that are not in the `private` section of the base class. You can demonstrate this very easily by changing all the CBox class data members to `private` and putting a Volume() function in the derived class CCandyBox, so that the class definition is as follows:

```
// Version of the classes that will not compile
class CBox
{
  public:
    CBox(double lv = 1.0, double wv = 1.0, double hv = 1.0):
    m_Length(lv), m_Width(wv), m_Height(hv){}

  private:
    double m_Length;
    double m_Width;
```

```
      double m_Height;
};

class CCandyBox: public CBox
{
  public:
    char* m_Contents;

    // Function to calculate the volume of a CCandyBox object
    double Volume() const            // Error - members not accessible
    { return m_Length*m_Width*m_Height; }

    CCandyBox(char* str = "Candy")      // Constructor
    {
      m_Contents = new char[ strlen(str) + 1 ];
      strcpy_s(m_Contents, strlen(str) + 1, str);
    }

    ~CCandyBox()                        // Destructor
    { delete[] m_Contents; }
};
```

A program using these classes does not compile. The function `Volume()` in the class `CCandyBox` attempts to access the `private` members of the base class, which is not legal, so the compiler will flag each instance with error number C2248.

TRY IT OUT Accessing Private Members of the Base Class

It is, however, legal to use the `Volume()` function in the base class, so if you move the definition of the function `Volume()` to the `public` section of the base class, `CBox`, not only will the program compile, but you can use the function to obtain the volume of a `CCandyBox` object. Create a new WIN32 project, `Ex9_02`, with the `Box.h` contents as the following:

```
// Box.h in Ex9_02
#pragma once

class CBox
{
  public:
    CBox(double lv = 1.0, double wv = 1.0, double hv = 1.0):
                          m_Length(lv), m_Width(wv), m_Height(hv){}

    //Function to calculate the volume of a CBox object
    double Volume() const
    { return m_Length*m_Width*m_Height; }

  private:
    double m_Length;
    double m_Width;
    double m_Height;
};
```

The `CandyBox.h` header in the project contains:

```
// Header file CandyBox.h in project Ex9_02
#pragma once
#include "Box.h"
class CCandyBox: public CBox
{
  public:
    char* m_Contents;

    CCandyBox(char* str = "Candy")                 // Constructor
    {
      m_Contents = new char[ strlen(str) + 1 ];
      strcpy_s(m_Contents, strlen(str) + 1, str);
    }

    ~CCandyBox()                                   // Destructor
    { delete[] m_Contents; };
};
```

The Ex9_02.cpp file in the project contains:

Available for
download on
Wrox.com

```
// Ex9_02.cpp
// Using a function inherited from a base class
#include <iostream>                      // For stream I/O
#include <cstring>                       // For strlen() and strcpy()
#include "CandyBox.h"                    // For CBox and CCandyBox
using std::cout;
using std::endl;

int main()
{
  CBox myBox(4.0,3.0,2.0);                          // Create CBox object
  CCandyBox myCandyBox;
  CCandyBox myMintBox("Wafer Thin Mints");          // Create CCandyBox object

  cout << endl
       << "myBox occupies " << sizeof  myBox      // Show how much memory
       << " bytes" << endl                        // the objects require
       << "myCandyBox occupies " << sizeof myCandyBox
       << " bytes" << endl
       << "myMintBox occupies " << sizeof myMintBox
       << " bytes";
  cout << endl
       << "myMintBox volume is " << myMintBox.Volume(); // Get volume of a
                                                        // CCandyBox object
  cout << endl;
  return 0;
}
```

code snippet Ex9_02.cpp

This example produces the following output:

```
myBox occupies 24 bytes
myCandyBox occupies 32 bytes
```

```
myMintBox occupies 32 bytes
myMintBox volume is 1
```

How It Works

The interesting additional output is the last line. This shows the value produced by the function Volume(), which is now in the public section of the base class. Within the derived class, it operates on the members of the derived class that are inherited from the base. It is a full member of the derived class, so it can be used freely with objects of the derived class.

The value for the volume of the derived class object is 1 because, in creating the CCandyBox object, the CBox() default constructor was called first to create the base class part of the object, and this sets default CBox dimensions to 1.

Constructor Operation in a Derived Class

Although I said the base class constructors are not inherited in a derived class, they still exist in the base class and are used for creating the base part of a derived class object. This is because creating the base class part of a derived class object is really the business of a base class constructor, not the derived class constructor. After all, you have seen that private members of a base class are inaccessible in a derived class object, even though they are inherited, so responsibility for these has to lie with the base class constructors.

The default base class constructor was called automatically in the last example to create the base part of the derived class object, but this doesn't have to be the case. You can arrange to call a particular base class constructor from the derived class constructor. This enables you to initialize the base class data members with a constructor other than the default, or, indeed, to choose to call a particular class constructor, depending on the data supplied to the derived class constructor.

TRY IT OUT **Calling Constructors**

You can see this in action through a modified version of the previous example. To make the class usable, you really need to provide a constructor for the derived class that allows you to specify the dimensions of the object. You can add an additional constructor in the derived class to do this, and call the base class constructor explicitly to set the values of the data members that are inherited from the base class.

In the Ex9_03 project, Box.h contains:

```
// Box.h in Ex9_03
#pragma once
#include <iostream>
using std::cout;
using std::endl;

class CBox
{
  public:
    // Base class constructor
```

```
        CBox(double lv = 1.0, double wv = 1.0, double hv = 1.0):
                            m_Length(lv), m_Width(wv), m_Height(hv)
        { cout << endl << "CBox constructor called"; }

        //Function to calculate the volume of a CBox object
        double Volume() const
        { return m_Length*m_Width*m_Height; }

    private:
        double m_Length;
        double m_Width;
        double m_Height;
};
```

The CandyBox.h header file should contain:

```
// CandyBox.h in Ex9_03
#pragma once
#include <iostream>
#include "Box.h"
using std::cout;
using std::endl;

class CCandyBox: public CBox
{
  public:
    char* m_Contents;

    // Constructor to set dimensions and contents
    // with explicit call of CBox constructor
    CCandyBox(double lv, double wv, double hv, char* str = "Candy")
                                                :CBox(lv, wv, hv)
    {
      cout << endl <<"CCandyBox constructor2 called";
      m_Contents = new char[ strlen(str) + 1 ];
      strcpy_s(m_Contents, strlen(str) + 1, str);
    }

    // Constructor to set contents
    // calls default CBox constructor automatically
    CCandyBox(char* str = "Candy")
    {
      cout << endl << "CCandyBox constructor1 called";
      m_Contents = new char[ strlen(str) + 1 ];
      strcpy_s(m_Contents, strlen(str) + 1, str);
    }

    ~CCandyBox()                                // Destructor
    { delete[] m_Contents; }
};
```

The #include directive for the <iostream> header and the two using declarations are not strictly necessary here because Box.h contains the same code, but it does no harm to put them in. On the contrary, putting these statements in here also means that if you were to remove this code from `Box.h` because it was no longer required there, `CandyBox.h` would still compile.

The contents of `Ex9_03.cpp` are:

```cpp
// Ex9_03.cpp
// Calling a base constructor from a derived class constructor
#include <iostream>                    // For stream I/O
#include <cstring>                     // For strlen() and strcpy()
#include "CandyBox.h"                  // For CBox and CCandyBox
using std::cout;
using std::endl;

int main()
{
  CBox myBox(4.0, 3.0, 2.0);
  CCandyBox myCandyBox;
  CCandyBox myMintBox(1.0, 2.0, 3.0, "Wafer Thin Mints");

  cout << endl
       << "myBox occupies " << sizeof  myBox      // Show how much memory
       << " bytes" << endl                        // the objects require
       << "myCandyBox occupies " << sizeof myCandyBox
       << " bytes" << endl
       << "myMintBox occupies " << sizeof myMintBox
       << " bytes";
  cout << endl
       << "myMintBox volume is "                   // Get volume of a
       << myMintBox.Volume();                      // CCandyBox object
  cout << endl;
  return 0;
}
```

code snippet Ex9_03.cpp

How It Works

As well as adding the additional constructor in the derived class, you have added an output statement in each constructor so you know when either gets called. The explicit call of the constructor for the CBox class appears after a colon in the function header of the derived class constructor. You have, perhaps, noticed that the notation is exactly the same as what you have been using for initializing members in a constructor, anyway:

```cpp
// Calling the base class constructor
CCandyBox(double lv, double wv, double hv, char* str= "Candy"):
                                             CBox(lv, wv, hv)
{
...
}
```

This is perfectly consistent with what you are doing here, because you are essentially initializing a CBox sub-object of the derived class object. In the first case, you are explicitly calling the default constructor for the `double` members `m_Length`, `m_Width`, and `m_Height` in the initialization list. In the second instance, you are calling the constructor for `CBox`. This causes the specific `CBox` constructor you have chosen to be called before the `CCandyBox` constructor is executed.

If you build and run this example, it produces the following output:

```
CBox constructor called
CBox constructor called
CCandyBox constructor1 called
CBox constructor called
CCandyBox constructor2 called
myBox occupies 24 bytes
myCandyBox occupies 32 bytes
myMintBox occupies 32 bytes
myMintBox volume is 6
```

The calls to the constructors are explained in the following table:

SCREEN OUTPUT	OBJECT BEING CONSTRUCTED
`CBox` constructor called	`myBox`
`CBox` constructor called	`myCandyBox`
`CCandyBox` constructor1 called	`myCandyBox`
`CBox` constructor called	`myMintBox`
`CCandyBox` constructor2 called	`myMintBox`

The first line of output is due to the `CBox` class constructor call, originating from the declaration of the `CBox` object, `myBox`. The second line of output arises from the automatic call of the base class constructor caused by the declaration of the `CCandyBox` object, `myCandyBox`.

Notice how the base class constructor is always called before the derived class constructor. The base class is the foundation on which the derived class is built, so the base class must be created first.

The following line is due to your version of the default derived class constructor being called for the `myCandyBox` object. This constructor is invoked because the object is not initialized. The fourth line of output arises from the explicit identification of the `CBox` class constructor to be called in our new constructor for `CCandyBox` objects. The argument values specified for the dimensions of the `CCandyBox` object are passed to the base class constructor. Next comes the output from the new derived class constructor itself, so constructors are again called for the base class first, followed by the derived class.

It should be clear from what you have seen up to now that when a derived class constructor is executed, a base class constructor is always called to construct the base part of the derived class object. If you don't specify the base class constructor to be used, the compiler arranges for the default base class constructor to be called.

The last line in the table shows that the initialization of the base part of the `myMintBox` object is working as it should be, with the `private` members having been initialized by the `CBox` class constructor.

Having the `private` members of a base class only accessible to function members of the base class isn't always convenient. There will be many instances where you want to have `private` members of a base class that *can* be accessed from within the derived class. As you surely have anticipated by now, C++ provides a way to do this.

Declaring Protected Class Members

In addition to the `public` and `private` access specifiers for members of a class, you can also declare members of a class as `protected`. Within the class, the `protected` keyword has the same effect as the `private` keyword: members of a class that are `protected` can only be accessed by member functions of the class, and by `friend` functions of the class (also by member functions of a class that is declared as a `friend` of the class — you will learn about `friend` classes later in this chapter). Using the `protected` keyword, you could redefine the CBox class as follows:

```
// Box.h in Ex9_04
#pragma once
#include <iostream>
using std::cout;
using std::endl;

class CBox
{
  public:
    // Base class constructor
    CBox(double lv = 1.0, double wv = 1.0, double hv = 1.0):
                       m_Length(lv), m_Width(wv), m_Height(hv)
    {  cout << endl << "CBox constructor called";  }

    // CBox destructor - just to track calls
    ~CBox()
    { cout << "CBox destructor called" << endl; }

  protected:
    double m_Length;
    double m_Width;
    double m_Height;
};
```

Now, the data members are still effectively `private`, in that they can't be accessed by ordinary global functions, but they'll still be accessible to member functions of a derived class.

TRY IT OUT   **Using Protected Members**

You can demonstrate the use of `protected` data members by using this version of the class CBox to derive a new version of the class CCandyBox, which accesses the members of the base class through its own member function, Volume():

```
// CandyBox.h in Ex9_04
#pragma once
#include "Box.h"
#include <iostream>
using std::cout;
using std::endl;

class CCandyBox: public CBox
{
  public:
    char* m_Contents;

    // Derived class function to calculate volume
    double Volume() const
    { return m_Length*m_Width*m_Height; }

    // Constructor to set dimensions and contents
    // with explicit call of CBox constructor
    CCandyBox(double lv, double wv, double hv, char* str = "Candy")
                                    :CBox(lv, wv, hv)  // Constructor
    {
      cout << endl <<"CCandyBox constructor2 called";
      m_Contents = new char[ strlen(str) + 1 ];
      strcpy_s(m_Contents, strlen(str) + 1, str);
    }

    // Constructor to set contents
    // calls default CBox constructor automatically
    CCandyBox(char* str = "Candy")                   // Constructor
    {
      cout << endl << "CCandyBox constructor1 called";
      m_Contents = new char[ strlen(str) + 1 ];
      strcpy_s(m_Contents, strlen(str) + 1, str);
    }

    ~CCandyBox()                                     // Destructor
    {
      cout << "CCandyBox destructor called" << endl;
      delete[] m_Contents;
    }
};
```

The code for main() in Ex9_04.cpp is:

```
// Ex9_04.cpp
// Using the protected access specifier
#include <iostream>                    // For stream I/O
#include <cstring>                     // For strlen() and strcpy()
#include "CandyBox.h"                  // For CBox and CCandyBox
using std::cout;
using std::endl;

int main()
{
  CCandyBox myCandyBox;
```

```
      CCandyBox myToffeeBox(2, 3, 4, "Stickjaw Toffee");

   cout << endl
         << "myCandyBox volume is " << myCandyBox.Volume()
         << endl
         << "myToffeeBox volume is " << myToffeeBox.Volume();

   // cout << endl << myToffeeBox.m_Length;   // Uncomment this for an error

   cout << endl;
   return 0;
 }
```

code snippet Ex9_04.cpp

How It Works

In this example, you calculate the volumes of the two `CCandyBox` objects by invoking the `Volume()` function that is a member of the derived class. This function accesses the inherited members `m_Length`, `m_Width`, and `m_Height` to produce the result. The members are declared as `protected` in the base class and remain `protected` in the derived class. The program produces the output shown as follows:

```
CBox constructor called
CCandyBox constructor1 called
CBox constructor called
CCandyBox constructor2 called
myCandyBox volume is 1
myToffeeBox volume is 24
CCandyBox destructor called
CBox destructor called
CCandyBox destructor called
CBox destructor called
```

The output shows that the volume is being calculated properly for both `CCandyBox` objects. The first object has the default dimensions produced by calling the default `CBox` constructor, so the volume is 1, and the second object has the dimensions defined as initial values in its declaration.

The output also shows the sequence of constructor and destructor calls, and you can see how each derived class object is destroyed in two steps.

Destructors for a derived class object are called in the reverse order of the constructors for the object. This is a general rule that always applies. Constructors are invoked starting with the base class constructor and then the derived class constructor, whereas the destructor for the derived class is called first when an object is destroyed, followed by the base class destructor.

You can demonstrate that the `protected` members of the base class remain `protected` in the derived class by uncommenting the statement preceding the `return` statement in the function `main()`. If you do this, you get the following error message from the compiler,

```
error C2248: 'm_Length': cannot access protected member declared in class 'CBox'
```

which indicates quite clearly that the member `m_Length` is inaccessible.

The Access Level of Inherited Class Members

You know that if you have no access specifier for the base class in the definition of a derived class, the default specification is private. This has the effect of causing the inherited public and protected members of the base class to become private in the derived class. The private members of the base class remain private to the base and, therefore, inaccessible to member functions of the derived class. In fact, they remain private to the base class regardless of how the base class is specified in the derived class definition.

You have also used public as the specifier for a base class. This leaves the members of the base class with the same access level in the derived class as they had in the base, so public members remain public and protected members remain protected.

The last possibility is that you declare a base class as protected. This has the effect of making the inherited public members of the base protected in the derived class. The protected (and private) inherited members retain their original access level in the derived class. This is summarized in Figure 9-3.

FIGURE 9-3

This may look a little complicated, but you can reduce it to the following three points about the inherited members of a derived class:

➤ Members of a base class that are declared as `private` are never accessible in a derived class.

➤ Defining a base class as `public` doesn't change the access level of its members in the derived class.

➤ Defining a base class as `protected` changes its `public` members to `protected` in the derived class.

Being able to change the access level of inherited members in a derived class gives you a degree of flexibility, but don't forget that you cannot relax the level specified in the base class; you can only make the access level more stringent. This suggests that your base classes need to have `public` members if you want to be able to vary the access level in derived classes. This may seem to run contrary to the idea of encapsulating data in a class in order to protect it from unauthorized access, but, as you'll see, it is often the case that you define base classes in such a manner that their only purpose is to act as a base for other classes, and they aren't intended to be used for instantiating objects in their own right.

THE COPY CONSTRUCTOR IN A DERIVED CLASS

Remember that the copy constructor is called automatically when you declare an object that is initialized with an object of the same class. Look at these statements:

```
CBox myBox(2.0, 3.0, 4.0);          // Calls constructor
CBox copyBox(myBox);                // Calls copy constructor
```

The first statement calls the constructor that accepts three arguments of type `double`, and the second calls the copy constructor. If you don't supply your own copy constructor, the compiler supplies one that copies the initializing object, member by member, to the corresponding members of the new object. So that you can see what is going on during execution, you can add your own version of a copy constructor to the class `CBox`. You can then use this class as a base for defining the `CCandyBox` class:

```
// Box.h in Ex9_05
#pragma once
#include <iostream>
using std::cout;
using std::endl;

class CBox                    // Base class definition
{
  public:
    // Base class constructor
    CBox(double lv = 1.0, double wv = 1.0, double hv = 1.0):
                    m_Length(lv), m_Width(wv), m_Height(hv)
    {  cout << endl << "CBox constructor called";  }

    // Copy constructor
    CBox(const CBox& initB)
    {
```

```
            cout << endl << "CBox copy constructor called";
            m_Length = initB.m_Length;
            m_Width = initB.m_Width;
            m_Height = initB.m_Height;
        }

        // CBox destructor - just to track calls
        ~CBox()
        { cout << "CBox destructor called" << endl; }

    protected:
        double m_Length;
        double m_Width;
        double m_Height;
};
```

Also recall that the copy constructor must have its parameter specified as a reference to avoid an infinite number of calls to itself, which would otherwise result from the need to copy an argument that is transferred by value. When the copy constructor in our example is invoked, it outputs a message to the screen, so you'll be able to see from the output when this is happening. All you need now is to add a copy constructor to the CCandyBox class.

TRY IT OUT   The Copy Constructor in a Derived Class

You can add the following code for the copy constructor to the public section of the derived CCandyBox class in Ex9_04:

```
    // Derived class copy constructor
    CCandyBox(const CCandyBox& initCB)
    {
        cout << endl << "CCandyBox copy constructor called";

        // Get new memory
        m_Contents = new char[ strlen(initCB.m_Contents) + 1 ];

        // Copy string
        strcpy_s(m_Contents, strlen(initCB.m_Contents) + 1, initCB.m_Contents);
    }
```

You can now run this new version (Ex9_05) of the last example with the following function main() to see how the new copy constructor works:

```
int main()
{
    CCandyBox chocBox(2.0, 3.0, 4.0, "Chockies");   // Declare and initialize
    CCandyBox chocolateBox(chocBox);                 // Use copy constructor

    cout << endl
         << "Volume of chocBox is " << chocBox.Volume()
         << endl
         << "Volume of chocolateBox is " << chocolateBox.Volume()
```

Available for
download on
Wrox.com

```
        << endl;

   return 0;
}
```

code snippet Ex9_05.cpp

How It Works

When you run this example, it produces the following output:

```
CBox constructor called
CCandyBox constructor2 called
CBox constructor called
CCandyBox copy constructor called
Volume of chocBox is 24
Volume of chocolateBox is 1
CCandyBox destructor called
CBox destructor called
CCandyBox destructor called
CBox destructor called
```

Although, at first sight, this looks okay, there is something wrong. The third line of output shows that the default constructor for the CBox part of the object chocolateBox is called, rather than the copy constructor. As a consequence, the object has the default dimensions rather than the dimensions of the initializing object, so the volume is incorrect. The reason for this is that when you write a constructor for an object of a derived class, you are responsible for ensuring that the members of the derived class object are properly initialized. This includes the inherited members.

The fix for this is to call the copy constructor for the base part of the class in the initialization list for the copy constructor for the CCandyBox class. The copy constructor then becomes:

```
// Derived class copy constructor
CCandyBox(const CCandyBox& initCB): CBox(initCB)
{
   cout << endl << "CCandyBox copy constructor called";

   // Get new memory
   m_Contents = new char[ strlen(initCB.m_Contents) + 1 ];

   // Copy string
   strcpy_s(m_Contents, strlen(initCB.m_Contents) + 1, initCB.m_Contents);
}
```

Now, the CBox class copy constructor is called with the initCB object. Only the base part of the object is passed to it, so everything works out. If you modify the last example by adding the base copy constructor call, the output is as follows:

```
CBox constructor called
CCandyBox constructor2 called
CBox copy constructor called
CCandyBox copy constructor called
Volume of chocBox is 24
Volume of chocolateBox is 24
```

```
CCandyBox destructor called
CBox destructor called
CCandyBox destructor called
CBox destructor called
```

The output shows that all the constructors and destructors are called in the correct sequence, and the copy constructor for the CBox part of chocolateBox is called before the CCandyBox copy constructor. The volume of the object chocolateBox of the derived class is now the same as that of its initializing object, which is as it should be.

You have, therefore, another golden rule to remember:

> **NOTE** *If you write any kind of constructor for a derived class, you are responsible for the initialization of all members of the derived class object, including all its inherited members.*

Of course, as you saw in the previous chapter, if you want to make a class that allocates memory on the heap as efficient as possible, you should overload the copy constructor with a version that uses an rvalue reference parameter. You could add the following to the CCandyBox class to take care of this:

```cpp
// Move constructor
CCandyBox(CCandyBox&& initCB): CBox(initCB)
{
  cout << endl << "CCandyBox move constructor called";
  m_Contents = initCB.m_Contents;
  initCB.m_Contents = 0;
}
```

You still have to call the base class copy constructor to get the base members initialized.

CLASS MEMBERS AS FRIENDS

You saw in Chapter 7 how a function can be declared as a friend of a class. This gives the friend function the privilege of free access to any of the class members. Of course, there is no reason why a friend function cannot be a member of another class.

Suppose you define a CBottle class to represent a bottle:

```cpp
#pragma once

class CBottle
{
  public:
    CBottle(double height, double diameter)
    {
      m_Height = height;
      m_Diameter = diameter;
    }

  private:
```

```
      double m_Height;                     // Bottle height
      double m_Diameter;                   // Bottle diameter
};
```

You now need a class to represent the packaging for a dozen bottles that automatically has custom dimensions to accommodate a particular kind of bottle. You could define this as:

```
#pragma once
class CBottle;                             // Forward declaration

class CCarton
{
  public:
    CCarton(const CBottle& aBottle)
    {
      m_Height = aBottle.m_Height;         // Bottle height
      m_Length = 4.0*aBottle.m_Diameter;   // Four rows of ...
      m_Width = 3.0*aBottle.m_Diameter;    // ...three bottles
    }

  private:
    double m_Length;                       // Carton length
    double m_Width;                        // Carton width
    double m_Height;                       // Carton height
};
```

The constructor here sets the height to be the same as that of the bottle it is to accommodate, and the length and width are set based on the diameter of the bottle so that 12 fit in the box. The forward declaration for the CBottle class is necessary because the constructor refers to CBottle. As you know by now, this won't work. The data members of the CBottle class are private, so the CCarton constructor cannot access them. As you also know, a friend declaration in the CBottle class fixes it:

```
#pragma once;
class CCarton;                             // Forward declaration

class CBottle
{
  public:
    CBottle(double height, double diameter)
    {
      m_Height = height;
      m_Diameter = diameter;
    }

  private:
    double m_Height;                       // Bottle height
    double m_Diameter;                     // Bottle diameter

  // Let the carton constructor in
  friend CCarton::CCarton(const CBottle& aBottle);
};
```

The only difference between the `friend` declaration here and what you saw in Chapter 7 is that you must put the class name and the scope resolution operator with the `friend` function name to identify it. You have a forward declaration for the `CCarton` class because the fried function refers to it.

You might think that this will compile correctly, but there is a problem. The `CCarton` class definition refers to the `CBottle` class, and the `CBottle` class with the friend function added refers to the `CCarton` class, so we have a cyclic dependency here. You can put a forward declaration of the `CCarton` class in the `CBottle` class, and vice versa, but this still won't allow the classes to compile. The problem is with the `CCarton` class constructor. This appears within the `CCarton` class definition and the compiler cannot compile this function without having first compiled the `CBottle` class. On the other hand, it can't compile the `CBottle` class without having compiled the `CCarton` class. The only way to resolve this is to put the `CCarton` constructor definition in a `.cpp` file. The header file holding the `CCarton` class definition will be:

```
#pragma once
class CBottle;                              // Forward declaration

class CCarton
{
  public:
    CCarton(const CBottle& aBottle);

  private:
    double m_Length;                       // Carton length
    double m_Width;                        // Carton width
    double m_Height;                       // Carton height
};
```

The contents of the `carton.cpp` file will be:

```
#include "carton.h"
#include "bottle.h"

CCarton::CCarton(const CBottle& aBottle)
{
  m_Height = aBottle.m_Height;             // Bottle height
  m_Length = 4.0*aBottle.m_Diameter;       // Four rows of ...
  m_Width = 3.0*aBottle.m_Diameter;        // ...three bottles
}
```

Now, the compiler is able to compile both class definitions and the `carton.cpp` file.

Friend Classes

You can also allow all the function members of one class to have access to all the data members of another by declaring it as a **friend class**. You could define the `CCarton` class as a friend of the `CBottle` class by adding a `friend` declaration within the `CBottle` class definition:

```
friend CCarton;
```

With this declaration in the `CBottle` class, all function members of the `CCarton` class now have free access to all the data members of the `CBottle` class.

Limitations on Class Friendship

Class friendship is not reciprocated. Making the CCarton class a friend of the CBottle class does not mean that the CBottle class is a friend of the CCarton class. If you want this to be so, you must add a friend declaration for the CBottle class to the CCarton class.

Class friendship is also not inherited. If you define another class with CBottle as a base, members of the CCarton class will not have access to its data members, not even those inherited from CBottle.

VIRTUAL FUNCTIONS

Let's look more closely at the behavior of inherited member functions and their relationship with derived class member functions. You could add a function to the CBox class to output the volume of a CBox object. The simplified class then becomes:

```
// Box.h in Ex9_06
#pragma once
#include <iostream>
using std::cout;
using std::endl;

class CBox                              // Base class
{
  public:

    // Function to show the volume of an object
    void ShowVolume() const
    {
      cout << endl
           << "CBox usable volume is " << Volume();
    }

    // Function to calculate the volume of a CBox object
    double Volume() const
    { return m_Length*m_Width*m_Height; }

    // Constructor
    CBox(double lv = 1.0, double wv = 1.0, double hv = 1.0)
                        :m_Length(lv), m_Width(wv), m_Height(hv) {}

  protected:
    double m_Length;
    double m_Width;
    double m_Height;
};
```

Now, you can output the usable volume of a CBox object just by calling the ShowVolume() function for any object for which you require it. The constructor sets the data member values in the initialization list, so no statements are necessary in the body of the function. The data members are as before and are specified as protected, so they are accessible to the member functions of any derived class.

Suppose you want to derive a class for a different kind of box called CGlassBox, to hold glassware. The contents are fragile, and because packing material is added to protect them, the capacity of the box is less than the capacity of a basic CBox object. You therefore need a different Volume() function to account for this, so you add it to the derived class:

```
// GlassBox.h in Ex9_06
#pragma once
#include "Box.h"

class CGlassBox: public CBox            // Derived class
{
  public:
    // Function to calculate volume of a CGlassBox
    // allowing 15% for packing
    double Volume() const
    { return 0.85*m_Length*m_Width*m_Height; }

    // Constructor
    CGlassBox(double lv, double wv, double hv): CBox(lv, wv, hv){}
};
```

There could conceivably be other additional members of the derived class, but we'll keep it simple and concentrate on how the inherited functions work, for the moment. The constructor for the derived class objects just calls the base class constructor in its initialization list to set the data member values. No statements are necessary in its body. You have included a new version of the Volume() function to replace the version from the base class, the idea being that you can get the inherited function ShowVolume() to call the derived class version of the member function Volume() when you call it for an object of the class CGlassBox.

TRY IT OUT   Using an Inherited Function

Now, see how your derived class works in practice. You can try this out very simply by creating an object of the base class and an object of the derived class with the same dimensions and then verifying that the correct volumes are being calculated. The main() function to do this is as follows:

```
// Ex9_06.cpp
// Behavior of inherited functions in a derived class
#include <iostream>
#include "GlassBox.h"                    // For CBox and CGlassBox
using std::cout;
using std::endl;

int main()
{
  CBox myBox(2.0, 3.0, 4.0);            // Declare a base box
  CGlassBox myGlassBox(2.0, 3.0, 4.0); // Declare derived box - same size

  myBox.ShowVolume();                   // Display volume of base box
```

```
    myGlassBox.ShowVolume();              // Display volume of derived box

  cout << endl;
  return 0;
}
```

code snippet Ex9_06.cpp

How It Works

If you run this example, it produces the following output:

```
    CBox usable volume is 24
    CBox usable volume is 24
```

This isn't only dull and repetitive, but it's also disastrous. It isn't working the way you want at all, and the only interesting thing about it is why. Evidently, the fact that the second call is for an object of the derived class CGlassBox is not being taken into account. You can see this from the incorrect result for the volume in the output. The volume of a CGlassBox object should definitely be less than that of a basic CBox with the same dimensions.

The reason for the incorrect output is that the call of the Volume() function in the function ShowVolume() is being set once and for all by the compiler as the version defined in the base class. ShowVolume() is a base class function, and when CBox is compiled, the call to Volume() is resolved at that time to the base class Volume() function; the compiler has no knowledge of any other Volume() function. This is called **static resolution** of the function call since the function call is fixed before the program is executed. This is also sometimes called **early binding** because the particular Volume() function chosen is bound to the call from the function ShowVolume() during the compilation of the program.

What we were hoping for in this example was that the question of which Volume() function call to use in any given instance would be resolved when the program was executed. This sort of operation is referred to as **dynamic linkage**, or **late binding**. We want the actual version of the function Volume() called by ShowVolume() to be determined by the kind of object being processed, and not arbitrarily fixed by the compiler before the program is executed.

No doubt, you'll be less than astonished that C++ does, in fact, provide you with a way to do this, because this whole discussion would have been futile otherwise! You need to use something called a **virtual function.**

What Is a Virtual Function?

A virtual function is a function in a base class that is declared using the keyword virtual. If you specify a function in a base class as virtual and there is another definition of the function in a derived class, it signals to the compiler that you don't want static linkage for this function. What you *do* want is the selection of the function to be called at any given point in the program to be based on the kind of object for which it is called.

TRY IT OUT   Fixing the CGlassBox

To make this example work as originally hoped, you just need to add the keyword `virtual` to the definitions of the `Volume()` function in the two classes. You can try this in a new project, `Ex9_07`. Here's how the definition of `CBox` should be:

```
// Box.h in Ex9_07
#pragma once
#include <iostream>
using std::cout;
using std::endl;

class CBox                              // Base class
{
  public:
    // Function to show the volume of an object
    void ShowVolume() const
    {
      cout << endl
           << "CBox usable volume is " << Volume();
    }

    // Function to calculate the volume of a CBox object
    virtual double Volume() const
    { return m_Length*m_Width*m_Height; }

    // Constructor
    CBox(double lv = 1.0, double wv = 1.0, double hv = 1.0)
                          :m_Length(lv), m_Width(wv), m_Height(hv) {}

  protected:
    double m_Length;
    double m_Width;
    double m_Height;
};
```

The `GlassBox.h` header file contents should be:

```
// GlassBox.h in Ex9_07
#pragma once
#include "Box.h"

class CGlassBox: public CBox            // Derived class
{
  public:
    // Function to calculate volume of a CGlassBox
    // allowing 15% for packing
    virtual double Volume() const
    { return 0.85*m_Length*m_Width*m_Height; }

    // Constructor
    CGlassBox(double lv, double wv, double hv): CBox(lv, wv, hv){}
};
```

The `Ex9_07.cpp` file version of `main()` is the same as for the previous example.

How It Works

If you run this version of the program with just the little word `virtual` added to the definitions of `Volume()`, it produces this output:

```
CBox usable volume is 24
CBox usable volume is 20.4
```

This is now clearly doing what you wanted in the first place. The first call to the function `ShowVolume()` with the `CBox` object `myBox` calls the `CBox` class version of `Volume()`. The second call with the `CGlassBox` object `myGlassBox` calls the version defined in the derived class.

Note that although you have put the keyword `virtual` in the derived class definition of the function `Volume()`, it's not essential to do so. The definition of the base version of the function as `virtual` is sufficient. However, I recommend that you *do* specify the keyword for virtual functions in derived classes because it makes it clear to anyone reading the derived class definition that they are virtual functions and that they are selected dynamically.

For a function to behave as virtual, it must have the same name, parameter list, and return type in any derived class as the function has in the base class, and if the base class function is `const`, the derived class function must be, too. If you try to use different parameters or return types, or declare one as `const` and the other not, the virtual function mechanism won't work and the functions operate with static linkage that is established and fixed at compile time.

The operation of virtual functions is an extraordinarily powerful mechanism. You may have heard the term **polymorphism** in relation to object-oriented programming, and this refers to the virtual function capability. Something that is polymorphic can appear in different guises, like a werewolf, or Dr. Jekyll, or a politician before and after an election, for example. Calling a virtual function produces different effects depending on the kind of object for which it is being called.

Note that the `Volume()` function in the derived `CGlassBox` class actually hides the base class version from the view of derived class functions. If you wanted to call the base version of `Volume()` from a derived class function, you would need to use the scope resolution operator to refer to the function as `CBox::Volume()`.

Using Pointers to Class Objects

Using pointers with objects of a base class and of a derived class is an important technique. You can use a pointer to a base class type to store the address of a derived class object as well as that of a base class object. You can thus use a pointer of the type "pointer to base" to obtain different behavior with virtual functions, depending on what kind of object the pointer is pointing to. You'll see more clearly how this works by looking at an example.

TRY IT OUT Pointers to Base and Derived Classes

You'll use the same classes as in the previous example, but make a small modification to the function main() so that it uses a pointer to a base class object. Create the Ex9_08 project with Box.h and GlassBox.h header files the same as in the previous example. You can copy the Box.h and Glassbox.h files from the Ex9_07 project to this project folder. Adding an existing file to a project is quite easy; you right-click Ex9_08 in the Solution Explorer tab, select Add ⇨ Existing Item. . . from the pop-up menu; then select a file to add it to the project. You can select multiple files to add, if you want. When you have added the headers, modify Ex9_08.cpp to the following:

```cpp
// Ex9_08.cpp
// Using a base class pointer to call a virtual function
#include <iostream>
#include "GlassBox.h"                     // For CBox and CGlassBox
using std::cout;
using std::endl;

int main()
{
  CBox myBox(2.0, 3.0, 4.0);             // Declare a base box
  CGlassBox myGlassBox(2.0, 3.0, 4.0);   // Declare derived box of same size
  CBox* pBox(nullptr);                   // Declare a pointer to base class objects

  pBox = &myBox;                         // Set pointer to address of base object
  pBox->ShowVolume();                    // Display volume of base box
  pBox = &myGlassBox;                    // Set pointer to derived class object
  pBox->ShowVolume();                    // Display volume of derived box

  cout << endl;
  return 0;
}
```

code snippet Ex9_08.cpp

How It Works

The classes are the same as in example Ex9_07.cpp, but the function main() has been altered to use a pointer to call the function ShowVolume(). Because you are using a pointer, you use the indirect member selection operator, ->, to call the function. The function ShowVolume() is called twice, and both calls use the same pointer to base class objects, pBox. On the first occasion, the pointer contains the address of the base object, myBox, and on the occasion of the second call, it contains the address of the derived class object, myGlassBox.

The output produced is as follows:

```
CBox usable volume is 24
CBox usable volume is 20.4
```

This is exactly the same as that from the previous example, where you used explicit objects in the function call.

You can conclude from this example that the virtual function mechanism works just as well through a pointer to a base class, with the specific function being selected based on the type of object being pointed to. This is illustrated in Figure 9-4.

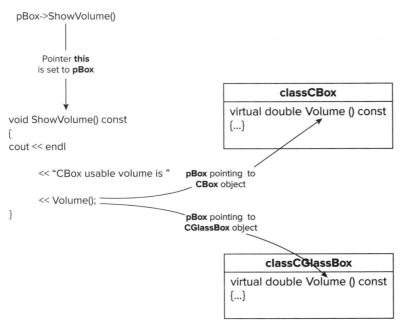

FIGURE 9-4

This means that, even when you don't know the precise type of the object pointed to by a base class pointer in a program (when a pointer is passed to a function as an argument, for example), the virtual function mechanism ensures that the correct function is called. This is an extraordinarily powerful capability, so make sure you understand it. Polymorphism is a fundamental mechanism in C++ that you will find yourself using again and again.

Using References with Virtual Functions

If you define a function with a reference to a base class as a parameter, you can pass an object of a derived class to it as an argument. When your function executes, the appropriate virtual function for the object passed is selected automatically. We could see this happening by modifying the function `main()` in the last example to call a function that has a reference as a parameter.

TRY IT OUT Using References with Virtual Functions

Let's move the call to `ShowVolume()` into a separate function and call that separate function from `main()`:

```
// Ex9_09.cpp
// Using a reference to call a virtual function
#include <iostream>
#include "GlassBox.h"              // For CBox and CGlassBox
using std::cout;
using std::endl;

void Output(const CBox& aBox);     // Prototype of function

int main()
{
  CBox myBox(2.0, 3.0, 4.0);            // Declare a base box
  CGlassBox myGlassBox(2.0, 3.0, 4.0); // Declare derived box of same size

  Output(myBox);                    // Output volume of base class object
  Output(myGlassBox);               // Output volume of derived class object
  cout << endl;
  return 0;
}

void Output(const CBox& aBox)
{
  aBox.ShowVolume();
}
```

code snippet Ex9_09.cpp

`Box.h` and `GlassBox.h` for this example have the same contents as for the previous example.

How It Works

The function `main()` now basically consists of two calls of the function `Output()`, the first with an object of the base class as an argument and the second with an object of the derived class. Because the parameter is a reference to the base class, `Output()` accepts objects of either class as an argument, and the appropriate version of the virtual function `Volume()` is called, depending on the object that is initializing the reference.

The program produces exactly the same output as the previous example, demonstrating that the virtual function mechanism does indeed work through a reference parameter.

Incomplete Class Definitions

At the beginning of the previous example, you have the prototype declaration for the `Output()` function. To process this declaration, the compiler needs to have access to the definition of the `CBox` class because the parameter is of type `CBox&`. In this case, the definition of the `CBox` class is available at this point because you have a #include directive for `GlassBox.h` that has its own #include directive for `Box.h`.

However, there may be situations where you have such a declaration and the class definition cannot be included in this way, in which case, you would need some other way to at least identify that the name `CBox` refers to a class type. In this situation, you could provide an **incomplete definition** of the class CBox preceding the prototype of the output function. The statement that provides an incomplete definition of the CBox class is simply:

```
class CBox;
```

The statement just identifies that the name CBox refers to a class that is not defined at this point, but this is sufficient for the compiler to know that CBox is the name of a class, and this allows it to process the prototype of the function Output(). Without some indication that CBox is a class, the prototype causes an error message to be generated.

Pure Virtual Functions

It's possible that you'd want to include a virtual function in a base class so that it may be redefined in a derived class to suit the objects of that class, but that there is no meaningful definition you could give for the function in the base class.

For example, you could conceivably have a class CContainer, which could be used as a base for defining the CBox class, or a CBottle class, or even a CTeapot class. The CContainer class wouldn't have data members, but you might want to provide a virtual member function Volume() to allow it to be called polymorphically for any derived classes. Because the CContainer class has no data members and, therefore, no dimensions, there is no sensible definition that you can write for the Volume() function. You can still define the class, however, including the member function Volume(), as follows:

```
// Container.h for Ex9_10
#pragma once
#include <iostream>
using std::cout;
using std::endl;

class CContainer           // Generic base class for specific containers
{
  public:
    // Function for calculating a volume - no content
    // This is defined as a 'pure' virtual function, signified by '= 0'
    virtual double Volume() const = 0;

    // Function to display a volume
    virtual void ShowVolume() const
    {
      cout << endl
           << "Volume is " << Volume();
    }
};
```

The statement for the virtual function Volume() defines it as having no content by placing the equals sign and zero in the function header. This is called a **pure virtual function**. Any class derived from this class must either define the Volume() function or redefine it as a pure virtual function. Because you have declared Volume() as const, its implementation in any derived class must also be const. Remember that const and non-const varieties of a function with the same name and parameter list are different functions. In other words, a const version of a function is an overload of a non-const version.

The class also contains the function ShowVolume(), which displays the volume of objects of derived classes. Because this is declared as virtual, it can be replaced in a derived class, but if it isn't, the base class version that you see here is called.

Abstract Classes

A class containing a pure virtual function is called an **abstract class**. It's called abstract because you can't define objects of a class containing a pure virtual function. It exists only for the purpose of defining classes that are derived from it. If a class derived from an abstract class still defines a pure virtual function of the base as pure, it, too, is an abstract class.

You should not conclude, from the previous example of the CContainer class, that an abstract class can't have data members. An abstract class can have both data members and function members. The presence of a pure virtual function is the only condition that determines that a given class is abstract. In the same vein, an abstract class can have more than one pure virtual function. In this case, a derived class must have definitions for every pure virtual function in its base; otherwise, it, too, will be an abstract class. If you forget to make the derived class version of the Volume() function const, the derived class will still be abstract because it contains the pure virtual Volume() member function that is const, as well as the non-const Volume() function that you have defined.

TRY IT OUT   An Abstract Class

You could implement a CCan class, representing beer or cola cans, perhaps, together with the original CBox class, and derive both from the CContainer class that you defined in the previous section. The definition of the CBox class as a subclass of CContainer is as follows:

```
// Box.h for Ex9_10
#pragma once
#include "Container.h"              // For CContainer definition
#include <iostream>
using std::cout;
using std::endl;

class CBox: public CContainer       // Derived class
{
  public:

    // Function to show the volume of an object
    virtual void ShowVolume() const
    {
      cout << endl
          << "CBox usable volume is " << Volume();
    }

    // Function to calculate the volume of a CBox object
    virtual double Volume() const
```

```
      { return m_Length*m_Width*m_Height; }

      // Constructor
      CBox(double lv = 1.0, double wv = 1.0, double hv = 1.0)
                              :m_Length(lv), m_Width(wv), m_Height(hv){}

  protected:
      double m_Length;
      double m_Width;
      double m_Height;
};
```

The unshaded lines are the same as in the previous version of the CBox class. The CBox class is essentially as we had it in the previous example, except this time, you have specified that it is derived from the CContainer class. The Volume() function is fully defined within this class (as it must be if this class is to be used to define objects). The only other option would be to specify it as a pure virtual function, since it is pure in the base class, but then we couldn't create CBox objects.

You could define the CCan class in the Can.h header file like this:

```
// Can.h for Ex9_10
#pragma once
#include "Container.h"          // For CContainer definition
extern const double PI;         // PI is defined elsewhere

class CCan: public CContainer
{
  public:
    // Function to calculate the volume of a can
    virtual double Volume() const
    { return 0.25*PI*m_Diameter*m_Diameter*m_Height; }

    // Constructor
    CCan(double hv = 4.0, double dv = 2.0): m_Height(hv), m_Diameter(dv){}

  protected:
    double m_Height;
    double m_Diameter;
};
```

The CCan class also defines a Volume() function based on the formula $h\pi r^2$ where h is the height of a can and r is the radius of the cross-section of a can. The volume is calculated as the height multiplied by the area of the base. The expression in the function definition assumes a global constant PI is defined, so we have the extern statement indicating that PI is a global variable of type const double that is defined elsewhere — in this program, it is defined in the Ex9_10.cpp file. Also notice that we redefined the ShowVolume() function in the CBox class, but not in the CCan class. You can see what effect this has when we get some program output.

You can exercise these classes with the following source file containing the main() function:

```
// Ex9_10.cpp
// Using an abstract class
#include "Box.h"               // For CBox and CContainer
#include "Can.h"               // For CCan (and CContainer)
```

```
#include <iostream>                    // For stream I/O
using std::cout;
using std::endl;

const double PI= 3.14159265;           // Global definition for PI

int main(void)
{
  // Pointer to abstract base class
  // initialized with address of CBox object
  CContainer* pC1 = new CBox(2.0, 3.0, 4.0);

  // Pointer to abstract base class
  // initialized with address of CCan object
  CContainer* pC2 = new CCan(6.5, 3.0);

  pC1->ShowVolume();                    // Output the volumes of the two
  pC2->ShowVolume();                    // objects pointed to
  cout << endl;

  delete pC1;                           // Now clean up the free store
  delete pC2;                           // ...

  return 0;
}
```

code snippet Ex9_10.cpp)

How It Works

In this program, you declare two pointers to the base class, CContainer. Although you can't define CContainer objects (because CContainer is an abstract class), you can still define a pointer to a CContainer, which you can then use to store the address of a derived class object; in fact, you can use it to store the address of any object whose type is a direct or indirect subclass of CContainer. The pointer pC1 is assigned the address of a CBox object created in the free store by the operator new. The second pointer is assigned the address of a CCan object in a similar manner.

Of course, because the derived class objects were created dynamically, you must use the delete operator to clean up the free store when you have finished with them. You learned about the delete operator back in Chapter 4.

The output produced by this example is as follows:

```
CBox usable volume is 24
Volume is 45.9458
```

Because you have defined ShowVolume() in the CBox class, the derived class version of the function is called for the CBox object. You did not define this function in the CCan class, so the base class version that the CCan class inherits is invoked for the CCan object. Because Volume() is a virtual function implemented in both derived classes (necessarily, because it is a pure virtual function in the base class), the call to it is resolved when the program is executed by selecting the version belonging to the class of the object being pointed to. Thus, for the pointer pC1, the version from the class CBox is called and, for the pointer pC2, the version in the class CCan is called. In each case, therefore, you obtain the correct result.

You could equally well have used just one pointer and assigned the address of the CCan object to it (after calling the Volume() function for the CBox object). A base class pointer can contain the address of *any* derived class object, even when several different classes are derived from the same base class, and so you can have automatic selection of the appropriate virtual function across a whole range of derived classes. Impressive stuff, isn't it?

Indirect Base Classes

At the beginning of this chapter, I said that a base class for a subclass could, in turn, be derived from another, "more" base class. A small extension of the last example provides you with an illustration of this, as well as demonstrating the use of a virtual function across a second level of inheritance.

TRY IT OUT   **More Than One Level of Inheritance**

All you need to do is add the class CGlassBox to the classes you have from the previous example. The relationship between the classes you now have is illustrated in Figure 9-5.

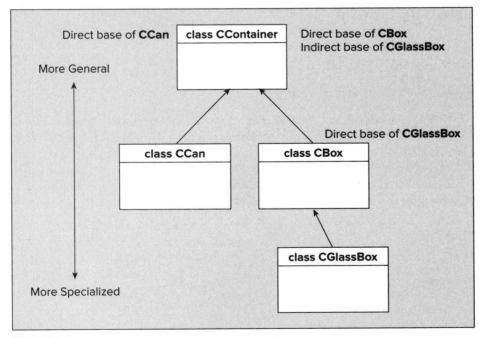

FIGURE 9-5

The class CGlassBox is derived from the CBox class exactly as before, but we omit the derived class version of ShowVolume() to show that the base class version still propagates through the derived classes. With the class hierarchy shown above, the class CContainer is an indirect base of the class CGlassBox, and a direct base of the classes CBox and CCan.

The `GlassBox.h` header file for the example contains:

```
// GlassBox.h for Ex9_11
#pragma once
#include "Box.h"                    // For CBox

class CGlassBox: public CBox        // Derived class
{
  public:

    // Function to calculate volume of a CGlassBox
    // allowing 15% for packing
    virtual double Volume() const
    { return 0.85*m_Length*m_Width*m_Height; }

    // Constructor
    CGlassBox(double lv, double wv, double hv): CBox(lv, wv, hv){}
};
```

The `Container.h`, `Can.h`, and `Box.h` header files contain the same code as those in the previous example, `Ex9_10`.

The source file for the new example, with an updated function `main()` to use the additional class in the hierarchy, is as follows:

```
// Ex9_11.cpp
// Using an abstract class with multiple levels of inheritance
#include "Box.h"              // For CBox and CContainer
#include "Can.h"              // For CCan (and CContainer)
#include "GlassBox.h"         // For CGlassBox (and CBox and CContainer)
#include <iostream>           // For stream I/O
using std::cout;
using std::endl;

const double PI = 3.14159265;              // Global definition for PI

int main()
{
  // Pointer to abstract base class initialized with CBox object address
  CContainer* pC1 = new CBox(2.0, 3.0, 4.0);

  CCan myCan(6.5, 3.0);                // Define CCan object
  CGlassBox myGlassBox(2.0, 3.0, 4.0); // Define CGlassBox object

  pC1->ShowVolume();                   // Output the volume of CBox
  delete pC1;                          // Now clean up the free store

  // initialized with address of CCan object
  pC1 = &myCan;                        // Put myCan address in pointer
  pC1->ShowVolume();                   // Output the volume of CCan

  pC1 = &myGlassBox;                   // Put myGlassBox address in pointer
  pC1->ShowVolume();                   // Output the volume of CGlassBox
```

```
    cout << endl;
    return 0;
}
```

code snippet Ex9_11.cpp

How It Works

You have the three-level class hierarchy shown in Figure 9-5 with CContainer as an abstract base class because it contains the pure virtual function, Volume(). The main() function now calls the ShowVolume() function three times using the same pointer to the base class, but with the pointer containing the address of an object of a different class type each time. Because ShowVolume() is not defined in either CCan or CGlassBox, the inherited version is called in each instance. A separate branch from the base CContainer defines the derived class CCan so CCan inherits ShowVolume() from CContainer and CGlassBox inherits the function from CBox.

The example produces this output:

```
CBox usable volume is 24
Volume is 45.9458
CBox usable volume is 20.4
```

The output shows that one of the three different versions of the function Volume() is selected for execution according to the type of object involved.

Note that you must delete the CBox object from the free store before you assign another address value to the pointer. If you don't do this, you won't be able to clean up the free store, because you would have no record of the address of the original object. This is an easy mistake to make when reassigning pointers and using the free store.

Virtual Destructors

One problem that arises when dealing with objects of derived classes using a pointer to the base class is that the correct destructor may not be called. You can see this effect by modifying the last example.

TRY IT OUT   Calling the Wrong Destructor

You just need to add a public destructor to each of the classes in the example that outputs a message so that you can track which destructor is called when the objects are destroyed. The destructor for the CContainer class in the Container.h file for this example is:

```
// Destructor
~CContainer()
{ cout << "CContainer destructor called" << endl; }
```

The destructor for the CCan class in Can.h in the example is:

```
                    // Destructor
                    ~CCan()
                    { cout << "CCan destructor called" << endl; }
```

The CBox class destructor in Box.h should be:

```
                    // Destructor
                    ~CBox()
                    { cout << "CBox destructor called" << endl; }
```

The CGlassBox destructor in the GlassBox.h header file should be:

```
                    // Destructor
                    ~CGlassBox()
                    { cout << "CGlassBox destructor called" << endl; }
```

Finally, the source file Ex9_12.cpp for the program should be as follows:

```
// Ex9_12.cpp
// Destructor calls with derived classes
// using objects via a base class pointer
#include "Box.h"                        // For CBox and CContainer
#include "Can.h"                        // For CCan (and CContainer)
#include "GlassBox.h"                   // For CGlassBox (and CBox and CContainer)
#include <iostream>                     // For stream I/O
using std::cout;
using std::endl;

const double PI = 3.14159265;           // Global definition for PI

int main()
{
  // Pointer to abstract base class initialized with CBox object address
  CContainer* pC1 = new CBox(2.0, 3.0, 4.0);

  CCan myCan(6.5, 3.0);                 // Define CCan object
  CGlassBox myGlassBox(2.0, 3.0, 4.0); // Define CGlassBox object

  pC1->ShowVolume();                    // Output the volume of CBox
  cout << endl << "Delete CBox" << endl;
  delete pC1;                           // Now clean up the free store

  pC1 = new CGlassBox(4.0, 5.0, 6.0);  // Create CGlassBox dynamically
  pC1->ShowVolume();                    // ...output its volume...
  cout << endl << "Delete CGlassBox" << endl;
  delete pC1;                           // ...and delete it

  pC1 = &myCan;                         // Get myCan address in pointer
  pC1->ShowVolume();                    // Output the volume of CCan

  pC1 = &myGlassBox;                    // Get myGlassBox address in pointer
```

```
      pC1->ShowVolume();                    // Output the volume of CGlassBox

      cout << endl;
      return 0;
}
```

code snippet Ex9_12.cpp

How It Works

Apart from adding a destructor to each class that outputs a message to the effect that it was called, the only other change is a couple of additions to the function `main()`. There are additional statements to create a CGlassBox object dynamically, output its volume, and then delete it. There is also a message displayed to indicate when the dynamically created CBox object is deleted. The output generated by this example is shown as follows:

```
CBox usable volume is 24
Delete CBox
CContainer destructor called

CBox usable volume is 102
Delete CGlassBox
CContainer destructor called

Volume is 45.9458
CBox usable volume is 20.4
CGlassBox destructor called
CBox destructor called
CContainer destructor called
CCan destructor called
CContainer destructor called
```

You can see from this that when you delete the CBox object pointed to by pC1, the destructor for the base class CContainer is called, but there is no call of the CBox destructor recorded. Similarly, when the CGlassBox object that you added is deleted, again, the destructor for the base class CContainer is called but not the CGlassBox or CBox destructors. For the other objects, the correct destructor calls occur with the derived class destructor being called first, followed by the base class destructor. For the first CGlassBox object created in a declaration, three destructors are called: first, the destructor for the derived class, followed by the direct base destructor, and, finally, the indirect base destructor.

All the problems are with objects created in the free store. In both cases, the wrong destructor is called. The reason for this is that the linkage to the destructors is resolved statically, at compile time. For the automatic objects, there is no problem — the compiler knows what they are and arranges for the correct destructors to be called. With objects created dynamically and accessed through a pointer, things are different. The only information that the compiler has when the delete operation is executed is that the pointer type is a pointer to the base class. The type of object the pointer is actually pointing to is unknown to the compiler because this is determined when the program executes. The compiler, therefore, simply ensures that the delete operation is set up to call the base class destructor. In a real application, this can cause a lot of problems, with bits of objects left strewn around the free store and possibly more serious problems, depending on the nature of the objects involved.

The solution is simple. You need the calls to be resolved dynamically — as the program is executed. You can organize this by using **virtual destructors** in your classes. As I said when I first discussed virtual functions, it's sufficient to declare a base class function as virtual to ensure that all functions in any derived classes with the same name, parameter list, and return type are virtual as well. This applies to destructors just as it does to ordinary member functions. You need to add the keyword `virtual` to the definition of the destructor in the class `CContainer` in `Container.h` so that the class definition is as follows:

```
class CContainer                    // Generic base class for containers
{
   public:

      // Destructor
      virtual ~CContainer()
      { cout << "CContainer destructor called" << endl; }

      // Rest of the class as before
};
```

Now, the destructors in all the derived classes are automatically virtual, even though you don't explicitly specify them as such. Of course, you're free to specify them as virtual if you want the code to be absolutely clear.

If you rerun the example with this modification, it produces the following output:

```
CBox usable volume is 24
Delete CBox
CBox destructor called
CContainer destructor called

CBox usable volume is 102
Delete CGlassBox
CGlassBox destructor called
CBox destructor called
CContainer destructor called

Volume is 45.9458
CBox usable volume is 20.4
CGlassBox destructor called
CBox destructor called
CContainer destructor called
CCan destructor called
CContainer destructor called
```

As you can see, all the objects are now destroyed with a proper sequence of destructor calls. Destroying the dynamic objects produces the same sequence of destructor calls as the automatic objects of the same type in the program.

The question may arise in your mind at this point, can constructors be declared as virtual? The answer is no — only destructors and other member functions.

> **NOTE** *It's a good idea always to declare your base class destructor as virtual as a matter of course when using inheritance. There is a small overhead in the execution of the class destructors, but you won't notice it in the majority of circumstances. Using virtual destructors ensures that your objects will be properly destroyed and avoids potential program crashes that might otherwise occur.*

CASTING BETWEEN CLASS TYPES

You have seen how you can store the address of a derived class object in a variable that is a pointer to a base class type, so a variable of type CContainer* can store the address of a CBox object, for example. So, if you have an address stored in a pointer of type CContainer*, can you cast it to type CBox*? Indeed, you can, and the dynamic_cast operator is specifically intended for this kind of operation. Here's how it works:

```
CContainer* pContainer = new CGlassBox(2.0, 3.0, 4.0);
CBox* pBox = dynamic_cast<CBox*>( pContainer);
CGlassBox* pGlassBox = dynamic_cast<CGlassBox*>( pContainer);
```

The first statement stores the address of the CGlassBox object created on the heap in a base class pointer of type CContainer*. The second statement casts pContainer up the class hierarchy to type CBox*. The third statement casts the address in pContainer to its actual type, CGlassBox*.

You can apply the dynamic_cast operator to references as well as pointers. The difference between dynamic_cast and static_cast is that the dynamic_cast operator checks the validity of a cast at runtime, whereas the static_cast operator does not. If a dynamic_cast operation is not valid, the result is null. The compiler relies on the programmer for the validity of a static_cast operation, so you should always use dynamic_cast for casting up and down a class hierarchy and check for a null result if you want to avoid abrupt termination of your program as a result of using a null pointer.

NESTED CLASSES

You can put the definition of one class inside the definition of another, in which case, you have defined a **nested class**. A nested class has the appearance of being a static member of the class that encloses it and is subject to the member access specifiers, just like any other member of the class. If you place the definition of a nested class in the private section of the class, the class can only be referenced from within the scope of the enclosing class. If you specify a nested class as public, the class is accessible from outside the enclosing class, but the nested class name must be qualified by the outer class name in such circumstances.

A nested class has free access to all the static members of the enclosing class. All the instance members can be accessed through an object of the enclosing class type, or a pointer or reference to an object. The enclosing class can only access the public members of the nested class, but in a nested class that is private in the enclosing class, the members are frequently declared as public to provide free access to the entire nested class from functions in the enclosing class.

A nested class is particularly useful when you want to define a type that is only to be used within another type, whereupon the nested class can be declared as private. Here's an example of that:

```cpp
// A push-down stack to store Box objects
class CStack
{
private:
  // Defines items to store in the stack
  struct CItem
  {
    CBox* pBox;                           // Pointer to the object in this node
    CItem* pNext;                         // Pointer to next item in the stack or null

    // Constructor
    CItem(CBox* pB, CItem* pN): pBox(pB), pNext(pN){}
  };

  CItem* pTop;                            // Pointer to item that is at the top
public:
  // Constructor
  CStack():pTop(nullptr){}

  // Push a Box object onto the stack
  void Push(CBox* pBox)
  {
    pTop = new CItem(pBox, pTop);        // Create new item and make it the top
  }

  // Pop an object off the stack
  CBox* Pop()
  {
    if(!pTop)                            // If the stack is empty
      return nullptr;                    // return null

    CBox* pBox = pTop->pBox;             // Get box from item
    CItem* pTemp = pTop;                 // Save address of the top item
    pTop = pTop->pNext;                  // Make next item the top
    delete pTemp;                        // Delete old top item from the heap
    return pBox;
  }

  // Destructor
  ~CStack()
  {
    CItem* pTemp(nullptr);
    while(pTop)                          // While pTop not null
    {
      pTemp = pTop;
      pTop = pTop->pNext;
      delete pTemp;
    }
  }
};
```

The CStack class defines a push-down stack for storing CBox objects. To be absolutely precise, it stores pointers to CBox objects so the objects pointed to are still the responsibility of the code making use of the Stack class. The nested struct, CItem, defines the items that are held in the stack. I chose to define CItem as a nested struct rather than a nested class because members of a struct are public by default. You could define CItem as a class and then specify the members as public so they can be accessed from the functions in the CStack class. The stack is implemented as a set of CItem objects, where each CItem object stores a pointer to a CBox object plus the address of the next CItem object down in the stack. The Push() function in the CStack class pushes a CBox object onto the top of the stack, and the Pop() function pops an object off the top of the stack.

Pushing an object onto the stack involves creating a new CItem object that stores the address of the object to be stored plus the address of the previous item that was on the top of the stack — this is null the first time you push an object onto the stack. Popping an object off the stack returns the address of the object in the item, pTop. The top item is deleted and the next item becomes the item at the top of the stack.

Because a CStack object creates CItem objects on the heap, we need a destructor to make sure any remaining CItem objects are deleted when a CStack object is destroyed. The process is to work down through the stack, deleting the top item after the address of the next item has been saved in pTop. Let's see if it works.

TRY IT OUT   **Using a Nested Class**

This example uses CContainer, CBox, and CGlassBox classes from Ex9_12, so create an empty WIN32 console project, Ex9_13, and add the header files containing those class definitions to it. Then add Stack.h to the project containing the definition of the CStack class from the previous section, and add Ex9_13.cpp to the project with the following contents:

```
// Ex9_13.cpp
// Using a nested class to define a stack
#include "Box.h"                    // For CBox and CContainer
#include "GlassBox.h"               // For CGlassBox (and CBox and CContainer)
#include "Stack.h"                  // For the stack class with nested struct Item

#include <iostream>                 // For stream I/O
using std::cout;
using std::endl;

int main()
{
  CBox* pBoxes[] = { new CBox(2.0, 3.0, 4.0),
                     new CGlassBox(2.0, 3.0, 4.0),
                     new CBox(4.0, 5.0, 6.0),
                     new CGlassBox(4.0, 5.0, 6.0)
                   };
  int nBoxes = sizeof pBoxes/sizeof pBoxes[0];
  cout << "The array of boxes have the following volumes:";
  for (int i = 0 ; i<nBoxes ; i++)
    pBoxes[i]->ShowVolume();        // Output the volume of a box

  cout << endl << endl
```

```
                   << "Now pushing the boxes on the stack..."
                   << endl;

        CStack* pStack = new CStack;        // Create the stack
        for (int i = 0 ; i<nBoxes ; i++)
          pStack->Push(pBoxes[i]);


        cout << "Popping the boxes off the stack presents them in reverse order:";
        CBox* pTemp(nullptr);
        while(pTemp = pStack->Pop())
          pTemp->ShowVolume();

        cout << endl;
        delete pStack;
        for(int i = 0 ; i<nBoxes ; ++i)
          delete pBoxes[i];
        return 0;
      }
```

code snippet Ex9_13.cpp

The output from this example is:

```
The array of boxes have the following volumes:
CBox usable volume is 24
CBox usable volume is 20.4
CBox usable volume is 120
CBox usable volume is 102

Now pushing the boxes on the stack...
Popping the boxes off the stack presents them in reverse order:
CBox usable volume is 102
CBox usable volume is 120
CBox usable volume is 20.4
CBox usable volume is 24
```

How It Works

You create an array of pointers to CBox objects so each element in the array can store the address of a CBox object or an address of any type that is derived from CBox. The array is initialized with the addresses of four objects created on the heap:

```
CBox* pBoxes[] = { new CBox(2.0, 3.0, 4.0),
                   new CGlassBox(2.0, 3.0, 4.0),
                   new CBox(4.0, 5.0, 6.0),
                   new CGlassBox(4.0, 5.0, 6.0)
                 };
```

The objects are two CBox objects and two CGlassBox objects with the same dimensions as the CBox objects.

After calculating the number of elements in the pBoxes array and listing the volumes of the four objects, you create a CStack object and push the objects onto the stack in a for loop:

```
CStack* pStack = new CStack;          // Create the stack
for (int i = 0 ; i<nBoxes ; i++)
  pStack->Push(pBoxes[i]);
```

Each element in the pBoxes array is pushed onto the stack by passing the array element as the argument to the Push() function for the CStack object. This results in the first element from the array being at the bottom of the stack, and the last element at the top.

You pop the objects off the stack in a while loop:

```
CBox* pTemp(nullptr);
while(pTemp = pStack->Pop())
  pTemp->ShowVolume();
```

The Pop() function returns the address of the element at the top of the stack, and you use this to call the ShowVolume() function for the object. The loop ends when the Pop() function returns null. Because the last element was at the top of the stack, the loop lists the volumes of the objects in reverse order. From the output, you can see that the CStack class does, indeed, implement a stack using a nested struct to define the items to be stored in the stack.

C++/CLI PROGRAMMING

All C++/CLI classes, including classes that you define, are derived classes by default. This is because both value classes and reference classes have a standard class, System::Object, as a base class. This means that both value classes and reference classes inherit from the System::Object class and, therefore, have the capabilities of the System::Object class in common. Because the ToString() function is defined as a virtual function in System::Object, you can override it in your own classes and have the function called polymorphically when required. This is what you have been doing in previous chapters when you defined the ToString() function in a class.

Because System::Object is a base class for all C++/CLI classes, the handle type System::Object^ fulfils a similar role to the void* type in native C++, in that it can be used to reference any type of object.

Boxing and Unboxing

The System::Object base class for all value class types is also responsible for enabling the boxing and unboxing of values of the fundamental types. Boxing a value type instance converts it to an object on the garbage-collected heap, so it will carry full type information along with the basic value. Unboxing is the reverse of boxing. The boxing/unboxing capability means that values of the fundamental types can behave as objects, but can participate in numerical operations without carrying the overhead of being objects. Values of the fundamental types are stored on the stack just as values for the purposes of normal operations and are only converted to an object on the heap that is referenced by a handle of type `System::Object^` when they need to behave as objects. For example, if you pass an unboxed value to a function with a parameter that is an appropriate value class type, the compiler will arrange for the value to be converted to an object on the heap; this is achieved by creating a new object on the heap containing the value. Thus, you get **implicit boxing** and the argument value will be boxed automatically.

Of course, **explicit boxing** is also possible. You can force a value to be boxed by assigning it to a variable of type `Object^`. For example:

```
double value = 3.14159265;
Object^ boxedValue = value;
```

The second statement forces the boxing of `value`, and the boxed representation is referenced by the handle `boxedValue`.

You can also force boxing of a value using `gcnew` to create a boxed value on the garbage-collected heap, for example:

```
long^ number = gcnew long(999999L);
```

This statement implicitly boxes the value `999999L` and stores it on the heap in a location referenced by the handle `number`.

You can unbox a value type using the dereference operator, for example:

```
Console::WriteLine(*number);
```

The value pointed to by the handle `number` is unboxed and then passed as a value to the `WriteLine()` function.

Finally, you can unbox a boxed value using `safe_cast`:

```
long n = safe_cast<long>(number);
```

This statement unboxes `number` and stores the value in n. Note that without the `safe_cast`, this statement will not compile because there is no implicit conversion in this situation.

Inheritance in C++/CLI Classes

Although value classes always have the `System::Object` class as a base, you cannot derive a value class from an existing class. To put it another way, when you define a value class, you are not allowed to specify a base class. This implies that polymorphism in value classes is limited to the functions that are defined as virtual in the `System::Object` class. These are the virtual functions that all value classes inherit from `System::Object`:

FUNCTION	DESCRIPTION
`String^` `ToString()`	Returns a `String` representation of an object, and the implementation in the `System::Object` class returns the class name as a string. You would typically override this function in your own classes to return a string representation of the value of an object.
`bool Equals(` `Object^ obj)`	Compares the current object to `obj` and returns `true` if they are equal and `false` otherwise. For reference types, equal, in this case, means referential equality — that is, the objects are one and the same. For value types, equal means that the objects have the same binary representation. Typically, you would override this function in your own classes to return `true` when the current object is the same value as the argument — in other words, when the fields are equal.
`int GetHashCode()`	Returns an integer that is a hash code for the current object. Hash codes are used as keys to store objects in a collection that stores `(key, object)` pairs. Objects are subsequently retrieved from such a collection by supplying the key that was used when the object was stored.

Of course, because `System::Object` is also a base class for reference classes, you may want to override these functions in reference classes, too. Note that if you override the `Equals()` function in a class, you must also implement the `operator==()` function in the class so that it returns the same result as the `Equals()` function.

You can derive a reference class from an existing reference class in the same way as you define a derived class in native C++. Let's re-implement Ex9_12 as a C++/CLI program as this also demonstrates nested classes in a CLR program. We can start by defining the `Container` class:

```
// Container.h for Ex9_14
#pragma once
using namespace System;

// Abstract base class for specific containers
ref class Container abstract
{
  public:
    // Function for calculating a volume - no content
    // This is defined as an "abstract" virtual function,
    // indicated by the "abstract" keyword
     virtual double Volume() abstract;

    // Function to display a volume
    virtual void ShowVolume()
    {
      Console::WriteLine(L"Volume is {0}", Volume());
    }
};
```

The first thing to note is the `abstract` keyword following the class name. If a C++/CLI class contains the equivalent of a native C++ pure virtual function, you must specify the class as abstract. You can, however, also specify a class as abstract that does not contain any abstract functions, which prevents you from creating objects of that class type. The `abstract` keyword also appears at the end of the `Volume()` function member declaration to indicate that it is not defined for this class. You could also add the " = 0" to the end of the member declaration for `Volume()` as you would for a native C++ member, but it is not required.

Both the `Volume()` and `ShowVolume()` functions are virtual here, so they can be called polymorphically for objects of class types that are derived from `Container`.

You can define the `Box` class like this:

```
// Box.h for Ex9_14
#pragma once
#include "Container.h"                   // For Container definition

ref class Box : Container               // Derived class
{
  public:
    // Function to show the volume of an object
    virtual void ShowVolume() override
    {
      Console::WriteLine(L"Box usable volume is {0}", Volume());
    }

    // Function to calculate the volume of a Box object
    virtual double Volume() override
    { return m_Length*m_Width*m_Height; }

    // Constructor
    Box() : m_Length(1.0), m_Width(1.0), m_Height(1.0){}

    // Constructor
    Box(double lv, double wv, double hv)
                            : m_Length(lv), m_Width(wv), m_Height(hv){}

  protected:
    double m_Length;
    double m_Width;
    double m_Height;
};
```

A base class for a ref class is always public and the `public` keyword is assumed by default. You can specify the base class explicitly as `public`, but it is not necessary to do so. A base class to a ref class cannot be specified as anything other than `public`. Because you cannot supply default values for parameters as in the native C++ version of the class, you define the no-arg constructor so that it initializes all three fields to 1.0. The `Box` class defines the `Volume()` function as an override to the inherited base class version. You must always specify the `override` keyword when you want to override a function in the base class. If the `Box` class did not implement the `Volume()` function, it would be abstract, and you would need to specify it as such to compile the class successfully.

Here's how the `GlassBox` class definition looks:

```
// GlassBox.h for Ex9_14
#pragma once
#include "Box.h"                    // For Box

ref class GlassBox : Box           // Derived class
{
  public:
    // Function to calculate volume of a GlassBox
    // allowing 15% for packing
    virtual double Volume() override
    { return 0.85*m_Length*m_Width*m_Height; }

    // Constructor
    GlassBox(double lv, double wv, double hv): Box(lv, wv, hv){}
};
```

The base class is `Box`, which is `public` by default. The rest of the class is essentially the same as the original.

Here's the `Stack` class definition:

```
// Stack.h for Ex9_14
// A push-down stack to store objects of any ref class type
#pragma once

ref class Stack
{
private:
  // Defines items to store in the stack
  ref struct Item
  {
    Object^ Obj;               // Handle for the object in this item
    Item^ Next;                // Handle for next item in the stack or nullptr

    // Constructor
    Item(Object^ obj, Item^ next): Obj(obj), Next(next){}
  };

  Item^ Top;                   // Handle for item that is at the top
public:
  // Push an object onto the stack
  void Push(Object^ obj)
  {
    Top = gcnew Item(obj, Top);    // Create new item and make it the top
  }

  // Pop an  object off the stack
  Object^ Pop()
  {
```

```
        if(Top == nullptr)              // If the stack is empty
          return nullptr;               // return nullptr

        Object^ obj = Top->Obj;         // Get object from item
        Top = Top->Next;                // Make next item the top
        return obj;
      }
    };
```

The first difference to notice is that the function parameters and fields are now handles, because you are dealing with ref class objects. The inner struct, Item, now stores a handle of type Object^, which allows objects of any CLR class type to be stored in the stack; this means either value class or ref class objects can be accommodated, which is a significant improvement over the native C++ CStack class. You don't need to worry about deleting Item objects when the Pop() function is called or when a Stack object is destroyed, because the garbage collector takes care of that.

Here's a summary of the differences from native C++ that these classes have demonstrated:

➤ Only ref classes can be derived class types.

➤ A base class for a derived ref class is always public.

➤ A function that has no definition for a ref class is an abstract function and must be declared using the abstract keyword.

➤ A class that contains one or more abstract functions must be explicitly specified as abstract by placing the abstract keyword following the class name.

➤ A class that does not contain abstract functions can be specified as abstract, in which case, instances of the class cannot be defined.

➤ You must explicitly use the override keyword when specifying a function that overrides a function inherited from the base class.

All you need to try out these classes is a CLR console project with a definition of main(), so let's do it.

TRY IT OUT   Using Derived Reference Classes

Create a CLR console program with the name Ex9_14 and add the classes in the previous section to the project; then add the following contents to Ex9_14.cpp:

Available for
download on
Wrox.com

```
// Ex9_14.cpp : main project file.
// Using a nested class to define a stack

#include "stdafx.h"
#include "Box.h"                       // For Box and Container
#include "GlassBox.h"                  // For GlassBox (and Box and Container)
#include "Stack.h"                     // For the stack class with nested struct Item

using namespace System;

int main(array<System::String ^> ^args)
{
```

```
array<Box^>^ boxes = { gcnew Box(2.0, 3.0, 4.0),
                       gcnew GlassBox(2.0, 3.0, 4.0),
                       gcnew Box(4.0, 5.0, 6.0),
                       gcnew GlassBox(4.0, 5.0, 6.0)
                     };

Console::WriteLine(L"The array of boxes have the following volumes:");
for each(Box^ box in boxes)
  box->ShowVolume();              // Output the volume of a box

Console::WriteLine(L"\nNow pushing the boxes on the stack...");

Stack^ stack = gcnew Stack;       // Create the stack
for each(Box^ box in boxes)
  stack->Push(box);

Console::WriteLine(
           L"Popping the boxes off the stack presents them in reverse order:");
Object^ item;
while((item = stack->Pop()) != nullptr)
  safe_cast<Container^>(item)->ShowVolume();


Console::WriteLine(L"\nNow pushing integers onto the stack:");
for(int i = 2 ; i<=12 ; i += 2)
{
  Console::Write(L"{0,5}",i);
  stack->Push(i);
}

Console::WriteLine(L"\n\nPopping integers off the stack produces:");
while((item = stack->Pop()) != nullptr)
  Console::Write(L"{0,5}",item);

Console::WriteLine();
  return 0;
}
```

code snippet Ex9_14.cpp

The output from this example is:

```
The array of boxes have the following volumes:
Box usable volume is 24
Box usable volume is 20.4
Box usable volume is 120
Box usable volume is 102

Now pushing the boxes on the stack...
Popping the boxes off the stack presents them in reverse order:
Box usable volume is 102
Box usable volume is 120
Box usable volume is 20.4
Box usable volume is 24
```

```
Now pushing integers onto the stack:
    2    4    6    8   10   12

Popping integers off the stack produces:
   12   10    8    6    4    2
```

How It Works

You first create an array of handles to Box objects:

```
array<Box^>^ boxes = { gcnew Box(2.0, 3.0, 4.0),
                       gcnew GlassBox(2.0, 3.0, 4.0),
                       gcnew Box(4.0, 5.0, 6.0),
                       gcnew GlassBox(4.0, 5.0, 6.0)
                     };
```

Because Box and GlassBox are ref classes, you create the objects on the CLR heap using gcnew. The addresses of the objects initialize the elements of the boxes array.

You then create a Stack object and push the boxes onto the stack:

```
Stack^ stack = gcnew Stack;            // Create the stack
for each(Box^ box in boxes)
    stack->Push(box);
```

The parameter to the Push() function is of type Object^, so the function accepts an object of any class type as the argument. The for each loop pushes each of the elements in the boxes array onto the stack.

Popping the elements off the stack occurs in a while loop:

```
Object^ item;
while((item = stack->Pop()) != nullptr)
    safe_cast<Container^>(item)->ShowVolume();
```

The loop condition stores the value returned from the Pop() function for the stack object in item, and compares it with nullptr. As long as item has not been set to nullptr, the statement that is the body of the while loop is executed. Within the loop, you cast the handle stored in item to type Container^. The item variable is of type Object^, and because the Object class does not define the ShowVolume() function, you cannot call the ShowVolume() function using a handle of this type; to call a function polymorphically, you must use a handle of a base class type that declares the function to be a virtual member. By casting the handle to type Container^, you are able to call the ShowVolume() function polymorphically, so the function is selected for the ultimate class type of the object that the handle references. In this case, you could have achieved the same result by casting item to type Box^. You use safe_cast here because you are casting up the class hierarchy, and it's just as well to use a checked cast operation in such circumstances. The safe_cast operator checks the cast for validity and, if the conversion fails, the operator throws an exception of type System::InvalidCastException. You could use dynamic_cast, but it is better to use safe_cast in CLR programs.

Finally, you push integers onto the stack and pop them off the stack again. You can see that the same `Stack` object can contain objects that are value types as well as reference types.

Interface Classes

The definition of an interface class looks quite similar to the definition of a ref class, but it is quite a different concept. An interface is a class that specifies a set of functions that are to be implemented by other classes to provide a standardized way of providing some specific functionality. Both value classes and ref classes can implement interfaces. An interface does not define any of its function members — these are defined by each class that implements the interface.

You have already met the `System::IComparable` interface in the context of generic functions where you specified the `IComparable` interface as a constraint. The `IComparable` interface specifies the `CompareTo()` function for comparing objects, so all classes that implement this interface have the same mechanism for comparing objects. You specify an interface that a class implements in the same way as a base class. For example, here's how you could make the `Box` class from the previous example implement the `System::IComparable` interface:

```
ref class Box : Container, IComparable              // Derived class
{
  public:
    // The function specified by IComparable interface
    virtual int CompareTo(Object^ obj)
    {
      if(Volume() < safe_cast<Box^>(obj)->Volume())
        return -1;
      else if(Volume() > safe_cast<Box^>(obj)->Volume())
        return 1;
      else
      return 0;
    }

  // Rest of the class as before...
};
```

The name of the interface follows the name of the base class, `Container`. If there were no base class, the interface name alone would appear here. A ref class can only have one base class, but it can implement as many interfaces as you want. The class must define every function specified by each of the interfaces that it claims to implement. The `IComparable` interface only specifies one function, but there can be as many functions in an interface as you want. The `Box` class now defines the `CompareTo()` function with the same signature as the `IComparable` interface specifies for the function. Because the parameter to the `CompareTo()` function is of type `Object^`, you have to cast it to type `Box^` before you can access members of the `Box` object it references.

Defining Interface Classes

You define an interface class using either of the keywords `interface class` or `interface struct`. Regardless of whether you use the `interface class` or the `interface struct` keyword to define an interface, all the members of an interface are always `public` by default, and you cannot specify them to be otherwise. The members of an interface can be functions, including operator functions, properties, static fields, and events, all of which you'll learn about later in this chapter. An interface can also specify a static constructor and can contain a nested class definition of any kind. In spite of all that potential diversity of members, most interfaces are relatively simple. Note that you can derive one interface from another in basically the same way as you use to derive one ref class from another. For example:

```
interface class IController : ITelevison, IRecorder
{
  // Members of IController...
};
```

The `IController` interface contains its own members, and it also inherits the members of the `ITelevision` and `IRecorder` interfaces. A class that implements the `IController` interface has to define the member functions from `IController`, `ITelevision`, and `IRecorder`.

You could use an interface instead of the `Container` base class in `Ex9_14`. Here's how the definition of this interface would look:

```
// IContainer.h for Ex9_15
#pragma once

interface class IContainer
{
  double Volume();                  // Function for calculating a volume
  void ShowVolume();                // Function to display a volume
};
```

By convention, the names of interfaces start with I in C++/CLI, so the interface name is `IContainer`. It has two members: the `Volume()` function and the `ShowVolume()` function, which are public because members of an interface are always public. Both functions are effectively abstract because an interface never includes function definitions — indeed, you could add the `abstract` keyword to both here, but it is not required. Instance functions in an interface definition can be specified as `virtual` and `abstract`, but it is not necessary to do so as they are anyway.

Any class that implements the `IContainer` interface must implement both functions if the class is not to be abstract. Let's see how the `Box` class looks:

```
// Box.h for Ex9_15
#pragma once

#include "IContainer.h"                 // For interface definition

using namespace System;

ref class Box : IContainer
{
  public:
    // Function to show the volume of an object
    virtual void ShowVolume()
```

```
    {
      Console::WriteLine(L"Box usable volume is {0}", Volume());
    }

    // Function to calculate the volume of a Box object
    virtual double Volume()
    { return m_Length*m_Width*m_Height; }

    // Constructor
    Box() : m_Length(1.0), m_Width(1.0), m_Height(1.0){}

    // Constructor
    Box(double lv, double wv, double hv)
                          : m_Length(lv), m_Width(wv), m_Height(hv){}

  protected:
    double m_Length;
    double m_Width;
    double m_Height;
};
```

The name of the interface goes after the colon in the first line of the class definition, just as if it were a base class. Of course, there could also be a base class, in which case, the interface name would follow the base class name, separated from it by a comma. A class can implement multiple interfaces, in which case, the names of the interfaces are separated by commas.

The Box class must implement both function members of the IContainer interface class; otherwise, it would be an abstract class and would need to be declared as such. The definitions for these functions in the Box class do not have the override keyword appended because you are not overriding existing function definitions here; you are implementing them for the first time.

The GlassBox class is derived from the Box class and, therefore, inherits the implementation of IContainer. The GlassBox class definition needs no changes at all to accommodate the introduction of the IContainer interface class.

The IContainer interface class has the same role as a base class in polymorphism. You can use a handle of type IContainer to store the address of an object of any class type that implements the interface. Thus, a handle of type IContainer can be used to reference objects of type Box or type GlassBox and obtain polymorphic behavior when calling the functions that are members of the interface class. Let's try it.

TRY IT OUT   Implementing an Interface Class

Create the CLR console project Ex9_15 and add the IContainer.h and Box.h header files with the contents from the previous section. You should also add copies of the Stack.h and GlassBox.h header files from Ex9_14 to the project. Finally, modify the contents of Ex9_15.cpp to the following:

```
// Ex9_15.cpp : main project file.
// Implementing an interface class
#include "stdafx.h"
#include "Box.h"                        // For Box and IContainer
#include "GlassBox.h"                   // For GlassBox (and Box and IContainer)
#include "Stack.h"                      // For the stack class with nested struct Item
```

```
using namespace System;

int main(array<System::String ^> ^args)
{
  array<IContainer^>^ containers = { gcnew Box(2.0, 3.0, 4.0),
                                     gcnew GlassBox(2.0, 3.0, 4.0),
                                     gcnew Box(4.0, 5.0, 6.0),
                                     gcnew GlassBox(4.0, 5.0, 6.0)
                                   };

  Console::WriteLine(L"The array of containers have the following volumes:");
  for each(IContainer^ container in containers)
    container->ShowVolume();        // Output the volume of a box

  Console::WriteLine(L"\nNow pushing the containers on the stack...");

  Stack^ stack = gcnew Stack;       // Create the stack
  for each(IContainer^ container in containers)
    stack->Push(container);

  Console::WriteLine(
        L"Popping the containers off the stack presents them in reverse order:");
  Object^ item;
  while((item = stack->Pop()) != nullptr)
    safe_cast<IContainer^>(item)->ShowVolume();

  Console::WriteLine();
  return 0;
}
```

code snippet Ex9_15.cpp

This example produces the following output:

```
The array of containers have the following volumes:
CBox usable volume is 24
CBox usable volume is 20.4
CBox usable volume is 120
CBox usable volume is 102

Now pushing the containers on the stack...
Popping the containers off the stack presents them in reverse order:
CBox usable volume is 102
CBox usable volume is 120
CBox usable volume is 20.4
CBox usable volume is 24
```

How It Works

You create an array of elements of type IContainer^ and initialize the elements with the addresses of Box and GlassBox objects:

```
array<IContainer^>^ containers = { gcnew Box(2.0, 3.0, 4.0),
```

```
                              gcnew GlassBox(2.0, 3.0, 4.0),
                              gcnew Box(4.0, 5.0, 6.0),
                              gcnew GlassBox(4.0, 5.0, 6.0)
                    };
```

The Box and GlassBox classes implement the IContainer interface, so you can store addresses of objects of these types in variables of type handle to IContainer. The advantage of doing this is that you'll be able to call the function members of the IContainer interface class polymorphically.

You list the volumes of the Box and GlassBox objects in a for each loop:

```
        for each(IContainer^ container in containers)
          container->ShowVolume();                // Output the volume of a box
```

The loop body shows polymorphism in action; the ShowVolume() function for the specific type of object referenced by container is called, as you can see from the output.

You push the elements of the containers array onto the stack in essentially the same way as the previous example. Popping the elements off the stack is also similar to the previous example:

```
        Object^ item;
        while((item = stack->Pop()) != nullptr)
          safe_cast<IContainer^>(item)->ShowVolume();
```

The loop body shows that you can cast a handle to an interface type using safe_cast in exactly the same way as you would cast to a ref class type. You are then able to use the handle to call the ShowVolume() function polymorphically.

Using interface classes is not only a useful way of defining sets of functions that represent standard class interfaces, but also a powerful mechanism for applying polymorphism in your programs.

Classes and Assemblies

A C++/CLI application always resides in one or more assemblies, so C++/CLI classes always reside in an assembly. The classes we have defined for each example up to now have all been contained in a single simple assembly that is the executable, but you can create assemblies that contain your own library classes. C++/CLI adds **visibility specifiers** for classes that determine whether a given class is accessible from outside the assembly in which it resides, which is referred to as its parent assembly. In addition to the public, private, and protected member access specifiers that you have in native C++, C++/CLI has additional access specifiers for class members that determine from where they may be accessed in different assemblies.

Visibility Specifiers for Classes and Interfaces

You can specify the visibility of a non-nested class, interface, or enum as private or public. A public class is visible and accessible outside the assembly in which it resides, whereas a private class is only accessible within its parent assembly. Classes, interfaces, and enum classes are private by default and, therefore, only visible within their parent assembly. To specify a class as public, you just use the `public` keyword, like this:

```
public interface class IContainer
{
  // Details of the interface...
};
```

The `IContainer` interface here is visible in an external assembly because you have defined it as public. If you omit the `public` keyword, the interface would be private by default and only usable within its parent assembly. You can specify a class, `enum`, or interface explicitly as `private` if you want, but it is not necessary.

Access Specifiers for Class and Interface Members

C++/CLI adds three more access specifiers for class members: `internal`, `public protected`, and `private protected`. The effects of these are described in the comments in the class definition:

```
public ref class MyClass        // Class visible outside assembly
{
public:
  // Members accessible from classes inside and outside the parent assembly

internal:
  // Members accessible from classes inside the parent assembly

public protected:
  // Members accessible in types derived from MyClass outside the parent assembly
  // and in any classes inside the parent assembly

private protected:
  // Members accessible in types derived from MyClass inside the parent assembly
};
```

Obviously, the class must be public for the member access specifiers to allow access from outside the parent assembly. Where the access specifier involves two keywords, such as `private protected`, the less restrictive keyword applies inside the assembly and the more restrictive keyword applies outside the assembly. You can reverse the sequence of the keyword pairs, so `protected private` has the same meaning as `private protected`.

To use some of these, you need to create an application that consists of more than one assembly, so let's recreate `Ex9_15` as a class library assembly plus an application assembly that uses the class library.

TRY IT OUT   Creating a Class Library

To create a class library, you can first create a CLR project with the name `Ex9_16lib` using the `Class Library` template. The project contains a header file, `Ex9_16lib.h`, with the following content:

```
// Ex9_16lib.h

#pragma once

using namespace System;

namespace Ex9_16lib
{
  public ref class Class1
  {
    // TODO: Add your methods for this class here.
  };
}
```

A class library has its own namespace, and here, the namespace name is Ex9_16lib by default. You could change this name to something more suitable if you want. The names of the classes in the library are qualified by the namespace name, so you need a using directive for the namespace name in any external source file that is accessing any of the classes in the library. The definitions of the classes that are to be in the library go between the braces for the namespace. There's a default ref class defined within the namespace, but you replace this with your own classes. Note that the Class1 class is public; all classes that are to be visible in another assembly must be specified as public.

Modify the contents of Ex9_16lib.h to:

```
// Ex9_16lib.h

#pragma once

using namespace System;

namespace Ex9_16lib
{
// IContainer.h for Ex9_16
public interface class IContainer
{
  virtual double Volume();              // Function for calculating a volume
  virtual void ShowVolume();            // Function to display a volume
};


// Box.h for Ex9_16
public ref class Box : IContainer
{
  public:
    // Function to show the volume of an object
    virtual void ShowVolume()
    {
      Console::WriteLine(L"CBox usable volume is {0}", Volume());
    }

    // Function to calculate the volume of a Box object
    virtual double Volume()
```

```
              { return m_Length*m_Width*m_Height; }

       // Constructor
       Box() : m_Length(1.0), m_Width(1.0), m_Height(1.0){}

       // Constructor
       Box(double lv, double wv, double hv)
                                : m_Length(lv), m_Width(wv), m_Height(hv){}

  public protected:
       double m_Length;
       double m_Width;
       double m_Height;
};

// Stack.h for Ex9_16
public ref class Stack
{
private:
  // Defines items to store in the stack
  ref struct Item
  {
    Object^ Obj;                      // Handle for the object in this item
    Item^ Next;                       // Handle for next item in the stack or nullptr

    // Constructor
    Item(Object^ obj, Item^ next): Obj(obj), Next(next){}
  };

  Item^ Top;                          // Handle for item that is at the top

public:
  // Push an object onto the stack
  void Push(Object^ obj)
  {
    Top = gcnew Item(obj, Top);       // Create new item and make it the top
  }

  // Pop an object off the stack
  Object^ Pop()
  {
    if(Top == nullptr)                // If the stack is empty
      return nullptr;                 // return nullptr

    Object^ obj = Top->Obj;           // Get box from item
    Top = Top->Next;                  // Make next item the top
    return obj;
  }
};
}
```

The IContainer interface class, the Box class, and the Stack class are now in this library. The changes to the original definitions for these classes are shaded. Each class is now public, which makes them accessible from an external assembly. The fields in the Box class are public protected, which means that they are inherited in a derived class as `protected` fields but are `public` so far as classes within the parent assembly are concerned. You don't actually refer to these fields from other classes within the parent assembly, so you could have left the fields in the `Box` class as `protected` in this case.

When you have built this project successfully, the assembly containing the class library is in a file `Ex9_16lib.dll` that is in the `debug` subdirectory to the project directory if you built a debug version of the project, or in a `release` subdirectory if you built the release version. The `.dll` extension means that this is a **dynamic link library**, or **DLL**. You now need another project that uses your class library.

TRY IT OUT   Using a Class Library

Add a new CLR console project with the name `Ex9_16` in its own solution as always. You can then modify `Ex9_16.cpp` as follows:

Available for download on Wrox.com

```cpp
// Ex9_16.cpp : main project file.
// Using a class library in a separate assembly

#include "stdafx.h"
#include "GlassBox.h"
#using <Ex9_16lib.dll>

using namespace System;
using namespace Ex9_16lib;

int main(array<System::String ^> ^args)
{
  array<IContainer^>^ containers = { gcnew Box(2.0, 3.0, 4.0),
                                     gcnew GlassBox(2.0, 3.0, 4.0),
                                     gcnew Box(4.0, 5.0, 6.0),
                                     gcnew GlassBox(4.0, 5.0, 6.0)
                                   };

  Console::WriteLine(L"The array of containers have the following volumes:");
  for each(IContainer^ container in containers)
    container->ShowVolume();                // Output the volume of a box

  Console::WriteLine(L"\nNow pushing the containers on the stack...");

  Stack^ stack = gcnew Stack;         // Create the stack
  for each(IContainer^ container in containers)
    stack->Push(container);


  Console::WriteLine(
          L"Popping the containers off the stack presents them in reverse order:");
  Object^ item;
  while((item = stack->Pop()) != nullptr)
```

```
        safe_cast<IContainer^>(item)->ShowVolume();

    Console::WriteLine();
    return 0;
}
```

code snippet Ex9_16.cpp

You also need to add the GlassBox.h header to the project with the same code as in Ex9_15, so you can copy the file to this project directory and then add it to the project by right-clicking Header Files in the Solution Explorer tab and selecting Add ➪ Existing Item. . . from the context menu. Of course, the GlassBox class is derived from the Box class, so the compiler needs to know where to find the Box class definition. In this case, it's in the library you created in the previous project, so add the following directive to the GlassBox.h header file after the #pragma once directive:

```
#using <Ex9_16lib.dll>
```

You should also remove the the #include directive for Box.h.

The Box class name is defined within the Ex9_16lib namespace, so you also need to add a using statement for that following the #using directive:

```
using namespace Ex9_16lib;
```

The Ex9_16lib.dll file must be available to build the project, so copy the file from the Ex9_16lib project to the subdirectory of the Ex9_16 project that contains the source files. Once the build is successful, you can move Ex9_16lib.dll to the directory that contains the Ex9_16.exe file so that the executable can find it when you run it. You could specify the full path to the assembly in the #using directive, but it is more usual to put any class libraries that a project uses in the directory that contains the executable for an application.

It's easy to get the directories muddled here. The Ex9_16lib.dll file is in the debug subdirectory of the Ex9_16lib *solution* directory, not the debug subdirectory of the Ex9_16lib project directory. You are copying the library file to the debug subdirectory of the Ex9_16 solution directory. Make sure you copy the .dll file to the correct directory, or the library won't be found.

Because the classes in the external assembly are in their own namespace, you have a using directive for the Ex9_16lib namespace name. Without this, you would have to qualify the IContainer, Box, and Stack names with the namespace name, so you would write Ex9_16lib::Box instead of just Box, for example.

The remainder of the code is exactly the same as in the main() function for Ex9_15; no changes are necessary because you are now using classes from an external assembly. If you execute the program, you'll see the output is the same as that from Ex9_15.

Functions Specified as new

You have seen how you use the override keyword to override a function in a base class. You can also specify a function in a derived class as new, in which case, it hides the function in the base class that has the same signature, and the new function does not participate in polymorphic behavior. To define the Volume() function as new in a class NewBox that is derived from Box, you code it like this:

```
ref class NewBox : Box                // Derived class
{
  public:
    // New function to calculate the volume of a NewBox object
    virtual double Volume() new
    { return 0.5*m_Length*m_Width*m_Height; }

    // Constructor
    NewBox(double lv, double wv, double hv): Box(lv, wv, hv){}
};
```

This version of the function hides the version of the Volume() function that is defined in Box, so if you call the Volume() function using a handle of type NewBox^, the new version is called. For example:

```
NewBox^ newBox = gcnew NewBox(2.0, 3.0, 4.0);
Console::WriteLine(newBox->Volume());  // Output is 12
```

The result is 12 because the new Volume() function hides the polymorphic version that the NextBox class inherits from Box.

The new Volume() function is not a polymorphic function, so for polymorphic calls using a handle to a base class type, the new version is not called. For example:

```
Box^ newBox = gcnew NewBox(2.0, 3.0,4.0);
Console::WriteLine(newBox->Volume());  // Output is 24
```

The only polymorphic Volume() function in the NewBox class is the one that is inherited from the Box class, so that is the function that is called in this case.

Delegates and Events

An **event** is a member of a class that enables an object to signal when a particular event has occurred, and the signaling process for an event involves a **delegate** that provides the mechanism for responding to the event in some way. A mouse click is a typical example of an event, and the object that originated the mouse-click event would signal that the event has occurred by calling one or more functions that are responsible for dealing with the event; a delegate would provide the means to access the function that is to respond to the event. Let's look at delegates first and return to events a little later in this chapter.

The idea of a delegate is very simple — it's an object that can encapsulate one or more pointers to functions that have a given parameter list and return type. A function that a delegate points to will deal with a particular kind of event. Thus, a delegate provides a similar facility in C++/CLI to a function pointer in native C++. Although the idea of a delegate is simple, however, the details of creating and using delegates can get a little confusing, so it's time to concentrate.

Declaring Delegates

The declaration for a delegate looks like a function prototype preceded by the `delegate` keyword, but, in reality, it defines two things: the reference type name for a delegate object, and the parameter list and return type of the functions that can be associated with the delegate. A delegate reference type has the `System::Delegate` class as a base class, so a delegate type always inherits the members of this class. Here's an example of a declaration for a delegate:

```
public delegate void Handler(int value);          // Delegate declaration
```

This defines a delegate reference type `Handler`, where the `Handler` type is derived from `System::Delegate`. An object of type `Handler` can contain pointers to one or more functions that have a single parameter of type `int` and a return type that is `void`. The functions pointed to by a delegate can be instance functions or static functions.

Creating Delegates

Having defined a delegate type, you can now create delegate objects of this type. You have a choice of two constructors for a delegate: one that accepts a single argument, and another that accepts two arguments.

The argument to the delegate constructor that accepts one argument must be a static function member of a class or a global function. The function you specify as the argument must have the same return type and parameter list as you specified in the delegate declaration. Suppose you define a class with the name `HandlerClass` like this:

```
public ref class HandlerClass
{
public:
  static void Fun1(int m)
  { Console::WriteLine(L"Function1 called with value {0}", m); }

  static void Fun2(int m)
  { Console::WriteLine(L"Function2 called with value {0}", m); }

  void Fun3(int m)
  { Console::WriteLine(L"Function3 called with value {0}", m+value); }

  void Fun4(int m)
  { Console::WriteLine(L"Function4 called with value {0}", m+value); }

  HandlerClass():value(1){}

  HandlerClass(int m):value(m){}
protected:
  int value;
};
```

The class has four functions, with a parameter of type `int` and a return type of `void`. Two of these are static functions, and two are instance functions. It also has two constructors, including a no-arg constructor. This class doesn't do much except produce output where you'll be able to determine which function was called and, for instance functions, what the object was.

You could create a delegate of the type `Handler` that we defined earlier like this:

```
Handler^ handler = gcnew Handler(HandlerClass::Fun1);    // Delegate object
```

The `handler` object contains the address of the static function, `Fun1`, in the `HandlerClass` class. If you call the delegate, the `HandlerClass::Fun1()` function is called, with the argument the same as you pass in the delegate call. You can write the delegate call like this:

```
handler->Invoke(90);
```

This calls all the functions in the invocation list for the handler delegate. In this case, there is just one function in the invocation list, `HandlerClass::Fun1()`, so the output is:

```
Function1 called with value 90
```

You could also call the delegate with the following statement:

```
handler(90);
```

This is shorthand for the previous statement that explicitly called the `Invoke()` function, and this is the form of delegate call you see generally.

The + operator is overloaded for delegate types to combine the invocation lists for two delegates into a new delegate object. For example, you could apparently modify the invocation list for the `handler` delegate with this statement:

```
handler += gcnew Handler(HandlerClass::Fun2);
```

The handler variable now references a delegate object with an invocation list containing two functions: `Fun1` and `Fun2`. However, this statement creates a new delegate object. The invocation list for a delegate cannot be changed, so the + operator works in a similar way to the way it works with `String` objects — you always get a new object created. You could invoke the delegate again with this statement:

```
handler(80);
```

Now, you get the output:

```
Function1 called with value 80
Function2 called with value 80
```

Both functions in the invocation list are called, and they are called in the sequence in which they were added to the delegate object.

You can effectively remove an entry from the invocation list for a delegate by using the subtraction operator:

```
handler -= gcnew Handler(HandlerClass::Fun1);
```

This creates a new delegate object that contains just `HandlerClass::Fun2()` in its invocation list. The effect of using the -= operator is to remove the functions that are in the invocation list on the right side (`HandlerClass::Fun1`) from the list for the handler, and create a new object pointing to the functions that remain.

 NOTE *The invocation list for a delegate must contain at least one function pointer. If you remove all the function pointers using the subtraction operator, then the result will be* `nullptr`.

When you use the delegate constructor that has two parameters, the first argument is a reference to an object on the CLR heap, and the second object is the address of an instance function for that object's type. Thus, this constructor creates a delegate that contains a pointer to the instance function specified by the second argument for the object specified by the first argument. Here's how you can create such a delegate:

```
HandlerClass^ obj = gcnew HandlerClass;
Handler^ handler2 = gcnew Handler (obj, &HandlerClass::Fun3);
```

The first statement creates an object of type `HandlerClass`, and the second statement creates a delegate of type `Handler` pointing to the `Fun3()` function for the `HandlerClass` object `obj`. The delegate expects an argument of type `int`, so you can invoke it with the statement:

```
handler2(70);
```

This results in `Fun3()` for `obj` being called with an argument value of 70, so the output is:

```
Function3 called with value 71
```

The value stored in the value field for `obj` is 1 because you create the object using the default constructor. The statement in the body of `Fun3()` adds the value field to the function argument — hence the 71 in the output.

Because they are both of the same type, you could combine the invocation list for `handler` with the list for the `handler2` delegate:

```
Handler^ handler = gcnew Handler(HandlerClass::Fun1);      // Delegate object
handler += gcnew Handler(HandlerClass::Fun2);

HandlerClass^ obj = gcnew HandlerClass;
Handler^ handler2 = gcnew Handler (obj, &HandlerClass::Fun3);
handler += handler2;
```

Here, you recreate `handler` to reference a delegate that contains pointers to the static `Fun1()` and `Fun2()` functions. You then create a new delegate referenced by `handler` that contains the static functions plus the `Fun3()` instance function for `obj`. You can now invoke the delegate with the statement:

```
handler(50);
```

This results in the following output:

```
Function1 called with value 50
Function2 called with value 50
Function3 called with value 51
```

As you see, invoking the delegate calls the two static functions plus the `Fun3()` member of `obj`, so you can combine static and non-static functions with a single invocation list for a delegate.

Let's put some of the fragments together in an example to make sure it really does work.

> ### TRY IT OUT   Creating and Calling Delegates

Here's a potpourri of what you have seen so far about delegates:

```cpp
// Ex9_17.cpp : main project file.
// Creating and calling delegates

#include "stdafx.h"

using namespace System;

public ref class HandlerClass
{
public:
  static void Fun1(int m)
  { Console::WriteLine(L"Function1 called with value {0}", m); }

  static void Fun2(int m)
  { Console::WriteLine(L"Function2 called with value {0}", m); }

  void Fun3(int m)
  { Console::WriteLine(L"Function3 called with value {0}", m+value); }

  void Fun4(int m)
  { Console::WriteLine(L"Function4 called with value {0}", m+value); }

  HandlerClass():value(1){}

  HandlerClass(int m):value(m){}
protected:
  int value;
};

public delegate void Handler(int value);          // Delegate declaration

int main(array<System::String ^> ^args)
{
```

```
    Handler^ handler = gcnew Handler(HandlerClass::Fun1); // Delegate object
    Console::WriteLine(L"Delegate with one pointer to a static function:");
    handler->Invoke(90);

    handler += gcnew Handler(HandlerClass::Fun2);
    Console::WriteLine(L"\nDelegate with two pointers to static functions:");
    handler->Invoke(80);

    HandlerClass^ obj = gcnew HandlerClass;
    Handler^ handler2 = gcnew Handler (obj, &HandlerClass::Fun3);
    handler += handler2;
    Console::WriteLine(L"\nDelegate with three pointers to functions:");
    handler(70);

    Console::WriteLine(L"\nShortening the invocation list...");
    handler -= gcnew Handler(HandlerClass::Fun1);
    Console::WriteLine
            (L"\nDelegate with pointers to one static and one instance function:");
    handler(60);
    return 0;
}
```

code snippet Ex9_17.cpp

This example produces the following output:

```
Delegate with one pointer to a static function:
Function1 called with value 90

Delegate with two pointers to static functions:
Function1 called with value 80
Function2 called with value 80

Delegate with three pointers to functions:
Function1 called with value 70
Function2 called with value 70
Function3 called with value 71

Shortening the invocation list...

Delegate with pointers to one static and one instance function:
Function2 called with value 60
Function3 called with value 61
```

How It Works

You saw all the operations that appear in main() in the previous section. You invoke a delegate using the Invoke() function explicitly, and by just using the delegate handle followed by its argument list. You can see from the output that everything works as it should.

Although the example shows a delegate that can contain pointers to functions with a single argument, a delegate can point to functions with as many arguments as you want. For example, you could declare a delegate type like this:

```
delegate void MyHandler(double x, String^ description);
```

This statement declares the `MyHandler` delegate type that can only point to functions with a `void` return type and two parameters, the first of type `double` and the second of type `String^`.

Unbound Delegates

The delegates you have seen up to now have been examples of **bound** delegates. They are called bound delegates because they each have a fixed set of functions in their invocation list. You can also create **unbound** delegates; an unbound delegate points to an instance function with a given parameter list and return type for a given type of object. Thus, the same delegate can invoke the instance function for any object of the specified type. Here's an example of declaring an unbound delegate:

```
public delegate void UBHandler(ThisClass^, int value);
```

The first argument specifies the type of the `this` pointer for which a delegate of type `UBHandler` can call an instance function; the function must have a single parameter of type `int` and a return type of `void`. Thus, a delegate of type `UBHandler` can only call a function for an object of type `ThisClass`, but for *any* object of that type. This may sound a bit restrictive but turns out to be quite useful; you could use the delegate to call a function for each element of type `ThisClass^` in an array, for example.

You can create an unbound delegate of type `UBHandler` like this:

```
UBHandler^ ubh = gcnew UBHandler(&ThisClass::Sum);
```

The argument to the constructor is the address of a function in the `ThisClass` class that has the required parameter list and return type.

Here's a definition for `ThisClass`:

```
public ref class ThisClass
{
public:
  void Sum(int n)
  { Console::WriteLine(L"Sum result = {0}", value + n); }

  void Product(int n)
  { Console::WriteLine(L"Product result = {0}", value*n); }

  ThisClass(double v) : value(v){}

private:
  double value;
};
```

The Sum() function is a public instance member of the ThisClass class, so invoking the ubh delegate can call the Sum() function for any given object of this class type.

When you call an unbound delegate, the first argument is the object for which the functions in the invocation list are to be called, and the subsequent arguments are the arguments to those functions. Here's how you might call the ubh delegate:

```
ThisClass^ obj = gcnew ThisClass(99.0);
ubh(obj, 5);
```

The first argument is a handle to a ThisClass object that you created on the CLR heap by passing the value 99.0 to the class constructor. The second argument to the ubh call is 5, so it results in the Sum() function being called with an argument of 5 for the object referenced by obj.

You can combine unbound delegates using the + operator to create a delegate that calls multiple functions. Of course, all the functions must be compatible with the delegate, so for ubh, they must be instance functions in the ThisClass class that have one parameter of type int and a void return type. Here's an example:

```
ubh += gcnew UBHandler(&ThisClass::Product);
```

Invoking the new delegate referenced by ubh calls both the Sum() and Product() functions for an object of type ThisClass. Let's see it in action.

TRY IT OUT   Using an Unbound Delegate

This example uses the code fragments from the previous section to demonstrate the operation of an unbound delegate:

```
// Ex9_18.cpp : main project file.
// Using an unbound delegate

#include "stdafx.h"

using namespace System;

public ref class ThisClass
{
public:
  void Sum(int n)
  { Console::WriteLine(L"Sum result = {0} ", value+n); }

  void Product(int n)
  { Console::WriteLine(L"product result = {0} ", value*n); }

  ThisClass(double v) : value(v){}

private:
  double value;
};
```

```
public delegate void UBHandler(ThisClass^, int value);

int main(array<System::String ^> ^args)
{
  array<ThisClass^>^ things = { gcnew ThisClass(5.0),gcnew ThisClass(10.0),
                                gcnew ThisClass(15.0),gcnew ThisClass(20.0),
                                gcnew ThisClass(25.0)
                              };

  UBHandler^ ubh = gcnew UBHandler(&ThisClass::Sum);   // Create a delegate object

  // Call the delegate for each things array element
  for each(ThisClass^ thing in things)
    ubh(thing, 3);

   ubh += gcnew UBHandler(&ThisClass::Product);   // Add a function to the delegate

  // Call the new delegate for each things array element
  for each(ThisClass^ thing in things)
    ubh(thing, 2);

  return 0;
}
```

code snippet Ex9_18.cpp

This example produces the following output:

```
Sum result = 8
Sum result = 13
Sum result = 18
Sum result = 23
Sum result = 28
Sum result = 7
product result = 10
Sum result = 12
product result = 20
Sum result = 17
product result = 30
Sum result = 22
product result = 40
Sum result = 27
product result = 50
```

How It Works

The UBHandler delegate type is declared by the following statement:

```
public delegate void UBHandler(ThisClass^, int value);
```

UBHandler delegate objects are unbound delegates that can call instance functions for objects of type ThisClass, as long as they have a single parameter of type int and a return type of void.

The ThisClass class definition in the example is the same as you saw in the previous section. It has two instance functions — Sum() and Product() — that have a parameter type of int and a return type of void, so either or both may be called by a delegate of type UBHandler.

You create an array of handles to ThisClass objects in main() with the statement:

```
array<ThisClass^>^ things = { gcnew ThisClass(5.0),gcnew ThisClass(10.0),
                              gcnew ThisClass(15.0),gcnew ThisClass(20.0),
                              gcnew ThisClass(25.0)
                            };
```

The five objects in the initialization list each encapsulate a different value of type double, so for Sum() and Product() function calls, the object involved will be easy to identify in the output.

You create a delegate object with the statement:

```
UBHandler^ ubh = gcnew UBHandler(&ThisClass::Sum);   // Create a delegate object
```

Invoking the delegate object referenced by the handle ubh calls the Sum() function for any object of type ThisClass, and you do this for each object in the things array:

```
for each(ThisClass^ thing in things)
  ubh(thing, 3);
```

The for each loop iterates over each element in the things array, so, in the loop body, you call the delegate with an element from the array as the first argument. This causes the Sum() function to be called for the thing object with an argument of 3. Thus, this loop produces the first five output lines.

Next, you create a new delegate:

```
ubh += gcnew UBHandler(&ThisClass::Product);   // Add a function to the delegate
```

This statement creates a new UBHandler delegate that points to the Product() function and combines this with the existing delegate referenced by ubh. The result is another delegate that has pointers to both the Sum() and Product() functions in its invocation list.

The last loop calls the ubh delegate for each element in the things array with the argument value 2. The result will be that both Sum() and Product() will be called for each ThisClass object with the argument value 2, so the loop produces the next ten lines of output.

Although you have used unbound delegates in a very simple way here, they provide immense flexibility in your programs. You could pass an unbound delegate as an argument to a function, for example, to enable the same function to call different combinations of instance functions at different times so the delegate becomes a kind of function selector. The sequence in which functions are called by a delegate is the sequence that they appear in the invocation list, so a delegate provides you with the means of controlling the sequence in which functions are called.

Creating Events

As I said earlier, the signaling of an event involves a delegate, and the delegate contains pointers to the functions that are to be called when the event occurs. Most of the events you work with in your programs are events associated with controls such as buttons or menu items, and these events arise from user interactions with your program, but you can also define and trigger events in your own program code.

An event is a member of a reference class that you define using the event keyword and a delegate class name:

```
public delegate void DoorHandler(String^ str);

// Class with an event member
public ref class Door
{
public:
  // An event that will call functions associated
  // with an DoorHandler delegate object
  event DoorHandler^ Knock;

  // Function to trigger events
  void TriggerEvents()
  {
    Knock("Fred");
    Knock("Jane");
  }
};
```

The Door class has an event member with the name Knock that corresponds to a delegate of type DoorHandler. Knock is an instance member of the class here, but you can specify an event as a static class member using the static keyword. You can also declare an event to be virtual. When a Knock event is triggered, it can call functions with the parameter list and return type that are specified by the DoorHandler delegate.

The Door class also has a public function, TriggerEvents(), that triggers two Knock events, each with different arguments. The arguments are passed to the functions that have been registered to receive notification of the Knock event. As you see, triggering an event is essentially the same as calling a delegate.

You could define a class that might handle Knock events like this:

```
public ref class AnswerDoor
{
public:
  void ImIn(String^ name)
  {
    Console::WriteLine(L"Come in {0}, it's open.",name);
  }

  void ImOut(String^ name)
  {
    Console::WriteLine(L"Go away {0}, I'm out.",name);
  }
};
```

The `AnswerDoor` class has two public function members that potentially could handle a `Knock` event, because they both have the parameter list and return type identified in the declaration of the `DoorHandler` delegate.

Before you can register functions that are to receive notifications of `Knock` events, you need to create a `Door` object. You can create a `Door` object like this:

```
Door^ door = gcnew Door;
```

Now, you can register a function to receive notification of the `Knock` event in the `door` object like this:

```
AnswerDoor^ answer = gcnew AnswerDoor;
door->Knock += gcnew DoorHandler(answer, &AnswerDoor::ImIn);
```

The first statement creates an object of type `AnswerDoor` — you need this because the `ImIn()` and `ImOut()` functions are not static class members. You then add an instance of the `DoorHandler` delegate type to the `Knock` member of class `Door`. This exactly parallels the process of adding function pointers to a delegate, and you could add further handler functions to be called when a `Knock` event is triggered in the same way. We can see it operating in an example.

TRY IT OUT   Handling Events

This example uses the classes from the preceding section to define, trigger, and handle events:

```cpp
// Ex9_19.cpp : main project file.
// Defining, triggering and handling events.
#include "stdafx.h"

using namespace System;

public delegate void DoorHandler(String^ str);

// Class with an event member
public ref class Door
{
public:
  // An event that will call functions associated
  // with a DoorHandler delegate object
  event DoorHandler^ Knock;

  // Function to trigger events
  void TriggerEvents()
  {
    Knock(L"Fred");
    Knock(L"Jane");
  }
};

// Class defining handler functions for Knock events
public ref class AnswerDoor
```

```
{
public:
  void ImIn(String^ name)
  {
    Console::WriteLine(L"Come in {0}, it's open.",name);
  }

  void ImOut(String^ name)
  {
    Console::WriteLine(L"Go away {0}, I'm out.",name);
  }
};

int main(array<System::String ^> ^args)
{
  Door^ door = gcnew Door;
  AnswerDoor^ answer = gcnew AnswerDoor;

  // Add handler for Knock event member of door
  door->Knock += gcnew DoorHandler(answer, &AnswerDoor::ImIn);

  door->TriggerEvents();                // Trigger Knock events

  // Change the way a knock is dealt with
  door->Knock -= gcnew DoorHandler(answer, &AnswerDoor::ImIn);
  door->Knock += gcnew DoorHandler(answer, &AnswerDoor::ImOut);
  door->TriggerEvents();                // Trigger Knock events
  return 0;
}
```

code snippet Ex9_19.cpp

Executing this example results in the following output:

```
Come in Fred, it's open.
Come in Jane, it's open.
Go away Fred, I'm out.
Go away Jane, I'm out.
```

How It Works

You first create two objects in main():

```
Door^ door = gcnew Door;
AnswerDoor^ answer = gcnew AnswerDoor;
```

The door object has an event member, Knock, and the answer object has member functions that can be registered to be called for Knock events.

The next statement registers the ImIn() member of the answer object to receive notification of Knock events for the door object:

```
door->Knock += gcnew DoorHandler(answer, &AnswerDoor::ImIn);
```

If it made sense to do so, you could register other functions to be called when a `Knock` event is triggered.

The next statement calls the `TriggerEvents()` member of the `door` object:

```
door->TriggerEvents();              // Trigger Knock events
```

This results in two `Knock` events, one with the argument `"Fred"` and the other with the argument `"Jane"`. The result is that the `ImIn()` function is called once for each event, which produces the first two lines of output.

Of course, you might want to respond differently to an event at different times, depending on the circumstances, and this is what the next three statements in `main()` demonstrate:

```
door->Knock -= gcnew DoorHandler(answer, &AnswerDoor::ImIn);
door->Knock += gcnew DoorHandler(answer, &AnswerDoor::ImOut);
door->TriggerEvents();              // Trigger Knock events
```

The first statement removes the pointer to the `ImIn()` function from the event, and the second statement registers the `ImOut()` function for the `answer` object to receive event notifications. When the `Knock` events are triggered by the third statement, the `ImOut()` function is called, so the results are a little different.

Destructors and Finalizers in Reference Classes

You can define a destructor for a reference class in the same way as you define a destructor for a native C++ class. The destructor for a reference class is called when the handle goes out of scope or the object is part of another object that is being destroyed. You can also apply the `delete` operator to a handle for a reference class object, and that results in the destructor being called. The primary reason for implementing a destructor for a native C++ class is to deal with data members allocated on the heap, but obviously, that doesn't apply to reference classes, so there is less need to define a destructor in a ref class. You might do this when objects of the class are using other resources that are not managed by the garbage collector, such as files that need to be closed in an orderly fashion when an object is destroyed. You can also clean up such resources in another kind of class member called a **finalizer**.

A finalizer is a special kind of function member of a reference class that is called automatically by the garbage collector when destroying an object. The purpose of a finalizer is to deal with unmanaged resources used by a reference class object that will not be dealt with by the garbage collector. Note that the finalizer is not called for a class object if the destructor was called explicitly, or was called as a result of applying the `delete` operator to the object. In a derived class, finalizers are called in the same sequence as destructor calls would be, so the finalizer for the most derived class is called first, followed by the finalizers for successive parent classes in the hierarchy, with the finalizer for the most base class being called last.

You define a finalizer in a class like this:

```
public ref class MyClass
{
  // Finalizer definition
  !MyClass()
  {
    // Code to clean-up when an object is destroyed...
  }

  // Rest of the class definition...
};
```

You define a finalizer function in a class in a similar way to a destructor, but with ! instead of the ~ that you use preceding the class name for a destructor. Similar to a destructor, you must not supply a return type for a finalizer, and the access specifier for a finalizer will be ignored. You can see how destructors and finalizers operate with a little example.

TRY IT OUT   **Finalizers and Destructors**

This example shows when destructors and finalizers get called in an application:

```
// Ex9_20.cpp : main project file.
// Finalizers and destructors

#include "stdafx.h"

using namespace System;

ref class MyClass
{
public:
  // Constructor
  MyClass(int n) : value(n){}

  // Destructor
  ~MyClass()
  {
    Console::WriteLine("MyClass object({0}) destructor called.", value);
  }

  // Finalizer
  !MyClass()
  {
    Console::WriteLine("MyClass object({0}) finalizer called.", value);
  }
private:
  int value;
};

int main(array<System::String ^> ^args)
{
  MyClass^ obj1 = gcnew MyClass(1);
```

```
        MyClass^ obj2 = gcnew MyClass(2);
        MyClass^ obj3 = gcnew MyClass(3);
        delete obj1;
        obj2->~MyClass();

        Console::WriteLine(L"End Program");
        return 0;
    }
```

code snippet Ex9_20.cpp

The output from this example is:

```
MyClass object(1) destructor called.
MyClass object(2) destructor called.
End Program
MyClass object(3) finalizer called.
```

How It Works

The MyClass class has a constructor, a destructor, and a finalizer. The destructor and finalizer just write output to the command line so you know when each is called. You are also able to tell for which object the finalizer or destructor was called, because they output the value of the value field.

In the main() function, you create three objects of type MyClass, encapsulating values 1, 2, and 3 to distinguish them. You then apply the delete operator to obj1 and then explicitly call the destructor for obj2. Making these calls results in the first two lines of the example output. This output is generated by the destructor calls for the objects that result from making the delete and explicit destructor calls.

The next line of output is produced by the statement preceding the return statement in main(), so the last line of output generated by the finalizer for obj3 occurs after the end of main(). The output shows that destructors are called when you delete an object or call its destructor explicitly, the destructor for the object will be executed, and these operations also suppress the execution of the finalizers for the objects. The object referenced by obj3 is destroyed by the garbage collector when the program ends, so the finalizer gets called to clean up any non-managed resources.

Thus, if a class has a finalizer and a destructor, only one of these is called when the object is destroyed, the destructor is called if you programmatically destroy the object, and the finalizer is called if it dies naturally by going out of scope. The finalizer won't necessarily be called immediately; it depends on when the garbage collector is doing its job. You can also deduce from this that if you rely on a finalizer to clean up after your objects have been destroyed, you should not explicitly delete the objects.

If you comment out the statements in main() that destroy obj1 and obj2, you will see that the finalizers for these objects are called by the garbage collector when the program ends. On the other hand, if you comment out the finalizer from MyClass, you will see that the destructor for obj3 does not get called by the garbage collector, so no clean-up occurs. You can conclude that if you want to be sure that unmanaged resources used by an object are taken care of regardless of how an object is terminated, you should implement both a destructor and a finalizer in the class.

NOTE *Implementing a finalizer in a class will result in considerable overhead, so you should define a finalizer in a class only when it is absolutely necessary.*

Generic Classes

C++/CLI provides you with the capability for defining generic classes where a specific class is instantiated from the generic class type at runtime. You can define generic value classes, generic reference classes, generic interface classes, and generic delegates. You define a generic class using one or more type parameters in a similar way to generic functions that you saw in Chapter 6.

For example, here's how you could define a generic version of the `Stack` class you saw in `Ex9_14`:

```
// Stack.h for Ex9_21
// A generic pushdown stack

generic<typename T> ref class Stack
{
private:
  // Defines items to store in the stack
  ref struct Item
  {
    T Obj;                        // Handle for the object in this item
    Item^ Next;                   // Handle for next item in the stack or nullptr

    // Constructor
    Item(T obj, Item^ next): Obj(obj), Next(next){}
  };

  Item^ Top;                      // Handle for item that is at the top

public:
  // Push an object onto the stack
  void Push(T obj)
  {
    Top = gcnew Item(obj, Top);   // Create new item and make it the top
  }

  // Pop an object off the stack
  T Pop()
  {
    if(!Top)                      // If the stack is empty
      return T();                 // return null equivalent

    T obj = Top->Obj;             // Get object from item
    Top = Top->Next;              // Make next item the top
    return obj;
  }
};
```

The generic version of the class now has a type parameter, `T`. Note that you could use the `class` keyword instead of the `typename` keyword when specifying the parameter — there is no difference between them in this context. A type argument replaces T when the generic class type is used; T is replaced by the type argument through the definition of the class, so a major advantage over the original version is that the generic class type is much safer without losing any of its flexibility. The Push() member of the original class accepts any handle, so you could happily push a mix of objects of type MyClass^, String^, or, indeed, any handle type onto the same stack, whereas an instance of the generic type accepts only objects of the type specified as the type argument or objects of a type that have the type argument as a base.

Look at the implementation of the Pop() function. The original version returned nullptr if the top item in the stack was null, but you can't return nullptr for a type parameter because the type argument could be a value type. The solution is to return T(), which is a no-arg constructor call for type T. This results in the equivalent of 0 for a value type and nullptr for a handle.

> **NOTE** You can specify constraints on a generic class type parameter using the *where* keyword in the same way as you did for generic functions in Chapter 6.

You could create a stack from the Stack<> generic type that stores handles to Box objects like this:

```
Stack<Box^>^ stack = gcnew Stack<Box^>;
```

The type argument Box^ goes between the angled brackets and the statement creates a Stack<Box^> object on the CLR heap. This object allows handles of type Box^ to be pushed onto the stack as well as handles of any type that have Box as a direct or indirect base class. You can try this out with a revised version of Ex9_14.

TRY IT OUT   Using a Generic Class Type

Create a new CLR console program with the name Ex9_21 and then copy the header files Container .h, Box.h, and GlassBox.h from Ex9_14 to the directory for this project. Add these headers to the project by right-clicking Header Files in the Solution Explorer tab and selecting Add ⇨ Existing Item from the context menu. You can then add a new header file, Stack.h, to the project and enter the generic Stack class definition that you saw in the previous section. Don't forget the #pragma once directive at the beginning of the file.

```
// Ex9_21.cpp : main project file.

// Using a nested class to define a stack

#include "stdafx.h"
#include "Box.h"                          // For Box and Container
#include "GlassBox.h"                     // For GlassBox (and Box and Container)
#include "Stack.h"                        // For the generic stack class

using namespace System;

int main(array<System::String ^> ^args)
```

```
{
   array<Box^>^ boxes = { gcnew Box(2.0, 3.0, 4.0),
                          gcnew GlassBox(2.0, 3.0, 4.0),
                          gcnew Box(4.0, 5.0, 6.0),
                          gcnew GlassBox(4.0, 5.0, 6.0)
                        };

   Console::WriteLine(L"The array of boxes have the following volumes:");
   for each(Box^ box in boxes)
     box->ShowVolume();                        // Output the volume of a box

   Console::WriteLine(L"\nNow pushing the boxes on the stack...");

   Stack<Box^>^ stack = gcnew Stack<Box^>;        // Create the stack
   for each(Box^ box in boxes)
     stack->Push(box);


   Console::WriteLine(
             L"Popping the boxes off the stack presents them in reverse order:");
   Box^ item;
   while((item = stack->Pop()) != nullptr)
     safe_cast<Container^>(item)->ShowVolume();

   // Try the generic Stack type storing integers
   Stack<int>^ numbers = gcnew Stack<int>;        // Create the stack
   Console::WriteLine(L"\nNow pushing integers onto the stack:");
   for(int i = 2 ; i<=12 ; i += 2)
   {
     Console::Write(L"{0,5}",i);
     numbers->Push(i);
   }
   int number;
   Console::WriteLine(L"\n\nPopping integers off the stack produces:");
   while((number = numbers->Pop()) != 0)
     Console::Write(L"{0,5}",number);

   Console::WriteLine();
   return 0;
}
```

code snippet Ex9_21.cpp

This example produces the following output:

```
The array of boxes have the following volumes:
CBox usable volume is 24
CBox usable volume is 20.4
CBox usable volume is 120
CBox usable volume is 102

Now pushing the boxes on the stack...
Popping the boxes off the stack presents them in reverse order:
```

```
CBox usable volume is 102
CBox usable volume is 120
CBox usable volume is 20.4
CBox usable volume is 24

Now pushing integers onto the stack:
    2    4    6    8   10   12

Popping integers off the stack produces:
   12   10    8    6    4    2
```

How It Works

The stack to store `Box` object handles is defined in the statement:

```
Stack<Box^>^ stack = gcnew Stack<Box^>;        // Create the stack
```

The type parameter is `Box^` so the stack stores handles to `Box` objects or handles to `GlassBox` objects. The code to push objects onto the stack and to pop them off again is exactly the same as in Ex9_14, and the output is the same, too. The difference here is that you could not push an object onto the stack if the type did not have `Box` as a direct or indirect base class, so the generic type guarantees that all the objects are `Box` objects.

Storing integers now requires a new `Stack<>` object:

```
Stack<int>^ numbers = gcnew Stack<int>;        // Create the stack
```

The original version used the same non-generic `Stack` object to store `Box` object references and integers, thus demonstrating how type safety was completely lacking in the operation of the stack. Here, you specify the type argument for the generic class as the value type `int`, so only objects of this type are accepted by the `Push()` function.

The loops that pop objects off the stack demonstrate that returning `T()` in the `Pop()` function does indeed return 0 for type `int` and `nullptr` for the handle type `Box^`.

Generic Interface Classes

You can define generic interfaces in the same way as you define generic reference classes, and a generic reference class can be defined in terms of a generic interface. To show how this works, you can define a generic interface that can be implemented by the generic class, `Stack<>`. Here's a definition for a generic interface:

```
// Interface for stack operations
generic<typename T> public interface class IStack
{
  void Push(T obj);      // Push an item onto the stack
  T Pop();
};
```

This interface has two functions identifying the push and pop operations for a stack.

The definition of the generic Stack<> class that implements the IStack<> generic interface is:

```
generic<typename T> ref class Stack : IStack<T>
{
private:
  // Defines items to store in the stack
  ref struct Item
  {
    T Obj;                          // Handle for the object in this item
    Item^ Next;                     // Handle for next item in the stack or nullptr

    // Constructor
    Item(T obj, Item^ next): Obj(obj), Next(next){}
  };

  Item^ Top;                        // Handle for item that is at the top

public:
  // Push an object onto the stack
  virtual void Push(T obj)
  {
    Top = gcnew Item(obj, Top);   // Create new item and make it the top
  }

  // Pop an  object off the stack
  virtual T Pop()
  {
    if(!Top)                        // If the stack is empty
      return T();                   // return null equivalent

    T obj = Top->Obj;               // Get object from item
    Top = Top->Next;                // Make next item the top
    return obj;
  }
};
```

The changes from the previous generic Stack<> class definition are shaded. In the first line of the generic class definition, the type parameter, T, is used as the type argument to the interface IStack, so the type argument used for the Stack<> class instance also applies to the interface. The Push() and Pop() functions in the class now have to be specified as virtual because the functions are virtual in the interface. You could add a header file containing the IStack interface to the previous example, and amend the generic Stack<> class definition to the example, and recompile the program to see it operating with a generic interface.

Generic Collection Classes

A **collection class** is a class that organizes and stores objects in a particular way; a linked list and a stack are typical examples of collection classes. The System::Collections::Generic namespace contains a wide range of generic collection classes that implement strongly typed collections. The generic collection classes available include the following:

TYPE	DESCRIPTION
List<T>	Stores items of type T in a simple list that can grow in size automatically when necessary
LinkedList<T>	Stores items of type T in a doubly linked list
Stack<T>	Stores item of type T in a stack, which is a first-in last-out storage mechanism
Queue<T>	Stores items of type T in a queue, which is a first-in first-out storage mechanism
Dictionary<K,V>	Stores key/value pairs where the keys are of type K and the values are of type V

I won't go into details of all these, but I'll mention briefly just three that you are most likely to want to use in your programs. I'll use examples that store value types for simplicity, but of course, the collection classes work just as well with reference types. The code fragments that follow assume a using directive for the System::Collections::Generic namespace is in effect.

List<T> — A Generic List

List<T> defines a generic list that automatically increases in size when necessary. You can add items to a list using the Add() function and you can access items stored in a List<T> using an index, just like an array. Here's how you define a list to store values of type int:

```
List<int>^ numbers = gcnew List<int>;
```

This has a default capacity, but you could specify the capacity you require. Here's a definition of a list with a capacity of 500:

```
List<int>^ numbers = gcnew List<int>(500);
```

You can add objects to the list using the Add() functions:

```
for(int i = 0 ; i<1000 ; i++)
  numbers->Add( 2*i+1);
```

This adds 1000 integers to the numbers list. The list grows automatically if its capacity is less than 1000. When you want to insert an item in an existing list, you can use the Insert() function to insert the item specified by the second argument at the index position specified by the first argument. Items in a list are indexed from zero, like an array.

You could sum the contents of the list like this:

```
int sum = 0;
for(int i = 0 ; i<numbers->Count ; i++)
  sum += numbers[i];
```

Count is a property that returns the current number of items in the list. The items in the list may be accessed through the default indexed property, and you can get and set values in this way. Note that you cannot increase the capacity of a list using the default indexed property. If you use an index outside the current range of items in the list, an exception is thrown.

You could also sum the items in the list like this:

```
for each(int n in numbers)
   sum +=n;
```

You have a wide range of other functions you can apply to a list, including functions for removing elements, and sorting and searching the contents of the list.

LinkedList<T> — A Generic Doubly Linked List

LinkedList<T> defines a linked list with forward and backward pointers so you can iterate through the list in either direction. You could define a linked list that stores floating-point values like this:

```
LinkedList<double>^ values = gcnew LinkedList<double>;
```

You could add values to the list like this:

```
for(int i = 0 ; i<1000 ; i++)
   values->AddLast(2.5*i);
```

The AddLast() function adds an item to the end of the list. You can add items to the beginning of the list by using the AddFirst() function. The Find() function returns a handle of type LinkedListNode<T>^ to a node in the list containing the value you pass as the argument to Find(). You could use this handle to insert a new value before or after the node that you found. For example:

```
LinkedListNode<double>^ node = values->Find(20.0);    // Find node containing 20.0
if(node)
   values->AddBefore(node, 19.9);                     // Insert 19.9 before node
```

The first statement finds the node containing the value 20.0. If it does not exist, the Find() function returns nullptr. The last statement that is executed if node is not nullptr adds a new value of 19.9 before node. You could use the AddAfter() function to add a new value after a given node. Searching a linked list is relatively slow because it is necessary to iterate through the elements sequentially.

You could sum the items in the list like this:

```
double sumd = 0;
for each(double v in values)
   sumd += v;
```

The for each loop iterates through all the items in the list and accumulates the total in sum.

The Count property returns the number of items in the linked list, and the First and Last properties return the values of the first and last items.

Dictionary<TKey, TValue> — A Generic Dictionary Storing Key/Value Pairs

The generic `Dictionary<>` collection class requires two type arguments; the first is the type for the key, and the second is the type for the value associated with the key. A dictionary is especially useful when you have pairs of objects that you want to store, where one object is a key to accessing the other object. A name and a phone number are an example of a key value pair that you might want to store in a dictionary, because you would typically want to retrieve a phone number using a name as the key. Suppose you have defined `Name` and `PhoneNumber` classes to encapsulate names and phone numbers, respectively. You can define a dictionary to store name/number pairs like this:

```
Dictionary<Name^, PhoneNumber^>^ phonebook = gcnew Dictionary<Name^, PhoneNumber^>;
```

The two type arguments are `Name^` and `PhoneNumber^`, so the key is a handle for a name and the value is a handle for a phone number.

You can add an entry in the `phonebook` dictionary like this:

```
Name^ name = gcnew Name("Jim", "Jones");
PhoneNumber^ number = gcnew PhoneNumber(914, 316, 2233);
phonebook->Add(name, number);          // Add name/number pair to dictionary
```

To retrieve an entry in a dictionary, you can use the default indexed property — for example:

```
try
{
  PhoneNumber^ theNumber = phonebook[name];
}
catch(KeyNotFoundException^ knfe)
{
  Console::WriteLine(knfe);
}
```

You supply the key as the index value for the default indexed property, which, in this case, is a handle to a `Name` object. The value is returned if the key is present, or an exception of type `KeyNotFoundException` is thrown if the key is not found in the collection; therefore, whenever you are accessing a value for a key that may not be present, the code should be in a `try` block.

A `Dictionary<>` object has a `Keys` property that returns a collection containing the keys in the dictionary, as well as a `Values` property that returns a collection containing the values. The `Count` property returns the number of key/value pairs in the dictionary.

Let's try some of these in a working example.

TRY IT OUT   **Using Generic Collection Classes**

This example exercises the three collection classes you have seen:

```
// Ex9_22.cpp : main project file.
// Using generic collection classes

#include "stdafx.h"

using namespace System;
```

Available for download on Wrox.com

```
using namespace System::Collections::Generic;    // For generic collections

// Class encapsulating a name
ref class Name
{
public:
  Name(String^ name1, String^ name2) : First(name1),Second(name2){}
  virtual String^ ToString() override{ return First + L" " + Second;}
private:
  String^ First;
  String^ Second;
};

// Class encapsulating a phone number
ref class PhoneNumber
{
public:
  PhoneNumber(int area, int local, int number):
      Area(area),Local(local), Number(number){}
  virtual String^ ToString() override
  { return Area + L" " + Local + L" " + Number; }

private:
  int Area;
  int Local;
  int Number;

};

int main(array<System::String ^> ^args)
{
  // Using List<T>
  Console::WriteLine(L"Creating a List<T> of integers:");
  List<int>^ numbers = gcnew List<int>;
  for(int i = 0 ; i<1000 ; i++)
    numbers->Add(2*i+1);

  // Sum the contents of the list
  int sum = 0;
  for(int i = 0 ; i<numbers->Count ; i++)
    sum += numbers[i];
  Console::WriteLine(L"Total = {0}", sum);

  // Using LinkedList<T>
  Console::WriteLine(L"\nCreating a LinkedList<T> of double values:");
  LinkedList<double>^ values = gcnew LinkedList<double>;
  for(int i = 0 ; i<1000 ; i++)
    values->AddLast(2.5*i);

  double sumd = 0.0;
  for each(double v in values)
    sumd += v;

  Console::WriteLine(L"Total = {0}", sumd);

  LinkedListNode<double>^ node = values->Find(20.0);  // Find node containing 20.0
```

```
    values->AddBefore(node, 19.9);
    values->AddAfter(values->Find(30.0), 30.1);

    // Sum the contents of the linked list again
    sumd = 0.0;
    for each(double v in values)
      sumd += v;

    Console::WriteLine(L"Total after adding values = {0}", sumd);

    // Using Dictionary<K,V>
    Console::WriteLine(L"\nCreating a Dictionary<K,V> of name/number pairs:");
    Dictionary<Name^, PhoneNumber^>^ phonebook =
                                        gcnew Dictionary<Name^, PhoneNumber^>;

    // Add name/number pairs to dictionary
    Name^ name = gcnew Name("Jim", "Jones");
    PhoneNumber^ number = gcnew PhoneNumber(914, 316, 2233);
    phonebook->Add(name, number);
    phonebook->Add(gcnew Name("Fred","Fong"), gcnew PhoneNumber(123,234,3456));
    phonebook->Add(gcnew Name("Janet","Smith"), gcnew PhoneNumber(515,224,6864));

    // List all numbers
    Console::WriteLine(L"List all the numbers:");
    for each(PhoneNumber^ number in phonebook->Values)
      Console::WriteLine(number);

    // List names and numbers
    Console::WriteLine(L"Access the keys to list all name/number pairs:");
    for each(Name^ name in phonebook->Keys)
      Console::WriteLine(L"{0} : {1}", name, phonebook[name]);

    return 0;
}
```

code snippet Ex9_22.cpp

The output from this example should be as follows:

```
Creating a List<T> of integers:
Total = 1000000

Creating a LinkedList<T> of double values:
Total = 1248750
Total after adding values = 1248800

Creating a Dictionary<K,V> of name/number pairs:
List all the numbers:
914 316 2233
123 234 3456
515 224 6864
Access the keys to list all name/number pairs:
Jim Jones : 914 316 2233
Fred Fong : 123 234 3456
Janet Smith : 515 224 6864
```

How It Works

Note the using namespace directive for the System::Collections::Generic namespace; this is essential when you want to use the generic collections classes without specifying fully qualified class names.

The first block of code in main() uses the List<> collection using the code from the previous section. It creates a class that stores integers in a list and then stores 1000 values in it. The loop that sums the contents of the list uses the default indexed property to retrieve the values. This could also be written as a for each loop. Don't forget — the default indexed property only accesses items already in the list. You can change the value of an existing item using the default indexed property, but you cannot add new items this way. To add an item to the end of the list, you use the Add() function; you can also use the Insert() function to insert an item at a given index position.

The next block of code in main() demonstrates the use of the LinkedList<> collection to store values of type double. Values of type double are added to the end of the linked list using the AddLast() function in a for loop. Values are retrieved and summed in a for each loop. Note that there is no default indexed property for accessing items in a linked list. The code also shows the use of the Find() and AddBefore() and AddAfter() functions to add new elements at a specific position in the linked list.

The last block of code in main() shows a Dictionary<> collection being used to store phone numbers with names as keys. The Name and PhoneNumber classes implement an override to the inherited ToString() function to enable the Console::WriteLine() function to output suitable representations of objects of these types. Three name/number pairs are added to the phonebook dictionary. The code then lists the numbers in the dictionary by using a for each loop to iterate over the values contained in the collection object that are returned by the Values property for phonebook. The last loop iterates over the names in the collection returned by the Keys property and uses the default indexed property for phonebook to access the values. No try block is necessary here because you are certain that all the keys in the Keys collection are present in the dictionary — if they are not, there's a serious problem with the implementation of the Dictionary<> generic class!

SUMMARY

This chapter covered the principal ideas involved in using inheritance for native C++ classes and C++/CLI classes.

You have now gone through all of the important language features of ISO/ANSI C++ and C++/CLI. It's important that you feel comfortable with the mechanisms for defining and deriving classes and the process of inheritance in both language versions. Windows programming with Visual C++ 2010 involves extensive use of all these concepts.

EXERCISES

You can download the source code for the examples in the book and the solutions to the following exercises from www.wrox.com.

1. What's wrong with the following code?

```
class CBadClass
{
private:
    int len;
    char* p;
public:
    CBadClass(const char* str): p(str), len(strlen(p)) {}
    CBadClass(){}
};
```

2. Suppose you have a class CBird, as follows, that you want to use as a base class for deriving a hierarchy of bird classes:

```
class CBird
{
protected:
    int wingSpan;
    int eggSize;
    int airSpeed;
    int altitude;
public:
    virtual void fly() { altitude = 100; }
};
```

Is it reasonable to create a CHawk by deriving from CBird? How about a COstrich? Justify your answers. Derive an avian hierarchy that can cope with both of these birds.

3. Given the following class,

```
class CBase
{
protected:
    int m_anInt;
public:
    CBase(int n): m_anInt(n) { cout << "Base constructor\n"; }
    virtual void Print() const = 0;
};
```

what sort of class is CBase and why? Derive a class from CBase that sets its inherited integer value, m_anInt, when constructed, and prints it on request. Write a test program to verify that your class is correct.

4. A binary tree is a structure made up of nodes, where each node contains a pointer to a "left" node and a pointer to a "right" node plus a data item, as shown in Figure 9-6.

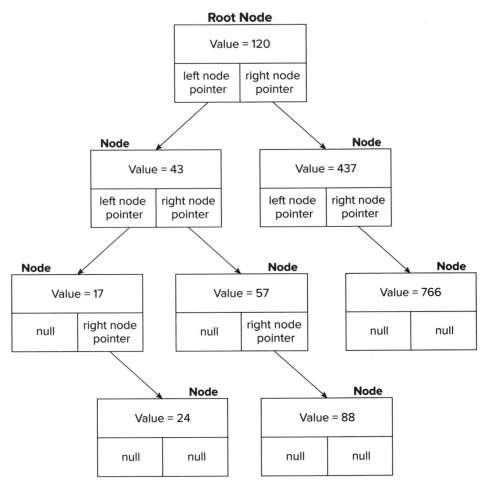

An Ordered Binary Tree

FIGURE 9-6

The tree starts with a root node, and this is the starting point for accessing the nodes in the tree. Either or both pointers in a node can be null. Figure 9-6 shows an ordered binary tree, which is a tree organized so that the value of each node is always greater than or equal to the value of the left node and less than or equal to the value of the right node.

Define a native C++ class to define an ordered binary tree that stores integer values. You also need to define a Node class, but that can be an inner class to the BinaryTree class. Write a program to test the operation of your `BinaryTree` class by storing an arbitrary sequence of integers in it and retrieving and outputting them in ascending sequence.

Hint: Don't be afraid to use recursion.

5. Implement Exercise 4 as a CLR program. If you did not manage to complete Exercise 4, look at the solution in the download and use that as a guide to doing this exercise.

6. Define a generic `BinaryTree` class for any type that implements the `IComparable` interface class, and demonstrate its operation by using instances of the generic class to store and retrieve first a number of random integers, and then the elements of the following array:

```
array<String^>^ words = {L"Success", L"is", L"the", L"ability", L"to",
                         L"go" , L"from", L"one", L"failure", L"to",
                         L"another", L"with", L"no", L"loss", L"of",
                         L"enthusiasm"};
```

Write the values retrieved from the binary tree to the command line.

▶ **WHAT YOU LEARNED IN THIS CHAPTER**

TOPIC	CONCEPT
Inherited members of a class	A derived class inherits all the members of a base class except for constructors, the destructor, and the overloaded assignment operator.
Accessibility of inherited members of a class	Members of a base class declared as `private` in the base class are not accessible in any derived class. To obtain the effect of the keyword `private` but allow access in a derived class, you should use the keyword `protected` in place of `private`.
Access specifiers for a base class	A base class can be specified for a derived class with the keyword `public`, `private`, or `protected`. If none is specified, the default is `private`. Depending on the keyword specified for a base, the access level of the inherited members may be modified.
Constructors in derived classes	If you write a derived class constructor, you must arrange for data members of the base class to be initialized properly, as well as those of the derived class.
Virtual functions	A function in a base class may be declared as `virtual`. This allows other definitions of the function appearing in derived classes to be selected at execution time, depending on the type of object for which the function call is made.
Virtual destructors	You should declare the destructor in a native C++ base class that contains a virtual function as `virtual`. This ensures correct selection of a destructor for dynamically-created derived class objects.
`friend` classes	A native C++ class may be designated as a `friend` of another class. In this case, all the function members of the `friend` class may access all the members of the other class. If class A is a `friend` of B, class B is not a `friend` of A unless it has been declared as such.
Pure virtual functions	A virtual function in a native C++ base class can be specified as pure by placing `= 0` at the end of the function declaration. The class then is an abstract class for which no objects can be created. In any derived class, all the pure virtual functions must be defined; if not, it, too, becomes an abstract class.
Derived classes in C++/CLI	A C++/CLI reference class can be derived from another reference class. Value classes cannot be derived classes.
Interface classes	An interface class declares a set of public functions that represent a specific capability that can be implemented by a reference class or value class. An interface class can contain public functions, events, and properties. An interface can also define static data members, functions, events, and properties, and these are inherited in a class that implements the interface.

TOPIC	CONCEPT
Derived interface classes	An interface class can be derived from another interface class, and the derived interface contains the members of both interfaces.
Delegates	A delegate is an object that encapsulates one or more pointers to functions that have the same return type and parameter list. Invoking a delegate calls all the functions pointed to by the delegate.
Event members of a class	An event member of a class can signal when the event occurs by calling one or more handler functions that have been registered with the event.
Generic C++/CLI classes	A generic class is a parameterized type that is instantiated at runtime. The arguments you supply for type parameters when you instantiate a generic type can be value class types or reference class types.
Collection classes	The `System::Collections::Generic` namespace contains generic collection classes that define type_safe collections of objects of any C++/CLI type.
C++/CLI class libraries	You can create a C++/CLI class library in a separate assembly, and the class library resides in a `.dll` file.

10

The Standard Template Library

At its name implies, the Standard Template Library (STL) is a library of standard class and function templates. You can use these templates to create a wide range of powerful general-purpose classes for organizing your data, as well as functions for processing that data in various ways. The STL is defined by the standard for native C++ and is therefore always available with a conforming compiler. Because of its broad applicability, the STL can greatly simplify programming in many of your C++ applications.

Of course, the STL for native C++ does not work with C++/CLI class types, but in Visual C++ 2010 you have an additional version of the STL available that contains templates and generic functions that you can instantiate with C++/CLI class types.

WHAT IS THE STANDARD TEMPLATE LIBRARY?

The STL is a large collection of class and function templates that is provided with your native C++ compiler. I'll first explain, in general terms, the kinds of resources the STL provides and how they interact with one another, before diving into the details of working examples. The STL contains six kinds of components: containers, container adapters, iterators, algorithms, function objects, and function adapters. Because they are part of the standard library, the names of the STL components are all defined within the std namespace.

The STL is a very large library, some of which is highly specialized, and to cover the contents fully would require a book in its own right. In this chapter, I'll introduce the fundamentals of how you use the STL and describe the more commonly used capabilities. Before getting into containers in depth, I'll introduce you to the primary components, concepts, and terminology you will find in the STL.

Containers

Containers are objects that you use to store and organize other objects. A class that implements a linked list is an example of a container. You create a container class from an STL template by supplying the type of the object that you intend to store. For example, vector<T> is a template for a container that is a linear array that automatically increases in size when necessary. T is the type parameter that specifies the type of objects to be stored. Here are a couple of statements that are examples of creating vector<T> containers:

```
vector<string> strings;    // Stores object of type string
vector<double> data;       // Stores values of type double
```

I chose the vector container as an example because it is probably used most often. The first statement creates the container class, strings, that stores objects of type string, while the second statement creates the data container that stores values of type double.

You can store items of a fundamental type, or of any class type, in a container. If your type argument for an STL container template is a class type, the container can store objects of that type, or objects of any derived class type. Typically, containers store copies of the objects that you store in them, and they automatically allocate and manage the memory that the objects occupy. When a container object is destroyed, the container takes care of deleting the objects it contains and freeing the memory they occupied. One advantage of using STL containers to store your objects is that it relieves you of the chore of managing the memory for them.

The templates for the STL container classes are defined in the standard headers shown in the following table.

HEADER FILE	CONTENTS
vector	A vector<T> container represents an array that can increase in capacity automatically when required. You can only add new elements efficiently to the end of a vector container. Adding elements to the middle of a vector can involve a lot of overhead.
deque	A deque<T> container implements a double-ended queue. This is equivalent to a vector but with the additional capability for you to efficiently add elements to the beginning.
list	A list<T> container is a doubly-linked list.

HEADER FILE	CONTENTS
map	A map<K, T> is an associative container that stores each object (of type T) with an associated key (of type K) that determines where the key/object pair is located. The value of each key in a map must be unique.
	This header also defines the multimap<K, T> container where the keys in the key/object pairs do not need to be unique.
set	A set<T> container is a map where each object serves as its own key. All objects in a set must be unique. A consequence of using an object as its own key is that you cannot change an object in a set; to change an object you must delete it and then insert the modified version.
	This header also defines the multiset<T> container, which is like a set container except that the entries do not need to be unique.
bitset	Defines the bitset<T> class template that represents a fixed number of bits. This is typically used to store flags that represent a set of states or conditions.

The containers in this table represent the complete set that is available with the STL. All the template names are defined within the std namespace. T is the template type parameter for the type of elements stored in a container; where keys are used, K is the type of key.

Microsoft Visual C++ also includes the headers hash_map and hash_set that define templates for the hash_map<K, T> and hash_set<K, T> containers. These are variations on the map<K, T> and set<K, T> containers. The standard map and set containers use an ordering mechanism to locate entries whereas the hash_map and hash_set containers use a hashing mechanism.

Container Adapters

The STL also defines **container adapters**. A container adapter is a template class that wraps an existing STL container class to provide a different, and typically more restricted, capability. The container adapters are defined in the headers in the following table.

HEADER FILE	CONTENTS
queue	A queue<T> container is defined by an adapter from a deque<T> container by default, but you could define it using a list<T> container. You can only access the first and last elements in a queue, and you can only add elements at the back and remove them from the front. Thus, a queue<T> container works more or less like the queue in your local coffee shop.
	This header also defines a priority_queue<T> container, which is a queue that orders the elements it contains so that the largest element is always at the front. Only the element at the front can be accessed or removed. A priority queue is defined by an adapter from a vector<T> by default, but you could use a deque<T> as the base container.

continues

(continued)

HEADER FILE	CONTENTS
stack	A stack<T> container is defined by an adapter from a deque<T> container by default, but you could define it using a vector<T> or a list<T> container. A stack is a last-in first-out container, so adding or removing elements always occurs at the top, and you can only access the top element.

Iterators

Iterators are objects that behave like pointers and are very important for accessing the contents of all STL containers, except for those defined by a container adapter; container adapters do not support iterators. You can obtain an iterator from a container, which you can use to access the objects you have previously stored. You can also create iterators that will allow input and output of objects, or data items of a given type, from, or to, a native C++ stream. Although basically all iterators behave like pointers, not all iterators provide the same functionality. However, they do share a base level of capability. Given two iterators, iter1 and iter2, accessing the same set of objects, the comparison operations iter1 == iter2, iter1 != iter2, and the assignment iter1 = iter2 are always possible, regardless of the types of iter1 and iter2.

There are four different categories of iterators; each category supports a different range of operations, as shown in the following table. The operations described for each category are in addition to the three operations that I mentioned in the previous paragraph.

ITERATOR CATEGORY	DESCRIPTION
Input and output iterators	These iterators read or write a sequence of objects and may only be used once. To read or write a second time, you must obtain a new iterator. You can perform the following operations on these iterators: ++iter or iter++ *iter For the dereferencing operation, only read access is allowed in the case of an input iterator, and only write access for an output iterator.
Forward iterators	Forward iterators incorporate the capabilities of both input and output iterators, so you can apply the operations shown above to them, and you can use them for access and store operations. Forward iterators can also be reused to traverse a set of objects in a forward direction as many times as you want.
Bidirectional iterators	Bidirectional iterators provide the same capabilities as forward iterators and additionally allow the operations --iter and iter--. This means you can traverse backward as well as forward through a sequence of objects.

ITERATOR CATEGORY	DESCRIPTION

Random access iterators	Random access iterators have the same capabilities as bidirectional iterators but also allow the following operations:
	
	`iter+n` or `iter-n`
	
	`iter += n` or `iter -= n`
	
	`iter1 - iter2`
	
	`iter1 < iter2` or `iter1 > iter2`
	
	`iter1 <= iter2` or `iter1 >= iter2`
	
	`iter[n]`
	
	Being able to increment or decrement an iterator by an arbitrary value n allows random access to the set of objects. The last operation using the `[]` operator is equivalent to `*(iter + n)`.

Thus, iterators in the four successive categories provide a progressively greater range of functionality. Where an algorithm requires an iterator with a given level of functionality, you can use any iterator that provides the required level of capability. For example, if a forward iterator is required, you must use at least a forward iterator; an input or an output operator will not do. On the other hand, you could also use a bidirectional iterator or a random access iterator because they both have the capability provided by a forward iterator.

Note that when you obtain an iterator to access the contents of a container, the kind of iterator you get will depend on the sort of container you are using. The types of some iterators can be complex, but as you'll see, in many instances the `auto` keyword can deduce the type for you if you initialize the iterator when you create it.

Algorithms

Algorithms are STL function templates that operate on a set of objects provided to them by an iterator. Because the objects are supplied by an iterator, an algorithm needs no knowledge of the source of the objects to be processed. The objects could be retrieved by the iterator from a container or even from a stream. Because iterators work like pointers, all STL template functions that accept an iterator as an argument will work equally well with a regular pointer.

As you'll see, you will frequently use containers, iterators, and algorithms in concert, in the manner illustrated in Figure 10-1.

FIGURE 10-1

When you apply an algorithm to the contents of a container, you supply iterators that point to objects within the container. The algorithm uses these iterators to access objects within the container and to write them back when appropriate. For example, when you apply the sort() algorithm to the contents of a vector, you pass two iterators to the sort() function. One points to the first object, and the other points to the position that is one past the last element in the vector. The sort() function uses these iterators to access objects for comparison, and to write the objects back to the container to establish the ordering. You see this working in an example later in this chapter.

Algorithms are defined in two standard header files, the algorithm header and the numeric header.

Function Objects in the STL

Function objects are objects of a class type that overloads the () operator (the function call operator), which means that the class implements the operator()() function. The STL defines a set of standard function objects as templates; you can use these to create a function object, where the overloaded () operator function works with your object type. For example, the STL defines the template less<T>. If you instantiate the template as less<myClass>, you have a type for function objects that implement operator()() to provide the less-than comparison for objects of type myClass.

Many algorithms make use of function objects to specify binary operations to be carried out, or to specify **predicates** that determine how or whether a particular operation is to be carried out. A predicate is a function that returns a value of type bool, and because a function object is an object of a type that implements the operator()() member function to return a value of type bool, a function object can also be a predicate. For example, suppose you have defined a class type Comp that implements the operator()() function to compare its two arguments and return a bool value. If you create an object f of type Comp, the expression f(a,b) returns a bool value that results from comparing a and b, and thus acts as a predicate.

Predicates come in two flavors, **binary predicates** that involve two operands, and **unary predicates** that require one operand. For example, comparisons such as less-than and equal-to, and logical operations such as AND and OR, are implemented as binary predicates that are members of function objects; logical negation, NOT, is implemented as a unary predicate member of a function object.

Function object templates are defined in the functional header; you can also define your own function objects when necessary. You'll see function objects in action with algorithms, and some container class functions, later in this chapter.

Function Adapters

Function adapters are function templates that allow function objects to be combined to produce a more complex function object. A simple example is the not1 function adapter. This takes an existing function object that provides a unary predicate and inverts it. Thus, if the function object function returns `true`, the function that results from applying `not1` to it will be `false`. I won't be discussing function adapters in depth, not because they are terribly difficult to understand — they aren't — but because there's a limit to how much I can cram into a single chapter.

THE RANGE OF STL CONTAINERS

The STL provides templates for a variety of container classes that you can use in a wide range of application contexts. **Sequence containers** are containers in which you store objects of a given type in a linear fashion, either as a dynamic array or as a list. **Associative containers** store objects based on a key that you supply with each object to be stored; the key is used to locate the object within the container. In a typical application, you might be storing phone numbers in an associative container, using names as the keys. This would enable you to retrieve a particular number from the container just by supplying the appropriate name.

I'll first introduce you to sequence containers, and then I'll delve into associative containers and what you can do with them.

SEQUENCE CONTAINERS

The class templates for the three basic sequence containers are shown in the following table.

TEMPLATE	HEADER FILE	DESCRIPTION
`vector<T>`	`vector`	Creates a class representing a dynamic array storing objects of type `T`.
`list<T>`	`list`	Creates a class representing a linked list storing objects of type `T`.
`deque<T>`	`deque`	Creates a class representing a double-ended queue storing objects of type `T`.

Which template you choose to use in any particular instance will depend on the application. These three kinds of sequence containers are clearly differentiated by the operations they can perform efficiently, as Figure 10-2 shows.

FIGURE 10-2

If you need random access to the contents of the container, and you are happy to always add or delete objects at the end of a sequence, then vector<T> is the container template to choose. It is possible to add or delete objects randomly within a vector, but the process will be very slow because all the objects past the insertion or deletion point will have to be moved. A deque<T> container is very similar to a vector<T> and supports the same operations, but it has the additional capability to add and delete at the beginning of the sequence. A list<T> container is a doubly-linked list, so adding and deleting at any position is efficient. The downside of a list is that there is no random access to the contents; the only way to access an object that is internal to the list is to traverse the contents from the beginning, or to run backward through the contents from the end.

Let's look at sequence containers in more detail and try some examples. I'll be introducing the use of some iterators, algorithms, and function objects along the way.

Creating Vector Containers

The simplest way to create a vector container is like this:

```
vector<int> mydata;
```

This creates a container that will store values of type int. The initial capacity to store elements is zero, so you will be allocating more memory right from the outset when you insert the first value. The push_back() function adds a new element to the end of a vector, so to store a value in this vector you would write:

```
mydata.push_back(99);
```

The argument to the push_back() function is the item to be stored. This statement stores the value 99 in the vector, so after executing this statement the vector contains one element.

Here's another way to create a vector to store integers:

```
vector<int> mydata(100);
```

This creates a vector that contains 100 elements that are all initialized to zero. If you add new elements to this vector, the memory allocated for storage in the vector will be increased automatically, so obviously it's a good idea to choose a reasonably accurate value for the number of integers you are likely to want to store. This vector already contains 100 elements and can be used just like an array. For example, to store a value in the third element, you can write:

```
mydata[2] = 999;
```

Of course, you can only use an index value to access elements within a vector that are within the range of elements that exist. You can't add new elements in this way, though. To add a new element, you should use the push_back() function.

You can initialize the elements in a vector to a different value, when you create it by using this statement:

```
vector<int> mydata(100, -1);
```

The second argument to the constructor is the initial value to be used, so all 100 elements in the vector will be set to -1.

If you don't want to create elements when you create the container, you can increase the capacity after you create it by calling its reserve() function:

```
vector<int> mydata;
mydata.reserve(100);
```

The argument to the reserve() function is the minimum number of elements to be accommodated. If the argument is less than the current capacity of the vector, then calling reserve() will have no effect. In this code fragment, calling reserve() causes the vector container to allocate sufficient memory for a total of 100 elements.

You can also create a vector with initial values for elements from an external array. For example:

```
double data[] = {1.5, 2.5, 3.5, 4.5, 5.5, 6.5, 7.5, 8.5, 9.5, 10.5};
vector<double> mydata(data, data+8);
```

Here the `data` array is created with 10 elements of type `double`, with the initial values shown. The second statement creates a vector storing elements of type `double`, with eight elements initially having the values corresponding to `data[0]` through `data[7]`. The arguments to the `vector<double>` constructor are pointers (and can also be iterators), where the first pointer points to the first initializing element in the array, and the second points to one past the last initializing element. Thus, the `mydata` vector will contain eight elements with initial values 1.5, 2.5, 3.5, 4.5, 5.5, 6.5, 7.5, and 8.5.

Because the constructor in the previous fragment can accept either pointer or iterator arguments, you can initialize a vector when you create it with values from another vector that contains elements of the same type. You just supply the constructor with an iterator pointing to the first element you want to use as an initializer, plus a second iterator pointing to one past the last element you want to use. Here's an example:

```
vector<double> values(mydata.begin(), mydata.end());
```

After executing this statement, the `values` vector will have elements that are duplicates of the `mydata` vector. As Figure 10-3 illustrates, the `begin()` function returns a random access iterator that points to the first element in the vector for which it is called, and the `end()` function returns a random access iterator pointing to one past the last element. A sequence of elements is typically specified in the STL by two iterators, one pointing to the first element in the sequence and the other pointing to one past the last element in the sequence, so you'll see this time and time again.

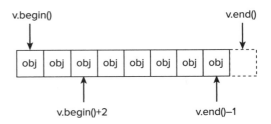

Iterators for a vector v

FIGURE 10-3

Because the `begin()` and `end()` functions for a vector container return random access iterators, you can modify what they point to when you use them. The type of the iterators that the `begin()` and `end()` functions return is `vector<T>::iterator`, where `T` is the type of object stored in the vector.

Here's a statement that creates a vector that is initialized with the third through the seventh elements from the `mydata` vector:

```
vector<double> values(mydata.begin()+2, mydata.end()-1);
```

Adding 2 to the first iterator makes it point to the third element in `mydata`. Subtracting 1 from the second iterator makes it point to the last element in `mydata`; remember that the second argument to the constructor is an iterator that points to a position that is *one past* the element to be used as the last initializer, so the object that the second iterator points to is not included in the set.

As I said earlier, it is pretty much standard practice in the STL to indicate a sequence of elements in a container by a begin iterator that points to the first element and an end iterator that points to one past the last element. This method allows you to iterate over all the elements in the sequence by incrementing the begin iterator until it equals the end iterator. This means that the iterators only need to support the equality operator to allow you to walk through the sequence.

Occasionally, you may want to access the contents of a vector in reverse order. Calling the `rbegin()` function for a vector returns an iterator that points to the last element, while `rend()` points to one past the first element (that is, the position preceding the first element), as Figure 10-4 illustrates.

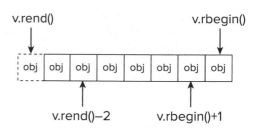

Reverse Iterators for a vector v

FIGURE 10-4

The iterators returned by `rbegin()` and `rend()` are called **reverse iterators** because they present the elements in reverse sequence. Reverse iterators are of type `vector<T>::reverse_iterator`. Figure 10-4 shows how adding a positive integer to the `rbegin()` iterator moves back through the sequence, and subtracting an integer from `rend()` moves forward through the sequence.

Here's how you could create a vector containing the contents of another vector in reverse order:

```
double data[] = {1.5, 2.5, 3.5, 4.5, 5.5, 6.5, 7.5, 8.5, 9.5, 10.5};
vector<double> mydata(data, data+8);
vector<double> values(mydata.rbegin(), mydata.rend());
```

Because you are using reverse iterators as arguments to the constructor in the last statement, the `values` vector will contain the elements from `mydata` in reverse order.

The Capacity and Size of a Vector Container

It's about time I explained the difference between the *capacity* and the *size* of a vector container. The *capacity* is the maximum number of objects a container can currently accommodate without allocating more memory. The *size* is the number of objects actually stored in the container. So, the size cannot be greater than the capacity.

You can obtain both the size and capacity of the container `data` at any time by calling the `size()` and `capacity()` member functions. For example:

```
cout << endl << "The current capacity of the container is: " << data.capacity()
     << endl << "The current size of the container is: " << data.size() << endl;
```

Calling the `capacity()` function for a vector returns the current capacity, and calling its `size()` function returns the current size, both values being returned as type `vector<T>::size_type`. This is an implementation-defined integer type that is defined within the `vector<T>` class template by a `typedef`. To create a variable to store the value returned from the `size()` or `capacity()` function, you specify it as type `vector<T>::size_type`, where you replace `T` with the type of object stored in the container. The following fragment illustrates this:

```
vector<double> values;
vector<double>::size_type cap = values.capacity();
```

NOTE. *The Microsoft Visual C++ library implementation of STL defines the* `vector<T>::size_type` *type as* `size_t`. `size_t` *is an unsigned integer type that is also a type of the result of the* `sizeof` *operator. You could use the* `auto` *keyword to specify the type of* `cap` *in the fragment above.*

If the value returned by the `size()` function is zero, then clearly the vector contains no elements; thus, you can use it as a test for an empty vector. You can also call the `empty()` function for a vector to test for this:

```
if(values.empty())
   cout << "No more elements in the vector."
```

The `empty()` function returns a value of type `bool` that is `true` when the vector is empty and `false` otherwise.

You are unlikely to need it very often, but you can discover the maximum possible number of elements in a vector by calling its `max_size()` function. For example:

```
vector<string> strings;
cout << "Maximum length of strings vector: " << strings.max_size();
```

Executing this fragment produces the output:

```
Maximum length of strings vector: 153391689
```

The maximum length is returned by the `max_size()` function as a value, in this case of type `vector<string>::size_type`. Note that the maximum length of a vector will depend on the type of element stored in the vector. If you try this out with a vector storing values of type `int`, you will get 1073741823 as the maximum length, and for a vector storing value of type `double` it is 536870911.

You can change the size of a vector by calling its `resize()` function, which can either increase or decrease the size of the vector. If you specify a new size that is less than the current size, sufficient elements will be deleted from the end of the vector to reduce it to its new size. If the new size is greater than the old, new elements will be added to the end of the vector to increase its length to the new size. Here's code illustrating this:

```
vector<int> values(5, 66);   // Contains 66 66 66 66 66
values.resize(7, 88);        // Contains 66 66 66 66 66 88 88
values.resize(10);           // Contains 66 66 66 66 66 88 88 0 0 0
values.resize(4);            // Contains 66 66 66 66
```

The first argument to `resize()` is the new size for the vector. The second argument, when it is present, is the value to be used for new elements that need to be added to make up the new size. If you are increasing the size and you don't specify a value to be used for new elements, the default value will be used. In the case of a vector storing objects of a class type, the default value will be the object produced by the no-arg constructor for the class.

You can explore the size and capacity of a vector through the following working example.

TRY IT OUT Exploring the Size and Capacity of a Vector

In this example, you will try out some of the ways you have seen for creating a vector, and you'll also see how the capacity changes as you add elements.

```cpp
// Ex10_01.cpp
// Exploring the size and capacity of a vector
#include <iostream>
#include <vector>
using std::cout;
using std::endl;
using std::vector;

// Template function to display the size and capacity of any vector
template<class T>
void listInfo(vector<T> &v)
{
  cout << "Container capacity: " << v.capacity()
       << " size: " << v.size() << endl;
}

int main()
{
  // Basic vector creation
  vector<double> data;
  listInfo(data);

  cout << endl << "After calling reserve(100):" << endl;
  data.reserve(100);
  listInfo(data);

  // Create a vector with 10 elements and initialize it
  vector<int> numbers(10,-1);
  cout << endl << "The initial values are:";
  for(vector<int>::size_type i = 0; i<numbers.size(); i++)
    cout << " " << numbers[i];

  // See how adding elements affects capacity increments
  auto oldC = numbers.capacity();    // Old capacity
  auto newC = oldC;                  // New capacity after adding element
  cout << endl << endl;
  listInfo(numbers);
  for(int i = 0; i<1000 ; i++)
  {
    numbers.push_back(2*i);
    newC = numbers.capacity();
    if(oldC < newC)
    {
      oldC = newC;
      listInfo(numbers);
    }
  }
  return 0;
}
```

code snippet Ex10_01.cpp

This example produces the following output:

```
Container capacity: 0 size: 0

After calling reserve(100):
Container capacity: 100 size: 0

The initial values are: -1 -1 -1 -1 -1 -1 -1 -1 -1 -1

Container capacity: 10 size: 10
Container capacity: 15 size: 11
Container capacity: 22 size: 16
Container capacity: 33 size: 23
Container capacity: 49 size: 34
Container capacity: 73 size: 50
Container capacity: 109 size: 74
Container capacity: 163 size: 110
Container capacity: 244 size: 164
Container capacity: 366 size: 245
Container capacity: 549 size: 367
Container capacity: 823 size: 550
Container capacity: 1234 size: 824
```

How It Works

The `#include` directive for the `vector` header adds the definition for the `vector<T>` template to the source file.

Following the `using` statement for the `std` namespace, you have a definition of the `listInfo()` function template:

```
template<class T>
void listInfo(vector<T> &v)
{
  cout << "Container capacity: " << v.capacity()
       << " size: " << v.size() << endl;
}
```

This function outputs the current capacity and size of any vector container. You will often find it convenient to write function templates when working with STL. The example shows how easy it is. The `T` parameter determines the type of argument the function expects. You can call this function with a vector container as the argument. Specifying the parameter as the reference type, `vector<T>&`, enables the code in the function body to access directly the container you pass as the argument to the function. If you specified the parameter as type `vector<T>`, then the argument would be copied each time the function is called, and this could be a time-consuming process for a large vector container.

The first action in `main()` is to create a vector and output its size and capacity:

```
vector<double> data;
listInfo(data);
```

You can see from the output that the size and the capacity are both zero for this container. Adding an element requires more space to be allocated.

Next you call the `reserve()` function for the container:

```
data.reserve(100);
```

You can see from the output that the capacity is now 100 and the size is zero. To put it another way, the container contains no elements but has memory allocated to accommodate up to 100 elements. Only when you add the 101st element will the capacity be increased automatically.

Next you create another container with this statement:

```
vector<int> numbers(10,-1);
```

This creates a container that contains 10 elements at the outset, each initialized with -1. To demonstrate that this is indeed the case, you output the elements in the container with the following loop:

```
for(vector<int>::size_type i = 0; i<numbers.size(); i++)
  cout << " " << numbers[i];
```

The upper limit for the loop variable, `i`, is the value returned by the `size()` function for the container (the number of elements currently stored). As you see, within the loop you access the container elements in the same way as an ordinary array.

Alternatively, you could write the loop using the `auto` keyword:

```
for(auto i = 0; i<numbers.size(); i++)
  cout << " " << numbers[i];
```

You could also use an iterator to access the elements. A loop to output the elements using an iterator looks like this:

```
for(auto iter = numbers.begin(); iter < numbers.end(); iter++)
  cout << " " << *iter;
```

The loop variable is an iterator, `iter`, of type `vector<int>::iterator`, that you initialize to the iterator returned by the `begin()` function. This is incremented on each loop iteration, and the loop ends when it reaches `numbers.end()`, which points to one past the last element. Note how you dereference the iterator just like a pointer to get at the value of the element.

The remaining statements in `main()` demonstrate how the capacity of a vector is increased as you add elements. The first two statements set up variables that store the current capacity and the new capacity after adding an element:

```
auto oldC = numbers.capacity();    // Old capacity
auto newC = oldC;                  // New capacity after adding element
```

After displaying the initial size and capacity, you execute the following loop:

```
for(int i = 0; i<1000 ; i++)
{
  numbers.push_back(2*i);
  newC = numbers.capacity();
```

```
      if(oldC < newC)
      {
        oldC = newC;
        listInfo(numbers);
      }
    }
```

This loop calls the `push_back()` function for the `numbers` vector, to add 1000 elements. We are only interested in seeing output when the capacity increases, so the `if` condition ensures that we only display the capacity and size when the capacity increases.

The output shows an interesting pattern in the way additional space is allocated in the container. As you would expect with the initial size and capacity at 10, the first capacity increase occurs when you add the 11th element. The increase in this case is half the capacity, so the capacity increases to 15. The next capacity increase is when the size reaches 15, and the increase is to 22, so the increment is again half the capacity. This process continues with each capacity increase being half the current capacity. Thus, you automatically get larger chunks of memory space allocated when required, the more elements the vector contains. On the one hand, this mechanism ensures that once the initial memory allocation in a container is occupied, you don't cause more memory to be allocated every time you add a new element. On the other hand, this also implies that you should take care when reserving space for a large number of elements in a vector. If you set up a container that provides initially for 100,000 elements for example, exceeding this by one element will cause space for another 50,000 to be allocated. In this sort of situation you could check for reaching the capacity, and use `reserve()` to increase the available memory by a more appropriate and less extravagant amount.

Accessing the Elements in a Vector

You have already seen that you can access the elements in a vector by using the subscript operator, just as you would for an array. You can also use the `at()` function where the argument is the index position of the element you want to access. Here's how you could list the contents of the `numbers` vector of integer elements in the previous example:

```
for(auto i = 0; i<numbers.size() ; i++)
  cout << " " << numbers.at(i);
```

So how does the `at()` function differ from using the subscript operator, `[]`? Well, if you use a subscript with the subscript operator that is outside the valid range, the result is undefined. If you do the same with the `at()` function, an exception of type `out_of_range` will be thrown. If there's the potential for subscript values outside the legal range to arise in a program, it's generally better to use the `at()` function and catch the exception than to allow the possibility for undefined results.

To access the first or last element in a vector container you can call the `front()` or `back()` function respectively:

```
cout << "The value of the first element is: " << numbers.front() << endl;
cout << "The value of the last element is: " << numbers.back() << endl;
```

Both functions come in two versions; one returns a reference to the object stored, and the other returns a const reference to the object stored. The latter option enables you to explicitly prevent modification of the object:

```
const int& firstvalue = numbers.front();    // firstvalue cannot be changed
int& lastvalue = numbers.back();            // lastvalue can be changed
```

Storing the reference that is returned in a const variable automatically selects the version of the function that returns a const reference.

Inserting and Deleting Elements in a Vector

In addition to the push_back() function you have seen, a vector container supports the pop_back() operation that deletes the last element. Both operations execute in **constant time**, that is, the time to execute will be the same, regardless of the number of elements in the vector. The pop_back() function is very simple to use:

```
vec.pop_back();
```

This statement removes the last element from the vector vec and reduces the size by 1. If the vector contains no elements, then calling pop_back() has no effect.

You could remove all the elements in a vector by calling the pop_back() function repeatedly, but the clear() function does this much more simply:

```
vec.clear();
```

This statement removes all the elements from vec, so the size will be zero. Of course, the capacity will be left unchanged.

You can call the insert() function to insert one or more new elements anywhere in a vector, but this operation will execute in **linear time**, which means that the time will increase in proportion to the number of elements in the container. This is because inserting new elements involves moving the existing elements. The simplest version of the insert() function inserts a single new element at a specific position in the vector, where the first argument is an iterator specifying the position where the element is to be inserted, and the second argument is the element to be inserted. For example:

```
vector<int> vec(5, 99);
vec.insert(vec.begin()+1, 88);
```

The first statement creates a vector with five integer elements, all initialized to 99. The second statement inserts 88 after the first element; so, after executing this, the vector will contain:

```
99 88 99 99 99 99
```

You can also insert several identical elements, starting from a given position:

```
vec.insert(vec.begin()+2, 3, 77);
```

The first argument is an iterator specifying the position where the first element is to be inserted, the second argument is the number of elements to be inserted, and the third argument is the element to be inserted. After executing this statement, vec will contain:

```
99 88 77 77 77 99 99 99 99
```

You have yet another version of the insert() function that inserts a sequence of elements at a given position. The first argument is an iterator pointing to the position where the first element is to be inserted. The second and third arguments are input iterators specifying the range of elements to be inserted from some source. Here's an example:

```
vector<int> newvec(5, 22);
newvec.insert(newvec.begin()+1, vec.begin()+1, vec.begin()+5);
```

The first statement creates a vector with five integer elements initialized to 22. The second statement inserts four elements from vec, starting with the second. After executing these statements, newvec will contain:

```
22 88 77 77 77 22 22 22 22
```

Don't forget that the second iterator in the interval specifies the position that is *one past* the last element, so the element it points to is not included.

The erase() function can delete one or more elements from any position within a vector, but this also is a linear time function and will typically be slow. Here's how you erase a single element at a given position:

```
newvec.erase(newvec.end()-2);
```

The argument is an iterator that points to the element to be erased, so this statement removes the second to last element from newvec.

To delete several elements, you supply two iterator arguments specifying the interval. For example:

```
newvec.erase(newvec.begin()+1, newvec.begin()+4);
```

This will delete the second, third, and fourth elements from newvec. The element that the second iterator argument points to is not included in the operation.

As I said, both the erase() and insert() operations are slow, so you should use them sparingly when working with a vector. If you find you need to use them often in your application, a list<T> is likely to be a better choice of container.

The swap() function enables you to swap the contents of two vectors, provided, of course, the elements in the two vectors are of the same type. Here's a code fragment showing an example of how this works:

```
vector<int> first(5, 77);        // Contains 77 77 77 77 77
vector<int> second(8, -1);       // Contains -1 -1 -1 -1 -1 -1 -1 -1
first.swap(second);
```

After executing the last statement, the contents of the vectors `first` and `second` will have interchanged. Note that the capacities of the vectors are swapped as well as the contents, and, of course, the size.

The `assign()` function enables you to replace the entire contents of a vector with another sequence, or to replace the contents with a given number of instances of an object. Here's how you could replace the contents of one vector with a sequence from another:

```
vector<double> values;
for(int i = 1 ; i <= 50 ; i++)
  values.push_back(2.5*i);
vector<double> newdata(5, 3.5);
newdata.assign(values.begin()+1, values.end()-1);
```

This code fragment creates the `values` vector and stores 50 elements that have the values 2.5, 5.0, 7.5,... 125.0. The `newdata` vector is created with five elements, each having the value 3.5. The last statement calls the `assign()` function for `newdata`, which deletes all elements from `newdata`, and then inserts copies of all the elements from `values`, except for the first and the last. You specify the new sequence to be inserted by two iterators, the first pointing to the first element to be inserted and the second pointing to one past the last element to be inserted. Because you specify the new elements to be inserted by two iterators, the source of the data can be from any sequence, not just a vector. The `assign()` function will also work with regular pointers, so you could also insert elements from an array of `double` elements.

Here's how you use the `assign()` function to replace the contents of a vector with a sequence of instances of the same element:

```
newdata.assign(30, 99.5);
```

The first argument is the count of elements in the replacement sequence, and the second argument is the element to be used. This statement will cause the contents of `newdata` to be deleted and replaced by 30 elements, each having the value 99.5.

Storing Class Objects in a Vector

So far, you have only seen vectors storing numerical values. You can store objects of any class type in a vector, but the class must meet certain minimum criteria. Here's a minimum specification for a given class `T` to be compatible with a vector, or, in fact, any sequence container:

```
class T
{
  public:
  T();                          // Default constructor
  T(const T& t);                // Copy constructor
  ~T();                         // Destructor
  T& operator=(const T& t);     // Assignment operator
};
```

Of course, the compiler will supply default versions of these class members if you don't supply them, so it's not difficult for a class to meet these requirements. The important thing to note is that they are required and are likely to be used, so when the default implementation that the compiler supplies will not suffice, you must provide your own implementation.

Note that the STL can make use of a move constructor and a move assignment operator when they are provided in a class, so the performance of your class may be increased if you implement these as well.

Let's try an example.

TRY IT OUT Storing Objects in a Vector

In this example you create `Person` objects that represent individuals by their name. Just to make it more interesting, I'm going to pretend that you have never heard of the `string` class, so you are stuck with using null-terminated strings to store names. This means you have to take care how you implement the class if you want to store objects in a `vector<Person>` container. In general, such a class might have lots of different data members relating to a person, but I'll keep it simple with just their first and second names.

Here's the definition of the `Person` class:

```
// Person.h
// A class defining people by their names
#pragma once
#include <cstring>
#include <iostream>
using std::cout;
using std::endl;

class Person
{
  public:
  // Constructor, includes no-arg constructor
  Person(const char* first = "John", const char* second = "Doe")
  {
    initName(first, second);
  }

  // Copy constructor
  Person(const Person& p)
  {
    initName(p.firstname, p.secondname);
  }

  // Destructor
  ~Person()
  {
    delete[] firstname;
    delete[] secondname;
  }

  // Assignment operator
  Person& operator=(const Person& p)
  {
    // Deal with p = p assignment situation
```

```
      if(&p == this)
        return *this;

      delete[] firstname;
      delete[] secondname;
      initName(p.firstname, p.secondname);
      return *this;
    }

    // Less-than operator
    bool operator<(const Person& p)
    {
      int result(strcmp(secondname, p.secondname));
      if(result < 0 || result ==  0 && strcmp(firstname, p.firstname) < 0)
        return true;
      return false;
    }

    // Output a person
    void showPerson() const
    {
      cout << firstname << " " << secondname << endl;
    }

    private:
    char* firstname;
    char* secondname;

    // Private helper function to avoid code duplication
    void initName(const char* first, const char* second)
    {
      size_t length(strlen(first)+1);
      firstname = new char[length];
      strcpy_s(firstname, length, first);
      length = strlen(second)+1;
      secondname = new char[length];
      strcpy_s(secondname, length, second);
    }
};
```

The #pragma once directive is there to ensure that the header does not get included in a program more than once.

The private initPerson() function is there because the constructors and the assignment operator function need to carry out the same operations to initialize the class data members. Using this helper function avoids having three occurrences of the same code.

Because the Person class allocates memory dynamically to store the first and second names of a person, you must implement the destructor to release the memory when an object is destroyed. You must also implement the assignment operator because this involves more memory allocation. Note the code at the beginning for dealing with the a = a assignment situation. Assigning an object to itself can arise in ways that are less than obvious, and can cause problems if you don't implement the operator=() function to take account of this.

The showPerson() function is a convenience function for outputting an entire name. It is declared as const to allow it to work with const and non-const Person objects. The operator<() function is there for use later.

The program to store Person objects in a vector looks like this:

```cpp
// Ex10_02.cpp
// Storing objects in a vector

#include <iostream>
#include <vector>
#include "Person.h"

using std::cin;
using std::cout;
using std::endl;
using std::vector;

int main()
{
  vector<Person> people;                  // Vector of Person objects
  const size_t maxlength(50);
  char firstname[maxlength];
  char secondname[maxlength];

  // Input all the people
  while(true)
  {
    cout << "Enter a first name or press Enter to end: ";
    cin.getline(firstname, maxlength, '\n');
    if(strlen(firstname) == 0)
      break;
    cout << "Enter the second name: ";
    cin.getline(secondname, maxlength, '\n');
    people.push_back(Person(firstname, secondname));
  }

  // Output the contents of the vector
  cout << endl;
  auto iter(people.begin());
  while(iter != people.end())
    iter++->showPerson();

  return 0;
}
```

code snippet Ex10_02.cpp

Here's an example of some output from this program:

```
Enter a first name or press Enter to end: Jane
Enter the second name: Fonda
Enter a first name or press Enter to end: Bill
Enter the second name: Cosby
Enter a first name or press Enter to end: Sally
Enter the second name: Field
Enter a first name or press Enter to end: Mae
```

```
Enter the second name: West
Enter a first name or press Enter to end: Oliver
Enter the second name: Hardy
Enter a first name or press Enter to end:

Jane Fonda
Bill Cosby
Sally Field
Mae West
Oliver Hardy
```

How It Works

You create a vector to store `Person` objects like this:

```
vector<Person> people;                    // Vector of Person objects
```

You then create two arrays of type `char[]` that you'll use as working storage when reading names from the standard input stream:

```
const size_t maxlength(50);
char firstname[maxlength];
char secondname[maxlength];
```

Each array accommodates a name up to `maxlength` characters long, including the terminating null.

You read names from the standard input stream in an indefinite loop:

```
while(true)
{
  cout << "Enter a first name or press Enter to end: ";
  cin.getline(firstname, maxlength, '\n');
  if(strlen(firstname) == 0)
    break;
  cout << "Enter the second name: ";
  cin.getline(secondname, maxlength, '\n');
  people.push_back(Person(firstname, secondname));
}
```

You read each name using the `getline()` member function for `cin`. This reads characters until a newline character is read, or until `maxlength-1` characters have been read. This ensures that you don't overrun the capacity of the input array because both arrays have `maxlength` elements, allowing for strings up to `maxlength-1` characters plus the terminating NULL. When an empty string is entered for the first name, the loop ends.

You create the `Person` object in the expression that is the argument to the `push_back()` function. This adds the objects to the end of the vector.

The last step is to output the contents of the vector:

```
cout << endl;
auto iter(people.begin());
while(iter != people.end())
  iter++->showPerson();
```

Here you use an iterator of type `vector<Person>::iterator` to output the elements of the vector with the type deduced automatically from the initial value. Within the body of the `while` loop, you output the element that the iterator points to, and then you increment the iterator using the postfix increment operator. The loop continues as long as `iter` is not equal to the iterator returned by `end()`.

Sorting Vector Elements

The `sort()` function template that is defined in the `algorithm` header will sort a sequence of objects identified by two random access iterators that point to the first and one-past-the-last objects in the sequence. Note that random access iterators are essential; iterators with lesser capability will not suffice. The `sort()` function template uses the < operator to order the elements. Thus, you can use the `sort()` template to sort the contents of any container that provides random access iterators, as long as the objects it contains can be compared using the less-than operator.

In the previous example, you implemented `operator<()` in the `Person` class, so you can sort a sequence of `Person` objects. Here's how you could sort the contents of the `vector<Person>` container:

```
sort(people.begin(), people.end());
```

This sorts the contents of the vector in ascending sequence. You can add an `#include` directive for `algorithm`, and put the statement in `main()` before the output loop, to see the sort in action. You'll also need a `using` declaration for `std::sort`.

Note that you can use the `sort()` template function to `sort()` arrays. The only requirement is that the < operator should work with the type of elements stored in the array. Here's a code fragment showing how you could use it to sort an array of integers:

```
const size_t max(100);
int data[max];
cout << "Enter up to " << max << " non-zero integers. Enter 0 to end." << endl;
int value(0);
size_t count(0);
for(size_t i = 0 ; i<max ; i++)          // Read up to max integers
{
  cin >> value;                          // Read a value
  if(value == 0)                         // If it is zero,
    break;                               // We are done
  data[count++] = value;
}
sort(data, data+count);                  // Sort the integers
```

Note how the pointer marking the end of the sequence of elements that are to be sorted must still be one past the last element.

When you need to sort a sequence in descending order, you can use a version of the `sort()` algorithm that accepts a function object that is a binary predicate, as the third argument to the function. The `functional` header defines a complete set of types for comparison predicates:

```
less<T>   less_equal<T>   equal<T>   greater_equal<T>   greater<T>
```

Each of these templates creates a class type for function objects that you can use with `sort()` and other algorithms. The `sort()` function used in the previous fragment uses a `less<int>` function object by default. To specify a different function object to be used as the sort criterion, you add it as a third argument, like this:

```
sort(data, data+count, greater<int>());      // Sort the integers
```

The third argument to the function is an expression that calls the constructor for the `greater<int>` type, so you are passing an object of this type to the `sort()` function. This statement will sort the contents of the `data` array in descending sequence. If you are trying these fragments out, don't forget that you need the `functional` header to be included for the function object, and that the `greater` name is defined in the `std` namespace.

Storing Pointers in a Vector

A vector container, like other containers, makes a copy of the objects you add to it. This has tremendous advantages in most circumstances, but it could be very inconvenient in some situations. For example, if your objects are large, there could be considerable overhead in copying each object as you add it to the container. This is an occasion where you might be better off storing pointers to the objects in the container rather than the objects themselves, and managing the objects externally. You could create a new version of the `Ex10_02.cpp` example to store pointers to `Person` objects in a container.

TRY IT OUT   Storing Pointers in a Vector

The `Person` class definition is exactly the same as before. Here's a revised version of the other source file:

Available for
download on
Wrox.com

```cpp
// Ex10_03.cpp
// Storing pointers to objects in a vector
#include <iostream>
#include <vector>
#include "Person.h"

using std::cin;
using std::cout;
using std::endl;
using std::vector;

int main()
{
  vector<Person*> people;              // Vector of Person objects
  const size_t maxlength(50);
  char firstname[maxlength];
  char secondname[maxlength];
  while(true)
  {
    cout << "Enter a first name or press Enter to end: ";
    cin.getline(firstname, maxlength, '\n');
```

```
      if(strlen(firstname) == 0)
        break;
      cout << "Enter the second name: ";
      cin.getline(secondname, maxlength, '\n');
      people.push_back(new Person(firstname, secondname));
    }

    // Output the contents of the vector
    cout << endl;
    auto iter(people.begin());
    while(iter != people.end())
      (*(iter++))->showPerson();

    // Release memory for the people
    iter = people.begin();
    while(iter != people.end())
      delete *(iter++);

    // Pointers in the vector are now invalid
    // so remove the contents
    people.clear();

    return 0;
  }
```

code snippet Ex10_03.cpp

The output is essentially the same as before.

How It Works

Only the shaded lines of code have been changed. The first change is in the definition of the container:

```
vector<Person*> people;                // Vector of Person objects
```

The vector<T> template type parameter is now Person*, which is a pointer to a Person object.

Within the input loop, each Person object is now created on the heap, and the address is passed to the push_back() function for the vector:

```
people.push_back(new Person(firstname, secondname));
```

It is important to take care when storing addresses of objects in a container. If you create objects on the stack, these objects will be destroyed when the function exits, and the pointers you have stored will be rendered invalid. With objects created on the heap using the new operator, the objects are only destroyed when you remove them using delete.

The iterator used to output the Person objects now has a different type, vector<Person*>::iterator, but it is still determined automatically:

```
auto iter(people.begin());
```

The way in which you output the Person object is also different:

```
(*(iter++))->showPerson();
```

The iterator now points to a pointer, so you must dereference the iterator to get to the pointer, and then use the pointer to call the `showPerson()` function for the `Person` object to produce the output. Note that the outer parentheses are essential because of operator precedence.

Because you created `Person` objects on the heap, you are responsible for deleting them:

```
iter = people.begin();
while(iter != people.end())
  delete *(iter++);
```

You obtain another random access iterator pointing to the first element in the vector, and then use this in the loop to delete each of the `Person` objects. Of course, you have to dereference the iterator to get the address of the object to be deleted.

Finally, because all the objects have been deleted, the pointers in the vector are no longer valid, so you empty the vector by calling its `clear()` function. This simply deletes everything stored in the container.

Double-Ended Queue Containers

The double-ended queue container template, `deque<T>`, is defined in the `deque` header. A double-ended queue container is very similar to a vector in that it can do everything a vector container can, and includes the same function members, but you can also add and delete elements efficiently at the beginning of the sequence as well as at the end. You could replace the vector used in `Ex10_02.cpp` with a double-ended queue, and it would work just as well:

```
deque<Person> people;              // Double-ended queue of Person objects
```

Of course, you would need to change the `#include` directive to include the `deque` header instead of the `vector` header.

The function to add an element to the front of the container is `push_front()`, and you can delete the first element by calling the `pop_front()` function. Thus, if you were using a `deque<Person>` container in `Ex10_02.cpp`, you could add elements at the front instead of the back:

```
people.push_front(Person(firstname, secondname));
```

The only difference in using this statement to add elements to the container would be that the order of the elements in the double-ended queue would be the reverse of what they are in the vector.

The range of constructors available for a `deque<T>` container is the same as for `vector<T>`. Here are examples of each of them:

```
deque<string> strings;             // Create an empty container
deque<int> items(50);              // A container of 50 elements initialized to
                                   // default value
deque<double> values(5, 0.5);      // A container with 5 elements 0.5
deque<int> data(items.begin(), items.end());  // Initialized with a sequence
```

Although a double-ended queue is very similar to a vector and does everything a vector can do, as well as allowing you to add to the front of the sequence efficiently, it does have one disadvantage compared to a vector. Because of the additional capability it offers, the memory management for a double-ended queue is more complicated than for a vector, so it will be slightly slower. Unless you need the ability to add elements to the front of the container, a vector is a better choice.

Let's see a double-ended queue in action.

TRY IT OUT **Using a Double-Ended Queue**

This example stores an arbitrary number of integers in a double-ended queue and then operates on them.

Available for
download on
Wrox.com

```cpp
// Ex10_04.cpp
// Using a double-ended queue

#include <iostream>
#include <deque>
#include <algorithm>
#include <numeric>

using std::cin;
using std::cout;
using std::endl;
using std::deque;
using std::sort;
using std::accumulate;

int main()
{
  deque<int> data;
  deque<int>::iterator iter;            // Stores an iterator
  deque<int>::reverse_iterator riter;   // Stores a reverse iteraotr

  // Read the data
  cout << "Enter a series of non-zero integers separated by spaces."
       << " Enter 0 to end." << endl;
  int value(0);
  while(cin >> value, value != 0)
    data.push_front(value);

  // Output the data using an iterator
  cout << endl << "The values you entered are:" << endl;
  for(iter = data.begin() ; iter != data.end() ; iter++)
    cout << *iter << "  ";
  cout << endl;

  // Output the data using a reverse iterator
  cout << endl << "In reverse order the values you entered are:" << endl;
  for(riter = data.rbegin() ; riter != data.rend() ; riter++)
    cout << *riter << "  ";

  // Sort the data in descending sequence
```

```
cout << endl;
cout << endl << "In descending sequence the values you entered are:" << endl;
sort(data.rbegin(), data.rend());
for(iter = data.begin() ; iter != data.end() ; iter++)
  cout << *iter << "   ";
cout << endl;

// Calculate the sum of the elements
cout << endl << "The sum of the elements in the queue is: "
     << accumulate(data.begin(), data.end(), 0)   << endl;

return 0;
}
```

code snippet Ex10_04.cpp

Here is some sample output from this program:

```
Enter a series of non-zero integers separated by spaces. Enter 0 to end.
405 302 1 23 67 34 56 111 56 99 77 82 3 23 34 111 89 0

The values you entered are:
89   111   34   23   3   82   77   99   56   111   56   34   67   23   1   302   405

In reverse order the values you entered are:
405   302   1   23   67   34   56   111   56   99   77   82   3   23   34   111   89

In descending sequence the values you entered are:
405   302   111   111   99   89   82   77   67   56   56   34   34   23   23   3   1

The sum of the elements in the queue is: 1573
```

How It Works

You create the double-ended queue container and two iterator variables at the beginning of main():

```
deque<int> data;
deque<int>::iterator iter;              // Stores an iterator
deque<int>::reverse_iterator riter;     // Stores a reverse iterator
```

The data container is empty to start with. You will be using the iter variable for storing an iterator that accesses the queue elements in a forward direction, and the riter variable for storing a reverse iterator. iter and riter are of different types, but they are both random access iterators in the case of a deque<T> container. This means you can increment or decrement them, or add or subtract integer values. The iterator types are defined within the container class, so you always get the type of iterator that is suited to the organization of the container. For vector and double-ended queue containers, you get random access iterators.

The input is read in a while loop:

```
int value(0);
while(cin >> value, value != 0)
  data.push_front(value);
```

The while loop condition makes use of the comma operator to separate two expressions, one that reads an integer from cin into value and another that tests whether the value read is non-zero. You saw in Chapter 2 that the value of a series of expressions separated by commas is the value of the rightmost expression, so the while loop continues as long as the expression value != 0 is true, and the value read is non-zero. Within the loop you store the value in the queue using the push_front() function.

The next loop lists the values contained in the queue:

```
cout << endl << "The values you entered are:" << endl;
for(iter = data.begin() ; iter != data.end() ; iter++)
  cout << *iter << "   ";
```

This uses iter as the loop control variable to output the values. The loop ends when iter is incremented to be equal to the iterator returned by the end() function. You could also write this as a while loop:

```
iter = data.begin();
while(iter != data.end())
  cout << *iter++ << "   ";
```

Here iter is incremented within the loop after the value it points to has been written to cout.

The next loop outputs the values in reverse order:

```
for(riter = data.rbegin() ; riter != data.rend() ; riter++)
  cout << *riter << "   ";
```

This uses a reverse iterator, so the loop starts with the last element and ends when riter is incremented to be equal to the iterator returned by rend(). The rbegin() function returns an iterator pointing to the last elements and the rend() function returns an iterator pointing to one before the first element.

Next you sort the elements in descending sequence and output them:

```
sort(data.rbegin(), data.rend());
for(iter = data.begin() ; iter != data.end() ; iter++)
  cout << *iter << "   ";
```

The default operation of the sort() algorithm is to sort the sequence, passed to it by the two random access iterator arguments, in ascending sequence. Here you pass reverse iterators to the functions, so it sees the elements in reverse order and sorts the reversed sequence in ascending order. The result is that the elements end up in descending sequence when seen in the normal forward order.

The last operation in main() is to output the sum of the elements:

```
cout << endl << "The sum of the elements in the queue is: "
       << accumulate(data.begin(), data.end(), 0)  << endl;
```

You could use a conventional loop to do this, but here you make use of the accumulate() algorithm that is defined in the numeric header. This accumulates the sum of the sequence of elements identified by the first two iterator arguments. The third argument specifies an initial value for the sum and must be the same type as the elements in the sequence. Supplying an initial value ensures that you always get a sensible result, even if the sequence to be summed is empty. The accumulate() function returns the result of the operation. You can apply the accumulate() function to a sequence of values of any numeric type.

Using List Containers

The List<T> container template that is defined in the list header implements a doubly-linked list. The big advantage a list container has over a vector or a double-ended queue is that you can insert or delete elements anywhere in the sequence in constant time. The range of constructors for a list container is similar to that for a vector or double-ended queue. This statement creates an empty list:

```
list<string> names;
```

You can also create a list with a given number of default elements:

```
list<string> sayings(20);              // A list of 20 empty strings
```

Here's how you create a list containing a given number of elements that are identical:

```
list<double> values(50, 2.71828);
```

This creates a list of 50 values of type double.

Of course, you can also construct a list initialized with values from a sequence specified by two iterators:

```
list<double> samples(++values.begin(), --values.end());
```

This creates a list from the contents of the values list, omitting the first and last elements in values. Note that the iterators returned by the begin() and end() functions for a list are bidirectional iterators, so you do not have the same flexibility as with a vector or a deque container that supports random access iterators. You can only change the value of a bidirectional iterator using the increment or decrement operator.

Just like the other sequence containers, you can discover the number of elements in a list by calling its size() member function. You can also change the number of elements in a list by calling its resize() function. If the argument to resize() is less than the number of elements in the list, elements will be deleted from the end; if the argument is greater, elements will be added using the default constructor for the type of elements stored.

Adding Elements to a List

You add an element to the beginning or end of a list by calling push_front() or push_back(), just as you would for a double-ended queue. To add elements to the interior of a list, you use the insert() function, which comes in three versions. Using the first version, you can insert a new element at a position specified by an iterator:

```
list<int> data(20, 1);                 // List of 20 elements value 1
data.insert(++data.begin(), 77);       // Insert 77 as the second element
```

The first argument to insert() is an iterator specified in the insertion position, and the second argument is the element to be inserted. The increment operator applied to the bidirectional iterator returned by begin() makes it point to the second element in the list. After executing this, the list contents will be:

```
1 77 1 1 1 1 1 1 1 1 1 1 1 1 1 1 1 1 1 1 1
```

You can see that the list now contains 21 elements, and that the elements from the insertion point on are simply displaced to the right.

You can also insert a number of copies of the same element at a given position:

```
list<int>::iterator iter = data.begin();
for(int i = 0 ; i<9 ; i++)
   ++iter;
data.insert(iter, 3, 88);    // Insert 3 copies of 88 starting at the 10th
```

The first argument to the insert() function is an iterator specifying the position, the second argument is the number of elements to be inserted, and the third argument is the element to be inserted repeatedly. To get to the tenth element you increment the iterator nine times in the for loop. Thus, this fragment inserts three copies of 88 into the list, starting at the tenth element. Now the contents of the list will be:

```
1 77 1 1 1 1 1 1 1 88 88 88 1 1 1 1 1 1 1 1 1 1 1 1
```

Now the list contains 24 elements.

Here's how you can insert a sequence of elements into a list:

```
vector<int> numbers(10, 5);               // Vector of 10 elements with value 5
data.insert(--(--data.end()), numbers.begin(), numbers.end());
```

The first argument to insert() is an iterator pointing to the second to last element position. The sequence to be inserted is specified by the second and third arguments to the insert() function, so this will insert all the elements from the vector into the list, starting at the second to last element position. After executing this, the contents of the list will be:

```
1 77 1 1 1 1 1 1 1 88 88 88 1 1 1 1 1 1 1 1 1 1 5 5 5 5 5 5 5 5 5 5 1 1
```

Inserting the 10 elements from numbers in the second-to-last element position displaces the last two elements in the list to the right. The list now contains 34 elements.

Accessing Elements in a List

You can obtain a reference to the first or last element in a list by calling the front() or back() function for the list. To access elements interior to the list you must use an iterator, and increment or decrement the iterator, to get to the element you want. As you have seen, the begin() and end() functions return a bidirectional iterator pointing at the first element, or one past the last element, respectively. The rbegin() and rend() functions return bidirectional iterators and enable you to iterate through the elements in reverse sequence.

Let's try out some of what we have seen in an example.

TRY IT OUT   **Working with a List**

In this example you read sentences from the keyboard and store them in a list.

Available for download on Wrox.com

```cpp
// Ex10_05.cpp
// Working with a list

#include <iostream>
#include <list>
#include <string>

using std::cin;
using std::cout;
using std::endl;
using std::list;
using std::string;

int main()
{
  list<string> text;
  list<string>::iterator iter;          // Stores an iterator

  // Read the data
  cout << "Enter a few lines of text. Just press Enter to end:"
       << endl;
  string sentence;
  while(getline(cin, sentence, '\n'), !sentence.empty())
    text.push_front(sentence);

  // Output the data using an iterator
  cout << endl << "Here is the text you entered:" << endl;
  for(iter = text.begin() ; iter != text.end() ; iter++)
    cout << *iter << endl;

  // Sort the data in ascending sequence
  cout << endl << "In ascending sequence the sentences you entered are:" << endl;
  text.sort();
  for(iter = text.begin() ; iter != text.end() ; iter++)
    cout << *iter << endl;

  return 0;
}
```

code snippet Ex10_05.cpp

Here is an example of some output from this program:

```
Enter a few lines of text. Just press Enter to end:
This sentance contains three erors.
This sentence is false.
People who live in glass houses might as well answer the door.
If all else fails, read the instructions.
Home is where the mortgage is.

Here is the text you entered:
Home is where the mortgage is.
```

```
If all else fails, read the instructions.
People who live in glass houses might as well answer the door.
This sentence is false.
This sentance contains three erors.

In ascending sequence the sentences you entered are:
Home is where the mortgage is.
If all else fails, read the instructions.
People who live in glass houses might as well answer the door.
This sentance contains three erors.
This sentence is false.
```

How It Works

You first create a list container to hold strings, followed by an iterator variable for use in outputting the contents of the list:

```
list<string> text;
list<string>::iterator iter;            // Stores an iterator
```

You then read an arbitrary number of text inputs from the standard input stream, `cin`:

```
string sentence;
while(getline(cin, sentence, '\n'), !sentence.empty())
  text.push_front(sentence);
```

This uses the same idiom for input as the previous example. The second expression in the `while` loop condition determines when the loop ends, which will be when calling `empty()` for `sentence` returns `true`. You add each input to the list using the `push_front()` function, but you could equally well use `push_back()`. The only difference would be that the order of elements in the list would be reversed.

You output the contents of the list in a loop:

```
for(iter = text.begin() ; iter != text.end() ; iter++)
  cout << *iter << endl;
```

This is exactly the same mechanism that you have used for a vector, but remember: A list does not support random access to the elements, so the iterators are bidirectional iterators, not random access iterators.

Lastly, you sort the contents of the list and output it:

```
text.sort();
for(iter = text.begin() ; iter != text.end() ; iter++)
  cout << *iter << endl;
```

This uses the `sort()` member of the `list<string>` object to sort the contents. Because a `list<T>` container does not provide random access iterators, you cannot use the `sort()` function that is defined in the `algorithm` header. This is why the `list<T>` template defines its own `sort()` function member.

Other Operations on Lists

The `clear()` function deletes all the elements from a list. The `erase()` function allows you to delete either a single element specified by a single iterator, or a sequence of elements specified by a pair of iterators in the usual fashion — the first in the sequence and one past the last.

```
int data[] = {10, 22, 4, 56, 89, 77, 13, 9};
list<int> numbers(data, data+8);

numbers.erase(++numbers.begin());        // Remove the second element

// Remove all except the first and the last two
numbers.erase(++numbers.begin(), --(--numbers.end()));
```

Initially, the list will contain all the values from the `data` array. The first `erase()` operation deletes the second element, so the list will contain:

```
10 4 56 89 77 13 9
```

For the second `erase()` operation, the first argument is the iterator returned by `begin()`, incremented by 1, so that it points to the second element. The second argument is the iterator returned by `end()`, decremented twice, so that it points to the second-to-last element. Of course, this is one past the end of the sequence, so the element that this iterator points to is not included in the set to be deleted, and the list contents after this operation will be:

```
10 13 9
```

The `remove()` function removes the elements from a list that match a particular value. With the `numbers` list defined as in the previous fragment, you could remove all elements equal to 22 with the following statement:

```
numbers.remove(22);
```

The `assign()` function removes all the elements from a list and copies either a single object into the list a given number of times, or copies a sequence of objects specified by two iterators. Here's an example:

```
int data[] = {10, 22, 4, 56, 89, 77, 13, 9};
list<int> numbers(data, data+8);

numbers.assign(10, 99);        // Replace contents by 10 copies of 99

// Remove all except the first and the last two
numbers.assign(data+1, data+4); // Replace contents by 22 4 56
```

The `assign()` function comes in the two overloaded versions illustrated here. The arguments to the first are the count of the number of replacement elements, and the replacement element value. The arguments to the second version are either two iterators or two pointers, specifying a sequence in the way you have already seen.

The unique() function will eliminate adjacent duplicate elements from a list, so if you sort the contents first, applying the function ensures that all elements are unique. Here's an example:

```
int data[] = {10, 22, 4, 10, 89, 22, 89, 10};
list<int> numbers(data, data+8);          // 10 22 4 10 89 22 89 10
numbers.sort();                           // 4 10 10 10 22 22 89 89
numbers.unique();                         // 4 10 22 89
```

The result of each operation is shown in the comments.

The splice() function allows you to remove all or part of one list and insert it in another. Obviously, both lists must store elements of the same type. Here's the simplest way you could use the splice() function:

```
int data[] = {1, 2, 3, 4, 5, 6, 7, 8};
list<int> numbers(data, data+3);                    // 1 2 3
list<int> values(data+4, data+8);                   // 5 6 7 8
numbers.splice(++numbers.begin(), values);          // 1 5 6 7 8 2 3
```

The first argument to the splice() function is an iterator specifying where the elements should be inserted, and the second argument is the list that is the source of the elements to be inserted. This operation removes all the elements from the values list and inserts them immediately preceding the second element in the numbers list.

Here's another version of the splice() function that removes elements from a given position in a source list and inserts them at a given position in the destination list:

```
int data[] = {1, 2, 3, 4, 5, 6, 7, 8};
list<int> numbers(data, data+3);                              // 1 2 3
list<int> values(data+4, data+8);                             // 5 6 7 8
numbers.splice(numbers.begin(), values, --values.end());     // 8 1 2 3
```

In this version, the first two arguments to the splice() function are the same as the previous version of the function. The third argument is an iterator specifying the position of the first element to be selected from the source list; all elements, from this position to the end, are removed from the source and inserted in the destination list. After executing this code fragment, values will contain 5 6 7.

The third version of splice() requires four arguments and selects a range of elements from the source list:

```
int data[] = {1, 2, 3, 4, 5, 6, 7, 8};
list<int> numbers(data, data+3);                    // 1 2 3
list<int> values(data+4, data+8);                   // 5 6 7 8
numbers.splice(++numbers.begin(), values, ++values.begin(), --values.end());

                                                    // 1 6 7 2 3
```

The first three arguments to the version of splice() are the same as the previous version, and the last argument is one past the last element to be removed from the source, values. After executing this, values will contain

5 8.

The merge() function removes elements from the list that you supply as an argument and inserts them in the list for which the function is called. The function then sorts the contents of the extended list into ascending order by default, or into some other order determined by a function object that you supply as a second argument to the merge() function. Both lists must be ordered appropriately before you call merge(); in other words, the lists must be ordered in the way that you want the final combined list to be ordered. Here's a fragment showing how you might use it:

```
int data[] = {1, 2, 3, 4, 5, 6, 7, 8};
list<int> numbers(data, data+3);           // 1 2 3
list<int> values(data+1, data+8);          // 2 3 4 5 6 7 8
numbers.merge(values);                      // 1 2 2 3 3 4 5 6 7 8
```

This merges the contents of values into numbers, so values will be empty after this operation. The merge() function that accepts a single argument orders the result in ascending sequence by default, and because the values in both lists are already ordered, you don't need to sort them. To merge the same lists in descending sequence, the code would be as follows:

```
numbers.sort(greater<int>());              // 3 2 1
values.sort(greater<int>());               // 8 7 6 5 4 3 2
numbers.merge(values, greater<int>());     // 8 7 6 5 4 3 3 2 2 1
```

Here you use the greater<int>() function object that is defined in the functional header to specify that the lists should be sorted in descending sequence and that they should be merged into the same sequence.

The remove_if() function removes elements from a list based on the result of applying a unary predicate; I'm sure you'll recall that a unary predicate is a function object that applies to a single argument and returns a bool value, true or false. If the result of applying the predicate to an element is true, then the element will be deleted from the list. Typically, you would define your own predicate to do this. This involves defining your own class template for the function object that you want, while the STL defines the unary_function<T, R> base template for use in this context. This template just defines types that will be inherited by the derived class that specifies your function object type. The base class template is defined as follows:

```
template<class _Arg, class _Result>
struct unary_function
{ // base class for unary functions
  typedef _Arg argument_type;
  typedef _Result result_type;
};
```

This defines argument_type and result_type as standardized types for use in your definition of the operator()() function. You must use this base template if you want to use your predicates with function adapters.

The way in which you can use the remove_if() function is best explained with a specific application, so let's try this in a working example.

TRY IT OUT   Defining a Predicate for Filtering a List

Here's how you could define a template for a function object based on the helper template from the STL, which you could then use to remove negative values from a list:

```
// function_object.h
// Unary predicate to identify negative values
#pragma once
#include <functional>

template <class T> class is_negative: public std::unary_function<T, bool>
{
  public:
  result_type operator()(argument_type& value)
  {
    return value < 0;
  }
};
```

This predicate works with any numeric type. The base template is very useful in that it standardizes the representation of the argument and return types for the predicate, and this is required if you want your function object to be usable with function adapters. Function adapters allow function objects to be used in combination to provide more complex functions. You should be able to see how you could define unary predicates for filtering a list in other ways — selecting even or odd numbers for example, or multiples of a given number, or numbers falling within a given range.

If you are not concerned about the use of your predicate with function adapters, you could define the template very easily without the base class template:

```
// function_object.h
// Unary predicate to identify negative values
#pragma once

template <class T> class is_negative
{
  public:
  bool operator()(T& value)
  {
    return value<0;
  }
};
```

You don't need the `#include` directive for `<functional>` here because you are not using the base template. This definition is simple, and perhaps easier to understand, but I included the original version just to show how you use the base template. You will want to do this if you intend to use your predicate in a more general context, in particular if you want to use it with function adapters. I'll create the example with the first version, but you can use either version, or perhaps try both.

To make the example more interesting, I'll include function templates both for inputting data to a list and for writing out the contents of a list. Here's the program to make use of your predicate:

```cpp
// Ex10_06.cpp
// Using the remove_if() function for a list

#include <iostream>
#include <list>
#include <functional>
#include "function_object.h"

using std::cin;
using std::cout;
using std::endl;
using std::list;
using std::greater;

// Template function to list the contents of a list
template <class T>
void listlist(list<T>& data)
{
  for(auto iter = data.begin() ; iter != data.end() ; iter++)
    cout << *iter << "   ";
  cout << endl;
}

// Template function to read data from cin and store it in a list
template<class T>
void loadlist(list<T>& data)
{
  T value = T();
  while(cin >> value , value != T())  //Read non-zero values
    data.push_back(value);
}

int main()
{
  // Process integers
  list<int> numbers;
  cout << "Enter non-zero integers separated by spaces. Enter 0 to end."
       << endl;
  loadlist(numbers);
  cout << "The list contains:" << endl;
  listlist(numbers);
  numbers.remove_if(is_negative<int>());
  cout << "After applying the remove_if() function the list contains:"
       << endl;
  listlist(numbers);

  // Process floating-point values
  list<double> values;
  cout << endl
       << "Enter non-zero values separated by spaces. Enter 0 to end."
       << endl;
  loadlist(values);
  cout << "The list contains:" << endl;
  listlist(values);
  values.remove_if(is_negative<double>());
  cout << "After applying the remove_if() function the list contains:" << endl;
```

```
        listlist(values);

        return 0;
    }
```

code snippet Ex10_06.cpp

Here's some sample output from this program:

```
Enter non-zero integers separated by spaces. Enter 0 to end.
23 -4 -5 66 67 89 -1 22 34 -34 78 62 -9 99 -19 0
The list contains:
23  -4  -5  66  67  89  -1  22  34  -34  78  62  -9  99  -19
After applying the remove_if() function the list contains:
23  66  67  89  22  34  78  62  99

Enter non-zero values separated by spaces. Enter 0 to end.
2.5 -3.1 5.5 100 -99 -.075 1.075 13 -12.1 13.2 0
The list contains:
2.5  -3.1  5.5  100  -99  -0.075  1.075  13  -12.1  13.2
After applying the remove_if() function the list contains:
2.5  5.5  100  1.075  13  13.2
```

How It Works

The output shows that the predicate works for values of type `int` and type `double`. The `remove_if()` function applies the predicate to each element in a list in turn, and deletes the elements for which the predicate returns `true`.

The body of the `loadlist<T>()` template function that reads the input is:

```
T value = T();
while(cin >> value , value != T())   //Read non-zero values
    data.push_back(value);
```

The local variable `value` is defined as type `T`, the type parameter for the template, so this will be of whatever type you use to instantiate the function. Because `value` is a template type, you initialize it using the no-arg constructor. The input is read in the `while` loop, and values continue to be read until you enter zero, in which case the last expression in the `while` loop condition will be `false`, thus ending the loop.

The body of the `listlist<T>()` function template is also very straightforward:

```
for(auto iter = data.begin() ; iter != data.end() ; iter++)
    cout << *iter << "  ";
cout << endl;
```

Note how you can use `auto`, even in a template. This deduces the type `list<T>::iterator` for the `for` loop control variable, which maps to the type required for the iterator for the list container that is passed as the argument. The output is produced by dereferencing the iterator in the way you have seen before.

If you wanted to try out the `merge()` function within this example, you could add the following code before the `return` statement in `main()`:

```
// Another list to use in merge
list<double> morevalues;
cout << endl
     << "Enter non-zero values separated by spaces. Enter 0 to end."
     << endl;
loadlist(morevalues);
cout << "The list contains:" << endl;
listlist(morevalues);
morevalues.remove_if(is_negative<double>());
cout << "After applying the remove_if() function the list contains:" << endl;
listlist(morevalues);

// Merge the last two lists
values.sort(greater<double>());
morevalues.sort(greater<double>());
values.merge(morevalues, greater<double>());
listlist(values);
```

Don't forget that you need an `#include` directive for `functional`, and a `using` directive for `std::greater`, for this to compile.

Using Other Sequence Containers

The remaining sequence containers are implemented through container adapters that I introduced at the beginning of this chapter. I'll discuss each of them briefly and illustrate their operation with an examples.

Queue Containers

A `queue<T>` container implements a first-in first-out storage mechanism through an adapter. You can only add to the end of the queue or remove from the front. Here's one way you can create a queue:

```
queue<string> names;
```

This creates a queue that can store elements of type `string`. By default, the `queue<T>` adapter class uses a `deque<T>` container as the base, but you can specify a different sequence container as a base, as long as it supports the operations `front()`, `back()`, `push_back()`, and `pop_front()`. These four functions are used to operate the queue. Thus, a queue can be based on a list or a vector container. You specify the alternate container as a second template parameter. Here's how you would create a queue based on a list:

```
queue< string, list<string> > names;
```

The second type parameter to the adapter template specifies the underlying sequence container that is to be used. The queue adapter class acts as a wrapper for the underlying container class and essentially restricts the range of operations you can carry out to those described in the following table.

FUNCTION	DESCRIPTION
`back()`	Returns a reference to the element at the back of the queue. There are two versions of the function, one returning a `const` reference and the other returning a non-`const` reference. If the queue is empty, then the value returned is undefined.
`front()`	Returns a reference to the element at the front of the queue. There are two versions of the function, one returning a `const` reference and the other returning a non-`const` reference. If the queue is empty, then the value returned is undefined.
`push()`	Adds the element specified by the argument to the back of the queue.
`pop()`	Removes the element at the front of the queue.
`size()`	Returns the number of elements in the queue.
`empty()`	Returns `true` if the queue is empty and `false` otherwise.

Note that there are no functions in the table that make iterators available for a queue container. The only way to access the contents of a queue is via the `back()` or `front()` functions.

TRY IT OUT   Using a Queue Container

In this example you read a succession of one or more sayings, store them in a queue, and then retrieve the sayings and output them.

Available for
download on
Wrox.com

```
// Ex10_07.cpp
// Exercising a queue container

#include <iostream>
#include <queue>
#include <string>

using std::cin;
using std::cout;
using std::endl;
using std::queue;
using std::string;

int main()
{
  queue<string> sayings;
  string saying;
  cout << "Enter one or more sayings. Press Enter to end." << endl;
  while(true)
  {
```

```
      getline(cin, saying);
      if(saying.empty())
        break;
      sayings.push(saying);
  }

  cout << "There are " << sayings.size()
       << " sayings in the queue."
       << endl << endl;
  cout << "The sayings that you entered are:" << endl;
  while(!sayings.empty())
  {
    cout << sayings.front() << endl;
    sayings.pop();
  }

  return 0;
}
```

code snippet Ex10_07.cpp

Here's an example of some output from this program:

```
Enter one or more sayings. Press Enter to end.
If at first you don't succeed, give up.
A preposition is something you should never end a sentence with.
The bigger they are, the harder they hit.
A rich man is just a poor man with money.
Wherever you go, there you are.
Common sense is not so common.

There are 6 sayings in the queue.

The sayings that you entered are:
If at first you don't succeed, give up.
A preposition is something you should never end a sentence with.
The bigger they are, the harder they hit.
A rich man is just a poor man with money.
Wherever you go, there you are.
Common sense is not so common.
```

How It Works

You first create a queue container that stores string objects:

```
queue<string> sayings;
```

You read sayings from the standard input stream and store them in the queue container in a `while` loop:

```
while(true)
{
  getline(cin, saying);
  if(saying.empty())
    break;
```

```
        sayings.push(saying);
    }
```

This version of the `getline()` function reads text from `cin` into the `string` object, `saying`, until a newline character is recognized. Newline is the default input termination character, and when you want to override this, you specify the termination character as the third argument to `getline()`. The loop continues until the `empty()` function for `saying` in the `if` statement returns `true`, which indicates an empty line was entered. When the input in `saying` is not empty, you store it in the `sayings` queue container by calling its `push()` function.

When input is complete, you output the count of the number of sayings that were stored in the queue:

```
    cout << "There are " << sayings.size()
         << " sayings in the queue."
         << endl << endl;
```

The `size()` function returns the number of elements in the queue.

You list the contents of the queue in another `while` loop:

```
    while(!sayings.empty())
    {
      cout << sayings.front() << endl;
      sayings.pop();
    }
```

The `front()` function returns a reference to the object at the front of the queue, but the object remains in its place. Because you want to access each of the elements in the queue in turn, you have to call the `pop()` function, after listing each element, to remove it from the queue.

The process of listing the elements in the queue also deletes them, so after the loop ends, the queue will be empty. What if you wanted to retain the elements in the queue? Well, one possibility is that you could put each saying back in the queue after you have listed it. Here's how you could do that:

```
    for(queue<string>::size_type i = 0 ; i < sayings.size() ; i++)
    {
      saying = sayings.front();
      cout << saying << endl;
      sayings.pop();
      sayings.push(saying);
    }
```

Here you make use of the value returned by `size()` to iterate over the number of sayings in the queue. After writing each saying to `cout`, you remove it from the queue by calling `pop()`, and then you return it to the back of the queue by calling `push()`. When the loop ends, the queue will be left in its original state. Of course, if you don't want to remove the elements when you access them, you could always use a different kind of container.

Priority Queue Containers

A `priority_queue<T>` container is a queue that always has the largest or highest priority element at the top. Here's one way to define a priority queue container:

```
priority_queue<int> numbers;
```

The default criterion for determining the relative priority of elements as you add them to the queue is the standard `less<T>` function object template. You add an element to the priority queue using the `push()` function:

```
numbers.push(99);                        // Add 99 to the queue
```

When you add an element to the queue, if the queue is not empty the function will use the `less<T>()` predicate to decide where to insert the new object. This will result in elements being ordered in ascending sequence from the back of the queue to the front. You cannot modify elements while they are in a priority queue, as this could invalidate the ordering that has been established.

The complete set of operations for a priority queue is shown in the following table.

FUNCTION	DESCRIPTION
`top()`	Returns a `const` reference to the element at the front of the priority queue, which will be the largest or highest priority element in the container. If the priority queue is empty, then the value returned is undefined.
`push()`	Adds the element specified by the argument to the priority queue at a position determined by the predicate for the container, which by default is `less<T>`.
`pop()`	Removes the element at the front of the priority queue, which will be the largest or highest priority element in the container.
`size()`	Returns the number of elements in the priority queue.
`empty()`	Returns `true` if the priority queue is empty and `false` otherwise.

Note that there is a significant difference between the functions available for the priority queue and for the queue container. With a priority queue, you have no access to the element at the back of the queue; only the element at the front is accessible.

By default, the base container used by the priority queue adapter class is `vector<T>`. You have the option of specifying a different sequence container as the base, and an alternative function object for determining the priority of the elements. Here's how you could do that:

```
priority_queue<int, deque<int>, greater<int>> numbers;
```

This statement defines a priority queue based on a deque<int> container, with elements being inserted using a function object of type greater<int>. The elements in this priority queue will be in descending sequence, with the smallest element at the top. The three template parameters are the element type, the container to be used as a base, and the type for the predicate to be used for ordering the elements.

You could omit the third template parameter if you want the default predicate to apply, which will be less<int> in this case. If you want a different predicate but want to retain the default base container, you must explicitly specify it, like this:

```
priority_queue<int, vector<int>, greater<int>> numbers;
```

This specifies the default base container vector<int> and a new predicate type, greater<int>, to be used to determine the ordering of elements.

TRY IT OUT   Using a Priority Queue Container

In this example you store Person objects in the container, with the Person class defined this time to hold the names as type string:

```cpp
// Person.h
// A class defining a person
#pragma once
#include <iostream>
#include <string>
using std::cout;
using std::endl;
using std::string;

class Person
{
public:
  Person(const string first, const string second)
  {
    firstname = first;
    secondname = second;
  }

  // No-arg constructor
  Person(){}

  // Copy constructor
  Person(const Person& p)
  {
    firstname = p.firstname;
    secondname = p.secondname;
  }

  // Less-than operator
  bool operator<(const Person& p)const
  {
    if(secondname < p.secondname ||
```

```
                ((secondname == p.secondname) && (firstname < p.firstname)))
            return true;

        return false;
    }

    // Greater-than operator
    bool operator>(const Person& p)const
    {
        return p < *this;
    }

    // Output a person
    void showPerson() const
    {
        cout << firstname << " " << secondname << endl;
    }

private:
    string firstname;
    string secondname;
};
```

Note that the > operator is overloaded here. This will make it possible to put objects in a priority queue that is ordered in either ascending or descending sequence.

Here's the program that stores `Person` objects in a priority queue:

```
// Ex10_08.cpp
// Exercising a priority queue container

#include <iostream>
#include <vector>
#include <queue>
#include <functional>
#include "Person.h"

using std::cin;
using std::cout;
using std::endl;
using std::vector;
using std::priority_queue;
using std::greater;

int main()
{
    priority_queue<Person, vector<Person>, greater<Person>> people;
    string first, second;
    while(true)
    {
        cout << "Enter a first name or press Enter to end: " ;
        getline(cin, first);
        if(first.empty())
```

```
          break;

        cout << "Enter a second name: " ;
        getline(cin, second);
        people.push(Person(first, second));
    }

    cout << endl << "There are " << people.size()
         << " people in the queue."
         << endl << endl;

    cout << "The names that you entered are:" << endl;
    while(!people.empty())
    {
        people.top().showPerson();
        people.pop();
    }

    return 0;
}
```

code snippet Ex10_08.cpp

Typical output from this example looks like this:

```
Enter a first name or press Enter to end: Oliver
Enter a second name: Hardy
Enter a first name or press Enter to end: Stan
Enter a second name: Laurel
Enter a first name or press Enter to end: Harold
Enter a second name: Lloyd
Enter a first name or press Enter to end: Mel
Enter a second name: Gibson
Enter a first name or press Enter to end: Brad
Enter a second name: Pitt
Enter a first name or press Enter to end:

There are 5 people in the queue.

The names that you entered are:
Mel Gibson
Oliver Hardy
Stan Laurel
Harold Lloyd
Brad Pitt
```

How It Works

The Person class is simpler than in the earlier version because the names are stored as string objects, and no dynamic memory allocation is necessary. You no longer need to define the assignment operator, as the default will be fine. Defining the < operator function is sufficient to allow Person objects to be stored in a default priority queue, and the overloaded > operator will permit Person objects to be ordered using the greater<Person> predicate type.

You define the priority queue in `main()` like this:

```
priority_queue< Person, vector<Person>, greater<Person>> people;
```

Because you want to specify the third template type parameter, you must supply all three, even though the base container type is the default. Incidentally, don't confuse the *type argument* you are using in the template instantiation here, `greater<Person>`, with the *object*, `greater<Person>()`, that you might supply as an argument to the `sort()` algorithm.

Of course, the third parameter to the priority queue template that defines the predicate for ordering the objects does not have to be a template type. You could use your own function object type as long as it has a suitable implementation of `operator()()` in the class:

```
// function_object.h
#pragma once
#include <functional>
#include "Person.h"
using std::binary_function;

class PersonComp: binary_function<Person, Person, bool>
{
public:
  result_type operator()(const first_argument_type& p1,
                          const second_argument_type& p2) const
  {
    return p1 > p2;
  }
};
```

For function objects that work with the STL, a binary predicate must implement `operator()()` with two parameters, and if you want the predicate to work with function adapters, your function object type must have an instance of the `binary_function<Arg1Type, Arg2Type, ResultType>` template as a base. Although you will typically make both arguments to a binary predicate of the same type, the base class does not require it, so when it is meaningful, your predicates can apply to arguments of different types.

If you don't want to use your function objects with function adapters, you could define the type as:

```
// function_object.h
#pragma once
#include "Person.h"

class PersonComp
{
public:
  bool operator()(const Person& p1, const Person& p2) const
  {
    return p1 > p2;
  }
};
```

With this function object type, you could define the priority queue object as:

```
priority_queue< Person, vector<Person>, PersonComp> people;
```

You read names from the standard input stream in an indefinite `while` loop:

```
while(true)
{
  cout << "Enter a first name or press Enter to end: " ;
  getline(cin, first);
  if(first.empty())
    break;

  cout << "Enter a second name: " ;
  getline(cin, second);
  people.push(Person(first, second));
}
```

An empty first name will terminate the loop. After reading a second name, you create the `Person` object in the argument expression to the `push()` function that adds the object to the priority queue. It will be inserted at a position determined by a `greater<Person>()` predicate. This will result in the objects being ordered in the priority queue with the smallest at the top. You can see from the output that the names are in ascending sequence.

After outputting the number of objects in the queue using the `size()` function, you output the contents of the queue in a `while` loop:

```
while(!people.empty())
{
  people.top().showPerson();
  people.pop();
}
```

The `top()` function returns a reference to the object at the front of the queue, and you use this reference to call the `showPerson()` function to output the name. You then call `pop()` to remove the element at the front of the queue; unless you do this, you can't access the next element.

When the loop ends, the priority queue will be empty. There's no way to access all the elements and retain them in the queue. If you want to keep them, you would have to put them somewhere else — perhaps in another priority queue.

Stack Containers

The `stack<T>` container adapter template is defined in the `stack` header and implements a pushdown stack based on a `deque<T>` container by default. A pushdown stack is a last-in first-out storage mechanism where only the object that was added most recently to the stack is accessible.

Here's how you can define a stack:

```
stack<Person> people;
```

This defines a stack to store `Person` objects.

The base container can be any sequence container that supports the operations `back()`, `push_back()`, and `pop_back()`. You could define a stack base on a list like this:

```
stack<string, list<string>> names;
```

The first template type argument is the element type, as before, and the second is the container type to be used as a base for the stack.

There are only five operations available with a `stack<T>` container, and they are shown in the following table.

FUNCTION	DESCRIPTION
`top()`	Returns a reference to the element at the top of the stack. If the stack is empty, then the value returned is undefined. You can assign the reference returned to a `const` or non-`const` reference and if it is assigned to the latter, you can modify the object in the stack.
`push()`	Adds the element specified by the argument to the top of the stack.
`pop()`	Removes the element at the top of the stack.
`size()`	Returns the number of elements in the stack.
`empty()`	Returns `true` if the stack is empty and `false` otherwise.

As with the other containers provided through container adapters, you cannot use iterators to access the contents of a stack.

Let's see a stack working in another example.

TRY IT OUT   Using a Stack Container

This example stores `Person` objects in a stack. The `Person` class is the same as in the previous example, so I won't repeat the code here.

```
// Ex10_09.cpp
// Exercising a stack container

#include <iostream>
#include <stack>
#include <list>
#include "Person.h"

using std::cin;
using std::cout;
using std::endl;
using std::stack;
using std::list;

int main()
```

```
{
  stack<Person, list<Person>> people;

  string first, second;
  while(true)
  {
    cout << "Enter a first name or press Enter to end: " ;
    getline(cin, first);
    if(first.empty())
      break;

    cout << "Enter a second name: " ;
    getline(cin, second);
    people.push(Person(first, second));
  }

  cout << endl << "There are " << people.size()
       << " people in the stack."
       << endl << endl;
  cout << "The names that you entered are:" << endl;
  while(!people.empty())
  {
    people.top().showPerson();
    people.pop();
  }

  return 0;
}
```

code snippet Ex10_09.cpp

Here is an example of the output:

```
Enter a first name or press Enter to end: Gordon
Enter a second name: Brown
Enter a first name or press Enter to end: Harold
Enter a second name: Wilson
Enter a first name or press Enter to end: Margaret
Enter a second name: Thatcher
Enter a first name or press Enter to end: Winston
Enter a second name: Churchill
Enter a first name or press Enter to end: David
Enter a second name: Lloyd-George
Enter a first name or press Enter to end:

There are 5 people in the stack.

The names that you entered are:
David Lloyd-George
Winston Churchill
Margaret Thatcher
Harold Wilson
Gordon Brown
```

How It Works

The code in `main()` is more or less the same as in the previous example. Only the container definition is significantly different:

```
stack<Person, list<Person>> people;
```

The stack container stores `Person` objects and is based on a `list<T>` container in this instance. You could also use a `vector<T>` container, and if you omit the second type parameter, the stack will use a `deque<T>` container as a base.

The output demonstrates that a stack is indeed a last-in first-out container, as the order of names in the output is the reverse of the input.

The array Container

The `array<T, N>` container that is defined in the `array` header stores an array of N elements of type `T`. The array<> container is very easy to use, and you can initialize it in the same way as an ordinary C++ array. For example:

```
std::array<int, 10> samples = { 1, 2, 3, 4, 5};
```

The `samples` container stores 10 elements of type `int`. The first five are initialized by the values in the initializer list; the elements without initial values will be zero. If the elements were of a class type, any elements that were not already initialized would be initialized using the no-arg constructor for the element type.

Like the `vector<>` and `list<>` containers, you can work through all the elements in an `array<>` using an iterator:

```
for(auto iter = samples.begin() ; iter != samples.end() ; ++iter)
  cout << *iter << "  ";
```

Because it also behaves like an ordinary array, you can also use an index value to access the elements in an `array<>` container:

```
for(size_t i = 0 ; i < samples.size() ; ++i)
  cout << samples[i] << "  ";
```

Elements are indexed from zero, just like an ordinary array. The `size()` member returns the number of elements in the container, and you just use this in the `for` loop to control indexing over all the elements.

A further possibility for accessing elements in an array is to use the `at()` function. The argument is the index position of the element you want to access, and the operation will throw an exception of type `out_of_range` if the argument is not a valid index. You could therefore write the previous loop as:

```
for(size_t i = 0 ; i < samples.size() ; ++i)
  cout << samples.at(i) << "  ";
```

Of course, if you want to deal with an index out-of-range condition you must put the statement in a try block and catch the exception.

There are overloaded operators for the full complement of comparison operators for array<> objects so you can use the operators <, <=, ==, !=, >= and > to compare array<> containers. Array containers are compared element by element, and the first pair of elements that differ determines that the arrays are unequal and whether one array<> object is greater or less than the other. Two array<> objects are equal if they have the same number of elements and corresponding elements are equal.

The tuple<> class template that is defined in the tuple header is a useful adjunct to the array<> container, and to other sequence containers such as the vector<>. As its name suggests, a tuple<> object encapsulates a number of different items of different types. If you were working with fixed records from a file, or possibly from an SQL database, you could use a vector<> or an array<> container to store tuple<> objects that encapsulate the fields in a record. Let's look at a specific example.

Suppose you are working with personnel records that contain an integer employee number, a first name, a second name, and the age of the individual in years. You could define a tuple<> instance to encapsulate an employee record like this:

```
typedef std::tuple<int, std::string, std::string, int> Record;
```

A typedef is very useful for reducing the verbosity of the type specification in this case. This typedef defines the Record type as being a tuple<> that stores values of type int, string, string, and int, corresponding to a person's ID, first name, second name, and age. You could now define an array<> container to store Record objects:

```
std::array<Record, 5> personnel = { Record(1001, "Joan", "Jetson", 35),
                                     Record(1002, "Jim" , "Jones" , 26),
                                     Record(1003, "June", "Jello" , 31),
                                     Record(1004, "Jack", "Jester", 39)};
```

This defines the personnel object, which is an array that can store five Record objects. If you wanted flexibility in the number of tuples you were dealing with, you could use a vector<> or a list<> container. Here you initialize four of the five elements in personnel from the initializer list. You could add elements explicitly though. Here's how you might add a fifth element:

```
personnel[4] = Record(1005, "Jean", "Jorell", 29);
```

This uses the index operator to access the fifth element in the array. You also have the option of creating a tuple<> object using the make_tuple() function template:

```
personnel[4] = std::make_tuple(1005, "Jean", "Jorell", 29);
```

The make_tuple() function creates a tuple<> instance that is equivalent to our Record type because the deduced type parameters are the same.

To access the fields in a tuple, you use the get() function template. The template parameter is the index position of the field you want, where fields in a tuple are indexed from zero. The argument to the `get()` function is the tuple that you are accessing. For example, here's how you could list the records in our `personnel` container:

```
cout << std::setiosflags(std::ios::left);      // Left align output
for(auto iter = personnel.begin() ; iter != personnel.end() ; ++iter)
   cout << std::setw(10) << get<0>(*iter) << std::setw(10) << get<1>(*iter)
        << std::setw(10) << get<2>(*iter) << std::setw(10) << get<3>(*iter)
        << endl;
```

This outputs the fields in each tuple in `personnel` on a single line, where the fields are left-justified in a field width of 10 characters, so it looks tidy. Note that the type parameter to the `get()` function template must be a compile-time constant. This implies that you cannot use a loop index variable as the type parameter, so you can't iterate over the fields in a loop. It is helpful to define some integer constants that you can use to identify the fields in a tuple in a more readable way. For example, you could define the following constants:

```
const size_t ID(0), firstname(1), secondname(2), age(3);
```

Now you can use these variables as type parameters in `get()` function instantiations making it much clearer which field you are retrieving.

Let's put some of the fragments together into something you can compile and run.

TRY IT OUT   Storing tuples in an array

Here's the code for the example:

```
// Ex10_10.cpp Using an array storing tuple objects
#include <array>
#include <tuple>
#include <string>
#include <iostream>
#include <iomanip>

using std::get;
using std::cout;
using std::endl;
using std::setw;
using std::string;

const size_t maxRecords(100);
typedef std::tuple<int, string, string, int> Record;
typedef std::array<Record, maxRecords> Records;

// Lists the contents of a Records array
void listRecords(const Records& people)
{
  const size_t ID(0), firstname(1), secondname(2), age(3);
  cout << std::setiosflags(std::ios::left);
  for(auto iter = people.begin() ; iter != people.end() ; ++iter)
  {
    if(*iter == Record()) break;
```

```
                cout << setw(6)   << get<ID>(*iter)           << setw(15) << get<firstname>(*iter)
                     << setw(15) << get<secondname>(*iter) << setw(5)   << get<age>(*iter)
                     << endl;
            }
        }

        int main()
        {
          Records personnel = {Record(1001,  "Clarke",  "Kent",  89),
                               Record(1002,  "Mary",  "Pickford",  55),
                               Record(1003,  "Mel",  "Smith",  34),
                               Record(1004,  "June",  "Whitfield",  74)};
          personnel[4] = std::make_tuple(1005, "Charles", "Chapin", 42);
          personnel.at(5) = Record(1006, "Lewis", "Hamilton", 22);

          listRecords(personnel);
          return 0;
        }
```

code snippet Ex10_10.cpp

This program produces the following output:

```
1001   Clarke        Kent            89
1002   Mary          Pickford        55
1003   Mel           Smith           34
1004   June          Whitfield       74
1005   Charles       Chapin          42
1006   Lewis         Hamilton        22
```

How It Works

To make the code easier to read, there are two typedef statements:

```
typedef std::tuple<int, string, string, int> Record;
typedef std::array<Record, maxRecords> Records;
```

The first typedef statement defines Record as equivalent to the tuple<> type that stores four fields of type int, string, string, and int. The second typedef defines Records as an array<> type, storing maxRecords elements of type Record. maxRecords is defined as a const value of type size_t. typedef statements are a great help in simplifying code that uses the STL.

The listRecords() function outputs the elements in a Records array:

```
void listRecords(const Records& people)
{
  const size_t ID(0), firstname(1), secondname(2), age(3);
  cout << std::setiosflags(std::ios::left);
  for(auto iter = people.begin() ; iter != people.end() ; ++iter)
  {
    if(*iter == Record()) break;
    cout << setw(6)   << get<ID>(*iter)           << setw(15) << get<firstname>(*iter)
         << setw(15) << get<secondname>(*iter) << setw(5)   << get<age>(*iter)
         << endl;
  }
}
```

The first statement in the function body defines constants for accessing the fields in a `Record` tuple. This enables meaningful names to be used, rather than numeric index values whose meaning would not be obvious. The next statement ensures that subsequent output to the standard output stream will be left-aligned. The `for` loop uses an iterator to run through the elements in the `Records` array that has been passed to the function. Elements that were not explicitly initialized will have been initialized using the no-arg constructor for the element type, `Record`. You don't want to see elements that are the equivalent of zero, so the `if` statement ends the loop when such an element is found. Fields in the tuple that each array element contains are accessed with the `get<>()` function using the constants that were defined for that purpose. The `setw()` manipulators set the width of the output field for the next item that is written to `cout`.

In `main()` you create the `personnel` array as type `Records` and initialize the first four elements with `Record` objects:

```
Records personnel = {Record(1001, "Clarke", "Kent", 89),
                     Record(1002, "Mary", "Pickford", 55),
                     Record(1003, "Mel", "Smith", 34),
                     Record(1004, "June", "Whitfield", 74)};
```

This is clearly a much more readable statement because of the `typedef` statements for `Records` and `Record`.

The next statement adds another `Record` to the array:

```
personnel[4] = std::make_tuple(1005, "Charles", "Chapin", 42);
```

This uses the `operator[]()` function overload for the `personnel` array to access the element, and uses the `make_tuple()` function to create a tuple that is similar to the tuple of type `Record` to be stored in the array.

Curiously, the next statement uses a different technique to set the value for an array element:

```
personnel.at(5) = Record(1006, "Lewis", "Hamilton", 22);
```

This uses the `at()` function for the array, and the argument value of 5 selects the sixth element in the array. Here, the tuple is created using the `Record` type name.

Finally, in `main()`, you call the `listRecords()` function to list the contents of `personnel`. The output shows that everything works as it should.

ASSOCIATIVE CONTAINERS

The most significant feature of the associative containers such as `map<K, T>` is that you can retrieve a particular object without searching. The location of an object of type `T` within an associative container is determined from a key of type `K` that you supply along with the object, so you can retrieve any object rapidly just by supplying the appropriate key. The key is actually a sort key that determines the order of the entries in the map.

For `set<T>` and `multiset<T>` containers, objects act as their own keys. You might be wondering what the use of a container is if, before you can retrieve an object, you have to have the object available. After all, if you already have the object, why would you need to retrieve it? The point of set and multiset containers is not so much to store objects for later retrieval, but to create an aggregation of objects that you can test to see whether or not a given object is already a member.

In this section, I'll concentrate on map containers. The set and multiset containers are used somewhat less frequently, and their operations are very similar to the map and multimap containers, so you should have little difficulty using these once you have learned how to apply the map containers.

Using Map Containers

The template for map containers is defined in the `map` header. When you create a `map<K, T>` container, you must supply type arguments for the type of key you will use, `K`, and the type of the object associated with a key, `T`. Here's an example:

```
map<Person, string> phonebook;
```

This defines an empty map container that stores entries that are key/object pairs, where the keys are of type `Person` and the objects are of type `string`.

> **NOTE** *Although you use class objects here for both keys and objects to be stored in the map, the keys and associated objects in a map can also be of any fundamental type, such as* int, *or* double *or* char.

You can also create a map container that is initialized with a sequence of key/object pairs from another map container:

```
map<Person, string> phonebook(iter1, iter2);
```

`iter1` and `iter2` are a pair of iterators defining a series of key/object pairs from another container in the usual way, with `iter2` specifying a position one past the last pair to be included in the sequence. You obtain iterators to access the contents of a map by calling the `begin()` and `end()` functions, just as you would for a sequence container. The iterators for a map are bidirectional iterators.

The entries in a map are ordered based on a function object of type `less<Key>` by default, so they will be stored in ascending key sequence. You can change the type function object used for ordering entries in a map by supplying a third template type parameter. For example:

```
map<Person, string, greater<Person>> phonebook;
```

This map stores entries that are `Person`/`string` pairs, where `Person` is the key with an associated string object. The ordering of entries will be determined by a function object of type `greater<Person>`, so the entries will be in descending key sequence.

Storing Objects

The objects that you store in a map are always a key/object pair that are of a template type pair<K, T>, where K is the type of key and T is the type of object associated with the key. The pair<K, T> type is defined in the utility header, which is included in the map header, so if you are using a map the type is automatically available. You can define a pair object like this:

```
auto entry = pair<Person, string>(Person("Mel", "Gibson"), "213 345 5678");
```

This creates the variable entry of type pair<Person,string> and initializes it to an object created from a Person object and a string object. I'm representing a phone number in a very simplistic way, just as a string, but of course it could be a more complicated class identifying the components of the number, such as country code and area code. The Person class is the class you used in the previous example.

An instance of the pair<K, T> class template defines two constructors, and the one you are using in the previous fragment defines an object from a key and its associated object. The other constructor is a copy constructor that allows you to construct a new pair from an existing one. You can access the elements in a pair through the members first and second; thus, in the example, entry.first references the Person object and entry.second references the string object.

You can also use a helper function, make_pair(), that is defined in the utility header to create a pair object:

```
auto entry = make_pair(Person("Mel", "Gibson"), "213 345 5678");
```

The make_pair() function is defined as a template, so it automatically deduces the type for the pair, from the argument types you supply.

All of the comparison operators are overloaded for pair objects, so you can compare them with any of the operators <, <=, ==, !=, >=, and >.

It's sometimes convenient to use a typedef statement to abbreviate the pair<K, T> type you are using in a particular instance. For example:

```
map<Person, string> phonebook;
typedef pair<Person, string> Entry;
```

The first statement defines a map container that will store string objects using Person objects as keys. The second statement defines Entry as the type for the key/object pair. Having defined the Entry type, you can create objects of this type. For example:

```
Entry entry1 = Entry(Person("Jack", "Jones"), "213 567 1234");
```

This statement defines a pair of type pair<Person, string>, using Person("Jack", "Jones") as the Person argument and "213 567 1234" as the string argument.

You can insert one or more pairs in a map using the insert() function. For example, here's how you insert a single object:

```
phonebook.insert(entry1);
```

This statement inserts the `entry1` pair into the phonebook container, as long as there is no other entry in the map that uses the same key. In fact, this version of the `insert()` function returns a value that is also a pair, where the first object in the pair is an iterator and the second is a value of type `bool`. The `bool` value in the pair will be `true` if the insertion was made, and `false` otherwise. The iterator value in the pair will point to the element if it was stored in the map, or the element that is already in the map if the insert failed. Therefore, you can check if the object was stored, like this:

```
auto checkpair = phonebook.insert(entry1);
if(checkpair.second)
  cout << "Insertion succeeded." << endl;
else
  cout << "Insertion failed." << endl;
```

The pair that the `insert()` function returns is stored in `checkpair`. The type for `checkpair` is `pair<map<Person,string>::iterator, bool>`, which corresponds to a pair encapsulating an iterator for our map of type `map<Person,string>::iterator`, which you could access as `checkpair.first`; and a value of type `bool`, which you access in the code as `checkpair.second`.

Dereferencing the iterator in the pair returned by the `insert()` function will give you access to the pair that is stored in the map; you can use the `first` and `second` members of that pair to access the key and object, respectively. This can be a little tricky, so let's see what it looks like for `checkpair` in the code above:

```
cout << "The key for the entry is:" << endl;
checkpair.first->first.showPerson();
```

The expression `checkpair.first` references the first member of the `checkpair` pair, which is an iterator, so you are accessing a pointer to the object in the map with this expression. The object in the map is another pair, so the expression `checkpair.first->first` accesses the first member of that pair, which is the `Person` object. You use this to call the `showPerson()` member to output the name. You could access the object in the pair in a similar way, with the expression `checkpair.first->second`.

You have another version of the `insert()` function for inserting a series of pairs in a map. The pairs are defined by two iterator arguments, and the series would typically be from another map container.

The `map<K,T>` template defines the `operator[]()` function, so you can also use the subscript operator to insert an object. Here's how you could insert the `entry1` object in the phonebook map:

```
phonebook[Person("Jack", "Jones")] = "213 567 1234";
```

The subscript value is the key to be used to store the object that appears to the right of the assignment operator. This is perhaps a somewhat more intuitive way to store objects in a map. The only disadvantage, compared to the `insert()` function, is that you lose the ability to discover whether the key was already in the map.

Accessing Objects

You can use the subscript operator to retrieve the object from a map that corresponds to a given key. For example:

```
string number = phonebook[Person("Jack", "Jones")];
```

This stores the object corresponding to the key

```
Person("Jack", "Jones")
```

in number. If the key is not in the map, then a pair entry will be inserted into the map for this key, with the object as the default for the object type; here, the no-arg Person class constructor will be called to create the object for this key if the entry is not there.

Of course, you may not want a default object inserted when you attempt to retrieve an object corresponding to a given key. In this case, you could use the find() function to check whether there's an entry for a given key, and then retrieve it:

```
string number;
Person key = Person("Jack", "Jones");
auto iter = phonebook.find(key);

if(iter != phonebook.end())
{
  number = iter->second;
  cout << "The number is " << number << endl;
}
else
{
  cout << "No number for the key ";
  key.showPerson();
}
```

The find() function returns an iterator of type map<Person,string>::iterator that points to the object corresponding to the key if the key is present in the map, or to one past the last entry in the map, which corresponds to the iterator returned by the end() function. Thus, if iter is not equal to the iterator returned by end(), the entry is present, and you can access the object through the second member of the pair. If you want to prevent the object in the map from being modified, you could define the iterator type explicitly as map<Person,string>::const_iterator.

Calling the count() function for a map with a key as the argument will return a count of the number of entries found corresponding to the key. For a map, the value returned can only be 0 or 1, because each key in a map must be unique. A multimap container allows multiple entries for a given key, so in this case other values are possible for the return value from count().

Other Map Operations

The erase() function enables you to remove a single entry, or a range of entries, from a map. You have two versions of erase() that will remove a single entry. One version requires an iterator as the argument pointing to the entry to be erased, and the other requires a key corresponding to the entry to be erased. For example:

```
Person key = Person("Jack", "Jones");
auto count = phonebook.erase(key);
if(count == 0)
  cout << "Entry was not found." << endl;
```

When you supply a key to the `erase()` function, it returns a count of the number of entries that were erased. With a map container, the value returned can only be `0` or `1`. A multimap container can have several entries with the same key, in which case the `erase()` function may return a value greater than 1.

You can also supply an iterator as an argument to `erase()`:

```
Person key = Person("Jack", "Jones");
auto iter = phonebook.find(key);
iter = phonebook.erase(iter);
if(iter == phonebook.end())
  cout << "End of the map reached." << endl;
```

In this case, the `erase()` function returns an iterator that points to the entry that remains in the map beyond the entry that was erased, or a pointer to the ends of the map if no such element is present.

The following table shows the other operations available with a map container.

FUNCTION	DESCRIPTION
`begin()`	Returns a bidirectional iterator pointing to the first entry in the map.
`end()`	Returns a bidirectional iterator pointing to one past the last entry in the map.
`rbegin()`	Returns a reverse iterator pointing to the last entry in the map.
`rend()`	Returns a reverse iterator pointing to one before the first entry in the map.
`lower_bound()`	Accepts a key as an argument and returns an iterator pointing to the first entry with a key that is greater than or equal to (the lower bound of) the specified key. If the key is not present, the iterator pointing to one past the last entry will be returned.
`upper_bound()`	Accepts a key as an argument and returns an iterator pointing to the first entry with a key that is greater than (the upper bound of) the specified key. If the key is not present, the iterator pointing to one past the last entry will be returned.
`equal_range()`	Accepts a key as an argument and returns a pair object containing two iterators. The first member of the pair points to the lower bound of the specified key, and the second member points to the upper bound of the specified key. If the key is not present, both iterators in the pair will point to one past the last entry in the map.
`swap()`	Interchanges the entries in the map you pass as the argument, with the entries in the map for which the function is called.
`clear()`	Erases all entries in the map.
`size()`	Returns the number of elements in the map.
`empty()`	Returns `true` if the map is empty and `false` otherwise.

The `lower_bound()`, `upper_bound()`, and `equal_range()` functions are not very useful with a map container. However, they come into their own with a multimap container, when you want to find all the elements with the same key.

Let's see a map in action.

TRY IT OUT   Using a Map Container

In this example you use a map container to store phone numbers, and provide a mechanism for finding a phone number for a person. You use a variation on the `Person` class:

```cpp
// Person.h
// A class defining a person
#pragma once
#include <iostream>
#include <string>
#include <functional>
using std::cout;
using std::endl;
using std::string;

class Person
{
public:
  Person(const string first = "", const string second = "")
  {
    firstname = first;
    secondname = second;
  }

  // Less-than operator
  bool operator<(const Person& p)const
  {
    if(secondname < p.secondname ||
      ((secondname == p.secondname) && (firstname < p.firstname)))
      return true;

    return false;
  }

  // Get the name
  string getName()const
  {
    return firstname + " " + secondname;
  }

private:
  string firstname;
  string secondname;
};
```

There are only a few minor changes from the previous version of the `Person` class. The no-arg constructor is now defined by providing default values for the constructor arguments. I have omitted the > operator function, the copy constructor, the assignment operator, and the `showPerson()` function. There is a new function, `getName()` that returns the complete name as a `string` object.

The source file containing `main()` and some helper functions looks like this:

```cpp
// Ex10_11.cpp
// Using a map container

#include <iostream>
#include <cstdio>
#include <iomanip>
#include <string>
#include <map>
#include "Person.h"

using std::cin;
using std::cout;
using std::endl;
using std::setw;
using std::ios;
using std::string;
using std::pair;
using std::map;
using std::make_pair;

// Read a person from cin
Person getPerson()
{
  string first;
  string second;
  cout << "Enter a first name: " ;
  getline(cin, first);
  cout << "Enter a second name: " ;
  getline(cin, second);
  return Person(first, second);
}

// Add a new entry to a phone book
void addEntry(map<Person, string>& book)
{
  string number;
  Person person = getPerson();

  cout << "Enter the phone number for "
    << person.getName() << ": ";
  getline(cin, number);
  auto entry = make_pair(person, number);
  auto pr = book.insert(entry);

  if(pr.second)
    cout << "Entry successful." << endl;
  else
  {
    cout << "Entry exists for " << person.getName()
```

```
                << ". The number is " << pr.first->second << endl;
    }
}

// List the contents of a phone book
void listEntries(map<Person, string>& book)
{
  if(book.empty())
  {
    cout << "The phone book is empty." << endl;
    return;
  }
  cout << setiosflags(ios::left);              // Left justify output
  for(auto iter = book.begin() ; iter != book.end() ; iter++)
  {
    cout << setw(30) << iter->first.getName()
         << setw(12) << iter->second << endl;
  }
  cout << resetiosflags(ios::right);           // Right justify output
}

// Retrieve an entry from a phone book
void getEntry(map<Person, string>& book)
{
  Person person = getPerson();
  auto iter = book.find(person);
  if(iter == book.end())
    cout << "No entry found for " << person.getName() << endl;
  else
    cout << "The number for " << person.getName()
         << " is " << iter->second << endl;
}

// Delete an entry from a phone book
void deleteEntry(map<Person, string>& book)
{
  Person person = getPerson();
  auto iter = book.find(person);
  if(iter == book.end())
    cout << "No entry found for " << person.getName() << endl;
  else
  {
    book.erase(iter);
    cout << person.getName() << " erased." << endl;
  }
}

int main()
{
  map<Person, string> phonebook;
  char answer = 0;

  while(true)
  {
    cout << "Do you want to enter a phone book entry(Y or N): " ;
```

```
      cin >> answer;
      cin.ignore();                       // Ignore newline in buffer
      if(toupper(answer) == 'N')
        break;
      if(toupper(answer) != 'Y')
      {
        cout << "Invalid response. Try again." << endl;
        continue;
      }
      addEntry(phonebook);
    }

    // Query the phonebook
    while(true)
    {
      cout << endl << "Choose from the following options:" << endl
           << "A  Add an entry    D Delete an entry   G  Get an entry" << endl
           << "L  List entries    Q  Quit" << endl;
      cin >> answer;
      cin.ignore();                       // Ignore newline in buffer

      switch(toupper(answer))
      {
        case 'A':
          addEntry(phonebook);
          break;
        case 'G':
          getEntry(phonebook);
          break;
        case 'D':
          deleteEntry(phonebook);
          break;
        case 'L':
          listEntries(phonebook);
          break;
        case 'Q':
          return 0;
        default:
          cout << "Invalid selection. Try again." << endl;
          break;
      }
    }
    return 0;
}
```

code snippet Ex10_11.cpp

Here is some output from this program:

```
Do you want to enter a phone book entry(Y or N): y
Enter a first name: Jack
Enter a second name: Bateman
Enter the phone number for Jack Bateman: 312 455 6576
Entry successful.
Do you want to enter a phone book entry(Y or N): y
Enter a first name: Mary
```

```
Enter a second name: Jones
Enter the phone number for Mary Jones: 213 443 5671
Entry successful.
Do you want to enter a phone book entry(Y or N): y
Enter a first name: Jane
Enter a second name: Junket
Enter the phone number for Jane Junket: 413 222 8134
Entry successful.
Do you want to enter a phone book entry(Y or N): n

Choose from the following options:
A  Add an entry   D Delete an entry   G  Get an entry
L  List entries   Q  Quit
a
Enter a first name: Bill
Enter a second name: Smith
Enter the phone number for Bill Smith: 213 466 7688
Entry successful.

Choose from the following options:
A  Add an entry   D Delete an entry   G  Get an entry
L  List entries   Q  Quit
g
Enter a first name: Mary
Enter a second name: Miller
No entry found for Mary Miller

Choose from the following options:
A  Add an entry   D Delete an entry   G  Get an entry
L  List entries   Q  Quit
g
Enter a first name: Mary
Enter a second name: Jones
The number for Mary Jones is 213 443 5671

Choose from the following options:
A  Add an entry   D Delete an entry   G  Get an entry
L  List entries   Q  Quit
d
Enter a first name: Mary
Enter a second name: Jones
Mary Jones erased.

Choose from the following options:
A  Add an entry   D Delete an entry   G  Get an entry
L  List entries   Q  Quit
L
Jack Bateman            312 455 6576
Jane Junket            413 222 8134
Bill Smith             213 466 7688

Choose from the following options:
A  Add an entry   D Delete an entry   G  Get an entry
L  List entries   Q  Quit
q
```

How It Works

You define a map container in `main()` like this:

```
map<Person, string> phonebook;
```

The object in an entry in the map is a `string` containing a phone number, and the key is a `Person` object.

You load up the map initially in a `while` loop:

```
while(true)
{
  cout << "Do you want to enter a phone book entry(Y or N): " ;
  cin >> answer;
  cin.ignore();                         // Ignore newline in buffer
  if(toupper(answer) == 'N')
    break;
  if(toupper(answer) != 'Y')
  {
    cout << "Invalid response. Try again." << endl;
    continue;
  }
  addEntry(phonebook);
}
```

You check whether an entry is to be read by reading a character from the standard input stream. Reading a character from `cin` leaves a newline character in the buffer, and this can cause problems for subsequent input. Calling `ignore()` for `cin` ignores the next character so that subsequent input will work properly. If `'n'` or `'N'` is entered, the loop is terminated. When `'y'` or `'Y'` is entered, an entry is created by calling the helper function `addEntry()` that is coded like this:

```
void addEntry(map<Person, string>& book)
{
  string number;
  Person person = getPerson();

  cout << "Enter the phone number for "
    << person.getName() << ": ";
    getline(cin, number);
    auto entry = make_pair(person, number);
    auto pr = book.insert(entry);

    if(pr.second)
      cout << "Entry successful." << endl;
    else
    {
      cout << "Entry exists for " << person.getName()
           << ". The number is " << pr.first->second << endl;
    }
}
```

Note that the parameter for addEntry() is a reference. The function modifies the container that is passed as the argument, so the function must have access to the original object. In any event, even if only access to the container argument was needed, it is important not to allow potentially very large objects, such as a map container, to be passed by value, because this can seriously degrade performance.

The process for adding an entry is essentially as you have seen in the previous section. The getPerson() helper function reads a first name and a second name, and then returns a Person object that is created using the names. The getName() member of the Person class returns a name as a string object, so you use this in the prompt for a number. Calling the make_pair() function returns a pair<Person, string> object that you store in entry, and the auto keyword avoids the necessity of explicitly spelling out the type. You then call insert() for the container object, and store the object returned in pr. The pr object enables you to check that the entry was successfully inserted into the map, by testing its bool member. The pr variable is of type pair<map<Person,string>::iterator,bool>, but the auto keyword works that out for you from the initial value. The first member of pr provides access to the entry, whether it's an existing entry or the new entry, and you use this to output a message when insertion fails.

After initial input is complete, a while loop provides the mechanism for querying and modifying the phone book. The switch statement in the body of the loop decides the action to be taken, based on the character that is entered and stored in answer. Querying the phone book is managed by the getEntry() function:

```
void getEntry(map<Person, string>& book)
{
  Person person = getPerson();
  auto iter = book.find(person);
  if(iter == book.end())
    cout << "No entry found for " << person.getName() << endl;
  else
    cout << "The number for " << person.getName()
         << " is " << iter->second << endl;
}
```

A Person object is created from a name that is read from the standard input stream by calling the getPerson() function. The Person object is then used as the argument to the find() function for the map object. This returns an iterator of type map<Person,string>::const_iterator that either points to the required entry, or points to one past the last entry in the map. If an entry is found, accessing the second member of the pair pointed to by the iterator provides the number corresponding to the Person object key.

The deleteEntry() function deletes an entry from the map. The process is similar to that used in the getEntry() function, the difference being that when an entry is found by the find() function, the erase() function is called to remove it. You could use another version of erase() to do this, in which case the code would be like this:

```
void deleteEntry(map<Person, string>& book)
{
  Person person = getPerson();
  if(book.erase(person))
    cout << person.getName() << " erased." << endl;
```

```
      else
        cout << "No entry found for " << person.getName() << endl;
    }
```

The code turns out to be much simpler if you pass the key to the `erase()` function.

The `listEntries()` function lists the contents of a phone book:

```
    void listEntries(map<Person, string>& book)
    {
      if(book.empty())
      {
        cout << "The phone book is empty." << endl;
        return;
      }
      cout << setiosflags(ios::left);                  // Left justify output
      for(auto iter = book.begin() ; iter != book.end() ; iter++)
      {
        cout << setw(30) << iter->first.getName()
             << setw(12) << iter->second << endl;
      }
      cout << resetiosflags(ios::right);               // Right justify output
    }
```

After an initial check for an empty map, the entries are listed in a `for` loop using an iterator whose type is determined from the initial value. The output is left-justified by the `setiosflags` manipulator to produce tidy output. This remains in effect until the `resetiosflags` manipulator is used to restore right-justification.

Using a Multimap Container

A multimap container works very much like the map container, in that it supports the same range of functions — except for the subscript operator, which you cannot use with a multimap. The principle difference between a map and a multimap is that you can have multiple entries with the same key in a multimap, and this affects the way some of the functions behave. Obviously, with the possibility of several keys having the same value, overloading the `operator[]()` function would not make much sense for a multimap.

The `insert()` function flavors for a multimap are a little different from the `insert()` functions for a map. The simplest version of `insert()` that accepts a `pair<K, T>` object as an argument, returns an iterator pointing to the entry that was inserted in the multimap. The equivalent function for a map returns a pair object, because this provides an indication of when the key already exists in the map and the insertion is not possible; of course, this cannot arise with a multimap. A multimap also has a version of `insert()` with two arguments: the second being the pair to be inserted, and the first being an iterator pointing to the position in the multimap from which to start searching for an insertion point. This gives you some control over where a pair will be inserted when the same key already exists. This version of `insert()` also returns an iterator pointing to the element that was inserted. The third version of `insert()` accepts two iterator arguments that specify a range of elements to be inserted from some other source.

When you pass a key to the `erase()` function for a multimap, it erases all entries with the same key, and the value returned indicates how many entries were deleted. The significance of having a version of `erase()` available that accepts an iterator as an argument should now be apparent — it allows you to delete a single element. You also have a version of `erase()` available that accepts two iterators to delete a range of entries.

The `find()` function can only find the first element with a given key in a multimap. You really need a way to find several elements with the same key and the `lower_bound()`, `upper_bound()`, and `equal_range()` functions provide you with a way to do this. For example, given a `phonebook` object that is type

```
multimap<Person, string>
```

rather than type `map<Person, string>`, you could list the phone numbers corresponding to a given key like this:

```
Person person = Person("Jack", "Jones");
auto iter = phonebook.lower_bound(person);
if(iter == phonebook.end())
  cout << "There are no entries for " << person.getName() << endl;
else
{
  cout << "The following numbers are listed for " << person.getName() << ":"
       << endl;
  for(  ;  iter != phonebook.upper_bound(person) ; iter++)
    cout << iter->second << endl;
}
```

It's important to check the iterator returned by the `lower_bound()` function. If you don't, you could end up trying to reference an entry one beyond the last entry.

MORE ON ITERATORS

The `iterator` header defines several templates for iterators that transfer data from a source to a destination. **Stream iterators** act as pointers to a stream for input or output, and they enable you to transfer data between a stream and any source or destination that works with iterators, such as an algorithm. **Inserter interators** can transfer data into a basic sequence container. The `iterator` header defines two stream iterator templates, `istream_iterator<T>` for input streams and `ostream_iterator<T>` for output streams, where `T` is the type of object to be extracted from, or written to, the stream. The header also defines three inserter templates, `inserter<T>`, `back_inserter<T>` and `front_inserter<T>`, where `T` is the type of sequence container in which data is to be inserted.

Let's explore some of these iterators in a little more depth.

Using Input Stream Iterators

Here's an example of how you create an input stream iterator:

```
istream_iterator<int> numbersInput(cin);
```

This creates the iterator `numbersInput` of type `istream_iterator<int>` that can point to objects of type `int` in a stream. The argument to the constructor specifies the actual stream to which the iterator relates, so this is an iterator that can read integers from `cin`, the standard input stream.

The default `istream_iterator<T>` constructor creates an end-of-stream iterator, which will be equivalent to the end iterator for a container that you have been obtaining by calling the `end()` function. Here's how you could create an end-of-stream iterator for `cin`, complementing the `numbersInput` iterator:

```
istream_iterator<int> numbersEnd;
```

Now you have a pair of iterators that defines a sequence of values of type `int` from `cin`. You could use these to load values from `cin` into a `vector<int>` container:

```
vector<int> numbers;
cout << "Enter integers separated by spaces then a letter to end:" << endl;
istream_iterator<int> numbersInput(cin), numbersEnd;
while(numbersInput != numbersEnd)
  numbers.push_back(*numbersInput++);
```

After defining the vector container to hold values of type `int`, you create two input stream iterators: `numbersInput` is an input stream iterator reading values of type `int` from `cin`, and `numbersEnd` is an end-of-stream iterator for the same input stream. The `while` loop continues as long as `numbersInput` is not equal to the end-of-stream iterator, `numbersEnd`. When you execute this fragment, input continues until end-of-stream is recognized for `cin`. But what produces that condition? The end-of-stream condition will arise if you enter `Ctrl+Z` to close the input stream, or if you enter an invalid character such as a letter.

Of course, you are not limited to using input stream iterators as loop control variables. You can use them to pass data to an algorithm, such as `accumulate()`, which is defined in the `numeric` header:

```
cout << "Enter integers separated by spaces then a letter to end:" << endl;
istream_iterator<int> numbersInput(cin), numbersEnd;
cout << "The sum of the input values that you entered is "
     << accumulate(numbersInput, numbersEnd, 0) << endl;
```

This fragment outputs the sum of however many integers you enter. You will recall that the arguments to the `accumulate()` algorithm are an iterator pointing to the first value in the sequence, an iterator pointing to one past the last value, and the initial value for the sum. Here you are transferring data directly from `cin` to the algorithm.

The `sstream` header defines the `basic_istringstream<T>` type that defines an object type that can access data from a stream buffer such as a `string` object. The header also defines the `istringstream` type as `basic_istringstream<char>`, which will be a stream of characters of type `char`. You can construct an `istringstream` object from a `string` object, which means you can read data from the `string` object, just as you read from `cin`. Because an `istringstream` object is a stream, you can pass it to an input iterator constructor and use the iterator to access the data in the underlying stream buffer. Here's an example of how you do that:

```
string data("2.4 2.5 3.6 2.1 6.7 6.8 94 95 1.1 1.4 32");
istringstream input(data);
istream_iterator<double> begin(input), end;
cout << "The sum of the values from the data string is "
     << accumulate(begin, end, 0.0) << endl;
```

You create the `istringstream` object, `input`, from the `string` object, `data`, so you can read from `data` as a stream. You create two stream iterators that can access `double` values in the `input` stream, and you use these to pass the contents of `data` to the `accumulate()` algorithm. Note that the type of the third argument to the `accumulate()` function determines the type of the result, so you must specify this as a value of type `double` to get the sum produced correctly.

Let's try a working example.

TRY IT OUT   Using an Input Stream Iterator

In this example you use a stream iterator to read text from the standard input stream and transfer it to a map container to produce a word count for the text. Here's the code:

Available for
download on
Wrox.com

```
// Ex10_12.cpp
// A simple word collocation
#include <iostream>
#include <iomanip>
#include <string>
#include <map>
#include <iterator>
using std::cout;
using std::cin;
using std::endl;
using std::string;

int main()
{
  std::map<string, int> words;            // Map to store words and word counts
  cout << "Enter some text and press Enter followed by Ctrl+Z then Enter to end:"
       << endl << endl;

  std::istream_iterator<string> begin(cin); // Stream iterator
  std::istream_iterator<string> end;        // End stream iterator

  while(begin != end )                      // Iterate over words in the stream
    words[*begin++]++;                      // Increment and store a word count

  // Output the words and their counts
  cout << endl << "Here are the word counts for the text you entered:" << endl;
  for(auto iter = words.begin() ; iter != words.end() ; ++iter)
    cout << std::setw(5) << iter->second << " " << iter->first << endl;

  return 0;
}
```

code snippet Ex10_12.cpp

Here's an example of some output from this program:

```
Enter some text and press Enter followed by Ctrl+Z then Enter to end:

Peter Piper picked a peck of pickled pepper
A peck of pickled pepper Peter Piper picked
If Peter Piper picked a peck of pickled pepper
Where's the peck of pickled pepper Peter Piper picked
^Z

Here are the word counts for the text you entered:
    1 A
    1 If
    4 Peter
    4 Piper
    1 Where's
    2 a
    4 of
    4 peck
    4 pepper
    4 picked
    4 pickled
    1 the
```

How It Works

You first define a map container to store the words and the word counts:

```
std::map<string, int> words;          // Map to store words and word counts
```

This container stores each word count of type `int`, using the word of type `string` as the key. This will make it easy to accumulate the count for each word when you read from the input stream using stream iterators.

```
std::istream_iterator<string> begin(cin); // Stream iterator
std::istream_iterator<string> end;        // End stream iterator
```

The `begin` iterator is a stream iterator for the standard input stream, and `end` is an end-of-stream iterator that you can use to detect when the end of the input is reached.

You read the words and accumulate the counts in a loop:

```
while(begin != end )                   // Iterate over words in the stream
  words[*begin++]++;                   // Increment and store a word count
```

This simple `while` loop does a great deal of work. The loop control expression will iterate over the words entered via the standard input stream until the end-of-stream state is reached. The stream iterator reads words from `cin` delimited by whitespace, just like the overloaded >> operator for `cin`. Within the loop, you use the subscript operator for the map container to store a count with the word as the key; remember, the argument to the subscript operator for a map is the key. The expression `*begin` accesses a word, and the expression `*begin++` increments the iterator after accessing the word.

The first time a word is read, it will not be in the map, so the expression words[*begin++] will store a new entry with the count having the default value 0, and increment the begin iterator to the next word, ready for the next loop iteration. The whole expression words[*begin++]++ will increment the count for the entry, regardless of whether it is a new entry or not. Thus, an existing entry will just get its count incremented, whereas a new entry will be created and then its count incremented from 0 to 1.

Finally, you output the count for each word in a for loop:

```
for(auto iter = words.begin() ; iter != words.end() ; ++iter)
    cout << std::setw(5) << iter->second << " " << iter->first << endl;
```

This uses the iterator for the container just as you have seen several times before. The loop control expressions are very much easier to read because of the use of the auto keyword. The loop control variable, iter, is of type std::map<string,int>::const_iterator, but the auto keyword enables the type to be deduced automatically.

Using Inserter Iterators

An inserter iterator is an iterator that can add new elements to the sequence containers vector<T>, deque<T>, and list<T>. There are three templates that create inserter iterators:

➤ back_insert_iterator<T> — inserts elements at the end of a container of type T. The container must provide the push_back() function for this to work.

➤ front_insert_iterator<T> — inserts elements at the beginning of a container of type T. This depends on push_front() being available for the container.

➤ insert_iterator<T> — inserts elements starting at a specified position within a container of type T. This requires that the container has an insert() function that accepts an iterator as the first argument, and an item to be inserted as the second argument.

The constructors for the first two types of inserter iterators expect a single argument specifying the container in which elements are to be inserted. For example:

```
list<int> numbers;
front_insert_iterator< list<int> > iter(numbers);
```

Here you create an inserter iterator that can insert data at the beginning of the list<int> container numbers.

Inserting a value into the container is very simple:

```
*iter = 99;                    // Insert 99 at the front of the numbers container
```

You could also use the front_inserter() function with the numbers container, like this:

```
front_inserter(numbers) = 99;
```

This creates a front inserter for the numbers list and uses it to insert 99 at the beginning of the list. The argument to the front_inserter() function is the container to which the iterator is to be applied.

The constructor for an `insert_iterator<T>` iterator requires two arguments:

```
insert_iterator<vector<int>> iter_anywhere(numbers, numbers.begin());
```

The second argument to the constructor is an iterator specifying where data is to be inserted — the start of the sequence, in this instance. You can use this iterator in exactly the same way as the previous one. Here's how you could insert a series of values into a vector container using this iterator:

```
for(int i = 0 ; i<100 ; i++)
   *iter_anywhere = i + 1;
```

This loop inserts the values from 1 to 100 in the `numbers` container at the beginning. After executing this, the first 100 elements will be 100, 99, and so on, through to 1.

You could also use the `inserter()` function to achieve the same result:

```
for(int i = 0 ; i<100 ; i++)
   inserter(numbers, numbers.begin()) = i + 1;
```

The first argument to `inserter()` is the container, and the second is an iterator identifying the position where data is to be inserted. The inserter iterators can be used in conjunction with the `copy()` algorithm in a particularly useful way. Here's how you could read values from `cin` and transfer them to a `list<T>` container:

```
list<double> values;
cout << "Enter a series of values separated by spaces"
     << " followed by Ctrl+Z or a letter to end:" << endl;
istream_iterator<double> input(cin), input_end;
copy(input, input_end, back_inserter<list<double>>(values));
```

You first create a list container that stores `double` values. After a prompt for input, you create two input stream iterators for values of type `double`. The first iterator points to `cin`, and the second iterator is an end-of-stream iterator created by the default constructor. You specify the input to the `copy()` function with the two iterators; the destination for the copy operation is a back inserter iterator that you create in the third argument to the `copy()` function. The back inserter iterator adds the data transferred by the copy operation to the list container, `values`. This is quite powerful stuff. If you ignore the prompt, in three statements you can read an arbitrary number of values from the standard input stream and transfer them to a list container.

Using Output Stream Iterators

Complementing the input stream iterator template, the `ostream_iterator<T>` template provides output stream iterators for writing objects of type `T` to an output stream. There are two constructors for creating an instance of the output stream iterator template. One creates an iterator that just transfers data to the destination stream:

```
ostream_iterator<int> out(cout);
```

The type argument, `int`, to the template, specifies the type of data to be handled, while the constructor argument, `cout`, specifies the stream that will be the destination for data, so the `out` iterator can write value of type `int` to the standard output stream. Here's how you might use this iterator:

```
int data[] = {1, 2, 3, 4, 5, 6, 7, 8, 9};
vector<int> numbers(data, data+9);        // Contents 1 2 3 4 5 6 7 8 9
copy(numbers.begin(), numbers.end(), out);
```

The `copy()` algorithm that is defined in the `algorithm` header copies the sequence of objects specified by the first two iterator arguments to the output iterator specified by the third argument. Here, the function copies the elements from the `numbers` vector to the `out` iterator, which will write the elements to `cout`. The result of executing this fragment will be:

```
123456789
```

As you can see, the values are written to the standard output stream with no spaces in between. The second output stream iterator constructor can improve on this:

```
ostream_iterator<int>  out(cout, ", ");
```

The second argument to the constructor is a string to be used as a delimiter for output values. If you use this iterator as the third argument to the `copy()` function in the previous fragment, the output will be:

```
1, 2, 3, 4, 5, 6, 7, 8, 9,
```

The delimiter string that you specify as a second constructor argument is written to the stream following each value.

Let's see how an output stream iterator works in practice.

TRY IT OUT   Using an Inserter Iterator

Suppose you want to read a series of integer values from `cin` and store them in a vector. You then want to output the values and their sum. Here's how you could do this with the STL:

Available for download on Wrox.com

```
// Ex10_13.cpp
// Using stream and inserter iterators
#include <iostream>
#include <numeric>
#include <vector>
#include <iterator>
using std::cout;
using std::cin;
using std::endl;
using std::vector;
using std::istream_iterator;
using std::ostream_iterator;
using std::back_inserter;
using std::accumulate;

int main()
{
  vector<int> numbers;
  cout << "Enter a series of integers separated by spaces"
```

```
                << " followed by Ctrl+Z or a letter:" << endl;

        istream_iterator<int> input(cin), input_end;
        ostream_iterator<int> out(cout, " ");

        copy(input, input_end, back_inserter<vector<int>>(numbers));

        cout << "You entered the following values:" << endl;
        copy(numbers.begin(), numbers.end(), out);

        cout << endl << "The sum of these values is "
                << accumulate(numbers.begin(), numbers.end(), 0) << endl;

        return 0;
    }
```

code snippet Ex10_13.cpp

Here's an example of some output:

```
Enter a series of integers separated by spaces followed by Ctrl+Z or a letter:
1 2 3 4 5 6 7 8 9 10 11 12 13 14 15 ^Z
You entered the following values:
1 2 3 4 5 6 7 8 9 10 11 12 13 14 15
The sum of these values is 120
```

How It Works

After creating the `numbers` vector to store integers and issuing a prompt for input, you create three stream iterators:

```
        istream_iterator<int> input(cin), input_end;
        ostream_iterator<int> out(cout, " ");
```

The first statement creates two input stream iterators for reading values of type `int` from the standard input stream, `input` and `input_end`, the latter being an end-of-stream iterator. The second statement creates an output stream iterator for transferring values of type `int` to the standard output stream, with the delimiter of a single space following each output value.

Data is read from `cin` and transferred to the vector container using the `copy()` algorithm:

```
        copy(input, input_end, back_inserter<vector<int>>(numbers));
```

You specify the source of data for the copy operation by the two input stream iterators, `input` and `input_end`, and the destination for the copy operation is a back inserter iterator for the `numbers` container. Thus, the copy operation will transfer data values from `cin` to the `numbers` container via the back inserter.

You output the values that have been stored in the container using another copy operation:

```
        copy(numbers.begin(), numbers.end(), out);
```

Here the source for the copy is specified by the `begin()` and `end()` iterators for the container, and the destination is the output stream iterator, `out`. This operation will therefore write the data from `numbers` to `cout`, with the values separated by a space.

Finally, you calculate the sum of the values in the `numbers` container in the output statement using the `accumulate()` algorithm:

```
cout << endl << "The sum of these values is "
     << accumulate(numbers.begin(), numbers.end(), 0) << endl;
```

You specify the range of values to be summed by the `begin()` and `end()` iterators for the container, and the initial value for the sum is zero. If you wanted the average rather than the sum, this is easy too, using the expression:

```
accumulate(numbers.begin(), numbers.end(), 0)/numbers.size()
```

MORE ON FUNCTION OBJECTS

The `functional` header defines an extensive set of templates for creating function objects that you can use with algorithms and containers. I won't discuss them in detail, but I'll summarize the most useful ones. The function objects for comparisons are shown in the following table.

FUNCTION OBJECT TEMPLATE	DESCRIPTION
`less<T>`	Creates a binary predicate representing the `<` operation between objects of type `T`. For example, `less<string>()` defines a function object for comparing objects of type `string`.
`less_equal<T>`	Creates a binary predicate representing the `<=` operation between objects of type `T`. For example, `less_equal<double>()` defines a function object for comparing objects of type `double`.
`equal<T>`	Creates a binary predicate representing the `==` operation between objects of type `T`.
`not_equal<T>`	Creates a binary predicate representing the `!=` operation between objects of type `T`.
`greater_equal<T>`	Creates a binary predicate representing the `>=` operation between objects of type `T`.
`greater<T>`	Creates a binary predicate representing the `>` operation between objects of type `T`.
`not2<B>`	Creates a binary predicate that is the negation of a binary predicate of type `B`. For example, `not2(less<int>)` creates a binary predicate for comparing objects of type `int` that returns `true` if the left operand is not less than the right operand. The template type parameter value `B` is deduced from the type of the constructor argument.

Here's how you could use the `not2<B>` template to define a binary predicate for use with the `sort()` algorithm:

```
sort(v.begin(), v.end(), not2(greater<string>()));
```

The argument to the `not2` constructor is `greater<string>()`, which is a call to the constructor for the `greater<string>` class type, so the `sort()` function will sort using "not greater than" as the comparison between objects in the container, v.

The `functional` header also defines function objects for performing arithmetic operations on elements. You would typically use these to apply operations to sequences of numerical values using the `transform()` algorithm that is defined in the `algorithm` header. These function objects are described in the following table, where the parameter `T` specifies the type of the operands.

FUNCTION OBJECT TEMPLATE	DESCRIPTION
`plus<T>`	Calculates the sum of two elements of type `T`.
`minus<T>`	Calculates the difference between two elements of type `T` by subtracting the second operand from the first.
`multiplies<T>`	Calculates the product of two elements of type `T`.
`divides<T>`	Divides the first operand of type `T` by the second operand of type `T`.
`modulus<T>`	Calculates the remainder after dividing the first operand of type `T` by the second.
`negate<T>`	Returns the negative of the operand of type `T`.

To make use of these you need to apply the `transform()` function, and I'll explain how this works in the next section.

MORE ON ALGORITHMS

The `algorithm` and `numeric` headers define a large number of algorithms. The algorithms in the `numeric` header are primarily devoted to processing arrays of numerical values, whereas those in the `algorithm` header are more general purpose and provide such things as the ability to search, sort, copy, and merge sequences of objects specified by iterators. There are far too many to discuss in detail in this introductory chapter, so I'll just introduce a few of the most useful algorithms from the `algorithm` header to give you a basic idea of how they can be used.

You have already seen the `sort()` and `copy()` algorithms from the `algorithm` header in action. Let's take a brief look at a few other of the more interesting functions in the `algorithm` header.

fill()

The `fill()` function is of this form:

```
fill(ForwardIterator begin, ForwardIterator end, const Type& value)
```

This fills the elements specified by the iterators `begin` and `end` with `value`. For example, given a vector v, storing values of type `string` containing more than 10 elements, you could write:

```
fill(v.begin(), v.begin()+10, "invalid");
```

This would set the first 10 elements in v to `"invalid"`, the value specified by the last argument to `fill()`.

replace()

The `replace()` algorithm is of the form:

```
replace(ForwardIterator begin, ForwardIterator end,
                          const Type& oldValue, const Type& newValue)
```

This function examines each element in the range specified by `begin` and `end`, and replaces each occurrence of `oldValue` by `newValue`. Given a vector v that stores `string` objects, you could replace occurrences of `"yes"` by `"no"` with the following statement:

```
replace(v.begin(), v.end(), string("yes"), string("no"));
```

Like all the algorithms that receive an interval defined by a couple of iterators, the `replace()` function will also work with pointers. For example:

```
char str[] =  "A nod is as good as a wink to a blind horse.";
replace(str, str+strlen(str), 'o', '*');
cout << str << endl;
```

This will replace every occurrence of `'o'` in the null-terminated string `str` by `'*'`, so the result of executing this fragment will be the output:

```
A n*d is as g**d as a wink t* a blind h*rse.
```

find()

The `find()` function is of the form:

```
find(InputIterator begin, InputIterator end, const Type& value)
```

This function searches the sequence specified by the first two arguments for the first occurrence of `value`. For example, given a vector v containing values of type `int`, you could write:

```
vector<int>::iterator iter = find(v.begin(), v.end(), 21);
```

Obviously, by using `iter` as the starting point for a new search, you could use the `find()` algorithm repeatedly to find all occurrences of a given value. Perhaps like this:

```
vector<int>::iterator iter = v.begin();
int value = 21, count = 0;
while((iter = find(iter, v.end(), value)) != v.end())
{
  iter++;
  count++;
}
cout << "The vector contains " << count << " occurrences of " << value << endl;
```

This fragment searches the vector v for all occurrences of `value`. On the first loop iteration, the search starts at `v.begin()`. On subsequent iterations, the search starts at one past the previous position that was found. The loop will accumulate the total number of occurrences of `value` in v. You could also code the loop as a `for` loop:

```
for((iter = find(v.begin(), v.end(), value)); iter != v.end() ;
                                  (iter = find(iter, v.end(), value))++, count++);
```

Now the find operation is in the third loop control expression, and you increment `iter` after the result from the `find()` function is stored. In my view, the `while` loop is a better solution because it's easier to understand.

transform()

The `transform()` function comes in two versions. The first version applies an operation specified by a unary function object to a set of elements specified by a pair of iterators, and is of the form:

```
transform(InputIterator begin, InputIterator end,
                            OutputIterator result, UnaryFunction f)
```

This version of `transform()` applies the unary function `f` to all elements in the range specified by the iterators `begin` and `end`, and stores the results, beginning at the position specified by the iterator `result`. The `result` iterator can be the same as `begin`, in which case the results will replace the original elements. The function returns an iterator that is one past the last result stored.

Here's an example:

```
double values[] = { 2.5, -3.5, 4.5, -5.5, 6.5, -7.5};
vector<double> data(values, values+sizeof values/sizeof values[0]);
transform(data.begin(), data.end(), data.begin(), negate<double>());
```

The `transform()` function call applies a `negate<double>` function object to all the elements in the vector `data`. The results are stored back in `data` and overwrite the original values; so, after this operation the vector will contain:

```
-2.5, 3.5, -4.5, 5.5, -6.5, 7.5
```

Because the operation writes the results back to the `data` vector, the `transform()` function will return the iterator `data.end()`.

The second version of `transform()` applies a binary function, with the operands coming from two ranges specified by iterators. The function is of the form:

```
transform(InputIterator1 begin1, InputIterator1 end1, InputIterator2 begin2,
                                 OutputIterator result, BinaryFunction f)
```

The range specified by `begin1` and `end1` represents the set of left operands for the binary function `f` that is specified by the last argument. The range representing the right operands starts at the position specified by the `begin2` iterator; an end iterator does not need to be supplied for this range because there must be the same number of elements as in the range specified by `begin1` and `end1`. The results will be stored in the range, starting at the `result` iterator position. The `result` iterator can be the same as `begin1` if you want the results stored back in that range, but it must not be any other position between `begin1` and `end1`. Here's an example of how you might use this version of the `transform()` algorithm:

```
double values[] = { 2.5, -3.5, 4.5, -5.5, 6.5, -7.5};
vector<double> data(values, values+ sizeof values/sizeof values[0]);
vector<double> squares(data.size());
transform(data.begin(), data.end(), data.begin(),
                                     squares.begin(), multiplies<double>());
ostream_iterator<double> out(cout, " ");
copy(squares.begin(), squares.end(), out);
```

You initialize the `data` vector with the contents of the `values` array. You then create a vector `squares` to store the results of the `transform()` operation with the same number of elements as `data`. The `transform()` function uses the `multiplies<double>()` function object to multiply each element of `data` by itself. The results are stored in the `squares` vector. The last two statements use an output stream iterator to list the contents of `squares`, which will be:

```
6.25 12.25 20.25 30.25 42.25 56.25
```

LAMBDA EXPRESSIONS

A **lambda expression** is a C++ language capability that provides you with an alternative programming mechanism to function objects in many instances. Lambda expressions are not specific to STL, but they can be applied extensively in this context, which is why I chose to discuss them here. A lambda expression defines a function object without a name, and without the need for an explicit class definition. You would typically use a lambda expression as the means of passing a function as an argument to another function. A lambda expression is much easier to use and understand, and requires less code, than defining and creating a regular function object. Of course, it is not a replacement for function objects in general.

Let's consider an example. Suppose you want to calculate the cubes (x^3) of the elements in a vector containing numerical values. You could use the `transform()` operation for this, except that there is no function object to calculate cubes. You can easily create a lambda expression to do it, though:

```
double values[] = { 2.5, -3.5, 4.5, -5.5, 6.5, -7.5};
vector<double> data(values, values+6);
vector<double> cubes(data.size());
transform(data.begin(), data.end(), cubes.begin(),
                          [](double x){ return x*x*x;} );
```

The last statement uses the `transform()` operation to calculate the cubes of the elements in the vector data and store the result in the vector cubes. The lambda expression is the last argument to the `transform()` function:

```
[](double x){ return x*x*x;}
```

The opening square brackets are called the **lambda introducer**, because they mark the beginning of the lambda expression. There's a bit more to this, but I'll come back to that a little later in this chapter.

The lambda introducer is followed by the lambda parameter list between parentheses, just like a normal function. In this case, there's just a single parameter, x. There are restrictions on the lambda parameter list, compared to a regular function: You cannot specify default values for the parameters to a lambda expression, and the parameter list cannot be of a variable length.

Finally, in the example, you have the body of the lambda expression between braces, again just like a normal function. In this case the body is just a single `return` statement, but in general, it can consist of as many statements as you like, just like a normal function. I'm sure you have noticed that there is no return type specification. When the body of the lambda expression is a single return statement that returns a value in the body, the return type defaults to that of the value returned. Otherwise, the default return type is `void`. Of course, you can specify the return type. To specify the return type you would write the lambda expression like this:

```
[](double x)->double { return x*x*x;}
```

The type `double` following the arrow specifies the return type as such.

If you wanted to output the values calculated, you could do so in the lambda expression, like this:

```
[](double x)->double {
                 double result(x*x*x);
                 cout << result << "   ";
                 return result;
                 }
```

This just extends the body of the lambda to provide for writing the value that is calculated to the standard output stream. In this case, the return type must be specified because the default return type would be `void`.

The Capture Clause

The lambda introducer can contain a **capture clause** that determines how the body of the lambda can access variables in the enclosing scope. In the previous section, the lambda expression had nothing between the square brackets, indicating that no variables in the enclosing scope can be accessed within the body of the lambda. The first possibility is to specify a **default capture clause** that applies to all variables in the enclosing scope. You have two options for this. If you place = between the square brackets, the body has access to all automatic variables in the enclosing scope by value — i.e., the values of the variables are made available within the lambda expression, but the original variables cannot be changed. On the other hand, if you put & between the square brackets, all the variables in the enclosing scope are accessible by reference, and therefore can be changed by the code in the body of the lambda. Look at this code fragment:

```
double factor = 5.0;
double values[] = { 2.5, -3.5, 4.5, -5.5, 6.5, -7.5};
vector<double> data(values, values+6);
vector<double> cubes(data.size());
transform(data.begin(), data.end(), cubes.begin(),
          [=](double x){ return factor*x*x*x;} );
```

In this fragment, the = capture clause allows all the variables in scope to be accessible by value from within the body of the lambda. Note that this is not quite the same as passing arguments by value. The value of the variable `factor` is available within the lambda, but you cannot update the copy of `factor` because it is effectively `const`. The following `transform()` statement will not compile, for example:

```
transform(data.begin(),data.end(),cubes.begin(),
          [=](double x)-> double{ factor += 10.0;        // Not allowed!
                         return factor*x*x*x;} );
```

If you want to modify the temporary copy of a variable in scope from within the lambda, adding the `mutable` keyword will enable this:

```
transform(data.begin(),data.end(),cubes.begin(),
          [=](double x)mutable -> double{ factor += 10.0;        // OK
                         return factor*x*x*x;} );
```

Now you can modify the copy of any variable within the enclosing scope without changing the original variable. After executing this statement, the value of `factor` will still be 5.0. The lambda remembers the local value of `factor` from one call to the next, so for the first element `factor` will be 5+10=15, for the second element it will be 15+10=25, and so on.

If you do want to change the original value of `factor` from within the lambda, just use & as the capture clause:

```
transform(data.begin(),data.end(),cubes.begin(),
          [&](double x)->double{ factor += 10.0;     // Changes original variable
                         return factor*x*x*x;} );
cout << "factor = " << factor << endl;
```

You don't need the `mutable` keyword here. All variables within the enclosing scope are available by reference, so you can use and alter their values. The result of executing this will be that `factor` has the value 65. If you thought it was going to be 15.0, remember that the lambda expression executes once for each element in `data`, and the cubes of the elements will be multiplied by successive values of `factor` from 15.0 to 65.0.

Capturing Specific Variables

There may be circumstances where you want to be more selective about how a lambda expression accesses variables in the enclosing scope. In this case, you can explicitly identify the variables to be accessed. You could rewrite the previous `transform()` statement as:

```
transform(data.begin(), data.end(), cubes.begin(),
        [&factor](double x)->double{ factor += 10.0;     // Changes original variable
                                     return factor*x*x*x;} );
```

Now, `factor` is the only variable from the enclosing scope that is accessible, and it is available by reference. If you omit the `&`, `factor` would be available by value and not updatable. If you want to identify multiple variables in the capture clause, you just separate them with commas. You could include `=` in the capture clause list, as well as explicit variable names. For example, with the capture clause `[=,&factor]` the lambda would have access to `factor` by reference and all other variables in the enclosing scope by value. Conversely, putting `[&,factor]` as the capture clause would capture `factor` by value and all other variables by reference. Note that in a function member of a class, you can include the `this` pointer in the capture clause for a lambda expression, which allows access to the other functions and data members that belong to the class.

A lambda expression can also include a `throw()` exception specification that indicates that the lambda does not throw exceptions. Here's an example:

```
transform(data.begin(), data.end(), cubes.begin(),
        [&factor](double x)throw() ->double{ factor += 10.0;
                                     return factor*x*x*x;} );
```

If you want to include the `mutable` specification, as well as the `throw()` specification, the `mutable` keyword must precede `throw()` and must be separated from it by one or more spaces.

Templates and Lambda Expressions

You can use a lambda expression inside a template. Here's an example of a function template that uses a lambda expression:

```
template <class T>
T average(const vector<T>& vec)
{
  T sum(0);
  for_each(vec.begin(), vec.end(),
    [&sum](const T& value){ sum += value; });
  return sum/vec.size();
}
```

This template generates functions for calculating the average of a set of numerical values stored in a vector. The lambda expression uses the template type parameter in the lambda parameter specification, and accumulates the sum of all the elements in a vector. The `sum` variable is accessed from the lambda by reference, so it is able to accumulate the sum there. The last line of the function returns the average, which is calculated by dividing `sum` by the number of elements in the vector. Let's try an example.

TRY IT OUT   Using lambda expressions

This example shows the use of a variety of lambda expressions:

```cpp
// Ex10_14.cpp Using lambda expressions
#include <algorithm>
#include <iostream>
#include <iomanip>
#include <vector>
#include <ctime>
#include <cstdlib>
using namespace std; // Just to avoid a lot of using directives in the example...

// Template function to return the average of the elements in a vector
template <class T> T average(const vector<T>& vec)
{
  T sum(0);
  for_each(vec.begin(), vec.end(),
    [&sum](const T& value){ sum += value; });
  return sum/vec.size();
}

// Template function to set a vector to values beginning with start
// and incremented by increment
template <class T> void setValues(vector<T>& vec, T start, T increment)
{
  T current(start);
  generate(vec.begin(), vec.end(),
    [increment, &current]()->T{T result(current);
                               current += increment;
                               return result;});
}

// Template function to set a vector to random values between min and max
template<class T> void randomValues(vector<T>& vec, T min, T max)
{
  srand(static_cast<unsigned int>(time(0)));   // Initialize random
                                               //   number generator
  generate(vec.begin(), vec.end(),
    [=](){ return static_cast<T>(static_cast<double>(rand())/
                                 RAND_MAX*(max-min)+min); });
}

// Template function to list the values in a vector
template<class T> void listVector(const vector<T>& vec)
{
  int count = 0;       // Used to control outputs per line
  for_each(vec.begin(), vec.end(),
    [&count](const T& n)->void{  cout << setw(10) << n;
                                 if(++count % 5)
                                   cout << "  ";
                                 else
                                   cout << endl;});
}

int main()
```

```
    {
        vector<int> integerData(50);
        randomValues(integerData, 1, 10);      // Set random integer values
        cout << "Vector contains:" << endl;
        listVector(integerData);
        cout << "Average value is "<< average(integerData) << endl;

        vector<double> realData(20);
        setValues(realData, 5.0, 2.5);    // Set real values starting at 5.0
        cout << "Vector contains:" << endl;
        listVector(realData);
        cout << "Average value is "<< average(realData) << endl;

        return 0;
    }
```

code snippet Ex10_14.cpp

This example produces output similar to the following:

```
Vector contains:
        1               7               7               6               6
        6               1               5               7               1
        2               9               5               5               1
        6               7               3               2               1
        1               8               7               7               9
        3               9               9               6               3
        9               4               2               3               5
        5               1               2               5               5
        3               2               7               3               7
        6               3               5               2               3
Average value is 4
Vector contains:
        5             7.5              10            12.5              15
     17.5              20            22.5              25            27.5
       30            32.5              35            37.5              40
     42.5              45            47.5              50            52.5
Average value is 28.75
```

Where the example uses random number generation, the values are likely to be different.

How It Works

There are four function templates that use lambda expressions in the implementation of the functions that operate on vector containers. The first template function in sequence, average(), calculates the average value of the elements in a vector by passing the following lambda expression as the last argument to the STL for_each() function:

```
[&sum](const T& value){ sum += value; }
```

The sum variable that is declared in the average() function is accessed by reference in the lambda to accumulate the sum of all the elements. The parameter to the lambda is value, which is of type reference to T, so the lambda automatically deals with whatever type of element is stored in the vector.

The next function template is `setValues()`. This sets the elements of a vector in sequence with the first element set to `start`, the next to `start+increment`, the next to `start+2*increment`, and so on. Thus, the function will set the vector elements to any set of equispaced values. The function calls the STL `generate()` function that is defined in the `algorithm` header. This function sets a sequence of elements, defined by the first two iterator arguments, to the value returned by the function object you specify as the third argument. In this case, the third argument is the lambda expression:

```
[increment, &current]()->T{T result(current);
                          current += increment;
                          return result;}
```

The lambda accepts no arguments, but it accesses `increment` by value and `current` by reference, the latter being used to store the next value to be set. The following lambda expression is exactly the same as the one above:

```
[=]()mutable->T{T result(current);
                current += increment;
                return result;}
```

The third function template is `randomValues()`, which stores random values of the appropriate type in the elements of a vector. The values will be in the range from `min` to `max`, the second and third arguments to the function.

The first statement in the function is:

```
srand(static_cast<unsigned int>(time(0)));   // Initialize random number generator
```

This calls the `srand()` function that is defined in the `cstdlib` header. This function initializes the sequence of random numbers generated by the `rand()` function, also defined in the `cstdlib` header. The argument to `srand()` is an unsigned integer value that is the seed for the random number generator. The same seed will always produce the same sequence of random numbers, so here the argument is the current time that is returned by the `time()` function (defined in the `ctime` header). This will always return a different integer each time it is called, so the sequence of random numbers will be different each time the `randomValues()` function is called.

The `randomValues()` function calls the `generate()` function to store values produced by the following lambda expression in the vector:

```
[=](){ return static_cast<T>(static_cast<double>(rand())/
                             RAND_MAX*(max-min)+min); }
```

All variables within scope are accessible by value, and this includes the `randomValues()` function parameters, `min` and `max`. The `RAND_MAX` constant represents the maximum integer that the `rand()` function can return, so the expression for the value to be returned evaluates to a value in the range `min` to `max`.

The last template function is `listVector()`, which outputs the values of the elements in a vector with five values on each line. It uses the following lambda expression as the argument to the `for_each()` function to do this:

```
[&count](const T& n)->void{  cout << setw(10) << n;
                             if(++count % 5)
                                cout << "  ";
                             else
                                cout << endl;}
```

The capture clause in the expression captures the variable `count` that is defined in the `listVector()` function by reference, and this variable is used to record the count of the number of values processed. The parameter is of type `const` reference to `T`, so any element type can be processed. The body of the lambda outputs the value of the current element, `n`, and the `if` statement ensures that after every fifth value, a newline is written to `cout`. The `setw()` manipulator ensures values are presented in the output in a field that is 10 characters wide, so we get nice neat columns of output.

In `main()`, you first create a vector that can store 50 integers, and then call `randomValues()` to set the elements to random values between one and 10:

```
vector<int> integerData(50);
randomValues(integerData, 1, 10);     // Set random integer values
cout << "Vector contains:" << endl;
listVector(integerData);
cout << "Average value is "<< average(integerData) << endl;
```

The call to `listVector()` outputs the values, five to a line, as you see in the output that was produced. The last statement above calls the `average()` template function to calculate the average of the values in the vector. In all three template functions, the type is deduced from the `vector<int>` argument that is passed, and this also determines the type in the lambda expression that each function uses.

The next block of code in `main()` is:

```
vector<double> realData(20);
setValues(realData, 5.0, 2.5);   // Set real values starting at 5.0
cout << "Vector contains:" << endl;
listVector(realData);
cout << "Average value is "<< average(realData) << endl;
```

This uses a vector storing values of type `double`, and its elements[1] values are set using the `setValues()` template. The output shows that everything works as expected.

Wrapping a Lambda Expression

An extension to the STL `functional` header defines the `function<>` class template that you can use to define a wrapper for a function object; this includes a lambda expression. The `function<>` template is referred to as a **polymorphic function wrapper** because an instance of the template can wrap a variety of function objects with a given parameter list and return type. I won't discuss all the details of the `function<>` class template, but I'll just show how you can use it to wrap a lambda expression. Using the `function<>` template to wrap a lambda expression effectively gives a name to the lambda expression, which not only provides the possibility of recursion within a lambda expression, it also allows you to use the lambda expression in multiple statements or pass it to several different functions. The same function wrapper could also wrap different lambda expressions at different times.

To create a wrapper object from the `function<>` template you need to supply information about the return type, and the types of any parameters, to a lambda expression. Here's how you could create an object of type `function` that can wrap a function object that has one parameter of type `double` and returns a value of type `int`:

```
function<int(double)> f = [](double x)->int{ return static_cast<int>(x*x); };
```

The type specification for the function template is the return type for the function object to be wrapped, followed by its parameter types between parentheses, and separated by commas. Let's try a working example.

TRY IT OUT Recursion in a Lambda Expression

This example will find the **highest common factor** (HCF) for a pair of integer values. The HCF is the largest number that will divide exactly into both integers. The HCF is also called the GCD, or greatest common divisor. Here's the code:

```cpp
// Ex10_15.cpp Wrapping a lambda expression
#include <iostream>
#include <functional>
using std::function;
using std::cout;
using std::endl;

int main()
{
  // Wrap the lambda expression to compute the HCF
  function<int(int,int)> hcf = [&](int m, int n) mutable ->int{
                                 if(m < n) return hcf(n,m);
                                 int remainder(m%n);
                                 if(0 == remainder) return n;
                                 return hcf(n, remainder);};
  int a(17719), b(18879);
  cout << "For numbers " << a << " and " << b
       << " the HCF is " << hcf(a, b) << endl;
  a = 103*53*17*97;
  b = 3*29*103;
  cout << "For numbers " << a << " and " << b
       << " the HCF is " << hcf(a, b) << endl;

  return 0;
}
```

code snippet Ex10_15.cpp

This produces the output:

```
For numbers 17719 and 18879 the HCF is 29
For numbers 9001891 and 8961 the HCF is 103
```

How It Works

The first statement in `main()` creates the `hcf` object using the `function` class template:

```
function<int(int,int)> hcf = [&](int m, int n) mutable ->int{
                                 if(m < n) return hcf(n,m);
                                 int remainder(m%n);
                                 if(0 == remainder) return n;
                                 return hcf(n, remainder);};
```

The lambda expression has two parameters of type int and returns a value of type int, so hcf is of type `function<int(int,int)>`.

The lambda expression uses Euclid's method for finding the highest common factor for two integer values. This involves dividing the larger number by the smaller number, and if the remainder is zero, the HCF is the smaller number. If the remainder is non-zero, the process continues by dividing the previous smaller number by the remainder, and this is repeated until the remainder is zero.

The code for the lambda expression assumes m is the larger of the two numbers that are passed as arguments, so if it isn't, it calls `hcf()` with the arguments reversed. If the first argument is the larger number, the remainder after dividing m by n is calculated. If the remainder is zero, then n is the highest common factor and is returned. If the remainder is not zero, `hcf()` is called with n and the remainder.

In `main()`, you call `hcf()` in the first output statement, with a and b as the arguments:

```
cout << "For numbers " << a << " and " << b
     << " the HCF is " << hcf(a, b) << endl;
```

The output shows that the HCF is 29.

You also call `hcf()` a second time, with new values for a and b, in a statement identical to that above. From the expressions defining the values stored in a and b, you can see that the lambda expression does indeed find the HCF for the two integers passed to it.

THE STL FOR C++/CLI PROGRAMS

The STL/CLR library is an implementation of the STL for use with C++/CLI programs and the CLR. The STL/CLR library covers all the capability that I have described for the STL for standard C++, so I won't go over the same ground again. I'll simply highlight some of the differences and illustrate how you use the STL/CLR with examples.

The STL/CLR library is contained within the `cliext` namespace, so all STL names are qualified by `cliext` rather than `std`. There are `cliext` include subdirectories that are equivalents for each of the standard C++ STL headers, including those for container adapters, algorithms and function objects, and the STL/CLR subdirectory name is the same in every case. Thus, the C++/CLI equivalents to the templates defined in a standard STL header, such as `functional`, can be found in `cliext/functional`. So, for example, if you want to use vector containers in your C++/CLI program you, need an `#include` directive for `cliext/vector`; to use the `queue<T>` adapter you must include the header file `cliext/queue`.

STL/CLR Containers

STL/CLR containers can store reference types, handles to reference types, and unboxed value types; they cannot store boxed value types. Most of the time, you will use STL/CLR containers with handles or value types. If you do choose to store reference types in a container, they will be passed by value, and the requirements for storing such objects in an STL/CLR container are essentially the same as for a native STL container. Any reference type stored in an STL/CLR container must at least implement a public copy constructor, a public assignment operator, and a public destructor. These requirements do not apply when you are storing value types or handles to reference types in an STL/CLR container.

Don't forget that the compiler does not supply default versions of the copy constructor and assignment operator for reference types, so when they are needed, you must always define them in your `ref` classes. Just to remind you, for a type `T` in a C++/CLI class, these functions will be of the form:

```
T(const T% t)                           // Copy constructor
{
  // Function body...
}

T% operator=(const T% t)                // Assignement operator
{
  // Function body...
}

~T()                                    // Destructor
{
  // Function body...
}
```

Some container operations also require a no-arg constructor and the `operator==()` function to be defined. A no-arg constructor may be used if space for elements in a container needs to be allocated when the container is storing objects rather than handles. If you are storing handles to reference types or value types in an associative container such as a set or a map, they must overload at least one comparison operator — the default requirement is for `operator<()`.

Using Sequence Containers

All the sequence containers provided by STL for native C++ are also available with the STL/CLR. The STL/CLR implements all the operations that the native STL containers support, so the differences tend to be notational, arising from the use of C++/CLI types. Let's explore the differences through some examples.

TRY IT OUT   Storing Handles in a Vector

First, define `Person` as a `ref` class type:

```
// Person.h
// A class defining a person
#pragma once
```

```
using namespace System;

ref class Person
{
public:
  Person():firstname(L""), secondname(L""){}

  Person(String^ first, String^ second):firstname(first), secondname(second) {}

    // Destructor
    ~Person(){}

    // String representation of a person
    virtual String^ ToString() override
    {
       return firstname + L" " + secondname;
    }

private:
  String^ firstname;
  String^ secondname;
};
```

The class has two constructors, including a no-arg constructor and a destructor. You will be only storing handles to Person objects in a vector, so you don't need to implement a copy constructor or an assignment operator. The ToString() function here overrides the version inherited from class Object and provides the way to get a String representation of a Person object for output purposes.

You can define a main() program that will store Person object handles in a vector like this:

```
// Ex10_16.cpp
// Storing handles in a vector
#include "stdafx.h"
#include "Person.h"
#include <cliext/vector>

using namespace System;
using namespace cliext;

int main(array<System::String ^> ^args)
{
  vector<Person^>^ people = gcnew vector<Person^>();
  String^ first;              // Stores a first name
  String^ second;             // Stores a second name
  Person^ person;             // Stores a Person

  while(true)
  {
    Console::Write(L"Enter a first name or press Enter to end: ");
    first = Console::ReadLine();
    if(0 == first->Length)
      break;
    Console::Write(L"Enter a second name: ");
    second = Console::ReadLine();
    person = gcnew Person(first->Trim(),second->Trim());
```

```
      people->push_back(person);
    }

    // Output the contents of the vector
    Console::WriteLine(L"\nThe persons in the vector are:");
    for each(Person^ person in people)
      Console::WriteLine("{0}",person);
    return 0;
  }
```

code snippet Ex10_16.cpp

Here is a sample of output from this program:

```
Enter a first name or press Enter to end: Marilyn
Enter a second name: Monroe
Enter a first name or press Enter to end: Nicole
Enter a second name: Kidman
Enter a first name or press Enter to end: Judy
Enter a second name: Dench
Enter a first name or press Enter to end: Sally
Enter a second name: Field
Enter a first name or press Enter to end:

The persons in the vector are:
Marilyn Monroe
Nicole Kidman
Judy Dench
Sally Field
```

How It Works

You create the vector container on the CLR heap like this:

```
vector<Person^>^ people = gcnew vector<Person^>();
```

The template type argument is `Person^`, which is a handle to a `Person` object. The container is also created on the CLR heap, so the `people` variable is a handle of type `vector<Person^>^`.

You create three handles for use as working storage in the input process:

```
String^ first;          // Stores a first name
String^ second;         // Stores a second name
Person^ person;         // Stores a Person
```

The first two refer to `String` objects, and the third is a handle to a `Person` object.

You read names from the standard input stream, and create `Person` objects in an indefinite `while` loop:

```
while(true)
{
  Console::Write(L"Enter a first name or press Enter to end: ");
  first = Console::ReadLine();
  if(0 == first->Length)
```

```
      break;
    Console::Write(L"Enter a second name: ");
    second = Console::ReadLine();
    person = gcnew Person(first->Trim(),second->Trim());
    people->push_back(person);
  }
```

After prompting for the input, the `Console::ReadLine()` function reads a name from the standard input stream and stores it in `first`. If just the `Enter` key is pressed, the length of the string will be zero, so you test for this to decide when to exit the loop. If the first name read is not of zero length, you read the second name. You then create a `Person` object on the CLR heap, and store the handle in `person`. For each `String^` argument to the constructor, you call the `Trim()` function to remove any leading or trailing spaces. Calling the `push_back()` function for the `people` container stores the `person` handle in the vector.

The objects exist independently of the container, so if you were to discard the container (by assigning `nullptr` to `people`, for example) it would not necessarily destroy the objects pointed to by the handles it contains. In our example, we do not retain any handles to the objects, so in this case destroying the container would result in the objects not being referenced anywhere; eventually the garbage collector would get around to destroying them and freeing the memory they occupy on the CLR heap.

After the input loop ends, you output the contents of a vector in a `for each` loop:

```
for each(Person^ person in people)
  Console::WriteLine("{0}",person);
```

The `for each` loop works directly with sequence containers, so you can use this to iterate over all the handles stored in the `people` vector. The `Console::WriteLine()` function calls the `ToString()` function for each `Person` object to produce the string to be inserted in the first argument string.

It is not normal usage, but let's look at another working example to explore how you can store `ref` class objects instead of handles in a sequence container.

TRY IT OUT   **Storing Reference Class Objects in a Double-Ended Queue**

You will use `Person` object again, but this time you will sort the contents of the container before you generate the output. Here's the new version of the `Person` class:

```
// Person.h
// A class defining a person
#pragma once
using namespace System;

ref class Person
{
public:
  Person():firstname(""), secondname(""){}

  Person(String^ first, String^ second):firstname(first), secondname(second)
```

```
    {}

     // Copy constructors
    Person(const Person% p):firstname(p.firstname),secondname(p.secondname){}
    Person(Person^ p):firstname(p->firstname), secondname(p->secondname){}

     // Destructor
     ~Person(){}

     // Assignment operator
     Person% operator=(const Person% p)
     {
       if(this != %p)
       {
         firstname = p.firstname;
         secondname = p.secondname;
       }
       return *this;
     }

     // Less-than operator
     bool operator<(Person^ p)
     {
       if(String::Compare(secondname, p->secondname) < 0 ||
          (String::Compare(secondname, p->secondname)== 0 &&
           String::Compare(firstname, p->firstname) < 0))
        return true;
       return false;
     }

     // String representation of a person
     virtual String^ ToString() override
     {
       return firstname + L" " + secondname;
     }

   private:
     String^ firstname;
     String^ secondname;
   };
```

You now have two copy constructors for Person objects, one accepting a Person object as an argument and the other accepting a handle to a Person object. A sequence container requires both copy constructors if it is to compile. You also have the assignment operator for Person objects, which is also required by the container. The operator<() function is needed for the sort() algorithm.

Here's the program code that will utilize this version of the Person class:

```
// Ex10_17.cpp
// Storing ref class objects in a double-ended queue
#include "stdafx.h"
#include "Person.h"
#include <cliext/deque>
```

```
#include <cliext/algorithm>

using namespace System;
using namespace cliext;

int main(array<System::String ^> ^args)
{

  deque<Person>^ people = gcnew deque<Person>();

  String^ first;                // Stores a first name
  String^ second;               // Stores a second name
  Person person;                // Stores a Person

  while(true)
  {
    Console::Write(L"Enter a first name or press Enter to end: ");
    first = Console::ReadLine();
    if(0 == first->Length)
      break;
    Console::Write(L"Enter a second name: ");
    second = Console::ReadLine();
    person = Person(first->Trim(),second->Trim());
    people->push_back(person);
  }

  sort(people->begin(), people->end());

  // Output the contents of the vector
  Console::WriteLine(L"\nThe persons in the vector are:");
  for each(Person^ p in people)
    Console::WriteLine(L"{0}",p);

  return 0;
}
```

code snippet Ex10_17.cpp

Here is some output, similar to that of the previous example, except that the objects have been sorted in ascending sequence:

```
Enter a first name or press Enter to end: Brad
Enter a second name: Pitt
Enter a first name or press Enter to end: George
Enter a second name: Clooney
Enter a first name or press Enter to end: Mel
Enter a second name: Gibson
Enter a first name or press Enter to end: Clint
Enter a second name: Eastwood
Enter a first name or press Enter to end:

The persons in the vector are:
George Clooney
Clint Eastwood
Mel Gibson
Brad Pitt
```

How It Works

You create the double-ended queue container like this:

```
deque<Person>^ people = gcnew deque<Person>();
```

The type parameter to the deque<T> template is now Person, so you will be storing Person objects, not handles.

The storage for the element to be inserted into the container is now defined like this:

```
Person person;                    // Stores a Person
```

You are now going to store Person objects, so the working storage is no longer a handle, as it was in the previous example.

The input loop is the same as in the previous example except for the last two statements in the while loop:

```
person = Person(first->Trim(),second->Trim());
people->push_back(person);
```

You create a Person object using the same syntax as in native C++. Although you don't use the gcnew keyword here, the compiler will arrange for the object to be created on the CLR heap because ref class objects cannot be created on the stack.

After the input loop, you sort the elements in the container:

```
sort(people->begin(), people->end());
```

The sort() algorithm expects two iterators to specify the range of elements to be sorted, and you obtain these by calling the begin() and end() functions for the container.

Finally, you list the contents of the container in a for each loop:

```
for each(Person^ p in people)
  Console::WriteLine(L"{0}",p);
```

Note that you still use a handle as the loop variable. Even though the container stores the objects themselves, you access them through a handle in a for each loop.

Of course, you could use the subscript operator for the container to access the objects. In this case, the output loop could be like this:

```
for(int i = 0 ; i<people->size() ; i++)
  Console::WriteLine("{0}", %people[i]);
```

The subscript operator returns a reference to an object in the container, and because the Console::WriteLine() function expects a handle, you have to use the % operator to obtain the address of the object.

You also have the possibility to use iterators:

```
deque<Person>::iterator iter;
for(iter = people->begin() ; iter < people->end() ; ++iter)
  Console::WriteLine(L"{0}", *iter);
```

The iterator type is defined in the `deque<Person>` class, as in native STL. The loop is very similar to a native STL iterator loop, but when you dereference the iterator, you get a handle to the element to which the iterator points. This gives a clue as to why the `for each` loop iterates over handles — because it uses an iterator.

Just to complete the set, let's see a sequence container storing elements that are value types.

TRY IT OUT   Storing Value Types in a List

This time you will use a list as the container and store values of type `double`. You will also try out the `sort()` member of the `list<T>` container.

```
// Ex10_18.cpp  Storing value class objects in a list
#include "stdafx.h"
#include <cliext/list>

using namespace System;
using namespace cliext;

int main(array<System::String ^> ^args)
{
  array<double>^ values = {2.5, -4.5, 6.5, -2.5, 2.5, 7.5, 1.5, 3.5};
  list<double>^ data = gcnew list<double>();
  for(int i = 0 ; i<values->Length ; i++)
    data->push_back(values[i]);

  Console::WriteLine(L"The list contains: ");
  for each(double value in data)
    Console::Write(L"{0} ", value);
  Console::WriteLine();

  data->sort(greater<double>());
  Console::WriteLine(L"\nAfter sorting the list contains: ");
  for each(double value in data)
    Console::Write(L"{0} ", value);
  Console::WriteLine();

  return 0;
}
```

code snippet Ex10_18.cpp

Here is the output from this example:

```
The list contains:
2.5 -4.5 6.5 -2.5 2.5 7.5 1.5 3.5

After sorting the list contains:
7.5 6.5 3.5 2.5 2.5 1.5 -2.5 -4.5
```

How It Works

You first create a handle to a `list<T>` object with this statement:

```
list<double>^ data = gcnew list<double>();
```

The elements to be stored are of type `double`, so the template type parameter is the same as for the native STL list.

The elements from the `values` array are stored in the `data` container in a loop:

```
for(int i = 0 ; i<sizeof values/sizeof values[0] ; i++)
  data->push_back(values[i]);
```

This is a straightforward loop that indexes through the `values` array and passes each element to the `push_back()` function for the list. Of course, you could also use a `for each` loop for this:

```
for each(double value in values)
  data->push_back(value);
```

You could also have initialized the list container with the contents of the `values` array:

```
list<double>^ data = gcnew list<double>(values);
```

Once the elements have been inserted into the list, and the list contents have been written to the standard output stream, you sort the contents of the list using the `sort()` function that is defined in the `list<double>` class:

```
data->sort(greater<double>());
```

The `sort()` function will use the default function object, `less<double>()`, to sort the list, unless you specify an alternative function object as the argument to the function. Here you specify `greater<double>()` as the function object to be used, sorting the contents of the list in descending sequence. Finally, you output the contents of the list to confirm that the sort does work as it should.

Using Associative Containers

All the associative containers in STL/CLR work in essentially the same way as the equivalent native STL containers, but there are some important small differences, generally to do with how pairs are represented.

First, the type of an element that you store in a map of type

```
map<K, T>
```

in native STL is of type `pair<K, T>`, but in an STL/CLR map container it is of type `map<K,T>::value_type`, which is a value type. This implies that you can no longer use the `make_pair()`

function to create a map entry in STL/CLR. Instead you use the static `make_value()` function that is defined in the `map<K, T>` class.

Second, the `insert()` function that inserts a single element in a `map<K, T>`, returns a value of type `pair<map<K, T>::iterator, bool>` for a native STL container, whereas for an STL/CLR `map<K, T>` container, the `insert()` function returns an object of type

```
map<K, T>::pair_iter_bool
```

which is a reference type. An object of type `map<K, T>::pair_iter_bool` has two public fields, `first` and `second`. `first` is a handle to an iterator of type

```
map<K, T>::iterator^
```

and second is of type `bool`. If `second` has the value `true`, then `first` points to the newly inserted element; otherwise it points to an element that already exists in the map with the same key.

I'll take one example to illustrate how associative containers in the STL/CLR work, and reproduce `Ex10_11` as a C++/CLI program.

TRY IT OUT   **Implementing a Phone Book Using a Map**

This example works in more or less the same way as the native STL example you saw earlier, `Ex10_11`. First, you must define a suitable version of the `ref` class `Person` that will represent keys in the map:

```cpp
// Person.h
// A class defining a person
#pragma once
using namespace System;

ref class Person
{
public:
 Person():firstname(L""), secondname(L""){}

 Person(String^ first, String^ second):
                firstname(first), secondname(second) {}

  // Destructor
  ~Person(){}

  // Less-than operator
  bool operator<(Person^ p)
  {
    if(String::Compare(secondname, p->secondname) < 0 ||
       (String::Compare(secondname, p->secondname)== 0 &&
        String::Compare(firstname, p->firstname) < 0))
      return true;
    return false;
  }

  // String representation of a person
```

```
      virtual String^ ToString() override
      {
        return firstname + L" " + secondname;
      }

  private:
    String^ firstname;
    String^ secondname;
  };
```

The `operator<()` member is essential because you will use `Person` objects as keys in the map, and to store a key/object pair, the map has to be able to compare keys.

Here is the content of `Ex10_19.cpp`, including the same helper functions as the native STL version:

```
// Ex10_19.cpp
// Storing phone numbers in a map
#include "stdafx.h"
#include "Person.h"
#include <cliext/map>

using namespace System;
using namespace cliext;

// Read a person from standard input
Person^ getPerson()
{
  String^ first;
  String^ second;
  Console::Write(L"Enter a first name: ") ;
  first = Console::ReadLine();
  Console::Write(L"Enter a second name: ") ;
  second = Console::ReadLine();
  return gcnew Person(first->Trim(), second->Trim());
}

// Add a new entry to a phone book
void addEntry(map<Person^, String^>^ book)
{
  map<Person^, String^>::value_type entry;        // Stores a phone book entry
  String^ number;
  Person^ person = getPerson();

  Console::Write(L"Enter the phone number for {0}: ", person);
  number = Console::ReadLine()->Trim();

  entry = book->make_value(person, number);
  map<Person^,String^>::pair_iter_bool pr = book->insert(entry);
    if(pr.second)
      Console::WriteLine(L"Entry successful.");
    else
      Console::WriteLine(L"Entry exists for {0}. The number is {1}",
                                    person, pr.first->second);
```

```
  }

  // List the contents of a phone book
  void listEntries(map<Person^, String^>^ book)
  {
    if(book->empty())
    {
      Console::WriteLine(L"The phone book is empty.");
      return;
    }
    map<Person^, String^>::iterator iter;
    for(iter = book->begin() ; iter != book->end() ; iter++)
      Console::WriteLine(L"{0, -30}{1,-12}",
                         iter->first, iter->second);
  }

  // Retrieve an entry from a phone book
  void getEntry(map<Person^, String^>^ book)
  {
    Person^ person = getPerson();
    map<Person^, String^>::const_iterator iter = book->find(person);
    if(book->end() == iter)
      Console::WriteLine(L"No entry found for {0}", person);
    else
      Console::WriteLine(L"The number for {0} is {1}",
                                          person, iter->second);
  }

  // Delete an entry from a phone book
  void deleteEntry(map<Person^, String^>^ book)
  {
    Person^ person = getPerson();
    map<Person^, String^>::iterator iter = book->find(person);

    if(book->end() == iter)
      Console::WriteLine(L"No entry found for {0}", person);
    else
    {
      book->erase(iter);
      Console::WriteLine(L"{0} erased.", person);
    }
  }

  int main(array<System::String ^> ^args)
  {
    map<Person^, String^>^ phonebook = gcnew map<Person^, String^>();
    String^ answer;

    while(true)
    {
      Console::Write(L"Do you want to enter a phone book entry(Y or N): ") ;
      answer = Console::ReadLine()->Trim();
      if(Char::ToUpper(answer[0]) == L'N')
        break;
      addEntry(phonebook);
```

```
    }

    // Query the phonebook
    while(true)
    {
      Console::WriteLine(L"\nChoose from the following options:");
      Console::WriteLine(L"A  Add an entry    D Delete an entry   G  Get an entry");
      Console::WriteLine(L"L  List entries    Q  Quit");

      // Check for an empty line being entered
      while(true)
      {
        answer = Console::ReadLine()->Trim();
        if(answer->Length)
          break;
        Console::WriteLine(L"\nYou must enter something - try again.");
      }

      switch(Char::ToUpper(answer[0]))
      {
        case L'A':
          addEntry(phonebook);
          break;
        case L'G':
          getEntry(phonebook);
          break;
        case L'D':
          deleteEntry(phonebook);
          break;
        case L'L':
          listEntries(phonebook);
          break;
        case L'Q':
          return 0;
        default:
          Console::WriteLine(L"Invalid selection. Try again.");
          break;
      }
    }

    return 0;
}
```

code snippet Ex10_19.cpp

Here's a sample of output from this example:

```
Do you want to enter a phone book entry(Y or N): y
Enter a first name: Jack
Enter a second name: Bateman
Enter the phone number for Jack Bateman: 312 455 6576
Entry successful.
Do you want to enter a phone book entry(Y or N): y
Enter a first name: Mary
Enter a second name: Jones
```

```
Enter the phone number for Mary Jones: 213 443 5671
Entry successful.
Do you want to enter a phone book entry(Y or N): y
Enter a first name: Jane
Enter a second name: Junket
Enter the phone number for Jane Junket: 413 222 8134
Entry successful.
Do you want to enter a phone book entry(Y or N): n

Choose from the following options:
A  Add an entry   D Delete an entry   G  Get an entry
L  List entries   Q  Quit
a
Enter a first name: Bill
Enter a second name: Smith
Enter the phone number for Bill Smith: 213 466 7688
Entry successful.

Choose from the following options:
A  Add an entry   D Delete an entry   G  Get an entry
L  List entries   Q  Quit
g
Enter a first name: Mary
Enter a second name: Miller
No entry found for Mary Miller

Choose from the following options:
A  Add an entry   D Delete an entry   G  Get an entry
L  List entries   Q  Quit
g
Enter a first name: Mary
Enter a second name: Jones
The number for Mary Jones is 213 443 5671

Choose from the following options:
A  Add an entry   D Delete an entry   G  Get an entry
L  List entries   Q  Quit
d
Enter a first name: Mary
Enter a second name: Jones
Mary Jones erased.

Choose from the following options:
A  Add an entry   D Delete an entry   G  Get an entry
L  List entries   Q  Quit
L
Jack Bateman              312 455 6576
Jane Junket               413 222 8134
Bill Smith                213 466 7688

Choose from the following options:
A  Add an entry   D Delete an entry   G  Get an entry
L  List entries   Q  Quit
q
```

How It Works

The first action in `main()` is to define a suitable map object:

```
map<Person^, String^>^ phonebook = gcnew map<Person^, String^>();
```

This map stores an object that combines a handle to a `Person` object as the key, and a handle to a `String` object as the associated object. Because this is an STL/CLR map, elements in the map are of type `map<Person^, String^>::value_type`; for a native STL map the elements would typically be of type `pair<Person, string>`.

Next, you define somewhere to store an input response:

```
String^ answer;
```

The `Console::ReadLine()` function that you will use to obtain input from the standard input stream always reads a line of input as a `String` object, so it's convenient to store a response as type `String^`.

Within the `while` loop that loads the map with new entries, you obtain a response to the first prompt like this:

```
answer = Console::ReadLine()->Trim();
```

The `Console::ReadLine()` call reads a line of input as a `String` object, and you call the `Trim()` function for the object returned to eliminate leading and trailing spaces. The result is stored in `answer` and the first character will be the input response.

You check for `L'n'` or `L'N'` being entered as the response, like this:

```
if(Char::ToUpper(answer[0]) == L'N')
  break;
```

This uses the `ToUpper()` function in the `Char` class to convert the first character in `answer` to uppercase before comparing it to `L'N'`. If the response is negative, you exit the loop. As it is coded, entering *any* response other than `L'n'` or `L'N'` is interpreted as `L'Y'`. To remove this anomaly, you could add this `if` statement following the one above:

```
if(Char::ToUpper(answer[0]) != L'Y')
{
  Console::WriteLine(L"'{0}' response is not valid. Try again.", answer[0]);
  continue;
}
```

With this amendment, you output a message and go to the next iteration, if an invalid response is entered.

If the response in `answer` is not in the negative, you call the `addEntry()` helper function to add a new entry to the map. The first statement in `addEntry()` defines a variable you will use to store a new map entry:

```
map<Person^, String^>::value_type entry;        // Stores a phone book entry
```

The `value_type` type is defined in the `map<K,T>` template and is the equivalent of a pair in native STL.

You obtain a handle to a new `Person` object by calling the `getPerson()` helper function. This uses `Console::ReadLine()` to read the names, and creates the `Person` object on the CLR heap. The phone number corresponding to the `Person` object is read in the `addEntry()` function, and you call the `make_value()` function for the map, with `person` and `number` as arguments, to create the new map entry. You insert the new entry using this statement:

```
map<Person^,String^>::pair_iter_bool pr = book->insert(entry);
```

The `insert()` function returns an object of type `pair_iter_bool`, which is similar to the pair object returned by the native STL version of the function. The `first` field in the `pr` object is a handle to an iterator, and the `second` field is a `bool` value that indicates whether or not the insert operation was successful. You use the `second` field in `pr` to output a suitable message, depending on how effective the insert operation was.

When the input loop ends, you prompt for operations on the map using a switch, as in the native version of the program. All the code for these operations is very similar to that in the native version. Note that the output in the `listEntries()` function could be coded like this:

```
for each(auto entry in book)
    Console::WriteLine(L"{0, -30}{1,-12}", entry->first, entry->second);
```

This iterates over all the entries in the map using a `for each` loop. You access the key and object in each entry via the `first` and `second` fields.

LAMBDA EXPRESSIONS IN C++/CLI

You can use lambda expression in your C++/CLI programs and with STL/CLR. There is one restriction, though. You cannot capture C++/CLI managed types, only standard C++ fundamental and class types. You, however, can specify a lambda parameter as a managed type, so you still have the potential for accessing variables of managed types in the enclosing scope from within the body of a lambda. Apart from this one exception, lambda expressions work exactly the same in C++/CLI code as they do with native C++.

SUMMARY

This chapter introduced the capabilities of the STL in native C++ and demonstrated how the same facilities are provided by STL/CLR for use in your C++/CLI programs.

My objective in this chapter was to introduce enough of the details of the STL and STL/CLR to enable you to explore the rest on your own. There's a great deal more there than I've been able to discuss here, so I encourage you to browse the documentation.

1. Write a native C++ program that will read some text from the standard input stream, possibly involving several lines of input, and store the letters from the text in a `list<T>` container. Sort the letters in ascending sequence and output them.

2. Use a `priority_queue<T>` container from the native STL to achieve the same result as in Exercise 1.

3. Implement Exercise 2 as a C++/CLI program.

4. Modify `Ex10_11.cpp` so that it allows multiple phone numbers to be stored for a given name. The functionality in the program should reflect this: the `getEntry()` function should display all numbers for a given name, and the `deleteEntry()` function should delete a particular person/number combination.

5. Modify `Ex10_19.cpp` to use an STL/CLR multimap to support multiple phone numbers for a person in the phone book.

6. Write a native C++ program to implement a phone book capability that will allow a name to be entered to retrieve one or more numbers, or a number to be entered to retrieve a name.

7. Implement the previous exercise solution as a C++/CLI program.

8. The Fibonacci series is an interesting sequence of integers that appears frequently in the natural world. You can see it in the way leaves and branches are arranged around the stems of plants, in the spirals on pine cones, and in the appearance of some seashells. It consists of the sequence of integers 0, 1, 1, 2, 3, 5, 8, 13, 21, ... where each integer after the first two is the sum of the two preceding integers (note the series sometimes omits the initial zero). Write a native C++ program that uses a lambda expression to initialize a vector of integers with values from the Fibonacci series.

▶ WHAT YOU LEARNED IN THIS CHAPTER

TOPIC	CONCEPT
Standard Template Libraries	The STL and STL/CLR capabilities include templates for containers, iterators, algorithms, and function objects.
Containers	A container is a class object for storing and organizing other objects. Sequence containers store objects in a sequence, like an array. Associative containers store elements that are key/object pairs, where the key determines where the pair is stored in the container.
Iterators	Iterators are objects that behave like pointers. Iterators are used in pairs to define a set of objects by a semi-open interval, where the first iterator points to the first object in the series, and the second iterator points to a position one past the last object in the series.
Stream iterators	Stream iterators are iterators that allow you to access or modify the contents of a stream.
Iterator categories	There are four categories of iterators: input and output iterators, forward iterators, bidirectional iterators, and random access iterators. Each successive category of iterator provides more functionality than the previous one; thus, input and output iterators provide the least functionality, and random access iterators provide the most.
Algorithms	Algorithms are template functions that operate on a sequence of objects specified by a pair of iterators.
Function objects	Function objects are objects of a type that overloads the `()` operator (by implementing the function `operator()()` in the class). The STL and STL/CLR define a wide range of standard function objects for use with containers and algorithms; you can also write your own classes to define function objects.
Lambda expressions	A lambda expression defines an anonymous function object without the need to explicitly define a class type. You can use a lambda expression as an argument to STL algorithms that expect a function object as an argument.
Polymorphic function wrappers	A polymorphic function wrapper is an instance of the `function<>` template that you can use to wrap a function object. You can also use a polymorphic function wrapper to wrap a lambda expression.

11

Debugging Techniques

WHAT YOU WILL LEARN IN THIS CHAPTER:

➤ How to run your program under the control of the Visual C++ 2010 debugger

➤ How to step through your program a statement at a time

➤ How to monitor or change the values of variables in your programs

➤ How to monitor the value of an expression in your program

➤ The call stack

➤ Assertions and how to use them to check your code

➤ How to add debugging specific code to a program

➤ How to detect memory leaks in a native C++ program

➤ How to use the execution tracing facilities and generate debugging output in C++/CLI programs

If you have been doing the exercises in the previous chapters, you have most likely been battling with bugs in your code. In this chapter you will explore how the basic debugging capabilities built into Visual C++ 2010 can help with this. You will also investigate some additional tools that you can use to find and eliminate errors from your programs, and see some of the ways in which you can equip your programs with specific code to check for errors.

UNDERSTANDING DEBUGGING

Bugs are errors in your program, and **debugging** is the process of finding and eliminating them. You are undoubtedly aware by now that debugging is an integral part of the programming process — it goes with the territory, as they say. The facts about bugs in your programs are rather depressing:

➤ Every program you write that is more than trivial will contain bugs that you need to try to expose, find, and eliminate if your program is to be reliable and effective. Note the three phases here — a program bug is not necessarily apparent; even when it is apparent you may not know where it is in your source code; and even when you know roughly where it is, it may not be easy to determine what exactly is causing the problem, and thus eliminate it.

➤ Many programs that you write will contain bugs even after you think you have fully tested them.

➤ Program bugs can remain hidden in a program that is apparently operating correctly — sometimes for years. They generally become apparent at the most inconvenient moments.

➤ Programs beyond a certain size and complexity always contain bugs, no matter how much time and effort you expend testing them. (The measure of size and complexity that guarantees the presence of bugs is not precisely defined, but Visual C++ 2010 and your operating system certainly are in this category!)

It is unwise to dwell on this last point if you are of a nervous disposition, especially if you fly a lot, or are regularly in the vicinity of any process, dependent on computers for proper operation, that can be damaging to your health in the event of failure.

Many potential bugs are eliminated during the compile and link phases, but there are still quite a few left even after you manage to produce an executable module for your program. Unfortunately, despite the fact that program bugs are as inevitable as death and taxes, debugging is not an exact science; however, you can still adopt a structured approach to eliminating bugs. There are four broad strategies you can adopt to make debugging as painless as possible:

➤ Don't re-invent the wheel. Understand and use the library facilities provided as part of Visual C++ 2010 (or other commercial software components you have access to) so that your program uses as much pre-tested code as possible. Note that while this will reduce the likelihood of bugs in your code, libraries, operating systems, and commercial software, components will still contain bugs in general, so your code can share those bugs.

➤ Develop and test your code incrementally. By testing each significant class and function individually, and gradually assembling separate code components after testing them, you can make the development process much easier, with fewer obscure bugs occurring along the way.

➤ Code defensively — which means writing code to guard against potential errors. For example, declare member functions of native C++ classes that don't modify an object as const. Use const parameters where appropriate. Don't use "magic numbers" in your code — define const objects with the required values.

➤ Include debugging code that checks and validates data and conditions in your program from the outset. This is something you will look at in detail later in this chapter.

Because of the importance of ending up with programs that are as bug-free as is humanly possible, Visual C++ 2010 provides you with a powerful armory of tools for finding bugs. Before you get into the detailed mechanics, however, let's look a little closer at how bugs arise.

Program Bugs

Of course, the primary originator of bugs in your program is you and the mistakes you make. These mistakes range from simple typos — just pressing the wrong key — to getting the logic completely wrong. I, too, find it hard to believe that I can make such silly mistakes so often, but no one has yet managed to come up with a credible alternative as to how bugs get into your code — so it must be true! Humans are creatures of habit so you will probably find yourself making some mistakes time and time again. Frustratingly, many errors are glaringly obvious to others, but invisible to you — this is just your computer's way of teaching you a bit of humility. Broadly, there are two kinds of errors you can make in your code that result in program bugs:

➤ **Syntactic errors** — These are errors that result from statements that are not of the correct form; for example, if you miss a semicolon from the end of a statement or use a colon where you should put a comma. You don't have to worry too much about syntactic errors. The compiler recognizes all syntactic errors, and you generally get a fairly good indication of what the error is so it's easy to fix.

➤ **Semantic errors** — These are errors where the code is syntactically correct, but it does not do what you intended. The compiler cannot know what you intended to achieve with your program, so it cannot detect semantic errors; however, you will often get an indication that something is wrong because the program terminates abnormally. The debugging facilities in Visual C++ 2010 are aimed at helping you find semantic errors. Semantic errors can be very subtle and difficult to find, for example, where the program occasionally produces the wrong results or crashes now and again. Perhaps the most difficult of such bugs arise in multi-threaded programs where concurrent paths of execution are not managed properly.

Of course, there are bugs in the system environment that you are using (Visual C++ 2010 included) but this should be the last place you suspect when your program doesn't work. Even when you do conclude that it *must* be the compiler or the operating system, nine times out of ten you will be wrong. There are certainly bugs in Visual C++ 2010, however, and if you want to keep up with those identified to date, together with any fixes available, you can search the information provided on the Microsoft Web site related to Visual C++ (`http://msdn2.microsoft.com/en-us/visualc/default.aspx`), or better still, if you can afford a subscription to Microsoft Developer Network, you get quarterly updates on the latest bugs and fixes.

It can be helpful to make a checklist of bugs you find in your code for future reference. By examining new code that you write for the kinds of errors you have made in the past, you can often reduce the time needed to debug new projects.

By the nature of programming, bugs are virtually infinite in their variety, but there are some kinds that are particularly common. You may be well aware of most of these, but take a quick look at them anyway.

Common Bugs

A useful way of cataloguing bugs is to relate them to the symptoms they cause because this is how you experience them in the first instance. The following list of five common symptoms is by no means exhaustive, and you are certainly able to add to it as you gain programming experience:

SYMPTOM	POSSIBLE CAUSES
Data corrupted	Failure to initialize variable.
	Exceeding integer type range.
	Invalid pointer.
	Error in array index expression.
	Loop condition error.
	Error in size of dynamically allocated array.
	Failing to implement class copy constructor, assignment operator, or destructor.
Unhandled exceptions	Invalid pointer or reference.
	Missing catch handler.
Program hangs or crashes	Failure to initialize variable.
	Infinite loop.
	Invalid pointer.
	Freeing the same free store memory twice.
	Failure to implement, or error in, class destructor.
	Failure to process unexpected user input properly.
Stream input data incorrect	Reading using the extraction operator and the `getline()` function.
Incorrect results	Typographical error: = instead of ==, or i instead of j, etc.
	Failure to initialize a variable.
	Exceeding the range of an integer type.
	Invalid pointer.
	Omitting break in a switch statement.

Look at how many different kinds of errors can be caused by invalid pointers and the myriad symptoms that bad pointers can generate. This is possibly the most frequent cause of those bugs that are hard to find, so always double-check your pointer operations. If you are conscious of the ways in which bad pointers arise, you can avoid many of the pitfalls. The common ways in which bad pointers arise are:

➤ Failing to initialize a pointer when you declare it

➤ Failing to set a pointer to free store memory to null when you delete the space allocated

➤ Returning the address of a local variable from a function

➤ Failing to implement the copy constructor and assignment operator for classes that allocate free store memory

Even if you do all this, there will still be bugs in your code, so now look at the tools that Visual C++ 2010 provides to assist debugging.

BASIC DEBUGGING OPERATIONS

So far, although you have been creating debug versions of the program examples, you haven't been using the **debugger**. The debugger is a program that controls the execution of your program in such a way that you can step through the source code one line at a time, or run to a particular point in the program. At each point in your code where the debugger stops, you can inspect or even change the values of variables before continuing. You can also change the source code, recompile, and then restart the program from the beginning. You can even change the source code in the middle of stepping through a program. When you move to the next step after modifying the code, the debugger automatically recompiles before executing the next statement.

To understand the basic debug capabilities of Visual C++ 2010, you will use the debugger on a program that you are reasonably sure works. You can then just pull the levers to see how things operate. Take a simple example from back in Chapter 4 that uses pointers:

```
// Ex4_05.cpp
// Exercising pointers
#include <iostream>
using namespace std;

int main()
{
  long* pnumber(nullptr);              // Pointer declaration & initialization
  long number1 = 55, number2 = 99;

  pnumber = &number1;                   // Store address in pointer
  *pnumber += 11;                       // Increment number1 by 11
  cout << endl
       << "number1 = " << number1
       << "   &number1 = " << hex << pnumber;

  pnumber = &number2;                   // Change pointer to address of number2
  number1 = *pnumber*10;                // 10 times number2

  cout << endl
       << "number1 = " << dec << number1
       << "   pnumber = " << hex << pnumber
```

```
          << "    *pnumber = " << dec << *pnumber;

   cout << endl;
   return 0;
}
```

code snippet Ex4_05.cpp

If you still have this example on your system, just open the project; otherwise, you need to download the code or enter it again.

When you write a program that doesn't behave as it should, the debugger enables you to work through a program one step at a time to find out where and how it's going wrong, and to inspect the state of your program's data at any time during execution. You'll execute this example one statement at a time and to monitor the contents of the variables that interest you. In this case you want to look at pnumber, the contents of the location pointed to by pnumber (which is *pnumber), number1, and number2.

First you need to be sure that the build configuration for the example is set to Win32 Debug rather than Win32 Release (Win32 Debug is the default, unless you've changed it). The build configuration selects the set of project settings for the build operation on your program that you can see when you select the Project/Settings menu option. The current build configuration in effect is shown in the pair of adjacent drop-down lists on the Standard toolbar. To display or remove a particular toolbar you just right-click the toolbar and select or deselect a toolbar in the list. Make sure you check the box against Debug to display the debugging toolbar. It comes up automatically when the debugger is operating, but you should take a look at what it contains before you start the debugger. You can change the build configuration by extending the drop-down list and choosing the alternative. You can also use the Build ⇨ Configuration Manager . . . menu option.

You can find out what the toolbar buttons are for by letting the mouse cursor linger over a toolbar button. A tool tip for that button appears that identifies its function.

The Debug configuration in a project causes additional information to be included in your executable program when you compile it so that the debugging facilities can be used. This extra information is stored in the .pdb file that will be in the Debug folder for your project. With the Professional version of Visual C++ 2010, the compiler also optimizes the code when compiling the release version of a program. Optimization is inhibited when the debug version is compiled because the optimization process can involve resequencing code to make it more efficient, or even omitting redundant code altogether. Because this destroys the one-to-one mapping between the source code and corresponding blocks of machine code, optimization makes stepping through a program potentially confusing, to say the least.

If you inspect the tooltips for the buttons on the Debug toolbar, you'll get a preliminary idea of what they do — you will use some of them shortly. With the example from Chapter 4, you won't use all the debugging facilities available to you, but you will try out some of the more important features. After you are familiar with stepping through a program using the debugger, you will explore more of the features with a program that has bugs.

You can start the debugger by clicking the leftmost button on the Debug toolbar, by selecting the Debug ⇨ Start Debugging menu item, or by pressing F5. I suggest that you use the toolbar for the example. The debugger has two primary modes of operation — it works through the code by single stepping (which is essentially executing one statement at a time), or runs to a particular point in the source code. The point in the source where the debugger is to stop is determined either by where you have placed the cursor or, more usefully, at a designated stopping point called a **breakpoint**. Let's look at how you define breakpoints.

Setting Breakpoints

A **breakpoint** is a point in your program where the debugger automatically suspends execution when in debugging mode. You can specify multiple breakpoints so that you can run your program, stopping at points of interest that you select along the way. At each breakpoint you can look at variables within the program and change them if they don't have the values they should. You are going to execute the Ex4_05 program one statement at a time, but with a large program this would be impractical. Usually, you will only want to look at a particular area of the program where you think there might be an error. Consequently, you would usually set breakpoints where you think the error is, and run the program so that it halts at the first breakpoint. You can then single step from that point if you want, where a single step implies executing a single source code statement.

To set a breakpoint at the beginning of a line of source code, you simply click in the grayed-out column to the left of the line for the statement where you want execution to stop. A red circular symbol called a **glyph** appears showing the presence of the breakpoint at that line. You can remove a breakpoint by clicking the glyph. Figure 11-1 shows the Editor pane with a couple of breakpoints set for Ex4_05.

```cpp
Ex4_05.cpp
(Global Scope)                                        main()
 1  // Ex4_05.cpp
 2  // Exercising pointers
 3  #include <iostream>
 4  using namespace std;
 5
 6  int main()
 7  {
 8    long* pnumber(nullptr);              // Pointer declaration & initialization
 9    long number1(55), number2(99);
10
11    pnumber = &number1;                  // Store address in pointer
12    *pnumber += 11;                      // Increment number1 by 11
13    cout << endl
14        << "number1 = " << number1
15        << "   &number1 = " << hex << pnumber;
16
17    pnumber = &number2;                  // Change pointer to address of number2
18    number1 = *pnumber*10;               // 10 times number2
19
20    cout << endl
21        << "number1 = " << dec << number1
22        << "   pnumber = " << hex << pnumber
23        << "   *pnumber = " << dec << *pnumber;
24
25    cout << endl;
26    return 0;
27  }
28
100 %
```

FIGURE 11-1

When debugging, you would normally set several breakpoints, each chosen to show when the variables that you think are causing a problem are changing. Execution stops *before* the statement indicated by the breakpoint is executed. Execution of the program can only break before a complete statement and not halfway through it. If you place a cursor in a line that doesn't contain any code (for example, the line above the second breakpoint in Figure 11-1), the breakpoint is set on that line, and the program stops at the beginning of the next executable line.

As I said, you can remove a breakpoint by clicking the red dot. You can also disable a breakpoint by right-clicking the line containing the breakpoint and selecting from the pop-up. You can remove all the breakpoints in the active project by selecting the Debug ⇨ Delete All Breakpoints menu item or by pressing Ctrl+Shift+F9. Note that this removes breakpoints from all files in the project, even if they're not currently open in the Editor pane. You can also disable all breakpoints by selecting the Debug ⇨ Disable All Breakpoints menu item.

Advanced Breakpoints

A more advanced way of specifying breakpoints is provided through a window you can display by pressing Alt+F9 or by selecting Breakpoints from the list displayed when you select the Windows button on the Debug toolbar — it's at the right end. This window is shown in Figure 11-2.

FIGURE 11-2

The Columns button on the toolbar enables you to add more columns to be displayed in the window. For example, you can display the source file name or the function name where the breakpoint is, or you can display what happens when the statement is reached.

You can set further options for a breakpoint by right-clicking the breakpoint line in the Breakpoints window and selecting from the pop-up. As well as setting a breakpoint at a location other than the beginning of a statement, you can set a breakpoint when a particular Boolean expression evaluates to true. This is a powerful tool but it does introduce very substantial overhead in a program, as the expression needs to be re-evaluated continuously. Consequently, execution is slow, even on the fastest machines. You can also set things up so that execution only breaks when the hit count, which is the number of times the breakpoint has been reached, reaches a given value. This is most useful for code inside a loop where you won't want to break execution on every iteration. If you set any condition on a breakpoint, the glyph changes so that a + appears in the center.

Setting Tracepoints

A **tracepoint** is a special kind of breakpoint that has a custom action associated with it. You create a tracepoint by right-clicking the line of code where you want the tracepoint to be set and selecting the Breakpoint ⇨ Insert Tracepoint menu item from the pop-up. Try this with line 17 of the program. You'll see the dialog window shown in Figure 11-3.

As you see, the tracepoint action can be to print a message and/or run a macro, and you can choose whether execution stops or continues at the tracepoint. The presence of a tracepoint on a source code line where execution does not stop is indicated by a red diamond-shaped glyph. The dialog text explains how to specify the message to be printed. For instance, you could print the name of the current function and the value of `pnumber` by specifying the following in the text box:

FIGURE 11-3

```
$FUNCTION, The value of pnumber is {pnumber}
```

The output produced by this when the tracepoint is reached is displayed in the Output pane in the Visual Studio application window.

When you check the `Run a macro:` checkbox, you'll be able to choose from a long list of standard macros that are available.

Starting Debugging

There are five ways of starting your application in debug mode from the options on the Debug menu, as shown in Figure 11-4:

1. The Start Debugging option (also available from a button on the Debug toolbar) simply executes a program up to the first breakpoint (if any) where execution will halt. After you've examined all you need to at a breakpoint, selecting the same menu item or toolbar button again will continue execution up to the next breakpoint. In this way, you can move through a program from breakpoint to breakpoint, and at each halt in execution have a look at critical variables, changing their values if you need to. If there are no breakpoints, starting the debugger in this way executes the entire program without stopping. Of course, just

FIGURE 11-4

because you started debugging in this way doesn't mean that you have to continue using it; at each halt in execution, you can choose any of the possible ways of moving through your code.

2.   The Attach to Process option on the Debug menu enables you to debug a program that is already running. This option displays a list of the processes that are running on your machine and you can select the process you want to debug. This is really for advanced users and you should avoid experimenting with it unless you are quite certain that you know what you are doing. You can easily lock up your machine or cause other problems if you interfere with critical operating system processes.

3.   The Step Into menu item (also available as a button on the Debug toolbar) executes your program one statement at a time, stepping into every code block — which includes every function that is called. This would be something of a nuisance if you used it throughout the debugging process because, for example, it would also execute all the code in the library functions for stream output — you're not really interested in this as you didn't write these routines. Quite a few of the library functions are written in Assembler language — including some of those supporting stream input/output. Assembler language functions execute one machine instruction at a time, which can be rather time consuming, as you might imagine.

4.   The Step Over menu item (also available as a button on the Debug toolbar) simply executes the statements in your program one at a time and runs all the code used by functions that might be called within a statement, such as stream operations, without stopping.

You have a sixth option for starting in debug mode that does not appear on the Debug menu. You can right-click any line of code and select Run to Cursor from the Context menu. This does precisely what it says — it runs the program up to the line where the cursor is and then breaks execution to allow you to inspect or change variables in the program. Whatever way you choose to start the debugging process, you can continue execution using any of the five options you have available from any intermediate breakpoint.

It's time to try it with the example. Start the program using the Step Into option, click the appropriate menu item or toolbar button, or press F11 to begin. After a short pause (assuming that you've already built the project), Visual C++ 2010 switches to debugging mode.

When the debugger starts, two tabbed windows appear below the Editor window. You can choose what is displayed at any time in either window by selecting one of the tabs. You can choose which windows appear when the debugger is started, and they can be customized. The complete list of windows is shown on the Debug ⇨ Windows menu drop-down. The Autos window that you can display by selecting from the menu shows current values for automatic variables in the context of the function that is currently executing. The Call Stack window on the right identifies the function calls currently in progress, but the Output tab in the same window is probably more interesting in this example. In the Editor pane, you'll see that the opening brace of your `main()` function is highlighted by an arrow to indicate that this is the current point in the program's execution. This is shown in Figure 11-5.

FIGURE 11-5

You can also see the breakpoint at line 11 and the tracepoint at line 17. At this point in the execution of the program, you can't choose any variables to look at because none exist at present. Until a declaration of a variable has been executed, you cannot look at its value or change it.

To avoid having to step through all the code in the stream functions that deal with I/O, you'll use the Step Over facility to continue execution to the next line. This simply executes the statements in your main() function one at a time, and runs all the code used by the stream operations (or any other functions that might be called within a statement) without stopping.

Inspecting Variable Values

Defining a variable that you want to inspect is referred to as **setting a watch** for the variable. Before you can set any watches, you must get some variables declared in the program. You can execute the declaration statements by invoking Step Over three times. Use the Step Over menu item, the toolbar icon, or press F10 three times so that the arrow now appears at the start of the line 11:

```
pnumber = &number1;                // Store address in pointer
```

If you look at the Autos window now, it should appear as shown in Figure 11-6 (although the value for &number1 may be different on your system as it represents a memory location). Note that the values for &number1 and pnumber are not equal to each other because the line in which pnumber is set to the address of number1 (the line that the arrow is pointing at) hasn't yet been executed. You initialized pnumber as a **null pointer** in the first line of the function, which is why the address it contains is zero. If you had not initialized the pointer, it would contain a junk value that still could be zero on occasion, of course, because it contains whatever value was left by the last program to use these particular four bytes of memory.

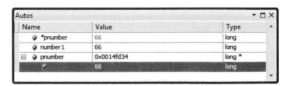

FIGURE 11-6

You can display the following five tabs in the bottom left window by selecting from the Debug ➪ Windows menu:

➤ The Autos tab shows the automatic variables in use in the current statement and its immediate predecessor (in other words, the statement pointed to by the arrow in the Editor pane and the one before it).

➤ The Locals tab shows the values of the variables local to the current function. In general, new variables come into scope as you trace through a program and then go out of scope as you exit the block in which they are defined. In this case, this window always shows values for `number1`, `number2` and `pnumber` because you have only one function, `main()`, consisting of a single code block.

➤ The Threads tab allows you to inspect and control threads in advanced applications.

➤ The Modules tab lists details of the code modules currently executing. If your application crashes, you can determine in which module the crash happened by comparing the address when the crash occurred with the range of addresses in the Address column on this tab.

➤ You can add variables to the Watch1 tab that you want to watch. Just click a line in the window and type the variable name. You can also watch the value of a C++ expression that you enter in the same way as a variable. You can add up to three additional Watch windows via the Debug ➪ Windows ➪ Watch menu item.

Notice that `pnumber` has a plus sign to the left of its name in the Autos window. A plus sign appears for any variable for which additional information can be displayed, such as for an array, or a pointer, or a class object. In this case, you can expand the view for the pointer variables by clicking the plus sign. If you press F10 twice more and click the + adjacent to `pnumber`, the debugger displays the value stored at the memory address contained in the pointer, as shown in Figure 11-7.

FIGURE 11-7

The Autos window automatically provides you with all the information you need, displaying both the memory address and the data value stored at that address. Integer values can be displayed as decimal or hexadecimal. To toggle between the two, right-click anywhere on the Autos tab and select from the pop-up menu. You can view the variables that are local to the current function by selecting the Locals tab. There are also other ways that you can inspect variables using the debugging facilities of Visual C++ 2010.

Viewing Variables in the Edit Window

If you need to look at the value of a single variable, and that variable is visible in the Text Editor window, the easiest way to look at its value is to position the cursor over the variable for a second. A tool tip pops up showing the current value of the variable. You can also look at more complicated expressions by highlighting them and resting the cursor over the highlighted area. Again, a tool tip pops up to display the value. Try highlighting the expression `*pnumber*10` a little lower down. Hovering the cursor over the highlighted expression results in the current value of the expression being displayed. Note that this won't work if the expression is not complete; if you miss the * that dereferences `pnumber` out of the highlighted text, for instance, or you just highlight `*pnumber*`, the value won't be displayed.

Changing the Value of a Variable

You can change the values of the variables you are watching in the Watch windows, and you can also change values in the Autos and Locals windows. You would use this in situations where a value displayed is clearly wrong, perhaps because there are bugs in your program, or maybe all the code is not there yet. If you set the "correct" value, your program staggers on so that you can test out more of it and perhaps pick up a few more bugs. If your code involves a loop with a large number of iterations, say, 30000, you could set the loop counter to 29995 to step through the last few to verify that the loop terminates correctly. It sure beats pressing F10 30,000 times! Another useful application of the ability to set values for variable during execution is to set values that cause errors. This enables you to check out the error handling code in your program, something almost impossible otherwise.

To change the value of a variable in a Watch window, double-click the variable value that is displayed, and type the new value. If the variable you want to change is an array element, you need to expand the array by clicking the + box alongside the array name and then changing the element value. To change the value for a variable displayed in hexadecimal notation, you can either enter a hexadecimal number, or enter a decimal value prefixed by 0n (zero followed by n), so you could enter a value as A9, or as 0n169. If you just enter 169 it is interpreted as a hexadecimal value. Naturally, you should be cautious about flinging new values into your program willy-nilly. Unless you are sure you know what effect your changes are going to have, you may end up with a certain amount of erratic program behavior, which is unlikely to get you closer to a working program.

You'll probably find it useful to run a few more of the examples you have seen in previous chapters in debug mode. It will enable you to get a good feel for how the debugger operates under various conditions. Monitoring variables and expressions is a considerable help in sorting out problems with your code, but there's a great deal more assistance available for seeking out and destroying bugs. Take a look at how you can add code to a program that provides more information about when and why things go wrong.

ADDING DEBUGGING CODE

For a program involving a significant amount of code, you certainly need to add code that is aimed at highlighting bugs wherever possible and providing tracking output to help you pin down where the bugs are. You don't want to be in the business of single stepping through code before you have any idea of what bugs there are, or which part of the code is involved. Code that does this sort of thing is only required while you are testing a program. You won't need it after you believe the program is fully working, and you won't want to carry the overhead of executing it or the inconvenience of seeing all the output in a finished product. For this reason, code that you add for debugging only operates in the debug version of a program, not in the release version (provided you implement it in the right way, of course).

The output produced by debug code should provide clues as to what is causing a problem, and if you have done a good job of building debug code into your program, it will give you a good idea of which part of your program is in error. You can then use the debugger to find the precise nature and location of the bug, and fix it.

The first way you can check the behavior of your program that you will look at is provided by a C++ library function.

Using Assertions

The standard library header `cassert` declares the `assert()` function that you can use to check logical conditions within your program when a special preprocessor symbol, `NDEBUG`, is not defined. The function is declared as:

```
void assert(int expression);
```

The argument to the function specifies the condition to be checked, but the effect of the `assert()` function is suppressed if a special preprocessor symbol, `NDEBUG`, is defined. The symbol `NDEBUG` is automatically defined in the release version of a program, but not in the debug version. Thus an assertion checks its argument in the debug version of a program but does nothing in a release version. If you want to switch off assertions in the debug version of a program, you can define `NDEBUG` explicitly yourself using a `#define` directive. For it to be effective, you must place the `#define` directive for `NDEBUG` preceding the `#include` directive for the `cassert` header in the source file:

```
#define NDEBUG                       // Switch off assertions in the code
#include <cassert>                   // Declares assert()
```

If the expression passed as an argument to `assert()` is non-zero (i.e. `true`), the function does nothing. If the expression is 0 (`false`, in other words) and `NDEBUG` are not defined, a diagnostic message is output showing the expression that failed, the source file name, and the line number in the source file where the failure occurred. After displaying the diagnostic message, the `assert()` function calls `abort()` to end the program. Here's an example of an assertion used in a function:

```
char* append(char* pStr, const char* pAddStr)
{
  // Verify non-null pointers
  assert(pStr != nullptr);
  assert(pAddStr != nullptr);

  // Code to append pAddStr to pStr...
}
```

Calling the `append()` function with a null pointer argument in a simple program produced the following diagnostic message on my machine:

```
Assertion failed: pStr != nullptr, file c:\beginning visual c++ 2010\examples
    visual studio project files\tryassertion\tryassertion\tryassertion.cpp, line 10
```

The assertion also displays a message box offering you the three options shown in Figure 11-8.

Clicking the Abort button ends the program immediately. The Retry button starts the Visual C++ 2010 debugger so you can step through the program to find out more about why the assertion failed. In principle, the Ignore button allows the program to continue in spite of the error, but this is usually an unwise choice as the results are likely to be unpredictable.

You can use any kind of logical expression as an argument to `assert()`. You can compare values, check pointers, validate object types, or whatever is a useful check on the correct operation of your code. Getting a message when some logical

FIGURE 11-8

condition fails helps a little, but in general you will need considerably more assistance than that to detect and fix bugs. Now take a look at how you can add diagnostic code of a more general nature.

Adding Your Own Debugging Code

Using preprocessor directives, you can add any code you like to your program so that it is only compiled and executed in the debug version. Your debug code is omitted completely from the release version, so it does not affect the efficiency of the tested program at all. You could use the absence of the `NDEBUG` symbol as the control mechanism for the inclusion of debugging code; that's the symbol used to control the `assert()` function operation in the standard library, as discussed in the last section. Alternatively, for a better and more positive control mechanism, you can use another preprocessor symbol, `_DEBUG`, that is always defined automatically in Visual C++ in the debug version of a program, but is not defined in the release version. You simply enclose code that you only want compiled and executed when you are debugging between a preprocessor `#ifdef/#endif` pair of directives, with the test applied to the `_DEBUG` symbol, as follows:

```
#ifdef _DEBUG

    // Code for debugging purposes...

#endif // _DEBUG
```

The code between the `#ifdef` and the `#endif` is compiled only if the symbol `_DEBUG` is defined. This means that once your code is fully tested, you can produce the release version completely free of any overhead from your debugging code. The debug code can do anything that is helpful to you in the debugging process, from simply outputting a message to trace the sequence of execution (each function might record that it was called for example) to providing additional calculations to verify and validate data, or calling functions providing debug output.

Of course, you can have as many blocks of debug code like this in a source file as you want. You also have the possibility of using your own preprocessor symbols to provide more selectivity as to what debug code is included. One reason for doing this is that some of your debug code may produce voluminous output, and you would only want to generate this when it was really necessary. Another is to provide granularity in your debug output, so you can pick and choose which output is produced on each run. But even in these instances it is still a good idea to use the _DEBUG symbol to provide overall control because this automatically ensures that the release version of a program is completely free of the overhead of debugging code.

Consider a simple case. Suppose you used two symbols of your own to control debug code: MYDEBUG that managed "normal" debugging code and VOLUMEDEBUG that you use to control code that produced a lot more output, and that you only wanted some of the time. The following directives will ensure that these symbols are defined only if _DEBUG is defined:

```
#ifdef _DEBUG

#define MYDEBUG
#define VOLUMEDEBUG

#endif
```

To prevent volume debugging output you just need to comment out the definition of VOLUMEDEBUG, and neither symbol is defined if _DEBUG is not defined. Where your program has several source files, you will probably find it convenient to place your debug control symbols together in a header file and then #include the header into each file that contains debugging code.

Examine a simple example to see how adding debugging code to a program might work in practice.

TRY IT OUT   **Adding Code for Debugging**

To explore these and some general debugging approaches, take an example of a program that, while simple, still contains quite a few bugs that you can find and eliminate. Thus you must regard all the code in the remainder of this chapter as suspect, particularly because it will not necessarily reflect good programming practice.

For experimenting with debugging operations, start by defining a class that represents a person's name and then proceed to test it in action. There is a lot wrong with this code, so resist the temptation to fix the obviously erroneous code here; the idea is to exercise the debugging operations to find them. However, in practice, a great many bugs are very evident as soon as you run a program. You don't necessarily need the debugger or additional code to spot them.

Create an empty Win32 console application, Ex11_01, and change the Character Set project property to Not Set. Next, add a header file, Name.h, to which you'll add the definition of the Name class. The class represents a name by two data members that are pointers to strings storing a person's first and second names. If you want to be able to declare arrays of Name objects you must provide a default constructor in addition to any other constructors. You want to be able to compare Name objects, so you should include overloaded operators in the class to do this. You also want to be able to retrieve the complete name as a single string for convenience. You can add a definition of the Name class to the Name.h file as follows:

```cpp
// Name.h - Definition of the Name class
#pragma once

// Class defining a person's name
class Name
{
public:
  Name();                                    // Default constructor
  Name(const char* pFirst, const char* pSecond); // Constructor

  char* getName(char* pName) const;          // Get the complete name
  size_t getNameLength() const;              // Get the complete name length

  // Comparison operators for names
  bool operator<(const Name& name) const;
  bool operator==(const Name& name) const;
  bool operator>(const Name& name) const;

private:
  char* pFirstname;
  char* pSurname;
};
```

code snippet Name.h

You can now add a `Name.cpp` file to the project to hold the definitions for the member functions of `Name`. The constructor definitions are shown here:

```cpp
// Name.cpp - Implementation of the Name class
#include "Name.h"           // Name class definitions
#include "DebugStuff.h"     // Debugging code control
#include <cstring>          // For C-style string functions
#include <cassert>          // For assertions
#include <iostream>
using namespace std;

// Default constructor
Name::Name()
{
#ifdef CONSTRUCTOR_TRACE
  // Trace constructor calls
  cerr << "\nDefault Name constructor called.";
#endif
  pFirstname = pSurname = "\0";
}

// Constructor
Name::Name(const char* pFirst, const char* pSecond):
                              pFirstname(pFirst), pSurname(pSecond)
{
  // Verify that arguments are not null
  assert(pFirst);
  assert(pSecond);
```

```
#ifdef CONSTRUCTOR_TRACE
  // Trace constructor calls
  cout << "\nName constructor called.";
#endif
}
```

code snippet Name.cpp

Of course, you don't particularly want to have Name objects that have null pointers as members, so the default constructor assigns empty strings for the names. You have used your own debug control symbol, CONSTRUCTOR_TRACE, to control output that traces constructor calls. You will add the definition of this symbol to the DebugStuff.h header a little later. You could put anything at all as debug code here, such as displaying argument values, but it is usually best to keep it as simple as your debugging requirements allow; otherwise, your debug code may introduce further bugs. Here you just identify the constructor when it is called.

You have two assertions in the constructor to check for null pointers being passed as arguments. You could have combined these into one, but by using a separate assertion for each argument, you can identify which pointer is null (unless they both are, of course).

You might also want to check that the strings are not empty in an application by counting the characters prior to the terminating '\0', for instance. However, you should not use an assertion to flag this. This sort of thing could arise as a result of user input, so ordinary program checking code should be added to deal with errors that may arise in the normal course of events. It is important to recognize the difference between bugs (errors in the code) and error conditions that can be expected to arise during normal operation of a program. The constructor should never be passed a null pointer, but a zero length name could easily arise under normal operating conditions (from keyboard input, for example). In this case it would probably be better if the code reading the names were to check for this before calling the Name class constructor. You want errors that arise during normal use of a program to be handled within the release version of the code.

The getName() function requires the caller to supply the address of an array that accommodates the name:

Available for
download on
Wrox.com

```
// Return a complete name as a string containing first name, space, surname
// The argument must be the address of a char array sufficient to hold the name
char* Name::getName(char* pName) const
{
    assert(pName);                                      // Verify non-null argument

#ifdef FUNCTION_TRACE
    // Trace function calls
    cout << '\n' << __FUNCTION__ << " called.";
#endif

    strcpy(pName, pFirstname);                          // copy first name
    pName[strlen(pName)] = ' ';                         // Append a space

    // Append second name and return total
    return strcpy(pName+strlen(pName)+1, pSurname);
}
```

code snippet Name.cpp

Here you have an assertion to check that the pointer argument passed is not null. Note that you have no way to check that the pointer is to an array with sufficient space to hold the entire name. You must rely on the calling function to do that. You also have debug code to trace when the function is called. This uses the `__FUNCTION__` preprocessor macro that is automatically replaced by the name of the function in which it appears. Note that the macro name has two underline characters at each end. Having a record of the complete sequence of calls up to the point where catastrophe strikes can sometimes provide valuable insights as to why and how the problem arose.

The `getNameLength()` member is a helper function that enables the user of a `Name` object to determine how much space must be allocated to accommodate a complete name:

```cpp
// Returns the total length of a name
size_t Name::getNameLength() const
{
#ifdef FUNCTION_TRACE
  // Trace function calls
  cout << '\n' << __FUNCTION__ << " called.";
#endif
  return strlen(pFirstname)+strlen(pSurname);
}
```

code snippet Name.cpp

A function that intends to call `getName()` is able use the value returned by `getNameLength()` to determine how much space is needed to accommodate a complete name. You also have trace code in this member function.

In the interests of developing the class incrementally, you can omit the definitions for the overloaded comparison operators. Definitions are only required for member functions that you actually use in your program, and in your initial test program you keep it very simple.

You can define the preprocessor symbols that control whether or not the debug code is executed in the `DebugStuff.h` header:

```cpp
// DebugStuff.h - Debugging control
#pragma once

#ifdef _DEBUG

#define CONSTRUCTOR_TRACE        // Output constructor call trace
#define FUNCTION_TRACE           // Trace function calls

#endif
```

code snippet DebugStuff.h

Your control symbols are defined only if `_DEBUG` is defined, so none of the debug code is included in a release version of the program.

You can now try out the `Name` class with the following `main()` function:

```cpp
// Ex11_01.cpp : Including debug code in a program

#include <iostream>
```

```
using namespace std;
#include "Name.h"

int main(int argc, char* argv[])
{
  Name myName("Ivor", "Horton");                    // Try a single object

  // Retrieve and store the name in a local char array
  char theName[10];
  cout << "\nThe name is " << myName.getName(theName);

  // Store the name in an array in the free store
  char* pName = new char[myName.getNameLength()];
  cout << "\nThe name is " << myName.getName(pName);

  cout << endl;
  return 0;
}
```

code snippet Ex11_01.cpp

Now that all the code has been entered, double-checked, and is completely correct, all you have to do is run it to make sure. Hardly seems necessary.

How It Works

Well, it doesn't — it doesn't even compile, does it? The major problem is the Name constructor. The parameters are const, as they should be, but the data members are not. You could declare the data members as const, but anyway, you should be copying the name strings, not just copying the pointers. Amend the constructor definition to:

```
// Constructor
Name::Name(const char* pFirst, const char* pSecond)
{
   // Verify that arguments are not null
   assert(pFirst);
   assert(pSecond);

#ifdef CONSTRUCTOR_TRACE
   // Trace constructor calls
   cout << "\nName constructor called.";
#endif
   pFirstname = new char[strlen(pFirst)+1];
   strcpy(pFirstname, pFirst);
   pFirstname = new char[strlen(pSecond)+1];
   strcpy(pSurname, pSecond);
}
```

Now you are copying the strings so you should be okay now, shouldn't you?

When you recompile the program there are some warnings about the strcpy() function being deprecated because it's much better to use strcpy_s() but strcpy() does work so ignore these in this exercise. However, when you rerun the program it fails almost immediately. You can see from the Console window that you got a message from the constructor, so you know roughly how far the execution went. Restart the program under the control of the debugger and you can see what happened.

DEBUGGING A PROGRAM

When the debugger starts, you get a message box indicating you have an unhandled exception. In the debugger, you have a comprehensive range of facilities for stepping through your code and tracing the sequence of events. Click Break in the dialog that indicates there is an unhandled exception to halt execution. The program is at the point where the exception occurred and the code currently executing is in the Editor window. The exception is caused by referring to a memory location way outside the realm of the program, so a rogue pointer in the program is the immediate suspect.

The Call Stack

The call stack stores information about functions that have been called and are still executing because they have not returned yet. As you saw earlier, the Call Stack window shows the sequence of function calls outstanding at the current point in the program. Refer to Figure 11-9.

Call Stack	
Name	**Language**
➡ msvcr100d.dll!strcat(unsigned char * dst=0x01247848, unsigned char * src=0x0033fb3c) Line 178	Asm
Ex11_01.exe!Name::Name(const char * pFirst=0x01247840, const char * pSecond=0x01247848) Line 33 + 0x10 bytes	C++
Ex11_01.exe!main(int argc=1, char * * argv=0x00984650) Line 13	C++
Ex11_01.exe!__tmainCRTStartup() Line 555 + 0x19 bytes	C
Ex11_01.exe!mainCRTStartup() Line 371	C
kernel32.dll!766736770	
[Frames below may be incorrect and/or missing, no symbols loaded for kernel32.dll]	
ntdll.dll!77789d720	
ntdll.dll!77789d450	

FIGURE 11-9

The sequence of function calls outstanding runs from the most recent call at the top, the library function `strcat()`, down to the `Kernel32` calls at the bottom of the window in Figure 11-9. Each function was called directly or indirectly by the one below it, and none of those displayed have yet executed a return. The `Kernel32` lines are all system routines that start executing prior to our `main()` function. Your interest is the role of your code in this, and you can see from the second line down in the window that the `Name` class constructor was still in execution (had not returned) when the exception was thrown. If you double-click on that line, the Editor window displays the code for that function, and indicates the line in the source code being executed when the problem arose, which in this case is:

```
strcpy(pSurname, pSecond);
```

This call caused the unhandled exception to be thrown — but why? The original problem is not necessarily here; it just became apparent here. This is typical of errors involving pointers. Double-click on the second line in the Call Stack window referencing the Name constructor call, and then take a look at the Locals window showing the values in the variables in the context of the Name constructor that is presently displayed in the Editor pane. Figure 11-10 shows how it looks.

FIGURE 11-10

Because the context is a function that is a member of the Name class, the Locals window displays the this pointer that contains the address of the current object. The pSurname pointer contains a weird address, 0xcccccccc, and it has been flagged with <Bad Ptr>. The debugger recognizes that pSurname has got to be a rogue pointer and has marked it as such. If you look at pFirstname, this is also in a mess. At the point where you are in the code (copying the surname) the first name should already have been copied, but the contents are rubbish.

The culprit is in the preceding line. Hasty copying of code has resulted in allocating memory for pFirstname for a second time, instead of allocating space for pSurname. The copy is to a junk address, and this causes the exception to be thrown. Don't you wish you had checked what you did properly? The line should be:

```
pSurname = new char[strlen(pSecond)+1];
```

It is typically the case that the code causing a bad pointer address is not the code where the error makes itself felt. In general it may be very far away. Just examining the pointer or pointers involved in the statement causing the error can often lead you directly to the problem, but sometimes it can involve a lot of searching. You can always add more debug code if you get really stuck.

Change the statement in the Editor window to what it should be and recompile the project with the change included. You can then restart the program inside the debugger after it has been recompiled by clicking the button on the Debug toolbar, but surprise, surprise, you get another unhandled exception. This undoubtedly means more pointer trouble, and you can see from the output in the Console window that the last function call was to getNameLength():

```
Name constructor called.
Name::getName called.
The name is Horton
Name::getNameLength called.
```

The output for the name is definitely not right; however, you don't know where exactly the problem is. Restarting and stepping through the program once more should provide some clues.

You can change the way numeric values are displayed in the Debugger windows. The default is to display values in hexadecimal format but you can change this to a decimal by right-clicking in a Debugger window and unchecking Hexadecimal Display. The change will apply to all Debugger windows.

Step Over to the Error

The `getNameLength()` function is currently displayed in the Editor pane and the debugger has indicated that the following line is where the problem arose:

```
return strlen(pFirstname)+strlen(pSurname);
```

In the Call Stack window, you can see that the program is in the `getNameLength()` function member, which merely calls the `strlen()` library function to get the overall length of the name. The `strlen()` function is unlikely to be at fault, so this must mean there is something wrong with part of the object. The Locals window showing the variables in the context of this function shows that the current object has been corrupted, as you can see in Figure 11-11.

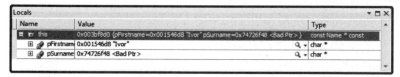

FIGURE 11-11

The current object is pointed to by `this`, and by clicking the plus symbol alongside `this`, you can see the data members. It's the `pSurname` member that is the problem. The address it contains should refer to the string "Horton," but it clearly doesn't. Further, the debugger has flagged it as a bad pointer.

On the assumption that this kind of error does not originate at the point where you experience the effect, you can go back, restart the program, and single step through, looking for where the `Name` object gets messed up. You can select Step Over or press F10 to restart the application, and single step through the statements by repeatedly pressing F10. After executing the statement that defines the `myName` object, the Locals window for the `main()` function shows that it has been constructed successfully, as you can see in Figure 11-12.

Locals			▾ □ ×
Name	**Value**	**Type**	
🔷 argc	1	int	
⊞ 🔷 argv	0x009b4650	char * *	
⊞ 🔷 myName	{pFirstname=0x009b46d8 "Ivor" pSurname=0x009b4720 "Horton" }	Name	
⊞ 🔷 pName	0xcccccccc <Bad Ptr>	char *	
⊞ 🔷 theName	0x004afbd8 "ÌÌÌÌÌÌÌÌÌÌÌÌÌÌÌÌØF›"	char [10]	

FIGURE 11-12

Executing the next statement that outputs the name corrupts the object `myName`. You can clearly see that this is the case from the Locals window for `main()` in Figure 11-13.

Locals			▾ ☐ ✕
Name	Value		Type
● argc	1		int
⊞ ● argv	0x009b4650		char **
⊟ ● myName	{pFirstname=0x009b46d8 "Ivor" pSurname=0x74726f48 <Bad Ptr>}		Name
⊞ ● pName	0xcccccccc <Bad Ptr>	🔍 ▾	char *
⊞ ● theName	0x004afbd8 "Ivor ÍÍÍÍÍÍÍÍÍÍÍÍÍØF;"	🔍 ▾	char [10]

FIGURE 11-13

On the reasonable assumption that the stream output operations work okay, it must be your `getName()` member doing something it shouldn't. Restart the debugger once more, but this time use Step Into when execution reaches the output statement. When execution is at the first statement of the `getName()` function, you can step through the statements in the `getName()` function using Step Over. Watch the Context window as you progress through the function. You will see that everything is fine until you execute the statement:

```
strcpy(pName+strlen(pName)+1, pSurname);    // Append second name after the space
```

This statement causes the corruption of `pSurname` for the current object, pointed to by `this`. You can see this in the Locals window in Figure 11-14.

Locals			▾ ☐ ✕
Name	Value		Type
⊟ ▣ this	0x003df894 {pFirstname=0x009e46d8 "Ivor" pSurname=0x74726f48 <Bad Ptr>}		const Name * const
⊞ ● pFirstname	0x009e46d8 "Ivor"	🔍 ▾	char *
⊞ ● pSurname	0x74726f48 <Bad Ptr>	🔍 ▾	char *
⊞ ● pName	0x003df880 "Ivor ÍÍÍÍÍÍÍÍÍÍÍÍÍØFƒ"	🔍 ▾	char *

FIGURE 11-14

How can copying from the object to another array corrupt the object, especially because `pSurname` is passed as an argument for a `const` parameter? You need to look at the address stored in `pName` for a clue. Compare it with the address contained in the `this` pointer. The difference is only 20 bytes — they could hardly be closer really! The address calculation for the position in `pName` is incorrect, simply because you forgot that copying a space to overwrite the terminating '\0' in the `pName` array means that `strlen(pName)` can no longer calculate the correct length of `pName`. The whole problem is caused by the statement:

```
pName[strlen(pName)] = ' ';              // Append a space
```

This is overwriting the '\0' and thus making the subsequent call to `strlen()` produce an invalid result.

This code is unnecessarily messy anyway; using the library function `strcat()` to concatenate a string is much better than using `strcpy()`, as it renders all this pointer modification unnecessary. You should rewrite the statement as:

```
strcat(pName, " ");                    // Append a space
```

Of course, the subsequent statement also needs to be changed to:

```
return strcat(pName, pSurname);        // Append second name and return total
```

With these changes you can recompile and give it another go. The program appears to run satisfactorily, as you can see from the output:

```
Name constructor called.
Name::getName() called.
The name is Ivor Horton
Name::getNameLength() called.
Name::getName() called.
The name is Ivor Horton
```

Getting the right output does not always mean that all is well, and it certainly isn't in this case. You get the message box displayed by the debug library shown in Figure 11-15 indicating that the stack is corrupted.

The following code shows where the problem lies:

FIGURE 11-15

```
int main(int argc, char* argv[])
{
  Name myName("Ivor", "Horton");                    // Try a single object

  // Retrieve and store the name in a local char array
  char theName[10];
  cout << "\nThe name is " << myName.getName(theName);

  // Store the name in an array in the free store
  char* pName = new char[myName.getNameLength()];
  cout << "\nThe name is " << myName.getName(pName);

  cout << endl;
  return 0;
}
```

Both the shaded lines are in error. The first shaded line provides an array of 10 characters to store the name. In fact, 12 are required: 10 for the two names, one for the space, and one for '\0' at the end. The second shaded line should add 1 to the value returned by the `getNameLength()` function to allow for the '\0' at the end. Thus, the code in `main()` should be:

```
int main(int argc, char* argv[])
{
  Name myName("Ivor", "Horton");                    // Try a single object

  // Retrieve and store the name in a local char array
  char theName[12];
  cout << "\nThe name is " << myName.getName(theName);

  // Store the name in an array in the free store
  char* pName = new char[myName.getNameLength()+1];
  cout << "\nThe name is " << myName.getName(pName);

  cout << endl;
  return 0;
}
```

There's a more serious problem in the definition `getNameLength()` member of the class. It omits to add 1 for the space between the first and second names, so the value returned is always one short. You can detect that something is wrong in the Locals window because the value for `pName` shows up in red. The definition of the `getNameLength()` function should be:

```
int Name::getNameLength() const
{
#ifdef FUNCTION_TRACE
  // Trace function calls
  cout << "\nName::getNameLength() called.";
#endif
  return strlen(pFirstname)+strlen(pSurname)+1;
}
```

That's not the end of it by any means. You may have already spotted that your class still has serious errors, but press on with testing to see if they come out in the wash.

TESTING THE EXTENDED CLASS

Based on the output, everything is working, so it's time to add the definitions for the overloaded comparison operators to the `Name` class. I'll assume this is a new Win32 console project, `Ex11_02`. To implement the comparison operators for `Name` objects, you can use the comparison functions declared in the `cstring` header. Start with the "less than" operator:

```
// Less than operator
bool Name::operator<(const Name& name) const
{
  int result = strcmp(pSurname, name.pSurname);
  if(result < 0)
    return true;
```

```
      if(result == 0 && strcmp(pFirstname, name.pFirstname) < 0)
        return true;
      else
        return false;
    }
```

You can now define the > operator very easily in terms of the < operator:

```
// Greater than operator
bool Name::operator>(const Name& name) const
{
  return name > *this;
}
```

For determining equal names, you use the strcmp() function from the standard library again:

```
// Equal to operator
bool Name::operator==(const Name& name) const
{
  if(strcmp(pSurname, name.pSurname) == 0 &&
                                  strcmp(pFirstname, name.pFirstname) == 0)
    return true;
  else
    return false;
}
```

Now you can extend the test program by creating an array of Name objects, initializing them in some arbitrary way, and then comparing the elements of the array using your comparison operators for a Name object. Here's main() along with a function, init(), to initialize a Name array:

```
// Ex11_02.cpp : Extending the test operation
#include <iostream>
#include "Name.h"
using namespace std;

// Function to initialize an array of random names
void init(Name* names, int count)
{
  char* firstnames[] = { "Charles", "Mary", "Arthur", "Emily", "John"};
  int firstsize = sizeof (firstnames)/sizeof(firstnames[0]);
  char* secondnames[] = { "Dickens", "Shelley", "Miller", "Bronte", "Steinbeck"};
  int secondsize = sizeof (secondnames)/sizeof(secondnames[0]);
  char* first = firstnames[0];
  char* second = secondnames[0];

  for(int i = 0 ; i<count ; i++)
  {
    if(i%2)
      first = firstnames[i%firstsize];
    else
      second = secondnames[i%secondsize];
```

```cpp
      names[i] = Name(first, second);
  }
}

int main(int argc, char* argv[])
{
  Name myName("Ivor", "Horton");                    // Try a single object

  // Retrieve and store the name in a local char array
  char theName[12];
  cout << "\nThe name is " << myName.getName(theName);

  // Store the name in an array in the free store
  char* pName = new char[myName.getNameLength()+1];
  cout << "\nThe name is " << myName.getName(pName);

  const int arraysize = 10;
  Name names[arraysize];                            // Try an array

  // Initialize names
  init(names, arraysize);

  // Try out comparisons
  char* phrase = nullptr;                           // Stores a comparison phrase
  char* iName = nullptr;                            // Stores a complete name
  char* jName = nullptr;                            // Stores a complete name

  for(int i = 0; i < arraysize ; i++)               // Compare each element
  {
    iName = new char[names[i].getNameLength()+1]; // Array to hold first name
    for(int j = i+1 ; j<arraysize ; j++)            // with all the others
    {
      if(names[i] < names[j])
        phrase = " less than ";
      else if(names[i] > names[j])
        phrase = " greater than ";
      else if(names[i] == names[j])     // Superfluous - but it calls operator==()
        phrase = " equal to ";

      jName = new char[names[j].getNameLength()+1]; // Array to hold second name
      cout << endl << names[i].getName(iName) << " is" << phrase
           << names[j].getName(jName);
    }
  }

  cout << endl;
  return 0;
}
```

code snippet Ex11_02.cpp

The `init()` function picks successive combinations of first and second names from the array of names to initialize the array `Name` objects. Names repeat after 25 have been generated, but you need only 10 here.

Finding the Next Bug

The Build output includes the following message:

```
warning C4717: 'Name::operator>' : recursive on all control paths, function will
cause runtime stack overflow
```

This is a strong indication that all is not well, but let's pretend that we didn't look that closely and assume that if the program builds okay, it must run okay.

If you start the program under the control of the debugger using the Start Debugging button on the Debug toolbar it fails again. The message box shown in Figure 11-16 is displayed.

The message box indicates you have exceeded the capacity of the stack memory available and if you select the Break button the Call Stack window tells you what is wrong. You have successive calls of the `operator>()`

FIGURE 11-16

function so it must be calling itself, as the missed message said it would. If you look at the code, you can see why: a typo. The single line in the body of the function should be:

```
bool Name::operator>(const Name& name) const
{
  return name < *this;
}
```

You can fix that, recompile, and try again. This time it works correctly, but unfortunately the class is still defective. It has a memory leak that exhibits no symptoms here, but in another context could cause mayhem. Memory leaks are hard to detect ordinarily, but you can get some extra help from Visual C++ 2010.

DEBUGGING DYNAMIC MEMORY

Allocating memory dynamically is a potent source of bugs, and perhaps the most common bugs in this context are memory leaks. Just to remind you, a memory leak arises when you use the `new` operator to allocate memory, but you never use the `delete` operator to free it again when you are done with it. Apart from just forgetting to delete memory that you have allocated, you should particularly be aware that non-virtual destructors in a class hierarchy can also cause the problem because they can cause the wrong destructor to be called when an object is destroyed, as you have seen. Of course, when your program ends, all the memory is freed; however, while it is running, it remains allocated to your program. Memory leaks present no obvious symptoms much of the time, maybe never in some cases, but memory leaks are detrimental to the performance of your machine because memory is being occupied to no good purpose. Sometimes, it can result in a catastrophic failure of the program when all available memory has been allocated.

For checking your program's use of the free store, Visual C++ 2010 provides a range of diagnostic routines; these use a special debug version of the free store. These are declared in the header `crtdbg.h`. All calls to these routines are automatically removed from the release version of your program, so you don't need to worry about adding preprocessor controls for them.

Functions for Checking the Free Store

Here's an overview of what's involved in checking free store operations and how memory leaks can be detected. The functions declared in `crtdbg.h` check the free store using a record of its status stored in a structure of type `_CrtMemState`. This structure is relatively simple, and is defined as:

```
typedef struct _CrtMemState
{
  struct _CrtMemBlockHeader* pBlockHeader; // Ptr to most recently allocated block
  unsigned long lCounts[_MAX_BLOCKS];      // Counter for each type of block
  unsigned long lSizes[_MAX_BLOCKS];// Total bytes allocated in each block type
  unsigned long lHighWaterCount;    // The most bytes allocated at a time up to now
  unsigned long lTotalCount;        // The total bytes allocated at present
} _CrtMemState;
```

You won't be concerned directly with the details of the state of the free store because you are using functions that present the information in a more readable form. There are quite a few functions involved in tracking free store operations, but you will only look at the five most interesting ones. These provide you with the following capabilities:

➤ To record the state of the free store at any point

➤ To determine the difference between two states of the free store

➤ To output state information

➤ To output information about objects in the free store

➤ To detect memory leaks

Here are the declarations of these functions together with a brief description of what they do:

```
void _CrtMemCheckpoint(_CrtMemState* state);
```

This stores the current state of the free store in a `_CrtMemState` structure. The argument you pass to the function is a pointer to a `_CrtMemState` structure in which the state is to be recorded.

```
int _CrtMemDifference(_CrtMemState* stateDiff,
                      const _CrtMemState* oldState,
                      const _CrtMemState* newState);
```

This function compares the state specified by the third argument, with a previous state that you specify in the second argument. The difference is stored in a `_CrtMemState` structure that you specify in the first argument. If the states are different, the function returns a non-zero value (`true`); otherwise, 0 (`false`) is returned.

```
void _CrtMemDumpStatistics(const _CrtMemState* state);
```

This dumps information about the free store state specified by the argument to an output stream. The state structure pointed to by the argument can be a state that you recorded using _CrtMemCheckpoint() or the difference between two states produced by _CrtMemDifference().

```
void _CrtMemDumpAllObjectsSince(const _CrtMemState* state);
```

This function dumps information on objects allocated in the free store, since the state of the free store is specified by the argument; this has been recorded by an earlier call in your program to _CrtMemCheckpoint(). If you pass null to the function, it dumps information on all objects allocated since the start of execution of your program.

```
int _CrtDumpMemoryLeaks();
```

This is the function you need for the example as it checks for memory leaks and dumps information on any leak that is detected. You can call this function at any time, but a very useful mechanism can cause the function to be called automatically when your program ends. If you enable this mechanism, you get automatic detection of any memory leaks that occurred during program execution, so let's see how you can do that.

Controlling Free Store Debug Operations

You control free store debug operations by setting a flag, _crtDbgFlag, which is of type int. This flag incorporates five separate control bits, including one to enable automatic memory leak checking. You specify these control bits using the following identifiers:

_CRTDBG_ALLOC_MEM_DF	When this bit is on, it turns on debug allocation so the free store state can be tracked.
_CRTDBG_DELAY_FREE_MEM_DF	When this is on, it prevents memory from being freed by delete, so that you can determine what happens under low-memory conditions.
_CRTDBG_CHECK_ALWAYS_DF	When this is on, it causes the _CrtCheckMemory() function to be called automatically at every new and delete operation. This function verifies the integrity of the free store, checking, for example, that blocks have not been overwritten by storing values beyond the range of an array. A report is output if any defect is discovered. This slows execution but catches errors quickly.
_CRTDBG_CHECK_CRT_DF	When this is on, the memory used internally by the run-time library is tracked in debug operations.
_CRTDBG_LEAK_CHECK_DF	Causes leak checking to be performed at program exit by automatically calling _CrtDumpMemoryLeaks(). You only get output from this if your program has failed to free all the memory that it allocated.

By default, the _CRTDBG_ALLOC_MEM_DF bit is on, and all the others are off. You must use the bitwise operators to set and unset combinations of these bits. To set the _crtDbgFlag flag you pass a flag of type int to the _CrtDbgFlag() function that implements the combination of indicators that you require. This puts your flag into effect and returns the previous status of _CrtDbgFlag. One way to set the indicators you want is to first obtain the current status of the _crtDbgFlag flag. Do this by calling the _CrtSetDbgFlag() function with the argument _CRTDBG_REPORT_FLAG as follows:

```
int flag = _CrtSetDbgFlag(_CRTDBG_REPORT_FLAG);            // Get current flag
```

You can then set or unset the indicators by combining the identifiers for the individual indicators with this flag using bitwise operators. To set an indicator on, OR the indicator identifier with the flag. For example, to set the automatic leak checking indicator on, in the flag, you could write:

```
flag |= _CRTDBG_LEAK_CHECK_DF;
```

To turn an indicator off, you must AND the negation of the identifier with the flag. For example, to turn off tracking of memory that is used internally by the library, you could write:

```
flag &= ~_CRTDBG_CHECK_CRT_DF;
```

To put your new flag into effect, you just call _CrtSetDbgFlag() with your flag as the argument:

```
_CrtSetDbgFlag(flag);
```

Alternatively, you can OR all the identifiers for the indicators that you want together, and pass the result as the argument to _CrtSetDbgFlag(). If you just want to leak check when the program exits, you could write:

```
_CrtSetDbgFlag(_CRTDBG_LEAK_CHECK_DF|_CRTDBG_ALLOC_MEM_DF);
```

If you need to set a particular combination of indicators, rather than setting or unsetting bits at various points in your program, this is the easiest way to do it. You are almost at the point where you can apply the dynamic memory debugging facilities to our example. You just need to look at how you determine where free store debugging output goes.

Free Store Debugging Output

The destination of the output from the free store debugging functions is not the standard output stream; by default it goes to the debug message window. If you want to see the output on stdout you must set this up. There are two functions involved in this: _CrtSetReportMode(), which sets the general destination for output, and _CrtSetReportFile(), which specifies a stream destination. The _CrtSetReportMode() function is declared as:

```
int _CrtSetReportMode(int reportType, int reportMode);
```

There are three kinds of output produced by the free store debugging functions. Each call to the _CrtSetReportMode() function sets the destination specified by the second argument for the output type specified by the first argument. You specify the report type by one of the following identifiers:

_CRT_WARN	Warning messages of various kinds. The output when a memory leak is detected is a warning.
_CRT_ERROR	Catastrophic errors that report unrecoverable problems.
_CRT_ASSERT	Output from assertions (not output from the assert() function that I discussed earlier).

The crtdbg.h header defines two macros, ASSERT and ASSERTE, that work in much the same way as the assert() function in the standard library. The difference between these two macros is that ASSERTE reports the assertion expression when a failure occurs, whereas the ASSERT macro does not.

You specify the report mode by a combination of the following identifiers:

_CRTDBG_MODE_DEBUG	This is the default mode, which sends output to a debug string that you see in the Debug window when running under control of the debugger.
_CRTDBG_MODE_FILE	Output is to be directed to an output stream.
_CRTDBG_MODE_WNDW	Output is presented in a message box.
_CRTDBG_REPORT_MODE	If you specify this, the _CrtSetReportMode() function just returns the current report mode.

To specify more than one destination, you simply OR the identifiers using the | operator. You set the destination for each output type with a separate call of the _CrtSetReportMode() function. To direct the output when a leak is detected to a file stream, you can set the report mode with the following statement:

```
CrtSetReportMode(_CRT_WARN, _CRTDBG_MODE_FILE);
```

This just sets the destination generically as a file stream. You still need to call the _CrtSetReportFile() function to specify the destination.

The _CrtSetReportFile() function is declared as:

```
_HFILE _CrtSetReportFile(int reportType, _HFILE reportFile);
```

The second argument here can either be a pointer to a file stream (of type _HFILE), which I will not go into further, or it can be one of the following identifiers:

_CRTDBG_FILE_STDERR	Output is directed to the standard error stream, stderr.
_CRTDBG_FILE_STDOUT	Output is directed to the standard output stream, stdout.
_CRTDBG_REPORT_FILE	If you specify this argument, the _CrtSetReportFile() function will just return the current destination.

To set the leak detection output to the standard output stream, you can write:

```
_CrtSetReportFile(_CRT_WARN, _CRTDBG_FILE_STDOUT);
```

The debugging output can be quite voluminous, so you might want to redirect the output stream to a file. You can redirect a standard stram to a file using the `freopen_s()` function that is defined in the `cstdio` header. It has the following prototype:

```
errno_t freopen(File** pFile, const char* filepath,  const char* mode,
                                                      File* stream);
```

`pFile` is a pointer to a file pointer in which the function will store the address of the file. `filepath` is the path to the file to which the stream is to be redirected. `mode` is the access mode permitted for the file and can be any of the following:

MODE	EFFECT
`"r"`	Opens the existing file specified by `filepath` for reading. If the file does not exist, the function will fail and return a non-zero error code.
`"w"`	Opens the file specified by `filepath` file for writing. If the file does not exist it will be created.
`"a"`	Opens the file specified by `filepath` for appending data after the EOF marker. If the file does not exist, it will be created.
`"r+"`	Opens the existing file specified by `filepath` for reading and writing.
`"w+"`	Opens an empty file specified by `filepath` for reading and writing. If the file exists, any contents will be overwritten.
`"a+"`	Opens the file specified by `filepath` for reading and appending data, overwriting the existing EOF marker. If the file does not exist, it will be created.

`stream` is the stream to be redirected to the file identified by `filepath`.

Here's how you could redirect `stdout` to a file with the name `debug_out.txt`:

```
FILE *pOut(nullptr);
errno_t err = freopen_s( &pOut, "debug_out.txt", "w", stdout );

if(err)
  cout << "error on freopen" << endl;
else
    cout << "successfully reassigned" << endl;
```

Supplying just the file name as the second argument uses the current default file path, so the file will be created in the same folder as the source file.

You now have enough knowledge of the free store debug routines to try out leak detection in your example.

TRY IT OUT   Memory Leak Detection

You can create a new project Ex11_02A that will be an extension of Ex11_02. You can copy the source files to the new project folder and then update them. Even though the example directs the standard output stream to a file, it's a good idea to reduce the volume of output, so reduce the size of the names array to five elements. Here's the new version of main() for Ex11_02A to use the free store debug facilities in general and leak detection in particular:

Available for download on Wrox.com

```cpp
int main(int argc, char* argv[])
{
  FILE *pOut(nullptr);
  errno_t err = freopen_s( &pOut, "debug_out.txt", "w", stdout );

  if(err)
    cout << "error on freopen" << endl;

  // Turn on free store debugging and leak-checking bits
  _CrtSetDbgFlag( _CRTDBG_LEAK_CHECK_DF|_CRTDBG_ALLOC_MEM_DF );

  // Direct warnings to stdout
  _CrtSetReportMode(_CRT_WARN, _CRTDBG_MODE_FILE);
  _CrtSetReportFile(_CRT_WARN, _CRTDBG_FILE_STDOUT);

  Name myName("Ivor", "Horton");                   // Try a single object

  // Retrieve and store the name in a local char array
  char theName[12];
  cout << "\nThe name is " << myName.getName(theName);

  // Store the name in an array in the free store
  char* pName = new char[myName.getNameLength()+1];
  cout << "\nThe name is " << myName.getName(pName);

  const int arraysize = 5;
  Name names[arraysize];                           // Try an array

  // Initialize names
  init(names, arraysize);

  // Try out comparisons
  char* phrase = nullptr;                          // Stores a comparison phrase
  char* iName = nullptr;                           // Stores a complete name
  char* jName = nullptr;                           // Stores a complete name

  for(int i = 0; i < arraysize ; i++)              // Compare each element
  {
    iName = new char[names[i].getNameLength()+1]; // Array to hold first name
    for(int j = i+1 ; j<arraysize ; j++)          // with all the others
    {
      if(names[i] < names[j])
        phrase = " less than ";
      else if(names[i] > names[j])
        phrase = " greater than ";
```

```
        else if(names[i] == names[j])    // Superfluous - but it calls operator==()
          phrase = " equal to ";
        jName = new char[names[j].getNameLength()+1]; // Array to hold second name
        cout << endl << names[i].getName(iName) << " is" << phrase
             << names[j].getName(jName);
      }
    }
    cout << endl;
    return 0;
}
```

code snippet Ex11_2A.cpp

To enable the heap debugging functions, you must add the following directives, in the order shown:

```
#include <stdlib.h>
#include <crtdbg.h>
```

You must also add an `#include` directive for `cstdio` because you use the `freopen_s()` function to redirect the standard output stream to a file.

To reduce output further, you could switch off the trace output by commenting out the control symbols in the `DebugStuff.h` header:

Available for download on Wrox.com

```
// DebugStuff.h - Debugging control
#pragma once

#ifdef _DEBUG

//#define CONSTRUCTOR_TRACE         // Output constructor call trace
//#define FUNCTION_TRACE            // Trace function calls
#endif
```

code snippet DebugStuff.h

You can recompile the example and run it again.

How It Works

It works just as expected. You get a report that your program does indeed have memory leaks, and you get a list of the objects in the free store at the end of the program. The output generated by the free store debug facility starts with:

```
Detected memory leaks!
Dumping objects ->
{160} normal block at 0x00039CB8, 16 bytes long.
 Data: <                > CD CD CD CD CD CD CD CD CD CD CD CD CD CD CD CD
{159} normal block at 0x00039C78, 16 bytes long.
 Data: <Emily Steinbeck > 45 6D 69 6C 79 20 53 74 65 69 6E 62 65 63 6B 00
{158} normal block at 0x00039C38, 13 bytes long.
...
```

and ends with:

```
...
{137} normal block at 0x000335F0, 8 bytes long.
 Data: <Dickens > 44 69 63 6B 65 6E 73 00
{136} normal block at 0x000335B8, 8 bytes long.
 Data: <Charles > 43 68 61 72 6C 65 73 00
{135} normal block at 0x00033580, 12 bytes long.
 Data: <Ivor Horton > 49 76 6F 72 20 48 6F 72 74 6F 6E 00
{133} normal block at 0x0029EFC8, 7 bytes long.
 Data: <Horton > 48 6F 72 74 6F 6E 00
{132} normal block at 0x00031488, 5 bytes long.
 Data: <Ivor > 49 76 6F 72 00
Object dump complete.
```

The objects reported as being left in the free store are presented with the most recently allocated first, and the earliest last. It is obvious from the output that the Name class is allocating memory for its data members, and never releasing it. The last three objects dumped correspond to the pName array allocated in main(), and the data members of the object myName. The blocks for the complete names are allocated in main(), and they too are left lying about. The problem our class has is that we forgot the fundamental rules relating to classes that allocate memory dynamically; they should always define a destructor, a copy constructor, and the assignment operator. The class should be declared as:

```
class Name
{
  public:
    Name();                                    // Default constructor
    Name(const char* pFirst, const char* pSecond);   // Constructor
    Name(const Name& rName);                   // Copy constructor

    ~Name();                                   // Destructor

    char* getName(char* pName) const;      // Get the complete name
    size_t getNameLength() const;          // Get the complete name length

  // Comparison operators for names
    bool operator<(const Name& name) const;
    bool operator==(const Name& name) const;
    bool operator>(const Name& name) const;

    Name& operator=(const Name& rName);            // Assignment operator

  private:
    char* pFirstname;
    char* pSurname;
};
```

You can define the copy constructor as:

```
Name:: Name(const Name& rName)
{
  pFirstname = new char[strlen(rName.pFirstname)+1];// Allocate space for 1st name
```

```
    strcpy(pFirstname, rName.pFirstname);                // and copy it.
    pSurname = new char[strlen(rName.pSurname)+1];        // Same for the surname...
    strcpy(pSurname, rName.pSurname);
}
```

The destructor just needs to release the memory for the two data members:

```
Name::~Name()
{
    delete[] pFirstname;
    delete[] pSurname;
}
```

In the assignment operator, you must make the usual provision for the left and right sides being identical:

```
Name& Name::operator=(const Name& rName)
{
    if(this == &rName)                                   // If lhs equals rhs
        return *this;                                    // just return the object

    delete[] pFirstname;
    pFirstname = new char[strlen(rName.pFirstname)+1];   // Allocate space for 1st name
    strcpy(pFirstname, rName.pFirstname);                // and copy it.
    delete[] pSurname;
    pSurname = new char[strlen(rName.pSurname)+1];       // Same for the surname...
    strcpy(pSurname, rName.pSurname);
    return *this;
}
```

You also should make the default constructor work properly. If the default constructor doesn't allocate memory in the free store, you have the possibility that the destructor will erroneously attempt to delete memory that was not allocated in the free store. You need to modify it to:

```
Name::Name()
{
#ifdef CONSTRUCTOR_TRACE
    // Trace constructor calls
    cout << "\nDefault Name constructor called.";
#endif

    // Allocate array of 1 for empty strings
    pFirstname = new char[1];
    pSurname = new char[1];

    pFirstname[0] = pSurname[0] = '\0';                  // Store null character
}
```

If you add statements to main() to delete the memory that is allocate dynamically there, the program should run without any messages relating to memory leaks. In main() you need to add the following statement to the end of the inner loop that is controlled by j:

```
delete[] jName;
```

You also need to add the following statement to the end of the outer loop that is controlled by i:

```
delete[] iName;
```

Finally, you still have to release the memory for pName after the loops in main():

```
delete[] pName;
```

DEBUGGING C++/CLI PROGRAMS

Life is simpler with C++/CLI programming. None of the complications of corrupted pointers or memory leaks arise in programs written for the CLR, so this reduces the debugging problem substantially, compared to native C++, at a stroke. You set breakpoints and tracepoints in a CLR program exactly the same way that you do for a native C++ code. You have a specific option that applies to C++/CLI code for preventing the debugger from stepping through library code. If you select the Tools ➪ Options menu item a dialog is displayed, and if you select the Debugging/General set of options the dialog looks as shown in Figure 11-17.

FIGURE 11-17

Checking the option highlighted in Figure 11-17 ensures that the debugger only steps through your source statements and executes the library code normally.

Using the Debug and Trace Classes

The Debug and Trace classes in the System::Diagnostics namespace are for tracing execution of a program for debugging purposes. The capabilities provided by the Debug and Trace classes are identical; the difference between them is that Trace functions are compiled into release builds, whereas `Debug` functions are not. Thus you can use `Debug` class functions when you are just debugging your code, and `Trace` class functions when you want to obtain `Trace` information in release versions of your code for performance monitoring or diagnostic and maintenance purposes. You also have control over whether the compile includes trace code in your program.

Because the functions and other members in the `Debug` and `Trace` classes are identical, I'll just describe the capability in terms of the `Debug` class.

Generating Output

You can produce output using the `Debug::WriteLine()` and `Debug::Write()` functions that write messages to an output destination; the difference between these two functions is that the `WriteLine()` function writes a newline character after the output whereas the `Write()` function does not. They both come in four overloaded versions; I'll use the `Write()` function as the example, but `WriteLine()` versions have the same parameter lists:

FUNCTION	DESCRIPTION
`Debug::Write(` `  String^ message)`	Writes `message` to the output destination.

`Debug::Write(`
`  String^ message,`
`  String^ category)`
	Writes `category` followed by `message` to the output destination. A category name is used to organize the output.

`Debug::Write(` `  Object^ value)`	Writes the string returned by `value->ToString()` to the output destination.

`Debug::Write(`
`  Object^ value,`
`  String^ category)`
	Writes `category` followed by the string returned by `value->ToString()` to the output destination.

The `WriteIf()` and `WriteLineIf()` are conditional versions of the `Write()` and `WriteLine()` functions in the `Debug` class:

FUNCTION	DESCRIPTION

`Debug::WriteIf(`
`  bool condition,`
`  String^ message)`
	Writes `message` to the output destination if `condition` is true; otherwise, no output is produced.

`Debug::WriteIf(`
`  bool condition,`
`  String^ message,`
`  String^ category)`
	Writes `category` followed by `message` to the output destination if `condition` is true; otherwise, no output is produced.

FUNCTION	DESCRIPTION
Debug::WriteIf(bool condition, Object^ value)	Writes the string returned by value->ToString() to the output destination if condition is true; otherwise, no output is produced.
Debug::WriteIf(bool condition, Object^ value, String^ category)	Writes category followed by the string returned by value->ToString() to the output destination if condition is true; otherwise, no output is produced.

As you see, the WriteIf() and WriteLineIf() functions have an extra parameter of type bool at the beginning of the parameter list for the corresponding Write() or WriteLine() function, and the argument for this determines whether or not output occurs.

You can also write output using the Debug::Print() function that comes in two overloaded versions:

FUNCTION	DESCRIPTION
Print(String^ message)	This writes message to the output destination followed by a newline character.
Print(String^ format, ...array<Object^>^ args)	This works in the same way as formatted output with the Console:: WriteLine() function. The format string determines how the arguments that follow it are presented in the output.

Setting the Output Destination

By default the output messages are sent to the Output window in the IDE, but you can change this by using a listener. A **listener** is an object that directs debug and trace output to one or more destinations. Here's how you can create a listener and direct debug output to the standard output stream:

```
TextWriterTraceListener^ listener = gcnew TextWriterTraceListener( Console::Out);
Debug::Listeners->Add(listener);
```

The first statement creates a TextWriterTraceListener object that directs the output to the standard output stream, which is returned by the static property Out in the Console class. (The In and Error properties in the Console class return the standard input stream and standard error stream respectively.) The Listeners property in the Debug class returns a collection of listeners for debug output, so the statement adds the listener object to the collection.

Alternatively, you could add a `ConsoleTraceListener` to direct output to the console screen, as follows:

```
ConsoleTraceListener^ myOutput = gcnew ConsoleTraceListener();
Debug::Listeners->Add(myOutput);
```

You could add other listeners that additionally direct output elsewhere (to a file perhaps).

The `Trace` and `Debug` classes share the same collection of listeners, so if you add a listener as described above for either the `Debug` class or the `Trace` class, it will also apply to output from both classes.

Indenting the Output

You can control the indenting of the debug and trace messages. This is particularly useful in situations where functions are called at various depths. By indenting the output at the beginning of a function and removing the indent before leaving the function, the debug or trace output is easily identified and you'll be able to see the depth of function call from the amount of indentation of the output.

To increase the current indent level for output by one (one indent unit is four spaces by default), you call the static `Indent()` function in the `Debug` class like this:

```
Debug::Indent();                    // Increase indent level by 1
```

To reduce the current indent level by one you call the static `Unindent()` function:

```
Debug::Unindent();                  // Decrease indent level by 1
```

The current indent level is recorded in the static `IndentLevel` property in the `Debug` class, so you can get or set the current indent level through this property. For example:

```
Debug::IndentLevel = 2*Debug::IndentLevel;
```

This statement doubles the current level of indentation for subsequent debug output.

The number of spaces in one indent unit is recorded in the static `IndentSize` property in the `Debug` class. You can retrieve the current indent size and change it to a different value. For example:

```
Console::WriteLine(L"Current indent unit = {0}", Debug::IndentSize);
Debug::IndentSize = 2;              // Set indent unit to 2 spaces
```

The first statement simply outputs the indent size and the second statement sets it to a new value. Subsequent calls to `Indent()` increases the current indentation by the new size, which is two spaces.

Controlling Output

Trace switches provide you with a way to switch any of the debug or trace output on and off. You have two kinds of trace switches you can use:

➤ The `BooleanSwitch` reference class objects provide you with a way to switch segments of output on or off depending on the state of the switch.

➤ The `TraceSwitch` reference class objects provide you with a more sophisticated control mechanism because each `TraceSwitch` object has four properties that correspond to four control levels for output statements.

You could create a `BooleanSwitch` object to control output as a static class member like this:

```
public ref class MyClass
{
private:
  static BooleanSwitch^ errors =
                      gcnew BooleanSwitch(L"Error Switch", L"Controls error
output");

public:
  void DoIt()
  {
    // Code...

    if(errors->Enabled)
      Debug::WriteLine(L"Error in DoIt()");

    // More code...
  }
  // Rest of the class...
};
```

This shows the errors object as a static member of `MyClass`. The first argument to the `BooleanSwitch` constructor is the display name for the switch that is used to initialize the `DisplayName` property, and the second argument sets the value of the `Description` property for the switch. There's another constructor that accepts a third argument of type `String^` that sets the `Value` property for the switch.

The `Enabled` property for a Boolean switch is of type `bool` and is `false` by default. To set it to `true`, you just set the property value accordingly:

```
errors->Enabled = true;
```

The `DoIt()` function in `MyClass` outputs the debug error message only when the `errors` switch is enabled.

The `TraceSwitch` reference class has two constructors that have the same parameters as the `BooleanSwitch` class constructors. You can create a `TraceSwitch` object like this:

```
TraceSwitch^ traceCtrl =
                      gcnew TraceSwitch(L"Update", L"Traces update operations");
```

The first argument to the constructor sets the value of the `DisplayName` property, and the second argument sets the value of the `Description` property.

The `Level` property for a `TraceSwitch` object is an enum class type, `TraceLevel`, and you can set this property to control trace output to any of the following values:

VALUE	DESCRIPTION
`TraceLevel::Off`	No trace output.
`TraceLevel::Info`	Output information, warning, and error messages.
`TraceLevel::Warning`	Output warning and error messages.
`TraceLevel::Error`	Output Error messages.
`TraceLevel::Verbose`	Output all messages.

The value you set determines the output produced. To get all messages, you set the property as follows:

```
traceCtrl->Level = TraceLevel::Verbose;
```

You determine whether a particular message should be issued by your trace and debug code by testing the state of one of four properties of type `bool` for the `TraceSwitch` object:

PROPERTY	DESCRIPTION
`TraceVerbose`	Returns the value `true` when all messages are to be output.
`TraceInfo`	Returns the value `true` when information messages are to be output.
`TraceWarning`	Returns the value `true` when warning messages are to be output.
`TraceError`	Returns the value `true` when error messages are to be output.

You can see from the significance of these property values that setting the `Level` property also sets the states of these properties. If you set the `Level` property to `TraceLevel::Warning` for instance, `TraceWarning` and `TraceError` is set to `true` and `TraceVerbose` and `TraceInfo` are set to `false`.

To decide whether to output a particular message, you just test the appropriate property:

```
if(traceCtrl->TraceWarning)
   Debug::WriteLine(L"This is your last warning!");
```

The message is output only if the `TraceWarning` property for `traceCtrl` is true.

Assertions

The `Debug` and `Trace` classes have static `Assert()` functions that provide a similar capability to the native C++ `assert()` function. The `Assert()` function in the `Debug` class only works in debug builds. The `Assert()` function in the `Trace` class works in release builds. The first argument to the `Debug::Assert()` function is a `bool` value or expression that causes the program to assert when the argument is `false`. The call stack is then displayed in a dialog as shown in Figure 11-18.

FIGURE 11-18

Figure 11-18 shows an assertion that is produced by the next example. When the program asserts, the call stack presented in the dialog shows the line numbers in the code and the names of the functions that are executing at that point. Here there are four functions executing, including `main()`.

You have three courses of action after an assertion. Clicking the Abort button ends the program immediately; clicking the Ignore button allows the program to continue; and clicking the Retry button gives you the option of executing the program in debug mode.

The following four overloaded versions of the `Assert()` function are available:

FUNCTION	DESCRIPTION
`Debug::Assert(` `  bool condition)`	When `condition` is `false`, a dialog displays showing the call stack at that point.
`Debug::Assert(` `  bool condition, String^ message)`	As above, but with `message` displayed in the dialog above the call stack information.

`Debug::Assert(`
`  bool condition, String^ message,`
`  String^ details)`
	As the preceding version, but with `details` displayed additionally in the dialog.

`Debug::Assert(`
`  bool condition, String^ message,`
`  String^ msgFormat, Object[] args)`
	When `condition` is `false`, it asserts as in the preceding version, but the `String.Format()` function is also called with `msgFormat` and `args` as arguments to produce additional output in the dialog.

The message argument and other output is directed to the message box that results from an assertion by the `DefaultTraceListener` object that is in the listeners collection that is shared by both the `Debug` and `Trace` classes. You can add your own listeners to direct output to other destinations.

Seeing it working is the best aid to understanding, so I put together an example that demonstrates debug and trace code in action.

TRY IT OUT Using Debug and Trace

This example is an exercise for some of the trace and debug functions I have described. Create a CLR console project and modify it to the following:

```cpp
// Ex11_03.cpp : main project file.
// CLR trace and debug output

#include "stdafx.h"

using namespace System;
using namespace System::Diagnostics;

public ref class TraceTest
{
public:
  TraceTest(int n):value(n){}

  property TraceLevel Level
  {
    void set(TraceLevel level) {sw->Level = level; }
    TraceLevel get(){return sw->Level; }
  }

  void FunA()
  {
    ++value;
    Trace::Indent();
    Trace::WriteLine(L"Starting FunA");
    if(sw->TraceInfo)
      Debug::WriteLine(L"FunA working...");
    FunB();
    Trace::WriteLine(L"Ending FunA");
    Trace::Unindent();
  }

  void FunB()
  {
    Trace::Indent();
    Trace::WriteLine(L"Starting FunB");
    if(sw->TraceWarning)
      Debug::WriteLine(L"FunB warning...");
    FunC();
    Trace::WriteLine(L"Ending FunB");
    Trace::Unindent();
  }

  void FunC()
  {
    Trace::Indent();
    Trace::WriteLine(L"Starting FunC");
    if(sw->TraceError)
```

```
        Debug::WriteLine(L"FunC error...");
      Debug::Assert(value < 4);
      Trace::WriteLine(L"Ending FunC");
      Trace::Unindent();
    }
  private:
    int value;
    static TraceSwitch^ sw =
                        gcnew TraceSwitch(L"Trace Switch", L"Controls trace output");
  };

int main(array<System::String ^> ^args)
{
  // Direct output to the command line
  TextWriterTraceListener^ listener = gcnew TextWriterTraceListener(Console::Out);
  Debug::Listeners->Add(listener);

  Debug::IndentSize = 2;                    // Set the indent size

  array<TraceLevel>^ levels = { TraceLevel::Off,      TraceLevel::Error,
                                TraceLevel::Warning ,TraceLevel::Verbose};
  TraceTest^ obj = gcnew TraceTest(0);

  Console::WriteLine(L"Starting trace and debug test...");
  for each(TraceLevel level in levels)
  {
    obj->Level = level;                    // Set level for messages
    Console::WriteLine(L"\nTrace level is {0}", obj->Level);
    obj->FunA();
  }
 return 0;
}
```

code snippet Ex11_03.cpp

This example results in an assertion dialog being displayed during execution. You can then choose to continue or abort execution or retry the program in debug mode by selecting the appropriate button in the dialog.

Depending on what you do when the program asserts, this example produces the following output:

```
Starting trace and debug test...

Trace level is Off
  Starting FunA
    Starting FunB
      Starting FunC
      Ending FunC
    Ending FunB
  Ending FunA
```

```
Trace level is Error
   Starting FunA
      Starting FunB
         Starting FunC
         FunC error...
         Ending FunC
      Ending FunB
   Ending FunA

Trace level is Warning
   Starting FunA
      Starting FunB
      FunB warning...
         Starting FunC
         FunC error...
         Ending FunC
      Ending FunB
   Ending FunA

Trace level is Verbose
   Starting FunA
   FunA working...
      Starting FunB
      FunB warning...
         Starting FunC
         FunC error...
         Fail:
         Ending FunC
      Ending FunB
   Ending FunA
```

How It Works

The `TraceTest` class defines three instance functions `FunA()`, `FunB()`, and `FunC()`. Each function contains a call to the `Trace::Indent()` function to increase indentation for debug output and `Debug::WriteLine()` function calls to track when the function is entered and exited. The `Trace::Unindent()` function is called immediately before exiting each function to restore the indent level to what it was when the function was called.

The `TraceTest` class defines a private `TraceSwitch` member, `sw`, which controls what level of debug output is displayed. Each of the three member functions also calls the `Debug::WriteLine()` function to issue a debug message depending on the level set in the `sw` member of the class.

The `FunA()` function increments the value member of the class object each time it is called and the `FunC()` function asserts if `value` exceeds 3.

In `main()` you create a `TextWriterTraceListener` object that directs trace and debug output to the command line:

```
TextWriterTraceListener^ listener = gcnew TextWriterTraceListener(Console::Out);
```

You then add the `listener` object to the collection of listeners in the `Debug` class:

```
Debug::Listeners->Add(listener);
```

This causes debug and trace output to be directed to `Console::Out`, the standard output stream.

You create an array of `TraceLevel` objects that represent various control levels for debug and trace output:

```
array<TraceLevel>^ levels = { TraceLevel::Off,      TraceLevel::Error,
                              TraceLevel::Warning ,TraceLevel::Verbose};
```

After creating the `TraceLevel` object you set the trace levels for it in a `for` each loop:

```
for each(TraceLevel level in levels)
{
  obj->Level = level;                // Set level for messages
  Console::WriteLine(L"\nTrace level is {0}", obj->Level);
  obj->FunA();
}
```

The level is set through the `Level` property for `obj`. This sets the `Level` property in the `TraceSwitch` member, `sw`, which is used in the instance functions to control output.

From the output you can see that the indent you set affects output from the static `WriteLine()` function in both the `Debug` and `Trace` classes. You can also see how the level that you set in the `TraceSwitch` class member affects the output. When the value member of the `TraceTest` class object `obj` reaches 4, the `FunC()` function asserts. You can rerun the example and try out the effects of the three buttons on the assertion dialog.

Getting Trace Output in Windows Forms Applications

It's often useful to be able to output trace information from a Windows Forms application. There are a couple of barriers in the way of doing this: Firstly, the output can be voluminous, particularly if you want to trace the execution of functions that execute very frequently, such as those dealing with mouse events, and secondly and more significantly, there is no console with a Windows Forms application to receive the output. You can get around this by adding some code to the constructor of the class encapsulating the form for the application, which reassigns output for `Console::Out` stream to a file. I won't explain every detail of the class objects involved and how this code works at this point but I'll just offer it here as something you can plug into a Windows Forms application:

```
FileStream^ fs = gcnew FileStream(L"Trace.txt", FileMode::Create);
StreamWriter^ sw = gcnew StreamWriter(fs);
sw->Autoflush = true;
Console::SetOut(sw);
```

The first statement creates a stream that encapsulates the file `Trace.txt` that will be created in the current directory. You can specify a full path if you want; just set the first argument to the `FileStream` constructor as `L"C\Debug Output\MyTrace.txt"`, for example. The next two statements set up an object that can write to the stream, `fs`, and make it flush data to the stream automatically. The last statement reassigns `Console::Out` to the `StreamWriter` object. To compile this code successfully you must add a `using` directive for the `System::IO` namespace to the header file containing the class definition for the form.

With this code in place you can put `Console` output statements anywhere in the code for the form to trace the execution sequence or to record data values. You can inspect the trace file with any simple text editor, such as Notepad.

SUMMARY

Debugging is a big topic, and Visual C++ 2010 provides many debugging facilities beyond what I have discussed here. If you are comfortable with what I have covered in this chapter, you should have little trouble expanding your knowledge of the debug capabilities through the Visual C++ 2010 documentation. Searching on "debugging" should generate a rich list of further information.

With the basics of debugging added to your knowledge of C++, you are ready for the big one: Windows programming!

▶ **WHAT YOU LEARNED IN THIS CHAPTER**

TOPIC	CONCEPT
Assertions	You can use the `assert()` library function that is declared in the `cassert` header to check logical conditions in your native C++ program that should always be `true`.
_DEBUG symbol	The preprocessor symbol `_DEBUG` is automatically defined in the debug version of a native C++program. It is not defined in the release version.
Debugging code	You can add your own debugging code by enclosing it between an `#ifdef`/`#endif` pair of directives testing for `_DEBUG`. Your debug code is then included only in the debug version of the program.
crtdbg.h header	The `crtdbg.h` header supplies declarations for functions to provide debugging of free store operations.
_crtDbgFlag flag	By setting the `_crtDbgFlag` appropriately, you can enable automatic checking of your program for memory leaks.
Debug output	To direct output messages from the free store debugging functions, you call the `_CrtSetReportMode()` and `_CrtSetReportFile()` functions.
C++/CLI debugging	Debugging operations using breakpoints and trace points in C++/CLI programs are exactly the same as in native C++ programs.
C++/CLI classes for debugging	The `Debug` and `Assert` classes defined in the `System::Diagnostics` namespace provide functions for tracing execution and generating debugging output in CLR programs.
Assertions in C++/CLI programs	The static `Assert()` function in the `Debug` and `Trace` classes provides an assertion capability in CLR programs.

12

Windows Programming Concepts

WHAT YOU WILL LEARN IN THIS CHAPTER:

➤   The basic structure of a window

➤   The Windows API and how it is used

➤   Windows messages and how you deal with them

➤   The notation that is commonly used in Windows programs

➤   The basic structure of a Windows program

➤   How you create an elementary program using the Windows API and how it works

➤   Microsoft Foundation Classes

➤   The basic elements of an MFC-based program

➤   Windows Forms

➤   The basic elements of a Windows Forms application

In this chapter, you will take a look at the basic ideas that are involved in every Windows program in C++. You'll first develop a very simple example that uses the Windows operating system API directly. This will enable you to understand how a Windows application works behinds the scenes, which will be useful to you when you are developing applications using the more sophisticated facilities provided by Visual C++ 2010. You will then see what you get when you create a Windows program using the Microsoft Foundation Classes, better known as the MFC. Finally, you'll create a basic program using Windows Forms that will execute with the CLR, so by the end of the chapter you'll have an idea of what each of the three approaches to developing a Windows application involves.

WINDOWS PROGRAMMING BASICS

With Visual C++ 2010 you have three basic ways of creating an interactive Windows application:

➤ Using the **Windows API.** This is the fundamental interface that the Windows operating system provides for communications between itself and the applications that are executing under its control.

➤ Using the **Microsoft Foundation Classes,** better known as the **MFC.** This is a set of C++ classes that encapsulate the Windows API.

➤ Using **Windows Forms.** This is a forms-based development mechanism for creating applications that execute with the CLR.

In a way, these three approaches form a progression from the most programming-intensive to the least programming-intensive. With the Windows API, you are writing code throughout — all the elements that make up the GUI for your application must be created programmatically. With MFC applications there's some help with GUI build in that you can assemble controls on a dialog form graphically and just program the interactions with the user; however, you still are involved in a lot of coding. With a Windows Forms application, you can build the complete GUI, including the primary application window, by assembling the controls that the user interacts with graphically. You just place the controls wherever you want them in a form window, and the code to create them is generated automatically. Using Windows Forms is by far the fastest and easiest mechanism for generating an application because the amount of code that you have to write is greatly reduced compared with the other two possibilities. The code for a Windows Forms application also gains all the benefits of executing with the CLR.

Using the MFC involves more programming effort than Windows Forms, but you have more control over how the GUI is created and you end up with a program that will execute natively on your PC. Because using the Windows API directly is the most laborious method for developing an application, I won't go into this in detail. However, you will put together a basic Windows API application so you'll have an opportunity to understand the principles of the mechanism that all Windows applications use to work with the operating system under the covers. You'll explore the fundamentals involved in all three possibilities for Windows application development in this chapter and investigate using MFC and Windows Forms in more detail later in the book. Of course, it also is possible to develop applications in C++ that do not require the Windows operating system, and games programs often take this approach when the ultimate in graphics performance is required. Although this is itself an interesting topic, it would require a whole book to do it justice, so I won't pursue this topic further.

Before getting to the examples in this chapter, I'll review the terminology that is used to describe an application window. You have already created a Windows program in Chapter 1 without writing a single line of code yourself, and I'll use the window generated by this to illustrate the various elements that go to make up a window.

Elements of a Window

You will inevitably be familiar with most, if not all, of the principal elements of the user interface to a Windows program. However, I will go through them anyway just to be sure we have a common understanding of what the terms mean. The best way to understand what the elements of a window can be is to look at one. An annotated version of the window displayed by the example that you saw in Chapter 1 is shown in Figure 12-1.

FIGURE 12-1

The example actually generated two windows. The larger window with the menu and the tool bars is the main, or **parent window**, and the smaller window is a **child window** of the parent. Although the child window can be closed without closing the parent window by double-clicking the title bar icon that is in the upper-left corner of the child window, closing the parent window automatically closes the child window as well. This is because the child window is owned by, and dependent upon, the parent window. In general, a parent window may have a number of child windows, as you'll see.

The most fundamental parts of a typical window are its **border**, the **title bar** that shows the name that you give to the window, the **title bar icon** that appears at the left end of the title bar, and the **client area**, which is the area in the center of the window not used by the title bar or borders. You can get all of these created for free in a Windows program. As you will see, all you have to do is provide some text for the title bar.

The border defines the boundary of a window and may be fixed or resizable. If the border is resizable, you can drag it to alter the size of the window. The window also may possess a size grip, which you can use to alter the size of a window. When you define a window, you can modify how the border behaves and appears if you want. Most windows will also have the maximize, minimize, and close buttons in the upper-right corner of the window. These allow the window to be increased to full screen size, reduced to an icon, or closed.

When you click the title bar icon with the left mouse button, it provides a standard menu for altering or closing the window called the **system menu** or **control menu**. The system menu also appears when you right-click the title bar of a window. Although it's optional, it is a good idea always to include the title bar icon in any main windows that your program generates. Including the title bar icon provides you with a very convenient way of closing the program when things don't work during debugging.

The client area is the part of the window where you usually want your program to write text or graphics. You address the client area for this purpose in exactly the same way as the yard that you saw in Figure 7-1 in Chapter 7. The upper-left corner of the client area has the coordinates (0, 0), with x increasing from left to right, and y increasing from top to bottom.

The menu bar is optional in a window but is probably the most common way to control an application. Each menu in the menu bar displays a drop-down list of menu items when you click it. The contents of a menu and the physical appearance of many objects that are displayed in a window, such as the icons on the toolbar that appear above, the cursor, and many others, are defined by a **resource file**. You will see many more resource files when we get to write some more sophisticated Windows programs.

The toolbar provides a set of icons that usually act as alternatives to the menu options that you use most often. Because they give a pictorial clue to the function provided, they can often make a program easier and faster to use.

I'll mention a caveat about terminology that you need to be conscious of before I move on. Users tend to think of a window as the thing that appears on the screen with a border around it, and, of course, it is, but it is only one kind of window; however, in Windows a window is a generic term covering a whole range of entities. In fact, almost any entity that is displayed is a window — for example, a dialog box is a window and each button is also a window. I will generally use terminology to refer to objects that describe what they are, buttons, dialogs, and so on, but you need to have tucked in the back of your mind that they are windows, too, because you can do things to them that you can do with a regular window — you can draw on a button, for instance.

Windows Programs and the Operating System

When you write a Windows program, your program is subservient to the operating system and Windows is in control. Your program must not deal directly with the hardware, and all communications with the outside world must pass through Windows. When you use a Windows program, you are interacting primarily with Windows, which then communicates with the application program on your behalf. Your Windows program is the tail, Windows is the dog, and your program wags only when Windows tells it to.

There are a number of reasons why this is so. First and foremost, because your program is potentially always sharing the computer with other programs that may be executing at the same time, Windows has to have primary control to manage the sharing of machine resources. If one application were allowed to have primary control in a Windows environment, this would inevitably make programming more complicated because of the need to provide for the possibility of other programs, and information intended for other applications could be lost. A second reason for Windows being in control is that Windows embodies a standard user interface and needs to be in charge to enforce that standard. You can only display information on the screen using the tools that Windows provides, and then only when authorized.

Event-Driven Programs

You have already seen, in Chapter 1, that a Windows program is **event-driven**, so a Windows program essentially waits around for something to happen. A significant part of the code required for a Windows application is dedicated to processing events that are caused by external actions of the user, but activities that are not directly associated with your application can nonetheless require that bits of your program code are executed. For example, if the user drags the window of another application that is active alongside your program and this action uncovers part of the client area of the window devoted to your application, your application may need to redraw that part of the window.

Windows Messages

Events in a Windows application are occurrences such as the user clicking the mouse or pressing a key, or a timer reaching zero. The Windows operating system records each event in a **message** and places the message in a **message queue** for the program for which the message is intended. Thus a Windows message is simply a record of the data relating to an event, and the message queue for an application is just a sequence of such messages waiting to be processed by the application. By sending a message, Windows can tell your program that something needs to be done, or that some information has become available, or that an event such as a mouse click has occurred. If your program is properly organized, it will respond in the appropriate way to the message. There are many different kinds of messages and they can occur very frequently — many times per second when the mouse is being dragged, for example.

A Windows program must contain a function specifically for handling these messages. The function is often called WndProc() or WindowProc(), although it doesn't have to have a particular name because Windows accesses the function through a pointer to a function that you supply. So the sending of a message to your program boils down to Windows calling a function that you provide, typically called WindowProc(), and passing any necessary data to your program by means of arguments to this function. Within your WindowProc() function, it is up to you to work out what the message is from the data supplied and what to do about it.

Fortunately, you don't need to write code to process every message. You can filter out those that are of interest in your program, deal with those in whatever way you want, and pass the rest back to Windows. You pass a message back to Windows by calling a standard function provided by Windows called DefWindowProc(), which provides default message processing.

The Windows API

All of the communications between any Windows application and Windows itself use the Windows application programming interface, otherwise known as the **Windows API**. This consists of literally hundreds of functions that are provided as a standard with the Windows operating system that provides the means by which an application communicates with Windows, and vice versa. The Windows API was developed in the days when C was the primary language in use, long before the advent of C++, and for this reason, structures rather than classes are frequently used for passing some kinds of data between Windows and your application program.

The Windows API covers all aspects of the communications between Windows and your application. Because there is such a large number of functions in the API, using them in the raw can be very difficult — just understanding what they all are is a task in itself. This is where Visual C++ 2010 makes the life of the application developer very much easier. Visual C++ 2010 packages the Windows API in a way that structures the API functions in an object-oriented manner, and provides an easier way to use the interface in C++ with more default functionality. This takes the form of the Microsoft Foundation Classes, MFC. Also, for applications targeting the CLR, you have a facility called Windows Forms where the code necessary to create a GUI is all created automatically. All you have to do is supply the code necessary to handle the events in the way that your application requires. You'll be creating a Windows Forms application a little later in this chapter.

Visual C++ also provides Application Wizards that create basic applications of various kinds, including MFC and Windows Forms-based applications. The Application Wizard can generate a complete working application that includes all of the boilerplate code necessary for a basic Windows application, leaving you just to customize this for your particular purposes. The example in Chapter 1 illustrated how much functionality Visual C++ is capable of providing without any coding effort at all on your part. I will discuss this in much more detail when we get to write some more practical examples using the MFC Application Wizard.

Windows Data Types

Windows defines a significant number of data types that are used to specify function parameter types and return types in the Windows API. These Windows-specific types also propagate through to functions that are defined in MFC. Each of these Windows types will map to some C++ type, but because the mapping between Windows types and C++ types can change, you should always use the Windows type where this applies. For example, in the past the Windows type WORD has been defined in one version of Windows as type `unsigned short` and in another Windows version as type `unsigned int`. On 16-bit machines these types are equivalent, but on 32-bit machines they are decidedly different so anyone using the C++ type rather than the Windows type could run into problems.

You can find the complete list of Windows data types in the documentation, but here are a few of the most common you are likely to meet:

BOOL or BOOLEAN	A Boolean variable can have the values TRUE or FALSE. Note that this is not the same as the C++ type `bool`, which can have the values true or false.
BYTE	An 8-bit byte.
CHAR	An 8-bit character.
DWORD	A 32-bit unsigned integer that corresponds to type `unsigned long` in C++.
HANDLE	A handle to an object — a handle being a 32-bit integer value that records the location of an object in memory, or 64-bit when compiling for 64 bit.
HBRUSH	A handle to a brush, a brush being used to fill an area with color.
HCURSOR	A handle to a cursor.

HDC	Handle to a device context — a device context being an object that enables you to draw on a window.
HINSTANCE	Handle to an instance.
LPARAM	A message parameter.
LPCTSTR	LPCWSTR if _UNICODE is defined, otherwise LPCSTR.
LPCWSTR	A pointer to a constant null-terminated string of 16-bit characters.
LPCSTR	A pointer to a constant null-terminated string of 8-bit characters.
LPHANDLE	A pointer to a handle.
LRESULT	A signed value that results from processing a message.
WORD	A 16-bit unsigned integer, so it corresponds to type unsigned short in C++.

I'll introduce any other Windows types we are using in examples as the need arises. All the types used by Windows, as well as the prototypes of the Windows API functions, are contained in the header file windows.h, so you need to include this header file when you put your basic Windows program together.

Notation in Windows Programs

In many Windows programs, variable names have a prefix, which indicates what kind of value the variable holds and how it is used. There are quite a few prefixes and they are often used in combination. For example, the prefix lpfn signifies a long pointer to a function. A sample of the prefixes you might come across is:

PREFIX	MEANING
b	a logical variable of type BOOL, equivalent to int
by	type unsigned char; a **byte**
c	type char
dw	type DWORD, which is unsigned long
fn	a **fun**ction
h	a **h**andle, used to reference something.
i	type int
l	type long
lp	long **p**ointer
n	type unsigned int

continues

(continued)

p	a **p**ointer
s	a **s**tring
sz	a **z**ero terminated **s**tring
w	type WORD, which is unsigned short

This use of these prefixes is called **Hungarian notation**. It was introduced to minimize the possibility of misusing a variable by interpreting it differently from how it was defined or intended to be used. Such misinterpretation was easily done in the C language, a precursor of C++. With C++ and its stronger type checking, you don't need to make such a special effort with your notation to avoid such problems. The compiler always flags an error for type inconsistencies in your program, and many of the kinds of bugs that plagued earlier C programs can't occur with C++.

On the other hand, Hungarian notation can still help to make programs easier to understand, particularly when you are dealing with a lot of variables of different types that are arguments to Windows API functions. Because Windows programs are still written in C, and, of course, because parameters for Windows API functions are still defined using Hungarian notation, the method is still used quite widely.

You can make up your own mind as to the extent to which you want to use Hungarian notation, as it is by no means obligatory. You may choose not to use it at all, but in any event, if you have an idea of how it works, you will find it easier to understand what the arguments to the Windows API functions are. There is a small caveat, however. As Windows has developed, the types of some of the API function arguments have changed slightly, but the variable names that are used remain the same. As a consequence, the prefix may not be quite correct in specifying the variable type.

THE STRUCTURE OF A WINDOWS PROGRAM

For a minimal Windows program that just uses the Windows API, you will write two functions. These are a WinMain() function, where execution of the program begins and basic program initialization is carried out, and a WindowProc() function that is called by Windows to process messages for the application. The WindowProc() part of a Windows program is usually the larger portion because this is where most of the application-specific code is, responding to messages caused by user input of one kind or another.

Although these two functions make up a complete program, they are not directly connected. WinMain() does not call WindowProc(), Windows does. In fact, Windows also calls WinMain(). This is illustrated in Figure 12-2.

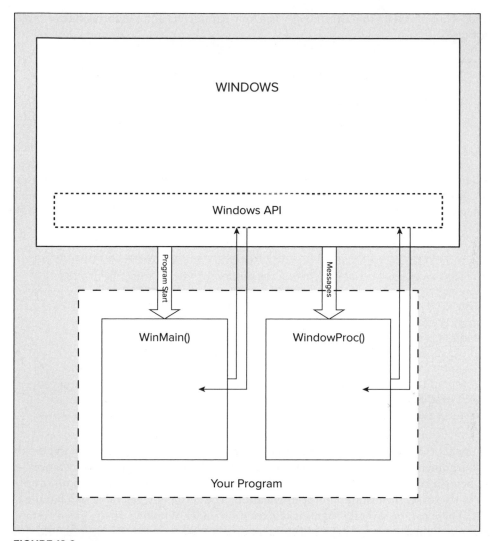

FIGURE 12-2

The function `WinMain()` communicates with Windows by calling some of the Windows API functions. The same applies to `WindowProc()`. The integrating factor in your Windows program is Windows itself, which links to both `WinMain()` and `WindowProc()`. You will take a look at what the pieces are that make up `WinMain()` and `WindowProc()` and then assemble the parts into a working example of a simple Windows program.

The WinMain() Function

The `WinMain()` function is the equivalent of the `main()` function in a console program. It's where execution starts and where the basic initialization for the rest of the program is carried out.

To allow Windows to pass data to it, `WinMain()` has four parameters and a return value of type `int`. Its prototype is:

```
int WINAPI WinMain(HINSTANCE hInstance,
                   HINSTANCE hPrevInstance,
                   LPSTR lpCmdLine,
                   int nCmdShow
                  );
```

Following the return type specifier, `int`, you have a specification for the function, `WINAPI`, which is new to you. This is a Windows-defined macro that causes the function name and arguments to be handled in a special way that is specific to Windows API functions. This is different from the way functions are normally handled in C++. The precise details are unimportant — this is simply the way Windows requires things to be, so you need to put the `WINAPI` macro name in front of the names of functions called by Windows.

> *If you really want to know about calling conventions, they are described in the documentation that comes with Visual C++ 2010.* `WINAPI` *is defined as* `__stdcall`*, and putting this modifier before a function name indicates that the standard Windows calling convention is to be used. This requires that the parameters are pushed on the stack in reverse order and that the function called will clean up the stack when it ends. The* `CALLBACK` *modifier that you will see later in this chapter is also defined as* `__stdcall` *and is therefore the equivalent of* `WINAPI`*. The standard C++ calling convention is specified by* `the __cdecl` *modifier.*

The four arguments that are passed by Windows to your `WinMain()` function contain important data. The first argument, `hInstance`, is of type `HINSTANCE`, which is a handle to an instance — an instance here being a running program. A **handle** is an integer value that identifies an object of some kind — in this case, the instance of the application. The actual integer value of a handle is not important. There can be several programs in execution under Windows at any given instant. This raises the possibility of several copies of the same application being active at once, and this needs to be recognized. Hence, the `hInstance` handle identifies a particular copy. If you start more than one copy of a program, each one has its own unique `hInstance` value. As you will see shortly, handles are also used to identify all sorts of other things. Of course, all handles in a particular context — application instance handles, for example — need to be different from one another.

The next argument passed to your `WinMain()` function, `hPrevInstance`, is a legacy from the 16-bit versions of the Windows operating system, and you can safely ignore it. On current versions of Windows, it is always null. The next argument, `lpCmdLine`, is a pointer to a string containing the command line that started the program. For instance, if you started it using the Run command from the Start button menu of Windows, the string contains everything that appears in the Open box. Having this pointer allows you to pick up any parameter values that may appear in the command line. The type `LPSTR` is another Windows type, specifying a 32-bit (long) pointer to a string, or 64-bit when compiling in 64-bit mode.

The last argument, nCmdShow, determines how the window is to look when it is created. It could be displayed normally or it might need to be minimized; for example, the shortcut for the program might specify that the program should be minimized when it starts. This argument can take one of a fixed set of values that are defined by symbolic constants such as SW_SHOWNORMAL and SW_SHOWMINNOACTIVE. There are a number of other constants like these that define the way a window is to be displayed, and they all begin SW_. Other examples are SW_HIDE or SW_SHOWMAXIMIZED. You don't usually need to examine the value of nCmdShow. You typically pass it directly to the Windows API function responsible for displaying your application window.

If you want to know what all the other constants are that specify how a window displays, you can find a complete list of the possible values if you search for WinMain in the MSDN Library. You can access the MSDN library online at http://msdn2.microsoft.com/en-us/library/default.aspx.

The function WinMain() in your Windows program needs to do four things:

➤ Tell Windows what kind of window the program requires

➤ Create the program window

➤ Initialize the program window

➤ Retrieve Windows messages intended for the program

We will take a look at each of these in turn and then create a complete WinMain() function.

Specifying a Program Window

The first step in creating a window is to define just what sort of window it is that you want to create. Windows defines a special struct type called WNDCLASSEX to contain the data specifying a window. The data that is stored in an instance of the struct defines a window class, which determines the type of window. Do not confuse this with a C++ class — the MFC defines a class that represents a window but, this is not the same at all. You need to create a variable of type WNDCLASSEX, and give values to each of its members (just like filling in a form). After you've filled in the variables, you can pass it to Windows (via a function that you'll see later) to register the class. When that's been done, whenever you want to create a window of that class, you can tell Windows to look up the class that you've already registered.

The definition of the WNDCLASSEX structure is as follows:

```
struct WNDCLASSEX
{
  UINT cbSize;              // Size of this object in bytes
  UINT style;              // Window style
  WNDPROC lpfnWndProc;     // Pointer to message processing function
  int cbClsExtra;          // Extra bytes after the window class
  int cbWndExtra;          // Extra bytes after the window instance
  HINSTANCE hInstance;     // The application instance handle
  HICON hIcon;             // The application icon
  HCURSOR hCursor;         // The window cursor
  HBRUSH hbrBackground;    // The brush defining the background color
  LPCTSTR lpszMenuName;    // A pointer to the name of the menu resource
```

```
    LPCTSTR lpszClassName;    // A pointer to the class name
    HICON hIconSm;            // A small icon associated with the window
};
```

You construct an object of type WNDCLASSEX in the way that you saw when I discussed structures, for example:

```
WNDCLASSEX WindowClass;                    // Create a window class object
```

All you need to do now is fill in values for the members of WindowClass. They are all public by default because WindowClass is a struct.

Setting the value for the cbSize member of the struct is easy when you use the sizeof operator:

```
WindowClass.cbSize = sizeof(WNDCLASSEX);
```

The style member of the struct determines various aspects of the window's behavior, in particular, the conditions under which the window should be redrawn. You can select from a number of options for this member's value, each defined by a symbolic constant beginning CS_.

 You'll find all the possible constant values for style if you search for WNDCLASSEX in the MSDN Library that you'll find at http://msdn2.microsoft.com/en-us/library.

Where two or more options are required, the constants can be combined to produce a composite value using the bitwise OR operator, |. For example:

```
WindowClass.style = CS_HREDRAW | CS_VREDRAW;
```

The option CS_HREDRAW indicates to Windows that the window is to be redrawn if its horizontal width is altered, and CS_VREDRAW indicates that it is to be redrawn if the vertical height of the window is changed. In the preceding statement, you have elected to have the window redrawn in either case. As a result, Windows sends a message to your program indicating that you should redraw the window whenever the width or height of the window is altered by the user. Each of the possible options for the window style is defined by a unique bit in a 32-bit word being set to 1. That's why the bitwise OR is used to combine them. These bits indicating a particular style are usually called **flags**. Flags are used very frequently, not only in Windows but also in C++, because they are an efficient way of representing and processing features that are either there or not, or parameters that are either true or false.

The member lpfnWndProc stores a pointer to the function in your program that handles messages for the window you create. The prefix to the name signifies that this is a long pointer to a function. If you followed the herd and called the function to handle messages for the application WindowProc(), you would initialize this member with the statement:

```
WindowClass.lpfnWndProc = WindowProc;
```

The next two members, cbClsExtra and cbWndExtra, allow you to ask that extra space be provided internally to Windows for your own use. An example of this could be when you want to associate additional data with each instance of a window to assist in message handling for each window instance. Normally you won't need extra space allocated for you, in which case you must set the cbClsExtra and cbWndExtra members to zero.

The hInstance member holds the handle for the current application instance, so you should set this to the hInstance value that was passed to WinMain() by Windows.

The members hIcon, hCursor, and hbrBackground are handles that in turn define the icon that represents the application when minimized, the cursor the window uses, and the background color of the client area of the window. (As you saw earlier, a handle is just a 32-bit integer (or 64-bit when compiled in 64-bit mode) used as an ID to represent something.) These are set using Windows API functions. For example:

```
WindowClass.hIcon = LoadIcon(0, IDI_APPLICATION);
WindowClass.hCursor = LoadCursor(0, IDC_ARROW);
WindowClass.hbrBackground = static_cast<HBRUSH>(GetStockObject(GRAY_BRUSH));
```

All three members are set to standard Windows values by these function calls. The icon is a default provided by Windows and the cursor is the standard arrow cursor used by the majority of Windows applications. A brush is a Windows object used to fill an area, in this case the client area of the window. The function GetStockObject() returns a generic type for all stock objects, so you need to cast it to type HBRUSH. In the preceding example, it returns a handle to the standard gray brush, and the background color for our window is thus set to gray. This function can also be used to obtain other standard objects for a window, such as fonts, for example. You could also set the hIcon and hCursor members to null, in which case Windows would provide the default icon and cursor. If you set hbrBackground to null, your program is expected to paint the window background, and messages are sent to your application whenever this becomes necessary.

The lpszMenuName member is set to the name of a resource defining the window menu, or to zero if there is no menu for the window. You will look into creating and using menu resources when you use the AppWizard.

The lpszClassName member of the struct stores the name that you supply to identify this particular class of window. You would usually use the name of the application for this. You need to keep track of this name because you will need it again when a window is created. This member would therefore be typically set with the statements:

```
static LPCTSTR szAppName = L"OFWin";       // Define window class name
WindowClass.lpszClassName = szAppName;     // Set class name
```

I have defined szAppName as a Unicode string here. In fact, the LPCTSTR type is defined as const wchar_t* if UNICODE is defined for the application, or const char* if it is not. Thus, the definition for szAppName here assumes a Unicode application.

The last member is hIconSm, which identifies a small icon associated with the window class. If you specify this as null, Windows searches for a small icon related to the hIcon member and uses that.

In fact, the WNDCLASSEX structure replaces another structure, WNDCLASS, that was used for the same purpose. The old structure did not include the cbSize member that stores the size of the structure in bytes or the hIconSm member.

Creating a Program Window

After all the members of your WNDCLASSEX structure have been set to the values required, the next step is to tell Windows about it. You do this using the Windows API function RegisterClassEx(). Given that your structure is WindowClass, the statement to do this would be:

```
RegisterClassEx(&WindowClass);
```

Easy, isn't it? The address of the struct is passed to the function, and Windows extracts and squirrels away all the values that you have set in the structure members. This process is called **registering** the window class. Just to remind you, the term *class* here is used in the sense of classification and is not the same as the idea of a class in C++, so don't confuse the two. Each instance of the application must make sure that it registers the window classes that it needs. If you were using the obsolete WNDCLASS structure that I mentioned, you would have to use a different function here, RegisterClass().

After Windows knows the characteristics of the window that you want, and the function that is going to handle messages for it, you can go ahead and create it. You use the function CreateWindow() for this. The window class that you've already created determines the broad characteristics of a window, and further arguments to the function CreateWindow() add additional characteristics. Because an application may have several windows in general, the function CreateWindow() returns a handle to the window created that you can store to enable you to refer to that particular window later. There are many API calls that require you to specify the window handle as a parameter if you want to use them. You will look at a typical use of the CreateWindow() function at this point. This might be:

```
HWND hWnd;                                // Window handle
...
hWnd = CreateWindow(
        szAppName,                        // the window class name
        "A Basic Window the Hard Way",    // The window title
        WS_OVERLAPPEDWINDOW,              // Window style as overlapped
        CW_USEDEFAULT,                    // Default screen position of upper left
        CW_USEDEFAULT,                    // corner of our window as x,y...
        CW_USEDEFAULT,                    // Default window size, width...
        CW_USEDEFAULT,                    // ...and height
        0,                                // No parent window
        0,                                // No menu
        hInstance,                        // Program Instance handle
        0                                 // No window creation data
      );
```

The variable hWnd of type HWND is a 32-bit integer handle to a window, or 64-bit in 64-bit mode. You'll use this variable to record the value that the CreateWindow() function returns that identifies the window. The first argument that you pass to the function is the class name. This is used by Windows to identify the WNDCLASSEX struct that you passed to it previously, in the RegisterClassEx() function call, so that the information from this struct can be used in the window creation process.

The second argument to `CreateWindow()` defines the text that is to appear on the title bar. The third argument specifies the style that the window has after it is created. The option specified here, `WS_OVERLAPPEDWINDOW`, actually combines several options. It defines the window as having the `WS_OVERLAPPED`, `WS_CAPTION`, `WS_SYSMENU`, `WS_THICKFRAME`, `WS_MINIMIZEBOX`, and `WS_MAXIMIZEBOX` styles. This results in an overlapped window, which is a window intended to be the main application window, with a title bar and a thick frame, which has a title bar icon, system menu, and maximize and minimize buttons. A window that you specify as having a thick frame has borders that can be resized.

The next four arguments determine the position and size of the window on the screen. The first two are the screen coordinates of the upper-left corner of the window, and the second two define the width and height of the window. The value `CW_USEDEFAULT` indicates that you want Windows to assign the default position and size for the window. This tells Windows to arrange successive windows in cascading positions down the screen. `CW_USEDEFAULT` only applies to windows specified as `WS_OVERLAPPED`.

The next argument value is zero, indicating that the window being created is not a child window (a window that is dependent on a parent window). If you wanted it to be a child window, you would set this argument to the handle of the parent window. The next argument is also zero, indicating that no menu is required. You then specify the handle of the current instance of the program that was passed to the program by Windows. The last argument for window creation data is zero because you just want a simple window in the example. If you wanted to create a multiple-document interface (MDI) client window, the last argument would point to a structure related to this. You'll learn more about MDI windows later in the book.

 The Windows API also includes a `CreateWindowEx()` *function that you use to create a window with extended style information.*

After calling the `CreateWindow()` function, the window now exists but is not yet displayed on the screen. You need to call another Windows API function to get it displayed:

```
ShowWindow(hWnd, nCmdShow);               // Display the window
```

Only two arguments are required here. The first identifies the window and is the handle returned by the function `CreateWindow()`. The second is the value `nCmdShow` that was passed to `WinMain()`, and that indicates how the window is to appear onscreen.

Initializing the Program Window

After calling the function `ShowWindow()`, the window appears onscreen but still has no application content, so you need to get your program to draw in the client area of the window. You could just put together some code to do this directly in the `WinMain()` function, but this would be most unsatisfactory: in this case, the contents of the client area are not considered to be permanent — if you want the client area contents to be retained, you can't afford to output what you want and forget about it. Any action on the part of the user that modifies the window in some way, such as dragging a border or dragging the whole window, typically requires that the window *and* its client area are redrawn.

When the client area needs to be redrawn for any reason, Windows sends a particular message to your program, and your `WindowProc()` function needs to respond by reconstructing the client area of the window. Therefore, the best way to get the client area drawn in the first instance is to put the code to draw the client area in the `WindowProc()` function and get Windows to send the message requesting that the client area be redrawn to your program. Whenever you know in your program that the window should be redrawn (when you change something, for example), you need to tell Windows to send a message back to get the window redrawn.

You can ask Windows to send your program a message to redraw the client area of the window by calling another Windows API function, `UpdateWindow()`. The statement to accomplish this is:

```
UpdateWindow(hWnd);                     // Cause window client area to be drawn
```

This function requires only one argument: the window handle `hWnd`, which identifies your particular program window. (In general, there can be several windows in an application.) The result of the call is that Windows sends a message to your program requesting that the client area be redrawn.

Dealing with Windows Messages

The last task that `WinMain()` needs to address is dealing with the messages that Windows may have queued for your application. This may seem a bit odd because I said earlier that you needed the function `WindowProc()` to deal with messages, but let me explain a little further.

Queued and Non-Queued Messages

I oversimplified Windows messaging when I introduced the idea earlier. There are, in fact, two kinds of Windows messages:

There are **queued messages** that Windows places in a queue, and the `WinMain()` function must extract these messages from the queue for processing. The code in `WinMain()` that does this is called the **message loop**. Queued messages include those arising from user input from the keyboard, moving the mouse, and clicking the mouse buttons. Messages from a timer and the Windows message to request that a window be redrawn are also queued.

There are **non-queued messages** that result in the `WindowProc()` function being called directly by Windows. A lot of the non-queued messages arise as a consequence of processing queued messages. What you are doing in the message loop in `WinMain()` is retrieving a message that Windows has queued for your application and then asking Windows to invoke your `WindowProc()` function to process it. Why can't Windows just call `WindowProc()` whenever necessary? Well, it could, but it just doesn't work this way. The reasons have to do with how Windows manages multiple applications executing simultaneously.

The Message Loop

As I said, retrieving messages from the message queue is done using a standard mechanism in Windows programming called the **message pump** or **message loop**. The code for this would be:

```
MSG msg;                                // Windows message structure
while(GetMessage(&msg, 0, 0, 0) == TRUE) // Get any messages
{
```

```
    TranslateMessage(&msg);              // Translate the message
    DispatchMessage(&msg);               // Dispatch the message
}
```

This involves three steps in dealing with each message:

➤   `GetMessage()`. Retrieves a message from the queue

➤   `TranslateMessage()`. Performs any conversion necessary on the message retrieved

➤   `DispatchMessage()`. Causes Windows to call the `WindowProc()` function in your application to deal with the message

The operation of `GetMessage()` is important because it has a significant contribution to the way Windows works with multiple applications, so we should explore it in a little more detail.

The `GetMessage()` function retrieves a message queued for the application window and stores information about the message in the variable `msg`, pointed to by the first argument. The variable `msg`, which is a `struct` of type `MSG`, contains a number of different members that you are not accessing here. Still, for completeness, the definition of the structure looks like this:

```
struct MSG
{
    HWND    hwnd;              // Handle for the relevant window
    UINT    message;          // The message ID
    WPARAM  wParam;           // Message parameter (32-bits)
    LPARAM  lParam;           // Message parameter (32-bits)
    DWORD   time;             // The time when the message was queued
    POINT   pt;               // The mouse position
};
```

The `wParam` member is an example of a slightly misleading Hungarian notation prefix that I mentioned was now possible. You might assume that it was of type `WORD` (which is a 16-bit unsigned integer), which used to be true in earlier Windows versions, but now it is of type `WPARAM`, which is a 32-bit integer value.

The exact contents of the `wParam` and `lParam` members are dependent on what kind of message it is. The message ID in the member `message` is an integer value and can be one of a set of values that are predefined in the header file, `windows.h`, as symbolic constants. Message IDs for general windows all start with `WM_`; typical examples are shown in the following table. General windows messages cover a wide variety of events and include messages relating to mouse and menu events, keyboard input, and window creation and management.

ID	DESCRIPTION
WM_PAINT	The window should be redrawn.
WM_SIZE	The window has been resized.
WM_LBUTTONDOWN	The left mouse button is down.
WM_RBUTTONDOWN	The right mouse button is down.

continues

(continued)

ID	DESCRIPTION
WM_MOUSEMOVE	The mouse has moved.
WM_CLOSE	The window or application should close.
WM_DESTROY	The window is being destroyed.
WM_QUIT	The program should be terminated.

The function GetMessage() always returns TRUE unless the message is WM_QUIT to end the program, in which case the value returned is FALSE, or unless an error occurs, in which case the return value is −1. Thus, the while loop continues until a quit message is generated to close the application or until an error condition arises. In either case, you need to end the program by passing the wParam value back to Windows in a return statement.

 There are prefixes other than WM for messages destined for other types of windows than a general window.

The second argument in the call to GetMessage() is the handle of the window for which you want to get messages. This parameter can be used to retrieve messages for one window separately from another. If this argument is 0, as it is here, GetMessage() retrieves all messages for an application. This is an easy way of retrieving all messages for an application regardless of how many windows it has. It is also the safest way because you are sure of getting all the messages for your application. When the user of your Windows program closes the application window, for example, the window is closed before the WM_QUIT message is generated. Consequently, if you only retrieve messages by specifying a window handle to the GetMessage() function, you cannot retrieve the WM_QUIT message and your program is not able to terminate properly.

The last two arguments to GetMessage() are integers that hold minimum and maximum values for the message IDs you want to retrieve from the queue. This allows messages to be retrieved selectively. A range is usually specified by symbolic constants. Using WM_MOUSEFIRST and WM_MOUSELAST as these two arguments would select just mouse messages, for example. If both arguments are zero, as you have them here, all messages are retrieved.

Multitasking

If there are no messages queued, the GetMessage() function does not come back to your program. Windows allows execution to pass to another application, and you only get a value returned from calling GetMessage() when a message appears in the queue. This mechanism was fundamental in enabling multiple applications to run under older versions of Windows and is referred to as **cooperative multitasking** because it depends on concurrent applications giving up their control of the processor from time to time. After your program calls GetMessage(), unless there is a message for your program, another application is executed and your program gets another opportunity to do something only if the other application releases the processor, perhaps by a call to GetMessage() when there are no messages queued for it, but this is not the only possibility.

With current versions of Windows, the operating system can interrupt an application after a period of time and transfer control to another application. This mechanism is called **pre-emptive multitasking** because an application can be interrupted in any event. With pre-emptive multitasking, however, you must still program the message loop in `WinMain()` using `GetMessage()` as before, and make provision for relinquishing control of the processor to Windows from time to time in a long-running calculation (this is usually done using the `PeekMessage()` API function). If you don't do this, your application may be unable to respond to messages to repaint the application window when these arise. This can be for reasons that are quite independent of your application — when an overlapping window for another application is closed, for example.

The conceptual operation of the `GetMessage()` function is illustrated in Figure 12-3.

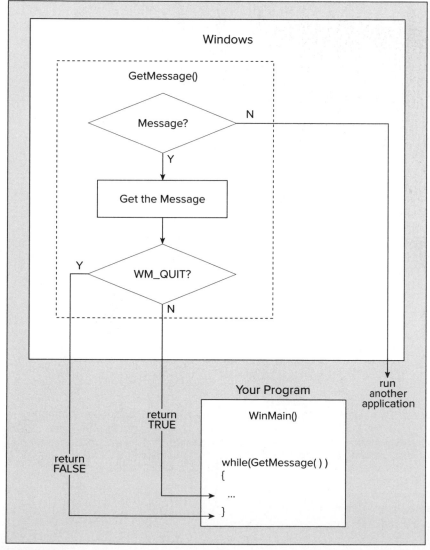

FIGURE 12-3

Within the `while` loop, the first function call to `TranslateMessage()` requests Windows to do some conversion work for keyboard-related messages. Then the call to the function `DispatchMessage()` causes Windows to **dispatch** the message or, in other words, to call the `WindowProc()` function in your program to process the message. The return from `DispatchMessage()` does not occur until `WindowProc()` has finished processing the message. The WM_QUIT message indicates that the program should end, so this results in FALSE being returned to the application that stops the message loop.

A Complete WinMain() Function

You have looked at all the bits that need to go into the function `WinMain()`. So now you can assemble them into a complete function:

```
// Listing OFWIN_1
int WINAPI WinMain(HINSTANCE hInstance, HINSTANCE hPrevInstance,
                   LPSTR lpCmdLine, int nCmdShow)
{
    WNDCLASSEX WindowClass;        // Structure to hold our window's attributes

    static LPCTSTR szAppName = L"OFWin";    // Define window class name
    HWND hWnd;                               // Window handle
    MSG msg;                                 // Windows message structure

    WindowClass.cbSize = sizeof(WNDCLASSEX);   // Set structure size

    // Redraw the window if the size changes
    WindowClass.style   = CS_HREDRAW | CS_VREDRAW;

    // Define the message handling function
    WindowClass.lpfnWndProc = WindowProc;

    WindowClass.cbClsExtra = 0;      // No extra bytes after the window class
    WindowClass.cbWndExtra = 0;      // structure or the window instance

    WindowClass.hInstance = hInstance;        // Application instance handle

    // Set default application icon
    WindowClass.hIcon = LoadIcon(0, IDI_APPLICATION);

    // Set window cursor to be the standard arrow
    WindowClass.hCursor = LoadCursor(0, IDC_ARROW);

    // Set gray brush for background color
    WindowClass.hbrBackground = static_cast<HBRUSH>(GetStockObject(GRAY_BRUSH));

    WindowClass.lpszMenuName = 0;             // No menu
    WindowClass.lpszClassName = szAppName;    // Set class name
    WindowClass.hIconSm = 0;                  // Default small icon

    // Now register our window class
    RegisterClassEx(&WindowClass);
```

```
    // Now we can create the window
    hWnd = CreateWindow(
            szAppName,                          // the window class name
            L"A Basic Window the Hard Way",     // The window title
            WS_OVERLAPPEDWINDOW,                // Window style as overlapped
            CW_USEDEFAULT,          // Default screen position of upper left
            CW_USEDEFAULT,          // corner of our window as x,y...
            CW_USEDEFAULT,          // Default window size
            CW_USEDEFAULT,          // ....
            0,                      // No parent window
            0,                      // No menu
            hInstance,              // Program Instance handle
            0                       // No window creation data
        );

    ShowWindow(hWnd, nCmdShow);     // Display the window
    UpdateWindow(hWnd);             // Cause window client area to be drawn

    // The message loop
    while(GetMessage(&msg, 0, 0, 0) == TRUE)   // Get any messages
    {
      TranslateMessage(&msg);                   // Translate the message
      DispatchMessage(&msg);                    // Dispatch the message
    }

    return static_cast<int>(msg.wParam);        // End, so return to Windows
}
```

code snippet Ex12_01.cpp

How It Works

After declaring the variables you need in the function, all the members of the WindowClass structure are initialized and the window is registered.

The next step is to call the CreateWindow() function to create the data for the physical appearance of the window, based on the arguments passed and the data established in the WindowClass structure that was previously passed to Windows using the RegisterClassEx() function. The call to ShowWindow() causes the window to be displayed according to the mode specified by nCmdShow, and the UpdateWindow() function signals that a message to draw the window client area should be generated.

Finally, the message loop continues to retrieve messages for the application until a WM_QUIT message is obtained, whereupon the GetMessage() function returns FALSE and the loop ends. The value of the wParam member of the msg structure is passed back to Windows in the return statement.

Message Processing Functions

The function WinMain() contained nothing that was application-specific beyond the general appearance of the application window. All of the code that makes the application behave in the way that you want is included in the message processing part of the program. This is the function

`WindowProc()` that you identify to Windows in the `WindowClass` structure. Windows calls this function each time a message for your main application window is dispatched.

This example is simple, so you will be putting all the code to process messages in the one function, `WindowProc()`. More generally, though, the `WindowProc()` function is responsible for analyzing what a given message was and which window it was destined for and then calling one of a whole range of functions, each of which would be geared to handling a particular message in the context of the particular window concerned. However, the overall sequence of operations, and the way in which the function `WindowProc()` analyses an incoming message, is much the same in most application contexts.

The WindowProc() Function

The prototype of our `WindowProc()` function is:

```
LRESULT CALLBACK WindowProc(HWND hWnd, UINT message,
                            WPARAM wParam, LPARAM lParam);
```

The return type is `LRESULT`, which is a type defined by Windows and is normally equivalent to type `long`. Because the function is called by Windows through a pointer (you set the pointer up in `WinMain()` in the `WNDCLASSEX` structure), you need to qualify the function as `CALLBACK`. I mentioned this specifier earlier, and its effect is the same as the `WINAPI` defined by Windows that determines how the function arguments are handled. Therefore, you could use `WINAPI` here instead of `CALLBACK`, although the latter expresses better what this function is about. The four arguments that are passed provide information about the particular message causing the function to be called. The meaning of each of these arguments is described in the following table:

ARGUMENT	MEANING
`HWND hWnd`	A handle to the window in which the event causing the message occurred.
`UINT message`	The message ID, which is a 32-bit value indicating the type of message.
`WPARAM wParam`	A 32-bit (or 64-bit in 64-bit mode) value containing additional information depending on what sort of message it is.
`LPARAM lParam`	A 32-bit (or 64-bit in 64-bit mode) value containing additional information depending on what sort of message it is.

The window that the incoming message relates to is identified by the first argument, `hWnd`, which is passed to the function. In this case, you have only one window, so you can ignore it.

Messages are identified by the value `message` that is passed to `WindowProc()`. You can test this value against predefined symbolic constants, each of which relates to a particular message. General windows messages begin with `WM_`, and typical examples are `WM_PAINT`, which corresponds to a request to redraw part of the client area of a window, and `WM_LBUTTONDOWN`, which indicates that the left mouse button was pressed. You can find the whole set of these by searching for `WM_` in the MSDN Library.

Decoding a Windows Message

The process of decoding the message that Windows is sending is usually done using a `switch` statement in the `WindowProc()` function, based on the value of `message`. Selecting the message types that you want to process is then just a question of putting a `case` statement for each case in the `switch`. The typical structure of such a `switch` statement, with arbitrary cases included, is as follows:

```
switch(message)
{
  case WM_PAINT:
    // Code to deal with drawing the client area
    break;

  case WM_LBUTTONDOWN:
    // Code to deal with the left mouse button being pressed
    break;

  case WM_LBUTTONUP:
    // Code to deal with the left mouse button being released
    break;

  case WM_DESTROY:
    // Code to deal with a window being destroyed
    break;

  default:
    // Code to handle any other messages
}
```

Every Windows program has something like this somewhere, although it may be hidden from sight in the Windows programs that you will write later using MFC. Each case corresponds to a particular value for the message ID and provides suitable processing for that message. Any messages that a program does not want to deal with individually are handled by the default statement, which should hand the messages back to Windows by calling `DefWindowProc()`. This is the Windows API function providing default message handling.

In a complex program dealing specifically with a wide range of possible Windows messages, this `switch` statement can become large and rather cumbersome. When you get to use the Application Wizard to generate a Windows application, you won't have to worry about this because it is all taken care of for you and you never see the `WindowProc()` function. All you need to do is to supply the code to process the particular messages in which you are interested.

Drawing the Window Client Area

Windows sends a `WM_PAINT` message to the program to signal that the client area of an application should be redrawn. So in your example, you need to draw the text in the window in response to the `WM_PAINT` message.

You can't go drawing in the window willy-nilly. Before you can write to the application window, you need to tell Windows that you want to do so, and get Windows' authority to go ahead.

You do this by calling the Windows API function `BeginPaint()`, which should only be called in response to a `WM_PAINT` message. It is used as follows:

```
HDC hDC;                            // A display context handle
PAINTSTRUCT PaintSt;                // Structure defining area to be redrawn

hDC = BeginPaint(hWnd, &PaintSt);   // Prepare to draw in the window
```

The type `HDC` defines what is called a **display context**, or more generally a **device context**. A device context provides the link between the device-independent Windows API functions for outputting information to the screen or a printer, and the device drivers that support writing to the specific devices attached to your PC. You can also regard a device context as a token of authority that is handed to you on request by Windows and grants you permission to output some information. Without a device context, you simply can't generate any output.

The `BeginPaint()` function provides you with a display context as a return value and requires two arguments to be supplied. The window to which you want to write is identified by the window handle, `hWnd`, which you pass as the first argument. The second argument is the address of a `PAINTSTRUCT` variable `PaintSt`, in which Windows places information about the area to be redrawn in response to the `WM_PAINT` message. I will ignore the details of this because you are not going to use it. You will just redraw the whole of the client area. You can obtain the coordinates of the client area in a `RECT` structure with the statements:

```
RECT aRect;                         // A working rectangle
GetClientRect(hWnd, &aRect);
```

The `GetClientRect()` function supplies the coordinates of the upper-left and lower-right corners of the client area for the window specified by the first argument. These coordinates are stored in the `RECT` structure aRect, which is passed through the second argument as a pointer. You can then use this definition of the client area for your window when you write the text to the window using the `DrawText()` function. Because your window has a gray background, you should alter the background of the text to be transparent, to allow the gray to show through; otherwise, the text appears against a white background. You can do this with this API function call:

```
SetBkMode(hDC, TRANSPARENT);        // Set text background mode
```

The first argument identifies the device context and the second sets the background mode. The default option is `OPAQUE`.

You can now write the text with the statement:

```
DrawText(hDC,                       // Device context handle
         L"But, soft! What light through yonder window breaks?",
         -1,                        // Indicate null terminated string
         &aRect,                    // Rectangle in which text is to be drawn
         DT_SINGLELINE|             // Text format - single line
         DT_CENTER|                 //              - centered in the line
         DT_VCENTER                 //              - line centered in aRect
        );
```

The first argument to the DrawText() function is your certificate of authority to draw on the window, the display context hDC. The next argument is the text string that you want to output. You could equally well have defined this in a variable and passed the pointer to the text as the second argument in the function call. The next argument, with the value -1, signifies that your string is terminated with a null character. If it weren't, you would put the count of the number of characters in the string here. The fourth argument is a pointer to a RECT structure defining a rectangle in which you want to write the text. In this case, it is the whole client area of the window defined in aRect. The last argument defines the format for the text in the rectangle. Here you have combined three specifications with a bitwise OR (|). The string is written as a single line, with the text centered on the line and the line centered vertically within the rectangle. This places it nicely in the center of the window. There are also a number of other options, which include the possibility to place text at the top or the bottom of the rectangle, and to left or right justify it.

After you have written all that you want to display, you must tell Windows that you have finished drawing the client area. For every BeginPaint() function call, there must be a corresponding EndPaint() function call. Thus, to end processing the WM_PAINT message, you need the statement:

```
EndPaint(hWnd, &PaintSt);          // Terminate window redraw operation
```

The hWnd argument identifies your program window, and the second argument is the address of the PAINTSTRUCT structure that was filled in by the BeginPaint() function.

Ending the Program

You might assume that closing the window closes the application, but to get this behavior, you actually have to add some more code. The reason that the application won't close by default when the window is closed is that you may need to do some clearing up. It is also possible that the application may have more than one window. When the user closes the window by double-clicking the title bar icon or clicking the Close button, this causes a WM_DESTROY message to be generated. Therefore, to close the application, you need to process the WM_DESTROY message in the WindowProc() function. You do this by generating a WM_QUIT message with the following statement:

```
PostQuitMessage(0);
```

The argument here is an exit code. This Windows API function does exactly what its name suggests: it posts a WM_QUIT message in the message queue for your application. This results in the GetMessage() function in WinMain() returning FALSE and ending the message loop, so ending the program.

A Complete WindowProc() Function

You have covered all the elements necessary to make up the complete WindowProc() function for your example. The code for the function is as follows:

Available for download on Wrox.com

```
// Listing OFWIN_2
LRESULT CALLBACK WindowProc(HWND hWnd, UINT message,
                  WPARAM wParam, LPARAM lParam)
{
```

```
HDC hDC;                          // Display context handle
PAINTSTRUCT PaintSt;             // Structure defining area to be drawn
RECT aRect;                       // A working rectangle

switch(message)                   // Process selected messages
{
  case WM_PAINT:                          // Message is to redraw the window
    hDC = BeginPaint(hWnd, &PaintSt);// Prepare to draw the window

    // Get upper left and lower right of client area
    GetClientRect(hWnd, &aRect);

    SetBkMode(hDC, TRANSPARENT);       // Set text background mode

    // Now draw the text in the window client area
    DrawText(
            hDC,                   // Device context handle
            L"But, soft! What light through yonder window breaks?",
            -1,                    // Indicate null terminated string
            &aRect,                // Rectangle in which text is to be drawn
            DT_SINGLELINE|         // Text format - single line
            DT_CENTER|             //                - centered in the line
            DT_VCENTER);           //                - line centered in aRect

    EndPaint(hWnd, &PaintSt);     // Terminate window redraw operation
    return 0;

  case WM_DESTROY:                // Window is being destroyed
    PostQuitMessage(0);
    return 0;

  default:                        // Any other message - we don't
                                  // want to know, so call
                                  // default message processing
    return DefWindowProc(hWnd, message, wParam, lParam);
  }
}
```

code snippet Ex12_01.cpp

How It Works

The entire function body is just a switch statement. A particular case is selected, based on the message ID that is passed to the function through the message parameter. Because this example is simple, you need to process only two different messages: WM_PAINT and WM_DESTROY. You hand all other messages back to Windows by calling the DefWindowProc() function in the default case for the switch. The arguments to DefWindowProc() are those that were passed to the function, so you are just passing them back as they are. Note the return statement at the end of processing each message type. For the messages you handle, a zero value is returned.

A Simple Windows Program

Because you have written `WinMain()` and `WindowProc()` to handle messages, you have enough to create a complete source file for a Windows program using just the Windows API. The complete source file simply consists of an `#include` directive for the `windows.h` header file, a prototype for the `WindowProc` function, and the `WinMain` and `WindowProc` functions that you have already seen:

```
// Ex12_01.cpp    Native windows program to display text in a window
#include <windows.h>

LRESULT CALLBACK WindowProc(HWND hWnd, UINT message,
                            WPARAM wParam, LPARAM lParam);

    // Insert code for WinMain() here (Listing OFWIN_1)

    // Insert code for WindowProc() here (Listing OFWIN_2)
```

code snippet Ex12_01.cpp

Of course, you'll need to create a project for this program, but instead of choosing Win32 Console Application as you've done up to now, you should create this project using the Win32 Project template. You should elect to create it as an empty project and then add the `Ex12_01.cpp` file to hold the code.

TRY IT OUT   A Simple Windows API Program

If you build and execute the example, it produces the window shown in Figure 12-4.

Note that the window has a number of properties provided by the operating system that require no programming effort on your part to manage. The boundaries of the window can be dragged to resize it, and the whole window can be moved about onscreen. The maximize and minimize buttons also work. Of course, all of these actions do affect the program. Every time you modify the position or size of the window, a `WM_PAINT` message is queued and your program has to redraw the client area, but all the work of drawing and modifying the window itself is done by Windows.

FIGURE 12-4

The system menu and Close button are also standard features of your window because of the options that you specified in the `WindowClass` structure. Again, Windows takes care of the management. The only additional effect on your program arising from this is the passing of a `WM_DESTROY` message if you close the window, as previously discussed.

WINDOWS PROGRAM ORGANIZATION

In the previous example, you saw an elementary Windows program that used the Windows API and displayed a short quote from the Bard. It's unlikely to win any awards, being completely free of any useful functionality, but it does serve to illustrate the two essential components of a Windows program: the `WinMain()` function that provides initialization and setup, and the `WindowProc()` function that services Windows messages. The relationship between these is illustrated in Figure 12-5.

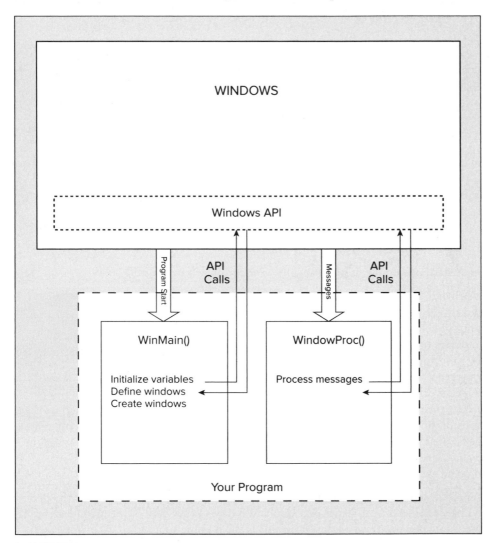

FIGURE 12-5

It may not always be obvious in the code that you will see, but this structure is at the heart of *all* Windows programs, including programs written for the CLR. Understanding how Windows applications are organized can often be helpful when you are trying to determine why things are not working as they should be in an application. The `WinMain()` function is called by Windows at the start of execution of the program, and the `WindowProc()` function, which you'll sometimes see with the name `WndProc()`, is called by the operating system whenever a message is to be passed to your application's window. In general, there typically is a separate `WindowProc()` function in an application for each window in an application.

The `WinMain()` function does any initialization that's necessary and sets up the window or windows that are the primary interface to the user. It also contains the message loop for retrieving messages that are queued for the application.

The `WindowProc()` function handles all the messages for a given window that aren't queued, which includes those initiated in the message loop in `WinMain()`. `WindowProc()`, therefore, ends up handling both kinds of messages. This is because the code in the message loop sorts out what kind of message it has retrieved from the queue, and then dispatches it for processing by `WindowProc()`. `WindowProc()` is where you code your application-specific response to each Windows message, which should handle all the communications with the user by processing the Windows messages generated by user actions, such as moving or clicking the mouse or entering information at the keyboard.

The queued messages are largely those caused by user input from either the mouse or the keyboard. The non-queued messages, for which Windows calls your `WindowProc()` function directly, are either messages that your program created, typically as a result of obtaining a message from the queue and then dispatching it, or messages that are concerned with window management — such as handling menus and scrollbars, or resizing the window.

THE MICROSOFT FOUNDATION CLASSES

The Microsoft Foundation Classes (**MFC**) are a set of predefined classes upon which Windows programming with Visual C++ is built. These classes represent an object-oriented approach to Windows programming that encapsulates the Windows API. MFC does not adhere strictly to the object-oriented principles of encapsulation and data hiding, principally because much of the MFC code was written before such principles were well established.

The process of writing a Windows program involves creating and using MFC objects or objects of classes derived from MFC. In the main, you'll derive your own classes from MFC, with considerable assistance from the specialized tools in Visual C++ 2010 that make this easy. The objects of these MFC-based class types incorporate member functions for communicating with Windows, for processing Windows messages, and for sending messages to each other. These derived classes, of course, inherit all of the members of their base classes. These inherited functions do practically all of the general grunt work necessary for a Windows application to work. All you need to do is to add data and function members to customize the classes to provide the application-specific functionality that you need in your program. In doing this, you'll apply most of the techniques that you've been grappling with in the preceding chapters, particularly those involving class inheritance and virtual functions.

MFC Notation

All the classes in MFC have names beginning with **C**, such as CDocument or CView. If you use the same convention when defining your own classes, or when deriving them from those in the MFC library, your programs will be easier to follow. Data members of an MFC class are prefixed with m_. I'll also follow this convention in the examples that use MFC.

You'll find that MFC uses Hungarian notation for many variable names, particularly those that originate in the Windows API. As you recall, this involves using a prefix of p for a pointer, n for an unsigned int, l for long, h for a handle, and so on. The name m_lpCmdLine, for example, refers to a data member of a class (because of the m_ prefix) that is of type 'pointer to long'. This practice of explicitly showing the type of a variable in its name was important in the C environment because of the lack of type checking; because you could determine the type from the name, you had a fair chance of not using or interpreting its value incorrectly. The downside is that the variable names can become quite cumbersome, making the code look more complicated than it really is. Because C++ has strong type checking that picks up the sort of misuse that used to happen regularly in C, this kind of notation isn't essential, so I won't use it generally for variables in the examples in the book. I will, however, retain the p prefix for pointers and some of the other simple type denotations because this helps to make the code more readable.

How an MFC Program Is Structured

You know from Chapter 1 that you can produce a Windows program using the Application Wizard without writing a single line of code. Of course, this uses the MFC library, but it's quite possible to write a Windows program that uses MFC without using the Application Wizard. If you first scratch the surface by constructing the minimum MFC-based program, you'll get a clearer idea of the fundamental elements involved.

The simplest program that you can produce using MFC is slightly less sophisticated than the example that you wrote earlier in this chapter using the raw Windows API. The example you'll produce here has a window, but no text displayed in it. This is sufficient to show the fundamentals, so try it out.

TRY IT OUT   A Minimal MFC Application

Create a new project using the File ➪ New ➪ Project menu option, as you've done many times before. You won't use the Application Wizard that creates the basic code here, so select the template for the project as Win32 Project and choose Windows Application and the Empty project options in the second dialog. After the project is created, select Project > Ex12_02 properties from the main menu, and on the General sub-page from Configuration Properties, click the Use of MFC property to set its value to Use MFC in a Shared DLL.

With the project created, you can create a new source file in the project as Ex12_02.cpp. So that you can see all the code for the program in one place, put the class definitions you need together with their implementations in this file. To achieve this, just add the code manually in the edit window — there isn't very much of it.

To begin with, add a statement to include the header file `afxwin.h`, as this contains the definitions for many MFC classes. This allows you to derive your own classes from MFC.

```
#include <afxwin.h>                    // For the class library
```

To produce the complete program, you'll only need to derive two classes from MFC: an **application class** and a **window class**. You won't even need to write a `WinMain()` function, as you did in the previous example in this chapter, because this is automatically provided by the MFC library behind the scenes. Take a look at how you define the two classes that you need.

THE APPLICATION CLASS

The class `CWinApp` is fundamental to any Windows program written using MFC. An object of this class includes everything necessary for starting, initializing, running, and closing the application. You need to produce the application to derive your own application class from `CWinApp`. You will define a specialized version of the class to suit your application needs. The code for this is as follows:

```
class COurApp: public CWinApp
{
   public:
       virtual BOOL InitInstance();
};
```

As you might expect for a simple example, there isn't a great deal of specialization necessary in this case. You've only included one member in the definition of the class: the `InitInstance()` function. This function is defined as a virtual function in the base class, so it's not a new function in your derived class; you are simply redefining the base class function for your application class. All the other data and function members that you need in the class, you'll inherit from `CWinApp` unchanged.

The application class is endowed with quite a number of data members defined in the base, many of which correspond to variables used as arguments in Windows API functions. For example, the member `m_pszAppName` stores a pointer to a string that defines the name of the application. The member `m_nCmdShow` specifies how the application window is to be shown when the application starts up. You don't need to go into all the inherited data members now. You'll see how they are used as the need arises in developing application-specific code.

In deriving your own application class from `CWinApp`, you must override the virtual function `InitInstance()`. Your version is called by the version of `WinMain()` that's provided for you by MFC, and you'll include code in the function to create and display your application window. However, before you write `InitInstance()`, I should introduce you to a class in the MFC library that defines a window.

THE WINDOW CLASS

Your MFC application needs a window as the interface to the user, referred to as a **frame window**. You derive a window class for the application from the MFC class `CFrameWnd`, which is designed specifically for this purpose. Because the `CFrameWnd` class provides everything for creating and managing a window for your application, all you need to add to the derived window class is a constructor. This enables you to specify a title bar for the window to suit the application context:

```
class COurWnd: public CFrameWnd
{
  public:
    // Constructor
    COurWnd()
    {
      Create(0, L"Our Dumb MFC Application");
    }
};
```

The `Create()` function that you call in the constructor is inherited from the base class. It creates the window and attaches it to the `COurWnd` object that is being created. Note that the `COurWnd` object is not the same thing as the window that is displayed by Windows — the class object and the physical window are distinct entities.

The first argument value for the `Create()` function, 0, specifies that you want to use the base class default attributes for the window — you'll recall that you needed to define window attributes in the previous example in this chapter that used the Windows API directly. The second argument specifies the window name that is used in the window title bar. You won't be surprised to learn that there are other parameters to the function `Create()`, but they all have default values that are quite satisfactory, so you can afford to ignore them here.

COMPLETING THE PROGRAM

Having defined a window class for the application, you can write the `InitInstance()` function in our `COurApp` class:

```
BOOL COurApp::InitInstance(void)
{
    // Construct a window object in the free store
    m_pMainWnd = new COurWnd;
    m_pMainWnd->ShowWindow(m_nCmdShow);        // ...and display it
    return TRUE;
}
```

This overrides the virtual function defined in the base class `CWinApp`, and as I said previously, it is called by the `WinMain()` function that's automatically supplied by the MFC library. The `InitInstance()` function constructs a main window object for the application in the free store by using the operator `new`. You store the address that is returned in the variable `m_pMainWnd`, which is an inherited member of your class `COurApp`. The effect of this is that the window object is owned by the application object. You don't even need to worry about freeing the memory for the object you have created — the supplied `WinMain()` function takes care of any cleanup necessary.

The only other item you need for a complete, albeit rather limited, program is to define an application object. An instance of our application class, `COurApp`, must exist before `WinMain()` is executed, so you must declare it at global scope with the statement:

```
COurApp AnApplication;     // Define an application object
```

The reason that this object needs to exist at global scope is that it is the application, and the application needs to exist before it can start executing. The `WinMain()` function that is provided by MFC calls the `InitInstance()` function member of the application object to construct the window object and, thus, implicitly assumes the application object already exists.

THE FINISHED PRODUCT

Now that you've seen all the code, you can add it to the `Ex12_02.cpp` source file in the project. In a Windows program, the classes are usually defined in `.h` files, and the member functions that are not defined within the class definitions are defined in `.cpp` files. Your application is so short, though, that you may as well put it all in a single `.cpp` file. The merit of this is that you can view the whole lot together. The program code is structured as follows:

```cpp
// Ex12_02.cpp  An elementary MFC program
#include <afxwin.h>                          // For the class library

// Application class definition
class COurApp:public CWinApp
{
   public:
       virtual BOOL InitInstance();
};

// Window class definition
class COurWnd:public CFrameWnd
{
   public:
       // Constructor
       COurWnd()
       {
          Create(0, L"Our Dumb MFC Application");
       }
};

// Function to create an instance of the main application window
BOOL COurApp::InitInstance(void)
{
   // Construct a window object in the free store
   m_pMainWnd = new COurWnd;
   m_pMainWnd->ShowWindow(m_nCmdShow);      // ...and display it
   return TRUE;
}

// Application object definition at global scope
COurApp AnApplication;                       // Define an application object
```

code snippet Ex12_02.cpp

That's all you need. It looks a bit odd because no `WinMain()` function appears, but as noted previously, there is a `WinMain()` function supplied by the MFC library.

How It Works

Now you're ready to roll, so build and run the application. Select the Build ⇨ Build Ex12_02.exe menu item, click the appropriate toolbar button, or just press Ctrl+Shift+B to build the solution. You should end up with a clean compile and link, in which case you can press Ctrl+F5 to run it. Your minimum MFC program appears as shown in Figure 12-6.

FIGURE 12-6

You can resize the window by dragging the border, move the whole thing around, and minimize or maximize it in the usual ways. The only other function that the program supports is "close," for which you can use the system menu, the Close button at the upper right of the window, or just key Alt+F4. It doesn't look like much, but considering that there are so few lines of code, it's quite impressive.

USING WINDOWS FORMS

A Windows form is an entity that represents a window of some kind. By a window, I mean window in its most general sense, being an area on the screen that can be a button, a dialog, a regular window, or any other kind of visible GUI component. A Windows form is encapsulated by a subclass of the System::Windows::Forms::Form class, but you don't need to worry about this much initially, because all the code to create a form is created automatically. To see just how easy it's going to be, create a basic window using Windows Forms that has a standard menu.

TRY IT OUT **A Windows Forms Application**

Choose the CLR project type in the New Project dialog and select the Windows Forms Application as the template for the project. Enter the project name as Ex12_03. When you click the OK button, the Application Wizard generates the code for the Windows form application and displays the design window containing the form as it is displayed by the application. This is shown in Figure 12-7.

You can now make changes to the form in the design pane graphically, and the changes are automatically reflected in the code that creates the form. For a start, you can drag the bottom corner of the form with the mouse cursor to increase the size of the form window. You can also change the text in the title bar — right-click in the client area of the form and select Properties from the context menu. This displays the Properties window that allows you to change the properties for the form. From the list of properties to the right of the

FIGURE 12-7

design pane, select Text, and then enter the new title bar text in the adjacent column showing the property value — I entered A Simple Form Window. When you press the Enter key, the new text appears in the title bar of the form.

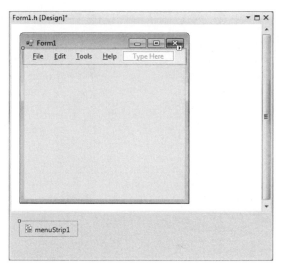

Just to see how easy it really is to add something to the form window, display the Toolbox pane by selecting the tab on the right of the window if it is present, or by pressing Ctrl+Alt+X or selecting Toolbox from the View menu. Find the MenuStrip option in the Menus and Toolbars list and drag it on to the form window in the Design tab pane. Right-click the MenuStrip1 that appears below the form window and select Insert Standard Items from the pop-up. You'll then have the menu in the form window populated with the standard File, Edit, Tools, and Help menus, each complete with its drop-down list of menu items. The result of this operation is shown in Figure 12-8.

FIGURE 12-8

How It Works

If you build the project by pressing the Ctrl+Shift+B and then execute it by pressing Ctrl+F5, you'll see the form window displayed complete with its menus. Naturally, the menu items don't do anything because you haven't added any code to deal with the events that result from clicking on them, but the icons at the right end of the title bar work, so you can close the application. You'll look into how to develop a Windows Forms application further, including handling events, later in the book.

SUMMARY

In this chapter you've seen three different ways of creating an elementary Windows application with Visual C++ 2010. You should now have a feel for the essential differences between these three approaches. In later chapters of the book, you'll be exploring in more depth how you develop applications using the MFC and using Windows Forms.

▶ **WHAT YOU LEARNED IN THIS CHAPTER**

TOPIC	CONCEPT
Windows API	The Windows API provides a standard programming interface by which an application communicates with the operating system.
The WinMain() function	All Windows applications include a `WinMain()` function that is called by the operating system to begin execution of the application. The `WinMain()` function also includes code to retrieve messages from the operating system.
Message processing	The Windows operating system calls a particular function in an application to handle processing of specific messages. An application identifies the message processing function for each window in an application by calling a Windows API function.
The MFC	The MFC consists of a set of classes that encapsulate the Windows API and simplify programming using the Windows API.
Windows Forms applications	A Windows Forms application executes with the CLR. The windows in a Windows Forms application can be created graphically with all the required code being generated automatically.

13

Programming for Multiple Cores

WHAT YOU WILL LEARN IN THIS CHAPTER:

➤ The principle features of the Parallel Patterns Library

➤ How to execute loop iterations in parallel

➤ How to execute two or more tasks concurrently

➤ How to manage shared resources in parallel operations

➤ How to indicate and manage sections in your parallel code that must not be executed by multiple processors

If your PC or laptop is relatively new, in all probability it has a processor chip with two or more cores. If it doesn't, you can skip this chapter and move on to the next chapter. Each core in a multi-core processor chip is an independent processing unit, so your computer can be executing code from more than one application at any given time. However, it is not limited to that. Having multiple cores or multiple processors provides you with the possibility of overlapping computations within a single application by having each processor handling a separate piece of the calculations required in parallel. Because at least some of the calculations in your application are overlapped, your application should execute faster.

This chapter will show you how you can use multiple cores within a single application. You will also get to use what you learned about the Windows API in the previous chapter in a significant parallel computation.

PARALLEL PROCESSING BASICS

Programming an application to use multiple cores or processors requires that you organize the computation differently from what you have been used to with serial processing. You must be able to divide the computation into a set of sub-tasks that can be executed independently of one another, and this is not always easy, or indeed possible. Sub-tasks that can run in parallel are usually referred to as **threads**.

Any interdependence between threads places serious constraints on parallel execution. Shared resources are a common limitation. Sub-tasks executing in parallel that access common resources, at best, can slow execution — potentially slower than if you programmed for serial execution — and, at worst, can produce incorrect results or cause the program to hang. A simple example is a shared variable that is accessed and updated by two or more threads. If one thread stored a result in the variable after the other thread has retrieved the value for updating, the result stored by the first thread will be lost and the result will be incorrect. The same kind of problem arises with updating files.

So, what are the typical characteristics of applications that may benefit from using more than one processor? First, these applications will involve operations that require substantial amount of processor time, measured in seconds rather than milliseconds. Second, the heavy computation will involve a loop of some kind. Third, the computation will involve operations that can be divided into discrete but significant units of calculation that can be executed independently of one another.

INTRODUCING THE PARALLEL PATTERNS LIBRARY

The **Parallel Patterns Library** (PPL) that is defined in the `ppl.h` header provides you with tools for implementing parallel processing in your applications, and these tools are defined within the `Concurrency` namespace. The PPL defines three kinds of facilities for parallel processing:

➤ Templates for algorithms for parallel operations

➤ A class template for managing shared resources

➤ Class templates for managing and grouping parallel tasks

In general, the PPL operates on a unit of work or task that is defined by a function object or, more typically, a lambda expression. You don't have to worry about creating threads of execution or allocating work to particular processors because in general the PPL takes care of this automatically. What you do have to do is to make sure your code is organized appropriately for parallel execution.

ALGORITHMS FOR PARALLEL PROCESSING

The PPL provides three algorithms for initiating parallel execution on multiple cores:

➤ The `parallel_for` algorithm is the equivalent of a `for` loop that executes loop iterations in parallel.

➤ The `parallel_for_each` algorithm executes repeated operations on a STL container in parallel.

➤ The `parallel_invoke` algorithm executes a set of two or more independent tasks in parallel.

These are defined as templates, but I won't go into the details of the definitions of the templates themselves. You can take a look at the `ppl.h` header file, if you are interested. Let's take a closer look at how you use each of them.

Using the parallel_for Algorithm

The `parallel_for` algorithm executes parallel loop iterations on a single task specified by a function object or lambda expression. The loop iterations are controlled by an integer index that is incremented on each iteration until a given limit is reached, just like a regular `for` loop. The function object or lambda expression that does the work must have a single parameter; the current index value will be passed as the argument corresponding to this parameter on each iteration. Because of the parallel nature of the operation, the iterations will not be executed in any particular order.

There are two versions of the `parallel_for` algorithm. The first has the form:

```
parallel_for(start_value, end_value, function_object);
```

This executes the task specified by the third argument, with index values running from `start_value` to `end_value-1`, and the default increment of 1. The first two arguments must be of the same integer type. If they are not, you will get a compile-time error. As I said, because iterations are executed in parallel, they will not be executed in sequence. This implies that each execution of the function object or lambda expression must be independent of the others, and the result must not depend on executing the task in a particular sequence.

Here's a fragment that shows how the `parallel_for` algorithm works:

```
const size_t count(100000);
long long squares[count];
Concurrency::parallel_for(static_cast<size_t>(0), count, [&squares](size_t n)
                          { squares[n] = (n+1)*(n+1); });
```

The computational task for each loop iteration is defined by the lambda expression, which is the third argument. The capture clause just accesses the squares array by reference. The function computes the square of n+1, where n is the current index value that is passed to the lambda, and stores the result in the nth element of the `squares` array. This will be executed for values of n, from 0 to `count-1`, as specified by the first two arguments. Note the cast for the first argument. Because `count` is of type `size_t`, the code will not compile without it. Because 0 is a literal of type `int`, without the cast, the compiler will not be able to decide whether to use type `int` or type `size_t` as a type parameter for the `parallel_for` algorithm template.

Although this fragment shows how the `parallel_for` algorithm can be applied, the increase in performance in this case may not be great, and indeed, you may find that things run more slowly than serial operations. The computation on each iteration in the example is very short, and inevitably there is some overhead in allocating the task to a processor on each iteration. The overhead may severely erode any reduction in execution time in computations that are relatively short. You should also not be misled by this simple example into thinking that implementing the use of parallel processing is trivial, and that you can just replace a `for` loop by a `parallel_for` algorithm. As you will see later in this chapter, all sorts of complications can arise in a more realistic situation.

Although with a `parallel_for` algorithm the index must always be ascending, you can arrange for descending index values inside the function that is being executed:

```
const size_t count(100000);
long long squares[count];
```

```
Concurrency::parallel_for(static_cast<size_t>(0), count,
                          [&squares, &count](size_t n)
                          {   squares[count-n-1] = (n+1)*(n+1);   });
```

Here, the squares of the index values passed to the lambda will be stored in descending sequence in the array.

The second version of the `parallel_for` algorithm has the following form:

```
parallel_for(start_value, end_value, increment, pointer_to_function);
```

Here, the second argument specifies the increment to use in iterating from `start_value` to `end_value-1`, so this provides for steps greater than 1. The second argument must be positive because only increasing index values are allowed in a `parallel_for` algorithm. The first three arguments must all be of the same integer type. Here's a fragment using this form of the `parallel_for` algorithm:

```
size_t start(1), end(300001), step(3);
vector<double> cubes(end/step + 1);
Concurrency::parallel_for(start, end, step, [&cubes](int n)
                          {   cubes[(n-1)/3] = static_cast<double>(n)*n*n;   });
```

This code fragment computes the cubes of integers from 1 to 300001 in steps of 3 and stores the values in the `cubes` vector. Thus, the cubes of 1, 4, 7, 10, and so on, up to 29998, will be stored. Of course, because this is a parallel operation, the values may not be stored in sequence in the vector.

Note that operations on STL containers are not thread-safe, so you must take great care when using them in parallel operations. Here, it is necessary to pre-allocate sufficient space in the vector to store the results of the operation. If you were to use the `push_back()` function to store values, the code would crash.

Because `parallel_for` is a template, you need to take care to ensure that the `start_value`, `end_value`, and `increment` arguments are of the same type. It is easy to get it wrong if you mix literals with variables. For example, the following will not compile:

```
size_t end(300001);
vector<double> cubes(end/3 + 1);
Concurrency::parallel_for(1, end, 3, [&cubes](size_t n)
                          {   cubes.push_back (static_cast<double>(n)*n*n);   });
```

This doesn't compile because the literals that are the first and third arguments are of type `int`, whereas `count` is of type `size_t`. The effect is that no compatible template instance can be found by the compiler.

Using the parallel_for_each Algorithm

The `parallel_for_each` algorithm works in a similar way to `parallel_for`, but the function operates on an STL container. The number of iterations to be carried out is determined by a pair of iterators. This algorithm is of the form:

```
Concurrency::parallel_for_each(start_iterator, end_iterator, function_object);
```

The function object specified by the third argument must have a single parameter of the type stored in the container that the iterators will access. This will enable you to access the object in the container that is referred to by the current iterator. Iterations run from `start_iterator` to `end_iterator-1`.

Here's a code fragment that illustrates how this works:

```
std::array<string, 6> people = {"Mel Gibson", "John Wayne", "Charles Chaplin",
                                "Clint Eastwood", "Jack Nicholson",  "George Clooney"};
Concurrency::parallel_for_each(people.begin(), people.end(), [](string& person)
{
  size_t space(person.find(' '));
  std::string first(person.substr(0, space));
  std::string second(person.substr(space + 1, person.length() - space - 1));
  person = second + ' ' + first;
});
std::for_each(people.begin(), people.end(), [](std::string& person)
{std::cout << person << std::endl; });
```

The `parallel_for_each` algorithm operates on the `people` array. Obviously, a real application would have more than 6 elements. The third argument specifies the function that does the work on each iteration. The parameter is a reference to type `string` because the elements in `people` are of type `string`. The function reverses the order of the names in each string. The last statement uses the STL `for_each` algorithm to list the contents of the `people` array. You can see that the PPL `parallel_for_each` algorithm has essentially the same syntax as the STL `for_each` algorithm.

Note that none of the parallel algorithms provide for premature termination of the operation. With a `for` loop, for example, you can use a `break` statement to terminate the loop, but this does not apply with the parallel algorithms. The only way to terminate the operation of a parallel algorithm before all concurrent operations have been completed is to throw an exception from within the function that defines the work to be done. This will stop all parallel operations immediately. Here's an example of how you can do that:

```
int findIndex(const std::array<string, 6>& people, const std::string& name)
{
  try
  {
    Concurrency::parallel_for(static_cast<size_t>(0), people.size(), [=](size_t n)
    {
      size_t space(people[n].find(' '));
      if(people[n].substr(0, space) == name)
        throw n;
    });
  } catch(size_t index) { return index;  }
  return -1;
}
```

This function searches the array from the previous fragment to find a particular name string. The `parallel_for` compares the name, up to the first space in the current `people` array element, with the second argument to the `findIndex()` function. If it's a match, the lambda expression throws an exception that will be the current index to the `people` array. This will be caught in the `catch` clause in the `findIndex()` function, and the value that was thrown will be returned. Throwing the exception terminates all current activity with the `parallel_for` operation. The `findIndex()`

function returns -1 if the `parallel_for` operation terminates with no exception having been thrown, because this indicates that name was not found. Let's see if it works.

TRY IT OUT   Terminating a parallel_for operation

To exercise the `findIndex()` function, you can append some code to the previous fragment that uses the `parallel_for_each` algorithm to reverse the sequence of names. Here's the complete program:

```cpp
// Ex13_01.cpp  Terminating a parallel operation
#include <iostream>
#include "ppl.h"
#include <array>
#include <string>
using namespace std;
using namespace Concurrency;

// Find name as the first name in any people element
int findIndex(const array<std::string, 6>& people, const string& name)
{
  try
  {
    parallel_for(static_cast<size_t>(0), people.size(), [=](size_t n)
    {
      size_t space(people[n].find(' '));
      if(people[n].substr(0, space) == name)
        throw n;
    });
  } catch(size_t index) { return index;  }
  return -1;
}

int main()
{
  array<string, 6> people = {"Mel Gibson", "John Wayne", "Charles Chaplin",
                     "Clint Eastwood", "Jack Nicholson",  "George Clooney"};
  parallel_for_each(people.begin(), people.end(), [](string& person)
  {
    size_t space(person.find(' '));
    string first(person.substr(0, space));
    string second(person.substr(space+1, person.length()-space-1));
    person = second +' ' + first;
  });
  for_each(people.begin(), people.end(), [](string& person)
  {cout << person << endl; });
  string name("Eastwood");
  size_t index(findIndex(people, name));
  if(index == -1)
    cout << name << " not found." << endl;
  else
    cout << name << " found at index position " << index << '.' << endl;
  return 0;
}
```

code snippet Ex6_01.cpp

Executing this example produces the following output:

```
Gibson Mel
Wayne John
Chaplin Charles
Eastwood Clint
Nicholson Jack
Clooney George
Eastwood found at index position 3.
```

How It Works

The `parallel_for_each` algorithm interchanges the first and second names in each element of the `people` array with operations working in parallel, as I explained in the previous section. The output produced by the STL `for_each` algorithm shows that this works as described.

You then create the `name` string that you are looking for. The `index` variable is initialized with the value returned from the `findIndex()` function call. The `if` statement outputs a message depending on the value stored in `index`, and the last line of output shows that `name` was indeed found in the `people` array.

Using the parallel_invoke Algorithm

The `parallel_invoke` algorithm is defined by a template that enables you to execute up to 10 tasks in parallel. Obviously, there is no point in attempting to execute more tasks in parallel than you have processors on your computer. You specify each task to be executed by a function object, which, of course, can be a lambda expression, so the arguments to the `parallel_invoke` algorithm are the function objects specifying the tasks to be executed in parallel. Here's an example:

```
std::array<double, 500> squares;
std::array<double, 500> values;
Concurrency::parallel_invoke(
  [&squares]
{  for(size_t i = 0 ; i<squares.size() ; ++i)
     squares[i] = (i+1)*(i+1);
},
  [&values]
{  for(size_t i = 0 ; i<values.size() ; ++i)
     values[i] = std::sqrt(static_cast<double>((i+1)*(i+1)*(i+1)));
});
```

The arguments to the `parallel_invoke` algorithm are two different lambda expressions. The first stores the squares of successive integers in the `squares` array, and the second stores the square root of the cube of successive integers in the `values` array. These lambdas are completely independent of one another and therefore can be executed in parallel.

The examples and code fragments that I have used up to now have not been computations that really take advantage of parallel execution. Let's look at something that does.

A REAL PARALLEL PROBLEM

To explore the practicalities of parallel processing, and to see the advantages, we need a computation that is chunky enough to warrant parallel processing. We also need something we can use to explore some of the pitfalls and problems that can arise with parallel operations.

The problem I have chosen does not involve a lot of code but does involve doing some calculations with **complex numbers**. In case you have never heard of complex numbers or maybe you did know something about them at one time but have since forgotten, I'll first give you a brief explanation of what they are and how operations on them work — just enough to understand what the calculations are about. Then we will get into the code. Take my word for it: it's not difficult, and the results are interesting.

A complex number is a number of the form $a + bi$, where i is the square root of –1. Thus, $1 + 2i$ and $0.5 - 1.2i$ are examples of complex numbers. The a is referred to as the real part of the complex number, and the b that is multiplied by i is referred to as the imaginary part. Complex numbers are often represented in the **complex plane**, as Figure 13-1 illustrates.

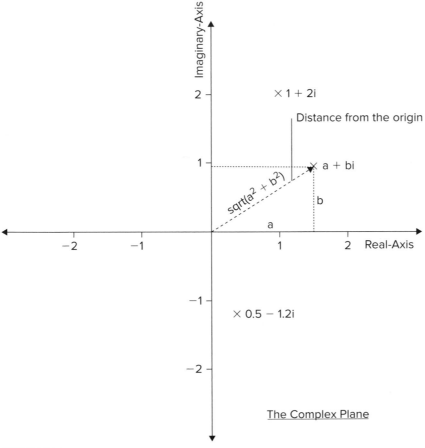

FIGURE 13-1

To add two complex numbers, you just add the real parts and the imaginary parts separately to get the real and imaginary parts for the result. Thus, adding *1 + 2i* and *0.5 − 1.2i* produces *(1+ 0.5) + (2 − 1.2)i*, so the result is *1.5 + 0.8i*.

Multiplying two complex numbers *a + bi* and *c + di* works like this:

$$a, c + di. + bi(c + di)$$

Remembering that *i* is the square root of −1, so i^2 is −1, you can expand the expression above to:

$$ac + adi + bci − bd$$

Thus, the final result is the complex number:

$$(ac − bd) + (ad + bc)i$$

Multiplying the two example numbers that I introduced at the beginning will therefore result in the number *(0.5 + 2.4) + (−1.2 + 1.0)i*, which is *2.9 − 0.2i*. Multiplying a number *a + bi* by itself results in

$$(a^2 − b^2) + 2abi$$

Now let's consider what the problem is about. The Mandelbrot set is a very interesting region of the complex plane that is defined by iterating the equation:

$$Z_{n+1} = Z^2_n + c \quad \text{where } Z_0 = c$$

for all points *c* over an area of the complex plane. By iterating, I mean that for any point c in the complex plane, you set Z_0 to *c* and use the equation to calculate Z_1 as c^2+c You then use Z_1 to calculate Z_2 using the equation, then Z_2 to calculate Z_3, and so on, repeating the operation for some large number of iterations. So how does this tell you which points are in the Mandelbrot set? If the distance from the origin (shown in Figure 13-1) of any Z_n exceeds 2, then continuing the iterations will result in the point moving further and further away from the origin towards infinity, so you don't need to iterate it further. All points that escape like this are *not* in the Mandelbrot set. Any point that does not diverge in this way after a given large number of iterations belongs to the Mandelbrot set. Any point that starts out more than a distance 2 from the origin will not belong to the Mandelbrot set, so this gives us an idea of the area in the complex plane in which to look.

Here's a function that iterates the equation for the Mandelbrot set:

```
size_t IteratePoint(double zReal, double zImaginary, double cReal, double cImaginary)
{
  double zReal2(0.0), zImaginary2(0.0); // z components squared
  size_t n(0);
  for( ; n < MaxIterations ; ++n)          // Iterate equation Zn = Zn-1**2 + K
  {                                        // for Mandelbrot K = c and Z0 = c
    zReal2 = zReal*zReal;
    zImaginary2 = zImaginary*zImaginary;
    if(zReal2 + zImaginary2 > 4)           // If distance from origin > 2, point will
      break;                               // go to infinity so we are done
```

```
    // Calculate next Z value
    zImaginary = 2*zReal*zImaginary + cImaginary;
    zReal = zReal2 - zImaginary2 + cReal;
  }
  return n;
}
```

The `IteratePoint()` function iterates the equation $z_{n+1}=z^2_n+c$ with the starting point, ,z-0., specified by the first two parameters and the complex constant c, specified by the last two parameters. `MaxIterations` is the maximum number of times to plug z back into the equation, and it needs to be defined as a global constant. The `for` loop calculates a new z, and if its distance from the origin is greater than 2, the loop is terminated and the current value of n is returned. The `if` expression actually compares the square of the distance from the origin to 4, to avoid having to execute the computationally expensive square root function. If the loop ends normally, then n will have the value `MaxIterations`, and this value will be returned.

So, maybe the `for` loop in the `IteratePoint()` function is a candidate for parallel operations? No, I'm afraid not. Each loop iteration requires the z from the previous iteration to be available, so this is essentially a serial operation. However, there are other possibilities. To figure out the extent of the Mandelbrot set, we will have to call this function for every point in a region of the complex plane. In that context, we will have lots of potential for parallel computation.

In order to visualize the Mandelbrot set, we will display it as an image in the client area of a window; we will treat the pixels in the client area as though they are points in the complex plane. This implies that we will need a loop to test every pixel in the client area to see whether it's in the Mandelbrot set. In broad terms, the loop will look like this:

```
for(int y = 0 ; y < imageHeight ; ++y)          // Iterate over image rows
{
  for(int x = 0 ; x < imageWidth ; ++x)         // Iterate over pixels in a row
      // Iterate current point x+yi. . .
}
  // Display the yth row. . .
}
```

Each pixel in the image will correspond to a particular point in a region of the complex plane. The pixel coordinates run from 0 to `imageWidth` along a row and from 0 to `imageHeight` down the y-axis of the client area. We need to map the pixels[1] coordinates to the area of the complex plane we are interested in. A good region to explore to find the Mandelbrot set is the area containing real parts — which will be the x-axis in the window — from –2.1 to +2.1 and the area containing the imaginary parts — the y-axis in the window — from –1.3 to +1.3. However, the client area of a window may not have the same aspect ratio as this, so ideally, we should make sure to map the pixels to the complex plane so that we maintain the same scale on both axes. This will prevent the shape of the Mandelbrot set from being squashed or elongated. To do this, we can calculate factors to convert from pixel coordinates to the complex plane as follows:

```
// Client area axes
const double realMin(-2.1);          // Minimum real value
double imaginaryMin(-1.3);           // Minimum imaginary value
double imaginaryMax(+1.3);           // Maximum imaginary value
```

```
    // Set maximum real so axes are the same scale
    double realMax(realMin+(imaginaryMax-imaginaryMin)*imageWidth/imageHeight);

    // Get scale factors to convert pixel coordinates
    double realScale((realMax-realMin)/(imageWidth-1));
    double imaginaryScale((imaginaryMax-imaginaryMin)/(imageHeight-1));
```

The `realMax` value is the maximum real value, and this is calculated so that the real and imaginary axes have the same scale. The `realScale` and `imaginaryScale` variables hold factors that we can use to multiply the x and y pixel coordinates, respectively, to convert them to complex plane values.

Let's put a working program together.

TRY IT OUT **Displaying the Mandelbrot Set**

You are going to create a Windows API program to do this. Create a new `Win32 Application` project with the default application settings, which will be for a Windows application. I called this `Ex13_02A`. When the project has been created, change the value for the `Character Set` project property to `Not Set`, because we won't be using Unicode. Rather than accept the default settings for the window that is to be created, modify the call to `CreateWindow()` in the `InitInstance()` function to:

```
    hWnd = CreateWindow(szWindowClass, szTitle, WS_OVERLAPPEDWINDOW,
        100, 100, 800, 600, NULL, NULL, hInstance, NULL);
```

The window will now be located at position 100,100, and its size will be 800x600. If you have a large screen with lots of pixels, by all means change the window size to suit your display. Remember, though, that the more pixels there are in the window, the longer it will take to execute the program.

Note that I use `NULL` for a null pointer in this example, and in the other examples in this chapter, just for consistency with the code that is generated automatically. Elsewhere in the book, I use the new language keyword, `nullptr`.

Now add the following definition at global scope:

```
    const size_t MaxIterations(8000);        // Maximum iterations before infinity
```

The appropriate value for `MaxIterations` depends on how finely the complex plane is represented. The more detail you can display, the higher this value needs to be. The value here is much higher than is necessary for the typical client area, but I set it this way so the elapsed time to compute the Mandelbrot set will be a significant number of seconds.

Next, you can add three global function prototypes, following the existing prototypes at the beginning of the source file:

```
    size_t IteratePoint(double zReal, double zImaginary, double cReal, double cImaginary);
    COLORREF Color(int n);                   // Selects a pixel color based on n
    void DrawSet(HWND hwnd);                 // Draws the Mandelbrot set
```

You can now add the definition for the `IteratePoint()` function to the end of the source file, exactly as it appears in the previous section.

Add the following `Color()` function definition:

```
COLORREF Color(int n)
{
  if(n == MaxIterations) return RGB(0, 0, 0);

  const int nColors = 16;
  switch(n%nColors)
  {
    case 0: return RGB(100,100,100);   case 1: return RGB(100,0,0);
    case 2: return RGB(200,0,0);       case 3: return RGB(100,100,0);
    case 4: return RGB(200,100,0);     case 5: return RGB(200,200,0);
    case 6: return RGB(0,200,0);       case 7: return RGB(0,100,100);
    case 8: return RGB(0,200,100);     case 9: return RGB(0,100,200);
    case 10: return RGB(0,200,200);    case 11: return RGB(0,0,200);
    case 12: return RGB(100,0,100);    case 13: return RGB(200,0,100);
    case 14: return RGB(100,0,200);    case 15: return RGB(200,0,200);
    default: return RGB(200,200,200);
  };
}
```

code snippet Ex13_02A.cpp

This function chooses a color for a pixel based on the value of the parameter n, which will be the value returned by the `IteratePoint()` function. The RGB macro forms a DWORD value specifying a color from three 8-bit values for intensities of the primary colors, red, green, and blue. The value of each color component can be from zero to 255. All values at zero will result in black, and all values at 255 will result in white.

The color-selection process based on n is arbitrary. I chose to use the remainder after dividing n by the number of colors, as this works reasonably well with the value I have set for MaxIterations. A more common approach is to select a color based on where the value of n lies in the interval 0 to MaxIterations-1, with the interval being divided into as many equal subdivisions as the number of colors you want to use, and MaxIterations representing black. However, this works better with a lower value for MaxIterations. You can try varying the mechanism for coloring pixels yourself.

You can also add the following definition for `DrawSet()` to the source file:

```
void DrawSet(HWND hWnd)
{
  // Get client area dimensions, which will be the image size
  RECT rect;
  GetClientRect(hWnd, &rect);
  int imageHeight(rect.bottom);
  int imageWidth(rect.right);

  // Create bitmap for one row of pixels in image
  HDC hdc(GetDC(hWnd));                         // Get device context
  HDC memDC = CreateCompatibleDC(hdc);          // Get device context to draw pixels
  HBITMAP bmp = CreateCompatibleBitmap(hdc, imageWidth, 1);
  HGDIOBJ oldBmp = SelectObject(memDC, bmp);    // Select bitmap into DC

  // Client area axes
  const double realMin(-2.1);        // Minimum real value
  double imaginaryMin(-1.3);         // Minimum imaginary value
  double imaginaryMax(+1.3);         // Maximum imaginary value
```

```cpp
      // Set maximum imaginary so axes are the same scale
      double realMax(realMin+(imaginaryMax-imaginaryMin)*imageWidth/imageHeight);

      // Get scale factors to convert pixel coordinates
      double realScale((realMax-realMin)/(imageWidth-1));
      double imaginaryScale((imaginaryMax-imaginaryMin)/(imageHeight-1));

      double cReal(0.0), cImaginary(0.0);              // Stores c components
      double zReal(0.0), zImaginary(0.0);              // Stores z components
      for(int y = 0 ; y < imageHeight ; ++y)           // Iterate over image rows
      {
        zImaginary = cImaginary = imaginaryMax - y*imaginaryScale;
        for(int x = 0 ; x < imageWidth ; ++x)          // Iterate over pixels in a row
        {
          zReal = cReal = realMin + x*realScale;
          // Set current pixel color based on n
          SetPixel(memDC, x, 0, Color(IteratePoint(zReal, zImaginary, cReal, cImaginary)));
        }
        // Transfer pixel row to client area device context
        BitBlt(hdc, 0, y, imageWidth, 1, memDC, 0, 0, SRCCOPY);
      }
      SelectObject(memDC, oldBmp);
      DeleteObject(bmp);                               // Delete bitmap
      DeleteDC(memDC);                                 // and our working DC
      ReleaseDC(hWnd, hdc);                            // and client area DC
    }
```

code snippet Ex13_02A.cpp

This version of the function is strictly serial execution. We will get to a parallel version once we have this working. The parameter of type HWND provides access within the function to the current window. You need this to be able to find out the size of the client area, and to draw on it. The call to the Windows API GetClientRect() function places data about the client area of the window you specify by the first argument, in a RECT structure that you supply as the second argument. The RECT structure will contain the coordinates of the top left and bottom right points of the client area of the window. The public members of the structure that will contain the x, y coordinates of the top-left corner, are left and top and right and bottom will contain the coordinates of the bottom-right corner. The coordinates of the top-left point will be 0,0, so the width and height of the client area are right and bottom, respectively.

To draw in the client area, we need a **device context** (DC). A device context is a structure that you use to draw or display text in a window. You obtain a DC from Windows by calling the GetDC() function with a handle to the window you want to work with as the argument. The function returns a handle to a DC that encapsulates the client area of the window. You won't be writing pixels to this DC directly. You will assemble the pixels for a row in the image in a bitmap, and then transfer this to the DC. To do this, you first have to create a compatible DC, memDC, which is a DC in memory with the same pixel color range as the window client area DC. Initially, this DC will be able to store only 1x1 pixels, so you'll need to adjust it. You then create a handle to a bitmap object, bmp, that can store one row of pixels (imageWidth long by 1 pixel high) by calling the CreateCompatibleBitmap() function. Calling the SelectObject() function replaces an existing object in the DC, specified by the first argument, with the one you pass as the second argument, so selecting bmp into memDC provides memDC with the capacity to hold an image row of pixels.

After you've created and initialized variables to hold Z and the constant c, you have two nested for loops. The outer loop iterates over the image rows, and the inner loop iterates over the pixels in a row.

The inner loop assembles a row of pixels in the image in memDC, using the SetPixel() API function to set each pixel to a color determined by the value returned by the IteratePoint() function. The arguments to SetPixel() are the DC, the x and y coordinates of the pixel to be set, and the color.

The memDC context is reused for each row of pixels in the client area, so before starting the next row, you write the contents of memDC to the client area DC, hdc; using the BitBlt() function (**Bit Block Transfer**). The arguments to this function are the destination DC (hdc); the coordinate of the first pixel; the number of pixels in a row (imageWidth) and the number of rows (1); the source DC (memDC); the x and y coordinates of the first pixel is the source DC (0,0); and a raster operation code (SRCCOPY) that determines how the source pixels are to be combined with the destination.

Finally, after the nested loops finish executing, you delete the bitmap and the DC resource you created, and release the DC you obtained from Windows, because they are no longer required.

The last bit of code you need to add is in the WndProc() function:

```
case WM_PAINT:
        hdc = BeginPaint(hWnd, &ps);
        // TODO: Add any drawing code here...
        DrawSet(hWnd);
        EndPaint(hWnd, &ps);
        break;
```

You just need to add the call to DrawSet() as the action for a WM_PAINT message.

When you compile and execute the example, you should get the window shown in Figure 13-2.

FIGURE 13-2

Of course, on your screen, it will be in glorious technicolor. The Mandelbrot set is the black region. The set is of finite area, clearly, because it lies inside a circle of radius 2, but its perimeter is of infinite length. Moreover, any segment of its perimeter, no matter how small, is also of infinite length, so there are unlimited possibilities for exploration of the boundaries of the set by scaling the image. The colored areas around the set produce some very interesting patterns, especially when they are scaled up.

TRY IT OUT Drawing the Mandelbrot Set Using parallel_invoke

You are going to create a new version of the DrawSet() function called DrawSetParallel(), but don't replace the original. Keep both versions in the source code for the example. You will be able to use both in a later evolution of this program. This version of the program is Ex13_02B in the code download.

To improve the performance of the program, you could use the parallel_invoke algorithm to compute two or more rows of the image simultaneously, depending on how many cores or processors your machine has. However, the fact that you must not write to a DC in parallel, because DCs are strictly serial facilities is a major limitation. This means that the SetPixel() and BitBlt() function calls are a problem.

One way to deal with the call SetPixel() is to create a separate memory DC and bitmap for each concurrent row computation. If you provide separate DCs and bitmaps for the concurrent tasks that you pass to parallel_invoke, they can execute without interfering with one another. I'll define the DrawSetParallel() function for two cores, because that's all I have in my computer. If you have more, you can extend the code accordingly. The code for a parallel version of DrawSet() might look like this:

```
void DrawSetParallel(HWND hWnd)
{
  HDC hdc(GetDC(hWnd));                    // Get device context

  // Get client area dimensions, which will be the image size
  RECT rect;
  GetClientRect(hWnd, &rect);
  int imageHeight(rect.bottom);
  int imageWidth(rect.right);

  // Create bitmap for one row of pixels in image
  HDC memDC1 = CreateCompatibleDC(hdc);   // Get device context to draw pixels
  HDC memDC2 = CreateCompatibleDC(hdc);   // Get device context to draw pixels
  HBITMAP bmp1 = CreateCompatibleBitmap(hdc, imageWidth, 1);
  HBITMAP bmp2 = CreateCompatibleBitmap(hdc, imageWidth, 1);
  HGDIOBJ oldBmp1 = SelectObject(memDC1, bmp1);   // Select bitmap into DC1
  HGDIOBJ oldBmp2 = SelectObject(memDC2, bmp2);   // Select bitmap into DC2

  // Client area axes
  const double realMin(-2.1);        // Minimum real value
  double imaginaryMin(-1.3);         // Minimum imaginary value
  double imaginaryMax(+1.3);         // Maximum imaginary value

  // Set maximum real so axes are the same scale
  double realMax(realMin+(imaginaryMax-imaginaryMin)*imageWidth/imageHeight);

  // Get scale factors to convert pixel coordinates
  double realScale((realMax-realMin)/(imageWidth-1));
  double imaginaryScale((imaginaryMax-imaginaryMin)/(imageHeight-1));
```

```
    // Lambda expression to create an image row
    std::function<void(HDC&, int)> rowCalc = [&] (HDC& memDC, int yLocal)
    {
      double zReal(0.0), cReal(0.0);
      double zImaginary(imaginaryMax - yLocal*imaginaryScale);
      double cImaginary(zImaginary);
      for(int x = 0 ; x < imageWidth ; ++x)            // Iterate over pixels in a row
      {
        zReal = cReal = realMin + x*realScale;
        // Set current pixel color based on n
        SetPixel(memDC, x, 0, Color(IteratePoint(zReal, zImaginary, cReal, cImaginary)));
      }
    };
  for(int y = 1 ; y < imageHeight ; y += 2)             // Iterate over image rows
  {
    Concurrency::parallel_invoke([&]{rowCalc(memDC1, y-1);}, [&]{rowCalc(memDC2, y);});
    // Transfer pixel rows to client area device context
    BitBlt(hdc, 0, y-1, imageWidth, 1, memDC1, 0, 0, SRCCOPY);
    BitBlt(hdc, 0, y, imageWidth, 1, memDC2, 0, 0, SRCCOPY);
  }
  // If there's an odd number of rows, take care of the last one
  if(imageHeight%2 == 1)
  {
    rowCalc(memDC1, imageWidth-1);
    BitBlt(hdc, 0, imageHeight-1, imageWidth, 1, memDC1, 0, 0, SRCCOPY);
  }
  SelectObject(memDC1, oldBmp1);
  SelectObject(memDC2, oldBmp2);
  DeleteObject(bmp1);                          // Delete bitmap 1
  DeleteObject(bmp2);                          // Delete bitmap 2
  DeleteDC(memDC1);                            // and our working DC 1
  DeleteDC(memDC2);                            // and our working DC 2
  ReleaseDC(hWnd, hdc);                        // Release client area DC
}
```

The bits that are new or changed from the `DrawSet()` function are shown in bold. You can see that there's quite a lot that's different from the original version of the function. You now create two memory DCs and two bitmaps, one for each of two parallel tasks. If you have four cores in your computer, you can create four of each of these.

The code for each task to run in parallel is the same, so rather than repeating the code in each of the arguments to `parallel_invoke`, you define a `function` variable, `rowCalc`, to encapsulate it. This uses the `function` template that I introduced in Chapter 10, defined in the `functional` header. The arguments to the `rowCalc` object are a memory DC and a value for `yLocal`, which will be the row index for the row to be calculated. The variables storing the components of Z and c are now inside the `rowCalc` function because these cannot be shared between parallel processes. The `rowCalc` function iterates over the pixels in a row, as before, and sets the pixel color in the memory DC that is passed to it, using the value returned by `IteratePoint()`.

In the loop over rows that is indexed by `y`, `y` now starts at 1 and proceeds in steps of 2 because you are going to compute rows `y` and `y-1` in parallel. You do this with the call to the `parallel_invoke` algorithm. The arguments to the algorithm are lambda expressions that call `rowCalc` with arguments that select the DC and the `y` value to be used. When the `parallel_invoke` algorithm returns, you transfer the pixels from each memory DC to the window DC, `hdc`, serially.

If `imageHeight` is odd, then the last row will not have been processed, so you have to treat this as a special case to complete the image. This just involves calling `rowCalc` for the last row with index value `imageHeight-1`. Finally, you delete the memory DCs and bitmaps when the computation is complete.

Before compiling and executing the new version, you should add a prototype for `DrawSetParallel()` to the source file and change the action for the `WM_PAINT` message in `WndProc()` to call this new function. You also need to add the following `#include` directives:

```
#include "ppl.h"
#include <functional>                 // For the function<> template
```

When you run this new version of the program, you should get the same image of the Mandelbrot set displayed, but faster. It would be nice to know how much faster though, wouldn't it?

Timing Execution

You will add a class to the application that defines a high-resolution timer that you can start when the computation begins and can stop when it ends. This version is in the code download as `Ex13_02C`. You will also add the capability to execute either `DrawSet()` for serial execution, or `DrawSetParallel()`, and see how long they take to execute. You'll be able to switch between serial and parallel execution by right-clicking the mouse. A good place to display the time will be in a status bar at the bottom of the application window, so you will add that to the application, too.

Defining a Timer

The `HRTimer` class will use the Windows API function for accessing a high-resolution timer. Not all systems have a high-resolution timer, so if yours doesn't, the timer will not work. I'll explain the bare bones of how this class works and leave you to research the fine detail.

Add a new header file, `HRTimer.h`, to the application and insert the following code:

```
#pragma once
#include "windows.h"

class HRTimer
{
public:
  // Constructor
  HRTimer(void) : frequency(1.0 / GetFrequency()) { }

  // Get the timer frequency - clock ticks per second
  double GetFrequency(void)
  {
    LARGE_INTEGER proc_freq;
    ::QueryPerformanceFrequency(&proc_freq);
    return static_cast<double>(proc_freq.QuadPart);
  }

  // Start the timer
  void StartTimer(void)
  {
    // Set thread to use processor 0
    DWORD_PTR oldmask = ::SetThreadAffinityMask(::GetCurrentThread(), 0);
```

```
      ::QueryPerformanceCounter(&start);
      ::SetThreadAffinityMask(::GetCurrentThread(), oldmask);  // Restore original
    }

    // Stop the timer and return elapsed time in seconds
    double StopTimer(void)
    {
      // Set thread to use processor 0
      DWORD_PTR oldmask = ::SetThreadAffinityMask(::GetCurrentThread(),0);
      ::QueryPerformanceCounter(&stop);
      ::SetThreadAffinityMask(::GetCurrentThread(), oldmask);  // Restore original
      return ((stop.QuadPart - start.QuadPart) * frequency);
    }
  private:

    LARGE_INTEGER start;                      // Stores start ime
    LARGE_INTEGER stop;                       // Stores stop time
    double frequency;                         // Time for one clock tick in seconds
  };
```

A high-resolution timer has a frequency — the clock tick rate per second — that can vary from one processor to another, so to use a timer, you must find out what the frequency is. The `::QueryPerformanceFrequency()` function does this, and stores the result in the `LARGE_INTEGER` variable you pass as the argument. You call this function in the `GetFrequency()` member function that is called by the class constructor to initialize the `frequency` member of the class. The `frequency` member stores the time in seconds, between one clock tick and the next, as a value of type `double`; this is calculated as the reciprocal of the timer frequency. The `LARGE_INTEGER` type is an 8-byte union that is defined in `Windows.h`. It combines two `struct`s as members, which I won't go into, because we won't be using them, plus a `QuadPart` member that is a signed 64-bit integer.

Once you have created a `HRTimer` object, you start the timer by calling its `StartTimer()` function. The start time is returned by the `::QueryPerformanceCounter()` function and stored in the `start` member. The call to `::SetThreadAffinityMask()`, before getting the start time, is to ensure the call is executed on a specific processor, processor 0. The `StopTimer()` member function that records the stop time and returns the elapsed time will execute on the same processor. This is to remove the possibility of problems arising from these calls executing on different processors.

To stop the timer, call `StopTimer()` for the timer object. This function computes the elapsed time from when you called `StartTimer()` by taking the difference between the two values (`QuadPart`, which treats the `stop` and `start` values as 64-bit signed integers) and multiplying by the `frequency` member. This will result in the elapsed time in seconds being returned as a value of type `double`.

To use an `HRTimer` object in `Ex13_02.cpp`, first add an `#include` directive for `HRTimer.h` to the source file. Then you can create a timer object at global scope by adding the following statement to the other global definitions in the file:

```
  HRTimer timer;                             // Timer object to calculate processor time
```

You'll add the code to use the timer after you have added a status bar to the application window.

Adding a Status bar

A status bar, like most entities that are displayed in Windows, is just another window, so you create a status bar by calling the `CreateWindowEx()` API function. The place to add the code that creates the status bar is in the `InitInstance()` function, so add the following code immediately before the call to `ShowWindow()`:

```
HWND hStatus = CreateWindowEx(0, STATUSCLASSNAME, NULL,
                          WS_CHILD | WS_VISIBLE | SBARS_SIZEGRIP, 0, 0, 0, 0,
                          hWnd, (HMENU)IDC_STATUS, GetModuleHandle(NULL), NULL);
if(!hStatus)                          // Make sure we have a status bar
  return FALSE;                       // and return false if we don't

// Set up the panels in the status bar
int statwidths[] = {100,200, -1};
SendMessage(hStatus, SB_SETPARTS, sizeof(statwidths)/sizeof(int), (LPARAM)statwidths);
SendMessage(hStatus, SB_SETTEXT, 0, (LPARAM)_T("Processor Time :"));
SendMessage(hStatus, SB_SETTEXT, 2, (LPARAM)_T(" Right-click for parallel execution"));
```

The second argument to `CreateWindowEx()` specifies the window to be a status bar with the standard class name `STATUSCLASSNAME`. There are many other standard class names for other kinds of controls (defined in the `commctrl.h` header), such as toolbars, buttons, and so on. The status bar will be a child window to the main window, `hWnd`. It will be visible, and it will have a size grip at the right end of the status bar. The size and position of the status bar will be determined by default to be along the bottom of the parent window and with a height to accommodate the default font. The `IDC_STATUS` symbol that appears in the 10th argument is a unique integer constant that identifies the status bar control. You need to add this to the resources for the project. Display the Resource View and right-click the .rc file name. Select Resource Symbols . . . from the popup to display the Resource Symbols dialog. Click on the New . . . button, enter the name as **IDC_STATUS,** and click on OK. Click on Close to close the dialog. The value for the new symbol will be chosen automatically to be different from the existing symbol values.

Each element in the `statwidths` array specifies the size, in logical units, of a **part** in the status bar, in which you will be displaying text. The array here defines three parts where the last part width is -1, which specifies that it takes up whatever space is left after the first two have been allocated space. The `SendMessage()` function sends a message to the window specified by its first argument — in this case, the status bar. You set the status bar parts by sending an `SB_PARTS` message to the status bar, with the third argument specifying the number of parts, and the fourth argument specifying the widths of the parts. The next two `SendMessage()` calls write text to a particular part of the status bar, the parts being indexed from the left, starting at zero. The first `SB_SETTEXT` message sets the text specified by the fourth argument in the part specified by the third argument. The last message that is sent sets the text for the third part. You'll use the second status bar part to show the elapsed time in seconds, when you have computed it.

In order to compile this code, you must add an `#include` directive for the `commctrl.h` header to the source file. If you execute the program at this point, you should see a status bar at the bottom of the application window.

Switching between Serial and Parallel Execution

First, add a global variable to `Ex13_02C.cpp` with the following definition:

```
bool parallel(false);                    // True for parallel execution
```

This is an indicator you will use to select which client area drawing function to call when the WM_PAINT message is received. You can toggle the value of this variable by handling the WM_RBUTTONDOWN message that is sent when the right mouse button is pressed. Add the following case statement in the switch in the WndProc() function:

```
case WM_RBUTTONDOWN:
    parallel = !parallel;           // Toggle the indicator
    // Now update the message in the status bar
    SendMessage(GetDlgItem(hWnd, IDC_STATUS), SB_SETTEXT, 2,
                            (LPARAM)(parallel ?
        _T(" Right-click for serial execution") :
        _T(" Right-click for parallel execution")));
    InvalidateRect (hWnd, NULL, TRUE);
    UpdateWindow (hWnd);
    break;
```

Here, you toggle the parallel variable and send a message to the status bar to update the text in the third status bar part to reflect the current value of parallel. The call to InvalidateRect() defines the region of the window specified by the first argument that needs to be redrawn when the next WM_PAINT message is received. The second argument is a RECT object that defines the region of the client area that is to be redrawn, but the NULL value here specifies the entire client area of the window. The third argument is TRUE if the client area is to be erased before being redrawn. The call to UpdateWindow() sends a WM_PAINT message to the application window, which will cause the Mandelbrot set to be recomputed either serially or in parallel, once we have finalized the code to do that.

Now you can update the code that processes the WM_PAINT message to draw the client area of the window:

```
case WM_PAINT:
hdc = BeginPaint(hWnd, &ps);
// TODO: Add any drawing code here...
if(parallel)
  DrawSetParallel(hWnd);
else
  DrawSet(hWnd);
EndPaint(hWnd, &ps);
break;
```

Handling the message now involves choosing which function to call to compute the Mandelbrot set, based on the value of parallel. When parallel is true, you run the parallel version of the function, and when it is false, the serial version.

Using the Timer

We can start and stop the global timer we have created in the code that handles the WM_PAINT message, but we have a slight problem. As you saw earlier, a HRTimer object returns elapsed time as a value of type double. Displaying this in the status bar requires that it be in the form of a null-terminated text string. Your first step in using a timer is to add a function that will accept a time value as type double and update the status bar with a text representation of the double value.

Add the following prototype to `Ex13_02C.cpp` at the end of the existing function prototypes:

```
void UpdateStatusBarTime(HWND hWnd, double time);
```

Here's the function definition to add to the source file:

```
void UpdateStatusBarTime(HWND hWnd, double time)
{
  std:: basic_ stringstream <TCHAR> ss;              // Create a string stream
  ss.setf(std::ios::fixed, std::ios::floatfield);    // Turn on fixed & turn off float
  ss.precision(2);                                   // Two decimal places
  ss << _T("  ") << time << _T(" seconds");          // Write time to ss
  SendMessage(GetDlgItem(hWnd, IDC_STATUS), SB_SETTEXT, 1, (LPARAM)(ss.str().c_str()));

}
```

The hard work is done by the `basic_stringstream` object, and the `basic_stringstream` class template is defined in the `sstream` header, so you need an `#include` directive for that. A `basic_stringstream <TCHAR>` object is a stream that transfers the data that you write to it to a string buffer storing characters of type `TCHAR`. This is very useful for formatting operations. Here, you set the flags for the `ss` object to transfer a floating-point value to the underlying buffer in a fixed-point representation instead of the default scientific representation. The first argument to the `setf()` function is the flags to be set, and the second argument is the flags to be unset. Calling the `precision()` function for `ss` with the argument as 2 causes floating-point values to have two decimal places after the point. You then write the time value to `ss`, along with the descriptive text.

You update the status bar with the time string by calling the `SendMessage()` function. The last argument to the function calls the `str()` function for `ss` to retrieve the contents of the stream as a `string` object. Calling the `c_str()` function for that produces a null-terminated string. The string pointer argument here has to be of type `LPARAM`, so you cast the pointer for this string to type `LPARAM`.

The last step is to amend the handling of the `WM_PAINT` message in the `WndProc()` function to use the timer:

```
case WM_PAINT:
  hdc = BeginPaint(hWnd, &ps);
  // TODO: Add any drawing code here...
  timer.StartTimer();
  if(parallel)
    DrawSetParallel(hWnd);
  else
    DrawSet(hWnd);
  UpdateStatusBarTime(hWnd, timer.StopTimer());
  EndPaint(hWnd, &ps);
  break;
```

You should now get the time displayed in the status bar. You can toggle between serial and parallel execution by clicking the right mouse button. This will enable you to see how much performance increase you are getting from parallel execution. I got the window shown in Figure 13-3 running parallel execution on my machine.

FIGURE 13-3

This is more than 3 seconds faster than the serial computation on my computer. Keep in mind that other programs running on your computer may have a significant effect on the timings. As well as various operating system services, your virus scanner may be executing in the background, for instance, so don't expect the execution times measured by our example to be necessarily consistent on different occasions. You will find the various stages of development of this example in the code download for the book as Ex13_02A, Ex13_02B, and Ex13_02C.

So, what about the parallel_for algorithm that I spent so much time discussing earlier in this chapter? Can we apply this to speed up the Mandelbrot set calculation, bearing in mind that the calculation consists almost entirely of for loops? Well, we could make the inner loop parallel by creating a new memDC for every image row, but it would be nice to make the outer loop parallel. However, the BitBlt() function call that has to be in the outer loop cannot be executed in parallel because it writes to a DC. This really prevents us from using parallel_for for the outer loop. However, with a little more help from the PPL, maybe we can crack it.

CRITICAL SECTIONS

A **critical section** is a contiguous sequence of statements that cannot be executed by more than one task at any given time. As you saw with the last example, concurrent execution of code that updates a device context will cause problems because a device context is not designed to be used in this way. Critical sections can arise in other contexts, too.

The PPL defines the `critical_section` class that you can use to identify sequences of statements that must not be executed in parallel.

Using critical_section Objects

There is only one constructor for the `critical_section` class, so creating an object is very simple:

```
Concurrency::critical_section cs;
```

This creates the object `cs`. A `critical_section` object is a **mutex**. The name mutex is a contraction of **mut**ual **ex**clusion object. A mutex allows multiple threads of execution to access a given resource, but only one at a time. It provides a mechanism for the thread to lock the resource that it is currently using. All other threads then must wait until the resource is unlocked before another thread can access it.

Locking and Unlocking a Section of Code

Once you have created a `critical_section` object, you can apply a lock to a section of code by calling the `lock()` member function as follows:

```
cs.lock();                    // Lock the statements that follow
```

The statements that follow this call to the `lock()` member function can be executed by only one thread at a time. All other threads are excluded until the `unlock()` method for the mutex is called, like this:

```
cs.lock();                    // Lock the statements that follow
// Code that must be single threaded. . .
cs.unlock();                  //  Release the lock
```

Once the `unlock()` method for the `critical_section` object has been called, another thread of execution may apply a lock to the code section and execute it.

If a task calls `lock()` for a `critical_section` object, and the code is already being executed by another task, the call to `lock()` will block. In other words, execution of the task trying to lock the code section cannot continue. In many situations this may be inconvenient. It can be the case that there are several different code sections controlled by other mutexes, and if another section is not locked, you could execute that section. In situations where you don't want the call to lock a section of code to block because there are other things you can do, you can use the `try_lock()` member function:

```
if(cs.try_lock())
{
  // Code that must be single threaded . . .
  cs.unlock();            // Release the lock
}
else

  // Do something else. . .
```

The `try_lock()` function does not block if a lock cannot be obtained, but returns a `bool` value that is `true` if a lock is obtained, and `false` otherwise.

I think we have enough additional capability to get over the problems in applying the `parallel_for` loop to the Mandelbrot set computation.

TRY IT OUT   Using the parallel_for for the Mandelbrot Set

You can just amend the previous example by replacing the `DrawSetParallel()` function with a new version. In the code download, this example will be `Ex13_03`.

The simplest approach to applying the `parallel_for` algorithm is to replace the outer loop in the original `DrawSet()` function, and then lock the code sections that must not execute concurrently. We will still need to rearrange some of the code though to allow parallel loop operations. Here's the code:

Available for download on Wrox.com

```cpp
void DrawSetParallel(HWND hWnd)
{
  HDC hdc(GetDC(hWnd));                          // Get device context

  // Get client area dimensions, which will be the image size
  RECT rect;
  GetClientRect(hWnd, &rect);
  int imageHeight(rect.bottom);
  int imageWidth(rect.right);

  // Client area axes
  const double realMin(-2.1);        // Minimum real value
  double imaginaryMin(-1.3);         // Minimum imaginary value
  double imaginaryMax(+1.3);         // Maximum imaginary value

  // Set maximum real so axes are the same scale
  double realMax(realMin+(imaginaryMax-imaginaryMin)*imageWidth/imageHeight);

  // Get scale factors to convert pixel coordinates
  double realScale((realMax-realMin)/(imageWidth-1));
  double imaginaryScale((imaginaryMax-imaginaryMin)/(imageHeight-1));
  Concurrency::critical_section cs;              // Mutex for BitBlt() operation
  Concurrency::parallel_for(0, imageHeight,[&](int y) // Iterate parallel over image rows
  {
    cs.lock();                                   // Lock for access to the client DC
    // Create bitmap for one row of pixels in image
    HDC memDC = CreateCompatibleDC(hdc);         // Get device context to draw pixels
    HBITMAP bmp = CreateCompatibleBitmap(hdc, imageWidth, 1);
    cs.unlock();                                 // We are done with hdc here so unlock
    HGDIOBJ oldBmp = SelectObject(memDC, bmp);   // Select bitmap into DC

  double cReal(0.0), cImaginary(0.0);            // Stores c components
  double zReal(0.0), zImaginary(0.0);            // Stores z components

    zImaginary = cImaginary = imaginaryMax - y*imaginaryScale;
    for(int x = 0 ; x < imageWidth ; ++x)              // Iterate over pixels in a row
    {
      zReal = cReal = realMin + x*realScale;
      // Set current pixel color based on n
      SetPixel(memDC, x, 0, Color(IteratePoint(zReal, zImaginary, cReal, cImaginary)));
```

```
    }
    cs.lock();                            // Lock for writing to hdc
    // Transfer pixel row to client area device context
    BitBlt(hdc, 0, y, imageWidth, 1, memDC, 0, 0, SRCCOPY);
    cs.unlock();                          // Release the lock
    SelectObject(memDC, oldBmp);
    DeleteObject(bmp);                    // Delete bitmap
    DeleteDC(memDC);                      // and our working DC
  });
  ReleaseDC(hWnd, hdc);                   // Release the client DC
  }
```

code snippet Ex13_03.cpp

When you substitute this function for the function of the same name in the previous example, you are ready to go. Executing the version that uses the `parallel_for` algorithm, you'll be able to see the non-sequential nature of the operation, with various rows in the image being displayed at different times. On my computer, it seemed to be slightly faster than the version using the `parallel_invoke` algorithm.

THE COMBINABLE CLASS TEMPLATE

The `combinable` class template is designed to help you with shared resources that can be segmented into thread-local variables and combined after the computation is complete. It offers advantages over using a mutex, like a `critical_section` object, in that you don't have to lock the shared resources and cause threads to wait. The way it works is that a `combinable` object can create duplicates of a shared resource, one for each thread that is to be executed in parallel. Each thread uses its own independent copy of the original shared resource. The only prerequisite is that you must be able to specify an operation that will combine the duplicates to form a single resource, once the parallel operation is complete. A very simple example of where `combinable` can help is a variable that is shared in a loop to accumulate a total. Consider the following fragment:

```
std::array<double, 100> values;
double sum(0.0);
for(size_t i = 0 ; i<values.size() ; ++i)
{
  values[i] = (i+1)*(i+1);
  sum += values[i];
}
std::cout << "Total = " << sum << std::endl;
```

You cannot make this loop parallel without doing something about `sum` because it is accessed and updated on each iteration. Allowing concurrent threads to do this is likely to corrupt the value of the result. Here's how the `combinable` class can help you execute the loop in parallel:

```
Concurrency::combinable<double> sums;
Concurrency::parallel_for(static_cast<size_t>(0) ,  values.size() ,
```

```
   [&values, &sums](size_t i)
   {
     values[i] = (i+1)*(i+1);
     sums.local() += values[i];
   });
 double sum = sums.combine([](double lSum, double rSum)
                             {return lSum + rSum;  });
```

The `combinable` object, `sums`, can create a local variable of type `double` for each concurrent thread. The template argument specifies the type of variable. Each concurrent thread uses its own local variable of the type specified, which you access by calling the `local()` function for `sums` in the lambda expression.

Once the `parallel_for` loop has executed, you combine the local variables that are owned by `sums` by calling its `combine()` function. The argument is a lambda expression that defines how any two local variables are to be combined. The lambda expression must have two parameters that are both of the same type, `T`, as you used for the `combinable` template argument, or both of type `const` reference to `T`. The lambda must return the result of combining its two arguments. The `combine()` function will use the lambda expression as often as necessary to combine all the local variables that were created, and return the result. In our case, this will be the sum of all the elements of `values`.

The `combinable` class also defines the `combine_each()` member function for combining local results that have a `void` return type. The argument to this function should be a lambda expression or a function object with a single parameter of type `T` or type `const T&`. With this function, it is up to you to assemble the combined result. Here's how you would use it to combine the local results for the previous fragment:

```
double sum(0.0);
sums.combine_each([&sum](double localSum)
                  { sum += localSum;  });
```

The lambda expression that is the argument to `combine_each()` will be called once for each local partial total owned by `sums`. Thus, you will accumulate the grand total in `sum`.

You can reuse a combinable object. To reset the value of the local variables for a combinable object, you just call its `clear()` function.

TRY IT OUT Using the combinable Class

Here's an example that uses the `combinable` class in summing a well-known series that converges to the value π^2:

```
// Ex13_04.cpp
// Computing pi by summing a series
#include <iostream>
#include <iomanip>
#include <cmath>
#include "ppl.h"

int main()
{
  Concurrency::combinable<double> piParts;
```

```
    Concurrency::parallel_for(1, 1000000, [&piParts](long long n)
                                    { piParts.local() += 6.0/(n*n);  });

    double pi2 = piParts.combine([](double left, double right)
                                    {  return left + right;  });
    std::cout << "pi squared = " << std::setprecision(10) << pi2 << std::endl;
    std::cout << "pi = " << std::sqrt(pi2) << std::endl;
    return 0;
}
```

This produces the following output:

```
pi squared = 9.869598401
pi = 3.141591699
```

How It Works

You first create a `combinable` object, `piParts`, to be used in the algorithm that follows. The `parallel_for` algorithm sums one million terms in the series:

$$,6\text{-},1\text{-}2..\text{+},6\text{-},2\text{-}2..\text{+},6\text{-},3\text{-}2..\text{+}\cdots$$

The algorithm will execute iterations in parallel on as many processors as you have available on your machine. The sums of terms computed on each processor are accumulated in a local copy of a variable of type `double` that is provided by the combinable object `piParts`. After the algorithm completes execution, you sum the local variables by calling the `combine()` function for `piParts`. The argument is a lambda expression that defines how any two local values are to be combined. The `combine()` function returns the sum of all the local variables used. You have to take the square root of the result to get the value you are looking for.

TASKS AND TASK GROUPS

You can use a `task_group` class object to manage the parallel execution of two or more tasks, where a task may be defined by a functor or a lambda expression. A `task_group` object is thread-safe, so you can use it to initiate tasks from different threads. If you only want to initiate parallel tasks from a single thread, then a `structured_task_group` object will be more efficient.

To execute a task in another thread, you first create your `task_group` object; then you pass the function object or lambda expression that defines the task to the `run()` function for the object. Here's a fragment that shows how this works:

```
    std::array<int, 50> odds;
    std::array<int, 50> evens;
    int n(0);
    std::generate(odds.begin(), odds.end(), [&n] { return ++n*2 - 1;  });
    n = 0;
    std::generate(evens.begin(), evens.end(), [&n] { return ++n*2;  });
    int oddSum(0), evenSum(0);
    Concurrency::task_group taskGroup;
```

```
taskGroup.run([&odds, &oddSum]
  { for(size_t i = 0 ; i<odds.size() ; ++i)
          oddSum += odds[i];
  });
for(size_t i = 0 ; i< evens.size() ; ++i)
  evenSum += evens[i];
taskGroup.wait();
```

The arrays odds and evens are initialized with sequential odd and even integers, respectively. The oddSum and evenSum variables are used to accumulate the sums of the elements in the two arrays. The first call to the run() function for the taskGroup object initiates the task specified by the lambda expression on a separate thread from the current thread — in other words, on a separate processor. The lambda expression sums the elements of the odds, and accumulates the result in oddSum. The for loop that follows sums the elements of the evens array and will execute concurrently with the task group lambda. Calling the wait() function for the taskGroup object suspends execution of the current thread until all tasks initiated by the taskGroup object — just one in our case — are complete.

Note how the current thread of execution can continue once a task group task has been initiated. The current thread will only pause execution when you call the wait() function for the task_group object. Of course, if you have more than two processors, you can use the task_group object to initiate more than one task to execute concurrently with the current thread.

A structured_task_group object can only be used to initiate tasks from a single thread. Unlike task_group objects, you cannot pass a lambda expression, or function object to the run() function, for a structured_task_group object. In this case, the argument specifying the task must be a task_handle object. task_handle is a class template where the type parameter is the type of the function object it encapsulates. It's easy to construct a task_handle object, though. Here's how the previous fragment can be coded to use the structured_task_group object to initiate a parallel task:

```
std::array<int, 50> odds;
std::array<int, 50> evens;
int n(0);
std::generate(odds.begin(), odds.end(), [&n] { return ++n*2 - 1;  });
n = 0;
std::generate(evens.begin(), evens.end(), [&n] { return ++n*2;  });
int oddSum(0), evenSum(0);
Concurrency::structured_task_group taskGroup;
auto oddsFun = [&odds, &oddSum]
  { for(size_t i = 0 ; i<odds.size() ; ++i)
          oddSum += odds[i];
  };
taskGroup.run(Concurrency::task_handle<decltype(oddsFun)>(oddsFun));
for(size_t i = 0 ; i< evens.size() ; ++i)
  evenSum += evens [i];
taskGroup.wait();
```

Here you create a function object, oddsFun, from a lambda expression. The auto keyword deduces the correct type for oddsFun from the lambda expression. The run() function for the taskGroup object requires the argument to be a task_handle object that encapsulates the task to be initiated. You create this by passing the oddsFun object as the argument, with the type argument for the task_handle template specified as the declared type of oddsFun. You use the decltype keyword to do this.

Note that the argument to the `task_handle` constructor must be a function object that has no parameters. Consequently, you cannot use a lambda expression here that requires arguments when it is executed. If you do need to use a lambda that requires parameters, you can usually wrap it in another lambda without parameters that calls your original lambda.

Another important consideration is that it is up to you to ensure that a `task_handle` object is not destroyed before the task associated with it has completed execution. This can come about if execution of the current thread, in which you create the `task_handle` object and initiated the parallel task execution, continues to a point where the destructor of the `task_handle` object is called, while the parallel task is still in progress.

TRY IT OUT   **Using a Task Group to Compute the Mandelbrot Set**

You can create a new version of the earlier Mandelbrot set example that will use a task group. I'll just show the code for the `DrawSetParallel()` function here because that's the only bit that's different. The rest of the code is exactly the same; the complete example is in the code download as `Ex13_05`. Here's how the function can be implemented to use a task group:

```
void DrawSetParallel(HWND hWnd)
{
  HDC hdc(GetDC(hWnd));                      // Get device context

  // Get client area dimensions, which will be the image size
  RECT rect;
  GetClientRect(hWnd, &rect);
  int imageHeight(rect.bottom);
  int imageWidth(rect.right);

  // Create bitmap for one row of pixels in image
  HDC memDC1 = CreateCompatibleDC(hdc);    // Get device context to draw pixels
  HDC memDC2 = CreateCompatibleDC(hdc);    // Get device context to draw pixels
  HBITMAP bmp1 = CreateCompatibleBitmap(hdc, imageWidth, 1);
  HBITMAP bmp2 = CreateCompatibleBitmap(hdc, imageWidth, 1);
  HGDIOBJ oldBmp1 = SelectObject(memDC1, bmp1);   // Select bitmap into DC1
  HGDIOBJ oldBmp2 = SelectObject(memDC2, bmp2);   // Select bitmap into DC2

  // Client area axes
  const double realMin(-2.1);        // Minimum real value
  double imaginaryMin(-1.3);         // Minimum imaginary value
  double imaginaryMax(+1.3);         // Maximum imaginary value

  // Set maximum real so axes are the same scale
  double realMax(realMin+(imaginaryMax-imaginaryMin)*imageWidth/imageHeight);

  // Get scale factors to convert pixel coordinates
  double realScale((realMax-realMin)/(imageWidth-1));
  double imaginaryScale((imaginaryMax-imaginaryMin)/(imageHeight-1));

    // Lambda expression to create an image row
    auto rowCalc = [&] (HDC& memDC, int yLocal)
```

```
    {
       double zReal(0.0), cReal(0.0);
       double zImaginary(imaginaryMax - yLocal*imaginaryScale);
       double cImaginary(zImaginary);
       for(int x = 0 ; x < imageWidth ; ++x)            // Iterate over pixels in a row
       {
         zReal = cReal = realMin + x*realScale;
         // Set current pixel color based on n
         SetPixel(memDC, x, 0, Color(IteratePoint(zReal, zImaginary,
                                        cReal, cImaginary)));
       }
    };
  Concurrency::task_group taskGroup;
  for(int y = 1 ; y < imageHeight ; y += 2)              // Iterate over image rows
  {
    taskGroup.run([&]{rowCalc(memDC1, y-1);});
    rowCalc(memDC2, y);
    taskGroup.wait();
    BitBlt(hdc, 0, y-1, imageWidth, 1, memDC1, 0, 0, SRCCOPY);
    BitBlt(hdc, 0, y, imageWidth, 1, memDC2, 0, 0, SRCCOPY);
  }
  // If there's an odd number of rows, take care of the last one
  if(imageHeight%2 == 1)
  {
    rowCalc(memDC1, imageWidth-1);
    BitBlt(hdc, 0, imageHeight-1, imageWidth, 1, memDC1, 0, 0, SRCCOPY);
  }

  SelectObject(memDC1, oldBmp1);
  SelectObject(memDC2, oldBmp2);
  DeleteObject(bmp1);                            // Delete bitmap 1
  DeleteObject(bmp2);                            // Delete bitmap 2
  DeleteDC(memDC1);                              // and our working DC 1
  DeleteDC(memDC2);                              // and our working DC 2
  ReleaseDC(hWnd, hdc);                          // Release client area DC
}
```

This will produce the same output as the earlier version of the program.

How It Works

The changes from the `parallel_invoke` version of the function are shown in bold. Only four lines are different. After creating a `task_group` object outside the loop, you pass a lambda expression to the `run()` function to execute it on another thread. The lambda expression that is the argument calls a `rowCalc` function object, which is defined by another lambda expression. The `rowCalc` function object computes the pixels for a single row in the client area of the window using the memory DC and y value that are passed as arguments. It is necessary to wrap `rowCalc` with another lambda expression because the argument to the `run()` function must be a function object that does not require arguments when it executes.

After the call to the `run()` function for the `taskGroup` object, you execute the `rowCalc` function object for the next row of pixels for the image. This executes concurrently with the computation initiated by the `run()` function for `taskGroup`. Calling `wait()` for the `taskGroup` object suspends execution of the current thread until the task executed by the `taskGroup` object is completed. You are then able to transfer the pixels from the memory DCs to the client area DC. Thus, the loop indexed by `y` computes two rows of the output image, concurrently, on each iteration.

SUMMARY

In this chapter, you have learned the basic elements provided by the Parallel Patterns Library for programming to use multiple processors in an application. The PPL is effective only if you have a substantial compute-intensive task that will run on a machine with multiple processors, but such tasks can crop up quite often. Many engineering and scientific applications come into this category, as do many image-processing operations, and you can find large-scale commercial data-processing tasks that may benefit from using the PPL.

EXERCISES

1. Define a function that will calculate the factorial of an integer of type `long long` using the `parallel_for` algorithm. (The factorial of an integer *n* is the product of all the integers from 1 to *n*.) Demonstrate that the function works with a suitable `main()` function.

2. Define a function that will compute the sum of squares of the elements of an `array<double>` container as a parallel computation using the `parallel_invoke` algorithm. The `array<double>` should be passed as an argument to the function. Demonstrate that the function works with a suitable `main()` function, first with a limited number of known values, then with a large number of random values.

3. Repeat the previous exercise, but this time use a `task_group` object to perform the computation in parallel.

▶ **WHAT YOU LEARNED IN THIS CHAPTER**

TOPIC	CONCEPT
The `parallel_for` algorithm	The `parallel_for` algorithm provides the equivalent of a `for` loop with iterations executing in parallel. You specify the task that is to be executed on each iteration by a function object or a lambda expression.
The `parallel_for_each` algorithm	The `parallel_for_each` algorithm provides a parallel loop that processes the contents of an STL container using iterators.
The `parallel_invoke` algorithm	You use the `parallel_invoke` algorithm to execute 2 to 10 tasks in parallel. You specify a task by a function object or a lambda expression.
The `combinable` class	You can use a `combinable` class object to manage resources that are accessed by tasks executing concurrently.
The `task_group` class	You can use a `task_group` object to execute one or more tasks in a separate thread of execution. A `task_group` object is thread-safe and can be used to initiate tasks from different threads.
The `structured_task_group` class	You can use a `structured_task_group` object to execute one or more tasks in separate threads of execution. A `structured_task_group` object is not thread-safe, and all tasks must be initiated from the same thread. Each task must be identified using a `task_handle` object.
High-resolution timers	You can use the `::QueryPerformanceFrequency()` and `::QueryPerformanceCounter()` functions provided by the Windows API to implement a high-resolution timer capability in an application.

14

Windows Programming with the Microsoft Foundation Classes

WHAT YOU WILL LEARN IN THIS CHAPTER:

➤ The basic elements of an MFC-based program

➤ How Single Document Interface (SDI) applications and Multiple Document Interface (MDI) applications differ

➤ How to use the MFC Application Wizard to generate SDI and MDI programs

➤ Files generated by the MFC Application Wizard and their contents

➤ How an MFC Application Wizard-generated program is structured

➤ The key classes in an MFC Application Wizard-generated program, and how they are interconnected

➤ The general approach to customizing an MFC Application Wizard-generated program

In this chapter, you start down the road of serious Windows application development using the MFC. You'll get an appreciation of what code the Application wizard generates for a Microsoft Foundation Class (MFC) program and what options you have for the features to be included in your code.

You'll be expanding the programs that you generate in this chapter by adding features and code incrementally in subsequent chapters. You will eventually end up with a sizable, working Windows program that incorporates almost all the basic user interface programming techniques you will have learned along the way.

THE DOCUMENT/VIEW CONCEPT IN MFC

When you write applications using MFC, it implies acceptance of a specific structure for your program, with application data being stored and processed in a particular way. This may sound restrictive, but it really isn't for the most part, and the benefits in speed and ease of implementation you gain far outweigh any conceivable disadvantages. The structure of an MFC program incorporates two application-oriented entities — a **document** and a **view** — so let's look at what they are and how they're used.

What Is a Document?

A **document** is the name given to the collection of data in your application with which the user interacts. Although the word *document* seems to imply something of a textual nature, a document isn't limited to text. It could be the data for a game, a geometric model, a text file, a collection of data on the distribution of orange trees in California, or, indeed, anything you want. The term *document* is just a convenient label for the application data in your program, treated as a unit.

You won't be surprised to hear that a document in your program is defined as an object of a document class. Your document class is derived from the CDocument class in the MFC library, and you'll add your own data members to store items that your application requires, and member functions to support processing of that data. Your application is not limited to a single document type; you can define multiple document classes when there are several different kinds of documents involved in your application.

Handling application data in this way enables standard mechanisms to be provided within MFC for managing a collection of application data as a unit and for storing and retrieving data contained in document objects to and from disk. These mechanisms are inherited by your document class from the base class defined in the MFC library, so you get a broad range of functionality built into your application automatically, without having to write any code.

Document Interfaces

You have a choice as to whether your program deals with just one document at a time, or with several. The **Single Document Interface**, abbreviated as **SDI**, is supported by the MFC library for programs that require only one document to be open at a time. A program using this interface is referred to as an **SDI application**.

For programs needing several documents to be open at one time, you can use the **Multiple Document Interface**, which is usually referred to as **MDI**. With the MDI, as well as being able to open multiple documents of one type, your program can also be organized to handle documents of different types simultaneously with each document displayed in its own window. Of course, you need to supply the code to deal with processing whatever different kinds of documents you intend to support. With an MDI application, each document is displayed in a child window of the application window. You have an additional application variant called the **multiple top-level document architecture** where each document window is a child of the desktop.

What Is a View?

A **view** always relates to a particular document object. As you've seen, a document contains a set of application data in your program, and a view is an object that provides a mechanism for displaying some or all of the data stored in a document. It defines how the data is to be displayed in a window and how the user can interact with it. Similar to the way that you define a document, you'll define your own view class by deriving it from the MFC class `CView`. Note that a view object and the window in which it is displayed are distinct. The window in which a view appears is called a **frame window**. A view is actually displayed in its own window that exactly fills the client area of a frame window. Figure 14-1 illustrates how the data in a document might be displayed in two views.

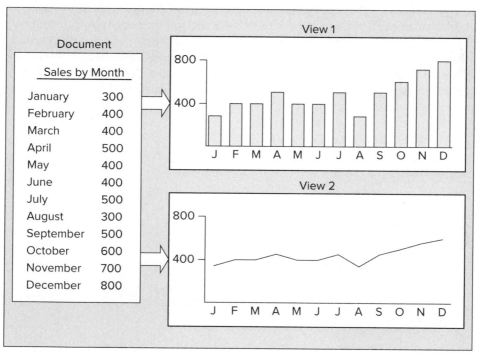

FIGURE 14-1

In the example in Figure 14-1, each view displays all the data that the document contains in a different form, although a view could display just part of the data in a document if that's what's required.

A document object can have as many view objects associated with it as you want. Each view object can provide a different presentation of the document data or a subset of the same data. If you were dealing with text, for example, different views could be displaying independent blocks of text from the same document. For a program handling graphical data, you could display all of the document data at different scales in separate windows, or in different formats, such as a textual representation of the elements that form the image. Figure 14-1 illustrates a document that contains numerical data — product sales data by month — where one view provides a bar chart representation of the sales performance and a second view shows the data in the form of a graph.

Linking a Document and Its Views

MFC incorporates a mechanism for integrating a document with its views, and each frame window with a currently active view. A document object automatically maintains a list of pointers to its associated views, and a view object has a data member holding a pointer to the document that it relates to. Each frame window stores a pointer to the currently active view object. The coordination among a document, a view, and a frame window is established by another MFC class of objects called **document templates**.

Document Templates

A **document template** manages the document objects in your program, as well as the windows and views associated with each of them. There is one document template for each type of document that you have in your application. If you have two or more documents of the same type, you need only one document template to manage them. To be more specific about the role of a document template, a document template object creates document objects and frame window objects, and views of a document are created by a frame window object. The application object that is fundamental to every MFC application creates the document template object itself. Figure 14-2 shows a graphical representation of these interrelationships.

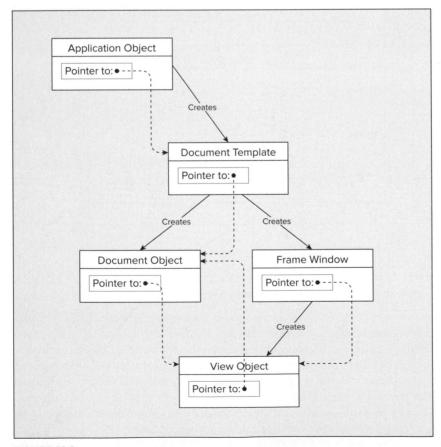

FIGURE 14-2

The diagram uses dashed arrows to show how pointers are used to relate objects. These pointers enable function members of one class object to access the **public** data or the function members in the interface of another object.

Document Template Classes

MFC has two classes for defining document templates. For SDI applications, the MFC library class CSingleDocTemplate is used. This is relatively straightforward because an SDI application has only one document and usually just one view. MDI applications are rather more complicated. They have multiple documents active at one time, so a different class, CMultiDocTemplate, is needed to define the document template. You'll see more of these classes as we progress into developing application code.

Your Application and MFC

Figure 14-3 shows the four basic classes that are going to appear in virtually all your MFC-based Windows applications:

➤ The application class CMyApp

➤ The frame window class CMyWnd

➤ The view class CMyView, which defines how data contained in CMyDoc is to be displayed in the client area of a window created by a CMyWnd object

➤ The document class CMyDoc, defining a document to contain the application data

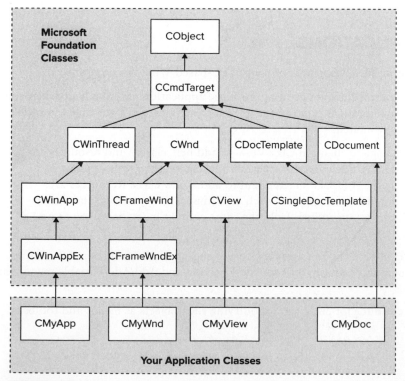

FIGURE 14-3

The actual names for these classes are specific to a particular application, but the derivation from MFC is much the same, although there can be alternative base classes, particularly with the view class. As you'll see a bit later, MFC provides several variations of the view class that provide a lot of functionality prepackaged for you, saving you lots of coding. You normally don't need to extend the class that defines a document template for your application, so the standard MFC class `CSingleDocTemplate` usually suffices in an SDI program. When you're creating an MDI program, your document template class is `CMultiDocTemplate`, which is also derived from `CDocTemplate`. An MDI application also contains an additional class, beyond the four that appear in Figure 14-3, that defines a child window.

The arrows in the diagram point from a base class to a derived class. The MFC library classes shown here form quite a complex inheritance structure, but, in fact, these are just a very small part of the complete MFC structure. You need not be concerned about the details of the complete MFC hierarchy, but it is important to have a general appreciation of it if you want to understand what the inherited members of your classes are. You will not see any of the definitions of the base classes in your program, but the inherited members of a derived class in your program are accumulated from the direct base class, as well as from each of the indirect base classes in the MFC hierarchy. To determine what members one of your program's classes has, you therefore need to know from which classes it inherits. After you know that, you can look up its members using the Help facility.

Another point you don't need to worry about is remembering which classes you need to have in your program and what base classes to use in their definition. As you'll see next, all of this is taken care of for you by Visual C++ 2010.

CREATING MFC APPLICATIONS

You use four primary tools in the development of your MFC-based Windows programs:

1. You use an Application Wizard for creating the basic application program code when you start. You use an Application Wizard whenever you create a project that results in code being automatically generated.

2. You use the project context menu in ClassView to add new classes and resources to your project. You display this context menu by right-clicking the project name in ClassView and using the Add/Class menu item to add a new class. Resources are things composed of non-executable data such as bitmaps, icons, menus, and dialog boxes. The Add/Resource menu item from the same context menu helps you to add a new resource.

3. You use the class context menu in ClassView for extending and customizing the existing classes in your programs. You use the Add/Add Function and Add/Add Variable menu items to do this.

4. You use a Resource Editor for creating or modifying such objects as menus and toolbars.

There are, in fact, several resource editors; the one used in any particular situation is selected depending on the kind of resource that you're editing. We'll look at editing resources in the next chapter, but for now, let's jump in and create an MFC application.

The process for creating an MFC application is just as straightforward as that for creating a console program; there are just a few more choices along the way. As you have already seen, you start by creating a new project by selecting the File ➪ New ➪ Project menu item, or you can use the shortcut and press Ctrl+Shift+N. The New Project dialog box is displayed, where you can then choose MFC as the project type and MFC Application as the template to be used. You also need to enter a name for the project, which can be anything you want — I've used TextEditor, as shown in Figure 14-4. You won't be developing this particular example into a serious application, so you can use any name you like.

FIGURE 14-4

As you know, the name that you assign to the project — TextEditor, in this case — is used as the name of the folder that contains all the project files, but it is also used as a basis for creating the names for classes that the Application Wizard generates for your project. When you click OK in the New Project dialog window, you'll see the MFC Application Wizard dialog, where you can choose options for the application, as shown in Figure 14-5.

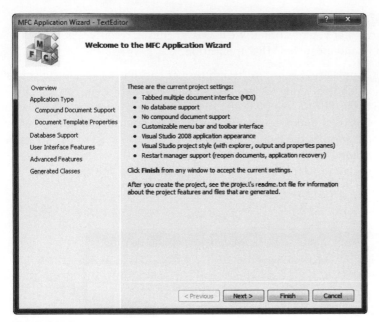

FIGURE 14-5

As you can see, the dialog explains the project settings that are currently in effect, and on the left of the dialog, you have a range of options you can select. You can select any of these to have a look if you want — you can always get back to the base dialog box for the Application Wizard by selecting the Overview option. Selecting any of the options on the left presents you with a whole range of further choices, so there are a lot of options in total. I won't discuss all of them — I'll just outline the ones that you are most likely to be interested in and leave you to investigate the others. Initially, the Application Wizard enables you to choose an SDI application, an MDI application that optionally can be tabbed, a dialog box-based application, or an application with multiple top-level frame windows. Let's create an SDI application first and explore what some of the choices are as we go along.

Creating an SDI Application

Select the Application Type option from the list to the left of the dialog window.

The default option selected is Multiple documents with the tabbed option selected, which selects the multiple document interface (MDI) with each document in its own tabbed page, and the appearance of this is shown at the top left in the dialog window so that you'll know what to expect. Select the Single document option, the MFC standard project style option, and the Windows Native/Default option from the drop-down list of visual styles, and the representation for the application that is shown top-left changes to a single window, as shown in Figure 14-6.

FIGURE 14-6

Consider some of the other options you have here for the application type:

OPTION	DESCRIPTION
Dialog based	The application window is a dialog window rather than a frame window.
Multiple top-level documents	Documents are displayed in child windows of the desktop rather than child windows of the application as they are with an MDI application.
Document/View architecture support	This option is selected by default so you get code built in to support the document/view architecture. If you uncheck this option, the support is not provided and it's up to you to implement whatever you want.
Resource language	The drop-down list box displays the choice of languages available that applies to resources such as menus and text strings in your application.
Use Unicode libraries	Support for Unicode is provided through Unicode versions of the MFC libraries. If you want to use them, you must check this option. Some functionality in MFC is only available when you elect to use Unicode libraries.
Project style	Here you can choose the visual appearance of the application window. Your choice will depend on the environment in which you want to run the application and the kind of application. For example, if your application relates to Microsoft Office, you would select the Office option.

If you hover the mouse cursor over any of the options in the dialog, a tooltip will be displayed explained what the option does. You can leave the Use Unicode libraries option checked by default. If you uncheck it when you create a new application, some of the capabilities that MFC offers in Visual C++ 2010 will not be available.

You have several options for the Project style. I'll select the MFC Standard option and suggest that you do the same. I also selected Windows Native /Default from the Visual style and colors drop-down list. This makes the application appearance the same as your current operating system. If you have Windows 7 installed, you can select the Windows 7 (Scenic) option.

You can also choose how MFC library code is used in your program. The default choice of using the MFC library as a shared DLL (Dynamic Link Library) means that your program links to MFC library routines at run time. This reduces the size of the executable file that you'll generate, but requires the MFC DLL to be on the machine that's running it. The two modules together (your application's .exe module and the MFC .dll) may be bigger than if you had statically linked the MFC library. If you opt for static linking, the MFC library routines are included in the executable module for your program when it is built. Statically linked applications run slightly faster than those that dynamically link to the MFC library, so it's a tradeoff between memory usage and speed of execution. If you keep the default option of using MFC as a shared DLL, several programs running simultaneously using the dynamic link library can all share a single copy of the library in memory.

If you select Document Template Properties in the left pane of the Application Wizard dialog, you can enter a file extension for files that the program creates in the right pane. The extension txt is a good choice for this example. You can also enter a Filter Name, which is the name of the filter that will appear in Open and Save As dialog boxes to filter the list of files so that only files with your file extension are displayed.

If you select User Interface Features from the list in the left pane of the MFC Application Wizard window, you get a further set of options that can be included in your application:

OPTION	DESCRIPTION
Thick Frame	This enables you to resize the application window by dragging a border. It is selected by default.
Minimize box	This option is also selected by default and provides a minimize box at the top right of the application window.
Maximize box	This option is also selected by default and provides a maximize box at the top right of the application window.
Minimized	If you select this option, the application starts with the window minimized so it appears as an icon.
Maximized	If you select this option, the application starts with the window maximized.
System Menu	This option provides the main window with a control-menu box in the title bar.
About box	This option provides your application with an About dialog.
Initial status bar	This option adds a status bar at the bottom of the application window containing indicators for CAPS LOCK, NUM LOCK, and SCROLL LOCK and a message line that displays help strings for menus and toolbar buttons. The option also adds menu commands to hide or show the status bar.
Split window	This option provides a splitter bar for each of the application's main views.

The Command bars options do not apply when you are using new appearance features, such as the Windows 7 option. The Command bars sub-options enable you to choose whether you use a classic style docking toolbar or an Internet Explorer style toolbar.

In this example, the Use a menu bar and toolbar option is selected by default. The User-defined toolbars and images sub-option allows the toolbar and images to be customized at runtime. The Personalized menu behavior sub-option enables menus to display only the items used most frequently. You can also choose to use a ribbon style for menus that is used in the latest releases of Microsoft Office, but you should only do this if it is appropriate to your application.

You should be aware of couple of features under the Advanced Features set of options. One is Printing and print preview, which is selected by default, and the other is Context-sensitive help, which you get if you check the box. Printing and print preview adds the standard Page Setup, Print Preview, and Print items to the File menu, and the Application Wizard also provides code to support these functions. Enabling the Context-sensitive help (HTML) option results in a basic set of facilities to support context-sensitive help. You'll obviously need to add the specific contents of the help files if you want to use this feature.

If you select the Generated Classes option in the MFC Application Wizard dialog box, you'll see a list of the classes that the Application Wizard will generate in your program code, as shown in Figure 14-7.

FIGURE 14-7

You can highlight any class in the list by clicking it, and the boxes below show the name given to the class, the name of the header file in which the definition will be stored, the base class used, and the name of the file containing the implementation of member functions in the class. The class definition is always contained in a .h file, and the member function source code is always included in a .cpp file.

In the case of the class CTextEditorDoc, you can alter everything except the base class; however, if you select CTextEditorApp, the only thing that you can alter is the class name. Try clicking the other classes in the list. For CMainFrame, you can alter everything except the base class, and for the CTextEditorView class shown in Figure 14-7, you can change the base class as well. Click the down arrow to display the list of other classes that you can have as a base class; the list appears in Figure 14-7. The capability built into your view class depends on which base class you select:

BASE CLASS	VIEW CLASS CAPABILITY
CEditView	Provides simple multiline text-editing capability, including find and replace and printing.
CFormView	Provides a view that is a form; a form is a dialog box that can contain controls for displaying data and for user input.
CHtmlEditView	Extends the CHtmlView class and adds the ability to edit HTML pages.
CHtmlView	Provides a view in which Web pages and local HTML documents can be displayed.
CListView	Enables you to use the document-view architecture with list controls.
CRichEditView	Provides the capability to display and edit documents containing rich edit text.
CScrollView	Provides a view that automatically adds scrollbars when the data that is displayed requires them.
CTreeView	Provides the capability to use the document-view architecture with tree controls.
CView	Provides the basic capability for viewing a document.

Because you've called the application TextEditor, with the notion that it is able to edit text, choose CEditView to get basic editing capability provided automatically.

You can now click Finish to have the program files for a fully working base program generated by MFC Application Wizard, using the options you've chosen.

MFC Application Wizard Output

All the program files generated by the Application Wizard are stored in the TextEditor project folder, which is a subfolder to the solution folder with the same name. There are also resource files in the res subfolder to the project folder. The IDE provides several ways for you to view the information relating to your project:

TAB/PANE	CONTENTS
Solution Explorer	Shows the files included in your project. The files are categorized in virtual folders with the names `Header Files`, `Resource Files`, and `Source Files`.
Class View	Class View displays the classes you have in your project and their members. It also shows any global entities you have defined. The classes are shown in the upper pane, and the lower pane displays the members for the class selected in the upper pane. By right-clicking entities in the Class View, you can display a menu that you can use to view the definition of the entity or where it is referenced.
Resource View	This displays the resources such as menu items and toolbar buttons used by your project. Right-clicking a resource displays a menu, enabling you to edit the resource or add new resources.
Property Manager	This displays the versions you can build for your project. The debug version includes extra facilities to make debugging your code easier. The release version results in a smaller executable, and you build this version when your code is fully tested for production use. By right-clicking a version — either Debug or Release — you can display a context menu where you can add a property sheet or display the properties currently set for that version. A property sheet enables you to set options for the compiler and linker.

You can switch to view any of these by selecting from the View menu or clicking on a tab label. If you right-click TextEditor in the Solution Explorer pane and select Properties from the pop-up, the project properties window is displayed, as shown in Figure 14-8.

FIGURE 14-8

The left pane shows the property groups you can select to be displayed in the right pane. Currently, the General group of properties is displayed. You can change the value for a property in the right pane by clicking it and selecting a new value from the drop-down list box to the right of the property name or, in some cases, by entering a new value.

At the top of the property pages window, you can see the current project configuration and the target platform when the project is built. You can change these by selecting from the drop-down list for each.

Viewing Project Files

If you select the Solution Explorer tab and expand the list by clicking the [unfilled] symbol for TextEditor files and then click the [unfilled] symbol for each of the Source Files, Header Files, and Resource Files folders, you'll see the complete list of files for the project, as shown in Figure 14-9. To collapse any expanded branch of the tree, just click the [filled] symbol.

FIGURE 14-9

 If you are still using Windows XP, the symbols to expand or collapse branches of the tree will be + and -.

Figure 14-9 shows the pane as a floating window to make the complete list of files visible at one time; you can arrange for any of the tabbed panes to be floating by clicking the down arrow at the top of the pane and selecting from the list of possible positions. As you can see, there are a total of 19 files shown in the project, excluding ReadMe.txt. You can view the contents of any of the files simply by double-clicking the file name. The contents of the file selected are displayed in the Editor window. Try it out with the ReadMe.txt file. You'll see that it contains a brief explanation of the contents of each of the files that make up the project. I won't repeat the descriptions of the files here, because they are very clearly summarized in ReadMe.txt.

Viewing Classes

The access to your project presented by the Class View tab is often much more convenient than that of Solution Explorer because classes are the basis for the organization of the application. When you want to look at the code, it's typically the definition of a class or the implementation of a member function you'll want to look at, and from Class View you can go directly to either. On occasions, however, Solution Explorer comes in handy. If you want to check the #include directives in a .cpp file, using Solution Explorer, you can open the file you're interested in directly.

In the Class View pane, you can expand the TextEditor classes item to show the classes defined for the application. Clicking the name of any class shows the members of that class in the lower pane. In the Class View pane shown in Figure 14-10, the `CTextEditorDoc` class has been selected.

Figure 14-10 shows the Class View pane in its docked state. The icons code the various kinds of things that you can display. You will find a key to what each icon indicates if you look at the Class View documentation.

You can see that you have the four classes that I discussed earlier that are fundamental to an MFC application: `CTextEditorApp` for the application, `CMainFrame` for the application frame window, `CTextEditorDoc` for the document, and `CTextEditorView` for the view. You also have a class `CAboutDlg` that defines objects that support the dialog box that appears when you select the menu item Help ➪ About in the application. If you select Global Functions and Variables, you'll see that it contains six items, as shown in Figure 14-11.

FIGURE 14-10

The application object, `theApp`, appears twice because there is an extern statement for `theApp` in `TextEditor.h` and the definition for `theApp` is in `TextEditor.cpp`. If you double-click either of the appearances of `theApp` in Class View, it will take you to the corresponding statement. `indicators` is an array of indicators recording the status of caps lock, num lock, and scroll lock that are displayed in the status bar. The remaining three variables relate to the management of the toolbars in the application. If you double-click any of these, you will see its definition.

To view the code for a class definition in the Editor pane, you just double-click the class name in the tree in Class View. Similarly, to view the code for a member function, double-click the function name. Note that you can drag the edges of any of the panes in an IDE window to view its contents or your

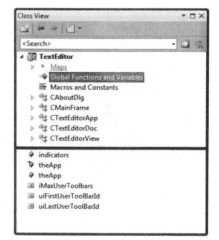

FIGURE 14-11

code more easily. You can hide or show the Solution Explorer set of panes by clicking the Autohide button at the right end of the pane title bar.

The Class Definitions

I won't go into the classes in complete detail here — you'll just get a feel for how they look and I'll highlight a few important aspects. Note that the precise content of each class that is generated by the Application Wizard depends on the options you select when creating the project. If you double-click the name of a class in the Class View, the code defining the class is displayed.

Take a look at the application class, `CTextEditorApp`, first. The definition for this class is shown here:

```
// TextEditor.h : main header file for the TextEditor application
//
#pragma once

#ifndef __AFXWIN_H__
        #error "include 'stdafx.h' before including this file for PCH"
#endif

#include "resource.h" // main symbols


// CTextEditorApp:
// See TextEditor.cpp for the implementation of this class
//

class CTextEditorApp : public CWinAppEx
{
public:
        CTextEditorApp();


// Overrides
public:
        virtual BOOL InitInstance();

// Implementation
        BOOL  m_bHiColorIcons;

        virtual void PreLoadState();
        virtual void LoadCustomState();
        virtual void SaveCustomState();

        afx_msg void OnAppAbout();
        DECLARE_MESSAGE_MAP()
};

extern CTextEditorApp theApp;
```

code snippet TextEditor.h

The `CTextEditorApp` class derives from `CWinAppEx` and includes a constructor, a virtual function `InitInstance()`, a function `OnAppAbout()`, three functions concerned with dealing with the application state, and a macro `DECLARE_MESSAGE_MAP()`.

A macro is not C++ code. It's a name defined by a `#define` pre-processor directive that will be replaced by some text that will normally be C++ code but could also be constants or symbols of some kind.

The DECLARE_MESSAGE_MAP() macro is concerned with defining which Windows messages are handled by which function members of the class. The macro appears in the definition of any class that may process Windows messages. Of course, our application class inherits a lot of functions and data members from the base class, and you will be looking further into these as you expand the program examples. If you take a look at the beginning of the code for the class definition, you will notice that the #pragma once directive prevents the file being included more than once. Following that is a group of preprocessor directives that ensure that the stdafx.h file is included before this file.

The application frame window for our SDI program is created by an object of the class CMainFrame, which is defined by the following code:

```cpp
class CMainFrame : public CFrameWndEx
{
protected: // create from serialization only
    CMainFrame();
    DECLARE_DYNCREATE(CMainFrame)

// Attributes
public:

// Operations
public:

// Overrides
public:
    virtual BOOL PreCreateWindow(CREATESTRUCT& cs);
    virtual BOOL LoadFrame(UINT nIDResource, DWORD dwDefaultStyle =
        WS_OVERLAPPEDWINDOW | FWS_ADDTOTITLE, CWnd* pParentWnd =
        NULL, CCreateContext* pContext = NULL);

// Implementation
public:
    virtual ~CMainFrame();
#ifdef _DEBUG
    virtual void AssertValid() const;
    virtual void Dump(CDumpContext& dc) const;
#endif

protected:  // control bar embedded members
    CMFCMenuBar       m_wndMenuBar;
    CMFCToolBar       m_wndToolBar;
    CMFCStatusBar     m_wndStatusBar;
    CMFCToolBarImages m_UserImages;

// Generated message map functions
protected:
    afx_msg int OnCreate(LPCREATESTRUCT lpCreateStruct);
    afx_msg void OnViewCustomize();
    afx_msg LRESULT OnToolbarCreateNew(WPARAM wp, LPARAM lp);
    DECLARE_MESSAGE_MAP()
};
```

This class is derived from `CFrameWndEx`, which provides most of the functionality required for our application frame window. The derived class includes four protected data members — `m_wndMenuBar`, `m_wndToolBar`, `m_wndStatusBar`, and `m_UserImages` — which are instances of the MFC classes `CMFCMenuBar`, `CMFCToolBar`, `CMFCStatusBar`, and `CMFCToolBarImages`, respectively. The first three of these objects create and manage the menu bar, the toolbar that provides buttons to access standard menu functions, and the status bar that appears at the bottom of the application window. The fourth objects hold the images that are to appear on toolbar buttons.

The definition of the `CTextEditorDoc` class that was supplied by the MFC Application wizard is:

```
class CTextEditorDoc : public CDocument
{
protected: // create from serialization only
      CTextEditorDoc();
      DECLARE_DYNCREATE(CTextEditorDoc)

// Attributes
public:

// Operations
public:

// Overrides
public:
      virtual BOOL OnNewDocument();
      virtual void Serialize(CArchive& ar);
#ifdef SHARED_HANDLERS
      virtual void InitializeSearchContent();
      virtual void OnDrawThumbnail(CDC& dc, LPRECT lprcBounds);
#endif // SHARED_HANDLERS

// Implementation
public:
      virtual ~CTextEditorDoc();
#ifdef _DEBUG
      virtual void AssertValid() const;
      virtual void Dump(CDumpContext& dc) const;
#endif

protected:

// Generated message map functions
protected:
      DECLARE_MESSAGE_MAP()

#ifdef SHARED_HANDLERS
      // Helper function that sets search content for a Search Handler
      void SetSearchContent(const CString& value);
#endif // SHARED_HANDLERS

#ifdef SHARED_HANDLERS
private:
```

```
        CString m_strSearchContent;
        CString m_strThumbnailContent;
#endif // SHARED_HANDLERS
};
```

As in the case of the previous classes, most of the meat comes from the base class and is therefore not apparent here. The DECLARE_DYNCREATE() macro that appears after the constructor (and was also used in the CMainFrame class) enables an object of the class to be created dynamically by synthesizing it from data read from a file. When you save an SDI document object, the frame window that contains the view is saved along with your data. This allows everything to be restored when you read it back. Reading and writing a document object to a file is supported by a process called **serialization**. You will see how to write your own documents to file using serialization and then reconstruct them from the file data in the examples we will develop.

The document class also includes the DECLARE_MESSAGE_MAP() macro in its definition to enable Windows messages to be handled by class member functions if necessary.

The view class in our SDI application is defined as:

```
class CTextEditorView : public CEditView
{
protected: // create from serialization only
        CTextEditorView();
        DECLARE_DYNCREATE(CTextEditorView)

// Attributes
public:
        CTextEditorDoc* GetDocument() const;

// Operations
public:

// Overrides
public:
        virtual BOOL PreCreateWindow(CREATESTRUCT& cs);
protected:
        virtual BOOL OnPreparePrinting(CPrintInfo* pInfo);
        virtual void OnBeginPrinting(CDC* pDC, CPrintInfo* pInfo);
        virtual void OnEndPrinting(CDC* pDC, CPrintInfo* pInfo);

// Implementation
public:
        virtual ~CTextEditorView();
#ifdef _DEBUG
        virtual void AssertValid() const;
        virtual void Dump(CDumpContext& dc) const;
#endif

protected:

// Generated message map functions
protected:
        afx_msg void OnFilePrintPreview();
```

```
        afx_msg void OnRButtonUp(UINT nFlags, CPoint point);
        afx_msg void OnContextMenu(CWnd* pWnd, CPoint point);
        DECLARE_MESSAGE_MAP()
};

#ifndef _DEBUG  // debug version in TextEditorView.cpp
inline CTextEditorDoc* CTextEditorView::GetDocument() const
    { return reinterpret_cast<CTextEditorDoc*>(m_pDocument); }
#endif
```

As you specified in the Application Wizard dialog box, the view class is derived from the class
`CEditView`, which already includes basic text handling facilities. The `GetDocument()` function
returns a pointer to the document object corresponding to the view, and you will be using this to
access data in the document object when you add your own extensions to the view class.

Creating an Executable Module

To compile and link the program, click Build ➪ Build Solution, press F7, or click the Build icon in
the toolbar.

There are two implementations of the `CTextEditorView` class member function `GetDocument()`
in the code generated by Application Wizard. The one in the `.cpp` file for the `CEditView`
class is used for the debug version of the program. You will normally use this during program
development because it provides validation of the pointer value stored for the document. (This is
stored in the inherited data member `m_pDocument` in the view class.) The version that applies to
the release version of your program you can find after the class definition in the `TextEditorView.h`
file. This version is declared as `inline` and it does not validate the document pointer.
The `GetDocument()` function just provides a link to the document object. You can call any
of the functions in the interface to the document class using the pointer to the document that
the function returns.

By default, you have debug capability included in your program. As well as the special version of
`GetDocument()`, there are lots of checks in the MFC code that are included in this case. If you
want to change this, you can use the drop-down list box in the Build toolbar to choose the release
configuration, which doesn't contain all the debug code.

Precompiled Header Files

The first time you compile and link a program, it will take some time. The second and
subsequent times should be quite a bit faster because of a feature of Visual C++ 2010 called
precompiled headers. During the initial compilation, the compiler saves the output from
compiling header files in a special file with the extension `.pch`. On subsequent builds, this file
is reused if the source in the headers has not changed, thus saving the compilation time for
the headers.

You can determine whether or not precompiled headers are used and control how they are handled
through the Properties tab. Right-click TextEditor and select Properties from the menu that is
displayed. If you expand the C/C++ node in the dialog box displayed, you can select Precompiled
Headers to set this property.

Running the Program

To execute the program, press Ctrl+F5. Because you chose `CEditView` as the base class for the `CTextEditorView` class, the program is a fully functioning, simple text editor. You can enter text in the window, as shown in Figure 14-12.

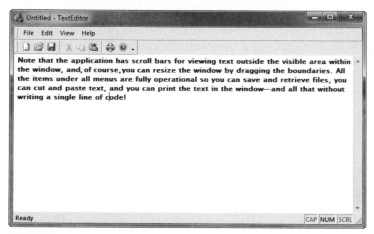

FIGURE 14-12

Note that the application has scroll bars for viewing text outside the visible area within the window, and, of course, you can resize the window by dragging the boundaries. All the items under all menus are fully operational so you can save and retrieve files, you can cut and paste text, and you can print the text in the window — and all that without writing a single line of code! As you move the cursor over the toolbar buttons or the menu options, prompts appear in the status bar describing the functions that are invoked, and if you let the cursor linger on a toolbar button, a tooltip is displayed showing its purpose. (You'll learn about tooltips in more detail in Chapter 15.)

How the Program Works

As in the trivial MFC example you looked at in an earlier chapter, the application object is created at global scope in our SDI program. You can see this if you expand the Global Functions and Variables item in the Class View, and then double-click theApp. In the Editor window, you'll see this statement:

```
CTextEditorApp theApp;
```

This declares the object `theApp` as an instance of our application class `CTextEditorApp`. The statement is in the file `TextEditor.cpp`, which also contains member function declarations for the application class, and the definition of the `CAboutDlg` class.

After the object `theApp` has been created, the MFC-supplied `WinMain()` function is called. This, in turn, calls two member functions of the `theApp` object. First, it calls `InitInstance()`, which provides for any initialization of the application that is necessary, and then `Run()`, which provides initial handling for Windows messages. The `WinMain()` function does not appear explicitly in the project source code, because it is supplied by the MFC class library and is called automatically when the application starts.

The InitInstance() Function

You can access the code for the `InitInstance()` function by double-clicking its entry in the Class View after highlighting the `CTextEditorApp` class — or, if you're in a hurry, you can just look at the code immediately following the line defining the `theApp` object. There's a lot of code in the version created by the MFC Application Wizard, so I just want to remark on a couple of fragments in this function. The first is:

```
SetRegistryKey(_T("Local AppWizard-Generated Applications"));
LoadStdProfileSettings(4);  // Load standard INI file options (including MRU)
```

The string passed to the `SetRegistryKey()` function is used to define a registry key under which program information is stored. You can change this to whatever you want. If I changed the argument to "`Horton`," information about our program would be stored under the registry key:

```
HKEY_CURRENT_USER\Software\Horton\TextEditor\
```

All the application settings are stored under this key, including the list of files most recently used by the program. The call to the function `LoadStdProfileSettings()` loads the application settings that were saved last time around. Of course, the first time you run the program, there aren't any.

A document template object is created dynamically within `InitInstance()` by the following statement:

```
pDocTemplate = new CSingleDocTemplate(
    IDR_MAINFRAME,
    RUNTIME_CLASS(CTextEditorDoc),
    RUNTIME_CLASS(CMainFrame),        // main SDI frame window
    RUNTIME_CLASS(CTextEditorView));
```

The first parameter to the `CSingleDocTemplate` constructor is a symbol, `IDR_MAINFRAME`, which defines the menu and toolbar to be used with the document type. The following three parameters define the document, main frame window, and View Class objects that are to be bound together within the document template. Because you have an SDI application here, there is only one of each in the program, managed through one document template object. `RUNTIME_CLASS()` is a macro that enables the type of a class object to be determined at run time.

There's a lot of other stuff here for setting up the application instance that you need not worry about. You can add any initialization of your own that you need for the application to the `InitInstance()` function.

The Run() Function

The CTextEditorApp class inherits the Run() function from the application base class CWinApp. Because the function is declared as **virtual**, you can replace the base class version of the function Run() with one of your own, but this is not usually necessary so you don't need to worry about it.

Run() acquires all the messages from Windows destined for the application and ensures that each message is passed to the function in the program designated to service it, if one exists. Therefore, this function continues executing as long as the application is running. It terminates when you close the application.

Thus, you can boil the operation of the application down to four steps:

1. Creating an application object, theApp.

2. Executing WinMain(), which is supplied by MFC.

3. WinMain() calling InitInstance(), which creates the document template, the main frame window, the document, and the view.

4. WinMain() calling Run(), which executes the main message loop to acquire and dispatch Windows messages.

Creating an MDI Application

Now let's create an MDI application using the MFC Application Wizard. Give it the project name **Sketcher** — and plan on keeping it. You will be expanding it into a sketching program during subsequent chapters. You should have no trouble with this procedure, because there are only a few things that you need to do differently from the process that you have just gone through for the SDI application. For the Application type group of options:

➤ Leave the default option, Multiple documents, but opt out of Tabbed documents.

➤ Select MFC standard as the project style and Windows Native/Default as the Visual style and colors option.

➤ Keep the Use Unicode libraries option.

Under the Document Template Properties set of options in the Application Wizard dialog box:

➤ Specify the file extension as ske. You'll see that you automatically get a filter for *.ske documents defined.

➤ Change the Generated Classes set of options at their default settings so that the base class for the CSketcherView class is CView.

You can see in the dialog box with Generated Classes selected that you get an extra class for your application compared with the TextEditor example, as Figure 14-13 shows.

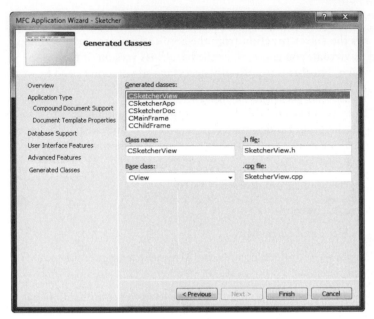

FIGURE 14-13

The extra class is `CChildFrame`, which is derived from the MFC class `CMDIChildWndEx`. This class provides a frame window for a view of the document that appears *inside* the application window created by a `CMainFrame` object. With an SDI application, there is a single document with a single view, so the view is displayed in the client area of the main frame window. In an MDI application, you can have multiple documents open, and each document can have multiple views. To accomplish this, each view of a document in the program has its own child frame window created by an object

of the class `CChildFrame`. As you saw earlier, a view is displayed in what is actually a separate window, but one which exactly fills the client area of a frame window.

Running the Program

You can build the program in exactly the same way as the previous example. Then, if you execute it, you get the application window shown in Figure 14-14.

In addition to the main application window, you have a separate document window with the caption Sketch1. `Sketch1` is the default name for the initial document, and it has the extension `.ske` if you save it. You can create additional views for the document by selecting the Window ⇨ New Window menu option.

FIGURE 14-14

You can also create a new document by selecting File ➪ New, so that there will be two active documents in the application. The situation with two documents active, each with two views open, is shown in Figure 14-15.

FIGURE 14-15

You can't yet actually create any data in the application because we haven't added any code to do that, but all the code for creating documents and views has already been included by the Application Wizard.

SUMMARY

In this chapter, you've been concerned mainly with the mechanics of using the MFC Application Wizard. You have seen the basic components of the MFC programs that the Application Wizard generates for both SDI and MDI applications. All our MFC examples are created by the MFC Application Wizard, so it's a good idea to keep the general structure and broad class relationships in mind. You probably won't feel too comfortable with the detail at this point, but don't worry about that now. You'll find that it becomes much clearer after you begin developing applications in the succeeding chapters.

EXERCISES

It isn't possible to give programming examples for this chapter, because it really just introduced the basic mechanics of creating MFC applications. There aren't solutions to all the exercises because you will either see the answer for yourself on the screen, or be able to check your answer back with the text.

However, you can download the source code for the examples in the book and the solutions to other exercises from `www.wrox.com`.

1. What is the relationship between a document and a view?

2. What is the purpose of the document template in an MFC Windows program?

3. Why do you need to be careful, and plan your program structure in advance, when using the Application Wizard?

4. Code up the simple text editor program. Build both debug and release versions, and examine the types and sizes of the files produced in each case.

5. Generate the text editor application several times, trying different window styles from the Advanced Options in Application Wizard.

► **WHAT YOU LEARNED IN THIS CHAPTER**

TOPIC	CONCEPT
The Application Wizard	The MFC Application Wizard generates a complete, working, framework Windows application for you to customize to your requirements.
SDI and MDI programs	The Application Wizard can generate single-document interface (SDI) applications that work with a single document and a single view, or multiple-document interface (MDI) programs that can handle multiple documents with multiple views simultaneously.
Classes in SDI programs	The four essential classes in an SDI application that are derived from the foundation classes are the application class, the frame window class, the document class, and the view class.
The application object	A program can have only one application object. This is defined automatically by the Application Wizard at global scope.
Document objects	A document class object stores application-specific data, and a view class object displays the contents of a document object.
Document templates	A document template class object is used to tie together a document, a view, and a window. For an SDI application, a `CSingleDocTemplate` class does this, and for an MDI application, the `CMultiDocTemplate` class is used. These are both foundation classes, and application-specific versions do not normally need to be derived.

15

Working with Menus and Toolbars

WHAT YOU WILL LEARN IN THIS CHAPTER:

➤ How an MFC-based program handles messages

➤ Menu resources, and how you can create and modify them

➤ Menu properties, and how you can create and modify them

➤ How to create a function to service the message generated when a menu item is selected

➤ How to add handlers to update menu properties

➤ How to add toolbar buttons and associate them with existing menu items

In the last chapter, you saw how a simple framework application generated by the MFC Application Wizard is made up and how the parts interrelate. In this chapter, you'll start customizing a Multiple Document Interface (MDI) framework application called Sketcher with a view to making it into a useful program. The first step in this process is to understand how menus are defined in Visual C++ 2010, and how functions are created to service the application-specific menu items that you add to your program. You'll also see how to add toolbar buttons to the application.

COMMUNICATING WITH WINDOWS

As you saw in Chapter 12, Windows communicates with your program by sending messages to it. In an MFC application, most of the drudgery of message handling is taken care of, so you don't have to worry about providing a WndProc() function at all. MFC enables you to provide functions to handle just the individual messages that you're interested in and to ignore the rest.

These functions are referred to as **message handlers** or just **handlers**. Because your application is MFC-based, a message handler is always a member function of one of your application's classes.

The association between a particular message and the function in your program that is to service it is established by a message map, and each class in your program that can handle Windows messages will have one. A message map for a class is simply a table of member functions that handle Windows messages bounded by a couple of macros. Each entry in the message map associates a function with a particular message; when a given message occurs, the corresponding function is called. Only the messages relevant to a class appear in the message map for the class.

A message map for a class is created automatically by the MFC Application Wizard when you create a project, or by ClassWizard when you add a class that handles messages to your program. Additions to, and deletions from, a message map are mainly managed by ClassWizard, but there are circumstances in which you need to modify the message map manually. The start of a message map in your code is indicated by a BEGIN_MESSAGE_MAP() macro, and the end is marked by an END_MESSAGE_MAP() macro. Let's look into how a message map operates using our Sketcher example.

Understanding Message Maps

A message map is established by the MFC Application Wizard for each of the main classes in your program. In the instance of an MDI program such as Sketcher, a message map is defined for each of CSketcherApp, CSketcherDoc, CSketcherView, CMainFrame, and CChildFrame. You can see the message map for a class in the .cpp file containing the implementation of the class. Of course, the functions that are included in the message map also need to be declared in the class definition, but they are identified here in a special way. Look at the definition for the CSketcherApp class shown here:

```
class CSketcherApp : public CWinAppEx
{
public:
      CSketcherApp();


// Overrides
public:
      virtual BOOL InitInstance();

// Implementation
      BOOL  m_bHiColorIcons;

      virtual void PreLoadState();
      virtual void LoadCustomState();
      virtual void SaveCustomState();

      afx_msg void OnAppAbout();
      DECLARE_MESSAGE_MAP()
};
```

Only one message handler, OnAppAbout(), is declared in the CSketcherApp class. The word afx_
msg at the beginning of the line declaring the OnAppAbout() function is there just to distinguish
a message handler from other member functions in the class. It is converted to white space by the
preprocessor, so it has no effect when the program is compiled.

The DECLARE_MESSAGE_MAP() macro indicates that the class can contain function members that are
message handlers. In fact, any class that you derive from the MFC class CCmdTarget can potentially
have message handlers, so such classes will have this macro included as part of the class definition
by the MFC Application Wizard or by the Add Class Wizard that you'll use to add a new class for
a project, depending on which was responsible for creating it. Figure 15-1 shows the MFC classes
derived from CCmdTarget that have been used in our examples so far.

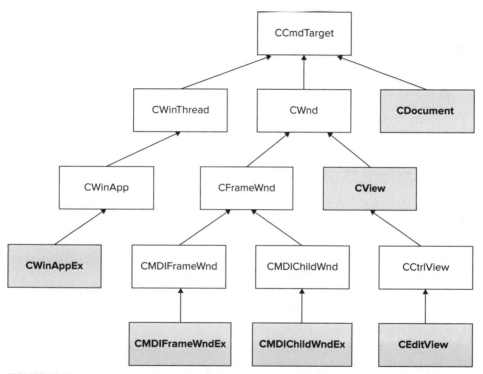

FIGURE 15-1

The classes that have been used directly, or as a direct base for our own application classes, are
shown shaded. Thus, the CSketcherApp class has CCmdTarget as an indirect base class and,
therefore, always includes the DECLARE_MESSAGE_MAP() macro. All the view (and other) classes
derived from CWnd also have it.

If you are adding your own members to a class directly, it's best to leave the DECLARE_MESSAGE_MAP()
macro as the last line in the class definition. If you do add members after DECLARE_MESSAGE_MAP(),
you'll also need to include an access specifier for them: public, protected, or private.

Message Handler Definitions

If a class definition includes the macro DECLARE_MESSAGE_MAP(), the class implementation must include the macros BEGIN_MESSAGE_MAP() and END_MESSAGE_MAP(). If you look in Sketcher.cpp, you'll see the following code as part of the implementation of CSketcherApp:

```
BEGIN_MESSAGE_MAP(CSketcherApp, CWinAppEx)
    ON_COMMAND(ID_APP_ABOUT, &CSketcherApp::OnAppAbout)
    // Standard file-based document commands
    ON_COMMAND(ID_FILE_NEW, &CWinAppEx::OnFileNew)
    ON_COMMAND(ID_FILE_OPEN, &CWinAppEx::OnFileOpen)
    // Standard print setup command
    ON_COMMAND(ID_FILE_PRINT_SETUP, &CWinAppEx::OnFilePrintSetup)
END_MESSAGE_MAP()
```

This is a message map. The BEGIN_MESSAGE_MAP() and END_MESSAGE_MAP() macros define its boundaries, and each of the message handlers in the class appears between these macros. In the preceding case, the code is handling only one category of message, the type of WM_COMMAND message called a **command message**, which is generated when the user selects a menu option or enters an accelerator key. (If that seems clumsy, it's because there's another kind of WM_COMMAND message called a **control notification message,** which provides information about the activity of a control.)

The message map knows which menu or key is pressed by the identifier (ID) that's included in the message. There are four ON_COMMAND macros in the preceding code, one for each of the command messages to be handled. The first argument to this macro is an ID associated with one particular command, and the ON_COMMAND macro ties the function name to the command specified by the ID. Thus, when a message corresponding to the identifier ID_APP_ABOUT is received, the function OnAppAbout() is called. Similarly, for a message corresponding to the ID_FILE_NEW identifier, the function OnFileNew() is called. This handler is actually defined in the base class, CWinApp, as are the two remaining handlers.

The BEGIN_MESSAGE_MAP() macro has two arguments. The first argument identifies the current class name for which the message map is defined, and the second provides a connection to the base class for finding a message handler. If a handler isn't found in the class defining the message map, the message map for the base class is then searched.

Note that command IDs such as ID_APP_ABOUT are standard IDs defined in MFC. These correspond to messages from standard menu items and toolbar buttons. The ID_ prefix is used to identify a command associated with a menu item or a toolbar button, as you'll see when I discuss resources later. For example, ID_FILE_NEW is the ID that corresponds to the selection of the File ⇨ New menu item, and ID_APP_ABOUT corresponds to Help ⇨ About.

There are symbols besides WM_COMMAND that Windows uses to identify standard messages. Each of them is prefixed with WM_ for "Windows message." These symbols are defined in Winuser.h, which is included in Windows.h. If you want to look at them, you'll find Winuser.h in the include subfolder of the VC folder containing your Visual C++ 2010 system.

 NOTE *There's a nice shortcut for viewing a .h file. If the name of the file appears in the editor window, you can just right-click it and select the menu item Open Document "Filename.h" from the pop-up menu. This works with standard library headers, too.*

Windows messages often have additional data values that are used to refine the identification of a particular message specified by a given ID. The WM_COMMAND message, for instance, is sent for a whole range of commands, including those originating from the selection of a menu item or a click on a toolbar button.

Note that when you are adding message handlers manually, you should not map a message (or, in the case of command messages, a command ID) to more than one message handler in a class. If you do, it won't break anything, but the second message handler is never called. Normally, you add message handlers through the Properties window, and, in this case, you will not be able to map a message to more than one message handler. If you want to see the Properties window for a class, right-click a class name in Class View and select Properties from the pop-up menu. You add a message handler by selecting the Messages button at the top of the Properties window that is displayed (see Figure 15-2). To determine which button is the Messages button, simply hover the cursor over each button until the tooltip displays.

FIGURE 15-2

Clicking the Messages button brings up a list of message IDs; however, before I go into what you do next, I need to explain a little more about the types of messages you may be handling.

Message Categories

There are three categories of messages that your program may be dealing with, and the category to which a message belongs determines how it is handled. The message categories are:

MESSAGE CATEGORY	DESCRIPTION
Windows messages	These are standard Windows messages that begin with the WM_ prefix, with the exception of WM_COMMAND messages, which we shall come to in a moment. Examples of Windows messages are WM_PAINT, which indicates that you need to redraw the client area of a window, and WM_LBUTTONUP, which signals that the left mouse button has been released.
Control notification messages	These are WM_COMMAND messages sent from controls (such as a list box) to the window that created the control, or from a child window to a parent window. Parameters associated with a WM_COMMAND message enable messages from the controls in your application to be differentiated.
Command messages	These are also WM_COMMAND messages that originate from the user interface elements, such as menu items and toolbar buttons. MFC defines unique identifiers for standard menu and toolbar command messages.

The standard Windows messages in the first category are identified by the WM_-prefixed IDs that Windows defines. You'll be writing handlers for some of these messages in the next chapter. The messages in the second category are a particular group of WM_COMMAND messages that you'll see in Chapter 18 when you work with dialog boxes. You'll deal with the last category, messages originating from menus and toolbars, in this chapter. In addition to the message IDs defined by MFC for the standard menus and toolbars, you can define your own message IDs for the menus and toolbar buttons that you add to your program. If you don't supply IDs for these items, MFC automatically generates IDs for you, based on the menu text.

Handling Messages in Your Program

You can't put a handler for a message anywhere you like. The permitted sites for a handler depend on what kind of message is to be processed. The first two categories of message that you saw earlier — that is, standard Windows messages and control notification messages — are always handled by objects of classes that are ultimately derived from CWnd. Frame window classes and view classes, for example, have CWnd as an indirect base class, so they can have member functions to handle Windows messages and control notification messages. Application classes, document classes, and document template classes are not derived from CWnd, so they can't handle these messages.

Using the Properties window for a class to add a handler solves the headache of remembering where to place handlers, as it offers you only the IDs allowed for the class. For example, if you select CSketcherDoc as the class, you won't be offered any of the WM_ messages in the Properties window for the class.

For standard Windows messages, the CWnd class provides default message handling. Thus, if your derived class doesn't include a handler for a standard Windows message, it is processed by the default handler defined in the base class. If you do provide a handler in your class, you'll sometimes still need to call the base class handler as well, so that the message is processed properly. When you're creating your own handler, a skeleton implementation of it is provided when you select the handler in the Properties window for a class, and this includes a call to the base handler where necessary.

Handling command messages is much more flexible. You can put handlers for these in the application class, the document and document template classes, and, of course, in the window and view classes in your program. So what happens when a command message is sent to your application, bearing in mind that there are a lot of options as to where it is handled?

How Command Messages Are Processed

All command messages are sent to the main frame window for the application. The main frame window then tries to get the message handled by routing it in a specific sequence to the classes in your program. If one class can't process the message, the main frame window passes it on to the next.

For an SDI program, the sequence in which classes are offered an opportunity to handle a command message is:

1. The view object

2. The document object

3. The document template object

4. The main frame window object

5. The application object

The view object is given the opportunity to handle a command message first, and, if no handler has been defined, the next class object has a chance to process it. If none of the classes has a handler defined, default Windows processing takes care of it, essentially throwing the message away.

For an MDI program, things are only a little more complicated. Although you have the possibility of multiple documents, each with multiple views, only the active view and its associated document are involved in the routing of a command message. The sequence for routing a command message in an MDI program is:

1. The active view object

2. The document object associated with the active view

3. The document template object for the active document

4. The frame window object for the active view

5. The main frame window object

6. The application object

It's possible to alter the sequence for routing messages, but this is so rarely necessary that I won't go into it in this book.

EXTENDING THE SKETCHER PROGRAM

You're going to add code to the Sketcher program you created in the previous chapter to implement the functionality you need to create sketches. You'll provide code for drawing lines, circles, rectangles, and curves with various colors and line thicknesses, and for adding annotations to a sketch. The data for a sketch is stored in a document, and you'll also allow multiple views of the same document at different scales.

It will take several chapters to learn how to add everything that you need, but a good starting point would be to add menu items to deal with the types of elements that you want to be able to draw, and to select a color for drawing. You'll make both the element type and color selection persistent in the program, which means that once you've selected a color and an element type, both of these will remain in effect until you change one or the other.

To add menus to Sketcher, you'll work through the following steps:

1. Define the menu items to appear on the main menu bar and in each of the menus.

2. Decide which of the classes in our application should handle the message for each menu item.

3. Add message handling functions to the classes for the menu messages.

4. Add functions to the classes to update the appearance of the menus to show the current selection in effect.

5. Add a toolbar button complete with tooltips for each of the menu items.

ELEMENTS OF A MENU

You'll be looking at two aspects of dealing with menus with the MFC: the creation and modification of the menu as it appears in your application, and the processing necessary when a particular menu item is selected — the definition of a message handler for it. Let's look first at how you create new menu items.

Creating and Editing Menu Resources

Menus are defined external to the program code in a **resource file**, and the specification of the menu is referred to as a **resource**. You can include several other kinds of resources in your application: typical examples include dialogs, toolbars, and toolbar buttons. You'll be seeing more on these as you extend the Sketcher application.

Having a menu defined in a resource allows the physical appearance of the menu to be changed without affecting the code that processes menu events. For example, you could change your menu items from English to French or Norwegian or whatever without having to modify or recompile the program code. The code to handle the message created when the user selects a menu item doesn't need to be concerned with how the menu looks, only with the fact that it was selected. Of course, if you do add items to the menu, you'll need to add some code for each of them to ensure that they actually do something!

The Sketcher program already has a menu, which means that it already has a resource file. You can access the resource file contents for the Sketcher program by selecting the Resource View pane, or, if you have the Solution Explorer pane displayed, you can double-click `Sketcher.rc`. This switches you to the Resource View, which displays the resources. If you expand the menu resource by clicking on the [unfilled] symbol, you'll see that it includes two menus, indicated by the identifiers `IDR_MAINFRAME` and `IDR_SketchTYPE`. The first of these applies when there are no documents open in the application, and the second when you have one or more documents open. MFC uses the `IDR_` prefix to identify a resource that defines a complete menu for a window.

You're going to be modifying only the menu that has the identifier `IDR_SketchTYPE`. You don't need to look at `IDR_MAINFRAME`, as your new menu items will be relevant only when a document is open. You can invoke a resource editor for the menu by double-clicking its menu ID in Resource View. If you do this for `IDR_SketchTYPE`, the Editor pane appears, as shown in Figure 15-3.

FIGURE 15-3

Adding a Menu Item to the Menu Bar

To add a new menu item, you can just click the menu box on the menu bar with the text "Type Here" to select it, and then type in your menu name. If you insert an ampersand (&) in front of a letter in the menu item, the letter is identified as a shortcut key to invoke the menu from the keyboard. Type the first menu item as **E&lement**. This selects l as the shortcut letter, so you will be able to invoke the menu item and display its pop-up by typing Alt+L. You can't use E because it's already used by Edit. When you finish typing the name, you can right-click the new menu item and select Properties from the pop-up to display its properties, as shown in Figure 15-4.

Properties are simply parameters that determine how the menu item will appear and behave. Figure 15-4 displays the properties for the menu item grouped by category. If you would rather have them displayed in alphabetical sequence, just click the second button from the left. Note that the Popup property is set to True by default; this is because the new menu item is at the top level on the menu bar, so it would normally present a pop-up menu when it

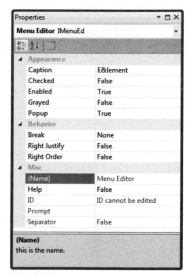

FIGURE 15-4

is selected. Clicking any property in the left column enables you to modify it in the right column. In this case, you want to leave everything as it is, so you can just close the Properties window. No ID is necessary for a pop-up menu item, because selecting it just displays the menu beneath and there's no event for your code to handle. Note that you get a new blank menu box for the first item in the pop-up menu, as well as one on the main menu bar.

It would be better if the Element menu appeared between the View and Window menus, so place the mouse cursor on the Element menu item and, keeping the left mouse button pressed, drag it to a position between the View and Window menu items, and release the left mouse button. After positioning the new Element menu item, the next step is to add items on the pop-up menu that corresponds to it.

Adding Items to the Element Menu

Select the first item (currently labeled "Type Here") in the Element pop-up menu by clicking it; then, type Line as the caption and press the Enter key. You can see the properties for this menu item by right-clicking it and selecting Properties; the properties for this first item in the pop-up menu are shown in Figure 15-5.

FIGURE 15-5

The properties modify the appearance of the menu item and also specify the ID of the message passed to your program when the menu item is selected. Here, we have the ID already specified as ID_ELEMENT_LINE, but you can change it to something else if you want. Sometimes it's convenient to specify the ID yourself, such as when the generated ID is too long or its meaning is unclear. If you choose to define your own ID, you should use the MFC convention of prefixing it with ID_ to indicate that it's a command ID for a menu item.

Because this item is part of a pop-up menu, the Popup property is False by default. You could make it another pop-up menu with a further list of items by setting the Popup property to True. As you see in Figure 15-5, you can display the possible values for the Popup property by selecting the down arrow. Don't you love the way pop-ups pop up all over the place?

You can enter a text string for the value of the Prompt property that appears in the status bar of your application when the menu item is highlighted. If you leave it blank, nothing is displayed in the status bar. I suggest you enter **Draw lines** as the value for the Prompt property. Note how you get a brief indication of the purpose of the selected property at the bottom of the Properties window. The Break property can alter the appearance of the pop-up by shifting the item into a new column. You don't need that here, so leave it as it is. Close the Properties window and click the Save icon in the toolbar to save the values that you have set.

Modifying Existing Menu Items

If you think you may have made a mistake and want to change an existing menu item, or even if you just want to verify that you set the properties correctly, it's very easy to go back to an item. Just double-click the item you're interested in, and the Properties window for that item is displayed. You can then change the properties in any way you want and close the window when you're done. If the item you want to access is in a pop-up menu that isn't displayed, just click the item on the menu bar to display the pop-up.

Completing the Menu

Now, you can go through and create the remaining Element pop-up menu items that you need: Rectangle, Circle, and Curve. You can accept the default IDs ID_ELEMENT_RECTANGLE, ID_ELEMENT_CIRCLE, and ID_ELEMENT_CURVE, respectively, for these. You could also set the values for the Prompt property value to Rectangle, Circle, and Curve, respectively.

You also need a Color menu on the menu bar, with pop-up menu items for Black, Red, Green, and Blue. You can create these, starting at the empty menu entry on the menu bar, using the same procedure that you just went through. You can use the default IDs (ID_COLOR_BLACK, etc.) as the IDs for the menu items. You can also add the status bar prompt for each as the value of the Prompt property. After you've finished, if you drag Color so that it's just to the right of Element, the menu should appear as shown in Figure 15-6.

FIGURE 15-6

Note that you need to take care not to use the same letter more than once as a shortcut in the main menu. There's no check made as you create new menu items, but if you right-click with the cursor on the menu bar when you've finished editing it, you'll get a pop-up that contains the item Check Mnemonics. Selecting this checks your menu for duplicate shortcut keys. It's a good idea to do this every time you edit a menu, because it's easy to create duplicates by accident.

That completes extending the menu for elements and colors. Don't forget to save the file to make sure that the additions are safely stored away. Next, you need to decide in which classes you want to deal with messages from your menu items, and add member functions to handle each of the messages. For that, you'll be using the Event Handler Wizard.

ADDING HANDLERS FOR MENU MESSAGES

To create an event handler for a menu item, right-click the item and select Add Event Handler from the pop-up displayed. If you try this with the Black menu item in the Color menu pop-up, you'll see the dialog shown in Figure 15-7.

FIGURE 15-7

As you can see, the wizard has already chosen a name for the handler function. You could change it, but OnColorBlack seems like a good name to me.

You obviously need to specify the message type as one of the choices shown in the dialog box. The "Message type:" box in the window in Figure 15-7 shows the two kinds of messages that can arise for a particular menu ID. Each type of message serves a distinct purpose in dealing with a menu item.

MESSAGE TYPE	DESCRIPTION
COMMAND	This type of message is issued when a particular menu item has been selected. The handler should provide the action appropriate to the menu item being selected, such as by setting the current color in the document object or setting the element type.
UPDATE_COMMAND_UI	This is issued when the menu should be updated — checked or unchecked, for example — depending on its status. This message occurs before a pop-up menu is displayed so you can set the appearance of the menu item before the user sees it.

The way these messages work is quite simple. When you click a menu item in the menu bar, an UPDATE_COMMAND_UI message is sent for each item in that menu before the menu is displayed. This provides the opportunity to do any necessary updating of the menu items' properties before the user sees it. When these messages are handled and any changes to the items' properties are completed, the menu is drawn. When you then click one of the items in the menu, a COMMAND message for that menu item is sent. I'll deal with the COMMAND messages now, and come back to the UPDATE_COMMAND_UI messages a little later in this chapter.

Because events for menu items result in command messages, you can choose to handle them in any of the classes that are currently defined in the Sketcher application. So how do you decide where you should process a message for a menu item?

Choosing a Class to Handle Menu Messages

Before you can decide which class should handle the messages for the menu items you've added, you need to decide what you want to do with the messages.

You want the element type and the element color to be modal — that is, whatever is set for the element type and element color should remain in effect until it is changed. This enables you to create as many blue circles as you want, and when you want red circles, you just change the color. You have two basic possibilities for handling the setting of a color and the selection of an element type: setting them by view or by document. You could set them by view, in which case, if there's more than one view of a document, each will have its own color and element set. This means that you might draw a red circle in one view, switch to another view, and find that you're drawing a blue rectangle. This would be confusing and in conflict with how you would probably want your tools to work.

It would be better, therefore, to have the current color and element selection apply to a document. You can then switch from one view to another and continue drawing the same element in the same color. There might be other differences between the views that you implement, such as the scale at which the document is displayed, perhaps, but the drawing operation will be consistent across multiple views.

This suggests that you should store the current color and element in the document object. These could then be accessed by any view object associated with the document object. Of course, if you had more than one document active, each document would have its own color and element type settings. It would therefore be sensible to handle the messages for your new menu items in the

CSketcherDoc class and to store information about the current selections in an object of this class. I think you're ready to dive in and create a handler for the Black menu item.

Creating Menu Message Functions

Highlight the CSketcherDoc class name in the Event Handler Wizard dialog box by clicking it. You'll also need to click the COMMAND message type. You can then click the Add and Edit button. This closes the dialog box, and the code for the handler you have created in the CSketcherDoc class is displayed in the edit window. The function looks like this:

```
void CSketcherDoc::OnColorBlack()
{
  // TODO: Add your command handler code here
}
```

The highlighted line is where you'll put your code that handles the event that results from the user's selecting the Black menu item. The wizard also has updated the CSketcherDoc class definition:

```
class CSketcherDoc : public CDocument
{
  ...

// Generated message map functions
protected:
  DECLARE_MESSAGE_MAP()
public:
  afx_msg void OnColorBlack();
};
```

The OnColorBlack() method has been added as a public member of the class, and the afx_msg prefix marks it as a message handler.

You can now add COMMAND message handlers for the other color menu IDs and all the Element menu IDs in exactly the same way as this one. You can create each of the handler functions for the menu items with just four mouse clicks. Right-click the menu item, click the Add Event Handler menu item, click the CSketcherDoc class name in the dialog box for the Event Handler Wizard, and click the Add and Edit button for the dialog box.

The Event Handler Wizard should now have added the handlers to the CSketcherDoc class definition, which now looks like this:

```
class CSketcherDoc: public CDocument
{
  ...

// Generated message map functions
protected:
  DECLARE_MESSAGE_MAP()
public:
  afx_msg void OnColorBlack();
  afx_msg void OnColorRed();
  afx_msg void OnColorGreen();
```

```
     afx_msg void OnColorBlue();
     afx_msg void OnElementLine();
     afx_msg void OnElementRectangle();
     afx_msg void OnElementCircle();
     afx_msg void OnElementCurve();
   };
```

A declaration has been added for each of the handlers that you've specified in the Event Handler Wizard dialog box. Each of the function declarations has been prefixed with afx_msg to indicate that it is a message handler.

The Event Handler Wizard also automatically updates the message map in your CSketcherDoc class implementation with the new message handlers. If you take a look in the file SketcherDoc.cpp, you'll see the message map, as shown here:

```
BEGIN_MESSAGE_MAP(CSketcherDoc, CDocument)
ON_COMMAND(ID_COLOR_BLACK, &CSketcherDoc::OnColorBlack)
ON_COMMAND(ID_COLOR_RED, &CSketcherDoc::OnColorRed)
ON_COMMAND(ID_COLOR_GREEN, &CSketcherDoc::OnColorGreen)
ON_COMMAND(ID_COLOR_BLUE, &CSketcherDoc::OnColorBlue)
ON_COMMAND(ID_ELEMENT_LINE, &CSketcherDoc::OnElementLine)
ON_COMMAND(ID_ELEMENT_RECTANGLE, &CSketcherDoc::OnElementRectangle)
ON_COMMAND(ID_ELEMENT_CIRCLE, &CSketcherDoc::OnElementCircle)
ON_COMMAND(ID_ELEMENT_CURVE, &CSketcherDoc::OnElementCurve)
END_MESSAGE_MAP()
```

The Event Handler Wizard has added an ON_COMMAND() macro for each of the handlers that you have identified. This associates the handler name with the message ID, so, for example, the member function OnColorBlack() is called to service a COMMAND message for the menu item with the ID ID_COLOR_BLACK.

Each of the handlers generated by the Event Handler Wizard is just a skeleton. For example, take a look at the code provided for OnColorBlue(). This is also defined in the file SketcherDoc.cpp, so you can scroll down to find it, or go directly to it by switching to the Class View and double-clicking the function name after expanding the tree for the class CSketcherDoc (make sure that the file is saved first):

```
void CSketcherDoc::OnColorBlue()
{
    // TODO: Add your command handler code here
}
```

As you can see, the handler takes no arguments and returns nothing. It also does nothing at the moment, but this is hardly surprising, because the Event Handler Wizard has no way of knowing what you want to do with these messages!

Coding Menu Message Functions

Now, let's consider what you should do with the COMMAND messages for our new menu items. I said earlier that you want to record the current element and color in the document, so you need to add a data member to the CSketcherDoc class for each of these.

Adding Members to Store Color and Element Mode

You could add the *data members* that you need to the CSketcherDoc class definition just by editing the class definition directly, but let's use the Add Member Variable Wizard to do it. Display the dialog box for the wizard by right-clicking the CSketcherDoc class name in the Class View and then selecting Add ⇨ Add Variable from the pop-up menu that appears. You then see the dialog box for the wizard, as shown in Figure 15-8.

FIGURE 15-8

I've already entered the information in the dialog box for the m_Element variable that stores the current element type to be drawn. I have selected protected as the access because it should not be accessible directly from outside the class. I have also entered the type as ElementType. You will define this type in the next section. When you click the Finish button, the variable is added to the class definition in the CSketcherDoc.h file.

Add the CSketcherDoc class member to store the element color manually just to show that you can. Its name is m_Color and its type is COLORREF, which is a type defined by the Windows API for representing a color as a 32-bit integer. You can add the declaration for the m_Color member to the CSketcherDoc class like this:

```
class CSketcherDoc : public CDocument
{
...
// Generated message map functions
protected:
  DECLARE_MESSAGE_MAP()
public:
```

```
     afx_msg void OnColorBlack();
     afx_msg void OnColorRed();
     afx_msg void OnColorGreen();
     afx_msg void OnColorBlue();
     afx_msg void OnElementLine();
     afx_msg void OnElementRectangle();
     afx_msg void OnElementCircle();
     afx_msg void OnElementCurve();
  protected:
     // Current element type
     ElementType m_Element;
     COLORREF m_Color;            // Current drawing color
  };
```

The m_Color member is also protected, as there's no reason to allow public access. You can always add functions to access or change the values of protected or private class members, with the advantage that you then have complete control over what values can be set. Of course, you could have used the Add Member Variable Wizard dialog as you did for m_Element; the difference is that you would type **COLORREF** in the "Variable type:" box, rather than selecting it from the drop-down list.

Initializing the New Class Data Members

You can define ElementType as an enum type, as follows:

```
// Element type definitions
enum ElementType{LINE, RECTANGLE, CIRCLE, CURVE};
```

Because it's an enum type, each of the possible values is automatically defined as a unique value. If you need to add further types in the future, it will obviously be very easy to add them here.

For the color values, it would be good to use constant variables that are initialized with the values Windows uses to define the colors in question. You could do this with the following lines of code:

```
// Color values for drawing
const COLORREF BLACK = RGB(0,0,0);
const COLORREF RED = RGB(255,0,0);
const COLORREF GREEN = RGB(0,255,0);
const COLORREF BLUE = RGB(0,0,255);
```

Each constant is initialized by RGB(), which is a standard macro, as you learned in Chapter 13. It is defined in the Wingdi.h header file that is included as part of Windows.h. Just to remind you, the three arguments to the macro define the red, green, and blue components of the color value, respectively. Each argument must be an integer between 0 and 255, 0 being no color component and 255 being the maximum color component. RGB(0,0,0) corresponds to black because there are no components of red, green, or blue. RGB(255,0,0) creates a color value with a maximum red component and no green or blue contribution. You can create other colors by combining red, green, and blue components.

You need somewhere to put the ElementType definition and the color constants, so create a new header file and call it **SketcherConstants.h**. You can create a new file by right-clicking the Header Files folder in the Solution Explorer tab and selecting the Add ⇨ Add New Item menu option from the pop-up. In the dialog box that appears, select the type to be Header file(.h), enter the header file name as **Sketcher Constants,** and then click the Add button. You'll then be able to enter the constant definitions in the editor window, as shown here:

```
//Definitions of constants

#pragma once

    // Element type definitions
enum ElementType{LINE, RECTANGLE, CIRCLE, CURVE};


    // Color values for drawing
    const COLORREF BLACK = RGB(0,0,0);
    const COLORREF RED = RGB(255,0,0);
    const COLORREF GREEN = RGB(0,255,0);
    const COLORREF BLUE = RGB(0,0,255);
    ////////////////////////////////////
```

As you'll recall, the pre-processor directive #pragma once is there to ensure that the definitions cannot be included more than once in a file.

After saving the header file, you can add the following #include statement to the beginning of the file Sketcher.h, after the #pragma once directive:

```
#include "SketcherConstants.h"
```

Any .cpp file that has an #include directive for Sketcher.h has the constants for the enum type available.

You can verify that the new color constants are now part of the project by expanding Global Functions and Variables in the Class View. You'll see that the names of the color constants that have been added now appear, along with the other global variables. The new element type now appears as a type in the Class View upper pane.

Modifying the Class Constructor

It's important to make sure that the data members you have added to the CSketcherDoc class are initialized appropriately when a document is created. You can add the code to do this to the class constructor as shown here:

```
CSketcherDoc::CSketcherDoc() : m_Element(LINE), m_Color(BLACK)
{
    // TODO: add one-time construction code here
}
```

Now, you're ready to add the code for the handler functions that you created for the Element and Color menu items. You can do this from the Class View. Click the name of the first handler function, OnColorBlack(). You just need to add one line to the function, so the code for it becomes:

```
void CSketcherDoc::OnColorBlack()
{
    m_Color = BLACK;              // Set the drawing color to black
}
```

The only job that the handler has to do is to set the appropriate color. In the interest of conciseness, the new line replaces the comment provided originally. You can go through and add one line to each of the `Color` menu handlers setting the appropriate color value.

The element menu handlers are much the same. The handler for the Element ⇨ Line menu item is:

```
void CSketcherDoc::OnElementLine()
{
    m_Element = LINE;            // Set element type as a line
}
```

With this model, it's not too difficult to write the other handlers for the Element menu. That's eight message handlers completed. You can now rebuild the example and see how it works.

Running the Extended Example

Assuming that there are no typos, the compiled and linked program should run without error. When you run the program, you should see the window shown in Figure 15-9.

FIGURE 15-9

The new menus are in place on the menu bar, and you can see that the items you have added to the menu are all there, and you should see the prompt message in the status bar that you provided in the properties box when the mouse cursor is over a menu item. You can also verify that Alt+C and Alt+L work. Ideally, the currently selected element of the color menu item should be checked as a cue to the current state. Let's look at how you can fix that.

Adding Message Handlers to Update the User Interface

To set the checkmark correctly for the new menus, you need to add the second kind of message handler, UPDATE_COMMAND_UI (signifying "update command user interface") for each of the new menu items. This sort of message handler is specifically aimed at updating the menu item properties before the item is displayed.

Go back to viewing the IDR_SketchTYPE menu in the editor window. Right-click the Black item in the Color menu and select Add Event Handler from the pop-up menu. You can then select CSketcherDoc as the class and UPDATE_COMMAND_UI as the message type, as shown in Figure 15-10.

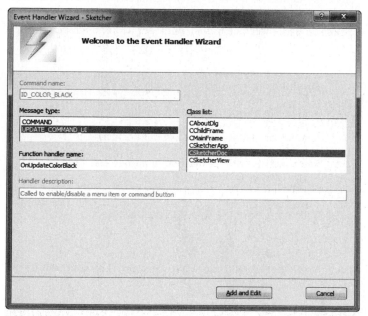

FIGURE 15-10

The name for the update function has been generated as OnUpdateColorBlack(). Because this seems a reasonable name for the function you want, click the Add and Edit button and have the Event Handler Wizard generate it. As well as the skeleton function definition in SketcherDoc.cpp being generated, its declaration is added to the class definition. An entry for it is also made in the message map in the SketcherDoc.cpp that looks like this:

```
ON_UPDATE_COMMAND_UI(ID_COLOR_BLACK, &CSketcherDoc::OnUpdateColorBlack)
```

This uses the ON_UPDATE_COMMAND_UI() macro that identifies the function you have just generated as the handler to deal with update messages corresponding to the ID shown. You could now enter the code for the new handler, but I'll let you add command update handlers for each of the menu items for both the Color and Element menus first.

Coding a Command Update Handler

You can access the code for the OnUpdateColorBlack() handler in the CSketcherDoc class by selecting the function in Class View. This is the skeleton code for the function:

```
void CSketcherDoc::OnUpdateColorBlack(CCmdUI* pCmdUI)
{
```

```
// TODO: Add your command update UI handler code here

}
```

The argument passed to the handler is a pointer to an object of the CCmdUI class type. This is an MFC class that is used only with update handlers, but it applies to toolbar buttons as well as menu items. The pointer points to an object that identifies the item that originated the update message, so you use this to operate on the item to update how it appears before it is displayed. The CCmdUI class has five member functions that act on user interface items. The operations that each of these provides are as follows:

FUNCTION	DESCRIPTION
ContinueRouting()	Passes the message on to the next priority handler.
Enable()	Enables or disables the relevant interface item.
SetCheck()	Sets a checkmark for the relevant interface item.
SetRadio()	Sets a button in a radio group on or off.
SetText()	Sets the text for the relevant interface item.

We'll use the third function, SetCheck(), as that seems to do what we want. The function is declared in the CCmdUI class as:

```
virtual void SetCheck(int nCheck = 1);
```

This function sets a menu item as checked if you pass 1 as the argument, and sets it as unchecked if you pass 0 as the argument. The parameter has a default value of 1, so if you just want to set a checkmark for a menu item regardless, you can call this function without specifying an argument.

In our case, you want to set a menu item as checked if it corresponds with the current color. You can, therefore, write the update handler for OnUpdateColorBlack() as:

```
void CSketcherDoc::OnUpdateColorBlack(CCmdUI* pCmdUI)
{
    // Set menu item Checked if the current color is black
    pCmdUI->SetCheck(m_Color==BLACK);
}
```

The statement you have added calls the SetCheck() function for the Color ⇨ Black menu item, and the argument expression m_Color==BLACK results in true if m_Color is BLACK, or false otherwise. The effect, therefore, is to check the menu item only if the current color stored in m_Color is BLACK, which is precisely what you want. You can implement the update handlers for the other Color pop-up menu items in the same way; just choose the appropriate COLORREF constant in the argument to SetCheck().

The update handlers for all the menu items in a menu are always called before the menu is displayed, so you can code the other handlers in the same way to ensure that only the item corresponding to the current color (or the current element) is checked.

A typical Element menu item update handler is coded as follows:

```
void CSketcherDoc::OnUpdateElementLine(CCmdUI* pCmdUI)
{
    // Set Checked if the current element is a line
    pCmdUI->SetCheck(m_Element==LINE);
}
```

You can now code all the other update handlers for items in the Element pop-up in a similar manner.

Exercising the Update Handlers

When you've added the code for all the update handlers, you can build and execute the Sketcher application again. Now, when you change a color or an element type selection, this is reflected in the menu, as shown in Figure 15-11.

FIGURE 15-11

When you click on a menu item, the default way the menu works is to display the most recently used menu item first without displaying the complete pop-up. You can change this by right-clicking the menu bar in the Sketcher application window and selecting Customize. . . from the pop-up. If you select the Options from the dialog that displays, you can uncheck the option "Menus show recently used commands first." Now, the full menu pop-up will display when you select a menu item.

You have completed all the code that you need for the menu items. Make sure that you have saved everything before embarking on the next stage. These days, toolbars are a must in any Windows program of consequence, so the next step is to take a look at how you can add toolbar buttons to support our new menus.

ADDING TOOLBAR BUTTONS

Select the Resource View and extend the toolbar resource. You'll see that there are two toolbars, one that has the same ID as the main menu, IDR_MAINFRAME, and another that has the ID IDR_MAINFRAME_256. The former provides you with toolbar icons that have four-bit color (16 colors) that will be displayed when small icons are selected the toolbar, whereas the latter provides icons with 24-bit color (256 colors) that correspond to the large icon toolbar. To implement Sketcher properly, you must add buttons to both toolbars.

If you right-click IDR_MAINFRAME_256 and select Open from the pop-up, the editor window appears, as shown in Figure 15-12.

FIGURE 15-12

If the toolbar displays as a contiguous image, rather than as shown in Figure 15-12, right-click in the editor window and select "Toolbar editor . . ." from the pop-up.

A toolbar button is a 16-by-15 array of pixels that contains a pictorial representation of the function it initiates. You can see in Figure 15-12 that the resource editor provides an enlarged view of a toolbar button so that you can see and manipulate individual pixels. It also provides you with a color palette to the right, from which you can choose the current working color. If you click the new button icon at the right end of the row as indicated, you'll be able to draw this icon. Before starting the editing, drag the new icon about half a button-width to the right. It separates from its neighbor on the left to start a new block.

You should keep the toolbar button icons in the same sequence as the items on the menu bar, so you'll create the element type selection buttons first. You'll probably want to use the following editing buttons provided by the resource editor, which appear in the toolbar for the Visual C++ 2010 application window:

- ➤ Pencil for drawing individual pixels
- ➤ Eraser for erasing individual pixels
- ➤ Fill an area with the current color
- ➤ Zoom the view of the button
- ➤ Draw a line
- ➤ Draw a rectangle
- ➤ Draw an ellipse
- ➤ Draw a curve

If it is not already visible, you can display the window that displays the palette, from which you can choose a color by right-clicking a toolbar button icon and selecting Show Colors Window from the pop-up. You select a foreground color by left-clicking a color from the palette, and a background color by right-clicking.

The first icon will be for the toolbar button corresponding to the Element ⇨ Line menu option. You can let your creative juices flow and draw whatever representation you like here to depict the act of drawing a line, but I'll keep it simple. If you want to follow my approach, make sure that black is selected as the foreground color and use the line tool to draw a diagonal line in the enlarged image of the new toolbar button icon. In fact, if you want the icon to appear a bit bigger, you can use the Magnification Tool editing button to make it up to eight times its actual size: just click the down arrow alongside the button and select the magnification you want. I drew a double black line then a very mute blue line as highlighting.

If you make a mistake, you can select the Undo button or you can change to the Erase Tool editing button and use that, but in the latter case, you need to make sure that the color selected corresponds to the background color for the button you are editing. You can also erase individual pixels by clicking them using the right mouse button, but again, you need to be sure that the background color is set correctly when you do this. After you're happy with what you've drawn, the next step is to edit the toolbar button properties.

Editing Toolbar Button Properties

Right-click your new button icon in the toolbar and select Properties from the pop-up to bring up its Properties window, as shown in Figure 15-13.

The Properties window shows a default ID for the button, but you want to associate the button with the menu item Element ⇨ Line that we've already defined, so click ID and then click the down arrow to display alternative values. You can then select ID_ELEMENT_LINE from the drop-down box. If you click

FIGURE 15-13

Prompt, you'll find that this also causes the same prompt to appear in the status bar because the prompt is recorded along with the ID. You can close the Properties window and click Save to complete the button definition.

You can now move on to designing the other three element buttons. You can use the rectangle editing button to draw a rectangle and the ellipse button to draw a circle. You can draw a curve using the pencil to set individual pixels, or use the curve button. You need to associate each button with the ID corresponding to the equivalent menu item that you defined earlier.

Now add the buttons for the colors. You should also drag the first button for selecting a color to the right, so that it starts a new group of buttons. You could keep the color buttons very simple and just color the whole button with the color it selects. You can do this by selecting the appropriate foreground color, then selecting the Fill editing button and clicking on the enlarged button image. Again, you need to use ID_COLOR_BLACK, ID_COLOR_RED, and so on as IDs for the buttons. The toolbar editing window should look like the one shown in Figure 15-14.

FIGURE 15-14

You now need to repeat the whole process for the IDR_MAINFRAME toolbar. Create equivalent buttons for the element types and colors, and assign the same IDs to the buttons that you assigned to the corresponding IDR_MAINFRAME_256 toolbar buttons.

That's all you need for the moment, so save the resource file and give Sketcher another spin.

Exercising the Toolbar Buttons

Build the application once again and execute it. You should see the application window shown in Figure 15-15.

FIGURE 15-15

There are some amazing things happening here. The toolbar buttons that you added already reflect the default settings that you defined for the new menu items, and the selected button is shown depressed. If you let the cursor linger over one of the new buttons, the prompt for the button appears in the status bar. The new buttons work as a complete substitute for the menu items, and any new selection made, with either the menu or the toolbar, is reflected by the toolbar button being shown depressed. The menu items now have the button icons in front of the text, with the selected menu item having the icon depressed. You can also enable large icons for the toolbar by right-clicking in the toolbar area or selecting Toolbars and Docking Windows from the View menu to display the Customize dialog.

If you close the document view window, Sketch1, you'll see that our toolbar buttons are automatically grayed and disabled. If you open a new document window, they are automatically enabled once again. You can also try dragging the toolbar with the cursor. You can move it to either side of the application window, or have it free-floating. You can also enable or disable it through the Customize dialog. You got all this without writing a single additional line of code!

Adding Tooltips

There's one further tweak that you can add to your toolbar buttons that is remarkably easy: tooltips. A tooltip is a small box that appears adjacent to the toolbar button when you let the cursor linger on the button. The tooltip contains a text string that is an additional clue to the purpose of the toolbar button.

To add a tooltip for a toolbar button, select the button in the toolbar editor tab. Select the Prompt property for the button in the Properties pane and enter \n followed by the text for the tooltip. For example, for the toolbar button with the ID ID_ELEMENT_LINE, you could enter the Prompt property value as \nDraw lines. The tooltip text will be displayed when you hover the mouse cursor over the toolbar button. If you put the \n after the text in the Prompt property value — for example, Draw lines\n — the text will be displayed in the status bar rather than as a tooltip when the mouse cursor is over the button.

You can have a different text in the status bar and in the tooltip. Set the value for the Prompt property for the Line menu item as **Draw Lines\nLine**.

This will display "Draw Lines" in the status bar when you hover the mouse cursor over the toolbar button. The tooltip will display the button icon image and the word "Line" with the status bar prompt text below it.

Change the Prompt property text for each of the toolbar buttons corresponding to the Element and Color menus in a similar way. That's all you have to do. After saving the resource file, you can now rebuild the application and execute it. Placing the cursor over one of the new toolbar buttons causes the prompt text to appear in the status bar and the tooltip to be displayed after a second or two.

MENUS AND TOOLBARS IN A C++/CLI PROGRAM

Of course, your C++/CLI programs can also have menus and toolbars. A good starting point for a Windows-based C++/CLI program is to create a Windows Forms application. The Windows Forms technology is oriented toward the development of applications that use the vast array of standard controls that are provided, but there's no reason you can't draw with a form-based application. There is much less programming for you to do with a Windows Forms application, because you add the standard components for the GUI using the Windows Forms Designer capability, and the code to generate and service the GUI components will be added automatically. Your programming activity will involve adding application-specific classes and customizing the behavior of the application by implementing event handlers.

Understanding Windows Forms

Windows Forms is a facility for creating Windows applications that execute with the CLR. A **form** is a window that is the basis for an application window or a dialog window to which you can add other controls that the user can interact with. Visual C++ 2010 comes with a standard set of more than 60 controls that you can use with a form. Because there is a very large number of controls, you'll get to grips only with a representative sample in this book, but that should give you enough of an idea of how they are used so you can explore the others for yourself. Many of the standard controls provide a straightforward interactive function, such as `Button` controls that represent buttons to be clicked, or `TextBox` controls that allow text to be entered. Some of the standard controls are **containers**, which means that they are controls that can contain other controls. For example, a `GroupBox` control can contain other controls such as `Button` controls or `TextBox` controls, and the function of a `GroupBox` control is simply to group the controls together for some purpose and optionally provide a label for the group in the GUI. There are also a lot of third-party controls available. If you can't find the control you want in Visual C++, it is very likely that you can find a third party that produces it.

A form and the controls that you use with a form are represented by a C++/CLI class. Each class has a set of properties that determines the behavior and appearance of the control or form. For example, whether or not a control is visible in the application window and whether or not a control is enabled to allow user interaction are determined by the property values that are set. You can set a control's properties interactively when you assemble the GUI using the IDE. You can also set property values at run time using functions that you add to the program, or via code that you add to existing functions through the code editor pane. The classes also define functions that you call to perform operations on the control.

When you create a project for a Windows Forms application, an application window based on the Form class is created along with all the code to display the application window. After you create a Windows Forms project, there are four distinct operations involved in developing a Windows Forms application:

➤ You create the GUI interactively in the Form Design tab that is displayed in the Editor pane by selecting controls in the Toolbox window and placing them on the form. You can also create additional form windows.

➤ You modify the properties for the controls and the forms to suit your application needs in the Properties window.

➤ You create click event handlers for a control by double-clicking the control on the Form Design tab. You can also set an existing function as the handler for an event for a control from its Properties window.

➤ You modify and extend the classes that are created automatically from your interaction with the Form Design tab to meet the needs of your application.

You'll get a chance to see how it works in practice.

Understanding Windows Forms Applications

You first need to get an idea of how the default code for a Windows Forms application works. Create a new CLR project using the Windows Forms Application template and assign the name CLR Sketcher to the project. The procedure is exactly the same as the one you used back in Chapter 12 when you created Ex12_03, so I won't repeat it here. The Design window for CLR Sketcher will show the form as it is defined initially, and you'll customize it to suit the development of a version of Sketcher for the CLR. It won't have the full capability of the MFC version, but it will demonstrate how you implement the major features in a C++/CLI context. You'll continue to add functionality to this application over the next four chapters.

The Editor pane displays a graphical representation of the application window because with a Windows Forms application, you build the GUI graphically. Even double-clicking Form1.h in the Solution Explorer pane does not display the code, but you can see it by right-clicking in the editor window and selecting View Code from the context menu.

The code defines the Form1 class that represents the application window, and the first thing to note is that the code is defined in its own namespace:

```
namespace CLRSketcher
{
 using namespace System;
 using namespace System::ComponentModel;
```

```
using namespace System::Collections;
using namespace System::Windows::Forms;
using namespace System::Data;
using namespace System::Drawing;

    // rest of the code
}
```

When you compile the project, it creates a new assembly, and the code for this assembly is within the namespace `CLRSketcher`, which is the same as the project name. The namespace ensures that a type in another assembly that has the same name as a type in this assembly is differentiated, because each type name is qualified by its own namespace name.

There are also six directives for .NET library namespaces, and these cover the library functionalities you are most likely to need in your application. These namespaces are:

NAMESPACE	CONTENTS
System	This namespace contains classes that define data types that are used in all CLR applications. It also contains classes for events and event handling, exceptions, and classes that support commonly used functions.
System::ComponentModel	This namespace contains classes that support the operation of GUI components in a CLR application.
System::Collections	This namespace contains collection classes for organizing data in various ways, and includes classes to define lists, queues, dictionaries (maps), and stacks.
System::Windows::Forms	This namespace contains the classes that support the use of Windows Forms in an application.
System::Data	This namespace contains classes that support ADO.NET, which is used for accessing and updating data sources.
System::Drawing	This namespace defines classes that support basic graphical operations such as drawing on a form or a component.

The `Form1` class is derived from the `Form` class that is defined in the `System::Windows::Forms` namespace. The `Form` class represents either an application window or a dialog window, and the `Form1` class that defines the window for CLR Sketcher inherits all the members of the `Form` class.

The section at the end of the `Form1` class contains the definition of the `InitializeComponent()` function. This function is called by the constructor to set up the application window and any components that you add to the form. The comments indicate that you must not modify this section of code using the code editor, and this code is updated automatically as you alter the application window interactively. It's important when you do use Form Design that you do not ignore these comments and modify the automatically generated code yourself; if you do, things are certain to go wrong at some point. Of course, you can write all the code for a Windows Forms application from the ground up, but it is much quicker and less error-prone to use the Form Design capability to set up the GUI for your application interactively. This doesn't mean you shouldn't know how it works.

The code for the `InitializeComponent()` function initially looks like this:

```cpp
void InitializeComponent(void)
{
    this->components = gcnew System::ComponentModel::Container();
    this->Size = System::Drawing::Size(300,300);
    this->Text = L"Form1";
    this->Padding = System::Windows::Forms::Padding(0);
    this->AutoScaleMode = System::Windows::Forms::AutoScaleMode::Font;
}
```

The `components` member of the `Form1` class is inherited from the base class, and its role is to keep track of components that you subsequently add to the form. The first statement stores a handle to a `Container` object in `components`, and this object represents a collection that stores GUI components in a list. Each new component that you add to the form using the Form Design capability is added to this `Container` object.

Modifying the Properties of a Form

The remaining statements in the `InitializeComponent()` function set properties for `Form1`. You must not modify any of these directly in the code, but you can choose your own values for these through the Properties window for the form, so return to the `Form1.h` (Design) tab for the form in the editor window and right-click it to display the Properties window shown in Figure 15-16.

Figure 15-16 shows the properties for the form categorized by function. You can also display the properties in alphabetical sequence by clicking the second button at the top of the window. This is helpful when you know the name of the property you want to change.

It's worth browsing through the list of properties for the form to get an idea of the possibilities. Clicking any of the properties displays a description at the bottom of

FIGURE 15-16

the window. Figure 15-16 shows the Properties window with the width increased to make the descriptions visible. You can select the cell in the right column to modify the property value. The properties that have an [unfilled] symbol to the left have multiple values, and clicking the symbol displays the values so you can change them individually. You can make the form a little larger by changing the value for the `Size` property in the Layout group to `500,350`. You don't want to make it too large at this point because that will make it difficult to work with when you have several windows open in the IDE, so just size the form so it's easy to work with on your display. You could also change the Text property (in the Appearance category) to CLRSketcher. This changes the text in the title bar for the application window. If you go back to the Form1.h tab in the editor window, you'll see that the code in the `InitializeComponent()` function has been altered to reflect the property changes you have made. As you'll see, the Properties window is a fundamental tool for implementing support for GUI components in a Forms-based application.

Note that you can also arrange for the application window to be maximized when the program starts by setting the value for the WindowState property. With the default Normal setting, the window is the size you have specified, but you can set the property to Maximized or Minimized by selecting from the list of values for this property.

How the Application Starts

Execution of the application begins, as always, in the `main()` function, and this is defined in the `CLRSketcher.cpp` file as follows:

```
int main(array<System::String ^> ^args)
{
    // Enabling Windows XP visual effects before any controls are created
    Application::EnableVisualStyles();
    Application::SetCompatibleTextRenderingDefault(false);

    // Create the main window and run it
    Application::Run(gcnew Form1());
    return 0;
}
```

The `main()` function calls three static functions that are defined in the `Application` class that is defined in the `System::Windows::Forms` namespace. The static functions in the `Application` class are at the heart of every Windows Forms application. The `EnableVisualStyles()` function that is called first in `main()` enables visual styles for the application. The `SetCompatibleTextRenderingDefault()` function determines how text is to be rendered in new controls based on the argument value. A value of `true` for the argument specifies that the `Graphics` class is to be used, and a `false` value specifies that the `TextRenderer` class is to be used. The `Run()` function starts a Windows message loop for the application and makes the `Form` object that is passed as the argument visible. An application running with the CLR is still ultimately a Windows application, so it works with a message loop in the same way as all other Windows applications.

Adding a Menu to CLR Sketcher

The IDE provides you with a standard set of controls that you can add to your application interactively through the Design window. Press Ctrl+Alt+X or select from the View menu to display the Toolbox window. The window containing the list of available groups of controls is displayed, as shown in Figure 15-17.

FIGURE 15-17

The block in the Toolbox window, labeled All Windows Forms, lists all the controls available for use with a form. You can click the [unfilled] symbol for the All Windows Forms tab (if it is not already expanded) to see what is in it. This shows all the controls that you can use with Windows Forms. You can collapse any expanded group by clicking the [filled] symbol to the left of the block heading. The controls are also grouped by type in the list, starting with the Common Controls block. You may find it most convenient, initially, to use the group containing all the controls at the beginning of the list, but after you are familiar with what controls are available, it will be easier to collapse the groups and just have one group expanded at one time.

A menu strip is a container for menu items, so add one to the form by dragging a MenuStrip from the Menus & Toolbars group in the Toolbox window to the form; the menu strip attaches itself to the top of the form, below the title bar. You'll see a small arrow at the top right of the control. If you click this, a pop-up window appears, as shown in Figure 15-18.

FIGURE 15-18

The first item in the MenuStrip Tasks pop-up embeds the menu strip in a `ToolStripContainer` control that provides panels on all four sides of the form plus a central area in which you can place another control. The second item generates four standard menu items: File, Edit, Tools, and Help, complete with menu item lists. As you'll see in a moment, you can also do this without displaying this pop-up. The RenderMode menu enables you to choose the painting style for the menu strip, and you can leave this at the default selection. The Dock option enables you to choose on which side of the form the menu strip is to be docked, or you can elect to have it undocked. The GripStyle option determines whether the grip for dragging the menu around is visible or not. The Visual C++ 2010 menu strips have visible grips that enable you to move them around. Selecting the final Edit Items. . . option displays a dialog box in which you can edit the properties for the menu strip or for any of its menu items.

If you right-click the menu strip and select Insert Standard Items from the pop-up, the standard menu items will be added; you'll be implementing only the File menu item, but you can leave the others there if you want. Alternatively, you can delete any of them by right-clicking the item and selecting Delete from the pop-up. I'll leave them in so they will appear in the subsequent figures.

To add the Element menu, click the box displaying "Type Here" and type **E&lement**. You can then click the box that displays below Element and type **Line** for the first submenu item. Continue to add the remaining submenu items by entering **Rectangle**, **Circle**, and **Curve** in successive boxes in the drop-down menu. To shift the Element menu to the left of the Help menu, select Element on the menu strip and drag it to the left of Help. Next, you can add the Color menu by typing **&Color** in the "Type Here" field on the menu strip. You can then enter **Black, Red, Green,** and **Blue**, successively, in the menu slots below Color to create the drop-down menu. After dragging Color to the left of Help, your application window should look like Figure 15-19.

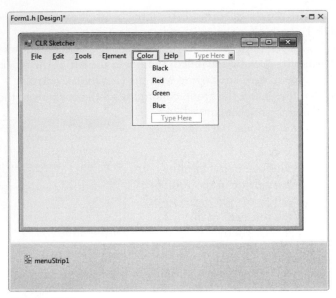

FIGURE 15-19

To check the default Color ⇨ Black menu item, right-click the menu item and select Checked from the pop-up. Do the same for the Element ⇨ Line menu item. All the code to create the menus is already in the application. You can see this if you select the Class View tab, select the [unfilled] symbol next to CLRSketcher to extend the tree, then click CLRSketcher in the tree, and finally double-click the `Form1` class name. The code for the `Form1` class displays in a new tabbed window. Around line 39, you'll see the class members that reference the menu items, and you'll see the code creating the objects that encapsulate the menu items in the body of the `InitializeComponent()` member of the `Form1` class. It's worth browsing the code in this function from time to time as you develop CLR Sketcher, because it will show you the code for creating GUI components as well as how delegates for events are created and registered. The code in the `Form1` class definition will grow considerably and look pretty daunting as you increase the capabilities of the application, but you always can navigate through it relatively easily using Class View.

You can add shortcut key combinations for menu items by setting the value of the `ShortcutKeys` property. Figure 15-20 shows this property for the Line menu item.

FIGURE 15-20

Select the modifier or modifiers by clicking the checkboxes, and select the key from the drop-down list. Figure 15-20 shows Ctrl+Shift+L specified as the shortcut key combination. You can control whether or not the shortcut key combination is displayed in the menu by setting the value of the ShowShortcutKeys property appropriately. Take care not to specify duplicate key combinations for shortcuts.

The next step is to add event handlers for the menu items.

Adding Event Handlers for Menu Items

Event handlers are delegates in a C++/CLI program, but you hardly need to be aware of this in practice because all the functions that are delegates will be created automatically. Return to the Design tab by clicking on it. You can start by adding handlers for the items in the Element menu.

If it is not already visible, extend the Element drop-down menu on the form by clicking it, then right-click the Line menu item and select Properties from the pop-up. Click the Events button in the Properties window (the one that looks like a lightning flash) and double-click the Click event at the top of the list. The IDE will switch to the code tab showing the delegate function for the menu item, which looks like this:

```
private: System::Void lineToolStripMenuItem_Click(System::Object^  sender,
                                                  System::EventArgs^  e)
{

}
```

I have rearranged the code slightly to make it easier to read. This function will be called automatically when you click the Line menu item in the application. The first parameter identifies the source of the event, the menu item object in this case, and the second parameter provides information relating to the event. You'll learn more about EventArgs objects a little later in this chapter. This function has already been identified as the event handler for the menu item with the following code:

```
this->lineToolStripMenuItem->Click += gcnew System::EventHandler(
                                      this, &Form1::lineToolStripMenuItem_Click);
```

This is in the InitializeComponent() function, located at about line 364 in the Form1.h listing on my system, but if you deleted the surplus standard menu items, it will be a different line; you'll find it in the section labeled in comments as // lineToolStripMenuItem.

You can add event handlers for all the menu items in the Element and Color menus in the same way. If you switch back to the Design tab and you have not closed the Properties window, clicking a new menu item will display the properties for that item in the window. You can then double-click the Click property to generate the handler function. Note that the names of the handler functions are created by default, but if you want to change the name, you can edit it in the value field to the right of the event name in the Properties window. The default names are quite satisfactory in this instance, though.

Implementing Event Handlers

Following the model of the MFC version of Sketcher, you need a way to identify different element types in the CLR version. An `enum` class will do nicely for this. Add the following line of code to the `Form1.h` file following the `using` directives at the beginning of the file, and immediately before the comments preceding the `Form1` class definition:

```
enum class ElementType {LINE, RECTANGLE, CIRCLE, CURVE};
```

This defines the four constants you need to specify the four types of elements in Sketcher. As soon as you have entered this code, you will see the new class appear in the Class View window as part of CLR Sketcher.

To identify the colors, you can use objects of type `System::Drawing::Color` that represent colors. The `System::Drawing` namespace defines a wide range of types for use in drawing operations, and you'll be using quite a number of them before CLR Sketcher is finished. The `Color` structure defines a lot of standard colors, including `Color::Black`, `Color::Red`, `Color::Green`, and `Color::Blue`, so you have everything you need.

The element type and the drawing color are modal, so you should add variables to the `Form1` class to store the current element type and color. You can do this manually or use a code wizard to do it. To use a code wizard, right-click Form1 in Class View and select Add ➪ Add Variable. . . from the pop-up. Select private for the access, double-click the default variable type and enter **ElementType**, and enter the variable name as **elementType**. You can also add a comment if you want, Current element type, and click Finish to add the variable to the class. Repeat the process for a private variable of type **Color** with the name **color**.

The new variables need to be initialized when the `Form1` constructor is called, so double-click the constructor name, `Form1(void)`, in the lower part of the Class View window. (For the members of `Form1` to be displayed, `Form1` must be selected in Class View.) Modify the code for the constructor to the following:

```
Form1(void) : elementType(ElementType::LINE), color(Color::Black)
{
        InitializeComponent();
        //
        //TODO: Add the constructor code here
        //
}
```

The new variables are initialized in the first line. You should see IntelliSense prompts for possible values for the `ElementType` and `Color` types as you type the initialization list. You now have enough in place to implement the menu event handlers. You can find the Line menu item handler toward the end of the code in `Form1.h`, or double-click the Line menu item in the Design window to go directly to it. Modify the handler code to the following:

```
private: System::Void lineToolStripMenuItem_Click(
                              System::Object^ sender, System::EventArgs^ e)
{
    elementType = ElementType::LINE;
}
```

This just sets the current element type appropriately. You can do the same for the other three Element menu handlers. Simple, isn't it?

The first Color menu handler should be modified as follows:

```
private: System::Void blackToolStripMenuItem_Click(
System::Object^  sender, System::EventArgs^  e)
{
        color = Color::Black;
}
```

The other Color menu handlers should set the value of color appropriately to Color::Red, Color::Green, or Color::Blue.

Setting Menu Item Checks

At present, selecting element and color menu items sets the mode in the program, but the checks don't get set on the menus. You don't have the COMMAND and COMMAND_UI message types with a CLR program that you have with the MFC, so you need a different approach to set the checkmark against the element and color menu items that are in effect. You can handle messages for the Element and Color menu items on the menu strip when one or the other is selected, and, conveniently, the handler for one of the messages is called before the corresponding drop-down menu is displayed. Right-click the Element menu item in the Design window and select Properties from the pop-up. When you select the Events button in the Properties window, the window should look like Figure 15-21.

The Action group shows the events relating to when the menu item is clicked. Double-click the DropDownOpening event in the Action group to create a handler for it. This handler will be executed before the drop-down Element menu is displayed, so you can set the checkmark in the function by modifying it like this:

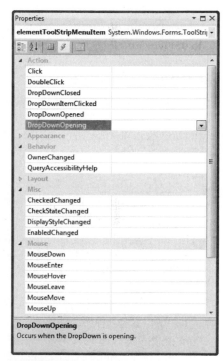

FIGURE 15-21

```
private: System::Void elementToolStripMenuItem_DropDownOpening(
                              System::Object^  sender, System::EventArgs^  e)
{
  lineToolStripMenuItem->Checked = elementType == ElementType::LINE;
  rectangleToolStripMenuItem->Checked = elementType == ElementType::RECTANGLE;
  circleToolStripMenuItem->Checked = elementType == ElementType::CIRCLE;
  curveToolStripMenuItem->Checked = elementType == ElementType::CURVE;
}
```

The four lines of code you add set the Checked property for each of the menu items in the drop-down list. The Checked property will be set to true for the case in which the value stored in `elementType` matches the element type set by the menu item, and all the others will be `false`. The drop-down will then be displayed with the appropriate menu item checked.

You can create a `DropDownOpening` event handler for the Color menu item and implement it like this:

```
private: System::Void colorToolStripMenuItem_DropDownOpening(
                              System::Object^ sender, System::EventArgs^ e)
{
  blackToolStripMenuItem->Checked = color == Color::Black;
  redToolStripMenuItem->Checked = color == Color::Red;
  greenToolStripMenuItem->Checked = color == Color::Green;
  blueToolStripMenuItem->Checked = color == Color::Blue;
}
```

If you recompile CLR Sketcher and execute it, you should see that the menu item checks are working as they should.

Adding a Toolbar

You can add a toolbar with buttons corresponding to the Element and Color menu items. To add a toolbar to the application, it's back to the Design window and the toolbox. Toolbar buttons sit on a tool strip, so drag a `ToolStrip` control from the Menus & Toolbars group in the Toolbox window onto the form; the tool strip will attach itself to the top of the form, below the menu strip. You can add a set of standard toolbar buttons by right-clicking the tool strip and selecting Insert Standard Items from the pop-up. You get more than you need, and, because you will be adding eight more buttons, remove all but the four on the left that control creating a new document, opening a file, saving a file, and printing. To remove a button, just right-click it and select Delete from the pop-up.

You will need bitmap images to display on the new toolbar buttons, so it's a good idea to create these first. Select the Resource View tab and expand the tree in the window so the app.rc file name is visible. The app.rc file contains resources such as icons and bitmaps that are used by the application, so you will add the bitmaps to this file. Right-click app.rc in the Resource View window, and then select Add Resource. . . from the pop-up. Select Bitmap in the dialog that displays and click the New button. You will then see a window with a default 48 × 48 pixel image that you can edit, and the Image Editor toolbar will be displayed for editing bitmap and icon images.

The bitmap will be identified in the Resource View window with a default ID, IDB_BITMAP1. It will be convenient to change the ID and file name for the bitmap to something more meaningful, so extend app.rc in the Resource pane, right-click the IDB_BITMAP1 resource ID, and select Properties from the pop-up. In the Properties window, you can change the Filename property value to **line .bmp** and the ID property value to **IDB_LINE**. The Filename property here contains the full path to the bitmap resource file, so change only the file name part of the property value to what you entered before, line.bmp. You can then click the pane displaying the bitmap itself and change the Height and Width property values to **16** instead of **48**, respectively. You can also change the Colors property value to 24-bit, but I will stick with four-bit color values. The new ID will enable you to identify the bitmap in Resource View in the event that you want to edit it. The new file name will make it easy to choose the correct bitmap for a given toolbar button.

If the Colors window that displays the color palette is not visible, right-click in the window displaying the bitmap and select Show Colors Window from the pop-up. As with the icon editor you used in the native version of Sketcher, right-clicking a color in the Colors window sets the background color, and left-clicking a color sets the foreground color. When using the Image Editor tools, holding the left mouse button down when drawing in the bitmap uses the foreground color, and holding the right button down uses the background color. Use the Image Editor toolbar buttons to draw your own image to represent the Line menu item action. You can then save the file before adding the next bitmap. You can add three more bitmaps corresponding to the Rectangle, Circle, and Curve menu item actions to complete the element set. To add each of these, you can right-click the Bitmap folder name in the Resource View window and select Insert Bitmap from the pop-up. You should end up with four items in the Bitmap folder in Resource View, as shown in Figure 15-22.

FIGURE 15-22

Create four more bitmap resources in app.rc for the color toolbar buttons. You can use the same principle for file names and IDs that you used for the element type bitmaps, so the files will be black.bmp, red.bmp, green.bmp, and blue.bmp, and the IDs will be IDB_BLACK, IDB_RED, IDB_GREEN, and IDB_BLUE.

You can now return to the Design window to add the toolbar buttons. Click the down arrow adjacent to the Add ToolStripButton icon on the tool strip to display the list shown in Figure 15-23.

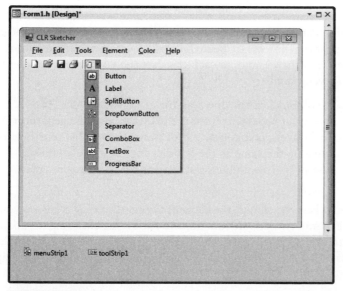

FIGURE 15-23

Select the Button item at the top of the list to add a button to the tool strip. You can then right-click the new button, select Set Image from the pop-up, and select line.bmp from the dialog that displays. Select the Open button in the dialog to set this image for the toolbar button.

Right-click the new line button and display its properties. In the Properties window, change the value of the (Name) property in the Design group to **toolStripLineButton**. You can also change the value of the ToolTipText property to something helpful, such as **Draw lines**.

The `DisplayStyle` property determines how the button is displayed on the toolbar. The default value is `Image`, which causes just the bitmap image to be displayed. You could change this to `Text`, which causes the value of the `Text` property to be displayed with no image. We need something short and meaningful for the value of the `Text` property, so I chose just the name of the shape, such as `Circles` for the button to draw circles. Setting the value of `DisplayStyle` to `ImageAndText` results in the image and the value of the `Text` property being displayed.

To be consistent with the standard buttons, you really want the new button to be transparent. To arrange this, set the ImageTransparentColor property value for each of the buttons to **White**.

Select the Events button to display the events for the button. You don't want to create a new handler for this button as the handler for the Line menu item will work perfectly well. Click the down arrow in the value column for the Click event for the button to display the available handler functions, as shown in Figure 15-24.

FIGURE 15-24

Select the lineToolStripMenuItem_Click handler from the list to register this function as the delegate for the Click event for the button. Repeat this process to create buttons to create the element toolbar buttons for drawing rectangles, circles, and curves, and, in each case, set the Click event handler to be the corresponding menu item Click event handler.

Before you add the buttons for element colors, click the down arrow at the side of the Add ToolStripButton icon on the toolbar and select Separator from the list; this inserts a separator to divide the element type button group from the colors group. You can now add the four buttons for colors, with the Click event handler being the same as the handler for the corresponding menu item. Don't forget to set the button properties in the same way as for the element type buttons.

The toolbar buttons don't get updated when you change the element type or drawing color, so you need to add some code for this. You can add two private functions to the `Form1` class, one to update the state of the element buttons and the other to update the state of the color buttons. You can add these by right-clicking `Form1` in Class View and selecting Add ⇨ Add Function. . . from the pop-up. Here's the code for the first function:

```
// Set the state of the element type toolbar buttons
void SetElementTypeButtonsState(void)
{
  toolStripLineButton->Checked = elementType == ElementType::LINE;
  toolStripRectangleButton->Checked = elementType == ElementType::RECTANGLE;
```

```
    toolStripCircleButton->Checked = elementType == ElementType::CIRCLE;
    toolStripCurveButton->Checked = elementType == ElementType::CURVE;
}
```

Calling this function will set the state of all four element type buttons based on the value of `elementType`. Thus the button matching `elementType` will be set as checked.

The function to set checks for the color buttons works in exactly the same way:

```
// Set the state of the color toolbar buttons
void SetColorButtonsState(void)
{
  toolStripBlackButton->Checked = color == Color::Black;
  toolStripRedButton->Checked = color == Color::Red;
  toolStripGreenButton->Checked = color == Color::Green;
  toolStripBlueButton->Checked = color == Color::Blue;
}
```

To set the initial state of the buttons correctly, you must call both functions in the `Form1` class constructor:

```
Form1(void) : elementType(ElementType::LINE), color(Color::Black)
{
  InitializeComponent();
  //
  SetElementTypeButtonsState();
  SetColorButtonsState();
  //
}
```

You must also update the state of the buttons whenever a change occurs to either the element type or the current drawing color. Each of the `Click` event handlers for the element type menu items must call the `SetElementTypeButtonsState()` function, so modify all four handler functions like this:

```
System::Void lineToolStripMenuItem_Click(
                            System::Object^  sender, System::EventArgs^  e)
{
  elementType = ElementType::LINE;
  SetElementTypeButtonsState();
}
```

You can add a statement to each of the functions that deal with `Click` events for the color menu items in a similar way:

```
System::Void blackToolStripMenuItem_Click(
                            System::Object^  sender, System::EventArgs^  e)
{
  color = Color::Black;
  SetColorButtonsState();
}
```

If you now recompile CLR Sketcher and execute it, you should see your version of the application as something like the window shown in Figure 15-25.

Figure 15-25 shows the tooltip text for the red button, and you should find that the menu items checks are all working regardless of whether you use the toolbar or the menus to select the element type and drawing color. You now have a CLR version of Sketcher that is essentially the same as the MFC version you developed earlier in this chapter. The two versions of Sketcher won't correspond exactly in subsequent chapters, but the main features will be in both.

FIGURE 15-25

SUMMARY

In this chapter, you learned how MFC connects a message with a class member function to process it, and you wrote your first message handlers. Much of the work in writing a Windows program is writing message handlers, so it's important to have a good grasp of what happens in the process. When we get to consider other message handlers, you'll see that the process for adding them is just the same.

You have also extended the standard menu and the toolbar in the MFC Application Wizard–generated program, which provides a good base for the application code that you add in the next chapter. Although there's no functionality under the covers yet, the menu and toolbar operation looks very professional, courtesy of the Application Wizard–generated framework and the Event Handler Wizard.

You learned about creating menus and toolbars in a CLR version of the Sketcher program and how you handle events to provide equivalent function to the MFC version.

In the next chapter, you'll add the code necessary to both versions of Sketcher to draw elements in a view, and use the menus and toolbar buttons that you created here to select what to draw and in which color. This is where the Sketcher program begins to live up to its name.

You can download the source code for the examples in the book and the solutions to the following exercises from www.wrox.com. You'll be developing both versions of Sketcher in subsequent chapters, so you need to retain the state of the program at the end of each chapter. The exercises involve modifying the existing Sketcher versions, but you can retain the original state quite easily by copying the entire contents of the project folder to another folder — say, one called Save Sketcher. When you have finished the exercises on the original project, you can delete the contents of the project file (or save it somewhere else if you want to keep it) and copy the contents of the Save Sketcher folder back to the original project directory.

1. Add the menu item Ellipse to the Element pop-up.

2. Implement the command and command update handlers for it in the document class.

3. Add a toolbar button corresponding to the Ellipse menu item, and add a tooltip for the button.

4. Modify the command update handlers for the color menu items so that the currently selected item is displayed in uppercase, and the others in lowercase.

5. Add an Ellipse menu item and toolbar button with a tooltip to CLR Sketcher.

▶ WHAT YOU LEARNED IN THIS CHAPTER

TOPIC	CONCEPT
Message maps	MFC defines the message handlers for a class in a message map that appears in the `.cpp` file for the class.
Handling command messages	Command messages that arise from menus and toolbars can be handled in any class that's derived from `CCmdTarget`. These include the application class, the frame and child frame window classes, the document class, and the view class.
Handling non-command messages	Messages other than command messages can be handled only in a class derived from `CWnd`. This includes frame window and view classes, but not application or document classes.
Identifying a message handler for command messages	MFC has a predefined sequence for searching the classes in your program to find a message handler for a command message.
Adding message handlers	You should always use the Event Handler Wizard to add message handlers to your program.
Resource files	The physical appearances of menus and toolbars are defined in resource files, which are edited by the built-in resource editor.
Menu IDs	Items in a menu that can result in command messages are identified by a symbolic constant with the prefix `ID`. These IDs are used to associate a handler with the message from the menu item.
Relating toolbar buttons to menu items	To associate a toolbar button with a particular menu item, give it the same ID as the menu item.
Adding tooltips	To add a tooltip to a toolbar button corresponding to a menu item in your MFC application, select the Prompt property for the button in the Properties pane and enter **\n**, followed by the text for the tooltip as the property value.
Creating menus and toolbars in CLR programs	You create menus and toolbars interactively in a CLR program through the Design window. Code is generated automatically to create menu items and toolbar buttons and display them on a form.
Handling events in CLR programs	You can create a delegate to handle a specific event for a control by double-clicking the event type in the Property window for the control. You can optionally select an existing delegate to handle the event. This is particularly relevant to handling toolbar button events that are equivalent to existing menu items events.

16

Drawing in a Window

WHAT YOU WILL LEARN IN THIS CHAPTER:

➤ What coordinate systems Windows provides for drawing in a window

➤ How to use the capabilities provided by a device context to draw shapes

➤ How and when your program draws in a window

➤ How to define handlers for mouse messages

➤ How to define your own shape classes

➤ How to program the mouse to draw shapes in a window

➤ How to get your program to capture the mouse

➤ How to implement Sketcher drawing capabilities in a C++/CLI program

In this chapter, you will add some meat to the Sketcher application. You'll focus on understanding how you get graphical output displayed in the application window. By the end of this chapter, you'll be able to draw all but one of the elements for which you have added menu items. I'll leave the problem of how to store them in a document until the next chapter.

BASICS OF DRAWING IN A WINDOW

As you learned in Chapter 12, if you want to draw in the client area of a window, you must obey the rules. In general, you must redraw the client area whenever a WM_PAINT message is sent to your application. This is because there are many events that require your application to redraw the window — such the user's resizing the window you're drawing in, or moving another window to expose part of your window that was previously hidden. The Windows operating system sends information along with the WM_PAINT message that enables you to determine which part of the client area needs to be re-created. This means that you don't have to draw all the client area in response to every WM_PAINT message, just the area identified as the update region. In an MFC application, MFC intercepts the WM_PAINT message and redirects it to a function in one of your classes. I'll explain how to handle this a little later in this chapter.

The Window Client Area

A window doesn't have a fixed position on-screen, or even a fixed visible area, because the user can drag a window around using the mouse and resize it by dragging its borders. How, then, do you know where to draw on-screen?

Fortunately, you don't. Because Windows provides you with a consistent way of drawing in a window, you don't have to worry about where it is on-screen; otherwise, drawing in a window would be inordinately complicated. Windows does this by maintaining a coordinate system for the client area of a window that is local to the window. It always uses the upper-left corner of the client area as its reference point. All points within the client area are defined relative to this point, as shown in Figure 16-1.

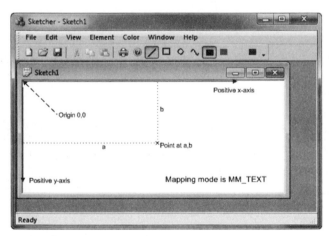

FIGURE 16-1

The horizontal and vertical distances of a point from the upper-left corner of the client area will always be the same, regardless of where the window is on-screen or how big it is. Of course, Windows needs to keep track of where the window is, and when you draw something at a point in the client area, it needs to figure out where that point actually is on-screen.

The Windows Graphical Device Interface

As you saw in Chapters 12 and 13, you don't actually write data to the screen in any direct sense. All output to your display screen is graphical, regardless of whether it is lines and circles or text. Windows insists that you define this output using the **Graphical Device Interface (GDI)**. The GDI enables you to program graphical output independently of the hardware on which it is displayed, meaning that your program works on different machines with different display hardware. In addition to display screens, the Windows GDI also supports printers and plotters, so outputting data to a printer or a plotter involves essentially the same mechanisms as displaying information on-screen.

Working with a Device Context

When you want to draw something on a graphical output device such as the display screen, you must use a **device context**. You used a device context back in Chapter 13 to draw the Mandelbrot set in the client area of a window. You also use a device context when you want to send output to other graphical devices, such as printers or plotters.

A device context is a data structure that's defined by Windows and contains information that allows Windows to translate your output requests, which are in the form of device-independent GDI function calls, into actions on the particular physical output device being used. You obtain a pointer to a device context by calling a Windows API function.

A device context provides you with a choice of coordinate systems called **mapping modes,** which are automatically converted to client coordinates. You can also alter many of the parameters that affect the output to a device context by calling GDI functions: such parameters are called **attributes**. Examples of attributes that you can change are the drawing color, the background color, the line thickness to be used when drawing, and the font for text output. There are also GDI functions that provide information about the physical device with which you're working, such as the resolution and aspect ratio of a display.

Mapping Modes

Each **mapping mode** in a device context is identified by an ID, much like Windows messages. Each symbol has the prefix MM_ to indicate that it defines a **m**apping **m**ode. The mapping modes provided by Windows are as follows:

MAPPING MODE	DESCRIPTION
MM_TEXT	A logical unit is one device pixel with positive x from left to right, and positive y from top to bottom of the window client area.
MM_LOENGLISH	A logical unit is 0.01 inches with positive x from left to right, and positive y from the top of the client area upward.
MM_HIENGLISH	A logical unit is 0.001 inches with the x and y directions as in MM_LOENGLISH.
MM_LOMETRIC	A logical unit is 0.1 millimeters with the x and y directions as in MM_LOENGLISH.
MM_HIMETRIC	A logical unit is 0.01 millimeters with the x and y directions as in MM_LOENGLISH.
MM_ISOTROPIC	A logical unit is of arbitrary length, but the same along both the x and y axes. The x and y directions are as in MM_LOENGLISH.
MM_ANISOTROPIC	This mode is similar to MM_ISOTROPIC, but allows the length of a logical unit on the x-axis to be different from that of a logical unit on the y-axis.
MM_TWIPS	A logical unit is a TWIP where a TWIP is 0.05 of a point and a point is 1/72 of an inch. Thus, a TWIP corresponds to 1/1440 of an inch, which is 6.9×10^{-4} of an inch. (A point is a unit of measurement for fonts.) The x and y directions are as in MM_LOENGLISH.

You will not use all these mapping modes with this book; however, the ones you will use form a good cross-section of those available, so you won't have any problem using the others when you need to.

MM_TEXT is the default mapping mode for a device context. If you need to use a different mapping mode, you have to take steps to change it. Note that the direction of the positive y-axis in the MM_TEXT mode is the opposite of what you saw in high-school coordinate geometry, as shown in Figure 16-1.

By default, the point at the upper-left corner of the client area has the coordinates (0,0) in *every* mapping mode, although it's possible to move the origin away from the upper-left corner of the client area if you want to. For example, some applications that present data in graphical form move the origin to the center of the client area to make plotting of the data easier. With the origin at the upper-left corner in MM_TEXT mode, a point 50 pixels from the left border and 100 pixels down from the top of the client area will have the coordinates (50,100). Of course, because the units are pixels, the point will be nearer the upper-left corner of the client area if your monitor is set to use a resolution of 1280×1024 than if it's working with the resolution set as 1024×768. An object drawn in this mapping mode will be smaller at the 1280×1024 resolution than at the 1024×768 resolution. Note that the DPI setting for your display affects presentation in all mapping modes. The default settings assume 96 DPI, so if the DPI for your display is set to a different value, this affects how things look. Coordinates are always 32-bit signed integers unless you are programming for the old Windows 95/98 operating systems, in which case, they are limited to 16 bits. The maximum physical size of the total drawing varies with the physical length of a coordinate unit, which is determined by the mapping mode.

The directions of the x and y coordinate axes are the same in MM_LOENGLISH and all the remaining mapping modes, but different in MM_TEXT. The coordinate axes for MM_LOENGLISH are shown in Figure 16-2. Although positive y is consistent with what you learned in high school (y values increase as you move up the screen), MM_LOENGLISH is still slightly odd because the origin is at the upper-left corner of the client area, so for points within the visible client area, y is always negative.

FIGURE 16-2

In the MM_LOENGLISH mapping mode, the units along the axes are 0.01 inches, so a point at the position (50,-100) is half an inch from the left border and one inch down from the top of the client area. An object is the same size in the client area, regardless of the resolution of the monitor on which it is displayed. If you draw anything in the MM_LOENGLISH mode with negative x or positive y coordinates, it is outside the client area and, therefore, not visible, because the reference point (0,0) is the upper-left corner by default. It's possible to move the position of the reference point, though, by calling the Windows API function SetViewportOrg() (or the SetViewportOrg() member of the CDC class that encapsulates a device context, which I'll discuss shortly).

THE DRAWING MECHANISM IN VISUAL C++

The MFC encapsulates the Windows interface to your screen and printer and relieves you of the need to worry about much of the details involved in programming graphical output. As you saw in the last chapter, the Application Wizard–generated program already contains a class derived from the MFC class CView that's specifically designed to display document data on-screen.

The View Class in Your Application

The MFC Application Wizard generated the class CSketcherView to display information from a document in the client area of a document window. The class definition includes overrides for several virtual functions, but the one of particular interest here is the function OnDraw(). This is called whenever the client area of the document window needs to be redrawn. It's the function that's called by the application framework when a WM_PAINT message is received in your program.

The OnDraw() Member Function

The implementation of the OnDraw() member function that's created by the MFC Application Wizard looks like this:

```
void CSketcherView::OnDraw(CDC* /*pDC*/)
{
   CSketcherDoc* pDoc = GetDocument();
   ASSERT_VALID(pDoc);
   if(!pDoc)
     return;

   // TODO: add draw code for native data here
}
```

A pointer to an object of the CDC class type is passed to the OnDraw() member of the view class. This object has member functions that call the Windows API functions, and these enable you to draw in a device context. Note that the parameter name is commented out: you must uncomment the name or replace it with your own name before you can use the pointer.

Because you'll put all the code to draw the document in this function, the Application Wizard has included a declaration for the pointer pDoc and initialized it using the function GetDocument(), which returns the address of the document object related to the current view:

```
   CSketcherDoc* pDoc = GetDocument();
```

The GetDocument() function that is defined in the CSketcherView class retrieves the pointer to the document from m_pDocument, an inherited data member of the view object. The function performs the important task of casting the pointer stored in this data member to the type corresponding to the document class in the application, CSketcherDoc. This is so you can use the pointer to access the members of the document class that you've defined; otherwise, you could use the pointer only to access the members of the base class. Thus, pDoc points to the document object in your application that is associated with the current view, and you will be using it to access the data that you've stored in the document object when you want to draw it.

The following line —

```
   ASSERT_VALID(pDoc);
```

— just makes sure that the pointer pDoc contains a valid address, and the if statement that follows ensures that pDoc is not null. ASSERT_VALID is ignored in a release version of the application.

The name of the parameter pDC for the OnDraw() function stands for "pointer to device context." The object of the CDC class pointed to by the pDC argument that's passed to the OnDraw()

function is the key to drawing in a window. It provides a device context, plus the tools you need to write graphics and text to it, so you clearly need to look at it in more detail.

The CDC Class

You should do all the drawing in your program using members of the CDC class. All objects of this class and classes derived from it contain a device context and the member functions you need for sending graphics and text to your display and your printer. There are also member functions for retrieving information about the physical output device you are using.

Because CDC class objects can provide almost everything you're likely to need in the way of graphical output, there are a lot of member functions of this class — in fact, well over a hundred. Therefore, in this chapter, you'll look only at the ones you're going to use in the Sketcher program; we'll go into others as you need them later on.

Note that MFC includes some more specialized classes for graphics output that are derived from CDC. For example, you will be using objects of CClientDC because it is derived from CDC and contains all the members we will discuss at this point. The advantage that CClientDC has over CDC is that it always contains a device context that represents only the client area of a window, and this is precisely what you want in most circumstances.

Displaying Graphics

In a device context, you draw entities such as lines, circles, and text relative to a **current position**. A current position is a point in the client area that was set either by the previous entity that was drawn or by your calling a function to set it. For example, you could extend the OnDraw() function to set the current position as follows:

```
void CSketcherView::OnDraw(CDC* pDC)
{
    CSketcherDoc* pDoc = GetDocument();
    ASSERT_VALID(pDoc);
    if(!pDoc)
      return;

    pDC->MoveTo(50, 50);     // Set the current position as 50,50
}
```

Note that the first line is bolded because it's necessary to uncomment the parameter name if this code is to compile. The second bolded line calls the MoveTo() function for the CDC object pointed to by pDC. This member function simply sets the current position to the x and y coordinates you specify as arguments. As you saw earlier, the default mapping mode is MM_TEXT, so the coordinates are in pixels and the current position will be set to a point 50 pixels from the inside-left border of the window, and 50 pixels down from the top of the client area.

The CDC class overloads the MoveTo() function to provide flexibility as to how you specify the position that you want to set as the current position. There are two versions of the function, declared in the CDC class as the following:

```
CPoint MoveTo(int x, int y);      // Move to position x,y
CPoint MoveTo(POINT aPoint);      // Move to position defined by aPoint
```

The first version accepts the x and y coordinates as separate arguments. The second accepts one argument of type POINT, which is a structure defined as follows:

```
typedef struct tagPOINT
{
    LONG x;
    LONG y;
} POINT;
```

The coordinates are members of the struct and are of type LONG (which is a type defined in the Windows API as a 32-bit signed integer). You may prefer to use a class instead of a structure, in which case, you can use objects of the class CPoint anywhere that a POINT object can be used. The class CPoint has data members x and y of type LONG, and using CPoint objects has the advantage that the class also defines member functions that operate on CPoint and POINT objects. This may seem weird because CPoint would seem to make POINT objects obsolete, but remember that the Windows API was built before MFC was around, and POINT objects are used in the Windows API and have to be dealt with sooner or later. I'll use CPoint objects in examples, so you'll have an opportunity to see some of the member functions in action.

The return value from the MoveTo() function is a CPoint object that specifies the current position as it was *before* the move. You might think this a little odd, but consider the situation in which you want to move to a new position, draw something, and then move back. You may not know the current position before the move, and after the move occurs, it is lost, so returning the position before the move makes sure it's available to you if you need it.

Drawing Lines

You can follow the call to MoveTo() in the OnDraw() function with a call to the function LineTo(), which draws a line in the client area from the current position to the point specified by the arguments to the LineTo() function, as illustrated in Figure 16-3.

The CDC class also defines two versions of the LineTo() function that have the following prototypes:

FIGURE 16-3

```
BOOL LineTo(int x, int y);    // Draw a line to position x,y
BOOL LineTo(POINT aPoint);    // Draw a line to position defined by aPoint
```

This offers you the same flexibility in specifying the argument to the function as with MoveTo(). You can use a CPoint object as an argument to the second version of the function. The function returns TRUE if the line was drawn and FALSE otherwise.

When the LineTo() function is executed, the current position is changed to the point specifying the end of the line. This enables you to draw a series of connected lines by just calling the LineTo() function for each line. Look at the following version of the OnDraw() function:

```
void CSketcherView::OnDraw(CDC* pDC)
{
    CSketcherDoc* pDoc = GetDocument();
```

```
    ASSERT_VALID(pDoc);
    if(!pDoc)
      return;

    pDC->MoveTo(50,50);          // Set the current position
    pDC->LineTo(50,200);         // Draw a vertical line down 150 units
    pDC->LineTo(150,200);        // Draw a horizontal line right 100 units
    pDC->LineTo(150,50);         // Draw a vertical line up 150 units
    pDC->LineTo(50,50);          // Draw a horizontal line left 100 units
  }
```

If you plug this code into the Sketcher program and execute it, it will display the document window shown in Figure 16-4. Don't forget to uncomment the parameter name.

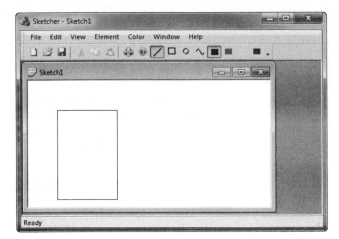

FIGURE 16-4

The four calls to the LineTo() function draw the rectangle shown counterclockwise, starting with the upper-left corner. The first call uses the current position set by the MoveTo() function; the succeeding calls use the current position set by the previous LineTo() function call. You can use this method to draw any figure consisting of a sequence of lines, each connected to the previous line. Of course, you are also free to use MoveTo() to change the current position at any time.

Drawing Circles

You have a choice of several function members in the CDC class for drawing circles, but they're all designed to draw ellipses. As you know from high-school geometry, a circle is a special case of an ellipse, with the major and minor axes equal. You can, therefore, use the member function Ellipse() to draw a circle. Like other closed shapes supported by the CDC class, the Ellipse() function fills the interior of the shape with a color that you set. The interior color is determined by a **brush** that is selected into the device context. The current brush in the device context determines how any closed shape is filled. There are two versions of the Ellipse() function:

```
BOOL Ellipse(int x1, int y1, int x2, int y2);
BOOL Ellipse(LPCRECT lpRect);
```

The first version draws an ellipse bounded by the rectangle defined by the points x1,y1, and x2,y2. In the second version, the ellipse is defined by a RECT object that is pointed to by the argument to the function. The function also accepts a pointer to an object of the MFC class CRect, which has four public data members: left, top, right, and bottom. These correspond to the x and y coordinates of the upper-left and lower-right points of the rectangle, respectively. The CRect class also provides a range of function members that operate on CRect objects, and we shall be using some of these later. The Ellipse() function returns TRUE if the operation was successful and FALSE if it was not.

With either function, the ellipse that is drawn extends up to, but does not include, the right and bottom sides of the rectangle. This means that the width and height of the ellipse are x2-x1 and y2-y1, respectively.

MFC provides the CBrush class that you can use to define a brush. You can set the color of a CBrush object and also define a pattern to be produced when you are filling a closed shape. If you want to draw a closed shape that isn't filled, you can select a null brush in the device context, which leaves the interior of the shape empty. I'll come back to brushes a little later in this chapter.

Another way to draw circles that aren't filled is to use the Arc() function, which doesn't involve brushes. This has the advantage that you can draw any arc of an ellipse, rather than the complete curve. There are two versions of this function in the CDC class, declared as follows:

```
BOOL Arc(int x1, int y1, int x2, int y2, int x3, int y3, int x4, int y4);
BOOL Arc(LPCRECT lpRect, POINT startPt, POINT endPt);
```

In the first version, (x1,y1) and (x2,y2) define the upper-left and lower-right corners of a rectangle enclosing the complete curve. If you make these coordinates into the corners of a square, the curve drawn is a segment of a circle. The points (x3,y3) and (x4,y4) define the start and end points of the segment to be drawn. The segment is drawn counterclockwise. If you make (x4,y4) identical to (x3,y3), you'll generate a complete, apparently closed curve, although it will not, in fact, be closed.

In the second version of Arc(), the enclosing rectangle is defined by a RECT object, and a pointer to this object is passed as the first argument. The POINT objects startPt and endPt in the second version of Arc() define the start and end of the arc to be drawn, respectively.

Here's some code that exercises both the Ellipse() and Arc() functions:

```
void CSketcherView::OnDraw(CDC* pDC)
{
    CSketcherDoc* pDoc = GetDocument();
    ASSERT_VALID(pDoc);
    if(!pDoc)
      return;

    pDC->Ellipse(50,50,150,150);              // Draw the 1st (large) circle

    // Define the bounding rectangle for the 2nd (smaller) circle
    CRect rect(250,50,300,100);
    CPoint start(275,100);                     // Arc start point
    CPoint end(250,75);                        // Arc end point
    pDC->Arc(&rect, start, end);               // Draw the second circle
}
```

Note that you used a `CRect` class object instead of a `RECT` structure to define the bounding rectangle, and that you used `CPoint` class objects instead of `POINT` structures. You'll also be using `CRect` objects later, but they have some limitations, as you'll see. The `Arc()` and `Ellipse()` functions do not require a current position to be set, as the position and size of the arc are completely defined by the arguments you supply. The current position is unaffected by the drawing of an arc or an ellipse — it remains exactly wherever it was before the shape was drawn. Now, try running Sketcher with this code in the `OnDraw()` function. You should get the results shown in Figure 16-5.

FIGURE 16-5

Try resizing the borders. The client area is automatically redrawn as you cover or uncover the arcs in the picture. Remember that screen resolution affects the scale of what is displayed. The lower the screen resolution you're using, the larger and farther from the upper-left corner of the client area the arcs will be.

Drawing in Color

Everything that you've drawn so far has appeared on the screen in black. Drawing always uses a **pen object** that has a color and a thickness, and you've been using the default pen object that is provided in a device context. You're not obliged to do this, of course — you can create your own pen with a given thickness and color. MFC defines the class `CPen` to help you do this.

All closed curves that you draw are filled with the current brush in the device context. As mentioned earlier, you can define a brush as an instance of the class `CBrush`. Take a look at some of the features of `CPen` and `CBrush` objects.

Creating a Pen

The simplest way to create a pen object is first to declare an object of the `CPen` class:

```
CPen aPen;                    // Declare a pen object
```

This object now needs to be initialized with the properties you want. You initialize it by calling the `CreatePen()` function for the object. The function is declared in the `CPen` class as follows:

```
BOOL CreatePen (int aPenStyle, int aWidth, COLORREF aColor);
```

The function returns TRUE as long as the pen is successfully initialized and FALSE otherwise. The first argument defines the line style that you want to use when drawing. You must specify it with one of the following symbolic values:

PEN STYLE	DESCRIPTION
PS_SOLID	The pen draws a solid line.
PS_DASH	The pen draws a dashed line. This line style is valid only when the pen width is specified as 1.
PS_DOT	The pen draws a dotted line. This line style is valid only when the pen width is specified as 1.
PS_DASHDOT	The pen draws a line with alternating dashes and dots. This line style is valid only when the pen width is specified as 1.
PS_DASHDOTDOT	The pen draws a line with alternating dashes and double dots. This line style is valid only when the pen width is specified as 1.
PS_NULL	The pen doesn't draw anything.
PS_INSIDEFRAME	The pen draws a solid line but, unlike with PS_SOLID, the points that specify the line occur on the edge of the pen rather than in the center, so that the drawn object never extends beyond the enclosing rectangle for closed shapes such as ellipses.

The second argument to the `CreatePen()` function defines the line width. If `aWidth` has the value 0, the line drawn is one pixel wide, regardless of the mapping mode in effect. For values of 1 or more, the pen width is in the units determined by the mapping mode. For example, a value of 2 for `aWidth` in MM_TEXT mode is two pixels; in MM_LOENGLISH mode, the pen width is 0.02 inches.

The last argument specifies the color to be used when drawing with the pen, so you could initialize a pen with the following statement:

```
aPen.CreatePen(PS_SOLID, 2, RGB(255,0,0));  // Create a red solid pen
```

Assuming that the mapping mode is MM_TEXT, this pen draws a solid red line that is two pixels wide.

You can also create a pen object with specified line type, width, and color:

```
CPen aPen(PS_SOLID, 2, RGB(255, 0, 0));
```

Using a Pen

To use a pen, you must select it into the device context in which you are drawing. To do this, you use the CDC class member function SelectObject(). To select the pen you want to use, you call this function with a pointer to the pen object as an argument. The function returns a pointer to the previous pen object being used, so that you can save it and restore the old pen when you have finished drawing. A typical statement selecting a pen is the following:

```
CPen* pOldPen = pDC->SelectObject(&aPen);    // Select aPen as the pen
```

You must always return a device context to its original state once you have finished with whatever you have selected into it. To restore the old pen when you're done, you simply call the function again, passing the pointer returned from the original call:

```
pDC->SelectObject(pOldPen);                  // Restore the old pen
```

When you create a pen of your own in this way, you are creating a Windows GDI PEN object that is encapsulated by the CPen object. When the CPen object is destroyed, the CPen class destructor will delete the GDI pen object automatically. If you create a GDI PEN object explicitly, you must delete the Windows GDI object by calling DeleteObject() with the PEN object as the argument.

You can see all this in action if you amend the previous version of the OnDraw() function in the CSketcherView class to the following:

```
void CSketcherView::OnDraw(CDC* pDC)
{
    CSketcherDoc* pDoc = GetDocument();
    ASSERT_VALID(pDoc);
    if(!pDoc)
      return;

    // Declare a pen object and initialize it as
    // a red solid pen drawing a line 2 pixels wide
    CPen aPen;
    aPen.CreatePen(PS_SOLID, 2, RGB(255, 0, 0));

    CPen* pOldPen = pDC->SelectObject(&aPen); // Select aPen as the pen
    pDC->Ellipse(50,50,150,150);              // Draw the 1st (large) circle

    // Define the bounding rectangle for the 2nd (smaller) circle
    CRect rect(250,50,300,100);
    CPoint start(275,100);                    // Arc start point
    CPoint end(250,75);                       // Arc end point
    pDC->Arc(&rect,start, end);               // Draw the second circle
    pDC->SelectObject(pOldPen);               // Restore the old pen
}
```

If you build and execute the Sketcher application with this version of the OnDraw() function, you get the same arcs drawn as before, but this time, the lines will be thicker and they'll be red. You could usefully experiment with this example by trying different combinations of arguments to the CreatePen() function and seeing their effects. Note that we have ignored the value returned from the `CreatePen()` function, so you run the risk of the function failing and not detecting it in the program. It doesn't matter here, as the program is still trivial, but as you develop the program, it becomes important to check for failures of this kind.

Creating a Brush

An object of the `CBrush` class encapsulates a Windows brush. You can define a brush to be solid, hatched, or patterned. A brush is actually an eight-by-eight block of pixels that's repeated over the region to be filled.

To define a brush with a solid color, you can specify the color when you create the brush object. For example:

```
CBrush aBrush(RGB(255,0,0));            // Define a red brush
```

This statement defines a red brush. The value passed to the constructor must be of type COLORREF, which is the type returned by the RGB() macro, so this is a good way to specify the color.

Another constructor is available to define a hatched brush. It requires two arguments to be specified, the first defining the type of hatching, and the second specifying the color, as before. The hatching argument can be any of the following symbolic constants:

HATCHING STYLE	DESCRIPTION
HS_HORIZONTAL	Horizontal hatching
HS_VERTICAL	Vertical hatching
HS_BDIAGONAL	Downward hatching from left to right at 45 degrees
HS_FDIAGONAL	Upward hatching from left to right at 45 degrees
HS_CROSS	Horizontal and vertical crosshatching
HS_DIAGCROSS	Crosshatching at 45 degrees

So to obtain a red, 45-degree crosshatched brush, you could define the CBrush object with the following statement:

```
CBrush aBrush(HS_DIAGCROSS, RGB(255,0,0));
```

You can also initialize a CBrush object much as you do a CPen object, by using the `CreateSolidBrush()` member function of the class for a solid brush, and the `CreateHatchBrush()` member for a hatched brush. They require the same arguments as the equivalent constructors. For example, you could create the same hatched brush as before with the following statements:

```
CBrush aBrush;                          // Define a brush object
aBrush.CreateHatchBrush(HS_DIAGCROSS, RGB(255,0,0));
```

Using a Brush

To use a brush, you select the brush into the device context by calling the SelectObject() member of the CDC class much as you would for a pen. This member function is overloaded to support selecting brush objects into a device context. To select the brush defined previously, you would simply write the following:

```
CBrush* pOldBrush = pDC->SelectObject(&aBrush);     // Select the brush into the DC
```

The SelectObject() function returns a pointer to the old brush, or NULL if the operation fails. You use the pointer that is returned to restore the old brush in the device context when you are done.

There are a number of standard brushes available. Each of the standard brushes is identified by a predefined symbolic constant, and there are seven that you can use. They are the following:

GRAY_BRUSH	LTGRAY_BRUSH	DKGRAY_BRUSH
BLACK_BRUSH	WHITE_BRUSH	
HOLLOW_BRUSH	NULL_BRUSH	

The names of these brushes are quite self-explanatory. To use one, call the SelectStockObject() member of the CDC class, passing the symbolic name for the brush that you want to use as an argument. To select the null brush, which leaves the interior of a closed shape unfilled, you could write this:

```
CBrush* pOldBrush = pDC->SelectStockObject(NULL_BRUSH);
```

Here, pDC is a pointer to a CDC object, as before. You can also use one of a range of standard pens through this function. The symbols for standard pens are BLACK_PEN, NULL_PEN (which doesn't draw anything), and WHITE_PEN. The SelectStockObject() function returns a pointer to the object being replaced in the device context. This enables you to restore it later, when you have finished drawing.

Because the function works with a variety of objects — you've seen pens and brushes in this chapter, but it also works with fonts — the type of the pointer returned is CGdiObject*. The CGdiObject class is a base class for all the graphic device interface object classes, and thus, a pointer to this class can be used to store a pointer to any object of these types. You could store the pointer returned by SelectObject() or SelectStockObject() as type CGdiObject* and pass that to SelectObject() when you want to restore it. However, it is better to cast the pointer value returned to the appropriate type so that you can keep track of the types of objects you are restoring in the device context.

The typical pattern of coding for using a stock brush and later restoring the old brush when you're done is this:

```
CBrush* pOldBrush = (CBrush*)pDC->SelectStockObject(NULL_BRUSH);

// draw something...

pDC->SelectObject(pOldBrush);                    // Restore the old brush
```

You'll be using this pattern in an example later in the chapter.

DRAWING GRAPHICS IN PRACTICE

You now know how to draw lines and arcs, so it's about time to consider how the user is going to define what he or she wants drawn in Sketcher. In other words, you need to decide how the user interface is going to work.

Because the Sketcher program is to be a sketching tool, you don't want the user to worry about coordinates. The easiest mechanism for drawing is using just the mouse. To draw a line, for instance, the user could position the cursor and press the left mouse button where he or she wanted the line to start, and then define the end of the line by moving the cursor with the left button held down. It would be ideal if you could arrange for the line to be continuously drawn as the cursor was moved with the left button down (this is known as "rubber-banding" to graphic designers). The line would be fixed when the left mouse button was released. This process is illustrated in Figure 16-6.

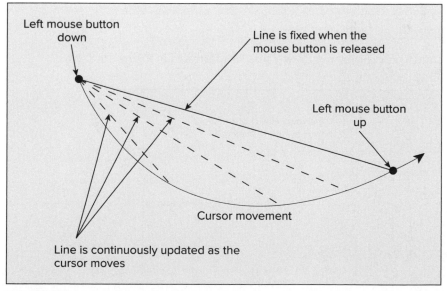

FIGURE 16-6

You could allow circles to be drawn in a similar fashion. The first press of the left mouse button would define the center, and as the cursor was moved with the button down, the program would track it. The circle would be continuously redrawn, with the current cursor position defining a point on the circumference of the circle. Like the line, the circle would be fixed when the left mouse button was released. You can see this process illustrated in Figure 16-7.

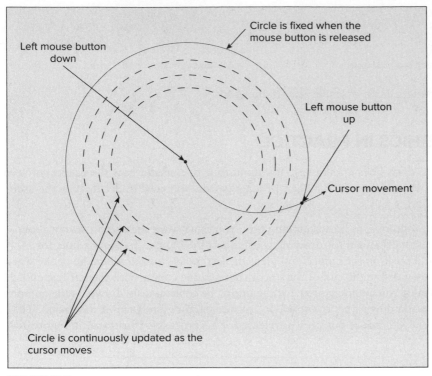

FIGURE 16-7

You can draw a rectangle as easily as you draw a line, as illustrated in Figure 16-8.

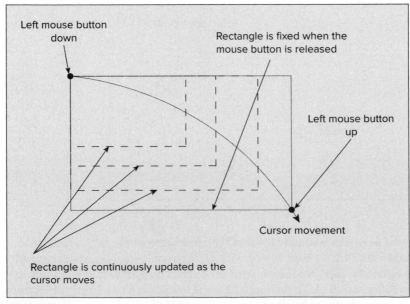

FIGURE 16-8

The first point is defined by the position of the cursor when the left mouse button is pressed. This is one corner of the rectangle. The position of the cursor when the mouse is moved with the left button held down defines the diagonal opposite corner of the rectangle. The rectangle actually stored is the last one defined when the left mouse button is released.

A curve is somewhat different. An arbitrary number of points may define a curve. The mechanism you'll use is illustrated in Figure 16-9.

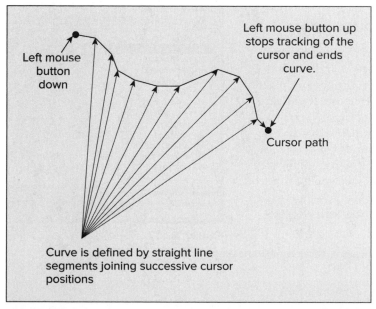

FIGURE 16-9

As with the other shapes, the first point is defined by the cursor position when the left mouse button is pressed. Successive positions recorded when the mouse is moved are connected by straight line segments to form the curve, so the mouse track defines the curve to be drawn.

Now that you know how the user is going to define an element, clearly, the next step in understanding how to implement this process is to get a grip on how the mouse is programmed.

PROGRAMMING FOR THE MOUSE

To be able to program the drawing of shapes in the way that I have discussed, you need to focus on how the mouse will be used:

➤ Pressing a mouse button signals the start of a drawing operation.

➤ The location of the cursor when the mouse button is pressed defines a reference point for the shape.

➤ A mouse movement after detecting that a mouse button has been pressed is a cue to draw a shape, and the cursor position provides a defining point for the shape.

➤ The mouse button's being released signals the end of the drawing operation and that the final version of the shape should be drawn according to the cursor position.

As you may have guessed, all this information is provided by Windows in the form of messages sent to your program. The implementation of the process for drawing lines and circles consists almost entirely of writing message handlers.

Messages from the Mouse

When the user of our program is drawing a shape, he or she will interact with a particular document view. The view class is, therefore, the obvious place to put the message handlers for the mouse. Right-click the `CSketcherView` class name in Class View and then display its properties window by selecting Properties from the context menu. If you then click the messages button (wait for the button tooltips to display if you don't know which it is) you'll see the list of message IDs for the standard Windows messages sent to the class, which are prefixed with `WM_` (see Figure 16-10).

FIGURE 16-10

You need to know about the following three mouse messages at the moment:

MESSAGE	DESCRIPTION
WM_LBUTTONDOWN	A message occurs when the left mouse button is pressed.
WM_LBUTTONUP	A message occurs when the left mouse button is released.
WM_MOUSEMOVE	A message occurs when the mouse is moved.

These messages are quite independent of one another and are being sent to the document views in your program even if you haven't supplied handlers for them. It's quite possible for a window to receive a `WM_LBUTTONUP` message without having previously received a `WM_LBUTTONDOWN` message. This can happen if the button is pressed with the cursor over another window and the cursor is then moved to your view window before being released, so you must keep this in mind when coding handlers for these messages.

If you look at the list in the Properties window, you'll see there are other mouse messages that can occur. You can choose to process any or all of the messages, depending on your application requirements. Let's define in general terms what we want to do with the three messages we are currently interested in, based on the process for drawing lines, rectangles, and circles that you saw earlier.

WM_LBUTTONDOWN

This starts the process of drawing an element. You should do the following:

1. Note that the element-drawing process has started.

2. Record the current cursor position as the first point for defining an element.

WM_MOUSEMOVE

This is an intermediate stage in which you want to create and draw a temporary version of the current element, but only if the left mouse button is down. Complete the following steps:

1. Check that the left button is down.

2. If it is, delete any previous version of the current element that was drawn.

3. If it isn't, then exit.

4. Record the current cursor position as the second defining point for the current element.

5. Cause the current element to be drawn using the two defining points.

WM_LBUTTONUP

This indicates that the process for drawing an element is finished. All that you need to do is as follows:

1. Store the final version of the element defined by the first point recorded, together with the position of the cursor when the button is released for the second point.

2. Record the end of the process of drawing an element.

Now you are ready to generate handlers for these three mouse messages.

Mouse Message Handlers

You can create a handler for one of the mouse messages by clicking the ID to select it in the Properties window for the view class and then selecting the down arrow in the adjacent column position; try selecting <add> OnLButtonUp for the WM_LBUTTONUP message, for example. Repeat the process for each of the messages WM_LBUTTONDOWN and WM_MOUSEMOVE. The functions generated in the CSketcherView class are OnLButtonDown(), OnLButtonUp(), and OnMouseMove(). You don't get the option of changing the names of these functions, because you're adding overrides for versions that are already defined in the base class for the CSketcherView class. Now, we can look at how you implement these handlers.

You can start by looking at the WM_LBUTTONDOWN message handler. This is the skeleton code that's generated:

```
void CSketcherView::OnLButtonDown(UINT nFlags, CPoint point)
{
    // TODO: Add your message handler code here and/or call default

    CView::OnLButtonDown(nFlags, point);
}
```

You can see that there is a call to the base class handler in the skeleton version. This ensures that the base handler is called if you don't add any code here. In this case, you don't need to call the base class handler when you handle the message yourself, although you can if you want to. Whether you need to call the base class handler for a message depends on the circumstances.

Generally, the comment indicating where you should add your own code is a good guide. Where it suggests, as in the present instance, that calling the base class handler is optional, you can omit it when you add your own message-handling code. Note that the position of the comment in relation to the call of the base class handler is also important, as sometimes you must call the base class message handler before your code, and other times afterward. The comment indicates where your code should appear in relation to the base class message handler call.

The handler in your class is passed two arguments: `nFlags`, which is of type `UINT` and contains a number of status flags indicating whether various keys are down, and the `CPoint` object `point`, which defines the cursor position when the left mouse button was pressed. The `UINT` type is defined in the Windows API and corresponds to a 32-bit unsigned integer.

The value of `nFlags` that is passed to the function can be any combination of the following symbolic values:

FLAG	DESCRIPTION
MK_CONTROL	Corresponds to the control key's being pressed
MK_LBUTTON	Corresponds to the left mouse button's being down
MK_MBUTTON	Corresponds to the middle mouse button's being down
MK_RBUTTON	Corresponds to the right mouse button's being down
MK_XBUTTON1	Corresponds to the first extra mouse button's being down
MK_XBUTTON2	Corresponds to the second extra mouse button's being down
MK_SHIFT	Corresponds to the shift key's being pressed

Being able to detect if a key is down in the message handler enables you to support different actions for the message, depending on what else you find. The value of `nFlags` may contain more than one of these indicators, each of which corresponds to a particular bit in the word, so you can test for a particular key using the bitwise AND operator. For example, to test for the control key's being pressed, you could write the following:

```
if(nFlags & MK_CONTROL)
    // Do something...
```

The expression `nFlags & MK_CONTROL` will have the value `true` only if the `nFlags` variable has the bit defined by `MK_CONTROL` set. In this way, you can perform different actions when the left mouse button is pressed, depending on whether or not the control key is also pressed. You use the bitwise AND operator here, so corresponding bits are AND-ed together. Don't confuse this operator with the logical and, &&, which would not do what you want here.

The arguments passed to the other two message handlers are the same as those for the OnLButtonDown() function; the code generated for them is as follows:

```
void CSketcherView::OnLButtonUp(UINT nFlags, CPoint point)
{
  // TODO: Add your message handler code here and/or call default

  CView::OnLButtonUp(nFlags, point);
}

void CSketcherView::OnMouseMove(UINT nFlags, CPoint point)
{
  // TODO: Add your message handler code here and/or call default

  CView::OnMouseMove(nFlags, point);
}
```

Apart from the function names, the skeleton code is more or less the same for each.

If you take a look at the end of the code for the CSketcherView class definition, you'll see that three function declarations have been added:

```
// Generated message map functions
protected:
  DECLARE_MESSAGE_MAP()
public:
  afx_msg void OnLButtonDown(UINT nFlags, CPoint point);
  afx_msg void OnLButtonUp(UINT nFlags, CPoint point);
  afx_msg void OnMouseMove(UINT nFlags, CPoint point);
};
```

These identify the functions that you added as message handlers.

Now that you have an understanding of the information passed to the message handlers you have created, you can start adding your own code to make them do what you want.

Drawing Using the Mouse

For the WM_LBUTTONDOWN message, you want to record the cursor position as the first point defining an element. You also want to record the position of the cursor after a mouse move. The obvious place to store these positions is in the CSketcherView class, so you can add data members to the class for these. Right-click the CSketcherView class name in Class View and select Add ⇨ Add Variable from the pop-up. You'll then be able to add details of the variable to be added to the class, as Figure 16-11 shows.

FIGURE 16-11

The drop-down list of types includes only fundamental types, so to enter the type as CPoint, you just highlight the type that is displayed by double-clicking it and then enter the type name that you want. The new data member should be protected to prevent direct modification of it from outside the class. When you click the Finish button, the variable will be created and an initial value will be set arbitrarily as 0 in the initialization list for the constructor. You'll need to amend the initial value to CPoint(0,0), so the code is as follows:

```
// CSketcherView construction/destruction

CSketcherView::CSketcherView():
      m_FirstPoint(CPoint(0,0))
{
   // TODO: add construction code here
}
```

This initializes the member to a CPoint object at position (0,0). You can now add m_SecondPoint as a protected member of type CPoint to the CSketcherView class that stores the next point for an element. You should also amend the initialization list for the constructor to initialize it to CPoint(0,0).

You can now implement the handler for the WM_LBUTTONDOWN message as follows:

```
void CSketcherView::OnLButtonDown(UINT nFlags, CPoint point)
{
   // TODO: Add your message handler code here and/or call default
   m_FirstPoint = point;                 // Record the cursor position
}
```

All the handler does is note the coordinates passed by the second argument. You can ignore the first argument in this situation altogether.

You can't complete the WM_MOUSEMOVE message handler yet, but you can have a stab at outlining the code for it:

```
void CSketcherView::OnMouseMove(UINT nFlags, CPoint point)
{
    // TODO: Add your message handler code here and/or call default
    if(nFlags & MK_LBUTTON)                 // Verify the left button is down
    {
        m_SecondPoint = point;              // Save the current cursor position

        // Test for a previous temporary element
        {
            // We get to here if there was a previous mouse move
            // so add code to delete the old element
        }

        // Add code to create new element
        // and cause it to be drawn
    }
}
```

It's important to check that the left mouse button is down because you want to handle the mouse move only when this is the case. Without the check, you would be processing the event when the right button was down or when the mouse was moved with no buttons pressed.

After verifying that the left mouse button is down, you save the current cursor position. This is used as the second defining point for an element. The rest of the logic is clear in general terms, but you need to establish a few more things before you can complete the function. You have no means of defining an element — you'll want to define an element as an object of a class, so some classes must be defined. You also need to devise a way to delete an element and get one drawn when you create a new one. A brief digression is called for.

Getting the Client Area Redrawn

Drawing or erasing elements involves redrawing all or part of the client area of a window. As you've already discovered, the client area gets drawn by the OnDraw() member function of the CSketcherView class, and this function is called when a WM_PAINT message is received by the Sketcher application. Along with the basic message to repaint the client area, Windows supplies information about the part of the client area that needs to be redrawn. This can save a lot of time when you're displaying complicated images because only the area specified actually needs to be redrawn, which may be a very small proportion of the total area.

As you saw in Chapter 13, you can tell Windows that a particular area should be redrawn by calling the Windows API function InvalidateRect(). There is an inherited member of your view class with the same name that calls the Windows API function. The view member function accepts two arguments, the first of which is a pointer to a RECT or CRect object that defines the rectangle in the client area to be redrawn. Passing a null for this parameter causes the whole client area to be redrawn. The second parameter is a BOOL value, which is TRUE if the background to the rectangle is to be erased and FALSE otherwise. This argument has a default value of TRUE, because you normally want the background erased before the rectangle is redrawn, so you can ignore it most of the time.

A typical situation in which you'd want to cause an area to be redrawn would be where something has changed in a way that makes it necessary for the contents of the area to re-created — the moving of a displayed entity might be an example. In this case, you want to erase the background to remove the old representation of what was displayed before you draw the new version. When you want to draw on top of an existing background, you just pass FALSE as the second argument to InvalidateRect().

Calling the InvalidateRect() function doesn't directly cause any part of the window to be redrawn; it just communicates to Windows the rectangle that you would like to have it redraw at some time. Windows maintains an update region — actually, a rectangle — that identifies the area in a window that needs to be redrawn. The area specified in your call to InvalidateRect() is added to the current update region, so the new update region encloses the old region plus the new rectangle you have indicated as invalid. Eventually, a WM_PAINT message is sent to the window, and the update region is passed to the window along with the message. When processing of the WM_PAINT message is complete, the update region is reset to the empty state.

Thus, all you have to do to get a newly created shape drawn is:

1. Make sure that the OnDraw() function in your view includes the newly created item when it redraws the window.

2. Call InvalidateRect() with a pointer to the rectangle bounding the shape to be redrawn passed as the first argument.

3. Cause the window to be redrawn by calling the inherited UpdateWindow() function for the view.

Similarly, if you want a shape removed from the client area of a window, you need to do the following:

1. Remove the shape from the items that the OnDraw() function will draw.

2. Call InvalidateRect() with the first argument pointing to the rectangle bounding the shape that is to be removed.

3. Cause the window to be redrawn by calling the inherited UpdateWindow() function for the view.

Because the background to the update region is automatically erased, as long as the OnDraw() function doesn't draw the shape again, the shape disappears. Of course, this means that you need to be able to obtain the rectangle bounding any shape that you create, so you'll include a function to provide this rectangle as a member of the classes that define the elements that can be drawn by Sketcher.

Defining Classes for Elements

Thinking ahead a bit, you will need to store elements in a document in some way. You must also be able to store the document in a file for subsequent retrieval if a sketch is to have any permanence. I'll deal with the details of file operations later on, but for now, it's enough to know that the MFC class CObject includes the tools for us to do this, so you'll use CObject as a base class for the element classes.

You also have the problem that you don't know in advance what sequence of element types the user will create. The Sketcher program must be able to handle any sequence of elements. This suggests that using a base class pointer for selecting a particular element class function might simplify things a bit. For example, you don't need to know what an element is to draw it. As long as you are accessing the element through a base class pointer, you can always get an element to draw itself by using a virtual function. This is another example of the polymorphism I talked about when I discussed virtual functions. All you need to do to achieve this is to make sure that the classes defining specific elements share a common base class and that, in this class, you declare all the functions you want to be selected automatically at run time as **virtual**. The element classes could be organized as shown in Figure 16-12.

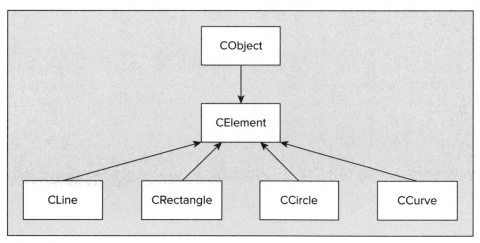

FIGURE 16-12

The arrows in the diagram point toward the base class in each case. If you need to add another element type, all you need to do is derive another class from CElement. Because these classes are closely related, you'll be putting the definitions for all these classes in a single new header file that you can call Elements.h. You can create the new CElement class by right-clicking Sketcher in Class View and selecting Add ➪ Class from the pop-up. Select MFC from the list of installed templates, and then select MFC Class in the center pane. When you click the Add button in the dialog, another dialog displays in which you can specify the class name and select the base class, as shown in Figure 16-13.

FIGURE 16-13

I have already filled in the class name as `CElement` and selected `CObject` from the drop-down list as the base class. I have also adjusted the names of the source files to be `Elements.h` and `Elements .cpp`, because eventually, these files will contain definitions for the other element classes you need. When you click the Finish button, the code for the class definition is generated:

```
#pragma once


// CElement command target

class CElement : public CObject
{
public:
  CElement();
  virtual ~CElement();
};
```

The only members that have been declared for you are a constructor and a virtual destructor, and skeleton definitions for these appear in the `Elements.cpp` file. You can see that the Class Wizard has included a `#pragma once` directive to ensure that the contents of the header file cannot be included into another file more than once.

You can add the other element classes using essentially the same process. Because the other element classes have `CElement` rather than an MFC class as the base class, you should set the class category as C++ and the template as "C++ class." For the `CLine` class, the Class Wizard window should look as shown in Figure 16-14.

FIGURE 16-14

The Class Wizard supplies the names of the header file and .cpp file as Line.h and Line.cpp by default, but you can change these to use different names for the files or use existing files. To have the CLine class code inserted in the files for the CElement class, just click the button alongside the file name and select the appropriate file to be used. I have already done this in Figure 16-14. You'll see a dialog displayed when you click the Finish button that asks you to confirm that you want to merge the new class into the existing header file. Just click Yes to confirm this, and do the same in the dialog that appears relating to the Elements.cpp file. When you have created the CLine class definition, do the same for CRectangle, CCircle, and CCurve. When you are done, you should see the definitions of all four subclasses of CElement in the Elements.h file, each with a constructor and a virtual destructor declared.

Storing a Temporary Element in the View

When I discussed how shapes would be drawn, it was evident that as the mouse was dragged after the left mouse button was pressed, a series of temporary element objects were created and drawn. Now that you know that the base class for all the shapes is CElement, you can add a pointer to the view class that you'll use to store the address of the temporary element. Right-click the CSketcherView class once more and again select the Add ➪ Add Variable option. The m_pTempElement variable should be of type CElement*, and it should be protected like the previous two data members that you added earlier. The Add Member Variable Wizard ensures that the new variable is initialized when the view object is constructed. The default value of NULL that is set will do nicely, but you could change it to nullptr if you wish.

You'll be able to use the m_pTempElement pointer in the WM_MOUSEMOVE message handler as a test for previous temporary elements because you'll arrange for it to be null when there are none.

Because you are creating `CElement` class objects in the view class member functions, and you refer to the `CElement` class in defining the data member that points to a temporary element, you should add a `#include` directive for `Elements.h` to `SketcherView.h`, immediately following the `#pragma once` directive.

The CElement Class

You can now start to fill out the element class definitions. You'll be doing this incrementally as you add more and more functionality to the Sketcher application — but what do you need right now? Some data items, such as color, are clearly common to all types of element, so you can put those in the `CElement` class so that they are inherited in each of the derived classes; however, the other data members in the classes that define specific element properties will be quite disparate, so you'll declare these members in the particular derived class to which they belong.

Thus, the `CElement` class will contain only virtual functions that are replaced in the derived classes, plus data and function members that are the same in all the derived classes. The virtual functions will be those that are selected automatically for a particular object through a pointer. You could use the Add Member Wizard you've used previously to add these members to the `CElement` class, but modify the class manually, for a change. For now, you can modify the `CElement` class definition to the following:

```
class CElement: public CObject
{
    protected:
        int m_PenWidth;                   // Pen width
        COLORREF m_Color;                 // Color of an element

    public:
        virtual ~CElement();
        virtual void Draw(CDC* pDC) {}    // Virtual draw operation

        CRect GetBoundRect() const;       // Get the bounding rectangle for an element

    protected:
        CElement();                       // Here to prevent it being called
};
```

I have changed the access for the constructor from `public` to `protected` to prevent it from being called from outside the class. At the moment, the members to be inherited by the derived classes are a data member storing the color, `m_Color`, a member storing the pen width, and a member function that calculates the rectangle bounding an element, `GetBoundRect()`. This function returns a value of type `CRect` that is the rectangle bounding the shape.

You also have a virtual `Draw()` function that is implemented in the derived classes to draw the particular object in question. The `Draw()` function needs a pointer to a `CDC` object passed to it to provide access to the drawing functions that you saw earlier that allow drawing in a device context.

You might be tempted to declare the `Draw()` member as a pure virtual function in the `CElement` class — after all, it can have no meaningful content in this class. This would also force its definition in any derived class. Normally, you would do this, but the `CElement` class inherits a facility from `CObject` called **serialization** that you'll use later for storing objects in a file, and this requires that it be possible for an instance of the CElement class to be created. A class with a pure virtual function member is an abstract class, and instances of an abstract class can't be created. If you want to use MFC's serialization capability for storing objects, your classes mustn't be abstract. You must also supply a no-arg constructor for a class to be serializable.

 NOTE *Note that serialization is a general term for writing objects to a file. Serialization in a C++/CLI application will work differently from serialization in the MFC.*

You might also be tempted to declare the GetBoundRect() function as returning a *pointer* to a CRect object — after all, you're going to pass a pointer to the InvalidateRect() member function in the view class; however, this could lead to problems. You'll be creating the CRect object as local to the function, so the pointer would be pointing to a nonexistent object on return from the GetBoundRect() function. You could get around this by creating the CRect object on the heap, but then, you'd need to take care that it's deleted after use; otherwise, you'd be filling the heap with CRect objects — a new one for every call of GetBoundRect().

The CLine Class

You can amend the definition of the CLine class to the following:

```
class CLine: public CElement
{
   public:
      ~CLine(void);
      virtual void Draw(CDC* pDC);        // Function to display a line

      // Constructor for a line object
      CLine(const CPoint& start, const CPoint& end, COLORREF aColor);

   protected:
      CPoint m_StartPoint;                // Start point of line
      CPoint m_EndPoint;                  // End point of line

      CLine(void);                        // Default constructor should not be used
};
```

The data members that define a line are m_StartPoint and m_EndPoint, and these are both declared to be protected. The class has a public constructor that has parameters for the values that define a line, and the no-arg default constructor has been moved to the protected section of the class to prevent its use externally. The first two constructor parameters are const references to avoid copying the CPoint objects when a CLine object is being created.

Implementing the CLine Class

You add the implementation of the member functions to the Elements.cpp file that was created by the Class Wizard when you created the CElement class. The stdafx.h file was included in this file to make the definitions of the standard system header files available. You're now ready to add the constructor for the CLine class to the Elements.cpp file.

The CLine Class Constructor

The code for the constructor is as follows:

```
// CLine class constructor
CLine::CLine(const CPoint& start, const CPoint& end, COLORREF aColor):
        m_StartPoint(start), m_EndPoint(end)
{
   m_PenWidth = 1;                        // Set pen width
   m_Color = aColor;                      // Set line color
}
```

You first initialize the m_StartPoint and m_EndPoint members with the object references that are passed as the first two arguments. The pen width is set to 1 in the inherited m_PenWidth member, and the color is stored in the m_Color member that is inherited from the CElement class.

Drawing a Line

The Draw() function for the CLine class isn't too difficult, either, although you do need to take into account the color that is to be used when the line is drawn:

```
// Draw a CLine object
void CLine::Draw(CDC* pDC)
{
   // Create a pen for this object and
   // initialize it to the object color and line width m_PenWidth
   CPen aPen;
   if(!aPen.CreatePen(PS_SOLID, m_PenWidth, m_Color))
   {
      // Pen creation failed. Abort the program
      AfxMessageBox(_T("Pen creation failed drawing a line"), MB_OK);
      AfxAbort();
   }

   CPen* pOldPen = pDC->SelectObject(&aPen);   // Select the pen

   // Now draw the line
   pDC->MoveTo(m_StartPoint);
   pDC->LineTo(m_EndPoint);

   pDC->SelectObject(pOldPen);                 // Restore the old pen
}
```

You create a new pen of the appropriate color and with a line thickness specified by m_Penwidth, only this time, you make sure that the creation works. In the unlikely event that it doesn't, the most likely cause is that you're running out of memory, which is a serious problem. This is almost invariably caused by an error in the program, so you have written the function to call AfxMessageBox(), which is an MFC global function to display a message box, and then call AfxAbort() to terminate the program. The first argument to AfxMessageBox() specifies the message that is to appear, and the second specifies that it should have an OK button. You can get more information on either of these functions by placing the cursor within the function name in the Editor window and then pressing F1.

After selecting the pen into the device context, you move the current position to the start of the line, defined in the m_StartPoint data member, and then draw the line from this point to the end point. Finally, you restore the old pen in the device context, and you are done.

Creating Bounding Rectangles

At first sight, obtaining the bounding rectangle for a shape looks trivial. For example, a line is always a diagonal of its enclosing rectangle, and a circle is *defined* by its enclosing rectangle, but there are a couple of slight complications. The shape must lie *completely* inside the rectangle; otherwise, part of the shape may not be drawn. Therefore, you must allow for the thickness of the line used to draw the shape when you create the bounding rectangle. Also, how you work out adjustments to the coordinates that define the bounding rectangle depends on the mapping mode, so you must take that into account too.

Look at Figure 16-15, which relates to the method for obtaining the bounding rectangle for a line and a circle.

FIGURE 16-15

I have called the rectangle that is used to draw a shape the **enclosing rectangle,** while the rectangle that takes into account the width of the pen I've called the **bounding rectangle** to differentiate it. Figure 16-15 shows the shapes with their enclosing rectangles, and with their bounding rectangles offset by the line thickness. This is obviously exaggerated here so you can see what's happening.

The differences in how you calculate the coordinates for the bounding rectangle in different mapping modes only concern the y coordinate; calculation of the x coordinate is the same for all mapping modes. To get the corners of the bounding rectangle in the MM_TEXT mapping mode, subtract the line thickness from the y coordinate of the upper-left corner of the defining rectangle, and add it to the y coordinate of the lower-right corner. However, in MM_LOENGLISH (and all the other mapping modes), the y-axis increases in the opposite direction, so you need to *add* the line thickness to the y coordinate of the upper-left corner of the defining rectangle, and *subtract* it from the y coordinate of the lower-right corner. For all the mapping modes, you subtract the line thickness from the x coordinate of the upper-left corner of the defining rectangle, and add it to the x coordinate of the lower-right corner.

To implement the element types as consistently as possible in Sketcher, you could store an enclosing rectangle for each shape in a member in the base class. The enclosing rectangle needs to be calculated when a shape is constructed. The job of the GetBoundRect() function in the base class will then be to calculate the bounding rectangle by offsetting the enclosing rectangle by the pen width. You can amend the CElement class definition by adding a data member to store the enclosing rectangle, as follows:

```
class CElement: public CObject
{
   protected:
     int m_PenWidth;                  // Pen width
     COLORREF m_Color;                // Color of an element
     CRect m_EnclosingRect;           // Rectangle enclosing an element

   public:
      virtual ~CElement();            // Virtual destructor
      virtual void Draw(CDC* pDC) {}  // Virtual draw operation

      CRect GetBoundRect();           // Get the bounding rectangle for an element

   protected:
      CElement();                     // Here to prevent it being called
};
```

You can add this data member by right-clicking the class name and selecting from the pop-up, or you can add the statements directly in the Editor window along with the comments.

You can now implement the GetBoundRect() member of the base class, assuming the MM_TEXT mapping mode:

```
// Get the bounding rectangle for an element
CRect CElement::GetBoundRect() const
{
   CRect boundingRect(m_EnclosingRect);         // Object to store bounding rectangle

   // Increase the rectangle by the pen width and return it
   boundingRect.InflateRect(m_PenWidth, m_PenWidth);
   return boundingRect;
}
```

This returns the bounding rectangle for any derived class object. You define the bounding rectangle by using the InflateRect() method of the CRect class to modify the coordinates of the enclosing rectangle stored in the m_EnclosingRect member so that the rectangle is enlarged all around by the pen width.

NOTE *As a reminder, the individual data members of a* CRect *object are* left *and* top *(storing the x and y coordinates, respectively, of the upper-left corner) and* right *and* bottom *(storing the coordinates of the lower-right corner). These are all public members, so you can access them directly. A mistake often made, especially by me, is to write the coordinate pair as* (top, left) *instead of in the correct order:* (left, top).

Normalized Rectangles

The InflateRect() function works by subtracting the values that you give it from the top and left members of the rectangle and adding those values to the bottom and right. This means that you may find your rectangle actually decreasing in size if you don't make sure that the rectangle is **normalized**. A normalized rectangle has a left value that is less than or equal to the right value, and a top value that is less than or equal to the bottom value. As long as your rectangles are normalized, InflateRect() will work correctly whatever the mapping mode. You can make sure that a CRect object is normalized by calling the NormalizeRect() member of the object. Most of the CRect member functions require the object to be normalized for them to work as expected, so you need to make sure that when you store the enclosing rectangle in m_EnclosingRect, it is normalized.

Calculating the Enclosing Rectangle for a Line

All you need now is code in the constructor for a line to calculate the enclosing rectangle:

```
CLine::CLine(const CPoint& start, const CPoint& end, COLORREF aColor)
   m_StartPoint(start), m_EndPoint(end)
{
   m_Color = aColor;                  // Set line color
   m_PenWidth = 1;                    // Set pen width

   // Define the enclosing rectangle
   m_EnclosingRect = CRect(start, end);
   m_EnclosingRect.NormalizeRect();
}
```

The arguments to the CRect constructor you are using here are the start and end points of the line. To ensure that the bounding rectangle has a top value that is less than the bottom value, regardless of the relative positions of the start and end points of the line, you call the NormalizeRect() member of the m_EnclosingRect object.

The CRectangle Class

Although you'll be defining a rectangle object with the same data that you use to define a line — a start point and an end point on a diagonal of the rectangle — you don't need to store the defining points. The enclosing rectangle in the data member that is inherited from the base class completely defines the shape, so you don't need any additional data members. You can therefore define the class like this:

```
// Class defining a rectangle object
class CRectangle: public CElement
{
```

```
   public:
      ~CRectangle(void);
      virtual void Draw(CDC* pDC);       // Function to display a rectangle

      // Constructor for a rectangle object
      CRectangle(const CPoint& start, const CPoint& end, COLORREF aColor);

   protected:
      CRectangle(void);                  // Default constructor - should not be used
};
```

The no-arg constructor is now `protected` to prevent its being used externally. The definition of the rectangle becomes very simple — just a constructor, the virtual `Draw()` function, plus the no-arg constructor in the `protected` section of the class.

The CRectangle Class Constructor

The code for the new `CRectangle` class constructor is somewhat similar to that for a `CLine` constructor:

```
// CRectangle class constructor
CRectangle:: CRectangle(const CPoint& start, const CPoint& end, COLORREF aColor)
{
   m_Color = aColor;           // Set rectangle color
   m_PenWidth = 1;             // Set pen width

   // Define the enclosing rectangle
   m_EnclosingRect = CRect(start, end);
   m_EnclosingRect.NormalizeRect();
}
```

If you modified the `CRectangle` class definition manually, there is no skeleton definition for the constructor, so you just need to add the definition directly to `Elements.cpp`. The constructor just stores the color and pen width and computes the enclosing rectangle from the points passed as arguments.

Drawing a Rectangle

There is a member of the `CDC` class called `Rectangle()` that draws a rectangle. This function draws a closed figure and fills it with the current brush. You may think that this isn't quite what you want because you want to draw rectangles as outlines only, but by selecting a `NULL_BRUSH` that is exactly what you will draw. Just so you know, there's also a function `PolyLine()`, which draws shapes consisting of multiple line segments from an array of points, or you could have used `LineTo()` again, but the easiest approach is to use the `Rectangle()` function:

```
// Draw a CRectangle object
void CRectangle::Draw(CDC* pDC)
{
   // Create a pen for this object and
   // initialize it to the object color and line width of m_PenWidth
   CPen aPen;
   if(!aPen.CreatePen(PS_SOLID, m_PenWidth, m_Color))
```

```
    {
        // Pen creation failed
        AfxMessageBox(_T("Pen creation failed drawing a rectangle"), MB_OK);
        AfxAbort();
    }

    // Select the pen
    CPen* pOldPen = pDC->SelectObject(&aPen);
    // Select the brush
    CBrush* pOldBrush = (CBrush*)pDC->SelectStockObject(NULL_BRUSH);

    // Now draw the rectangle
    pDC->Rectangle(m_EnclosingRect);

    pDC->SelectObject(pOldBrush);         // Restore the old brush
    pDC->SelectObject(pOldPen);           // Restore the old pen
}
```

After setting up the pen and the brush, you simply pass the whole rectangle directly to the
Rectangle() function to get it drawn. All that remains to do is to clear up afterward and restore
the device context's old pen and brush.

The CCircle Class

The interface of the CCircle class is no different from that of the CRectangle class. You can define
a circle solely by its enclosing rectangle, so the class definition is as follows:

```
// Class defining a circle object
class CCircle: public CElement
{
    public:
        ~CCircle(void);
        virtual void Draw(CDC* pDC);      // Function to display a circle

        // Constructor for a circle object
        CCircle(const CPoint& start, const CPoint& end, COLORREF aColor);

    protected:
        CCircle(void);                    // Default constructor - should not be used
};
```

You have defined a public constructor that creates a circle from two points, and the no-arg
constructor is protected to prevent its being used externally. You have also added a declaration for
the draw function to the class definition.

Implementing the CCircle Class

As discussed earlier, when you create a circle, the point at which you press the left mouse button
is the center, and after you move the cursor with the left button down, the point at which you
release the button is a point on the circumference of the final circle. The job of the constructor is to
convert these points into the form used in the class to define a circle.

The CCircle Class Constructor

The point at which you release the left mouse button can be anywhere on the circumference, so the coordinates of the points specifying the enclosing rectangle need to be calculated, as illustrated in Figure 16-16.

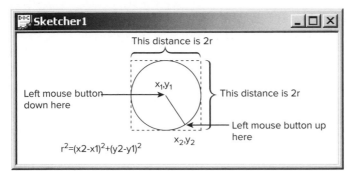

FIGURE 16-16

From Figure 16-16, you can see that you can calculate the coordinates of the upper-left and lower-right points of the enclosing rectangle relative to the center of the circle (x_1, y_1), which is the point you record when the left mouse button is pressed. Assuming that the mapping mode is MM_TEXT, for the upper-left point, you just subtract the radius from each of the coordinates of the center. Similarly, you obtain the lower-right point by adding the radius to the x and y coordinates of the center. You can, therefore, code the constructor as follows:

```
// Constructor for a circle object
CCircle::CCircle(const CPoint& start, const CPoint& end, COLORREF aColor)
{
    // First calculate the radius
    // We use floating point because that is required by
    // the library function (in cmath) for calculating a square root.
    long radius = static_cast<long> (sqrt(
                static_cast<double>((end.x-start.x)*(end.x-start.x)+
                                    (end.y-start.y)*(end.y-start.y))));

    // Now calculate the rectangle enclosing
    // the circle assuming the MM_TEXT mapping mode
    m_EnclosingRect = CRect(start.x-radius, start.y-radius,
                            start.x+radius, start.y+radius);
    m_EnclosingRect.NormalizeRect();    // Normalize-in case it's not MM_TEXT

    m_Color = aColor;                   // Set the color for the circle
    m_PenWidth = 1;                     // Set pen width to 1
}
```

To use the `sqrt()` function, you must add the line to the beginning of the `Elements.cpp` file:

```
#include <cmath>
```

You can place this after the #include directive for stdafx.h.

The maximum coordinate values are 32 bits, and the CPoint members x and y are declared as long, so evaluating the argument to the sqrt() function can safely be carried out as an integer. The result of the square root calculation is of type double, so you cast it to long because you want to use it as an integer.

Drawing a Circle

The implementation of the Draw() function in the CCircle class is as follows:

```
// Draw a circle
void CCircle::Draw(CDC* pDC)
{
   // Create a pen for this object and
   // initialize it to the object color and line width of m_PenWidth
   CPen aPen;
   if(!aPen.CreatePen(PS_SOLID, m_PenWidth, m_Color))
   {
      // Pen creation failed
      AfxMessageBox(_T("Pen creation failed drawing a circle"), MB_OK);
      AfxAbort();
   }

   CPen* pOldPen = pDC->SelectObject(&aPen);   // Select the pen

   // Select a null brush
   CBrush* pOldBrush = (CBrush*)pDC->SelectStockObject(NULL_BRUSH);

   // Now draw the circle
   pDC->Ellipse(m_EnclosingRect);

   pDC->SelectObject(pOldPen);                 // Restore the old pen
   pDC->SelectObject(pOldBrush);               // Restore the old brush
}
```

After selecting a pen of the appropriate color and a null brush, you draw the circle by calling the Ellipse() function. The only argument is the CRect object that encloses the circle you want.

The CCurve Class

The CCurve class is different from the others in that it needs to be able to deal with a variable number of defining points. A curve is defined by two or more points, which can be stored in either a list or a vector container. It won't be necessary to remove points from a curve, so a vector<CPoint> STL container is a good candidate for storing the points. You already looked at the vector<T> template in some detail back in Chapter 10, so this should be easy. However, before we can complete the definition of the CCurve class, we need to explore in more detail how a curve will be created and drawn by a user.

Drawing a Curve

Drawing a curve is different from drawing a line or a circle. With a line or a circle, as you move the cursor with the left button down, you are creating a succession of different line or circle elements that share a common reference point — the point at which the left mouse button was pressed. This is not the case when you draw a curve, as shown in Figure 16-17.

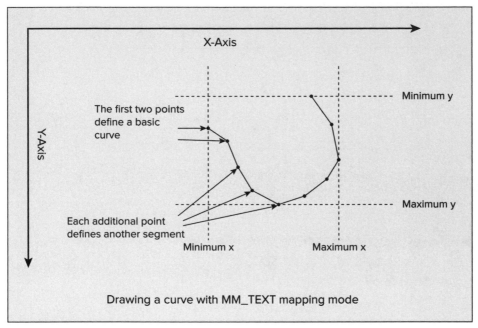

FIGURE 16-17

When you move the cursor while drawing a curve, you're not creating a sequence of new curves, but rather extending the same curve, so each successive point adds another segment to the curve's definition. Therefore, you need to create a curve object as soon as you have the two points from the WM_LBUTTONDOWN message and the first WM_MOUSEMOVE message. Points defined with subsequent mouse move messages then define additional segments to the existing curve object. You'll need to add a function, AddSegment(), to the CCurve class to extend the curve once it has been created by the constructor.

A further point to consider is how you are to calculate the enclosing rectangle. You can define this by getting the minimum-x-and-minimum-y pair from all the defining points to establish the upper-left corner of the rectangle, and the maximum-x-and-maximum-y pair for the bottom right. The easiest way of generating the enclosing rectangle is to compute it in the constructor based on the first two points and then re-compute it incrementally in the AddSegment() function as points are added to the curve.

In Elements.h, you can modify the CCurve class definition to this:

```
// Class defining a curve object
class CCurve: public CElement
{
  public:
    ~CCurve(void);
```

```
    virtual void Draw(CDC* pDC);    // Function to display a curve

    // Constructor for a curve object
    CCurve(const CPoint& first, const CPoint& second, COLORREF aColor);
    void AddSegment(const CPoint& point); // Add a segment to the curve

protected:
    std::vector<CPoint> m_Points;    // Points defining the curve
    CCurve(void);                    // Default constructor - should not be used
};
```

Don't forget to add a #include directive for the vector header to Elements.h. You can add the following definition for the constructor in Elements.cpp:

```
// Constructor for a curve object
CCurve::CCurve(const CPoint& first, const CPoint& second, COLORREF aColor)
{
    // Store the points
    m_Points.push_back(first);
    m_Points. push_back(second);
    m_Color = aColor;
    m_EnclosingRect = CRect(min(first.x, second.x), min(first.y, second.y),
                            max(first.x, second.x), max(first.y, second.y));
    m_PenWidth = 1;
}
```

The constructor has the first two defining points and the color as parameters, so it defines a curve with only one segment. You use the min() and max() functions defined in the cmath header in the creation of the enclosing rectangle. I'm sure you recall that the push_back() function adds an element to the end of a vector.

The Draw() function can be defined as follows:

```
// Draw a curve
void CCurve::Draw(CDC* pDC)
{
    // Create a pen for this object and
    // initialize it to the object color and line width of m_PenWidth
    CPen aPen;
    if(!aPen.CreatePen(PS_SOLID, m_PenWidth, m_Color))
    {
        // Pen creation failed
        AfxMessageBox(_T("Pen creation failed drawing a curve"), MB_OK);
        AfxAbort();
    }

    CPen* pOldPen = pDC->SelectObject(&aPen);  // Select the pen

    // Now draw the curve
    pDC->MoveTo(m_Points[0]);
    for(size_t i = 1 ; i<m_Points.size() ; ++i)
      pDC->LineTo(m_Points[i]);

    pDC->SelectObject(pOldPen);                // Restore the old pen
}
```

The `Draw()` function has to provide for a curve with an arbitrary number of points. Once the pen has been set up, the first step is to move the current position in the device context to the first point in the vector, `m_Points`. Line segments for the curve are drawn in the `for` loop. A `LineTo()` operation moves the current position to the end of the line it draws, and each call of the function here draws a line from the current position to the next point in the vector. In this way, you draw all the segments that make up the curve in sequence.

You can implement the `AddSegment()` function like this:

```
// Add a segment to the curve
void CCurve::AddSegment(const CPoint& point)
{
    m_Points. push_back(point);                    // Add the point to the end

    // Modify the enclosing rectangle for the new point
    m_EnclosingRect = CRect(min(point.x, m_EnclosingRect.left),
                            min(point.y, m_EnclosingRect.top),
                            max(point.x, m_EnclosingRect.right),
                            max(point.y, m_EnclosingRect.bottom));
}
```

You add the point that is passed to the function to the end of the vector and adjust the enclosing rectangle by ensuring the top-left point is the minimum x and y, and the bottom-right is the maximum x and y.

Completing the Mouse Message Handlers

You can now come back to the `WM_MOUSEMOVE` message handler and fill out the details. You can get to it through selecting `CSketcherView` in the Class View and double-clicking the handler name, `OnMouseMove()`.

This handler is concerned only with drawing a succession of temporary versions of an element as you move the cursor because the final element is created when you release the left mouse button. You can therefore treat the drawing of temporary elements to provide rubber-banding as being entirely local to this function, leaving the final version of the element that is created to be drawn by the `OnDraw()` function member of the view. This approach results in the drawing of the rubber-banded elements being reasonably efficient because it won't involve the `OnDraw()` function that ultimately is responsible for drawing the entire document.

You can execute this approach very easily with the help of a member of the `CDC` class that is particularly effective in rubber-banding operations: `SetROP2()`.

Setting the Drawing Mode

The `SetROP2()` function sets the **drawing mode** for all subsequent output operations in the device context associated with a `CDC` object. The "ROP" bit of the function name stands for **Raster OPeration**, because the setting of drawing modes applies to raster displays. In case you're wondering what `SetROP1()` is — it doesn't exist. The function name stands for **Set Raster OPeration to**, not the number two!

The drawing mode determines how the color of the pen that you use for drawing is to combine with the background color to produce the color of the entity you are displaying. You specify the drawing mode with a single argument to the function that can be any of the following values:

DRAWING MODE	EFFECT
R2_BLACK	All drawing is in black.
R2_WHITE	All drawing is in white.
R2_NOP	Drawing operations do nothing.
R2_NOT	Drawing is in the inverse of the screen color. This ensures that the output is always visible because it prevents your drawing in the same color as the background.
R2_COPYPEN	Drawing is in the pen color. This is the default drawing mode if you don't set a mode.
R2_NOTCOPYPEN	Drawing is in the inverse of the pen color.
R2_MERGEPENNOT	Drawing is in the color produced by OR-ing the pen color with the inverse of the background color.
R2_MASKPENNOT	Drawing is in the color produced by AND-ing the pen color with the inverse of the background color.
R2_MERGENOTPEN	Drawing is in the color produced by OR-ing the background color with the inverse of the pen color.
R2_MASKNOTPEN	Drawing is in the color produced by AND-ing the background color with the inverse of the pen color.
R2_MERGEPEN	Drawing is in the color produced by OR-ing the background color with the pen color.
R2_NOTMERGEPEN	Drawing is in the color that is the inverse of the R2_MERGEPEN color.
R2_MASKPEN	Drawing is in the color produced by AND-ing the background color with the pen color.
R2_NOTMASKPEN	Drawing is in the color that is the inverse of the R2_MASKPEN color.
R2_XORPEN	Drawing is in the color produced by exclusive OR-ing the pen color and the background color.
R2_NOTXORPEN	Drawing is in the color that is the inverse of the R2_XORPEN color.

Each of these symbols is predefined and corresponds to a particular drawing mode. There are a lot of options here, but the one that can work some magic for us is the last of them, R2_NOTXORPEN.

When you set the mode as R2_NOTXORPEN, the first time you draw a particular shape on the default white background, it is drawn normally in the pen color you specify. If you draw the same shape again, overwriting the first, the shape disappears because the color that the shape is drawn in corresponds to that produced by exclusive OR-ing the pen color with itself. The drawing color that results from this is white. You can see this more clearly by working through an example.

White is formed from equal proportions of the "maximum" amounts of red, blue, and green. For simplicity, I'll represent this as 1,1,1 — the three values represent the RGB components of the color. In the same scheme, red is defined as 1,0,0. These combine as follows:

	R	G	B
Background — white	1	1	1
Pen — red	1	0	0
XOR-ed	0	1	1
NOT XOR (produces red)	1	0	0

So, the first time you draw a red line on a white background, it comes out red, as the last line above indicates. If you now draw the same line a second time, overwriting the existing line, the background pixels you are writing over are red. The resultant drawing color works out as follows:

	R	G	B
Background (red)	1	0	0
Pen (red)	1	0	0
XOR-ed	0	0	0
NOT XOR (produces white)	1	1	1

As the last line indicates, the line comes out as white, and because the rest of the background is white, the line disappears.

You need to take care to use the right background color here. You should be able to see that drawing with a white pen on a red background is not going to work too well, as the first time you draw something, it is red and, therefore, invisible. The second time, it appears as white. If you draw on a black background, things appear and disappear as on a white background, but they are not drawn in the pen color you choose.

Coding the OnMouseMove() Handler

You can start by adding the code that creates the element after a mouse move message. Because you are going to draw the element from within the handler function, you need to create a device context that you can draw in. The most convenient class to use for this is CClientDC, which is derived from CDC. As I said earlier, the advantage of using this class rather than CDC is that it automatically takes care of creating the device context for you and destroying it when you are done. The device context that it creates corresponds to the client area of a window, which is exactly what you want.

The logic for drawing an element is somewhat complicated. You can draw a shape using the R2_NOTXORPEN mode as long as the shape is not a curve. When a curve is being created, you don't want to draw a new curve each time the mouse moves. You just want to extend the curve by a new segment. This means you must treat the case of drawing a curve as an exception in the OnMouseMove() handler. You also want to delete an old element when it exists, but only when it is not a curve. Here's how that functionality can be implemented:

```
void CSketcherView::OnMouseMove(UINT nFlags, CPoint point)
{
  // Define a Device Context object for the view
  CClientDC aDC(this);                    // DC is for this view
  if(nFlags & MK_LBUTTON)
  {
    m_SecondPoint = point;                // Save the current cursor position
    if(m_pTempElement)
    {
      if(CURVE == GetDocument()->GetElementType())    // Is it a curve?
      { // We are drawing a curve so add a segment to the existing curve
        static_cast<CCurve*>(m_pTempElement)->AddSegment(m_SecondPoint);
        m_pTempElement->Draw(&aDC);       // Now draw it
        return;                           // We are done
      }

      // If we get to here it's not a curve so
      // redraw the old element so it disappears from the view
      aDC.SetROP2(R2_NOTXORPEN);          // Set the drawing mode
      m_pTempElement->Draw(&aDC);         // Redraw the old element
      delete m_pTempElement;              // Delete the old element
      m_pTempElement = nullptr;           // Reset the pointer
    }

    // Create a temporary element of the type and color that
    // is recorded in the document object, and draw it
    m_pTempElement = CreateElement();  // Create a new element
    m_pTempElement->Draw(&aDC);        // Draw the element
  }
}
```

The first new line of code creates a local CClientDC object. The this pointer that you pass to the constructor identifies the current view object, so the CClientDC object has a device context that corresponds to the client area of the current view. As well as the characteristics I mentioned, this object has all the drawing functions you need because they are inherited from the CDC class.

A previous temporary element exists if the pointer m_pTempElement is not nullptr. If it's not a curve, you need to redraw the element to which it points to remove it from the client area of the view, so you first check whether the user is drawing a curve. You call the function GetElementType() for the document object to get the current element type (you'll add this function to the CSketcherDoc class in a moment). If the current element type is CURVE, you cast m_pTempElement to type CCurve so you can call the AddSegment() function for the object to add the next segment to the curve. You then draw the curve and return.

When the current element is not a curve, you redraw the old element after calling the SetROP2() function of the aDC object to set the mode to R2_NOTXORPEN. This erases the old temporary element.

You then delete the element object and reset m_pTempElement to null. The new element is then created and drawn. This combination automatically rubber-bands the shape being created, so it appears to be attached to the cursor position as the cursor moves. You must not forget to reset the pointer m_pTempElement back to nullptr in the WM_LBUTTONUP message handler after you create the final version of the element.

If there is no temporary element, this is the first time through the OnMouseMove() handler and you need to create a temporary element. To create a new element, you call a view member function, CreateElement(). (You'll define the CreateElement() function as soon as you have finished this handler.) This function will create an element using the two points stored in the current view object, with the color and type specification stored in the document object, and return the address of the element. You store the pointer to the new element that is returned in m_pTempElement.

Using the pointer to the new element, you call its Draw() member to get the object to draw itself. The address of the CClientDC object is passed as the argument. Because you defined the Draw() function as virtual in the CElement base class, the function for whatever type of element m_pTempElement is pointing to is automatically selected. The new element is drawn normally with the R2_NOTXORPEN mode, because you are drawing it for the first time on a white background.

Creating an Element

You should add the CreateElement() function as a protected member to the Operations section of the CSketcherView class:

```
class CSketcherView: public CView
{

    // Rest of the class definition as before...

    // Operations
    public:

    protected:
        CElement* CreateElement(void) const;    // Create a new element on the heap

     // Rest of the class definition as before...

};
```

To do this, you can either amend the class definition directly by adding the bolded line, or you can right-click on the class name, CSketcherView, in Class View, select Add ➪ Add Function from the context menu, and add the function through the dialog that is displayed. The function is protected because it is called only from inside the view class.

If you added the declaration to the class definition manually, you'll need to add the complete definition for the function to the .cpp file. This is as follows:

```
// Create an element of the current type
CElement* CSketcherView::CreateElement(void) const
{
    // Get a pointer to the document for this view
    CSketcherDoc* pDoc = GetDocument();
```

```
        ASSERT_VALID(pDoc);                      // Verify the pointer is good

   // Now select the element using the type stored in the document
   switch(pDoc->GetElementType())
   {
      case RECTANGLE:
         return new CRectangle(m_FirstPoint, m_SecondPoint,
                                              pDoc->GetElementColor());

      case CIRCLE:
         return new CCircle(m_FirstPoint, m_SecondPoint, pDoc->GetElementColor());

      case CURVE:
         return new CCurve(m_FirstPoint, m_SecondPoint, pDoc->GetElementColor());

      case LINE:
         return new CLine(m_FirstPoint, m_SecondPoint, pDoc->GetElementColor());

      default:
         // Something's gone wrong
         AfxMessageBox(_T("Bad Element code"), MB_OK);
         AfxAbort();
         return nullptr;
   }
}
```

The first thing you do here is get a pointer to the document by calling GetDocument(), as you've seen before. For safety, you use the ASSERT_VALID() macro to ensure that a good pointer is returned. In the debug version of MFC that is used in the debug version of your application, this macro calls the AssertValid() member of the object, which is specified as the argument to the macro. This checks the validity of the current object, and if the pointer is NULL or the object is defective in some way, an error message is displayed. In the release version of MFC, the ASSERT_VALID() macro does nothing.

The switch statement selects the element to be created based on the type returned by a function in the document class, GetElementType(). Another function in the document class is used to obtain the current element color. You can add the definitions for both these functions directly to the CSketcherDoc class definition, because they are very simple:

```
class CSketcherDoc: public CDocument
{

   // Rest of the class definition as before...

   // Operations
public:
   unsigned int GetElementType() const     // Get the element type
      { return m_Element; }
   COLORREF GetElementColor() const        // Get the element color
      { return m_Color; }

   // Rest of the class definition as before...

};
```

Each of the functions returns the value stored in the corresponding data member. Remember that putting a member function definition in the class definition is equivalent to a request to make the function `inline`; so as well as being simple, these functions should be fast.

Dealing with WM_LBUTTONUP Messages

The `WM_LBUTTONUP` message completes the process of creating an element. The job of the handler for this message is to pass the final version of the element that was created to the document object, and then to clean up the view object data members. You can access and edit the code for this handler as you did for the previous one. Add the following lines to the function:

```
void CSketcherView::OnLButtonUp(UINT nFlags, CPoint point)
{
    // Make sure there is an element
    if(m_pTempElement)
    {
        // Call a document class function to store the element
        // pointed to by m_pTempElement in the document object

        delete m_pTempElement;          // This code is temporary
        m_pTempElement = nullptr;       // Reset the element pointer
    }
}
```

The `if` statement verifies that `m_pTempElement` is not zero before processing it. It's always possible that the user could press and release the left mouse button without moving the mouse, in which case, no element would have been created. As long as there is an element, the pointer to the element is passed to the document object; you'll add the code for this in the next chapter. In the meantime, you just delete the element here, so as not to pollute the heap. Finally, the `m_pTempElement` pointer is reset to `nullptr`, ready for the next time the user draws an element.

EXERCISING SKETCHER

Before you can run the example with the mouse message handlers, you must update the `OnDraw()` function in the `CSketcherView` class implementation to get rid of any old code that you added earlier.

To make sure that the `OnDraw()` function is clean, go to Class View and double-click the function name to take you to its implementation in `SketcherView.cpp`. Delete any old code that you added, but leave in the first four lines that the wizard provided to get a pointer to the document object. You'll need this later to get to the elements when they're stored in the document. The code for the function should now be as follows:

```
void CSketcherView::OnDraw(CDC* pDC)
{
    CSketcherDoc* pDoc = GetDocument();
    ASSERT_VALID(pDoc);
    if(!pDoc)
        return;
}
```

Because you have no elements in the document as yet, you don't need to add anything to this function at this point. When you start storing data in the document in the next chapter, you'll add code to draw the elements in response to a WM_PAINT message. Without it, the elements just disappear whenever you resize the view, as you'll see.

Running the Example

After making sure that you have saved all the source files, build the program. If you haven't made any mistakes entering the code, you'll get a clean compile and link, so you can execute the program. You can draw lines, circles, rectangles, and curves in any of the four colors the program supports. A typical window is shown in Figure 16-18.

FIGURE 16-18

Try experimenting with the user interface. Note that you can move the window around and that the shapes stay in the window as long as you don't move it so far that they're outside the borders of the application window. If you do, the elements do not reappear after you move it back. This is because the existing elements are never redrawn. When the client area is covered and uncovered, Windows sends a WM_PAINT message to the application that causes the OnDraw() member of the view object to be called. As you know, the OnDraw() function for the view doesn't do anything at present. This gets fixed when you use the document to store the elements.

When you resize the view window, the shapes disappear immediately, but when you move the whole view around, they remain (as long as they don't slide beyond the application window border). How come? Well, when you resize the window, Windows invalidates the whole client area and expects your application to redraw it in response to the WM_PAINT message. If you move the view around, Windows takes care of relocating the client area as it is. You can demonstrate this by moving the view so that a shape is partially obscured. When you slide it back, you still have a partial shape, with the bit that was obscured erased.

If you try drawing a shape while dragging the cursor outside the client view area, you'll notice some peculiar effects. Outside the view window, you lose track of the mouse, which tends to mess up the rubber-banding mechanism. What's going on?

Capturing Mouse Messages

The problem is caused by the fact that Windows is sending the mouse messages to the window under the cursor. As soon as the cursor leaves the client area of your application view window, the WM_MOUSEMOVE messages are being sent elsewhere. You can fix this by using some inherited members of the CSketcherView class.

The view class inherits a function, SetCapture(), that you can call to tell Windows that you want your view window to get *all* the mouse messages until such time as you say otherwise by calling another inherited function in the view class, ReleaseCapture(). You can capture the mouse as soon as the left button is pressed by modifying the handler for the WM_LBUTTONDOWN message:

```
// Handler for left mouse button down message
void CSketcherView::OnLButtonDown(UINT nFlags, CPoint point)
{
   m_FirstPoint = point;           // Record the cursor position
   SetCapture();                   // Capture subsequent mouse messages
}
```

Now, you must call the ReleaseCapture() function in the WM_LBUTTONUP handler. If you don't do this, other programs cannot receive any mouse messages as long as your program continues to run. Of course, you should release the mouse only if you've captured it earlier. The GetCapture() function that the view class inherits returns a pointer to the window that has captured the mouse, and this gives you a way of telling whether or not you have captured mouse messages. You just need to add the following to the handler for WM_LBUTTONUP:

```
void CSketcherView::OnLButtonUp(UINT nFlags, CPoint point)
{
   if(this == GetCapture())
      ReleaseCapture();            // Stop capturing mouse messages

   // Make sure there is an element
   if(m_pTempElement)
   {
      // Call a document class function to store the element
      // pointed to by m_pTempElement in the document object

   delete m_pTempElement;          // This code is temporary
      m_pTempElement = nullptr;    // Reset the element pointer
   }
}
```

If the pointer returned by the GetCapture() function is equal to the pointer this, your view has captured the mouse, so you release it.

The final alteration you should make is to modify the WM_MOUSEMOVE handler so that it deals only with messages that have been captured by the view. You can do this with one small change:

```
void CSketcherView::OnMouseMove(UINT nFlags, CPoint point)
{
   // Define a Device Context object for the view
```

```
CClientDC aDC(this);                // DC is for this view
if((nFlags & MK_LBUTTON) && (this == GetCapture()))
{
  m_SecondPoint = point;            // Save the current cursor position
  if(m_pTempElement)
  {
    if(CURVE == GetDocument()->GetElementType())   // Is it a curve?
    {  // We are drawing a curve so add a segment to the existing curve
       static_cast<CCurve*>(m_pTempElement)->AddSegment(m_SecondPoint);
       m_pTempElement->Draw(&aDC);   // Now draw it
       return;                       // We are done
    }
    // If we get to here it's not a curve so
    // redraw the old element so it disappears from the view
    aDC.SetROP2(R2_NOTXORPEN);       // Set the drawing mode
    m_pTempElement->Draw(&aDC);      // Redraw the old element
    delete m_pTempElement;           // Delete the old element
    m_pTempElement = nullptr;        // Reset the pointer to 0
  }

  // Create a temporary element of the type and color that
  // is recorded in the document object, and draw it
  m_pTempElement = CreateElement();// Create a new element
  m_pTempElement->Draw(&aDC);       // Draw the element
}
}
```

The handler now processes only the message if the left button is down *and* the left-button-down handler for your view has been called so that the mouse has been captured by your view window.

If you rebuild Sketcher with these additions you'll find that the problems that arose earlier when the cursor was dragged off the client area no longer occur.

DRAWING WITH THE CLR

It's time to augment the CLR Sketcher application from the previous chapter with some drawing capability. I won't discuss the principles of drawing shapes using the mouse again, because they are essentially the same in both environments.

The MFC is a set of classes that wraps the Windows API, so inevitably, most of the processes are very similar to those of the Windows API. Of course, the CLR is a virtual machine that insulates you from the host environment, so there is no need for the CLR to follow the patterns for handling events and drawing in a window that are in the Windows API. There are significant differences, as you'll see, but the CLR is not so different from the MFC that you will have any problems understanding it. Indeed, in a CLR program, things are typically somewhat simpler.

Drawing on a Form

In a CLR program, you have none of the complications of mapping modes when you are drawing on a form. The origin, for drawing purposes, is at the top left of the form, with the positive x-axis running from left to right and the positive y-axis running from top to bottom. The classes that enable you to draw on a form are within the `System::Drawing` namespace, and drawing on the form is carried out by a function in the `Form1` class that handles the `Paint` event. Right-click on the form in the Design window for CLR Sketcher and select Properties from the pop-up. Select the Events button to display the events for the form, and double-click the `Paint` event; it's the only event in the Appearance group in the Properties window. This generates the `Form1_Paint()` function that will be called in response to a `Paint` event that occurs when the form must be redrawn. You'll implement this method to draw a sketch in the next chapter.

One thing you can do at this point is change the background color for the form. By default, the background color is a shade of gray that is not ideal as a drawing background; white would be better. Change the value of the `BackColor` property for the form in the Properties window by selecting White from the Custom or Web tab on the drop-down list to the right. The form will now display with a nice white background to draw on.

FIGURE 16-19

Adding Mouse Event Handlers

As I said, the drawing principles in CLR Sketcher are essentially the same as in MFC Sketcher, so you need handlers for the corresponding mouse events. If you scroll down the list of events in the `Form1` Properties window, you can find the Mouse group of events, as shown in Figure 16-19.

The ones that are of particular interest for drawing operations are the `MouseDown`, `MouseMove`, and `MouseUp` events. The `MouseDown` event occurs when a mouse button is pressed and you determine which mouse button it is from information passed to the event handler. Similarly, the `MouseUp` event occurs when any mouse button is released and the arguments passed to the handler for the event enable you to figure out which. You need handlers for these two events as well as the `MouseMove` event, so double-click each in the Properties window to generate the event handler functions for them. The handler for the `MouseDown` event looks like this:

```
private: System::Void Form1_MouseDown(
System::Object^  sender, System::Windows::Forms::MouseEventArgs^  e)
{
}
```

The first parameter identifies the source of the event and the second parameter provides information about the event itself. The `MouseEventArgs` object that is passed to this handler function (in fact, all the mouse event handlers have a parameter of this type) contains several properties that provide information you can use in handling the event, and these are described in the following table.

PROPERTY NAME	DESCRIPTION
Button	A property of enum type `System::Windows::Forms::MouseButtons` that identifies which mouse button was pressed. The `MouseButtons` enum defines the following possible values for the property: `MouseButtons::Left`: The left mouse button `MouseButtons::Right`: The right mouse button `MouseButtons::None`: None of the mouse buttons `MouseButtons::Middle`: The middle mouse button `MouseButtons::XButton1`: The first XButton `MouseButtons::XButton2`: The second XButton
Location	A property of type `System::Drawing::Point` that identifies the location of the mouse cursor. The `X` and `Y` properties of a `Point` object are the integer x and y coordinate values.
X	The x coordinate of the mouse cursor, as a value of type `int`.
Y	The y coordinate of the mouse cursor, as a value of type `int`.
Clicks	A count of the number of times the mouse button was pressed and released, as a value of type `int`.
Delta	A signed count of the number of detents (a detent being one notch on the mouse wheel) the mouse wheel has rotated, as a value of type `int`.

Following the same logic you used in the MFC Sketcher program, the MouseDown event handler needs to check that the left mouse button is pressed and record the current cursor position somewhere for use in the MouseMove handler. It also should record that the drawing of an element is in progress. To support this, you can add two private data members to the Form1 class, a bool variable with the name drawing to record when drawing an element is in progress, and a variable of type Point with the name firstPoint to record the initial mouse cursor position. You can do this manually, or from Class View using the Add ➪ Add Variable capability. Make sure that the variables are initialized by the Form1 constructor, drawing to false and firstPoint to 0; the wizard should insert these values automatically. The Point class is defined in the System::Drawing namespace, and you should already have a using directive for the System::Drawing namespace at the beginning of Form1.h.

You can now add the code for the MouseDown delegate like this:

```
private: System::Void Form1_MouseDown(
System::Object^  sender, System::Windows::Forms::MouseEventArgs^  e)
{
  if(e->Button == System::Windows::Forms::MouseButtons::Left)
  {
    drawing = true;
    firstPoint = e->Location;
  }
}
```

As long as the left mouse button is pressed, drawing an element has started, so you set `drawing` to true. The `Location` property for the parameter `e` supplies the cursor location as a `Point` object so you can store it directly in `firstPoint`.

The `MouseMove` event handler will take care of creating elements for the sketch, and the `MouseUp` event handler will finalize the process, but before you complete the code for these two mouse event handlers, you need to take a little detour to define the classes that encapsulate the elements you can draw.

Defining C++/CLI Element Classes

The pattern for the classes that define elements will be similar to those in the MFC version of Sketcher; an `Element` base class with the specific element types defined by classes derived from `Element`. Go to the Solution Explorer window, right-click the Header Files folder, and select Add ⇨ New Item from the pop-up. Use the dialog to add a header file with the name `Elements.h`. Add the code for `Element` base class definition to `Elements.h`, like this:

```
// Elements.h
// Defines element types
#pragma once

using namespace System;
using namespace System::Drawing;

namespace CLRSketcher
{

  public ref class Element abstract
  {
  protected:
    Point position;
    Color color;
    System::Drawing::Rectangle boundRect;

  public:
    virtual void Draw(Graphics^ g) abstract;
  };
}
```

You are using classes from the `System` and `System::Drawing` namespaces in the element class definitions, so there are `using` directives for both. The code for the application is defined within the `CLRSketcher` namespace, so you put the definitions for the element classes in the same namespace. The `Element` class and its subclasses have to be ref classes because value classes cannot be derived classes. The `Element` class also must be defined as `abstract` because there is no implementation for the `Draw()` function. The `Draw()` function will be overridden in each of the derived classes to draw a specific type of element, and you will call the function polymorphically, just as you did in MFC Sketcher.

The `position` member is of type `System::Drawing::Point`, which is a value type that defines a point object with two members, `X` and `Y`. The `position`, `color`, and `boundRect` members will be inherited in the derived classes and will store the position of the element in the client area, the element color, and the bounding rectangle for the element. All elements will be drawn relative to the point `position`. For the moment, you won't worry about the distinction between a bounding rectangle and an enclosing rectangle. Incidentally, the type name for the `boundRect` variable,

System::Drawing::Rectangle, is fully qualified here because you will add a derived class with the name Rectangle; without the qualified name here, the compiler would assume you meant the Rectangle class in this header file, which is not what you want.

Defining a Line

Next, you can add an initial definition for the Line class to Elements.h. Make sure you add this code before the closing brace for the CLRSketcher namespace block:

```
public ref class Line : Element
{
  protected:
    Point end;

  public:
    // Constructor
    Line(Color color, Point start, Point end)
    {
      this->color = color;
      position = start;
      this->end = end;
      boundRect = System::Drawing::Rectangle(Math::Min(position.X, end.X),
                                             Math::Min(position.Y, end.Y),
                    Math::Abs(position.X - end.X), Math::Abs(position.Y - end.Y));

      // Provide for lines that are horizontal or vertical
      if(boundRect.Width < 2) boundRect.Width = 2;
      if(boundRect.Height < 2) boundRect.Height = 2;
    }

    // Function to draw a line
    virtual void Draw(Graphics^ g) override
    {
      // Code to draw a line...
    }
};
```

The constructor sets the value for the color member that is inherited from the base class. It also stores the start and end points of the line that are passed as arguments in the inherited position member and the end member, respectively. The inherited boundRect member is initialized from the position and end points. You have several ways to create a System::Drawing::Rectangle object. Here, the first two arguments to the Rectangle constructor are the coordinates of the top-left corner of the rectangle. The third and fourth arguments are the width and height of the rectangle. You use the Min() function from the System::Math class to obtain the minimum values of the coordinates of position and end, and the Abs() function to obtain the absolute (positive) value for the difference between pairs of corresponding coordinates, to get the width and height, respectively. The Math class defines several other static utility functions that are very handy when you want to carry out basic mathematical operations.

If a line is exactly horizontal or vertical, the bounding rectangle will have a width or height that is 0, so the last two if statements in the constructor ensure that the rectangle always has a width and height of greater than 0.

Defining a Color

`System::Drawing::Color` is a value class that encapsulates an ARGB color value. An ARGB color is a 32-bit value comprising four eight-bit components, an **alpha** component that determines transparency and three primary color components, **red**, **green**, and **blue**. Each of the component values can be from 0 to 255, where an alpha of 0 is completely transparent and an alpha of 255 is completely opaque; an eight-bit color component value represents the intensity of that color, where 0 is zero intensity (i.e. no color) and 255 is the maximum. A lot of the time, you can make use of standard color constants that the `Color` class defines, such as `Color::Blue` or `Color::Red`. If you look at the documentation for members of the `Color` class, you'll see the complete set. I haven't listed them here because there are more than 130 predefined colors.

Drawing Lines

The `Draw()` function will use the `System::Drawing::Graphics` object that is passed as the argument to draw the line in the appropriate color. The `Graphics` class defines a large number of functions that you use for drawing shapes, including those in the following table.

FUNCTION	DESCRIPTION
`DrawLine(Pen pen,` `    Point p1, Point p2)`	Draws a line from p1 to p2 using pen. A `Pen` object draws in a specific color and line thickness.

`DrawLine(Pen pen,`
`    int x1, int y1,`
`    int x2, int y2)`
	Draws a line from (x1,y1) to (x2,y2) using pen.

`DrawLines(Pen pen, Point[] pts)`	Draws a series of lines connecting the points in the `pts` array using pen.
`DrawRectangle(Pen pen,` `    Rectangle rect)`	Draws the rectangle `rect` using pen.

`DrawRectangle(Pen pen,`
`    int X, int Y,`
`    int width, int height)`
	Draws a rectangle at (x, y) using pen with the rectangle dimensions specified by `width` and `height`.

`DrawEllipse(Pen pen,` `    Rectangle rect)`	Draws the ellipse that is specified by the bounding rectangle `rect` using pen.

`DrawEllipse(Pen pen,`
`    int x, int y,`
`    int width, int height)`
	Draws an ellipse using pen. The ellipse is specified by the bounding rectangle at (x, y) with the dimensions `width` and `height`.

In each case, the `Pen` parameter determines the color and style of line used to draw the shape, so we'll explore the `Pen` class in a little more depth.

Defining a Pen for Drawing

The `System::Drawing::Pen` class represents a pen for drawing lines and curves. The simplest `Pen` object draws in a specified color with a default line width, for example:

```
Pen^ pen =  gcnew Pen(Color::CornflowerBlue);
```

This defines a `Pen` object that you can use to draw in cornflower blue.

You can also define a `Pen` with a second argument to the constructor that defines the thickness of the line as a `float` value:

```
Pen^ pen =  gcnew Pen(Color::Green, 2.0f);
```

This defines a `Pen` object that will draw green lines with a thickness of `2.0f`. Note that the pen width is a public property, so you can always set the width for a given `Pen` object explicitly:

```
pen->Width = 3.0f;
```

You can now conceivably complete the definition of the `Draw()` function in the `Line` class, like this:

```
virtual void Draw(Graphics^ g) override
{
  g->DrawLine(gcnew Pen(color), position, end);
}
```

This implementation of the function draws a line from position to end with a default line width of 1 and in the color specified by `color`. However, don't add this to CLR Sketcher yet, as there's a better approach.

The default `Pen` object draws a continuous line of a default thickness of `1.0f`, but you can draw other types of lines by setting properties for a `Pen` object; the following table shows some of the `Pen` properties.

PEN PROPERTY	DESCRIPTION
Color	Gets or sets the color of the pen as a value of type `System::Drawing::Color`. For example, to set the drawing color for a `Pen` object, pen, to red, you set the property like this: `pen->Color = Color::Red;`
Width	Gets or sets the width of the line drawn by the pen as a value of type `float`.

DashPattern	Gets or sets an array of `float` values specifying a dash pattern for a line. The array values specify the lengths of alternating dashes and spaces in a line. For example:
	`array<float>^ pattern = { 5.0f, 2.0f, 4.0f, 3.0f};`
	`pen->DashPattern = pattern;`
	This defines a pattern that will be a dash of length 5 followed by a space of length 2 followed by a dash of length 4 followed by a space of length 3; the pattern repeats as often as necessary along a line.

continues

(continued)

PEN PROPERTY	DESCRIPTION
DashOffset	Specifies the distance from the start of a line to the beginning of a dash pattern as a value of type `float`.

StartCap	Specifies the cap style for the start of a line. Cap styles are defined by the `System::Drawing::Drawing2D::LineCap` enumeration that defines the following possible values: `Flat`, `Square`, `Round`, `Triangle`, `NoAnchor`, `SquareAnchor`, `RoundAnchor`, `DiamondAnchor`, `ArrowAnchor`, `Custom`, `AnchorMask`. For example, to draw lines with a round line cap at the start, set the property as follows:
	
	`pen->StartCap =`
	
	`       System::Drawing::Drawing2D::LineCap::Round;`

EndCap	Specifies the cap style for the end of a line. The possible values for the cap style for the end of a line are the same as for `StartCap`.

When you are drawing with different line styles and colors, you have the option of creating a new `Pen` object for each drawing operation or using a single `Pen` object and changing the properties to provide the line you want. It will be useful later to adopt the latter approach in CLR Sketcher, so add a protected `Pen` member to the `Element` base class:

```
Pen^ pen;
```

This will be inherited in each of the concrete derived classes, and each derived class constructor will initialize the pen member appropriately. This will preempt the need to create a new `Pen` object each time an element is drawn. Modify the `Line` class constructor like this:

```
Line(Color color, Point start, Point end)
{
  pen = gcnew Pen(color);
  this->color = color;
  position = start;
  this->end = end;
  boundRect = System::Drawing::Rectangle(Math::Min(position.X, end.X),
                                Math::Min(position.Y, end.Y),
              Math::Abs(position.X - end.X), Math::Abs(position.Y - end.Y));
}
```

With the pen set up, you can now implement the `Draw()` function for the `Line` class:

```
virtual void Draw(Graphics^ g) override
{
  g->DrawLine(pen, position, end);
}
```

It's important to the performance of the application that the `Draw()` function does not carry excess overhead when it executes, because it will be called many times, sometimes very frequently. Now the

Draw() function doesn't create a new Pen object each time it is called. A positive side effect is that adding the ability to draw using different line styles will now be a piece of cake, because all that's needed is to change the pen's properties.

Standard Pens

Sometimes, you don't want full flexibility to change the properties of a Pen object you use. In this case, you can use the System::Drawing::Pens class that defines a large number of standard pens that draw a line of width 1 in a given color. For example, Pens::Black and Pens::Beige are standard pens that draw in black and beige, respectively. Note that you cannot modify a standard pen — what you see is what you get. Consult the documentation for the Pens class for the full list of standard pen colors.

Defining a Rectangle

Add the definition of the class encapsulating CLR Sketcher rectangles to Elements.h:

```
public ref class Rectangle : Element
{
protected:
  int width;
  int height;

public:
  Rectangle(Color color, Point p1, Point p2)
  {
    pen = gcnew Pen(color);
    this->color = color;
    position = Point(Math::Min(p1.X, p2.X), Math::Min(p1.Y,p2.Y));
    width = Math::Abs(p1.X - p2.X);
    height = Math::Abs(p1.Y - p2.Y);
    boundRect = System::Drawing::Rectangle(position, Size(width, height));
  }

      virtual void Draw(Graphics^ g) override
  {
    g->DrawRectangle(pen, position.X, position.Y, width, height);
  }
};
```

A rectangle is defined by the top-left corner position and the width and height so you have defined class members to store these. As in the MFC version of Sketcher, you need to figure out the coordinates of the top-left corner of the rectangle from the points supplied to the constructor. Here, you define the value of the inherited boundRect member of the class as a System::Drawing::Rectangle using a constructor that accepts a Point object specifying the top-left corner as the first argument. The second argument is a System::Drawing::Size object encapsulating the width and height of the rectangle. The Draw() function draws the rectangle on the form using the DrawRectangle() function for the Graphics object, g, which is passed to the Draw() function.

Defining a Circle

The definition of the `Circle` class in `Elements.h` is also very straightforward:

```
public ref class Circle : Element
{
protected:
  int width;
  int height;

public:
  Circle(Color color, Point center, Point circum)
  {
    pen = gcnew Pen(color);
    this->color = color;
    int radius = safe_cast<int>(Math::Sqrt(
                  (center.X-circum.X)*(center.X-circum.X) +
                              (center.Y-circum.Y)*(center.Y-circum.Y)));
    position = Point(center.X - radius, center.Y - radius);
    width = height = 2*radius;
    boundRect = System::Drawing::Rectangle(position, Size(width, height));
  }

  virtual void Draw(Graphics^ g) override
  {
    g->DrawEllipse(pen, position.X, position.Y, width, height);
  }
};
```

The two points that are passed to the constructor are the center and a point on the circumference of the circle. The radius is the distance between these two points, and the `Math::Sqrt()` function calculates this. You need the width and height of the rectangle enclosing the circle to draw it, and the value of each of these is twice the radius. To draw the circle, you use the `DrawEllipse()` function for the `Graphics` object, `g`.

Defining a Curve

A class to represent a curve is a little trickier, as you will draw it as a series of line segments joining a set of points. As in the MFC version of Sketcher, you need a way to store an arbitrary number of points in a `Curve` object. An STL/CLR container looks to be a promising solution, and a `vector<Point>` container is a good choice for storing the points on a curve. Here's how the `Curve` class definition looks based on that:

```
public ref class Curve : Element
{
private:
  vector<Point>^ points;

public:
  Curve(Color color, Point p1, Point p2)
  {
    pen = gcnew Pen(color);
    this->color = color;
```

```
      points = gcnew vector<Point>();
      position = p1;
      points->push_back(p2 - Size(position));

      // Find the minimum and maximum coordinates
      int minX = p1.X < p2.X ? p1.X : p2.X;
      int minY = p1.Y < p2.Y ? p1.Y : p2.Y;
      int maxX = p1.X > p2.X ? p1.X : p2.X;
      int maxY = p1.Y > p2.Y ? p1.Y : p2.Y;
      int width = Math::Max(2, maxX - minX);
      int height = Math::Max(2, maxY - minY);
      boundRect = System::Drawing::Rectangle(minX, minY, width, height);
    }

  // Add a point to the curve
  void Add(Point p)
  {
    points->push_back(p - Size(position));

    // Modify the bounding rectangle to accommodate the new point
    if(p.X < boundRect.X)
    {
      boundRect.Width = boundRect.Right - p.X;
      boundRect.X = p.X;
    }
    else if(p.X > boundRect.Right)
      boundRect.Width = p.X - boundRect.Left;

    if(p.Y < boundRect.Y)
    {
      boundRect.Height = boundRect.Bottom - p.Y;
      boundRect.Y = p.Y;
    }
    else if(p.Y > boundRect.Bottom)
      boundRect.Height = p.Y - boundRect.Top;
  }

   virtual void Draw(Graphics^ g) override
  {
    Point previous(position);
    Point temp;
    for each(Point p in points)
    {
      temp = position + Size(p);
      g->DrawLine(pen, previous, temp);
      previous = temp;
    }
  }
};
```

Don't forget to add a `#include` directive for the `cliext/vector` header to `Elements.h`. You will also need a using directive for the `cliext` namespace.

You create a `Curve` object initially from the first two points on the curve. The first point, `p1`, defines the position of the curve, so you store it in `position`. Because you draw the curve relative to the origin, the second point must be specified relative to `position`, so you calculate this by subtracting a `Size` object you construct from p2 and store the result in the `points` container. The addition and subtraction operators that the `Point` class defines provide for adding or subtracting a `Size` object, respectively. `Size` is a value class with properties `Width` and `Height`, typically of a rectangle. `Width` is treated as the `X` component and `Height` as the `Y` component for the purposes of the addition and subtraction operators in the `Point` class. You add subsequent points to the `vector<Point>` container by calling the `Add()` member function after modifying the coordinates of each point so it is defined relative to position.

The constructor creates the initial bounding rectangle for the curve from the first two points by obtaining the minimum and maximum coordinate values and using these to determine the top-left point coordinates and the width and height of the rectangle, respectively. A curve could conceivably be a vertical or horizontal line that would result in a width or height of 0, so the width and height are always set to at least 2. The `Add()` function updates the object referenced by `boundRect` to accommodate the new point that it adds to the container.

The `Right` property of a `System::Drawing::Rectangle` object corresponds to the sum of the x coordinate for the top-left position and the width. The `Bottom` property is the sum of the y coordinate and the height. These properties are get-only. There are also `Left` and `Top` properties that are get-only, and these correspond to the x coordinate of the left edge and the y coordinate of the top edge of the rectangle, respectively. The `X`, `Y`, `Width`, and `Height` properties of a `System::Drawing::Rectangle` object are the x and y coordinates of the top-left corner and the width and height, respectively; you can get and set these properties.

You commence drawing the curve in the `Draw()` method by first initializing the `previous` variable to `position`, which defines the start point for the first line segment. You then iterate through the points in the `points` container, obtaining the absolute coordinates of each point by adding a `Size` object constructed from p to position. The `DrawLine()` member of the `Graphics` object draws the line; then, you store the last absolute point in `previous` so it becomes the first point for the next line segment. You will be able to improve this rather cumbersome mechanism for drawing a curve considerably in the next chapter.

Implementing the MouseMove Event Handler

The `MouseMove` event handler creates a temporary element object of the current type. Add a private member, `tempElement`, to the `Form1` class of type `Element^` to store the reference to the temporary element, and initialize it to `nullptr` in the initialization list for the `Form1` constructor. This temporary element will be stored eventually in the sketch by the `MouseUp` event handler, because the `MouseUp` event signals the end of the drawing process for an element, but you'll deal with this in the next chapter. Don't forget to add a `#include` directive for the `Elements.h` header at the beginning of the `Form1.h` header file; otherwise, the compiler will not recognize the `Element` type and the code won't compile.

You want to create an element in the `MouseMove` event handler only when the `drawing` member of the `Form1` class is `true`, because this is how the `MouseDown` event handler records that the drawing of an element has started. Here's the code for implementing the `MouseMove` event handler that you added to the `Form1` class earlier:

```
private: System::Void Form1_MouseMove(System::Object^  sender,
System::Windows::Forms::MouseEventArgs^  e)
{
```

```
if(drawing)
{
  switch(elementType)
  {
    case ElementType::LINE:
      tempElement = gcnew Line(color, firstPoint, e->Location);
      break;
    case ElementType::RECTANGLE:
      tempElement = gcnew Rectangle(color, firstPoint, e->Location);
      break;
    case ElementType::CIRCLE:
      tempElement = gcnew Circle(color, firstPoint, e->Location);
      break;
    case ElementType::CURVE:
      if(tempElement)
        safe_cast<Curve^>(tempElement)->Add(e->Location);
      else
        tempElement = gcnew Curve(color, firstPoint, e->Location);
      break;
  }
  Invalidate();
  }
}
```

If `drawing` is `false`, the handler does nothing. The `switch` statement determines which type of element is to be created from the `elementType` member of the `Form1` object. Creating lines, rectangles, and circles is very simple: just use the appropriate class constructor. You obtain the current mouse cursor position as you did in the `MouseDown` event handler — by using the `Location` property for the `MouseEventArgs` object.

Creating a curve is different. You create a new `Curve` object only if `tempElement` is `nullptr`, which will occur the first time this handler is called when you are drawing a curve. On all subsequent occasions, `tempElement` won't be `nullptr`, and you cast the reference to type `Curve` so that you can call the `Add()` function for the `Curve` object.

Calling `Invalidate()` for the `Form1` object causes the form to be redrawn, which results in the `Paint` event handler for the form being called. Obviously, this is where you will draw the entire sketch eventually, and you'll implement that mechanism properly in the next chapter.

Implementing the MouseUp Event Handler

The task of the `MouseUp` event handler is to store the new element in the sketch, to reset `tempElement` back to `nullptr` and the `drawing` indicator back to `false`, and to redraw the sketch. Here's the code to do that:

```
private: System::Void Form1_MouseUp(System::Object^  sender,
    System::Windows::Forms::MouseEventArgs^  e)
{
  if(!drawing)
    return;
  if(tempElement)
  {
    // Store the element in the sketch...
```

```
      tempElement = nullptr;
//    Invalidate();
    }
    drawing = false;
  }
```

If `drawing` is `false`, you return immediately, because the element drawing process has not started. The second `if` statement verifies that `tempElement` is not `nullptr` before adding the element to the sketch. You might think that if you get to this point, `tempElement` must exist, but this is not so; apart from the fact that the ability to draw a curve is not yet implemented, a user might press the left mouse button and release it immediately, in which case, the `MouseMove` handler would not be invoked at all. Of course, you need to call `Invalidate()` only to redraw the form when you have added a new element to the sketch. The call to `Invalidate()` is commented out for the moment because there is no sketch at present, and redrawing the form here would cause the temporary element to disappear as soon as you released the mouse button.

Implementing the Paint Event Handler for the Form

The `Paint` event delegate that you generated earlier has two parameters: the first parameter, of type `Object^`, identifies the source of the event, and the second, of type `System::Windows::Forms::PaintEventArgs`, provides information about the event. In particular, the `Graphics` property for the second parameter provides the `Graphics` object that you use to draw on the form.

You call the `Invalidate()` function for the form in the `MouseUp` event handler to draw the sketch, and in the `MouseMove` event handler to draw the temporary element. Therefore, the `Paint` event handler must eventually do two things: it must draw the sketch and it must draw the temporary element, but only if there is one. Here's the code:

```
private: System::Void Form1_Paint(System::Object^ sender,
                                  System::Windows::Forms::PaintEventArgs^ e)
{
  Graphics^ g = e->Graphics;
  // Code to draw the sketch...
  if(tempElement != nullptr)
  {
    tempElement->Draw(g);
  }
}
```

You initialize the local variable, `g`, with the value obtained from the `Graphics` property for the `PaintEventArgs` object, e. If `tempElement` is not `nullptr`, you call the `Draw()` function to display the element.

If you compile and execute CLR Sketcher, you'll see that you can create elements in any color. Of course, the elements are not displayed on an ongoing basis because there is no sketch object. As soon as you draw a new element, the existing one disappears. You will fix that in the next chapter.

SUMMARY

After completing this chapter, you should have a good grasp of how to write message handlers for the mouse, and how to organize drawing operations in your Windows programs. You have seen how using polymorphism with the shape classes makes it possible to operate on any shape in the same way, regardless of its actual type. The C++/CLI version of Sketcher demonstrates how much easier the .NET environment is to work with than native C++ with the MFC.

EXERCISES

You can download the source code for the examples in the book and the solutions to the following exercises from www.wrox.com. Don't forget to back up the MFC Sketcher and CLR Sketcher projects before you modify them for the exercises, because you will be extending them further in the next chapter.

1. Add the menu item and Toolbar button to MFC Sketcher for an element of type `ellipse`, as in the exercises from Chapter 15, and define a class to support drawing ellipses defined by two points on opposite corners of their enclosing rectangle.

2. Which functions now need to be modified to support the drawing of an ellipse? Modify the program to draw an ellipse.

3. Which functions must you modify in the example from the previous exercise so that the first point defines the center of the ellipse, and the current cursor position defines a corner of the enclosing rectangle? Modify the example to work this way. (Hint: look up the `CPoint` class members in Help.)

4. Add a new menu pop-up to the `IDR_SketcherTYPE` menu for Pen Style, to allow solid, dashed, dotted, dash-dotted, and dash-dot-dotted lines to be specified.

5. Which parts of the program need to be modified to support the operation of the menu, and the drawing of elements in the line types listed in the previous exercise?

6. Implement support for the new menu pop-up and drawing elements in any of the line types.

7. Modify CLR Sketcher to support the drawing of an ellipse defined by two points on opposite corners of the enclosing rectangle. Add a toolbar button as well as a menu item to select ellipse mode.

8. Implement a Line Style menu in CLR Sketcher with menu items Solid, Dashed, and Dotted. Add toolbar buttons with tooltips for the menu items. Implement the capability in CLR Sketcher for drawing elements in any of the three line styles in the new menu. Create your own representation for the line styles by setting the `DashPattern` property for the pen appropriately.

▶ **WHAT YOU LEARNED IN THIS CHAPTER**

TOPIC	CONCEPT
The client coordinate system	By default, Windows addresses the client area of a window using a client coordinate system with the origin in the upper-left corner of the client area. The positive x direction is from left to right, and the positive y direction is from top to bottom.
Drawing in the client area	You can draw in the client area of a window only by using a device context.
Device contexts	A device context provides a range of logical coordinate systems called mapping modes for addressing the client area of a window.
Mapping modes	The default origin position for a mapping mode is the upper-left corner of the client area. The default mapping mode is MM_TEXT, which provides coordinates measured in pixels. The positive x-axis runs from left to right in this mode, and the positive y-axis from top to bottom.
Drawing in a window	Your program should always draw the permanent contents of the client area of a window in response to a WM_PAINT message, although temporary entities can be drawn at other times. All the drawing for your application document should be controlled from the OnDraw() member function of a view class. This function is called when a WM_PAINT message is received by your application.
Redrawing a window	You can identify the part of the client area you want to have redrawn by calling the InvalidateRect() function member of your view class. The area passed as an argument is added by Windows to the total area to be redrawn when the next WM_PAINT message is sent to your application.
Mouse messages	Windows sends standard messages to your application for mouse events. You can create handlers to deal with these messages by using the Class Wizard.
Capturing mouse messages	You can cause all mouse messages to be routed to your application by calling the SetCapture() function in your view class. You must release the mouse when you're finished with it by calling the ReleaseCapture() function. If you fail to do this, other applications are unable to receive mouse messages.
Rubber-banding	You can implement rubber-banding during the creation of geometric entities by drawing them in the message handler for mouse movements.
Selecting a drawing mode	The SetROP2() member of the CDC class enables you to set drawing modes. Selecting the right drawing mode greatly simplifies rubber-banding operations.
Adding event handlers	The Properties window for a GUI component also enables you to add event handler functions automatically.
The Graphics class	The System::Drawing::Graphics class defines functions that enable you to draw on a form.
The Pen class	The System::Drawing::Pen class defines an object for drawing in a given color and line style.

17

Creating the Document and Improving the View

WHAT YOU WILL LEARN IN THIS CHAPTER:

➤ How to use an STL list container and an STL/CLR list container to store sketch data

➤ How to implement drawing a sketch in the MFC and CLR versions of Sketcher

➤ How to implement scrolling in a view in MFC Sketcher

➤ How to create a context menu at the cursor

➤ How to highlight the element nearest the cursor to provide feedback to the user for moving and deleting elements

➤ How to program the mouse to move and delete elements

In this chapter, you'll extend the MFC version of Sketcher to make the document view more flexible, introducing several new techniques in the process. You'll also extend the MFC and CLR versions of Sketcher to store elements in an object that encapsulates a complete sketch.

CREATING THE SKETCH DOCUMENT

The document in the Sketcher application needs to be able to store a sketch consisting of an arbitrary collection of lines, rectangles, circles, and curves in any sequence, and an excellent vehicle for handling this is a list. Using a list will also enable you to change an element's position in the list or to delete an element easily if it becomes necessary to do so. Because all the element classes that you've defined include the capability for the objects to draw themselves, the user will be able to a draw a sketch easily by stepping through the list.

Using a list<T> Container for the Sketch

You can define an STL `list<CElement*>` container that stores pointers to instances of the shape classes that make up a sketch. You just need to add the list declaration as a new member in the `CSketcherDoc` class definition. You also need a member function to add an element to the list, and `AddElement()` is a good, if unoriginal, name for this:

```cpp
// SketcherDoc.h : interface of the CSketcherDoc class
//

#pragma once
#include <list>
#include "Elements.h"
#include "SketcherConstants.h"

class CSketcherDoc: public CDocument
{
protected: // create from serialization only
    CSketcherDoc();
    DECLARE_DYNCREATE(CSketcherDoc)

// Attributes
public:

// Operations
public:
    unsigned int GetElementType() const      // Get the element type
        { return m_Element; }
    COLORREF GetElementColor() const         // Get the element color
        { return m_Color; }
    void AddElement(CElement* pElement)       // Add an element to the list
        { m_ElementList.push_back(pElement); }
// Rest of the class as before...

protected:
    ElementType m_Element;                   // Current element type
    COLORREF m_Color;                        // Current drawing color
    std::list<CElement*> m_ElementList;      // List of elements in the sketch

// Rest of the class as before...

};
```

code snippet SketcherDoc.h

The `CSketcherDoc` class now refers to the `CElement` class, so there is an `#include` directive for `Elements.h` in `SketcherDoc.h`. There is also one for the `list` header because you are using the STL `list<>` template.

You create shape objects on the heap, so you can just pass a pointer to the `AddElement()` function. Because all this function does is add an element, you have put the implementation of `AddElement()` in the class definition. Adding an element to the list requires only one statement, which calls the `push_back()` member function. That's all you need to create the document, but you still have to consider what happens when a document is closed. You must ensure that the list of pointers and all the elements they point to are destroyed properly. To do this, you need to add code to the destructor for CSketcherDoc objects.

Implementing the Document Destructor

In the destructor, you'll first go through the list deleting the element pointed to by each entry. After that is complete, you must delete the pointers from the list. The code to do this is as follows:

```
CSketcherDoc::~CSketcherDoc(void)
{
  // Delete the element pointed to by each list entry
  for(auto iter = m_ElementList.begin() ; iter != m_ElementList.end() ; ++iter)
    delete *iter;

  m_ElementList.clear();    // Finally delete all pointers
}
```

You should add this code to the definition of the destructor in SketcherDoc.cpp. You can go directly to the code for the destructor through the Class View.

The for loop iterates over all the elements in the list. The auto keyword ensures the correct type is specified for the iterator iter. When the for loop ends, you call the clear() function for the list to remove all the pointers from the list.

Drawing the Document

Because the document owns the list of elements and the list is protected, you can't use it directly from the view. The OnDraw() member of the view does need to be able to call the Draw() member for each of the elements in the list, though, so you need to consider how best to arrange this. One possibility is to make some const iterators for the m_ElementList member of the document class available. This will allow the view class object to call the Draw() function for each element, but will prevent the list from being changed. You can add two more functions to the CSketcherDoc class definition to provide for this:

```
class CSketcherDoc: public CDocument
{

// Rest of the class as before...

// Operations
public:
    unsigned int GetElementType() const // Get the element type
        { return m_Element; }
    COLORREF GetElementColor() const    // Get the element color
        { return m_Color; }
    void AddElement(CElement* pElement) // Add an element to the list
        { m_ElementList.AddTail(pElement); }
    std::list<CElement*>::const_iterator begin() const // Get list begin iterator
                    { return m_ElementList.begin(); }
    std::list<CElement*>::const_iterator end() const    // Get list end iterator
                    { return m_ElementList.end(); }

// Rest of the class as before...

};
```

The `begin()` function returns an iterator that points to the first element in the list, and the `end()` function returns an iterator that points to one past the last element in the list. The iterator type is defined in the `list<>` class template as `const_iterator`, but because the iterator type is specific to a particular instance of the template, you must qualify the type name with the list instance type.

By using the two functions you have added to the document class, the `OnDraw()` function for the view will be able to iterate through the list, calling the `Draw()` function for each element. This implementation of `OnDraw()` is as follows:

Available for
download on
Wrox.com

```
void CSketcherView::OnDraw(CDC* pDC)
{
    CSketcherDoc* pDoc = GetDocument();
    ASSERT_VALID(pDoc);
    if(!pDoc)
        return;

    CElement* pElement(nullptr);
    for(auto iter = pDoc->begin() ; iter != pDoc->end() ; ++iter)
    {
        pElement = *iter;
        if(pDC->RectVisible(pElement->GetBoundRect())) // If the element is visible
            pElement->Draw(pDC);                       // ...draw it
    }
}
```

Code snippet SketcherView.cpp

Frequently, when a `WM_PAINT` message is sent to your program, only part of the window needs to be redrawn. When Windows sends the `WM_PAINT` message to a window, it also defines an area in the client area of the window, and only this area needs to be redrawn. The `CDC` class provides a member function, `RectVisible()`, which determines whether a rectangle you supply to it as an argument overlaps the area that Windows requires to be redrawn. Here, you use this function to make sure that you draw only the elements that are in the area Windows wants redrawn, thus improving the performance of the application.

You use the `begin()` and `end()` members of the document object in the `for` loop to iterate over all the elements in the list. The `auto` keyword determines the type of `iter` appropriately. Within the loop, you dereference `iter` and store it in the `pElement` variable. You retrieve the bounding rectangle for each element using the `GetBoundRect()` member of the object, and pass it to the `RectVisible()` function in the `if` statement. If the value returned by `RectVisible()` is true, you call the `Draw()` function for the current element pointed to by `pElement`. As a result, only elements that overlap the area that Windows has identified as invalid are drawn. Drawing on the screen is a relatively expensive operation in terms of time, so checking for just the elements that need to be redrawn, rather than drawing everything each time, improves performance considerably.

Adding an Element to the Document

The last thing you need to do to have a working document in our program is to add the code to the `OnLButtonUp()` handler in the `CSketcherView` class to add the temporary element to the document:

```
void CSketcherView::OnLButtonUp(UINT nFlags, CPoint point)
{
   if(this == GetCapture())
      ReleaseCapture();          // Stop capturing mouse messages

   // If there is an element, add it to the document
   if(m_pTempElement)
   {
      GetDocument()->AddElement(m_pTempElement);
      InvalidateRect(nullptr);   // Redraw the current window
      m_pTempElement = nullptr;  // Reset the element pointer
   }
}
```

Of course, you must check that there really is an element before you add it to the document. The user might just have clicked the left mouse button without moving the mouse. After adding the element to the list in the document, you call `InvalidateRect()` to get the client area for the current view redrawn. The argument of 0 invalidates the whole of the client area in the view. Because of the way the rubber-banding process works, some elements may not be displayed properly if you don't do this. If you draw a horizontal line, for instance, and then rubber-band a rectangle with the same color so that its top or bottom edge overlaps the line, the overlapped bit of line disappears. This is because the edge being drawn is XORed with the line underneath, so you get the background color back. You also reset the pointer `m_pTempElement` to avoid confusion when another element is created. Note that the statement deleting `m_pTempElement` has been removed.

Exercising the Document

After saving all the modified files, you can build the latest version of Sketcher and execute it. You'll now be able to produce art such as "The Happy Programmer," shown in Figure 17-1.

FIGURE 17-1

The program is now working more realistically. It stores a pointer to each element in the document object, so they're all automatically redrawn as necessary. The program also does a proper cleanup of the document data when it's deleted.

There are still some limitations in the program that you can address. For instance:

➤ You can open another view window by using the Window ⇨ New Window menu option in the program. This capability is built into an MDI application and opens a new view to an existing document, not a new document. If you draw in one window, however, the elements are not drawn in the other window. Elements never appear in windows other than the one in which they were drawn, unless the area they occupy needs to be redrawn for some other reason.

➤ You can draw only in the client area you can see. It would be nice to be able to scroll the view and draw over a bigger area.

➤ You can't delete an element, so if you make a mistake, you either live with it or start over with a new document.

These are all quite serious deficiencies that, together, make the program fairly useless as it stands. You'll overcome all of them before the end of this chapter.

IMPROVING THE VIEW

The first item that you can try to fix is the updating of all the document windows that are displayed when an element is drawn. The problem arises because only the view in which an element is drawn knows about the new element. Each view is acting independently of the others, and there is no communication between them. You need to arrange for any view that adds an element to the document to let all the other views know about it, and they need to take the appropriate action.

Updating Multiple Views

The document class conveniently contains a function, UpdateAllViews(), to help with this particular problem. This function essentially provides a means for the document to send a message to all its views. You just need to call it from the OnLButtonUp() function in the CSketcherView class whenever you have added a new element to the document:

```
void CSketcherView::OnLButtonUp(UINT nFlags, CPoint point)
{
   if(this == GetCapture())
      ReleaseCapture();                    // Stop capturing mouse messages

   // If there is an element, add it to the document
   if(m_pTempElement)
   {
      GetDocument()->AddElement(m_pTempElement);
      GetDocument()->UpdateAllViews(nullptr, 0, m_pTempElement); // Tell the views
      m_pTempElement = nullptr;            // Reset the element pointer
   }
}
```

When the m_pTempElement pointer is not nullptr, the specific action of the function has been extended to call the UpdateAllViews() member of your document class. This function communicates with the views by causing the OnUpdate() member function in each view to be called. The three arguments to UpdateAllViews() are described in Figure 17-2.

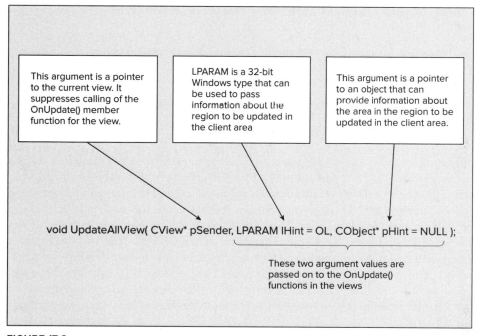

This argument is a pointer to the current view. It suppresses calling of the OnUpdate() member function for the view.

LPARAM is a 32-bit Windows type that can be used to pass information about the region to be updated in the client area

This argument is a pointer to an object that can provide information about the area in the region to be updated in the client area.

void UpdateAllView(CView* pSender, LPARAM lHint = OL, CObject* pHint = NULL);

These two argument values are passed on to the OnUpdate() functions in the views

FIGURE 17-2

The first argument to the UpdateAllViews() function call is often the this pointer for the current view. This suppresses the call of the OnUpdate() function for the current view. This is a useful feature when the current view is already up to date. In the case of Sketcher, because you are rubber-banding, you want to get the current view redrawn as well, so by specifying the first argument as 0 you get the OnUpdate() function called for all the views, including the current view. This removes the need to call InvalidateRect() as you did before.

You don't use the second argument to UpdateAllViews() here, but you do pass the pointer to the new element through the third argument. By passing a pointer to the new element, you allow the views to figure out which bit of their client area needs to be redrawn.

To catch the information passed to the UpdateAllViews() function, you must add an override for the OnUpdate() member function to the view class. You can do this from the Class View through the Properties window for CSketcherView. As I'm sure you recall, you display the properties for a class by right-clicking the class name and selecting Properties from the pop-up. If you click the Overrides button in the Properties window, you'll be able to find OnUpdate in the list of functions you can override. Click the function name, then the <Add> OnUpdate option that shows in the drop-down list in the adjacent column. You'll be able to edit the code for the

`OnUpdate()` override you have added in the Editor pane. You only need to add the highlighted code below to the function definition:

```
void CSketcherView::OnUpdate(CView* pSender, LPARAM lHint, CObject* pHint)
{
    // Invalidate the area corresponding to the element pointed to
    // if there is one, otherwise invalidate the whole client area
    if(pHint)
    {
        InvalidateRect(static_cast<CElement*>(pHint)->GetBoundRect());
    }
    else
    {
        InvalidateRect(nullptr);
    }
}
```

Note that you must uncomment at least the name of the third parameter in the generated version of the function; otherwise, it won't compile with the additional code here. The three arguments passed to the `OnUpdate()` function in the view class correspond to the arguments that you passed in the `UpdateAllViews()` function call. Thus, `pHint` contains the address of the new element. However, you can't assume that this is always the case. The `OnUpdate()` function is also called when a view is first created, but with a null pointer for the third argument. Therefore, the function checks that the `pHint` pointer isn't `nullptr` and only then gets the bounding rectangle for the element passed as the third argument. It invalidates this area in the client area of the view by passing the rectangle to the `InvalidateRect()` function. This area is redrawn by the `OnDraw()` function in this view when the next `WM_PAINT` message is sent to the view. If the `pHint` pointer is `nullptr`, the whole client area is invalidated.

You might be tempted to consider redrawing the new element in the `OnUpdate()` function. This isn't a good idea. You should do permanent drawing only in response to the Windows `WM_PAINT` message. This means that the `OnDraw()` function in the view should be the only thing that's initiating any drawing operations for document data. This ensures that the view is drawn correctly whenever Windows deems it necessary.

If you build and execute Sketcher with the new modifications included, you should find that all the views are updated to reflect the contents of the document.

Scrolling Views

Adding scrolling to a view looks remarkably easy at first sight; the water is, in fact, deeper and murkier than it at first appears, but jump in anyway. The first step is to change the base class for `CSketcherView` from `CView` to `CScrollView`. This new base class has the scrolling functionality built in, so you can alter the definition of the `CSketcherView` class to this:

```
class CSketcherView: public CScrollView
{
    // Class definition as before...
};
```

You must also modify two lines of code at the beginning of the SketcherView.cpp file that refer to the base class for CSketcherView. You need to replace CView with CScrollView as the base class:

```
IMPLEMENT_DYNCREATE(CSketcherView, CScrollView)

BEGIN_MESSAGE_MAP(CSketcherView, CScrollView)
```

However, this is still not quite enough. The new version of the view class needs to know some things about the area you are drawing on, such as the size and how far the view is to be scrolled when you use the scroller. This information has to be supplied before the view is first drawn. You can put the code to do this in the OnInitialUpdate() function in the view class.

You supply the information required by calling a function that is inherited from the CScrollView class: SetScrollSizes(). The arguments to this function are explained in Figure 17-3.

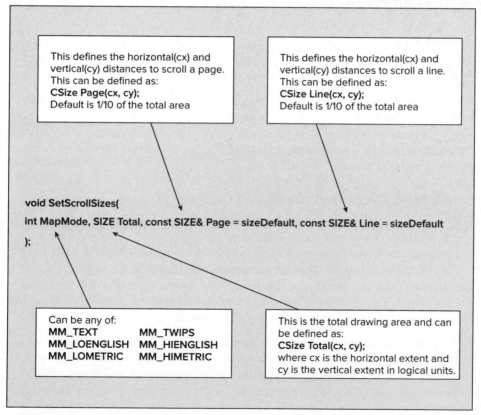

FIGURE 17-3

Scrolling a distance of one line occurs when you click on the up or down arrow on the scroll bar; a page scroll occurs when you click the scrollbar itself. You have an opportunity to change the mapping mode here. MM_LOENGLISH would be a good choice for the Sketcher application, but first get scrolling working with the MM_TEXT mapping mode because there are still some difficulties to be uncovered. (Mapping modes were introduced in Chapter 16.)

To add the code to call SetScrollSizes(), you need to override the default version of the OnInitialUpdate() function in the view. You access this in the same way as for the OnUpdate() function override — through the Properties window for the CSketcherView class. After you have added the override, just add the code to the function where indicated by the comment:

```
void CSketcherView::OnInitialUpdate()
{
    CScrollView::OnInitialUpdate();

    // Define document size
    CSize DocSize(20000,20000);

    // Set mapping mode and document size
    SetScrollSizes(MM_TEXT, DocSize, CSize(500,500), CSize(50,50));
}
```

This maintains the mapping mode as MM_TEXT and defines the total extent that you can draw on as 20,000 pixels in each direction. It also specifies a page scroll increment as 500 pixels in each direction and a line scroll increment as 50 pixels, because the defaults would be too large.

This is enough to get the scrolling mechanism working after a fashion. Build the program and execute it with these additions, and you'll be able to draw a few elements and then scroll the view. However, although the window scrolls OK, if you try to draw more elements with the view scrolled, things don't work as they should. The elements appear in a different position from where you draw them and they're not displayed properly. What's going on?

Logical Coordinates and Client Coordinates

The problem is the coordinate systems you're using — and that plural is deliberate. You've actually been using *two* coordinate systems in all the examples up to now, although you may not have noticed. As you saw in the previous chapter, when you call a function such as LineTo(), it assumes that the arguments passed are **logical coordinates**. The function is a member of the CDC class that defines a device context, and the device context has its own system of logical coordinates. The mapping mode, which is a property of the device context, determines what the unit of measurement is for the coordinates when you draw something.

The coordinate data that you receive along with the mouse messages, on the other hand, has nothing to do with the device context or the CDC object — and outside of a device context, logical coordinates don't apply. The points passed to the OnLButtonDown() and OnMouseMove() handlers have coordinates that are always in device units — that is, pixels — and are measured relative to the upper left corner of the client area. These are referred to as **client coordinates**. Similarly, when you call InvalidateRect(), the rectangle is assumed to be defined in terms of client coordinates.

In MM_TEXT mode, the client coordinates and the logical coordinates in the device context are both in pixels, and so they're the same — *as long as you don't scroll the window*. In all the previous examples, there was no scrolling, so everything worked without any problems. With the latest version of Sketcher, it all works fine until you scroll the view, whereupon the logical coordinates origin (the 0,0 point) is moved by the scrolling mechanism, so it's no longer in the same place as the client coordinates origin. The *units* for logical coordinates and client coordinates are the same here, but the *origins* for the two coordinates systems are different. This situation is illustrated in Figure 17-4.

The left side shows the position in the client area where you draw, and the points that are the mouse positions defining the line. These are recorded in client coordinates. The right side shows where the line is actually drawn. Drawing is in logical coordinates, but you have been using client coordinate values. In the case of the scrolled window, the line appears displaced because the logical origin has been relocated.

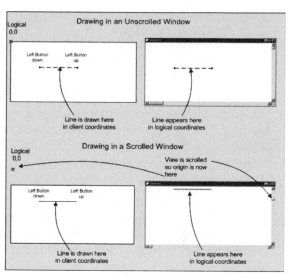

FIGURE 17-4

This means that you are actually using the wrong values to define elements in the Sketcher program, and when you invalidate areas of the client area to get them redrawn, the rectangles passed to the function are also wrong — hence, the weird behavior of the program. With other mapping modes, it gets worse, because not only are the units of measurement in the two coordinate systems different, but the *y* axes also may be in opposite directions!

Dealing with Client Coordinates

Consider what needs to be done to fix the problem. There are two things you may have to address:

➤ You need to convert the client coordinates that you got with mouse messages to logical coordinates before you can use them to create elements.

➤ You need to convert a bounding rectangle that you created in logical coordinates back to client coordinates if you want to use it in a call to InvalidateRect().

These amount to making sure you always use logical coordinates when using device context functions, and always use client coordinates for other communications about the window. The functions you have to apply to do the conversions are associated with a device context, so you need to obtain a device context whenever you want to convert from logical to client coordinates or vice versa. You can use the coordinate conversion functions of the CDC class inherited by CClientDC to do the work.

The new version of the OnLButtonDown() handler incorporating this is as follows:

```
// Handler for left mouse button down message
void CSketcherView::OnLButtonDown(UINT nFlags, CPoint point)
{
```

```
        CClientDC aDC(this);           // Create a device context
        OnPrepareDC(&aDC);             // Get origin adjusted
        aDC.DPtoLP(&point);           // Convert point to logical coordinates
        m_FirstPoint = point;         // Record the cursor position
        SetCapture();                 // Capture subsequent mouse messages
    }
```

You obtain a device context for the current view by creating a `CClientDC` object and passing the pointer `this` to the constructor. The advantage of `CClientDC` is that it automatically releases the device context when the object goes out of scope. It's important that device contexts are not retained, as there are a limited number available from Windows and you could run out of them. If you use `CClientDC`, you're always safe.

As you're using `CScrollView`, the `OnPrepareDC()` member function inherited from that class must be called to set the origin for the logical coordinate system in the device context to correspond with the scrolled position. After you have set the origin by this call, you use the function `DPtoLP()`, which converts from **Device Points to Logical Points**, to convert the `point` value that's passed to the handler to logical coordinates. You then store the converted point, ready for creating an element in the `OnMouseMove()` handler.

The new code for the `OnMouseMove()` handler is as follows:

```
void CSketcherView::OnMouseMove(UINT nFlags, CPoint point)
{
    CClientDC aDC(this);               // Device context for the current view
    OnPrepareDC(&aDC);                 // Get origin adjusted
    aDC.DPtoLP(&point);                // Convert point to logical coordinates
    if((nFlags&MK_LBUTTON)&&(this==GetCapture()))
    {
        m_SecondPoint = point;         // Save the current cursor position

    // Rest of the function as before...
}
```

The code for the conversion of the point value passed to the handler is essentially the same as in the previous handler, and that's all you need here for the moment. The last function that you must change is easy to overlook: the `OnUpdate()` function in the view class. This needs to be modified to the following:

```
void CSketcherView::OnUpdate(CView* pSender, LPARAM lHint, CObject* pHint)
{
    // Invalidate the area corresponding to the element pointed to
    // if there is one, otherwise invalidate the whole client area
    if(pHint)
    {
        CClientDC aDC(this);           // Create a device context
        OnPrepareDC(&aDC);             // Get origin adjusted

        // Get the enclosing rectangle and convert to client coordinates
        CRect aRect = static_cast<CElement*>(pHint)->GetBoundRect();
        aDC.LPtoDP(aRect);
        InvalidateRect(aRect);         // Get the area redrawn
    }
```

```
    else
  {
    InvalidateRect(nullptr);            // Invalidate the client area
  }
}
```

The modification here creates a `CClientDC` object and uses the `LPtoDP()` function member to convert the rectangle for the area that's to be redrawn to client coordinates.

If you now compile and execute Sketcher with the modifications I have discussed and are lucky enough not to have introduced any typos, it will work correctly, regardless of the scroller position.

Using MM_LOENGLISH Mapping Mode

Now, we will look into what you need to do to use the `MM_LOENGLISH` mapping mode. The advantage of using this mapping mode is that it provides drawings in logical units of 0.01 inches, which ensures that the drawing size is consistent on displays at different resolutions. This makes the application much more satisfactory from the user's point of view.

You can set the mapping mode in the call to `SetScrollSizes()` made from the `OnInitialUpdate()` function in the view class. You also need to specify the total drawing area: if you define it as 3,000 by 3,000, this provides a drawing area of 30 inches by 30 inches, which should be adequate. The default scroll distances for a line and a page are satisfactory, so you don't need to specify those. You can use the Class View to get to the `OnInitialUpdate()` function and then change it to the following:

```
void CSketcherView::OnInitialUpdate(void)
{
    CScrollView::OnInitialUpdate();

    // Define document size as 30x30ins in MM_LOENGLISH
    CSize DocSize(3000,3000);

    // Set mapping mode and document size.
    SetScrollSizes(MM_LOENGLISH, DocSize);
}
```

You just alter the arguments in the call to `SetScrollSizes()` for the mapping mode and the document size that you want. That's all that's necessary to enable the view to work in `MM_LOENGLISH`.

Note that you are not limited to setting the mapping mode once and for all. You can change the mapping mode in a device context at any time and draw different parts of the image to be displayed using different mapping modes. A function, `SetMapMode()`, is used to do this, but I won't be going into this any further here. You can get your application working just using `MM_LOENGLISH`. Whenever you create a `CClientDC` object for the view and call `OnPrepareDC()`, the device context that it owns has the mapping mode you've set in the `OnInitialUpdate()` function.

That should do it for the program as it stands. If you rebuild Sketcher, you should have scrolling working, with support for multiple views.

DELETING AND MOVING SHAPES

Being able to delete shapes is a fundamental requirement in a drawing program. One question relating to this is how you're going to select the element you want to delete. Of course, after you decide how you are going to select an element, your decision also applies to how you move an element, so you can treat moving and deleting elements as related problems. But first, consider how you're going to bring move and delete operations into the user interface for the program.

A neat way of providing move and delete functions would be to have a pop-up **context menu** appear at the cursor position when you click the right mouse button. You could then include Move and Delete as items on the menu. A pop-up that works like this is a very handy tool that you can use in lots of different situations.

How should the pop-up be used? The standard way that context menus work is that the user moves the mouse over a particular object and right-clicks it. This selects the object and pops up a menu containing a list of items relating to actions that can be performed on that object. This means that different objects can have different menus. You can see this in action in Developer Studio itself. When you right-click a class icon in Class View, you get a menu that's different from the one you get if you right-click the icon for a member function. The menu that appears is sensitive to the context of the cursor, hence the term "context menu." You have two contexts to consider in Sketcher. You could right-click with the cursor over an element, or you could right-click when there is no element under the cursor.

So how can you implement this functionality in the Sketcher application? You can do it simply by creating two menus: one for when you have an element under the cursor and one for when you don't. You can check if there's an element under the cursor when the user clicks the right mouse button. If there *is* an element under the cursor, you can highlight the element so that the user knows exactly which element the context pop-up is referring to.

First, take a look at how you can create a pop-up at the cursor, and, after that works, you can come back to how to implement the details of the move and delete operations.

IMPLEMENTING A CONTEXT MENU

You will need two context menu pop-ups: one for when there is an element under the mouse cursor, and another for when there isn't.

The first step is to create a menu containing Move and Delete as menu items that will apply to the element under the cursor. The other pop-up will contain a combination of menu items from the Element and Color menus. So change to Resource View and expand the list of resources. Right-click the Menu folder to bring up a context menu — another demonstration of what you are now trying to create in the Sketcher application. Select Insert Menu to create a new menu. This has a default ID `IDR_MENU1` assigned, but you can change this. Select the name of the new menu in the Resource View and display the Properties window for the resource by pressing Alt+Enter (this is a shortcut to the View ⇨ Other Windows ⇨ Properties Window menu item). You can then edit the resource ID in the Properties window by clicking the value for the ID. You could change it to something more suitable, such as `IDR_ELEMENT_MENU`, in the right column. Note that the name for a menu resource must start with `IDR`. Pressing the Enter key saves the new name.

You can now create a new item on the menu bar in the Editor pane. This can have any old caption because it won't actually be seen by the user; the caption element will be OK. Now you can add the Move and Delete items to the element pop-up. The default IDs of ID_ELEMENT_MOVE and ID_ELEMENT_DELETE will do fine, but you can change them if you want in the Properties window for each item. Figure 17-5 shows how the new element menu looks.

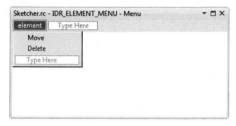

FIGURE 17-5

Save the menu and create another with the ID IDR_NOELEMENT_MENU; you can make the caption no element this time. The second menu will contain the list of available element types and colors, identical to the items on the Element and Color menus on the main menu bar, but here separated by a separator. The IDs you use for these items must be the same as the ones you applied to the IDR_SketcherTYPE menu. This is because the handler for a menu is associated with the menu ID. Menu items with the same ID use the same handlers, so the same handler is used for the Line menu item regardless of whether it's invoked from the main menu pop-up or from the context menu.

You have a shortcut that saves you from having to create all these menu items one by one. If you display the IDR_SketcherTYPE menu and extend the Element menu, you can select all the menu items by clicking the first item and then clicking the last item while holding down the Shift key. You can then right-click the selection and select Copy from the pop-up or simply press Ctrl+C. If you then return to the IDR_NOELEMENT_MENU and right-click the first item on the no element menu, you can insert the complete contents of the Element menu by selecting Paste from the pop-up or by pressing Ctrl+V. The copied menu items will have the same IDs as the originals. To insert the separator, just right-click the empty menu item and select Insert Separator from the pop-up. Repeat the process for the Color menu items and you're done.

Close the properties box and save the resource file. At the moment, all you have is the definition of the context menus in a resource file. It isn't connected to the code in the Sketcher program. You now need to associate these menus and their IDs with the view class. You also must create command handlers for the menu items in the pop-up corresponding to the IDs ID_ELEMENT_MOVE and ID_ELEMENT_DELETE.

Associating a Menu with a Class

Context menus are managed in an MFC program by an object of type CContextManager. The CSketcherApp class object already has a member of type CContextManager defined, and you can use this object to manage your context menus. Go to the CSketcherApp class in the Class View and go to the definition of the PreLoadState() member function. Add the following lines of code:

```
void CSketcherApp::PreLoadState()
{
/*
  BOOL bNameValid;
  CString strName;
  bNameValid = strName.LoadString(IDS_EDIT_MENU);
  ASSERT(bNameValid);
```

```
        GetContextMenuManager()->AddMenu(strName, IDR_POPUP_EDIT);
*/

    GetContextMenuManager()->AddMenu(_T("Element menu"), IDR_ELEMENT_MENU);
    GetContextMenuManager()->AddMenu(_T("No element menu"), IDR_NOELEMENT_MENU);
}
```

Code snippet SketcherApp.cpp

 NOTE *I have commented out the original lines of code that were there, to show that they are no longer required. You should remove these lines because they display the Edit menu as a context menu, and you don't want that to happen.*

Calling the `GetContextManager()` function for the application object returns a pointer to the `CContextManager` object. The `AddMenu()` function adds the menu specified by the second argument to the `CContextManager` object. The first argument specifies a name for the new menu. You can specify the name explicitly, as in the code here, or you can specify a resource ID for the string that is the name.

Note how the text strings in the first argument to the `AddMenu()` function are enclosed within the `_T()` macro. This is because we are using the Unicode version of the MFC libraries. The `_T()` macro selects the correct type for the string, depending on whether or not the `_UNICODE` symbol is defined for the project. You may remember we left the `Use Unicode libraries` option checked when we first created the Sketcher project. You should always use the `_T()` macro when defining string literals in a Unicode program. When you are using the MFC Unicode libraries, you should also use the `TCHAR` type instead of the `char` type in your code, `LPTSTR` instead of `char*`, and `LPCTSTR` instead of `const char*`.

A context menu can be displayed in response to a `WM_CONTEXTMENU` message, but the default code generated by the wizard calls the `OnContextMenu()` handler from the `OnRButtonUp()` handler. If you look at the `CSketcherView` class implementation, there should already be a definition of the `OnRButtonUp()` handler and the `OnContextMenu()` handler, and this is where you'll put the code to display the new context menus you have just defined. Note that the default code for the `OnRButtonUp()` handler calls `ClientToScreen()` to convert the coordinates of the current cursor position to screen coordinates.

You can then add the following code to the `OnContextMenu()` handler:

```
    void CSketcherView::OnContextMenu(CWnd* pWnd, CPoint point)
    {
#ifndef SHARED_HANDLERS

//  theApp.GetContextMenuManager()->ShowPopupMenu(IDR_POPUP_EDIT,
//                                      point.x, point.y, this, TRUE);
    if(m_pSelected)
      theApp.GetContextMenuManager()->ShowPopupMenu(IDR_ELEMENT_MENU,
                                    point.x, point.y, this);
    else
      theApp.GetContextMenuManager()->ShowPopupMenu(IDR_NOELEMENT_MENU,
                                    point.x, point.y, this);
#endif
}
```

The first line of code was already present, and I have commented it out to indicate that it is not required for Sketcher. You should remove this line because it displays the Edit menu as a context menu, and you don't want that to happen.

The new code chooses between the two context menus you have created based on whether or not the m_pSelected member is null. m_pSelected will store the address of the element under the mouse cursor, or nullptr if there isn't one. You will add this member to the view class in a moment. Calling the ShowPopupMenu() function for the CContextMenuManager object displays the pop-up identified by the first argument at the position in the client area specified by the second and third arguments.

Add m_pSelected as a protected member of the CSketcherView class as type CElement*. You can initialize this member to nullptr in the view class constructor.

Now, you can add the handlers for the items in the element pop-up menu. Return to the Resource View and double-click IDR_ELEMENT_MENU. Right-click the Move menu item and then select Add Event Handler from the pop-up. You can then specify the handler in the dialog for the Event Handler wizard. It's a COMMAND handler and you create it in the CSketcherView class. Click the Add and Edit button to create the handler function. You can follow the same procedure to create the hander for the Delete menu item.

You don't have to do anything for the no element context menu, as you already have handlers written for it in the document class. These automatically take care of the messages from the pop-up items.

Identifying a Selected Element

We will create a very simple mechanism for selecting an element. An element in a sketch will be selected whenever the mouse cursor is within the bounding rectangle for an element. For this to be effective, Sketcher must track at all times, whether or not there is an element under the cursor.

To keep track of which element is under the cursor, you can add code to the OnMouseMove() handler in the CSketcherView class. This handler is called every time the mouse cursor moves, so all you have to do is add code to determine whether there's an element under the current cursor position and set m_pSelected accordingly. The test for whether a particular element is under the cursor is simple: if the cursor position is within the bounding rectangle for an element, that element is under the cursor. Here's how you can modify the OnMouseMove() handler to determine whether there's an element under the cursor:

```
void CSketcherView::OnMouseMove(UINT nFlags, CPoint point)
{
  // Define a Device Context object for the view
  CClientDC aDC(this);              // DC is for this view
  OnPrepareDC(&aDC);                // Get origin adjusted
  aDC.DPtoLP(&point);               // Convert point to logical coordinates
  if((nFlags & MK_LBUTTON) && (this == GetCapture()))
  {
    // Code as before...
  }
```

```
      else
      {  // We are not creating an element, so select an element
        CSketcherDoc* pDoc=GetDocument();        // Get a pointer to the document
        m_pSelected = pDoc->FindElement(point);  // Set selected element
      }
    }
```

The new code is very simple and is executed only when we are not creating a new element. The `else` clause in the `if` statement calls the `FindElement()` function for the document object that you'll add shortly and stores the element address that is returned in `m_pSelected`. The `FindElement()` function has to search the document for the first element that has a bounding rectangle that encloses `point`. You can add `FindElement()` to the document class as a public member and implement it like this:

```
// Finds the element under the point
CElement* CSketcherDoc::FindElement(const CPoint& point)const
{
  for(auto rIter = m_ElementList.rbegin() ; rIter != m_ElementList.rend() ; ++rIter)
  {
    if((*rIter)->GetBoundRect().PtInRect(point))
      return *rIter;
  }
  return nullptr;
}
```

You use a reverse-iterator to search the list from the end, which means the most recently created and, therefore, last-drawn element will be found first. The `PtInRect()` member of the `CRect` class returns `TRUE` if the point you pass as the argument lies within the rectangle, and `FALSE` otherwise. Here, you use this function to test whether or not the point lies within any bounding rectangle for an element in the sketch. The address of the first element for which this is true is returned. If no element in the sketch is found, the loop will end and `nullptr` will be returned. The code is now in a state where you can test the context menus.

Exercising the Pop-Ups

You have added all the code you need to make the pop-ups operate, so you can build and execute Sketcher to try it out. When you right-click the mouse, or press Shift+F10, a context menu will be displayed. If there are no elements under the cursor, the second context pop-up appears, enabling you to change the element type and color. These options work because they generate exactly the same messages as the main menu options, and because you have already written handlers for them.

If there is an element under the cursor, the first context menu will appear with Move and Delete on it. It won't do anything at the moment, as you've yet to implement the handlers for the messages it generates. Try right-button clicks outside the view window. Messages for these are not passed to the document view window in your application, so the pop-up is not displayed.

Highlighting Elements

Ideally, the user will want to know which element is under the cursor *before* right-clicking to get the context menu. When you want to delete an element, you want to know which element you are operating on. Equally, when you want to use the other context menu — to change color, for example — you need to be sure no element is under the cursor when you right-click the mouse. To show precisely which element is under the cursor, you need to highlight it in some way before a right-button click occurs.

You can change the Draw() member function for an element to accommodate this. All you need to do is pass an extra argument to the Draw() function to indicate when the element should be highlighted. If you pass the address of the currently-selected element that you save in the m_pSelected member of the view to the Draw() function, you will be able to compare it to the this pointer to see if it is the current element.

All highlights will work in the same way, so let's take the CLine member as an example. You can add similar code to each of the classes for the other element types. Before you start changing CLine, you must first amend the definition of the base class CElement:

```cpp
class CElement : public CObject
{
   protected:
      int m_PenWidth;                 // Pen width
      COLORREF m_Color;               // Color of an element
      CRect m_EnclosingRect;          // Rectangle enclosing an element
   public:
      virtual ~CElement();
      // Virtual draw operation
      virtual void Draw(CDC* pDC, CElement* pElement=nullptr) {}

      CRect GetBoundRect() const;     // Get the bounding rectangle for an element

   protected:
      CElement();                     // Here to prevent it being called
};
```

Code snippet Elements.h

The change is to add a second parameter to the virtual Draw() function. This is a pointer to an element. The reason for initializing the second parameter to nullptr is that this allows the use of the function with just one argument; the second will be supplied as nullptr by default.

You need to modify the declaration of the Draw() function in each of the classes derived from CElement in exactly the same way. For example, you should change the CLine class definition to the following:

```cpp
class CLine :
   public CElement
{
   public:
      CLine(void);
      // Function to display a line
      virtual void Draw(CDC* pDC, CElement* pElement=nullptr);

      // Constructor for a line object
      CLine(const CPoint& Start, const CPoint& End, COLORREF aColor);
```

```
    protected:
        CPoint m_StartPoint;          // Start point of line
        CPoint m_EndPoint;            // End point of line

        CLine(void);                  // Default constructor - should not be used
};
```

The implementation for each of the `Draw()` functions for the classes derived from `CElement` needs to be extended in the same way. The function for the `CLine` class is as follows:

```
void CLine::Draw(CDC* pDC, CElement* pElement)
{
    // Create a pen for this object and
    // initialize it to the object color and line width m_PenWidth
    CPen aPen;
    if(!aPen.CreatePen(PS_SOLID, m_PenWidth,this==pElement ? SELECT_COLOR : m_Color))
    {
        // Pen creation failed. Abort the program
        AfxMessageBox(_T("Pen creation failed drawing a line"), MB_OK);
        AfxAbort();
    }

    CPen* pOldPen = pDC->SelectObject(&aPen);    // Select the pen

    // Now draw the line
    pDC->MoveTo(m_StartPoint);
    pDC->LineTo(m_EndPoint);

    pDC->SelectObject(pOldPen);                  // Restore the old pen
}
```

Code snippet Elements.cpp

This is a very simple change. The third argument to the `CreatePen()` function is now a conditional expression. You choose the color for the pen based on whether or not `pElement` is the same as the current `CLine` element pointer, `this`. If it is, you choose `SELECT_COLOR` for the pen rather than the original color for the line.

When you have updated the `Draw()` functions for all the subclasses of `CElement`, you can add the definition for `SELECT_COLOR` to the `SketcherConstants.h` file:

```
// SketcherConstants.h : Definitions of constants
//Definitions of constants

#pragma once

// Element type definitions
enum ElementType{LINE, RECTANGLE, CIRCLE, CURVE};

// Color values for drawing
const COLORREF BLACK = RGB(0,0,0);
const COLORREF RED = RGB(255,0,0);
const COLORREF GREEN = RGB(0,255,0);
const COLORREF BLUE = RGB(0,0,255);
```

```
const COLORREF SELECT_COLOR = RGB(255,0,180);
/////////////////////////////////////
```

Code snippet SketcherConstants.h

You have nearly implemented the highlighting. The derived classes of the CElement class are now able to draw themselves as selected when required — you just need a mechanism to cause an element to *be* selected. So where should you create this? You can determine which element, if any, is under the cursor in the OnMouseMove() handler in the CSketcherView class, so that's obviously the place to expedite the highlighting.

The amendments to the OnMouseMove() handler are as follows:

```
void CSketcherView::OnMouseMove(UINT nFlags, CPoint point)
{
  // Define a Device Context object for the view
  CClientDC aDC(this);                       // DC is for this view
  OnPrepareDC(&aDC);                         // Get origin adjusted
  aDC.DPtoLP(&point);                        // Convert point to logical coordinates
  if((nFlags & MK_LBUTTON) && (this == GetCapture()))
  {
    // Code as before...
  }
  else
  { // We are not creating an element to do highlighting
    CSketcherDoc* pDoc=GetDocument();        // Get a pointer to the document
    CElement* pOldSelected(m_pSelected);
    m_pSelected = pDoc->FindElement(point);   // Set selected element
    if(m_pSelected != pOldSelected)
    {
      if(m_pSelected)
        InvalidateRect(m_pSelected->GetBoundRect(), FALSE);
      if(pOldSelected)
        InvalidateRect(pOldSelected->GetBoundRect(), FALSE);
      pDoc->UpdateAllViews(nullptr);
    }
  }
}
```

You must keep track of any previously highlighted element because, if there's a new one, you must un-highlight the old one. To do this, you save the value of m_pSelected in pOldSelected before you check for a selected element. You then store the address returned by the FindElement() function for the document object in m_pSelected.

If pOldSelected and m_pSelected are equal, then either they both contain the address of the same element or they are both zero. If they both contain a valid address, the element will already have been highlighted last time around. If they are both zero, nothing is highlighted and nothing needs to be done. Thus, in either case, you do nothing.

Thus, you want to do something only when m_pSelected is not equal to pOldSelected. If m_pSelected is not nullptr, you need to get it redrawn, so you call InvalidateRect() with the first argument as the bounding rectangle for the element, and the second argument as FALSE so as not to erase the background. If pOldSelected is also not null, you must un-highlight the old element by invalidating its bounding rectangle in the same way. Finally, you call UpdateAllViews() for the document object to get the views updated.

Drawing Highlighted Elements

You still need to arrange that the highlighted element is actually drawn highlighted. Somewhere, the m_pSelected pointer must be passed to the draw function for each element. The only place to do this is in the OnDraw() function in the view:

```
void CSketcherView::OnDraw(CDC* pDC)
{
  CSketcherDoc* pDoc = GetDocument();
  ASSERT_VALID(pDoc);
  if (!pDoc)
    return;

  CElement* pElement(nullptr);
  for(auto iter = pDoc->begin() ; iter != pDoc->end() ; ++iter)
  {
    pElement = *iter;
    if(pDC->RectVisible(pElement->GetBoundRect())) // If the element is visible
        pElement->Draw(pDC, m_pSelected);          // ...draw it
  }
}
```

You need to change only one line. The Draw() function for an element has the second argument added to communicate the address of the element to be highlighted.

Exercising the Highlights

This is all that's required for the highlighting to work all the time. It wasn't trivial but, on the other hand, it wasn't terribly difficult. You can build and execute Sketcher to try it out. Any time there is an element under the cursor, the element is drawn in magenta. This makes it obvious which element the context menu is going to act on before you right-click the mouse, and means that you know in advance which context menu will be displayed.

Servicing the Menu Messages

The next step is to provide code in the bodies of the handlers for the Move and Delete menu items that you added earlier. You can add the code for Delete first, as that's the simpler of the two.

Deleting an Element

The code that you need in the OnElementDelete() handler in the CSketcherView class to delete the currently selected element is simple:

```
void CSketcherView::OnElementDelete()
{
  if(m_pSelected)
  {
    CSketcherDoc* pDoc = GetDocument();// Get the document pointer
    pDoc->DeleteElement(m_pSelected);  // Delete the element
    pDoc->UpdateAllViews(nullptr);     // Redraw all the views
    m_pSelected = nullptr;             // Reset selected element ptr
  }
}
```

The code to delete an element is executed only if m_pSelected contains a valid address, indicating that there is an element to be deleted. You get a pointer to the document and call the function DeleteElement() for the document object; you'll add this member to the CSketcherDoc class in a moment. When the element has been removed from the document, you call UpdateAllViews() to get all the views redrawn without the deleted element. Finally, you set m_pSelected to nullptr to indicate that there isn't an element selected.

You can add a declaration for DeleteElement() as a public member of the CSketcherDoc class:

```
class CSketcherDoc : public CDocument
{
protected: // create from serialization only
       CSketcherDoc();
       DECLARE_DYNCREATE(CSketcherDoc)

// Attributes
public:

// Operations
public:
       unsigned int GetElementType() const       // Get the element type
          { return m_Element; }
       COLORREF GetElementColor() const          // Get the element color
          { return m_Color; }
    void AddElement(CElement* pElement)          // Add an element to the list
       { m_ElementList.push_back(pElement); }
    std::list<CElement*>::const_iterator begin() const
       { return m_ElementList.begin(); }
    std::list<CElement*>::const_iterator end() const
       { return m_ElementList.end(); }
  CElement* FindElement(const CPoint& point) const;

  void DeleteElement(CElement* pElement);        // Delete an element

// Rest of the class as before...
};
```

It accepts as an argument a pointer to the element to be deleted and returns nothing. You can implement it in SketcherDoc.cpp as the following:

```
// Delete an element from the sketch
void CSketcherDoc::DeleteElement(CElement* pElement)
{
  if(pElement)
  {
    m_ElementList.remove(pElement);      // Remove the pointer from the list
    delete pElement;                     // Delete the element from the heap
  }
}
```

You shouldn't have any trouble understanding how this works. You use pElement with the remove() member of the list<CElement*> object to delete the pointer from the list, then you delete the element pointed to by the parameter pElement from the heap.

That's all you need in order to delete elements. You should now have a Sketcher program in which you can draw in multiple scrolled views, and delete any of the elements in your sketch from any of the views.

Moving an Element

Moving the selected element is a bit more involved. As the element must move along with the mouse cursor, you must add code to the OnMouseMove() method to provide for this behavior. As this function is also used to draw elements, you need a mechanism for indicating when you're in "move" mode. The easiest way to do this is to have a flag in the view class, which you can call m_MoveMode. If you make it of type BOOL, the Windows API Boolean type, you use the value TRUE for when move mode is on, and FALSE for when it's off. Of course, you can also define it as the C++ fundamental type, bool, with the values true and false.

You'll also have to keep track of the cursor during the move, so you can add another data member in the view for this. You can call it m_CursorPos, and it will be of type CPoint. Another thing you should provide for is the possibility of aborting a move. To do this, you must remember the first position of the cursor when the move operation started, so you can move the element back when necessary. This is another member of type CPoint, and it is called m_FirstPos. Add the three new members to the protected section of the view class:

```
class CSketcherView: public CScrollView
{
  // Rest of the class as before...

  protected:
    CPoint m_FirstPoint;        // First point recorded for an element
    CPoint m_SecondPoint;       // Second point recorded for an element
    CElement* m_pTempElement;   // Pointer to temporary element
    CElement* m_pSelected;      // Currently selected element
    bool m_MoveMode;            // Move element flag
    CPoint m_CursorPos;         // Cursor position
    CPoint m_FirstPos;          // Original position in a move

    // Rest of the class as before...
};
```

These must also be initialized in the constructor for CSketcherView, so modify it to the following:

```
CSketcherView::CSketcherView()
: m_FirstPoint(CPoint(0,0))
, m_SecondPoint(CPoint(0,0))
, m_pTempElement(nullptr)
, m_pSelected(nullptr)
, m_MoveMode(false)
, m_CursorPos(CPoint(0,0))
, m_FirstPos(CPoint(0,0))
{
  // TODO: add construction code here
}
```

The element move process starts when the Move menu item from the context menu is selected. Now, you can add the code to the message handler for the Move menu item to set up the conditions necessary for the operation:

```
void CSketcherView::OnElementMove()
{
    CClientDC aDC(this);
    OnPrepareDC(&aDC);                  // Set up the device context
    GetCursorPos(&m_CursorPos);         // Get cursor position in screen coords
    ScreenToClient(&m_CursorPos);       // Convert to client coords
    aDC.DPtoLP(&m_CursorPos);           // Convert to logical
    m_FirstPos = m_CursorPos;           // Remember first position
    m_MoveMode = true;                  // Start move mode
}
```

You are doing four things in this handler:

1. Getting the coordinates of the current position of the cursor, because the move operation starts from this reference point.

2. Converting the cursor position to logical coordinates, because your elements are defined in logical coordinates.

3. Remembering the initial cursor position in case the user wants to abort the move later.

4. Setting the move mode on as a flag for the OnMouseMove() handler to recognize.

The GetCursorPos() function is a Windows API function that stores the current cursor position in m_CursorPos. Note that you pass a reference to this function. The cursor position is in screen coordinates (that is, coordinates measured in pixels relative to the upper-left corner of the screen). All operations with the cursor are in screen coordinates. You want the position in logical coordinates, so you must do the conversion in two steps. The ScreenToClient() function (which is an inherited member of the view class) converts from screen to client coordinates, and then you apply the DPtoLP() function member of the aDC object to the result to convert to logical coordinates.

After saving the initial cursor position in m_FirstPos, you set m_MoveMode to true so that the OnMouseMove() handler can deal with moving the element.

Now that you have set the move mode flag, it's time to update the mouse move message handler to deal with moving an element.

Modifying the WM_MOUSEMOVE Handler

Moving an element only occurs when move mode is on and the cursor is being moved. Therefore, all you need to do in OnMouseMove() is add code to handle moving an element in a block that gets executed only when m_MoveMode is TRUE. The new code to do this is as follows:

```
void CSketcherView::OnMouseMove(UINT nFlags, CPoint point)
{
    CClientDC aDC(this);                // DC is for this view
    OnPrepareDC(&aDC);                  // Get origin adjusted

    aDC.DPtoLP(&point);                 // Convert point to logical coordinates
```

```
  // If we are in move mode, move the selected element and return
  if(m_MoveMode)
  {
    MoveElement(aDC, point);          // Move the element
    return;
  }

  // Rest of the mouse move handler as before...
}
```

This addition doesn't need much explaining, really, does it? The `if` statement verifies that you're in move mode and then calls a function `MoveElement()`, which does what is necessary for the move. All you have to do now is implement this function.

Add the declaration for `MoveElement()` as a `protected` member of the `CSketcherView` class by adding the following at the appropriate point in the class definition:

```
void MoveElement(CClientDC& aDC, const CPoint& point); // Move an element
```

As always, you can also right-click the class name in Class View to do this, if you want to. The function needs access to the object encapsulating a device context for the view, aDC, and the current cursor position, point, so both of these are reference parameters. The implementation of the function in the `SketcherView.cpp` file is as follows:

```
void CSketcherView::MoveElement(CClientDC& aDC, const CPoint& point)
{
  CSize distance = point - m_CursorPos;   // Get move distance
  m_CursorPos = point;                    // Set current point as 1st for
                                          // next time

  // If there is an element selected, move it
  if(m_pSelected)
  {
    aDC.SetROP2(R2_NOTXORPEN);
    m_pSelected->Draw(&aDC, m_pSelected); // Draw the element to erase it
    m_pSelected->Move(distance);          // Now move the element
    m_pSelected->Draw(&aDC, m_pSelected); // Draw the moved element
  }
}
```

The distance to move the element that is currently selected is stored locally as a `CSize` object, `distance`. The `CSize` class is specifically designed to represent a relative coordinate position and has two public data members, `cx` and `cy`, which correspond to the x and y increments. These are calculated as the difference between the current cursor position, stored in `point`, and the previous cursor position, saved in `m_CursorPos`. This uses the subtraction operator, which is overloaded in the `CPoint` class. The version you are using here returns a `CSize` object, but there is also a version that returns a `CPoint` object. You can usually operate on `CSize` and `CPoint` objects combined. You save the current cursor position in `m_CursorPos` for use the next time this function is called, which occurs if there is a further mouse move message during the current move operation.

You implement moving an element in the view using the `R2_NOTXORPEN` drawing mode, because it's easy and fast. This is exactly the same as what you have been using during the creation of an element. You redraw the selected element in its current color (the selected color) to reset it to the background color, and then call the function `Move()` to relocate the element by the distance specified by `distance`. You'll add this function to the element classes in a moment. When the element has moved itself, you simply use the `Draw()` function once more to display it highlighted at the new position. The color of the element will revert to normal when the move operation ends, as the `OnLButtonUp()` handler will redraw all the windows normally by calling `UpdateAllViews()`.

Getting the Elements to Move Themselves

Add the `Move()` function as a virtual member of the base class, `CElement`. Modify the class definition to the following:

```
class CElement : public CObject
{
   protected:
     int m_PenWidth;                    // Pen width
     COLORREF m_Color;                  // Color of an element
     CRect m_EnclosingRect;             // Rectangle enclosing an element
   public:
     virtual ~CElement();

     // Virtual draw operation
     virtual void Draw(CDC* pDC, CElement* pElement=nullptr) {}
     virtual void Move(const CSize& aSize){} // Move an element

     CRect GetBoundRect();              // Get the bounding rectangle for an element

   protected:
     CElement();                        // Here to prevent it being called
};
```

As discussed earlier in relation to the `Draw()` member, although an implementation of the `Move()` function here has no meaning, you can't make it a pure virtual function because of the requirements of serialization.

You can now add a declaration for the `Move()` function as a `public` member of each of the classes derived from `CElement`. It is the same in each:

```
     virtual void Move(const CSize& aSize); // Function to move an element
```

Next, you can add the implementation of the `Move()` function in the `CLine` class to `Elements.cpp`:

```
void CLine::Move(const CSize& aSize)
{
  m_StartPoint += aSize;              // Move the start point
  m_EndPoint += aSize;               // and the end point
  m_EnclosingRect += aSize;          // Move the enclosing rectangle
}
```

This is easy because of the overloaded `+=` operators in the `CPoint` and `CRect` classes. They all work with `CSize` objects, so you just add the relative distance specified by `aSize` to the start and end points for the line and to the enclosing rectangle.

Moving a CRectangle object is even easier:

```
void CRectangle::Move(const CSize& aSize)
{
  m_EnclosingRect+= aSize;              // Move the rectangle
}
```

Because the rectangle is defined by the m_EnclosingRect member, that's all you need to move it.

The Move() member of the CCircle class is identical:

```
void CCircle::Move(const CSize& aSize)
{
  m_EnclosingRect+= aSize;              // Move rectangle defining the circle
}
```

Moving a CCurve object is a little more complicated, because it's defined by an arbitrary number of points. You can implement the function as follows:

```
void CCurve::Move(const CSize& aSize)
{
  m_EnclosingRect += aSize;            // Move the rectangle
  // Now move all the points
  std::for_each(m_Points.begin(), m_Points.end(),
                        [&aSize](CPoint& p){ p += aSize; });
}
```

So that you don't forget about them, I have used an algorithm and a lambda expression here. You will need to add an #include directive for the algorithm header to Elements.cpp.

There's still not a lot to it. You first move the enclosing rectangle stored in m_EnclosingRect, using the overloaded += operator for CRect objects. You then use the STL for_each algorithm to apply the lambda expression that is the third argument to all the points defining the curve. The capture clause for the lambda expression accesses the aSize parameter by reference. Of course, the lambda parameter must be a reference so the original points can be updated.

Dropping the Element

Once you have clicked on the Move menu item, the element under the cursor will move around as you move the mouse. All that remains now is to add the capability to drop the element in position once the user has finished moving it, or to abort the whole move. To drop the element in its new position, the user clicks the left mouse button, so you can manage this operation in the OnLButtonDown() handler. To abort the operation, the user clicks the right mouse button — so you can add the code to the OnRButtonDown() handler to deal with this.

You can take care of the left mouse button first. You'll have to provide for this as a special action when move mode is on. The changes are highlighted in the following:

```
void CSketcherView::OnLButtonDown(UINT nFlags, CPoint point)
{
  CClientDC aDC(this);                 // Create a device context
  OnPrepareDC(&aDC);                   // Get origin adjusted
```

```
    aDC.DPtoLP(&point);                    // convert point to Logical

  if(m_MoveMode)
  {
    // In moving mode, so drop the element
    m_MoveMode = false;                    // Kill move mode
    m_pSelected = nullptr;                 // De-select the element
    GetDocument()->UpdateAllViews(0);      // Redraw all the views
    return;
  }
    m_FirstPoint = point;                  // Record the cursor position
    SetCapture();                          // Capture subsequent mouse messages
}
```

The code is pretty simple. You first make sure that you're in move mode. If this is the case, you just set the move mode flag back to `false` and then de-select the element. This is all that's required because you've been tracking the element with the mouse, so it's already in the right place. Finally, to tidy up all the views of the document, you call the document's `UpdateAllViews()` function, causing all the views to be redrawn.

Add a handler for the `WM_RBUTTONDOWN` message to `CSketcherView` using the Properties window for the class. The implementation for aborting a move must do two things. It must move the element back to where it was and turn off move mode. You can move the element back in the right-button-down handler, but you must leave switching off move mode to the right-button-up handler to allow the context menu to be suppressed. The code to move the element back is as follows:

```
void CSketcherView::OnRButtonDown(UINT nFlags, CPoint point)
{
  if(m_MoveMode)
  {
    // In moving mode, so drop element back in original position
    CClientDC aDC(this);
    OnPrepareDC(&aDC);                       // Get origin adjusted
    MoveElement(aDC, m_FirstPos);            // Move element to original position
    m_pSelected = nullptr;                   // De-select element
    GetDocument()->UpdateAllViews(nullptr);  // Redraw all the views
  }
}
```

You first create a `CClientDC` object for use in the `MoveElement()` function. You then call the `MoveElement()` function to move the currently selected element the distance from the current cursor position to the original cursor position that we saved in `m_FirstPos`. After the element has been repositioned, you just deselect the element and get all the views redrawn.

The last thing you must do is switch off move mode in the button-up handler:

```
void CSketcherView::OnRButtonUp(UINT /* nFlags */, CPoint point)
{
  if(m_MoveMode)
  {
    m_MoveMode = false;
    return;
  }
```

```
    ClientToScreen(&point);
    OnContextMenu(this, point);
}
```

Now, the context menu gets displayed only when move mode is not in progress.

Exercising the Application

Everything is now complete for the context pop-ups to work. If you build Sketcher, you can select the element type and color from one context menu, or if you are over an element, you can move that element or delete it from the other context menu.

DEALING WITH MASKED ELEMENTS

There's still a limitation that you might want to get over. If the element you want to move or delete is enclosed by the rectangle of another element that is drawn after the element you want, you won't be able to highlight it because Sketcher always finds the outer element first. The outer element completely masks the element it encloses. This is a result of the sequence of elements in the list. You could fix this by adding a Send to Back item to the context menu that would move an element to the beginning of the list.

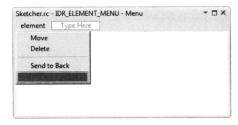

Add a separator and a menu item to the element drop-down in the IDR_ELEMENT_MENU resource, as shown in Figure 17-6.

FIGURE 17-6

You can add a handler for the item to the view class through the Properties window for the CSketcherView class. It's best to handle it in the view because that's where you record the selected element. Select the Events toolbar button in the Properties window for the class and double-click the message ID ID_ELEMENT_SENDTOBACK. You'll then be able to select COMMAND below and <Add>OnElementSendtoback in the right column. You can implement the handler as follows:

```
void CSketcherView:: OnElementSendtoback()
{
  GetDocument()->SendToBack(m_pSelected);   // Move element to start of list
}
```

You'll get the document to do the work by passing the currently selected element pointer to a public function, SendToBack(), that you implement in the CSketcherDoc class. Add it to the class definition with a void return type and a parameter of type CElement*. You can implement this function as follows:

```
void CSketcherDoc::SendToBack(CElement* pElement)
{
  if(pElement)
  {
```

```
        m_ElementList.remove(pElement);      // Remove the element from the list
        m_ElementList.push_front(pElement);  // Put it back at the beginning of the list
    }
}
```

After checking that the parameter is not `null`, you remove the element from the list by calling `remove()`. Of course, this does not delete the element from memory; it just removes the element pointer from the list. You then add the element pointer back at the beginning of the list, using the `push_front()` function.

With the element moved to the beginning of the list, it cannot mask any of the others because you search for an element to highlight from the end. You will always find one of the other elements first if the applicable bounding rectangle encloses the current cursor position. The Send to Back menu option is always able to resolve any element masking problem in the view.

EXTENDING CLR SKETCHER

It's time to extend CLR Sketcher by adding a class encapsulating a complete sketch. You'll also implement element highlighting and a context menu with the ability to move and delete elements. You can adopt a different approach to drawing elements in this version of Sketcher that will make the move element operation easy to implement. Before you start extending CLR Sketcher and working with the element classes, let's explore another feature of the `Graphics` class that will be useful in the application.

Coordinate System Transformations

The `Graphics` class contains functions that can move, rotate, and scale the entire drawing coordinate system. This is a very powerful capability that you can use in the element drawing operations in Sketcher. The following table describes the most useful functions that transform the coordinate system.

TRANSFORM FUNCTION	DESCRIPTION
`TranslateTransform(` `    float dx, float dy)`	Translates the coordinate system origin by `dx` in the x-direction and `dy` in the y-direction.
`RotateTransform(` `    float angle)`	Rotates the coordinate system about the origin by `angle` degrees. A positive value for `angle` represents rotation from the x-axis toward the y-axis, a clockwise rotation in other words.

`ScaleTransform(`
`    float scaleX,`
`    float scaleY)`
	Scales the x-axis by multiplying by `scaleX` and scales the y-axis by multiplying by `scaleY`.

`ResetTransform()`	Resets the current transform state for a `Graphics` object so no transforms are in effect.

You will be using the `TranslateTransform()` function in the element drawing operations. To draw an element, you can translate the origin for the coordinate system to the position specified by the inherited `position` member of the `Element` class, draw the element relative to the origin (0,0) and then restore the coordinate system to its original state. This process is illustrated in Figure 17-7, which shows how you draw a circle.

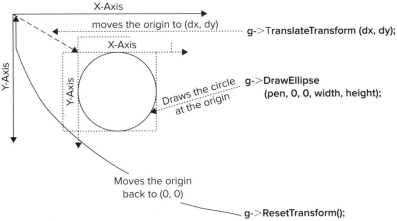

FIGURE 17-7

You can change the `Draw()` function in the `Circle` class to use the `TranslateTransform()` function:

```
virtual void Draw(Graphics^ g) override
{
    g->TranslateTransform(safe_cast<float>(position.X),
                          safe_cast<float>(position.Y));
```

```
    g->DrawEllipse(pen, 0, 0, width,height);
    g->ResetTransform();
}
```

The `TranslateTransform()` function requires arguments of type `float`, so you cast the coordinates to this type. This is not absolutely necessary, but you will get warning messages from the compiler if you don't, so it is a good idea to always put the casts in.

To make the most efficient use of the `TranslateTransform()` function when drawing a line, you could change the `Line` class constructor to store the end point relative to `position`:

```
Line(Color color, Point start, Point end)
{
  pen = gcnew Pen(color);
  this->color = color;
  position = start;
  this->end = end - Size(start);
  boundRect = System::Drawing::Rectangle(Math::Min(position.X, end.X),
                                         Math::Min(position.Y, end.Y),
                      Math::Abs(position.X - end.X), Math::Abs(position.Y - end.Y));

  // Provide for lines that are horizontal or vertical
  if(boundRect.Width < 2) boundRect.Width = 2;
  if(boundRect.Height < 2) boundRect.Height = 2;
}
```

The subtraction operator for the `Point` class enables you to subtract a `Size` object from a `Point` object. Here, you construct the `Size` object from the `start` object that is passed to the constructor. This results in the `end` member coordinates being relative to `start`.

Change the `Draw()` function in the `Line` class to the following:

```
virtual void Draw(Graphics^ g) override
{
  g->TranslateTransform(safe_cast<float>(position.X),
                        safe_cast<float>(position.Y));
  g->DrawLine(pen, 0, 0, end.X, end.Y);
  g->ResetTransform();
}
```

The `DrawLine()` function now draws the line relative to 0,0 after the `TranslateTransform()` function moves the origin of the client area to `position`, the start point for the line.

The `Draw()` function for the `Rectangle` class is very similar to that for the `Circle` class:

```
virtual void Draw(Graphics^ g) override
{
  g->TranslateTransform(safe_cast<float>(position.X),
                        safe_cast<float>(position.Y));
  g->DrawRectangle(pen, 0, 0, width, height);
  g->ResetTransform();
}
```

The `Draw()` function for the `Curve` class is simpler than before:

```
virtual void Draw(Graphics^ g) override
{
  g->TranslateTransform(safe_cast<float>(position.X),
                        safe_cast<float>(position.Y));
  Point previous(0,0);
  for each(Point p in points)
  {
    g->DrawLine(pen, previous, p);
    previous = p;
  }
  g->ResetTransform();
}
```

The points in the `points` vector all have coordinates relative to `position`, so once you transfer the client area origin to `position` using the `TranslateTransform()` method, each line can be drawn directly by means of the points in the `points` vector.

With the existing element classes updated, you are ready to define the object that will encapsulate a sketch.

Defining a Sketch Class

Using Solution Explorer, create a new header file with the name `Sketch.h` to hold the `Sketch` class; just right-click the Header Files folder and select from the pop-up. A sketch is an arbitrary sequence of elements of any type that has `Element` as a base class. An STL/CLR container looks a good bet to store the elements in a sketch, and this time you can use a `list<T>` container. To allow any type of element to be stored in the list, you can define the container class as type `list<Element^>`. Specifying that the container stores references of type `Element^` will enable you to store references to objects of any type that is derived from `Element`.

Initially, the `Sketch` class will need a constructor, an `Add()` function that adds a new element to a sketch, and a `Draw()` function to draw a sketch. Here's what you need to put in `Sketch.h`:

Available for
download on
Wrox.com

```
// Sketch.h
// Defines a sketch

#pragma once
#include <cliext/list>
#include "Elements.h"

using namespace System;
using namespace cliext;

namespace CLRSketcher
{
  public ref class Sketch
  {
  private:
    list<Element^>^ elements;

  public:
    Sketch()
```

```
      {
      elements = gcnew list<Element^>();
      }

      // Add an element to the sketch
      Sketch^ operator+=(Element^ element)
      {
        elements->push_back(element);
        return this;
      }

      // Remove an element from the sketch
      Sketch^ operator-=(Element^ element)
      {
        elements->remove(element);
        return this;
      }

      void Draw(Graphics^ g)
      {
        for each(Element^ element in elements)
          element->Draw(g);
      }
  };
}
```

code snippet Sketch.h

The #include directive for the <cliext/list> header is necessary for accessing the STL/CLR
list<T> container template, and the #include for the Elements.h header enables you to reference
the Element base class. The Sketch class is defined within the CLRSketcher namespace, so it can be
referenced without qualification from anywhere within the CLRSketcher application. The elements
container that the constructor creates stores the sketch. You add elements to a Sketch object by calling
its += operator overload function, which calls the push_back() function for the elements container
to store the new element. Drawing a sketch is very simple. The Draw() function for the Sketch object
iterates over all the elements in the elements container and calls the Draw() function for each of them.

To make the current Sketch object a member of the Form1 class, add a member of type Sketch^
with the name sketch to the class. You can add the initialization for sketch to the Form1
constructor:

```
Form1(void) : drawing(false), firstPoint(0),
              elementType(ElementType::LINE), color(Color::Black),
              tempElement(nullptr), sketch(gcnew Sketch())
  {
    InitializeComponent();
    //
    SetElementTypeButtonsState();
    SetColorButtonsState();
    //
  }
```

Code snippet Form1.h

Don't forget to add an `#include` directive for the `Sketch.h` header at the beginning of the `Form1.h` header. Now that you have the `Sketch` class defined, you can modify the `MouseUp` event handler in the `Form1` class to add elements to the sketch:

```
private: System::Void Form1_MouseUp(System::Object^  sender,

System::Windows::Forms::MouseEventArgs^  e)
{
  if(!drawing)
    return;
  if(tempElement)
  {
    sketch += tempElement;
    tempElement = nullptr;
    Invalidate();
  }
  drawing = false;
}
```

The function uses the `operator+=()` function for the `sketch` object when `tempElement` is not `nullptr`. After resetting `tempElement` to `nullptr`, you call the `Invalidate()` function to redraw the form. The final piece of the jigsaw in creating a sketch is the implementation of the `Paint` event handler to draw the sketch.

Drawing the Sketch in the Paint Event Handler

Amazingly, you need only one extra line of code to draw an entire sketch:

```
private: System::Void Form1_Paint(System::Object^  sender,
                                  System::Windows::Forms::PaintEventArgs^  e)
{
  Graphics^ g = e->Graphics;
  sketch->Draw(g);
  if(tempElement != nullptr)
    tempElement->Draw(g);
}
```

You pass the `Graphics` object, `g`, to the `Draw()` function for the `sketch` object to draw the sketch. This will result in `g` being passed to the `Draw()` function for each element in the sketch to enable each element to draw itself. Finally, if `tempElement` is not `nullptr`, you call the `Draw()` function for that, too. With the `Paint()` event handler complete, you should have a working version of CLR Sketcher.

A little later in this chapter, you will add the capability to pop up a context menu to allow elements to be moved as in the MFC version of Sketcher, but first, you need to get the element highlighting mechanism working.

Implementing Element Highlighting

You want to highlight an element when the mouse cursor is within the element's bounding rectangle, just like the MFC version of Sketcher. You will implement the mechanism to accomplish this in CLR Sketcher in a slightly different way.

The `MouseMove` event handler in `Form1` is the prime mover in highlighting elements because it tracks the movement of the cursor, but highlighting should occur only when there is not a drawing operation in progress. The first thing you need to do, before you can modify the `MouseMove` handler, is to implement a way for an element to draw itself in a highlight color when it is under the cursor. Add `highlighted` as a public property of the `Element` class of type `bool` to record whether an element is highlighted.

```
public:
  property bool highlighted;
```

You can also add a protected member to the `Element` class to specify the highlight color for elements:

```
Color highlightColor;
```

Add a public constructor to the `Element` class to initialize the new members:

```
Element() : highlightColor(Color::Magenta) {    highlighted = false;  }
```

You cannot initialize a property in the initialization list, so it must go in the body of the constructor.

As you will see, you will need external access to the bounding rectangle for an element, so you can add a public property to the `Element` class to provide this:

```
property System::Drawing::Rectangle bound
{
  System::Drawing::Rectangle get() { return boundRect; }
}
```

This makes `boundRect` accessible without endangering its integrity, because there is no `set()` function for the `bound` property.

Now, you can change the implementation of the `Draw()` function in each of the classes derived from `Element`. Here's how the function looks for the `Line` class:

```
virtual void Draw(Graphics^ g) override
{
  pen->Color = highlighted ? highlightColor : color;
  g->TranslateTransform(safe_cast<float>(position.X),
                        safe_cast<float>(position.Y));
  g->DrawLine(pen, 0, 0, end.X, end.Y);
  g->ResetTransform();
}
```

The extra statement sets the `Color` property for `pen` to `highlightColor` whenever `highlighted` is true, or to `color` otherwise. You can add the same statement to the `Draw()` function for the other element classes.

Finding the Element to Highlight

To highlight an element, you must discover which element, if any, is under the cursor at any given time. It would be helpful if an element could tell you if a given point is within the bounding rectangle. This process will be the same for all types of element, so you can add a public function to the `Element` base class to implement this:

```
bool Hit(Point p)
  {
    return boundRect.Contains(p);
    }
```

The `Contains()` member of the `System::Drawing::Rectangle` structure returns `true` if the `Point` argument lies within the rectangle, and `false` otherwise. There are two other versions of this function: one accepts two arguments of type `int` that specify the x and y coordinates of a point, and the other accepts an argument of type `System::Drawing::Rectangle` and returns `true` if the rectangle for which the function is called contains the rectangle passed as an argument.

You can now add a public function to the `Sketch` class to determine if any element in the sketch is under the cursor:

```
Element^ HitElement(Point p)
{
      for (auto riter = elements->rbegin(); riter != elements->rend(); ++riter)
      {
        if((*riter)->Hit(p))
          return *riter;
      }
    return nullptr;
}
```

This function iterates over the elements in the sketch in reverse order, starting with the last one added to the container, and returns a reference to the first element for which the `Hit()` function returns `true`. If the `Hit()` function does not return `true` for any of the elements in the sketch, the `HitElement()` function returns `nullptr`. This provides a simple way to detect whether or not there is an element under the cursor.

Highlighting the Element

Add a private member, `highlightedElement`, of type `Element^` to the `Form1` class to record the currently highlighted element and initialize it to `nullptr` in the `Form1` constructor. Because there's such a lot of code in the `Form1` class, it is best to do this by right-clicking the class name and selecting Add ⇨ Add variable. . . from the pop-up. Now, you can add code to the `MouseMove` handler to make the highlighting work:

```
private: System::Void Form1_MouseMove(System::Object^  sender,
    System::Windows::Forms::MouseEventArgs^  e)
{
  if(drawing)
  {
    if(tempElement)
      Invalidate(tempElement->bound);            // Invalidate old element area
    switch(elementType)
    {
      case ElementType::LINE:
```

```
            tempElement = gcnew Line(color, firstPoint, e->Location);
            break;
          case ElementType::RECTANGLE:
            tempElement = gcnew Rectangle(color, firstPoint, e->Location);
            break;
          case ElementType::CIRCLE:
            tempElement = gcnew Circle(color, firstPoint, e->Location);
            break;
          case ElementType::CURVE:
            if(tempElement)
              safe_cast<Curve^>(tempElement)->Add(e->Location);
            else
              tempElement = gcnew Curve(color, firstPoint, e->Location);
            break;
        }
        Invalidate(tempElement->bound);              // Invalidate new element area
        Update();                                    // Repaint
      }
      else
      {
        // Find the element under the cursor - if any
        Element^ element(sketch->HitElement(e->Location));
        if(highlightedElement == element)            // If the old is same as the new
          return;                                    // there's nothing to do

        // Reset any existing highlighted element
        if(highlightedElement)
        {
          Invalidate(highlightedElement->bound);  // Invalidate element area
          highlightedElement->highlighted = false;
          highlightedElement = nullptr;
        }
        // Find and set new highlighted element, if any
        highlightedElement = element;
        if(highlightedElement)
        {
          highlightedElement->highlighted = true;
          Invalidate(highlightedElement->bound);  // Invalidate element area
        }
        Update();                                    // Send a paint message
      }
    }
}
```

There's a change to the original code that is executed to improve performance when `drawing` is `true`. The old code redraws the entire sketch to highlight an element when, in fact, only the regions occupied by the un-highlighted element and the newly highlighted element need to be redrawn. The `Invalidate()` member of the `System::Windows::Forms::Form` class has an overloaded version that accepts an argument of type `System::Drawing::Rectangle` to add the rectangle specified by the argument to the currently invalidated region for the form. Thus, you can call `Invalidate()` repeatedly to accumulate a composite of rectangles to be redrawn.

Calling `Invalidate()` with a rectangle argument does not redraw the form, but you can get the invalid region redrawn by calling the `Update()` function for the form. You must pass the *enclosing* rectangle for an element to `Invalidate()`, rather than the bounding rectangle, to get elements redrawn properly, because the shapes extend beyond the right and bottom edges of the bounding rectangle by the thickness of the pen. You will therefore have to adjust the existing bounding rectangles to take the pen width into account if this is to work properly; you'll get to that in a moment.

You now pass the bounding rectangle of the old temporary element to the `Invalidate()` function to get just that area added to the region to be repainted. When you have created a new temporary element, you add its bounding rectangle to the region to be repainted. You finally call `Update()` for the `Form1` object to send a `WM_Paint` message. The effect of all this is that only the region occupied by the old and new temporary elements will be repainted, so the operation will be much faster than drawing the whole of the client area.

If `drawing` is `false`, you execute the highlighting code in the `else` clause. First, you get a reference to a new element under the cursor by calling the `HitElement()` function for the sketch. If the return value is the same as `highlightedElement`, either they are both `nullptr` or both reference the same element — either way, there's nothing further to be done.

If you don't return from the handler, you test for an existing highlighted element, and if there is one, you invalidate the rectangle it occupies and reset it by setting the value of its `highlighted` property to `false`. You then set `highlightedElement` back to `nullptr`. You store the `element` value in `highlightedElement`, and if this is not `null`, you set the `highlighted` member for the element to `true` and call `Invalidate()` with the bounding rectangle as the argument. Finally, you call `Update()` to redraw the invalid region.

The highlight code will execute repeatedly for every movement of the mouse cursor, so it needs to be efficient.

Adjusting the Bounding Rectangle for an Element

The existing bounding rectangles for the elements need to be inflated by the width of the pen. The pen width is available as a floating point value, as the `Width` property of a `Pen` object. Here's how you can modify the `Line` class constructor to inflate the bounding rectangles appropriately:

```
Line(Color color, Point start, Point end)
{
  pen = gcnew Pen(color);
  this->color = color;
  position = start;
  this->end = end - Size(start);
  boundRect = System::Drawing::Rectangle(Math::Min(position.X, end.X),
                                   Math::Min(position.Y, end.Y),
              Math::Abs(position.X - end.X), Math::Abs(position.Y - end.Y));
  int penWidth(safe_cast<int>(pen->Width));         // Pen width as an integer
  boundRect.Inflate(penWidth, penWidth);
}
```

There are just two additional statements. The first converts the `Width` property value for the pen to an integer and stores it locally. The second calls `Inflate()` for the `Rectangle` object. This inflates the width of the rectangle in both directions by the first argument value, and the height in both directions by the second argument value. Thus, both the width and height will increase by twice the pen width. Note that the statements that were there previously to ensure the width and height were greater than zero are no longer required, because both will always be at least twice the pen width.

You can add the same two statements to the end of the constructors for the `Rectangle` and `Circle` classes. The `Curve` constructor should be changed to the following:

```
Curve(Color color, Point p1, Point p2)
{
  pen = gcnew Pen(color);
  this->color = color;
  points = gcnew vector<Point>();
  position = p1;
  points->push_back(p2 - Size(position));

  // Find the minimum and maximum coordinates
  int minX = p1.X < p2.X ? p1.X : p2.X;
  int minY = p1.Y < p2.Y ? p1.Y : p2.Y;
  int maxX = p1.X > p2.X ? p1.X : p2.X;
  int maxY = p1.Y > p2.Y ? p1.Y : p2.Y;
  int width = maxX - minX;
  int height = maxY - minY;
  boundRect = System::Drawing::Rectangle(minX, minY, width, height);
  int penWidth(safe_cast<int>(pen->Width));        // Pen width as an integer
  boundRect.Inflate(penWidth, penWidth);
}
```

You also need to change the `Add()` member of the `Curve` class:

```
void Add(Point p)
{
  points->push_back(p - Size(position));

  // Modify the bounding rectangle to accommodate the new point
  int penWidth(safe_cast<int>(pen->Width));        // Pen width as an integer
  boundRect.Inflate(-penWidth, -penWidth);         // Reduce by the pen width
  if(p.X < boundRect.X)
  {
    boundRect.Width = boundRect.Right - p.X;
    boundRect.X = p.X;
  }
  else if(p.X > boundRect.Right)
    boundRect.Width = p.X - boundRect.Left;

  if(p.Y < boundRect.Y)
  {
    boundRect.Height = boundRect.Bottom - p.Y;
    boundRect.Y = p.Y;
  }
  else if(p.Y > boundRect.Bottom)
    boundRect.Height = p.Y - boundRect.Top;

  boundRect.Inflate(penWidth, penWidth);           // Inflate by the pen width
}
```

Once you have done this, you should find CLR Sketcher works with element highlighting in effect.

Creating Context Menus

You use the Design window to create context menus interactively by dragging a `ContextMenuStrip` control from the Toolbox window to the form. You need to display two different context menus, one for when there is an element under the cursor and one for when there isn't, and you can arrange for both possibilities using a single context menu strip. First, drag a `ContextMenuStrip` control from the Toolbox window to the form in the Design window; this will have the default name `ContextMenuStrip1`, but you can change this if you want. To make the context menu strip display when the form is right-clicked, display the Properties window for the form and set the `ContextMenuStrip` property in the Behavior group by selecting `ContextMenuStrip1` from the drop-down in the value column.

The drop-down for the context menu is empty at present, and you are going to control what menu items it contains programmatically. When an element is under the cursor, the element-specific menu items should display, and when there is no element under the cursor, menu items equivalent to those from the Element and Color menus should display. First, add a Send to Back menu item, a Delete menu item, and a Move menu item to the drop-down for the context menu by typing the entries into the design window. Change the (name) properties for the items to `sendToBackContextMenuItem`, `deleteContextMenuItem`, and `moveContextMenuItem`.

A menu item can belong to only one menu strip, so you need to add new ones to the context menu matching those in the Element and Color menus. Add a separator and then add menu items Line, Rectangle, Circle, and Curve, and Black, Red, Green, and Blue. Change the (name) property for each in the same way as the others, to `lineContextMenuItem`, `rectangleContextMenuItem`, and so on. Also change the (name) property for the separator to `contextSeparator` so you can refer to it easily.

You need `Click` event handlers for all the menu items in the context menu, but the only new ones you need to create are for the Move, Delete, and Send to Back items; you can set the handlers for all the other menu items to be the same as the corresponding items in the Element and Color menus.

You can control what displays in the drop-down for the context menu in the `Opening` event handler for the context menu strip, because this event handler is called before the drop-down displays. Open the Properties window for the context menu strip by right-clicking it and selecting Properties. Click the Events button in the Properties window and double-click the `Opening` event to add a handler. You are going to add different sets of menu items to the context menu strip, depending on whether or not an element is under the cursor; so how can you determine if anything is under the cursor? Well, the `MouseMove` handler for the form has already taken care of it. All you need to do is check to see whether the reference contained in the `highlightElement` member of the form is `nullptr` or not.

You have added items to the drop-down for `contextMenuStrip1` to add the code to create the objects in the `Form1` class that encapsulates them, but you want to start with a clean slate for the drop-down menu when it is to display, so you can set it up the way you want. In the Opening event handler, you want to remove any existing menu items before you add back the specific menu items you want. A ContextMenuStrip object that encapsulates a context menu stores its drop-down menu items in an Items property that is of type ToolStripItemsCollection^. To remove existing items from the drop-down, simply call Clear() for the Items property. To add a menu item to the context menu, call the Add() function for the Items property with the menu item as the argument.

The implementation of the Opening handler for the context menu strip is as follows:

```
private: System::Void contextMenuStrip1_Opening(System::Object^  sender,
System::ComponentModel::CancelEventArgs^  e)
{
  contextMenuStrip1->Items->Clear();     // Remove existing items
  if(highlightedElement)
  {
    contextMenuStrip1->Items->Add(moveContextMenuItem);
    contextMenuStrip1->Items->Add(deleteContextMenuItem);
    contextMenuStrip1->Items->Add(sendToBackContextMenuItem);
  }
  else
  {
    contextMenuStrip1->Items->Add(lineContextMenuItem);
    contextMenuStrip1->Items->Add(rectangleContextMenuItem);
    contextMenuStrip1->Items->Add(circleContextMenuItem);
    contextMenuStrip1->Items->Add(curveContextMenuItem);
    contextMenuStrip1->Items->Add(contextSeparator);
    contextMenuStrip1->Items->Add(blackContextMenuItem);
    contextMenuStrip1->Items->Add(redContextMenuItem);
    contextMenuStrip1->Items->Add(greenContextMenuItem);
    contextMenuStrip1->Items->Add(blueContextMenuItem);

    // Set checks for the menu items
    lineContextMenuItem->Checked = elementType == ElementType::LINE;
    rectangleContextMenuItem->Checked = elementType == ElementType::RECTANGLE;
    circleContextMenuItem->Checked = elementType == ElementType::CIRCLE;
    curveContextMenuItem->Checked = elementType == ElementType::CURVE;
    blackContextMenuItem->Checked = color == Color::Black;
    redContextMenuItem->Checked = color == Color::Red;
    greenContextMenuItem->Checked = color == Color::Green;
    blueContextMenuItem->Checked = color == Color::Blue;
  }
}
```

After clearing the context menu, you add a set of items to it depending on whether or not highlightedElement is null. You set the checks for the element and color menu items in the same way you did for the main menu, by setting the Checked property for each of the menu items.

All the element and color menu items in the context menu should now work, so try it out. All that remains is to implement the element-specific operations. Let's do the easiest one first.

Implementing the Element Delete Operation

The overloaded `-=` operator in the `Sketch` class already provides you with a way to delete an element. You can use the `operator-=()` function in the implementation of the `Click` event handler for the `Delete` menu item:

```
private: System::Void deleteContextMenuItem_Click(System::Object^ sender,
                                                  System::EventArgs^ e)
{
  if(highlightedElement)
  {
    sketch -= highlightedElement;              // Delete the highlighted element
    Invalidate(highlightedElement->bound);
    highlightedElement = nullptr;
    Update();
  }
}
```

As well as deleting the element from the sketch, the event handler also invalidates the region it occupies to remove it from the display, and resets `highlightedElement` back to `nullptr`.

Implementing the "Send to Back" Operation

The Send to Back operation works much as in MFC Sketcher. You remove the highlighted element from the list in the `Sketch` object and add it to the end of the list. Here's the implementation of the handler function:

```
private: System::Void sendToBackContextMenuItem_Click(System::Object^ sender,
                                                       System::EventArgs^ e)
{
  if(highlightedElement)
  {
    sketch -= highlightedElement;                  // Delete the highlighted
                                                   // element
    sketch->push_front(highlightedElement);        // Then add it back to the
                                                   // beginning

    highlightedElement->highlighted = false;
    Invalidate(highlightedElement->bound);
    highlightedElement = nullptr;
    Update();
  }
}
```

You delete the highlighted element using the `operator-=()` function, and then add it back to the beginning of the list using the `push_front()` function that you will define in the `Sketch` class in a moment. You reset the `highlighted` member of the element to `false` and `highlightedElement` to `nullptr` before calling `Invalidate()` for the form to redraw the region occupied by the previously highlighted element.

You can implement `push_front()` as a public function in the `Sketch` class definition as follows:

```
    void push_front(Element^ element)
    {
      elements->push_front(element);
    }
```

Implementing the Element Move Operation

You'll move an element by dragging it with the left mouse button down. This implies that a move operation needs a different set of functions from normal to be carried out by the mouse event handlers, so a move will have to be modal, as in the MFC version of Sketcher. You can identify possible modes with an enum class that you can add following the ElementType enum in Form1.h:

```
    enum class Mode {Normal, Move};
```

This defines just two modes, but you could add more if you wanted to implement other modal operations. You can now add a private member of type Mode with the name mode to the Form1 class. Initialize the new variable to Mode::Normal in the Form1 constructor.

The only thing the Click event handler for the Move menu item has to do is set mode to Mode::Move:

```
    private: System::Void moveContextMenuItem_Click(System::Object^  sender,

    System::EventArgs^  e)
    {
      mode = Mode::Move;
    }
```

The mouse event handlers for the form must take care of moving an element. Change the code for the MouseDown handler so it sets drawing to true only when mode is Mode::Normal:

```
    private: System::Void Form1_MouseDown(System::Object^  sender,

    System::Windows::Forms::MouseEventArgs^  e)
    {
      if(e->Button == System::Windows::Forms::MouseButtons::Left)
      {
        if(mode == Mode::Normal)
        {
          drawing = true;
        }
        firstPoint = e->Location;
      }
    }
```

This sets drawing to true only when mode has the value Mode::Normal. If mode has a different value, only the point is stored for use in the MouseMove event handler. The MouseMove event handler will not create elements when drawing is false, so this functionality is switched off for all modes except Mode::Normal. The MouseUp event handler will restore mode to Mode::Normal when a move operation is complete.

Moving an Element

Because you now draw all elements relative to a given position, you can move an element just by changing the inherited `position` member to reflect the new position and to adjust the location of the bounding rectangle in a similar way. You can add a public `Move()` function to the `Element` base class to take care of this:

```
void Move(int dx, int dy)
{
  position.Offset(dx, dy);
  boundRect.X += dx;
  boundRect.Y += dy;
}
```

Calling the `Offset()` function for the `Point` object, `position`, adds `dx` and `dy` to the coordinates stored in the object. To adjust the location of `boundRect`, just add `dx` to the `Rectangle` object's `X` field and `dy` to its `Y` field.

The `MouseMove` event handler will expedite the moving process:

```
private: System::Void Form1_MouseMove(System::Object^  sender,
 System::Windows::Forms::MouseEventArgs^  e) {
   if(drawing)
  {
    if(tempElement)
      Invalidate(tempElement->Bound);  // The old element region
    switch(elementType)
    {
       // Code to create a temporary element as before...
    }
    Invalidate(tempElement->bound);    // The new element region
    Update();
  }
    else if(mode == Mode::Normal)
  {
     // Code to highlight the element under the cursor as before
  }
  else if(mode == Mode::Move &&
                      e->Button ==
 System::Windows::Forms::MouseButtons::Left)
   { // Move the highlighted element
     if(highlightedElement)
     {
       Invalidate(highlightedElement->bound);     // Region before move
       highlightedElement->Move(e->X - firstPoint.X, e->Y - firstPoint.Y);
       firstPoint = e->Location;
       Invalidate(highlightedElement->bound);     // Region after move
       Update();
     }
   }
 }
```

This event handler now provides three different functions: it creates an element when `drawing` is true, it does element highlighting when `drawing` is `false` and `mode` is `Mode::Normal`, and it moves the currently highlighted element when mode is Mode::Move and the left mouse button is down. This means that moving an element in this version of Sketcher will work a little differently from in the native version. To move an element, you select Move from the context menu, then drag the element to its new position with the left button down.

The new else if clause executes only when mode has the value Mode::Move and the left button is down. Without the button test, moving would occur if you moved the cursor after clicking the menu item. This would happen without a MouseDown event occurring, which would create some confusion, as firstPoint would not have been initialized. With the code as you have it here, the moving process is initiated when you click the menu item and release the left mouse button. You then press the left mouse button and drag the cursor to move the highlighted element.

If there is a highlighted element, you invalidate its bounding rectangle before moving the element the distance from firstPoint to the current cursor location. You then update firstPoint to the current cursor position, ready for the next move increment, and invalidate the new region the highlighted element occupies. You finally call Update() to redraw the invalid regions of the form.

The last part you must implement to complete the ability to move elements is in the MouseUp event handler:

```
private: System::Void Form1_MouseUp(System::Object^  sender,
  System::Windows::Forms::MouseEventArgs^  e)
{
  if(!drawing)
  {
    mode = Mode::Normal;
    return;
  }
  if(tempElement)
  {
    sketch += tempElement;
    tempElement = nullptr;
    Invalidate();
  }
  drawing = false;
}
```

Releasing the left mouse button ends a move operation. The drawing variable is false when an element is being moved, and the only thing the handler has to do when this is the case is reset mode to Mode::Normal to end the move operation.

With that done, you should now have a version of CLR Sketcher in which you can move and delete elements, as illustrated in Figure 17-8.

The Send to Back facility ensures that any element can always be highlighted to be moved or deleted; if an element will not highlight,

FIGURE 17-8

just Send to Back any elements enclosing the element you want to move or delete. In Chapter 19, you will implement the capability to save a sketch in a file.

SUMMARY

In this chapter, you've seen how to apply STL collection classes to the problems of managing objects and managing pointers to objects. Collections are a real asset in programming for Windows, because the application data you store in a document often originates in an unstructured and unpredictable way, and you need to be able to traverse the data whenever a view needs to be updated.

You have also seen how to create document data and manage it in a pointer list in the document, and, in the context of the Sketcher application, how the views and the document communicate with each other.

You have improved the view capability in Sketcher in several ways. You've added scrolling to the views using the MFC class CScrollView, and you've introduced a pop-up at the cursor for moving and deleting elements. You have also implemented an element-highlighting feature to provide the user with feedback during the moving or deleting of elements.

CLR Sketcher has most of the features of MFC Sketcher, including drawing operations and a context menu, but you implemented some things a little differently because the characteristics of the CLR are not the same as the characteristics of MFC. The coding effort was considerably less than for MFC Sketcher because of the automatic code generation provided by the Forms Designer capability. The downside of using Forms Designer is that you can't control how the code is organized, and the Form1 class becomes rather unwieldy because of the sheer volume of code in the definition. However, the Class View is a great help in navigating around the class definition.

EXERCISES

You can download the source code for the examples in the book, and the solutions to the following exercises, from www.wrox.com.

1. Implement the CCurve class so that points are added to the head of a list instead of the back of a vector.

2. Implement the CCurve class in the Sketcher program using list of pointers instead of a vector of objects to represent a curve.

3. Look up the CArray template collection class in Help, and use it to store points in the CCurve class in the Sketcher program.

4. Add the capability in CLR Sketcher to change the color of an existing element. Make this capability available through the context menu.

▶ WHAT YOU LEARNED IN THIS CHAPTER

TOPIC	CONCEPT
Windows coordinate systems	When you draw in a device context using the MFC, coordinates are in logical units that depend on the mapping mode set. Points in a window that are supplied along with Windows mouse messages are in client coordinates. The two coordinate systems are usually not the same.
Screen coordinates	Coordinates that define the position of the cursor are in screen coordinates that are measured in pixels relative to the upper-left corner of the screen.
Converting between coordinate systems	Functions to convert between client coordinates and logical coordinates in an MFC application are available in the CDC class.
WM_PAINT messages	Windows requests that a view be redrawn by sending a WM_PAINT message to your MFC application. This causes the OnDraw() member of the affected view to be called.
The OnDraw() function	You should always do any permanent drawing of a document in the OnDraw() member of the view class in your MFC application. This ensures that the window is drawn properly when that is required by Windows.
Drawing efficiently	You can make your OnDraw() implementation more efficient by calling the RectVisible() member of the CDC class to check whether an entity needs to be drawn.
Updating multiple views	To get multiple views updated when you change the document contents, you can call the UpdateAllViews() member of the document object. This causes the OnUpdate() member of each view to be called.
Updating efficiently	You can pass information to the UpdateAllViews() function to indicate which area in the view needs to be redrawn. This makes redrawing the views faster.
Context menus	You can display a context menu at the cursor position in an MFC application in response to a right mouse click. This menu is created as a normal pop-up.
Menus and toolbars in Windows Forms applications	You create menu strips, context menus, and toolbars in a Windows Forms application by dragging the appropriate component from the Toolbox window to the form in the Forms Designer window. You cause the context menu to be displayed on the form in response to a right click by setting the ContextMenuStrip property for the form.
Creating event handlers in Windows Forms applications	You create event handlers for a component in a Windows Forms application through the Properties window for the component. You can change the name of the event handler function that is created by changing the value of its (name) property.
Controlling what is displayed in a menu	Implementing the DropDownOpening event handler for a menu item enables you to modify the drop-down before it displays.

18

Working with Dialogs and Controls

WHAT YOU WILL LEARN IN THIS CHAPTER:

➤ How to create dialog resources

➤ How to add controls to a dialog

➤ The basic varieties of controls available

➤ How to create a dialog class to manage a dialog

➤ How to program the creation of a dialog box, and how to get information back from the controls in it

➤ Modal and modeless dialogs

➤ How to implement and use direct data exchange and validation with controls

➤ How to implement view scaling

➤ How to add a status bar to an application

Dialogs and controls are basic tools for user communication in the Windows environment. In this chapter you'll learn how to implement dialogs and controls by applying them to extend the Sketcher program.

UNDERSTANDING DIALOGS

Of course, dialog boxes are not new to you. Most Windows programs of consequence use dialogs to manage some of their data input. You click a menu item and up pops a **dialog box** with various **controls** that you use for entering information. Just about everything that appears in a dialog box is a control. A dialog box is actually a window and, in fact, each of the controls in a dialog is also a specialized window. Come to think of it, most things you see on the screen under Windows are windows.

There are two things needed to create and display a dialog box in an MFC program: the physical appearance of the dialog box, which is defined in a resource file, and a dialog class object, used to manage the operation of the dialog and its controls. MFC provides a class called `CDialog` for you to use after you have defined your dialog resource.

UNDERSTANDING CONTROLS

Many different controls are available to you in Windows, and in most cases there's flexibility to how they look and operate. Most of them fall into one of the six categories shown in the following table.

CONTROL TYPE	WHAT THEY DO
Static controls	These are used to provide titles or descriptive information.
Button controls	Buttons provide a single-click input mechanism. There are basically three flavors of button controls: simple push buttons, radio buttons (of which only one may be in a selected state at any one time), and checkboxes (of which several may be in a selected state at one time).
Scrollbars	Scrollbars are typically used to scroll text or images, either horizontally or vertically, within another control.
List boxes	These present a list of choices of which one or more selections can be in effect at one time.
Edit controls	Edit controls allow text input or editing of text that is displayed.
Combo boxes	Combo boxes present a list of choices from which you can select, combined with the option of entering text yourself.

A control may or may not be associated with a class object. Static controls don't do anything directly, so an associated class object may seem superfluous; however, there's an MFC class, `CStatic`, that provides functions to enable you to alter the appearance of static controls. Button controls can also be handled by the dialog object in many cases, but again, MFC does provide the `CButton` class for use in situations where you need a class object to manage a control. MFC also provides a full complement of classes to support the other controls. Because controls are windows, they are all derived from `CWnd`.

> ### COMMON CONTROLS
>
> The set of standard controls supported by MFC and the Resource editor are called **common controls**. Common controls include all the controls you have just seen, as well as other more complex ones such as the **animate control**, for example, which has the capability to play an AVI (Audio Video Interleaved) file, and the **tree control**, which can display a hierarchy of items in a tree.
>
> Another useful control in the set of common controls is the **spin button**. You can use this to increment or decrement values in an associated edit control. To go into all of the possible controls that you might use is beyond the scope of this book, so I'll just take a few illustrative examples (including one that uses a spin button) and implement them in the Sketcher program.

CREATING A DIALOG RESOURCE

Here's a concrete example. You could add a dialog to Sketcher to provide a choice of pen widths for drawing elements. This ultimately involves modifying the current pen width in the document, as well as in the CElement class, and adding or modifying functions to manage pen widths. You'll deal with all that, though, after you've gotten the dialog together.

Display the Resource View, expand the resource tree for Sketcher by clicking ▷ twice, and right-click the Dialog folder in the tree; then click Insert Dialog from the pop-up to add a new dialog resource to Sketcher. This results in the Dialog Resource editor swinging into action and displaying the dialog in the Editor pane, and the Toolbox showing a list of controls that you can add; if the Toolbox is not displayed, click Toolbox in the right-hand sidebar or press Ctrl+Alt+X.

The dialog has OK and Cancel button controls already in place. Adding more controls to the dialog is simplicity itself: you can just drag the control from the list in the Toolbox window to the position at which you want to place it in the dialog. Alternatively, you can click a control from the list to select it, and then click in the dialog where you want the control to be positioned. When it appears you'll still be able to move it around to set its exact position, and you'll also be able to resize it by dragging handles on the boundaries.

The dialog has a default ID assigned, IDD_DIALOG1, but it would be better to have an ID that's a bit more meaningful. You can edit the ID by right-clicking the dialog name in the Resource View pane and selecting Properties from the pop-up; this displays the properties for the dialog node. Change the ID to something that relates to the purpose of the dialog, such as IDD_PENWIDTH_DLG. You can also display the properties for the dialog itself by right-clicking in the Dialog Editor pane and selecting from the pop-up. Here you can change the Caption property value that appears in the title bar of the dialog window to Set Pen Width.

Adding Controls to a Dialog Box

To provide a mechanism for entering a pen width, you can add controls to the basic dialog that is displayed initially until it looks like the one shown in Figure 18-1. The figure shows the grid that you can use to position controls. If the grid is not displayed, you can select the appropriate toolbar button to display it; the toolbar button toggles the grid on and off.

FIGURE 18-1

Alternatively, you can display rules along the side and top of the dialog, which you can use to create guide lines, by clicking the Toggle Guides button. You create a horizontal guide by clicking in the appropriate rule where you want the guide to appear. Controls placed in contact with a guide will be attached to it and move with the guide. You can reposition a guide line by dragging the arrow for it along the rule. You can use one or more guides when positioning a control. You can toggle guides on and off by clicking the Toggle Guides toolbar button.

The dialog shown has six radio buttons that provide the pen width options. These are enclosed within a **group box** with the caption `Pen Widths`. The group box serves to enclose the radio buttons and make them operate as a group, for which only one member of the group can be checked at any given time. Each radio button has an appropriate label to identify the pen width that is set when it is selected. There are also the default OK and Cancel buttons that close the dialog. Each of the controls in the dialog has its own set of properties that you can access and modify, just as for the dialog box itself. Let's press on with putting the dialog together.

The next step in the creation of the dialog shown in Figure 18-1 is to add the group box. As I said, the group box serves to associate the radio buttons in a group from an operational standpoint, and to provide a caption and a boundary for the group of buttons. Where you need more than one set of radio buttons, a means of grouping them is essential if they are to work properly. You can select the button corresponding to the group box from the common controls palette by clicking it; then click the approximate position in the dialog box where you want to place the center of the group box. This places a group box of default size onto the dialog. You can then drag the borders of the group box to enlarge it to accommodate the six radio buttons that you add. To set the caption for the group box, type the caption you want while the group box is selected (in this case, type **Pen Widths**).

The last step is to add the radio buttons. Select the radio button control by clicking it, and then clicking the position in the dialog where you want to place a radio button within the group box. Do the same for all six radio buttons. You can select each button by clicking it; then type in the caption to change it. You can also drag the border of the button to set its size, if necessary. To display the Properties window for a control, select it by right-clicking it; then select Properties from the pop-up. You can change the ID for each radio button in the Properties window for the control, in order to make the ID correspond better to its purpose: `IDC_PENWIDTH0` for the one-pixel-width pen, `IDC_PENWIDTH1` for the 0.01-inch-width pen, `IDC_PENWIDTH2` for the 0.02-inch-pen, and so on.

You can position individual controls by dragging them around with the mouse. You can also select a group of controls by selecting successive controls with the Shift key pressed, or by dragging the cursor with the left button pressed to create an enclosing rectangle. To align a group of controls, or to space them evenly horizontally or vertically, select the appropriate button from the Dialog Editor toolbar. If the Dialog Editor toolbar is not visible, you can show it by right-clicking in the toolbar area and selecting it from the list of toolbars that is displayed. You can also align controls in the dialog by selecting from the Format menu.

Testing the Dialog

The dialog resource is now complete. You can test it by selecting the toolbar button that appears at the left end of the toolbar or by pressing Ctrl+T. This displays the dialog window with the basic operations of the controls available, so you can try clicking on the radio buttons. When you have a group of radio buttons, only one can be selected at a time. As you select one, any other that was previously selected is reset. Click either the OK or Cancel button, or even the close icon in the title bar of the dialog, to end the test. After you have saved the dialog resource, you're ready to add some code to support it.

PROGRAMMING FOR A DIALOG

There are two aspects to programming for a dialog: getting it displayed, and handling the effects of its controls. Before you can display the dialog corresponding to the resource you've just created, you must first define a dialog class for it. The Class Wizard helps with this.

Adding a Dialog Class

Right-click in the Resource Editor pane for the dialog and then select Add Class from the pop-up to display the Class Wizard dialog. You'll define a new dialog class derived from the MFC class CDialog, so select that class name from the "Base class" drop-down list box, if it's not already selected. You can enter the class name as **CPenDialog** in the Class name edit box. The Class Wizard dialog should look as shown in Figure 18-2. Click the Finish button to create the new class.

The CDialog class is a window class (derived from the MFC class CWnd) that's specifically for displaying and managing dialogs. The dialog resource that you have created

FIGURE 18-2

automatically associates with an object of type CPenDialog because the IDD class member is initialized with the ID of the dialog resource:

```
class CPenDialog : public CDialog
{
  DECLARE_DYNAMIC(CPenDialog)

public:
  CPenDialog(CWnd* pParent = NULL);   // standard constructor
  virtual ~CPenDialog();

// Dialog Data
  enum { IDD = IDD_PENWIDTH_DLG };

protected:
  virtual void DoDataExchange(CDataExchange* pDX);    // DDX/DDV support

  DECLARE_MESSAGE_MAP()
};
```

The boldfaced statement defines IDD as a symbolic name for the dialog ID in the enumeration. Incidentally, using an enumeration is one of two ways to get an initialized data member into a native C++ class definition. The other way is to define a static const integral member of the class, so the Class Wizard could have used the following in the class definition:

```
static const int IDD = IDD_PENWIDTH_DLG;
```

If you try putting an initial value for any regular non-static data member declaration in a class, it won't compile.

Having your own dialog class derived from CDialog means that you get all the functionality that that class provides. You can also customize the dialog class by adding data members and functions to suit your particular needs. You'll often want to handle messages from controls within the dialog class, although you can also choose to handle them in a view or a document class if this is more convenient.

Modal and Modeless Dialogs

There are two different types of dialogs, **modal** and **modeless**, and they work in completely different ways. While a modal dialog is displayed, all operations in the other windows in the application are suspended until the dialog box is closed, usually by the user clicking an OK or Cancel button. With a modeless dialog you can move the focus back and forth between the dialog window and other windows in your application just by clicking them, and you can continue to use the dialog at any time until you close it. The Class Wizard is an example of a modal dialog; the Properties window is modeless.

You can create a modeless dialog box by calling the Create() member of the CDialog class in your dialog class constructor. You create a modal dialog box by creating an object on the stack from your dialog class and calling its DoModal() function.

Displaying a Dialog

Where you put the code to display a dialog in your program depends on the application. In the Sketcher program, it will be convenient to add a menu item that, when selected, results in the pen width dialog's being displayed. You can put this item in the IDR_SketcherTYPE menu bar. As both the pen width and the drawing color are associated with a pen, you can rename the Color menu as Pen. You do this just by double-clicking the Color menu item in the Resource Editor pane to open its Properties window and changing the value of the Caption property to &Pen.

When you add the Width menu item to the Pen menu, it would be a good idea to separate it from the colors in the menu. You can add a separator after the last color menu item by right-clicking the empty menu item and selecting the Insert Separator menu item from the pop-up. You can then enter the new Width item as the next menu item after the separator. The Width menu item ends with an ellipsis (three periods) to indicate that it displays a dialog; this is a standard Windows convention. Double-click the menu to display the menu properties for modification, as shown in Figure 18-3.

The default ID, ID_PEN_WIDTH, is fine, so you don't need to change that. You can add a status bar prompt for the menu item, and because

FIGURE 18-3

you'll also add a toolbar button, you can include text for the tooltip as well. Remember, you just put the tooltip text after the status bar prompt text, separated from it by \n. Here, the value for the Prompt property is "Change pen width\nShow pen width options."

You need to add toolbar buttons to both toolbars corresponding to the Width menu item. To add the toolbar button to the toolbar that is displayed when you check "Large icons" in the Customize dialog for the application toolbar, open the toolbar resource by extending the Toolbar folder in the Resource View and double-clicking IDR_MAINFRAME_256. You can add a toolbar button to represent a pen width. The one shown in Figure 18-4 tries to represent a pen drawing a line.

FIGURE 18-4

To associate the new button with the menu item that you just added, open the Properties box for the button and specify its ID as ID_PEN_WIDTH, the same as that for the menu item. You then need to repeat the process for the IDR_MAINFRAME toolbar.

Code to Display the Dialog

The code to display the dialog goes in the handler for the Pen ⇨ Width menu item. So, in which class should you implement this handler? The `CSketcherView` class is a candidate for dealing with pen widths, but following the previous logic with colors and elements, it would be sensible to have the current pen width selection in the document, so the handler should go in the `CSketcherDoc` class.

Right-click the Width menu item in the Resource View pane for the `IDR_SketcherTYPE` menu and select Add Event Handler from the pop-up. You can then create a function for the COMMAND message handler corresponding to `ID_PEN_WIDTH` in the `CSketcherDoc` class. Now edit this handler and enter the following code:

```
// Handler for the pen width menu item
void CSketcherDoc::OnPenWidth()
{
    CPenDialog aDlg;                     // Create a local dialog object

    // Display the dialog as modal
    aDlg.DoModal();
}
```

There are just two statements in the handler at the moment. The first creates a dialog object that is automatically associated with your dialog resource. You then display the dialog by calling the `DoModal()` function for the `aDlg` object.

Because the handler creates a `CPenDialog` object, you must add a `#include` directive for `PenDialog.h` to the beginning of `SketcherDoc.cpp` (after the `#include` directives for `stdafx.h` and `Sketcher.h`); otherwise, you'll get compilation errors when you build the program. After you've done that, you can build Sketcher and try out the dialog. It should appear when you click the pen-width toolbar button. Of course, if the dialog is to do anything, you still have to add the code to support the operation of the controls; to close the dialog, you can use either of the buttons or the close icon in the title bar.

Code to Close the Dialog

The OK and Cancel buttons (and the close icon on the title bar) already close the dialog. The handlers to deal with the `BN_CLICKED` event handlers for the OK and Cancel button controls have been implemented for you. However, it's useful to know how the action of closing the dialog is implemented, in case you want to do more before the dialog is finally closed, or if you are working with a modeless dialog.

The `CDialog` class defines the `OnOK()` method that is called when you click the default OK button, which has `IDOK` as its ID. This function closes the dialog and causes the `DoModal()` method to return the ID of the default OK button, `IDOK`. The `OnCancel()` function is called when you click the default Cancel button in the dialog; this closes the dialog, and `DoModal()` returns the button ID, which is `IDCANCEL`. You can override either or both of these functions in your dialog class to do what you want. You just need to make sure you call the corresponding base class function at the end of your function implementation. You'll probably remember by now that you can add an override class by clicking the override button in the Properties window for the class.

For example, you could implement an override for the `OnOK()` function as follows:

```
void CPenDialog::OnOK()
{
  // Your code for data validation or other actions...

  CDialog::OnOK();                      // Close the dialog
}
```

In a complicated dialog, you might want to verify that the options selected, or the data that has been entered, is valid. You could put code here to check the state of the dialog and fix up the data, or even to leave the dialog open if there are problems.

Calling the OnOK() function defined in the base class closes the dialog and causes the DoModal() function to return IDOK. Thus, you can use the value returned from DoModal() to detect when the dialog was closed via the OK button.

As I said, you can also override the OnCancel() function in a similar way if you need to do extra cleanup operations before the dialog closes. Be sure to call the base class method at the end of your function implementation.

When you are using a modeless dialog you must implement the OnOK() and OnCancel() function overrides so that they call the inherited DestroyWindow() to terminate the dialog. In this case, you must not call the base class OnOK() or OnCancel() functions, because they do not destroy the dialog window, but merely render it invisible.

SUPPORTING THE DIALOG CONTROLS

For the pen dialog you'll store the selected pen width in a data member, m_PenWidth, of the CPenDialog class. You can either add the data member by right-clicking the CPenDialog class name and selecting from the context menu, or you can add it directly to the class definition as follows:

```
class CPenDialog : public CDialog
{
// Construction
public:
    CPenDialog(CWnd* pParent = NULL);   // standard constructor

// Dialog Data
    enum { IDD = IDD_PENWIDTH_DLG };

    int m_PenWidth;                        // Record the current pen width

// Plus the rest of the class definition....

};
```

 NOTE *If you do use the context menu for the class to add* m_PenWidth, *be sure to add a comment to the member variable definition. This is a good habit to get into, even when the member name looks self-explanatory.*

You'll use the m_PenWidth data member to set as checked the radio button corresponding to the current pen width in the document. You'll also arrange for the pen width selected in the dialog to be stored in this member, so that you can retrieve it when the dialog closes. At this point you could arrange to initialize m_PenWidth to 0 in the CPenDialog class constructor.

Initializing the Controls

You can initialize the radio buttons by overriding the OnInitDialog() function defined in the base class, CDialog. This function is called in response to a WM_INITDIALOG message, which is sent during the execution of DoModal() just before the dialog box is displayed. You can add the function to the CPenDialog class by selecting OnInitDialog in the list of overrides in the Properties window for the CPenDialog class. The implementation for the new version of OnInitDialog() is:

```
BOOL CPenDialog::OnInitDialog()
{
   CDialog::OnInitDialog();

   // Check the radio button corresponding to the pen width
   switch(m_PenWidth)
   {
      case 1:
         CheckDlgButton(IDC_PENWIDTH1,1);
         break;
      case 2:
         CheckDlgButton(IDC_PENWIDTH2,1);
         break;
      case 3:
         CheckDlgButton(IDC_PENWIDTH3,1);
         break;
      case 4:
         CheckDlgButton(IDC_PENWIDTH4,1);
         break;
      case 5:
         CheckDlgButton(IDC_PENWIDTH5,1);
         break;
      default:
         CheckDlgButton(IDC_PENWIDTH0,1);
   }
   return TRUE;   // return TRUE unless you set the focus to a control
                  // EXCEPTION: OCX Property Pages should return FALSE
}
```

You should leave the call to the base class function there because it does some essential setup for the dialog. The switch statement checks one of the radio buttons, depending on the value set in the m_PenWidth data member. This implies that you must arrange to set m_PenWidth to a suitable value before you execute DoModal() because the DoModal() function causes the WM_INITDIALOG message to be sent, resulting in your version of OnInitDialog() being called.

The CheckDlgButton() function is inherited indirectly from CWnd through CDialog. The first argument identifies the button, and the second argument, of type UINT, sets its check status. If the second argument is 1, it checks the button corresponding to the ID you specify in the first argument. If the second argument is 0, the button is unchecked. This function works with both checkboxes and radio buttons.

Handling Radio Button Messages

After the dialog box is displayed, every time you click one of the radio buttons a message is generated and sent to the application. To deal with these messages, you can add handlers to the CPenDialog class. Return to the dialog resource that you created, right-click each of the radio buttons in turn, and select Add Event Handler from the pop-up to create a handler for the BN_CLICKED message. Figure 18-5 shows the event handler dialog window for the button that has IDC_PENWIDTH0 as its ID. Note that I have edited the name of the handler, as the default name was a little cumbersome.

The implementations of the BN_CLICKED event handlers for all of these radio buttons are similar because each just sets the pen

FIGURE 18-5

width in the dialog object. As an example, the handler for IDC_PENWIDTH0 is as follows:

```
void CPenDialog::OnPenwidth0()
{
    m_PenWidth = 0;
}
```

You need to add the code for all six handlers to the CPenDialog class implementation, setting m_PenWidth to 1 in OnPenwidth1(), to 2 in OnPenwidth2(), and so on.

COMPLETING DIALOG OPERATIONS

You must now modify the OnPenWidth() handler in CSketcherDoc to make the dialog effective. Add the following code to the function:

```
// Handler for the pen width menu item
void CSketcherDoc::OnPenWidth()
{
    CPenDialog aDlg;       // Create a local dialog object

    // Set the pen width in the dialog to that stored in the document
    aDlg.m_PenWidth = m_PenWidth;

    // Display the dialog as modal
    // When closed with OK, get the pen width
    if(aDlg.DoModal() == IDOK)
    {
        m_PenWidth = aDlg.m_PenWidth;
    }
}
```

The m_PenWidth member of the aDlg object is passed a pen width stored in the m_PenWidth member of the document; you still have to add this member to CSketcherDoc. The call of the DoModal() function now occurs in the condition of the if statement, which is true if the DoModal() function returns IDOK. In this case you retrieve the pen width stored in the aDlg object and store it in the m_PenWidth member of the document. If the dialog box is closed by means of the Cancel button, the escape key on the keyboard, or the close icon, IDOK won't be returned by DoModal(), and the value of m_PenWidth in the document will not be changed.

Note that even though the dialog box is closed when DoModal() returns a value, the aDlg object still exists, so you can call its member functions without any problem. The aDlg object is destroyed automatically, on return from OnPenWidth().

All that remains to do to support variable pen widths in your application is to update the affected classes: CSketcherDoc, CElement, and the four shape classes derived from CElement.

Adding Pen Widths to the Document

You need to add the m_PenWidth member to the document class, and the GetPenWidth() function to allow external access to the value stored. You should add the following bolded statements to the CSketcherDoc class definition:

```
class CSketcherDoc : public CDocument
{
// the rest as before...

protected:
// the rest as before...
   int m_PenWidth;                        // Current pen width

// Operations
public:
// the rest as before...
   int GetPenWidth() const                // Get the current pen width
      { return m_PenWidth; }

// the rest as before...
};
```

Because it's trivial, you can define the GetPenWidth() function in the definition of the class and gain the benefit of its being implicitly inline. You still need to add initialization for m_PenWidth to the constructor for CSketcherDoc, so modify the constructor in SketcherDoc.cpp to initialize m_PenWidth to 0.

Adding Pen Widths to the Elements

You have a little more to do to the CElement class and the shape classes that are derived from it. You already have a member m_PenWidth in CElement to store the width to be used when you are drawing an element, and you must extend each of the constructors for elements to accept a pen width as an argument, and set the member in the class accordingly. The GetBoundRect() function in CElement must be altered to deal with a pen width of 0. You can modify the CElement class first. The new version of the GetBoundRect() function in the CElement class is as follows:

```
// Get the bounding rectangle for an element
CRect CElement::GetBoundRect() const
{
    CRect boundingRect(m_EnclosingRect);      // Object to store bounding rectangle

    //Increase the bounding rectangle by the pen width
    int Offset = m_PenWidth == 0 ? 1 : m_PenWidth; // Width must be at least 1
    boundingRect.InflateRect(Offset, Offset);
    return BoundingRect;
}
```

You use the local variable Offset to ensure that you pass the InflateRect() function a value of 1 if the pen width is 0 (a pen width of 0 always draws a line one pixel wide), and that you pass the actual pen width in all other cases.

Each of the constructors for CLine, CRectangle, CCircle, and CCurve must be modified to accept a pen width as an argument, and to store it in the inherited m_PenWidth member of the class. The declaration for the constructor in each class definition needs to be modified to add the extra parameter. For example, in the CLine class, the constructor declaration becomes:

```
CLine(const CPoint& start, const CPoint& end, COLORREF aColor, int penWidth);
```

And the constructor implementation should be modified to this:

```
CLine::CLine(const CPoint& start, const CPoint& end, COLORREF aColor, int penWidth)
 :m_StartPoint(start), m_EndPoint(end)
{
    m_PenWidth = penWidth;              // Set pen width
    m_Color = aColor;                  // Set line color

    // Define the enclosing rectangle
    m_EnclosingRect = CRect(Start, End);
    m_EnclosingRect.NormalizeRect();
}
```

You should modify each of the class definitions and constructors for the shapes in the same way, so that each initializes m_PenWidth with the value passed as the last argument.

Creating Elements in the View

The last change you need to make is to the CreateElement() member of CSketcherView. Because you have added the pen width as an argument to the constructors for each of the shapes, you must update the calls to the constructors to reflect this. Change the definition of CSketcherView::CreateElement() to the following:

```
CElement* CSketcherView::CreateElement()
{
    // Get a pointer to the document for this view
```

```
      CSketcherDoc* pDoc = GetDocument();
      ASSERT_VALID(pDoc);                              // Verify the pointer is good

      // Now select the element using the type stored in the document
      switch(pDoc->GetElementType())
      {
         case RECTANGLE:
            return new CRectangle(m_FirstPoint, m_SecondPoint,
                                 pDoc->GetElementColor(), pDoc->GetPenWidth());
         case CIRCLE:
            return new CCircle(m_FirstPoint, m_SecondPoint,
                                 pDoc->GetElementColor(), pDoc->GetPenWidth());
         case CURVE:
            return new CCurve(m_FirstPoint, m_SecondPoint,
                                 pDoc->GetElementColor(), pDoc->GetPenWidth());
         case LINE:
            return new CLine(m_FirstPoint, m_SecondPoint,
                                 pDoc->GetElementColor(), pDoc->GetPenWidth());
         default:                              // Something's gone wrong
            AfxMessageBox(_T("Bad Element code"), MB_OK);
            AfxAbort();
            return nullptr;
      }
   }
```

Each constructor call now passes the pen width as an argument. This is retrieved from the document with the GetPenWidth() function that you added to the document class.

Exercising the Dialog

You can now build and run the latest version of Sketcher to see how the pen dialog works out. Selecting the Pen ⇨ Width menu option or the associated toolbar button displays the dialog box so that you can select the pen width. The screen shown in Figure 18-6 is typical of what you might see when the Sketcher program is executing.

Note that the dialog box is a completely separate window. You can drag it around to position it where you want. You can even drag it outside the Sketcher application window.

FIGURE 18-6

USING A SPIN BUTTON CONTROL

Now you can move on to looking at how the spin button can help in the Sketcher application. The spin button is particularly useful when you want to constrain an input within a given integer range. It's normally used in association with another control, called a **buddy control**, that displays the value that the spin button modifies. The associated control is usually an edit control, but it doesn't have to be.

It would be nice to be able to draw at different viewing scales in Sketcher. If you had a way to change the scale, you could scale up whenever you wanted to fill in the fine detail in your masterpiece, and scale down again when working across the whole vista. You could apply the spin control to managing scaling in a document view. A drawing scale would be a view-specific property, and you would want the element drawing functions to take the current scale of a view into account. Altering the existing code to deal with view scaling requires rather more work than setting up the control, so first look at how you create a spin button and make it work.

Adding the Scale Menu Item and Toolbar Button

The first step is to provide a means of displaying the scale dialog. Go to Resource View and open the IDR_SketcherTYPE menu. You are going to add a Scale menu item to the end of the View menu. Enter the caption for the unused menu item as **Scale. . . .** This item will bring up the scale dialog, so you end the caption with an ellipsis (three periods) to indicate that it displays a dialog. Next you can add a separator before the new menu item by right-clicking it and selecting Insert Separator from the pop-up. The menu should now look as shown in Figure 18-7.

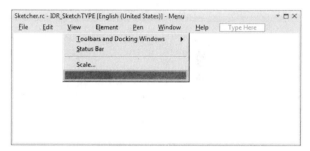

FIGURE 18-7

You can also add toolbar buttons to both toolbars for this menu item. All you need to do is make sure that the ID for each new button is also set to ID_VIEW_SCALE.

Creating the Spin Button

You've got the menu item; you better have a dialog to go with it. In Resource View, add a new dialog by right-clicking the Dialog folder on the tree and selecting Insert Dialog from the pop-up. Change the ID to IDD_SCALE_DLG and the Caption property to Set Drawing Scale.

Click the spin control in the palette, and then click on the position in the dialog where you want it to be placed. Next, right-click the spin control to display its properties. Change its ID to something more meaningful than the default, such as IDC_SPIN_SCALE. Now take at look at the properties for the spin button. They are shown in Figure 18-8.

FIGURE 18-8

The `Arrow Keys` property is already set to True, enabling you to operate the spin button by using arrow keys on the keyboard. You should also set to true the value for both the Set Buddy Integer property, which specifies the buddy control value as an integer, and Auto Buddy, which provides for automatic selection of the buddy control. The effect of the latter is that the control selected as the buddy is automatically the previous control defined in the dialog. At the moment this is the Cancel button, which is not exactly ideal, but you'll see how to change this in a moment. The Alignment property determines how the spin button is displayed in relation to its buddy. You should set this to Right Align so that the spin button is attached to the right edge of its buddy control.

Next, add an edit control at the left side of the spin button by selecting the edit control from the list in the toolbox pane and clicking in the dialog where you want it positioned. Change the ID for the edit control to IDC_SCALE.

To make the contents of the edit control quite clear, you could add a static control just to the left of the edit control in the dialog and enter **View Scale:** as the caption. You can select all three controls by clicking them while holding down the Shift key. Pressing the F9 function key aligns the controls tidily, or you can use the Format menu.

The Controls' Tab Sequence

Controls in a dialog have what is called a **tab sequence**. This is the sequence in which the focus shifts from one control to the next when you press the tab key, determined initially by the sequence in which controls are added to the dialog. You can see the tab sequence for the current dialog box by selecting Format ⇨ Tab Order from the main menu, or by pressing Ctrl+D. Figure 18-9 shows the tab order required for the spin control to work with its buddy control.

FIGURE 18-9

If the tab order you see is different, you have to change it. You really want the edit control to precede the spin button in the tab sequence, so you need to select the controls by clicking them in the order in which you want them to be numbered: OK button; Cancel button; edit control; spin button; and finally the static control. So, the tab order will be as shown in Figure 18-9. Now the edit control is selected as the buddy to the spin button.

Generating the Scale Dialog Class

After saving the resource file, you can right-click the dialog and select Add Class from the pop-up at the cursor. You'll then be able to define the new class associated with the dialog resource that you have created. You should name the class `CScaleDialog` and select the base class as `CDialog`. Clicking the Finish button adds the class to the Sketcher project.

You need to add a variable to the dialog class that stores the value returned from the edit control, so right-click the `CScaleDialog` class name in the Class View and select Add ⇨ Add Variable from the pop-up. The new data member of the class is a special kind, called a **control variable**, so first check the "Control variable" box in the window for the Add Member Variable wizard. A control variable is a variable that is to be associated with a control in the dialog. Select IDC_SCALE as the ID from the Control ID drop-down list and Value from the Category list box. Enter the variable name as **m_Scale**. You'll be storing an integer scale value, so select int as the variable type. The Add Member Variable wizard displays edit boxes in which you can enter maximum and minimum values for the variable m_Scale. For our application, a minimum of 1 and a maximum of 8 would be good values. Note that this constraint applies only to the edit box; the spin control is independent of it.

Figure 18-10 shows how the window for the Add Member Variable Wizard should look when you are done.

FIGURE 18-10

When you click the Finish button, the wizard takes care of entering the code necessary to support your new control variable.

You will also need to access the spin control in the dialog, and you can use the Add Member Variable Wizard to create that, too. Right-click CScaleDialog in Class View once again and click the "Control variable" checkbox. Leave the Category selection as Control and select IDC_SPIN_SCALE as the control ID: this corresponds to the spin control. You can now enter the variable name as **m_Spin** and add a suitable comment. When you click the Finish button, the new variable will be added to the CScaleDialog class.

The class definition you'll end up with after the wizard has added the new members is as follows:

```
class CScaleDialog : public CDialog
{
  DECLARE_DYNAMIC(CScaleDialog)

public:
  CScaleDialog(CWnd* pParent = NULL);   // standard constructor
  virtual ~CScaleDialog();

// Dialog Data
  enum { IDD = IDD_SCALE_DLG };

protected:
  virtual void DoDataExchange(CDataExchange* pDX);    // DDX/DDV support

  DECLARE_MESSAGE_MAP()
public:
  // Stores the current drawing scale
  int m_Scale;
  // Spin control for view scale
  CSpinButtonCtrl m_Spin;

};
```

The interesting bits of the class definition are bolded. The class is associated with the dialog resource through the enum statement, initializing IDD with the ID of the resource. It contains the variable m_Scale, which is specified as a public member of the class, so you can set and retrieve its value in a CScaleDialog object directly. There's also some special code in the implementation of the class to deal with the new m_Scale member. The m_Spin variable references the CSpinButtonCtrl object so you can call functions for the spin control.

Dialog Data Exchange and Validation

A virtual function called DoDataExchange() has been included in the class by the Class Wizard. If you look in the ScaleDialog.cpp file, you'll find that the implementation looks like this:

```
void CScaleDialog::DoDataExchange(CDataExchange* pDX)
{
    CDialog::DoDataExchange(pDX);
    DDX_Text(pDX, IDC_SCALE, m_Scale);
    DDV_MinMaxInt(pDX, m_Scale, 1, 8);
    DDX_Control(pDX, IDC_SPIN_SCALE, m_Spin);
}
```

This function is called by the framework to carry out the exchange of data between variables in a dialog and the dialog's controls. This mechanism is called **dialog data exchange**, usually abbreviated to **DDX**. This is a powerful mechanism that can provide automatic transfer of information between a dialog and its controls in most circumstances, thus saving you the effort of programming to get the data yourself, as you did with the radio buttons in the pen width dialog.

In the scale dialog, DDX handles data transfers between the edit control and the variable m_Scale in the CScaleDialog class. The variable pDX, passed to the DoDataExchange() function, controls the direction in which data is transferred. After the base class DoDataExchange() function is called, the DDX_Text() function is called. The latter actually moves data between the variable m_Scale and the edit control.

The call to the DDV_MinMaxInt() function verifies that the value transferred is within the limits specified. This mechanism is called **dialog data validation**, or **DDV**. The DoDataExchange() function is called automatically before the dialog is displayed to pass the value stored in m_Scale to the edit control. When the dialog is closed with the OK button, it is automatically called again to pass the value in the control back to the variable m_Scale in the dialog object. All this is taken care of for you. You need only to ensure that the right value is stored in m_Scale before the dialog box is displayed, and arrange to collect the result when the dialog box closes.

Initializing the Dialog

You'll use the OnInitDialog() function to initialize the dialog, just as you did for the pen width dialog. This time you'll use it to set up the spin control. You'll initialize the m_Scale member a little later when you create the dialog in the handler for a Scale menu item, because it should be set to the value of the scale stored in the view. For now, add an override for the OnInitDialog() function to the CScaleDialog class, using the same mechanism you used for the previous dialog, and add code to initialize the spin control as follows:

```
BOOL CScaleDialog::OnInitDialog()
{
   CDialog::OnInitDialog();

   // If you have not checked the auto buddy option in
   // the spin control's properties, you can set the buddy control here

   // Set the spin control range
   m_Spin.SetRange(1, 8);

   return TRUE;   // return TRUE unless you set the focus to a control
                  // EXCEPTION: OCX Property Pages should return FALSE
}
```

There is only one line of code to add. This sets the upper and lower limits for the spin button by calling the `SetRange()` member of the spin control object. Although you have set the range limits for the edit control, this doesn't affect the spin control directly. If you don't limit the values in the spin control here, you allow the spin control to insert values outside the limits in the edit control, and there will be an error message from the edit control. You can demonstrate this by commenting out the statement that calls `SetRange()` here and trying out Sketcher without it.

If you want to set the buddy control using code, rather than by setting the value of `Auto buddy` in the spin button's properties to `True`, the `CSpinButtonCtrl` class has a function member to do this. You need to add the statement

```
mSpin.SetBuddy(GetDlgItem(IDC_SCALE));
```

at the point indicated by the comments.

> **NOTE** *You can also access controls in a dialog programmatically. The function* `GetDlgItem()` *is inherited from* `CWnd` *via* `CDialog`, *and you can use it to retrieve the address of any control from the ID you pass as the argument. Thus, calling* `GetDlgItem()` *with* `IDC_SPIN_SCALE` *as the argument would return the address of the spin control. As you saw earlier, a control is just a specialized window, so the pointer returned is of type* `CWnd*`; *you therefore have to cast it to the type appropriate to the particular control, which would be* `CSpinButtonCtrl*` *in this case.*

Displaying the Spin Button

The dialog is to be displayed when the Scale menu option (or its associated toolbar button) is selected, so you need to add a COMMAND event handler to the `CSketcherView` class corresponding to the `ID_VIEW_SCALE` message through the Properties window for the class. You can then add code as follows:

```
void CSketcherView::OnViewScale()
{
  CScaleDialog aDlg;                    // Create a dialog object
  aDlg.m_Scale = m_Scale;               // Pass the view scale to the dialog
  if(aDlg.DoModal() == IDOK)
```

```
  {
    m_Scale = aDlg.m_Scale;          // Get the new scale
    InvalidateRect(0);               // Invalidate the whole window
  }
}
```

You create the dialog as a modal dialog, just as you did the pen width dialog. Before the dialog box is displayed by the `DoModal()` function call, you store the scale value provided by the `m_Scale` member of `CSketcherView` in the dialog member with the same name; this ensures that the control displays the current scale value when the dialog is displayed. If the dialog is closed with the OK button, you store the new scale from the `m_Scale` member of the dialog object in the view member with the same name. Because you have changed the view scale, you need to get the view redrawn with the new scale value applied. The call to `InvalidateRect()` does this. Don't forget to add an `#include` directive for `ScaleDialog.h` to `SketcherView.cpp`.

Of course, you must not forget to add the `m_Scale` data member to the definition of `CSketcherView`, so add the following line at the end of the other data members in the class definition:

```
    int m_Scale;                     // Current view scale
```

You should also modify the `CSketcherView` constructor to initialize `m_Scale` to 1. This results in a view always starting out with a scale of one to one.

That's all you need to get the scale dialog and its spin control operational. You can build and run Sketcher to give it a trial spin before you add the code to use a view scale factor in the drawing process.

USING THE SCALE FACTOR

Scaling with Windows usually involves using one of the scalable mapping modes, MM_ISOTROPIC or MM_ANISOTROPIC. By using one of these mapping modes you can get Windows to do most of the work. Unfortunately, it's not as simple as just changing the mapping mode, because neither is supported by `CScrollView`. If you can get around that, however, you're home and dry. You'll use MM_ANISOTROPIC for reasons that you'll see in a moment, so let's first understand what's involved in using this mapping mode.

Scalable Mapping Modes

As I've said, there are two mapping modes that allow the mapping between logical coordinates and device coordinates to be altered, and these are the MM_ISOTROPIC and MM_ANISOTROPIC modes. The MM_ISOTROPIC mode has a property that forces the scaling factor for both the x- and y-axes to be the same, which has the advantage that your circles will always be circles. The disadvantage is that you can't map a document to fit into a rectangle of a different aspect ratio. The MM_ANISOTROPIC mode, on the other hand, permits scaling of each axis independently. Because it's the more flexible mode of the two, you'll use MM_ANISOTROPIC for scaling operations in Sketcher.

The way in which logical coordinates are transformed to device coordinates is dependent on the following parameters, which you can set:

PARAMETER	DESCRIPTION
Window Origin	The logical coordinates of the upper left corner of the window. You set this by calling the function `CDC::SetWindowOrg()`.
Window Extent	The size of the window specified in logical coordinates. You set this by calling the function `CDC::SetWindowExt()`.
Viewport Origin	The coordinates of the upper left corner of the window in device coordinates (pixels). You set this by calling the function `CDC::SetViewportOrg()`.
Viewport Extent	The size of the window in device coordinates (pixels). You set this by calling the function `CDC::SetViewportExt()`.

The **viewport** referred to here has no physical significance by itself; it serves only as a parameter for defining how coordinates are transformed from logical coordinates to device coordinates.

Remember the following:

➤ **Logical coordinates** (also referred to as **page coordinates**) are determined by the mapping mode. For example, the MM_LOENGLISH mapping mode has logical coordinates in units of 0.01 inches, with the origin in the upper left corner of the client area, and the positive y-axis direction running from bottom to top. These are used by the device context drawing functions.

➤ **Device coordinates** (also referred to as **client coordinates** in a window) are measured in pixels in the case of a window, with the origin at the upper left corner of the client area, and with the positive y-axis direction from top to bottom. These are used outside a device context — for example, for defining the position of the cursor in mouse message handlers.

➤ **Screen coordinates** are measured in pixels and have the origin at the upper left corner of the screen, with the positive y-axis direction from top to bottom. These are used for getting or setting the cursor position.

The formulae used by Windows to convert from logical coordinates to device coordinates are:

$$xDevice = (xLogical - xWindowOrg) * \frac{xViewportExt}{xWindowExt} + xViewportOrg$$

$$yDevice = (yLogical - yWindowOrg) * \frac{yViewportExt}{yWindowExt} + yViewportOrg$$

With coordinate systems other than those provided by the MM_ISOTROPIC and MM_ANISOTROPIC mapping modes, the window extent and the viewport extent are fixed by the mapping mode and can't be changed. Calling the functions SetWindowExt() or SetViewportExt() in the CDC object to change them has no effect, although you can still move the position of (0,0) in your logical reference frame by calling SetWindowOrg() or SetViewportOrg(). However, for a given document size that is expressed by the window extent in logical coordinate units, you can adjust the scale at which elements are displayed by setting the viewport extent appropriately. By using and setting the window and viewport extents, you can get the scaling done automatically.

Setting the Document Size

You need to maintain the size of the document in logical units in the document object. You can add a protected data member, m_DocSize, to the CSketcherDoc class definition to store the size of the document:

```
CSize m_DocSize;                    // Document size
```

You will also want to access this data member from the view class, so add a public function to the CSketcherDoc class definition as follows:

```
CSize GetDocSize() const         // Retrieve the document size
   { return m_DocSize; }
```

You must initialize the m_DocSize member in the constructor for the document; modify the implementation of CSketcherDoc() as follows:

```
CSketcherDoc::CSketcherDoc()
: m_Element(LINE)
, m_Color(BLACK)
, m_PenWidth(0)
, m_DocSize(CSize(3000,3000))
{
   // TODO: add one-time construction code here
}
```

You'll be using notional MM_LOENGLISH coordinates, so you can treat the logical units as increments of 0.01 inches, and the value set gives you an area of 30 square inches to draw on.

Setting the Mapping Mode

You can set the mapping mode to MM_ANISOTROPIC in an override for the inherited OnPrepareDC() function in the CSketcherView class. This function is always called for any WM_PAINT message, and you have arranged to call it when you draw temporary objects in the mouse message handlers; however, you have to do a little more than just set the mapping mode.

You'll need to create the function override in CSketcherView before you can add the code. Just open the Properties window for the CSketcherView class and click the Overrides toolbar button. You can then add the override by selecting OnPrepareDC from the list and clicking on <Add> OnPrepareDC in the adjacent column. You are now able to type the code directly into the Editor pane. The implementation of `OnPrepareDC()` is as follows:

```
void CSketcherView::OnPrepareDC(CDC* pDC, CPrintInfo* pInfo)
{
  CScrollView::OnPrepareDC(pDC, pInfo);
  CSketcherDoc* pDoc = GetDocument();
  pDC->SetMapMode(MM_ANISOTROPIC);       // Set the map mode
  CSize DocSize = pDoc->GetDocSize();    // Get the document size

  pDC->SetWindowExt(DocSize);            // Now set the window extent

  // Get the number of pixels per inch in x and y
  int xLogPixels = pDC->GetDeviceCaps(LOGPIXELSX);
  int yLogPixels = pDC->GetDeviceCaps(LOGPIXELSY);

  // Calculate the viewport extent in x and y
  int xExtent = (DocSize.cx*m_Scale*xLogPixels)/100;
  int yExtent = (DocSize.cy*m_Scale*yLogPixels)/100;

  pDC->SetViewportExt(xExtent,yExtent); // Set viewport extent
}
```

The override of the base class function is unusual here in that you have left in the call to `CScrollView::OnPrepareDC()` and added the modifications after it, rather than where the comment in the default code suggests. If the class was derived from `CView`, you would replace the call to the base class version because it does nothing, but in the case of `CScrollView`, this isn't the case. You need the base class function to set some attributes before you set the mapping mode. Don't make the mistake of calling the base class function at the end of the override version, though — if you do, scaling won't work.

The `CDC` member function `GetDeviceCaps()` supplies information about the device with which the device context is associated. You can get various kinds of information about the device, depending on the argument you pass to the function. In this case the arguments `LOGPIXELSX` and `LOGPIXELSY` return the number of pixels per logical inch in the x and y directions, respectively. These values are equivalent to 100 units in your logical coordinates.

You use these values to calculate the x and y values for the viewport extent, which you store in the local variables `xExtent` and `yExtent`, respectively. The document extent along an axis in logical units, divided by 100, gives the document extent in inches. If this is multiplied by the number of logical pixels per inch for the device, you get the equivalent number of pixels for the extent. If you then use this value as the viewport extent, you get the elements displayed at a scale of one to one. If you simplify the equations for converting between device and logical coordinates by assuming that the window origin and the viewport origin are both (0,0), they become the following:

$$xDevice = xLogical * \frac{xViewportExt}{xWindowExt}$$

$$yDevice = yLogical * \frac{yViewportExt}{yWindowExt}$$

If you multiply the viewport extent values by the scale (stored in m_Scale), the elements are drawn according to the value of m_Scale. This logic is exactly represented by the expressions for the x and y viewport extents in your code. The simplified equations, with the scale included, are as follows:

$$xDevice = xLogical * \frac{xViewportExt * m\_Scale}{xWindowExt}$$

$$yDevice = yLogical * \frac{yViewportExt * m\_Scale}{yWindowExt}$$

You should be able to see from this that a given pair of device coordinates varies in proportion to the scale value. The coordinates at a scale of three are three times the coordinates at a scale of one. Of course, as well as making elements larger, increasing the scale also moves them away from the origin.

That's all you need in order to scale the view. Unfortunately, at the moment scrolling won't work with scaling, so you need to see what you can do about that.

Implementing Scrolling with Scaling

CScrollView just won't work with the MM_ANISOTROPIC mapping mode, so clearly you must use another mapping mode to set up the scrollbars. The easiest way to do this is to use MM_TEXT, because in this case the units of logical coordinates are the same as the client coordinates — pixels, in other words. All you need to do, then, is figure out how many pixels are equivalent to the logical document extent for the scale at which you are drawing, which is easier than you might think. You can add a function to CSketcherView to take care of the scrollbars and implement it to work out the number of pixels corresponding to the logical document extent. Right-click the CSketcherView class name in Class View and add a public function, ResetScrollSizes(), with a void return type and no parameters. Add the code to the implementation, as follows:

```
void CSketcherView::ResetScrollSizes(void)
{
  CClientDC aDC(this);
  OnPrepareDC(&aDC);                        // Set up the device context
  CSize DocSize = GetDocument()->GetDocSize();  // Get the document size
  aDC.LPtoDP(&DocSize);                     // Get the size in pixels
  SetScrollSizes(MM_TEXT, DocSize);         // Set up the scrollbars
}
```

After creating a local CClientDC object for the view, you call OnPrepareDC() to set up the MM_ANISOTROPIC mapping mode. Because this takes scaling into account, the LPtoDP() member of the aDC object converts the document size stored in the local variable DocSize to the correct number of pixels for the current logical document size and scale. The total document size in pixels defines how large the scrollbars must be in MM_TEXT mode — remember, MM_TEXT logical coordinates are in pixels. You can then get the SetScrollSizes() member of CScrollView to set up the scrollbars based on this by specifying MM_TEXT as the mapping mode.

It may seem strange that you can change the mapping mode in this way, but it's important to keep in mind that the mapping mode is nothing more than a definition of how logical coordinates are to be converted to device coordinates. Whatever mode (and therefore coordinate conversion algorithm) you've set up applies to all subsequent device context functions until you change it, and you can change it whenever you want. When you set a new mode, subsequent device context function calls just use the conversion algorithm defined by the new mode. You figure out how big the document is in pixels with MM_ANISOTROPIC because this is the only way you can get the scaling into the process; you then switch to MM_TEXT to set up the scrollbars because you need units for this in pixels for it to work properly. Simple really, when you know how.

Setting Up the Scrollbars

You must set up the scrollbars initially for the view in the OnInitialUpdate() member of CSketcherView. Change the previous implementation of the function to the following:

```
void CSketcherView::OnInitialUpdate()
{
  ResetScrollSizes();                    // Set up the scrollbars
  CScrollView::OnInitialUpdate();
}
```

All you do is call the ResetScrollSizes() function that you just added to the view. This takes care of everything — well, almost. The CScrollView object needs an initial extent to be set in order for OnPrepareDC() to work properly, so you need to add one statement to the CSketcherView constructor:

```
CSketcherView::CSketcherView()
: m_FirstPoint(CPoint(0,0))            // Set 1st recorded point to 0,0
, m_SecondPoint(CPoint(0,0))           // Set 2nd recorded point to 0,0
, m_pTempElement(NULL)                 // Set temporary element pointer to 0
, m_pSelected(NULL)                    // No element selected initially
, m_MoveMode(FALSE)                    // Set move mode off
, m_CursorPos(CPoint(0,0))             // Initialize as zero
, m_FirstPos(CPoint(0,0))              // Initialize as zero
, m_Scale(1)                           // Set scale to 1:1
{
    SetScrollSizes(MM_TEXT, CSize(0,0));     // Set arbitrary scrollers
}
```

The additional statement just calls SetScrollSizes() with an arbitrary extent to get the scrollbars initialized before the view is drawn. When the view is drawn for the first time, the ResetScrollSizes() function call in OnInitialUpdate() sets up the scrollbars properly.

Of course, each time the view scale changes, you need to update the scrollbars before the view is redrawn. You can take care of this in the OnViewScale() handler in the CSketcherView class:

```
void CSketcherView::OnViewScale()
{
  CScaleDialog aDlg;                    // Create a dialog object
  aDlg.m_Scale = m_Scale;              // Pass the view scale to the dialog
  if(aDlg.DoModal() == IDOK)
```

```
    {
      m_Scale = aDlg.m_Scale;              // Get the new scale
      ResetScrollSizes();                  // Adjust scrolling to the new scale
      InvalidateRect(0);                   // Invalidate the whole window
    }
  }
```

With the `ResetScrollSizes()` function, taking care of the scrollbars isn't complicated. Everything is covered by the one additional line of code.

Now you can build the project and run the application. You'll see that the scrollbars work just as they should. Note that each view maintains its own scale factor, independently of the other views.

USING THE CTASKDIALOG CLASS

The `CTaskDialog` class is a new feature of Visual C++ 2010 that enables you to create and display a wide range of message boxes and input dialogs programmatically. Although `CTaskDialog` is easy to use, it has a couple of limitations. First, it works only if your application is running under Windows Vista or later. If you want to use it, and also support earlier versions of Windows, you have to program the old-fashioned way as an alternative, so it doesn't save you any effort. Second, you have much more flexibility in how your input dialogs look and work if you create dialog resources for them in the way you have seen. Because of these limitations, I'll only discuss the class briefly, and we won't be integrating it into Sketcher.

To use the `CTaskDialog` class in a source file, you need an `#include` directive for `afxTaskDialog.h`. You can program to use this class, but only when it is supported, like this:

```
  if(CTaskDialog::IsSupported)
  {
    // Use CTaskDialog
  }
  else
  {
    // Use a dialog derived from CDialog or use AfxMessageBox()
  }
```

The static `IsSupported()` function in `CTaskDialog` returns `TRUE` if the operating system environment on which the application is running supports it.

Displaying a Task Dialog

The simplest way to create a `CTaskDialog` dialog and display it is to call the static `ShowDialog()` member of the class. Because you have no explicit `CTaskDialog` object, you can't do anything beyond the basic options offered by the `ShowDialog()` function, so this is primarily a more sophisticated alternative to calling `AfxMessageBox()`. The prototype of the `ShowDialog()` function is as follows:

```
  static INT_PTR ShowDialog(
  const CString& content,                         // Content of the dialog
```

```
const CString& mainInstr,                           // Main instruction in the dialog
const CString& title,                               // Title bar text
int nIDCommandFirst,                                // String ID of the first command
int nIDCommandLast,                                 // String ID of the last command
int buttons = TDCBF_YES_BUTTON|TDCBF_NO_BUTTON,     // Buttons in the dialog
int nOptions = TDF_ENABLE_HYPERLINKS|TDF_USE_COMMAND_LINKS,  // Dialog options
const CString& footer=_T(""));                      // Footer string in the dialog
```

The `nIDCommandFirst` and `nIDCommandLast` parameters specify a range of IDs that should identify entries in the string table resource in your application. For each valid ID, a command button will be created, and the string from the table will appear as the caption for the command button. You need to make sure that the value for the `nIDCommandFirst` parameter is greater than the IDs for any other buttons you may be using, such as `IDOK` and `IDCANCEL`. If you create the IDs through the resource editor for the string table, this should not be a problem.

The `buttons` parameter specifies the common buttons that the user can click to close the dialog. In addition to the defaults, you can also use `TDCBF_OK_BUTTON`, `TDCBF_CANCEL_BUTTON`, `TDCBF_RETRY_BUTTON`, and `TDCBF_CLOSE_BUTTON`. These are single-bit masks that identify the buttons. When you want to have two or more buttons displayed in the dialog, you OR them together.

There are many standard options you can specify via the `nOptions` parameter, in addition to the default values shown. You can find these in the documentation for the `SetOptions()` function in the dialog class.

The integer value that is returned reflects the selection made by the user to close the dialog. This will be the ID for the control that was clicked to close the dialog. In the case of a command button being clicked, the ID will be the ID that identifies the entry in the string table. If a common button is clicked to close the dialog, the value returned will be one of `IDYES`, `IDNO`, `IDOK`, `IDCANCEL`, `IDRETRY`, or `IDCLOSE`.

Here's a code fragment showing how you might use the `ShowDialog()` function:

```
CString content(_T("Modal Line Type Options"));
   CString mainInst(
            _T("Choose the line type you want to use or click Cancel to exit:"));
   CString title(_T("Line Type Chooser"));
   int result = CTaskDialog::ShowDialog(
     content,
     mainInst,
     title,
     IDS_SOLID_LINE,
     IDS_DASHED_LINE,
     TDCBF_CANCEL_BUTTON
     );
```

For this fragment to compile and execute successfully, you would need to have defined the symbols `IDS_SOLID_LINE`, `IDS_DOTTED_LINE`, `IDS_DOTDASH_LINE`, and `IDS_DASHED_LINE` with consecutive values. You can create new symbols by clicking on the string table resource on the Resources pane and pressing the insert key to add a new string. You will then be able to edit the `Caption`, `ID`, and `Value` properties for the new entry.

The dialog that is displayed is shown in Figure 18-11.

To get the data from this dialog when it closes, you could use the following code:

FIGURE 18-11

```
switch(result)
{
  case IDS_SOLID_LINE:
   m_LineType = SOLID;
   break;
  case IDS_DOTTED_LINE:
   m_LineType = DOTTED;
   break;
  case IDS_DOTDASH_LINE:
   m_LineType = DOTDASH;
   break;
  case IDS_DASHED_LINE:
   m_LineType = DASHED;
   break;
  case IDCANCEL:
   break;
  default:
    CTaskDialog::ShowDialog(
     _T("Error Choosing Line Type"),
     _T("Invalid return from dialog!"),
     _T("Error"),
     0,
     0,
     TDCBF_OK_BUTTON
     );
   break;
}
```

This fragment sets the value of a member variable, `m_LineType`, depending on the value returned from the `ShowDialog()` function. The function returns the symbol value corresponding to the command or common button that was clicked to terminate the dialog. There's a provision in the default case for displaying an error dialog using the `ShowDialog()` function. This supplies string arguments as literals rather than creating `CString` objects.

Creating CTaskDialog Objects

When you create a `CTaskDialog` object using the class constructor, you have increased flexibility in what you can do with the dialog because you have functions available that enable you to customize the dialog object. There are two constructors that have parameters similar to those of the `ShowDialog()` function. One has parameters for specifying a range of IDs for command controls, and the other doesn't. The prototype for the constructor without command control parameters is as follows:

```
CTaskDialog(
const CString& content,                              // Content of the dialog
const CString& mainInstr,                            // Main instruction in the dialog
const CString& title,                                // Title bar text
int buttons = TDCBF_OK_BUTTON|TDCBF_CANCEL_BUTTON,   // Buttons in the dialog
int nOptions = TDF_ENABLE_HYPERLINKS|TDF_USE_COMMAND_LINKS,  // Dialog options
const CString& footer=_T("")                         // Footer string in the dialog
};
```

Note that the default button values are different from those of the ShowDialog() function. Here the defaults are for OK and Cancel buttons rather than Yes and No buttons. Here's how you could use this constructor:

```
CTaskDialog scaleDlg(
_T("Choose the View Scale"),
_T("Click on the view scale you want:"),
_T("View Scale Selector") );
```

When you use this constructor, you typically customize the object by calling member functions before displaying the dialog.

The more comprehensive constructor adds two parameters that specify the IDs for a range of command controls:

```
CTaskDialog(
const CString& content,                              // Content of the dialog
const CString& mainInstr,                            // Main instruction in the dialog
const CString& title,                                // Title bar text
int nIDCommandFirst,                                 // String ID of the first command
int nIDCommandLast,                                  // String ID of the last command
int buttons,                                         // Buttons in the dialog
int nOptions = TDF_ENABLE_HYPERLINKS|TDF_USE_COMMAND_LINKS,  // Dialog options
const CString& footer=_T("")                         // Footer string in the dialog
};
```

As you see, there are no default button values in this case. This constructor produces an object that encapsulates a dialog that is similar to the one produced by the ShowDialog() function.

Adding Radio Buttons

You can add radio buttons to a CTaskDialog object using the AddRadioButton() function. Here's how you could add radio buttons to the scaleDlg object that was created in the previous section:

```
  const int SCALE_1(1001), SCALE_2(1002), SCALE_3(1003), SCALE_4(1004);
scaleDlg.AddRadioButton(SCALE_1, _T("View scale 1"));
scaleDlg.AddRadioButton(SCALE_2, _T("View scale 2"));
scaleDlg.AddRadioButton(SCALE_3, _T("View scale 3"));
scaleDlg.AddRadioButton(SCALE_4, _T("View scale 4"));
int result = scaleDlg.DoModal();
```

The first statement defines four integer constants that you use to identify the radio buttons. The `AddRadioButton()` function calls add four radio buttons, each identified by the first argument, with the annotation for each radio button specified by the second argument. Executing this fragment, following the statement in the previous section that creates `scaleDlg`, will display the dialog shown in Figure 18-12.

The first radio button is selected by default. If you wanted to have a different radio button selected by default, you could call the `SetDefaultRadioButton()` function for the dialog before you display it. For example:

FIGURE 18-12

```
scaleDlg.SetDefaultRadioButton(SCALE_3);
```

The argument to the function is the ID of the button you want to set as the default selection.

You can remove all the radio buttons from a `CTaskDialog` object by calling its `RemoveAllRadioButtons()` function. You would do this if you wanted to add a different set of radio buttons before you re-display the dialog.

Getting Output from Radio Buttons

You can obtain the ID of the radio button that is selected when the dialog closes by calling the `GetSelectedRadioButtonID()` function for the dialog object. Here's how you can get output from `scaleDlg`:

```
if(scaleDlg.DoModal() == IDOK)
{
  switch(scaleDlg.GetSelectedRadioButtonID())
  {
  case SCALE_1:
    m_Scale = 1;
    break;
  case SCALE_2:
    m_Scale = 2;
    break;
  case SCALE_3:
    m_Scale = 3;
    break;
  case SCALE_4:
    m_Scale = 4;
    break;
  }
}
```

You display the dialog by calling `DoModal()` for `scaleDlg`. You want to check the state of the radio buttons in the dialog only when the OK button is used to close the dialog, and the if statement verifies that the return from `DoModal()` corresponds to the OK button. The `GetSelectedRadioButtonID()` function returns the ID of the radio button that is selected, so the `switch` statement sets the value of the `m_Scale` member, depending on the ID that is returned.

The CTaskDialog class is a convenient and more flexible alternative to the AfxMessageBox() function, especially when you want to get user input in addition to communicating a message. There are also many more functions that the CTaskDialog class defines for manipulating and updating the dialog that I have described here. However, creating a dialog resource using the toolbox provides you with a much wider range of controls that you can use and gives you complete flexibility in how the dialog is laid out. Furthermore, when you do use the CTaskDialog class in an application that you want to run with Windows XP or earlier operating systems, you must call the IsSupported() function to verify that the class is supported before you attempt to use it, and you will need to program for an alternative dialog creation process when it isn't. For these reasons, you will find that most dialogs are best created as a dialog resource or through AfxMessageBox().

WORKING WITH STATUS BARS

With each view now being scaled independently, there's a real need to have some indication of what the current scale in a view is. A convenient way to do this would be to display the scale in the status bar for each view window. A status bar was created by default in the Sketcher main application window. Usually, the status bar appears at the bottom of an application window, below the horizontal scrollbar, although you can arrange for it to be at the top of the client area. The status bar is divided into segments called **panes**; the status bar in the main application window in Sketcher has four panes. The one on the left contains the text "Ready," and the other three are the recessed areas on the right that are used as indicators to record when Caps Lock, Num Lock, and Scroll Lock are in effect.

It's possible for you to write to the status bar that the Application Wizard supplied by default, but you need access to the m_wndStatusBar member of the CMainFrame object for the application, as this represents it. As it's a protected member of the class, you must either add a public member function to modify the status bar from outside the class, or add a member to return a reference to m_wndStatusBar.

You may well have several views of the same sketch, each with its own view scale, so you really want to associate displaying the scale with each view. Our approach will be to give each child window its own status bar. The m_wndStatusBar object in CMainFrame is an instance of the CMFCStatusBar class. You can use the same class to implement your own status bars in the view windows.

Adding a Status Bar to a Frame

The CMFCStatusBar class defines a control bar with multiple panes in which you can display information. We will be using this in a very simple way, but the CMFCStatusBar class provides a great deal of advanced capability, including the ability to display icons in status bar panes. Consult the Visual C++ 2010 documentation for the CMFCStatusBar class for more information on this.

The first step to using CMFCStatusBar is to add a data member for the status bar to the definition of CChildFrame, which is the frame window for a view. Add the following declaration to the public section of the class:

```
CMFCStatusBar m_StatusBar;                   // Status bar object
```

NOTE *Status bars should be part of the frame, not part of the view. You don't want to be able to scroll the status bars or draw over them. They should just remain anchored to the bottom of the window. If you added a status bar to the view, it would appear inside the scrollbars and would be scrolled whenever you scrolled the view. Drawing over the part of the view containing the status bar would cause the bar to be redrawn, leading to an annoying flicker. Having the status bar as part of the frame avoids these problems.*

Creating Status Bar Panes

To create the panes in the status bar, you call the SetIndicators() function for the status bar object. This function requires two arguments, a const array of indicators of type UINT and the number of elements in the array. Each element in the array is a resource symbol that will be associated with a pane in the status bar, and each resource symbol must have an entry in the resource string table that will be the default text in the pane. There are standard resource symbols, such as ID_INDICATOR_CAPS and ID_INDICATOR_NUM, which are used to identify indicators for the Caps Lock and Num Lock keys respectively, and you can see these in use if you look at the implementation of the OnCreate() function in the CMainFrame class. They also appear in the string table resource.

You can create your own indicator resource symbol by extending the String Table resource in Resource View: click the ▷ symbol, double-click the String Table entry to display the table, and then press the insert key. If you right-click the new entry in the table and select Properties from the menu, you will be able to change the ID to ID_INDICATOR_SCALE and the caption to View Scale :   1.

You should initialize the m_StatusBar data member just before the visible view window is displayed. So, using the Properties window for the CChildFrame class, you can add a function to the class that will be called in response to the WM_CREATE message that is sent to the application when the window is to be created. Add the following code to the OnCreate() handler:

```
int CChildFrame::OnCreate(LPCREATESTRUCT lpCreateStruct)
{
  if(CMDIChildWndEx::OnCreate(lpCreateStruct) == -1)
    return -1;

  // Create the status bar
  m_StatusBar.Create(this);
  static UINT indicators[] = {ID_INDICATOR_SCALE};
  m_StatusBar.SetIndicators(indicators, sizeof(indicators)/sizeof(UINT));
  m_StatusBar.SetPaneStyle(0, SBPS_STRETCH);      // Stretch the first pane
  return 0;
}
```

The generated code isn't bolded. There's a call to the base class version of the OnCreate() function, which takes care of creating the definition of the view window. It's important not to delete this function call; otherwise, the window is not created.

Calling the `Create()` function for the `CMFCStatusBar` object creates the status bar. You pass the `this` pointer for the current `CChildFrame` object to the `Create()` function, setting up a connection between the status bar and the window that owns it. The indicators that define the panes in the status bar are typically defined as an array of `UINT` elements. Here you are interested only in setting up a single pane, so you define `indicators` as an array that is initialized just with the symbol for your status pane. When you want to add multiple panes to a status bar, you can separate them by including `ID_SEPARATOR` symbols between your symbols in the `indicators` array. You call the `SetIndicators()` function for the status bar object with the address of `indicators` as the first argument and a count of the number of elements in the array as the second argument. This will create a single pane to the left in the status bar. The call to `SetPaneStyle()` for the first pane causes this pane to be stretched as necessary, the first argument being the pane index and the second a `UINT` value specifying the style or styles to be set. Without this, the sizing grip would not remain in the correct position when you resized the window. Only one pane can have the `SBPS_STRETCH` style. Other styles you can set for a pane are as follows:

SBPS_NORMAL	No stretch, borders, or pop-out styles set.
SBPS_POPOUT	Border reversed, so text pops out.
SBPS_NOBORDERS	No 3D borders.
SBPS_DISABLED	No text drawn in the pane.

You just OR the styles together when you want to set more than one style for a pane.

Updating the Status Bar

If you build and run the code now, the status bars appear, but they show only a scale factor of one, grayed out, no matter what scale factor is actually being used — not very useful. This is because there is no mechanism in place for updating the status bar. What you need to do is add code somewhere that changes the text in the status bar pane each time a different scale is chosen. The obvious place to do this is in the `CSketcherView` class because that's where the current view scale is recorded.

You can update a pane in the status bar by adding an `UPDATE_COMMAND_UI` handler that is associated with the indicator symbol for the pane. Right-click `CSketcherView` in Class View, and select Class Wizard from the pop-up. This will display the MFC Class Wizard dialog. As you can see, this enables you to create and edit a whole range of functions in a class and provides an alternative way to access any class member.

If it is not already visible, select the Commands tab in the dialog: this enables you to add command handlers to the class. Select `ID_INDICATOR_SCALE` in the Object IDs pane; this ID identifies the status bar pane you want to update. Then, select `UPDATE_COMMAND_UI` in the Messages pane. The dialog should look like Figure 18-13.

FIGURE 18-13

Click the Add Handler button to add the command handler to the class. Another dialog will be displayed that gives you the opportunity to change the handler function name to OnUpdateScale, which is a little more concise than the default. You can then click OK to close the dialog, and OK again to close the MFC Class Wizard dialog.

All you need is to complete the definition for the handler that was added, so add the following code to the function in SketcherView.cpp:

```
void CSketcherView::OnUpdateScale(CCmdUI *pCmdUI)
{
    pCmdUI->Enable();
    CString scaleStr;
    scaleStr.Format(_T(" View Scale : %d"), m_Scale);
    pCmdUI->SetText(scaleStr);
}
```

The parameter is a pointer to a CCmdUI object that encapsulates the status bar pane as a command target. You create a CString object and call its Format() function to generate the text string to be displayed in the pane. The first argument to Format() is a format control string in which you can embed conversion specifiers for subsequent arguments. The format string with the embedded specifiers is the same as for the C function, printf(). Each of the subsequent arguments is converted according to the corresponding format specifier in the first argument, so there must be one format specifier in the format string for each argument after the first. Here the %d specifier converts the value of m_Scale to a decimal string, and this is incorporated into the format string. Other common specifiers you can use are %f for floating point values and %s for string values. Calling SetText() for the CCmdUI object sets the string you supply as the argument in the status bar pane. Calling Enable() for the CCmdUI object causes the pane text to be displayed normally because the BOOL paramcter has a default value of TRUE. An explicit argument of FALSE would make the pane text grayed out.

That's all you need for the status bar. If you build Sketcher again, you should have multiple, scrolled windows, each at different scales, with the scale displayed in the status bar in each view.

USING A LIST BOX

Of course, you don't have to use a spin button to set the scale. You could also use a list box control, for example. The logic for handling a scale factor would be exactly the same, and only the dialog box and the code to extract the value for the scale factor from it would change. If you want to try this out without messing up the development of the Sketcher program, you can copy the complete Sketcher project to another folder and make the modifications to the copy. Deleting part of a Class Wizard–managed program can be a bit messy, so it's a useful experience to have before you really need to do it.

Removing the Scale Dialog

You first need to delete the definition and implementation of CScaleDialog from the copy of the Sketcher project, as well as the resource for the scale dialog. To do this, go to the Solution Explorer pane, select ScaleDialog.cpp, and press the delete key. Click the Delete button in the dialog that is displayed, unless you want to keep the file; then select ScaleDialog.h and remove it from the project in the same way. Go to Resource View, expand the Dialog folder, click IDD_SCALE_DLG, and press the delete key to remove the dialog resource. Delete the #include directive for ScaleDialog.h from SketcherView.cpp.

At this stage, all references to the original dialog class have been removed from the project. Are you all done yet? Almost. The IDs for the resources should have been deleted for you. To verify this, right-click Sketcher.rc in Resource View and select the Resource Symbols menu item from the pop-up; you can check that IDC_SCALE and IDC_SPIN_SCALE are no longer in the list. Of course, the OnViewScale() handler in the CSketcherView class still refers to CScaleDialog, so the Sketcher project won't compile yet. You'll fix that when you have added the list box control.

Select the Build ➪ Clean Solution menu item to remove any intermediate files from the project that may contain references to CScaleDialog. After that's done, you can start recreating the dialog resource for entering a scale value.

Creating a List Box Control

Right-click the Dialog folder in Resource View, and
add a new dialog with a suitable ID and caption. You
could use the same ID as before, IDD_SCALE_DLG.

Select the list box button in the list of controls, and
click where you want the list box to be positioned in
the dialog box. You can enlarge the list box and adjust
its position in the dialog by dragging it appropriately.
Right-click the list box and select Properties from the
pop-up. You can set the ID to something suitable, such
as IDC_SCALE_LIST, as shown in Figure 18-14.

The Sort property will be True by default, so make
sure you set it to False. This means that strings that
you add to the list box are not automatically sorted.
Instead, they're appended to the end of the list in the
box, and are displayed in the sequence in which you
enter them. Because you will be using the position
of the selected item in the list to indicate the scale,
it's important not to have the sequence changed. The
list box has a vertical scrollbar for the list entries by
default, and you can accept the defaults for the other

FIGURE 18-14

properties. If you want to look into the effects of the other properties, you can click each of them in
turn to display text at the bottom of the Properties window explaining what the property does.

Now that the dialog is complete, you can save it, and you're ready to create the class for the dialog.

Creating the Dialog Class

Right-click the dialog and select Add Class from the pop-up. Again, you'll be taken to the dialog
to create a new class. Give the class an appropriate name, such as the one you used before,
CScaleDialog, and select CDialog as the base class. If, when you click Finish, you get a message
box saying that ScaleDialog.cpp already exists, you forgot to explicitly delete the .h and .cpp
files. Go back and do that now, or rename the files if you want to keep them. Everything should then
work as it's supposed to. After you've completed that, all you need to do is add a public control
variable called m_Scale to the class, corresponding to the list box ID, IDC_SCALE_LIST. The type
should be int and the limits should be 0 and 7. Don't forget to set the Category as Value; otherwise,
you won't be able to enter the limits. Because you have created it as a control variable, DDX is
implemented for the m_Scale data member, and you will use the variable to store a zero-based
index to one of the eight entries in the list box.

You need to initialize the list box in the OnInitDialog() override in the CScaleDialog class,
so add an override for this function using the Properties window for the class. Add code to the
function as follows:

```
BOOL CScaleDialog::OnInitDialog()
{
  CDialog::OnInitDialog();

  CListBox* pListBox = static_cast<CListBox*>(GetDlgItem(IDC_SCALE_LIST));
  CString scaleStr;
  for(int i = 1 ; i <= 8 ; ++i)
  {
    scaleStr.Format(_T("Scale %d"), i);
    pListBox->AddString(scaleStr);
  }
  pListBox->SetCurSel(m_Scale);            // Set current scale

  return TRUE;   // return TRUE unless you set the focus to a control
                 // EXCEPTION: OCX Property Pages should return FALSE
}
```

The first line that you have added obtains a pointer to the list box control by calling the `GetDlgItem()` member of the dialog class. This is inherited from the MFC class, `CWnd`. It returns a pointer of type `CWnd*`, so you cast this to type `CListBox*`, which is a pointer to the MFC class defining a list box.

Using the pointer to the dialog's `CListBox` object, you then use the `AddString()` member repeatedly in the `for` loop to add the lines defining the list of scale factors. Each entry in the list box is formed by a call to the `Format()` member of the `scaleStr` object. The statement following the `for` loop sets the currently selected entry in the list box to correspond to the value of `m_Scale`. These entries appear in the list box in the order in which you enter them, so that the dialog is displayed as shown in Figure 18-15.

FIGURE 18-15

Each entry in the list is associated with a zero-based index value that is automatically stored in the `m_Scale` member of `CScaleDialog` through the DDX mechanism. Thus, if you select the third entry in the list, `m_Scale` is set to 2.

Displaying the Dialog

The dialog is displayed by the `OnViewScale()` handler that you added to `CSketcherView` in the previous version of Sketcher. You need only to amend this function to deal with the new dialog, using a list box, the code for it is as follows:

```
void CSketcherView::OnViewScale()
{
  CScaleDialog aDlg;                    // Create a dialog object
  aDlg.m_Scale = m_Scale - 1;           // Pass the view scale to the dialog
  if(aDlg.DoModal() == IDOK)
  {
    m_Scale = 1 + aDlg.m_Scale;         // Get the new scale

    ResetScrollSizes();                 // Adjust scrolling to the new scale
    InvalidateRect(0);                  // Invalidate the whole window
  }
}
```

Because the index value for the entry selected from the list is zero-based, you must decrement the current scale value by one when setting the value in the CScaleDialog object. You also need to add one to the value obtained from the dialog to get the actual scale value to be stored in the view. The code to display this value in the view's status bar is exactly as before. The rest of the code to handle scale factors is already complete and requires no changes. After you've added back the #include directive for ScaleDialog.h, you can build and execute this version of Sketcher to see the list box in action.

USING AN EDIT BOX CONTROL

You could use an edit box control to add annotations to a sketch in Sketcher. You'll need a new element type, CText, that corresponds to a text string, and an extra menu item to set a TEXT mode for creating elements. Because a text element needs only one reference point, you can create it in the OnLButtonDown() handler in the view class. You'll also need a new item in the Element menu to set TEXT mode. You'll add this text capability to Sketcher in the following sequence:

1. Create a dialog resource and its associated class with an edit box control for input.

2. Add the new menu item.

3. Add the code to open the dialog for creating an element.

4. Add the support for a CText class.

Creating an Edit Box Resource

Create a new dialog resource in Resource View by right-clicking the Dialog folder and selecting Insert Dialog from the pop-up. Change the ID for the new dialog to IDD_TEXT_DLG, and the caption text to Enter Text.

To add an edit box, select the edit control icon from the list of controls and then click the position in the dialog where you want to place it. You can adjust the size of the edit control by dragging its borders, and you can alter its position in the dialog by dragging the whole thing around. You can display the properties for the edit box by right-clicking it and selecting Properties from the pop-up. You could first change its ID to IDC_EDIT_TEXT, as shown in Figure 18-16.

Some of the properties for this control are of interest at this point. First, select the Multiline property. Setting the value for this as True creates a multiline edit box in which the text you enter can span more than one line. This enables you to enter a long line of text that will still remain visible in its entirety in the edit box. The Align text property determines

FIGURE 18-16

how the text is to be positioned in the multiline edit box. The value Left is fine here, but you also have the options for Center and Right.

If you were to change the value for the Want return property to True, pressing Enter on the keyboard while entering the text in the control would insert a return character into the text string. This enables you to analyze the string if you want to break it into multiple lines for display. You don't want this effect, so leave the property value as False. In this state, pressing enter has the effect of selecting the default control (which is the OK button), so pressing enter closes the dialog.

If you set the value of the Auto HScroll property to False, there is an automatic spill to the next line in the edit box when you reach the edge of the control while entering text. However, this is just for visibility in the edit box — it has no effect on the contents of the string. You could also change the value of the Auto VScroll property to True to allow text to continue beyond the number of lines that are visible in the control. If you set the Vertical Scroll property to True, the edit control will be supplied with a scrollbar that will allow you to scroll the text.

When you've finished setting the properties for the edit box, close its Properties window. Make sure that the edit box is first in the tab order by selecting the Format ⇨ Tab Order menu item or by pressing Ctrl+D. You can then test the dialog by selecting the Test Dialog menu item or by pressing Ctrl+T. The dialog is shown in Figure 18-17.

FIGURE 18-17

You can even enter text into the dialog in test mode to see how it works. Clicking the OK or Cancel button closes the dialog.

Creating the Dialog Class

After saving the dialog resource, you can create a suitable dialog class corresponding to the resource, which you could call **CTextDialog**. To do this, right-click the dialog in Resource View and select Add Class from the pop-up. The base class should be CDialog. Next you can add a control variable to the CTextDialog class by right-clicking the class name in Class View and selecting Add ⇨ Add Variable from the pop-up. Select IDC_EDIT_TEXT as the control ID and Value as the category. Call the new variable **m_TextString** and leave its type as CString — you'll take a look at this class after you've finished the dialog class. You can also specify a maximum length for it in the Max chars edit box, as shown in Figure 18-18.

FIGURE 18-18

A length of `100` is more than adequate for your needs. The variable that you have added here is automatically updated from the data entered into the control by the DDX mechanism. You can click Finish to create the variable in the `CTextDialog` class, and close the Add Member Variable wizard.

The CString Class

You have already used `CString` objects a couple of times in Sketcher, but there's more to it than you have seen so far. The `CString` class provides a very convenient and easy-to-use mechanism for handling strings that you can use just about anywhere a string is required. To be more precise, you can use a `CString` object in place of strings of type `const char*`, which is the usual type for a character string in native C++, or of type `LPCTSTR`, which is a type that comes up frequently in Windows API functions.

The `CString` class provides several overloaded operators, as shown in the following table, that make it easy to process strings.

OPERATOR	USAGE

=	Copies one string to another, as in:
	 `str1 = str2;`
	 `str1 = _T("A normal string");`

+	Concatenates two or more strings, as in: `str1 = str2 + str3 + _T(" more");`
+=	Appends a string to an existing `CString` object, as in: `str1 += str2;`
==	Compares two strings for equality, as in: `if(str1 == str2)  // do something...`
<	Tests if one string is less than another.
<=	Tests if one string is less than or equal to another.
>	Tests if one string is greater than another.
>=	Tests if one string is greater than or equal to another.

The variables `str1` and `str2` in the preceding table are `CString` objects.

`CString` objects automatically grow as necessary, such as when you add an additional string to the end of an existing object. For example:

```
CString str = _T("A fool and your money ");
str += _T("are soon partners.");
```

The first statement declares and initializes the object `str`. The second statement appends an additional string to `str`, so the length of `str` automatically increases.

Adding the Text Menu Item

Adding a new menu item should be easy by now. You just need to open the menu resource with the ID IDR_SketcherTYPE in Resource View by double-clicking it, and add a new menu item, Text, to the Element menu. The default ID, ID_ELEMENT_TEXT, that appears in the Properties window for the item is fine, so you can leave that as it is. You can add a prompt to be displayed on the status bar corresponding to the menu item, and because you'll also want to add an additional toolbar button corresponding to this menu item, you can add a tooltip to the end of the prompt line, using \n to separate the prompt and the tooltip.

Don't forget the context menu. You can copy the menu item from IDR_SketcherTYPE. Right-click the Text menu item and select Copy from the pop-up. Open the menu IDR_NOELEMENT_MENU, right-click the empty item at the bottom, and select Paste. All you need to do then, is drag the item to the appropriate position — above the separator — and save the resource file.

Add the toolbar button to the IDR_MAINFRAME_256 toolbar and set its ID to the same as that for the menu item, ID_ELEMENT_TEXT. You can drag the new button so that it's positioned at the end of the block defining the other types of elements. Do the same for the IDR_MAINFRAME toolbar that is used for small toolbar icons. When you've saved the resources, you can add an event handler for the new menu item.

In the Class View pane, right-click CSketcherDoc and display its Properties window. Add a COMMAND handler for the ID_ELEMENT_TEXT ID and add code to it as follows:

```
void CSketcherDoc::OnElementText()
{
  m_Element = TEXT;
}
```

Only one line of code is necessary to set the element type in the document to TEXT.

You also need to add a function to check the menu item if it is the current mode, so add an UPDATE_COMMAND_UI handler corresponding to the ID_ELEMENT_TEXT ID, and implement the code for it as follows:

```
void CSketcherDoc::OnUpdateElementText(CCmdUI* pCmdUI)
{
  // Set checked if the current element is text
  pCmdUI->SetCheck(m_Element == TEXT);
}
```

This operates in the same way as the other Element pop-up menu items. Of course, you could also have added both of these handlers through the Class Wizard dialog that you display by selecting Class Wizard from the context menu in Class View.

You must also add an additional entry to the ElementType enum in the SketcherConstants.h header file:

```
enum ElementType{LINE, RECTANGLE, CIRCLE, CURVE, TEXT};
```

The next step is to define the CText class for an element of type TEXT.

Defining a Text Element

You can derive the class `CText` from the `CElement` class as follows:

```cpp
// Class defining a text object
class CText: public CElement
{
  public:
    // Function to display a text element
    virtual void Draw(CDC* pDC, CElement* pElement=0);

    // Constructor for a text element
    CText(const CString& aString, const CRect& rect, COLORREF aColor);
    virtual void Move(const CSize& size);  // Move a text element

  protected:
    CString m_String;                       // Text to be displayed
    CText(){}                               // Default constructor
};
```

I added this manually, but I'll leave it to you to decide how you want to do it. This definition should go at the end of the `Elements.h` file, following the other element types. This class definition declares the virtual `Draw()` and `Move()` functions, as the other element classes do. The data member `m_String` of type `CString` stores the text to be displayed.

The `CText` constructor declaration defines three parameters: the string to be displayed, the rectangle in which the string is to be displayed, and the color. The pen width doesn't apply to an item of text, because the appearance is determined by the font. Although you do not need to pass a pen width as an argument to the constructor, the constructor needs to initialize the `m_PenWidth` member inherited from the base class because it is used in the computation of the bounding rectangle for the text.

Implementing the CText Class

You have three functions to implement for the `CText` class:

➤   The constructor for a `CText` object

➤   The virtual `Draw()` function to display it

➤   The `Move()` function to support moving a text object by dragging it with the mouse

I added these directly to the `Elements.cpp` file.

The CText Constructor

The constructor for a `CText` object needs to initialize the class and base class data members:

```cpp
// CText constructor
CText::CText(const CString& aString, const CRect& rect, COLORREF aColor)
{
  m_PenWidth = 1;                    // Set the pen width
```

```
    m_Color = aColor;                       // Set the color for the text
    m_String = aString;                     // Make a copy of the string

    m_EnclosingRect = rect;
    m_EnclosingRect.NormalizeRect();
}
```

You set the pen width to 1, and store the color and the text string to be displayed. The second parameter is the rectangle in which the text is to be displayed, so this is stored as the enclosing rectangle.

Creating a Text Element

After the element type has been set to TEXT, a text object should be created at the cursor position whenever you click the left mouse button and enter the text you want to display. You therefore need to display the dialog that permits text to be entered in the OnLButtonDown() handler, but only when the element type is TEXT. Add the following code to this handler in the CSketcherView class:

```
void CSketcherView::OnLButtonDown(UINT nFlags, CPoint point)
{
  CClientDC aDC(this);             // Create a device context
  OnPrepareDC(&aDC);               // Get origin adjusted
  aDC.DPtoLP(&point);              // convert point to Logical
  // In moving mode, so drop the element
  if(m_MoveMode)
  {
    m_MoveMode = false;                    // Kill move mode
    m_pSelected = nullptr;                 // De-select element
    GetDocument()->UpdateAllViews(nullptr);  // Redraw all the views
    return;
  }
  CSketcherDoc* pDoc = GetDocument();// Get a document pointer
  if(pDoc->GetElementType() == TEXT)
  {
    CTextDialog aDlg;
    if(aDlg.DoModal() == IDOK)
    {
      // Exit OK so create a text element
      CSize textExtent = aDC.GetTextExtent(aDlg.m_TextString);
      CRect rect(point, textExtent);       //Create enclosing rectangle
      CText* pTextElement = new CText(
                          aDlg.m_TextString, rect, pDoc->GetElementColor());

      // Add the element to the document
      pDoc->AddElement(pTextElement);

      // Get all views updated
      pDoc->UpdateAllViews(nullptr, 0, pTextElement);
    }
    return;
  }

  m_FirstPoint = point;             // Record the cursor position
  SetCapture();                     // Capture subsequent mouse messages
}
```

The code to be added is bolded. It creates a CTextDialog object and then opens the dialog using the DoModal() function call. The m_TextString member of aDlg is automatically set to the string entered in the edit box, so you can use this data member to pass the string entered back to the CText constructor if the OK button is used to close the dialog. The color is obtained from the document using the GetElementColor() member that you have used previously.

You also need to determine the rectangle that bounds the text. Because the size of the rectangle for the block of text depends on the font used in a device context, you use the GetTextExtent() function in the CClientDC object, aDC, to initialize the CSize object, textExtent, with the width and height of the text string in logical coordinates. You then use a CRect constructor that creates a rectangle from a point that is the top right corner of the rectangle, and a CSize object that specifies the width and height of the rectangle.

The CText object is created on the heap because the list in the document maintains only pointers to the elements. You add the new element to the document by calling the AddElement() member of CSketcherDoc, with the pointer to the new text element as an argument. Finally, UpdateAllViews() is called with the first argument 0, which specifies that all views are to be updated.

Drawing a CText Object

Drawing text in a device context is different from drawing a geometric figure. The implementation of the Draw() function for a CText object is as follows:

```
void CText::Draw(CDC* pDC, CElement* pElement)
{
  COLORREF Color(m_Color);              // Initialize with element color

  if(this==pElement)
    Color = SELECT_COLOR;               // Set selected color

  // Set the text color and output the text
  pDC->SetTextColor(Color);
  pDC->DrawText(m_String, m_EnclosingRect, DT_CENTER|DT_VCENTER|
DT_SINGLELINE|DT_NOCLIP);
}
```

You don't need a pen to display text. You just need to specify the text color using the SetTextColor() function member of the CDC object, and then use the DrawText() member to output the text string. This displays the string, specified by the first argument, in the rectangle specified by the second argument, using the default font. The third argument specifies how the text is to be formatted. You specify the third argument as one or more standard formatting constants of type UINT combined together with logical ORs.

Many of these constants correspond to the ones defined for use with the Windows API DrawText() function. The following table lists some of the more common constants:

CONSTANT	MEANING
DT_LEFT	Text is aligned with the left of the rectangle.
DT_CENTER	Text is centered horizontally in the rectangle.
DT_RIGHT	Text is aligned with the right of the rectangle.
DT_TOP	Text is aligned with the top of the rectangle.
DT_VCENTER	Text is centered vertically in the rectangle. This is used only with DT_SINGLELINE.
DT_BOTTOM	Text is aligned with the bottom of the rectangle. This is used only with DT_SINGLELINE.
DT_SINGLELINE	Text is displayed on a single line. CR and LF do not break the line.
DT_NOCLIP	Inhibits clipping of the text, and drawing is faster.
DT_WORDBREAK	The string will be broken between words if it would otherwise extend beyond the sides of the rectangle.

Because the TextOut() function doesn't use a pen, it isn't affected by setting the drawing mode of the device context. This means that the raster operations (ROP) method that you use to move the elements leaves temporary trails behind when applied to text. Remember that you used the SetROP2() function to specify the way in which the pen would logically combine with the background. By choosing R2_NOTXORPEN as the drawing mode, you could cause a previously drawn element to disappear by redrawing it — it would then revert to the background color and thus become invisible. Fonts aren't drawn with a pen, so it won't work properly with the text elements. You'll see how to fix this problem a little later in this chapter.

Moving a CText Object

The Move() function for a CText object is simple:

```
void CText::Move(const CSize& size)
{
  m_EnclosingRect += size;              // Move the rectangle
}
```

All you need to do is alter the enclosing rectangle by the distance specified in the size parameter.

To fix the trails problem when moving a text element, you have to treat it as a special case in the MoveElement() function in the CSketcherView class. Providing an alternative move mechanism for text elements requires that you can discover when the m_pSelected pointer contains the address of a CText object. The typeid operator in native C++ that you met back in Chapter 2 can help with this.

By comparing the expression `typeid(*m_pSelected)` with `typeid(CText)`, you can determine whether or not `m_pSelected` is pointing to a `CText` object. To be able to use the `typeid` operator in your code, you must change the `Enable Run-Time Type Information` property value for the project to `Yes(/GR)`. You can open the project's Properties dialog by pressing Alt+F7; you will find the property to change by selecting Configuration Properties ⇨ C/C++ ⇨ Language in the left pane of the dialog.

Here's how you can update the `MoveElement()` function to eliminate the trails when moving text:

```
void CSketcherView::MoveElement(CClientDC& aDC, CPoint& point)
{
  CSize distance = point - m_CursorPos;   // Get move distance
  m_CursorPos = point;            // Set current point as 1st for next time

  // If there is an element, selected, move it
  if(m_pSelected)
  {
    // If the element is text use this method...
    if (typeid(*m_pSelected) == typeid(CText))
    {
      CRect oldRect=m_pSelected->GetBoundRect(); // Get old bound rect
      aDC.LPtoDP(oldRect);                        // Convert to client coords
      m_pSelected->Move(distance);                // Move the element
      InvalidateRect(&oldRect);                   // Invalidate combined area
      UpdateWindow();                             // Redraw immediately
      m_pSelected->Draw(&aDC,m_pSelected);        // Draw highlighted

      return;
    }

    // ...otherwise, use this method
    aDC.SetROP2(R2_NOTXORPEN);
    m_pSelected->Draw(&aDC,m_pSelected);    // Draw the element to erase it
    m_pSelected->Move(distance);            // Now move the element
    m_pSelected->Draw(&aDC,m_pSelected);    // Draw the moved element
  }
}
```

When `m_pSelected` points to a text element, you obtain the bounding rectangle for the old element before moving the element to its new position, and convert the rectangle to client coordinates, because that's what `InvalidateRect()` expects. After the move, you call `InvalidateRect()` to redraw the rectangle where the element used to be.

You can see that the code for invalidating the rectangles that you must use for moving the text is a little less elegant than the ROP code that you use for all the other elements. It works, though, as you'll see for yourself if you make this modification, and then build and run the application. Because you use the `typeid` operator for testing the type, you must add an `#include` directive for the `typeinfo` header to `SketcherView.cpp`. This header provides the definition for the `type_info` class, and you need this because the `typeid` operator returns a reference to a `const type_info` object.

For the program to compile successfully, you need to add a #include directive for TextDialog.h to the SketcherView.cpp file. You should now be able to produce annotated sketches using multiple scaled and scrolled views, such as the ones shown in Figure 18-19.

FIGURE 18-19

You can see that the text does not scale along with the shapes. You could scale the text by adjusting the font size in the device context based on the scale. Of course, you would have to adjust the rectangle enclosing the text when you draw it, too.

DIALOGS AND CONTROLS IN CLR SKETCHER

There is a full range of dialogs and controls available for use in a CLR program, but the procedure for adding them to an application is often different from what you have seen in the MFC version of Sketcher. Extending CLR Sketcher will allow you to try out some of the ways in which you can use dialogs and controls in a Windows Forms application. You will not necessarily end up with the GUI for CLR Sketcher that you would want in practice because you will inevitably duplicate some functions in a way that is not needed in the application.

Adding a Dialog

It would be useful to add a dialog that you can use to enter pen widths, to allow elements to be drawn with lines of different thicknesses. Your first thought as to how to do this is likely to involve the Design window for the form — and indeed, for some predefined dialogs this is the place to start. However, when you want to create your own dialog from the ground up, the starting point is Solution Explorer.

To add a dialog, you actually add a form to the project that you then modify to make it a dialog window. In Solution Explorer, right-click your project, click the Add menu item, then click New Item. In the dialog that displays, select the UI group in the left pane; then select Windows Form in the right pane. Enter the name as **PenDialog.cs** and click the OK button. The `.cs` extension identifies that the dialog is for a C++/CLI program. A new Design window will display showing the dialog. In the Properties window for the dialog, change the `FormBorderStyle` property in the Appearance group to `FixedDialog` and set the `ControlBox`, `MinimizeBox`, and `MaximizeBox` properties in the Window Style group to `false`. Change the value of the `Text` property to `Set Pen Width`. You now have a modal dialog for setting the pen width, so next you can add the controls you need to the dialog.

Customizing the Dialog

You'll use radio buttons to allow a pen width to be chosen, and place them within a group box that serves to keep them in a group in which only one radio button can be checked at one time. Drag a `GroupBox` control from the Containers group in the Toolbox window onto the dialog you have created. Change the value of the `Text` property for the group box to `Select Pen Width` and change the value of the `(name)` property to `penWidthGroupBox`. Adjust the size of the group box by dragging its border so that it fits nicely within the dialog frame. Drag six `RadioButton` controls from the Toolbox window to the group box and arrange them in a rectangular configuration as you did in the MFC Sketcher program. You'll notice that alignment guides to help you position the controls display automatically for each `RadioButton` control after the first. Change the text properties for the radio button controls to `Pen Width 1` through `Pen Width 6`, and the corresponding `(name)` property values to `penWidthButton1` through `penWidthButton6`. Change the value of the `Checked` property for `penWidthButton1` to `true`.

Next you can add two buttons to the dialog and change their `Text` properties to `OK` and `Cancel`, and the `(name)` properties to `penWidthOK` and `penWidthCancel`. Return to the dialog's Properties window and set the `AcceptButton` and `CancelButton` property values to `penWidthOK` and `penWidthCancel` by selecting from the list in the values column. Verify that the `DialogResult` property values for the buttons are `OK` and `Cancel`; this will cause the appropriate `DialogResult` value to be returned when the dialog is closed by the user clicking one button or the other. You should now have a dialog in the Design window that looks similar to Figure 18-20.

FIGURE 18-20

The code for the dialog class is part of the project and is defined in the PenDialog.h header file. However, there are no instances of the PenDialog class anywhere at the moment, so to use the dialog you must create one. You will create a PenDialog object in the Form1 class; add an #include directive for PenDialog.h to Form1.h. Add a new private variable of type PenDialog^ to the Form1 class with the name penDialog and initialize it in the Form1 constructor to gcnew PenDialog().

You need a way to get information about which radio button is checked from the PenDialog object. One way to do this is to add a public property to the class to make the information available. It can be a read-only property, so you need only to implement get() for the property. The code that the Windows Form Designer generates is delimited by a #pragma region and a #pragma endregion directive, and you should not modify this manually or add in your own code. Add the following code to the PenDialog class definition immediately after the #pragma endregion directive:

```
public: property float PenWidth
{
  float get()
  {
    if(penWidthButton1->Checked)
      return 1.0f;
    if(penWidthButton2->Checked)
      return 2.0f;
    if(penWidthButton3->Checked)
      return 3.0f;
    if(penWidthButton4->Checked)
      return 4.0f;
    if(penWidthButton5->Checked)
      return 5.0f;
    return 6.0f;
  }
}
```

The System::Drawing::Pen class defines a pen where the pen width is a floating-point value; hence, the PenWidth property is floating-point.

Now that the dialog is complete, and you have a Form1 member that references a dialog object, you need a mechanism to open the dialog. Another toolbar button on the Form1 window is a good choice.

Displaying the Dialog

You need a bitmap to display on the new toolbar button. Switch to the Resource View, right-click the Bitmap folder, and click Insert Bitmap. Set the Height and Width property values for the bitmap to 16, the Filename property value to penwidth.bmp, and the ID to IDB_PENWIDTH. You can now create a bitmap of your choosing to represent a line width; I'll use a symbol that looks like a pen drawing a line, as in MFC Sketcher.

In the Design window for Form1.h, add a separator to the toolbar, followed by a new toolbar button. Change the (name) property value to **penWidthButton** and the ToolTipText property value to **Change pen width**. Set the image for the new button to **penwidth.bmp**, and then create a Click event handler for the toolbar button by double-clicking the Click event in its Properties window. You can add the following code to the new event handler to display the pen dialog:

```
private: System::Void penWidthButton _Click(
                                 System::Object^ sender, System::EventArgs^ e)
{
  if(penDialog->ShowDialog() == System::Windows::Forms::DialogResult::OK)
  {
    // Get the pen width ...
  }
}
```

Calling `ShowDialog()` for the `PenDialog` object displays the dialog. Because it is a modal dialog, it remains visible until a button is clicked to close it. The `ShowDialog()` function returns a value that is an enumerator from the `System::Windows::Forms::DialogResult` enumeration. This enumeration defines the following enumerator values:

```
None, OK, Cancel, Abort, Retry, Ignore, Yes, No
```

These provide for a variety of buttons being identified to close a dialog, and you can set any of these values from the drop-down list of values for the `DialogResult` property of a button. You must fully qualify the `DialogResult` type name here because the `Form1` class has an inherited member with the name `DialogResult`.

You need somewhere to record the current pen width in the `Form1` class, so add a private `penWidth` variable of type `float` to the class and initialize it to `1.0f` in the constructor. You can now replace the comment in the preceding `Click` event handler with the following:

```
penWidth = penDialog->PenWidth;
```

This will set the current pen width to the value returned by the `PenWidth` property for the dialog.

All that remains to do is to implement creating and drawing elements with a given pen width.

Creating Elements with a Pen Width

This will involve modifying the constructor in each of the derived element classes. The modifications are essentially the same in each class, so I'll just show how the `Line` class constructor changes, and you can do the rest.

The changes to the `Line` class constructor to allow for different pen widths are as follows:

```
Line(Color color, Point start, Point end, float penWidth)
{
  pen = gcnew Pen(color, penWidth);
this->color = color;
position = start;
this->end = end - Size(start);
boundRect = System::Drawing::Rectangle(Math::Min(position.X, end.X),
                                      Math::Min(position.Y, end.Y),
           Math::Abs(position.X - end.X), Math::Abs(position.Y - end.Y));
```

```
        boundRect.Inflate(safe_cast<int>(penWidth), safe_cast<int>(penWidth));

    }
```

The only changes are to add an extra parameter to the `Line` constructor, to use the `Pen` constructor that accepts a second argument of type `float` that specifies the pen width, and to increase the size of the bounding rectangle by the `penWidth` argument value. Make the same change to the constructors for the other element classes.

Because you have changed the parameter list for the element class constructors, you must change the `MouseMove` event handler that creates elements:

```
private: System::Void Form1_MouseMove(System::Object^  sender,
System::Windows::Forms::MouseEventArgs^  e) {
  if(drawing)
 {
   if(tempElement)
     Invalidate(tempElement->Bound);   // The old element region
   switch(elementType)
   {
     case ElementType::LINE:
       tempElement = gcnew Line(color, firstPoint, e->Location, penWidth);
       break;
     case ElementType::RECTANGLE:
       tempElement = gcnew Rectangle(color, firstPoint, e->Location, penWidth);
       break;
     case ElementType::CIRCLE:
       tempElement = gcnew Circle(color, firstPoint, e->Location, penWidth);
       break;
     case ElementType::CURVE:
       if(tempElement)
         safe_cast<Curve^>(tempElement)->Add(e->Location);
       else
         tempElement = gcnew Curve(color, firstPoint, e->Location, penWidth);
       break;
   }
   // Rest of the code as before...
 }
```

You should now have CLR Sketcher with pen widths fully working, as Figure 18-21 illustrates.

Using a Combo Box Control

You can add a combo box to the toolbar in the Form1 Design window to provide a way to enter a line style. ComboBox is an option in the list that displays when you click the down arrow for the toolbar item that adds new entries in the Design window. You can customize this option to do what you want.

FIGURE 18-21

Set the DropDownStyle property to **DropDownList**; the effect of this is to only allow values to be selected from the list. A value of DropDown allows any value to be typed in the combo box. Change (name) to something more relevant, such as **lineStyleComboBox**. You want to add a specific set of items to be displayed in the combo box, and the Items property holds these. Select the Items property, click (Collection) in the value column, and select the ellipsis at the right to open the String Collection Editor dialog. You can then enter strings, as shown in Figure 18-22.

FIGURE 18-22

These are the entries that will be displayed in the drop-down for the combo box; they are indexed from 0 to 4.

Because the default size for the combo box is not as wide as you need for the longest string, change the value of the Size property to 150,25. You can also change the FlatStyle property to Standard, so that the combo box will be more visible on the toolbar. You can set the ToolTipText property to Choose line style.

At present the combo box will not show anything when it is first displayed, but you can fix that in the `Form1` constructor. Add the following line of code to the constructor after the `// TODO` comment:

```
lineStyleComboBox->SelectedIndex = 0;
```

The `SelectedIndex` property determines which of the entries in the `Items` collection is displayed in the combo box, and because the entries in the combo box `Items` property collection are indexed from 0, this causes the first entry to be displayed initially. That will continue to be the entry displayed until you select a new entry from the combo box, so the combo box will always show the currently selected line width.

You need somewhere to store the current line style, so add a private member, `lineStyle`, to the `Form1` class of type `System::Drawing::Drawing2D::DashStyle`. This is an enum type used by the `Pen` class to specify a style for drawing lines. If you add a `using` directive for the `System::Drawing::Drawing2D` namespace, you can specify the type for `lineStyle` as just `DashStyle`.

The `DashStyle` enum defines the members `Solid`, `Dash`, `Dot`, `DashDot`, `DashDotDot`, and `Custom`. The meaning for the first five are obvious. The `Custom` style gives you complete flexibility in specifying a line style as virtually any sequence of line segments and spaces of differing lengths that you want. You specify how the line style is to appear by setting the `DashPattern` property for the `Pen` object. You specify the pattern with an array of `float` values that specify the lengths of the line segments and intervening spaces. Here's an example:

```
array<float>^ pattern = {5.0f, 3.0f};
pen->DashPattern = pattern;
```

This specifies a dashed line for the `Pen` object `pen`, consisting of segments of length `5.0f` separated by spaces of length `3.0f`. The pattern you specify is repeated as often as necessary to draw a given line. Obviously, by specifying more elements in the array, you can define patterns as complicated as you like.

You need to know when an entry from the combo box is selected so that you can update the `lineStyle` member of the `Form1` class. An easy way to arrange this is to add a handler for the `SelectedIndexChanged` event for the `ComboBox` object; add this handler through the Properties window and implement it like this:

```
private: System::Void lineStyleComboBox_SelectedIndexChanged(
                           System::Object^  sender, System::EventArgs^ e)
{
  switch(lineStyleComboBox->SelectedIndex)
  {
    case 1:
     lineStyle = DashStyle::Dash;
     break;
    case 2:
     lineStyle = DashStyle::Dot;
     break;
    case 3:
     lineStyle = DashStyle::DashDot;
     break;
    case 4:
     lineStyle = DashStyle::DashDotDot;
     break;
    default:
     lineStyle = DashStyle::Solid;
     break;
  }
}
```

This just sets the value of `lineStyle` to one of the `DashStyle` enum values based on the value of the `SelectedIndex` property for the combo box object.

To draw elements with different line styles you must add another parameter of type `DashStyle` to each of the element constructors. First, add the following `using` directive to `Elements.h`:

```
using namespace System::Drawing::Drawing2D;
```

Here's how you update the `Line` class constructor to support drawing lines in different styles:

```
Line(Color color, Point start, Point end, float penWidth, DashStyle style)
{
  pen = gcnew Pen(color, penWidth);
  pen->DashStyle = style;
  // Rest of the code for the function as before...
}
```

There's just one new line of code, which sets the `DashStyle` property for the pen to the property passed as the last argument to the constructor. Change the other element class constructors in the same way.

The last thing you must do is update the constructor calls in the mouse move event handler in the `Form1` class:

```
private: System::Void Form1_MouseMove(System::Object^  sender,
System::Windows::Forms::MouseEventArgs^  e)
{
  if(drawing)
  {
    if(tempElement)
      Invalidate(tempElement->bound);                  // Invalidate old element area
    switch(elementType)
    {
      case ElementType::LINE:
        tempElement = gcnew Line(color, firstPoint, e->Location, penWidth,
                                                                   lineStyle);
        break;
      case ElementType::RECTANGLE:
        tempElement = gcnew Rectangle(color, firstPoint, e->Location, penWidth,
                                                                   lineStyle);
        break;
      case ElementType::CIRCLE:
        tempElement = gcnew Circle(color, firstPoint, e->Location, penWidth,
                                                                   lineStyle);
        break;
      case ElementType::CURVE:
        if(tempElement)
          safe_cast<Curve^>(tempElement)->Add(e->Location);
        else
          tempElement = gcnew Curve(color, firstPoint, e->Location, penWidth,
                                                                   lineStyle);
        break;
    }

    // Rest of the code for the function as before...
  }
}
```

If you recompile CLR Sketcher and run it again, the combo box will enable you to select a new line style for drawing elements. The line styles don't really work for curves because of the way they are drawn — as a series of very short line segments. With the other elements, the line styles look better if you draw with a pen width greater than the default.

Creating Text Elements

Drawing text in CLR Sketcher will be similar to drawing text in MFC Sketcher. Selecting a Text menu item or clicking a text toolbar button will set `Text` as the element drawing mode, and in this mode clicking anywhere on the form will display a modal dialog that allows some text to be entered; closing the dialog with the OK button will display the text at the cursor position. There are many ramifications to drawing text, but in the interest of keeping the book to a modest weight, I'll limit this discussion to the basics.

Add a TEXT enumerator to the ElementType enum class, then add a Text menu item to the Elements menu, and a corresponding toolbar button in the Form1 Design window; you will need to create a bitmap resource for the button. Change the value of the (name) property for the menu item to textToolStripMenuItem if necessary, and create a Click event handler for it. You can also add a value for the ToolTipText property for the menu item and the toolbar button. You can create a bitmap for the toolbar button to indicate text mode, and select the Click event handler for the toolbar button to be the Click event handler for the menu item. You can implement the Click event handler like this:

```
private: System::Void textToolStripMenuItem_Click(
                                System::Object^ sender, System::EventArgs^ e)
{
    elementType = ElementType::TEXT;
    SetElementTypeButtonState();
}
```

The function just sets elementType to the ElementType enumerator that represents text drawing mode.

Update the SetElementTypeButtonsState() function to check the text button. You will need to update the DropDownOpening event handler for the tool strip to ensure that the new text menu item gets checked. Don't forget to add a Text menu item to the context menu, too. This will involve amending the handler for the Opening event for the context menu to add the Text menu item, and set it as checked when appropriate.

Drawing Text

You need to look into several things before you can make CLR Sketcher create and draw text. Let's start with how you draw text. The Graphics class defines a DrawString() function for drawing text. There are several overloaded versions of this function, as described in the following table.

FUNCTION	DESCRIPTION

DrawString(
 	
  String^ str,
 	
  Font^ font,
 	
  Brush^ brush,
 	
  PointF point)
	Draws str at the position point using font, with the color determined by brush. Type Windows::Drawing::PointF is a point represented by coordinates of type float. You can use a Point object as an argument in any of the functions for a PointF parameter.

DrawString(
 	
  String^ str,
 	
  Font^ font,
 	
  Brush^ brush,
 	
  float X,
 	
  float Y)
	Draws str at the position (X,Y) using font, with the color determined by brush. You can also use coordinate arguments of type int when you call this function.

continues

(continued)

```DrawString(\n String^ str,\n Font^ font,\n Brush^ brush,\n RectangleF rect)```	Draws `str` within the rectangle `rect` using `font`, with the color determined by `brush`. Type `Windows::Drawing::RectangleF` defines a rectangle with its position width and height specified by values of type `float`. You can use a `Rectangle` object as an argument in any of the functions for a `RectangleF` parameter.
```DrawString(\n String^ str,\n Font^ font,\n Brush^ brush,\n PointF point,\n StringFormat^ format)```	Draws `str` at the position `point` using `font`, with the color determined by `brush` and the formatting of the string specified by `format`. A `StringFormat` object determines the alignment and other formatting properties for a string.
```DrawString(\n String^ str,\n Font^ font,\n Brush^ brush,\n float X,\n float Y,\n StringFormat^ format)```	Draws `str` at the position `(X,Y)` using `font`, with the color determined by `brush` and the formatting of the string specified by `format`.
```DrawString(\n String^ str,\n Font^ font,\n Brush^ brush,\n RectangleF rect,\n StringFormat^ format)```	Draws `str` within the rectangle `rect` using `font`, with the color determined by `brush` and the formatting of the string determined by `format`.

Clearly, you need to understand a bit about fonts and brushes in order to use the `DrawString()` function, so I'll briefly introduce those before returning to how you can create and display `Text` elements.

Creating Fonts

You specify the font to be used when you draw a string by a `System::Drawing::Font` object that defines the typeface, style, and size of the drawn characters. An object of type `System::Drawing::FontFamily` defines a group of fonts with a given typeface, such as `"Arial"` or `"Times New Roman"`. The `System::Drawing::FontStyle` enumeration defines possible font styles, which can be any of the following: `Regular`, `Bold`, `Italic`, `Underline`, and `Strikeout`.

You can create a `Font` object like this:

```
FontFamily^ family = gcnew FontFamily(L"Arial");
System::Drawing::Font^ font = gcnew System::Drawing::Font(family, 10,
                                       FontStyle::Bold,  GraphicsUnit::Point);
```

You create the `FontFamily` object by passing the name of the font to the constructor. The arguments to the `Font` constructor are the font family, the size of the font, the font style, and an enumerator from the `GraphicUnit` enumeration that defines the units for the font size. The possible enumerator values are as follows:

`World`	The world coordinate system is the unit of measure.
`Display`	The unit of measure is that of the display device: pixels for monitors, and 1/100 inch for printers.
`Pixel`	A device pixel is the unit of measure.
`Point`	The unit of measure is a point (1/72 inch).
`Inch`	The unit of measure is the inch.
`Document`	The unit of measure is the document unit, which is 1/300 inch.
`Millimeter`	The millimeter is the unit of measure.

Thus, the previous code fragment defines a 10-point bold Arial font. Note that the `Font` type name is fully qualified in the fragment because a form object in a Windows Forms application inherits a property with the name `Font` from the `Form` base class that identifies the default font for the form. Windows Forms applications support TrueType fonts primarily, so it is best not to choose Open Type fonts. If you attempt to use a font that is not supported, or the font is not installed on your computer, the Microsoft Sans Serif font will be used.

Creating Brushes

A `System::Drawing::Brush` object determines the color used to draw a string with a given font; it is also used to specify the color and texture used to fill a shape. You can't create a `Brush` object directly because `Brush` is an abstract class. You create brushes using the `SolidBrush`, the `TextureBrush`, and the `LinearGradientBrush` class types derived from `Brush`. A `SolidBrush` object is a brush of a single color, a `TextureBrush` object is a brush that uses an image to fill the interior of a shape, and a `LinearGradientBrush` is a brush defining a color gradient blend, usually between two colors, but also possibly among several colors. You will use a `SolidBrush` object to draw text, which you create like this:

```
SolidBrush^ brush = gcnew SolidBrush(Color::Red);
```

This creates a solid brush that will draw text in red.

Choosing a Font

You can store a reference to the current `Font` object, to be used when CLR Sketcher is creating `Text` elements, by adding a `private` variable of type `System::Drawing::Font^`, and with the name textFont, to the Form1 class. You must use the fully qualified type name to avoid confusion with the inherited property with the name Font. Initialize textFont in the Form1 constructor to Font, which is a form property specifying the default font for the form. Be sure to do this in the body of the constructor following the // TODO: comment; if you attempt to initialize it in the initialization list, the program will fail because Font is not defined at this point.

You can add a toolbar button to allow the user to select a font for entering text, perhaps a button with a bitmap representation of F for font. Give the button a suitable value for the (name) property, such as toolStripFontButton, and add a Click event handler for it.

The Toolbox window has a standard dialog for choosing a font that will display all the fonts available on your system and allow selection of the font style and size. Select the Design window for Form1.h and drag a FontDialog control from the Toolbox window to the form. The Click event handler for the toolStripFontButton can display the font dialog:

```
private: System::Void toolStripFontButton_Click(
                                System::Object^ sender, System::EventArgs^ e)
{
  if(fontDialog1->ShowDialog() == System::Windows::Forms::DialogResult::OK)
  {
    textFont = fontDialog1->Font;
  }
}
```

You display the dialog by calling its ShowDialog() function, as you did for the pen dialog. If the function returns DialogResult::OK, you know the dialog was closed with the OK button. In this case, you retrieve the chosen font from the Font property for the dialog object, and store it in the textFont variable in the Form1 class object. You can try this out if you want. The Font dialog will look like Figure 18-23.

You need a class to represent a Text element, so let's define that next.

FIGURE 18-23

Defining the Text Element Class

The TextElement element type will have Element as a base class like the other element types, so you can call the Draw() function polymorphically. Basic information about the location and color of the text element will be recorded in the members inherited from the base class, but you need to add extra members to store the text and information relating to the font. Here's the initial definition of the class:

```
public ref class TextElement : Element
{
  protected:
    String^ text;
    SolidBrush^ brush;
    Font^ font;
```

```
    public:
      TextElement(Color color, Point p, String^ text, Font^ font)
      {
        this->color = color;
        brush = gcnew SolidBrush(color);
        position = p;
        this->text = text;
        this->font = font;
        int height = font->Height;                // Height of text string
        int width = static_cast<int>(font->Size*text->Length); // Width of string
        boundRect = System::Drawing::Rectangle(position, Size(width, height));
        boundRect.Inflate(2,2);                   // Allow for descenders
      }

      virtual void Draw(Graphics^ g) override
      {
        brush->Color = highlighted ? highlightColor : color;
        g->TranslateTransform(safe_cast<float>(position.X),
                              safe_cast<float>(position.Y));
        g->DrawString(text, font, brush, Point(0,0));
        g->ResetTransform();
      }
  };
```

I chose the `TextElement` type name, rather than just `Text`, to avoid confusion with a member of the `Form` class with the name `Text`. A `TextElement` object has members to store the text string, the font, and the brush to be used to draw the text.

Determining the bounding rectangle for a text element introduces a slight complication in that it depends on the point size of the font, and you have to figure out the width and height from the font size. The height is easy because the `font` object has a `Height` property that makes the font's line spacing available, which is a good estimate for the height of the text string. The `Size` property returns the em size of the font (which is the width of the letter *M*), so you can get a generous estimate of the width of the rectangle the string will occupy by multiplying the em size by the number of characters in the string. I have inflated the rectangle by two because the line spacing doesn't always result in a bounding rectangle that takes account of descenders such as in lowercase *p*s and *q*s.

Creating the Text Dialog

You'll want to enter text from the keyboard when you create a `TextElement` element, so you need a dialog to manage this. Go to the Solution Explorer window, and add a new form to CLR Sketcher by right-clicking the project name and clicking Add ⇨ New Item from the menu. Enter the name as TextDialog. Change the `Text` property for the form to `Create Text Element`, and change the properties to make it a dialog as you did for `PenDialog`; this involves changing the `FormBorderStyle` property to `FixedDialog` and setting `MaximizeBox`, `MinimizeBox`, and `ControlBox` properties to `false`.

The next step is to add buttons to close the dialog. Add an OK button and a Cancel button to the text dialog with the `DialogResult` property values set appropriately. Change the (name) property values to `textOKButton` and `textCancelButton` respectively. Set the `AcceptButton` property value for `TextDialog` to `textOKButton` and the `CancelButton` property value to `textCancelButton`.

Using a Text Box

A TextBox control allows a single line or multiple lines of text to be entered, so it certainly covers what you want to do here. Add a TextBox to the text dialog by dragging it from the Toolbox window to the dialog in the Design window. By default, a TextBox allows a single line of text to be entered, and you can stick with that here. When you want to allow multiple lines of input, you click the arrow to the right on the TextBox in the Design window, and click the checkbox to enable Multiline. The Text property for the TextBox provides access to the input and makes it available as a String object.

Ideally, you want the text dialog to open with the focus on the box for entering text. Then you can enter the text immediately after the dialog opens, and press enter to close it as if you had selected the OK button. The control that has the focus initially is determined by the tab order of the controls on the dialog, which depends on the value of the TabIndex property for the controls. If you set the TabIndex property for the text box to 0 and the OK and Cancel buttons to 1 and 2 respectively, this will result in the text box having the focus when the dialog initially displays. The tab order also defines the sequence in which the focus changes when you press the tab key. You can display the tab order for the controls in the Design window for the dialog by selecting View ➪ Tab Order from the main menu; selecting the menu item again removes the display of the tab order.

The textBox1 control will store the string you enter, but because this is a private member of the dialog object, it is not accessible directly. You must add a mechanism to retrieve the string from the dialog object. Another problem is that the textBox1 control will retain the text you enter and display it the next time the dialog is opened. You probably don't want this to occur, so you need a way to reset the Text property of textBox1. You can add a public property to the TextDialog class that will deal with both difficulties. Add the following code to the TextDialog class definition, following the #pragma endregion directive:

```
// Property to access the text in the edit box
public: property String^ TextString
{
  String^ get() {return textBox1->Text; }
  void set(String^ text) { textBox1->Text = text; }
}
```

The get() function for the TextString property makes the string you enter available, and the set() function enables you to reset it.

It would be nice if the text appeared in the edit box in the current font so that the user could tell whether it's what he or she wants. This will provide an opportunity to cancel the text entry and change to another font. Add the following property to the TextDialog class, following the preceding one:

```
// Set the edit box font
public: property System::Drawing::Font^ TextFont
{
  void set(System::Drawing::Font^ font) { textBox1->Font = font; }
}
```

This is a set-only property that you can use to set the font for the edit box object textBox1.

You need an extra data member in the `Form1` class to help you create text elements. Add an `#include` directive for `TextDialog.h` to `Form1.h`, then add a `textDialog` member of type `TextDialog^`. You can initialize it to `gcnew TextDialog()` in the initialization list for the `Form1` class constructor.

Displaying the Dialog and Creating a Text Element

The process for creating an element that is text is different from the process for geometric elements, so to understand the sequence of events in the code, let's describe the interactive process. Text element mode is in effect when you select the Text menu item or toolbar button. To create an element, you click at the position on the form where you want the top left corner of the text string to be. This will display the text dialog; you type the text you want in the text box, and press Enter to close the dialog. The `MouseMove` handler is not involved in the process at all. Clicking the mouse to define the position of the element embodies the whole process. This implies that you must display the dialog and create the text element in the `MouseDown` event handler. Here's the code to do that:

```
private: System::Void Form1_MouseDown(System::Object^ sender,
System::Windows::Forms::MouseEventArgs^ e) {
  if(e->Button == System::Windows::Forms::MouseButtons::Left)
  {
    firstPoint = e->Location;
    if(mode == Mode::Normal)
    {
      if(elementType == ElementType::TEXT)
      {
        textDialog->TextString = L"";        // Reset the text box string
        textDialog->TextFont = textFont;     // Set the font for the edit box
        if(textDialog->ShowDialog() == System::Windows::Forms::DialogResult::OK)
        {
          tempElement = gcnew TextElement(color, firstPoint,
                                          textDialog->TextString, textFont);
          sketch += tempElement;
          Invalidate(tempElement->bound);    // The text element region
          tempElement = nullptr;
          Update();
        }
        drawing = false;
      }
      else
      {
        drawing = true;
      }
    }

  }
}
```

You create text elements only when the `elementType` member of the form has the value `ElementType::TEXT` and the `mode` is `Mode::Normal`; the second condition is essential to avoid displaying the dialog when you are in move mode. When a text element is being created, the first action is to reset the `Text` property for the `textBox1` control to an empty string by setting it as

the value for the `TextString` property for the
dialog. You also set the font for the edit box
to the value stored in the `textFont` member
of the form.

You display the dialog by calling
`ShowDialog()` in the `if` condition
expression. If the `ShowDialog()` function
returns `DialogResult::OK`, you retrieve
the string from the dialog, use it to create
the `TextElement` object, and add the object
to the sketch. You then invalidate the
region occupied by the new element and
call `Update()` to display it. You also reset
`tempElement` to `nullptr` when you are done
with it. Finally, you set `drawing` to `false`
to prevent the `MouseMove` handler from
attempting to create an element.

FIGURE 18-24

If you recompile Sketcher, you should be able to create text elements using a font of your choice.
Not only that, but you can move and delete them too. Figure 18-24 shows Sketcher displaying text
elements.

SUMMARY

In this chapter you've seen several different dialogs using a variety of controls. Although you haven't
created dialogs involving several different controls at once, the mechanism for handling them is the
same as what you have seen, because each control can operate independently of the others. Dialogs
are a fundamental tool for managing user input in an application. They provide a way for you to
manage the input of multiple related items of data. You can easily ensure that an application only
receives valid data. Judicious choice of the controls in a dialog can force the user to choose from a
specific set of options. You can also check the data after it has been entered in a dialog and prompt
the user when it is not valid.

EXERCISES

You can download the source code for the examples in the book and the solutions to the following
exercises from www.wrox.com.

1. Implement the scale dialog in MFC Sketcher using radio buttons.

2. Implement the pen width dialog in MFC Sketcher using a list box.

3. Implement the pen width dialog in MFC Sketcher as a combo box with the drop list type selected
on the Styles tab in the Properties box. (The drop list type allows the user to select from a drop-
down list but not to enter alternative entries in the list.)

▶ **WHAT YOU LEARNED IN THIS CHAPTER**

TOPIC	CONCEPT
Dialogs	A dialog involves two components: a resource defining the dialog box and its controls, and a class that is used to display and manage the dialog.
Extracting data from a dialog	Information can be extracted from controls in a dialog by means of the DDX mechanism. The data can be validated with the DDV mechanism. To use DDX/DDV you need only use the Add Control Variable option for the Add Member Variable wizard to define variables in the dialog class associated with the controls.
Modal dialogs	A modal dialog retains the focus in the application until the dialog box is closed. As long as a modal dialog is displayed, all other windows in an application are inactive.
Modeless dialogs	A modeless dialog allows the focus to switch from the dialog box to other windows in the application and back again. A modeless dialog can remain displayed as long as the application is executing, if required.
Common controls	Common Controls are a set of standard Windows controls supported by MFC and the resource editing capabilities of Developer Studio.
Adding controls	Although controls are usually associated with a dialog, you can add controls to any window.
Adding a new form in a Windows Forms application	You add a form to a Windows Forms application using the Solutions Explorer pane; you right-click the project name and select Add ⇨ New Item from the menu.
Converting a form into a modal dialog	You convert a form into a modal dialog window by changing the value of the `FormBorderStyle` property to `FixedDialog`, and changing the values of the `MaximizeBox`, `MinimizeBox`, and `ControlBox` properties to `false`.
Adding controls to a dialog	You populate a dialog with controls by dragging them from the Toolbox window onto the dialog in the Design pane.
Displaying a dialog	You display a dialog by calling its `ShowDialog()` function.
The `DialogResult` property for a button	The value that you set for the `DialogResult` property for a button in a dialog determines the value returned by the `ShowDialog()` function when that button is used to close the dialog.
Using standard dialogs	The toolbox has several complete standard dialogs available, including a dialog for choosing a font.
Drawing test on a form	You can draw a string on a form by calling the `DrawString()` function for the `Graphics` object that encapsulates the drawing surface of a form. A `Font` object argument to the function determines the typeface, style, and size of the characters drawn, and a `Brush` object argument determines the color.

19

Storing and Printing Documents

WHAT YOU WILL LEARN IN THIS CHAPTER:

➤ How serialization works

➤ How to make objects of a class serializable

➤ The role of a `CArchive` object in serialization

➤ How to implement serialization in your own classes

➤ How to implement serialization in the Sketcher application

➤ How printing works with MFC

➤ Which view class functions you can use to support printing

➤ What a `CPrintInfo` object contains and how it's used in the printing process

➤ How to implement multipage printing in the Sketcher application

With what you have accomplished so far in the Sketcher program, you can create a reasonably comprehensive document with views at various scales, but the information is transient because you have no means of saving a document. In this chapter, you'll remedy that by seeing how you can store a document on disk. You'll also investigate how you can output a document to a printer.

UNDERSTANDING SERIALIZATION

A document in an MFC-based program is not a simple entity — it's a class object that can be very complicated. It typically contains a variety of objects, each of which may contain other objects, each of which may contain still more objects . . . and that structure may continue for a number of levels.

You want to be able to save a document in a file, but writing a class object to a file represents something of a problem because it isn't the same as a basic data item like an integer or a character string. A basic data item consists of a known number of bytes, so to write it to a file only requires that the appropriate number of bytes be written. Conversely, if you know a value of type int was written to a file, to get it back, you just read the appropriate number of bytes.

Writing objects is different. Even if you write away all the data members of an object, that's not enough to be able to get the original object back. Class objects contain function members as well as data members, and all the members, both data and functions, have access specifiers; therefore, to record objects in an external file, the information written to the file must contain complete specifications of all the class structures involved. The read process must also be clever enough to synthesize the original objects completely from the data in the file. MFC supports a mechanism called **serialization** to help you to implement input from and output to disk of your class objects with a minimum of time and trouble.

The basic idea behind serialization is that any class that's serializable must take care of storing and retrieving itself. This means that for your classes to be serializable — in the case of the Sketcher application, this will include the CElement class and the shape classes you have derived from it — they must be able to write themselves to a file. This implies that for a class to be serializable, all the class types that are used to declare data members of the class must be serializable, too.

SERIALIZING A DOCUMENT

This all sounds rather tricky, but the basic capability for serializing your document was built into the application by the Application Wizard right at the outset. The handlers for the File ⇨ Save, File ⇨ Save As, and File ⇨ Open menu items all assume that you want serialization implemented for your document, and already contain the code to support it. Take a look at the parts of the definition and implementation of CSketcherDoc that relate to creating a document using serialization.

Serialization in the Document Class Definition

The code in the definition of CSketcherDoc that enables serialization of a document object is shown shaded in the following fragment:

```
class CSketcherDoc : public CDocument
{
protected: // create from serialization only
    CSketcherDoc();
    DECLARE_DYNCREATE(CSketcherDoc)

// Rest of the class...

// Overrides
    public:
    virtual BOOL OnNewDocument();
    virtual void Serialize(CArchive& ar);

// Rest of the class...

};
```

There are three things here that relate to serializing a document object:

1. The `DECLARE_DYNCREATE()` macro.

2. The `Serialize()` member function.

3. The default class constructor.

`DECLARE_DYNCREATE()` is a macro that enables objects of the `CSketcherDoc` class to be created dynamically by the application framework during the serialization input process. It's matched by a complementary macro, `IMPLEMENT_DYNCREATE()`, in the class implementation. These macros apply only to classes derived from `CObject`, but as you will see shortly, they aren't the only pair of macros that can be used in this context. For any class that you want to serialize, `CObject` must be a direct or indirect base because it adds the functionality that enables serialization to work. This is why the `CElement` class was derived from `CObject`. Almost all MFC classes are derived from `CObject` and, as such, are serializable.

 NOTE *The Hierarchy Chart in the Microsoft Foundation Class Reference for Visual C++ 2010 shows those classes, which aren't derived from* `CObject`. *Note that* `CArchive` *is in this list.*

The class definition also includes a declaration for a virtual function `Serialize()`. Every class that's serializable must include this function. It's called to perform both input and output serialization operations on the data members of the class. The object of type `CArchive` that's passed as an argument to this function determines whether the operation that is to occur is input or output. You'll explore this in more detail when considering the implementation of serialization for the document class.

Note that the class explicitly defines a default constructor. This is also essential for serialization to work because the default constructor is used by the framework to synthesize an object when reading from a file, and the synthesized object is then filled out with the data from the file to set the values of the data members of the object.

Serialization in the Document Class Implementation

There are two bits of the `SketcherDoc.cpp` file containing the implementation of `CSketcherDoc` that relate to serialization. The first is the macro `IMPLEMENT_DYNCREATE()` that complements the `DECLARE_DYNCREATE()` macro:

```
// SketcherDoc.cpp : implementation of the CSketcherDoc class
//

#include "stdafx.h"
// SHARED_HANDLERS can be defined in an ATL project implementing preview, thumbnail
// and search filter handlers and allows sharing of document code with that project.
#ifndef SHARED_HANDLERS
#include "Sketcher.h"
```

```
#include "PenDialog.h"
#endif

#include "SketcherDoc.h"

#include <propkey.h>

#ifdef _DEBUG
#define new DEBUG_NEW
#endif

// CSketcherDoc


IMPLEMENT_DYNCREATE(CSketcherDoc, CDocument)

// Message maps and the rest of the file...
```

This macro defines the base class for `CSketcherDoc` as `CDocument`. This is required for the proper dynamic creation of a `CSketcherDoc` object, including members that are inherited from the base class.

The Serialize() Function

The class implementation also includes the definition of the `Serialize()` function:

```
void CSketcherDoc::Serialize(CArchive& ar)
{
   if (ar.IsStoring())
   {
      // TODO: add storing code here
   }
   else
   {
      // TODO: add loading code here
   }
}
```

This function serializes the data members of the class. The argument passed to the function, `ar`, is a reference to an object of the `CArchive` class. The `IsStoring()` member of this class object returns TRUE if the operation is to store data members in a file, and FALSE if the operation is to read back data members from a previously stored document.

Because the Application Wizard has no knowledge of what data your document contains, the process of writing and reading this information is up to you, as indicated by the comments. To understand how you do this, let's look a little more closely at the `CArchive` class.

The CArchive Class

The `CArchive` class is the engine that drives the serialization mechanism. It provides an MFC-based equivalent of the stream operations in C++ that you used for reading from the keyboard and writing to the screen in the console program examples. An object of the MFC class `CArchive` provides a mechanism for streaming your objects out to a file, or recovering them again as an input stream, automatically reconstituting the objects of your class in the process.

A CArchive object has a CFile object associated with it that provides disk input/output capability for binary files, and provides the actual connection to the physical file. Within the serialization process, the CFile object takes care of all the specifics of the file input and output operations, and the CArchive object deals with the logic of structuring the object data to be written or reconstructing the objects from the information read. You need to worry about the details of the associated CFile object only if you are constructing your own CArchive object. With the document in Sketcher, the framework has already taken care of it and passes the CArchive object that it constructs, ar, to the Serialize() function in CSketcherDoc. You'll be able to use the same object in each of the Serialize() functions you add to the shape classes when you implement serialization for them.

The CArchive class overloads the extraction and insertion operators (>> and <<) for input and output operations, respectively, on objects of classes derived from CObject, plus a range of basic data types. These overloaded operators work with the object types and primitive types shown in the following table.

TYPE	DEFINITION
bool	Boolean value, true or false
float	Standard single precision floating point
double	Standard double precision floating point
BYTE	8-bit unsigned integer
char	8-bit character
wchar_t	16-bit character
short	16-bit signed integer
LONG and long	32-bit signed integer
LONGLONG	64-bit signed integer
ULONGLONG	64-bit unsigned integer
WORD	16-bit unsigned integer
DWORD and unsigned int	32-bit unsigned integer
CString	A CString object defining a string
SIZE and CSize	An object defining a size as a **cx**, **cy** pair
POINT and CPoint	An object defining a point as an **x**, **y** pair
RECT and CRect	An object defining a rectangle by its upper-left and lower-right corners
CObject*	Pointer to CObject

For basic data types in your objects, you use the insertion and extraction operators to serialize the data. To read or write an object of a serializable class that you have derived from `CObject`, you can either call the `Serialize()` function for the object, or use the extraction or insertion operator. Whichever way you choose must be used consistently for both input and output, so you should not output an object using the insertion operator and then read it back using the `Serialize()` function, or vice versa.

Where you don't know the type of an object when you read it, as in the case of the pointers in the list of shapes in our document, for example, you must *only* use the `Serialize()` function. This brings the virtual function mechanism into play, so the appropriate `Serialize()` function for the type of object pointed to is determined at runtime.

A `CArchive` object is constructed either for storing objects or for retrieving objects. The `CArchive` function `IsStoring()` returns `TRUE` if the object is for output, and `FALSE` if the object is for input. You saw this used in the `if` statement in the `Serialize()` member of the `CSketcherDoc` class.

There are many other member functions of the `CArchive` class that are concerned with the detailed mechanics of the serialization process, but you don't usually need to know about them to use serialization in your programs.

Functionality of CObject-Based Classes

There are three levels of functionality available in your classes when they're derived from the MFC class `CObject`. The level you get in your class is determined by which of three different macros you use in the definition of your class:

MACRO	FUNCTIONALITY
`DECLARE_DYNAMIC()`	Support for runtime class information
`DECLARE_DYNCREATE()`	Support for runtime class information and dynamic object creation
`DECLARE_SERIAL()`	Support for runtime class information, dynamic object creation, and serialization of objects

Each of these macros requires that a complementary macro, named with the prefix `IMPLEMENT_` instead of `DECLARE_`, be placed in the file containing the class implementation. As the table indicates, the macros provide progressively more functionality, so I'll concentrate on the third macro, `DECLARE_SERIAL()`, because it provides everything that the preceding macros do and more. This is the macro you should use to enable serialization in your own classes. It requires that the macro `IMPLEMENT_SERIAL()` be added to the file containing the class implementation.

You may be wondering why the document class uses `DECLARE_DYNCREATE()` and not `DECLARE_SERIAL()`. The `DECLARE_DYNCREATE()` macro provides the capability for dynamic creation of the objects of the class in which it appears. The `DECLARE_SERIAL()` macro provides the capability for serialization of the class, plus the dynamic creation of objects of the class, so it incorporates the effects of `DECLARE_DYNCREATE()`. Your document class doesn't need serialization because the framework only has to synthesize the document object and then restore the values of its data members; however, the data members of a document *do* need to be serializable, because this is the process used to store and retrieve them.

The Macros Adding Serialization to a Class

With the `DECLARE_SERIAL()` macro in the definition of your `CObject`-based class, you get access to the serialization support provided by `CObject`. This includes special `new` and `delete` operators that incorporate memory leak detection in debug mode. You don't need to do anything to use this because it works automatically.

The macro requires the class name to be specified as an argument, so for serialization of the `CElement` class, you would add the following line to the class definition:

```
DECLARE_SERIAL(CElement)
```

 NOTE *There's no semicolon required here because this is a macro, not a C++ statement.*

It doesn't matter where you put the macro within the class definition, but if you always put it as the first line, you'll always be able to verify that it's there, even when the class definition involves a lot of lines of code.

The `IMPLEMENT_SERIAL()` macro, which you place in the implementation file for the class, requires three arguments to be specified. The first argument is the name of the class, the second is the name of the direct base class, and the third argument is an unsigned 32-bit integer identifying a **schema number,** or version number, for your program. This schema number allows the serialization process to guard against problems that can arise if you write objects with one version of a program and read them with another, in which the classes may be different.

For example, you could add the following line to the implementation of the `CElement` class:

```
IMPLEMENT_SERIAL(CElement, CObject, 1)
```

If you subsequently modify the class definition, you would change the schema number to something different, such as 2. If the program attempts to read data that was written with a different schema number from that in the currently active program, an exception is thrown. The best place for this macro is as the first line following the `#include` directives and any initial comments in the `.cpp` file.

Where `CObject` is an indirect base class, as in the case of the `CLine` class, for example, each class in the hierarchy must have the serialization macros added for serialization to work in the top-level class. For serialization in `CLine` to work, the macros must also be added to `CElement`.

How Serialization Works

The overall process of serializing a document is illustrated in a simplified form in Figure 19-1.

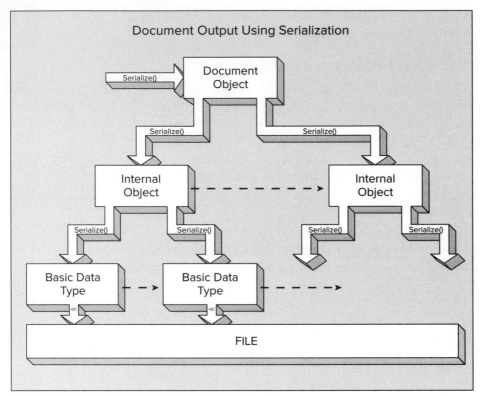

FIGURE 19-1

The Serialize() function in the document object calls the Serialize() function (or uses an overloaded insertion operator) for each of its data members. Where a member is a class object, the Serialize() function for that object serializes each of its data members in turn until, ultimately, basic data types are written to the file. Because most classes in MFC ultimately derive from CObject, they contain serialization support, so you can almost always serialize objects of MFC classes.

The data that you'll deal with in the Serialize() member functions of your classes and the application document object are, in each case, just the data members. The structure of the classes that are involved and any other data necessary to reconstitute your original objects are automatically taken care of by the CArchive object.

Where you derive multiple levels of classes from CObject, the Serialize() function in a class must call the Serialize() member of its direct base class to ensure that the direct base class data members are serialized. Note that serialization doesn't support multiple inheritance, so there can only be one base class for each class defined in a hierarchy.

How to Implement Serialization for a Class

From the previous discussion, I can summarize the steps that you need to take to add serialization to a class:

1. Make sure that the class is derived directly or indirectly from CObject.

2. Add the DECLARE_SERIAL() macro to the class definition (and to the direct base class if the direct base is not CObject or another standard MFC class).

3. Declare the Serialize() function as a member function of your class.

4. Add the IMPLEMENT_SERIAL() macro to the file containing the class implementation.

5. Implement the Serialize() function for your class.

Now, take a look at how you can implement serialization for documents in the Sketcher program.

APPLYING SERIALIZATION

To implement serialization in the Sketcher application, you must implement the Serialize() function in CSketcherDoc so that it deals with all of the data members of that class. You need to add serialization to each of the classes that specify objects that may be included in a document. Before you start adding serialization to your application classes, you should make some small changes to the program to record when a user changes a sketch document. This isn't absolutely necessary, but it is highly desirable because it enables the program to guard against the document being closed without saving changes.

Recording Document Changes

There's already a mechanism for noting when a document changes; it uses an inherited member of CSketcherDoc, SetModifiedFlag(). By calling this function consistently whenever the document changes, you can record the fact that the document has been altered in a data member of the document class object. This causes a prompt to be automatically displayed when you try to exit the application without saving the modified document. The argument to the SetModifiedFlag() function is a value of type BOOL, and the default value is TRUE. If you have occasion to specify that the document was unchanged, you can call this function with the argument FALSE, although circumstances where this is necessary are rare.

There are only three occasions when you alter a document object:

➤ When you call the AddElement() member of CSketcherDoc to add a new element.

➤ When you call the DeleteElement() member of CSketcherDoc to delete an element.

➤ When you move an element.

You can handle these three situations easily. All you need to do is add a call to `SetModifiedFlag()` to each of the functions involved in these operations. The definition of `AddElement()` appears in the `CSketcherDoc` class definition. You can extend this to:

```
void AddElement(CElement* pElement)      // Add an element to the list
{
  m_ElementList. push_back (pElement);
  SetModifiedFlag();                      // Set the modified flag
}
```

You can get to the definition of `DeleteElement()` in `CSketcherDoc` by clicking the function name in the Class View pane. You should add one line to it, as follows:

```
void CSketcherDoc::DeleteElement(CElement* pElement)
{
  if(pElement)
  {
    m_ElementList.remove(pElement);     // Remove the pointer from the list
    delete pElement;                    // Delete the element from the heap
    SetModifiedFlag();                  // Set the modified flag
  }
}
```

Note that you must only set the flag if `pElement` is not `nullptr`, so you can't just stick the function call anywhere.

In a view object, moving an element occurs in the `MoveElement()` member called by the handler for the `WM_MOUSEMOVE` message, but you only change the document when the left mouse button is pressed. If there's a right-button click, the element is put back to its original position, so you only need to add the call to the `SetModifiedFlag()` function for the document to the `OnLButtonDown()` function, as follows:

```
void CSketcherView::OnLButtonDown(UINT nFlags, CPoint point)
{
  CClientDC aDC(this);                  // Create a device context
  OnPrepareDC(&aDC);                    // Get origin adjusted
  aDC.DPtoLP(&point);                   // convert point to Logical

  if(m_MoveMode)
  {
    // In moving mode, so drop the element
    m_MoveMode = false;                 // Kill move mode
    m_pSelected = nullptr;              // De-select the element
    GetDocument()->UpdateAllViews(0);   // Redraw all the views
    GetDocument()->SetModifiedFlag();   // Set the modified flag
    return;
  }
  // Rest of the function as before...
}
```

You call the inherited `GetDocument()` member of the view class to get access to a pointer to the document object and then use this pointer to call the `SetModifiedFlag()` function. You now have all the places where you change the document covered.

If you build and run Sketcher, and modify a document or add elements to it, you'll now get a prompt to save the document when you exit the program. Of course, the File ⇨ Save menu option doesn't do anything yet except clear the modified flag and save an empty file to disk. You must implement serialization to get the document written away to disk properly, and that's the next step.

Serializing the Document

The first step is the implementation of the `Serialize()` function for the `CSketcherDoc` class. Within this function, you must add code to serialize the data members of `CSketcherDoc`. The data members that you have declared in the class are as follows:

```
protected:
  int m_PenWidth;                      // Current pen width
  CSize m_DocSize;                     // Document size
  ElementType m_Element;               // Current element type
  COLORREF m_Color;                    // Current element color
  std::list<CElement*> m_ElementList;  // List of elements in the sketch
```

These are the data members that have to be serialized to allow a `CSketcherDoc` object to be deserialized. All that's necessary is to insert the statements to store and retrieve these five data members in the `Serialize()` member of the class. However, there is a slight problem. The `list<CElement*>` object is not serializable because the template is not derived from `CObject`. In fact, *none* of the STL containers are serializeable, so you always have to take care of serializing STL containers yourself.

All is not lost, however. If you can serialize the objects that the pointers in the container point to, you will be able to reconstruct the container when we want to read it back.

 NOTE *The MFC does define container classes such as* `CList` *that are serializable. However, if you used these in Sketcher, you would not learn about how you can make a class serializable.*

You can implement serialization for the document object with the following code:

```
void CSketcherDoc::Serialize(CArchive& ar)
{
  if (ar.IsStoring())
  {
    ar << m_Color                      // Store the current color
       << static_cast<int>(m_Element)  // the current element type as an integer
       << m_PenWidth                   // and the current pen width
       << m_DocSize;                   // and the current document size

    ar << m_ElementList.size();        // Store the number of elements in the list

    // Now store the elements from the list
    for(auto iter =  m_ElementList.begin() ; iter != m_ElementList.end() ; ++iter)
```

```
      ar << *iter;                    // Store the element
  }
  else
  {
    int elementType(0);              // Stores element type
    ar >> m_Color                    // Retrieve the current color
       >> elementType                // the current element type as an integer
       >> m_PenWidth                 // and the current pen width
       >> m_DocSize;                 // and the current document size

    m_Element = static_cast<ElementType>(elementType);

    size_t elementCount(0);          // Count of number of elements
    CElement* pElement(nullptr);     // Element pointer
    ar >> elementCount;              // retrieve the element count
    // Now retrieve all the elements and store in the list
    for(size_t i = 0 ; i < elementCount ; ++i)
    {
      ar >> pElement;
      m_ElementList.push_back(pElement);
    }
  }
}
```

For three of the data members, you just use the extraction and insertion operators that are overloaded in the CArchive class. This works for the data member m_Color, even though its type is COLORREF, because type COLORREF is the same as type long. The m_Element member is of type ElementType, and the serialization process won't handle this directly. However, an enum type is an integer type, so you can cast it to an integer for serialization, and then just deserialize it as an integer before casting the value back to ElementType.

For the list of elements, m_ElementList, you first store the count of the number of elements in the list in the archive, because you will need this to be able to read the elements back. You then write the elements from the list to the archive in the for loop. You use the << operator to write *iter, which is a pointer of type CElement*, to the archive. The serialization mechanism will recognize that *iter is a pointer and take care of writing the element pointed to by *iter to the archive.

The else clause for the if deals with reading the document object back from the archive. You use the extraction operator to retrieve the first four members from the archive in the same sequence that they were written. The element type is read into the local integer variable, elementType, and then stored in m_Element as the correct type.

You read the number of elements recorded in the archive and store it locally in elementCount. Finally, you use elementCount to control the for loop that reads the elements back from the archive and stores them in the list. Note that you don't need to do anything special to take account of the fact that the elements were originally created on the heap. The serialization mechanism takes care of restoring the elements on the heap automatically.

In case you are wondering where the list<CElement*> object comes from when you are deserializing an object, it will be created by the serialization process using the default constructor for the CSketcherDoc class. This is how the basic document object and its uninitialized data members get created. Like magic, isn't it?

That's all you need for serializing the document class data members, but serializing the elements from the list causes the `Serialize()` functions for the element classes to be called to store and retrieve the elements themselves, so you also need to implement serialization for those classes.

Serializing the Element Classes

All the shape classes are serializable because you derived them from their base class, `CElement`, which, in turn, is derived from `CObject`. The reason that you specified `CObject` as the base for `CElement` was solely to get support for serialization. Make sure that the default constructor is actually defined for each of the shape classes. The deserialization process requires that this constructor be defined.

You can now add support for serialization to each of the shape classes by adding the appropriate macros to the class definitions and implementations, and adding the code to the `Serialize()` function member of each class to serialize its data members. You can start with the base class, `CElement`, where you need to modify the class definition as follows:

```
class CElement: public CObject
{
DECLARE_SERIAL(CElement)
  protected:
      int m_PenWidth;                          // Pen width
      COLORREF m_Color;                        // Color of an element
      CRect m_EnclosingRect;                   // Rectangle enclosing an element

    public:
      virtual ~CElement();
      virtual void Draw(CDC* pDC, CElement* pElement=0) {} // Virtual draw operation
      virtual void Move(const CSize& aSize){}             // Move an element

      CRect GetBoundRect() const;        // Get the bounding rectangle for an element
      virtual void Serialize(CArchive& ar);  // Serialize function for the class

  protected:
    CElement(void);                                 // Here to prevent it being called
};
```

You add the `DECLARE_SERIAL()` macro and a declaration for the virtual function `Serialize()`. You already have the default constructor that was created by the Application Wizard. You changed it to `protected` in the class, although it doesn't matter what its access specification is as long as it appears explicitly in the class definition. It can be `public`, `protected`, or `private`, and serialization still works. If you forget to include a default constructor in a class, though, you'll get an error message when the `IMPLEMENT_SERIAL()` macro is compiled.

You should add the `DECLARE_SERIAL()` macro to each of the derived classes `CLine`, `CRectangle`, `CCircle`, `CCurve`, and `CText`, with the relevant class name as the argument. You should also add a declaration for the `Serialize()` function as a `public` member of each class.

In the file `Elements.cpp`, you must add the following macro at the beginning:

```
IMPLEMENT_SERIAL(CElement, CObject, VERSION_NUMBER)
```

You can define the constant VERSION_NUMBER in the `SketcherConstants.h` file by adding the lines:

```
// Program version number for use in serialization
const UINT VERSION_NUMBER = 1;
```

You can then use the same constant when you add the macro for each of the other shape classes. For instance, for the `CLine` class you should add the line,

```
IMPLEMENT_SERIAL(CLine, CElement, VERSION_NUMBER)
```

and similarly for the other shape classes. When you modify any of the classes relating to the document, all you need to do is change the definition of VERSION_NUMBER in the `SketcherConstants.h` file, and the new version number applies in all your `Serialize()` functions. You can put all the IMPLEMENT_SERIAL() statements at the beginning of the file if you like. The complete set is:

```
IMPLEMENT_SERIAL(CElement, CObject, VERSION_NUMBER)
IMPLEMENT_SERIAL(CLine, CElement, VERSION_NUMBER)
IMPLEMENT_SERIAL(CRectangle, CElement, VERSION_NUMBER)
IMPLEMENT_SERIAL(CCircle, CElement, VERSION_NUMBER)
IMPLEMENT_SERIAL(CCurve, CElement, VERSION_NUMBER)
IMPLEMENT_SERIAL(CText, CElement, VERSION_NUMBER)
```

The Serialize() Functions for the Shape Classes

You can now implement the `Serialize()` member function for each of the shape classes. Start with the `CElement` class:

```
void CElement::Serialize(CArchive& ar)
{
  CObject::Serialize(ar);            // Call the base class function

  if (ar.IsStoring())
    {
      ar << m_PenWidth             // the pen width
         << m_Color                // Store the color,
         << m_EnclosingRect;       // and the enclosing rectangle
    }
  else
    {
      ar >> m_PenWidth             // the pen width
         >> m_Color                // the color
         >> m_EnclosingRect;       // and the enclosing rectangle
    }
}
```

This function is of the same form as the one supplied for you in the CSketcherDoc class. All of the data members defined in CElement are supported by the overloaded extraction and insertion operators, and so, everything is done using those operators. Note that you must call the Serialize() member for the CObject class to ensure that the inherited data members are serialized.

For the CLine class, you can code the function as:

```
void CLine::Serialize(CArchive& ar)
{
  CElement::Serialize(ar);             // Call the base class function

  if (ar.IsStoring())
  {
    ar << m_StartPoint                 // Store the line start point,
       << m_EndPoint;                  // and the end point
  }
  else
  {
    ar >> m_StartPoint                 // Retrieve the line start point,
       >> m_EndPoint;                  // and the end point
  }
}
```

Again, the data members are all supported by the extraction and insertion operators of the CArchive object ar. You call the Serialize() member of the base class CElement to serialize its data members, and this calls the Serialize() member of CObject. You can see how the serialization process cascades through the class hierarchy.

The Serialize() function member of the CRectangle class is simple:

```
void CRectangle::Serialize(CArchive& ar)
{
  CElement::Serialize(ar);             // Call the base class function
}
```

This only calls the direct base class Serialize() function because the class has no additional data members.

The CCircle class doesn't have additional data members beyond those inherited from CElement, either, so its Serialize() function also just calls the base class function:

```
void CCircle::Serialize(CArchive& ar)
{
  CElement::Serialize(ar);             // Call the base class function
}
```

For the CCurve class, you have rather more work to do. The CCurve class uses a vector<CPoint> container to store the defining points, and because this is not directly serializable, you must take care of it yourself. Having serialized the document, this is not going to be terribly difficult. You can code the `Serialize()` function as follows:

```
void CCurve::Serialize(CArchive& ar)
{
  CElement::Serialize(ar);              // Call the base class function
  // Serialize the vector of points
  if (ar.IsStoring())
  {
    ar << m_Points.size();              // Store the point count
    // Now store the points
    for(size_t i = 0 ; i< m_Points.size() ; ++i)
      ar << m_Points[i];
  }
  else
  {
    size_t nPoints(0);                  // Stores number of points
    ar >> nPoints;                      // Retrieve the number of points
    // Now retrieve the points
    CPoint point;
    for(size_t i = 0 ; i < nPoints ; ++i)
    {
      ar >> point;
      m_Points.push_back(point);
    }
  }
}
```

You first call the base class `Serialize()` function to deal with serializing the inherited members of the class. Storing the contents of the vector is basically the same as the technique you used for serializing the document. You first write the number of elements to the archive, then the elements themselves. The `CPoint` class is serializable, so it takes care of itself. Reading the points back is equally straightforward. You just store each object read from the archive in the vector, `m_Points`, in the `for` loop. The serialization process uses the no-arg constructor for the `CCurve` class to create the basic class object, so the `vector<CPoint>` member is created within this process.

The last class for which you need to add an implementation of `Serialize()` to `Elements.cpp` is `CText`:

```
void CText::Serialize(CArchive& ar)
{
  CElement::Serialize(ar);              // Call the base class function

  if (ar.IsStoring())
  {
    ar << m_String;                     // Store the text string
  }
  else
  {
    ar >> m_String;                     // Retrieve the text string
  }
}
```

After calling the base class function, you serialize the m_String data member using the insertion and extraction operators for ar. The CString class, although not derived from CObject, is still fully supported by CArchive with these overloaded operators.

EXERCISING SERIALIZATION

That's all you have to do to implement the storing and retrieving of documents in the Sketcher program! The Save and Open menu options in the file menu are now fully operational without adding any more code. If you build and run Sketcher after incorporating the changes I've discussed in this chapter, you'll be able to save and restore files and be automatically prompted to save a modified document when you try to close it or exit from the program, as shown in Figure 19-2.

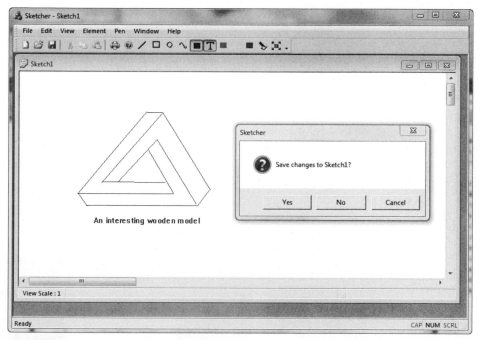

FIGURE 19-2

The prompting works because of the SetModifiedFlag() calls that you added everywhere you updated the document. If you click the Yes button in the screen shown in Figure 19-2, you'll see the File ⇨ Save As dialog box shown in Figure 19-3.

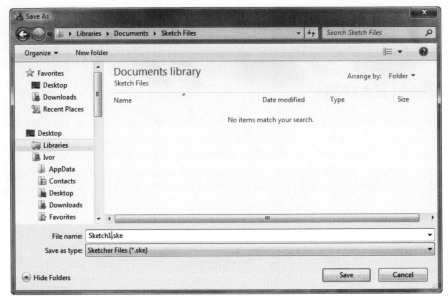

FIGURE 19-3

This is the standard dialog box for this menu item under Windows. If yours looks a little different, it's probably because you are using a different version of the Windows operating system from mine. The dialog is all fully working, supported by code supplied by the framework. The file name for the document has been generated from that assigned when the document was first opened, and the file extension is automatically defined as .ske. The application now has full support for file operations on documents. Easy, wasn't it?

PRINTING A DOCUMENT

It's time to take a look at how you can print a sketch. You already have a basic printing capability implemented in the Sketcher program, courtesy of the Application Wizard and the framework. The File ⇨ Print, File ⇨ Print Setup, and File ⇨ Print Preview menu items all work. Selecting the File ⇨ Print Preview menu item displays a window showing the current Sketcher document on a page, as shown in Figure 19-4.

Whatever is in the current document is placed on a single sheet of paper at the current view scale. If the document's extent is beyond the boundary of the paper, the section of the document off the paper won't be printed. If you select the Print button, this page is sent to your printer.

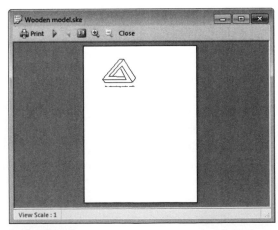

FIGURE 19-4

As a basic capability that you get for free, it's quite impressive, but it's not adequate for our purposes. A typical document in our program may well not fit on a page, so you would either want to scale the document to fit, or, perhaps more conveniently, print the whole document over as many pages as necessary. You can add your own print processing code to extend the capability of the facilities provided by the framework, but to implement this, you first need to understand how printing has been implemented in MFC.

The Printing Process

Printing a document is controlled by the current view. The process is inevitably a bit messy because printing is inherently a messy business, and it potentially involves you in implementing your own versions of quite a number of inherited functions in your view class.

Figure 19-5 shows the logic of the process and the functions involved. It also shows how the sequence of events is controlled by the framework and how printing a document involves calling five inherited members of your view class, which you may need to override. The CDC member functions shown on the left side of the diagram communicate with the printer device driver and are called automatically by the framework.

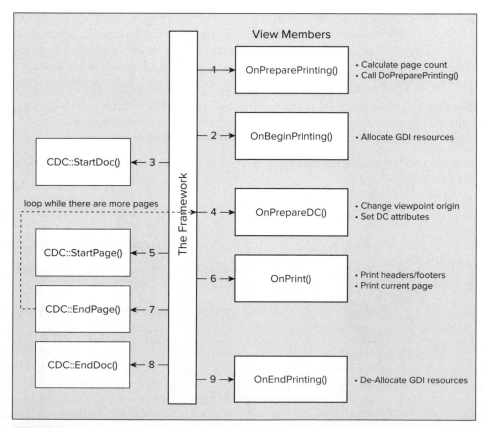

FIGURE 19-5

The typical role of each of the functions in the current view during a print operation is specified in the notes alongside it. The sequence in which they are called is indicated by the numbers on the arrows. In practice, you don't necessarily need to implement all of these functions, only those that you want to for your particular printing requirements. Typically, you'll want at least to implement your own versions of OnPreparePrinting(), OnPrepareDC(), and OnPrint(). You'll see an example of how these functions can be implemented in the context of the Sketcher program a little later in this chapter.

The output of data to a printer is done in the same way as outputting data to the display — through a device context. The GDI calls that you use to output text or graphics are device-independent, so they work just as well for a printer as they do for a display. The only difference is the device that the CDC object applies to.

The CDC functions in Figure 19-5 communicate with the device driver for the printer. If the document to be printed requires more than one printed page, the process loops back to call the OnPrepareDC() function for each successive new page, as determined by the EndPage() function.

All the functions in your view class that are involved in the printing process are passed a pointer to an object of type CPrintInfo as an argument. This object provides a link between all the functions that manage the printing process, so take a look at the CPrintInfo class in more detail.

The CPrintInfo Class

A CPrintInfo object has a fundamental role in the printing process because it stores information about the print job being executed and details of its status at any time. It also provides functions for accessing and manipulating this data. This object is the means by which information is passed from one view function to another during printing, and between the framework and your view functions.

An object of the CPrintInfo class is created whenever you select the File ⇨ Print or File ⇨ Print Preview menu options. After being used by each of the functions in the current view that are involved in the printing process, it's automatically deleted when the print operation ends.

All the data members of CPrintInfo are public. The ones we are interested in for printing sketches are shown in the following table.

MEMBER	USAGE
m_pPD	A pointer to the CPrintDialog object that displays the Print dialog box.
m_bDirect	This is set to TRUE by the framework if the print operation is to bypass the Print dialog box; otherwise, FALSE.
m_bPreview	A member of type BOOL that has the value TRUE if File ⇨ Print Preview was selected; otherwise, FALSE.
m_bContinuePrinting	A member of type BOOL. If this is set to TRUE, the framework continues the printing loop shown in the diagram. If it's set to FALSE, the printing loop ends. You only need to set this variable if you don't pass a page count for the print operation to the CPrintInfo object (using the SetMaxPage() member function). In this case, you'll be responsible for signaling when you're finished by setting this variable to FALSE.

continues

(continued)

MEMBER	USAGE
m_nCurPage	A value of type UINT that stores the page number of the current page. Pages are usually numbered starting from 1.
m_nNumPreviewPages	A value of type UINT that specifies the number of pages displayed in the Print Preview window. This can be 1 or 2.
m_lpUserData	This is of type LPVOID and stores a pointer to an object that you create. This allows you to create an object to store additional information about the printing operation and associate it with the CPrintInfo object.
m_rectDraw	A CRect object that defines the usable area of the page in logical coordinates.
m_strPageDesc	A CString object containing a format string used by the framework to display page numbers during print preview.

A CPrintInfo object has the public member functions shown in the following table.

FUNCTION	DESCRIPTION
SetMinPage(UINT nMinPage)	The argument specifies the number of the first page of the document. There is no return value.
SetMaxPage(UINT nMaxPage)	The argument specifies the number of the last page of the document. There is no return value.
GetMinPage() const	Returns the number of the first page of the document as type UINT.
GetMaxPage() const	Returns the number of the last page of the document as type UINT.
GetFromPage() const	Returns the number of the first page of the document to be printed as type UINT. This value is set through the print dialog.
GetToPage() const	Returns the number of the last page of the document to be printed as type UINT. This value is set through the print dialog.

When you're printing a document consisting of several pages, you need to figure out how many printed pages the document will occupy, and store this information in the CPrintInfo object to make it available to the framework. You can do this in your version of the OnPreparePrinting() member of the current view.

To set the number of the first page in the document, you need to call the function `SetMinPage()` in the `CPrintInfo` object, which accepts the page number as an argument of type `UINT`. There's no return value. To set the number of the last page in the document, you call the function `SetMaxPage()`, which also accepts the page number as an argument of type `UINT` and doesn't return a value. If you later want to retrieve these values, you can call the `GetMinPage()` and `GetMaxPage()` functions for the `CPrintInfo` object.

The page numbers that you supply are stored in the `CPrintDialog` object pointed to by the `m_pPD` member of `CPrintInfo`, and displayed in the dialog box that pops up when you select File ⇨ Print... from the menu. The user is then able to specify the numbers of the first and last pages that are to be printed. You can retrieve the page numbers entered by the user by calling the `GetFromPage()` and `GetToPage()` members of the `CPrintInfo` object. In each case, the value returned is of type `UINT`. The dialog automatically verifies that the numbers of the first and last pages to be printed are within the range you supplied by specifying the minimum and maximum pages of the document.

You now know what functions you can implement in the view class to manage printing for yourself, with the framework doing most of the work. You also know what information is available through the `CPrintInfo` object that is passed to the functions concerned with printing. You'll get a much clearer understanding of the detailed mechanics of printing if you implement a basic multipage print capability for Sketcher documents.

IMPLEMENTING MULTIPAGE PRINTING

You use the `MM_LOENGLISH` mapping mode in the Sketcher program to set things up and then switch to `MM_ANISOTROPIC`. This means that the unit of measure for the shapes and the view extent is one hundredth of an inch. Of course, with the unit of size being a fixed physical measure, ideally, you want to print objects at their actual size.

With the document size specified as 3000 by 3000 units, you can create documents up to 30 inches square, which spreads over quite a few sheets of paper if you fill the whole area. It requires a little more effort to work out the number of pages necessary to print a sketch than with a typical text document because in most instances, you'll need a two-dimensional array of pages to print a complete sketch document.

To avoid overcomplicating the problem, assume that you're printing on a normal sheet of paper (either A4 size or 8 1/2 by 11 inches) and that you are printing in portrait orientation (which means the long edge is vertical). With either paper size, you'll print the document in a central portion of the paper measuring 7.5 inches by 10 inches. With these assumptions, you don't need to worry about the actual paper size; you just need to chop the document into 750 by 1000–unit chunks, where a unit is 0.01 inches. For a document larger than one page, you'll divide up the document as illustrated in the example in Figure 19-6.

FIGURE 19-6

As you can see, you'll be numbering the pages row-wise, so in this case, pages 1 to 4 are in the first row and pages 5 to 8 are in the second. A sketch occupying the maximum size of 30×30 inches will print on 12 pages.

Getting the Overall Document Size

To figure out how many pages a particular document occupies, you need to know how big the sketch is, and for this, you want the rectangle that encloses everything in the document. You can do this easily by adding a function GetDocExtent() to the document class, CSketcherDoc. Add the following declaration to the public interface for CSketcherDoc:

```
CRect GetDocExtent();        // Get the bounding rectangle for the whole document
```

The implementation is no great problem. The code for it is:

```
// Get the rectangle enclosing the entire document
CRect CSketcherDoc::GetDocExtent()
{
  CRect docExtent(0,0,1,1);                // Initial document extent
  for(auto iter = m_ElementList.begin() ; iter != m_ElementList.end() ; ++iter)
    docExtent.UnionRect(docExtent, (*iter)->GetBoundRect());

  docExtent.NormalizeRect();
  return docExtent;
}
```

You can add this function definition to the SketcherDoc.cpp file, or simply add the code if you used the Add ➪ Add Function capability from the pop-up in Class View. The process loops through every element in the document, getting the bounding rectangle for each element and combining it with docExtent. The UnionRect() member of the CRect class calculates the smallest rectangle that contains the two rectangles passed as arguments, and puts that value in the CRect object for which the function is called. Therefore, docExtent keeps increasing in size until all the elements are contained within it. Note that you initialize DocExtent with **(0,0,1,1)** because the UnionRect() function doesn't work properly with rectangles that have zero height or width.

Storing Print Data

The OnPreparePrinting() function in the view class is called by the application framework to enable you to initialize the printing process for your document. The basic initialization that's required is to provide information about how many pages are in the document for the print dialog that displays. You'll need to store information about the pages that your document requires, so you can use it later in the other view functions involved in the printing process. You'll originate this in the OnPreparePrinting() member of the view class, too, store it in an object of your own class that you'll define for this purpose, and store a pointer to the object in the CPrintInfo object that the framework makes available. This approach is primarily to show you how this mechanism works; in many cases, you'll find it easier just to store the data in your view object.

You'll need to store the number of pages running the width of the document, m_nWidths, and the number of rows of pages down the length of the document, m_nLengths. You'll also store the upper-left corner of the rectangle enclosing the document data as a CPoint object, m_DocRefPoint, because you'll use this when you work out the position of a page to be printed from its page number. You can store the file name for the document in a CString object, m_DocTitle, so that you can add it as a title to each page. It will also be useful to record the size of the printable area within the page. The definition of the class to accommodate these is:

```
#pragma once

class CPrintData
{
  public:
    UINT printWidth;            // Printable page width - units 0.01 inches
    UINT printLength;           // Printable page length - units 0.01 inches
    UINT m_nWidths;             // Page count for the width of the document
    UINT m_nLengths;            // Page count for the length of the document

    CPoint m_DocRefPoint;       // Top-left corner of the document contents
    CString m_DocTitle;         // The name of the document

    // Constructor
    CPrintData():
      printWidth(750)           // 7.5 inches
    , printLength(1000)         // 10 inches
      {}
};
```

The constructor sets default values for the printable area that corresponds to an A4 page with half-inch margins all round. You can change this to suit your environment, and, of course, you can change the values programmatically in a CPrintData object.

You can add a new header file with the name `PrintData.h` to the project by right-clicking the Header Files folder in the Solution Explorer pane and then selecting Add ⇨ New Item from the pop-up. You can now enter the class definition in the new file.

You don't need an implementation file for this class. Because an object of this class is only going to be used transiently, you don't need to use `CObject` as a base or to consider any other complication.

The printing process starts with a call to the view class member `OnPreparePrinting()`, so check out how you should implement that.

Preparing to Print

The Application Wizard added versions of `OnPreparePrinting()`, `OnBeginPrinting()`, and `OnEndPrinting()` to `CSketcherView` at the outset. The base code provided for `OnPreparePrinting()` calls `DoPreparePrinting()` in the `return` statement, as you can see:

```
BOOL CSketcherView::OnPreparePrinting(CPrintInfo* pInfo)
{
    // default preparation
    return DoPreparePrinting(pInfo);
}
```

The `DoPreparePrinting()` function displays the Print dialog box using information about the number of pages to be printed that's defined in the `CPrintInfo` object. Whenever possible, you should calculate the number of pages to be printed and store it in the `CPrintInfo` object before this call occurs. Of course, in many circumstances, you may need information from the device context for the printer before you can do this — when you're printing a document where the number of pages is going to be affected by the size of the font to be used, for example — in which case, it won't be possible to get the page count before you call `OnPreparePrinting()`. In this case, you can compute the number of pages in the `OnBeginPrinting()` member, which receives a pointer to the device context as an argument. This function is called by the framework after `OnPreparePrinting()`, so the information entered in the Print dialog box is available. This means that you can also take account of the paper size selected by the user in the Print dialog box.

Assume that the page size is large enough to accommodate a 7.5-inch by 10-inch area to draw the document data, so you can calculate the number of pages in `OnPreparePrinting()`. The code for it is:

```
BOOL CSketcherView::OnPreparePrinting(CPrintInfo* pInfo)
{
    CPrintData*p(new CPrintData);                // Create a print data object
    CSketcherDoc* pDoc = GetDocument();          // Get a document pointer
    CRect docExtent = pDoc->GetDocExtent();      // Get the whole document area

    // Save the reference point for the whole document
    p->m_DocRefPoint = CPoint(docExtent.left, docExtent.top);

    // Get the name of the document file and save it
    p->m_DocTitle = pDoc->GetTitle();

    // Calculate how many printed page widths are required
```

```
      // to accommodate the width of the document
      p->m_nWidths = static_cast<UINT>(ceil(
                    static_cast<double>(docExtent.Width())/p->printWidth));

      // Calculate how many printed page lengths are required
      // to accommodate the document length
      p->m_nLengths = static_cast<UINT>(
                    ceil(static_cast<double>(docExtent.Height())/p->printLength));

      // Set the first page number as 1 and
      // set the last page number as the total number of pages
      pInfo->SetMinPage(1);
      pInfo->SetMaxPage(p->m_nWidths*p->m_nLengths);
      pInfo->m_lpUserData = p;               // Store address of PrintData object

    return DoPreparePrinting(pInfo);
  }
```

You first create a `CPrintData` object on the heap and store its address locally in the pointer. After getting a pointer to the document, you get the rectangle enclosing all of the elements in the document by calling the function `GetDocExtent()` that you added to the document class earlier in this chapter. You then store the corner of this rectangle in the `m_DocRefPoint` member of the `CPrintData` object, and put the name of the file that contains the document in `m_DocTitle`.

The next two lines of code calculate the number of pages across the width of the document, and the number of pages required to cover the length. The number of pages to cover the width is computed by dividing the width of the document by the width of the print area of a page and rounding up to the next highest integer using the `ceil()` library function that is defined in the `cmath` header. For example, `ceil(2.1)` returns `3.0`, `ceil(2.9)` also returns `3.0`, and `ceil(-2.1)` returns `-2.0`. A similar calculation to that for the number of pages across the width of a document produces the number to cover the length. The product of these two values is the total number of pages to be printed, and this is the value that you'll supply for the maximum page number. The last step is to store the address of the `CPrintData` object in the `m_lpUserData` member of the `pInfo` object.

Don't forget to add a `#include` directive for `PrintData.h` to the `SketcherView.cpp` file.

Cleaning Up after Printing

Because you created the `CPrintData` object on the heap, you must ensure that it's deleted when you're done with it. You do this by adding code to the `OnEndPrinting()` function:

```
    void CSketcherView::OnEndPrinting(CDC* /*pDC*/, CPrintInfo* pInfo)
    {
      // Delete our print data object
      delete static_cast<CPrintData*>(pInfo->m_lpUserData);
    }
```

That's all that's necessary for this function in the Sketcher program, but in some cases, you'll need to do more. Your one-time final cleanup should be done here. Make sure that you remove the comment delimiters (**/* */**) from the second parameter name; otherwise, your function won't compile. The default implementation comments out the parameter names because you may not need to refer to them in your code. Because you use the pInfo parameter, you must uncomment it; otherwise, the compiler reports it as undefined.

You don't need to add anything to the OnBeginPrinting() function in the Sketcher program, but you'd need to add code to allocate any GDI resources, such as pens, if they were required throughout the printing process. You would then delete these as part of the clean-up process in OnEndPrinting().

Preparing the Device Context

At the moment, the Sketcher program calls OnPrepareDC(), which sets up the mapping mode as MM_ANISOTROPIC to take account of the scaling factor. You must make some additional changes so that the device context is properly prepared in the case of printing:

```
void CSketcherView::OnPrepareDC(CDC* pDC, CPrintInfo* pInfo)
{
  int scale = m_Scale;                      // Store the scale locally
  if(pDC->IsPrinting())
    scale = 1;                              // If we are printing, set scale to 1

  CScrollView::OnPrepareDC(pDC, pInfo);
  CSketcherDoc* pDoc = GetDocument();
  pDC->SetMapMode(MM_ANISOTROPIC);          // Set the map mode
  CSize DocSize = pDoc->GetDocSize();       // Get the document size
  pDC->SetWindowExt(DocSize);               // Now set the window extent

  // Get the number of pixels per inch in x and y
  int xLogPixels = pDC->GetDeviceCaps(LOGPIXELSX);
  int yLogPixels = pDC->GetDeviceCaps(LOGPIXELSY);

  // Calculate the viewport extent in x and y
  int xExtent = (DocSize.cx*scale*xLogPixels)/100;
  int yExtent = (DocSize.cy*scale*yLogPixels)/100;

  pDC->SetViewportExt(xExtent, yExtent);    // Set viewport extent
}
```

This function is called by the framework for output to the printer as well as to the screen. You should make sure that a scale of 1 is used to set the mapping from logical coordinates to device coordinates when you're printing. If you left everything as it was, the output would be at the current view scale, but you'd need to take account of the scale when calculating how many pages you needed, and how you set the origin for each page.

You determine whether or not you have a printer device context by calling the IsPrinting() member of the current CDC object, which returns TRUE if you are printing. All you need to do when you have a printer device context is set the scale to 1. Of course, you must change the statements lower down that use the scale value so that they use the local variable scale rather than the m_Scale member of the view. The values returned by the calls to GetDeviceCaps() with the arguments LOGPIXELSX and LOGPIXELSY return the number of logical points per inch in the x and *y* directions for your printer when you're printing, and the equivalent values for your display when you're drawing to the screen, so this automatically adapts the viewport extent to suit the device to which you're sending the output.

Printing the Document

You can write the data to the printer device context in the `OnPrint()` function. This is called once for each page to be printed. You need to add an override for this function to `CSketcherView`, using the `Properties` window for the class. Select `OnPrint` from the list of overrides and then click `<Add>` `OnPrint` in the right column.

You can obtain the page number of the current page from the `m_nCurPage` member of the `CPrintInfo` object and use this value to work out the coordinates of the position in the document that corresponds to the upper-left corner of the current page. The way to do this is best understood using an example, so imagine that you are printing page seven of an eight-page document, as illustrated in Figure 19-7.

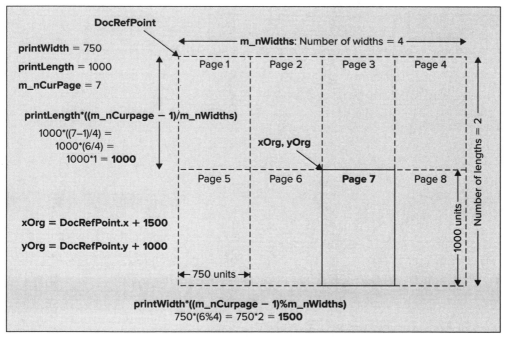

FIGURE 19-7

You can get an index to the horizontal position of the page by decrementing the page number by 1 and taking the remainder after dividing by the number of page widths required for the width of the printed area of the document. Multiplying the result by `printWidth` produces the *x* coordinate of the upper-left corner of the page, relative to the upper-left corner of the rectangle enclosing the elements in the document. Similarly, you can determine the index to the vertical position of the document by dividing the current page number reduced by 1 by the number of page widths required for the horizontal width of the document. By multiplying the remainder by `printLength`, you get the relative *y* coordinate of the upper-left corner of the page. You can express this in the following statements:

```
CPrintData* p(static_cast<CPrintData*>(pInfo->m_lpUserData));
int xOrg = p->m_DocRefPoint.x + p->printWidth*
                              ((pInfo->m_nCurPage - 1)%(p->m_nWidths));
int yOrg = p->m_DocRefPoint.y + p->printLength*
                              ((pInfo->m_nCurPage - 1)/(p->m_nWidths));
```

It would be nice to print the file name of the document at the top of each page and, perhaps, a page number at the bottom, but you want to be sure you don't print the document data over the file name and page number. You also want to center the printed area on the page. You can do this by moving the origin of the coordinate system in the printer device context *after* you have printed the file name. This is illustrated in Figure 19-8.

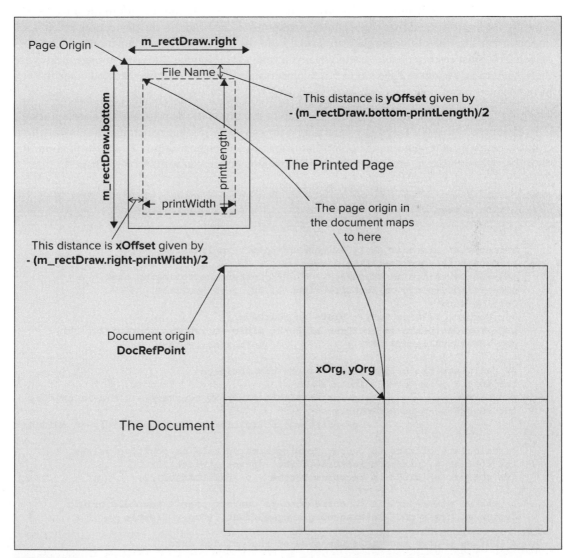

FIGURE 19-8

Figure 19-8 illustrates the correspondence between the printed page area in the device context and the page to be printed in the reference frame of the document data. Remember that these are in logical coordinates — the equivalent of MM_LOENGLISH in Sketcher — so *y* is increasingly negative from top to bottom. The page shows the expressions for the offsets from the page origin for the printWidth by printLength area where you are going to print the page. You want to print the information from the document in the dashed area shown on the page, so you need to map the xOrg, yOrg point in the document to the position shown in the printed page, which is displaced from the page origin by the offset values xOffset and yOffset.

By default, the origin in the coordinate system that you use to define elements in the document is mapped to the origin of the device context, but you can change this. The CDC object provides a SetWindowOrg() function for this purpose. This enables you to define a point in the document's logical coordinate system that you want to correspond to the origin in the device context. It's important to save the old origin that's returned from the SetWindowOrg() function as a CPoint object. You must restore the old origin when you've finished drawing the current page; otherwise, the m_rectDraw member of the CPrintInfo object is not set up correctly when you come to print the next page.

The point in the document that you want to map to the origin of the page has the coordinates xOrg-xOffset,yOrg-yOffset. This may not be easy to visualize, but remember that by setting the window origin, you're defining the point that maps to the viewport origin. If you think about it, you should see that the xOrg, yOrg point in the document is where you want it on the page.

The complete code for printing a page of the document is:

```
// Print a page of the document
void CSketcherView::OnPrint(CDC* pDC, CPrintInfo* pInfo)
{
  CPrintData* p(static_cast<CPrintData*>(pInfo->m_lpUserData));
  // Output the document file name
  pDC->SetTextAlign(TA_CENTER);          // Center the following text
  pDC->TextOut(pInfo->m_rectDraw.right/2, 20, p->m_DocTitle);
  CString str;
  str.Format(_T("Page %u") , pInfo->m_nCurPage);
  pDC->TextOut(pInfo->m_rectDraw.right/2, pInfo->m_rectDraw.bottom-20, str);
  pDC->SetTextAlign(TA_LEFT);            // Left justify text

  // Calculate the origin point for the current page
  int xOrg = p->m_DocRefPoint.x +
                     p->printWidth*((pInfo->m_nCurPage - 1)%(p->m_nWidths));
  int yOrg = p->m_DocRefPoint.y +
                     p->printLength*((pInfo->m_nCurPage - 1)/(p->m_nWidths));

  // Calculate offsets to center drawing area on page as positive values
  int xOffset = (pInfo->m_rectDraw.right - p->printWidth)/2;
  int yOffset = (pInfo->m_rectDraw.bottom - p->printLength)/2;

  // Change window origin to correspond to current page & save old origin
  CPoint OldOrg = pDC->SetWindowOrg(xOrg-xOffset, yOrg-yOffset);

  // Define a clip rectangle the size of the printed area
```

```
    pDC->IntersectClipRect(xOrg, yOrg, xOrg+p->printWidth, yOrg+p->printLength);

    OnDraw(pDC);                           // Draw the whole document
    pDC->SelectClipRgn(nullptr);           // Remove the clip rectangle
    pDC->SetWindowOrg(OldOrg);             // Restore old window origin
  }
```

The first step is to initialize the local pointer, p, with the address of the CPrintData object that is stored in the m_lpUserData member of the object to which pInfo points. You then output the file name that you squirreled away in the CPrintData object. The SetTextAlign() function member of the CDC object allows you to define the alignment of subsequent text output in relation to the reference point you supply for the text string in the TextOut() function. The alignment is determined by the constant passed as an argument to the function. You have three possibilities for specifying the alignment of the text, as shown in the following table.

CONSTANT	ALIGNMENT
TA_LEFT	The point is at the left of the bounding rectangle for the text, so the text is to the right of the point specified. This is default alignment.
TA_RIGHT	The point is at the right of the bounding rectangle for the text, so the text is to the left of the point specified.
TA_CENTER	The point is at the center of the bounding rectangle for the text.

You define the x coordinate of the file name on the page as half the page width, and the y coordinate as 20 units, which is 0.2 inches, from the top of the page.

After outputting the name of the document file as centered text, you output the page number centered at the bottom of the page. You use the Format() member of the CString class to format the page number stored in the m_nCurPage member of the CPrintInfo object. This is positioned 20 units up from the bottom of the page. You then reset the text alignment to the default setting, TA_LEFT.

The SetTextAlign() function also allows you to change the position of the text vertically by OR-ing a second flag with the justification flag. The second flag can be any of those shown in the following table.

CONSTANT	ALIGNMENT
TA_TOP	Aligns the top of the rectangle bounding the text with the point defining the position of the text. This is the default.
TA_BOTTOM	Aligns the bottom of the rectangle bounding the text with the point defining the position of the text.
TA_BASELINE	Aligns the baseline of the font used for the text with the point defining the position of the text.

The next action in `OnPrint()` uses the method that I discussed for mapping an area of the document to the current page. You get the document drawn on the page by calling the `OnDraw()` function that is used to display the document in the view. This potentially draws the entire document, but you can restrict what appears on the page by defining a **clip rectangle**. A clip rectangle encloses a rectangular area in the device context within which output appears. Output is suppressed outside of the clip rectangle. It's also possible to define irregularly shaped areas for clipping, called **regions**.

The initial default clipping area defined in the print device context is the page boundary. You define a clip rectangle that corresponds to the `printWidth` by `printLength` area centered in the page. This ensures that you draw only in this area and the file name and page number will not be overwritten.

After the current page has been drawn by the `OnDraw()` function call, you call `SelectClipRgn()` with a `NULL` argument to remove the clip rectangle. If you don't do this, output of the document title is suppressed on all pages after the first, because it lies outside the clip rectangle that would otherwise remain in effect in the print process until the next time `IntersectClipRect()` gets called.

Your final action is to call `SetWindowOrg()` again to restore the window origin to its original location, as discussed earlier in this chapter.

Getting a Printout of the Document

To get your first printed Sketcher document, you just need to build the project and execute the program (once you've fixed any typos). If you try File ➪ Print Preview, you should get something similar to the window shown in Figure 19-9.

FIGURE 19-9

You get print preview functionality completely for free. The framework uses the code that you've supplied for the normal multipage printing operation to produce page images in the Print Preview window. What you see in the Print Preview window should be exactly the same as appears on the printed page.

SERIALIZATION AND PRINTING IN CLR SKETCHER

As you know, serialization is the process of writing objects to a stream, and deserialization is the reverse: reconstructing objects from a stream. The .NET Framework offers several different ways to serialize and deserialize your C++/CLI class objects. **XML serialization** serializes objects into an XML stream that conforms to a particular XML schema. You can also serialize objects into XML streams that conform to the Simple Object Access Protocol (SOAP) specification, and this is referred to as **SOAP serialization**. A discussion of XML and SOAP is beyond the scope of this book, not because it's difficult — it isn't — but because to cover it adequately requires more pages than I can possibly include in this book. I'll therefore show you how to use the third and, perhaps, simplest form of serialization provided by the .NET Framework, **binary serialization**.

You'll also investigate how you can print sketches from CLR Sketcher. With the help given by the Form Designer, this is going to be easy.

Understanding Binary Serialization

Before you get into the specifics of serializing a sketch, let's get an overview of what's involved in binary serialization of your class objects. For binary serialization of your class objects to be possible, you have to make your classes serializable. You can make a ref class or value class serializable by marking it with the `Serializable` attribute, like this:

```
[Serializable]
public ref class MyClass
{
  // Class definition...
};
```

Of course, in practice, there may be a little more to it. For serialization to work with `MyClass`, all the class fields must be serializable, too, and often, there are fields that are not serializable by default, or fields that it does not make sense to serialize because the data stored will not be valid when it is deserialized, or fields that you just don't want serialized for security reasons. In this case, special measures are necessary to take care of the non-serializable class members.

Dealing with Fields That Are Not Serializable

Where a class has members that are not serializable, you can mark them with the `NonSerialized` attribute to prevent them from being serialized. For example:

```
[Serializable]
public ref class MyClass
{
```

```
  public:
  [NonSerialized]int value;
  // Rest of the class definition...
};
```

Here, the serialization process will not attempt to serialize the value member of a MyClass object. For this to compile, you need a using declaration for the System::Runtime::Serialization namespace.

Although marking a data member as non-serializable avoids the possibility of the serialization process failing with types you cannot serialize, it does not solve the problem of serializing the objects unless the non-serialized data can be happily omitted when you come to reconstruct the object when it is deserialized. You will typically want to take some special action in relation to the non-serialized fields.

You use the OnSerializing attribute to mark a class function that you want to be called when the serialization of an object begins. You can also identify a function that is to be called after an object has been serialized, by marking it with the OnSerialized attribute. This gives you an opportunity to do something about the non-serialized fields. For example:

```
[Serializable]
public ref class MyClass
{
  public:
  [NonSerialized]
   ProblemType anObject;

  [OnSerializing]
  void FixNonSerializedData(StreamingContext context)
  {
     // Code to do what is necessary for anObject before serialization...
  }

  [OnSerialized]
  void PostSerialization(StreamingContext context)
  {
     // Code to do what is necessary after serialization...
  }

  // Rest of the class definition...
};
```

When a MyClass object is serialized, the FixNonSerializedData() function will be called before the object is serialized, and the code in here will deal with the problem of anObject not being serialized, perhaps by allowing some other data to be serialized that will enable anObject to be reconstructed when the MyClass object is deserialized. The PostSerialization() function will be called after a MyClass object has been serialized. The function that you mark with either the OnSerializing or the OnSerialized attribute must have a void return type and a parameter of type StreamingContext. The StreamingContext object that is passed to the function when it is called is a struct containing information about the source and destination, but you won't need to use this in CLR Sketcher.

You can also arrange for a member function to be called after an object is deserialized. The OnDeserializing and OnDeserialized attributes identify functions that are to be called before or after deserialization, respectively. For example:

```
[Serializable]
public ref class MyClass
{
  public:
  [NonSerialized]
   ProblemType anObject;

  [OnSerializing]
  void FixNonSerializedData(StreamingContext context)
  {
     // Code to do what is necessary for anObject before serialization...
  }

  [OnSerialized]
  void PostSerialization(StreamingContext context)
  {
     // Code to do what is necessary after serialization...
  }

  [OnDeserializing]
  void PreSerialization(StreamingContext context)
  {
     // Code to do stuff before deserialization...
  }

  [OnDeserialized]
  void ReconstructObject(StreamingContext context)
  {
     // Code to reconstruct anObject...
  }

  // Rest of the class definition...
};
```

The PreSerialization() function will be called immediately before the deserialization process for a MyClass object starts. The ReconstructObject() function will be executed after the deserialization process for the object is complete, so this function will have the responsibility for setting up anObject appropriately. Functions that you mark with the OnDeserializing or OnDeserialized attributes must also have a void return type and a parameter of type StreamingContext.

To summarize, typically, you can prepare a class to allow objects of that class type to be serialized through the following five steps:

1. Mark the class to be serialized with the Serializable attribute.

2. Identify any data members that cannot or should not be serialized and mark them with NonSerialized attributes.

3. Add a public function with a return type of void and a single parameter of type StreamingContext to deal with the non-serializable fields when an object is serialized, and mark the function with the OnSerializing attribute.

4. Add a public function with a return type of void and a single parameter of type StreamingContext to deal with the non-serialized fields when an object is deserialized, and mark the function with the OnDeSerialized attribute.

5. Add a using declaration for the System::Runtime::Serialization namespace to the header file containing the class.

Serializing an Object

Serializing an object means writing it to a stream, so you first must define the stream that is the destination for the data defining the object. A stream is represented by a System::IO::Stream class, which is an abstract ref class type. A stream can be any source or destination for data that is a sequence of bytes; a file, a TCP/IP socket, and a pipe that allows data to be passed between two processes are all examples of streams.

You will usually want to serialize your objects to a file, and the System::IO::File class contains static functions for creating objects that encapsulate files. You use the File::Open() function to create a new file or open an existing file for reading and/or writing. The Open() function returns a reference of type FileStream^ to an object that encapsulates the file. Because FileStream is a type that is derived from Stream, you can store the reference that the Open() function returns in a variable of type Stream^. The Open() function comes in three overloaded versions, and the version you will be using has the following form:

```
FileStream^ Open(String^ path, FileMode mode)
```

The path parameter is the path to the file that you want to open and can be a full path to the file, or just the file name. If you just specify an argument that is just a file name, the file will be assumed to be in the current directory.

The mode parameter controls whether the file is created if it does not exist, and whether the data can be overwritten if the file does exist. The mode argument can be any of the FileMode enumeration values described in the following table.

FILEMODE ENUMERATOR	DESCRIPTION
CreateNew	Requests that a new file specified by path be created. If the file already exists, an exception of type System::IO::IOException is thrown. You use this when you are writing a new file.
Truncate	Requests that an existing file specified by path be opened and its contents discarded by truncating the size of the file to zero bytes. You use this when you are writing an existing file.
Create	Specifies that if the file specified by path does not exist, it should be created, and if the file does exist, it should be overwritten. You use this when you are writing a file.

continues

(continued)

FILEMODE ENUMERATOR	DESCRIPTION
Open	Specifies that the existing file specified by `path` should be opened. If the file does not exist, an exception of type `System::IO::FileNotFoundException` is thrown. You use this when you are reading a file.
OpenOrCreate	Specifies that the file specified by `path` should be opened if it exists, and created if it doesn't. You can use this to read or write a file, depending on the access argument.
Append	The file specified by `path` is opened if it exists and the file position set to the end of the file; if the file does not exist, it will be created. You use this to append data to an existing file or to write a new file.

Thus, you could create a stream encapsulating a file in the current directory that you can write with the following statement:

```
Stream^ stream = File::Open(L"sketch.dat", FileMode::Create);
```

The file `sketch.dat` will be created in the current directory if it does not exist; if it exists, the contents will be overwritten.

The static `OpenWrite()` function in the `File` class will open the existing file that you specify by the string argument with write access, and return a `FileStream^` reference to the stream you use to write the file.

To serialize an object to a file encapsulated by a `FileStream` object that you have created, use an object of type `System::Runtime::Serialization::Formatters::Binary::BinaryFormatter`, which you can create as follows:

```
BinaryFormatter^ formatter = gcnew BinaryFormatter();
```

You need a `using` declaration for `System::Runtime::Serialization::Formatters::Binary` if this statement is to compile. The `formatter` object has a `Serialize()` function member that you use to serialize an object to a stream. The first argument to the function is a reference to the stream that is the destination for the data, and the second argument is a reference to the object to be serialized to the stream. Thus, you can write a `sketch` object to `stream` with the following statement:

```
formatter->Serialize(stream, sketch);
```

You read an object from a stream using the `Deserialize()` function for a `BinaryFormatter` object:

```
Sketch^ sketch = safe_cast<Sketch^>(formatter->Deserialize(stream));
```

The argument to the `Deserialize()` function is a reference to the stream that is to be read. The function returns the object read from the stream as type `Object^`, so you must cast it to the appropriate type.

Serializing a Sketch

You have to do two things to allow sketches to be serialized in the CLR Sketcher application: make the `Sketch` class serializable and add code to enable the `File` menu items and toolbar buttons to support saving and retrieving sketches.

Making the Sketch Class Serializable

Add a using directive for `System::Runtime::Serialization` to the `Sketch.h` header file. While you are about it, you can copy the directive to the `Elements.h` header because you will need it there, too. Add the `Serializable` attribute immediately before the `Sketch` class definition to specify that the class is serializable:

```
[Serializable]
 public ref class Sketch
{
  // Class definition as before...
};
```

Although this indicates that the class is serializable, in fact, it is not. Serialization will fail because the STL/CLR container classes are not serializable by default. You must specify that the `elements` class member is not serializable, like this:

```
[Serializable]
 public ref class Sketch
{
  private:
    [NonSerialized]
    list<Element^>^ elements;

  // Rest of the class definition as before...
};
```

The class really is serializable now, but not in a useful way, because none of the elements in the sketch will get written to the file. You must provide an alternative repository for the elements in the `list<Element^>` container that is serializable to get the sketch elements written to the file. Fortunately, a regular C++/CLI array is serializable, and even more fortunately, the list container has a `to_array()` function that returns the entire contents of the container as an array. You can therefore add a public function to the class with the `OnSerializing` attribute that will copy the contents of the elements container to an array, and that you can arrange to be called before serialization begins. You can also add a public function with the `OnDeserialized` attribute that will recreate the `elements` container when the array containing the elements is deserialized. Here are the changes to the `Sketch` class that will accommodate that:

```
[Serializable]
 public ref class Sketch
{
  private:
    [NonSerialized]
    list<Element^>^ elements;
```

```
          array<Element^>^ elementArray;

      public:
        Sketch() : elementArray(nullptr)
        {
        elements = gcnew list<Element^>();
        }

        [OnSerializing]
        void ListToArray(StreamingContext context)
        {
          elementArray = elements->to_array();
        }

        [OnDeserialized]
        void ArrayToList(StreamingContext context)
        {
          elements = gcnew list<Element^>(elementArray);
          elementArray = nullptr;
        }

      // Rest of the class definition as before...
    };
```

You have a new private data member, `elementArray`, that holds all the elements in the sketch when it is serialized to a file. You initialize this to `nullptr` in the constructor. When a `Sketch` object is serialized, the `ListToArray()` function will be called first, so this function transfers the contents of the list container to the `elementArray` array before serialization of the object takes place. The `Sketch` object containing the `elementArray` object is then written to the file. When a `Sketch` object is deserialized, the object is recreated containing the `elementArray` member, after which the `ArrayToList()` function is called to restore the contents of the `elements` container from the array. The array is no longer required, so you set it to `nullptr` in the function.

So far, so good, but you are not quite there yet. For a sketch to be serializable, all the elements in the sketch must be serializable, too, and there's the small problem of the `Curve` class that has an STL/CLR container as a member. `Pen` and `Brush` objects are not serializable, so something must be done about those before a sketch can be serialized.

First, though, you can add the `Serializable` attribute to the `Element` class and all its subclasses. You can also mark the `pen` member of the `Element` class with the `NonSerialized` attribute.

Dealing with Pen and Brush Objects

You can't serialize/deserialize a `Pen` or `Brush` object, but if you serialize the attributes of the pen or brush, you will be able to reconstruct it. You can add some members to the `Element` base class to store the attributes you need:

```
[Serializable]
public ref class Element abstract
{
  protected:
    Point position;
```

```
       Color color;
       System::Drawing::Rectangle boundRect;
       Color highlightColor;
       float penWidth;
       DashStyle dashStyle;

       [NonSerialized]
       Pen^ pen;

    // Rest of the class as before...
  };
```

I have shown all the additions for serialization as bold. There are two extra protected members of the class that store the pen width and the DashStyle property value for the element.

Pen objects are not used by the TextElement class, so you should only reconstruct the pen member of the Element class in the classes that define geometric shapes. You can add the following public functions to the Line, Rectangle, and Circle classes:

```
       [OnSerializing]
       void SavePenAttributes(StreamingContext context)
       {
           penWidth = pen->Width;
           dashStyle = pen->DashStyle;
       }

       [OnDeserialized]
       void CreatePen(StreamingContext context)
       {
         pen = gcnew Pen(color, penWidth);
         pen->DashStyle = dashStyle;
       }
```

The SavePenAttributes() function will be called immediately before an object is serialized to fill out the penWidth and dashStyle members ready for serialization. The CreatePen() function will be called after an object has been deserialized, and it will re-create the pen object from the attributes saved by the serialization process.

In the TextElement class, you should mark the brush member with the NonSerialized attribute. You then must provide for reconstructing this object after deserializing a TextElement object.

The changes to the class definition for this are as follows:

```
    [Serializable]
      public ref class TextElement : Element
      {
        protected:
          String^ text;
          Font^ font;

          [NonSerialized]
          SolidBrush^ brush;

        public:
          [OnDeserialized]
```

```
      void CreateBrush(StreamingContext context)
      {
        brush = gcnew SolidBrush(color);
      }

  // Rest of the class as before...
};
```

The `CreateBrush()` function is called to reconstruct the `brush` member after an object is deserialized. No additional information is required to reconstruct the `SolidBrush` object, because it only needs to have the `color` member available, and that is serializable, anyway.

Making the Curve Class Serializable

The `Curve` class needs to deal with the inherited pen member, and it must also take care of the vector container that isn't serializable. You can pull the same trick with the container in the `Curve` class as you did with the `Sketch` class container, so amend the class definition to the following:

```
[Serializable]
public ref class Curve : Element
{
private:
  [NonSerialized]
  vector<Point>^ points;
  array<Point>^ pointsArray;

public:
  Curve(Color color, Point p1, Point p2, float penWidth) : pointsArray(nullptr)
  {
      // Code for the constructor as before...
  }

  [OnSerializing]
  void SavePenAndVectorData(StreamingContext context)
  {
    penWidth = pen->Width;
    dashStyle = pen->DashStyle;
    pointsArray = points->to_array();
  }

  [OnDeserialized]
  void RestorePenAndVectorData(StreamingContext context)
  {
    pen = gcnew Pen(color, penWidth);
    pen->DashStyle = dashStyle;
    points = gcnew vector<Point>(pointsArray);
    pointsArray = nullptr;
  }

  // Rest of the class definition as before...
};
```

It should be easy to see how this works. The `points` member is now non-serialized, but you have a new member of the class, `pointsArray`, that will store the points in a serializable form.

The `SavePenAndVectorData()` function that is called immediately prior to serialization of an object sets up the `penWidth`, `dashStyle`, and `pointsArray` members ready for serialization. The `RestorePenAndVectorData()` function restores the pen and the vector container after a `Curve` object has been deserialized. Don't forget to add the `using` declaration for the `System::Runtime::Serialization` namespace to `Sketch.h` and `Elements.h`.

Implementing File Operations for a Sketch

The menu items and toolbar buttons for file operations are already in place in CLR Sketcher. If you double-click the `Click` event property in the Properties window for the File ⇨ Save, File ⇨ Save As..., and File ⇨ Open menu items, you'll put the event handlers in place for all of them. Then just select the appropriate event handler from the drop-down list of values for the `Click` event for each of the toolbar buttons. All you have to do now is supply the code to make them do what you want.

Creating Dialogs for File Operations

The Toolbox has standard dialogs for opening and saving files and you can use both of these. Drag an `OpenFileDialog` and a `SaveFileDialog` from the Toolbox to the Design window for `Form1`. You can change the `(name)` property values to `saveFileDialog` and `openFileDialog`. Change the values for the `Title` properties for both dialogs to whatever you want displayed in the title bar. You can also change the `FileName` property in the `saveFileDialog` to sketch; this is the default file name that will be displayed when the dialog is first used. It's a good idea to define a folder that will hold your sketches, so create one now; you could use something like `C:\CLR Sketches`. You can specify the default directory as the value for the `InitialDirectory` property for both dialogs. Both dialogs have a `Filter` property that specifies the filters for the list of files that are displayed by the dialogs. The `DefaultExt` property value specifies a default extension for files, so set this to `ske`. You can set the value for the `Filter` property for both dialogs to

```
"CLR Sketches|*.ske| All files|*.*".
```

The default value of 1 for the `FilterIndex` property determines that the first file filter applies by default. If you want the second file filter to apply, set the value for `FilterIndex` to 2. Verify that the values for the `ValidateNames` and `OverwritePrompt` properties for the `saveFileDialog` have default values of `true`; this results in the user being prompted when an existing sketch is about to be overwritten.

Recording the Saved State of a Sketch

Before you get into implementing the event handler for the File ⇨ Save menu item, let's consider what the logic is going to be. When you click the File ⇨ Save menu item, what happens depends on whether the current sketch has been saved before. If the sketch has never been saved, you want the file save dialog to be displayed; if the sketch has been saved previously, you just want to write the sketch to the file without displaying the dialog. To allow this to work, you need a way to record whether or not the sketch has been saved. One way to do this is to add a public member of type `bool` with the name `saved` to the `Sketch` class. You can initialize it to `true` in the `Sketch` class constructor because you don't want to save an empty sketch. Any change to a sketch should result in `saved` being set to `false`, and it should be set to `true` whenever the sketch is saved. The `Form1_MouseUp()` handler adds new elements to the sketch, so this needs to be updated:

```
private: System::Void Form1_MouseUp(System::Object^  sender,
         System::Windows::Forms::MouseEventArgs^  e)
```

```
  {
    if(!drawing)
    {
      mode = Mode::Normal;
      return;
    }
    if(tempElement)
    {
      sketch += tempElement;
      sketch->saved = false;            // Sketch has changed so mark it not saved
      tempElement = nullptr;
      Invalidate();
    }
    drawing = false;
  }
```

The `Form1_MouseDown()` handler adds the `TextElement` object to the sketch, so `saved` should be set to `false` there:

```
  private: System::Void Form1_MouseDown(System::Object^  sender,
  System::Windows::Forms::MouseEventArgs^  e)
  {
    if(e->Button == System::Windows::Forms::MouseButtons::Left)
    {
      firstPoint = e->Location;
      if(mode == Mode::Normal)
      {
        if(elementType == ElementType::TEXT)
        {
          textDialog->TextString = L"";      // Reset the text box string
          textDialog->TextFont = textFont;    // Set the font for the edit box
          if(textDialog->ShowDialog() == System::Windows::Forms::DialogResult::OK)
          {
            tempElement = gcnew TextElement(color, firstPoint,
                                            textDialog->TextString, textFont);
            sketch += tempElement;
            sketch->saved = false;           // Sketch has changed so mark it not saved
            Invalidate(tempElement->bound); // The text element region
            tempElement = nullptr;
            Update();
          }
          drawing = false;
        }
        else
        {
          drawing = true;
        }
      }
    }
  }
```

The Form1_MouseMove() function changes the sketch, so you must set saved to false in here, too:

```
private: System::Void Form1_MouseMove(System::Object^  sender,
  System::Windows::Forms::MouseEventArgs^  e)
{
  if(drawing)
  {
    // Code as before...
  }
  else if(mode == Mode::Normal)
  {
    // Code as before...
  }
  else if(mode == Mode::Move &&
                     e->Button == System::Windows::Forms::MouseButtons::Left)
  {  // Move the highlighted element
    if(highlightedElement)
    {
      sketch->saved = false;                      // Mark sketch as not saved
      Invalidate(highlightedElement->bound);      // Region before move
      highlightedElement->Move(e->X - firstPoint.X, e->Y - firstPoint.Y);
      firstPoint = e->Location;
      Invalidate(highlightedElement->bound);      // Region after move
      Update();
    }
  }
}
```

The handler for the Delete context menu item changes the sketch, so that has to be updated:

```
private: System::Void deleteContextMenuItem_Click(System::Object^  sender
System::EventArgs^  e)
{
  if(highlightedElement)
  {
    sketch->saved = false;                      // Mark sketch as not saved
    sketch -= highlightedElement;               // Delete the highlighted element
    Invalidate(highlightedElement->bound);
    highlightedElement = nullptr;
    Update();
  }
}
```

Finally, the sendToBack() handler needs to be changed:

```
private: System::Void sendToBackContextMenuItem_Click(System::Object^  sender,
System::EventArgs^  e) {
  if(highlightedElement)
  {
    sketch->saved = false;                      // Mark sketch as not saved
    // Rest of the code as before...
  }
}
```

That's covered the saved state of the sketch. Now, you can implement the process of saving it.

Saving a Sketch

You need a `BinaryFormatter` object to save a sketch, and a good place to keep it is in the `Form1` class. Add a `using` declaration for the `System::Runtime::Serialization::Formatters::Binary` namespace to `Form1.h`, and add a new private member, `formatter`, of type `BinaryFormatter^`, to the `Form1` class. You can initialize it to `gcnew BinaryFormatter()` in the initialization list for the `Form1` class constructor.

Before you implement the `Click` event handler for the File ⇨ Save menu item, add a `using` declaration for the `System::IO` namespace to the `Form1.h` header file. Add a private `String^` member, `sketchFilePath`, to the `Form1` class to store the file path for a sketch, and initialize this to `nullptr` in the `Form1` constructor. You can add the following code to implement the `Click` event handler for save operations:

```
private: System::Void saveToolStripMenuItem_Click(
                                System::Object^ sender, System::EventArgs^ e)
{
   SaveSketch();
}
```

This just calls a helper function that you will add shortly.

Here's how you can implement the handler for the Save As... menu item using another helper function:

```
private: System::Void saveAsToolStripMenuItem_Click(System::Object^ sender,
System::EventArgs^ e)
{
   SaveSketchAs();
}
```

The reason for using helper functions in this way is because the process for dealing with a Save operation can use the functionality that is required for a Save As... operation.

Add the `SaveSketch()` function as a `private` member of the `Form1` class and implement it like this:

```
void SaveSketch(void)
{
  if(sketch->saved)
    return;                     // Nothing to do because the sketch was not modified

  if(sketchFilePath == nullptr)
  {
    // File has not yet been saved before, so show the save dialog
    SaveSketchAs();
  }
  else
  {
    // File has been saved before, so just save it using the same name
    Stream^ stream = File::OpenWrite(sketchFilePath);
```

```
        formatter->Serialize(stream, sketch);
        stream->Close();
    }
}
```

There are two courses of action, depending on whether the sketch has been saved previously. If the sketch is unchanged, there's nothing to do, so the function returns. If saved indicates that the sketch needs to be saved, there are two further possibilities:

1. The sketch has never been saved previously, which is indicated by sketchFilePath having the value nullptr. In this case, you call SaveSketchAs() to use the save dialog to save the sketch.

2. The sketch has been saved before, in which case, sketchFilePath will refer to a valid path. In this case, you can save it using the existing file path.

To save the sketch when it has been saved previously, you obtain a reference to a FileStream object that you can use to serialize the sketch by calling the static OpenWrite() function that is defined in the File class. The argument to OpenWrite() is the existing file path for the sketch. You then serialize the sketch by calling the Serialize() function for the BinaryFormatter object. Finally, you call Close() for the stream to close the stream and release the resources.

You can add the SaveSketchAs() function to the Form1 class as a private function implemented like this:

```
// Saves the current sketch
void SaveSketchAs(void)
{
  if(saveFileDialog->ShowDialog() == System::Windows::Forms::DialogResult::OK)
  {
    Stream^ stream = File::Open(saveFileDialog->FileName, FileMode::Create);
    if(stream != nullptr)
    {
      formatter->Serialize(stream, sketch);
      stream->Close();
      sketchFilePath = saveFileDialog->FileName;
      sketch->saved = true;
    }
    else
    {
      MessageBox::Show(L"Failed to create sketch file stream!");
    }
  }
}
```

You display the file save dialog by calling its ShowDialog() function in the if condition. If the OK button closes the dialog, the user wants to complete the save operation, so you call the static Open() function to create a FileStream object for the file using the file name provided by the FileName property for the dialog object. You serialize the sketch to the file by calling the Serialize() function for the BinaryFormatter object, and close the stream. You save the file path from the dialog for use next time around, and set the saved member of the Sketch object to true.

If calling the `Open()` function in the `File` class fails, `nullptr` is stored in `stream`. In this case, you use the `System::Windows::Forms::MessageBox` class to display a message. The `MessageBox` class `Show()` function provides you with the opportunity to display a wide range of message boxes. You will see more of the possibilities later in this chapter.

Retrieving a Sketch from a File

Retrieving a sketch from a file is a little more complicated, because you have to consider the possibility for the current sketch to be overwritten. If there is a current sketch that has not been saved, you should give the user an opportunity to save it before reading the new sketch from a file. The `Click` handler for the File ⇨ Open menu item deals with reading a sketch from a file. You can implement it like this:

```
private: System::Void openToolStripMenuItem_Click(
                          System::Object^ sender, System::EventArgs^ e)
{
  Stream^ stream;
  if(!sketch->saved)
  {
    String^ message = L"The current sketch is not saved.\nSave the current sketch?";
    String^ caption = L"Sketch Not Saved";
    MessageBoxButtons buttons = MessageBoxButtons::YesNo;

    // Displays the MessageBox to warn about unsaved sketch
    if (MessageBox::Show(this, message, caption, buttons) ==
                              System::Windows::Forms::DialogResult::Yes)
    {
      SaveSketch();
    }
  }

  // Now open a new sketch
  if(openFileDialog->ShowDialog() == System::Windows::Forms::DialogResult::OK)
  {
    stream = openFileDialog->OpenFile();
    if(stream != nullptr)
    {
      sketch = safe_cast<Sketch^>(formatter->Deserialize(stream));
      stream->Close();
      sketch->saved = true;
      sketchFilePath = openFileDialog->FileName;
      Invalidate();
    }
  }
}
```

If the `saved` member of the current `Sketch` object is `false`, the current sketch has not been saved. Therefore, you display a message box offering the user the opportunity to save the current sketch. This version of the `Show()` function in the `MessageBox` class accepts four arguments: a reference to the current window, the message to be displayed, the caption for the message box, and a `MessageBoxButtons` value that determines the buttons to be included in the message box. `MessageBoxButtons` is an enumeration that includes the members `OK`, `OKCancel`, `AbortRetryIgnore`, `YesNoCancel`, `YesNo`, and `RetryCancel`. If the value returned from the `Show()` function in the `MessageBox` class corresponds to the `Yes` button being clicked, you call the `SaveSketch()` function to allow it to save the sketch.

The `OpenFileDialog` class provides an `OpenFile()` function that returns a reference to the stream encapsulating the file selected in the dialog. You deserialize the sketch from the file by calling the `Deserialize()` function for the `formatter` object, and close the stream. The sketch is obviously in a file, so you set the `saved` member of the sketch to `true`. You store the file name in `sketchFilePath` for use by subsequent save operations, and call `Invalidate()` to get the form repainted to display the sketch you have just loaded.

Implementing the File New Operation

The File ➪ New menu item should create a new empty sketch, but only after checking that the current sketch has been saved. Add a `Click` event handler for the menu item and implement it like this:

```
private: System::Void newToolStripMenuItem_Click(
                                  System::Object^  sender, System::EventArgs^  e)
{
  SaveSketchCheck();
  sketch = gcnew Sketch();
  sketchFilePath = nullptr;
  Invalidate();
  Update();
}
```

The implementation is very simple. You call `SaveSketchCheck()` to check whether the current sketch needs to be saved and provide the opportunity for the user to do so. You then create a new `Sketch` object, rest the `sketchFilePath` member, and redraw the client area by calling `Invalidate()`, then `Update()`.

Add `SaveSketchCheck()` as a `private` member of the `Form1` class and implement it like this:

```
void SaveSketchCheck()
{
  if(!sketch->saved)
  {
    String^ message = L"The current sketch is not saved.\nSave the current sketch?";
    String^ caption = L"Sketch Not Saved";
    MessageBoxButtons buttons = MessageBoxButtons::YesNo;

    // Displays the MessageBox to warn about unsaved sketch
    if ( MessageBox::Show(this, message, caption, buttons) ==
                                    System::Windows::Forms::DialogResult::Yes)
    {
      SaveSketch();
    }
  }
}
```

Dealing with Closing the Form

At the moment, you can close the application by clicking on the close icon in the top-right corner of the form. This will close the application and lose the current sketch, if there is one. You really want to provide the possibility of saving the sketch before the application shuts down. Add a `FormClosing` event handler for the form by displaying the Property window for the form and double-clicking the `FormClosing` event. You can implement the event handler like this:

```
private: System::Void Form1_FormClosing(
        System::Object^ sender, System::Windows::Forms::FormClosingEventArgs^ e)
{
  SaveSketchCheck();
}
```

You just call `SaveSketchCheck()` to provide for the sketch being saved when necessary. That's all there is to it.

Supporting the Toolbar Buttons

The toolbar buttons for saving and opening files and creating a new sketch do nothing at the moment. However, to make them work is trivial. All you have to do is to select the `Click` event handler for the File menu item corresponding to a button as the event handler for the button.

You now have a version of CLR Sketcher with saving and retrieving sketches fully operational.

Printing a Sketch

You have a head start on printing a sketch because the Toolbox provides five components that support printing operations, including a page setup dialog and print and print preview dialogs. To print a sketch, you create an instance of the `PrintDocument` component, implement a `PrintPage` event handler for the `PrintDocument`, and call the `Print` function for the `PrintDocument` object to actually print the sketch. Of course, you also need to create `Click` event handlers for the menu items that are involved and display a few dialogs along the way, but let's start with the `PrintDocument` component.

Using the PrintDocument Component

Drag a `PrintDocument` component from the Toolbox window to the form in the Design window. This adds a `PrintDocument` member to the `Form1` class. If you display the `Properties` window for the `PrintDocument` object, you can change the value of its `(name)` property to `printDocument`. Click the `Events` button and double-click the `PrintPage` event to create a handler for it. The `PrintPageEventArgs^` parameter has a `Graphics` property that supplies a `Graphics` object that you can use to draw the sketch ready for printing, like this:

```
private: System::Void printDocument_PrintPage(
        System::Object^ sender, System::Drawing::Printing::PrintPageEventArgs^ e)
{
  sketch->Draw(e->Graphics);
}
```

It couldn't be much easier, really, could it?

Implementing the Print Operation

You need a print dialog to allow the user to select the printer and initiate printing, so drag a `PrintDialog` component from the Toolbox window to the form and change the `(name)` property value to `printDialog`. To associate the `printDocument` object with the dialog, select `printDocument` as the value of the `Document` property for the dialog from the drop-down list in the value column. Add a `Click` event handler for the File ⇨ Print menu item, and set this handler as the handler for the toolbar button for printing. All you have to do now is add code to the handler to display the dialog to allow printing:

```
private: System::Void printToolStripMenuItem_Click(
                                       System::Object^  sender, System::EventArgs^  e)
{
   if(printDialog->ShowDialog() == System::Windows::Forms::DialogResult::OK)
      printDocument->Print();
}
```

You display the dialog and, if the value returned from `ShowDialog()` is `DialogResult::OK`, you call the `Print()` function for the `printDocument` object to print the sketch. That's it! You added two lines of code here plus one line of code in the `PrintPage` event handler, and a basic printing capability for sketches is working.

Displaying the print dialog allows the user to choose the printer and change preferences for the print job before printing starts. Of course, you don't have to display the dialog to print the sketch. If you wanted to print the sketch immediately without displaying the dialog, you could just call the `Print()` function for the `PrintDocument` object.

SUMMARY

In this chapter, you have implemented the capability to store a document on disk in a form that allows you to read it back and reconstruct its constituent objects using the serialization processes supported by MFC and the CLR. You have also implemented the capability to print sketches in the native C++ and C++/CLI versions of the Sketcher application. If you are comfortable with how serialization and printing work in the two versions of Sketcher, you should have little difficulty with implementing serialization and printing in any MFC or Windows Forms application.

EXERCISES

You can download the source code for the examples in the book and the solutions to the following exercises from www.wrox.com.

1. Update the code in the OnPrint() function in Sketcher so that the page number is printed at the bottom of each page of the document in the form "Page *n* of *m*," where *n* is the current page number and *m* is the total number of pages.

2. As a further enhancement to the CText class in Sketcher, change the implementation so that scaling works properly with text. (*Hint*: Look up the CreatePointFont() function in the online help.)

3. Modify CLR Sketcher so that the user can choose a custom color for elements. (*Hint*: This will involve adding a new menu item and toolbar button. Look in the Toolbox for help with custom color selection.)

4. Add a line type option to CLR Sketcher for a line style pattern that is two dashes, then two dots, then one dash, then one dot.

▶ **WHAT YOU LEARNED IN THIS CHAPTER**

TOPIC	CONCEPT
Serialization	Serialization is the process of transferring objects to a file. Deserialization reconstructs object from data in a file.
MFC Serialization	To serialize objects in an MFC application, you must identify the class as serializable. To do this you use the `DECLARE_SERIALIZABLE()` macro in the class definition and the `IMPLEMENT_SERIALIZABLE()` macro in the file containing the class implementation.
Serializable classes in an MFC application.	For a class to be serializable in an MFC application, it must have `CObject` as a base class, it must implement a no-arg constructor and implement the `Serialize()` function as a class member.
C++/CLI Serialization	To identify a C++/CLI class as serializable you must mark in with the Serialiable attribute.
Serializing C++/CLI classes	For a class to be serializable in a C++/CLI application, you must: ➤ mark any fields that cannot or should not be serialized with the `NonSerialized` attribute, ➤ add a public member function to deal with non-serializable fields when serializing an object that has a `void` return type and a single parameter of type `StreamingContext` and mark it with the `OnSerializing` attribute, ➤ add a public member function to handle non-serialized fields when deserializing an object that has a `void` return type and a single argument of type `StreamingContext` and mark the function with the `OnDeserialized` attribute, ➤ add a using declaration for the `System::Runtime::Serialization` namespace to each header file containing serializable classes.
Printing with the MFC	To provide the ability to print a document in an MFC application, you must implement your versions of the `OnPreparePrinting()`, `OnBeginPrinting()`, `OnPrepareDC()`, `OnPrint()` and `OnEndPrinting()` functions in the document view class.
The `CPrintInfo` object	A `CPrintInfo` object is created by the MFC framework to store information about the printing process. You can store the address of your own class object that contains print information in a pointer in the `CPrintInfo` object.
Printing in a C++/CLI application	To implement printing in a Windows Forms application, add a `PrintDocument` component to the form and implement the handler for the `PrintPage` event to print the form.
Implementing the printing user-interface in a C++/CLI application	To implement the printing UI in a Windows Forms application, add a `PrintDialog` component to the form and display it in the `Click` handler for the menu item/toolbar button that initiates printing. When the print dialog is closed using the OK button, call the `Print()` function for the `PrintDocument` object to print the form.

20

Writing Your Own DLLs

WHAT YOU WILL LEARN IN THIS CHAPTER:

➤ DLLs and how they work

➤ When you should consider implementing a DLL

➤ What varieties of DLLs are possible and what they are used for

➤ How to extend MFC using a DLL

➤ How to define what is accessible in a DLL

➤ How to access the contents of a DLL in your programs

Chapter 9 discussed how a C++/CLI class library is stored in a .dll file. Dynamic link libraries (DLLs) are also used extensively with native C++ applications. A complete discussion of DLLs in native C++ applications is outside the scope of a beginner's book, but they are important enough to justify including an introductory chapter on them.

UNDERSTANDING DLLS

Almost all programming languages support libraries of standard code modules for commonly used elements such as functions. In native C++, you've been using lots of functions that are stored in standard libraries, such as the `ceil()` function that you used in the previous chapter, which is declared in the cmath header. The code for this function is stored in a library file with the extension .lib, and when the executable module for the Sketcher program was created, the linker retrieved the code for this standard function from the library file and integrated a copy of it into the .exe file for the Sketcher program. If you write another program and use the same function, it will also have its own copy of the `ceil()` function. The `ceil()` function is **statically linked** to each application and is an integral part of each executable module, as illustrated in Figure 20-1.

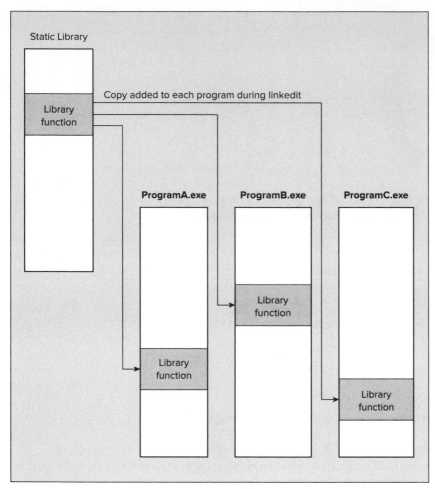

FIGURE 20-1

Although this is a very convenient way of using a standard function with minimal effort on your part, it does have its disadvantages as a way for several concurrently executing programs to make use of the same function in the Windows environment. A statically linked standard function being used by more than one program concurrently is duplicated in memory for each program using it. This may not seem to matter much for the ceil() function, but some functions — input and output, for instance — are invariably common to most programs and are likely to occupy sizable chunks of memory. Having these statically linked would be extremely inefficient.

Another consideration is that a standard function from a static library may be linked into hundreds of programs in your system, so identical copies of the code for them will be occupying disk space in the .exe file for each program. For these reasons, an additional library facility is supported by Windows for standard functions. It's called a **dynamic link library,** and it's usually abbreviated to **DLL.** This allows one copy of a function to be shared among several concurrently executing programs and avoids the need to incorporate a copy of the code for a library function into the executable module for a program that uses it.

How DLLs Work

A dynamic link library is a file containing a collection of modules that can be used by any number of different programs. The file for a DLL usually has the extension .dll, but this isn't obligatory. When naming a DLL, you can assign any extension you like, but this can affect how it's handled by Windows. Windows automatically loads dynamic link libraries that have the extension .dll. If they have some other extension, you will need to load them explicitly by adding code to do this to your program. Windows itself uses the extension .exe for some of its DLLs. You have likely seen the extensions .vbx (Visual Basic Extension) and .ocx (OLE Custom Extension), which are applied to DLLs containing specific kinds of controls.

You might imagine that you have a choice about whether or not you use dynamic link libraries in your program, but you don't. The Win32 API is used by every Windows program, and the API is implemented in a set of DLLs. DLLs are fundamental to Windows programming.

Connecting a function in a DLL to a program is different from the process used with a statically linked library, where the code is incorporated once and for all when the program is linked to generate the executable module. A function in a DLL is connected only to a program that uses it when the application is run, and this is done each time the program is executed, as Figure 20-2 illustrates.

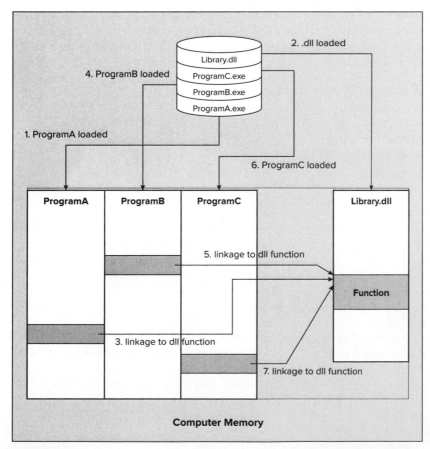

FIGURE 20-2

Figure 20-2 shows the sequence of events when three programs that use a function in a DLL are started successively and then all execute concurrently. No code from the DLL is included in the executable module of any of the programs. When one of the programs is executed, the program is loaded into memory, and if the DLL it uses isn't already present, it, too, is loaded separately. The appropriate links between the program and the DLL are then established. If, when a program is loaded, the DLL is already there, all that needs to be done is to link the program to the required function in the DLL.

Note particularly that when your program calls a function or uses a class that is defined in a DLL, Windows will automatically load the DLL into memory. Any program subsequently loaded into memory that uses the same DLL can use any of the capabilities provided by the *same copy* of the DLL, because Windows recognizes that the library is already in memory and just establishes the links between it and the program. Windows keeps track of how many programs are using each DLL that is resident in memory, so that the library remains in memory as long as at least one program is still using it. When a DLL is no longer used by any executing program, Windows automatically deletes it from memory.

MFC is provided in the form of a number of DLLs that your program can link to dynamically, as well as a library that your program can link to statically. By default, the Application Wizard generates programs that link dynamically to the DLL form of MFC.

Having a function stored in a DLL introduces the possibility of changing the function without affecting the programs that use it. As long as the interface to the function in the DLL remains the same, the programs can use a new version of the function quite happily, without the need for recompiling or relinking them. Unfortunately, this also has a downside: it's easy to end up using the wrong version of a DLL with a program. This can be a particular problem with applications that install DLLs in the Windows System folder. Some commercial applications arbitrarily write the DLLs associated with the program to this folder without regard for the possibility of a DLL with the same name being overwritten. This can interfere with other applications that you have already installed and, in the worst case, can render them inoperable.

 NOTE *DLLs are not the only means of sharing classes or functions among several applications. COM (Component Object Model) objects provide another, more powerful way for you to create reusable software components. Using COM can be quite complicated, but the ATL (Active Template Library), which is a template-based class library, can make COM programming easier. There is quite a lot to learn if you want to use COM and/or ATL; however, both topics are outside the scope of this book.*

Runtime Dynamic Linking

The DLL that you'll create in this chapter is automatically loaded into memory when the program that uses it is loaded into memory for execution. This is referred to as **load-time dynamic linking** or **early binding**, because the links to the functions used are established as soon as the program and DLL have been loaded into memory. This kind of operation was illustrated in Figure 20-2; however, this isn't the only choice available. It's also possible to cause a DLL to be loaded after execution of a program has started. This is called **runtime dynamic linking** or **late binding**. The sequence of operations that occurs with late binding is illustrated in Figure 20-3.

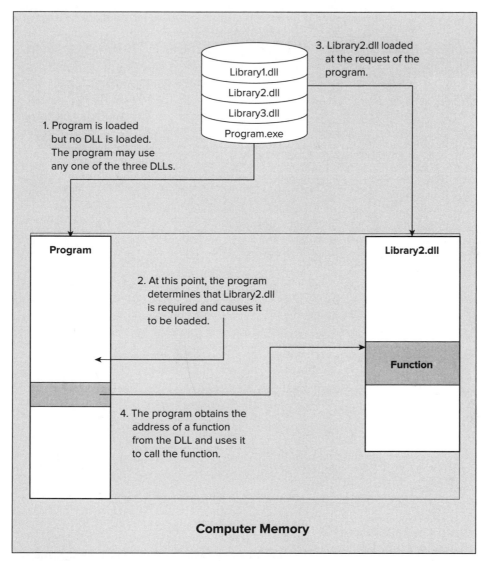

1. Program is loaded but no DLL is loaded. The program may use any one of the three DLLs.

Library1.dll
Library2.dll
Library3.dll
Program.exe

3. Library2.dll loaded at the request of the program.

Program

2. At this point, the program determines that Library2.dll is required and causes it to be loaded.

4. The program obtains the address of a function from the DLL and uses it to call the function.

Library2.dll

Function

Computer Memory

FIGURE 20-3

Runtime dynamic linking enables a program to defer linking of a DLL until it's certain that the functions in a DLL are required. This enables you to write a program that can choose to load one or more of a number of DLLs based upon input to the program, so that only those functions that are necessary are actually loaded into memory. In some circumstances, this can drastically reduce the amount of memory required to run a program.

A program implemented to use runtime dynamic linking calls the Windows API function LoadLibrary() to load the DLL when it's required. The address of a function within the DLL can then be obtained via the function GetProcAddress(). When the program no longer has a need to use the DLL, it can detach itself from the DLL by calling the `FreeLibrary()` function. If no other program is using the DLL, it will be deleted from memory. I won't be going into further details of how this works in this book.

Contents of a DLL

A DLL isn't limited to storing code for functions. You can also put other global entities such as classes, global variables, and resources into a DLL, including such things as bitmaps and fonts. The Solitaire game that comes with Windows uses a dynamic link library called `Cards.dll`, which contains all the bitmap images of the cards and functions to manipulate them. If you wanted to write your own card game, you could conceivably use this DLL as a base and save yourself the trouble of creating all the bitmaps needed to represent the cards. Of course, to use it, you would need to know specifically which functions and resources are included in the DLL.

You can also define static global variables in a DLL, including C++ class objects, so that these can be accessed by programs using it. The constructors for global static class objects are called automatically when such objects are created. You should note that each program using a DLL gets its own copy of any static global objects defined in the DLL, even though they may not necessarily be used by a program. For global class objects, this involves the overhead of calling a constructor for each. You should, therefore, avoid introducing such objects into a DLL unless they are absolutely essential.

The DLL Interface

You can't access just anything that's contained in a DLL. Only items that have been specifically identified as **exported** from a DLL are visible to the outside world. Functions, classes, global static variables, and resources can all be exported from a DLL, and those that are make up the **interface** to it. Anything that isn't exported can't be accessed from the outside. You'll see how to export items from a DLL later in this chapter.

The DllMain() Function

Even though a DLL isn't executable as an independent program, it does contain a special variety of the `main()` function, called `DllMain()`. This is called by Windows when the DLL is first loaded into memory to allow the DLL to do any necessary initialization before its contents are used. Windows will also call `DllMain()` just before it removes the DLL from memory to enable the DLL to clean up after itself if necessary. There are also other circumstances in which `DllMain()` is called, but these situations are outside the scope of this book.

DLL Varieties

There are three different kinds of DLL that you can build with Visual C++ 2010 using MFC: an MFC extension DLL, a regular DLL with MFC statically linked, and a regular DLL with MFC dynamically linked.

MFC Extension DLL

You build this kind of DLL whenever it's going to include classes derived from the MFC. Your derived classes in the DLL effectively extend the MFC. The MFC must be accessible in the environment in which your DLL is used, so all the MFC classes are available together with your derived classes — hence the name "MFC extension DLL." However, to derive your own classes from the MFC isn't the only reason to use an MFC extension DLL. If you're writing a DLL that includes functions that pass pointers to MFC class objects to functions in a program using it, or that receive such pointers from functions in the program, you must create it as an MFC extension DLL.

Accesses to classes in the MFC by an extension DLL are always resolved dynamically by a link to the shared version of MFC that is itself implemented in DLLs. An extension DLL is created with the shared DLL version of the MFC, so when you use an extension DLL, the shared version of MFC must be available. An MFC extension DLL can be used by a normal Application Wizard–generated application. It requires the option Use MFC in a Shared DLL to be selected under the General set of properties for the project, which you access through the Project ⇨ Properties menu option. This is the default selection with an Application Wizard–generated program. Because of the fundamental nature of the shared version of the MFC in an extension DLL, an MFC extension DLL can't be used by programs that are statically linked to MFC.

Regular DLL — Statically Linked to MFC

This is a DLL that uses MFC classes linked statically. Use of the DLL doesn't require MFC to be available in the environment in which it is used, because the code for all the classes it uses is incorporated into the DLL. This bulks up the size of the DLL, but the big advantage is that this kind of DLL can be used by any Win32 program, regardless of whether or not it uses MFC.

Regular DLL — Dynamically Linked to MFC

This is a DLL that uses dynamically linked classes from MFC but doesn't add classes of its own. This kind of DLL can be used by any Win32 program, regardless of whether it uses MFC itself; however, use of the DLL does require the MFC to be available in the environment.

You can use the Application Wizard to build all three types of DLL that use MFC. You can also create a project for a DLL that doesn't involve MFC at all, by creating a Win32 project type using the Win32 Project template and selecting DLL in the application settings for the project.

DECIDING WHAT TO PUT IN A DLL

How do you decide when you should use a DLL? In most cases, the use of a DLL provides a solution to a particular kind of programming problem, so if you have the problem, a DLL can be the answer. The common denominator is often sharing code among a number of programs, but there are other instances in which a DLL provides advantages. The kinds of circumstances in which putting code or resources in a DLL is a very convenient and efficient approach include the following:

➤ You have a set of functions or resources on which you want to standardize and that you will use in several different programs. The DLL is a particularly good solution for managing these, especially if some of the programs using your standard facilities are likely to be executing concurrently.

➤ You have a complex application that involves several programs and a lot of code, but that has sets of functions or resources that may be shared among several of the programs in the application. Using a DLL for common functionality or common resources enables you to manage and develop these with a great deal of independence from the program modules that use them, and can simplify program maintenance.

➤ You have developed a set of standard application-oriented classes derived from MFC that you anticipate using in several programs. By packaging the implementation of these classes in an extension DLL, you can make using them in several programs very straightforward, and, in the process, provide the possibility of being able to improve the internals of the classes without affecting the applications that use them.

➤ You have developed a brilliant set of functions that provide an easy-to-use but amazingly powerful toolkit for an application area that just about everybody wants to dabble in. You can readily package your functions in a regular DLL and distribute them in this form.

There are also other circumstances in which you may choose to use DLLs, such as when you want to be able to dynamically load and unload libraries, or to select different modules at run time. You could even use them to make the development and updating of your applications easier generally.

The best way of understanding how to use a DLL is to create one and try it out. Let's do that now.

WRITING DLLS

This section examines two aspects of writing a DLL: how you actually write a DLL, and how you define what's to be accessible in the DLL to programs that use it. As a practical example of writing a DLL, you'll create an extension DLL to add a set of application classes to the MFC. You'll then extend this DLL by adding variables available to programs using it.

Writing and Using an Extension DLL

You can create an MFC extension DLL to contain the shape classes for the Sketcher application. Although this will not bring any major advantages to the program, it demonstrates how you can write an extension DLL without involving yourself in the overhead of entering a lot of new code.

The starting point is the Application Wizard, so create a new project by pressing Ctrl+Shift+N and choosing the project type as MFC and the template as MFC DLL.

This selection identifies that you are creating a project for an MFC-based DLL with the name ExtDLLExample. Click the OK button and select Application Settings in the next window displayed. The window looks as shown in Figure 20-4.

FIGURE 20-4

Here, you can see three radio buttons corresponding to the three types of MFC-based DLL that I discussed earlier. You should choose the third option, as shown in the figure.

The two checkboxes below the first group of three radio buttons enable you to include code to support Automation and Windows sockets in the DLL. These are both advanced capabilities within a Windows program, so you don't need either of them here. **Automation** provides the potential for hosting objects created and managed by one application inside another. **Windows sockets** provide classes and functionality to enable your program to communicate over a network, but you won't be getting into this as it's beyond the scope of the book. You can click the Finish button and complete creation of the project.

Now that the MFC DLL wizard has done its stuff, you can look into the code that has been generated on your behalf. If you look at the contents of the project in the Solution Explorer pane, you'll see that the MFC DLL wizard has generated several files, including a .txt file that contains a description of the other files. You can read what they're all for in the .txt file, but the two shown in the following table are the ones of immediate interest.

FILE NAME	CONTENTS
dllmain.cpp	This contains the function DllMain() and is the primary source file for the DLL.
ExtDLLExample.def	The information in this file is used during compilation. It contains the name of the DLL, and you can also add to it the definitions of those items in the DLL that are to be accessible to a program using the DLL. You'll use an alternative and somewhat easier way of identifying such items in the example.

When your DLL is loaded, the first thing that happens is that DllMain() is executed, so perhaps you should take a look at that first.

Understanding DllMain()

If you look at the contents of dllmain.cpp, you will see that the MFC DLL wizard has generated a version of DllMain() for you, as shown here:

```
extern "C" int APIENTRY
DllMain(HINSTANCE hInstance, DWORD dwReason, LPVOID lpReserved)
{
    // Remove this if you use lpReserved
    UNREFERENCED_PARAMETER(lpReserved);

    if (dwReason == DLL_PROCESS_ATTACH)
    {
        TRACE0("EXTDLLEXAMPLE.DLL Initializing!\n");

        // Extension DLL one-time initialization
        if (!AfxInitExtensionModule(ExtDLLExampleDLL, hInstance))
            return 0;
```

```
        // Insert this DLL into the resource chain
        // NOTE: If this Extension DLL is being implicitly linked to by
        //   an MFC Regular DLL (such as an ActiveX Control)
        //   instead of an MFC application, then you will want to
        //   remove this line from DllMain and put it in a separate
        //   function exported from this Extension DLL.  The Regular DLL
        //   that uses this Extension DLL should then explicitly call that
        //   function to initialize this Extension DLL.  Otherwise,
        //   the CDynLinkLibrary object will not be attached to the
        //   Regular DLL's resource chain, and serious problems will
        //   result.

        new CDynLinkLibrary(ExtDLLExampleDLL);
    }
    else if (dwReason == DLL_PROCESS_DETACH)
    {
        TRACE0("EXTDLLEXAMPLE.DLL Terminating!\n");
        // Terminate the library before destructors are called
        AfxTermExtensionModule(ExtDLLExampleDLL);
    }
    return 1;    // ok
}
```

There are three arguments passed to `DllMain()` when it is called. The first argument, `hInstance`, is a handle that has been created by Windows to identify the DLL. Every task under Windows has an instance handle that identifies it uniquely. The second argument, `dwReason`, indicates the reason why `DllMain()` is being called. You can see this argument being tested in the `if` statements in `DllMain()`. The first `if` tests for the value `DLL_PROCESS_ATTACH`, which indicates that a program is about to use the DLL, and the second `if` tests for the value `DLL_PROCESS_DETACH`, which indicates that a program has finished using the DLL. The third argument is a pointer that's reserved for use by Windows, so you can ignore it.

When the DLL is first used by a program, it's loaded into memory, and the `DllMain()` function is executed with the argument `dwReason` set to `DLL_PROCESS_ATTACH`. This results in the Windows API function `AfxInitExtensionModule()` being called to initialize the DLL and an object of the class `CDynLinkLibrary` created on the heap. Windows uses objects of this class to manage extension DLLs. If you need to add initialization of your own, you can add it to the end of this block. Any cleanup you require for your DLL can be added to the block for the second `if` statement.

Adding Classes to the Extension DLL

You will use the DLL to contain the implementation of the Sketcher shape classes. Move the files `Elements.h` and `Elements.cpp` from the folder containing the source for Sketcher to the folder containing the DLL. Be sure that you *move* rather than *copy* the files. Because the DLL is going to supply the shape classes for Sketcher, you don't want to leave them in the source code for Sketcher.

You'll also need to remove `Elements.cpp` from the Sketcher project once you have copied it to the DLL project. To do this, open the Sketcher project, highlight `Elements.cpp` in the Solution Explorer pane by clicking the file, and then press Delete. If you don't do this, the compiler complains that it can't find the file when you try to compile the project. Follow the same procedure to get rid of `Elements.h` from the Header Files folder in the Solution Explorer pane.

You now need to add `Elements.h` and `Elements.cpp` to the extension DLL project, so open the `ExtDLLExample` project, select the menu option Project ➪ Add Existing Item, and choose the files Elements.cpp and Elements.h from the list box in the dialog box, as shown in Figure 20-5.

You can add multiple files in a single step by holding down the control key while you select from the list of files in the Add Existing Item dialog box. You should eventually see the files you have added in the Solution Explorer pane and all the shape classes displayed in the Class View pane for the project.

FIGURE 20-5

The shape classes use the constants VERSION_NUMBER and SELECT_COLOR that you have defined in the file `SketcherConstants.h`, so copy the definitions for these from the `SketcherConstants.h` file in the Sketcher project folder to the `Elements.cpp` file in the folder containing the DLL; you can place them immediately after the `#include` directives. Note that the VERSION_NUMBER and SELECT_COLOR variables are used exclusively by the shape classes, so you can delete them from the `SketcherConstants.h` file used in the Sketcher program or just comment them out.

Exporting Classes from the Extension DLL

The collection of entities in a DLL that can be accessed by a program that is using it is referred to as the **interface** to the DLL. The process of making an object part of the interface to a DLL is referred to as **exporting** the object, and the process of accessing an object that is exported from a DLL is described as **importing** the object.

The names of the classes defined in the DLL that are to be accessible in programs that use it must be identified in some way so that the appropriate links can be established between a program and the DLL. As you saw earlier, one way of doing this is by adding information to the `.def` file for the DLL. This involves adding what are called **decorated names** to the DLL and associating each decorated name with a unique identifying numeric value called an **ordinal**. A decorated name for an object is a name generated by the compiler, which adds an additional string to the name you gave to the object. This additional string provides information about the type of the object or, in the case of a function (for example), information about the types of the parameters to the function. Among other things, it ensures that everything has a unique identifier and enables the linker to distinguish overloaded functions from each other.

Obtaining decorated names and assigning ordinals to export items from a DLL is a lot of work and isn't the best or the easiest approach. A much easier way to identify the classes that you want to export from the DLL is to modify the class definitions in `Elements.h` to include the MFC macro `AFX_EXT_CLASS` before each class name, as shown in the following for the `CLine` class:

```
// Class defining a line object
class AFX_EXT_CLASS CLine: public CElement
{
  // Details of the class definition as before...
};
```

The `AFX_EXT_CLASS` macro indicates that the class is to be exported from the DLL. This has the effect of making the complete class available to any program using the DLL and automatically allows access to any of the data and functions in the public interface of the class.

`AFX_EXT_CLASS` is defined as `__declspec(dllexport)` when it appears within an extension DLL and `__declspec(dllimport)` otherwise. This means that you can use the same macro for exporting entities from a DLL and importing entities into an application. However, the `dllexport` and `dllimport` attributes provide a more general mechanism for exporting and importing entities in a DLL that you can use regardless of whether or not your DLL is an MFC extension, so I will use these in the example, rather than `AFX_EXT_CLASS`, which is available only with MFC.

Here's how you can use `__declspec(dllexport)` to export the `CLine` class from the DLL:

```
// Macro to make the code more readable
#define SKETCHER_API   __declspec(dllexport)

// Class defining a line object
class SKETCHER_API CLine: public CElement
{
  // Details of the class definition as before...
};
```

You need to add `SKETCHER_API` to all the other shape classes, including the base class `CElement`, in exactly the way as with the `CLine` class. Why is it necessary to export `CElement` from the DLL? After all, programs create only objects of the classes derived from `CElement`, and not objects of the class `CElement` itself. One reason is that you have declared `public` members of `CElement` that form part of the interface to the derived shape classes, and that are almost certainly going to be required by programs using the DLL. If you don't export the `CElement` class, functions such as `GetBoundRect()` will not be available. Another reason is that you create variables of type `CElement` or `CElement*` in Sketcher, so you need the class definition available for such a definition to compile.

You have done everything necessary to add the shape classes to the DLL. All that remains is for you to compile and link the project to create the DLL.

Building a DLL

You build the DLL in exactly the same way that you build any other project — by using the Build ⇨ Build Solution menu option or selecting the corresponding toolbar button. The output produced is somewhat different, though. You can see the files that are produced in the debug subfolder of the project folder for a Debug build, or in the release subfolder for a Release build. The executable code for the DLL is contained in the file `ExtDLLExample.dll`. This file needs to be available to execute a program that uses the DLL. The file `ExtDLLExample.lib` is an import library file that contains the definitions of the items that are exported from the DLL, and it must be available to the linker when a program using the DLL is linked.

> **NOTE** *If you find the DLL build fails because* `Elements.cpp` *contains an* `#include` *directive for* `Sketcher.h`, *just remove it. On my system, the Class Wizard added the* `#include` *directive for* `Sketcher.h` *when creating the code for the* `CElement` *class, but it is not required.*

Importing Classes from a DLL

You now have no information in the Sketcher program on the shape classes because you moved the files containing the class definitions and implementations to the DLL project. However, the compiler still must know where the shape classes are coming from in order to compile the code for the Sketcher program. The Sketcher application needs to include a header file that defines the classes that are to be imported from the DLL. It must also identify the classes as external to the project by using the `__declspec(dllimport)` qualification for the class names in the class definitions.

An easy way to do this is to modify the file `Elements.h` in the DLL project so that it can be used in the Sketcher project as well. What you need is for the class definitions in `Elements.h` to be qualified with `__declspec(dllexport)` when they are in the DLL project and qualified with `__declspec(dllimport)` when they are in the Sketcher project. You can achieve this by replacing the `#define` macro for the `SKETCHER_API` symbol in `Elements.h` with the following:

```
#ifdef ELEMENT_EXPORTS
#define SKETCHER_API    __declspec(dllexport)
#else
#define SKETCHER_API    __declspec(dllimport)
#endif
```

If the symbol `ELEMENT_EXPORTS` is defined, then `SKETCHER_API` will be replaced by `__declspec(dllexport)`; otherwise, it will be replaced by `__declspec(dllimport)`. `ELEMENT_EXPORTS` is not defined in Sketcher, so using the header in Sketcher will do what you want. All you need is to define `ELEMENT_EXPORTS` in the `ExtDLLExample` project. You can do this by adding the following to the `stdafx.h` header in the DLL project, immediately following the `#pragma once` directive:

```
#define ELEMENT_EXPORTS
```

Now you can rebuild the DLL project.

Using the Extension DLL in Sketcher

Now that you have copied the new version of the `Elements.h` file to the project, you should add it back into the project by right-clicking the Header Files folder in the Solution Explorer pane and selecting Add ➪ Existing Item from the context menu.

When you rebuild the Sketcher application, the linker needs to have the `ExtDLLExample.lib` file identified as a dependency for the project, because this file contains information about the contents of the DLL. Right-click Sketcher in the Solution Explorer pane and select Properties from the pop-up. You can then expand the Linker folder and select Input in the left pane of the Properties window. Then enter the name of the `.lib` file as an additional dependency, as shown in Figure 20-6.

FIGURE 20-6

Figure 20-6 shows the entry for the debug version of Sketcher. The `.lib` file for the DLL is in the Debug folder within the DLL project folder. If you create a release version of Sketcher, you'll also need the release version of the DLL available to the linker and its `.lib` file, so you'll have to enter the fully qualified name of the `.lib` file for the release version of the DLL, corresponding to the release version of Sketcher. The file to which the properties apply is selected in the Configuration drop-down list box in the Properties window. You have only one external dependency, but you can enter several when necessary by clicking the button to the right of the text box for input. Because the full path to the `.lib` file has been entered here, the linker will know not only that `ExtDLLExample.lib` is an external dependency, but also where it is.

For the Sketcher application to compile and link correctly, the `.lib` file for the DLL must be available to the application. When you execute Sketcher, the `.dll` file is required. To enable Windows to find and load a DLL for a program when it executes, it's usual to place the DLL in your Windows `System32` folder. If it's not in this folder, Windows searches the folder containing the executable (`Sketcher.exe` in this case). If it isn't there, you'll get an error message. To avoid cluttering up your System32 folder unnecessarily, you can copy `ExtDllExample.dll` from the Debug folder of the DLL project to the Debug folder for Sketcher. If you now build the Sketcher application once more, you'll find there is a problem. In particular, the `Serialize()` member of `CSketcherDoc` causes a `LNK2001` linker error. The problem is with the `operator>>()` member of the `CArchive` class. There is a version of this function defined in the `CArchive` class that supports type `CObject`, and, in the original version of Sketcher, the compiler was happy to use this to deserialize `CElement` objects before storing them in the list container. With the `CElement` class now imported from a DLL, this no longer works. However, you can get around this quite easily. You can change the code in the `Serialize()` function that reads shape objects to the following:

```
size_t elementCount(0);              // Count of number of elements
CObject* pElement(nullptr);          // Element pointer
ar >> elementCount;                  // retrieve the element count
// Now retrieve all the elements and store in the list
for(size_t i = 0 ; i < elementCount ; ++i)
{
  ar >> pElement;
  m_ElementList.push_back(static_cast<CElement*>(pElement));
}
```

Now, you store the address of the shape object that is to be deserialized as type `CObject*`. You then cast this to type `CElement*` before storing it in the list. With these changes, the `Serialize()` function will compile and work as before. Sketcher should now execute exactly as before, except that now it uses the shape classes in the DLL you have created.

Files Required to Use a DLL

From what you have just seen in the context of using the DLL you created in the Sketcher program, you can conclude that three files must be available to use a DLL in a program, as shown in the following table.

EXTENSION	CONTENTS
.h	Defines those items that are exported from a DLL and enables the compiler to deal properly with references to such items in the source code of a program using the DLL. The .h file needs to be added to the source code for the program using the DLL.
.lib	Defines the items exported by a DLL in a form, which enables the linker to deal with references to exported items when linking a program that uses a DLL.
.dll	Contains the executable code for the DLL, which is loaded by Windows when a program using the DLL is executed.

If you plan to distribute program code in the form of a DLL for use by other programmers, you need to distribute all three files in the package. For applications that already use the DLL, only the .dll file is required to go along with the .exe file that uses it.

SUMMARY

In this chapter, you've learned the basics of how to construct and use a DLL.

EXERCISE

You can download the source code for the examples in the book and the solutions to the following exercise from `www.wrox.com`.

1. This is the last time you'll be amending this version of the Sketcher program, so try the following. Using the DLL we've just created, implement a Sketcher document viewer — in other words, a program that simply opens a document created by Sketcher and displays the whole thing in a window at once. You need not worry about editing, scrolling, or printing, but you will have to work out the scaling required to make a big picture fit in a little window!

▶ WHAT YOU LEARNED IN THIS CHAPTER

TOPIC	CONCEPT
Dynamic link libraries	Dynamic link libraries provide a means of linking to standard functions dynamically when a program executes, rather than incorporating them into the executable module for a program.
MFC DLLs	An Application Wizard–generated program links to a version of MFC stored in DLLs by default.
Using DLLs	A single copy of a DLL in memory can be used by several programs executing concurrently.
Extension DLLs	An extension DLL is so called because it extends the set of classes in MFC. An extension DLL must be used if you want to export MFC-based classes or objects of MFC classes from a DLL. An extension DLL can also export ordinary functions and global variables.
Regular DLLs	A regular DLL can be used if you want to export only ordinary functions or global variables that aren't instances of MFC classes.
Exporting classes from a DLL	You can export classes from an extension DLL by using the keyword `AFX_EXT_CLASS` before the class name in the DLL.
Importing classes from a DLL	Using the `AFX_EXT_CLASS` keyword, you can import the classes exported from an extension DLL by using the .h file from the DLL that contains the class definitions.

INDEX

M

U